T0334548

SHIPBROKING AND CHARTERING PRACTICE

LLOYD'S PRACTICAL SHIPPING GUIDES

SHIPBROKING AND CHARTERING PRACTICE

Dr. EVI PLOMARITOU

Shipping Consultant at Lloyd's Maritime Academy
Lecturer of Chartering at Frederick University (Cyprus)

and

ANTHONY PAPADOPOULOS

Senior Shipping Analyst

EIGHTH EDITION

Routledge
Taylor & Francis Group

LONDON AND NEW YORK

Eighth edition published 2018
by Informa Law from Routledge

2 Park Square, Milton Park, Abingdon, Oxfordshire OX14 4RN
52 Vanderbilt Avenue, New York, NY 10017

Routledge is an imprint of the Taylor & Francis Group, an informa business

First issued in paperback 2019

First edition published 1980 by Informa Law
Seventh edition published by Informa 2009

British Library Cataloguing-in-Publication Data
A catalogue record for this book is available from the British Library

Library of Congress Cataloging-in-Publication Data
Names: Plomaritou, Evi, author. | Papadopoulos, Antonis, author.
Title: Shipbroking and chartering practice / by Evi Plomaritou and Antonis Papadopoulos.
Description: Eighth edition. | Milton Park, Abingdon, Oxon ; New York, NY : Informa
    Law from Routledge, 2018. | Series: Lloyd's practical shipping guides |
    Includes bibliographical references.
Identifiers: LCCN 2017034512 | ISBN 9781138826946 (hbk) | ISBN 9781315689609 (ebk)
Subjects: LCSH: Charter-parties. | Ship brokers—Legal status, laws, etc.
Classification: LCC K1182 .G67 2018 | DDC 343.09/65—dc23
LC record available at https://lccn.loc.gov/2017034512

ISBN: 978-1-138-82694-6 (hbk)
ISBN: 978-0-367-87101-7 (pbk)

Typeset in Times New Roman
by Apex CoVantage, LLC

To our beloved daughter,
Anna Maria

CONTENTS

DETAILED CONTENTS

PREFACE

The first edition of this book dates back in 1980. The idea was based on a project launched by the Swedish Shipowners' Association and it was first published in the Swedish language in conjunction with Liber Hermods, a Swedish editor. At the same time, the first English edition was published by Lloyd's of London Press Ltd., being rather different from the basic Swedish text. The authors of the original version, Professor Lars Gorton, Mr. Rolf Ihre and the recently passed away Captain Arne Sandevärn, together with the Lloyd's of London Press, went on publishing successfully the next editions of this work up to 2009, when Mr. Patrick Hillenius joined the author team. Now, on the eighth edition, Professor Lars Gorton and Mr. Rolf Ihre have decided to leave behind this project, thus giving a heavy legacy to us.

As the new authors of the present volume, having being taught as University students by past editions of "Shipbroking & Chartering Practice", our goal is to continue the "journey", by adopting the same philosophy and seeking the same targets.

The intention of this substantially revised edition is to strengthen the competitive edge of this book, namely:

- To retain the comprehensive, concise, authoritative and easily conceivable writing style.
- To expand the scope, by providing a wide and fully updated coverage of the subject of shipbroking and chartering practice from a commercial, financial/economical, managerial, operational and, to some extent, legal point of view, analysing all charter markets and addressing to both market practitioners and students.
- To base this work on professional orientation, personal experience, primary research, extensive bibliography and market data sourced from expert research providers.
- To enrich the text with practical examples on voyage estimations, laytime calculations and chartering negotiations, provide an expanded analysis of charter markets, an illustration of freight rates for all major vessel types from 1980 to 2015, a detailed description of Worldscale principles applying to tanker spot charters, an enlightening presentation of marketing as a critical tool of improving the chartering policy and a complete "glossary and abbreviations" section at the end of the text.
- To make an updated and thorough review of common charterparty clauses, based on current, reputable standard document forms for all major types of charter (e.g. NYPE 2015).

It should be mentioned that the reader who needs precise information on specific legal points should refer to specialised literature. Few legal cases, mainly selected from English and American common law, have been included intending to illustrate certain principles.

We would like to point out that comments and suggestions are more than welcome. We would appreciate it if the readers shared with us their experience in the field, as well as highlighting parts of the book which are superfluous or superficial. All such information may be addressed to Informa Law from Routledge, 2 Park Square, Milton Park, Abingdon OX14 4RN.

Finally, we wish to express our gratitude to the Informa group for confiding to us the substantial revision of this edition.

Dr. Evi Plomaritou, Anthony Papadopoulos.
This edition pays tribute to Professor Lars Gorton,
Mr. Rolf Ihre and in the memory of Captain Arne Sandevärn.

INTRODUCTION

Chartering is the part of international shipping business which broadly deals with the proper matching of cargoes' transport needs and vessels' commercial trading for the safe carriage of goods by sea. This business activity requires multi-faceted knowledge and professional experience.

This volume is concerned with the commercial, economical/financial, operational, managerial and legal aspects of chartering, offering numerous case studies and practical examples which clearly link theory to practice.

More specifically, the book is structured as follows:

- Chapter 1 intends to familiarise the reader with basic definitions of chartering, such as the types of charter, which are considered as a prerequisite knowledge to help reading throughout the book. Then, the *fundamentals of chartering* are given; namely the vessels, the cargoes, the trades and the respective market segmentation.
- Chapter 2 completes the charter market analysis, focusing on the *freight rates* side. It illustrates how the general state of freight rates is determined in the open market, which factors affect the fixture rate of an individual charter, and discusses the fundamental elements of the four major freight markets – dry bulk, tanker, gas and containerships. The picture is complemented with tables presenting the freight rates for all major vessel types from 1980 to 2015. Freight indices are briefly described and freight derivatives are introduced at the end of chapter.
- Chapter 3 presents the major sources of *chartering information,* the most important information centres in the world, how this information is transmitted within the chartering network and what the means of communication are. Great emphasis is placed on the description of the role of the *shipbrokers and agents* in handling this business data.
- Chapter 4 aims at tracking the location of chartering within the ship management field. It first introduces some main aspects of shipowning and ship management. Then, the importance of *commercial management* of vessels is highlighted, as well as its relationship with chartering and shipbroking practice.

- Chapter 5 investigates modern and innovative managerial aspects of chartering. *Marketing* is introduced as the strategic tool which helps a shipping company improves its chartering policy and profitability. The chartering policy of shipowners and charterers in bulk and liner markets is also examined. The stages of marketing implementation are further presented. Various shipping marketing strategies are illustrated through real case studies and commercial examples.
- Chapter 6 intends to show the *general trading context*, by searching how chartering business is related with the international laws and practices of sales of goods and their transport by sea. Significant subjects are examined, such as the contract of sale of goods, Incoterms® 2010 rules, the charterparty and the bill of lading as main contracts of sea carriage, the documentary letter of credit, the carriage of goods by sea international cargo conventions, etc.
- Chapter 7 deals with the most important *types of charter* and explains how they function. Emphasis is given to the most popular types of vessels' charter, namely the voyage charter, the time charter, the bareboat charter and the contract of affreightment. *Allocation of obligations, duties, liabilities, rights and costs* of the involved parties are briefly presented per type of charter. Furthermore, standard forms of charterparties per type of charter are introduced.
- Chapter 8 is concerned with a substantial subject of shipbroking and chartering practice; the *chartering negotiations*. It provides an analytical and comprehensive description of chartering negotiation procedure, comprising three stages; investigation, negotiation and drawing-up of the charterparty. This chapter is enriched with real practical examples of orders, position lists and offers, illustrating the cases and the differences among various charter types.
- Chapter 9 introduces the *legal perspectives of the charterparties*. Initially, some of the fundamental legal principles applying to charterparties are presented, while the reader gets also familiarised with the contracting parties, the applicable law and the legislation of the charter documents. Dispute settlement procedures are discussed and relevant clauses are commented. Finally, critical rules are examined in respect to the construction and interpretation of charterparties.
- Chapter 10 is focused on general questions, *concepts and clauses commonly applying to all different charter types and shipping contracts*. Various topics of considerable interest are examined, such as the layout of a charterparty, the identity of the contracting parties, the importance of a vessel's description, the vessel's "seaworthiness" etc.
- Chapter 11 examines in detail typical clauses found and critical matters accruing from a *voyage charter*. Issues such as the accurate vessel's description, the nomination of safe ports, the execution of the voyage with utmost despatch and with no deviation, the problems related to the

quantity or the quality of the cargo, the allocation of costs between the shipowner and charterer etc. are highlighted. The content of the chapter is enriched with examples from real clauses sourced from standard forms of voyage charterparties; dry and wet.

- Chapter 12 discusses the typical clauses and critical matters of *time charter*. Aspects such as the description of the vessel, the trading limitations, the period of the contract, the vessel's delivery and redelivery, the last voyage, the overlapping/underlapping situations, the key position of the master etc. are some of the matters that are thoroughly presented. The text is enriched with examples of clauses sourced from standard forms of time charterparties; dry and wet.
- Chapter 13 presents two specialised forms of chartering; the *bareboat charter* and the *contract of affreightment (CoA)*. Critical topics of the bareboat charter, such as the vessel, the allocation of obligations and costs, the vessel's commercial operation, the vessel's delivery and redelivery, the manning, the maintenance and repair, the insurance, the hire payment etc., are presented. Then, analysis is focused on the crucial subjects of CoA, such as peculiarities and clauses about the period, the cargo, the vessels, the shipments, the nominations of ports, the charterparty construction, the role of shipbrokers, etc.
- Chapter 14 deals with the practical aspects of *chartering calculations*, concerning different charter forms and vessel types. Initially, the *voyage estimation* principles and stages are examined. Then, focus is placed on various important terms, but above all on the explanation of the *Time Charter Equivalent (TCE)*. Tanker chartering calculation particularities are finally highlighted by following a thorough analysis of *Worldscale*. Practical examples are presented throughout the chapter to enlighten the commercial aspects of chartering and shipbroking business.
- Chapter 15 presents the commercial and practical aspects of *laytime calculations*. The rules and principles of handling time risks are initially presented. Then, emphasis is given on the explanation of terminology, methodology and calculations of laytime, based on the official "*Laytime Definitions 2013*". A comparative analysis of the latest "Laytime Definitions 2013" against the previous "Voylayrules '93" follows. Finally, some practical examples are presented to analytically explain and enlighten the laytime subjects.
- An analytical glossary contains typical *terms and abbreviations*, commonly used in chartering business.

For better cohesion across the whole manuscript, a short *summary* has been inserted at the beginning of each chapter, while *links* and *explanatory references* have been added throughout the text. *Practical examples* have been used to further elaborate the concepts and practices of chartering business where it was considered necessary. At the end of the book, there is an extensive *bibliography* for every reader who wishes to broaden his knowledge in the field of chartering and shipbroking.

After the study of this book, the reader should be able to understand the *fundamentals* in respect of the *commercial practices*, the *economic and financial issues*, the *managerial aspects* and the *legal matters* of shipbroking and chartering business *before, during and after the execution of a vessel's charter*.

SHORT BIOGRAPHIES

Dr. Evi Plomaritou is a Shipping Consultant specialising in Chartering and Shipping Marketing. She undertakes the planning of chartering policy and marketing strategy of shipping companies, as well as the in-company professional training in Greece and abroad. Since 2011, Dr. Plomaritou has been working as a Shipping Consultant for the Lloyd's Maritime Academy (Informa Group). Moreover, since 2008, she has been a Lecturer at the Department of Maritime Studies of Frederick University (Cyprus) teaching Chartering and Commercial Ship Management in the BSc and MSc programmes of study.

In 2001–2008, she worked for the Institute of Chartered Shipbrokers (ICS) providing consulting and training services to shipping practitioners, while she was actively involved with the foundation of the ICS Greek Branch. She has taught at the following institutions: Frederick University (Cyprus), European University (Switzerland), Middlesex University (UK), National & Kapodistrian University of Athens (Greece), University of Piraeus (Greece) etc. Her writing experience includes five books and 14 e-books on the fields of her expertise. In addition, she has had her research published in leading international academic journals and conferences. Furthermore, she has a three-year research experience in maritime projects (funded by the European Commission) at the Research Centre of the University of Piraeus, as well as a nine-month practical experience onboard bulk carriers.

Dr. Plomaritou was awarded with distinction her "PhD in Chartering Policy and Marketing Strategy of Shipping Companies" (University of Piraeus). She holds the "MSc in International Transport" (University of Cardiff, Wales), the "Advanced Diploma in Transport & Logistics" (Chartered Institute of Logistics and Transport, UK) and the "Professional Diploma in Dry Cargo Chartering" (Cambridge Academy of Transport, UK). She has graduated with distinction from the Department of Maritime Studies of the University of Piraeus (BSc in Maritime Business).

Mr. Anthony Papadopoulos has been working for the National Bank of Greece since 2000. For the last ten years he has been serving as Shipping Credit Officer & Senior Shipping Analyst, responsible for the evaluation of all shipping finance proposals and the monitoring of the Bank's entire shipping portfolio in respect of credit risk. Before that, he held other challenging positions in the Bank, being a Shipping Account Officer & Corporate Underwriter in 2000–2006 and a Shipping Loan Administration Officer in 2006–2007, assuming responsibilities related to the management of relations with shipping clients, the submission of financial proposals to the credit committees, the financial statement analysis of shipping companies and the review of loan agreements, ship mortgages and other security documents. Moreover, Mr. Papadopoulos has been an in-house NBG certified instructor on the subject of shipping finance since 2013.

In 1998–2000, he worked as a Post Fixture Officer & Operations Assistant for Danaos Shipping, having tasks related to the freight & hire collection, the post-fixture control, the disbursements accounts, the handling of all financial aspects arising from charterparties and the operational assistance on the managed vessel fleet. In 1997–1998, he worked also as a Chartering Assistant for Zenith Ocean Navigation Ltd. In addition, during 1997–2001, Mr. Papadopoulos collaborated with the University of Piraeus Research Centre as a Scientific Associate in EU international research programmes.

His work has been published in professional international journals and conferences. It is worth noting that Mr. Papadopoulos, together with Dr. E. Plomaritou of Lloyd's Maritime Academy and Professor K. Giziakis of the University of Piraeus, are the authors of the Greek book titled *Chartering* (3rd edition, 2010, reprint 2012, Stamoulis Publications, 1319 pages, with accompanying DVD / 2nd edition 2006 / 1st edition 2002). This has been used as the main academic textbook in the fields of chartering and maritime economics at the University of Piraeus and the University of the Aegean, while it has also been a popular title in the Greek shipping market since 2002.

Mr. Papadopoulos graduated with distinction from the Department of Maritime Studies at the University of Piraeus (1995), he also graduated from the Department of Banking & Financial Management of the same University (2010), while he has obtained his postgraduate degree from the University of Wales, Cardiff, Department of International Transport (MSc in International Transport, 1996).

LIST OF FIGURES

LIST OF TABLES

ACKNOWLEDGEMENTS

In our attempt to complete this work, a valuable support was offered by various parties. It would be an omission if we did not express our sincere thanks to the following people, companies, organisations and professional bodies:

- BIMCO and in particular Mr. Grant Hunter, for their kind permission to reproduce a series of BIMCO documents and the "Laytime Definitions 2013" in an appendix. All these have formed the basis of our commentary in chapters 10, 11, 12, 13 and 15.
- Drewry Shipping Consultants Limited and in particular Ms. Antonia Mitsana, not only for their kind permission to use their market data, but also because we highly appreciate their efforts to create – on a tailor-made and exclusive basis for this edition – the tables which depict the evolution of time charter rates for all major ship types, from 1980 up to 2015. All this information has been included in chapter 2.
- Clarksons Research and Mr. Hashim Abbas, for their kind permission to use their data as the basis of our commentary on market coverage in chapters 1 and 2, as well as for allowing us to reproduce two practical tanker examples in chapter 14.
- The Baltic Exchange and Mr. Bill Lines, for their kind permission to reproduce a dry cargo voyage estimation example as presented in the Baltic Code 2014 and to use that as a basis of our analysis and commentary in chapter 14.
- Worldscale Association (London) Limited and Mr. Ian McCarthy, for their kind permission to present and explain the Worldscale methodology in chapter 14.
- Federation of National Associations of Ship Brokers and Agents (FONASBA) and Mr. Jonathan C. Williams, for their kind permission to include FONASBA Time Charter Interpretation Code 2000 as an appendix.
- Association of Ship Brokers and Agents (USA) Inc. (ASBA) and Ms. Jeanne L. Cardona, for their kind permission to include NYPE 2015 as an appendix.

- Shell International Trading & Shipping Company Limited and Ms. Karen Heslop, for their kind permission to include Shellvoy 6 and Shelltime 4 as appendices.
- International Chamber of Commerce (ICC) and Ms. Marie-Dominique Fraidérik, for their kind permission to let us describe the official Incoterms® rules in chapter 6 and the glossary.
- Simpson Spence & Young (SSY) and Mr. John Kearsey, for their kind permission to reproduce their dry cargo market reports in chapter 3.
- P.F. Bassoe AS, for their kind permission to reproduce their tanker market report in chapter 3.
- Shipping Guides Ltd., Ms. Barbara Forrest and Mr. Tony Gawn, for their kind permission to reproduce a world map of international load line zones and areas in chapter 14.
- UK P&I Club and Mr. Paul Knight, for their kind permission to reproduce a figure about vessels' load lines in chapter 14.
- IHRDC and Ms. Anne Barton, for their kind permission to reproduce a figure about specific gravity and API gravity correlation for different crude oil varieties in chapter 1.

Last but not least, we would like to express our appreciation and gratitude to all our colleagues from the Informa Group. Special thanks are deserved to Mr. Stephen Wrench and Ms. Gina Taylor who first believed in us, Ms. Faye Mousley who initiated this project with great enthusiasm, Ms. Amy Jones and Ms. Caroline Church who then took over the edition of the book and always remained so supportive until final completion, but also to Ms. Zoe Everitt who supervised the smooth production of the book. Finally, it would be an omission to forget Ms. Marie-Louise Roberts from Apex CoVantage, who undertook the technical part of this publication, for her excellent co-operation.

CHAPTER 1

Charter market

Chartering is the part of international shipping business which broadly deals with the proper matching of cargoes' transport needs and vessels' commercial trading. Thus, this chapter starts by presenting in short a few basic definitions in respect of chartering, considered as a prerequisite knowledge to help reading throughout this book. Focus is then turned to the fundamentals of chartering; namely the vessels, the cargoes, the geography and the types of charter, showing how they are placed in the international transport scene to form crucial charter market segments. In respect of the cargoes, emphasis is given on cargo groups schemed according to their physical attributes, handling requirements, types of transport, loading factors etc. Concerning the vessels, analysis examines the various types and sub-segments structured, according to their size and characteristics, cargoes carried, commercial trades and market elements seen from a chartering viewpoint. The last but no less important aspect of charter market analysis concerns the financial element, namely the freight rates which are presented in the subsequent chapter.

1.1 Segmentation of the charter market

This section intends to present how the charter market may be structured according to a variety of criteria. Before proceeding to this type of analysis, a few critical chartering definitions will be presented.

1.1.1 Chartering definitions

A *"charter"* is the agreement for commercial employment of a ship. It is contracted between two involved parties, the *"shipowner"* and the *"charterer"*, the former representing the ship's interests and the latter using the ship's services either for a specific cargo voyage or for a period of time. In exchange for that, the charterer undertakes to pay a financial compensation called *"freight"* or *"hire"* in accordance with the selected type of charter, as described below. The chartering agreement is confirmed by the chartering contract which is called *"charterparty"*. From this short definition of a charter, the type of vessel employment which concerns the provision of liner services may rather be excepted and the reasoning will be clear later on in this chapter (see section 1.1.3).

In order to facilitate the understanding of this book, the reader should always bear in mind that the commercial employment of a vessel may basically be

1

distinguished in four major *"charter types or forms"*[1] (for an in-depth analysis the reader should refer to chapters 7, 11, 12 and 13):

- *Voyage (Spot) Charter:* A short-term type of charter. The shipowner undertakes to carry on his ship a specific cargo quantity between specific ports, in other words for a specific voyage. The charterer is obliged to pay the "freight" which is typically calculated in USD per tonne[2] of cargo carried (see appendix 16 about measurements).
- *Time Charter:* It may be a short, medium or long-term type of charter. The shipowner concedes the use of his ship to the charterer for an agreed period of time. The owner keeps the commercial operation of the vessel (crewing, insurance, repair and maintenance, supplies and stores), whilst the charterer undertakes the commercial employment (except navigation) of the vessel (i.e. nomination of ports, payment of voyage costs etc.). The charterer is obliged to pay the agreed daily "hire" in regular intervals, for example in USD per day, payable every 15 days or monthly in advance.
- *Bareboat or Demise Charter:* It is a medium to long-term type of charter. The shipowner charters the vessel's hull and machinery for an agreed period of time. The charterer undertakes the full control of the ship (crewing, insurance, repair and maintenance, supplies and stores, as well as the commercial employment), as he was the shipowner. The charterer is obliged to pay an agreed daily "hire" in regular intervals to the owner, for example in USD per day, payable every 15 days or monthly in advance. The shipowner undertakes only the vessel's capital cost (for an analytical cost breakdown per type of charter see section 7.6).
- *Contract of Affreightment (CoA):* It is a medium to long-term, hybrid type of charter. The shipowner undertakes to serve charterer's needs by carrying specific quantities of homogeneous cargo, in specific dates and within an agreed period of time (e.g. four shiploads of steam coal per year), in specific voyages, with no determined ship. The charterer usually pays the "freight" in USD per tonne of cargo carried in each executed voyage. It is considered a "hybrid" form of charter.

---

1 Wilson, J. (2010) *Carriage of Goods by Sea* (Pearson Education Ltd, 7th edition, pp. 7–8); Baughen, S. (2015) *Shipping Law* (Routledge-Cavendish, 6th edition, pp. 188–190).

2 To avoid any misunderstanding, it is clarified from the outset that the metric system will be followed throughout this book, except otherwise specified. This is the most widely used system of cargo measurement in everyday chartering practice. It is noted, therefore, that the terms "tonne", "metric tonne", "metric ton", "ton" and the respective abbreviated forms "mt" or "MT" are considered synonyms in the context of this book, expressing the metric measurement. Any reference made to other types of "ton" (e.g. "long ton", "registered ton") is denoted specifically in the text. Finally, it is explained that this book follows the British way of expressing the English language, thus the terms "tonne" or "metric tonne" are preferred in some parts of the text. However, in chartering practice where "time is money", simplified terms often prevail in daily communication, thus the term "metric ton" (which is the American way of expressing the same metric neasurement) is commonly used in chartering negotiations, shipping publications and therefore in other parts of this book.

The term *"charter market"* refers mostly to a common place where various types of charters are fixed, whereas the term *"freight market"* describes the freight rate levels of these fixtures. However, both terms may be interpreted as synonyms in general. The "freight market" or "charter market"[3] may be simply defined as the whole system of freight rate determination by making charter fixtures. The analysis of such a system should comprise four components: the geographical place of the market; the persons and legal entities acting in that; the methodology and business practice of the market; and finally, the rationale of the market, namely the reasoning behind acts, behaviours and processes, as well as the inter-change among persons and conditions within the market. More specifically, the "charter" or "freight" market may be defined as one or all of the following[4]:

- The geographical place where charter fixtures are made, freight rates are determined and sea transport is bought, sold and executed.
- The individuals and the legal entities which, by expressing their different shipping interests and acting in various ways to achieve their goals, they finally interact to *"close fixtures"* (i.e. vessel charters) and form the freight rate levels.
- A system composed of interdependent persons, entities, factors and conditions, which through financial mechanisms and business procedures, leads in making vessel charters and forming the freight rate levels of international sea transport.

Within the shipping business practice, *"chartering"* may be simplistically defined as this act or procedure which deals with vessels' commercial employment, cargoes' international transport and in many times the appropriate matching of them. Furthermore, *"shipbroking"* is the act and the mediating profession which facilitates the business contacts between shipowners and charterers in order vessel charters to be fixed (the role of shipbrokers is analytically presented in section 3.5). From the above, the significance of cargoes and vessels in forming shipping market segments becomes obvious.

1.1.2 Charter market segments

The charter (freight) market is not a uniform market following a single trend. Instead, it consists of a number of different part-markets, which are not necessarily dependent on one another and can often develop very differently. The charter (freight) market does not have a homogeneous connection with a specific

---

3 This book is to interpret those terms as synonyms. However, this chapter focuses on the market segmentation and thus the term "charter market" is mostly preferred, whilst the second chapter deals more with freight rate determination and the state of the markets, so the term "freight market" will be widely used.

4 Giziakis, K., Papadopoulos, A. and Plomaritou, E. (2010) *Chartering* (Athens, Stamoulis Publications, 3rd edition, in Greek, pp. 56–57).

geographical area but rather with ships that can carry similar types of cargo. The trend or state of the market is determined by the balance between the supply and demand of shipping services of various kinds. A measure of the state of the market is the freight rate level which a certain type of vessel can obtain in various standard trades or charter forms. The freight market is dependent on the state of world trade and influenced by a plethora of global factors (see further chapter 2). It should be mentioned also that there is an inter-relation between the new-building market, the second-hand tonnage market and the freight rate level, although these are not synchronised in detail. This also means that, like new-building, scrapping also affects the freight market.

To define shipping markets a small part of the timeless "Rochdale Report" written in 1967 may be quoted as follows: *"Shipping is a complex industry . . . the conditions which govern its operations in one sector do not necessarily apply in another . . . it might even be better regarded as a group of related industries. Its main assets, ships themselves, vary widely in size and type; they provide the whole range of services which are needed to carry passengers and a great variety of goods, whether over shorter or longer distances"*.

The shipping market and the charter market accordingly are constituted of separate segments differentiated as to the type of cargo, the type and size of ship, the trade routes, the type and duration of charter.[5] More specifically:

1. *According to the type of cargo, the charter market may be broadly divided into* the dry bulk cargo markets, the liquid bulk cargo markets, the specialised cargo markets and the general cargo/container markets. Moreover, according to the various kinds of commodities, the above mentioned markets are sub-divided further into sub-categories (see section 1.2).

2. *According to the type of vessel, the charter market may be broadly divided into* the bulk carrier markets, the tanker markets, the gas carrier markets, the chemical carrier markets, the combined carrier markets, the containership markets, the ro/ro markets, the reefer markets, the general cargo vessel markets, the multi-purpose vessel markets, the offshore markets and the specialised vessels markets. Moreover, *according to the size of vessels, the shipping and charter markets are further sub-divided into sub-categories* (see section 1.3).

   Table 1.1 shows that the world cargo fleet consisted of over 58,600 vessels with a total tonnage of about 1.7 billion deadweight tonnes (dwt, see glossary), as of January 2016. Tankers (including chemical tankers) represented about 13,800 units of 548 m. dwt accounting for 32% of the total cargo tonnage. About 7,700 units of these tankers were smaller than 10,000 dwt in size. Bulkers represented about 10,700 units of 776 m. dwt, accounting for 45% of the world cargo tonnage.

5 Giziakis, K., Papadopoulos, A. and Plomaritou, E. (2010) *Chartering* (Athens, Stamoulis Publications, 3rd edition, in Greek, p. 57).

Table 1.1 World Cargo Fleet

Total Cargo Fleet	*Vessels (01.01.2016)*	
	No.	*m. dwt*
Oil Tankers > 10k dwt	4,510	490.1
Oil Tankers < 10k dwt	5,063	13.3
Chemical Tankers	3,521	40.7
Other Tankers	673	3.6
Bulkers	10,662	776.1
Combos	19	2.8
LPGs	1,341	19.4
LNGs	443	35.0
Containerships	5,249	244.3
Multi-Purpose	3,211	29.3
General Cargo	14,292	31.6
Ro-Ro	1,271	7.7
Car Carriers	785	12.4
Reefers	1,401	5.0
Offshore (AHTS/PSV)	5,430	10.0
Other Cargo	772	5.9
Total World Cargo Fleet	*58,643*	*1,727.2*

Source: Clarksons Research, *Shipping Intelligence Weekly* (8 January 2016)

There were also almost 5,250 containerships of 19.7 m. TEU[6] or 244 m. dwt, amounting to 14% of the total capacity in tonnage terms. Gas carriers amounted to almost 1,800 vessels of a small percentage in tonnage terms, as their cargo carrying capacity is commonly measured in volume terms (cubic metres). Apart from pure bulk carriers and containerships, there are also other types of vessels carrying dry cargoes (multi-purpose, general cargo, ro/ro, car carriers and reefers) which amounted to almost 21,000 vessels of 86 m. dwt collectively as per January 2016. Finally, over 5,400 vessels of 10 m. dwt were activating in the offshore market (this number includes only AHTS and PSVs which support the offshore market, but excludes platforms, drillships and other types of vessels used for oil extraction). All numbers were mentioned only to show an indication of the world cargo fleet breakdown at a specific moment in time, not for a current market update. Regarding that, the contribution of expert market data providers should always be sought.

3. *According to the type of trade routes, the charter market may be divided geographically into* many segments, for example the Black

---

6 TEU: Twenty-foot Equivalent Unit is the cargo carrying capacity measure for containerships. It practically shows how many containers equivalent to the standard 20-foot box can be carried by a containership. A TEU is equivalent to one 20-foot shipping container. Thus, a 40-foot container is equal to two TEUs.

Sea – Mediterranean Sea suezmax tankers market, the Pacific or the Atlantic basin capesize market etc.

4. *According to the type and duration of charter, the charter market may be generally divided into* the voyage charter or spot market, the time charter market, the bareboat charter market, as well as other hybrid charter forms such as the contract of affreightment, the trip time charter and the consecutive voyages markets.

The type of ship and the type of cargo could be named as the fundamental criteria of charter (freight) market segmentation because ship and cargo are the "major players" in every commercial sea transport. Trade routes and types of charter could be defined as the complementary or secondary or determinative criteria of charter (freight) market segmentation as their meaning is explanatory, constituting the basis for sub-apportionment of every main market segment ensued from the fundamental criteria. For example, if someone refers to the Mediterranean market, this by itself is not sufficient to lend meaning and to determine a market section with common characteristics. A meaning may be obtained only if the secondary distinction is referred to as determinative factor for some of the sections ensuing from the fundamental distinctions, for example the Med Sea feeder containership market. At this point, it should be noted that the two fundamental criteria do not operate cumulatively in forming the market segments. What happens in practice is that a group of cargoes is transported by one or some categories of ships, or vice versa, it may also be said that a ship market usually services one or some cargo markets.

Within each charter market segment the transportation requirements of charterers and shippers, as well as the vessel particulars, present common or similar characteristics. Furthermore, each market segment has different interested parties (shipowners, charterers, shippers, brokers, agents, etc.) and thus separate networks or channels of information. Contact and interchange among the different markets may be more or less extensive depending on the type and size of ships (how specialised or versatile they are), the commodities involved, the distance of transportation and the type of vessel's employment.

Charter market segmentation may be depicted in Table 1.2 below. It is a simplified mind-map attempting to show the trading matching between the fundamental types of cargoes and vessels, as well as the orientation of each major segment in broad terms (i.e. bulkers are cost-oriented, tankers are safety-oriented and liner market is quality-oriented). In addition, it must be noted that the last right column describes various charter types and the last bottom line shows different examples of vessels' geographical trading. All types of charter and all types of trading may apply to all types of vessels and cargoes without any limitation.

In every market segment the transportation needs, requirements and behaviours of charterers and shippers present some common characteristics. A necessary precondition for the commercial success of a shipping company is the understanding of the different needs the charterers-shippers have in the market segments. Shipping companies ought to adjust their chartering policy and marketing strategy in accordance with those needs. This subject is analysed in chapter 5.

Table 1.2 Segmentation of the Charter Market

Type of Vessel ↓	Dry Bulk	Liquid Bulk	General Cargo/ Containers	Special Cargo	Type of Cargo ←
Bulk Carriers	C				Voyage (Spot) Charter
Tankers		S			Consecutive Voyages
LPG, LNG Carriers		S			Trip Time Charter
Chemical Vessels		S			Contract of Affreightment
Containerships			Q		
RO/RO & LO/LO Vessels			Q	Q	Round Voyage Time Charter
Multi-purpose Vessels	C		Q	Q	
Reefer Vessels			Q	Q	Time Charter
Specialised Vessels				Q	
Combined Carriers	C	S			Bareboat Charter
Type of Trade →	Global	Regional	Local/Short Sea	Specific	↑ Type of Charter

Q: Quality Oriented Market   C: Cost Oriented Market   S: Safety Oriented Market

1.1.3 Bulk shipping v liner shipping

Fundamental is also the segmentation of the shipping market into two major shipping industrial segments; the bulk shipping industry and the liner shipping industry. The segmentation criterion used is the size of the cargo consignment transported by sea. Consequently, the bulk shipping industry transports ship-sized parcels of homogeneous cargoes transported in bulk (see section 1.2.1) while the liner shipping industry transports small general cargo parcels that have to be grouped for shipment to be carried in containers (see section 1.2.2). The main differences between the liner and bulk or tramp[7] markets are the following[8]:

- *The employment of ships:* Bulk (tramp) vessels may be employed in almost any geographical area depending on the demand for sea transport.

---

7 The term "bulk" describes the nature of the cargo carried, whilst the term "tramp" refers to the way of finding vessel's employment, i.e. vessel's trading worldwide to serve demand requests. The terms have similar meaning and are considered synonyms, but the word "bulk" is preferable throughout this book.

8 Giziakis, K., Papadopoulos, A. and Plomaritou, E. (2010) *Chartering* (Athens, Stamoulis Publications, 3rd edition, in Greek, pp. 46–47).

Liner vessels are employed in predetermined routes (lines) among specific ports with fixed timetable schedules of sailings and arrivals.

- *Charter types and contracts:* Liner companies typically own some vessels, but also charter-in ships owned to independent shipowners, on a period charter basis (e.g. time or bareboat charter). Liner vessels work on a "common carrier basis", i.e. various cargoes are booked by many shippers to be carried (typically in a containership) at the same time by one ship. *"Cargo bookings"* are made through an extensive liner agency network. In other words, liner operators may charter-in ships based on charterparty agreements, they book cargoes in accordance with booking note terms, and cargoes are carried in accordance with bill of lading terms. In bulk shipping, there is a great variety of all charter types and contracts, such as spot charters, time charters, bareboat charters, hybrid charter forms etc. Vessel chartering is made through shipbrokers' networks. It may be said that the contract of carriage in bulk shipping is mainly the charterparty, while the contract of carriage in liner shipping is the bill of lading (see appendices 1–2, 4–11, 13–14).

- *The type of cargo:* The cargoes of bulk shipping are mainly big parcels (over 2,000–3,000 tonnes) which are sufficiently large to fill a whole ship or hold. Such cargoes may be dry, liquid or specialised bulks. The cargoes of liner shipping are basically small parcels (under 2,000–3,000 tonnes) which are not sufficiently large to fill a whole ship or hold. Liner vessels carry the general cargoes, main types of which are the containers, the loose (break-bulk) cargo, the pallets, the pre-slung, the wheeled cargoes etc.

- *The kind of carriage:* Bulk shipping industry provides transport for ship-loads of cargo on "one ship, one cargo" basis, while the liner shipping industry provides transport for small cargo parcels on "common carrier" basis.

- *The type of vessels:* Bulk fleet mainly includes bulk carriers, tankers, gas carriers, combined carriers and specialised bulk vessels (e.g. cement carriers, chemical tankers etc.). Bulk fleet provides transport for bulk cargoes. Liner fleet is mainly composed of pure containerships. However, there is a variety of other vessel types, such as multi-purpose vessels, car carriers, ro/ro and lo/lo, reefers, con-bulkers etc. which can trade either in liner or in tramp services. Liner fleet provides transport for general cargoes.

- *The freight:* In bulk shipping the freight is negotiable between the parties depending mostly on the supply and demand of vessels and therefore on the prevailing general state of the market, as well as on individual conditions of each charter. In liner shipping the freight paid for the carriage of a container is more or less predetermined by fixed methods of pricing. Liner traffic is a firmly controlled business where remuneration is geared more to the long term than to single voyages. The freight rates in the pricing tables are by definition not subject to the large variations

and fluctuations that characterise the so-called open market.[9] Nevertheless, liner traffic is susceptible to market variations, depending on market competition, availability of cargo and load factors on each voyage,
where:

$$\text{Load Factor} = \frac{\text{Loaded Cubic Capacity}}{\text{Available Cubic Capacity}} \times 100(\%)$$

The load factor indicates how much of the available cubic capacity of a
container and the whole containership is made use of. Even though the
liner market has nowadays been concentrated around very few major
shipping alliances, it must be stressed that by law alliance members are
not permitted to jointly set freight rates or share profits, but only to co-
operate in providing shipping services.

- *The type of market:* Liner market may be characterised as a competitive market with strong elements of oligopoly (oligopolistic competition) and high concentration of ownership and operation, while the bulk
  market may be characterised in general as an almost perfectly competitive market with more dispersed ownership. As an indicative example, in 2015 the top-25 liner operators owned around 43% of the world
  liner fleet in TEU terms but, if charter-in capacity had been added, they
  seemed to control/operate more than 90% of the global TEU capacity.
  Further to that, the top-25 independent containership owners (so-called
  "charter owners") owned around 29% of the world liner fleet in TEU
  terms. On the other hand, in bulk carriers market, there are many owners
  around the globe (e.g. the top-30 owned almost 26% of the total bulkers
  fleet in dwt terms in 2015). Finally, in tankers market, the top-30 independent shipowners (excluding government fleets) owned almost 35%
  of the total tankers fleet in dwt terms in 2015.[10]
- *The seeking of cargo, the type of charter and the chartering business:*
  In bulk shipping the fixture of charter is carried out by the shipbrokers
  through the chartering investigation and negotiation stages (see chapter 8). In liner shipping the seeking of cargo is fulfilled by the cargo
  canvassers (e.g. liner agents or freight forwarders) through the adver-
  tisement of schedules, ports and dates of arrivals and departures of
  liner vessels. Liner vessels get the larger share of their cargo through
  an extensive network of liner agents, which either form subsidiaries
  of a holding company of the liner group, or are individual agencies

---

9 In the context of this book, open market is meant to include all the chartering procedures,
people and places where vessels are chartered through brokers' channels. Therefore, it may be interpreted as comprising the bulk market and the part of the liner market which refers to vessels' charters
by independent shipowners to liner companies, whereas excluding the part of the liner market which
refers to the provision of vessels' liner services through cargo bookings

10 Clarksons Research, *Shipping Review & Outlook* (Autumn 2015, pp. 160–162), www.
alphaliner.com/top100 (accessed 19 June 2015).

contracted to work (as exclusive agents or not) representing geographically a liner company or an alliance. Sometimes, a liner company may also book part-cargoes or special commodities just to fill empty space. This may be done on charterparty terms through broker connections in the open market. Imbalances in cargo volumes between the outward and homeward legs of a round voyage often make the lines competitors with the multi-purpose, con-bulker, ro/ro, reefer or other tonnage working in the open market at the same geographical areas.

- *The type of ownership/management:* Bulk vessels are privately-owned or publicly-owned carriers chartered for a particular period or a cargo voyage, by clients who are called charterers. The ships are usually individually contracted under negotiated terms which are set down in the charterparty. A simple structure of a bulk shipping group, either a public or a private one, contains typically the single-ship owning companies (each shipowning company has only one ship as main asset), the owned managing company which manages the owned/operated fleet and possibly a holding company which holds the shares of the shipowning companies (see chapter 4). On the other hand, the typical liner service requires the use of several vessels for providing a wide coverage of regular services. This type of service is typically operated by "alliances" of liner companies.[11] They pool their shipping resources to provide a jointly operated liner service, however they must not set common prices. The vessels may be under a single owner or under common ownership. It must be said that liner shipping was always a controlled shipping business. In the past the market was structured around the so-called "liner conferences" or "rate agreements" which formed types of cartel or monopoly for particular liner trades. Today, due to strong anti-monopolistic policies in the USA and Europe, the liner market is organised with other forms of market control and consolidation, arising from mergers and acquisitions, takeovers, alliances, freight pools, consortiums etc. Strategically, some liner operators decide to charter-in vessels from independent shipowners, against preferring a 100% owned fleet policy. Shipowning and chartering policy of liners may be determined by various reasons, for example the financial results of the company, a possible need of increasing liquidity or repaying part of a heavy debt by selling owned fleet and chartering-back vessels, liner service needs and shippers' requirements, prevailing and forecasted freight rates, sale and charter back or charter-in opportunities, etc. Finally, liner companies are usually publicly listed mega-carriers offering integrated, door-to-door logistics services to their clients. Liner operators are usually more involved than other shipowners in the improvement of cargo-handling

---

11 It is worth knowing that global carriers had mutated into four big alliances composed as follows in 2015 (Lloyd's List, 9.3.2015): "2M" (Maersk, MSC), "Ocean Three" (CMA CGM, UASC, China Shipping), "G6" (Hapag Lloyd, APL, HMM, MOL, NYK, OOCL) and "CKYHE" (COSCO, "K" Line, Yang Ming, Hanjin, Evergreen).

techniques and they often participate actively in developing those ports at which they call regularly (particularly their hub ports).

Up to this point it must have been clear that bulk and liner markets differ greatly and structurally. From a chartering and shipbroking perspective, bulk shipping is far more significant than liner. The following sections of this chapter will attempt to familiarise the reader with the most known cargoes, vessels and respective market segments, since this is a fundamental knowledge when speaking about chartering and shipbroking matters.

1.2 Cargoes

This section describes the predominant cargoes carried by the bulk and liner fleet. Bulk cargo is any cargo that is transported by sea in bulk and in large consignments so as to reduce the unit cost of transport due to economies of scale. Most often only one bulk cargo is carried at a time, although some ships can carry various bulk cargoes in different holds or on different legs of a voyage. General cargo concerns smaller quantities of various cargoes. These are shipped together either in containers or on pallets, in bales, or some other method of assembly (unitisation). The goal is common, to achieve reduced unit cost of transport through economies of scale, however the means is different, as in the carriage of general cargo economies of scale are achieved through the cargo unitisation.

1.2.1 Bulk cargoes

Bulk cargo (a big parcel over 2,000–3,000 tonnes) is any individual cargo consignment which is sufficiently large to fill a whole ship or a hold of a vessel and for that reason it is transported in bulk.[12] There are three main categories of bulk cargoes. The first one includes the dry bulk cargoes, the second one includes the liquid bulk cargoes and the last one includes the specialised bulk cargoes. Most of the bulk cargoes concern the major raw material, energy and food trades, such as oil, iron ore, coal, grain, gas etc. These cargoes may be described as bulk cargoes on the assumption that most of them are shipped in bulk. The bulk cargoes are transported by suitable vessels of the bulk fleet. Generally speaking, the dry bulk cargoes are transported by the bulk carriers, the liquid bulk cargoes (including gas) are transported by the tankers and gas carriers and the specialised bulk cargoes are transported by specialised ships. The bulk fleet is employed in the bulk shipping industry, which provides transport for ship loads of cargo "*on one ship-one cargo basis*". The most important categories of bulk cargo are[13]:

- The "*five major dry bulks*": It covers the most important five homogeneous bulk cargoes – iron ore, coal, grain, phosphates and bauxite/alumina – which can be transported satisfactorily in a conventional dry bulk carrier

---

12 Stopford, M. (2009) *Maritime Economics* (London, Routledge Publications, 3rd edition, p. 419).
13 Stopford, M. (2009) *Maritime Economics* (London, Routledge Publications, 3rd edition, p. 64).

or a multi-purpose vessel. Iron ore and coal form almost two-thirds of the globally dry bulk market and China has been the largest influencer.

- *Minor dry bulks:* It concerns a great number of various industrial and agricultural materials that travel in shiploads. The most important types of minor bulks are steel products, sugar, salt, gypsum, non-ferrous metal ores etc. They are transported either by bulk carriers or multi-purpose vessels in bulk, or by liner vessels in modes of unitised transport (e.g. containers, bags, pallets, sacks etc.).
- *Major liquid bulks:* It includes the crude oil, oil products, liquefied natural gas, liquefied petroleum gas and liquid chemicals such as caustic soda, ammonia, phosphoric acid etc. The size of individual consignments varies from a few thousand tonnes up to almost half a million tonnes in the case of crude oil. They are carried in crude or product tankers or gas carriers or chemical tankers.
- *Minor liquid bulks:* It includes all other liquid bulk cargoes such as wine, vegetable oil, water etc. They are carried in small size or specialised tankers.
- *Specialised bulk or neobulk cargoes:* This refers to any bulk cargoes with specific handling or storage requirements. Steel products, refrigerated cargo, cement, cars and special heavy cargo, for example a prefabricated building, fall into this category. They are carried by specialised bulk vessels, such as reefers, cement carriers, car carriers, heavy lift vessels or by containerships in liner trades.

1.2.2 General cargoes

General cargo (a small parcel under 2,000–3,000 tonnes) is any individual cargo consignment which is not sufficiently large to fill a whole ship or a hold of a vessel and therefore, too small to justify setting up a bulk shipping operation.[14] In addition, there are often high-value or delicate cargoes that require a special shipping service and for which the shipper requires an almost fixed price of transport rather than a fluctuating freight market rate. The main categories of general cargoes are the containerised cargo, the loose or break-bulk cargo, the palletised cargo, the pre-slung cargo and the heavy cargo. General cargo, either loose or unitised, is transported by liner vessels which offer regular transport schedules. The general cargoes are transported by fully cellular containerships (FCC) as well as the suitable vessels of the wider liner fleet which comprise the conventional general cargo vessels, the multi-purpose vessels (MPP), or even other types that may be employed occasionally in the liner trades, such as the con-bulkers, the vehicle carriers, the roll-on/roll-off vessels (ro/ro), the reefers and the barge/heavy lift vessels.

The liner fleet is employed in the liner shipping industry, which provides transport for ship loads of cargo *"on a common carrier basis"*.[15] The liner fleet

---

14 Stopford, M. (2009) *Maritime Economics* (London, Routledge Publications, 3rd edition, pp. 36, 41).

15 Many shippers carry their cargoes at the same time on the same ship (common carrier).

transports small parcels of general cargo (which includes manufactured and semi-manufactured goods) as well as many small quantities of bulk commodities (such as malting barley, steel products, non-ferrous metal ores). Because there are so many parcels to handle on each voyage, this is a very organisation-intensive business. In addition, the transport leg often forms part of an integrated production operation, so speed, reliability and high service levels are important (see section 5.1.3). However, cost is also important because the whole business philosophy of international manufacturing depends on cheap transport. With so many transactions, the business relies on published prices, though nowadays prices are generally negotiated with major customers as part of a service agreement. The main categories of general cargo are[16]:

- *Containerised cargo:* The standard boxes, usually 8 feet wide, 8 feet 6 inches high and 20, 30, or 40 feet long, filled with cargo. This is the dominating form of general cargo transport currently. It must be stressed that the variety of container types is very extensive. For example, some of the most popular types are the dry cargo containers, the reefer containers, the "open tops", "flat racks", "high cubes" etc.
- *Loose or break-bulk cargo:* Non-unitised individual items, such as boxes, bags, sacks, pieces of machinery etc., each of which to be handled and stowed separately. All general cargo used to be shipped this way in the past, but now almost all has been unitised in one way or another.
- *Palletised cargo:* Cargo packed onto a pallet for stacking and handling.
- *Heavy and awkward cargo:* Large cargo, difficult to stow.
- *Liquid cargo:* It travels in liquid containers, deep tanks, drums etc.
- *Refrigerated cargo:* Perishable goods that must be shipped, chilled or frozen, in insulated holds of specialised ships called "reefer vessels" or in refrigerated containers on board containerships.
- *Pre-slung cargo:* Small items such as planks of wood lashed together into standard-sized packages.

Table 1.3 presents a snapshot of the world seaborne trade breakdown for the most important commodities in 2014. It is only to show an indication, not a current update.

1.2.3 Factors affecting whether a cargo is suitable for bulk or liner shipment

The factors which affect whether a cargo is suitable for bulk or liner shipment are[17]:

- Volume: Many commodities travel partly in bulk and partly as general cargo. For example, 50,000 tonnes of sugar would be carried in bulk

---

16 Stopford, M. (2009) *Maritime Economics* (London, Routledge Publications, 3rd edition, p. 65).

17 Plomaritou, E. (2015) *Vessels and Voyage Operations* (London, Lloyd's Maritime Academy, Module 2 of Distance Learning Course "Certificate in Ship Operations", p. 40).

Table 1.3 World Seaborne Trade

Cargo		2014 (in mil. tonnes)
Iron Ore		1,337
Coal	Coking (Metallurgical)	262
	Steam (Thermal)	950
Grain		432
Bauxite/Alumina		105
Phosphate Rock		30
Minor Bulk		1,434
Container		1,631
Other Dry		969
Total Dry		*7,150*
Crude Oil		1,799
Oil Products		994
Total Oil		*2,793*
Gas	LPG	71
	LNG	248
Chemical		264
Grand Total		*10,527*

Source: Clarksons Research, *Shipping Review & Outlook*, (Autumn 2015, p. 113)

with a bulk carrier, but 500 tonnes of sugar might be carried in sacks with a general cargo vessel.

- Handling: Several aspects of the cargo are important, such as its handling and stowage characteristics, its susceptibility to damage and some special requirements from the vessel (for example low temperature, high pressure, corrosion resistance etc.).
- Seasonality: Some cargoes are seasonal (e.g. grain, sugar etc.) due to the fact that their production depends on each year's harvest. For example, the sugar trade may be carried out either in containers or bags or sacks by liner vessels or in bulk by tramp vessels, depending on varying needs of shippers, pattern of trade, vessels' availability, freight rate levels etc.
- State of the market and expectations of the parties for the market.

1.2.4 Loading factors for dry and liquid bulks

The *stowage factor* (*s.f.*) is a crucial term for dry bulk and specialised bulk cargo stowage and handling operations. It is the ratio of a cargo's volume (cubic) measurement to its weight, expressed in cubic feet per long ton of 2,240 lb or cubic metres per metric tonne. It shows how much space a metric tonne or a long ton of a particular type of cargo occupies in a hold of a cargo ship. The stowage factor is used in conjunction with a ship's grain or bale capacities, as well as with a proper allowance for broken stowage and dunnage, to determine the total quantity of cargo which can be loaded and how it should be stowed (see chapter 14 and glossary). While most commonly used for dry bulk cargoes, stowage factor can also be calculated for liquid bulk cargoes and other commodities such as containers or cars.

Table 1.4 presents indicatively the stowage factors of main types of cargoes. It may be seen that iron ore cargoes are the heaviest of all quoted ones, therefore having by far the smallest stowage factors in the table, whereas bulky and/or light cargoes, such as cork, pulpwood, woodchips or cars, require much higher volume in relation to their weight to get stowed.[18] The following conversion factors should always be remembered (see also appendix 16 and glossary):

- 1 cubic foot per long ton = 0.02788 cubic metres per tonne
- 1 cubic metre per tonne = 35.88 cubic feet per long ton

On the other hand, liquids fill the tank into which they are put. For this reason, liquid cargoes which are generally handled and loaded in bulk are typically described by *"specific gravity"* (abbrev: s.g., synonym: relative density) and not by stowage factor. The specific gravity of liquids is defined as a dimensionless

Table 1.4 Stowage Factors of Important Cargoes

Commodity	cub. ft/long ton	cub. mt/metric tonne
Asphalt (bulk)	33–36	0.94–0.98
Bauxite (bulk)	25–31	0.70–0.85
Cement (bulk)	20–36	0.60–1.00
Coal (bulk)	38–50	1.08–1.39
Coke (bulk)	45–65	1.25–1.80
Cork (pressed bales)	200	5.57
Fertilizers (bags)	50–60	1.39–1.67
Grain – Barley (bulk)	48–54	1.34–1.50
Grain – Barley (bags)	52–60	1.45–1.67
Grain – Wheat (bulk)	45–50	1.25–1.39
Grain – Wheat (bags)	48–53	1.34–1.48
Grain (heavy)	45	1.30
Iron Ore (bulk)	14	0.40
Iron, Pig (bulk)	10–12	0.28–0.33
Pulpwood (average)	120–150	3.34–4.18
Salt	29–40	0.81–1.12
Wood Chips	110–160	3.07–4.46
Containers (TEU)	56–105	1.6–3.0
Cars	150	4.2
Light Crude Oil	37.6	1.07
Heavy Crude Oil	33.7	0.95
Water	35.3	1

18 Rankin, K. (1995) *Thomas' Stowage: The Properties and Stowage of Cargoes* (pp. 125–350); Alderton, P. (1984) *Sea Transport: Operations and Economics* (Thomas Reed Publications, p. 238); Giziakis, K., Papadopoulos, A. and Plomaritou, E. (2010) *Chartering* (Athens, Stamoulis Publications, 3rd edition, in Greek, pp. 575–576).

unit which is the ratio of density of a liquid material to the density of water at a given temperature (4° C or 39.2° F), where density is defined as the material's mass per unit volume and is measured in kg/m³. After mathematical inferences, specific gravity is defined also as the ratio of the weight of a liquid to its cubic capacity. Therefore, in shipping terms, the fluid's volume to be carried can be calculated using the specific gravity of the fluid and the weight. Conversely, the weight of the cargo can be calculated if the volume and the specific gravity are known. Specific gravity is unique to every fluid material and has a very wide range of application.[19]

It is important to note further that crude oil's density is an important measure of its overall quality, as lighter oils are generally easier to refine than heavy oils, therefore tending to have higher value. Even though oil density is sometimes expressed in terms of its specific gravity, more often it is given as API gravity. As it was mentioned, the specific gravity of a liquid is defined as the density of that liquid divided by the density of fresh water. Fresh water has a density of 62.4 pounds per cubic foot. Therefore, for example, an oil variety with a density of 53 pounds per cubic foot would have a specific gravity of 0.85 (53/62.4). Fresh water, by definition, has a specific gravity of 1.0. The American Petroleum Institute (API) has developed a special measure that expresses oil density in terms of *API gravity* (*API degrees or °API*) which is related to the specific gravity as follows[20]:

$$S.G. = 141.5 / (131.5 + °API)$$
or
$$°API = (141.5 / S.G.) - 131.5$$

From these relationships, it is determined that fresh water, with a specific gravity of 1.0, has an API gravity of 10 degrees, while our 0.85 S.G. oil above has an API gravity of 35 degrees; almost all crude oils are lighter than water and so they will have higher API gravities. Figure 1.1 shows the correlation between specific gravity and API gravity for various crude oil and condensate samples, namely crude oils from different fields, such as Lagunillas (Venezuela), Prudhoe Bay (Alaska), Ghawar (Saudi Arabia), Ninian (offshore UK), and the very light condensate produced from the Arun Field (Indonesia) which has higher °API therefore higher quality.

1.3 Vessels

This section goes further to examine the most common vessel types, used either in bulk or liner transport.

1.3.1 Bulk carriers

The bulk carrier is a ship specifically designed to transport quantities of bulk cargoes such as iron ore, coal, grain, steel products, sugar etc. Cargo carrying capacity

---

19 www.calculator.org (accessed 31 June 2015).
20 www.ihrdc.com (accessed 20 May 2015).

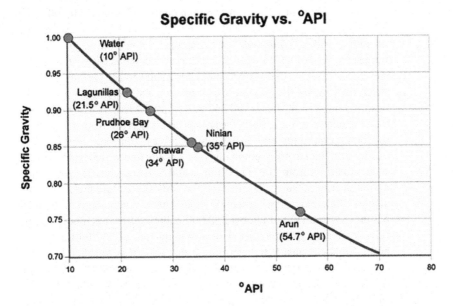

Figure 1.1 Specific Gravity and API Gravity Correlation for Crude Oil Varieties
Courtesy of IHRDC (www.ihrdc.com, accessed 20 May 2015).

varies from about 1,000 to over 400,000 dwt, trading worldwide. Although a division into size-classes cannot be very distinct, there are certain differences which are recognised in day-to-day market discussions.

According to the size of bulkers, the following sub-segments may be distinguished:

- *Capesize:* Gearless bulk carriers of 100,000 to over 400,000 dwt. They carry iron ore in long-haul transportation on routes such as Brazil or Australia to China, as well as coal on various long-haul routes. Due to their size, they are not able to pass through the Panama Canal, therefore they sail round the "Cape of Good Hope" or "Cape Horn", taking their name from that. In the daily communication brokers sometimes use subdivisions for this class, like *"Small Capes"* for the capacity up to 150,000 dwt, *"Normal Capes"* for ships of 160,000–180,000 dwt, *"Large Capes"* for capacities over 180,000 dwt, *"Wozmax"* vessels of around 250,000–260,000 dwt,[21] reserving *"Very Large Bulk Carriers"* (*VLBC*) or *"Very Large Ore Carriers"* (*VLOC*) for sizes above 200,000 dwt in general. Some types are named from the ports they mainly serve, such as *"Newcastlemax"* of around 200,000–210,000 dwt because they serve the port of Newcastle in Australia, *"Dunkirkmax"* of around 175,000

---

21 Clarksons Research, *Shipping Intelligence Network* (accessed 7 April 2015).

dwt for Dunkirk in France and "*Setouchmax*" of around 205,000 dwt which serve the ports of Setouch Sea in Japan. The largest capesizes are nowadays called "*Chinamax*" or "*Valemax*". Their deadweight tonnage ranges from 380,000 to over 400,000 dwt. Chinamax is a standard of ship measurements that allows conforming ships to use various harbours when fully laden, the maximum size of such a ship being 24 m. (79 ft.) draft, 65 m. (213 ft.) beam and 360 m. (1,180 ft.) length. The Chinamax name is related to these port restrictions and is derived from the massive dry-bulk (ore) shipments that China receives from around the globe.

The Brazilian iron ore company Vale was the first which gradually put orders (starting from 2008) in Chinese and S. Korean yards for building a total fleet of 35 such vessels, therefore this size is commonly referred also as "Valemax" type. Valemax vessels have seven cargo holds with a total gross volume of almost 220,000 cubic metres. Each hold can be fully loaded by a shiploader with a loading rate of 13,500 tonnes per hour. The space inside the cargo hold that cannot be reached by grabs during discharging, the so-called "dead spots", is minimised. With a deadweight tonnage of 400,000 tonnes, a fully laden Valemax vessel is carrying as much iron ore as around 11,150 trucks. These ships have a service speed of around 15 knots while burning almost 100 tonnes of heavy fuel oil per day. Due to the large size of the vessels the emissions per cargo ton-mile are very low and the vessels are among the most efficient long-distance dry bulk carriers in service. Valemax use was extremely controversial and subject to heavy criticism, as it was blamed for "killing" the already oversupplied dry cargo market, driving down further the freight rates, thus prolonging the shipping market depression which started after the global financial crisis in the last financial quarter of 2008, consequently stalling the freight recovery.

- *Panamax:* Bulk carriers of 60–65,000 to 100,000 dwt, most of them gearless except some of the older and smaller ones which are geared. They are mainly used for transporting coal, grain, iron ore and minor bulks. "Panamax bulkers" means vessels representing the largest vessels' measurements allowed in length, beam and draught for passage through the Panama Canal in loaded condition. The size of the canal locks determines the maximum size of a ship that can pass through them. Because of the importance of the canal to international trade, many ships are built to the maximum size allowed. For many years, the typical deadweight range for a panamax bulker was up to 80,000 dwt and concentrated within the 68,000–76,000 dwt bracket, whilst its actual cargo capacity was restricted to about 52,500 tonnes because of the 12.1 m. (39.6 ft.) draft restrictions within the old locks of the canal. The largest ship ever transited the old locks of the canal was an Ore/Bulk/Oil (OBO) vessel 296.6 m. (973 ft.) long and 32.3 m. (106 ft.) wide, comparing with locks' width of 33.5 m (110.0 ft.). Besides, in the last decade, the so-called "Kamsarmax" vessels of 80,000–90,000 dwt

18

were built, which have also the proper dimensions for passage through the old locks of the Panama Canal and thus included in this segment of the analysis. These ships serve the bauxite exporting trade from the port Kamsar in Guinea of West Africa, taking their name from that.

For many years, bulkers' sizes of 90,000–130,000 dwt used to be called *"Post-Panamax"* or *"Over-Panamax"* or *"Mini-Capes"* and formed an interim category between typical panamax/kamsarmax and capesize vessels. Their role was somewhat restricted in the market place, however it will get increased in the future after the completion of expansion works in the Panama Canal, as these vessels will then be able to cross the passage. After the construction of a third lane of locks in 2016, which is wider, longer and deeper than the two old ones still working alongside, bulk carriers of up to 130,000 dwt are now able to cross the Canal. Except from changes in vessel sizes, the Panama Canal expansion is expected to bring about major alterations in cargo shiploads, vessel trade routes etc.

- *Ultramax or Supramax or Super-handymax:* Vessels of 50,000–65,000 dwt, almost all of them geared. They carry grain, coal, minor bulks, phosphates, bauxite/alumina etc. on medium-haul routes. Vessels of around 60,000–65,000 dwt are usually called *"Ultramax"* and vessels of 50,000–60,000 dwt *"Supramax"* or *"Super-Handymax"*.
- *Handymax:* Vessels of 35–40,000 to 50,000 dwt, typically geared. They carry grain, coal, minor bulks, phosphates, bauxite/alumina etc. trading worldwide, usually on relatively short- or medium-haul routes. Larger vessels of this category compete for cargoes with supramaxes, whilst smaller ones compete with handies.
- *Handysize:* Vessels of 20,000 up to 35–40,000 dwt, most of them geared, trading worldwide, usually on relatively short-haul routes. They principally carry a wide range of minor bulks and smaller quantities of grain, phosphates, bauxite/alumina etc. Many vessels are properly equipped to transport specialised cargoes, such as logs, woodchips and cement.
- *Small bulkers:* Vessels of 300–20,000 dwt, geared or gearless. They carry minor bulks, grain etc. Within this category, the smaller vessels (300–3,000 dwt) serve coastal and/or short sea trades, therefore they are called *"coasters"* or *"short sea traders"*.

Although generalisations should be avoided in the dynamic environment of the shipping markets, the following *financial characteristics of the bulk carriers' market* may be distinguished:

- The structure of the market almost follows the perfect competition principles in most sub-markets (the target is profit maximisation for both shipowners and charterers, no party may affect the market, great number of market players exists, transport service is uniform with little margins of differentiation, few barriers to entry and exit, participants are well-informed about market developments, emphasis is on cost control etc.).

- The larger the vessels:

  ○ the more barriers to entry exist and the "players" are (i.e. shipowners and operators, charterers, brokers);
  ○ the higher is the sensitivity/volatility of freight rates and vessels' values to the economic cycles;
  ○ the less easily liquidated the vessels are.

- Concentration of ownership is relatively low.
- There is a great number of players (owners, charterers, brokers, agents etc.) located worldwide.
- Vessels are trading worldwide wherever employment opportunities arise.
- A great variety of charterparty contracts exists.

Bulk carriers can also be used for the transportation of unitised cargoes of various kinds, like paper and pulp, logs, woodchip, containers etc. A type of bulk carrier which is able to carry both bulk cargoes in the holds as well as containers is called *"con-bulker"* (10,000–60,000 dwt). A bulk carrier equipped with fixed or portable upright stanchions and lashing points to allow logs to be loaded on deck is called *"log-fitted bulk carrier"* (10,000–60,000 dwt). *"Lumber Carriers"* are similarly able to carry packaged wood products (boards, sheets, plywoods, planks) in their specially designed holds, which are box shaped to avoid broken stowage. They have their own gear (gantry cranes) and their size ranges between 15,000–50,000 dwt.

Ships fitted with specialised equipment or designed for a particular cargo, trade or area have to look to their own specific section of the market in order to charge the extra rate on top of the current freight rate, which is required to pay off investments in equipment and construction. Examples of these may be bulkers with a wide hatch called *"open-hatch bulkers"* (10,000–105,000 dwt), bulk carriers equipped with their own grabs or conveyor belts systems for discharge of bulk commodities called *"self-dischargers"* or *"self-unloaders"* (10,000–105,000 dwt), vessels specially constructed with the measurements and fittings required for passage through the St. Lawrence Seaway during the season called *"Lakes traders"* or *"Lakes-fitted vessels"* (10,000–50,000 dwt) or restricted only to Great Lakes navigation (*"Lakes only"* of 10,000–85,000 dwt) and "ice-class" vessels which are suitable for trading into the Baltic Sea or to Canada during winter conditions.

Finally, there is a specialised dry cargo market which includes the so-called *"cement carriers"*. These are fully enclosed vessels which handle cement pneumatically, discharging via pipes in which the powdered cement behaves as a fluid. The size ranges between 10,000–50,000 dwt.

1.3.2 Tankers

The tanker is a ship designed for the carriage of liquid cargo (oil and other petrochemicals) in bulk. Tankers load their cargo by gravity from the shore or by shore pumps and discharge using their own pumps.[22] Oil tankers vary in size from small coastal vessels of 1,000 dwt, through medium-sized ships of about 60,000 dwt, to the giant ULCCs (Ultra Large Crude Carriers) of over 320,000 dwt. *According to the size of tanker vessels*, the following sub-markets (sub-segments) may be mentioned:

- *ULCC (Ultra Large Crude Carriers):* Tankers of 320,000–565,000 dwt. They carry only crude oil. ULCCs are difficult to enter in ports when fully loaded. The oil tanker *Seawise Giant* was built in 1979 and was in service up to 2009 (with various names) when it was scrapped. It was the largest ship ever by deadweight tonnage (565,000 dwt), length (458 m.) and displacement (657,000 tonnes). Nowadays, there are only about 50 ULCCs still in operation.[23] In 2015, the largest tankers in service were two sister ships, built in 2002–2003, each carrying 442,000 dwt (3.1 mil. barrels of oil), whilst the mammoth vessels of over 500,000 dwt had been removed from the market.
- *VLCC (Very Large Crude Carriers):* Tankers of 200,000–320,000 dwt. They principally carry crude oil on long-haul voyages from the Middle East and West Africa to the Far East and North America. Since the 1950s, when the tanker market was divided into a "crude" or "dirty" sector and a "product" sector, there had been a continuous trend towards increasingly larger tankers, a development which escalated during the late 1970s when ULCCs were built. Now, the "jumboisation" phenomenon of building tankers of 400,000–500,000 dwt has gradually faded, so it may be said that the largest crucial vessels of the tanker market are those of around 320,000 dwt which are able to carry about 2 million oil barrels.
- *Suezmax:* Tankers of 120,000–200,000 dwt. They carry mostly crude and rarely oil products when their tanks are coated (only 3% of the respective fleet was able to carry products in 2015[24]), trading on long and medium-haul voyages. Suezmaxes represent the vessels with largest measurements allowed for passage through the Suez Canal in loaded condition. Besides, they are called "*one million barrel vessels*" because of their oil-carrying capacity. Since 2016, suezmax vessels have been able to pass through the new lane of the Panama Canal, leaving only the VLCCs/ULCCs as the only tankers without ability to cross this passage.
- *Aframax:* Tankers of 80,000–120,000 dwt. They carry mostly crude, but also oil products when their tanks are coated (about 30% of the respective fleet in 2015[25]). An aframax tanker has the capacity to carry around 750–800,000 oil barrels.
- *Panamax:* Tankers of 60,000–80,000 dwt. They carry both crude and oil products since most of them are coated (about 80% of the respective fleet

---

22 Brodie, P. (2013) *Commercial Shipping Handbook* (London, Routledge, 2nd edition).
23 Clarksons Research, *Shipping Intelligence Network* (accessed 15 April 2015).
24 Clarksons Research, *Shipping Intelligence Network* (accessed 15 April 2015).
25 Clarksons Research, *Shipping Intelligence Network* (accessed 15 April 2015).

in 2015[26]). These vessels are the largest allowed to pass through the Panama Canal in loaded condition. A panamax tanker was typically able to carry up to 550,000 oil barrels, whilst this capacity has increased up to 680,000 barrels after the completion of expansion works in the Panama Canal.

- *Handysize:* Tankers of 10,000–60,000 dwt. They include products, chemical and other specialised tankers (about 96% of the respective fleet was coated in 2015[27]). Their capacity ranges from 100,000–300,000 oil barrels. Since the 2000s vegetable oil has become a popular product for handysize tankers.
- *Small Tankers:* Tankers of 100–10,000 dwt able to carry oil products, chemicals or other specialised liquid cargoes.

According to the nature of cargo, the following categories may be recognised:

- *Crude Tankers:* They include all uncoated tankers above 60,000 dwt carrying crude oil or dirty petroleum products. Their size can theoretically reach over 500,000 dwt, but practically over 400,000 dwt currently.
- *Product Tankers:* They have coated tanks (e.g. most commonly by epoxy, less frequently by zinc or polymer), which enable them to carry refined petroleum products (clean or dirty). Their size can typically reach up to the Aframax size of 120,000 dwt, with the exception of some coated suezmaxes of up to 160,000 dwt.

  Furthermore, according to the haul (distance) of cargo carriage and the size of the vessels, product tankers may also be categorised as follows:

(a) *Long Range 3 (LR3):* Tankers of 120,000–160,000 dwt (suezmax size).

(b) *Long Range 2 (LR2):* Tankers of 80,000–120,000 dwt (aframax size). LR2 aframax product tankers serve the petrochemical industry, typically carrying naphtha and other clean petroleum products in long-haul distances, such as from the Middle East to Japan or Korea or Europe. Instead, most newbuilt suezmax tankers are typically used to carry either crude oil or even middle distillates of oil products, e.g. gasoil. Thus, very few of these tankers are built with such specifications to be capable of carrying clean products. For this reason, the LR3 product tanker is still rather rare in the tanker market.

(c) *Long Range 1 (LR1):* Tankers of 60,000–80,000 dwt (panamax size). Most of them are used to transport clean petroleum products on long to medium-haul routes, such as from the Middle East and China to the Far East and Europe.

(d) *Medium Range (MR):* Tankers of 45,000–60,000 dwt.

---

26 Clarksons Research, *Shipping Intelligence Network* (accessed 15 April 2015).
27 Clarksons Research, *Shipping Intelligence Network* (accessed 15 April 2015).

(e) *Handy Products Tankers:* Tankers of 10,000–45,000 dwt.

The last two categories concern flexible vessels involved in the short to medium-haul petroleum products trade on intra-Asian routes, as well as trade from the Middle East Gulf and Indian subcontinent to the Indo-Pacific basin and Europe.

• *Chemical Tankers:* They are defined as tankers that are suitable for chemical trades, because they have either stainless steel or coated tanks. Types of coating include epoxy/phenolic coating and zinc/marine line coating. These ships can often carry a great number of petrochemical products of different kinds in separate holds at the same time (parcelling). The size of a chemical tanker approximately equals that of a small to medium product tanker (10,000–60,000 dwt). There are also small chemical tankers for coastal trading able to carry less than 10,000 tonnes.

In accordance with the respective IMO grade of the chemical cargoes carried, the chemical tankers are typically classified as[28]:

(a) *IMO I* vessels which are modern, fully segregated parcel tankers with fully stainless steel or coated tanks, carrying cargoes of major hazard (MARPOL Annex II category "X" cargoes);

(b) *IMO II* vessels which are modern, (not fully) segregated tankers, with sophisticated coated tanks, carrying cargoes of medium hazard (MARPOL Annex II category "Y" cargoes);

(c) *IMO III* vessels which are chemical/product tankers, carrying chemicals of minor hazard (MARPOL Annex II category "Z" cargoes).

As far as the oil cargoes are segmented within the tanker market in accordance with their quality and clarity, chemicals are the cleaner cargoes, followed by clean petroleum products (CPP) such as naphtha, kerosene etc., then dirty petroleum products (DPP) such as fuel oil, diesel oil etc. and finally crude oil. From a chartering perspective, it is noted that chemical cargoes require high degree of vessels' sophistication thus they are transported by specialised chemical tankers, while both clean and dirty oil products are able to be carried by product tankers when tanks are carefully cleaned between loadings, and crude oil is typically carried only by large double-hull crude tankers.

• *Specialised Tankers:* They carry specialised liquid cargoes (other than chemicals). Typical such vessels are *asphalt and bitumen carriers* (200–30,000 dwt), *shuttle tankers* (35,000–120,000 dwt) and *small tankers* (100–10,000 dwt) carrying water, wine, edible oils, waste and slops, sulphur, methanol, palm oil etc. Sometimes, gas carriers (mainly LNG, LPG) or offshore vessels may be regarded as specialised tankers. For the purpose of this book these are analysed separately in sections 1.3.3 and 1.3.4.

---

28 IMO *Carriage of Chemicals by Ship and IBC Code* (www.imo.org, accessed 12 November 2016).

Although generalisations should be avoided, some *characteristics of the tankers' market* may be found below:

- Most sub-markets of the tanker market follow the principles of perfect competition.
- The larger and more sophisticated or more specialised the tankers:
  - the more barriers to entry exist and thus fewer market participants (owners, operators, charterers and their respective brokers);
  - the higher the sensitivity/volatility of freight rates and vessels' values to the economic cycles;
  - the less easily liquidated the vessels are.

- Safety and prevention of oil pollution are of paramount importance for all involved parties. Regulatory framework is a major determinant of the tanker market developments. International regulations for tanker ship safety have become much stricter and oil pollution in any form is not acceptable. All these rules and regulations are followed by the majority of tanker shipowners competing for charters, whilst charterers have adopted strict vetting processes for carefully selecting the vessels which move their cargoes. The crucial regulatory influence in the tanker sector has been clearly seen by the compulsory and extensive IMO phase-out schedule of all single-hull tankers which was fulfilled up to the end of 2015. It goes without saying that currently all newly built tankers are double hull constructions.
- Concentration of ownership is relatively low in the tanker market, whilst in specialised segments or larger vessel sizes the concentration of ownership usually gets higher. A very important characteristic of the tanker market has been the dominating position held historically by a comparatively small number of big charterers called "oil majors"; that is, the large oil companies. However, in the last 30–40 years the control of oil transport has changed and their role in transport has been diluted. In the past it had been typical for the big oil companies to own a considerable fleet of tankers being under their management, but now the trend is for these companies to sell off and cease business as owners and ship operators. Instead, independent tanker owners build vessels to charterers' specifications and place them on charters with them. Oil producers, especially in the Middle East, now actively market their oil through distribution organisations in the consuming markets and only several have built their own tanker fleets. New oil companies have emerged in the rapidly growing Asian markets, with their own transport policies. The number of smaller private firms (often known as "traders") and state organisations engaged in the chartering of tankers increased considerably during the 1980s and their role remains important today. Moreover, large volumes of oil are now handled by oil traders.
- From a technical point of view, the sea transport of crude oil is carried out in virtually the same way all over the world. The transport of

oil derivatives is a more complicated activity. Regarding the transport tasks, oil cargoes may differ in two important respects; specific gravity (see section 1.2.4) and standards of cleanliness required.[29]

- The comparatively small number of loading areas and the offshore loading terminals are also typical features of the tanker market, although there has been a significant increase in the number of loading sites since the late 1990s.
- Oil trades may be affected by the completion of expansion works in the Panama Canal.
- Tankers – especially those carrying crude oil – practically have difficulty in getting return cargoes. Therefore, they are usually forced to proceed in ballast over an ocean route to a loading area.
- Many shipowners prefer to place their ships on time charter for a long period, but there is also an important spot market for tankers. It is typical that the volume of spot business becomes comparatively larger during a low-market period, as owners prefer to take the upside potential of a future freight rate increase.
- Tanker charterers, owners and brokers are working with elaborate and standardised documents, the design of which has been influenced by the oil companies over the years and which may be used, more or less, on a "take-it-or-leave-it" basis. Therefore, the negotiations for a tanker charter are less complicated than, for example, negotiations in dry cargo chartering and are normally carried out within a very short space of time. The problems encountered in tanker chartering are, however, even greater than those found in other forms of chartering. The art is to hit the right time for the fixture at a freight level well in tune with the prevailing market. The fluctuations normally occur very rapidly and with strong deflections, which may cause the situation to change radically from one day to the next. This fast movement is due mainly to the quick changes in oil prices, so the chartering closely reflects the commodity trading. This relationship was very characteristic at end of 2014 and 2015 when the slump in oil prices and the "*contango*"[30] oil market led to an increase in oil trading, the strategic stockbuilding of oil reserves by major economies, the use of older tankers as "*floating storage*" vessels and consequently to booming tanker freight rates, particularly for the larger sizes. Owing to the dominating position of oil majors and the comparatively limited number of parties involved in some segments of the tanker market, every occurrence has a great effect, which sometimes means that one single fixture may affect the total state of the market for the day. This is particularly the case in the sub-markets of larger vessels (e.g. VLCCs).

---

29 Stopford, M. (2009) *Maritime Economics* (London, Routledge Publications, 3rd edition, p. 441).
30 Contango is a situation where the futures price (or forward price) of a commodity is higher than the expected spot price (Source: Black, J., Hashimzade, N. and Myles, G. (2009) *Contango. A Dictionary of Economics* (Oxford University Press, 3rd edition)).

1.3.3 Gas carriers

In the past, gas carriers used to be reported as part of the tanker sector analysis, mentioned as the most important specialised tankers, as long as gas carriers have certain features common with other tankers used for the carriage of bulk liquids. Since 2000's they form an independent, constantly growing market due to their rapid development and their special features. These are ships designed for the transport of condensed (liquefied) gases. A liquefied gas is the liquid form of a substance which, at ambient temperature and at atmospheric pressure, would be a gas. All gas cargoes are transported in liquid form (i.e. they are not carried as a gas in its vapour form) and, because of their physical and chemical properties, they are carried either at[31]:

- pressures greater than atmospheric, or
- temperatures below ambient, or
- a combination of both.

Liquefied Petroleum Gas (LPG) typically includes a variety of petroleum gases which are stored and transported as liquids under pressure. Unlike liquefied natural gas (LNG), LPG does not require cooling to be liquefied. The most common LPG cargoes are butane and propane, however LPG carriers may also carry ammonia and petrochemicals such as ethylene, propylene, olefins (e.g. butadiene) and vinyl chloride monomer (VCM). *Liquefied Natural Gas (LNG)* is the cargo category which includes natural gases (typically methane and ethane) compressed at moderate pressure but (unlike LPG) cooled to -259°F (-162°C) to remain liquid. The volume of natural gas as liquid is 1/600th of its volume as gas. LNG is a clear, colourless, odourless liquid. It is neither corrosive nor toxic. LNG is stored and transported in insulated pressure tanks or containers.[32]

The LPG carrier and the LNG carrier are ships specially designed for the safe carriage of liquefied gas cargoes. The design in cargo tank construction of LNG and LPG ships can be prismatic, membrane or spherical. Cargo tanks can be made from aluminium, nickel steel, stainless steel or other highly insulating materials. An almost unique feature to the gas carrier is that the cargo is kept under positive pressure to prevent air entering the cargo system. Therefore, only cargo liquid and cargo vapour are present in the cargo tank and flammable atmospheres cannot develop. All gas carriers utilise closed cargo systems when loading or discharging, preventing vapour from escaping out in to the atmosphere. In order to virtually eliminate cargo release to the atmosphere and minimise the risk of vapour ignition, equipment requirements are of very high standards and include temperature and pressure monitoring, gas detection and cargo tank liquid level indicators.[33] Because of the requirement for heavy insulation at these

---

31 www.liquefiedgascarrier.com (accessed 25 May 2015).
32 www.businessdictionary.com (accessed 19 February 2016); www.energy.ca.gov (accessed 13 November 2016).
33 www.liquefiedgascarrier.com (accessed 25 May 2015).

extremely low cargo temperatures and the variation of equipment, the construction cost of these specialised ships is extremely high. All gas carriers are highly sophisticated, however the LNG carrier is considered the most sophisticated of all commercial ships. It is worth saying that an LNG carrier may cost about twice as much as an oil tanker of the same size. As an indication, an LNG cost around USD 200 million to be built in early 2016.[34]

According to the size of vessels, the following sub-segments may be distinguished in the LPG market:

- *Very Large Gas Carriers (VLGC):* LPG vessels of about 65,000 cbm or above. These vessels are fully-refrigerated and mainly employed on long-haul trade routes, e.g. from Middle East Gulf (MEG) and the United States to Asia. Modern vessels of this size may be called *"Very Large Ethane Carriers"* (*VLECs*) designed to transport ethane in significant quantities.
- *Large Gas Carriers (LGC):* LPG vessels of about 45,000–65,000 cbm, mainly carrying LPG and ammonia between ports where limitations deter VLGCs' entrance. West Africa is a major loading area for these vessels. It is a "niche market" with a limited number of players.
- *Mid-Sizes:* LPG vessels of about 20,000–45,000 cbm, typically fully-refrigerated, carrying ammonia or LPG, on intra-regional routes (e.g. within the Americas or Asia) and medium-haul cross-trades (e.g. in the North Sea and Europe). This is a "core" sector for global ammonia trades.
- *Handy Gas Carriers:* LPG vessels of about 300–20,000 cbm. A diverse segment which includes semi-refrigerated, fully-refrigerated and some larger, pressurised ships that carry a wide range of cargoes such as ethylene, petrochemicals, LPG and ammonia on short to medium-haul routes.

According to their specifications the following types of gas carriers may be recognised, starting from the simplest to the more sophisticated ones[35]:

- *Fully Pressurised Gas Carriers:* LPG vessels with cargo capacity of less than 11,000 cbm, having fully pressurised tanks. It is the simplest type of a gas carrier, carrying propane, butane and chemical gases.
- *Semi or Fully-Refrigerated and Semi-Pressurised Gas Carriers:* LPG vessels with cargo capacity of less than 28,000 cbm, carrying a variety of petrochemical gases except ethylene. Initially with semi-refrigerated, but nowadays with fully-refrigerated and semi-pressurised tanks. A refrigeration plant is installed on the vessel to provide a fully-refrigerated ability while having a high pressure for the cargo tanks, though below that required for fully pressurised carriage. A reliquefaction plant on

---

34 Clarksons Research *Shipping Intelligence Weekly* (8 January 2016, p. 10).
35 www.liquefiedgascarrier.com (accessed 10 June 2015).

these vessels generally has a substantial capacity and can, if required, load the cargo as a gas and then reliquefy it onboard.

- *Ethylene Gas Carriers:* LPG vessels with cargo capacity reaching up to 22,000 cbm. Similar to the semi-pressurised vessels described before, but most sophisticated and able to carry also ethylene, fully-refrigerated at its atmospheric pressure boiling point. These vessels carry most liquefied gas cargoes except LNG. Having thermal insulation and a high capacity reliquefaction plant in their cylindrical or bi-lobe tanks, they can load or discharge at pressurised and refrigerated terminals, making them the most versatile gas carriers in terms of cargo-handling ability.
- *Fully-Refrigerated Gas Carriers:* LPG vessels with cargo capacity of 18,000–86,000 cbm, with fully refrigerated tanks. They carry liquefied gases, such as LPG, ammonia and vinyl chloride, at low temperature and atmospheric pressure, in large volumes, over long distances, between terminals equipped with fully refrigerated storage tanks. Their prismatic-shaped cargo tanks, fabricated from nickel steel, allow the carriage of cargoes at temperatures as low as -48°C.
- *Insulated Gas Carriers (LNG):* LNG vessels have a cargo capacity which ranges widely from 1,000–267,000 cbm. Fitted with independent membrane cargo tanks, they are able to transport LNG at its atmospheric pressure boiling point of approximately -162°C, depending on the cargo grade. Typically, these ships are highly specialised and sophisticated, but in smaller sizes they may also carry basic LPG cargoes. If an LNG ship is capable of carrying basic LPG cargoes, a reliquefaction plant is installed to handle the boil-off LPG cargo vapours. LNG carriers are typically fully insulated because it is not cost effective to liquefy methane onboard, although the first vessels with reliquifaction plants have already appeared in the market. The LNG sector has been one of the fastest growing shipping markets since 2010, driven by a robust demand expansion in some geographical areas (e.g. in Asia, South America), the increased regasification terminal capacity (e.g. in China, India) and the opening of new LNG exporting projects (e.g. in Angola, Papua New Guinea, Algeria, Australia etc.).

Some *general characteristics of the gas carriers' market* may be mentioned as follows:

- Seaborne transportation of liquefied gases began in the 1930s.
- Gas carriers trade worldwide and their useful life may extend over 25 years.
- The gas carrier market is a closed, specialised and highly sophisticated market, since:
  - Barriers to entry are high.
  - Cost of investment is high. Due to that, gas shipping companies may be listed to stock exchanges, so as to broaden their sources of

required capital. As most gas carriers are employed in period charter contracts with major charterers, this offers a clearer "visibility"
as concern as the expected revenues of the shipping company and
accordingly it provides the stakeholder with an increased possibility
of earning income from dividends.

- Sensitivity/volatility of freight rates and vessels' values to the economic cycles is high.
- Vessels are not easily liquidated due to high cost of investment and
  great specialisation needed.
- Specialised know-how in cargo handling and operations is a
  pre-requisite.
- The number of owners, operators, shipbrokers and charterers is relatively small.
- Gas carriers, particularly LNG vessels, are commonly built against
  long-term chartering contracts (extending even to the whole ship's
  life) from first-class charterers. In 2015 almost 70% of the LNGs was
  employed in period contracts and only a 30% in the spot market.
- Owners and charterers, particularly in the LNG market, are almost
  long-standing business partners. Chartering contracts may follow
  standard types issued by BIMCO (e.g. *Gasvoy* for gas voyage charters or *Gastime* for time charters of gas carriers), or more commonly
  follow private contracts issued by major charterers.

• A great effect is expected from Panama Canal expansion in gas trades,
cargo shiploads and vessel sizes.

1.3.4 Offshore vessels

A field related to the oil and tanker market is the offshore sector, concerned with
exploration and exploitation of oil in the open sea with more or less permanently
anchored *oil platforms, drilling vessels* and *drilling rigs*. Since the 2000s a special charter market has been developed for such "ships" and for their offshore
servants; the supply ships. The activity on the offshore market varies greatly and
consequently so does the market for supply vessels. To some extent supply ships
can compete for cargoes with smaller tonnage in the short-sea trades and they
may also be used for towing works.

There are also the technically sophisticated *shuttle tankers*, the so-called *buoy
loaders* and the *FPSO/FSO* units (Floating Production Storage and Offloading/
Floating Storage and Offloading respectively), which are normally built by owners exclusively for operation under a chartering contract with a specific oil company during a medium to long-time period. These types may in certain situations
be freed for competing in the open market with the regular tanker tonnage.

The offshore vessels' market is crucially affected by the oil prices. In a global
geopolitical and economic environment of high oil prices, interest for oil exploitation is increasing and so does demand for offshore vessels. Therefore, freight or

hire rates are increasing. The contrary occurs in an environment of lower oil prices, for example as from the second-half of 2014.

The offshore market comprises a great variety of numerous vessels as follows[36]:

- *Mobile Offshore Drilling Units (MODUs):* Units engaged in drilling activities, including oil platforms, submersible and semi-submersible units, jack-up drilling rigs and drillships. A *platform* is built on concrete or steel legs, or both, anchored directly onto the seabed, supporting a deck with space for drilling rigs, production facilities and crew quarters. A *submersible drilling rig* can be floated to location and lowered onto the sea floor for offshore drilling activities. A *jack-up rig* or a *self-elevating unit* is a type of mobile platform that consists of a buoyant hull fitted with a number of movable legs, capable of raising its hull over the surface of the sea. A *drillship* is a conventional ship-shaped structure, fitted with drilling apparatus, powerful engines and sophisticated propulsion systems. The maximum water depth where all these units may be active ranges from 1,000–12,000 feet.
- *Construction Vessels/Platforms:* Vessels involved in the installation of the infrastructure required for production to start on an oilfield, or conducting inspection, repair and maintenance activities. They include various types, such as *derrick crane vessels* which perform heavy lift operations, *pipe or cable layers, heavy lift vessels, dive support vessels and dredgers.*
- *Mobile Offshore Production Units (MOPUs):* Units engaged in production and processing of oil in remote, deepwater areas, where it would be impractical to install a fixed, production platform or a pipeline to shore. The most popular ones are called *"Floating Production Storage and Offloading"* (*FPSOs*). A large number of these structures are converted oil tankers, although some are purpose-built.
- *Logistics Units:* This sector includes floating storage units and shuttle tankers. A *"Floating Storage and Offloading unit"* (*FSO*) is a vessel that is normally moored to the seabed adjacent to a Mobile Offshore Production Unit (MOPU). The MOPU will offload processed oil into the FSO via a *Single Point Mooring* (*SPM*), and the oil will typically remain in the FSO until it can be exported to shore via a pipeline or a shuttle tanker. FSOs are generally converted from merchant tankers that have been retired. Their size ranges from 10,000–450,000 dwt. A *"shuttle tanker"* is a ship designed to transport oil and condensates produced at offshore units or floating structures to onshore terminals and refineries. Shuttle tankers differ from conventional tankers in their ability to load in open water, through their bow-loading and submerged turret equipment, as well as dynamic positioning systems. Their size ranges from 30,000–160,000 dwt.
- *Anchor Handling Tugs (AHT):* Tugs for offshore rig anchor handling with towing capacity ranging between 1,000–25,000 bhp.

---

36 Segmentation in accordance with Clarksons Research, *Shipping Intelligence Network* (accessed 26 July 2015). Description is based on various sources.

- *Anchor Handling Tug Supply vessels (AHTS):* Dual-purpose tugs designed for offshore rig anchor handling and towage, along with offshore supply duties, with towing capacity ranging between 1,000–35,000 bhp. They are the backbone of offshore operations and constitute the largest proportion of offshore vessels. Not only do they deliver supplies (e.g. water, fuel, drilling fluids etc.) to oil rigs and platforms, but also they provide anchor handling services, towage duties and in some cases serve as *"Emergency Towing Rescue and Recovery Vessels"* *(ETRRV)*. The largest vessels are primarily utilised in regions with harsh conditions (e.g. North Sea) or in ultra-deepwater (e.g. Brazil).
- *Platform Supply Vessels (PSV):* Vessels with cargo capacity of up to 8,500 dwt, which support rigs and platforms by delivering materials to them from onshore. Large PSVs are capable of transporting supplies over longer distances in harsher conditions, as well as at frontier areas such as the Arctic and the Barents Sea. Smaller in size but faster ships typically operate closer to shore in benign sea conditions.
- *Rescue Salvage Vessels* involved in emergency response activities on oil & gas fields, or in offshore salvage activities, or in barge tows. For instance, an *"Emergency Response and Rescue Vessel"* (ERRV) responds to emergency situations on offshore structures and its capacity may reach up to 20,000 bhp. An *"Ocean Going Tug"* is equipped with large engines and powerful thrusters providing a high level of manoeuvrability and pulling power, required to tow large offshore units (e.g. from a shipyard to an offshore location), or even save vessels in distress. Its towing capacity may reach up to 33,000 bhp.
- *Survey Units* conducting a range of survey activities (e.g. seismic, geophysical, oceanographic), or *Utility Support Vessels* including a range of small vessel types which support the operations of larger and more sophisticated offshore vessel types.

Some general characteristics of the offshore market are as follows:

- It is a closed, highly specialised and sophisticated market.
- There is an absolute dependence of freight/hire rates and vessels' values to the oil prices and economic cycles. In an environment of abundant oil supply and low oil prices (e.g. as it was the case in 2014–2017), oil exploitation becomes unprofitable and offshore vessels get idle whilst paying huge amounts for fixed running costs.
- Barriers to entry are high, due to high cost of investment. For example, a 7th generation drillship might have cost over USD 700–800 million to be constructed in 2013 (in a period of high oil prices).
- Shipowning companies may be listed to shipping exchanges, so as to secure wider sources of capital.
- Specialised know-how in operations is a pre-requisite.

- Vessels/units are not easily liquidated due to high cost of investment, great specialisation needed and absolute dependence of earnings on oil prices.
- Drillships and oil platforms are typically chartered to the oil majors for medium to long charter periods. Owners typically build offshore vessels (particularly the most expensive ones, such as oil platforms and drill-ships) against secured charter employment from the oil charterers. Spot chartering activity is very rare.
- Number of owners, operators, shipbrokers and charterers is very limited.

1.3.5 Combined carriers

Combined carriers are the ships that can carry either liquid or dry bulk cargoes. Most common types of such vessels are:

- *OBO: Ore/Bulk/Oil*
- *PROBO: Products/Ore/Bulk/Oil*
- *O/O: Ore/Oil*

The size of these vessels varies from 30,000–320,000 dwt.

The combination carriers have still a market position, although not in the way originally intended (about 20 such ships were trading in July 2015). The initial intention was that those ships would perform combined voyages; for example carrying dry bulk cargo in one direction and oil cargo on the return leg, thus improving the round voyage result by reducing the time in ballast and increasing the earning time. Such an operation requires a high degree of flexibility and skill in the owner's management and teamwork of staff. The great majority of "combo" operators, however, prefer to use their ships either as pure tankers or as pure bulk carriers, depending on which market is offering the best financial result at the time. This development was also created by the difficulty of combining freight contracts and also by such practical problems as costs for cleaning the ships' holds between the different commodities. Thus, in the past the combination carriers' role was crucial as they could increase the supply of tonnage on the market where they were employed and could, therefore, contribute in weakening an upward trend in freight levels or strengthening a downward trend. This influence has gradually decreased since few combos have been built since the 2000s, and the older ones are being scrapped without replacements.

1.3.6 Containerships

Fully cellular containerships are the ocean-going merchant ships, designed and constructed in such a way to easily stack containers near and on top of each other in the holds as well as on deck. They carry only standard-sized intermodal containers enabling efficient loading, unloading and transport to and from the vessel. There is a great variety of container types, however the most common container has the following dimensions: 8 feet (2.4 m.) width, 8 feet 6 inches (2.6 m.) height and 20 or 40 feet length (6.1 m. or 12.2 m. respectively). The vessel's hull is divided into cells that are easily accessible through large hatches, but more containers can be loaded on deck atop the closed hatches. Loading and unloading can proceed simultaneously using giant traveling cranes at special container berths.

The *pure fully cellular containerships* are extremely specialised ships trading only in the liner sector, being subject to competition from versatile ships such as *cellular containerships with Ro/Ro capability* which carry containers either in cells or on truck trailers, *modern tween-deckers* of standard type or *multi-purpose vessels* which carry general or dry bulk cargo and containers, *con-bulkers* which carry dry bulk cargoes and containers, or even pure *Ro/Ro vessels, reefers, car carriers* and the *LASH and SeaBee floating barge systems* (called "lighters") able to carry containers.

Panama Canal restrictions are of utmost importance for the containership market. Thus, the market is in a transition phase and *according to the size of containerships*, there are the following, rather vaguely distinguished, sub-markets:

- *Post-Panamax and Neo-Panamax:* The critical point for a containership to be named as "Panamax" or "Post-Panamax" is not its size (i.e. container carrying capacity in TEU), but its beam, thus its ability to cross the Panama Canal. "Post-Panamax" vessels are those not able to pass the Canal. Most of them serve the long-haul deep sea liner trades and are gearless. On 26 June 2016, "*COSCO Shipping Panama*", a 9,443 TEU fully cellular containership, became the first ship which sailed through the new locks of the Panama Canal.[37] Before this, long and narrow containerships carrying up to max. 5,300 TEU were the largest able to pass the Canal. However, after the construction of the third lane of locks working alongside the two existing ones (built in 1914 when the Canal opened), containerships of up to 14,500 TEU are now able to cross this crucial passage. This has created a new segment, the so-called "*Neo-Panamax*" containerships of 8,000–15,000 TEU, leaving only those vessels still not able to cross the Canal (over 14,000–15,000 TEU and depending on their designed dimensions) to be named "*Post-Panamax*" or "*Ultra Large Container Vessels – ULCV*". The sizes of the larger container vessels have been continually increasing to provide economies of scale. As a result, the total number and carrying capacity of ships in the world container fleet increased very rapidly. As of September 2017, the biggest containerships in service were two sisterships built by OOCL in 2017 with each having a carrying capacity reaching 21,413 TEU, whereas orders had been placed for vessels of over 22,000 TEUs. Vessels of over 8,000 TEU are trading in major liner routes, such as the Far East – European or Trans-Pacific trades.

---

37 www.theguardian.com (accessed 26 June 2016).

- *Intermediary and Old Panamax:* Vessels of 3,000–8,000 TEU, either too wide or not to cross the old locks of the Panama Canal, are currently deployed on a wide variety of routes, such as Trans-Pacific and Trans-Atlantic main lanes, North–South, non-mainlane East–West trades and intra-regional services. Most of them are gearless. The future of these boxships looks somewhat uncertain and it remains to be seen whether they will find new trading alternatives or be scrapped.
- *Sub-Panamax:* Their cargo capacity varies from about 2,000–3,000 TEU. Most of them are gearless. They mainly serve North–South and intra-regional services, used to link main lane services with important secondary ports not covered by direct liner calls.
- *Handysize:* Their cargo capacity varies from about 1,000–2,000 TEU and they are involved with regional, short sea, draught restricted or feeder liner trades, similarly to the "sub-panamaxes". Most of them are geared.
- *Feeder/Feedermax:* Their cargo capacity varies from about 100–1,000 TEU and they are trading in smaller, niche, regional, short sea, draught restricted or feeder liner trades. Most of them are geared.

There is a positive correlation between vessel's size and speed. For example, the feeder ships of 100–1,000 TEU may have an average speed of 15–17 knots, while the biggest ships of over 3,000 TEU an average speed of 21–26 knots. This reflects the fact that smaller ships generally operate on shorter routes where high speed brings fewer economic benefits. Whereas a general cargo ship may spend much of its life in port loading and discharging cargo, a modern containership can be turned around in 36 hours or less, spending little of its time in port.

In general, *the most important features of the containerships' market* are the following:

- Containerships are always employed in regular lines. The ships are either owned and operated by liner companies which run their own liner network, or they may be owned by independent shipowners who charter them out (typically in period or bareboat charters) to these lines. As a consequence of this structure, the spot charter market is of little importance to the containerships. Furthermore, the time charter market for containerships has proved to be one of the first which can react to a change in the state of the world trade. This is probably so, because these ships are employed in the world-wide movement of finished, semi-finished and some agricultural products.
- The larger the containerships:

  ○ the more barriers to entry exist either for the liner operators or for the independent shipowners;
  ○ the higher is the sensitivity/volatility of vessels' values to the economic cycles;
  ○ the less easily liquidated they are.

- The current trend is to build bigger and bigger ships, for the liner companies to reduce unit cost of transport through economies of scale and respond to huge fixed costs.
- Concerning the involved parties, the containerships market has a twofold dimension. On the one hand, in the liner business aspect the involved parties are the liner operators (companies), the shippers, the liner agents and the freight forwarders. Their scope is to book cargoes under a "booking note" and transport them by regular lines under a "bill of lading" (see appendices 11 and 14). On the other hand, liner companies charter-in vessels from independent shipowners through specialised shipbrokers' networks in the open market, typically under a period charterparty (time charter or bareboat). This is the most important part of the containerships market from a chartering/shipbroking perspective.
- Containerships are employed in a global liner network, having long established their place, especially in traffic plying among highly industrialised areas (USA, Europe, Asia) with a technically advanced inland transportation system in both the exporting and the importing areas. This traffic requires large investment in specially equipped vessels, port installations and terminal equipment. The liner network is expanded through "*hub and spoke*" systems, where the containers are initially transported in main lanes (e.g. Trans-Atlantic, Trans-Pacific, Asia-Europe etc.) and then trans-shipped in smaller feeder vessels trading in regional routes (e.g. in the Mediterranean Sea) to reach their destination.
- Containerships are often operated by international alliances, joint venture organisations, consortia and pools, because of the high investment costs involved, for multi-national marketing purposes and to meet the customers' demand for total and value-added services.

It must be noted that there is some overlapping between the employment of liner and tramp vessels. When freight rates for various dry cargoes increase, charterers look at alternative shipping solutions. Thus, some trades that used to be reserved for the bulk carriers or multi-purpose vessels or reefers etc. in pure bulk/tramp markets, they may become fully containerised and executed by pure containerships or general cargo liners or reefers etc, in a liner network. This applies not only to unitised cargoes, but also to pure bulk cargoes.

1.3.7 Multi-purpose vessels

A multi-purpose vessel (MPP) is capable of carrying at the same time different types of dry (bulk or general) cargo and containers, requiring different methods of handling. Con-bulkers and barge carriers are not included in this segment. MPPs are small and versatile ships. They are non-fully cellular container capable vessels, thus not equipped with fixed cell guides in all holds but with partial coverage and/or portable guides. Their container carrying capacity is at least 100 TEU, whereas their typical cargo-carrying capacity in tonnage terms varies from

8,000–25,000 dwt. They normally have a relatively high TEU/Dwt ratio. There are several types of ships falling into this category, for instance the ships which can carry roll on/roll off (ro/ro) cargo together with containers. Concerning the dry cargoes carried, particularly minor bulks are those transported either as dry bulk cargoes or as general cargoes.

MPPs are trading worldwide, by offering either tramp or liner services. They can be single-deckers or tween-deckers and they are always geared. Their market structure follows the principles of perfect competition. Cost control is of importance for all involved parties. Concentration of ownership is very low. Ownership, charterers and brokers are extremely dispersed around the globe. MPPs are subject to fierce competition by containerships, general cargo vessels, small bulkers, con-bulkers, ro/ro vessels, reefers and other types of liner and tramp ships.

1.3.8 General cargo vessels

In this wide category, various types of vessels may be included, such as tween-deckers, break bulk freighters, cattle carriers, pallet carriers, timber carriers etc. Sophisticated general cargo vessels are mostly built with a certain type of trading in mind, for example, forest products may be carried by "*timber carriers*" within the capacity brackets of about 6,000–20,000 dwt, or livestock may be carried by "*cattle carriers*". A standard type *tween-decker* now generally means a vessel of 17,000–23,000 dwt with her own gear of derricks and/or cranes and with one tween-deck throughout. Tween-deckers may be categorised either as multipurpose or as general cargo vessels.

Prior to the days of containerisation, all cargo was carried on what were known as general cargo ships. The cargo was known as break-bulk cargo, i.e. non-unitised general cargo including bags, sacks, individual items etc. With the advent of containerisation there are fewer general cargo ships. Generally, they carry cargo that is too large to be carried in a container, for example, steel, rolls of wire and machinery. However, they also carry boxed goods that are too small to justify the use of a full container.

Conventional general cargo vessels mostly trade in regional, secondary lines, though they may be also employed in tramp markets. Vessels ownership may belong to the liner companies or to independent shipowners which charter them either to liner operators or in the open market. Within this sector, the "*general cargo liners*" are faster tween-deckers designed for liner trades before containerisation (usually over 5,000 dwt, with a high Dwt/TEU ratio and high service speeds), whereas "*general cargo tramps*" are slower general cargo vessels.

1.3.9 Reefer vessels

The reefer is designed to carry goods requiring refrigeration, such as meat and fruits. This ship has insulated holds into which cold air is passed at the temperature appropriate to the goods being carried. Reefers are trading worldwide and their carrying capacity is measured in volume terms reaching up to 460,000 cu.ft. They may be operated in the open market, when their operation is similar to that of a bulk carrier, or in secondary/regional/short-sea trades of the liner market (in complement or in competition to the container-ships). Most reefers being built today have permanent fittings on deck and on top of the weather deck hatches for reefer containers, to increase the carrying capacity and to meet special requirements from customers. This also enables the owners to compete with the regular lines, or even to be employed in certain liner trades.

The major competitor to specialised reefer ships is the ever-growing container fleet. The comparison between the total boxship reefer capacity and the reefer capacity of pure reefer vessels shows an overwhelming predominance of the con-tainerships over the years. Due to that, the reefer fleet is rather aged and orders for new vessels are dwindling.

In order to improve profitability and survive in this fierce competition, if the freight levels permit, reefers are able to carry also a variety of dry products, such as bagged cargoes, paper, lightweight unitised cargoes, containers or even cars. The vessels will then be in straight competition with various other ships, such as tween-deckers and multi-purpose ships operating in the open market, general cargo liners, small bulkers, ro/ro, or even car carriers.

Within this sector there are various vessel types, however the most popular ones are the "*pure reefers*" with fully refrigerated holds, the "*freezers*" being able to carry frozen cargo, the *container capable reefer vessels* which carry contain-erised refrigerated cargo, the "*general cargo reefers*" being capable of carrying also break-bulk cargoes, as well as the *reefers with ro/ro capability* which may load wheeled cargoes.

Some general characteristics of the reefer vessels' market are the following:

- The reefer market is closed, specialised and highly seasonal. There is intense seasonality, since demand for such vessels peaks on first-half of the year when the products of the southern hemisphere are bound for shipment to Europe, the USA and Japan. Bananas, and to a large extent meat, are transported year round, while fish, citrus and other fruits, veg-etables and potatoes are seasonal.
- Barriers to entry are high.
- Sensitivity/volatility of freight rates and vessels' values to the economic cycles is relatively high.
- The number of owners, operators and reefer shipbrokers is small. Char-terers are often large organisations, state or private. Sometimes a reefer charter is made directly between owners and charterers without the assistance of brokers.
- Reefer ships are employed to a large extent in contract trading, but there is also an important spot market. Demand for transport depends on crop outcome in various geographical areas. Sudden problems in some supplying areas may cause drastic re-routing of reefer vessels even

overnight but, in general, the shipping programmes and the contractual engagements follow very strict schedules and require perfect timing.

- The loading areas are worldwide but the discharging areas are concentrated primarily in Europe, the USA and Japan. Thus, the routes are "one way" and there is a huge imbalance geographically in the distribution of the loading/discharging areas.
- Reliable technical equipment, great skill in cargo handling and treatment during the sea voyage are very important. Economy is achieved by reducing ballasting to a minimum and by always using a vessel's maximum cargo capacity. In order to reduce the time and costs in port, reefer trades use palletisation.
- The future of reefers is uncertain, since containership reefer capacity has long outreached the capacity of conventional reefers. Since a 1999 peak, the reefer fleet has been steadily declining.

1.3.10 Ro/Ro vessels and passenger ships

The ro/ro vessel is designed to accommodate wheeled cargo that is rolled-on and rolled-off aboard through the ramps of the vessel, cargo that is shipped aboard by lift-on/lift-off (lo/lo) equipment (e.g. fork-lift trucks), containers and/or break bulk cargo. A ro/ro vessel can be self-sustaining. Equipped with large openings at bow and stern and sometimes also in the side, the ship permits rapid loading and discharge with hydraulically operated ramps providing easy access. Fully loaded trucks or trailers carrying containers are accommodated on inside decks.

The ro/ro market as a sector of its own was established rather late. Initially these ships were typical short-trade carriers in trades between highly industrialised countries. Several circumstances have, however, transformed these vessels to whole ocean traffic "players".

During the 1970s the movement overseas of industrial products, machinery, vehicles and building materials increased considerably, especially from Europe and the United States to the Middle East, as well as from Europe to West Africa. The ports in the importing countries had a low capacity at the time and, therefore, ran into serious congestion caused by too many vessel arrivals and the inability to cope with the increasing quantity of cargo. At the same time, the liner companies trading to these areas with conventional general cargo ships began to renew their fleets. One solution to these problems was the ocean-going ro/ro ship, requiring a minimum of port installations, with a very fast and flexible cargo-handling system and able to accommodate a mixture of commodities, not restricted to rolling units but able to load all goods movable by fork-lift truck and also containers.

In respect of passenger traffic, large-size tonnage with accommodation only for passengers is now primarily engaged in cruising. Most passenger vessels are operated in short-distance routes with consecutive trips on tight schedules, the so-called "ferry traffic". These ships mostly have a good capacity for rolling goods and they are a supplement to the pure cargo ro/ro ships operating in the same trading area. The market for passenger ships is very much dependent on seasonal variations.

Apart from cruise ships and pure passenger ships that do not carry cargoes, within this sector there is a great variety of other merchant vessels, as for example the *"ro/ro freighters"* with roll-on roll-off ramps and accommodation for few drivers/passengers, the *"passenger/car ferries"* with high passenger capacity in respect to cargo carried, or the *"ro/pax vessels"* with a higher emphasis on carrying cargo than passengers.

Some general characteristics of the Ro/Ro vessels' market are as follows:

- Although ro/ro vessels are flexible and versatile in their trading, their market is rather a closed and extremely specialised one, since:
  - Barriers to entry are relatively high, particularly for the larger vessels which are more expensive to be built. Thus, ship ownership is relatively concentrated.
  - Sensitivity/volatility of freight rates and vessels' values to the economic cycles is high.
  - Smaller vessels are more easily liquidated than larger ones.
  - The wide range of transported cargoes may sometimes require specialised know-how in cargo handling. Each trade has its own peculiarities which vary greatly. Ports of call vary widely too.
  - The vessels have to compete with the containerships and survive within this market.
- Ro/Ro ships are able to trade globally. Their use is important where port facilities are not well developed. Therefore, they usually operate in liner services such as in the North–South (e.g. USA–South America, Europe-Africa) and regional trades (e.g. Intra-Asian) or in short-sea/coastal services or even in the open (tramp) market.
- There are specialised shipbrokers for the chartering of these vessels and some even specialise in only one of the ro/ro segments.

1.3.11 Car carriers

Car carriers are designed to transport fully assembled vehicles and cars. They are able to carry 2,000–8,500 vehicles by roll-on/roll-off type of loading. Such ships are typically characterised by hoistable and strengthened decks to enable the transportation of "high and heavy" vehicle cargoes. Most vehicles are medium-sized passenger cars, but lorries, trucks, tractors and buses are also transported. This sector of the market has gained importance in the last few decades. In addition and parallel to the trade of fully assembled vehicles, there is a trade in used cars from Europe, the USA and Japan to Africa, South America and Asia, as well as an important volume of car parts, so-called *"Cars Knocked Down"* (CKD), for assembly in factories at the receiving countries. These cargoes may be carried either by car carriers or by other liner vessels.

The overseas transportation of cars in the big-volume trades is carried out by very large purpose-built vessels, so-called *"Pure Car Carriers"* (*PCC*), whilst the car carriers specially built to accommodate also large vehicles are called *"Pure Car Truck Carriers"* (*PCTC*). Each has a typical capacity of 2,000–7,000 *"Car Equivalent Units"* (*CEU*), although the *"Large Car Truck Carrier"* has been introduced which is able to accommodate over 8,000 CEU. The loading/unloading of a PCC/PCTC is procured by ro/ro methods and is extremely fast. All mass transportation of fully built-up vehicles is done by the ro/ro mode in PCCs, ro/ro ships and ferries. One good reason for this is that shippers of cars normally refuse shipment by lo/lo tonnage (lifting methods) when ro/ro is available. Smaller volumes of cars (from just a few up to about 100–150 per shipment) are taken care of by the lines at liner prices, but for trades where the volumes are increasing up to anything between 200 and 900 units per shipment the charterers may sometimes employ reefer tonnage, which, with many "tween-decks" can provide the deck space required.

The most important trades of fully assembled vehicles are from Japan and South Korea to the USA and Europe and vice versa, from Europe to the USA, whilst there is also an inter-European trade covering important volumes. Secondary trades in respect of volumes carried are from Europe and the United States to countries in the Middle East, Africa, Central and South America, as well as from Japan to the same areas, plus Australia. China is also starting to play an important role more as an importer and less as an exporter of new cars.

The car carrier market is very closed and specialised. It is characterised by:

- A small number of owners, operators, shipbrokers and charterers.
- There were almost 780 car carriers employed on a worldwide basis in 2015.[38] It is a closed market using very little broker assistance, where business is concluded mostly on the basis of long-term chartering contracts between a few ship operators and the exporting companies (car manufacturers). The vessels are often built against time charters of 10–15 years. The orderbook shows a preference for larger ships, the majority being of 6,000 CEUs or more.[39]
- Except typical time charters, contracts of affreightment (CoA) are also used as a common charter form in this market (see chapter 13).
- High sensitivity/volatility of freight rates and vessels' values to economic cycles.
- No seasonality, as the market follows its own patterns, depending on changes of World GDP, consumption and growth rates in major economies etc.
- Vessels are not easily liquidated. The second-hand market is practically "shallow".
- High barriers to entry.

---

38 Clarksons Research, *Shipping Intelligence Network* (accessed 26 July 2015).
39 Clarksons Research, *Shipping Intelligence Network* (accessed 26 July 2015).

1.3.12 Small vessels

There is a large number of vessels of 10,000 dwt and less. Dry cargoes may be carried by small pure bulkers or multi-purpose or general cargo vessels possibly having also a small container capacity. Specialised liquid cargoes are carried by small tankers correspondingly. Such liquid cargoes may be water, wine, edible oils, asphalt and bitumen, waste and slops, palm oil, sulphur etc.

Most of this tonnage is engaged in short-sea and coastal trading. Sometimes, coastal shipping may be reserved particularly for vessels of the coastal state ("*cabotage trade*"). The charter markets of small vessels have their own information systems and channels of communication which function independently (e.g. the market of small bulkers differs to that of small tankers), whilst their freight market variations and freight rate fluctuations do not necessarily coincide with those of the respective ocean-going tonnage (e.g. the freight rate trends of small tankers may differ from those of ocean-going tankers).

In dry cargo markets, many shipping companies carry on independent trading with smaller-sized vessels, but the trend is now to employ small single-deckers or tween-deckers in some sort of regularly scheduled feeder traffic. The result is that these vessels find themselves in competition with other carriers in the short-sea trades, including larger ships carrying part-cargoes, as well as road and rail traffic.

One may find typical feeder vessels (small containerships or multi-purpose vessels) looking for employment in the open market depending on the casual need. It is, however, also common for ocean liner companies or forwarding agents or charterers who trade with their own products to operate feeder ships as a part of their transport scheme.

Owners and operators of coasters and feeder vessels frequently work together, pooling their fleets and administrative resources in order to undertake chartering contracts and to optimise vessels' scheduling, employment earnings and costs.

Some owners specialise in tailoring their ships and operation for so-called industrial shipping, in close co-operation over a longer period of time with a big exporter/importer or industry to provide an integrated link in the industry's overall logistics system.

1.3.13 Specialised vessels

In addition to the above-mentioned types of vessels, some of which regarded as specialised ones forming separate markets on their own (e.g. offshore vessels, gas carriers, car carriers etc.), there are a number of extremely specialised ships which serve special transport needs. Among such vessels, the following types are worth mentioning:

- *Heavy-lift carriers*
Some companies have specialised in heavy-lift cargoes and technically complicated transports, where the movements between quay and ship are the most

difficult parts of the operation. For such purposes vessels must be built with heavy lifting gear. Special demands on stability and constructional strength are required, particularly with regard to vessels' gear.

• *Barges and pontoons*
This is a transport system also used for the carriage of heavy material, for example a ready-built drilling rig, but they are further used as floating quays, as feeders in short-sea traffic and as discharging platforms between an ocean-going ship and the quay. The tug-barge system requires a combination of logistics, where a detachable pushing tug unit is used as an engine for a number of "cargo-hold" units. The most known such systems are called "*LASH*" and "*Seabee*".

• *Tugs*
The demand for towing vessels has grown with their increased use by the offshore industry (see section 1.3.4). Apart from this, towing work for the merchant fleet has been relatively stable worldwide, as tugs are regularly used not only for assisting vessels in arriving at and departing from ports of call, but also for salvage purposes.

CHAPTER 2

Charter rates and state of the freight market

Freight is considered to be the most crucial part of a charter agreement. This chapter completes the charter market analysis, focusing on the freight rates perspective. Firstly, it shows how the general state of freight rates is determined in the open market. This is compared with liner pricing aspects for which a short reference is made. Then, factors affecting the fixture rate of an individual charter are discussed. Analysis goes further to examine the fundamentals of the four major freight markets; dry bulk, tanker, gas and containerships. In order to show an overall view of the charter market, for each market segment some interesting chartering topics are considered, such as the preferred types of vessel fixtures, the indicative voyage/trade routes, the major cargo exporting and importing areas, the typical cargo shiploads, the expression and reporting of spot and time charter rates, the key indicators of ships' demand and supply, together with examples of real charter fixtures (spot and time charter). The state of each freight market is discussed and the long-term historical evolution of time charter rates is illustrated for all the representative types of vessels, ranging from 1980 up to 2015. In the last section of this chapter, freight indices are described to show how the state of the market is measured and expressed, while freight derivatives are introduced to present how the freight market risk may be managed. Finally, it is worth noting that freight markets are dynamic, thus an updated market data coverage is beyond the scope of this book. Therefore, freight rates have been intentionally omitted from the respective tables.

2.1 Freight market mechanism

In all sectors of the open chartering market, the price for a sea transport, namely the *freight*, is determined on the basis of the negotiating power of the involved parties (the shipowner and the charterer), at a specific time, under the prevailing charter (freight) market conditions and in accordance with the special requirements of the charter. The *fixture rate* of a specific charter is typically ranging close to the current general state of the market for respective vessels and types of charter. The *general state of the freight market* is determined from the interchange of demand and supply for sea transport services at a specific point of time. A huge variety of factors, predictable or not, may possibly affect the demand or supply of global sea transport and consequently the level of freight rates. Besides, as the demand for sea transport is derived from the demand for the goods carried, it may be said that the freight levels are effectively formed by the business balance and the bargaining power between buyers and sellers in the competitive field of international trade.[1]

There is a considerable difference between the *liner freight market* and the *open freight market*. The latter is the market where tonnage is principally fixed voyage by voyage, the so-called *spot market*, where the buyers of sea transport find the tonnage (vessels) required to carry the available cargoes. The open market also includes the time charter segment and an important part covering other more long-term contractual engagements of various natures (e.g. bareboat, CoA etc.). Freight rates are determined through a chartering negotiation process, made among the shipowners, charterers and their brokers (see chapter 8). On the other hand, the liner freight market is formed in accordance with freight contracts made between liner operators and shippers, typically on a regular basis (e.g. annually). Liner pricing is based on complicated pricing schemes where cargoes are classified in group or classes and each group is priced in accordance with pre-determined tables.

A great percentage of the world volume of goods transported by sea is fixed in the open market. The balance is taken care of by the liner services in their strictly directed and scheduled traffic with controlled freight terms and conditions. The total volume of open market fixtures is mostly dispersed between spot fixtures and time charters. The spot market increases its percentage share of chartered ships during periods of general economic recession, when there is a low demand for sea transport.

The open market is influenced by the "laws" of ships' supply and demand, but it would be an over-simplification to state that the freight market is generated and directed only by this. The fluctuations in freight levels are very large and intense, particularly for tankers and bulkers. This will be commented below in the specific market analysis (see section 2.4 and Tables 2.12, 2.13). Dry bulk and tanker markets are the two most important freight markets. In the long run their freight rate fluctuations tend to coincide – but not always – with world industrial output, whilst in the short run there are seasonal variations, not only arising from the shipping market fundamentals, but also from major exogenous geo-political, social and other factors (e.g. wars, embargoes, natural disasters, strikes, etc. of a global or local nature). The connection of freight rates to world industrial activity is greatly reflected by the two so-called "leading" dry bulk commodities, namely iron ore and coal (raw materials for the steel industry), whereas seasonal variations are clearly depicted by the demand for ships to carry grain (including soya beans and rice), which is the third leading commodity in the dry bulk cargo sector and certainly affected by the "crop season" on a global or local level.

A part of the total available cargoes and ships of the world freight markets is negotiated, more or less secretly, between the owners and charterers, finally being fixed for time charters and other long-term period contracts. What remains is a number of cargoes looking for ships and a number of ships looking for

---

1 McConville, J. (1999) *Economics of Maritime Transport – Theory and Practice* (London, Witherby and Co. Ltd., 1st edition, pp. 9, 11).

employment. This constitutes the so-called *spot market* which develops and changes on a day-by-day basis; the spot market affects any geographical area and covers the whole spectrum of types, sizes and features of ships. It is this market situation, the fixing and the terms obtained in the spot market of shipping sectors, that are being reported continuously by brokers and shipping publications. The spot market still reacts quickly to various exogenous factors (e.g. war or armed conflict). However, today, when information is readily available to all parties, there tend to be fewer surprises and the volatility in the freight markets, even remaining high, has been reduced compared to the past.

An illustration in Figure 2.1 shows how operative forces work in practice in a miniature spot market. If, for a specific loading date within a limited geographical area, there are 10 ships open for employment, but there are only nine cargoes offered, then it is likely that none of the vessels will obtain a higher freight rate than the lowest rate that anyone of the respective shipowners is willing to accept. In the reverse situation, where there are 10 cargoes available but only nine ships, one can expect every ship that is fixed to obtain better terms than the preceding one.

Various factors may influence the general freight conditions, the ship costs and the development of the open market, such as the general state of the world economy, sudden changes in demand for specific commodities, an economic boom within special market areas, a state of war, a closure of important routes, a crop failure, an extreme congestion in important ports, an oversupply of specific types of ships, or an unusually late or early closure of ice-bound waters etc.

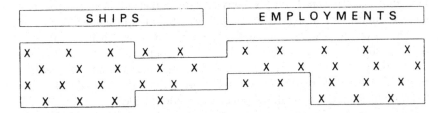

NOTE: *This is a simplified picture of the open market status at any one time. The ships and employments within the frame are finding each other directly in some kind of long-term engagement, in other words they are fixed away and covered and the ships concerned are trading. The ships and employments remaining open outside the frame constitute the spot market at this particular time and in this specific area or market sector. Brokers will be trying to match the respective Owners and Charterers. The freight rates and other terms obtainable will reflect the unbalance between supply of ships and demand for transport. That status will tell brokers and other parties involved whether the market is going up or down, and the circulated fixture reports and market gossip will advise about the freight levels and terms actually fixed.*

Figure 2.1 The Spot Market

It is practically impossible to predict with any degree of certainty future developments in the freight market. In general, periods of low freight market conditions are substantially longer than periods when high freight rates can be obtained. There is really no such thing as a "normal" market level and it would be more accurate to say that the freight market constantly oscillates between extremes.

There are always, even during periods of general economic recession, market areas where there may exist a more or less temporarily high demand for tonnage. In 1977, for instance, dry bulk and tanker freight rates were weak as there was a great excess of tonnage in both markets, caused by continuing deliveries of vessels from the shipyards. At the same time, however, there was a strong demand for ocean-going ro/ro vessels and reefer ships, which thus obtained very high time charter rates. More recently, a similar market divergence was observed in 2014–2016. Dry bulk spot rates remained depressed, greatly influenced by the reduced growth rate of China and an oversupply of vessels, whereas on the contrary, tanker spot market was extremely strong, positively affected by the low oil price environment and a low orderbook of new vessels.

Other factors which contribute to the uncertainty in forecasting and always have a decisive influence on the freight market development, are changes in economic conditions in critical countries and geographical areas, such as China, the USA, Europe, Japan, Russia, Brazil, India, Middle East, Latin America and Australia. A farmers' strike in Argentina creating a massive congestion in the Argentinean ports certainly has an influence in the dry bulk freight rates, as does flooding which affects the production in Australian coal mines. Another remarkable example concerns the United Nations' embargoes that may be imposed against various countries for various reasons (e.g. Libya, Iran, Iraq), having rather a sudden impact on the tanker freight markets. Information about such matters tends to hit the shipping market suddenly, although not quite unexpectedly. The most remarkable example in this century is the absolute collapse of the international trade and thus of all freight markets, which occurred after the outbreak of the "Global Financial Crisis" in the last financial quarter of 2008.

During a general low freight market period, every sign is noted which may indicate a change toward an increase in demand for sea transport, such as the state of the world economy and its key drivers, or the development of the geopolitical situation or the market trends within special sectors (e.g. steel output, production of cars, outcome of harvest, developments in important consuming areas etc.). When there seem to be small but firm indications of higher freight rates shown simultaneously by most important market indicators, the charterers and shippers will try to belittle such signs of forthcoming changes, while shipowners then adopt a "wait and see" approach. If it becomes evident that there is substance in these market trends, charterers become more and more active in the time charter markets, trying to secure long-term charter contracts at low freight levels. Thereby, the supply of tonnage on the spot market will decrease and the freight levels generally start to rise, albeit slowly.

If there arises a sudden increase in demand for tonnage in a special trade, as for instance the iron ore trade between Australia and China, a scarcity of tonnage may occur in other areas and in other trades dependent on the same type and size of ship, for example in the iron ore trade between Brazil and China (as Australia and Brazil are competing major iron ore exporters). The rising trend in freight levels will then become further accentuated. At this point, certain psychological factors will start to contribute to the development of the market. Charterers and shippers, in fear of running into a situation of acute scarcity of tonnage, will try to conclude their shipping arrangements as soon as possible. Shipowners can ask for increasingly higher freight rates and if, for example, a sudden political crisis arises, then those interested in the shipping market may find themselves in a real freight boom. The trading in Forward Freight Agreements (FFAs) will no doubt have an impact on owners' expectations of the market. Before fixing away the ship for a period employment, an owner will carefully study the FFA figures for the time span in question (see section 2.5).

A frequent consequence of such a development is that the owners of older vessels, which may have been laid up during the low market period, will start trading their ships again instead of sending them to the scrapyards. The shipowners will now start to offer part of the previously time-chartered tonnage for employment on the rising spot market.

Another factor which will affect the market with a delay of some two or three years is that a number of owners are now ordering new-builds, which, if they have bad luck, will be delivered during the next period of a low freight market. Due to heavy ordering of new ships, a recession in the shipping market may now be "en route", although its precise timing cannot be predicted exactly. Shipowners will show an increasing interest in fixing their ships for long-term charter contracts and freight levels will gradually move downwards, as new vessels are gradually entering the market. Charterers will hold out to obtain even lower freight levels and, as suddenly as the freight rates started to rise to very high levels, the market will drop.

The effects of the above-described cycle were highlighted in 2008. The period 2003–2008 was by far the most profitable six-year period in the entire history of shipping. Freight rates increased unthinkably in all major freight markets, namely dry bulk, tanker and containerships. As a result, a huge amount of new-builds were ordered. However, during the "Global Financial Crisis" which broke out in autumn 2008, the shipping market came to a total standstill and the freight rates dropped drastically. At the same time the new-builds that had been previously ordered had been planned for delivery in 2009 and onwards, putting further pressure on a freight market already in distress.

The year 2008 formed a milestone for shipowners, since it marked the end of the most profitable period ever, as well as the start of a sore and protracted shipping recession (or even depression) for most of the vessel types and for so many years. That year fully demonstrated the unpredictability of the market, due to the unprecedented volatility of freight rates. After the unique culmination of the freight markets in May 2008 and the best summer ever, the bankruptcy of the investment bank Lehman Brothers on 16 September 2008 marked the reversal of the flow of things for all global markets. Looking at the dry bulk market, at the beginning of the year, a capesize earned in the spot market $130,000/day, whilst in February the freight had decreased by 40%. Then, the need to stockbuild ore reserves and some port congestion incidents fired the spot rates to $320,000/day in June. In early September the spot earnings dropped to $80,000/day, however, as the financial crisis was intensified, still mills stocks accumulated and trade collapsed, the capesize spot earnings tumbled to $6,000/day in October and just $2,000/day in November. Although the 2008 average annual profitability of dry cargo vessels closed slightly below the all-time high recorded in 2007, the year ended in an absolutely devastating manner. For the tanker market, things were equally unpredictable and highly volatile. A VLCC who earned in the spot market $195,000/day in early January, earned only $50,000/day at the end of the same month. Although the demand for crude and petroleum products remained sluggish, the market defied the fundamentals, resulting in VLCCs earning $170,000/day in July, due to the need for stockbuilding and the marginalisation of single hull tankers from the market. In general, the average annual tanker spot rates increased by 30% compared with 2007.[2]

2.2 Liner pricing aspects

Although from the perspective of shipbroking and chartering practice focus should be given on the open market freight determination mechanism, before proceeding further, and for the sake of completeness, a few liner pricing issues will be examined at this point.

As a result of containerisation, in liner trade routes the freight of carrying a container may be composed of the following five parts[3]:

1. Inland haulage outbound from shipper to terminal, i.e. from the point where the shipper delivers the cargo to the carrier (shipping line) up to the loading terminal.
2. Terminal charge at port of loading.
3. Ocean freight for sea transport.
4. Terminal charge at port of discharge.
5. Inland haulage inbound from terminal to consignee (recipient), i.e. from the discharging terminal up to the point where the cargo is delivered to the consignee.

Although freight of inland haulage and terminal charges are calculated on a container basis, ocean freight is a function of the cargo carried inside the container. As a consequence of the numerous cargoes carried by the liner vessels, each liner company has established its own complicated pricing system of sea transport services. In accordance with that, each cargo is classified in a group or class of commodities

---

2 Clarksons Research *Shipping Intelligence Weekly* (9 January 2009).

3 Cambridge Academy of Transport (2000) *Anatomy of Shipping* (seminar proceedings, 10–22 September 2000, sessions 31 & 32, pp. 19–20).

on the basis of its particular properties and characteristics. Each group of commodities is priced in accordance with a pre-determined pricing scheme.

There are a number of factors influencing the freight determination in liner shipping; however two of them are critical: the unit value of commodity and the cargo stowage factor. Even though pricing mechanisms have been simplified by far due to the extensive use of advanced IT systems, the rationale remains unchanged; different types of cargoes are carried on different freight rates even if almost all liner cargoes are carried in containers today. On the other hand, cargoes may be carried on *"Freight All Kinds"* (*FAK*) terms, when various kinds of goods are pooled and shipped together at one single freight rate which is irrespective of each individual commodity. Ocean freight is typically surcharged with the so-called *"Currency Adjustment Factors"* (*CAF*) and *"Bunker Adjustment Factors"* (*BAF*), where it is agreed that the freight is adjusted in accordance with the currency exchange fluctuations and the bunkers prices respectively.

In the past, liner *conferences* used to offer better prices in major shippers, either by the so-called "deferred rebate schemes" where the shippers should prove that they used only the liner services of the specific conference members to receive a special rebate, or by the "exclusive contract" or "dual rate schemes", where shippers should co-operate on an exclusive basis with the liner conference in exchange for receiving better freight rates.[4] Loyal customers may still enjoy better pricing from liner companies today, even though liner conferences have vanished and methods of preferential treatment or market control are nowadays prohibited by most countries. Nevertheless, liner companies have adopted other modern methods of co-operation and market consolidation, such as shipping alliances or merger and acquisition techniques. After a period of significant mergers and acquisitions starting at the end of the 1990s, now all major liner companies have been consolidated to operate under only a few major shipping alliances in main trades, which are allowed to co-operate mostly on terms of vessels' scheduling, slots' interchange etc., but not on controlling freight rates (see section 1.1.3).

When pricing their services, liner companies face fierce competition and considerable restrictions, the most important of them coming from shippers' strategic decisions, the elimination of the role of conferences and other monopolistic practices of the liner companies due to global anti-trust rules, the over-supply of the liner market from the shipbuilding of huge containerships, the competition from air transport and bulk shipping, or even from problems of co-operation arising from inside a shipping alliance.[5]

In general, since early 2000s freight rate determination in liner shipping has been converted from *"tariff-based"* to *"contract-based"* and the reform of

---

4 Sjostrom, W. "Liner Shipping: Modelling Competition and Collusion" in Grammenos, C.T. (2002) *The Handbook of Maritime Economics and Business* (London, LLP, 1st edition, p. 318); McConville, J. (1999) *Economics of Maritime Transport – Theory and Practice* (London, Witherby and Co. Ltd., 1st edition, pp. 348–349).

5 Heaver, T. "Supply Chain and Logistics Management: Implications for Liner Shipping" in Grammenos, C.T. (2002) *The Handbook of Maritime Economics and Business* (London, LLP, 1st edition, p. 380).

institutional business framework in the USA and Europe has been the major influencing factor to this. Liner market has eliminated price enforcement methods or practices of oligopolistic control, encouraging carriers and shippers to freely and individually negotiate and agree on contract of carriage terms, in accordance to their commercial needs. Therefore, even if each liner operator may have retained its own "tariff" which determines the groups of cargo pricing classification in accordance with the cargoes' particulars, the freight rates are not imposed monopolistically, but formed as a result of the negotiating power of the involved parties; carriers and shippers. Final prices offered from carriers to shippers come after the evaluation of the transport services required, the types of containers and the cargoes carried (e.g. reefer containers are priced higher) and the current balance between the ships' supply and demand in the market. Liner companies' offers usually apply for a specific period (e.g. up to one year), so shippers are able to control the transport costs and plan their transport needs. Under such circumstances, the negotiating position of the shippers seems to have been strengthened in comparison to the past.

Liner freight rates are not subject to as much volatility as freight rates in the open market. Freight changes are slow and fluctuations are smoother in the liner market. It goes without saying that liner shipping is clearly a market of less interest as far as chartering and shipbroking are concerned. Therefore, liner pricing will not be commented on further in this text. Instead, analysis will revert to principles followed on the open market, discussing the determinants of a fixture in the following section, before proceeding to a freight market presentation in section 2.4.

2.3 Determinants of the fixture rate in the open chartering market

Freight or hire rate is the most crucial subject of chartering negotiations. The fixture rate of an individual charter is negotiated through brokers' channels in the open market and may be influenced or determined by the following important factors:

1. The *type of vessel* sought to be fixed. As a general rule, freight rates of the most common vessel types (e.g. tankers, bulkers) present higher volatility and sharper fluctuations than more specialised types of vessels. This is a crucial factor in all types of charter (spot and period).
2. *Ship's specification and condition.* Vessel particulars, such as the cargo-carrying capacity, speed, draught, beam, age, fuel efficiency (e.g. eco-ships), class, cargo gear etc. affect the chartering opportunities and the freight rates achieved. This is also affected by the status of ship's maintenance. A charterer's opinion for the future performance of the ship is much influenced by such parameters. This is a crucial factor in all charter types (spot and period).
3. The *geographical location* of vessel. In voyage charters the distance between the geographical position of the ship and the cargo to be carried

may seriously affect the freight rate of a fixture. In period charters the geographical position of the vessel in relation to the agreed delivery place to the charterer may also play a role in calculating the charter hire.

4. *Charter period.* Spot freight rates are more volatile compared to time charter rates, due to the shorter time of vessel's employment in the first case. Spot rates reflect the daily fluctuations of the freight market, whilst time charter rates reflect the long-term trend of the freight market.

5. The *overall cost of providing the vessel.* Cost allocation between the involved parties is of utmost importance when selecting a type of charter and fixing a chartering rate. For example, in a voyage charter the ship's voyage costs, operating expenses, capital costs and possibly the cargo-handling expenses are all for the shipowner's account, in a time charter the voyage and cargo-handling costs are passed to the charterer, whereas in a bareboat charter only the ship's capital costs are owner's responsibility.

6. *Market anticipation.* Market forecast and expectations of the negotiating parties in respect of the future freight rates are critical. This is important in all aspects of decision-making in shipping, thus it affects considerably all types of charter (spot and period).

7. *Current state of the market.* It is one of the most important factors when fixing the freight rate for a specific charter. Market reports, shipping publications and freight indices are valuable tools for all chartering and shipbroking practitioners, in order to form their view for the state of the freight market and adjust their policy accordingly.

8. *Customer satisfaction and retention.* Modern marketing principles (see chapter 5) require from the shipowners to form their chartering strategy in accordance to their customers' (charterers'/shippers') needs. This is more important today than in the past within the shipping industry. It may be a critical factor when considering the determination of freight rates. It applies in all types of a ship's charter, whilst it is also important for liner shipping.

9. *Bargaining (negotiation) power of the parties.* Determination of a fixture rate is a matter of chartering negotiation between a shipowner and a charterer. This balance is affected by various parameters, such as financial standing of the parties, timing, long-term relationships and the needs or priorities of the parties, etc.

2.4 Freight market analysis and state of the market

This section attempts to chart the most important freight markets and comprehensively describe the fundamental parameters which determine the state of the freight rates. Each of the following sections presents the types of preferable vessel fixtures, benchmark voyage routes, major ports of loading and discharging, examples of how spot freight rates and time charter rates are measured and expressed in the market, as well as the key indicators in respect of ships' demand

and supply. This methodology is followed for each of the four crucial freight markets of the shipping industry: dry bulk, tankers, gas carriers and containerships. Tables and figures are provided to familiarise the reader with types of vessels' employment, important cargoes, shipload quantities and trade routes, as well as with the way that freight rates are expressed. As the market is dynamic, numbers are constantly changing, thus there is no point for this section to focus on freight rates of the markets. The market practitioner should always consult expertised maritime research companies, shipbrokers and shipping publications in order to get a fully and constantly updated view of the freight markets. However, the reader may refer to Tables 2.12 and 2.13 at the end of this section, to find a historical evolution of the yearly average time charter rates of all major ship types, ranging from 1980 up to 2015, as kindly provided by Drewry Maritime Research on an exclusive basis for this edition.

2.4.1 Dry bulk market

A large variety of cargoes are carried on bulk carriers but, as a rule, the larger the vessel the bigger the shiploads are and the fewer commodities are commonly loaded. For example, capesize ships carry mostly iron ore and coal in large shiploads. Panamax sizes are commonly employed on coal and grain trades but also for the carriage of fertilisers, sulphur, salt, bauxite, alumina and steel slabs. The smaller handysize to supramax sizes, in addition to the above, are also often employed in carrying smaller quantities of cargoes such as steel products, scrap and sugar.

In all dry bulk markets, spot charters concern vessel fixtures made on a voyage basis and thus freight rates are typically expressed or reported in US Dollars per tonne of cargo carried, as well as on a time charter equivalent basis[6] (average earnings in US Dollars per day) which enables a comparison with time charter employment alternatives. On the other hand, time charter hire rates are always expressed and reported in US Dollars per day. The most prominent shipping reviews may report average hire rates for different vessel types and sizes (e.g. capesize, panamax, supramax/handymax, handysize) and for a variety of charter durations (e.g. six-month, one-year, three-year, five-year time charters) and vessels' age (e.g. modern vessels of five years old, or elder ones of 10 or 15 years old).

An analytical presentation of the main dry bulk markets is set out below.

2.4.1.1 Capesize market

Capesize vessels (> 100,000 dwt) are mostly employed in spot charters, i.e. being fixed on a voyage-by-voyage basis, but also period charters are not uncommon. Table 2.1 presents indicative trade routes for spot (voyage) employment of capesize vessels, the typical cargoes carried and some of the major ports of loading and discharging. As the market is dynamic, emphasis is given on these factors, not on the respective charter rates which are constantly changing. It may be seen that these vessels typically carry iron ore and coal.

---

6 See section 14.1.2.5 for Time Charter Equivalent (TCE).

Table 2.1 Capesize Bulk Carriers Indicative Spot Trades

Cargo Shipment (tons)		Single Voyage
100–150,000	Iron Ore	Tubarao (Brazil) – Japan
160,000	Iron Ore	Brazil – ARA (Antwerp/Rotterdam/Amsterdam)
160–170,000	Iron Ore	Tubarao (Brazil) – Qingdao (China)
160–170,000	Iron Ore	Dampier (Australia) – Qingdao (China)
120–160,000	Iron Ore	W. Australia – ARA
160,000	Iron Ore	Saldanha Bay (South Africa) – China
150,000	Coal	Richards Bay (South Africa) – ARA
160,000	Coal	Richards Bay (South Africa) – China
150,000	Coal	E. Australia – South Korea
150,000	Coal	Hay Point (Eastern Australia) – Japan
150,000	Coal	Puerto Bolivar (Colombia) – ARA

Source: Drewry Maritime Research *Shipping Insight* (February 2016, p. 14) and Baltic Exchange *Manual for Panellists: A Guide to Freight Reporting and Index Production* (January 2015, p. 34), data compiled by A. Papadopoulos.

The most interesting iron ore trade concerns China imports either from Brazil or Australia in quantities of about 175,000 mt. Major iron ore trades may be summarised as follows[7]:

- Australia to Far East and Europe
- India to Far East
- South Africa to Far East and Europe
- Brazil to Far East, Europe and Argentina
- Chile to Far East
- Norway to Europe
- Black Sea to Far East

Coal is mostly exported from South Africa, Colombia or Australia to Europe, China etc. in quantities of about 168,000 tonnes. Major coal trades may be summarised as follows[8] (this concerns all coal trades, thus includes also smaller coal shipments that may be carried by panamax, supramax and handymax vessels):

- Australia to Far East and Europe, with some cargoes also to Brazil and Argentina
- Australia to India and South Africa to India
- Indonesia to Far East and Europe
- South Africa to Far East and Europe
- Colombia to Europe
- USA (East Coast) to Far East and Europe
- Canada (West Coast) to Far East

---

7 The Baltic Exchange (2014) *The Baltic Code 2014* (p. 11).
8 The Baltic Exchange (2014) *The Baltic Code 2014* (p. 11).

An example of a spot (voyage) charter concerns a fixture made in mid-July 2015 about a capesize vessel (177,000 dwt, built 2010) owned by a respectable Hong Kong based shipowner which chartered his vessel to a first-class charterer, for a cargo voyage from Tubarao (Brazil) to Qingdao (China), in order to transport 170,000 mt of iron ore, at USD 13.5/mt of cargo carried, with lay/can[9] dates on 10/18 August 2015.

An example of a time charter fixture was reported as made in mid-July 2015, concerning a capesize vessel (181,000 dwt, built 2014) owned by a respectable Greek-based shipowner which chartered his vessel to a first-class charterer, for a short period of 4–7 months, in order to trade it worldwide, for $14,750/day, with lay/can dates on 25/30 July 2015 and agreed delivery place in China, redelivery worldwide.

2.4.1.2 Panamax market

Panamax vessels (65–100,000 dwt) are mostly employed in spot charters, but also period charters are found. Table 2.2 presents indicative types of spot (voyage) employment for panamaxes, the typical cargoes carried and some major ports of loading and discharging. It is shown that these vessels usually carry coal and grain. Coal that is loaded in panamaxes is mostly exported from Australia, South Africa, the USA, Colombia, Russia, Indonesia and imported mostly in Europe, China, Japan and India in quantities of about 65–74,000 mt. Some major coal trades were also mentioned before (see Capesize market, section 2.4.1.1). Grain quantities for panamaxes are loaded in the North Pacific area and the USA to China, Japan and Europe in quantities of about 55–60,000 mt. For example, major wheat trades may be summarised as follows (this concerns all trades, thus includes also smaller shipments that may be carried by supramax, handymax and handysize vessels)[10]:

- North America to Far East, Middle East and Europe
- Australia to Far East and Middle East
- East Coast of South America to Far East and Europe with some cargoes also to Middle East
- UK/Continent to Middle East and North Africa
- Black Sea to Middle East

Another typical grain cargo is soya beans. Its major trades may be summarised as follows (this concerns all trades, thus includes also smaller shipments that may be carried by supramax, handymax and handysize vessels):

- USA (Gulf/Mississippi) to Far East, Middle East and Europe
- Brazil to Far East and Europe
- Argentina to Far East and Europe

---

9 Lay/Can term here determines the agreed period within which the loading process must start.
10 The Baltic Exchange (2014) *The Baltic Code 2014* (p. 11).

Table 2.2 Panamax Bulk Carriers Indicative Spot Trades

Cargo Shipment (tons)		Single Voyage
70,000	Coal	Eastern Australia – Japan
70,000	Coal	Richards Bay (South Africa) – Mediterranean Sea
74,000	Coal	Newcastle (Australia) – Qingdao (China)
55,000	Grain	US Gulf – Japan
55,000	Grain	US Gulf – ARA

Source: Drewry Maritime Research *Shipping Insight* (February 2016, p. 15), data compiled by A. Papadopoulos.

Table 2.3 Handymax/Supramax Bulk Carriers Indicative Time Charter Trips

Vessel Size (dwt)	Trip Charter/Trading Area
40–60,000	Transpacific trip
40–60,000	FE (Far East) – Australia
40–60,000	Continent (Western mainland Europe excl. UK) – FE (Far East)
40–60,000	FE (Far East) – Continent
40–60,000	US Gulf – Continent

Source: Drewry Maritime Research *Shipping Insight* (February 2016, p. 16), data compiled by A. Papadopoulos.

An example of a spot (voyage) charter concerns a fixture made in June 2015 about an older panamax vessel (70,000 dwt, built 1997) which was chartered to carry a cargo of 53,000 mt of grain from US Gulf to China, for a high rate of $31.75/mt of cargo carried, with lay/can dates on 10/15 July 2015.

An example of a time charter fixture was reported as made in July 2015, concerning a panamax vessel (73,000 dwt, built 2006) owned by a respectable Greek-based shipowner which chartered his vessel to a first-class charterer, for a period of 11–14 months, in order to trade it worldwide, for $7,000/day, with lay/can dates on 12/20 July 2015 and agreed delivery place in China, redelivery worldwide.

2.4.1.3 Handymax and supramax / ultramax market
Handymax and supramax/ultramax vessels (40–65,000 dwt) are usually employed in spot charters and time charter trips. Table 2.3 presents indicative types of trip time charters for handymax and supramax/ultramax bulkers, as well as some major trading areas. This does not downgrade at all the importance of the spot market for this sector. These vessels usually carry coal and grain in similar (spot) trade routes but in smaller quantities than panamax vessels. The most important coal and grain trades worldwide were mentioned above (see 2.4.1.2, 2.4.1.1).

An example of a voyage charter concerns a fixture made in July 2015 for a modern Ultramax vessel (63,000 dwt, built 2013) which was fixed to carry a cargo of 54,000 mt HSS grain (HSS: heavy grain, soya, sorghums) from Texas

Gulf (USA) to Northern China, at $37/mt of cargo carried, with lay/can dates on 25 July/5 August 2015.

It must be mentioned here that supramax/ultramax vessels are commonly chartered on a time charter trip (TCT) basis, which is a hybrid form of charter where the owner commits his vessel for such a time period as it lasts for a specific voyage to be executed. In such a charter the owner is paid in US Dollars per day, not in US Dollars per ton of cargo carried. An example of a time charter trip fixture was reported as made in July 2015, concerning a modern supramax vessel (56,000 dwt, built 2014) which was agreed to be delivered to the charterers in Rio Grande (Brazil) to load in the ECSA (East Coast South America) area, so as to execute a cargo voyage and discharge in the Singapore–Japan area where it should be redelivered to the owners. The charter hire was for $13,000/day and a ballast bonus of $300,000 was agreed, i.e. an extra amount paid to the owner as compensation for moving his vessel in ballast to the delivery area.

2.4.1.4 Handysize market

Handysize bulkers (10–40,000 dwt) typically trade on a spot basis, as well as in time charter trips. Table 2.4 presents indicative types of trip time charters for handysize bulkers and some major trading areas. These vessels are trading world-wide, able to carry a great variety of cargoes, so only some representative time charter trips are shown instead of typical spot trades. This does not downgrade at all the importance of the spot market for this sector.

It must be stressed that time charter trips are fixed, paid and reported in US Dollars per day, even though they concern specific cargo voyages.

An example of a voyage charter concerns a fixture made in July 2015 for a modern handysize vessel (33,000 dwt, built 2014) which was fixed to carry a cargo of 25,000 mt sugar from Maputo (Mozambique) to Rotterdam (Netherlands), for $25/mt of cargo carried, with lay/can dates on 21–25 July 2015.

Another example of a time charter trip fixture was reported as made in July 2015, concerning an older handysize vessel (30,000 dwt, built 1999) which was agreed to be delivered to the charterers in Bejaia (Algeria) to load in the Black Sea area, so as to execute a cargo voyage and discharge in the Mediterranean Sea area where it should be redelivered to the owners. The charter hire rate was agreed for $8,000/day.

Table 2.4 Handysize Bulk Carriers Indicative Time Charter Trips

Vessel Size (dwt)	*Trip Charter/Trading Area*
10–40,000	Continent (Western mainland Europe excl. UK) – Transatlantic rv (round voyage)
10–40,000	FE (Far East)/Australia rv (round voyage)

Source: Drewry Maritime Research *Shipping Insight* (February 2016, p. 17), data compiled by A. Papadopoulos.

2.4.1.5 Dry bulk market: demand factors

The demand for bulk carriers is crucially affected by numerous, constantly changing, global factors. At this point, only the most important key drivers for the dry bulk demand will be addressed below (the list is indicative, not exhaustive):

- The most significant driver of dry bulk demand is China, more precisely Chinese policy in respect of overall industrial activity, steel production, iron ore production and imports, metallurgical (coking) and steam (thermal) coal demand, grain imports and efforts to combat pollution. Together with that, China's selection of its basic iron ore supplier between the traditional rivals, Brazil and Australia, is always crucial.
- GDP growth on a global level and particularly in the two key drivers of the world economy, China and North America, as well as other economic areas such as the European countries of OECD, Japan, India, other Asian countries, Latin America.
- Global imports of the five major bulks, namely iron ore, metallurgical and steam coal, grain, phosphates, bauxite/alumina, as well as imports of steel products and minor bulks.
- Steel production on a global level, but also particularly in Japan, Western Europe and developing Asia, including India which plays a critical role (China is excepted as mentioned separately above). In relation to that, critical factors are also Japanese, European and Asian iron ore and metallurgical coal imports. The role of India in importing steam coal is expected to increase in the future.
- In respect of the steel products trades, critical factors are exports from China, Japan and countries of the former Soviet Union, as well as imports in the US, Middle East and developing Asia.
- In respect of the grain trade, critical factors are exports from the US, Latin America and Australia, imports in Japan, other Asian countries (except China imports which mentioned separately before), Middle East and Africa, as well as seasonality and weather conditions which affect "crop years".
- Demand expressed in ton-mile terms, so as the distance of trades to be taken into consideration in correlation to the volumes of cargo carried. Iron ore trade is mostly affected by this. For example, if China imports a quantity of iron ore from Australia and substitutes this supplier for Brazil, this would create much more demand in ton-mile terms for the same cargo quantity carried.
- Seasonality.

2.4.1.6 Dry bulk market: supply factors

There are some "key indicators" about the supply of dry bulk vessels. These critical factors are listed below (the list is indicative, not exhaustive):

- Fleet annual growth, which is determined by ships' ordering and deliveries on the one hand and scrapping on the other.

- Fleet structure. In respect of this, the following points may be examined:

  ○ *Orderbook to existing fleet:* This ratio measures the number or tonnage capacity of the vessels that are expected to be built in the next 2–3 years, as a percentage to the existing fleet. A "heavy" orderbook, either in absolute terms or as a percentage to an existing fleet, denotes that many ships are to enter in the market in the next few years, increasing the possibility of an "over-supply" and a drop of the freight rates if demand does not prove sufficient. As an example, the orderbook for all dry bulk vessels stood at a moderate 16% of the whole fleet in January 2016, with the heaviest orderbook among the sub-sectors being for the handymax/supramax segment.[11]

  ○ *Age breakdown:* This shows the age structure of a fleet. As a general and widely accepted market perception, the vessels' useful life is estimated at approximately 25 years. Thus, vessels of up to 10 years old are generally considered modern ones and ships over 20 years old are generally considered scrapping "candidates". It is obvious however that, in periods of shipping recession, vessels may be scrapped even at the age of 15 years old, whereas in periods of booming markets vessels of 30 years old or more may keep on trading as owners defer their decision to scrap them. The fleet age structure indicates if a fleet is modern or aged. In periods of low rates, the freight markets may be more easily relieved in cases of aged fleets rather than in cases of modern fleets, as in the former situation more vessels are possible to move to the scrapyards. In relation to the above, a ratio showing which percentage of the fleet is over 15 or 20 years old shows how aged a fleet is and how many vessels may be scrapped in the next years. As an example, it may be commented that the bulk carrier fleet in total was modern enough in January 2016, as only 8% of the fleet was over 20 years old.[12]

  ○ *Replacement ratio:* This measures the orderbook (number of ships or tonnage capacity in dwt) of the vessels to be built, as a percentage to the existing fleet which is over 15 years old. Essentially, it is a ratio which combines the above-mentioned aspects (orderbook and age structure) to show how the older vessels are expected to be replaced by the newbuildings. As an example, it may be mentioned that in January 2016 the replacement ratio (orderbook to fleet of over 15 years old) stood at 105% for the total dry bulk fleet, showing a considerable orderbook in relation to a relatively modern dry bulk fleet.[13]

- Fleet productivity, technological factors and innovation. The so-called "productivity" of the fleet is increased when a fleet's average speed is

---

11 Clarksons Research *Dry Bulk Trade Outlook* (January 2016).
12 Clarksons Research *Dry Bulk Trade Outlook* (January 2016).
13 Clarksons Research *Dry Bulk Trade Outlook* (January 2016).

improved. Slow steaming may be preferred in periods of low or flat freight rates when this is combined with high oil prices and costly bunkers, as this tactic saves costs and keeps the fleet employed for a longer time period. In such a case vessels' supply is "technically" decreased and freight rates are not further deteriorated. Besides, technological factors, such as automation, innovation, cost-effective fuel management (e.g. eco-ships), may crucially affect the ships' productivity, operation and chartering ability.

- Fleet utilisation and vessels' lay-up. In periods of strong freight markets, the utilisation of vessels is increased, whilst in periods of weak markets the contrary occurs. When Baltic Dry Index (BDI) recorded a new all-time low at 290 points in February 2016, the dry bulk fleet utilisation rate stood at 82.5%, the lowest level since 1980.[14] This reflected the poor state of the respective freight market in 2015 which finally collapsed in early 2016, mostly due to a typical "over-supply" phenomenon and China's economic slowdown. In such periods of shipping crisis, lay-up of vessels gets radically increased as ship operators are unable to find satisfactory chartering alternatives for their ships. When vessels' earnings are far below their operating costs, then the owners are forced to examine the alternative of lay-up, by taking into account the relevant costs compared to the freight market prospects and the chartering ability of their vessels. This was a growing situation in 2016, when the owners had the choice of the so-called *"warm lay-up"* (a more temporary option where the vessel is kept at anchorage, fully functioning and ready for employment with her crew stand-by) and the *"cold lay-up"* (a more permanent option that may last for months or even years).

2.4.1.7 State of the dry bulk market

The dry bulk market was at historical lows in 2015 and collapsed in early 2016. Baltic Dry Index (BDI)[15] recorded an all-time low at 290 points on 11 February 2016, after a protracted recession period which began in the last financial quarter of 2008. This in turn had followed a booming six-year period of shipowners' extraordinary profits which lasted from 2003 till 2008, when BDI recorded its all-time high at 11,793 points on 20 May 2008. It is remarkable that a modern capesize vessel could have been chartered for over USD 160,000 per day in a one-year time charter at the end of 2007 and mid-2008, whilst a similar vessel would have fetched only USD 6,250 per day in a one-year time charter and about USD 3,000 per day on spot employment in March 2016. From the historical development of freight rates, the long-term cyclical pattern of the dry bulk market may be obvious, as well as the high volatility of bulk carrier freight rates.

---

14 Marsoft *Dry Bulk Market Report* (February 2016, p. 4).
15 BDI is the most representative shipping index measuring the daily state of the dry bulk market. It is published by the Baltic Exchange of London. See also section 2.5.

Tables 2.12 and 2.13 at the end of this section depict the historical development of the average one-year time charter rates for the most indicative types of bulk carriers (handysize, handymax, panamax and capesize) ranging from 1980 to 2015, as kindly provided by Drewry Maritime Research.

2.4.2 Tanker market

Tankers are mainly designed to carry all variations of oil cargoes. The larger vessels are specialised in carrying crude oil, whilst the smaller sizes are focusing on the products trades. An analytical presentation of tanker sub-sectors follows, including a separate section for the chemical tankers. All tanker freight markets (particularly the crude trades) remained very strong for both spot and time charters from the last financial quarter of 2014 up to the end of 2015 and the first-half of 2016. This was mainly caused by the decrease of oil prices and the consequent stockbuilding of oil reserves by the major economies of the world.

In all tanker markets spot charters concern vessel fixtures made on a voyage basis. Freight rates are expressed and reported either in Worldscale terms (see chapter 14 and www.worldscale.co.uk), or in US Dollars per ton of cargo carried, or on a time charter equivalent basis ($ per day) to be able to get compared with time charter employment alternatives. On the other hand, time charters concern vessel fixtures made on a period basis and thus hire rates are expressed in US Dollars per day. The most prominent shipping reviews may report average hire rates for different vessel types and sizes (e.g. VLCC, suezmax, LR1, MR etc.) and for a variety of charter durations (e.g. six-month, one-year, three-year, five-year time charters) and vessels' age (e.g. modern vessels of five years old, or older ones of 10 or 15 years old).

An analytical presentation of the main tanker markets follows.

2.4.2.1 VLCC market

VLCCs (> 200,000 dwt) mostly trade on a spot basis, typically carrying crude and other dirty oil cargoes, while period charters are not uncommon. Table 2.5 presents indicative types of spot (voyage) employment for VLCCs, typical cargoes and sizes, as well as some major ports/areas of loading and discharging. It is clearly seen that these vessels carry crude oil which is loaded in quantities of about 260–280,000 mt and mainly exported from the ports of the Arabian Gulf area and secondary from the West Africa or the Caribbean Sea. Major importers are Europe, the USA, Japan, China, South Korea, India and Singapore.

The most important crude oil trades worldwide may be summed up as follows (this concerns all trades, thus includes also smaller shipments that may be carried by suezmax, aframax or panamax tankers)[16]:

- Middle East to Far East, NW Europe, USA, Indian subcontinent, South Africa, Brazil, Red Sea, Mediterranean and Australasia
- Red Sea to Far East, USA, NW Europe and Mediterranean

---

16 The Baltic Exchange (2014) *The Baltic Code 2014* (p. 12).

- West Africa to Far East, NW Europe, Mediterranean, Indian subcontinent, USA and South America
- North Africa to Mediterranean, NW Europe, USA and Far East
- North Sea to USA and Far East
- Baltic Sea to UK/Continent, Mediterranean, USA and Far East
- Black Sea to UK/Continent, Mediterranean, USA and Far East
- E. Coast Mexico to USA, Europe and South America
- Caribbean to USA, Europe, South America, Indian subcontinent and Far East
- South America to USA, Europe and Far East
- Indonesia/Malaysia to Far East and Australasia

Table 2.5 VLCC Tankers Indicative Spot Trades

Cargo Shipment (tons)		Single Voyage
280,000	Crude	AG (Arabian Gulf) – US Gulf
270,000	Crude	AG (Arabian Gulf) – Singapore
265,000	Crude	AG (Arabian Gulf) – Japan
260,000	Crude	WAF (West Africa) – US Gulf
260,000	Crude	WAF (West Africa) – China
280,000	Crude	AG (Arabian Gulf) – NW Europe
280,000	Crude	AG (Arabian Gulf) – RS (Red Sea)

Source: Drewry Maritime Research *Shipping Insight* (February 2016, p. 26) and Baltic Exchange *Manual for Panellists: A Guide to Freight Reporting and Index Production* (January 2015, pp. 38–39), data compiled by A. Papadopoulos.

An example of a spot (voyage) charter concerns a fixture made in July 2015 involving a VLCC tanker (298,000 dwt, built 2008, double hull) owned by a respectable Chinese shipping group which chartered the vessel to a first-class charterer, for a cargo voyage from Basrah Oil Terminal (Iraq) to Yingkou (China), in order to transport 270,000 mt of crude oil, for a worldscale rate of 75, with lay/can dates on 8/10 August 2015.

An example of a time charter fixture was reported as made in July 2015, concerning a VLCC vessel (317,000 dwt, built 2003, double hull) owned by a respectable Greek-based shipowner which chartered his vessel to a first-class charterer, for a period of three years at $40,300/day, to trade it worldwide.

2.4.2.2 Suezmax market

Suezmaxes (120–200,000 dwt) are also typically chartered on a spot basis, mainly carrying crude and other dirty oil cargoes (e.g. fuel oil), but also period charters are commonly found. Table 2.6 presents indicative types of spot employment for suezmaxes, typical cargoes and sizes, as well as some major ports/areas of loading and discharging. These vessels normally carry crude oil which is loaded in quantities of about 130–140,000 mt. They are mainly trading in the Black Sea – Mediterranean Sea area, but also from the West Africa to the USA and from the Arabian Gulf to India.

Table 2.6 Suezmax Tankers Indicative Spot Trades

Cargo Shipment (tons)		Single Voyage
130,000	Crude	WAF (West Africa) – Caribs/USAC (US Atlantic Coast) or USEC (US East Coast) or USES
135,000	Crude	Black Sea – Med
130,000	Crude	WAF – UKC (United Kingdom or Continent)
130,000	Crude	AG (Arabian Gulf) – East
130–140,000	Crude	Med – NW Europe
130–140,000	Crude	NW Europe – Caribs/USAC or USEC or USES
130–140,000	Crude	NW Europe – NW Europe

Source: Drewry Maritime Research *Shipping Insight* (February 2016, p. 27) and Baltic Exchange *Manual for Panellists: A Guide to Freight Reporting and Index Production* (January 2015, pp. 38–39), data compiled by A. Papadopoulos.

An example of a spot (voyage) charter concerns a fixture made in July 2015 for a suezmax tanker (164,000 dwt, built 2002, double hull) owned by a respectable Greek shipowner which chartered the vessel to a first-class charterer, for a cargo voyage from CPC Novorossiysk (Russia) to a port in the Mediterranean Sea area, in order to transport 135,000 mt of crude oil, at a Worldscale rate of 85.

An example of a time charter fixture was reported as made in April 2015, concerning a suezmax tanker (167,000 dwt, built 2007, double hull) owned by a respectable Greek-based shipowner which chartered his vessel to a first-class charterer, for a fixed period of two years plus charterers' option for one more year, at $29,000/day for the fixed and the optional period.

2.4.2.3 Aframax market

Aframaxes (80–120,000 dwt) are usually chartered on a spot basis too, without period charters being uncommon. Spot chartering is more balanced here between crude oil carriage and other petroleum products, for example dirty cargoes such as fuel oil or dirty petroleum products (DPP), or clean cargoes such as naphtha, clean petroleum products (CPP), ultra low sulphur diesel, jetoil, gasoil etc. for the coated vessels.

The most important dirty petroleum products trades worldwide may be summarised as follows (this concerns all trades, thus includes also bigger shipments that may be carried by suezmax or rarely by VLCC tankers, but also smaller shipments most commonly carried by specialised panamax or handy product tankers):

- Middle East to Far East
- NW Europe to Far East and USA
- Mexico and Caribs to USA, NW Europe and Far East
- Baltic Sea to UK/Continent, Mediterranean, USA and Far East
- Singapore to Far East
- Inter-regional trade within Europe/Mediterranean
- Inter-regional trade within SE Asia and Far East

The most important clean petroleum products trades worldwide may be summed up as follows (this concerns all trades, thus may include also bigger shipments that are rarely carried by suezmax, but also smaller shipments that most commonly are carried by specialised panamax or handy product tankers)[17]:

- Middle East to USA, Mediterranean, Europe and Far East
- NW Europe to USA, Mediterranean, West Africa and Far East
- Mediterranean to NW Europe, USA and Far East
- US Gulf to South America and Europe
- Caribbean to USA and Europe
- Indian sub-continent to USA, Mediterranean, Europe and Far East
- NE Asia to USWC (US West Coast) and WC South America
- Singapore to worldwide destinations
- Inter-regional trade within Europe/Mediterranean
- Inter-regional trade within Middle East and Indian sub-continent
- Inter-regional trade within SE Asia and Far East

Table 2.7 presents indicative types of spot employment for aframaxes, typical cargoes and sizes, as well as major ports/areas of loading and discharging. Typical trades of these vessels concern the transport of crude oil from various loading areas, such as Baltic Sea, Egypt, Libya, Mediterranean Sea, Arabian Gulf, Europe, Indonesia or the Caribbean Sea. The cargo is loaded in quantities of about 70–100,000 mt and is imported in various areas of the world, such as Europe, the USA and Asia. It may be stressed that aframax tankers with coated tanks are able to activate in clean petroleum products trades. They are called *"Long Range 2" (LR2)* product tankers as they carry clean cargoes on long distances and large quantities.

An example of a spot (voyage) charter concerns a fixture made in July 2015 for an aframax tanker (103,000 dwt, built 2006, double hull) owned by a respectable

Table 2.7 Aframax Tankers Indicative Spot Trades

Cargo Shipment (tons)		Single Voyage
100,000	Crude	Baltic Sea – UKC (United Kingdom or Continent)
80,000	Crude	Med – Med
80,000	Crude	North Sea – Continent
70,000	Crude	Caribs (Caribbean Sea) – US Gulf
80,000	Crude and/or DPP	Kuwait – Singapore
70,000	Crude	EC Mexico – USAC or USEC or USES
80,000	Crude	Med – NW Europe
80,000	Crude	Indonesia – Far East

Source: Drewry Maritime Research *Shipping Insight* (February 2016, p. 28) and Baltic Exchange *Manual for Panellists: A Guide to Freight Reporting and Index Production* (January 2015, pp. 38–39), data compiled by A. Papadopoulos.

---

17 The Baltic Exchange (2014) *The Baltic Code 2014* (p. 13).

Greek shipowner which chartered the vessel to a first-class charterer, for a cargo voyage from Primorsk (Russia) to a port in the UKC (United Kingdom or Continent) area, in order to transport 100,000 mt of crude oil, at a Worldscale rate of 85.

An example of a time charter fixture was reported as made in July 2015, concerning a modern aframax tanker (110,000 dwt, built 2014, double hull) owned by a respectable Norwegian-based shipowner which chartered his vessel to a first-class charterer, for a period of 30 months, at $27,600/day. The vessel was to be delivered to the charterers on 31 July 2015 at WCCA (West Coast Central America) area.

2.4.2.4 Product tankers: Panamax and Handy market

Although aframaxes or even suezmaxes may be able to carry oil product cargoes, the cornerstone of the oil product trades are these two markets which are examined here together; the panamax vessels and the handies.

Panamaxes (60–80,000 dwt) are mostly chartered on a spot basis (time charters are not uncommon). This mainly concerns the transport of clean cargoes such as naphtha, clean petroleum products (CPP), ultra-low sulphur diesel, jetoil, gasoil etc., but also in a less extent the transport of dirty cargoes such as fuel oil or dirty petroleum products. Panamax product tankers are called *"Long Range 1"* (*LR1*) vessels as they are able to carry clean cargoes on relatively long distances.

Handies (10–60,000 dwt) are also chartered mostly on a spot basis, overwhelmingly for the transport of clean cargoes and rarely for carrying dirty petroleum products. Handy product tankers are called also *"Medium Range"* (*MR*) vessels as they are able to carry clean cargoes on medium distances. Sometimes they may be seen in terminology as sub-divided in *"Medium Range 1"* (*MR1*) vessels of 25–40,000 dwt and *"Medium Range 2"* (*MR2*) vessels of 40–55,000 dwt. The typical MR product tanker is considered nowadays as that with a size of about 48–53,000 dwt.

Table 2.8 presents indicative spot trades for petroleum cargoes (clean and dirty), their cargo load quantities, as well as some major ports/areas of loading and discharging. Clean products are loaded from various areas of the world, such as Arabian Gulf, Europe, US Gulf, Singapore, India, the Mediterranean Sea and the Black Sea. The cargo is loaded in typical quantities ranging between 30–75,000 tons and is imported in various areas of the world, such as Japan, Europe, the USA, Africa, Australia and South America. Dirty products are loaded from various areas of the world, such as the Mediterranean Sea and the Black Sea, UK, Continental Europe and the Caribbean Sea. The cargo is loaded in typical quantities ranging between 30–55,000 tons and is imported mostly in the US Gulf and the Mediterranean Sea areas.

An example of a spot (voyage) charter concerns a fixture made in April 2015 for a panamax tanker (75,000 dwt, built 2011, double hull) owned by a respectable Chinese shipowner which chartered the vessel to a first-class charterer, for a cargo voyage from Arabian Gulf to Japan, in order to transport 55,000 mt of naphtha, at a Worldscale rate of 98.

An example of a time charter fixture was reported as made in July 2015, concerning a modern panamax tanker (75,000 dwt, built 2010, double hull) owned by a respectable Chinese-based shipowner which chartered his vessel to a first-class

Table 2.8 Product Tankers Indicative Spot Trades

Cargo Shipment (tons)		Single Voyage
75,000	Clean	AG (Arabian Gulf) – Japan
55,000	Clean	AG (Arabian Gulf) – Japan
55,000	Dirty	Caribs – US Gulf or USAC
55,000	Dirty	Med – Caribs/USES/US Gulf
50,000	Dirty	NW Europe (ARA) – Caribs or US Gulf
50,000	Dirty	Med – Med
50,000	Dirty	EC Mexico/Caribs – USAC/USES
38,000	Clean	US Gulf – NW Europe/Continent/ARA or ECSA (East Coast South America)
37,000	Clean	Continent (NW Europe) – USAC/Caribs
30,000	Clean	Med – Med
30,000	Clean	Singapore – East/Japan
30,000	Clean	Singapore – E. Australia
30,000	Clean or Dirty	Black Sea – Med

Source: Drewry Maritime Research *Shipping Insight* (February 2016, pp. 29–30) and Baltic Exchange *Manual for Panellists: A Guide to Freight Reporting and Index Production* (January 2015, pp. 38–40), data compiled by A. Papadopoulos.

charterer, for a period of one year, at $20,000/day. The vessel was to be delivered to the charterers on 28 July 2015 at South China area.

For the handy sector an example of a spot (voyage) charter concerns a fixture made in July 2015 for an MR product tanker (50,000 dwt, built 2013, double hull) owned by a respectable Norwegian shipowner which chartered the vessel to a first-class charterer, for a cargo voyage from Arabian Gulf to UKC (a port in UK or Continent), in order to transport 40,000 mt of jetoil (clean product), at a fixed lumpsum freight amount of USD 1,837,500.

An example of a time charter fixture was reported as made in July 2015, concerning a handymax tanker (46,000 dwt, built 2004, double hull) which was chartered for a period of one year plus 12 months at charterers' option (chopt), at $18,750/day for the fixed period and $20,250/day for the optional one.

2.4.2.5 Chemical tankers

Chemical cargoes are categorised by IMO to categories I, II and III, with cargoes of category I being the most hazardous. Chemical vessels are categorised to respective categories according to the quality of their tanks in order to carry such cargoes. Most chemical tankers are categorised as IMO II and III vessels, as the volume of IMO I cargoes is very limited.

The special feature of these vessels is called "*parceling*", as they normally have separate cargo tanks able to load and carry different cargo parcels of chemicals at the same time in the ships' *coated or stainless steel tanks*. The coating or cargo tank material determines what types of cargo a particular tank can carry: stainless steel tanks are required for aggressive acid cargoes such as sulphuric and phosphoric acid, while "easier" cargoes – such as vegetable oils – can be carried in epoxy-coated tanks. The coating or tank material also influences how quickly tanks can be cleaned. Typically, ships with stainless steel tanks can carry a wider range of cargoes and can clean more quickly between one cargo and another, which justifies the additional cost of their construction and the higher charter rates earned.

Chemical tankers are either chartered on a spot basis or on time charters. Table 2.9 presents indicative types of spot employment for chemical tankers, indicative cargo parcel quantities, as well as some of the major trading routes and ports/areas of loading and discharging. It may be pointed out that, when comparing the time charter rates between coated and stainless steel vessels of the same size, the latter seem to enjoy a considerable chartering premium. For example, a 30–32,000 dwt IMO II chemical tanker with stainless steel tanks earned on average $22,800/day in 2014, whereas a similar vessel with coated tanks had an average time charter rate of $13,400/day for the same year.

Typical cargo parcel sizes are those of 1,000 mt, 3,000 mt, 5,000 mt, 10,000 mt or 15,000 mt, whilst typical vessel sizes range from 5–50,000 dwt. Major spot routes concern the exports from the Middle East Gulf to various destinations, the USA exports due to the *"shale oil revolution"*, trades among developed and developing areas of the world, as well as the transatlantic routes between the USA and Europe, the transpacific routes between the USA and Asia and the Far East–Europe trades. Spot rates are typically expressed in US Dollars per mt of cargo carried (not in Worldscale rates as in other tanker trades). Chemical tankers' freight rates present lower volatility and less abrupt fluctuations than other tanker markets, both in spot and time charter terms.

Table 2.9 Chemical Tankers Indicative Spot Trades

Cargo Shipment (tons)		Single Voyage
5,000	Chem.	Houston – Rotterdam (transatlantic eastbound)
5,000	Chem.	Rotterdam – Houston (transatlantic westbound)
5,000	Chem.	Houston – Ulsan (transpacific westbound)
5,000	Chem.	Far East – NW Europe

Source: Drewry Maritime Research *Shipping Insight* (February 2016, p. 32), data compiled by A. Papadopoulos.

2.4.2.6 Tanker market: demand factors

The demand for tankers is crucially affected by numerous, constantly changing, global factors. At this point, only some of the most important key drivers for the tanker demand will be discussed below (the list is indicative, not exhaustive)[18]:

- Global imports of crude oil and oil products, as well as yearly growth rate. Furthermore, seaborne oil imports monitored per geographical

---

18 Marsoft *Tanker Market Report* (May 2015), Giziakis, K., Papadopoulos, A. and Plomaritou, E. (2010) *Chartering* (Athens, Stamoulis Publications, 3rd edition, in Greek, pp. 200–207).

area, i.e. North America, OECD Europe, Japan, China, other Asia/ Pacific, Latin America, Africa, East Europe and Middle East.

- Oil prices and stockbuilding. For example, the collapse in oil prices which started in the fourth financial quarter of 2014 and continued in 2015, brought about a strong oil inventory building in both the US and China. In the US, crude inventories reached an 80-year high by April 2015.[19] The sharp rise in US inventories was driven also by a contango oil market phenomenon witnessed in early 2015. Besides, the low oil price environment led to a level-off of oil production in the US and other geographical areas, changing the seaborne oil trade patterns.
- GDP growth in a global level and particularly in China and North America, as well as other major economical areas, such as European countries of OECD, Japan and developing Asia.
- Oil consumption globally and in specific geographical areas, such as North America, OECD Europe, Japan and China.
- Oil production in North America, OECD Europe and OPEC countries (Saudi Arabia is the leading producer). For example, rising OPEC output was the catalyst behind the increase of oil trade demand in 2015.
- Refineries' output and location.
- Geopolitical factors (e.g. lifting of Iranian sanctions in respect of oil production in 2016, political unrest in Libya since 2011 etc.).
- Demand in ton-mile terms for crude oil and products, as well as triangular chartering opportunities. For example, in 2015 West African and Latin American exports shifted from North America to longer-haul Asia/Pacific destinations, whilst crude exports from the Middle East to North America increased significantly. This not only boosted ton-mile demand and fleet productivity, but also created triangular chartering opportunities (limited backhaul ballast voyages).
- Seasonality.

2.4.2.7 Tanker market: supply factors
Some key indicators about the supply of tanker vessels may be summarised below (the list is not exhaustive):

- Fleet annual growth, which is determined by ordering and deliveries on the one hand and scrapping on the other.
- Fleet structure. In respect of that, the following indicators may be examined:
  - *Orderbook to existing fleet:* This ratio measures (at the time of measurement) the number or tonnage capacity of the vessels that are expected to be built in the next 2–3 years, as a percentage of the existing fleet. As an example of that, the orderbook for all tanker vessels stood at an historically moderate 19% of the whole fleet in January 2016.[20]

---

19 Marsoft *Tanker Market Report* (May 2015).
20 Clarksons Research *Oil and Tanker Trades Outlook* (January 2016).

    ° *Age breakdown:* This shows the age structure of a fleet. For example, a ratio showing which percentage of the fleet is over 15 or 20 years old shows how aged a fleet is and how many vessels may be scrapped in the next years. It is worth to mention that the tanker fleet in total was exceptionally modern in January 2016, as only 4% of the fleet was over 20 years old.[21] This was due to the fact that the tanker fleet had already been renewed by newbuildings, as IMO imposed the completion of a phasing out scheme of all single-hull tankers up to the end of 2015.

    ° *Replacement ratio:* This measures the orderbook (number of vessels or tonnage capacity in dwt) of the vessels to be built, as a percentage to the existing fleet which is over 15 years old. As an example, it may be mentioned that in January 2016 the replacement ratio (orderbook to fleet of over 15 years old) stood at 114% for the total tanker fleet, showing a rising orderbook after a previous two-year freight boom, in relation to a relatively modern tanker fleet.[22]

- Fleet productivity, technological factors and innovation. Fleet productivity increases when average fleet speed gets increased. Due to strong tanker freight rates in 2014–2015 fleet productivity increased significantly, offsetting some of the benefits from the rise in ton-miles demand. Besides, this is always influenced by technological factors, such as automation, innovation and cost-effective fuel management (e.g. eco-ships) etc.
- Floating storage. Larger and older vessels may be used for oil storage purposes. When this occurs, tankers' available supply for transport is essentially decreased, thus freight rates may be positively affected.
- Fleet utilisation and vessels' lay-up. The crude tanker fleet utilisation rate stood at about 90% in early 2015, the highest level since mid-2010.[23] This is contrary to what happened in the dry bulk market in the same period and reflects the strong tanker freight market which happened in 2014–2016. In respect of tankers' lay-up, the market reached its all-time highs during the period of the two oil crises which occurred in the late 1970s and early 1980s.

2.4.2.8 State of the tanker market

From the last financial quarter of 2014 up to the end of 2016 the tanker market recovered well after a six-year deeply recessive period which resulted in continuously falling freight rates after the financial crisis began at the end of 2008. This in turn had followed a booming six-year period which lasted from 2003 till 2008. It is remarkable that a modern VLCC tanker could have been chartered for over USD 90,000 per day on a one-year time charter in mid-2008, whilst the same charter type rates were formed at less than USD 20,000 per day on average for a similar vessel in 2013. In March 2016 the one-year time charter rate of a modern VLCC tanker

---

21 Clarksons Research *Oil and Tanker Trades Outlook* (January 2016).
22 Clarksons Research *Oil and Tanker Trades Outlook* (January 2016).
23 Marsoft *Tanker Market Report* (May 2015, p. 3).

was standing at a very decent amount of USD 45,000 per day, whilst the average rates for spot employment of such a tanker type were at about USD 40,000 per day. From the historical development of freight rates, the long-term cyclical pattern of the tanker market may become obvious, as well as the high volatility of crude tanker rates. It is worth commenting that the level of tankers' lay-up was amazing during the oil crises of the 1970s and the protracted shipping depression in 1980s.

Tables 2.12 and 2.13 towards the end of this section present the historical development of the yearly average one-year time charter rates for the most indicative types of crude tankers (aframax, suezmax and VLCC), product tankers (handysize, handymax and panamax), as well as various sizes of chemical tankers, ranging from 1980 up to 2015, as kindly provided by Drewry Maritime Research.

2.4.3 Gas carriers market

LPG vessels vary greatly in respect of their size and cargoes carried. They are either chartered on a spot basis or on period charters. Table 2.10 presents indicative types of spot trades for LPG carriers, indicative cargoes and quantities carried, as well as some major trading routes and ports/areas of loading and discharging. There is a wide variety of gas cargoes carried (LPG, ammonia, fuel gas etc.), cargo shiploads, trade routes and vessel sizes ranging between 3,000–85,000 cubic metres of cargo carrying capacity. For Very Large Gas Carriers (VLGCs > 60,000 cbm) the benchmark trade is from Ras Tanura (Arabian Gulf) to Chiba (Japan). Major other exporters are the USA and Qatar, whilst other importers are China, India and South Korea. As these vessels are capable of crossing the new locks of Panama Canal, their role is of great importance nowadays. Large Gas Carriers (LGCs 40–60,000 cbm) are few in number and commonly fixed on time charters. They are capable of crossing even the old, narrower locks of the Panama Canal, however the completion of the Canal's expansion is going to affect this vessel size. For midsized vessels (20–40,000 cbm), LPG and ammonia are the most important cargoes. Major exporters are located in the Black Sea, Trinidad and Tobago, Middle East and North Africa, whilst major importers are in India, Morocco and Europe. The smaller LPGs (3–23,000 cbm) are semi-refrigerated or ethylene or pressurised

Table 2.10 LPG Indicative Spot Trades

Cargo Shipment (tons)		Single Voyage
43,000	LPG	Arabian Gulf – Japan
35,000	NH3 (ammonia)	Baltic Sea – US Gulf
20,000	NH3 (ammonia)	Baltic Sea – Med
4,000	Ethylene	US Gulf – NWE (NW Europe)
4,000	Btd (butadiene)	NWE (NW Europe) – US Gulf
3,000	LPG	North Sea – Portugal
1,800	LPG	North Sea – ARA

Source: Drewry Maritime Research *Shipping Insight* (February 2016, pp. 36, 38), data compiled by A. Papadopoulos.

vessels able to carry various cargoes which have their own market fundamentals. For example, petrochemicals are traded between the USA and Europe when arbitrage conditions come up, ethylene is mainly produced in Europe and imported in Asia, whilst propylene remains popular in local and intra-regional trades.[24] Spot rates are contracted and reported in US Dollars per mt of cargo carried.

LNG vessels are together with some offshore vessel types the most technologically advanced, highly sophisticated and expensive ships of the shipping industry. It is roughly estimated that in the middle of 2015 about 70% of the fleet was employed in long-term period charters and only the remaining 30% was trading spot. The cargo for such vessels (LNG) is highly specialised, without any diversification. Most of the vessels are exclusively serving specific LNG projects requiring regular transport services. As per mid-2015 LNG charter rates were in a continuously falling mode, deteriorating gradually, this reflecting the softer demand growth, a considerable increase in the LNG fleet and most of all the lower energy price global environment. For example, the one-year time charter rate for a modern 160,000 cbm ship averaged at $35,000/day in April 2015, compared to $70,000/day in 2014 as average and $150,000/day in July 2012.[25] The technological development and delivery of new vessels have led to the evolution of a two or three tier charter market, based on vessel specifications. Initially, conventional LNGs had steam turbines for their propulsion, whereas other modern and highly advanced propulsion systems were gradually developed, first the *DFDE* (*Dual Fuel Diesel Electric*) and then the *TFDE* (*Tri-Fuel Diesel Electric*) systems. The word "tri-fuel" originates from the fact that the power generation engines are able to use three different types of fuel. Major LNG exporters are Middle East, Australia, Asia and North/West Africa. Major LNG importers are Japan, South Korea, China, Europe, whilst the role of other countries is growing, such as India, Mexico and Brazil.

Tables 2.12 and 2.13 towards the end of this section depict the historical development of the average one-year time charter rates for various sizes of LPG carriers, ranging from 1980 up to 2015, as kindly provided by Drewry Maritime Research.

2.4.4 Containerships market

Almost all the fixtures of containerships concern period charters, mostly vessels' time charters from the independent shipowners (also called *"charter owners"*) to the liner operators (also called *"operating owners"*). It is known that no or extremely limited spot chartering activity exists in liner shipping as vessels are employed/utilised by the lines in pre-determined routes and schedules (liner services). Table 2.11 presents indicative types of time charters for various size categories of containerships.

---

24 Clarksons Research *Shipping Review & Outlook* (Spring 2015 pp. 48–52); Drewry *Shipping Insight* (7 May 2015, pp. 36–40).
25 Clarksons Research *Shipping Review & Outlook* (Spring 2015 pp. 54–55); Drewry *Shipping Insight* (7.5.2015, pp. 42–45).

Table 2.11 Containerships Indicative Types of Employment

Liner Services or (scarce) Spot Charters or Time Charters	
Vessel Type	*Time Charter Duration*
Neo-Panamax, 9,000 TEU, gearless	3-year Time Charter (T/C)
Intermediate, (wide beam, old post-panamax) 4,500–5,500 TEU, gearless	12-month Time Charter (T/C)
Intermediate (old panamax), 4,250 TEU, gearless	12-month Time Charter (T/C)
Intermediate (old panamax), 3,500 TEU, gearless	12-month Time Charter (T/C)
Sub-Panamax, 2,500 TEU, geared	12-month Time Charter (T/C)
Handysize, 1,700 TEU, geared	12-month Time Charter (T/C)
Handysize, 1,100 TEU, geared	12-month Time Charter (T/C)
Feeder, 700 TEU, gearless	12-month Time Charter (T/C)

2.4.4.1 Post-panamax market

This category comprises all the container vessels that are not able to cross the Panama Canal. After the completion of expansion works, containerships able to pass from the new locks of the Canal have a maximum carrying capacity of about 15,000 TEUs. Although this size borderline is not strict, vessels larger than this may safely be called "Post-Panamax" containerships.

This is the fastest growing segment of the containership market having attained the newbuilding attention amongst liner operators. These vessels are often called *"Ultra Large Container Vessels" (ULCVs)*. Such boxships are almost exclusively deployed on the Far East–Europe trade where the major liners are now fiercely competing through alliances and vessel sharing agreements (see sections 1.1.3 and 1.3.6). The freight rate for carrying a 20-foot container at the Shanghai–Europe trade averaged at $620 per TEU in 2015, suffering a significant drop from the respective average of $1,172 per TEU in 2014.[26] Backhaul trade from Europe to the Far East is typically the weaker leg of this trade lane. Port restraints currently limit the trading of these vessels on other routes. These ships represented about 15% of the total boxship fleet capacity in mid-2015. Newbuilding interest in these vessels picked up in 2015, including six 20,150 TEU boxships reported ordered, breaching the 20,000 TEU barrier. While deployment of mega-vessels on other routes is limited, opportunities may eventually spread to other trades in the long run. This segment of the market is overwhelmed by vessels belonging to the liner operators, thus time charter fixtures are scarce.

2.4.4.2 Neo-panamax market

This rapidly growing segment concerns vessels of 8–15,000 TEUs and is characterised by vessels' efficiency derived from size and deployment flexibility. Such ships are principally trading on Transpacific, Far East–Europe and North–South

---

26 Clarksons Research *Shipping Intelligence Weekly* (15 January 2016).

trades (mostly with Latin America). Vessels of 12–15,000 TEUs are often characterised as *"Very Large Container Vessels"* (*VLCVs*), whereas vessels of 8–12,000 TEUs as *"Large Container Vessels"* (*LCVs*).

The completed expansion of the Panama Canal allows for the passage of larger container vessels, potentially reducing the cost of trans-ocean shipping services between the Far East and US East and Gulf Coast ports. The maximum size of a containership that can transit through the Canal has increased from that of about 5,000 TEU capacity (previous *"panamax"* size) to about 14–15,000 TEU (the so-called *"neo-panamax"* size), bringing about a major breakthrough to this market sector, as well as a requirement of a considerable investment for the improvement of US East Coast port infrastructure.[27]

Asia–US West Coast route (transpacific trade) is significantly serviced by this category of vessels. The freight rate for carrying a 40-foot container from Shanghai to US West Coast averaged $1,482 per FEU in 2015, much lower than the average of $1,975 per FEU in 2014. On the contrary, box freight rates from Shanghai to US East Coast (another transpacific trade) averaged at $3,727 per FEU in 2014 (13% higher than their average 2013 level), but kept rather strong in 2015 averaging $3,669 up until the September of the year. This stresses the point that the "state" of a market as a whole may be even mixed within a specific period and the reasons for these diversifications may be varied. In our reference above, a number of cargoes were diverted from the US West Coast to the US East Coast, partly as a result of port congestion. On North–South trades, freight rates performed weakly in 2014, due to supply matters arising from vessel upsizing and "cascading".[28]

It may be pointed out here that the state of the liner market, i.e. the freight rate paid by shippers to liner operators for carrying a box to its destination, affects significantly the state of the containerships charter market, namely the hire rates paid from the liner operators to the independent containership owners to charter-in vessels on period charters (mostly time charters). This is due to the fact that liner operators are willing to pay more to charter-in vessels from the open market (i.e. from the independent charter owners), when they expect that such vessels will be commercially capable of serving their liner transport requirements against their clients (shippers), with a profit. In other words, one expects that time charter rates for containerships would rather be higher in periods of higher liner freight rates.

With regards to this segment of vessels, an example of a time charter fixture made in January 2015 was concerning a containership of 9,000 TEU (new-building delivery at her first charter), owned by a specialised Greek containership shipping company which chartered his vessel to a Chinese first-class charterer (liner operator), for a period of five years, at $39,200/day. This vessel was then called "post-panamax", but now it is included in the "neo-panamax" category.

---

27 US Department of Transportation, Maritime Administration *Panama Canal Expansion Study* (November 2013, pp. 130–131).
28 Clarksons Research *Shipping Review & Outlook* (Autumn 2015, p. 70).

2.4.4.3 Intermediary and old panamax market

This category of vessels ranging between 3–8,000 TEUs includes both the previously called "panamax" and the wide-beam, shallow draft previously called "post-panamax" vessels, which now, after the construction of the third larger lane in the Panama Canal, are all able to cross this critical sea passage. All these medium-sized vessels are usually employed on North–South and non-core East–West trades. Two examples of such trades are the Shanghai–Santos trade lane and the Shanghai–Durban trade lane. This vessel category was influenced by the "cascading" effect, which occurs when higher-capacity vessels are employed on the non-mainlanes, generally exerting downward pressures on freight earnings.

Newbuilding contracts for the ex-panamax size were minimum in previous years, with just few orders reported, as containership newbuilding interest has concentrated on the huge size sectors. The Panama Canal expansion has been responsible for the reduction in ex-panamax ordering. Although many of these vessels were re-directed in other trades, their narrow-beam and fuel-inefficiency make them less competitive over more modern and fuel efficient wide-beam designs. While it initially seems that ex-panamax vessels of about 4–5,000 TEUs may be negatively influenced by the expansion of the Panama Canal, in contrast new trading and chartering opportunities for the whole segment of the 3–8,000 TEU intermediate fleet may be explored in the future.

An example of a time charter fixture for such an intermediate-sized containership was reported as made in March 2015, concerning a vessel of 5,086 TEU, built in 2010, owned by a specialised in containerships German owner which chartered his vessel to a French first-class charterer (liner operator), for a period of 12 months, at $12,700/day.

2.4.4.4 Small containerships market

Vessels of 2–3,000 TEU are often called "sub-panamax", those of 1–2,000 TEU are called "handysize" and those carrying less than 1,000 TEU are called "feeders". The segment of the smaller sizes often suffers supply pressures coming from the "cascade" effect, as well as being restrained by port and operational limitations. As seen in Table 2.11, the benchmark one-year time charter rates are for geared vessels of 2,500 TEU, 1,700 TEU, 1,100 TEU and 700 TEU within this category. Intra-Asian and intra-European routes are some of the most common forms of liner trading for these vessels. The fleet has been decreasing since 2012, as a result of both accelerated demolition levels and relatively limited investment.

An example of a time charter fixture for a sub-panamax containership was reported in June 2015, concerning a vessel of 2,546 TEU, built in 2010, owned by a specialised in containership operation Hong Kong based public company which chartered his vessel to a Swiss-based first-class charterer (liner operator), for a period of 11–12 months, at $11,700/day.

Another example of a time charter fixture for a handy containership was reported in July 2015, concerning a vessel of 1,100 TEU, built in 2015, owned by a Greek company which chartered his vessel to a Japanese first-class charterer (liner operator), for a very short period of 20–40 days, at $10,750/day. This is to illustrate that even short time charters may be agreed in the charter market of containerships between independent charter owners and liner operators.

Another example of a time charter fixture for a feedermax containership was reported in May 2015, concerning a vessel of 830 TEU, built in 2005, owned by a German company which chartered his vessel to a Swiss-based first-class charterer (liner operator), for 24 months, at $6,500/day.

2.4.4.5 Containerships market: demand factors

The demand for containerships is crucially affected by numerous, constantly changing, global factors. At this point, some of the most important key drivers for the containership demand will be shortly commented below (the list is indicative, not exhaustive)[29]:

- GDP growth in a global level and particularly in China, the USA, European countries of OECD and Japan.
- Global container trade and in particular TEU imports in North America, Europe, Japan, Southeast Asia, China, S. Korea, Taiwan, Hong Kong, Australia, Latin America, Africa.
- Commodity prices.
- Global manufacturing and location of manufacturing capacity.
- Geopolitical risks.
- Currency exchange and interest rates.
- Seasonality.

2.4.4.6 Containerships market: supply factors

The key indicators about the supply of container vessels may be summarised below (the list is not exhaustive):

- Cellular and non-cellular fleet annual growth, which is determined by ordering and deliveries on the one hand and scrapping on the other.
- Fleet structure. In respect of this, the following points may be examined:
  - *Orderbook to existing fleet:* As it has been explained before, this ratio measures the number or carrying capacity of the vessels that (at the time of measurement) are expected to be built in the next 2–3 years, as a percentage to the existing fleet. As an example of that, the orderbook for all container vessels stood at 19% of the whole fleet in January 2016, where by far the heaviest orderbook was for the largest sizes (orderbook 70% for vessels over 12,000 TEU).[30]
  - *Age breakdown:* This shows the age structure of a fleet. For instance, the containership fleet was considered as a very modern one in early 2016, since only 4% of the total fleet was over 20 years old (note:

29 Marsoft *Container Market Report* (March 2015).
30 Clarksons Research *Container Intelligence Monthly* (January 2016).

all of the aged vessels were under 5,000 TEU).[31] This was due to the heavy ordering activity of the previous years and the predominance of mega-containerships in the newbuilding market.

○ *Replacement ratio:* This measures the orderbook (number of ships or tonnage capacity in TEU) of the vessels to be built, as a percentage of the existing fleet which is over 15 years old.

- Idle (laid-up) fleet. The lower the idle tonnage the faster the market recovery when market fundamentals improve.
- Fleet productivity, technological factors and innovation. Due to weak freight rates in 2014–2016 fleet productivity remained low, regardless of the low fuel prices environment which could otherwise have led to an increase of fleet average speed.
- Fleet utilisation. The liner fleet utilisation rate stood at about 82% in 2015,[32] reflecting the weak state of the market.
- Vessels' cascading.
- Major shipping alliances controlling the liner services offered in main trades. For example, in 2015 only few global alliances controlled nearly 100% of capacity deployed in the two premier markets of Asia–Europe and Transpacific routes, as well as a substantial share in the Transatlantic routes. By this form of co-operation each alliance controls a sizeable presence and reaps operating savings induced by fleet efficiency and improved vessel utilisation.[33] Further to that, the liner market is consolidated by mergers and acquisitions of shipping companies and this may influence also the effective vessels' supply.
- Oil prices as a significant part of vessels' cost.
- Port and terminal productivity (congestion problems).

2.4.4.7 State of the containerships market

The containership market passed a six-year period of extraordinary profits in 2003–2008 (similarly to the other major shipping markets), then slumped in 2009 when the world trade collapsed, this was followed by a two-year short recovery of rates in 2010–2011 and then a phase of low freight rates, mostly due to the heavy ordering and deliveries of mega-ships. It is remarkable that a modern gearless containership of 4,400 TEU could have been chartered for USD 50,000 per day on a one-year time charter at the end of 2004/early 2005, whilst a similar vessel would have fetched less than USD 7,800 per day on average in 2009 and only USD 5,800 per day in March 2016.

Tables 2.12 and 2.13 present the historical development of the yearly average one-year time charter rates for various sizes of containerships, ranging from 1980 up to 2015, as kindly provided by Drewry Maritime Research.

---

31 Clarksons Research *Container Intelligence Monthly* (January 2016).
32 Marsoft *Container Market Report* (March 2015, p. 9).
33 Marsoft *Container Market Report* (March 2015, p. 42).

Table 2.12 Average One-Year Time Charter Rates of Major Ship Types (US$ per day): 1980–1997

	1980	1981	1982	1983	1984	1985	1986	1987	1988	1989	1990	1991	1992	1993	1994	1995	1996	1997
Bulk Carriers																		
Handysize	8,330	7,665	4,405	3,820	4,150	3,605	3,415	4,595	7,405	8,670	7,240	8,020	7,240	7,705	7,690	9,625	6,625	8,165
Handymax	10,350	9,390	4,775	4,040	4,715	4,075	3,535	5,500	8,455	10,010	8,470	9,130	8,355	10,300	12,910	11,790	9,710	9,400
Panamax	14,165	12,320	5,600	4,830	6,220	5,650	4,840	7,550	12,350	13,585	10,915	12,115	9,815	12,300	11,865	15,200	10,990	11,000
Capesize	16,165	12,960	4,890	5,460	8,795	7,860	7,260	9,090	15,525	18,460	15,930	16,160	12,850	15,835	17,295	20,730	14,050	16,625
Chemical Tankers																		
8,000 dwt (IMO 2)	-	-	-	-	-	6,300	6,300	7,800	7,600	8,300	9,700	8,800	6,500	6,300	7,250	10,800	9,500	9,200
14,000 dwt (IMO 2)	-	-	-	-	-	8,900	8,800	11,000	10,700	11,600	13,700	12,300	9,200	8,500	10,000	15,800	12,400	10,400
24,000 dwt (IMO 2)	-	-	-	-	-	13,400	13,200	16,500	16,000	17,400	20,500	18,400	13,700	10,500	12,100	16,500	15,000	14,200
32,000 dwt (IMO 2)	-	-	15,500	15,500	17,000	15,300	15,100	18,800	18,300	19,900	23,500	21,000	18,000	16,500	19,000	25,000	24,000	22,000
Container Ships																		
500 teu (geared)																		
1,000 teu (geared)	-	-	-	-	-	8,500	6,375	5,100	6,400	7,300	7,200	7,100	7,200	7,000	7,100	7,400	7,125	6,100
1,500 teu (geared)	-	-	-	-	-	11,250	7,875	7,650	9,550	11,550	11,350	11,050	11,450	10,900	10,700	11,400	10,800	9,200
2,500 teu (gearled)	-	-	-	-	-	13,600	9,200	9,675	12,375	15,750	15,225	14,850	15,720	15,150	14,385	16,050	15,375	12,450
3,500 teu (gearless)	-	-	-	-	-	-	-	11,400	15,000	19,000	18,400	19,075	19,925	17,800	17,650	18,875	18,500	18,875
LPG Carriers																		
6,000 cu.m	14,539	12,072	12,961	9,145	9,375	6,086	6,086	6,743	8,651	12,007	14,178	11,447	11,513	5,800	7,800	12,500	9,100	7,900
10,000 cu.m	13,783	13,849	11,118	11,414	7,204	7,895	8,224	11,678	15,789	19,342	18,200	15,100	10,060	9,800	14,000	11,900	14,300	13,000
30,000 cu.m	13,980	15,888	12,072	9,605	7,697	7,500	9,737	12,928	17,599	22,697	26,000	22,800	16,300	13,000	15,200	23,000	17,600	19,000
75,000 cu.m	16,546	19,342	15,164	7,730	6,776	8,947	13,388	21,217	24,770	47,303	38,900	27,500	19,600	19,400	23,100	21,200	18,600	25,500
Oil Tankers																		
Products (30,000 dwt)	13,675	9,450	8,600	7,650	6,525	4,700	7,300	7,800	7,900	9,700	11,000	10,300	9,700	9,300	10,900	10,900	11,500	12,300
Products (45,000 dwt)	-	-	-	-	-	-	-	-	-	-	13,200	14,500	11,700	12,100	13,800	13,100	13,800	14,300
Panamax (50-60,000 dwt)	-	-	-	-	-	-	-	-	-	-	15,000	14,700	12,300	12,000	12,100	13,800	13,600	15,300
Aframax (80-90,000 dwt)	13,200	9,610	5,830	9,300	6,250	5,300	9,970	9,500	11,900	14,300	19,200	20,700	15,400	14,300	15,200	17,450	17,500	19,000
Suezmax (120-140,000 dwt)	-	-	-	-	-	-	-	-	-	-	24,600	24,500	18,100	19,100	17,500	18,800	20,900	23,300
VLCC (M/T 250-280,000 dwt)	3,250	6,200	5,300	8,500	5,500	6,100	10,900	13,600	12,700	15,100	34,300	38,000	24,900	24,000	21,000	23,000	25,700	31,200

Source: Drewry Maritime Research (2016)

Table 2.13 Average One-year Time Charter Rates of Major Ship Types (US$ per day): 1998–2015

	1998	1999	2000	2001	2002	2003	2004	2005	2006	2007	2008	2009	2010	2011	2012	2013	2014	2015
Bulk Carriers																		
Handysize	6,020	5,835	7,371	5,629	4,829	8,289	14,413	12,021	12,558	23,021	24,110	9,425	14,025	7,900	7,100	6,700	6,800	5,800
Handymax	7,355	7,430	9,433	8,472	7,442	13,736	31,313	23,038	21,800	43,946	48,310	15,179	20,779	13,700	8,700	8,800	9,600	7,000
Panamax	7,775	8,500	11,063	9,543	9,102	17,781	36,708	27,854	22,475	52,229	56,480	19,650	25,317	14,900	9,600	9,600	10,600	7,600
Capesize	13,040	11,425	18,021	14,431	13,608	30,021	55,917	49,333	45,646	102,875	116,180	35,285	40,308	17,500	11,400	9,400	12,100	8,900
Chemical Tankers																		
8,000 dwt (IMO 2)	8,200	8,478	8,463	8,500	7,025	7,025	7,131	7,881	8,838	9,825	8,600	6,563	5,650	5,875	5,900	6,700	6,800	9,300
14,000 dwt (IMO 2)	10,450	10,550	10,050	10,800	8,841	8,620	9,350	11,834	13,313	14,563	12,563	9,063	7,875	8,200	8,000	8,900	9,205	12,300
24,000 dwt (IMO 2)	13,200	13,400	14,400	16,000	10,937	11,074	12,550	13,889	14,875	17,688	16,763	11,913	11,175	12,250	10,900	12,000	12,236	15,500
32,000 dwt (IMO 2)	21,000	21,038	20,817	22,000	11,970	12,509	14,237	16,017	18,388	21,675	20,175	12,938	11,750	12,550	12,600	13,300	13,373	23,000
Container Ships																		
500 teu (geared)	5,675	4,175	4,600	4,500	4,932	5,028	7,102	8,750	6,871	7,451	7,116	3,007	3,193	4,367	4,029	4,546	4,483	5,000
1,000 teu (geared)	7,450	6,275	7,700	7,767	5,462	8,136	13,143	15,763	11,429	11,292	10,260	4,168	5,890	7,708	5,013	5,854	5,725	5,600
1,500 teu (geared)	9,275	7,100	11,625	10,370	7,276	11,693	20,156	24,790	16,492	15,775	13,640	4,566	6,486	9,992	6,125	6,692	7,533	6,800
2,500 teu (geared)	14,250	12,975	18,094	16,467	10,366	17,777	24,250	28,154	20,496	21,336	19,677	5,679	9,013	12,688	6,958	7,255	7,967	7,600
3,500 teu (gearless)					14,470	23,456	30,625	32,277	24,233	27,479	28,088	10,232	11,957	15,046	7,267	7,454	8,058	7,300
LPG Carriers																		
6,000 cu.m	7,400	7,000	6,414	5,658	5,230	5,757	7,138	9,507	9,868	10,329	10,033	8,816	9,046	9,539	8,816	8,750	7,270	16,677
10,000 cu.m	11,800	11,500	14,638	15,559	13,882	14,770	18,158	22,072	22,697	23,947	23,783	19,046	16,020	17,500	19,605	20,850	23,550	23,280
30,000 cu.m	17,800	18,400	21,941	22,664	20,395	21,020	23,487	29,737	32,928	30,724	28,388	20,428	19,112	21,283	23,586	25,650	30,100	35,550
75,000 cu.m	24,500	23,500	25,428	26,447	17,467	21,217	26,447	31,250	35,362	24,539	23,289	16,678	18,158	25,296	29,276	30,590	50,650	60,900
Oil Tankers																		
Products (30,000 dwt)	11,300	10,400	12,454	15,583	11,417	13,267	15,629	18,854	21,417	22,200	21,438	13,675	11,038	12,208	12,013	12,944	13,071	15,000
Products (45,000 dwt)	13,000	11,400	13,958	17,563	13,288	14,845	19,029	25,271	26,792	25,367	23,092	14,850	12,388	13,633	13,325	14,411	14,571	17,400
Panamax (50-60,000 dwt)	15,000	12,500	14,854	19,708	15,292	14,163	18,813	21,833	23,225	22,292	19,704	13,675	11,738	10,275	9,808	11,028	11,786	21,900
Aframax (80-90,000 dwt)	17,900	13,900	18,854	23,125	16,896	19,146	29,500	34,771	35,150	33,413	34,708	19,663	18,571	15,208	13,588	13,306	15,361	26,300
Suezmax (120-140,000 dwt)	23,200	19,300	27,042	30,500	18,349	26,104	37,875	42,292	42,667	43,042	46,917	27,825	25,967	19,700	17,504	15,944	19,056	34,700
VLCC (M/T 250-280,000 dwt)	31,900	25,800	35,250	37,958	23,458	33,604	53,875	60,125	55,992	53,333	74,663	38,533	36,083	24,642	20,996	20,250	24,528	46,500

Source: Drewry Maritime Research (2016).

2.5 Freight indices

The *freight indices or indexes* are financial tools created to monitor the current state, conditions and trends of the freight market. As previously mentioned, the freight or charter market is not a single, homogeneous market in which all trends follow a uniform pattern. It consists of different individual markets, which are neither strictly secluded from each other nor necessarily interdependent, often resulting in diverse directions within the entire freight market. This diversification of the freight markets brings about the need for creation of respective freight rate indicators.

As part of the shipping market practice, the creation of freight indices is mainly based on the four fundamental criteria of charter market segmentation, namely the type and size of *vessels*, the kind and nature of *cargoes* carried, the type and duration of *charters*, as well as the *geographical aspect of vessels' trading*.[34] Since freight indices are measuring the current state of the freight markets, their configuration is always so variable as the shipping market itself is. Therefore, an extensive presentation of freight indices can not be fully exhaustive and up to date. For this reason, only a brief discussion of the Baltic Exchange indices will be set out below.

The Baltic Exchange publishes on a daily basis a series of freight indices for the dry and wet bulk markets, based on the professional assessments of independent shipbrokers who are located in major shipping centres worldwide. For the dry bulk market, the most important indices are the *Baltic Dry Index* (*BDI*) which measures the overall freight rate level in the dry bulk market, together with the *Baltic Capesize Index* (*BCI*), the *Baltic Panamax Index* (*BPI*), the *Baltic Supramax Index* (*BSI*) and the *Baltic Handysize Index* (*BHSI*), each of which expressing the general state of the respective freight market segment. For the tanker market, the most important such indices are the *Baltic Dirty Tanker Index* (*BDTI*), which expresses the general state of the tanker freight market in dirty cargo trades (e.g. crude oil, fuel oil, other dirty products), as well as the *Baltic Clean Tanker Index* (*BCTI*), which expresses the level of the tanker freight market in clean cargo trades.

A freight index is typically based on a weighted calculation system whereby selected chartering alternatives (e.g standard voyage routes, time charters, trip charters, round voyages etc.) of a specific vessel group participate in the index formation at a predetermined weighting factor. The level of freight rates on these benchmark chartering options are examined daily, either through the actual chartering fixtures or from estimates of authorised shipbrokers. The weighting factor of each chartering option in the calculation of the index is determined in accordance with the importance of this type of charter. The current level of the index is then shaped by a daily examination of freight rates on the benchmark charters which make up the index, in accordance with the predetermined weighting factor contribution. A freight index is usually expressed either in terms of index points or US Dollars per day.

---

34 Giziakis, K., Papadopoulos, A. and Plomaritou, E. (2010) *Chartering* (Athens, Stamoulis Publications, 3rd edition, in Greek, pp. 281–282).

All the above may be illustrated by a short example. As per January 2015, BCI was a basket of 11 benchmark chartering options, with standard trading specifications determined by the Baltic Exchange, composed of seven standard voyage routes weighing in total 50% of the index and four standard period charters (time charters or round voyages) weighing the rest 50% of the index.[35] Similarly, all other indices are typically composed of benchmark charter types per vessel grouping.

Finally, it is worth emphasising on the most important freight index of our days. Since 1 November 1999, *"Baltic Dry Index"* (*BDI*), as the successor of *"Baltic Freight Index"* (*BFI*),[36] has been the representative indicator of the freight rate levels in the entire dry bulk market. BDI measures the overall state of the dry bulk freight market and often is regarded as a forerunner of the industrial output and world economy trends. BDI is expressed as index points and calculated daily by the following formula[37]:

$$[(BCI\ TCavg + BPI\ TCavg + BSI\ TCavg + BHSI\ TCavg) / 4] * 0,113473601$$

where:
BCI = Baltic Capesize Index
BPI = Baltic Panamax Index
BSI = Baltic Supramax Index
BHSI = Baltic Handysize Index
TCavg = Time Charter average = the average rate of time charters involved in determining each individual freight index.

The multiplier was first applied when the BDI replaced BFI and has changed over the years as the contributing indices and the methods of BDI calculation have been modified.

2.6 Freight derivatives

At this last part of the chapter, a short reference will be made to a highly sophisticated, modern, specialised and advanced tool of managing the freight market risk; the freight derivatives. It is noted that analysis of this subject will be restricted only to familiarising the reader with basic principles, since presenting the full spectrum would require extensive econometric and financial knowledge which goes beyond the scope of this book.

The story started from the Baltic Exchange which initially undertook an important role as an international freight exchange centre when, in 1985, it first

---

35 The Baltic Exchange *Manual for Panellists: A Guide to Freight Reporting and Index Production* (January 2015, pp. 34–35).

36 BFI was for many years the most significant shipping index, as it measured the daily freight rate level in the dry bulk market from 4 January 1985 to 1 November 1999, when it was replaced by BDI.

37 The Baltic Exchange *Manual for Panellists: A Guide to Freight Reporting and Index Production* (January 2015, p. 37).

inaugurated the *Baltic International Freight Futures Exchange* (*BIFFEX*). On this exchange there were two daily sessions for trading charterparties and futures contracts which were to be performed at some later date (up to two years) against a weighted freight index. This index was then called *Baltic Freight Index* (*BFI*), the predecessor of BDI, reflecting the state of the dry bulk freight market. By trading the BIFFEX freight futures contracts, owners, charterers and other parties on the shipping scene, including speculators, could protect themselves (*"hedge"*) against the risk of or play on the volatility of freight rates and time charter hires.

In 1991 an additional, more advanced, freight derivatives methodology was introduced; the *Forward Freight Agreement* (*FFA*) which gradually replaced the BIFFEX contracts. This system met the need to make contracts that were more specific rather than to settle against a global freight index. The FFAs are *"over the counter (OTC) forward products traded principal to principal"*, as opposed to the BIFFEX contracts which were *"futures"* traded via an exchange. Should more security for the performance of the contract be required, the FFA deal can also be done through a clearing-house, such as the Norwegian Futures and Options Clearing House (NOS), the London Clearing House (LCH), the Singapore Exchange (SGX), the Chicago Mercantile Exchange (CME) and the Intercontinental Exchange (ICE). When a trade is cleared through an exchange, then the clearing house becomes the counter-party to each of the original parties to the transaction, thus credit risk is minimised.

It should be emphasised that an FFA is often tailor-made to suit an owner's or charterer's particular need for a hedge. The following example is a classic and simple form of how the FFA trade works.

A buyer of an FFA (charterer) and a seller of an FFA (shipowner) agree to trade an FFA contract. The Baltic Exchange today produces a broad series of daily assessments and indices broken down into wet and dry freight markets, so there is a variety of cargoes and routes to be chosen from in order to be used as the *"underlying object"* of the derivative. Through their FFA broker, the charterer and the owner will agree:

- the agreed route;
- the day, month and year of settlement;
- the contract quantity; and
- the contract rate at which differences will be settled.

Typically, the actual settlement price (i.e. the future freight level against which the FFA settlement will be made) is normally agreed as the average value of an agreed freight index or a specific route of that, at a specific future time (e.g. the average value of a specific route of Baltic Panamax Index on the last seven days of an agreed month).

Assume that the FFA buyer (charterer) has a panamax cargo Continent/Far East to move two months ahead from now and is concerned that the time charter (T/C) market will go up within the near future. The FFA seller (shipowner) has four ships coming open on the Continent in the relevant period and is seeking to safeguard a minimum T/C rate for at least one of his ships. Negotiations start and the parties finally agree an FFA contract rate at $12,800 per day. FFA settlement will probably be made against the Route P2A_03 of the Baltic Panamax Index (BPI).

Two months later, at the date of settlement, the average value of the last seven days of the agreed BPI route turns out to be $14,000 per day, which is higher than the agreed FFA contract rate. Thus, the seller (shipowner) pays the buyer (charterer) the difference of $1,200 × 65 days (total time of voyage) = $78,000 that the charterer will use to offset against the high rate he will have to pay for a vessel on the real spot market. The shipowner should be able to fix his ship close to the $14,000 per day on the prevailing physical market and, although the shipowner is losing some on the FFA, he has safeguarded an income for one of the ships. The other three ships will benefit from the improved rates on the physical (spot) market.

CHAPTER 3

Chartering information

A basic element of shipbroking and chartering practice is the exchange of information. In respect of that, accuracy, reliability, speed, timing and other qualitative aspects are of utmost importance. This chapter presents the major sources of chartering information, the most important information centres in the world, how this information is transmitted within the chartering network, what the means of communication are and how significant the time factor is. Great emphasis is given on the description of the role of the shipbrokers and agents in handling this business data. It is underlined that chartering negotiations through orders, position lists, indications, offers, counter-offers etc. form information channels of paramount importance, thus this chapter is closely related with chapter 8, where chartering negotiations are analysed.

3.1 Types and importance of information

Those who are engaged in chartering and shipbroking practice are important receivers and distributors of information. The continuous flow of information and the treatment and evaluation of the collected material are necessary elements for a correct judgment of the current situation and trends in the freight markets. Quality of information (correctness, reliability, accuracy, speed, timing etc.) is always of utmost importance. The main sources of such information are described in detail below.

3.1.1 Market reports

These are reports circulated by the Baltic Exchange or other influential organisations such as BIMCO, Intertanko, ASBA, on a membership basis, or by specialised market analysts on a subscription basis (e.g. Drewry, Clarkson, Marsoft), or by big shipbroking firms/houses to shipowners, charterers, other brokers and agents, banks etc. giving a concentrated picture of the prevailing situation of the shipping market for a day, a week, a month or even a year. By comparing the conclusions made in various market reports with one's own judgment of the situation, it is possible to form a fairly accurate view of the state of the market in the sectors of particular interest. A comprehensive market report contains comments primarily focused on the most important freight markets, that is, dry cargo or tanker or container or gas, but also, for example, on the sale and purchase of ships or on more specialised markets. Generally, the different tonnage sizes are also dealt with separately (e.g. a dry bulk market report usually contains separate analysis for capes, panamaxes, supramaxes, handies). The comments are illustrated by examples of recently made representative fixtures.[1] Furthermore, the market developments within different geographical chartering areas may be commented on separately (e.g. a dry bulk market report focusing either on the Atlantic or on the Pacific basin), or for different commodities (e.g. fixtures concerning grain, coal, iron ore etc. are grouped and presented together).

Examples of market reports may be seen in Figures 3.1, 3.2, 3.3 and 3.4. Figure 3.1 presents a dry cargo report specialising in panamax and kamsarmax bulk carriers in 2016, whilst Figure 3.2 is a tanker market report from 2011. Figures 3.3 and 3.4 are of high historical importance as describing the dry bulk freight markets situation just before the outbreak of the Global Financial Crisis at the last financial quarter of 2008.

3.1.2 Orders

The following sections discuss the orders, position lists, indications and offers/counter-offers only as major sources of chartering information. As these also form the fundamental parts of a chartering negotiation, their analysis and respective examples are presented in chapter 8. An order is the common denominator for every request for transportation of a specific cargo from one port to another. An order may also concern a requirement from a shipper or owner of cargo to time charter a ship for short or long duration. Between charterers and their brokers, between owners and their brokers and between the broking firms, such orders are circulated one by one or by lists covering a number of orders. The party requesting chartering service is said to "*place an order on the market*" and will then await reactions from the tonnage that may be interested in the order.

An example of an order is the following:

OUR DIR CHRS IMPERIAL SHIPPING, LONDON
35/45,000 DWT – GRD
DELY SOUTH SWEDEN
27TH OCTOBER
1 TC TRIP VIA BALTIC TO EAST MED
CARGO – SAWN TIMBER UNDER/ON DECK
DURATION ABT 40 DAYS WOG
REDELY DLOSP 1SP EGYPT MED (INTN ALEXANDRIA)
3.75 PCT ADDCOM PAST US

This order concerns the charterers' interest for a geared vessel of 35–45,000 dwt to make a trip charter carrying timber from Sweden to the East Mediterranean Sea.

---

1 When a ship is chartered and a freight (or hire) rate is agreed between the shipowner and the charterer, then the vessel is said to be "fixed".

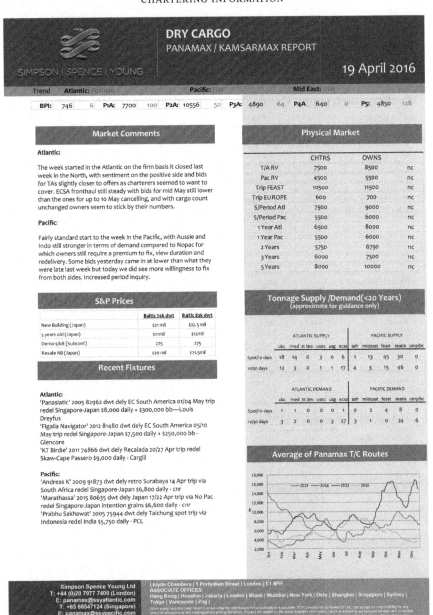

Figure 3.1 Dry Cargo Market Report

Source: Simpson Spence Young (SSY), 19 April 2016

Bassøe Friday Report

Week 11 – 18.03.2011   www.pfbassoe.no   Nr 11. Vol 34

Tanker chartering – Crude

It has been an active week in the VLCC market ex MEG with a high number of fixtures being reported. However, rates have continued to soften since last week due to the amount of ships available in the MEG. During the week rates have dropped abt 5 point to ws62.5 for MEG/East, while west is unchanged at ws42.5. The situation in Japan is still going to have a negative impact on the market and with the amount of available ships next 30 days, we expect this market to continue softening. Smaxes has gone a bit quiet at the end of the week, but in Wafr rate levels are still holding up despite lack of activity. Rates are now at abt ws110 for Wafr/Usac. The Med market going through the same slow pattern and after charterers took a step back, the rates soften and Blsea/Ukcmed have eased off to around ws130. Owners eyes are at Libya and how the problems will develop, and any turn to the worse will Influence the market. In comparison to last week, its been an active week for Aframax owners in the Med and Blsea. We have seen a high number of fixtures in both areas, and rates have moved abt 10 points to ws105 for cross Med and ws110 for Bl Sea/Med. We expect this trend to continue in next week, but it remains to see how many cargoes that is left for the month. The Baltic market with its ice conditions haven been firm and stable throughout the week, but the non ice Nsea market have seen rates drop down to abt ws 107,5 for XNsea.

VLCC (DH)	Current trend: Softer		
Route	WS today	Last week	USD/day
270' MEG – Korea	62,5	67,5	24 865
275' MEG – UKC	42,5	45	2 350
260' Bonny – LOOP	75,0	80,0	38 091

Suezmax (DH)	Current trend: Softer		
Route	WS	Last	USD/day
130' Bonny – Phila.	110,0	110,0	33 113
135' Novo–Augusta	130,0	142,5	43 792

Aframax (DH)	Current trend: Mixed		
Route	WS today	Last week	USD/day
80' TEES – R.dam	107,5	110,0	12 903
70' PLC – Texas	110,0	120	5 350
80' MEG–Singapore	115,0	115,0	6 430

VLCC availability in MEG (# vessels)		
	Single hull	Double hull
Spot	6	5
Next 30 days	20	90

Bunkers (USD/mt)			
Fujairah	641	Rotterdam	606

VLCC earnings

Suezmax earnings

Aframax earnings

VLCC availability in MEG

vessels next 30 days ex. FRO and TI

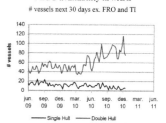

P.F. Bassøe AS	P O Box 1723 Vika	Phone +47 22 01 08 00	E-mail Internet	crude@pfbassoe.no
Enterprise Number:	N-0121 Oslo, Norway	Fax +47 22 01 08 10	E-mail Comtext	A43NN076
NO-927161052	Dronning Mauds gt. 3	Telex +56 76766 basso n	www.pfbassoe.no	

Figure 3.2 Tanker Market Report

Source: www.pareto.no/p.-f.bassoe (accessed 18 March 2011)

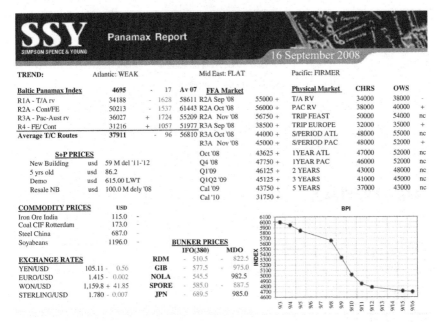

SSY
SIMPSON SPENCE & YOUNG

Panamax Report

16 September 2008

TREND:		Atlantic: WEAK			Mid East: FLAT		Pacific: FIRMER		

Baltic Panamax Index	4695	-	17	**Av 07**	**FFA Market**		**Physical Market**	**CHRS**	**OWS**
R1A - T/A rv	34188	-	1628	58611	R2A Sep '08	55000 +	T/A RV	34000	38000	-
R2A - Cont/FE	50213	-	1537	61443	R2A Oct '08	56000 +	PAC RV	38000	40000	+
R3A - Pac-Aust rv	36027	+	1724	55209	R2A Nov '08	56750 +	TRIP FEAST	50000	54000	nc
R4 - FE/ Cont	31216	+	1057	51977	R3A Sep '08	38500 +	TRIP EUROPE	32000	35000	+
Average T/C Routes	**37911**	-	96	56810	R3A Oct '08	44000 +	S/PERIOD ATL	48000	55000	nc
					R3A Nov '08	45000 +	S/PERIOD PAC	48000	52000	+
					Oct '08	43625 +	1YEAR ATL	47000	52000	nc
S+P PRICES					Q4 '08	47750 +	1YEAR PAC	46000	52000	nc
New Building	usd	59 M del '11-'12			Q1'09	46125 +	2 YEARS	43000	48000	nc
5 yrs old	usd	86.2			Q1Q2 '09	45125 +	3 YEARS	41000	45000	nc
Demo	usd	615.00 LWT			Cal '09	43750 +	5 YEARS	37000	43000	nc
Resale NB	usd	100.0 M dely '08			Cal '10	31750 +			

COMMODITY PRICES	**USD**	
Iron Ore India	115.0	-
Coal CIF Rotterdam	173.0	-
Steel China	687.0	-
Soyabeans	1196.0	-

BPI

BUNKER PRICES		
	IFO(380)	MDO
RDM	- 510.5	- 822.5
GIB	- 577.5	- 975.0
NOLA	- 545.5	982.5
SPORE	- 585.0	- 887.5
JPN	- 689.5	985.0

EXCHANGE RATES		
YEN/USD	105.11 -	0.56
EURO/USD	1.415 -	0.002
WON/USD	1,159.8 +	41.85
STERLING/USD	1.780 -	0.007

MAX 20 YEARS AGE TONNAGE SUPPLY (Approximate for guidance only)

	ATLANTIC						PACIFIC					
(ATL TTL SPOT=53+TTL51 10-30DAYS=60+)							(PAC TTL SPOT=68+/TTL 10-30DAY=61+)					
	ukc	med	st law	usec	usg	ecsa	safr	mideast	feast	seasia	isnp/bc	
Spot/10days	24	19	1	1	4	4	3	15	32	18	0	121
10/30 days	26	13	3	1	9	8	0	16	21	22	2	121

MAX 20 YEARS AGE TONNAGE DEMAND (Approximate for guidance only)

	ATLANTIC						PACIFIC				
(ATL TTL SPOT=9+/TL 10-30DAYS=21-)							(PAC TTL SPOT=18-/TTL 10-30DAYS=19+)				
	ukc	med	st law	usec	usg	ecsa	safr	mideast	feast	seasia	isnp/bc
Spot/10days	1	5	0	1	0	2	0	1	4	13	0
10/30 days	1	2	3	1	3	11	1	2	0	8	8

Baltic Exchange Panamax Index 2005-08

REPORTED FIXTURES

Pacific
SEAS/SEAS - 'Cemtex Venture' Glencore relet 2006 73546 dwt dely Phu My 16/20 Sept trip via Indonesia redel Malaysia $32000 daily - U Ming
SEAS/FEAST - 'Felicia' 1997 72456 dwt dely Hong Kong 19/21 Sept trip via Villaneuva redel Japan $35500 daily - NYK
SEAS/SEAS - 'Greta R' 1989 68722 dwt dely Shanghai 16/18 Sept trip via Indonesia redel Philippines $22000 daily - Baumarine
AUS/ECSA - 'Ligari' relet 2000 73288 dwt dely Longkou 20/24 Sept trip via Queensland redel Brazil $21000 daily - Cargill

Atlantic
NCSA/FEAST - 'Waimea' Cargill relet 1997 70000/10 Ponta da Madeira/Kaohsiung ely Oct $48.50 fio 40000sc/38000sc 12 hours tt bends - CSE
ECSA/CONT - 'Ilenao' 1987 60000/10 Norfolk/Antwerp 25 Sept/5 Oct $20.00 fio 25000sc/30000sc - Mittal

Atlantic - Some fresh enquiry today and drop in levels slowing.
Pacific - Strong demand on early panamaxes firming market somewhat. Some short period activity also.
BDI 4760 (UP 13) **BCI 6471** (UP 102) **BPI 4695** (DOWN 17) **BSI 3086** (DOWN 16) **BHSI 1711** (DOWN 26)

Figure 3.3 Daily Panamax Bulker Market Report

Source: Simpson Spence Young (SSY), 16 September 2008

CAPESIZE

An extremely tough week for owners with rates tumbling in both the Atlantic and Pacific, the average of the four timecharter routes having shed over $31,000 through the week. There has been precious little transatlantic enquiry to give the market much needed support, leaving fronthaul to bear the brunt and consequently rates have suffered. Earlier in the week a 171,000- dwt built 2003, open in the UK, agreed $145,000 daily for a trip via Brazil to China and subsequently a 14 year old 150,000 tonner accepted $95,000 daily for a similar run. Voyage rates have also fallen, a Korean charterer is trading Ponta Da Madeira/China around $55, a drop of about $10 since early this week, although lower bunker costs have softened the blow. In the East, there has been no shortage of activity but owners have been unable to make any headway and rates here have also slumped, West Australia/China has been traded at $21 and subsequently a charterer bid $18. Earlier a 177,000 dwt, open north China, agreed a lower $95,000 daily however this was quickly overtaken by events as a similar size newbuilding accepted $79,000 for a round via Australia.

A bright spot lies in the period market, where charterers do not appear to be deterred in looking forward, a 170,000-dwt fixed a year with a Chinese charterer around $130,000. Also for the longer term 180,000-dwt secured $87,000 daily for five years with delivery later this year.

PANAMAX

The Pacific has fought hard to improve however with capes struggling. Panamaxes in turn were restrained, a 2 year old 76,000-dwt, open south Japan fixed a round voyage via New South Wales at $34,500 daily. Short trip activity includes a 74,000-dwt in China fixing a trip via Indonesia back to China at $28,000 daily. Backhaul levels were also not very exciting a modern 75,000, open China, agreed $24,250 daily for a trip to the US east coast. The Atlantic has struggled to maintain impetus although rates remain appreciably higher than the Pacific, a 75,000 tonner, open Continent, obtained $70,000 daily for a trip via Baltimore to Japan. Short haul activity includes a 73,000-dwt, open in the UK, fixing a trip from the Baltic Sea to the Continent around $57,500 daily.

HANDY/ SUPRAMAX

A week of sharply declining rates in the Atlantic as tonnage lists continued to grow. One sector that was previously bucking the easier trend was the East Med/Black Sea area but even here conditions became much more difficult. It was reported that the 2004 built 50,619 dwt RM Power was booked with spot delivery at Canakkale for a trip via the Black Sea to Pakistan at $40,000 daily; although in mitigation it was thought that the vessel only had about 40 days remaining on the balance of her charter. Across the pond it was thought that a 2008 built 56,000 dwt vessel in ballast from the East Med had been booked delivery North Coast South America mid September for a trip to Spain at $59,000 daily.

It was also thought that the vessel may have to wait a few days before going on hire. In the Far East, the market also looked easier, however with a reasonable amount of enquiry in the North Pacific area, owners were having more chance of offering some sort of resistance. One report suggested that a 2001 built 50,200 dwt vessel open North China spot had been booked for a long duration trip to West Africa at $33,000 daily.

The Indian Ocean however was proving to be a graveyard and although a few cargoes were now being quoted, the Charterers were able to take their pick from a large number of available vessels. Earlier in the week, the 2002 built 50,200 dwt Legend Phoenix was booked for a trip from Chennai to China at $22,000 daily.

Figure 3.4 Weekly Dry Cargo Market Commentary (12 September 2008)
Source: Baltic Exchange, 12 September 2008

3.1.3 Position lists

This contains information about where and when vessels are expected to become available (open) for new employment. Positions are circulated by shipowners and operators as a guide to brokers and charterers. The intention is that these position lists will generate interest and suggestions for next charter employment of the ships mentioned.

An example of a position list is the following:

PLSE PROPOSE FOR OUR LOCAL OWNS:
M/V ILYA 6.964 MTS DWAT ON 6.972 M, DWCC 6200 ON WINTERMARK
ST VINCENT FLAG, BUILT 1994, ITF ICE 1A SUPER
SINGLEDECK/OPEN HATCH BULK CARRIER
134.2 M LOA/19.90 M BEAM 4 HOLDS/4 HATCHES
10610 CBM BALE/10720 CBM GRAIN
OPEN EAST MED – BEG. NOVEMBER
PREFERS DIRECTION CONT/BALTIC

This position list seeks for the next charter of a vessel. It gives the ship's short description, expressing that the vessel will be "open" at East Mediterranean in the beginning of November with preferred next direction to Continent/Baltic Sea area.

3.1.4 Indications

An initial indication of the intentions, terms and conditions under which the ship-owner or the charterer is willing to start chartering negotiations. This term is used by chartering brokers and concerns information such as quantity of cargo to be carried, dates that a ship or a cargo will be available, the amount of freight that a charterer is willing to pay or the shipowner is willing to receive.

3.1.5 Offers/counter-offers

These are the most important pieces of information exchanged during chartering nego-tiations between the parties involved. Shipowners, charterers and their brokers partic-ipate in influencing the state of the freight market, and the information interchanged in relation to the business in question is as important as the agreement reached. For a judgment of the state of the market and the influence on the market development, this type of information is of equal importance whether a fixture is concluded or not. The crucial elements of a chartering negotiation are the offers and counter-offers exchanged between the negotiating parties, leading in a charter agreement.

3.1.6 General sources of information

Other necessary information concerns cost-related items about the operation and despatch of vessels, for example, costs for the handling of certain cargoes in various ports, port dues and charges associated with the ship's call, costs for canal passages, notes about bunker prices etc. Information about port congestion, hindrances from ice, opening and closing of canals and other important passages, notes on maximum draught allowed in ports, ships' cargo-handling equipment and its capacity for different commodities, as well as availability of labour to load/unload a vessel, constitute other valuable pieces of information. Moreover, various sudden geo-political occurrences and general economic and social circumstances always have a decisive effect on the development of the international shipping market. Such pieces of information, as described above, may be sourced either directly from shipowners, charterers, brokers and port/ship agents, commonly through private communications, or by specific information circulated publicly via the internet or on a membership basis by major organisations (e.g. BIMCO).

Some examples of other sources of information are the following:

- *Shipbroking and Agency Network:* Chartering information sourced from the global network of shipbrokers is always of utmost importance, whereas valuable information in respect of the ports (e.g. port restrictions, dues, expenses, fees etc.) should be traced from local agents.
- *Databases:* Some maritime organisations (e.g. BIMCO, Intertanko etc.), or maritime research experts (e.g. Lloyd's List Intelligence, Clarksons' Shipping Intelligence Network, Drewry, Fearnleys, Barry Rogliano Salles, RS Platou etc.) publish databases and reports on a membership or subscription or free of charge basis with important information regarding shipping companies, ships, freight rates, vessel values, cargo volumes and trade routes, ports, costs etc.
- *Commodity Reports:* Some international organisations issue reports related to the developments of world trade, such as the "Grain Market Report" which is issued monthly by the IGC (International Grains Council), the "Bunker Report" issued by the Baltic Exchange, the "Statistical Review of World Energy" by BP, the "Market Reports" by Clarksons, the "Market Intelligence" by Barry Rogliano Salles, the "Fertilizers Quarterly" by RS Platou, reports for oil and energy matters issued by the International Energy Agency or the US Energy Information Administration, etc.
- *Commodity Price Bulletins & Handbook on International Trade and Development Statistics:* UNCTAD (United Nations Conference on Trade and Development) publishes a monthly newsletter with product prices and an annual handbook with statistical data concerning the development of international trade.
- *Country Reports:* Researches regarding the economic situation of various countries are carried out by embassies, ministries and other state agencies. Such researches are also carried out by UNCTAD in co-operation with OECD (Organisation for Economic Co-operation and Development).

- *Reports on the Global Economy:* For instance, IMF (International Monetary Fund) issues a series of researches regarding the developments in world economy.
- *Lloyd's Publications and Informa Group services:* Highly specialised information is provided to shipping market practitioners and organisations around the world, through publishing (books, reports, magazines, newspapers), events (conferences, seminars), training, market research intelligence and expertise (consulting, in-house training, distance learning courses). From a chartering and shipbroking aspect, the most valuable Lloyd's publications and services are considered to be the "Lloyd's List" electronic newspaper, the "Lloyd's Law Reports", the "Lloyd's Shipping Economist" and most of all the "Lloyd's List Intelligence" electronic database network, together with a plethora of shipping book titles etc.
- *Internet network:* Web pages compose a major source of shipping information. The reader may find a list of widely recognised shipping links at the end of the bibliography for further research.

3.2 Information centres

London, New York and Tokyo are of primary interest as information centres, but Oslo, Piraeus, Hamburg, Copenhagen, Geneva and Paris also play a crucial role in the distribution of shipping information. In the last few decades, due to the growth of Asian economies, Singapore, Hong Kong, Shanghai, Seoul and Taipei have grown rapidly in importance, whilst other shipping locations worth mentioning are Vancouver, Hamilton, Istanbul, Monte Carlo, Antwerp, Rio de Janeiro and Mumbai.[2] Shipowners who operate their ships worldwide are also in daily contact with shipping centres in many other countries. At this point emphasis will be given to specific maritime organisations which play an influencing role in chartering matters on a global level, on one way or another.

3.2.1 Baltic Exchange

This is a unique and very old institution focusing on the exchange of shipping information. It is headquartered in London, with regional offices in Athens, Singapore and Shanghai. In the past, owners, charterers and brokers used to meet there regularly for a few hours around noon to distribute cargo circulars and to exchange information in absolute confidentiality and trust. The prevailing state of the market was discussed, formal freight negotiations could take place and fixtures were sometimes concluded on "the floor". Today, this part of the work relating to the Baltic is normally done via telephone, e-mail and internet. However, the Baltic Exchange still plays an important role, with a total membership of over 600 companies. Membership is not just limited to shipbrokers, charterers

---

2 Clarkson Research Services *Shipping Intelligence Weekly* (27 March 2015, p. 20).

and shipowners, but expanded to financial institutions, maritime lawyers, educators, insurers and related associations.

Baltic's international community reflects the majority of world shipping interests and commits to a code of business conduct encapsulated in the motto "*our word our bond*". Baltic Exchange members are responsible for a large proportion of the total dry cargo and tanker fixtures as well as for most of the global sale and purchase activity of merchant vessels.

The members benefit from the shipping market information produced. This information is based on assessments made by a global panel of recognised shipbrokers. Daily reporting is provided on freight rates of over 50 trade routes, as well as market guidance on second-hand values, demolition prices and fixtures of ships. Independent, high quality dry, wet and gas freight market information is provided by the Baltic Exchange, whilst the freight derivatives market (FFAs) is also covered. In addition, training courses about chartering and freight derivates are organised.

Baltic Exchange contribution is decisive on international chartering matters, mainly through the publication of a series of shipping and freight indices. These are used as general indicators of the freight markets' performance, as benchmarks against physical charter contracts and as settlement tools for freight derivative trades. The role of the Baltic Exchange in publishing freight indices has been described in section 2.5. Further to that, it is worth adding that the Baltic Exchange is one out of four organisations which created the "Laytime Definitions for Charter Parties 2013", together with BIMCO, FONASBA and CMI (see chapter 15 and appendix 3).

3.2.2 Baltic and International Maritime Council (BIMCO)

The Baltic and International Maritime Council (BIMCO) in Copenhagen is a leading maritime organisation with around 2,300 members, being shipowners, operators, managers, brokers and agents spread all over the world. BIMCO's core objective is to facilitate the commercial operations of its members by developing standard contracts and clauses, providing a system of document editing (called BIMCO "Idea"), as well as offering quality information, advice and education. BIMCO promotes fair business practices, free trade and open access to markets, having a strong commitment to the harmonisation and standardisation of all shipping-related activities.

Its documentary committee is dealing with the design and development of shipping documents. Today, there is a list of about 100 printed standard charterparty and other document forms, as well as 100 standard clauses that have in one way or another been approved by BIMCO. Due to its wide membership, influence and global coverage, BIMCO may also be asked to provide information on, for example, congestion in a certain port, requested port dues and charges, port regulations and practices (rules of the trade) etc. If somebody in shipping circles repeatedly and deliberately violates the rules of the trade or has otherwise acted improperly (e.g. when there is slow-paced settlement of outstanding amounts), then he may be officially reported to BIMCO, which in turn can put pressure on such parties to remedy the fault. Owners and charterers quite frequently use the opportunity to ask for a BIMCO consultancy on dispute matters.

From a chartering and shipbroking view, BIMCO's influence is wide and absolute. It is worth noting that almost all the relevant standard shipping documents used worldwide (e.g. charterparties, bills of lading, booking notes, timesheets and statements of facts used in laytime practice, or even agency agreements, ship management or sale & purchase contracts etc.) are either issued or approved by BIMCO. Charterparty drafting concerns all types of charter and covers the whole spectrum of shipping markets, for example, from the commonly used and famous general-purpose voyage charterparty *"Gencon"*, the general time charterparty *"Gentime"*, the *"Barecon"* a typical contract for bareboat charters and the *"Gencoa"* a typical one for contracts of affreightment, to less popular but very specialised documents, as for instance the *"LNGvoy"*, a first published in 2016, voyage charterparty created to reflect the developing spot market of LNG vessels. BIMCO's role is similarly broad, extensive and crucial in drafting of balanced bills of lading and wording of charterparty clauses. Finally, it must be stressed that BIMCO is the leading organisation behind the issuance of "Laytime Definitions 2013" (see chapter 15 and appendix 3).

3.2.3 International Association of Dry Cargo Shipowners (INTERCARGO)

INTERCARGO members mostly operate bulk carriers in the international dry bulk trades. Its main role is to work with its members, the regulators and other shipping associations to ensure that the dry bulk industry operates safely, efficiently, profitably and in an environmentally friendly manner. To achieve this, it actively participates in the development of global legislation through the International Maritime Organisation (IMO) and other similar bodies.

INTERCARGO's publications are important sources of information for the shipping market practitioners. The "INTERCARGO Benchmarking Bulk Carriers Report", which is issued annually, contains statistical and benchmarking information on bulk carriers. It provides guidance to owners, port state control authorities, flag states, financiers, terminal operators, charterers and other industry stakeholders.

3.2.4 International Association of Independent Tanker Owners (INTERTANKO)

INTERTANKO has been representing the interests of independent tanker owners since 1970, seeking to ensure that oil is always shipped and carried by sea safely, responsibly and competitively. INTERTANKO functions as a forum where the tanker industry meets, policies are discussed and statements are created. It is a valuable source of first-hand information, opinions and guidance about tanker and oil matters.

Membership is open to independent tanker owners and operators, i.e. non-oil companies and non-state controlled tanker owners, who fulfil the Association's membership criteria. The organisation has over 200 members, whilst associate membership stands at some 240 companies related to the tanker industry.

INTERTANKO has opened offices in Singapore and Washington DC, in addition to its principal offices in Oslo and London. Within the shipping industry itself, INTERTANKO participates in discussions within the International Maritime Organisation (IMO) where it has non-governmental status, and the International Oil Pollution Compensation Fund (IOPC). In addition, it has a consultative status at the United Nations Conference on Trade and Development.

INTERTANKO is actively involved in a wide range of tanker topics, which include commercial, technical, legal, operational, environmental, documentary and market issues. Direct contact with the members and original sources enables it to select and promulgate the information which is essential to the tanker industry. INTERTANKO's information and advisory services include the "*Weekly News*", courses, seminars, free access to a range of web-based services and various publications. Members and associate members are also entitled to direct expert opinions from resourceful and experienced lawyers, mariners, naval architects, marine engineers, economists and other specialists within the association.

Focusing on the chartering matters, in a tanker market traditionally dominated by the charterers (oil majors) which follow their own standard charterparty forms, INTERTANKO has historically played a key role in shaping more balanced standard charterparties for various charter types. Namely, it has issued in the past the "*Tankervoy '87*" for tanker voyage charters, the "*Interconsec '76*" for consecutive voyages charters and the "*Intertanktime '80*" for tanker time charters.

3.2.5 *Federation of National Associations of Shipbrokers & Agents (FONASBA)*

FONASBA provides a "united voice" for the world's shipbrokers and agents. As a federation, its membership is made up of the national associations of shipbrokers and agents of 49 countries, 43 of which as full members with a further six countries represented by associate or candidate members. Individual companies are also eligible to join. All members of the national associations which make up FONASBA are encouraged to obtain the *FONASBA Quality Standard*, proving their financial standing and commitment to quality.

Founded in 1969, the organisation promotes fair and equitable practices and ensures that the needs of its members are understood at both a governmental level and across the maritime industry. It focuses on liner and tramp agency matters, chartering and shipbroking issues, sale and purchase and documentary affairs across all shipping markets. FONASBA is based at London's Baltic Exchange.

FONASBA has a consultative status at the International Maritime Organisation (IMO), United Nations Conference on Trade & Development (UNCTAD) and the World Customs Organisation (WCO). It also works closely with shipowning bodies such as BIMCO, Intercargo and Intertanko.

FONASBA's relationship with the European Union is handled through its sub-committee, the European Community Association of Ship Brokers & Agents (ECASBA) established in 1990 to represent European shipbrokers and agents. ECASBA provides critical input about European seaports and their services, short-sea shipping, shipping safety and EDI policies, as well as for customs and administrative procedures.

It is worth pointing out that FONASBA was one out of the four organisations which co-operated in issuing the "Laytime Definitions 2013" (see chapter 15 and appendix 3). Moreover, it has published the "Time Charter Interpretation Code 2000" attempting to help in eliminating charterparty disputes often arising from time charters (see chapter 12 and appendix 7).

3.2.6 Institute of Chartered Shipbrokers (ICS)

The Institute of Chartered Shipbrokers (ICS) is an internationally recognised professional body representing shipbrokers, ship managers and agents. The Institute was founded in 1911 and awarded a British Royal Charter in 1920. With 24 branches in key shipping areas and 4,000 individual members, ICS membership represents a high professional standard across the shipping industry, particularly within chartering and shipbroking cycles. As a major provider of shipping-related education and training, ICS delivers its main educational programme – tutor ship – directly from its London head office and under agreement through its distance learning centres worldwide.

3.2.7 Association of Ship Brokers and Agents (USA) Inc. (ASBA)

ASBA is an independent membership trade association, established in 1934, currently with offices in the USA and Canada. Its purpose is to bring together the members, namely shipbrokers (dry cargo, tanker, sale & purchase) and agents, as well as affiliate members (shipowners, operators, charterers and tug companies), which all shall have to operate in the USA or Canada for at least one year. ASBA advances and fosters the ideals and standards of professional conduct and practices and is a means through which members with common interests can communicate.

ASBA organises conferences and offers distance learning courses and live seminars designed to give participants a broad and comprehensive understanding of shipping industry's developments. ASBA is well known for the publication of a widely used, balanced standard form of time charterparty, under the title *"NYPE" (New York Produce Exchange)*, which was updated in 2015 and its sample may be found in appendix 6. Besides, ASBA sells its charterparty editor software, a licensed, annually renewed product which intends to facilitate chartering negotiations, charterparty drafting and finalisation. This system supports a wide range of documents (dry cargo and tanker, voyage and time charterparties, together with few miscellaneous other forms) and offers advantages to the shipbrokers and their principals.

3.3 Information network

It is of great importance for shipowners, charterers, brokers and agents to establish a network of contacts which catches all interesting business opportunities and by which adequate information is quickly transmitted. Different brokers specialise in different markets or market sectors. By communicating with those brokers who are specialists in the chartering of, for example, grain, and who have good and direct contacts with the big grain houses in London, Paris, Geneva, Hamburg or New York, an owner can keep well abreast of the availability of grain cargoes worldwide. He can also get current information through the brokers about the freight levels that may at any time be interesting to the potential charterers and – no less important – he can get information about the freight rates asked for by the competing tonnage.

In this way the owners follow continuously all the market sectors of interest. Charterers find their information in a corresponding way. For them, it is important to communicate with brokers who have contact with all owners operating suitable ships and who have an interest in the cargo or trade or charter type in question.

What has been said above is valid mainly for tonnage operated in the open market. The information network for liner trading has a different set-up. The individual liner company (shipowner, carrier, operator) or a liner alliance, maintaining traffic in a certain trade, will have a number of liner agents as integrated part of the shipping service (see section 3.5.3). These agents divide the areas that generate cargoes for booking into geographical areas of interest, within which each individual agent keeps in contact with the local customers (shippers), either directly or through forwarding agents (freight forwarders). The liner agents and the shipowner (liner company) normally enter into a formal agreement, a so-called "*exclusivity agreement*", by which the agents are guaranteed certain rights and benefits but at the same time they agree not to book any cargo or otherwise work for the account of competing lines. In principle, the liner operator cannot book cargo on his own, from the area covered by the agreement, without indemnifying his agent.

3.4 Information coverage

From the owner's point of view, one might think that it would be convenient not to use an intermediary, but instead to keep direct contact with interested charterers. Such contacts do exist, but then it is often a question of a very restricted market where a reasonably good view can be maintained through a small number of contacts. In the dry cargo or in tanker market this is not possible, since owners would then miss important or, on certain occasions, even crucial market information.

In order to keep the chartering staff as small as possible and to reduce his business inquiry expenses, the owner may even decide to channel all information through one or two brokers only. These brokers will then act as more or less exclusive "agents" for this owner and will be responsible for the necessary information, that is, collecting, treating and evaluating material to present to the owner. The disadvantage with such an arrangement is that the owner gets information which is trimmed, thus important judgments are then made by the middleman instead of the owner himself.

The other extreme is the owner working through a very large number of broker contacts without especially favouring any of them. Possibly one would thereby get most of the orders circulating in the market and the same order could be received from a number of different sources. Such an arrangement may, however, result in the work at the owner's office becoming slow and laborious. Another disadvantage is that the owner may also find that none of the brokers will put in the amount of effort which an exclusively appointed broker is supposed to.

In principle, the same approach is applicable from the charterer's point of view, but at the same time the charterer's position is somewhat different. Especially with respect to the important commodities, the charterers do keep a fairly careful check on tonnage available and freight levels through their own contacts. For various administrative reasons, they may also decide to separate their shipping division from the original body of the company and name it as their exclusive agent with authority to seek for tonnage and fix the company's cargoes. On the other hand, a charterer or shipper of cargoes able to be carried either as bulk or general cargoes (e.g. shipments of salt that may be carried in bags or in bulk at holds) must communicate both with liner agents working in the trade concerned and with brokers dealing with suitable tonnage in the open market, so as to find out the proper way of moving the cargo.

3.5 Information handlers

Information management is paramount in all business aspects of the modern era. Although many people may know the same piece of information, only some may be able to create added value by handling that information. In chartering and shipbroking business, the role of shipbrokers and agents is crucial in that perspective. Chartering brokers and port agents play an influential role in the chartering process (from the negotiation to the closing and execution of a charter), while the role of liner agents and freight forwarders is important in the cargo booking procedure of the liner industry. It goes without saying that the shipbrokers' role is the most important of all, thus it is analysed in greater depth below.

3.5.1 Shipbrokers (chartering brokers)

In the open charter market (including bulk business, tramp operations and vessel charters of the liner market) the shipowner and the charterer will often come in contact through *shipbrokers (chartering brokers)*[3], although in today's electronic

---

3 A shipbroker either specialises in chartering matters, then called "chartering broker", or in ship sale and purchase transactions, then called "s&p broker". Within the context of this book, the words "broker" and "shipbroker" shall always mean the chartering broker.

world the traditional role of the shipbroker has changed gradually and the negotiations are usually carried out by e-mail. Brokers have informative, intermediary, consultative and co-ordinating functions along the transportation chain.

A chartering broker acts on behalf, in the name of, and for the account of, one principal, either an owner or a charterer, and this is made known to all the parties concerned at an initial stage of discussions. A chartering broker brings the parties in contact, negotiates the contract of carriage, gives advice and recommendations with respect to appropriate offers and proposals, draws up the charterparty, follows up on contractual matters, arranges financial matters and assists in case of disputes. Normally, a shipbroker does not have the authority to conclude an agreement for the principal, but only to negotiate. The situation is quite different where a broker makes a contract in his own name but for the account of someone else. In such cases there is an "undisclosed principal" situation. It is not unusual that the principal's name is not made known initially, but the broker presents himself for example as "*agent for first-class charterer*", which, of course, is a rather risky undertaking from the broker's side. In an English case the House of Lords found that one broker involved had no "*usual or apparent authority*" and that a person acting for one of the parties lacked "*actual as well as ostensible authority*" (see *Armagas Ltd v Mundogas S.A. (The Ocean Frost) [1986] 2 Lloyd's Rep. 109 (HL)*).

A chartering broker ordinarily specialises in a certain market or in a sector of a market. In chartering, an owner and a charterer have real interest in the broker's sources of information, his particular knowledge and his skill at negotiation. Normally, both parties will have their own broker – the "*owner's broker*" and the "*charterer's broker*". Thus, both parties negotiate through their representatives, who should do their best to preserve their respective principal's interests and intentions. Sometimes the broker will have a certain authority to bind his principal, but normally the negotiations will be carried out in close co-operation between the principal, the broker and the respective counter-parties. When the agreement has been concluded, the broker may obtain specific authority to sign it (as recap or charterparty), which he does sometimes "*as agent only*" without mentioning the party or parties, or sometimes "*as agent for X*". In the former case, certain legal problems may arise as to who has really entered into the agreement. An owner may choose to do his business through one sole *confidential* or *exclusive* broker, or he may prefer to work through a number of brokers, who will then have equal opportunities to do the business.

Sometimes the broker introduces a "*first-class charterer*" or a "*first-class owner/carrier*" without mentioning a name. Should it appear later that the carrier or charterer is not first-class, the broker may become liable for the consequences of his wrong description. Both parties have good reasons and rights to check on their counterparts. Several years ago a carrier entered into a charterparty with, as he believed, an entity named "Indian Shippers". When, after the voyage, the owner claimed deadfreight, he discovered that there was no entity called "Indian Shippers", but that this was merely a collective description for a number of shippers. This illustrates the importance of identifying the other contracting party.

In a market with such widely differing sectors, one broker cannot possibly cover all sectors with his direct connections. He will then leave his order with other brokers, who in their turn may have good connections with colleagues representing an interested counter-party. A broker thus engaged in efforts to bring together an owner's confidential broker with the broker of a suitable charterer is engaged in "competitive chartering" and is called a "*competitive broker*". However, it must be said that in today's competitive shipping market these fixtures are becoming very difficult to make. All brokers endeavour to tie to themselves a number of principals (owners or charterers) for whom they may work as one of some few confidential brokers. As broker, it is an advantage to work on such a confidential or exclusive basis, since the broker may thereby have a fairly secure employment and a certain continuity in his activities.

The main function of the broker is to represent his principal in charter negotiations (see chapter 8). The broker has to work for and protect his principal's interests in the following ways:

1. *The broker should keep his principal continuously informed* about the market situation, the market development, the current freight rates, the available cargo proposals and shipment possibilities. He should, in the best possible way, cover the market for the given positions and orders. Furthermore, the broker provides his views on the market with respect to future freight rate movements. If a chartering broker of a shipowner expects freight rates to increase in the short term, he will most likely advise his principal to wait a few days before fixing. If he expects a decline of freight rates in short term, he will advise his principal to fix as soon as possible, before the decline. If the chartering broker represents a charterer then his advice will be the opposite of that given to the shipowner. Some shipbroking companies publish regularly market reports (see section 3.1) and undertake tailor-made researches for their clients.

2. *The broker should act strictly within given authorities* in connection with the negotiations. Sometimes the broker may have a fairly wide framework – a wide discretion – within which to work when carrying out the negotiations, however he should always take into account some absolute limits which must not be exceeded.

3. *The broker should in all respects work loyally for his principal* and carry out scrupulously and skilfully the negotiations and other work connected with the charter.

4. *The broker may not withhold any information from his principal nor give him wrong information.* Nor may he reveal his principal's business "secrets" or act to the advantage of the counter-party in the negotiations in order to reach an agreement.

5. *A "first-class broker" should not advance cargo shipment or vessel employment proposals to his principal if the business is not seriously founded or if there may be doubts about the counter-party's honesty or solvency.*

6. *The broker should also protect his principal's interests by preventing wrongfully worded or incomplete orders from being forwarded* until they have been corrected or completed. The broker also has a *duty to preserve his principal's reputation.*

7. *The broker has a duty to take an active part in the negotiations and give advice and recommendations* with respect to appropriate offers, proposals and compromises. He should also try to find out the actions of competitors in order to secure as many advantages as possible for his principal. A "mailbox" broker who only furthers information, offers and counter-offers without judging and processing them can hardly count on a high degree of appreciation from the owner or the charterer.

Chartering brokers are classified into various categories depending on the person they represent, the charter market in which they operate, their personality and temper etc. More specifically:

- Brokers who act on behalf of shipowners seeking cargoes (*"chartering brokers seeking cargoes"*) and those who act on behalf of charterers seeking ships (*"chartering brokers seeking ships"*).

- In accordance with the broker's personality and temper, somewhat informally a distinction is often made between a *"freight broker"* and a *"charterparty broker"*. The former is the broker who is always successful in contracting somewhat above the market level, but who will never risk losing business due to the details of a particular charterparty clause. The latter will contract at the actual market level, but he will always try to phrase every single charterparty clause so that it will be as advantageous as possible to his principal. It must be stressed that a charterparty that has not been carefully drafted may cause considerable losses to one of the parties, but a business result can only be determined after the post-fixture calculation, disbursement of expenses and final settlement. One may say that every clause has a value and a price.

- *"Dry cargo broker"* is the chartering broker who specialises in the dry cargo market or in a sector of this market. *"Tanker broker"* is the chartering broker who specialises in the liquid cargo market or in a sector of this market.

- *"Competitive broker"* is the broker who works freely and individually in the charter market, while *"in-house broker"* is the broker who acts exclusively for a shipowner or a charterer. It is common for at least the large shipping companies to have within their own organisations separate departments or divisions or even companies working as their brokers. Besides, large brokers may also be directly involved in operating or even owning fleets. Having an in-house broker within a shipping group or a shipping company is not always a guarantee that an order given to the broker will also be brought out into the open market, or vice versa. Therefore, when the owner and the broker are in the same group of companies, certain orders may be prevented from going out into the open market and instead they will be reserved for the "house" tonnage, if the broker is not fully *independent*.

- In order to entice an owner to work "his way", the charterer's broker may draw up the order in such a way that it indicates, more or less, that he has a close or particularly good relationship with the charterer. In this context, *"exclusive"* means that a broker is the only one who works on the order, thus instructed directly and preferentially by the charterer. Exclusivity has the same meaning when it concerns the relationship of the broker with the shipowner. The expression *"local charterers"* indicates a geographically close connection of brokers with charterers. The word *"friends"* may also be used under different circumstances by brokers to indicate a special connection.

A broker will hardly ever have full liberty to "go out on the market" with an order to *"fix best possible"*. Instead, he will normally have an *authority* to negotiate on behalf of his principal within a framework of certain specified terms and conditions, which, if they are not accepted by the counter-party, the broker must get new instructions. This will be repeated until both parties are in total agreement.

When an owner or a charterer, having received an order or a position, demands additional information or wishes to look more carefully into the possibility of a charter agreement, he is regarded as being *"committed"* to this broker. If the principal wants to open up negotiations, it is regarded as good practice to work through the broker to whom he (the principal) is already "committed". Sometimes brokers try to commit a principal on the telephone by advancing the order and trying at the same time to discuss the possibility of the order. Such a way of proceeding is not regarded as a first-class method.

Normally, the privilege of choosing a broker channel is considered to belong to the owner. But then again regard should be given to factors such as: Who first presented the order or position? Who has the most "direct" connection? Which of the brokers seems to have the best and most complete information and background with respect to the business in question? Who has better bargaining power? Consideration is also normally given to whether a previous connection with the same customer has been made through a certain broker with respect to similar charters. Further, personal relations naturally play an important role.

Sometimes the owner and the charterer, after having concluded one agreement through a broker, may do subsequent business directly with each other. Such direct business may be a consequence of their wish to avoid paying commissions. It may happen also that a *competitive broker* has presented an order which for some reason the owner's *confidential broker* has not received via his direct channel or which he has not observed. The owner may then be tempted to inform his direct (exclusive) channel about the order thereby "committing himself" through this channel instead of giving the competitive broker a chance. Such or similar methods are considered improper and not quite acceptable from an ethical point of view.

Charterer's shipbroker will also have as one of his duties, to make out the original charterparty in accordance with the agreed terms and conditions, immediately after the charter negotiations have been concluded. Another important duty of both brokers is to follow up how the transport undertaking is performed, so that the parties receive continuous information, notices are given correctly, freight or hire are duly paid etc.

A number of standard forms of charterparties contain a printed term on brokerage (i.e. the broker's remuneration for providing his services), but leave it to the parties to fill in the percentage, for instance, *Gencon '94* (see appendix 1, *part II, clause 15 "brokerage"*):

> *A brokerage commission at the rate stated in Box 24 on the freight, dead-freight and demurrage earned is due to the party mentioned in Box 24. In case of non-execution 1/3 of the brokerage on the estimated amount of freight to be paid by the party responsible for such non-execution to the Brokers as indemnity for the latter's expenses and work. In case of more voyages the amount of indemnity to be agreed.*

Instead of the agency fees that are usually agreed and paid to the agents on a lump sum agency fee basis, brokers typically receive remuneration calculated as a certain percentage of the gross freight figure. The intermediaries involved will normally be entitled to remuneration only when the charter agreement has been concluded and/or connected contracts have been signed. The broker's income is thus dependent on the freight market and the size of the deal involved. Such size may be measured in terms of the cargo quantity (in a spot charter) or the length of the charter period (in a period charter). Normally, every broker involved in a charter deal will get an amount corresponding to 1¼ per cent (1.25%) of the gross freight. Unless otherwise agreed (which is very rare in practice), such broker's remuneration is generally referred to as the *"commission"* or *"brokerage"*. It is paid by the owner and the total actual percentage for a certain deal, the *total commission*, should be specified in every order presented to the owner. The brokerage should cover broker's expenses and give him a net profit. As mentioned, the commission or brokerage is always calculated on a percentage of the gross freight or hire and, depending on what is agreed during the negotiations, the so-called "demurrage", "ballast bonus" and "deadfreight" (see chapters 14 and 15) may also be the basis of commission, in addition to the gross freight at a voyage charter. Thus, it is common in the dry cargo sector that every broker gets 1.25% and the relevant freight calculations will normally be based on 2.5% or 3.75% depending on the number of brokers involved. It is, however, not uncommon for the total commission to be even higher, but in those cases a so-called "*address commission*" will almost invariably be involved. In many trades and with time charters it is usual that part of the commission is "returning to the house" (charterer) which in practice thus reduces the freight or hire to be paid. Such address commissions may be up to 5% (heavy address). The reason for this practice is said to be that the charterers' shipping department, for book-keeping purposes, must show some kind of income from their activities. State trading companies regularly include a 5% address commission in their orders. Furthermore, it is quite common to find that a charterer's broker, who is working on an exclusive basis for his principal, will be entitled to 2.5% brokerage. As mentioned, the owners will pay all commissions and therefore, they may try to cover such costs by a corresponding freight or hire increase.

Finally, it must be added that continuing structural change in the shipping industry has also led to changes for brokers, port agents and other intermediaries in shipping. There is a tendency for intermediaries to be more often involved in disputes. A consequence is that the need for insurance of intermediaries has increased. P&I Clubs for shipbrokers, port agents, managers and other intermediaries in shipping have been founded, and these clubs seem to be well established as a necessary complement to the traditional P&I Clubs.

3.5.2 Port agents

In bulk shipping (including also tramp operations of all vessel types), the task of the port agent is to represent the owner and assist the vessel for the owner's account, so that the ship will have the best possible despatch during a port call. It is important that the owner employs a reliable and energetic agent. Port agent will be remunerated by a fixed *agency fee* which varies considerably between different ports and also depends on the tonnage of the vessel.

The port agent should in all respects assist the master in his contacts with all local authorities, including harbour authorities, and he also has to procure cash to master (CTM), provisions and other necessities, assist in medical matters, boarding and expatriation of the crew, co-ordinate possible repairs and maintenance of the ship, communicate orders and messages to and from the owners etc. Loading and discharging will often be for the charterer's account (in period charters and when FIO terms or similar variations are agreed in the voyage charterparty). The charterer should then prefer to be entitled to nominate the *port agent* in order to further his interests. The question of appointing an agent may be an important detail in the charter negotiations, since the parties have to establish whether the charterparty shall stipulate *"owner's agents"* or *"charterer's agents"*. If a charterer's agent is to be appointed it may be an advantage from the owner's point of view that the actual clause states, for example, *"charterer's agent to be nominated, but if actually appointed by the owner, the latter will do so only by authority of and for the account of the charterer"*. If the owner has to accept the charterer's agent he may protect his interests to a certain extent by appointing a *"husbandry agent"* or *"protective agent"* who will then assist the master and look after the owner's interests in order that the charterer's agent will not act to the disadvantage of the owner and the ship.

The agent arranges on behalf of the shipowner *services* relevant to the ship and its cargo, such as[4]:

- *Allocating ship's berthing* place to load and/or unload, as well as ensuring that the master is well aware of port requirements and vice versa.

---

4 Plomaritou, E. (2015) *What Agents Need to Know about Chartering* (London, Lloyd's Maritime Academy, Module 6 of Distance Learning Course "Diploma for Ship and Port Agents", p. 15).

- Arranging the *pilot and tug boat* services.
- Organising the safe and effective *loading and/or unloading* of merchandise.
- *Liaising* with the people involved in the actual loading or discharging, who would be stevedores (the case of dry cargo) or the jetty management (the case of liquid cargo).
- Preparing the *cargo manifest*; this gives detailed information on cargo to be handled. Sometimes, the agent may even sign the bill of lading on behalf of the ship's master.
- Advising import/export *cargo owners.*
- Advising the *customs office* of the ship's arrival and reporting the cargo on board.
- Ensuring that the *ship's documentation* complies with international and local regulations, as this will be inspected by port state control, customs, classification societies or other authorities when they board the ship.
- Providing information on the crew and any passengers to the department of *immigration* and citizenship.
- Organising *ship repairs and maintenance.*
- Arranging the delivery of *stores, supplies, charts and spares* to the ship.
- Organising *crew* changes, any associated immigration documentation and arrangements such as booking flights, as well as catering for medical treatment of crew members.
- Handling the *mail* of the crew.
- Handling the amount of cash required by the master of the ship (*Cash to Master – CTM*).
- Preparing the *statement of facts*; this is a record of events occurring during a ship's port call that can affect the counting of laytime and forwarding it to the shipowner upon the ship's departure (see chapter 15).
- Undertaking the payment of ship's expenses at the port, preparing the *disbursements account (D/A)* and submitting it to the shipowner.

3.5.3 Liner agents

Liner agents form an important group of intermediaries in liner shipping. Whereas brokers and port agents seldom enter into written contracts with their principals, liner agents often enter into long-term written agreements. There are even some standard liner agency contracts in the market practice.

Liner agents may be employed as a shipowner's/liner operator's branch office at the port-of-call soliciting cargoes on behalf of the line, typically within a defined geographical area. The agent may be independent and represent more than one principal, but in many cases he is tied to, or is often a subsidiary of, one specific principal.[5] Normally, the liner agent involved in a booking deal will get an amount corresponding to 3–5% of the gross freight.

---

5 FONASBA (2012) *The Role, Responsibilities and Obligations of the Ship Agent in the International Transport Chain.*

The liner agent arranges on behalf of the liner operator services relevant to the ship and its cargo, such as:

- *Securing cargo for the liner operator.* This requires from the agent to be in regular contact with local shippers and be ready to provide information on vessel schedules, competitive rates and conditions of carriage. The booking will normally be made without special negotiations, through a quotation in accordance with the pricing scheme in force. As soon as the booking has been noted and confirmed by the agent, there is an agreement on the carriage of goods and a booking note is normally issued (see appendix 11).
- *Booking up with or without the authorisation from the operator.* The agent will normally have from the liner operator – before every loading occasion – an allocation of space for booking up without any further authorisation from the owner. However, for certain cargoes such as unusual goods (heavy lifts etc.), approval must be obtained from the liner operator in every single case.
- *Ensuring the cargo is at the right place and time.* The liner agent undertakes also to ensure that the cargo is available at the right place and time and makes arrangements for it to be loaded and – in the case of an inbound ship – ensures that the cargo is delivered to the correct consignees. He undertakes the co-ordination of delivery of inward shipments and of receipt of outward shipments, keeping close contact with the liner operator, the terminal and port vendors, as well as with other transport operators (truck operators, rail operators etc.). In addition, liner agents have to make their utmost effort in each port of call to expedite the despatch, so that the vessel keeps to her schedule.
- *Checking documentation.* Since every item of cargo generates the need for paperwork, the liner agent undertakes also to check the documentation (e.g. booking note, bill of lading etc.).
- *Arranging container tracking and control.* The procedure of container tracking and control is an important element of the liner agent's duties. Container tracking is to monitor the status and location of every container within the agent's territory. Container control is the function of ensuring, in collaboration with the principal, that containers are where they are needed.
- Settling the proper *supply of containers' seals, labels, numbering and documents.*
- Undertaking the *arrangement of tasks related to containers' maintenance* in accordance with the guidelines of liner operator.
- Undertaking *services related to inland transportation, customs clearance* and other services.
- *Keeping shippers advised of vessel's schedule, cargoes' status* etc.
- *Arranging marketing and sales matters.* Liner agent deals with the day-to-day contacts with the customers and is always trying to create new clientele. Therefore, it is routine to travel and to visit customers. Great

emphasis is given on making marketing research, providing periodical market analysis, as well as placing advertisements in trade magazines and daily newspapers. Additional advertising may be carried out from time to time through big advertising campaigns.

- Undertaking *financial matters*, such as the collection of money from shippers and the payment of various expenses on behalf of the vessel.
- Arranging *operational tasks,* such as ship's repairing, ship's provision with stores, spares and lubricants, ship's bunkering. Furthermore, he undertakes crew changes and medical matters.
- *Settling various claims* in accordance with the instructions of the liner operator.

Finally, the case of chartered vessels must be commented. When vessels serving a line have been chartered-in from independent owners, then the ship (i.e. the owners) may also use the liner agency network for their own purposes, even though such agents are appointed by the charterer (liner operator).

3.5.4 Forwarding agents (freight forwarders)

In the liner market forwarding agents (or freight forwarders) play an important role in creating the contract of carriage between the shipowner (carrier) and the cargo owner. The freight forwarder is the person or company that organises shipments for individuals or corporations to get goods from the manufacturer or producer to a market, customer or final point of distribution. The forwarder does not move the goods, but acts as an expert in the logistics network. In other words, the freight forwarder arranges for the carriage of goods and associated formalities on behalf of a shipper. Therefore, he undertakes the booking of space onboard the vessel, the provision of the necessary documentation, the arrangement of customs clearance etc.

The changing structure of modern liner business has brought about increasing co-operation among the various carriers (various transport mode providers, including ships, airplanes, trucks and railroads) involved in cargo carriage from the seller to the buyer. Thus, large freight forwarders often offer "through carriage", performing as carriers throughout the whole cargo transit. In liner traffic, there is a growing tendency for freight forwarders to establish themselves as logistics companies taking over responsibility for all their customers' transports needs and other ancillary services (e.g. warehousing).

International freight forwarders typically perform activities pertaining to international shipments. They have additional expertise in preparing and processing customs documentation.

3.6 Means of communication

People engaged in day-to-day chartering work have to use various technical means of communication. The shipping community has been quick to adopt and gear up with modern IT tools and techniques although the telephone remains the most popular means. Telex was a very safe method of communication exchange, but has been replaced by chat forums and today's social media. Although the internet, Skype and e-mail are fully adopted for day-to-day shipping communication, as well as for marketing via, for example, websites, the safety factors and the legal implications still remain to be fully defined and ascertained.

In the shipowner's chartering and marketing departments as well as at the brokers' offices, new chartering opportunities, the present state of the market and shipping developments are always discussed on the basis of the daily inflow of information. Face-to-face contact is so important that chartering and shipbroking people working for the same or adjacent market sectors often prefer to be seated in the same room, although the environment may be very noisy from time to time. As mentioned above, the telephone (facilitated by mobiles) is the most frequently used medium for daily discussions with intermediaries and principals, so negotiations are frequently carried out over this instrument. Information about orders, position lists, market reports and various other matters are primarily received by e-mail, which is also widely used during the negotiations. Shipping documents, letters and signed charterparties are, of course, distributed by post mail. At this point it should be mentioned that various forms of electronic trade are nowadays applied to a broad field of shipping activities, which include chartering negotiation, charterparty editing (e.g. BIMCO Idea), issuance of shipping documents (e.g. bills of lading issued through EDI systems in liner shipping), the follow-up of ship's movements, the communication of ship with manager's/shipowner's office and the charterer, the general flow of information, the advertising of sea transport services, the support of the shipowner's or carrier's client (charterer/ shipper/freight forwarder), as well as the electronic payments.[6]

Irrespective of how sophisticated all communication means are, the old truth prevails, that the *quality of the input determines the quality of the output* in all information systems.

3.7 Information flow and time factor

In a shipping company which operates ships worldwide, the chartering work may continue day and night because of the time differences between various countries. It is important to remember that, due to competition, both owners and charterers can normally choose among a number of alternative business partners. These may also be domiciled at diametrically opposite places on Earth.

During negotiations every offer and counter-offer is submitted with a time limit for reply within which the party offering or countering is committed. If no reply from the counter-party is received within the time allowed, then the first party is free to start firm negotiations with any other party. The time for reply is often short, that is, anything from immediate reply up to a couple of hours.

---

6 Plomaritou, E. (2008) *Marketing of Shipping Companies* (Athens, Stamoulis Publications, p. 84).

Normally, the parties try to avoid staying firmly committed overnight or over a weekend. In a business opportunity where firm negotiations have started, the parties would normally try to conclude without interruptions, at least the main terms.

In bulk shipping, it is quite impossible to judge the tonnage position and foresee the alternative chartering opportunities during a period of time that lays a couple of months ahead. Therefore, it is not unusual to work with various notice time renewals lasting for as long as six months after the fixture.

In liner shipping, the lines do not normally alter their pricing tables without a pre-notice. However, when they give freight quotations a long time ahead of shipment, they possibly make a reservation (disclaimer) that any price changes may arise at short notice because of unforeseen circumstances.

CHAPTER 4

Chartering business and ship management

This chapter aims to track the location of chartering within the ship management field. It first introduces some general aspects of shipowning, describing various structures of shipping group organisation and how those may be related with chartering and shipbroking matters. Then, the ship management function is defined and the difference with shipowning is discussed. Ship management services and types of managerial models are presented. Not only the importance of commercial management of vessels, but also the relation with chartering and shipbroking practice, is highlighted. Emphasis is placed on showing some of the owners' and managers' most critical commercial decisions, most of all seen from a chartering perspective. Finally, it is worth reading an example illustrating how an owner may evaluate the routing plan and the chartering alternatives for one of his vessels.

4.1 Ship ownership

In a legal and strict interpretation, a shipowner is the person, either a physical presence or a legal entity, which holds the ownership of the vessel. However, in a broader sense, shipowning may sometimes be interpreted as comprising also the ship management/operation function, apart from pure ship ownership. This is so, because it is very common for both the shipowning and ship managing companies to belong to the same shipping group. Moreover, from a chartering and shipbroking perspective, it is important to note that the term "shipowner" describes the contracting party which represents the vessel's interests in a charterparty, either on a voyage or a period charter.

There is a wide variety of shipowners. Some owners operate a single ship while others larger fleets. Some concentrate on ships of a particular type (*fleet specialisation*), while others operate a varied collection of vessels (*fleet diversification*). The type of vessel's employment (spot or period charters) depends upon the market's circumstances, the shipowner's intentions, expectations and policies, as well as social and international geopolitical forces. Whilst in bulk shipping single-vessel shipowning companies form the international rule of ship ownership, in liner shipping the need for cost minimisation requires co-operation among operators and results in the pooling of shipping resources and common ownership or management of vessels.[1]

---

1 Giziakis, K., Papadopoulos, A. and Plomaritou, E. (2010) *Chartering* (Athens, Stamoulis Publications, 3rd edition, in Greek, pp. 349–363).

Business confidentiality and difficulty in lifting the "corporate veil"[2] of a shipping company are two good motives for the creation of *"single-vessel shipowning companies"* structure. Tax avoidance and cost control are the reasons why most shipowning companies are offshore. Current managerial trends are towards more transparency in organisational structures of shipping groups (e.g. holding companies, corporate structures and public shipping companies are more common now than in the past, audited financial statements of the shipping groups are now the standard business practice, etc.).

A modern shipping group activating in the ocean-going market would possibly comprise, for example, as many offshore, single-vessel shipowning companies as the vessels of the group are, with each vessel belonging to a separate, special purpose, shipowning company. Besides, the group would include one owned ship management company managing the vessels of the group, as well as presumably a holding company owning the shares of the shipowning companies. This holding company of the group might be listed to an international stock exchange (e.g. NYSE, Nasdaq, AIM). Within the shipping group there may be any other companies, relevant (or not) to the shipping activities of the sponsor (shipowner), for example cash management companies, investment "vehicles", real estate companies etc. Private (i.e. not listed) shipping groups may select to issue audited consolidated or combined financial statements, but they are not obliged to do so. However, there is an obligation on the publicly listed companies to publish audited accounts.

The concept of who a shipowner is has greatly changed over the years. Nowadays, several different types of company structures are used, including sole proprietorship, partnerships (e.g. *Master Limited Partnerships – MLPs*) and corporate structures. Within the bulk and liner shipping industries there are many different types of business, each with its own distinctive organisational structure, commercial aims and strategic objectives. Stopford M. gives some enlightening examples of typical shipping group structures, which have been slightly altered or expanded in this text to illustrate also possible differences on chartering/shipbroking matters, as follows[3]:

- *Private bulk shipping group*: A shipping group of companies owned by two Greek brothers. They operate a fleet of five ships, three product tankers and two small bulk carriers trading worldwide. The group has a small office in London, run by a chartering manager. Its main office is in Athens, where a few individuals facilitate the accounts and the administration. The three product tankers are on time charters and the two bulkers are on the spot market. One of the brothers is now more or less retired and all the important decisions are taken by the other brother,

---

2 Under most legal jurisdictions it is difficult to break the independence of the legal entity of a company, thus proving for example that two or more ships and their owning companies belong to the same shipping group/shipowner.

3 Stopford, M. (2009) *Maritime Economics* (London, Routledge Publications, 3rd edition, p. 86).

who knows from experience that the real profits are made from buying and selling ships, rather than from trading them on the charter market. Ships are fixed through a few competitive shipbrokers with whom long-established relationships of trust exist. Ship agents are selected in each port of call on a case-by-case basis. As bulk carriers are chartered on the spot market, clients (charterers and shippers) are dispersed and located worldwide, whereas various standard voyage charterparty forms are used depending mostly on the cargo carried. On the other hand, the tanker vessels are sought to get employed on time charters, thus clientele is smaller in number, more specific and concentrated around few charterers which typically use their own charter forms.

- *Shipping corporate:* A liner company in the container business. The company operates a fleet of 20 containerships (ten owned and ten chartered-in from independent owners) from a large modern office block, housing about 1,000 staff. All major decisions are taken by the main board, which consists of 12 executive board members along with representatives of major stockholders. In addition to the head office, the company runs an extensive network of local offices and agencies, owned or working on an "exclusive" basis, which look after their affairs in the various ports worldwide. The head office has large departments dealing with ship operations, marketing, documentation, secretariat, personnel and legal. In total the company has 3,500 people on its payroll, 2,000 shore staff and 1,500 sea staff. Ship's space and cargo transport are booked by shippers or freight forwarders through the liner agency network of the company. Such agreements are confirmed by documents called "booking notes". Liner shipping clients are numerous and widely dispersed worldwide, whilst cargoes are carried on the basis of various bill of lading forms.

- *Shipping division:* The shipping division of an international oil company. The company has a policy of transporting 30% of its oil shipments in company-owned vessels. The division is responsible for the acquisition and operation of these vessels. There is a divisional board, responsible for day-to-day decisions, but major decisions about the sale and purchase of ships or any strategic matters must be approved by the main board. Any items of capital expenditure in excess of $2 million must have main board approval. Currently, the division is operating a fleet of ten VLCCs and 36 small tankers. As long as the company serves 70% of its transport needs by chartered-in vessels, the shipping division has established an in-house chartering/shipbroking team, so as to secure that their cargoes are shipped on modern, well-maintained ships belonging to first-class independent owners. An absolute condition of co-operation is for the chartered-in vessels to pass the company's strict vetting process. The division has a freedom to decide whether to charter vessels on the spot market or on period charters depending on company's needs, market view and prevailing conditions. The company has established and always uses its own standard charterparty forms (voyage and time charter).

- *Public diversified shipping group:* A holding company with a fleet of more than 60 ships of different types and sizes, owned by a respective number of single-vessel shipowning subsidiaries. Financial matters are managed from its head office in New York, though technical management, manning, operations and chartering are carried out from offices in other more cost-effective locations. The company is quoted on the New York Stock Exchange and the majority of shares are owned by institutional investors, so its financial and managerial performance is closely followed by investment analysts who specialise in shipping. In recent years the problems of operating in the highly cyclical shipping market have resulted in strenuous efforts to diversify into other activities. Recently the company was the subject of a major takeover bid, which was successfully resisted, but management is under constant pressure to increase the return on capital employed in the business. Ships are chartered through a combination of both in-house and competitive shipbrokers. Ship agents are selected in each port of call on a case-by-case basis. The group has developed an advanced credit control system evaluating the creditworthiness of its clients, thus in all markets of activation it shows a preference in working with reliable, first-class charterers, typically established names, located worldwide. Vessels are chartered either spot or on period charters, depending on market opportunities and prospects. The in-house chartering and legal division has obtained a high and wide experience in using the most suitable standard charterparty forms, depending on the situation.

- *Semi-public shipping group:* A Scandinavian shipping group started by a Norwegian who purchased small tankers in the early 1920s. Although the holding company is quoted on the Stock Exchange, the family still owns a controlling interest in that. Since the Second World War the group has followed a strategy of progressively moving into more sophisticated markets. Thus, apart from oil tankers, it is involved with the ownership of container vessels and the carriage of specialist bulk cargoes, such as motor vehicles and forest products, in both of which markets it has a sizeable ownership market share and a reputation for quality and reliability of the transport service provided. To improve managerial control and investment prospects the tanker business was floated as a separate company. The group runs a large fleet of modern merchant ships designed to give operating performance. It is based in an Oslo office with a sizeable staff. All vessels, activating in different markets, are sought to secure time charters or other forms of long-term employment (e.g. bareboat, CoA), with first-class charterers and for long durations, particularly on periods of strong freight markets. This matches with the relatively conservative profile of the group as it increases its cashflow "visibility" and "stability". Clients (charterers) of the group are relatively few, but co-operating as long-standing partners in all markets of activity. NYPE, Gentime or other more specialised time charterparties are used for the containerships and specialised vessels of the fleet, whilst charterers' forms are preferred for the tankers. The group has one small, in-house, broking team for each market segment of activation.

4.2 Ship management

Ship management is a different function than the ship ownership and this may become clear by a definition.

4.2.1 Ship management definition

According to Willingale M., *"ship management is the professional supply of a single or range of services by a management company separate from the vessel's ownership"*.

"Professional supply" means that the ship manager provides services to the shipowner according to contracted terms and in return for a remuneration called *"management fee"*. In doing so the ship manager is required to ensure that the vessel always complies with international rules and regulations, is run in a safe, cost-efficient and profitable manner without threat to the environment and is properly maintained so as to be seaworthy and preserve as far as possible its asset value.[4]

Ship management involves crucial tasks such as manning, training and appointment of both ship and shore-based personnel, advice on most suitable type of vessel to be purchased and method of financing, provisions of ship's supplies and stores, advice on the available options of ship's registration, trading, operations and commercial employment, maintenance etc.[5] Thus, "a single or a range of services" describes a comprehensive range or just one service offered by the ship manager to the shipowner. These services break down into some main and typical groups, such as the technical management, the crew management, the commercial management (chartering and post-fixture) and the ancillary services.[6] The way in which these management services are dealt with and how they are grouped together differs extensively.

All these managerial activities are provided either by a managing company within the shipping group of the shipowner or may be transferred (synonyms: outsourced, contracted-out) to specialised companies so-called *"third-party ship management companies"*. Such companies primarily become involved in the efficient manning, chartering and maintenance/repair of ships.[7] Outsourcing of

---

4 Willingale, M. (1998) *Ship Management* (London, LLP Publishing, 3rd edition, pp. 11–14).

5 Branch, A. and Robarts, M. (2014) *Branch's Elements of Shipping* (London, Routledge, 9th edition, p. 291).

6 Willingale, M. (1998) *Ship Management* (London, LLP Publishing, 3rd edition, p. 11).

7 Branch, A. and Robarts, M. (2014) *Branch's Elements of Shipping* (London, Routledge, 9th edition, p. 291).

ship management provides the shipping companies with opportunities to focus on core competencies, to access best management practices and to increase competitiveness in implementing new technologies.[8]

"Management company separate from the vessel's ownership" means that the managing company is a different legal entity from the shipowning company. In cases of third-party ship management, the offices of the management company may be located several thousand miles away from where the shipowner is domiciled and in a completely different time zone to where the vessel in question normally trades. In such cases, there is no common shareholding interest between the shipowner and the manager. In practice, however, common shareholding interests exist in many instances, where ship management and shipowning companies belong to the same shipping group. In every case the manager (ship management company) will function as a separate cost centre and will provide equitable services to all clients (shipowning companies) according to a well-defined contract and detailed budget agreed between the two main contracting parties.

The contract signed between a shipowner and a ship manager (even if both belong to the same shipping group) is called *"ship management agreement"*. One of the best known and most used ship management contracts is the BIMCO standard ship management agreement, known as *Shipman 2009* (see appendix 15). It concerns a typical contract that can then be amended as needed to fit the unique requirements of each completed ship management agreement.

4.2.2 Ship management services

Ship management is an umbrella term encompassing miscellaneous types of services. These are typically grouped as technical management, crew management (manning), commercial management and ancillary services (see Table 4.1). Chartering is a crucial service element of commercial management, affecting both the revenues earned and the cost structures of a ship. On the other hand, technical management, manning and ancillary services are extremely important managerial aspects when controlling the ship costs, specifically the most important category of the so-called operating expenses ("opex") of a ship. "Operating" or "running" costs (e.g. crewing, insurance, maintenance and repair etc.) form one out of the two fixed cost categories in managing a ship, the other one being the capital expenses ("capex"), e.g. the loan instalments and the interest payments arising from the acquisition of a vessel through debt. The last major ship cost category is that comprising the variable cost elements[9], such as bunkers, port and canal dues etc. The ship cost structure and the allocation of expenses between the shipowner and the charterer in various types of charter is presented in section 7.4. It is worth noting that ship management decisions finally affect the earning capability of vessels, their cost structure and levels, as well as the quality of the transport

---

8 Cariou, P. and Wolff, F.-C. (2011) "Ship-owners' Decision to Outsource Vessel Management" *Transport Reviews* 31(6), 709–724.

9 Variable costs are those depending on the voyage executed, whilst fixed costs are running daily irrespective of the vessel's employment.

Table 4.1 Ship Management Services

Service Group	Technical Management	Crew Management	Commercial Management	Ancillary
Service Elements	Maintenance/Repair	Selection/ Engagement	Marketing/ Advertising	Consultancy
	Inspection	Manning Levels	Voyage Estimating	Insurance of Vessels
	Budgeting	Certification Control	Chartering	Legal/Claims
	Purchasing (Spares/Stores)	Performance Appraisal	Operations/ Bunkering	Financial
	Performance Monitoring	Payroll	Post-Fixture	Audit
	Reporting	Travel	Freight/Hire Collection	
	Safety & Quality (S&Q)	Welfare	Laytime Calculating	
	Drydocking	Drugs and Alcohol	Disbursements	
	Certification	Training	Accounting/ Payments	
	Emergency Contingency	Insurance of Crew	Master General Account (MGA)	
	Insurance of Machinery	Reporting	Shipbroking/ Agency	
			Investment/ Disinvestment	

Source: Willingale M. (1998) *Ship Management* (London, LLP Publishing, 3rd edition, p. 16), adjusted by E. Plomaritou and A. Papadopoulos.

services provided, thus such decisions are so crucial in forming the profitability margins of a shipping company and its market profile.

The management services are analysed in the following sections.

4.2.2.1 Technical management services
The primary objective of technical management is to provide all the services required to ensure the safe, environmentally friendly and cost-efficient vessel operation in accordance with the international rules and regulations. Technical management has to do with the proper maintenance and repair of a ship and is sub-divided into various service elements which are related to[10]:

- The supply and provision of all stores, spares, lubricants, chemicals and other miscellaneous products which are required by a vessel on a day-to-day basis in order to be maintained in a seaworthy and cargoworthy

10 Willingale, M. (1998) *Ship Management* (London, LLP Publishing, 3rd edition, pp. 14–23).

condition, together with the inventory control and the control of suppliers. Additionally, stores department cares for the adequate supplies of various special foods in order to satisfy different crew nationalities with different eating habits.

- The inspection of the vessel through regular visits of the superintendent on board, in order to monitor the level of vessel's maintenance and operating performance, the technical condition of the ship's structure and equipment, to ensure the ship's staff compliance with company policies and to assist ship's staff resolve any technical and operational problems.
- The repair of a vessel or its drydocking which includes the pre-docking activities, such as the preparation of the drydock work lists, assessment of the selection criteria of a repair yard (including quality, price, terms of payment, delivery and redelivery costs), as well as the drydocking activities, such as the management of drydock operation, the assessment of any unbudgeted items or services and the approval of the work carried out.

Repair and maintenance costs may concern on the one hand scheduled repairs such as routine onboard works or programmed drydocks and on the other hand unscheduled, major or minor, repairs. Stores and Supplies costs may concern a great variety of items, such as marine and deck stores (e.g. paints, ropes, safety equipment and clothing etc.), engine room stores (e.g. greases, gases, electrical items etc.), steward's stores (e.g. cleaning equipment and materials, clothing, galley and laundry supplies, recreational items etc.), as well as lubricating oils (lubes), which is the dominant cost component in this category. In a typical ship operating cost profile, repair and maintenance costs, including an allowance for intermediate and special surveys, account for 15–20% of total operating costs. Stores, spares and lubricants typically account for another 20–25% of total operating costs. It has been ascertained that in periods of weak freight rates, as for example the dry bulk market in 2009–2016, owners possibly postpone the maintenance of their vessels. This combined with excess availability of repair capacity lead in maintenance and repair costs being kept at relatively low levels in periods of depressed markets.[11]

4.2.2.2 Crew management services

The primary objective of crew management is the provision of well-trained and suitably experienced crew of the nationality required by the shipowner to a vessel, so as to ensure safe, efficient and economical operation according to international regulations. Crew management is made up of different service elements such as:

- Crew selection which includes the management of large amounts of data concerning seamen's records and application forms.
- Liaison between different persons who are involved in the sourcing of sea staff at various locations, typically the master, the crew manager and

---

11 Drewry Maritime Research *Ship Operating Costs 2015/16 Annual Review and Forecast* (November 2015, pp. 15, 53 and 61).

the recruitment officer, as well as other interested parties (port agents, medical practitioners etc.).

- Assessment of sea staff performance during their period of employment and policies for the avoidance of human error. Human error can be reduced by increasing communication, training, fatigue management and by eliminating the causes or the conditions which induce human error, e.g. improved shore-based management could decrease the commercial pressure of the seafarers.
- Crew training and career development.
- Control of drugs and alcohol.
- Medical matters.

Apart from crew wages and various forms of extras (e.g. overtime), manning costs typically include also victualling and travel/repatriation expenses. All are affected by external factors such as crew nationality and the trading status of the ship. Manning accounts for 35–40% of total ship operating costs, therefore having a major impact on ship management.[12]

4.2.2.3 Commercial and operational management services
Chartering and shipbroking have a direct relation with the commercial management of vessels. This group involves the provision of ship management services for the employment of a vessel, such as:

- *Pre-fixture services*, provided during the stages of chartering investigation and negotiation (see chapter 8). Evaluation of chartering alternatives is generally called "voyage estimation" and is also included at this category of services (see chapter 14 for voyage estimation analysis).
- *Fixture services*, provided during the stage of the fixture of a charter. Typically, the commercial manager, after the negotiation of the required terms and conditions, undertakes to finalise and sign the agreed charterparty, representing the ship's/shipowner's interests in the agreement (see chapters 7, 9–13).
- *Operational (post-fixture) services*, provided during the execution of the charter. Once the vessel's employment has been determined, the commercial manager instructs the ship's master accordingly for the execution of the charter. Operational management ensures that the ship carries out the tasks to which it has been committed by the commercial people who arranged employment through chartering brokers. Operational post-fixture management is composed of critical service elements, such as bunker management, appointment of port agents and advice for their actions as concern as the vessel, the monitoring of income collection (freight, hire, demurrage, other), the maintenance of vessels accounts,

---

12 Drewry Maritime Research *Ship Operating Costs 2015/16 Annual Review and Forecast* (November 2015, pp. 12, 24).

the checking of invoices (*"disbursements"* or *"D/As"* in short), the resolution of any disputes involving the charter, as well as specialist matters which must be accomplished in liaison with other departments (e.g. the drydocking of a vessel, an accident). This group of services comprises also the laytime calculation, a crucial, post-fixture process of high practical, commercial and legal importance, closely related to the chartering and shipbroking business (see analytically chapter 15).

• *Marketing services*, provided during the marketing implementation process (see analytically chapter 5). Marketing is a tool for the improvement of chartering policy and thus it constitutes a means helping to increase the shipping company's profitability and customer retention.

• *Services related to the purchase of a ship (second hand or newbuilding), the sale of a ship (scrap or second hand), the lay-up of a ship etc.*

Shipowners may sometimes sub-contract all the management of their ships with the exception of the actual arranging of the ships' commercial management. In these cases, the contact with brokers, the fixing of charter and the marketing process all remain under the owner's total control.

4.2.2.4 Ancillary management services
This group of services is mainly focused on the management of financial matters (e.g. advice on the publication of financial accounts or monitoring of the credit risk of prospective charterers), as well as on the management of special technical projects (e.g. consulting for the construction of a newbuilding vessel or a ship conversion and monitoring the relevant works).

Furthermore, insurance services may be handled by a ship management company. Insurance for ships generally falls into two major categories; the insurance against loss or damage to the ship itself known as *"Hull & Machinery (H&M) insurance"* and the insurance for claims made against the ship by other persons or companies (third parties), such insurance broadly known as *"Protection and Indemnity (P&I) Club insurance"*. These two elements normally account for about 90% of insurance costs, with the remaining expenses to concern war risk, freight demurrage and defense (FD&D) etc. Insurance costs typically account for 8–10% of total ship operating costs.[13]

In this category of ancillary services some other kinds may also be included, such as handling of legal claims or auditing of financial accounts.

4.2.3 Ship management models

The above-mentioned analysis does not reflect the complexity of the relationship which often exists between the shipowner and the ship manager. The following sections describe shortly the most significant types of ship management

---

13 Drewry Maritime Research *Ship Operating Costs 2015/16 Annual Review and Forecast* (November 2015, pp. 15, 38).

models. One fundamental consideration is the choice between keeping the management (mostly technical and crew) in-house or outsourcing to an independent, third-party ship manager. However, the selection is not solely related with cost. It depends on how much decision-making the owner is prepared to concede. In other words, it takes on a strategic risk and an evaluation of counter-party risk.[14]

4.2.3.1 Traditional ship management model

This is a fully integrated management system where the owner (i.e. the person or the group of shipping companies) creates an in-house management system for the ship or ships. The owner retains the full responsibility of managing/operating the ships and employs personnel to work directly for him. Typically, office and staff are common for the managing company and the shipowning companies of the group. There exists an organisational structure to deal on his own with all aspects of the ships' operation and management, including meeting the requirements of the ISM Code and achieving the relevant certification for the office and each ship.[15]

This is the most common form of ship management because in this case privacy of decision-making is retained. For this reason, the terms "shipowner" or "owner" or "shipping company" are often meant to include also the function of the ship manager. For the sake of simplification and alignment with current practice, this book uses the word "shipowner" as containing also the role of the commercial manager or operator of vessels, unless otherwise stated.

4.2.3.2 Outsourcing or third-party ship management model

This is where the management of the ship is contracted out to a third-party company. As a result, all the day-to-day management of the ships is carried out by a specialist company. In this model all of the following functions are outsourced: technical, crewing, operations, commercial (chartering and post-fixture), accounting and financing, safety and quality. In effect, the management company takes control of the ship and reports to the owner how this is progressing. The owner still has the final say, being responsible for funding the operation of the ship and paying a monthly fee for the services contained in the management contract.

The need for using the services of a third-party ship manager arises from various causes. Sometimes ships are owned by a group of companies that have combined to fund their purchase but have no shipping knowledge or experience to run them (e.g. pension or investment funds). Therefore, in many cases, the people, companies or organisations which own the ships have no expertise in shipping. If this is the case, the need to find a competent ship management company becomes extremely important to ensure that there is a return on the investment.[16]

---

14 Drewry Maritime Research *Ship Operating Costs 2014/15 Annual Review and Forecast* (January 2015, p. 52).

15 Dickie, J.W. (2014) *21st Century Ship Management* (London, Bloomsbury Publishing, p. 2).

16 Dickie, J.W. (2014) *21st Century Ship Management* (London, Bloomsbury Publishing, pp. 1–2).

Another important reason for using a third-party ship management company (apart from lack of expertise) is the cost of managing ships. The complexity of shipping has progressed and shipping groups have amended their strategy to respond to new requirements (such as changes in legislation or in safety matters). In addition, modern communication systems have also changed the way ships are operated and have implications on the monthly budget of a shipping company. To meet these challenges, the shipowning companies may decide to co-operate with third-party ship management companies with a large number of ships under their care, which can deliver cost-effective management services comparing with the self-owned managing companies which form part of smaller private shipping groups.

If a shipowner has very few ships, the cost to be allocated against each ship to cover the in-house management function becomes uneconomical. This is not the problem in large fleets as the management costs are spread over more units. The owner of a small fleet, apart from the obvious solution of buying more ships, may employ the services of independent ship management companies in order to reduce operating costs. These companies contain all departments needed to provide an efficient service, charging a fee for that. Because of their size they may be able to attract top-class executives or have best access to crew and the large numbers of ships under their management enable them to enjoy economies of scale. In this case, the shipowner may agree to have the "final word" on how his ships are used or may let that decision to the managing company. Last but not least, the shipowner will be the ultimate beneficiary of the net income generated by each ship.

There is a dilemma for the medium sized shipowner who will have to consider the benefits of using his own staff over which he has direct control, balancing this against the economies in using a third party to manage his ships. Sometimes that problem is solved by sub-contracting only parts of the total management function (see section 4.2.3.3). This is possible in case of a clear demarcation of different business activities in ship management. Moreover, the medium sized shipowner has another choice to successfully overcome the lack of economies of scale. That is, contracting to manage ships belonging to other owners, by his personnel which in any case is employed to run his own vessels.

In conclusion, there can be many reasons why a shipowner may select to outsource the ship management. More specifically[17]:

- Cost savings (overheads reduced by an economy of scale).
- Flexibility of investment (allows the freedom and provides opportunities to invest, divest or diversify or any combination of them).
- Benchmarking (it is easier to evaluate how well and cost-effectively the ship is operated).

17 Dickie, J.W. (2014) *21st Century Ship Management* (London, Bloomsbury Publishing, p. 3); Branch, A. and Robarts, M. (2014) *Branch's Elements of Shipping* (London, Routledge, 9th edition, p. 291); Cariou, P. and Wolff, F.-C. (2011) "Ship-owners' Decision to Outsource Vessel Management" *Transport Reviews* 31(6), 709–724.

- Compliance to international maritime laws and regulatory measures (reducing the problems of legislative demands and the resources needed to meet them).
- No in-house expertise to operate the ships (this may be because the shipowner has no experience of managing ships).
- Settlement of operational matters (the management company ensures that daily operation and maintenance of the vessel are correctly superintended).
- Improvement of quality and reliability of services.
- Increase of speed and flexibility of services.

4.2.3.3 Hybrid ship management model

In this case there is a partial outsourcing of the functions from the owner to the management company. Spruyt illustrates this complexity by providing a number of specific examples of what can be described as hybrid shipowner–ship manager relationships. These include situations where[18]:

1. The shipowner retains control over a number of critical functions in the management of his ships, including, for example the selection of senior ship officers, safety auditing, the negotiation and management of drydockings etc., while outsourcing the remaining day-to-day ship management activities.
2. The shipowner retains a technical department to run a "core" fleet (e.g. bulk carriers), but in acquiring a fleet of specialist vessels such as chemical tankers, uses a ship manager that is able to provide the appropriate technical management, including the maintenance of tank coatings, the sourcing of skilled and experienced crew relevant to the ships in question etc.
3. The shipowner does not have the in-house staff to handle a sudden increase in his fleet, perhaps via an opportunistic purchase. In this case a ship manager will be used only until the shipowner recruits extra personnel to cope with the additional workload.
4. A ship manager has a shareholding position in a vessel under management or has some kind of equity association with the shipowner.

Consequently, a shipowner may manage his entire group of companies or sub-contract all or some parts, such as ship operation or crewing or commercial or technical management to other companies. In special cases, he may almost sub-contract even the "ownership" of the ship by making a bareboat charter, known also as "demise charter" (see chapter 13). In this charter type the charterer is called "quasi-owner" as undertaking fully the responsibility for vessel's operation and commercial employment. It must be emphasised that the risk of a

---

18 Spruyt, J. (1994) *Ship Management* (London, LLP Publishing).

bareboat charter is extremely high for the shipowner, as long as severe problems may be faced by him even though they were caused by bad ship operation and insolvency from the bareboat charterer.

4.3 Importance of commercial management

In previous sections an attempt was made to locate the position of chartering within the field of ship management. From the above-mentioned analysis it was inferred that chartering business forms a significant part of commercial management.

It is known that the main parties involved in the chartering business are the shipowner, the charterer and the shipbroker. The shipowner executes a cargo transport by his vessel or gives the vessel for hire (in order to carry cargoes by sea), the charterer needs that vessel either because he has or he may find cargoes for transport, and the brokers act on behalf of the shipowner and the charterer, bringing together the two parties in order to have a charter deal. The role of the shipbrokers was described extensively in section 3.5.1, whilst the chartering negotiation procedure will be presented analytically in chapter 8. Types of charter were briefly discussed in chapter 1, whilst they are analysed further in chapters 11–13. The following parts of this chapter will focus on some of the managerial aspects of chartering business, most of all on crucial decision making examined basically from the operational, day-by-day viewpoint, as well as on showing why commercial management and therefore chartering are so important for the success of a shipping group. The strategic thinking and the chartering policy formation by the shipowners and the charterers/shippers are analysed in chapter 5.

4.3.1 Decision-making in commercial management

Adequate information and a great deal of flexibility are always required from companies and organisations engaged in shipping. Apart from the daily fluctuations in freight rate levels and trading conditions, depending on the supply–demand situation, there is a constant development towards new techniques in shipbuilding and propulsion, cargo handling, terminal operations etc. Due to the ever-changing conditions in international commerce, the overseas trading patterns are changing and new cargoes and loading–discharging areas emerge, sometimes quite drastically diminishing the importance of previously busy ports and critical cargo movements. Such changes will occur over periods of a few years and probably several times during a vessel's commercial lifespan (typically 20–25 years, although sometimes ships may trade up to 30 years, or even more). Irrespective of the freight market being booming, flat or depressed, there are also some seasonal changes in cargo volumes to be shipped. In such a dynamic commercial environment, shipowners, ship managers, fleet operators, charterers and shippers, shipbrokers and agents have to be able to take advantage of new opportunities so as to survive and remain competitive.

In order to maintain maximum flexibility on a daily and a long-term basis, thereby staying safe and sound economically, shipowners may decide to renew their fleets when they consider that conditions are favourable. Shipowners operate the number, type and size of vessels necessary to meet the requirements of their chartering contract engagements. They may hire (charter-in) extra tonnage whenever their shippers or charterers require, or because of other temporary or sudden increases in demand for shipping space in the market sectors of participation. This means that an owner who runs a fleet of ships may operate owned vessels as a more or less permanent base, plus an additional fleet capacity of chartered-in tonnage (under time or bareboat charterparties) to suit the market and customer requirements over a period of time. He may further operate supplementary tonnage chartered on a spot basis to meet temporary increases in cargo offerings or fill unexpected gaps in liner or contract schedules.

Obviously the shipowning business has to do with decision-making. Crucial commercial decisions concern ship investment and disinvestment, employment of vessels and of course the timing of such decisions. Therefore, ship ownership (as influenced by ship sale and purchase, newbuilding orders and scrapping), as well as ship management and chartering decisions are of paramount importance for the entire shipping community. The investment/disinvestment decisions, though of utmost importance for the success of a shipping group, are beyond the scope of this book. However, in respect of chartering business, owners, ship operators and managers should be able to make critical commercial decisions; strategic and operational ones. There is a great variety of *day-by-day chartering and ships' employment decisions*. Some indicative examples are seen below:

- *Securing employment for owned vessels at the open market* by fixing full or part cargoes on either a voyage-by-voyage basis or by long-term contract engagements.
- *Engaging owned ships in so-called "industrial shipping"* with a charterer, under a chartering contract lasting several years (e.g. time charter, bareboat, CoA, consecutive voyages charter), with a fleet of ships specially built and equipped to suit the charterer's needs, and for a transport service to be offered as an integrated link in the customer's business production and distribution chain.
- *Chartering-in tonnage* for a longer period (e.g. under a time or a bareboat charterparty) or for a shorter period (e.g. under a trip time charter) to supplement the owned fleet of vessels, intending to satisfy the expected market requirements, fulfil the chartering/transport contract commitments or even keep the standards of a liner service engagement, generally by obtaining maximum efficiency, economy and customer satisfaction over a period of time.
- *Time chartering "out" owned or period-chartered tonnage* to other owners or ship operators, for longer or shorter periods, against a fixed daily hire, for those parties to operate the vessels in the open (spot) market or in the liner trades.

- *In pure liner trades, securing bookings of so-called "parcels"* (typically smaller consignments of various commodities transported in containers), intending to fill empty spaces of vessels employed in a liner service, at fixed itinerary.

4.3.2 Example of vessel routing and chartering alternatives

To explain how difficult, complicated and fast decision-making could be on commercial management, Figure 4.1 illustrates a hypothetical example presenting an owner's possible chartering alternatives about the deployment of one of his vessels, as well as the combinations of cargo and ballast voyages that will be considered and calculated on. A similar evaluation process is always followed by owners operating cargo vessels in the open market. It is assumed that the ship in question is a modern "con-bulker" of 30,000 dwt, able to operate either as a bulk carrier in tramp (bulk) trades or as a supplementary feeder vessel carrying containers in smaller liner trades. The vessel is "open" at point A (i.e. having no fixed chartering commitment). One option would be to let the vessel out for a time charter (T/C)

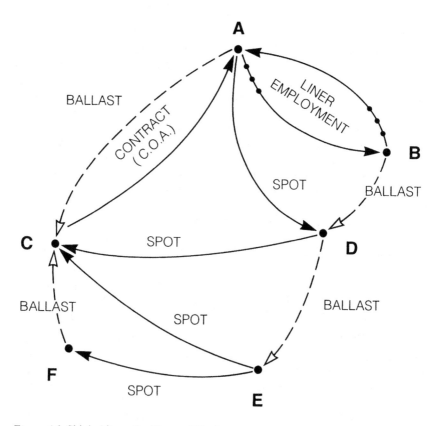

Figure 4.1 Ship's Alternative Types of Deployment

trip on behalf of a liner company looking for extra tonnage. The owners would then consider redelivery at point B, or, if the charterers were interested in extending the charter to a full round trip, the vessel would be open again at point A. If in position B, the next opportunity could be a voyage from D to C. In such a case the vessel would proceed from B to D in ballast. If in position A, the owners might be lucky enough to find a cargo available at A for discharge at D, where next a new cargo might be fixable to C or the vessel would have to ballast from D to E for the cargo destined to F or another employment to C. These owners might have a long-term transport contract running (e.g. a Contract of Affreightment, see chapter 13), which requires cargoes to be lifted at certain intervals from C for discharge at A. The ship coming in to C from D or E with cargo, or in ballast from F, could be in just the right position to lift one of the CoA cargoes. After discharge, the owners would find this ship open again at position A.

The above is just an example, complicated even before discussing anything about the earning income (i.e. freight or hire rates) of each chartering alternative. Imagine then how challenging and demanding it could be in real life conditions. Evaluation of ship employment alternatives is always the starting point in the chartering process, and is therefore valuable. Voyage estimation methodology is analysed in chapter 14.

There are a number of factors that owners have to consider in this continuous scheduling, evaluation and calculation process. The next open position in lieu of new employment possibilities, as well as the duration of the employment in relation to the freight market outlook are the most prominent factors to consider in such a decision-making process. Other crucial questions to ask could include the following: Is the cargo dirty or of a dangerous nature? Could this cargo damage the ship's holds and gear? Is it a well-known trade with well-established chartering routines and clean charterparty clauses, or are there unknown conditions and risks which cannot be easily pre-calculated? Are the charterers reputable in the market and considered as first-class charterers (FCC)? Is the ship due for special survey or drydocking, and whereabouts in the world would it be most economic and appropriate to have this job done? How this could be programmed among chartering alternatives and other commitments of the vessel?

The owners should also consider fleet optimisation, in other words the efficient and economical routing of the entire fleet in operation. That means, to minimise the total ballasting and off-hire periods and to maximise the total earnings of the group, by a suitable combination of period contracts and spot market trading, chartering extra tonnage as and when required. This could include also the investment point of view, in other words buying or selling ships when needs or opportunities arise.

4.3.3 Commercial management highlights from a chartering business perspective

From a chartering and shipbroking viewpoint, the importance of commercial management lies in the fact that it decisively determines the particulars of a vessel's employment. It is mainly concerned with deciding the type of charter and the consequent cost allocation between the shipowner and the charterer, the duration of charter engagement, the freight or hire rate fixed and income earned, the trading areas and the timing of decisions. Whereas all other day-to-day managerial aspects (e.g. crewing, technical, ancillary services etc.) directly affect only the cost element of managing a ship, commercial management has a direct effect on both ships' revenues and costs; thus it influences the profitability of a shipping company. For example, if a vessel is fixed on a voyage charter, the freight is paid on a $ per ton of cargo carried basis and the owner bears the voyage costs (bunkers, port dues etc.), whilst in a time charter revenue is earned on a $ per day basis and voyage costs are transferred to the charterer. In addition, whereas the ship's operating costs (manning, maintenance, insurance etc.) are borne by the owner on a time charter, they are transferred to the charterer on a bareboat charter (for the ship cost allocation between the shipowner and the charterer in various types of charter, see section 7.4). It should be very clear that the choice of charter affects crucially the financial results of a shipping company.

Another point to remember has to do with the need for recognition of roles among the "players" within the shipping market. Chartering is about meeting the cargo transport needs with the vessel employment alternatives on a day-by-day business routine. This matching is always concluded by important documents such as charterparties and bills of lading. For all participants of the shipping market it is crucial to be able to recognise the roles and distinctions of others. When contracting in a shipping document, it is imperative to know who the counter-party is, what his role is, what business he serves and which interests he represents. For example, in a charterparty (voyage or period) the party which represents the vessel's interests might possibly be a shipowning or a managing company (owned or third-party) or a ship operator. On the contrary, the party which represents the cargo's interests in a charterparty or a bill of lading could be a shipper, a charterer or even a freight forwarder. This is equally important for the shipbrokers who should know their customers before promoting and representing them in a chartering negotiation procedure. Knowing well the counter-party or the customer helps preventing from problems, as well as better perceiving situations, interpreting business behaviours and understanding how far the responsibility of each contracting party may reach. This is a rather qualitative aspect of ships' commercial management playing a great role in chartering and shipbroking matters.

It was seen also in this chapter that differences in shipowning structures and vessel types operated usually bring about differences to the chartering policy adopted, as well as to the shipbroking and agency network followed. It is important to note that each market segment has its own structures, persons and peculiarities to handle from a commercial management standpoint.

When making decisions about ship management, the state of the freight market in relation to the continuous need for cost control are also of high importance. For example, in periods of depressed freight earnings, shipowners may resist as much as possible to cost increases seeking ways to cut operating costs. Moreover, another critical point from a chartering perspective is the cost of bunkers. In periods of low freight levels and high oil prices, an owner could possibly prefer to time charter a vessel for a relatively short or medium period, thus passing the high bunkers cost to the charterer, instead of chartering his vessel on the spot market where such costs are borne by the owner.

Furthermore, commercial management comprises also two basic practical and calculative aspects of chartering. The first one is done before fixing a ship and concerns the evaluation of chartering alternatives, the so-called "voyage estimation" process, which crucially examines the vessel's profitability (see chapter 14). The second one is about "laytime calculation", a significant field of chartering as it concerns a complicated, practical matter with serious legal implications. Laytime is the period of time agreed in a charterparty during which the owner shall make and keep his vessel available to the charterer for loading or discharging without payment additional to the freight. Laytime is a matter of high importance and often a subject of dispute in chartering practice (see chapter 15).

As a conclusion, it may be said that the commercial management of vessels is formed from two parts: one operational and the other strategic. The operational aspect essentially comprises the chartering decisions and the control of income streams. In this context, shipbroking is the intermediary profession which facilitates chartering business, namely the decisions and procedures about fixing of vessels. On the other hand, the strategic aspect of commercial management is not only based on investment and disinvestment decisions (e.g. buying and selling of ships), but also, from a chartering perspective, on marketing which is considered a valuable strategic tool for advancing the chartering policy of shipping companies. The next chapter is devoted to that modern instrument of chartering policy formation.

CHAPTER 5

Chartering policy and marketing strategy

This chapter goes on analysing further the commercial management of ships. Marketing is introduced as the strategic tool which helps a shipping company improve its chartering policy. At first, factors affecting the chartering policy of charterers, shippers and shipowners in both bulk and liner shipping are discussed. This is followed by a comprehensive presentation of the marketing principles and how these may be applied to a shipping company. Finally, various shipping marketing strategies are illustrated through real-life case studies and commercial examples.

5.1 Chartering policy of charterers and shippers

In bulk markets a charterer decides to work with a shipowner after considering a series of selection criteria. Thus, the charterer's requirements and the determinants of his decision-making process play a decisive role in the formation of charterer's chartering policy. A similar process is followed by a shipper in the liner market when selecting a carrier to work with. The following sections present the chartering policy of charterers and shippers in bulk and liner market.

5.1.1 Charterers' requirements in the liquid bulk (tanker) market

In the tanker market seven categories of criteria have been recognised as playing a critical role in the charterer's selection process of a shipowner. These criteria represent the *requirements of charterers in liquid bulk (tanker) markets* and are classified in order of importance as follows[1]:

1. *Compliance of shipping company with the international regulations for safety management.*

This includes, for example:

- Well-designed and built tankers.
- Well-maintained tankers.
- Training and competence of crew.
- Training and competence of employees.

---

1 Plomaritou, E. (2008) *Marketing of Shipping Companies: A Tool for Improvement of Chartering Policy* (Athens, Stamoulis Publications, pp. 127–133); Plomaritou, E. (2006) *Marketing of Shipping Companies* (Athens, Stamoulis Publications, in Greek, pp. 216–229).

This criterion is related to the application of international rules and standards recommended by the International Maritime Organisation (IMO), state authorities (e.g. port state controls) and recognised registers (classification societies), for avoiding marine accidents, marine pollution, vessels' and/or cargoes' losses and/or damages. From the early 1990s, an increasing national and international concern over tanker safety and environmental aspects was observed, resulting in new rules and conditions for tanker owners (e.g. US Oil Pollution Act known as OPA '90), which affect the market and the marketing of tankers, especially older vessels. The above-mentioned rules may refer to the construction, maintenance and trading of ships, as well as to the training of crew and personnel. The most prominent such example was the IMO single-hull tanker vessels phase-out programme which dictated that all such tankers should have been banned from international trading up to the end of 2015.

The so-called "oil majors", together with a few smaller companies, control a significant percentage of the production, trading and – particularly – seaborne transportation of crude oil and refined petroleum products worldwide. The oil companies, acting as charterers in the market, are specially careful and sensitised in environmental matters. Accordingly, they have established strict operational and financial standards that they use to pre-qualify, or vet, tanker owners prior to entering into charters. The oil companies require previous inspection of the tankers they are about to charter, in order to ascertain that they are suitable for their transportation needs. This investigation process is widely known as the "*vetting*" of tankers. Many independent tanker owners believe that it is necessary for a charterer to know in every detail what he is about to charter. However, some owners think the above charterers' stand is excessive, since an extensive inspection has already been carried out on the vessel by the register or by the flag state or by the port states or the shipping company itself.

Oil companies constantly evaluate the shipping companies they work with, as well as the quality of the vessels they charter. While numerous factors are considered and evaluated prior to a commercial decision, the "oil majors", through their association called *"Oil Companies International Marine Forum"* or *"OCIMF"*,[2] have developed two basic tools: the Ship Inspection Report programme (SIRE) and the Tanker Management & Self Assessment programme (TMSA).

The *SIRE programme*[3] was launched in 1993 to provide a standardised tanker inspection format, with objective reports capable of being shared. The SIRE Programme is a unique tanker risk assessment tool of value to charterers, ship operators, terminal operators and government bodies concerned with ship safety. At the heart of the SIRE system is a large database of objective technical and operational information about a range of vessels used for carrying oil, gas and chemicals. This information helps in vetting decisions on vessels ahead of charter, as well as focusing attention on the importance of improvements in vessel quality and safety. OCIMF member companies commission vessel inspections

---

2 www.ocimf.org (accessed 5 June 2017).
3 www.ocimf.org/sire (accessed 5 June 2017).

and appoint an accredited SIRE inspector to conduct an inspection. The inspector accesses the vessel particulars from the SIRE database along with the appropriate "Vessel or Barge Inspection Questionnaires" (VIQ/BIQ) before carrying out an on-board inspection of activities ranging from cargo-handling processes to the vessel's pollution prevention measures. The resultant report contributes to the member company's risk assessment in advance of charter. The report is also uploaded to the SIRE database, where, for a nominal fee, it can be accessed by registered companies who charter tankers or operate terminals. Free access to all SIRE reports is provided to government agencies engaged in port state control activities. By establishing a standardised, objective inspection process that systematically examines tanker operations and that is shared by OCIMF members and other authorised recipients, SIRE has been instrumental in driving up expectations and behaviours relating to chartering, operational and safety standards in the industry.

The *TMSA programme*[4] was introduced in 2004 as a tool to help vessel operators assess, measure and improve their safety management systems. The programme encourages vessel operators to assess their own safety management systems against listed key performance indicators (KPIs) and provides best practice guidance on how to attain appropriate standards of safety performance. Vessel operators are encouraged to use their assessment results to develop phased improvement plans that can be applied, as appropriate, across their entire fleet and to share feedback with potential charterers via the TMSA database. The TMSA programme offers a standard framework for assessment of a vessel operator's safety management systems. The framework is based on 13 elements of management practice, each one associated with a clear objective and a set of supporting KPIs to help operators assess the level of attainment in their company. The 13 elements are:

1. Management, leadership and accountability.
2. Recruitment and management of shore-based personnel.
3. Recruitment and management of vessel personnel.
4. Reliability and maintenance standards.
5. Navigational safety.
6. Cargo, ballast, tank cleaning, bunkering, mooring and anchoring operations
7. Management of change.
8. Incident investigation analysis.
9. Safety management.
10. Environmental and energy management.
11. Emergency preparedness and contingency planning.
12. Measurement, analysis and improvement.
13. Maritime security

---

4 www.ocimf.org/sire/about-tmsa (accessed 3 September 2017).

2. *Reputation and image of the shipowner in the shipping market.*

This includes, for example:

- Loss and damage track record of shipping company.
- Reputation, experience and reliability of the shipowner.

The oil companies maintain the view that the reliability, honesty and integrity of the shipowner are more important than the most attractive charterparty terms that may be offered to them. Thus, the oil companies, during the chartering negotiations, take seriously into account the reputation of the shipping company within the freight market, the marine insurance market, the sale and purchase market, the newbuilding market etc. The "track record" or in other words the history of losses and damages of the shipping company crucially affects the decision process of charterers in making a fixture.

3. *Low cost sea transport operations.*

For example:

- Transportation solutions that reduce charterers' costs and maximise financial results.

In the past the tanker market was characterised by a small number of big charterers – the oil majors – that largely had the ability to fully control the oil transport operations. Nowadays, top oil companies may be state-owned (e.g. Saudi Aramco, Rosneft, ADNOC, CNPC, KPC, PDVSA, NNPC),[5] state-controlled (e.g. Gazprom, Petrobras) or multi-national companies (e.g. Exxon-Mobil Corporation, BP P.L.C., Royal Dutch Shell, Chevron Corporation, Total S.A.), being either publicly traded or private ones. It is worth noting that national oil companies accounted for 75% of global oil production and controlled 90% of proven oil reserves in 2010.

In the 1950s it was typical for the big oil companies to own and manage a considerable fleet of tankers. By the end of 1960s the oil companies owned about 36% of the tanker fleet, they time-chartered another 52% and they topped up their seasonal requirements from the spot market which accounted for about 12% of supply.[6] Until the 1970s the seven major oil companies, known as the "seven sisters", were responsible for around 80% of all oil processing in the world and they operated or controlled, through long-term charters, most of the seaborne oil transport. In the early 1970s, due to the fact that the oil trade fell sharply and the supply got out of control, the trend for these companies was to reduce their share as tanker

---

5 Carpenter, W. (2015) *The World's Biggest State Owned Oil Companies* (www.investopedia. com).

6 Stopford, M. (2009) *Maritime Economics* (London, Routledge Publications, 3rd edition, p. 436).

owners or operators and enter into long-term ship charter engagements of two or three years. More specifically, 80% of oil tankers owned by independent shipowners were on time charter to oil companies. As a result, independent tanker owners built vessels to charterers' specifications and placed them on long-term charters. In 1990s due to the fact that the oil trade changed from a predictable to a more risky business, the chartering policy of oil majors changed again and only 20% of tankers owned by independent shipowners were on time charter to oil companies. It has been conclusively proven that the policy of oil companies may change rapidly and continuously in response to the dynamic circumstances in the tanker market.

In the last 30 years the control of oil transport has changed and the role of oil majors in transport has been diluted. The number of smaller private firms (often known as "oil traders") and state organisations engaged in the chartering of tankers increased considerably during the 1980s. Oil producers, especially in the Middle East, market their oil through distribution organisations in the consuming markets and several have built their own tanker fleets. New oil companies have emerged in the rapidly growing Asian markets, with their own transport policies. Large volumes are now handled by oil traders, some of them working for the oil companies and others for independent diversified traders. Oil traders own much of the oil during shipment and since they are constantly buying and selling oil cargoes, it suits their business model to charter ships as required on a voyage by voyage basis, and this has encouraged the growth of the spot market.

Within this framework, the freight cost is always important, but the greater the proportion of freight in the overall cargo cost equation, the more emphasis charterers are likely to place on it. For example, in the 1950s the cost of transporting a barrel of oil from the Middle East to Europe represented 49% of the CIF cost. As a result, oil companies devoted great effort to finding ways to reduce the cost of transport. By the 1990s, the price of oil had increased and the cost of transport had fallen to just 2.5% of the CIF price, so transport costs became less important.[7]

4. *Appropriate (fair and unselfish) chartering negotiating process.*

This includes, for example:

- Compliance with widely accepted chartering negotiation rules.
- Provision of accurate and reliable information regarding the ship.
- Co-operation and response to charterers' requirements.

The charterers wish to ensure that appropriate chartering negotiations are followed. This means prompt negotiations with the application of proper negotiation rules. The negotiating parties should comply with the standards and principles, as generally proposed by crucial institutions, such as BIMCO, Baltic Exchange, FONASBA etc. The charterers require from the shipowners to provide true,

---

7 Stopford, M. (2009) *Maritime Economics* (London, Routledge Publications, 3rd edition, pp. 7–8).

precise and reliable information concerning the vessels. The ship's description is of a great importance to the degree it influences the charterer to sign the chartering contract. All information must be exchanged in good faith.

In addition, the charterers require from the shipowners to comply with the time limits for the submission of offers and counter-offers (see chapter 8). During negotiations, the parties' offers and counter-offers are submitted within logical time limits. Obviously, aimless delays during chartering negotiations are not desirable.

The shipowner should not offer the same ship to more than one charterer at the same time, because if all charterers accepted the offers, then the shipowner would not be able to fulfil his obligations and make his vessel available concurrently. Sometimes, during the negotiation of a ship the shipowner uses phrases such as "*subject open*" or "*subject free*" or "*subject unfixed*", which means that the ship is subject to a negotiation with more than one charterer at the same time. However, such a tactic is not desirable from the charterer.

   5.   *Provision of high quality transport services.*

This includes, for example:

- Safe transportation of cargo to its destination. No cargo loss or damage. No claims.
- Trade and schedule flexibility.
- Appropriate voyage planning.
- Speedy voyage execution.
- Quick despatch. Proper loading and discharging operations without stoppages.
- Reduction of turn-around time to the minimum.

Charterers' requirement for high quality transport services includes the appropriate planning of the voyage, speedy and faultless loading and unloading operations, therefore the reduction of "turn around" time to the minimum. Charterers desire the same high quality of transport service irrespective of the type of trade, the type of vessel, the geographical area and economic developments.

The oil companies also wish to do business with shipowners who offer trading flexibility, without commercial or geographical limitations concerning the vessel's usage, even in extremely sensitive environmental regions. Charterers want to charter universally accepted vessels. So far as it is possible they wish to avoid any trading limitations included in charterparties due to political or economical reasons. However, it is almost impossible for a charterparty to have absolutely no trading limitations.

Charterers also require shipowners to execute the determined voyages with utmost dispatch and without unjustifiable delays or deviations. It is difficult to determine which delay is justifiable and which is not. If a logical master, who has the voyage's control and knows the prevailing conditions at trades and ports, judges that a delay is necessary for the ship's, crew's and cargoes' safety then the delay is considered justifiable. Furthermore, the market conditions play a vital role in the determination of the desired sailing speed. For example, at the worst of the economic downturn and in a high oil price environment, slow steaming was implemented in the tanker sector as a fuel-saving measure accepted by the charterers.

During the loading and unloading operation, the charterer requires the shipowner to exercise due diligence for the appropriate, safe and speedy receipt, loading, unloading and delivery of cargo. In order to ensure the ship's safety, the shipowner has the duty to supervise the loading and unloading operation. If he allows inappropriate loading methods, the shipowner is rendered responsible for his actions or omissions. Loading and discharging must be performed in such a manner, so that the cargo will not be damaged and the ship will not lose her stability. In addition, the avoidance of stoppages during loading and unloading operations is deemed necessary. The master should reduce the time of vessel's arriving–loading and unloading–departing, i.e. the ship's "turn-around" time, to the minimum. The vessel's stay in port is considered as non-productive time, since the productivity of a ship is measured in tonne-miles per dwt, in other words it is a function of the quantity of cargo carried and the distance of carriage. The minimisation of ship's delay at a port is the result of team-work performed by the ship's master and crew, the port agent, the charterer, the cargo owner and the cargo receiver, as well as other persons such as stevedores, port and custom officers etc.

The charterer desires his cargo to be transported with safety, to be delivered on time and at the port of destination. All persons involved in oil transportation must be appropriately trained according to the IMO's requirements, in order to ensure the appropriate loading, transportation, unloading and delivery of cargo.

6. *Maintenance of good relationships with charterer.*

For example:

- Good master–crew–charterer relationships.
- Good company–charterer relationships.

The charterer wishes to maintain excellent relations and reliable communication channels with the ship's master and crew, especially in the case of time or bareboat charters. The charterer should be satisfied by the master's behaviour and actions, mostly regarding the ship's compliance to commercial employment orders and navigational instructions. It should be mentioned that in the case of a bareboat charter, where the charterer undertakes the commercial operation and employment of the ship, the master is obliged to comply with the orders and instructions of the charterer regarding navigation, employment and operation. In the case of a time charter, however, the charterer has only the commercial employment of the ship, so the master is obliged to comply with the charterer's employment orders and not with his navigational instructions. Even though the charterer has no right to give navigational instructions, he would expect the master to respond to his logical demands on that. On the other hand, the master is obliged to act logically when he receives the charterer's orders, some of which might require immediate execution while others could need negotiation before executing.

Additionally, the charterer aims to maintain good relations with the shipping company; more specifically he seeks optimum communication and co-operation with shore personnel, for satisfying his requirements, to the extent that shipowner's interests are not damaged.

7. *System of informing the client–charterer.*

This includes, for example:

- Updated information system.
- Informative nature of shipowner's advertising programmes.

The charterer finally considers that a modern ship information system could also be essential in order to be aware of the voyage situations and ship's monitoring. The system should be appropriately designed to provide, on a daily basis, useful and updated information concerning the ship's performance – in technical and financial terms – such as fuel consumption, vessel's service speed, ship's movements, estimation of arrival at ports, etc.

From this analysis, it is inferred that the charterers' requirements in the tanker market – and therefore their chartering policy – are largely dictated by safety and environmental protection issues.

5.1.2 Charterers' requirements in the dry bulk market

Dry bulk ships operating in the spot market must satisfy the charterers' needs concerning the vessel type and size, while also providing sea transport at a low cost. Over the 20th century, improved efficiency, bigger ships and more effective organisation of the shipping operation brought about a steady reduction in transport costs combined with a higher quality of service. The vessel must be available to the charterer at the right position (area, port or dock), at the right time and at a competitive freight rate compared to what other interested parties may offer and what currently prevails in the present market.

Although a charterer's selection criteria when choosing a shipowner in the dry bulk market are similar to those in the tanker market, the order of importance is different. In the dry bulk market the criteria which play a decisive role in the selection process of a shipowner by the charterer are classified in order of importance as follows[8]:

1. *Low cost sea transport operations.*
2. *Appropriate (fair and unselfish) chartering negotiating process.*

---

8 Plomaritou, E. (2008) *Marketing of Shipping Companies: A Tool for Improvement of Chartering Policy* (Athens, Stamoulis Publications, pp. 133–134); Plomaritou, E. (2006) *Marketing of Shipping Companies* (Athens, Stamoulis Publications, in Greek, pp. 216–229).

3. *Compliance of shipping company with the international regulations for safety management.*
4. *Reputation and image of the shipowner in the shipping market.*
5. *Provision of high quality transport services.*
6. *Maintenance of good relationship with charterer.*
7. *System of informing the client – charterer.*

From this analysis, it arises that the charterers' requirements in the dry bulk market and therefore their chartering policy are cost-oriented.

5.1.3 Shippers' requirements in the liner market

In the liner market a shipper typically follows completely different criteria in the selection process of a carrier.[9] These criteria are classified in order of importance as follows[10]:

1. *Provision of high quality transport services.*

Quality of service mainly includes the following:

- Schedule flexibility and wide geographical coverage.
- Directness and regularity of sailings.
- Reduction of turn-around time to minimum.
- On-time pick up and delivery of the cargo.
- Appropriate cargo handling.
- Fast and safe execution of the voyage.

Given the nature of logistics today, shippers look for carriers who can offer global coverage, frequency of sailings and flexible trade routes. Sea transport is only one stage of the entire production process. Frequent sailings allow shippers to plan correctly and reduce the level of stock kept at each end of the transport chain.

Due to the high value of general cargo (typically containers), shippers need carriers to execute trade routes directly without unjustifiable delays. Trans-shipments and container movements must be reduced to the minimum, so as to drop costs and eliminate the possibility of cargo damage. Masters should also aim to reduce the "turn-around" time to the minimum. As it has been mentioned, the minimum stay at ports is a result of teamwork by the ship, the agent, the owner, the shipper, the receiver of cargo and other parts (e.g. stevedores, port and custom officers etc.). The role of the agency network is of utmost importance in liner business.

---

9 In liner market the contract of cargo carriage is the bill of lading, where the contracting parties are the carrier (shipping company) and the shipper, not the shipowner and the charterer as it is the case in a charterparty.

10 Plomaritou, E. (2008) *Marketing of Shipping Companies: A Tool for Improvement of Chartering Policy* (Athens, Stamoulis Publications, pp. 134–139); Plomaritou, E. (2006) *Marketing of Shipping Companies* (Athens, Stamoulis Publications, in Greek, pp. 246–259).

Time in transit incurs an inventory cost, so shippers of high-value commodities value speed. The cost of holding high-value commodities in stock may make it cheaper to ship small quantities frequently even if the freight cost is higher. For example, a European manufacturer ordering spare parts from the Far East may be happy to pay 10 times the ocean freight for delivery in three days by air, if the alternative is to have machinery out of service for five or six weeks while the spares are delivered by sea. In the case of long journeys, the reliability of the schedule, as well as the on-time pick up and delivery of cargo are highly important. Unfortunately, due to various circumstances, tasks are not always fulfilled as scheduled and issues occur during the trip causing serious delays. With *"just in time"* stock control systems, transport reliability has taken on great significance. Some shippers may be prepared to pay more for a service, which is guaranteed to operate to time and as promised.

Shippers need carriers to facilitate the appropriate, safe and speedy receipt, loading, unloading, protection and delivery of cargo. The master has the duty to supervise the loading and unloading operations. If he allows inappropriate loading methods, the carrier is rendered responsible for his actions or omissions. Furthermore, the avoidance of loading and unloading stoppages is crucial, as long as time is money. Moreover, the cargo must be shipped onboard the vessel in accordance with the terms of the booking note. In some cases of over-booked vessels, a shipping company may not load the cargo on board as agreed in the booking note, but instead warehouse it in the port until next departure. Similarly, a shipping company may unload a container in a trans-shipment port, where it is stored instead of trans-shipped to the connecting vessel as agreed. Finally, shippers request increased free time[11] in addition to the days allowed according to the customs of the ports.

Liner operators manage to strengthen their competitive position in the liner shipping market by offering package solutions to transport problems, such as the arrangement of *door-to-door* services. According to shippers the ability of carriers to provide inland transport is a prerequisite to be selected by them.

2. *Compliance of shipping company with international regulations of safety management.*

Shippers require from the carriers to care for the suitability of their vessels and of their equipment in order to fulfil the safe transportation of the cargo. The carriers are obliged to provide ships designed, constructed, equipped, supplied and staffed in accordance with the international regulations, in order to execute the voyage safely and overcome those risks which could be met during the voyage (ordinary perils of the sea).

Shippers also need clean and well-maintained containers without deficiencies, for the safe transport of their cargo. Moreover, shippers request that the containers should comply with the global equipment quality standards. However, in some ports there are some differences in what is considered as approved quality

---

11 Free time is the time period (calendar days) allowed to the goods to be stored at the port after arrival and before pick-up.

for containers. Consequently, containers that are approved in the departing port may not be approved in the destination port, making the shipper obliged to pay an extra fee to the operator for the alleged quality deficiencies. Shippers do not want to undertake the extra cost when such situations arise.

3. *Reputation and image of the liner operator in the market.*

Shippers take seriously into account the reputation and image of the liner operator (carrier). Liner companies create for themselves a reputation in shipping circles, which is very quickly spread internationally. In the day-to-day exchange of information, certain expressive wordings are used like "first-class people", "unprofessional operators", "good performers", etc. Being labeled as "difficult" indicates that the party in question is hard to co-operate with, showing lack of flexibility. Additionally, any experience of past loss or damage of cargo caused by a shipping company affects the shipper's decision. Shippers consider that a very crucial selection criterion of a carrier and the renewal of a contract is the ability of the carrier/operator to comply with what has been promised and what has been agreed in the contract of carriage.

4. *Low cost sea transport operations.*

Regarding the shippers' requirement for the provision of transport services at reduced cost, this does not necessarily constitute the decisive selection factor of a carrier, although shippers always consider it seriously. Shippers may lose much more money in case of damage of high value cargoes – due to poor quality of transport service – compared to what they could have gained by compressing their transportation cost. As a consequence, shippers place more importance on the high quality of transport services than on the low cost of sea transport operations. Therefore, liner operators are involved much more than other shipowners in improving cargo-handling equipment and in developing port facilities, so as to satisfy their customers' needs. As a result, automation of cargo handling and investment in specialist terminals has transformed the liner business.

However, some shippers consider that a fixed rate on a yearly basis is very important in order to be able to budget their transport cost throughout the year. This is particularly important for shippers who own cargoes and price their goods on the basis of budgeted costs over the year. That is one of the reasons why the liner pricing has been transformed to "*contract-based*", where shippers and carriers agree for their annual transport contracts.

5. *Satisfactory co-operation with carrier's personnel and ship's crew.*

This includes, for example:

- Co-operation with shore personnel (liner agents' network).
- Master–crew–shipper relationship.

- Liner company–shipper relationship.
- Co-operation and response to shippers' demands.
- Settlement of cargo claims.
- Efficient handling of cargo bookings.

Shippers seek satisfactory co-operation with the shipping company. The immediacy of master of the ship, crew and shore personnel constitutes basic precondition of maintaining the client relationship. The relationships between the master/crew and the shipper must be excellent, in order to achieve smooth execution of the cargo transport. It must be emphasised that the same applies when the liner vessel is chartered-in by the liner operator. In such a case, which is not at all unusual in the containership market, an independent owner has time chartered his vessel to a liner company and bears the manning cost and the responsibility of selecting the master and crew. Thus, the perfect relationship must be kept and coordinated among the master and crew, the shippers, the shipowner of the vessel and the liner operator.

Shippers ask for the understanding of their needs and the satisfaction of their requirements. Such a requirement may be the flexibility of the liner operator to carry more cargo than what has been committed in the contract of carriage. This request may be expressed by shippers who experience seasonal demand for their cargoes. The marketing philosophy generates and builds up long-term relationships between the shipowners and the shippers. The shipping companies must also maintain and strengthen contacts with old clients.

The skill and diplomacy exercised by the personnel of the claims department are especially important. Such matters must be dealt with in accordance with law and good practice, so that the liner operator does not lose the client. Shippers today value more the effective management of a shipping company that can resolve problems presented during the cargo transport and respond efficiently to reasonable shippers' needs and requirements.

6. *Information system for shippers.*

This includes, for example:

- Information to shippers/Tracking communications system.
- Informative nature of advertising programmes of liner services.

Systems of electronic cargo booking, follow-up of the carriage and continuous updating are also demanded by shippers. A proper information system provides shippers with increased sense of control and decreased sense of uncertainty.

Furthermore, informative advertising of liner services is deemed crucial for attracting new clients and informing existing ones. Advertising material, such as folders, annual reports, advertisements in trade magazines together with an interesting website, are used by shipowners and/or liner operators to create new business opportunities.

From the above analysis, it is concluded that shippers' requirements in the liner market (and therefore their chartering policy) are more oriented to quality.

5.1.4 Decision-making process and buying behaviour of charterers and shippers in bulk and liner markets

The decision-making process of the charterer (in bulk market) and shipper (in liner market) is a sequence of thinking, evaluating and finally deciding. This process helps a shipping company (bulk or liner) to structure its approach and form its chartering policy and marketing strategy accordingly. More specifically, the basic *stages of the charterer's or shipper's decision-making process* are the following[12]:

1. *The pre-purchase choice among alternatives during the pre-fixture stage (in bulk market) or pre-booking stage (in liner market).*
   This stage refers to all charterer's or shipper's activities occurring before the acquisition of the transport service, in other words before the fixture of the charter in the case of bulk market or before the booking of space onboard in the case of liner market. This stage begins when the contract of sale of goods is signed and the cargo has to be carried from the port of origin to the port of destination. During this stage, the charterer or the shipper, who may act on behalf of the cargo owner or be the cargo owner himself, examines his transportation needs and collects information regarding possible alternative vessels. The charterer or the shipper seeks the appropriate ship that will undertake the cargo carriage. The charterer in the bulk (tramp) market shows his interest for a specific type of vessel and for a particular type of charter by drawing out the cargo order and by exchanging offers and counter-offers with interested shipowners. Charterers have a list of transport options on the basis of their experience, convenience and knowledge. On the other hand, the shipper in the liner market shows his interest for a specific vessel by searching for appropriate liner services according to his experience, market research, contacts with liner agents or freight forwarders or from information sourced in the shipping press and from the internet. The pre-purchase stage includes transportation need awareness, information and market search, as well as the evaluation of alternatives. An important outcome of the pre-purchase stage is the decision of the charterer to fix a certain charter and the decision of the shipper to book space on a certain vessel.
2. *The charterer's or shipper's behaviour during the carriage of goods.*
   Charterers and shippers have expectations about the performance of the chartered vessel. The vessel must execute the voyage as quickly as

---

12 Plomaritou, E., Plomaritou, V. and Giziakis, K. (2011) "Shipping Marketing and Customer Orientation: The Psychology and Buying Behaviour of Charterer and Shipper in Tramp and Liner Market" *Management – Journal of Contemporary Management Issues*, Vol. 16, No. 1, pp. 57–89.

possible and must deliver the cargo safely at the port of discharge. Additionally, the charterer and shipper have obligations during the charter, which depend on the type of charter (see chapter 7). This stage is characterised by the prolonged interaction between charterer (or shipper), shipowner, shore personnel, master and crew. It is from these interpersonal interactions that the transport service experience is acquired.

3. *The post-purchase evaluation of satisfaction during the post-fixture stage (in bulk market) – or post-booking stage (in liner market) – and after the delivery of cargo to the consignee.*

During this stage, charterer or shipper may experience varying levels of doubt that the correct fixture or booking was made. Due to the extended delivery process of service, the post-choice evaluation occurs both during and after the use of services rather than only afterward. There are two ways of evaluating the quality of transportation services; the compliance of the shipping company (and vessel) with the safety rules, as well as the satisfaction of charterer's requirements. Further to that, compliance of the vessel to port state controls and minimum delays due to vessel detentions can be added.

At this point of analysis, emphasis should be given to the external factors caused by social forces and physical causes, which affect positively or negatively the decision-making process of charterers and shippers, as well as their chartering policy. More specifically[13]:

- *Physical causes* mainly concern physical catastrophes and weather conditions. For example, a heavy winter in Europe will increase the demand for oil, the demand for tankers and consequently it may affect the chartering policy of tanker charterers.
- *Social forces* include political, technological and economic events. The term political events is used to refer to such occurrences as localised wars, revolutions, political nationalisations of foreign assets, strikes, canal closures, flag boycotts, embargoes, oil crises, government changes and similar events. The unforeseen political events bring about a sudden and unexpected change in demand for sea transport services and consequently in the charterers' policy.
- *Technological events* are mainly related to the great technological developments in cargo-handling methods, as well as in navigational practices. Technical developments, such as the "no ballast system", the "LNG fuel for propulsion and auxiliary engine", the "sulphur scrubber system", the "advanced rubber and propeller system", the "speed nozzle", the "exhaust gas recirculation" etc. which if used together would result in the Green Ship of the future. The transition from one technology to

---

13 Plomaritou, E. (2008) *Marketing of Shipping Companies: A Tool for Improvement of Chartering Policy* (Athens, Stamoulis Publications, pp. 53–56).

another may affect the decision-making process and chartering policy of charterers and shippers. For example, technological developments in shipbuilding may lead to an increase of demand for the new type of vessel and to a decrease of demand for the existing technologically disdained tonnage.

The charterer's and shipper's buying behaviour is complex because it passes through the decision-making process comprising of:

- the recognition of the need for cargo transportation,
- the seeking of information (e.g. through the cargo orders),
- the evaluation of alternative vessel employments,
- the decision for negotiation,
- the chartering pre- and post-fixture behaviour (in bulk market) or pre- and post-booking behaviour (in liner market).

The charterer's and shipper's buying behaviour involves risk in the sense that any action taken by the charterer or shipper will produce consequences that he cannot anticipate with any certainty, and some of which are likely to be unpleasant. With respect to uncertainty, the charterer (or shipper), for example, may have never chartered the vessel X and may have never co-operated with the shipping company which manages the vessel X. Moreover, even though the shipowner has performed the carriage of similar cargoes successfully in the past, the charterer (or shipper) is not guaranteed that this particular voyage will end with the same successful outcome. In addition, uncertainty is likely to increase if the charterer (or shipper) lacks sufficient knowledge before the execution of the charter, concerning the particulars of the vessel, the business profile of the shipping company, past loss and damage experience of the company, etc. The consequences of a poor decision regarding the chartering of a vessel could cause damages or loss of cargo.

The charterer and the shipper perceive three types of risk. More specifically:

- *Financial risk* assumes that financial loss could occur in the case of the vessel's poor performance. Loss or damage of cargo in transit is an insurable risk, but raises many difficulties for the shipper, who may not be well prepared to pay more against the risk of damage for securing the transportation of his product.
- *Social risk* relates to the idea that there might be a loss of the charterer's or shipper's social status, associated mostly with the carriage of oil or dangerous goods by sea.
- *Shipping risk* is described by the possibility of not recovering the investment in a merchant ship (including the anticipated return on the capital employed) during a period of ship ownership. When shippers are able to forecast the demand of their cargoes in future (for example in iron ore trades), or if they believe that sea transport is of great strategic

importance, they may decide to take the shipping risk themselves by acquiring ships or by chartering on a long-term basis the vessels of independent shipowners. However, there are many cases where shippers never know how many cargoes they will have in future and consequently they do not know how many ships they will need in the future (for example in grain trades). As a result, the shippers enter into the market and charter vessels when they need them. The shipping risk then is undertaken by the shipowners.

By taking into consideration that charterers and shippers usually do not like taking the above-mentioned risks, then it seems obvious that they will try, whenever possible, to reduce risk before fixture. One strategy of risk minimisation is the brand loyalty. Brand loyalty is based on the degree to which the charterer (or shipper) has obtained satisfaction in the past. If charterers (or shippers) have been satisfied in the past with the transport services, they have little incentive to risk trying a new shipping company. Having been satisfied in a high-risk charter, a charterer is less likely to experiment with a different owner. Maintaining a long-term relationship with the same shipping company helps to reduce the perceived risk associated with the charter. This is why it is common to observe charterers and shippers chartering vessels from the same shipping company over long periods of time or for repeated or renewed charters.

Another strategy of risk minimisation is the collection of information about the vessel's particulars, the shipowner's reputation, the shipping company's profile and its past loss/damage experience. Considerable information is provided to the tanker charterers by the SIRE reports (see section 5.1.1).

5.2 Chartering policy of shipowners

5.2.1 Chartering policy of shipowners in bulk and liner markets

In bulk market the shipowner's chartering policy defines the type of vessel's employment and vice versa. The shipowner comes to the freight market with a ship available, free of cargo, with no employment. In small shipping groups, the shipowner makes all the decisions about the employment of his vessels. In large shipping companies, top management is more remote from the daily operation of the business. Decisions are made by more complicated managerial schemes composed of more than one person (for example a board of directors composed of five or seven persons). In the case of listed companies, time charters may be preferable so as to give some income visibility and provide the stockholder with a possible dividend payout. During periods of strong or booming freight markets, chartering policy is usually focused more on spot charters, so as to reap the benefits of this growth and give value to the shareholder of the company. On the contrary, during times of freight rate recession, either short-term time charters or spot employment may be preferred, to avoid locking the vessel earnings at low levels for a long period. It should be underlined that in the liquid bulk market, the role of oil companies is crucial. These companies are relatively few in number, often huge in size and form the main clients of the tanker shipping companies. Within this framework, the tanker shipping company should be in a position to persuade an oil company to select and charter its vessels.

The daily and periodical fluctuations of freight rates in the bulk market occur very quickly, thus the market situation changes from one moment to the next. Consequently, the key factors in chartering tankers and bulk carriers are synchronisation and optimisation in decision-making, so that the fixture is achieved at the best possible freight levels. The success of the shipowner in the bulk market[14] results from matching the free vessel with the available cargo, fixing the appropriate type of charter, discovering the client's needs, offering suitable transport services that satisfy those needs, providing operating efficiency, communicating effectively with the target market and negotiating the freight as a function to the services provided and what the current state of the market dictates.

Ships operated in the spot market must comply with charterers' demands concerning vessels' type, size, specifications and compliance with international safety management regulations. Furthermore, the vessel must be available at the right area, port or dock, at the right time and ask for a competitive freight level compared to freight quotes from other interested shipowners. If the employment in question is for a longer duration on a time charter contract basis, then the importance of a shipowner's solvency, financial strength, integrity, reliability and reputation for good performance will increase correspondingly.

Fleet utilisation is another important point to mention. Most tankers and large bulkers rarely find cargoes for their return voyages to the loading ports. This means that they may be forced to execute the return leg in ballast. The shipowner achieves the most appropriate and efficient commercial usage of his vessels when he reduces "ballast legs" (voyages) to the minimum, eliminates off-hire periods and maximises the total earnings by a suitable combination of period contracts and spot market trading.

Chartering policy of shipowners depends on the phase of the shipping market and the respective expectations. In the case of a sharp increase in ships' demand, which cannot be immediately counter-balanced by increasing supply through new shipbuilding deliveries,[15] the carriers will be placed into a strong position, as charterers are in a period of excessive cargoes' availability. Then, instead of offering their ships for time charters, owners may seek to charter them per voyage in order to take advantage of the high spot freight rates. Shipowners committed beforehand to long-term charters gain little in such a situation of a growing or booming spot market. On the other hand, when ships' demand starts to fade and the spot market is expected to weaken in the near future, owners wish to fix their vessels for longer periods in order to secure higher earnings than what otherwise might be earned from the spot market.

---

14 Plomaritou, E. (2017) *Chartering Policy of Shipping Companies* (London, Lloyd's Maritime Academy, Module 7 of Distance Learning Course "Diploma in Maritime Business Management").

15 There is a time lag of 1.5–3 years between the placing of an order and the delivery of a new-built vessel.

In the liner market, the structure is completely different, since shipowners (carriers or liner operators) typically have a large and complex office staff and a geographically wide agency network to manage, so there is an unavoidable emphasis on administration (see section 4.1). When the shipowner employs his ship in the liner market, by providing services to anyone who wishes to transport cargoes by sea (becoming "common carrier"), then the chartering policy is applied in a different way than that in the bulk market. The chartering business in the liner market is completely different to that of the bulk market. In the liner market no lengthy and detailed chartering negotiations take place. General cargo in the liner market finds most of its business through agents whose role differs greatly from the role of chartering brokers or ship agents in the tramp shipping market (see section 3.5). The shipper wishes to transport his cargo and for that reason "books" space on a vessel through an agent. If the liner operator cannot transport the cargoes with his own vessels, then he charters-in containerships or other types of liner vessels from independent shipowners. In this case, the charterparty verifies this chartering agreement of the vessel between the liner operator and the independent shipowner. Typically, this occurs in the form of a time charter or less frequently with a bareboat charter. Spot charters fixed between liner operators and independent shipowners are rare. It may be broadly said that, what is known as spot (voyage) charters in bulk shipping have only few similarities to the liner services offered by the lines to the shippers in the liner market, in the sense that both concern a specific cargo voyage.

When booking cargoes in the liner market, the success factors of the shipowner/liner operator/carrier are the geographical coverage, frequency of sailings, regularity, reliability, short transit times, safety of cargo shipped, compliance with international safety management regulations, efficient handling of cargo bookings and settlement of cargo claims. Further strengthening of the carrier's competitive position can be achieved by offering package solutions to transport problems, such as the arrangement of door-to-door transport etc.

5.2.2 Commercial risks faced by shipowners in chartering

Shipowners face increased exposure to commercial risks arising from charterparties, operations and claim issues. In certain circumstances, these risks are large enough to undermine or destroy the financial base of shipowners. Successful commercial decisions, chartering policies and marketing strategies assist them to limit or even to avoid some types of risk.

With regard to chartering matters, the *nature of commercial/business risks* may be[16]:

- *Financial:* At the end of the day, each aspect of chartering results in a financial allocation of risks. There are some risks of purely financial

---

16 Plomaritou, E. and Nikolaides, M. (2016) "Commercial Risks arising from Chartering Vessels" *Journal of Shipping & Ocean Engineering* Vol. 6, Issue 4, pp. 261–268.

nature, e.g. the risk of hire payment default by a time charterer. However, even the risks of operational or legal nature almost always lead to a financial claim or motive.

- *Chartering oriented, operational, navigational and geographical:* It comprises all those risks that arise from pure chartering orientation (e.g. wrong chartering policy), as well as from operational matters of a charter, such as for example cargo handling, shipowner's delivery of a seaworthy vessel to the charterer, provision of the cargo from the charterer etc. Besides, commercial risks may be of navigational or geographical nature, e.g. navigating in dangerous seas (e.g. piracy areas) or employing the vessel outside the agreed trading limits in a time charter etc.
- *Legal:* All the risks related to the law of the charter are included in this category. Legal matters may concern and affect the whole process of a charter, comprising the pre-fixture stages of investigation and negotiation of the charter, the fixture stages of drafting and signing the charterparty, the stage of the execution of the charter, as well as the post-fixture stages of the allocation of disbursements and the legal claims that may arise from the charter.
- *Ethical:* The image and reputation of a company may be radically affected from a charter. Considerable risks of ethical nature sometimes arise. For example, a tanker owner is at risk of being liable for making oil pollution when he employs a substandard vessel with a drunkard master on board. Consequently, apart from the financial penalties, he is subject to a huge risk of an ethical nature, as long as his reputation and image will be badly harmed.

The most significant *commercial risks arising from chartering matters* are the following[17]:

- *The market risk:* Every part of the shipping industry is always moving around the spot freight market of the vessels. All major shipping decisions (chartering spot or in period charters, evaluation of alternative charters, selling or scrapping a vessel etc.) are directly based and affected by the prevailing conditions of the freight market and the future expectations of the involved parties. For example, if a shipowner fixes his vessel for a three-year time charterparty at USD 10,000/day and during that time the average rate of the respective spot market climbs at USD 30,000/day, the shipowner will suffer a huge loss of earnings.
- *The risk of timing at decision-making:* The same decision (e.g. chartering vessels on the spot market) may be right at a specific point of time,

---

17 Plomaritou, E. (2017) *Commercial Risks arising from Charterparties, Operations and Claim Issues* (London, Lloyd's Maritime Academy, Module 2 of Distance Learning Course "Certificate in Commercial Risks in Shipping").

whereas it may be wrong at another. The freight market is highly volatile and cyclical. So, perfect timing of decisions is the initial key to success.

- *The chartering strategy and policy risk:* The selected chartering strategy and policy of a company determines the amount of risk undertaken. When chartering a vessel, some important questions must be placed and then answered, for example, as follows:

  - Should we charter spot, taking the whole risk of high volatility of the spot market? In other words, should we take on our own all the potential upside but also all the downside risk of the market?
  - Should we put the vessel in some form of period charter (time charter, bareboat), in such case fixing our future earnings, whilst taking the risk of losing the upside potential of the spot market?
  - Who is the counter-party? Is he credible? What is his track record and reputation? The longer the charter, the most important these questions become.
  - What is the market forecast? What are our expectations? What is our character, mentality, temperament and psychology?
  - When is the perfect timing for a decision?
  - What are the available chartering alternatives at a specific point of time and at a specific geographical location?
  - Should we hedge or insure some chartering risks?

- *The currency risk:* The currency of the charterparty puts a significant risk on the involved parties. Most charterparties provide that freight or hire payment is to be made in US Dollars. When earnings of a party denominated in a different currency than the costs and expenses, then a currency exchange risk exists. Taking into account that the exchange rate of some currencies may have high volatility, this risk may sometimes be considerable.

- *The bunkers risk:* In a period of high oil prices cost of bunkers may even form 60% of a ship's total cost. In a voyage charter, such cost is borne by the shipowner, whereas in a time or a bareboat charter the charterer is responsible. It is self-explanatory how critical bunker prices may be in parallel with the selected type of charter. Besides, bunkers risk may have qualitative aspects. The optimum choice of a bunkering company ensures the good quality of fuel for the ship in order to avoid a damaged engine. The geographical optimisation of bunkering in order to avoid deviations is also crucial for chartering purposes. Moreover, the optimisation of bunkers quantity in relation to the carried cargo quantity is always of paramount importance. Finally, a ship's damage or loss may lead to bunkers' loss, for which settlement must be made between the contracting parties of the charterparty in accordance with the facts of the case.

- *The risk of loss:* Vessel, cargo, bunkers and income may be lost, in full or in part. Settlement will be made in accordance with the risk allocation between the parties of the charterparty, the execution of the charter, shipping operations and claims disputes.

- *The risk of damage:* Similarly, vessel and cargo may be damaged.
- *The risk of delay:* It is a considerable aspect of commercial risk. Vessel and cargo may be delayed during a charter. The risk and cost of such delay are allocated between the contracting parties of the charterparty. In chartering matters "time is money"!
- *The risk of death or injury:* Shipping operations are extremely tough and may sometimes cause the death or injury of involved persons (e.g. crewmen, stevedores). Liability is allocated between the contracting parties of the charterparty, depending on the type and the applicable law of the charter.
- *The freight risk:* It is the risk which lies with the owner when he, fully or partly, fails to fulfil his obligation to carry the cargo and thereby lose his right to collect freight, in full, or in part, respectively.
- *The credit risk:* It is the shipowner's counter-party risk. It concerns the risk of charterer's default in payment of freight or hire.
- *The interest rates risk, the inflation risk and the opportunity cost risk:* A charter agreement concerns a commitment of capital in the shipping business. Therefore, such risks should not get underestimated when a vessel is chartered.

5.2.3 Factors affecting shipowners' chartering policy in bulk and liner markets

The way in which a shipowner operates the vessels under his control will vary according to various parameters, such as trading intentions, requirements and expectations, the global economy, current and anticipated charter market conditions and freight rate levels, as well as according to political and shipping regulations enforced by governments and international bodies, flags, ports, classification societies etc.

Thinking more strategically about chartering, some of the most important *factors playing a critical role in the decision-making process of the shipowner* are the following[18]:

- *State of freight market and expectations:* When trade is buoyant and spot freight rates are rising, shipowners, in anticipation of further rises, tend to contract for shorter periods. When rates are expected to fall, shipowners tend to charter for longer periods so as to "secure" higher earnings for the future. Therefore, the current time charter rate tends to reflect the expected trend of spot rates in the future. If spot rates are expected to rise, the current time charter rate may tend to be above the current voyage rates; if spot rates are expected to fall, the current time charter rate may tend to be below the current voyage rates. The duration of ship's employment depends clearly on market outlook which is a significant factor that shipowners have to consider before the final decision of a charter.

---

18 Plomaritou, E. (2008) *Marketing of Shipping Companies: A Tool for Improvement of Chartering Policy* (Athens, Stamoulis Publications, pp. 141–144).

- *State of the world economy and seaborne trade:* The demand for shipping services is a derived demand, arising as a direct result of the demand for the commodities which are hauled by sea. Shipping is therefore demanded not for itself, but because it is part of the production process of goods. Like all productive factors, demand for shipping derives from the consumers' ultimate want of goods and services. The level of seaborne trade determines the amount and quality of shipping and cargo space required as well as the type of ship's employment and charter. Fluctuations in the level of international trade may be caused by a number of factors. The aim of the shipowner is to respond on demand for tonnage, adjust his strategic decisions and operational policies, finally serving charterers' transportation needs.

- *Voyage estimations:* Shipping companies have departments whose job is to assess comparative costs and earnings between various alternative ways of employing their ships. The object is to find the most suitable charter. Although it might seem an easy matter to calculate the cost of a specific cargo voyage from one port to another, or to calculate the rate of freight or hire which will cover a shipowner's costs, plus a reasonable profit, these calculations can in fact turn out to be somewhat complex. Market outlook, duration of charter, trading areas, charterers' credibility, suitable charterparty and laytime terms, cargo sizes etc. are basic factors that shipowners have to consider in this continuous evaluation, calculation and decision-making process (see analytically chapter 14 for voyage estimation).

- *Attraction of sub-contract:* There are three reasons why sub-contracting may be attractive.[19] First, a large industrial player may not wish to become a shipowner, but its business requires the use of a ship under his control. Second, in such cases of major industrial players, the time charter may work out cheaper than buying vessels, especially in depressed freight markets and if the shipowner may have lower costs, due to lower overheads and larger fleet size. Third, the time or bareboat charterer may speculate by taking a position in anticipation of a change in the spot market. So, for instance, he may time or bareboat charter a ship, anticipating to earn more by sub-contracting in higher spot rates. It is advisable that sub-charters should always be treated with absolute caution by shipowners. One of the causes of the deep shipping crisis, which burst up in the last quarter of 2008 in the aftermath of the Global Financial Crisis, was the extensive sequence of charters and sub-charters. After a booming, all-time record, six-year freight market in 2003–2008, the freight rates collapsed at the end of 2008 and sub-charters brought about a "domino effect" in the shipping market. Some shipping companies went bankrupt, because the depressed spot freight markets lasted for

---

19 Stopford, M. (2009) *Maritime Economics* (London, Routledge Publications, 3rd edition, p. 184).

so long that shipowners and charterers of "chain charters" were not able at last to respond to their committed liabilities, for example from 10-year period charters that should be paid in very high hire rates.

- *Policy of the shipowner as approved by investors/shareholders:* The timing of decisions about chartering ships is crucial. Shipowners should have the investors' approval concerning the ships' employment. This is the case either in public or in private shipping companies. For example, a public company may attract investors' interest by chartering its vessels on long period charters with first-class charterers on above market hire rates, therefore offering the possibility of earnings visibility, fixed dividend payouts and higher capital gains to its shareholders. On the other hand, a privately held family-owned shipping company may be focused on being flexible in chartering decisions by making a mixed balance of spot and period charters depending on the freight expectations.

- *Relationship and experience with certain charterers/shippers:* It is strongly felt by the shipping community that personal contact and trust between parties are becoming increasingly important. Charterers prefer to fix vessels owned by shipowners with whom they have excellent business relations and very good past experience. Transport services are "experience-based" and charterers or shippers seek to co-operate with shipowners who have already offered high quality services and have satisfied their requirements in the past. On the other hand, the shipowner keeps lists of charterers which have a good reputation on the market and are considered "first-class". The charter will tend to be fixed for as long as the shipowner approves the charterer's credibility. In other words, when vessels are fixed for long period charters of 10–15 years, the shipowner and the charterer overcome a simple customer relationship, becoming long-standing shipping partners.

- *Type of vessels and quality of fleet:* Shipowners are free to use whatever ships they think will provide the transport service most profitably. When a shipowner decides which vessels to operate, a number of determinants should be taken into consideration, such as the type of cargo, the type of shipping operation and the cargo trades. Furthermore, size, age, specifications and state of maintenance all play a vital role in determining a vessel's earning potential and chartering ability.

- *Geographical and trading limits of ship's employment:* The vessel's technical design characteristics and specifications (e.g. ship's draught and length, ice-class etc.), as well as its flag, affect the geographical and trading limits of ship's employment and commercial performance. For example, Very Large Bulk Carriers (VLBCs) cannot approach ports with draught restrictions and old cargo-handling technology, whilst tankers flying black-listed flags are banned from approaching the environmentally sensitive US coasts.

- *Type of cargo and trade:* The shipowner has to take into consideration some basic questions about the cargo and the trade. For example:

- ○ What is the cargo nature and its handling requirements? Could it damage the ship?
- ○ What is the trade? Is it known and well-established?
- ○ What is the proposed charterparty?
- ○ Are there any risks which cannot be assessed?
- ○ What are the next obligations of the ship? Is it due for special survey or drydocking?

Similar questions must be answered on a daily basis and chartering decisions should be adjusted accordingly.

5.3 Marketing of shipping companies as a tool for improvement of chartering policy

The marketing of a merchant shipping company deals with the satisfaction of charterer's or shipper's transport needs, with the main aim being the profit maximisation of the enterprise. This satisfaction presupposes on the one hand correct diagnosis of the shipping market to better understand and forecast client's (charterer's/shipper's) needs; and on the other hand appropriate planning, organisation and control of shipping company's means to improve its chartering policy. A misunderstanding of the needs of various customer groups and the inability of implementing the proper chartering policy may result in substandard provision of the desired transport services at non-acceptable freight levels. This in turn leads to the dissatisfaction of charterers/shippers and the incapability of retaining them, resulting in the commercial failure of the enterprise. Shipping marketing is a considerable tool for improving the chartering policy, offering better transport services, satisfying the clients' needs, meliorating the customer relationships and maximising the profit of the shipping company.[20]

The procedure of shipping marketing implementation includes the systematic analysis of all chartering alternatives in respect of vessel's employment, the choice of some of them, the determination of goals and finally the planning and implementation of the necessary actions (strategies) for the goals' achievement. This process must be regarded as continuous and is included in the functions of commercial management (see chapter 4). More specifically, *the process of marketing implementation in a shipping company includes mainly the following stages* (see Figure 5.1)[21]:

- • *Diagnosis:* The shipping company, through a marketing information system, collects updated data regarding the economic and business climate.

---

20 Plomaritou, E. (2005) *Marketing of Shipping Companies as a Tool for Improvement of Chartering Policy. A Comparative Analysis of Marketing Implementation in Bulk and Liner Shipping Companies Worldwide and in Greece: A Case Study in Containership Market and Tanker Market* (PhD Thesis, University of Piraeus, Greece).

21 Plomaritou, E. (2008) *Marketing of Shipping Companies: A Tool for Improvement of Chartering Policy* (Athens, Stamoulis Publications, pp. 45–102).

START

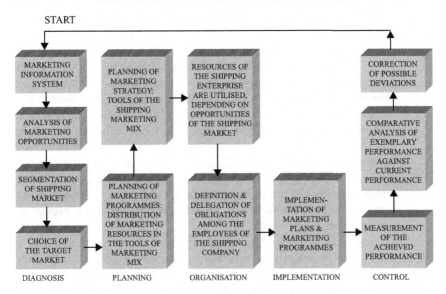

Figure 5.1 Process of Marketing Implementation in Shipping Companies

Source: Plomaritou, E. (2008) *Marketing of Shipping Companies: A Tool for Improvement of Chartering Policy* (Athens, Stamoulis Publications, p. 47).

Necessary information is sourced as concern as the position of the company within the shipping market (strengths, weaknesses, opportunities and threats). Furthermore, the company evaluates every market segment, examines the chartering policy and transportation needs of charterers and shippers at the various market segments and selects its target market(s). This stage assists the company to understand the requirements of its clients, as well as to recognise its competitive position in the shipping market.

- *Planning:* The shipping company determines a mixture of objectives, such as the improvement of market share, the fixture of profitable period charters, the interception of shipping risk etc. The main aim of shipping marketing always remains the maximisation of company's profit through the satisfaction of charterer's and shipper's transportation needs. Moreover, during this stage the marketing strategies and programmes are planned carefully. *Marketing strategies* are the means and actions by which the objectives are achieved and the chartering policy is improved. The marketing strategies are divided into the shipping marketing mix strategies, the differentiation strategies and the positioning strategies (see section 5.5). The *marketing programmes* include the basic decisions concerning the budget used for the implementation of strategies. This stage assists the shipping company to determine the means (strategies) by which its objectives may be achieved and its chartering policy may be improved.

- *Organisation:* The shipping company defines which objectives will be met and by whom. Marketing is not done just by a marketing department.

153

Chartering and operation departments also undertake the stages of marketing process. However, the real task of doing marketing is part of everyone's job in the shipping company.

- *Implementation:* At this stage of marketing process, the marketing plans (strategies and programmes) are applied. In marketing-oriented shipping companies, the charterer (or shipper) is at the centre of all activities. The client is the concern not simply of marketing, chartering and operation departments, but also of administrative personnel whose actions move towards meeting his requirements. The *marketing plans* must be applied correctly, so that the proper transport service is provided to the appropriate charterer/shipper, at the right time and geographical area with the appropriate vessel and at freight levels that satisfy not only the shipping enterprise, but also the client, always keeping in mind the prevailing market conditions.

- *Control:* During this stage the performance achieved is measured, a comparative analysis of exemplary performance of marketing plans against current performance is carried out, causes of possible deviations are sought and business measures are taken for their correction.

The *marketing of shipping companies is* the provision of appropriate transport services by the right people (personnel), to right clients (charterers/shippers), with the appropriate vessel (seaworthy and cargoworthy), at the proper time and place (loading – discharging ports or trading areas), at a fair price (freight or hire) with a suitable promotion.

It should be mentioned that marketing becomes even more necessary during periods of shipping crises, where the oversupply of vessels puts the charterers in the advantageous position of selecting the shipping company for the carriage of their goods by sea. Consequently, in times of crises those shipping companies with marketing strategies in place have more possibilities for chartering their vessels than laying up them, because they have built good customer relationships and an enhanced reputation in the shipping market. As competitive pressures in global shipping, economical, political and social environments are broadened, the need for effective marketing plans becomes more and more imperative.[22]

5.4 Shipping marketing with customer orientation

Shipping marketing is not only concerned with the planning and implementation of successful programmes and strategies. For marketing to be successful there needs to be a unique orientation throughout the company, which fosters the marketing concept and demonstrates an identical approach to all chartering activities.

---

22 Plomaritou, E. and Goulielmos, A. (2009) A Review of Marketing in Tramp Shipping *International Journal of Shipping and Transport Logistics* (Vol. 1, No. 2, pp. 119–155); Plomaritou, E. (2005) "Marketing: the Greek Way" *Shipping Network* (London, Institute of Chartered Shipbrokers, No. 1, Issue 6, p. 7).

Customer orientation is the sufficient understanding of the target clients and the ability to create superior value for them continuously. The term "*customer-oriented firms*" is frequently used to describe how knowledgeable a firm is about its client needs and how responsive it is in terms of a continuous value creation and delivery. The essence of customer orientation is the successful management of a relationship between the shipping company and the charterer/shipper. Strong business relationships must be developed with those clients that are able to assess the value created and offered by the shipping company.

Shipping marketing orientation is based around a philosophy, which places the client (charterer or shipper) first, and it recognises that every action taken by the company ultimately affects the customer relationship.

Every interaction between the shipping company and the charterers/shippers can affect the quality of the transportation service and the benefits provided. The main types of interaction are indicatively the following:

- The direct interaction between the service provider, such as a member of staff or master or crew of the company, and the charterer (or shipper).
- The interaction between the charterer and the shipowner's broker.
- The interaction between the shipowner and the charterer's broker.
- The interaction between the charterer's broker and the shipowner's broker.
- The interaction between the charterer (or shipper) and service facilities (provided by the shipowner), such as the formation of bill of lading by electronic means (e.g. EDI system).
- The interaction between the liner agent and the liner operator.
- The interaction between the liner agent and the independent shipowner, when the latter has time-chartered his vessel to a liner operator.
- The interaction between the liner agent and the master.
- The interaction between the liner agent and the shipper and/or the freight forwarder.
- The interaction between the charterer and other sub-charterers or shippers.

If a true marketing orientation is to be achieved, all members of personnel and crew need to know the main aims of shipping marketing and what marketing really means.

The main *aims of shipping marketing* are:

- To understand the transportation needs of charterers and/or shippers.
- To improve the chartering policy of the shipping company, in order to offer the appropriate services and provide clients with benefits which meet the above transportation needs.
- To ensure consistent quality of offered services.
- To retain existing and attract new clients (charterers or shippers).
- To achieve the shipping company's objectives.

- To build a good reputation of the shipping company in the market.
- To maximise the profit of the enterprise.

Customer orientation places the charterer (or shipper) at the centre of the company's activities. Being close to the client is the focal point of the marketing concept. All personnel as well as the crew need to be aware of the way in which they can contribute to customer satisfaction, even when they do not have personal direct contact (e.g. the employees of the accounting department). Positive feedback from charterers should be relayed to everyone in the shipping company through internal messages. Similarly, any quality problems or customer complaints should also be discussed at all levels to see if systems or processes within the shipping company can be improved. A necessary precondition of an effective shipping marketing system is the understanding of charterers' – shippers' requirements, their buying behaviour, as well as their chartering policy (see section 5.1).

5.5 Marketing strategy and chartering policy of shipping companies

Marketing strategies are the means and actions by which the company's objectives are achieved and the chartering policy is improved. The marketing strategies are classified into the shipping marketing mix strategies, the differentiation strategies and the positioning strategies (see Figure 5.2). The overall aim of marketing strategies is to increase the profitability of the shipping company through the improvement of its chartering policy, the provision of the appropriate transport services and the satisfaction of charterers' and shippers' needs.

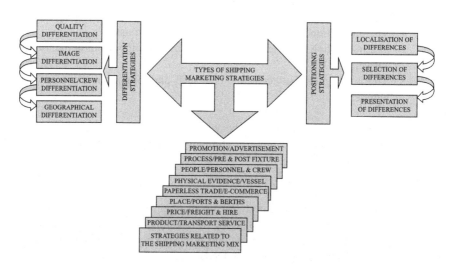

Figure 5.2 Shipping Marketing Strategies

Source: Plomaritou, E. (2008) *Marketing of Shipping Companies: A Tool for Improvement of Chartering Policy* (Athens, Stamoulis Publications, p. 97).

For each market segment, appropriate marketing strategies must be planned so that the proper transport service is provided to the appropriate charterer/shipper, at the right time and place, with the appropriate vessel and at freight levels that satisfy not only the shipping company but also the client. It would be much simpler for a shipping company if all factors that influence the charterers' and shippers' buying behaviour were under its own full control. However, the shipping industry is a globally complex sector and as a result the charterers' and shippers' buying behaviour and in a wider sense their chartering policy are shaped by many influences from exogenous factors which are beyond the control of the shipping company.

5.5.1 Strategies related to shipping marketing mix

The shipping marketing mix refers to the set of tools that a shipping company uses to improve its chartering policy, meliorate its services, satisfy its clients' needs, promote its image in the shipping market, establish good customer relationships and maximise profitability. Shipping marketing mix includes eight tools which are used for the planning of the appropriate marketing strategies (see Figure 5.3). More specifically, the *eight tools of shipping marketing mix – known as "the 8Ps of shipping marketing mix"* – are described below[23]:

1. *Product – Service:* The most important tool of the shipping marketing mix is the maritime transport service which represents the offer of the shipping enterprise to the client and includes the quality of the service provided. The fundamental difference is between bulk and liner service. However, even within the same shipping market there may be important differentiations (see section 1.1 for market segmentation). Characteristic examples of product/service strategies are the expansion strategies of company activities in bulk or liner markets. It is generally defined that shipping groups which focus on the operation of a specific type and/or size of vessel follow a *"specialisation strategy"*, whereas those companies operating various vessel types and/or sizes are said to follow a *"diversification strategy"*. Very few mega-carriers in the world are able to be active in both bulk and liner markets. They may implement such expansion strategies by possessing a large and modern fleet of bulk as well as liner vessels, thereby servicing the needs of trade throughout the world. Besides, it must be stressed that some ships (e.g. multi-purpose vessels, con-bulkers, OBOs, PROBOs etc.) are designed to operate in several different markets, whereas other vessels are specialising in the carriage of one cargo category (e.g. containerships, tankers, bulk carriers,

---

23 Plomaritou, E. (2008) "A Proposed Application of the Marketing Mix Concept to Tramp and Liner Shipping Companies" *Management – Journal of Contemporary Management Issues*, Vol. 13, No. 1, pp. 59–71; Plomaritou, E. (2005) *Marketing of Shipping Companies as a Tool for Improvement of Chartering Policy. A Comparative Analysis of Marketing Implementation in Bulk and Liner Shipping Companies Worldwide and in Greece: A Case Study in Containership Market and Tanker Market* (PhD Thesis, University of Piraeus).

gas carriers etc.). It must be recognised that in a depressed freight market, shipowners may move their investment from one market sector to another in order to avoid market threats and to exploit opportunities. As a result, supply/demand imbalances in one part of the market can ripple across to other sectors. For example, in 2015, due to a deep freight market recession and a negative outlook for dry bulk markets in contrast with a strong freight market for tankers, some newbuilding orders for bulk carriers were converted to tanker orders, resulting in an increase of tanker supply and a drop of tanker freight rates. At this point, some general conclusions and examples may be commented in respect of the product/service strategies followed throughout the shipping market:

- Most shipping companies prefer to focus on either bulk or liner operations.
- In bulk shipping, small companies (1–5 vessels), medium companies (6–15 vessels) and large companies (15+ vessels) may all follow strategies of either specialisation or diversification. Typically, for larger companies it is easier to diversify in various sectors.
- Public (listed) companies may be specialised or diversified. As long as they have to "sell an investment and growth story" to the shareholders, they often seek fixed employment for their vessels, income "visibility", stable dividend payout and capital gains. In that way, it is more common for the public shipping companies to follow specialisation strategies (i.e. companies focusing only on tankers or bulk carriers or containerships or gas carriers, not in many markets at the same time). However, there are also cases of diversified listed shipping companies.
- Private companies may be specialised or diversified. They are in general person-oriented or family-oriented groups, more independent in taking decisions and more flexible when selecting their chartering mix strategy.
- In liner shipping, large operators are fully diversified mega-carriers, seeking global coverage for their transport networks, following strategies of integration, horizontally (through forming shipping alliances with other companies) and vertically (by offering for example intermodal door-to-door services, terminal and depot management, freight forwarding, logistics and agency services etc.). On the contrary, small to medium liner operators usually focus on more specific parts of the business and are more restricted geographically (e.g. a niche operator offering only feeder services in the Black Sea–Mediterranean Sea region).
- Independent shipowners of containerships typically follow a specialisation strategy, seeking for ships' operational accuracy, so as to be able to charter (in period contracts) their specialised vessels to the liner operators. They aim at minimising off-hire periods and

building excellent relationships with their long-term clients (liner companies).

- Gas carriers typically require a high degree of specialised, sophisticated and accurate operation. Such owners typically concentrate on this segment, building close and long-standing relationships with their charterers, usually chartering their specialised vessels for very long periods.

- Marketing strategies, as shortly described above, are always closely related with the chartering policies adopted from the shipping companies.

2. *Price – Freight:* In all sectors of bulk market, the price of maritime transport service (i.e. the freight) depends on the negotiating power of involved parties (charterer and shipowner) at a given moment, under the general conditions of the market and under the special requirements of the specific fixture. However, the freight of an individual fixture fluctuates around the general freight level of the market, which is determined by supply and demand for sea transport services globally and regionally. A great number of factors, predictable or unpredictable, affect the supply of sea transport and the demand for sea transport at any moment and therefore the corresponding freight level (see chapter 2). Bulk shipping freight rates are characterised by high volatility and daily fluctuations. On the other hand, in the liner market, the freight level is determined more or less by fixed price tables which remain relatively stable for long periods (e.g. yearly shipping contracts between shippers and liner operators), thus diminishing market volatility and giving shippers the ability of planning transportation costs more accurately. In bulk shipping, as far as the price strategies are concerned, the following example may be mentioned: A big ship operator might be able to charter one of his vessels at lower freight rate than the prevailing rate at the market, compressing his profit margins, due to vessel's lower operating costs arising from achieved economies of scale of larger fleets. This could be done for various reasons, perhaps for keeping a good charterer "happy", or preferring to work with a credible charterer even at lower rates, or for positioning well his vessel for the next charter etc.

3. *Process:* The process includes all the stages of the service offer. In the bulk market, the process includes the pre-fixture, fixture and post-fixture phases. More specifically, the pre-fixture and fixture phases include the following stages[24]:

- The stage of sale of goods during which the relevant contract is signed.

- The investigation stage during which the charterer seeks for an appropriate ship to transport his cargo.

---

24 Giziakis, K., Papadopoulos, A. and Plomaritou, E. (2010) *Chartering* (Athens, Stamoulis Publications, 3rd edition, in Greek, pp. 399–401).

- The stage of chartering negotiation during which offers and counter-offers are made by the shipowner and charterer via their brokers.
- The stage of fixture during which the charterparty is signed.

The post-fixture phase concerns the execution of charter and includes the following stages:

- The preliminary (ballast) voyage.
- The loading operation.
- The carrying (laden) voyage.
- The discharging operation.
- The delivery of cargo to the recipient (consignee).

In the liner market, the process includes the pre-booking, booking and post-booking phases and is similar to the process of the bulk (tramp) market. The basic difference between a pre-fixture phase and a pre-booking phase is that in the latter case, instead of the negotiation procedure, a booking procedure takes place which leads to the issue of the booking note and not to the signature of the charterparty. Besides, this procedure takes place between the liner agent and the shipper or the freight forwarder, instead of the shipowner, the charterer and their brokers. Additionally, the basic difference between a "bulk market" post-fixture phase and a "liner market" post-booking phase is that the latter may include integration solutions and door-to-door services offered to the consignee of the cargo.

Examples of process strategies are those intended to improve the negotiation procedures and skills, as well as strategies of voyage execution with safety and speed. The chartering industry is very demanding. Contracts are negotiated within a few days, if not hours. Under the pressure of difficult negotiations conducted at speed, by people located around the globe, often by telephone or e-mail, mistakes and errors can have disastrous consequences. In this demanding and competitive environment, care must be taken to present a professional image, negotiations must be conducted in a serious and businesslike way and charterparty clauses must express the will of contracting parties. When the principles of negotiation are ignored, the parties may well become liable for substantial claims. Moreover, the strategies of voyage execution may concern various aspects. For example, an optimum process in a specific liner service (trade) comprises frequency and directness of sailings, scheduling flexibility, on-time pick-up and delivery of cargo, fast execution of the voyage, reduction of turn-around time to a minimum, appropriate cargo-handling procedures during the loading and discharging operations, safe transport of goods, door-to-door delivery to the recipient etc. Liner companies compete to each other for various "quality awards", such as for example the "Sailing Schedule Reliability Reward on Australia–East Asia Trade", in respect of applying improved process strategies. Focusing on improving processes may be used as a powerful marketing tool to achieve the enhancement of a company's reputation.

4. *People:* Human resources are vital for the provision of an appropriate sea transport service to the charterer or shipper. Human resources comprise the office (shore) personnel, the master and the ship's crew. The relations of the master/crew with the charterers must be excellent, especially in the case of time charters where the charterer has the commercial employment of the vessel. On the contrary, for a vessel operating in the liner market no remarkable relations of the crew with the shippers can be developed, as there are too many shippers in each voyage leg, so many port calls and so fast "transit" and "turn-around" times of the containerships. However, liner operator–shipper relationship is enforced by the implementation of EDI systems which enables the shipper to monitor his cargo from loading to delivery. Office personnel and ship's crew must be qualified both in their professional skills and experience, so that the smooth operation of the vessel and its efficiency are achieved. The shipowning company must abide by the relevant codes, standards or instructions recommended by the international maritime organisations, the relevant state authorities and the registers (classification societies). The above-mentioned standards concern professional training of the seamen, in order that their skills meet the required certificates, safety regulations and recent business developments in the industry. Characteristic examples of people strategies are the programmes of continuous shore personnel and crew training. According to these strategies, a company's office personnel and crew participate in training programmes in order to be aware of new developments in the world shipping industry, for example in fields of interest, such as charter's legal framework, cargo handling and port customs, master's duties etc. Some big shipping companies maintain their own training centres for the continuous training of their personnel and crew.

5. *Place – Ports:* This tool of marketing mix includes the geographical position of the ship in comparison to the geographical position of the cargo to be transported, the ports of loading and unloading in a voyage charter, the ports of delivery and redelivery of the vessel in a time charter, the geographical and commercial trading limits of the ship etc. In case of a time charter engagement the charterers wish to employ vessels without trading and geographical limits. Instead of that, the time charterparty usually specifies that the vessel must be used only within a certain geographical area and that the charterers have the right of breaching the trading limits only by paying an extra insurance premium and after shipowners' consent. Where a charterparty states that loss of time caused by average (i.e. damage) due to a breach of International Navigating Limits is to be for the charterer's account, this provision refers not only to the time lost on passage due to average but also to the time wasted by the shipowner while the damage is being repaired. A place strategy includes the policy of operating vessels with minimum possible trading and geographical limits, for example the operation of

well-designed, well-built and well-maintained ice-class tankers which can be navigated through sea ice in environmentally sensitive or dangerous trading areas. Leading tanker companies follow this example by investing in large and modern fleets of tankers, with advanced specifications, which can meet the strict legislations of the environmentally sensitive regions and be employed at any sea, almost without any trading and geographical restrictions, therefore gaining a sustainable competitive edge in the market. Moreover, a place strategy concerns of course the case where a shipowner, who charters his vessel in the spot market, strategically selects a specific port rotation or a geographical area which positions optimally his vessel for the next voyage or the next charter, or even is safer for vessel's trading than another geographical option.

6. *Promotion:* Distribution of a shipping service cannot take place in the same way that a product is distributed, since in the case of services there is nothing tangible to be delivered. Promotion represents the various actions the shipping company undertakes in order to propagate to the charterers/shippers the advantages of its fleet and to convince them to fix a charter (in bulk shipping) or make a cargo booking (in liner shipping). This tool of shipping marketing mix should emphasise the benefits of specific services which are provided. The possible benefits will be evaluated by the charterer or the shipper. The charterer will decide if he wishes to commence negotiations with the shipowning company by making an official proposal (firm offer) to the shipowner. The shipper will decide which liner company he chooses to transport his cargo. The promotion of benefits can be made through advertising, personal contacts, shipping press, participation in exhibitions etc. Advertising is considered one of the main factors of non-price competition. Maritime transport services are considered to be experience-based, namely their characteristics are made known after the execution of a charter. Advertising can provide charterers or shippers – who may not have a previous professional co-operation with the shipping enterprise – with the necessary information, in order to sign a chartering or shipping agreement with the company. Advertising operates at three levels; it informs, persuades and reinforces. In order to inform, advertising normally relates to the promotion of new or existing transportation services offered by vessels of the company. There is also the public relations side of advertising, which includes media relations and exhibitions. However, it must be emphasised that advertising is a highly developed marketing tool throughout the liner market, but instead this is not the case for bulk markets, where only the biggest companies may follow such strategies. This divergence is due to the nature of the service provided and the structure of each market. Liner companies "sell" quality-oriented shipping services (speed, reliability, accuracy, regularity, safety of transport etc.) to a

wide spectrum of shippers worldwide. Bulk companies "sell" safety-oriented (for tankers) or cost-oriented (for bulkers) shipping services to far fewer charterers and shippers. Instead of advertising, bulk companies promote themselves through personal contacts and build their reputation mainly on two critical factors: (a) the increased size of operated modern fleets, which offers better capabilities for economies of scale, broader geographical coverage and scope for improved freight negotiations; and/or (b) the operational efficiency of the fleet, irrespective of the number of operated vessels. Nowadays, it goes without saying that all shipping companies should have integrated promotion programmes, possibly including a web page on the Internet, brochures, advertisements in the shipping press, participation at maritime exhibitions and regular personal contacts.

7. *Physical Evidence – Ship:* This is the physical environment in which the service is provided, i.e. the ship and its characteristics such as name, year and country of shipbuilding, flag, class, cargo capacity, service speed, draught, width, length, cargo-handling equipment, number and type of holds, fuel consumption, etc. Before a charterparty is signed between the charterer and the shipowner for a carriage of goods by sea, the shipowner must check the ship's suitability for fulfilling the transportation, which is designated by the term "seaworthiness". The suitability of the vessel for seaway (*seaworthiness*) and the suitability of the ship to receive and carry cargo (*cargoworthiness*) are related terms. The obligation of the shipowner to provide a seaworthy ship includes obligations concerning all sections of the vessel and engine, the supplies and spares, as well as crewing. The shipowner is obliged to provide a ship built, equipped, supplied and manned in such a manner, as to carry the cargo safely to its destination and to overcome the ordinary perils of the seas. The charterers' satisfaction from the ship's good performance will lead to a possible repetition of the charter and a wider co-operation between the shipowner and the charterer. In liner shipping the concept of seaworthiness is similar to that described above. Characteristic examples of physical evidence strategies concern the improvement of vessels' performance and efficiency, the company's compliance to the international regulations in respect of vessel's design, management and maintenance of fleet etc.

8. *Paperless Trade:* A basic tool that the shipping enterprise must use in order to achieve its marketing objectives is called "paperless trade" and constitutes the *eighth "P" of the shipping marketing mix*.[25] The global character of the shipping industry means ships operation requires vigilant follow-up on a 24-hour basis. In addition, the shipping business

---

25 Plomaritou, E. (2005) *Marketing of Shipping Companies as a Tool for Improvement of Chartering Policy. A Comparative Analysis of Marketing Implementation in Bulk and Liner Shipping Companies Worldwide and in Greece: A Case Study in Containership Market and Tanker Market* (PhD Thesis, University of Piraeus, Greece).

Figure 5.3 The Tools of Shipping Marketing Mix ("8 Ps")

Source: Plomaritou, E. (2008) *Marketing of Shipping Companies: A Tool for Improvement of Chartering Policy* (Athens, Stamoulis Publications, p. 86).

is characterised by the voluminous and time-consuming exchange of documents. Shipping companies, in order to respond fully to the demands of the competitive shipping market, use modern electronic communication means by which time, cost and effort are saved and service quality is improved. Electronic trade is a combination of business activity and practices, which allows the accomplishment of commercial processes via electronic means. Electronic methods are applied to a broad field of shipping activities, which includes charterparty editing and chartering negotiation (e.g. the BIMCO IDEA electronic system of drafting charterparty clauses, structuring charterparties and facilitating negotiations), issuance of shipping documents (e.g. bills of lading), follow-up of the ship's movements, communication between ship – office – charterer, flow of information, advertising of sea transport services, support of the client (charterer/shipper), as well as electronic payments. Enterprises which use electronic paperless trade gain functional and strategic advantages, whilst improving their competitiveness and status. By using an electronic data interchange system, the shipping company provides improved high-quality services to its clients, maintains better business relations with them and gains a competitive advantage in the shipping market. Paperless trade was initially adopted in liner shipping in the 1990s, whilst bulk shipping companies followed in the 2000s.

5.5.2 Differentiation and positioning strategies

During the marketing planning stage, special emphasis should be given on designing the differentiation and positioning strategies for gaining competitive advantage. Once the target-market[26] is selected, successful shipping firms establish a differentiation strategy, which sets them apart from competitors in their clients' eyes. Success through differentiation demands skills that completely diverge from those needed for cost leadership. The differentiator wins by offering a transportation service that is unique or superior to competitors. Shipping companies aim to achieve superior performance by adding value to the sea transport services. One way in which firms seek to gain an advantage over their competitors is by providing greater quality service. Added value can also be achieved by offering completely new services which are not yet available from competitors, by modifying existing services or by making them more easily available to customers in order to gain a competitive advantage.[27] The shipping company can differentiate its offer from that of its competitors through the following *differentiation approaches*[28]:

- *Qualitative Differentiation:* According to charterers and shippers, the quality of services offered includes mainly the reliability, frequency, flexibility, immediacy and speed of service, as well as the safe carriage of goods by sea. A shipping enterprise can achieve a qualitative differentiation with the offer of special services to its client – charterer or shipper – in comparison to the package of benefits that its competitors offer. In this framework, this is more important and frequent in the liner market than in the bulk market. In bulk shipping, qualitative differentiation is almost identical to the operational supremacy, adequate fleet size with modern vessels, market status and character of the shipowner.

- *Geographical Differentiation:* The enterprise may achieve geographical differentiation with its ability to obtain a competitive advantage arising from a geographical parameter. An example of geographical differentiation is the case of a liner operator, who possesses and operates a modern fleet of containerships, managing the largest route network and serving the needs of trade worldwide. This is a strategy followed by the leading companies of the liner market. Furthermore, geographical differentiation may be achieved even by a smaller niche liner operator which focuses on a specific geographical region, for example a Latin America or an intra-Asian or a Mediterranean Sea liner service. Even in bulk shipping, there are ship operators trading their vessels in specific

---

26 The target-market is the sum of charterers/shippers that have the same transportation needs, they express eagerness in buying the transport services and show a high degree of buying force.

27 Plomaritou, E., Goulielmos, A. (2014) "The Shipping Marketing Strategies within the Framework of Complexity Theory" *British Journal of Economics, Management & Trade* Vol. 4, Issue 7, pp. 1128–1142.

28 Plomaritou, E. (2017) *Marketing Strategy of Shipping Companies* (London, Lloyd's Maritime Academy, Module 7 of Distance Learning Course "Diploma in Maritime Business Management").

geographical regions, e.g. dry bulk operators which activate their fleet either in the Atlantic or the Pacific basin.

- *Personnel and Crew Differentiation:* In this case the enterprise excels by employing the appropriately trained personnel and crew at company's offices and vessels. A shipping company may achieve that by providing crew with continuous development at its training and simulation centres.

- *Image Differentiation:* This is achieved by maintaining the best possible profile of the enterprise to the bankers, insurers, suppliers, brokers and agents, charterers and shippers or even investors and personnel (ashore and onboard). To build a very good image in the market possibly needs years; however it may be ruined in just a few minutes, either from an operational mistake (e.g. an accident causing heavy oil pollution to the environment) or from a strategic error. This is the case in tanker and gas carrier markets in particular, as the environmental risk is higher than in other sectors. Image should be matched with reality, in the sense that a good reputation is substantiated by vessels' operational efficiency and excellence, quality services provided to the customer, as well as integrity and character of the shipowner.

The more effective an enterprise is in differentiating its transportation services from competitors, the greater its power is. The quality, personnel/crew, image and geographical differentiation aim to reduce the competition on freight rates, even if in any case price differentiation does not apply largely in shipping companies.

A shipping company can realistically aim to be leader or competitively strong enough in one of the above-mentioned fields, but not in all at the same time. It therefore enforces those strengths, which will give it a differential performance advantage in one of these benefit areas. A characteristic of the differentiation strategy of a shipping company is that innovation of a sea transport service cannot be easily copied due to the high capital cost of vessels. So, a shipping company seeking to differentiate by innovation should not find its innovatory service copied quickly by competitors.

The *positioning strategy* refers to the selection of differential advantage, which defines how the company will compete with rivals in its target segment(s). In this way, positioning strategy designates what the company is in relation to its competitors. The appropriateness and effectiveness of the positioning strategy is the major determinant of business growth and profit performance. The positioning process of a shipping company includes the following stages[29]:

- First, the shipping company spots the possible differences in its sea transport services compared to other competitive enterprises.

---

29 Plomaritou, E. (2017) *Marketing Strategy of Shipping Companies* (London, Lloyd's Maritime Academy, Module 7 of Distance Learning Course "Diploma in Maritime Business Management").

- Second, the shipping company selects the most important differences leading to a comparative advantage over its competitors. Some firms prefer the selection of only one competitive advantage – and no more – in the target market.
- Finally, the company shows and promotes that difference within its target market.

Differentiation and positioning strategies play a vital role in improving the chartering policy of a shipping company, creating a competitive advantage, providing added-value transport services, satisfying the charterers' and shippers' needs in a more efficient way than that of competitors and finally maximising the profitability of the company.

CHAPTER 6

Sales contract, carriage of goods by sea and bill of lading

Up to this point, analysis has been focused primarily on the presentation of the charter/freight markets, the nature of chartering business and the critical managerial or practical perspectives. Chartering is a part of commercial management of ships, which, however, cannot exist by itself. The operative force is always a sales contract of goods and subsequently the need for sea transport. First, there is a sale/purchase of merchandise; second, a need for sea transport; and third, a need for chartering a vessel. Before proceeding to the "core" chartering matters, this chapter intends to show the general context, by investigating how chartering business is related with the international laws and practices of sales of goods and their transport by sea. Therefore, significant subjects are examined, such as: the importance of the sales contract; Incoterms® 2010 rules, a practical, widely recognised set of internationally accepted trade terms, defining by whom and how sea transport is organised, performed and paid for; the contractual relations among sellers and buyers of goods and sea carriers; the charterparty and the bill of lading as main contracts of sea carriage; the documentary letter of credit as the most commonly used method of payment for exports; the carriage of goods by sea international cargo conventions; the critical functions of bills of lading or other similar transport documents; the carrier's liability for damage to or loss of goods; and finally how major risks are insured.

6.1 General remarks

It is supposed that a buyer in Holland wishes to buy some pieces of machinery from a manufacturer in Singapore. When making their sales/purchase contract the parties will consider a number of critical questions: When will property of the goods pass from the seller to the buyer? When will risk for the goods is transferred? Who is responsible to arrange and pay for the transportation and the insurance of the goods? What is the financing scheme of the sale? By what date should the goods be delivered or actually reach the buyer? When and how will payment be made? From this example it is inferred that the sales contract is the "legal instrument" which induces a set of legal relations. The sales contract is thus decisive not only for the relation between the seller and the buyer of goods, but also for a number of ancillary reasons; it sets out rules for the price determination, the payment methods (e.g. documentary letters of credit), as well as principles for delivery of cargo and risk allocation which affect transportation and insurance issues, etc. Several parties may be involved in such international transactions and, depending on the agreed distribution of risks and costs in the sales contract, a number of duties will be put on the seller and the buyer, respectively, who will then enter into the various ancillary agreements, for example the vessel charter agreement or the contract of cargo carriage, the insurance contract or a letter of credit. Thus, the contractual relations differ and there is a need for co-ordinating the respective rights and obligations of the various parties involved in the different transactions and contracts. Even if the sales contract is practically decisive for the ancillary contracts, all of them are separate from each other and are governed by different legal jurisdictions.

6.2 The sales contract as the basic agreement in the export transaction

The sales contract stipulates the object of the agreement (namely the sale and purchase of the goods), the price, the method, the terms and the conditions of payment, the means of transport and the delivery, the risk distribution between the parties which in turn affects also the insurance of goods, the financing of the purchase, etc. Purely domestic sales are regulated by national laws, but the international sale transactions are mostly governed by the rules of a widely accepted convention, known as the *"United Nations Convention on Contracts for the International Sale of Goods"* (*abbrev.* *"CISG"* or the *"Vienna Convention"* in *short*) and developed by the United Nations Commission on International Trade Law (UNCITRAL) in Vienna in 1980. This is a treaty providing a uniform international sales law, being adopted by a large number of countries which account for a significant proportion of world trade. In this sense there has been a harmonisation in this particular area of law. The UK, India, Hong Kong, Taiwan and South Africa were the major trading countries which had not ratified the CISG convention as per 2016.[1]

The sales contract sets out the framework of the sale, including the type of goods, the quantity, the time of delivery, the price etc. The sales contract deals also with the related contracts, e.g. the agreements on financing, insurance and transport. Some of the principal questions which arise in connection with the sales contract are answered in the so-called *transport* or *delivery clause*, in which the parties agree on the apportionment of the risks and expenses involved in the transportation of the goods. Within this context, internationally accepted rules called "Incoterms" have been established and may be used to facilitate the commercial practice, the cost allocation and risk transfer of the sale transactions. For example, the parties may agree to follow either an FOB or a CIF or another Incoterms rule in a cargo sale (see analytically section 6.3 for Incoterms® 2010 rules). However, such clauses do not directly regulate the payment terms and conditions, that is, when, where and how payment is going to be effected or the way the collection of money is secured by the seller.

---

1 www.uncitral.org/uncitral/en/uncitral_texts/sale_goods/1980CISG.html (accessed 11 June 2017).

Many difficulties and disputes that arise in international trade law and practice may be explained by a lack of synchronisation between sales contracts, financing contracts, contracts of carriage and insurance terms and conditions. In practice, it is rather inconceivable that all parties involved in the different connected transactions have knowledge of all the other related transactions, but normally they only know in detail about their own contracts. However, it is essential that all the parties involved make sure from the beginning that, as far as practically possible, their various contracts are designed in such a way that the delivery from the seller to the buyer can be performed without too many problems occurring. Therefore, the sales contract may be either sufficiently wide to allow for various alternatives to be followed, or narrow enough since it is already clear that there will have to be a particular solution. For example, a payment clause in a sales contract could only call for payment to be made by a letter of credit, or specifically state that "*an irrevocable letter of credit to be opened by X bank not later than Y day and valid for a period up to and including Z day and available for payment against the presentation of the following documents: clean bills of lading, invoice, insurance documents*". This being said, it has to be reiterated that the various contracts are separate and it is rare that any of the different contractual parties, except the seller and the buyer, has an overall view of the basic contract and the ancillary ones.

6.3 Incoterms® rules[2]

Most legal systems contain legislation dealing with the sales of goods or provisions concerning the relationship between the seller and the buyer, although in practice the parties normally regulate their relationship by agreement. Different legal systems may deal with similar questions in slightly different ways. This has led to certain difficulties in international trade, requiring special efforts to harmonise the sales law provisions of different countries. As mentioned, in the field of sales law a great effort has been made to improve harmonisation through the international sales convention called CISG and issued in 1980, the rules of which having been adopted by a large number of countries – with the exception of the UK and a few other major nations.

Further to that, another practically important set of rules which have a considerable impact on the passing of risk between the seller and the buyer of goods are the *Incoterms® rules*, which determine the meaning and effects of certain transport clauses used in international trade (e.g. FOB, CIF etc.). Incoterms definitions are published by the International Chamber of Commerce (ICC). Their first version dated back in the 1930s, while the latest version was published in 2010, thus it is known as "Incoterms® 2010 rules". Since the 1990s, the last revisions of the Incoterms rules were gradually amended to bring them in line with modern transportation methods and to mirror new transportation risks. For example, the traditional FOB and CIF Incoterms® concepts had to adapt to the modern cargo

---

2 "Incoterms" is a trademark of the International Chamber of Commerce (ICC). Available on www.iccwbo.org.

equipment traffic and new terms were created to reflect those changes (e.g. the "Free Carrier – named destination" Incoterms® rule). The Incoterms® rules were revised, restructured, expanded and divided over time. Some supplementary clauses were introduced, other terms were deleted as outdated and Incoterms® rules were grouped into C, D, E and F clauses according to their meaning and commercial practice. These will be explained further in section 6.3.2.

6.3.1 Risk, cost and liability distribution in the transport chain

Incoterms® rules define by whom and also how the sea transport will be organised, performed and paid for. FOB and CIF are still probably the most used traditional Incoterms clauses in bulk transportation. Under traditional FOB terms, the buyer of the goods will basically be organising the sea transport and acting as charterer of the ship, thus being the counterpart of the shipowner and a signing party to the charterparty in the open bulk market or to the booking note in the liner market. Besides, in such a case the buyer may also be acting as the shipper of the cargo to the bill of lading. On the contrary, when CIF terms are agreed in the sales contract, the seller of the goods plays the above-mentioned roles.

At this point it should be cleared out that a charterparty (C/P) in the bulk market or a booking note (B/N) in the liner market, in either case supplemented by a bill of lading (B/L), are the principal contracts which cover the part of the carriage of goods by sea following a cargo sale transaction. In charterparties the division of responsibilities and costs between the shipowner and the charterer (the "contracting parties") is often well defined and the points related to "the passing of the risk and costs" are very clearly set out. Although the relevant terms and their differences (e.g. between FIO and liner terms in deciding the allocation of cargo-handling costs) are discussed below in section 11.6 and in the glossary, some major points are briefly introduced here.

In the bulk market the individual voyage charterparty is often based on "fio terms" (free in and out) or similar, whereas in liner trades the so-called "liner terms" are frequently used, though there are occasions when full liner terms (synonym: "gross terms") may also apply in open market fixtures. Under FIO terms the charterers are organising and paying for the loading and discharging of the goods, and the charterers also guarantee the cargo-handling operation during the time the ship spends in port (see chapter 15 for analysis). On the contrary, traditional "liner terms" means that the owner will be organising and paying for cargo handling; this service is often extended by mutual agreement to cover a range of activities on the shore side. Under liner terms the owners will bear the risk and responsibility for the duration of the ship's stay in port, but owners may request that charterers (shippers) accept FAC ("fast as can") terms, meaning that cargo must be delivered alongside for loading, received alongside on discharge as fast as the vessel can actually receive onboard, take out from the holds. Finally, in regular liner services shipowners (carriers) may undertake a full door-to-door intermodal transport, from the warehouse of the seller to the warehouse of the buyer. All the above are illustrated in Figure 6.1.

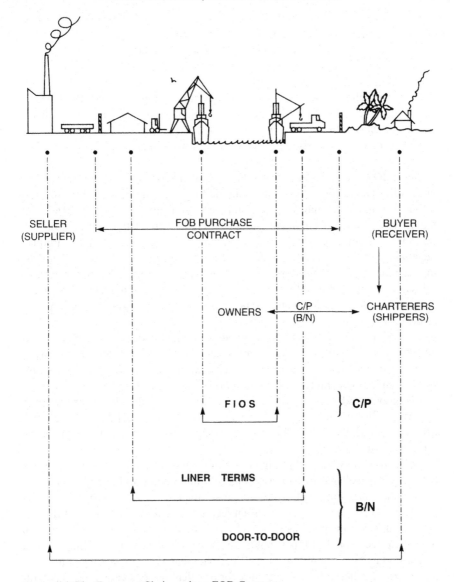

Figure 6.1 The Transport Chain under a FOB Contract

Every *export transaction* gives rise to several *relationships*, namely between:

- the seller and the buyer of cargo, which is governed by the *sales contract*;
- the seller or the buyer of cargo (depending on the agreement of the sales contract) and the carrier, which is governed by the contract of carriage and more specifically by the *charterparty* in the open or bulk market,

173

the *booking note* in the liner market and is supplemented in either case by the *bill of lading* or similar (e.g. *waybill*);

- the seller or the buyer of cargo (depending on the agreement of the sales contract) and the insurance underwriter, which is governed by the *cargo insurance policy*;
- the seller or the buyer of cargo (depending on the agreement of the sales contract) and the financier/bank, which is governed by the *financing contract*, the *documentary credit* etc.
- one of these parties and other ancillary suppliers of service.

Depending on the contractual relationship, the parties are also referred to under different headings; for example in the cargo carriage relationship the seller or buyer of the cargo may appear as shipper or consignee contracting to a bill of lading, or as charterer contracting to a charterparty; in a letter of credit transaction the buyer of cargo will be the instructing party and the seller of cargo the beneficiary, etc. This means that the various contracting parties may be involved in different ways in the different contractual relations, e.g. the seller in a cargo sales agreement may also be the charterer in a ship charter agreement, a beneficiary under a letter of credit and the insured party under a cargo insurance policy as the case may be.

The risk of damage to or loss of goods or the delay damages may thus pass through several levels. Basically, there is a distribution of costs and risks between the *seller* and the *buyer*, but also the other relationships contain risk allocations. Even if under the contract of sale and in relation to the seller the buyer is liable for the goods sold, he may in turn claim damages from the *carrier* or the *cargo underwriter* in case of delay, loss or damage to the goods, depending on the risk distribution formula applied and following applicable contractual provisions and relevant legal rules.

The parties may understand their positions and their relationships in different ways. The seller is often not willing to grant a credit to the buyer unless he knows and trusts him well or has adequate financial security. When goods are sold within a country, a seller will often regard the goods he sells as a sufficiently good security for the purchase price. He will not wish to lose possession of them until the price is paid. If this is not possible, he will seek to retain some interest in the goods which he might then sell if payment fails. In international sales, however, the seller in this respect may for practical reasons be in a less favourable position. Security interests in the goods may be of little value to a seller who might have to try to enforce a right over property several thousands of miles away in another jurisdiction. He often feels that he must have rights which are more predictable and more easily accessible. Thus, a purchase on terms, such as cash on delivery (COD) prevents the buyer from getting delivery of the goods before he has paid – often through a bank – but it does not protect the seller from expenses for sending the goods, unless payment for such costs is secured. This may be done through advance payment. The buyer, in his turn, is not in a very much better position if he is asked to pay before the goods have even been sent and, even worse, when they have been sent, if they do not conform to the terms and conditions of the sales contract. Therefore, the buyer is often not willing to effect payment before delivery of goods has taken place.

International commerce has over the years worked out a number of measures to mitigate such trading risks. To that effect, an important role has been played by the use of the documents exchanged in international sales transactions, the evolution and adjustment of Incoterms® rules and the payment by documentary letters of credit. When the seller has fulfilled his obligations under the sales contract, he is entitled to be paid upon the presentation of the documents involved. At this point the buyer, in his turn, should have made financial arrangements so that he can meet this requirement. The procedure may vary but, in international trade, payment by letter of credit (see below, section 6.4) is important to create a balance of security interest for the seller and buyer.

Figure 6.2 illustrates an example of an international sale transaction between a Belgian seller based in Liege and a British buyer based in Leeds. Depending on the agreement and the situation, a sales contract may involve various transport stages, transport clauses, different involved parties and several contractual relations.

6.3.2 Incoterms® 2010 rules

Incoterms® 2010 rules is the eighth set of pre-defined international contract terms published by the International Chamber of Commerce (ICC), with the first set having been published in 1936. In an effort to reflect the current commercial practice in the latest version, some of the clauses were amended and others were deleted or replaced. Incoterms® 2010 rules contain 11 terms, slightly fewer than the 13 defined by Incoterms® 2000 rules. Four rules of the 2000 version have been replaced by two new rules in the 2010 set.

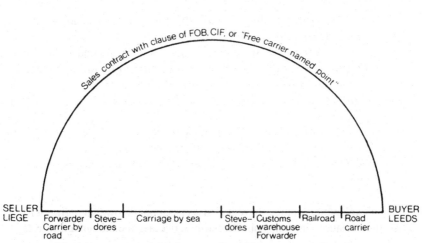

The sales contract may involve several underlying contractual relations.

Figure 6.2 Contractual Relations under the Sales Contract

In the revisions made in 1990 and 2000, the rules had been divided into four categories, the C, D, E and F groups, according to the criterion of the increasing responsibility and risk of the seller (the one E term had the least responsibility for the seller, growing to F, C and D terms accordingly). However, in the latest edition the 11 pre-defined terms are subdivided only into two categories based on the method of transport delivery. This means that seven of the rules may apply at all modes of transport, while the other four are applicable only to cargo sales that solely involve transportation by water, where the condition of the goods can be verified at the point of loading on board the ship. Therefore, those four terms are not able to be used for containerised freight, other combined transport methods, or for transport by road, rail or air.

It is important that the sales agreement explicitly refers to the Incoterms® rules of a certain year of publication, since otherwise a problem may occur with respect to which set or specific clause shall apply. The parties should be aware of the differences between the different versions. It may be mentioned that the FOB and the CIF Incoterms® rules are traditionally the most common ones in international sales, but they are currently, to a large extent, confined to the sale of bulk products. For container trades CPT and FCA Incoterms® rules should be used instead. In present sales contracts reference should be made to the latest edition of Incoterms® 2010 rules, unless the parties intend another version to apply.

Among Incoterms® rules, there are certain provisions that have a special meaning – some of the more important ones are defined below[3]:

- *Delivery:* The point in the transaction where the risk of loss or damage to the goods is transferred from the seller to the buyer.
- *Arrival:* The point named in the Incoterms® rule up to which carriage has been paid.
- *Free:* Seller has an obligation to deliver the goods to a named place for transfer to a carrier.
- *Carrier:* Any person who, in a contract of carriage, undertakes to perform or to procure the performance of transport by rail, road, air, sea, inland waterway or by a combination of such modes.
- *Freight forwarder:* A firm that makes or assists in the making of shipping arrangements.
- *Terminal:* Any place, whether covered or not, such as a dock, warehouse, container yard or road, rail or air cargo terminal.
- *To clear for export:* To file shipper's export declaration and get export permit.

A brief explanation of the different clauses is set out below, but parties wishing to use these clauses in their commercial practice are recommended to refer to

---

3 Mayer, R.A. (2013) *International Business Law: Text, Cases and Readings* (Harlow, 6th edition, Pearson).

the official Incoterms® definitions commentary, published by ICC.[4] Some of the clauses are no longer part of the Incoterms® 2010 rules, but may still have some practical importance; thus they are also discussed.

6.3.2.1 EXW (Ex Works)
Incoterms® 2010 rule applying to any mode of transport. "Ex works" means that the seller's only responsibility is to make the goods available at his premises or at another named place (i.e. works, factory, warehouse). In particular, the seller is not responsible for loading the goods onto the vehicle provided by the buyer, unless otherwise agreed, nor does he need to clear the goods for export, where such clearance is applicable. The buyer bears the full cost and risk involved in bringing the goods from there to the desired destination. This term thus represents the minimum obligation for the seller.

6.3.2.2 FCA (Free Carrier – Named Point)
Incoterms® 2010 rule applying to any mode of transport. This term has been designed to meet the requirements of modern transport, particularly such "multi-modal" transport as container or ro/ro traffic by trailers and ferries. It is based on the same main principle as FOB, except that the seller fulfils his obligations when he delivers the goods into the custody of the carrier at the named point. The parties are advised to specify as clearly as possible the point within the named place of delivery, as the risk passes to the buyer at that point. If no precise point can be stipulated at the time of the contract of sale, the parties should refer to the place or range where the carrier should take the goods into his charge. The risk of loss or damage to the goods is transferred from seller to buyer at that time and not at the ship's rail. When the seller has to furnish a bill of lading, waybill or carrier's receipt, he duly fulfils this obligation by presenting such a document issued by a person so defined.

6.3.2.3 FAS (Free Alongside Ship)
Incoterms® 2010 rule applying only to sea and inland waterway transport. Under this term the seller's obligations are fulfilled when the goods have been placed alongside the ship on the quay or in lighters nominated by the buyer at the named port of shipment. This means that the buyer has to bear all costs and risks of loss or damage to the goods from that moment. It should be noted that, unlike FOB, the term FAS requires the buyer to clear the goods for export.

6.3.2.4 FOB (Free on Board)
Incoterms® 2010 rule applying only to sea and inland waterway transport. The goods are placed on board a ship by the seller at a port of shipment nominated by the buyer at the sales contract. The risk of loss or damage to the goods is transferred from the seller to the buyer when the goods pass the ship's rail, and the

---

4 International Chamber of Commerce *The Incoterms® Rules* (www.iccwbo.org, accessed 1 January 2017).

buyer bears all costs from that moment onwards. A particular variation is "FOB airport", where the seller fulfils his obligations by delivering the goods to the air carrier at the airport of departure.

6.3.2.5 CFR (Cost and Freight)
Incoterms® 2010 rule applying only to sea and inland waterway transport. The seller must pay the costs and freight necessary to bring the goods to the named destination, but the risk of loss or damage to the goods, as well as of any cost increases, is transferred from the seller to the buyer when the goods pass the ship's rail in the port of shipment.

6.3.2.6 CIF (Cost, Insurance and Freight)
Incoterms® 2010 rule applying only to sea and inland waterway transport. This term is basically the same as CFR but with the addition that the seller has to procure marine insurance against the risk of loss or damage to the goods during the carriage. The seller contracts with the insurer and pays the insurance premium. Under CIF the seller is required to obtain insurance only on minimum cover. Should the buyer wish to have more insurance protection, it will need either to agree it as much expressly with the seller or to make its own extra insurance arrangements.

6.3.2.7 CPT (Freight or Carriage Paid to – Named Place)
Incoterms® 2010 rule applying to any mode of transport. Like CFR, "freight or carriage paid to" means that the seller contracts and pays the freight for the carriage of the goods to the agreed destination (nominated by the seller). However, the risk of loss or damage to the goods, as well as of any cost increases, is transferred from the seller to the buyer when the goods have been delivered into the custody of the first carrier and not at the ship's rail. It can be used for all modes of transport including multi-modal operations and container or ro/ro traffic by trailers and ferries. When the seller has to furnish a bill of lading, waybill or carrier's receipt, he duly fulfils this obligation by presenting such a document issued by the person with whom he has contracted for carriage to the named destination.

6.3.2.8 CIP (Freight or Carriage and Insurance Paid to – Named Place)
Incoterms® 2010 rule applying to any mode of transport. This term is the same as "freight or carriage paid to", but with the addition that the seller has to procure transport insurance against the risk of loss or damage to the goods during the carriage. The seller contracts with the insurer and pays the insurance premium, having also a minimum cover obligation.

6.3.2.9 DAF (Delivered at Frontier)
Incoterms® 2000 rule. "Delivered at frontier" means that the seller's obligations are fulfilled when the goods have arrived at the frontier – but before "the customs border" – of the country named in the sales contract. The term is primarily intended to be used when goods are to be carried by rail or road, but it may be

used irrespective of the mode of transport. *Note that this clause is no longer a part of the current Incoterms® definitions.*

6.3.2.10 DAP (Delivered at Place)

Incoterms® 2010 rule applying to any mode of transport. The seller delivers when the goods are placed at the disposal of the buyer on the arriving means of transport ready for unloading at a named place of destination. The seller bears all risks involved in bringing the goods to the named place and then are taken over by the buyer.

6.3.2.11 DAT (Delivered at Terminal)

Incoterms® 2010 rule applying to any mode of transport. Similar to DAP, but the seller delivers when the goods, once unloaded from the arriving means of transport, are placed at the disposal of the buyer at a named terminal at the named port or place of destination. The seller bears all risks involved in bringing the goods to and unloading them at the terminal at the named port or place of destination.

6.3.2.12 DES (Delivered ex Ship)

Incoterms® 2000 rule. The seller makes the goods available to the buyer on board the ship at the destination named in the sales contract. The seller has to bear the full cost and risk involved in bringing the goods there. *Note that this clause is no longer a part of the current Incoterms® definitions.*

6.3.2.13 DEQ (Delivered ex Quay)

Incoterms® 2000 rule. The seller makes the goods available to the buyer on the quay (wharf) at the destination named in the sales contract. The seller has to bear the full cost and risk involved in bringing the goods there.

There are two "ex quay" contracts in use, namely *"ex quay (duty paid)"*, and *"ex quay (duties on buyer's account)"*, in which the liability to clear the goods for import are to be met by the buyer instead of by the seller. Parties are recommended always to use the full descriptions of these terms, namely "ex quay (duty paid)" or "ex quay (duties on buyer's account)", or else there may be uncertainty as to who is to be responsible for the liability to clear the goods for import. *Note that this clause is no longer a part of the current Incoterms® definitions.*

6.3.2.14 DDU (Delivered Duty Unpaid) and DDP (Delivered Duty Paid)

The former is an Incoterms® 2000 rule and the latter is an Incoterms® 2010 rule applying to any mode of transport. While the term "ex works" signifies the seller's minimum obligation, the term "delivered duty paid" followed by words naming the buyer's premises denotes the other extreme; the seller's maximum obligation. The seller delivers when the goods are placed at the disposal of the buyer, cleared for import on the arriving means of transport ready for unloading at the named place of destination. The seller bears all the costs and risks involved in bringing the goods to the place of destination and has an obligation to clear the goods not only for export but also for import, to pay any duty for both export and import and to carry out all customs formalities. If the parties wish that the seller should clear the goods for import but that some of the costs payable upon the import of the goods should be excluded – such as value added tax (VAT) and/or other similar taxes – this should be made clear by adding words to this effect (e.g., *"exclusive of VAT and/or taxes"*). *Note that DDU is no longer a part of the current Incoterms® definitions.*

6.4 Documentary Letter of Credit

6.4.1 Introduction

Except for *cash in advance*, the *export letter of credit (L/C)* gives the seller the highest degree of financial protection among all the commonly used methods of payment for exports. A letter of credit is essentially an undertaking by the buyer's bank that, upon the instructions of the buyer, it will pay the agreed amount to the seller/exporter (the *"beneficiary"*) against the latter's provision and presentation of certain agreed documents, for example the invoice, the transport documents etc. When a letter of credit is issued in an international transaction, at least two banks are normally involved. Typically, one bank is in the buyer's/importer's country, called the *"opening bank"* or the *"issuing bank"*, which undertakes to establish (open) the letter of credit in favour of the beneficiary, forward it to the bank of the beneficiary and commit itself to honour demand drafts drawn by the beneficiary against the amount specified in the L/C if the agreed conditions have been met. The other bank is in the seller's/exporter's country, called the *"advising bank"* or the *"confirming bank"*, which guarantees that the letter of credit established by the importer will be honoured once the conditions therein are fully complied with and undertakes this responsibility on an arrangement called "confirmation".

The value of the letter of credit to the exporter (seller) is that, when presenting the prescribed supporting documents, he is entitled to draw drafts on a bank or to be paid in cash by the bank, and thereby he receives the agreed payment for the goods.

The basis for the whole transaction is the sales agreement. It generally follows from the sales agreement that the goods have to be paid for, they have to be moved from the seller to the buyer and they have to be insured in accordance with the terms and conditions of the purchase agreement. Depending on the transportation clause used (e.g. FOB, CIF or other Incoterms® rules), the seller or the buyer, as the case may be, will be obliged to arrange insurance and carriage and pay for them. If the parties to the sales agreement have agreed that payment shall be made by a letter of credit, a basic precondition of the seller's obligation to deliver the cargo is that the buyer will have arranged with a bank – in a timely manner – to open the documentary credit. This letter of credit shall almost invariably be an *irrevocable letter of credit (ILOC)*. Under an irrevocable letter of credit, the issuing (or confirming) bank undertakes and guarantees to pay the seller, if the documents presented meet the requirements of the letter of credit. An irrevocable letter of credit cannot be cancelled, nor in any way modified, except with the explicit agreement of all parties involved; the buyer, the seller and the issuing bank. For example, the issuing bank does not have the authority by itself to change any of the terms of an ILOC once it is issued. The buyer's financial protection lies in the fact that the bank will pay under the documentary credit only if the seller presents documents which contain information and particulars in conformity with the documentary credit provisions. The general idea is that all documentation will be synchronised (sales agreement, letter of credit, bill of lading and insurance documents).

Because a letter of credit is typically a negotiable document, the issuing bank pays the beneficiary or any bank nominated by the beneficiary. If a letter of credit is transferable, the beneficiary may assign the right to draw to another entity, e.g. a corporate parent or a third party. A *transferable letter of credit* permits the beneficiary of the letter to make some or all of the credit available to another party, thereby creating a secondary beneficiary. The issuing bank must approve the transfer. The carrier's demand for freight may sometimes be secured by the use of a transferable credit, whereby part of the original transferable letter of credit will be available for payment to the carrier under a separate credit.

The sales/purchase agreement is thus the source of several ancillary contracts setting out various obligations to different parties. The buyer will have to arrange an agreed or customary type of documentary credit at the agreed time and with a first-class (or named) bank, and the provisions of the documentary credit must correspond with those agreed in the purchase agreement. The purchase agreement should thus contain an explicit provision in respect of the letter of credit, its type, the time for opening, the expiry date etc. Furthermore, the documentary credit normally makes reference to the *"UCP"* (*Uniform Customs and Practice for Documentary Credits*) to be followed, meaning a universal set of rules on the issuance and use of letters of credit. The UCP standard is utilised by bankers and commercial parties in trade finance almost all over the globe. This standard has been established by the ICC (International Chamber of Commerce) by publishing the first UCP in 1933 and subsequently updating it throughout the years. The latest version is the sixth revision of the rules, which was published in 2006 and is called *"UCP 600"*[5] (see section 6.5.3.3). The UCP rules have gained worldwide recognition and use in the field of international trade.

Very often the payment clause in the sales agreement is not very elaborate and may give rise to a number of problems. It is therefore necessary for the beneficiary, immediately upon receipt of the documentary credit, to make a thorough check of its provisions and reject it if it is not in conformity with the purchase agreement or with his understanding of it.

Under an irrevocable letter of credit the bank instructed by the buyer undertakes to pay the seller when he has performed his part of the deal, which he will do by presenting the documents prescribed in the letter of credit, normally at least

---

5 International Chamber of Commerce *ICC's New Rules on Documentary Credits Now Available* (www.iccwbo.org, accessed 4 December 2006).

an invoice, an insurance policy and, if an ocean carriage is involved, a bill of lading. From the seller's point of view the bill of lading is essential, since it gives him a right to assert and support delivery of the goods at the port of discharge, while from the buyer's side the bill of lading is also important since it contains information related to the goods (type, quantity, loading time, loading condition etc.), which form documentary evidence of the goods bought. The bill of lading "representing" the cargo, together with the insurance policy, is what the buyer pays for. The buyer's bank will take up the documents from the seller, on behalf of the buyer, which can be used as the basis for further transactions or as financial security for the financing bank.

It is thus evident that the documents used in international sales contracts play a significant role both in the relationship between the seller and the buyer, as well as between the carrier and the shipper/consignee. This is particularly true for the *bill of lading* which is often described as a *document of title* and used to enable consignor and consignee to deal in the goods being carried. The carrier is lawfully in possession of the goods of another party, and he is sometimes described in legal terms as a *bailee*. The important role of the bill of lading also means that far-reaching and unpredictable liability exclusions on the part of the carrier may impair the interest of the consignee to receive cargo of the right kind, weight, quantity and condition. This also means that there may be a discrepancy between the description of the goods in the bill of lading and the actual quantity and state of the goods upon delivery to the consignee. Such discrepancy may cause loss to one or more of the parties involved (the bill of lading will be discussed further below in section 6.4.3).

6.4.2 *How the documentary credit works*

The principal advantages connected with the use of a documentary credit are the following:

- the buyer shall not have to make any payment until and unless the goods are shipped and evidence to this effect is produced by means of the documents which are to be surrendered, according to the documentary credit being based on the presentation of a clean shipped bill of lading to the paying bank; and
- the seller is in a position to proceed with the execution of the order and the shipment of the goods as soon as he is in possession of the advice that the documentary credit has been established by the buyer's bank. On the strength of an irrevocable documentary credit, the seller (beneficiary) is assured of payment by the bank, upon due presentation of the documents, provided that they are in conformity with the terms of the letter of credit and the UCP.

The handling of a documentary credit involves a minimum of three, but in many cases four, parties as Figure 6.3 illustrates.

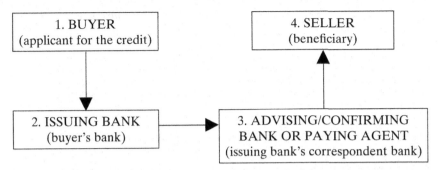

Figure 6.3 Documentary Credit Process

When the parties to a business transaction agree to payment terms involving a documentary credit, the buyer instructs his bank to open a credit in favour of the seller and to advise the latter to this effect either directly or through a correspondent bank (which will be either an advising bank or a confirming bank) in the country of the seller.

When the terms and conditions of the purchase contract provide that payment shall be made by irrevocable documentary credit, the buyer arranges with his bank for the issuance ("opening") of the required credit. The buyer informs its bank of the nature of the transaction and the amount to be paid, gives a brief description of the merchandise to be shipped, specifies the documents required as evidence of shipment and sets an expiration date for the credit. On the basis of this information, the bank issues the irrevocable letter in a form that meets the requirements of the sales contract.

The issuing bank normally uses a correspondent bank, in the exporter's country, and the next step will thus be that the issuing bank instructs its correspondent bank to advise the beneficiary that the letter of credit has been established. The importer's bank may also request its correspondent to *confirm* the letter of credit; such confirmation binds the correspondent bank as well as the importer's bank to honour the credit. Alternatively, the importer's bank may request the correspondent bank itself to open the letter of credit, in which case only the correspondent bank is bound.

It should be pointed out that, instead of using letters of credit, the parties to an export transaction may agree that the buyer arranges for the issuance of an on-demand *guarantee* or a *standby letter of credit* (*SLOC*), which will serve as financial security in case the buyer is defaulting on payment.

6.4.3 Documents required in the documentary credit

The payment clause in the sales contract, depending on the payment method used, may prescribe along the following lines:

"*Payment in the amount of USD . . . shall be made by irrevocable letter of credit opened by X bank not later than Y day. The letter of credit shall be valid until and including Q day. Payment shall be available against beneficiary presenting the following documents:*

(a) Invoice; (b) Marine and War Risk Insurance Policy (Certificate) covering 110% of the CIF value of the goods; (c) Full set of clean "on board" (or "received for shipment") Bills of Lading to order, evidencing shipment from Tokyo to Gothenburg latest 30th June 2017, and marked "Freight paid"; (d) Certificate of Origin in duplicate; (e) Weight Note in duplicate. The letter of credit shall be subject to UCP 600".

The letter of credit should mirror the terms and conditions of the sales agreement. The documentary credit transaction is based on the idea that the bank pays the agreed amount to the beneficiary after it has examined the documents presented and found them to be in accordance with the terms and conditions of the documentary credit and with UCP. The duty to examine the documents submitted to the bank gives to the buyer some certainty that the goods covered by the particular bill of lading are the goods purchased under the contract of sale. If the examining bank is negligent when carrying out the examination, this may have an effect on the buyer (and consequently on the seller/beneficiary for that matter). Following the UCP, the bank therefore has a duty to use due diligence in its examination of the documents presented. It should be emphasised that the bank only examines the documents; the bank is not liable for the actual quality, quantity and condition of the goods, nor the authenticity of the documents, but only for their accuracy, that is that they correspond to the requirements of the letter of credit (see also sections 6.5.3.3 and 6.5.4).

Thus, the bank has a duty to follow carefully the individual instructions as well as the provisions of the UCP, and it may have a certain liberty within strict limits to make the examination at its own discretion in order to avoid problems. Should the bank be negligent, it may be liable in damages to the beneficiary or to the buyer, as the case may be. In cases of fraud the bank will have no liability for having paid the beneficiary unless it is aware of such fraud. Under such circumstances the bank may be relieved of its duty to pay under the documentary credit. During recent years the instances of documentary credit fraud seem to have increased.

6.5 Carriage of goods by sea, transport documents and bill of lading

At this point, emphasis will be given to a crucial part of international transport practice and law; the carriage of goods by sea conventions will be examined and the critical functions of bills of lading and other transport documents will be highlighted. These aspects are closely inter-related and essentially affect chartering and charterparty matters.

6.5.1 Introduction to the carriage of goods by sea international conventions

Over the years, four major sets of international rules have been established to govern the international carriage of goods by sea. As reference will be made to them throughout the following course of the chapter and the rest of the book, a brief description of the sea transport *"cargo conventions"* is introduced below[6] (this is mainly sourced by the Standard P&I Club commentary, further analysis follows in section 6.6.2):

- The *"Hague Rules"* (formally the "International Convention for the Unification of Certain Rules of Law relating to Bills of Lading, and Protocol of Signature") represented the first attempt by the international sea transport community to establish a workable and uniform set of rules governing the carriage of goods by sea and identifying the rights and responsibilities of carriers and owners of cargo. These Rules were published in 1924 following an international convention and were subsequently given the force of law in many maritime countries. It is the first effort to impose minimum standards upon commercial carriers of goods by sea, on an international basis, while previously only common law or national statutes (e.g. the Harter Act in the USA) provided protection to cargo-owners.

- The *"Hague-Visby Rules"* (officially the "Protocol to Amend the International Convention for the Unification of Certain Rules of Law Relating to Bills of Lading") was an agreement to amend the Hague Rules. The first protocol amendment was made in 1968, whilst a second and final protocol was made in 1979. The Visby amendment to the Hague Rules added two main elements; an increase to the limitation of liability amounts and a specific provision of limitation relating to containers. Many countries declined to adopt the Hague-Visby Rules and stayed with the 1924 Hague Rules, whereas some other countries which upgraded to Hague-Visby then did not adopt the 1979 SDR protocol. The *"Carriage of Goods by Sea Act (COGSA) 1971"* incorporated the Hague-Visby Rules into English Law. The subsequent *"Carriage of Goods by Sea Act (COGSA) 1992"*, even though not amending the Hague-Visby Rules, upgraded the status of a bill of lading to be conclusive evidence of receipt for shipment.

- The *"Hamburg Rules"* (officially the "United Nations Convention on the Carriage of Goods by Sea") were adopted in 1978. The Rules sought to redress the apparent imbalance between carriers' and shippers' interests by adopting a new approach to cargo liability where the carrier is held responsible for the loss of or damage to goods whilst in their charge, unless they can prove that all reasonable measures to avoid damage or loss were taken. The convention entered into force in 1992 when the pre-requisite number of countries acceded to the convention. However, these Rules have proved unpopular, as many of the world's trading nations failed to sign up.

- The *"Rotterdam Rules"* (formally, the "United Nations Convention on Contracts for the International Carriage of Goods Wholly or Partly by Sea") is a treaty comprising international rules that revise the legal and

---

6 The Standard Club *Cargo Conventions* (www.standard-club.com, accessed 6 January 2017).

political framework for maritime carriage of goods. The convention attempts to establish a comprehensive, uniform legal regime governing the rights and obligations of shippers, carriers and consignees under a contract for door-to-door shipments that involve international sea transport. The stated aim of the convention is to extend and modernise international rules already in existence and achieve uniformity of admiralty law in the field of maritime carriage, by updating and/or replacing many provisions in the Hague Rules, Hague-Visby Rules and Hamburg Rules, containing among other things some provisions relating to electronic documents. The final draft of the Rules was adopted by UNCITRAL (United Nations Commission on International Trade Law) in 2008. Signatories included countries said to make up 25% of world trade by volume. However, as of October 2015 the Rules had not yet come into force as they had only been ratified by three states – 20 states have to ratify in order for the Rules to come into effect.

6.5.2 Relationship between carriage of goods by sea and other means of transportation

In modern international trade it is increasingly common that the goods are carried not only by sea, but also by an additional mode of transport (this is the idea behind the "Rotterdam Rules"). This occurs on a daily basis with respect to containerised cargo which is carried by sea, but also by road/railway before and/or after the sea transport. The sea leg is often the most significant part (at least the longest one) and in such a case the carriage by road and/or by railway is a carriage which is ancillary to the carriage by sea. There has been a recognised need for uniform rules applicable to the carriage by sea and to the carriage by other modes preceding or following the sea transport. This is due to the fact that in many cases no inspection is carried out with respect to the condition of the containers either at the commencement or at the end of the sea leg. Therefore, it is far simpler and clearer for all parties to the contract of carriage if the condition of the goods is established when the containers are taken in charge by the carrier, whether this takes place inland or in a port or in the place where the goods are handed over by the carrier to the consignee, irrespective of where this takes place.

Ever since efforts were made to introduce a new separate convention on multimodal transport, there has been a problem in finding a common solution which could be acceptable to all the different legal regimes in use. The problem is, among other things, whether the same rules concerning the liability of the carrier should apply throughout the whole transport, or whether particular rules should apply only with respect to that particular part of the combined transport where the damage occurred. One difficulty which has been identified is the method of applying universally agreed evidence rules, i.e. to define exactly where the actual damage took place, how liability is allocated and who is responsible. The second problem comes from the fact that the liability rules are different among ocean, road and railway carriage worldwide. Thus, failing to find an internationally accepted solution in legislation, the involved parties have instead tried to work out practical alternatives. The use of the ICC rules on combined transport or other individual agreements are such practical solutions usually followed.

6.5.3 Bill of lading and other transport documents

The bill of lading is the best known ocean transport document still in use. It has a very long heritage dating back to the old "lex mercatoria" or the "Roman times". The need for the bill of lading arose when merchants first decided that they would no longer accompany their goods during maritime transport but, instead, placed them in the custody of the master for transportation to overseas destinations and then sent the bill of lading by another ship in order for it to reach the buyer, so that he would be able to present it and receive the goods. This sea journey became unnecessary with the development of ever faster mail and courier services.

While the *charterparty (C/P)* is the document which embodies the written form of the vessel's charter agreement, containing the terms and conditions which govern the relationship between the *shipowner* and the *charterer*, the *bill of lading (B/L)* is that transport document which relates to the cargo carriage, governs the relationship between the *shipper* and the *carrier* and it is issued either upon the goods being received for shipment (*received for shipment bill of lading*) or, traditionally, upon their shipment on board the ship (*shipped bill of lading*).

The bill of lading, in practice often filled in by the shipper or by a forwarding agent, is issued and signed by a representative of the carrier/shipowner, for instance the master of the vessel or the owner's agent. Instead of that, the charterparty may sometimes stipulate that the charterer's agent will sign the bill of lading. From the owner's point of view it is then important that the bill of lading shall be in conformity with the mate's receipt and the cargo manifest.

A *mate's receipt* is issued by the mate of the vessel after the cargo has been tallied into the ship by tally clerks. In a charterparty a clause will require the master to sign bills of lading in accordance with mate's receipts. For example, the *NYPE 2015* form, *clause 8(a) "performance of voyages"* (see appendix 6) states that "*Charterers shall perform all cargo handling, including but not limited to loading, stowing, trimming, lashing, securing, dunnaging, unlashing, discharging, and tallying, at their risk and expense, under the supervision of the Master*", while it complements further in *clause 31(a) "bills of lading"* that "*. . . the Master shall sign bills of lading or waybills for cargo as presented in conformity with mates' receipts*". A copy of the "mate's receipt" will be given to the shipowner, and the bill of lading will be given to the shipper. The bill of lading acknowledges that the goods have been "*shipped in apparent good order and condition*" if the "mate's receipt" is clean. Otherwise, comments are transferred to the bill of lading.

The complete list of cargo loaded, as compiled from the bill of lading, forms the *cargo manifest* of the ship issued by the port agent. Customs regulations at most ports require at least one copy of the manifest. Copies of the cargo manifest are also required from stevedores at discharging ports.

The bill of lading is sent to the shipper usually after the goods have been loaded on board the vessel. The shipper, after examining the content of the bill of lading, forwards the original bill of lading to the cargo owner. A properly endorsed original bill of lading is a negotiable instrument carrying the right to demand and have possession of the goods described in it. Provided they have no notice of any other claim to the goods, the agent of the vessel is justified in delivering the goods to the first person who presents the original bill of lading to him.

The cargo owner or his forwarding agent shall, as holder of the bill of lading, present himself to the shipping agent and receive the delivery order and the necessary information regarding the quay and the time where the goods will be discharged. Upon arrival of the goods and after payment of the reception costs and eventually of the freight, the cargo receiver presents the *delivery order* to the person in possession of the goods (i.e. the carrier or a warehouseman), directing that person to deliver the cargo to himself, as being the person named in the order.

In liner trading, where numerous bills of lading are issued, the traditional signature has been increasingly replaced by electronic means, such as facsimile signature, perforated signature, stamp, symbol or any other method of mechanical or electronic authentication.

In general, a bill of lading contains all the information that serves to identify the carriage and the cargo, such as the name of the shipper of the goods, the name of the consignee (if known, but quite frequently the bill of lading will be made out *"to order"* of a person where in such case the document is negotiable and might be pledged as security to a bank which has financed the purchase under a letter of credit), the port of loading, the port of discharge, the name of the ship, a description of the cargo (e.g. in terms of loading marks, description of packages, weight or measurement and contents), the amount of freight, as well as the place and time for payment, etc.

Even in today's modern transportation, the traditional bill of lading is still the most used shipping document in bulk and oil transportation, basically serving three main purposes:

(1) the bill of lading is the *master's confirmation that he has received or shipped on board goods* in a certain quantity and condition;

(2) the bill of lading is (prima facie or conclusive) *evidence of the contract of carriage* between the shipper and the carrier; and

(3) the bill of lading is a *negotiable document of title* enabling the seller, who has shipped the goods for delivery to the buyer, to transfer the right to obtain delivery of the goods to the buyer or the holder of the document.

It is obvious that all three main functions aim to link crucial information and rights deriving from the contract of carriage as well as from the contract of sale, allowing the consignee/receiver to be in a position to collect the cargo at the place of destination.

Transport documents need certain legal qualities in order to meet all the above-mentioned requirements. Such documents which meet all three requirements provide the *holder* with the right to take delivery of the goods and entitle the holder of the documents to dispose of the goods while in transit. They are often considered to be *"documents of title"* as they are *"negotiable documents"* (or at least *"quasi-negotiable"*). This means that such documents represent the cargo and may be traded. This is the case with the traditional bill of lading. However, to an ever-growing extent, the traditional bill of lading in modern cargo transportation has been replaced by a "sea waybill" or by other documents which do not have the same legal qualities as the bill of lading (e.g. consignment notes, waybills).

The bill of lading may be made out *"to a named person"*, *"to a named person or order"*, *"to the holder"* or *"to a named person not to order"*. In the first three cases the bills of lading are regarded as *"negotiable"* or *"quasi-negotiable"* documents of title (except in the United States where in some cases the first one is not). On the other hand, consignment notes and waybills set out the name of the party entitled to receive the goods mentioned in the document and also identify the type and quantity of the goods, but they are not negotiable documents and thus they are not documents of title. Increasingly, sea waybill has replaced the traditional bill of lading as the main transport document in ocean carriage.

A *consignment note* is a transport document containing particulars of goods for shipment, prepared by a consignor and countersigned by the carrier as a proof of receipt of consignment for delivery at the destination. It is an alternative to the bill of lading (especially in inland transport), however, without being either a contract of carriage or a document of title, it is therefore a non-negotiable instrument.

A *waybill* is a transport document that travels with a shipment, identifies its consignor, consignee, origin and destination, describes the goods and shows their weight and freight. It is prepared by the shipping company (carrier) for its internal record and control, without being either a contract of carriage or a document of title, therefore it is not a negotiable instrument.

A *seawaybill or sea waybill* is a transport document that serves as evidence of the contract of carriage and as a receipt of cargo taken "on board" a vessel. Unlike a bill of lading, the sea waybill is a non-negotiable form of bill of lading (thus not a document of title) where delivery is to be made to the named consignee. The *named person*, not the holder of the document, is here entitled to claim delivery of the goods. In practice this is typically the case when electronic documentation is being used. Furthermore, the sea waybill is used in many trades (such as the container trade) where it is not expected that the goods will be resold while afloat. The use of the traditional bill of lading can cause problems if the goods reach the port of discharge before the bill of lading comes into the hands of the buyer. The latter will only be able to persuade the shipowner to deliver if he provides a suitable guarantee to indemnify the shipowner against any misdelivery claims. Apart from the inconvenience caused by arranging such guarantees, there will also be some cost involved for the buyer if the shipowner insists on a bank providing the guarantee. The above-mentioned problems can be avoided by using a sea waybill.[7]

---

7 Baughen, S. (2015) *Shipping Law* (Routledge, 8th edition, p. 8).

Although the term "bill of lading" is well-established in international trading practice, it would not be impossible if it became obsolete in the years to come. The Rotterdam Rules (article 1.14) introduce the new general term "transport document" as follows[8]:

> "*Transport document means a document issued under a contract of carriage by the carrier that:*
> (a) *Evidences the carrier's or a performing party's receipt of goods under a contract of carriage; and*
> (b) *Evidences or contains a contract of carriage*".

It becomes clear that, according to this definition, modern transport documents (whether bills of lading or sea waybills) should share only two out of three basic functions of a traditional negotiable bill of lading. The third function of a "negotiable document of title" is connected only with the traditional bill of lading which is generally "*a negotiable instrument, entailing the right to demand the goods described therein and to take possession of them*". If a "bill of lading" is declared to be "non-negotiable", then it should be treated as a sea waybill.

Therefore, assuming the Rotterdam Rules come into force, it remains to be seen how trading practice will be transformed in the future. For someone to conceive this evolution, it is worth reading also other interesting definitions of the Rotterdam Rules (article 1: "contract of carriage", "liner transportation", "carrier", "performing party and maritime performing party", "shipper and documentary shipper", "holder", "consignee", "negotiable and non-negotiable transport document", "electronic communication and electronic transport record", etc.).

In liner shipping, the bill of lading (or substitute documents/methods) is the main document regulating the relationship between the carrier, the shipper (frequently the customer) and the consignee. The cargo carriage is normally booked by telephone or e-mail, sometimes resulting in a *booking note* (see appendix 11) whereby the agent of the carrier promises space to the customer in a particular vessel and/or within a certain period of time. The bill of lading will thereafter be issued upon the shipment of the cargo (*shipped bill of lading*) or upon receipt thereof (*received for shipment bill of lading*).

In bulk/tramp shipping, the vessel's charter relationship is regulated in a charterparty signed by the charterer and the shipowner. The bill of lading will first be a receipt for the goods shipped, but then it will retain its other functions to a large degree, particularly in relation to the "bona fide" third party (consignee) who acquires the bill of lading in good faith so as to receive the goods. The bill of lading may also refer to the charterparty as the underlying document.

It has already been mentioned that a sale and purchase of goods typically forms the basis of, inter alia, the contract of carriage. In the sales contract the parties normally agree on whether the seller or the buyer will arrange and/or pay for the transportation and other ancillary costs, as well as take on certain

---

8 United Nations (2008) *United Nations Convention on Contracts for the International Carriage of Goods Wholly or Partly by Sea (Rotterdam Rules)*.

risks related with the sales transaction. The so-called *"transport clauses"* (see above Incoterms® definitions) are therefore of importance in the transportation relationship, particularly since the carrier will have to deal with the shipper, the consignee and the charterer.

A large number of bill of lading clauses govern the carrier's (shipowner's) relationship with the shipper and the consignee. Whether *freight* will be payable in advance or at a later stage is very important from a seller/buyer point of view. In a CIF transaction the seller has an obligation to pay the freight, in which case the bill of lading should thus be marked *"freight prepaid"*. However, practical problems may occur in an FOB sale, when the different parties have not made clear that the shipper is not entitled to ask for a bill of lading freight prepaid, as long as in an FOB sale it will be the buyer who pays for the freight.

Due to this relationship between the seller and the carrier, in case of a negotiated bill of lading, the holder of the bill of lading which is a "bona fide" third party (i.e. acting in good faith and unless he is both the shipper of the bill of lading and the charterer of the charterparty) will be typically protected by mandatory rules to avoid the carrier exempting himself from his responsibilities with regard to the cargo liability. Such legislation, based on international conventions (e.g. Hague Rules, Hague-Visby Rules, Hamburg Rules and Rotterdam Rules, see section 6.5.1), aims at placing on the carrier a minimum liability for damage to, or loss of, the cargo. This mandatory legislation (commonly the Hague-Visby Rules) may be incorporated in a charterparty by a specific clause. In such a situation the carrier may be vested with a more far-reaching liability than he would have had under the charterparty.

It is important that the terms and conditions of the bill of lading and the charterparty are synchronised as far as possible. Otherwise the result may be that the carrier may become liable for damage to cargo under the bill of lading without being able to invoke agreed exemptions under the charterparty or to seek redress from the charterer. Correspondingly, imbalances may appear if laws of different countries apply to the different agreements.

The carrier (shipowner) usually tries to make the terms and conditions of the charterparty applicable to the bill of lading by reference to the charter, for example by stamping on the bill of lading a clause of the following type:

> *"This bill of lading shall be subject to the terms and conditions of charterparty between . . . and . . . dated. . . .".*

Frequently, the seller of goods is not prepared to accept such a clause because, when payment is to be made under a documentary credit, the paying bank may, following the provisions of UCP, refuse to accept a bill of lading making reference to a charterparty, unless it has been expressly instructed to accept such a bill of lading.

Bills of lading and other transport documents are printed documents. BIMCO has designed various standard forms of bills of lading, such as the general purpose *Congenbill* (see appendix 13 for the latest version of 2016) and the liner *Conlinebill* (see appendix 14 for the latest version of 2016).

The following sections will discuss more specifically the functions and the importance of a traditional bill of lading.

6.5.3.1 Bill of lading as a document of title

The particular challenge in maritime transport is that a trader may want to be able to buy a cargo overseas, have it shipped on board a vessel and then, while the goods move over the oceans towards their overseas destination, look to sell to another trader or an ultimate receiver. He may not be planning to take actual physical delivery himself, but sell the cargo in order to make some trading profit.

In order that the buyer does not have to wait for the actual arrival of the vessel at the port of discharge before being able to resell the cargo, the transport document (typically a bill of lading) has developed into a document of title over time. The traditional bill of lading, usually called an "order" bill of lading, is recognised as a negotiable or at least a quasi-negotiable document. This means that, by transferring the document to a third party, all rights deriving from the bill of lading are transferred to the new holder of the document. Since it is a traditional principle of maritime law that the carrier is only obliged to deliver the goods to the holder of a bill of lading, the actual holder of the document is entitled to have delivery of the goods.

Moreover, the holder of a full set of bills of lading is authorised to deal with the goods (right of disposal/right of instructions) while they are still on board the vessel. This is particularly important when agreeing with the carrier to change the port of discharge.

Furthermore, a second type of bill of lading that can perform as document of title is the "straight" bill of lading which is issued to a named consignee. In this case, however, the bill of lading is not a negotiable document, thus it is a document of title only for the one specific consignee indicated on the document.

To put it simply, the *"bill of lading confers prima facie title over the goods to the named consignee or the lawful holder"*.

Due to technical improvements and speedier services in the maritime industry, it frequently happens that the vessel arrives at its destination before traders are able to negotiate the documents through the L/C channels. The goods will therefore reach the port of discharge before the documents arrive, creating a lot of problems that have to be sorted out.

6.5.3.2 Bill of lading as a confirmation of receipt of goods for transport

The bill of lading as evidence for the quantity and condition of the goods

One of the traditional functions of a bill of lading is to evidence the exact quantity and the apparent condition of the goods at the time of delivery to the carrier. Once the carrier has stated the quantity and condition in the receipt, which in this context means the bill of lading, then it is assumed that the goods were in fact given to him in this quantity and in the condition stated. If the cargo is found to be in good order and there is no remark entered into the bill of lading, it will be a so-called *"clean bill of lading"*.

The reason behind the need of such a clean bill of lading is for the merchant (consignee) to prove the so-called prima facie case leading to a presumed liability of the carrier under the current international cargo conventions (see 6.5.1). Thus, the receipt function of the bill of lading becomes a crucial instrument of the shipper and/or the consignee when claiming compensation in the context of maritime claims, because the information given in the transport document is presumed to evidence the true nature/quantity of the goods.

The bill of lading as proof of delivery of the goods in conformity with the contract of sale

The receipt function of the bill of lading has thus great implications in the context of an international sale. When receiving the bill of lading (which states the condition and quantity of the goods), the shipper, who is often at the same time the seller under the contract of sale, is able to prove to the buyer that he has in fact delivered the goods in full conformity with the contract of sale.

This is important in many contexts, and as indicated above it becomes crucial where the payment for the goods is being made by letter of credit, since the bill of lading is often one of the relevant documents to be presented by the seller (beneficiary) for payment by the letter of credit bank. A bill of lading which gives description of the goods which is not in conformity with the provisions of the letter of credit, or a bill of lading with remarks making it unclean will not be accepted by the bank.

A bill of lading established by the master with some reservations regarding the apparent condition or quantity of the goods will thus greatly affect the trading value of the document. This is because the document is no longer "clean" and will cause some problems for the shipper when negotiating it through the L/C channel. This is where the use of letters of indemnity (LOI) have come up in international trade. The importance of a clean bill of lading is analysed further in section 6.5.3.3.

Mandatory content of a bill of lading

As a consequence of this function as a receipt and as a proof of the delivery of the goods to the carrier, it soon became necessary to establish mandatory rules obliging the carrier to provide at least minimum information on the "front" of the bill of lading. This is defined in the cargo liability conventions (Hague Rules, Hague-Visby Rules; Hamburg Rules). However, if the latest convention (Rotterdam Rules) comes into force, covering carriage of goods by sea and ancillary contracts, the use of transport documents will be governed rather by even more complex and detailed rules, as the new instrument contains clauses which may have an effect on the value of the bill of lading as a negotiable document. Regulation is expected to increase with respect to the information given in a bill of lading or a similar transport document.

"Weight unknown" and "said to contain" clauses

International maritime law has burdened the carrier with the obligation to confirm the quantity and the condition of the goods before he establishes a clean bill of lading. This duty is in no way unlimited since he is obliged only to state the *apparent* condition of the goods. Where goods are sealed, because they are packaged or containerised, the carrier has of course no realistic means of inspecting the cargo and thus under most national laws he is allowed up to a certain point to insert "weight unknown" or "said to contain" clauses in the bill of lading. It follows that the evidential value of bills of lading containing such clauses is more limited than if the bill of lading contains clear statements.

Importance of the receipt function for the consignee

If only two parties were involved in the transaction, then the receipt function of the bill of lading would have been only marginally important. This is because the receipt would have been only a prima facie evidence that the carrier had received the goods in that quantity and condition. The actual problem arises in international trade because the people relying on the statements made in the bill of lading are often *third parties*. Thus, the consignee, when receiving a bill of lading, wishes to rely fully on the statements made by the master because he will typically release the funds of the contractual sales price to the seller upon transfer of document as if he had physically received the goods. The same applies in a letter of credit transaction.

That is why the Hague-Visby Rules of 1968 state that the carrier will not be able to disprove the prima facie evidence of the bill of lading towards third parties and will be bound by his statements made in the bill of lading.

6.5.3.3 "Clean" bill of lading and documentary credit

It has been clear that bills of lading and transport documents in general play a fundamental role in international trade serving important functions in different contractual relations. The basis for the letter of credit transaction is that the bank pays the agreed amount to the beneficiary after it has examined the documents presented and has found them to be in accordance with the terms and conditions of the documentary credit as well as with the terms of the applied UCP set of rules. As already emphasised, the bank examines that the documents seem correct; the bank has no liability to examine the actual quality, quantity and condition of the goods shipped, but only to ensure that the documents are in accordance with the instructions given to the bank. UCP 600 (article 5) states that *"banks deal with documents and not with goods, services or performance to which the documents may relate"*. This setting explains why the information in the bill of lading is so important in order for the letter of credit transaction to function. Under a documentary credit transaction most legal problems emanate from the documents tendered and examined, since they may set out information which is not in fact correct. It is obvious that the relationship among the sales agreement, the law of transport and the letter of credit transaction is crucial.

From the buyer's point of view, it is important that the transport document gives critical information about the cargo, since the buyer may have only the bill of lading and the seller's invoice to rely on when asked to pay. Hence, the buyer actually pays against the documents without previously having had a chance to examine the goods. Furthermore, the buyer gets an indication of when the goods have been shipped on board or, at least, when they have been received for shipment.

For the seller/shipper it is significant to have a *clean bill of lading* issued by the carrier – that is a bill of lading which does not contain any remarks with respect to the condition and quantity of the goods. Otherwise, the buyer or the paying bank (under a documentary credit) will be entitled to refuse to pay against a "claused" or "qualified" document when tendered, since such qualification is an indication that the actual goods do not conform with the requirements of the sales agreement. Under the terms and conditions of the sales agreement, the buyer is generally under no duty to pay for an unclean bill of lading, at least in cases where a remark gives reason to presume that the goods are not in customary or agreed condition or quantity. Under payment by documentary credit, UCP 600 (article 27) stipulates that "*a bank will only accept a clean transport document*". A clean transport document is one bearing no clause or notation expressly declaring a defective condition of the goods or their packaging or a shortfall of quantity. The word "clean" need not appear on a transport document, even if a credit has a requirement for that transport document to be "*clean on board*".

The seller's interest in clean bills of lading has thus, in some instances, caused pressure on the carrier to issue clean bills of lading, although remarks should be entered with respect to the quantity of the goods or their quality as it appears (e.g. a box may be torn or damaged by water). The carrier has a duty to note such remarks in the bill of lading, and under the Hague-Visby Rules he is not entitled to produce evidence conflicting with the remarks of the bill of lading against a third person who has acquired the bill of lading in good faith. The carrier's liability for wrong statements in the bill of lading may become extensive. The various transport conventions have somewhat different solutions in this respect. In exchange for the clean bill of lading the seller/shipper may issue a "*letter of indemnity*" (*LOI*) in favour of the carrier, whereby it assumes liability for all consequences of the carrier (owner) issuing a clean bill of lading. Such a back-letter may have a limited value and it should be underlined that the P&I insurance does not give the owner any protection in case of damages due to incorrect statements in a bill of lading. The Hamburg Rules and the Rotterdam Rules contain express provisions in this regard, disallowing the carrier to rely upon the terms of such indemnity.

6.5.3.4 Bill of lading as evidence of the contract of carriage
The bill of lading is an evidence of the contract of carriage of goods by sea between the shipper and the carrier. The bill of lading also sets out vital information for the buyer under the sales agreement. Various pieces of information will be found in the bill of lading, such as type of goods, quantity of cargo, weight, remarks, destination, name of vessel (in case of on board bills of lading) and possibly substitution of the vessel, as well as consignee and provisions on liability. All these items are important, not only for the shipper, but probably even more for the consignee (receiver, buyer) since he will, at the end of the voyage

and at the port of discharge, claim the goods from the carrier. Again, it is the third party, namely the consignee, who needs to be able to rely on the contractual terms entered into between the shipper and the carrier. Due to this need on the part of the consignee, he, as the buyer of the goods, will require bills of lading with specific contractual wording and entries when formulating the contract of sale. Upon discharge of the cargo at the port of discharge the buyer/consignee is entitled to receive cargo which is in conformity with the description in the bill of lading. Failing such conformity, the carrier may be liable in damages according to the liability regime applicable and the contractual provisions.

When the bill of lading is negotiated to a bona fide third party (consignee), then the bill of lading becomes *conclusive evidence of the contract of carriage*. It is because the third party cannot examine the actual shipment and can only be based on the transport document itself.

The shipper in its turn needs to present to the consignee or to the L/C bank a document which is in full conformity with the requirements of the contract of sale. In order to obtain such a document the shipper may put the carrier under some commercial pressure, inducing him to enter into the bill of lading certain information which is not completely truthful, for example an early date for the issuing of the bill of lading or the note "*shipped on board in apparently good condition*" even though it may be suspected or known that a portion of the goods is damaged or missing. Sometimes, the quantity mentioned in the bill of lading is not correct. Here again, the carrier induced by this erratic information will ask for a letter of indemnity as cover for potential liabilities. This practice has been denounced in many jurisdictions.

6.5.4 Bankability of transport documents

The importance of the bill of lading in international trade has been enhanced in the context of letter of credit transactions. In overseas trade the bill of lading is traditionally the key document in the list of documents to be provided under a letter of credit. As has been illustrated, this is so for a number of reasons. First, the bill of lading is a document evidencing the receipt of the goods and eventually the shipment on board by the carrier, indicating the condition and the quantity of the goods at that time. Second, it is a document of title enabling the rightful holder to claim the goods at destination.

The document and the rights deriving therefrom are transferable to third parties. This means that the bill of lading may be used as financial security for a bank extending credit to the buyer. Where waybills (e.g. airwaybill, sea waybill, CMR waybill etc.) are the transport documents used for the transaction, the bank does not obtain security by holding the waybill, but by being mentioned in the document as consignee. It is through these functions that banks use the transport documents as security for the financing of the underlying trade. Because of the lack of uniformity in this respect, it will depend on the applicable law whether and to what extent the bank receives financial security over the goods by holding the documents or by being named as consignee in the bill of lading. Similarly, it seems that the use of electronic documents have gradually gained acceptance and this has also been reflected in the Rotterdam Rules (see section 6.5.7).

6.5.5 Interface between the contract of carriage and sales of cargo

The contract of carriage is ancillary to the contract of sale insofar as the party requested to provide transportation from the sales contract is the actual party involved in the contract of carriage. For example, in the traditional FOB clause the buyer of goods is typically involved in the contract of carriage against the carrier, while in a CIF clause this role is undertaken by the seller of goods. Transportation of cargo is one of the key elements of performance next to the delivery of the goods and the payment of the price. However, for the two cardinal performances (delivery of the goods and payment of the price) the contract of carriage has a crucial function.

As trade and transport have evolved since the creation of the bill of lading, many functions have been added to its usage. The carrier now certifies (for the purpose of the sales contract) in a transport document:

(a) the fact that he has received the goods and later that the goods have been loaded on board;

(b) the date of shipment;

(c) the fact that the goods are of apparent good condition and in the requested quantity, when received;

(d) that the goods were put on a transportation vehicle/ship for a contracted voyage up to the place agreed in the contract of sale; and

(e) the cost of transportation and possibly the distribution of it between the seller and the buyer (e.g. CAD/freight prepaid, CIF, CIP etc.).

Further, the contract of sale requires the seller to provide transportation documents, first of all as proof of shipment, but also in order to allow the buyer to freely trade the goods to third parties. By handing out the transport document, which first of all should be the document as between the carrier and his contracting party, the carrier becomes (indirectly) highly involved in the underlying transaction, namely the sales contract, without being party to it. The carrier is also involved in the paramount obligation of the buyer. His document will trigger the payment by the buyer to the seller, for example, under a letter of credit.

Finally, in dispute situations between the seller and the buyer, the carrier is involved; for example, in a buyer's bankruptcy situation, by the right invoked by the seller to *stop the goods in transit*. In disputes regarding the quality of the cargo, the carrier is involved since the goods may not be accepted for delivery at the port of discharge.

For these reasons it is evident that there is a close relation between the various contractual relations mentioned, although each of them is particular and governed by its own contractual and legal rules.

6.5.6 Types of bills of lading

Summing up at this point, some distinctions may be made among various types of bill of lading. Traditionally, the *shipped bill of lading* has been the most common one, a document issued by the master or often in practice by the carrier's agent, when the goods have been loaded on board the vessel. Thus, this is a decisive point with respect to the passing of risk from the shipper to the carrier, but it may also be important with respect to the relation between the seller and the buyer.

The *received for shipment bill of lading* is issued when the goods have been received by the carrier for loading on a ship. This has come to play a much more important role where unit transport is involved, particularly container transports and ro/ro traffic. The received for shipment bill of lading is issued by the carrier when the goods have been received at the terminal. Later on, it may be stamped "*shipped*" or "*on board*" once the goods have been loaded to the ship.

Carriage of general cargo (mostly containers) is now increasingly performed in co-operation among different carriers, who each perform one part of transport immediately following upon the preceding part. Either the same means of transportation or different modes (e.g. sea, road, rail, air) may be used to perform the total transport. Terms such as "*through transport*", "*combined transport*", "*intermodal transport*" or "*multi-modal transport*" are used to describe the latter case, where combined transport documents (e.g. CT bills of lading) are issued, often electronically. Sometimes, shipping documents may be issued by freight forwarders (e.g. forwarder's certificates of transport – FCT), undertaking the role of the carrier, then often referred to as "Non-Vessel Operating Common Carriers" (NVOCC). These developments are particularly important in liner shipping. It must be pointed out that under through bills of lading, the principal carrier or freight forwarder who issued the through B/L is liable under a contract of carriage only for its own phase of the transport journey, acting as an agent for the carriers executing the other phases. On the other hand, under multi-modal or intermodal or combined transport bills of lading the carrier or freight forwarder who issued the B/L takes on full liability under a contract of carriage for the entire journey and over all modes of transportation.

Carriage involving several steps or parts may give rise to problems. As the document covering the whole transport may be issued either by a non-vessel-owning operator or by a freight forwarder conducting business "*as a carrier*" or "*as agent only for a carrier*" or by one of the carriers (e.g. the shipowner), new documents and procedures have been introduced. Electronic devices (often the terminology speaks of electronic documents) are frequently in use, not the least in container transportation. One of the practical problems arising is that different mandatory rules apply in respect of different means of transport, governing the relation between the carrier(s) and the cargo owner (the shipper or the consignee as the case may be).

Another aspect may also have a critical bearing in modern times of transportation. Bills of lading are frequently delayed in the bank handling, with the result that they do not arrive until after the relevant goods have been delivered. This problem can occur not only when short-sea transits are involved (e.g. in North Sea trades). In documentary credit sales, documents are also often delayed in the course of bank handling. From the ocean carrier's point of view this creates problems, since his duty to deliver the goods is based on the obligation of the receiver to surrender the bills of lading. This is a legal implication due to the nature and function of the bill of lading and this is also where the bill of lading differs from the consignment note/waybill. If the carrier delivers the cargo without the bill of lading being surrendered by the receiver of the cargo, the carrier may be liable for any resulting loss or damage, if another person turns up with an original bill of lading claiming delivery of the cargo. In such circumstances, as previously mentioned, the carrier is not covered by his P&I Club with respect to losses that may occur. What commonly happens in such a situation is that the consignee may put up a *bank guarantee* to cover any loss or expense incurred by the carrier as a result of his delivering the cargo without the bills of lading being surrendered. Such guarantee is not unlawful per se, but the growing use of such guarantees illustrates the deterioration of the bill of lading system. It has become common that tanker charterparties, or dry cargo charterparties where large charterers are involved, provide that the shipowner has to release the cargo against the *charterer's guarantee* (not a bank's guarantee) even without the surrender by the consignee of the bill of lading at the port of discharge. Therefore, charterparties increasingly contain a clause saying something along the following lines: *"The owner shall deliver the cargo to the consignee without the presentation of an original bill of lading against the charterer's guarantee"*. There are various ways of construing such clauses. Even if some of these clauses are hardly sufficient to deal with the problems that may occur, P&I Clubs have to a growing extent accepted that such guarantees issued by well-known, reputable companies of good financial standing will be acceptable.

For carriage over short distances there is usually less need for financing by documentary credit. In some trades it has become usual practice to issue *destination bills of lading*. In these cases, the bill of lading is either issued at the destination in order to avoid loss of time, or else one bill of lading is carried on board to be signed by the consignee as a receipt when the goods are delivered. Legally, this is a questionable custom.

As already mentioned, a critical distinction is made between *negotiable* (or rather *quasi-negotiable*) and *non-negotiable* bills of lading. Most bills of lading used in ocean carriage are of the former type. The carrier is bound to deliver the goods at the discharge port only to the legal holder of at least one original bill of lading and by the same token only such holder is entitled to claim delivery of the goods in exchange for surrendering the bill of lading. If two people, each with an original bill of lading, claim delivery at the destination, then neither of them is entitled to have the goods. The goods must then have to be stored until a court decides who is the "true owner".

Only a holder of all the original bills of lading may dispose of the goods at a place which is not the destination. Thus, the carrier can only agree to re-route the goods, when all the original bills of lading are produced to him. Similarly, the carrier may only issue a new set of bills of lading in exchange for all the old originals. However, it is not uncommon in practice for cargoes (especially oil) to be delivered without bills of lading being surrendered, as well as for new bills of lading to be issued without the old originals being produced. It is also important to keep in mind that, particularly in the oil trade, the goods may be sold several times during the voyage and the destination may change several times. It is inevitable that frequent conflicts between the legal rules and the practical requirements arise.

All these features have led to a need for document simplification and replacement. One step has been the use of *non-negotiable sea waybills* or similar documents used instead of traditional bills of lading (modelled upon the waybills in use in other transport modes). This system works well where the shipper does not demand the issuance of a traditional bill of lading. Another step was the use of electronic devices rather than the paper documents.

The difficulty is to create a system which preserves all the functions of the bill of lading without maintaining the disadvantages. Computerisation appears to allow such a system, but there is still much suspicion in the trade among both banks and traders regarding documentary replacement. The use of electronic arrangements has increased. The impression is that trade has gradually adapted to the situation, even though all the difficulties of adopting this have not yet been overcome.

6.5.7 Electronic commerce

The transition from the traditional paper documents to the use of electronic documents is tied to other technical, social and financial developments, including, for example, the improvement of navigational equipment, the growing use of containers which led to changes in transport patterns, the new financing methods, the construction of huge containerships that are trading between a limited number of high developed ports, and the new trade routes (such as the Northern Sea Route passage north of Russia), etc. All these have brought about considerable changes in the area of shipping and transportation, particularly in the liner business.

The traditional paper-based distribution of transport data presupposes an efficient mailing service in order to forward the pieces of paper, as physical objects, to the place of destination before the goods arrive. When this system no longer meets the practical requirements, since cargo transports are often quicker than the transfer of the documents, the transport industry must search for and adopt new routines and processes. This is therefore what has happened in practice. It is worth noting that, in 2008, United Nations Commission on International Trade Law (UNCITRAL) established the "Rotterdam Rules" (see section 6.5.1) which form a uniform and modern legal regime governing the rights and obligations of shippers, carriers and consignees under a contract for door-to-door carriage that includes an international sea leg, containing among other things some provisions about electronic documents.

Modern technology offers new infrastructure, based on the optimised combination of computerisation and telecommunication. In order to switch from traditional paper-based methods to electronic ones, the first step required was to re-define the term "document". The word implies a "paper document" rather than an "electronic document". A document in a strict sense of the word refers to the information contained in a paper document, in other words to the totality of what has been written down as one entity. The paper itself is only the means by which this information is distributed. Talking about paperless transfer (see section 5.5.1) of transport information, does not mean that paper transport documents are eliminated from commercial procedures, but only that the traditional means of transport information, a piece of paper, is replaced by a digital file on a computer. Paper-administrated operations are thus transformed into computer-based operations. The structured network intended to support the international carriage of goods geographically is therefore serviced through sophisticated and highly advanced telecommunication systems.

In an electronic network, there exists only one document in the strict sense of the word, namely the "electronic document" stored in the memory disk of a machine. All print-outs produced are copies of the one and only electronic document. A print-out is a proof of what in fact was stored on the computer. Print-outs can be made at any time and for any number of copies, while their contents might be altered as soon as the electronic document is amended.

Moreover, when paper documents are issued by the carrier, these will be handed over to the shipper and other individuals (e.g. one copy kept for himself as carrier's copy, one copy sent to the master). After that, the carrier can no longer influence the contents of the document. Where an electronic document has been issued, typically only the carrier still holds access to the one and only document during the whole transit of the goods. This fact makes it necessary for the shipper to be provided with some sort of proof of what was stored on the computer at the time the goods were delivered to the carrier. In other words, it shows how important it is to get the first print-out. Obviously paperless methods are in practice not 100% paperless. *The first print-out creates the necessary link between the electronic recording and real life.* The delivery by the shipper of the goods to be carried against the first print-out means that this is the first recording of what in fact has been delivered. In this way the first print-out constitutes a receipt and as such it is prima facie evidence of the particulars of the goods. This means that the legal concept of "document" should not be narrowed down to paper documents, but must be appropriately adjusted and understood in a broader sense, meaning both any data medium and a group or set of data recorded.

The *BOLERO project*,[9] standing for "Bill of Lading Electronic Registry Organisation", was set up on a pilot basis by the European Union in 1999, so as to suggest a practical solution, study the feasibility and promote the application of electronic commerce and the respective documents. This did not prove to be the final solution, even though it has been a step forward. According to Carr and

---

9 See www.bolero.net.

Stone,[10] BOLERO is a closed network available on a subscription basis, undertaking the role of a trusted third party and providing a platform of secure exchange of electronic transport documents (e.g. bills of lading, documentary credits, guarantees). The subscribers – some of the most important corporations, financial institutions, carriers, traders, shipping and logistics companies worldwide – are subject to the BOLERO rulebook which provides the legally-binding framework for paperless transactions. The BOLERO title registry plays a vital role in respect of bills of lading; it is a centrally operated database of information relating to bills of lading. Transfer is made using a combination of notification, confirmation and authentication through digital signatures. The title registry records the current holder of the electronic document ensuring its uniqueness. The registry can only be updated by the current holder. Without the title registry record, the document has no status and is just a copy of the data.

The bill of lading is a key instrument in global trade and is likely to remain in the future. However, it is definitely a part of the digital revolution in trade documentation. Similarly to its paper equivalent, the *electronic bill of lading* (*eBL*) contains respective information (e.g. description of cargo, ports of loading and discharge, date of shipment, terms and conditions of carriage etc.), it replicates the three basic functions of a paper bill of lading (receipt from the carrier for the goods to be carried, contract for the carriage of the goods, document of title entitling the rightful holder to claim delivery of the goods) and provides the holder with the respective rights, obligations and limitations. The benefits of switching to eBLs are numerous, immediate and concern improvements on speed, ease of use, accuracy and cost of trade. Automation reduces overheads, document transmission has no basic constraints, fast processing reduces the likelihood of goods being discharged prior to the arrival of the bill of lading thus cutting the need for letters of indemnity, trade settlements have been accelerated, enterprises improve their working capital and credit line management, while transactions are more secure, reducing the risk of fraud, since eBLs enjoy protection from digital signature and encryption technology similar to that used in banking for the transfer of electronic funds. Finally, in a globalised market era, where increasing emphasis is placed on speed, eBLs are indispensable tools for carriers, shippers, commodity companies and banks in their effort to digitise their international trade operations and gain competitive edge.[11]

As the advantages of electronic bills of lading have become apparent and their role have been increased, they have been recognised around the globe. It is worth to be mentioned that BIMCO has issued a relevant standard charterparty clause. Additionally, P&I clubs of the International Group typically provide a standard coverage for eBLs on the same basis as for paper bills. Besides, as mentioned already, the "Rotterdam Rules" contain provisions which deal with electronic

---

10 Carr, I., Stone, P. (2014) *International Trade Law* (Routledge, 5th edition, pp. 194–195).

11 Bolero International *Electronic Bills of Lading are Part of the Quiet Revolution in World Trade* (www.bolero.net, accessed 21 November 2016).

documents. Whether the solutions suggested will prove to be efficient remains to be seen.

6.6 Carrier's liability

The ocean carrier's liability for damage to or loss of the goods is regulated in different ways depending mostly on the means of transportation and the particular trade, since different rules may apply as long as international conventions use somewhat differentiating approaches. In a charter relationship the owner and the charterer are basically free to agree on and distribute between themselves the liability for cargo damage. In liner service, where the bill of lading is the main document governing the relationship between the cargo owner and the carrier, mandatory legislation – based on the certain international conventions mentioned above (see section 6.5.1) – has been introduced in many countries. The idea behind these rules is to place a minimum liability on the ocean carriers for damage to cargo, primarily where the bill of lading is the governing document. Under these regimes the carrier is vested with a compulsory liability in relation to the shipper as well as to the consignee. On the other hand, where a charterparty governs the relationship between a carrier and a shipper who acts also as charterer in the charterparty, then the mandatory rules do not take precedence over their parties' contractual intentions as between a shipowner and a charterer contracted in the charterparty. However, a "bona fide" (i.e. acting in good faith) third party holder of the bill of lading can invoke the mandatory rules which apply.

When making claims for cargo lost or damaged in a carriage by sea, various questions may need to be asked in order to ascertain whether liability can be established against one or more of the parties involved. The main questions are:

- What are the grounds of liability?
- Against whom can a claim be made?
- Will the shipowner or the charterer be held ultimately liable?

These questions will be discussed below, particularly the basis for the liability of the carrier. With respect to the last question, it can be briefly mentioned here that, even if the charterer and the owner have between themselves agreed on the distribution of cargo liability, a cargo receiver may nevertheless, under the bill of lading, have a claim against either of them. In such a situation there may be a question of redress between the owner and the charterer.

6.6.1 Liability for cargo under charterparties

The questions concerning allocation of liability for cargo under voyage charterparties and time charterparties will be dealt with separately under respective chapters (see chapters 11 and 12). It is known that a bill of lading is usually issued for each lot of cargo and the liability for cargo under the bill of lading is governed by national rules based on one of the international conventions which are not immediately applicable to charterparties. Therefore, as a base for the next chapters, the following sections will attempt to explain the fundamental rules of liability for cargo under a bill of lading, on which cargo receivers usually found their claim.

6.6.2 Sea carrier's liability statutory regime

An initial reference to the international cargo conventions has been made in section 6.5.1. Here, focus is given in the evolution of the sea carrier liability regimes worldwide.

Even from the 19th century, the bill of lading regime used in different cargo trades was amended with new liability clauses appearing against the shipowners. The question of the ocean carrier's liability was historically tied to the characteristics of the bill of lading as a document of title "representing" the goods, as well as to the need of transferring the document and thereby the title to the cargo. In English law, those questions were dealt with in the *Bill of Lading Act 1855*, which was much later replaced by a new *UK Carriage of Goods by Sea Act 1992 (UK COGSA)*. The new Act deals with various transport documents, not only with the traditional bill of lading.

In the USA, where cargo interests were traditionally strong, compulsory legislation was introduced through the *Harter Act of 1893*. Under this statute, for the first time a minimum liability was put on sea carriers loading or discharging cargo in the USA. This legislation still forms a basis for the carrier's liability in the USA, despite being superseded in some parts by the *US Carriage of Goods by Sea Act 1936* (*US GOGSA*) which formally implemented the Hague Rules 1924. In fact, the Harter Act formed the forerunner for the Hague Rules. The US COGSA 1936 still applies only from loading to discharge of a sea carriage concerning ports of the USA, whereas the Harter Act is still effective before loading and after discharging of the goods (unless the bill of lading expressly makes COGSA fully applicable to such shipments), as well as for coastal trades within the United States. According to the Harter Act, the shipowner is prohibited to insert any clause in a bill of lading that reduces or eliminates his responsibility to exercise due diligence, properly man, equip and supply the ship and to make the ship seaworthy. The shipowner's negligence or exception clauses of bills of lading are thus conditional, meaning that they do not relieve the shipowner (or his servants such as the manager, the agent and the master) from liability for loss or damage to the cargo, arising from "*negligence, fault or failure in proper loading, stowage, custody, care or proper delivery . . .*" of goods in the charge of the shipowner or their servants, unless they exercise due diligence to make the ship seaworthy in all respects. The Act also exempts shipowners from liability for errors in navigation and management of the ship.[12]

During the 1920s the time came for an international convention aimed at some protection for the cargo owners and of the bill of lading as a negotiable document,

---

12 www.shipinspection.eu (accessed 10 January 2017).

therefore the *Hague Rules* were formed. This fundamental convention was created in 1924 to set a minimum mandatory liability of carriers acting worldwide. Under the Hague Rules the shipper bears the cost of lost or damaged goods if he cannot prove that the vessel was unseaworthy. In other words, the carrier can avoid liability for risks resulting from human error provided he exercises due diligence and his vessel is seaworthy. The Hague Rules form the basis of modern international shipping, having influenced the national legislation in almost all of the world's major trading nations.

This convention was slightly amended and updated by two protocols, the first one in 1968 and the second in 1979, but neither improved the basic liability provisions, which remained essentially unchanged. The amended convention is usually referred to as the *Hague-Visby Rules* which were incorporated into English law by the *Carriage of Goods by Sea Act 1971* (*UK COGSA 1971*). Having been issued 44 years after the Hague Rules, the amended convention was kept short and consisted of only ten articles, but it failed to cover important issues such as multi-modal transport (i.e. the convention covers sea carriage only), the container revolution etc.

During the 1970s, after pressure from several developing countries, work began within the United Nations (UNCITRAL) to develop a new convention aimed at replacing the previous ones. In 1978, a new convention, the *Hamburg Rules*, was signed, placing on the carrier a more far-reaching liability than do the Hague/Hague-Visby Rules. The new rules were embraced by many developing countries, but they were largely ignored by ship-operating nations, thus not having received wide acceptance. It must be said that the Hamburg Rules require the contracting states to denounce the earlier conventions within five years after the entry into force of the Hamburg Rules. The Nordic countries have denounced the Hague Rules.

In 2008, the *Rotterdam Rules* were adopted by UNCITRAL. Even though they are detailed – having 96 articles and a wider scope, covering also multi-modal/ancillary transport, expanding provisions on the transport documents and liability of the shipper, increasing the limitation amounts, dealing with the question of delay etc. – they are still a long way from obtaining worldwide recognition.

Both the Hamburg Rules and the Rotterdam Rules refuse carrier's exemption for negligent navigation and management. Also, whereas the Hague-Visby Rules require a ship to be seaworthy only "before and at the beginning" of the voyage, under the Rotterdam Rules the carrier will have to keep the ship seaworthy throughout the voyage.

The Hague Rules and the Hague-Visby Rules have been made national legislation in several countries.

Since these conventions are rather complicated, they have not been adopted in the same way in all countries and they are interpreted differently, a detailed discussion about the carrier's liability for cargo under the bill of lading is beyond the scope of this book. However, there will be an effort to outline the basic rules and the differences among various conventions.

Different countries follow various methods to incorporate these international conventions in their legal systems. In this respect, the legislation may look different between the countries, since there are national rules based on one or another convention or maybe a mixture of them.

Finally, it is very common practice for a bill of lading or a charterparty to incorporate an international cargo convention by the use of a so-called "*Paramount clause*". Typically, the main purpose of such a clause is to incorporate an international cargo liability regime, such as the Hague or Hague-Visby Rules (or less frequently the Hamburg Rules) into the document which is (or which evidences) the contract of carriage of goods by sea. Where the Rules are incorporated so as to generally apply to a contract of carriage (bill of lading or charterparty), their application will not be limited only to cargo claims. As the word "paramount" means "supreme" or "above all others", the clause is related to some feature that prevails over everything else. Therefore, the paramount clause may incorporate any particular legislation. The clause implies that the whole contract of carriage would be subject to the terms incorporated by the paramount clause. For example, if the clause states that the carriage of goods is subject to the Hague-Visby Rules, these Rules then become part of the contract of carriage and establish express, contractual obligations and rights of the parties. Without the incorporation of the Hague Rules/Hague-Visby Rules or Hamburg Rules, the parties to a contract of carriage are free to allocate the obligations and rights between themselves.[13]

6.6.3 Compulsory nature of liability rules

As already mentioned, the different conventions are mandatory in their nature. This is expressed in the *Hague-Visby Rules (art. III, par. 8)* in the following way:

> "*Any clause, covenant, or agreement in the contract of carriage relieving the carrier or the ship from liability for loss or damage to, or in connection with, goods arising from negligence, fault, or failure in the duties and obligations provided in this article or lessening such liability otherwise than as provided in this Convention shall be null and void and of no effect*".

The *Hamburg Rules (part VI, art. 23, par. 1)* use the following language:

> "*Any stipulation in a contract of carriage by sea, in a bill of lading, or in any other document evidencing that contract of carriage by sea is null and void to the extent that it derogates, directly or indirectly, from the provisions of this Convention. The nullity of such a stipulation does not affect the validity of the other provisions of the contract or document of which it forms a part. A clause assigning benefit of insurance of the goods in favour of the carrier, or any similar clause, is null and void*".

The cargo liability conventions determine risk allocation schemes between the carrier and the cargo owner. The relevant articles of these sets of rules concern the basis for liability distribution, defining also the exemptions of liability, the liability regime for damage to, or loss of, goods or for delay, the extension of liability in time and in transport stages (e.g. from which point to which point a set

---

13 www.shipinspection.eu (accessed 10 January 2017).

of rules applies), etc. Thus, in general, more risk is placed on the carrier under the Hamburg Rules than under the Hague Rules. The risk allocation scheme under the Hague/Hague-Visby Rules exempted the carrier from liability under certain circumstances and limited his liability substantially. These Rules imposed on the carrier a general duty of care in relation to the goods throughout the applicable period of carriage and provided that the cargo should not be exposed to a high degree of risk, for example when carrying deck cargo or live animals (i.e. the two main exceptions in Hague-Visby rules' application). The Hague/Hague-Visby Rules apply mandatorily only from the loading of the goods onto the ship until their discharge from the ship.

Nothing in the conventions prevents the carrier from accepting a more extensive liability than the minimum prescribed, but this should be made in agreement. This frequently happens in container and ro/ro trades. Furthermore, as already mentioned, the Hague/Hague-Visby Rules' liability is commonly introduced through a *Paramount clause* into bills of lading covering shipments where the Rules would not otherwise apply. Paramount clauses are also commonly inserted into charterparties, where the Hague/Hague-Visby Rules are otherwise not applicable.

6.6.4 Scope of application of the international cargo conventions

The international cargo conventions may apply automatically or by agreement. The rules are automatically applicable mainly when the agreement for carriage is included in a bill of lading and when there is a carriage from a country which has signed the bill of lading convention. In some cases the rules are automatically applicable when the carriage is destined to a country which has signed the convention. There are also other supplementary rules which may complicate the picture. Particular legal problems may come to the fore in the future if the different conventions all remain in force but operate to various extents in different countries.

It should be noted that, in cases where the basic agreement is set out in a charterparty containing provisions as to cargo liability less severe to the carrier than those found in the compulsory regulations, the latter will nevertheless apply in the relationship between the carrier and a third-party consignee acting in good faith. This means that the parties under the charterparty may have contracted for less cargo liability than the compulsory conventions call for. However, as soon as a bill of lading covering the shipment has reached a holder who has not accepted, or has not been able to take note of and accept the charterparty liability, the compulsory liability becomes applicable.

The period of liability in the Hague/Hague-Visby Rules is based on the so-called "*tackle-to-tackle*" principle, that is, from the moment when the cargo is hooked onto the vessel's gear upon loading until it is again hooked off upon discharge. However, this tackle-to-tackle principle is not applied in the same manner to all countries. In some cases an extension of the scope of application of the Rules may occur towards a principle providing that, even if the goods have in fact been discharged, the carrier still may have a duty to ensure that the goods are not unloaded and stored in such a manner that damage is likely to occur after the discharge. There is also a general duty on the master to protect the cargo owner's interest and he may have an obligation to intervene if he becomes aware (or more precisely he ought to have become aware) that the goods are not being properly taken care of immediately after discharge. Thus, for example, a reefer carrier cannot be sure of relying on the tackle-to-tackle principle if refrigerated cargo is discharged onto a pier where there are no refrigeration facilities. Numerous factors may be relevant in determining the carrier's extent of obligations in such a case, depending for example on who the actual receiver is; how the port and warehouse system in the harbour functions; what influence the carrier has on the situation, etc. In some countries additional compulsory legislation has been introduced covering the terminal period.

The Hamburg Rules have also adopted the more extensive application, so that they apply from the time the carrier *"has taken over the goods from the shipper. . . until the time he has delivered the goods. . ."*. Transport documents involving container or ro/ro trades etc. commonly use this more extensive liability period. It is also used when there is no mandatory legislation to such effect. Finally, the same applies also to the Rotterdam Rules.

6.6.5 Liability system

Damage to the goods may arise in different ways. There may be a physical damage or goods may be short-landed or may be delayed or they may never arrive at the port of destination. Another type of damage is related to wrong statements being made in the bill of lading. Under any international cargo convention, the liability system is primarily geared at physical damage and short-landing, but damage due to delay is also often covered in some way. Moreover, if wrong statements have been made intentionally in the bill of lading, then there may be a criminal case.

The liability system under the Hague/Hague-Visby Rules will be used as a basis of the next discussion, since this is still the most applied cargo liability regime in international carriage of goods by sea. This liability system is based upon several different factors.

First of all, the carrier has a duty to make the vessel *seaworthy*. This is expressed in the *Hague-Visby Rules (art. III, par. 1)* in the following way:

> *"The carrier shall be bound before and at the beginning of the voyage to exercise due diligence to:*
> *(a) Make the ship seaworthy;*
> *(b) Properly man, equip and supply the ship;*
> *(c) Make the holds, refrigerating and cool chambers, and all other parts of the ship in which goods are carried, fit and safe for their reception, carriage and preservation".*

It must be emphasised that there is *no absolute liability on the carrier to make the vessel seaworthy, but he shall "exercise due diligence"*. If he can later prove that he has acted properly in this respect, he is relieved from liability for loss of or damage to goods as a result of the vessel's unseaworthiness.

In a next provision (*art. III, par. 2*) it is also stated that the carrier's obligation is to "*properly and carefully load, handle, stow, carry, keep, care for, and discharge the goods carried*".

The principal rule in the *Hague-Visby Rules* liability system is expressed in the following way (*art. IV, par. 2q*):

> "*Neither the carrier nor the ship shall be responsible for loss or damage arising or resulting from:*
> *(q) Any other cause arising without the actual fault or privity of the carrier, or without the fault or neglect of the agents or servants of the carrier, but the burden of proof shall be on the person claiming the benefit of this exception to show that neither the actual fault or privity of the carrier nor the fault or neglect of the agents or servants of the carrier contributed to the loss or damage*".

This rule is fundamental to the liability provisions. The principle is that the carrier is responsible for loss or damage arising or resulting from the fault or privity of him or his servants or agents. The burden of proof is on the carrier, which means that he has to prove that he, his servants or agents, *have not* caused the loss or damage by negligence.

There are a number of specific *exceptions* which relieve the carrier of responsibility for loss or damage resulting from (*art. IV, par. 2(c)–(p)*):
" . . .

> *(c) Perils, dangers and accidents of the sea or other navigable waters.*
> *(d) Act of God.*
> *(e) Act of war.*
> *(f) Act of public enemies.*
> *(g) Arrest or restraint of princes, rulers or people, or seizure under legal process.*
> *(h) Quarantine restrictions.*
> *(i) Act or omission of the shipper or owner of the goods, his agent or representative.*
> *(j) Strikes or lockouts or stoppage or restraint of labour from whatever cause, whether partial or general.*
> *(k) Riots and civil commotions.*
> *(l) Saving or attempting to save life or property at sea.*
> *(m) Wastage in bulk or weight or any other loss or damage arising from inherent defect, quality or vice of the goods.*
> *(n) Insufficiency of packing.*
> *(o) Insufficiency or inadequacy of marks.*
> *(p) Latent defects not discoverable by due diligence*".

The above exemptions actually illustrate situations where the carrier is not negligent, but there are also two "true" exceptions of the carrier from the principal rule. These are "*error in navigation*" and "*fire*". As per the *Hague-Visby Rules* (*art. IV, par. 2(a)–(b)*):

> *"Neither the carrier nor the ship shall be responsible for loss or damage arising or resulting from:*
>
> *(a)   Act, neglect, or default of the master, mariner, pilot, or the servants of the carrier in the navigation or in the management of the ship.*
>
> *(b)   Fire, unless caused by the actual fault or privity of the carrier".*

As regards (a) above, it should be noted that *only negligence etc. in the navigation or the management of the ship relieves the carrier of liability*. It is sometimes difficult to draw the distinction between "management of the ship" (error in navigation) and "management and handling of the cargo" (commercial error).

A contractual principle is that a party may not one-sidedly change his fundamental contractual obligations (fundamental breach). In the law of carriage of goods by sea the carrier may thus *not "deviate"* from the agreed or normal route. The doctrine of deviation may sometimes cause problems when it comes to striking a balance between what is commercially suitable but legally not permitted. If the cargo is lost or damaged further to ship's deviation (causing also a delay as a consequence), the carrier is not liable provided the deviation was made *"in saving or attempting to save life or property at sea"* or else provided the deviation was *"reasonable"* (*Hague-Visby Rules, art. IV, par. 4*). If the deviation is not regarded as reasonable considering both the carrier's and the cargo owner's interests, the carrier will risk facing liability without keeping any of the defences or limitations of an applicable cargo convention. Most charterparties and bills of lading contain "scope of voyage" (or similar) clauses, which allow the carrier to change the ship's route. This may be a commercial cost-saving right for the carrier not least in liner operation. However, in bill of lading relations such a "scope of voyage" clause may, depending on the circumstances, be in conflict with the mandatory rules on deviation. Thus, clear and non-contradictory wording should always be used.

There are also some other important exceptions. The *Hague-Visby Rules (art. I, par. c)* do not apply to the carriage of *"live animals and cargo which by the contract of carriage is stated as being carried on deck and is so carried"*. Furthermore, it should be mentioned that in modern container traffic a number of containers are always placed on what may be described as *"deck cargo"*. To avoid the above-mentioned problems, the carrier may agree in the bill of lading to take on the same liability for cargo on deck as under-deck.

Summing up, the Hague-Visby Rules did not essentially change the fundamental solutions proposed by the Hague Rules, but rather introduced a change in the limitation rules, increased liability amounts and established rules specifically oriented to solve problems arising from the use of containers.

6.6.6 Cargo claims and time limits

A cargo owner who intends to claim against the carrier for loss of or damage to the goods should do this in writing and enclose the necessary documents and supporting evidence, such as a copy of the bill of lading, survey or tally reports from discharging, invoices stating the value of the cargo, etc. It is important for the claimant to be aware of the *one-year time limit* which, in the *Hague-Visby Rules (art. III, par. 6)*, has the following wording:

"*. . . the carrier and the ship shall in any event be discharged from all liability what-soever in respect of the goods, unless suit is brought within one year of their delivery or of the date when they should have been delivered. This period, may however, be extended if the parties so agree after the cause of action has arisen*".

It is not sufficient to make sure that the claim has been sent to the carrier before the year has ended. Unless the claimant gets payment, he must either get time extension from the carrier or file a suit before the year has ended as otherwise his claim will be time-barred.

In the *Hague-Visby Rules (art. III, par. 6 bis)*, but not in the Hague Rules, there is a special section dealing with the redress situation by which the claimant gets additional time when the claim is an action for indemnity against a third person. The Hamburg Rules extend the initial limitation period to two years, as do the Rotterdam Rules.

6.6.7 Limitation of carrier's liability

All international cargo conventions specifying carrier's liability also contain rules limiting the carrier's liability. These rules, which limit the carrier's liability to a certain amount per package or per unit or per kilo, are fairly complicated. It may be difficult to define "package or unit" and it has also been difficult to find an international monetary base for the limitation. As a result of these complications, the final outcome of the claimant's action may vary depending on the particular law that is applicable. In the case *River Gurara [1998] 1 Lloyd's Rep. 225*, the question discussed was whether, under the Hague Rules, the container would be regarded as the unit for the limitation or instead whether the various packages within the container should be regarded as the units for limitation. In this case the Court of Appeal adopted the latter view, which is close to the solution adopted in the *Hague-Visby Rules (art. IV, par. 5(c))*.

The Hague-Visby Rules have supplemented the Hague Rules in certain respects. As per *art. III, par. 5(a)*, the limitation figure was increased and the claimant may use either the package/unit limitation or a limitation per kilo of the weight of the goods, whichever is preferable to him (i.e. higher). Furthermore, even though the limitation amounts were previously based on common denominators used in the international regulation of liability, such as Poincaré francs (a fictitious monetary standard), *Hague Visby Rules (art. III, par. 5(d))* adopted Special Drawing Rights – SDRs (a "basket" of different major currencies) as the measuring unit for the limitation of liability.

The Hamburg Rules in their turn increased further the limitation amounts, while the Rotterdam Rules have followed suit.

6.6.8 Carrier's liability for inspection and description of the goods

The importance to shippers of getting a clean bill of lading has already been mentioned (see section 6.5.3.3). According to the cargo conventions, the master or the carrier's agents shall, at the request of the shipper, issue a bill of lading after the goods have been received. The bill of lading should contain a statement concerning leading marks for identification of the goods, quantity, as well as apparent order and condition of the goods. According to the Hague-Visby Rules the carrier is not entitled to bring in counter-evidence to the particulars entered into the bill of lading, against the third person who has acquired the bill of lading in good faith. Thus, it is important for the carrier that the master and the ship's officers make proper examination and description of the goods. The goods will be inspected and tallied before loading, but exactly how inspection and tallying are arranged is dependent on the type of cargo, method of loading etc., decided from case to case. The usual wording in the bill of lading is that the cargo "*has been received in apparent good order and condition*". This indicates that the carrier is not strictly liable for the cargo and thus, for instance, not liable for hidden defects.

The sequence of events is that, while the bulk cargoes are loaded in the traditional way, the ship officers carry out the supervision and make a note in the mate's receipt of any particulars related to the cargo, such as defects in the packing. All such remarks in the mate's receipts should then be inserted into the bill of lading. This is where the practical problem arises. The shippers are not happy to have an "unclean bill of lading", but if shippers are properly advised, they may have the chance to take back defective cargo and deliver substitute cargo free from defects.

If the carrier fails to insert a remark or to make an annotation in the bill of lading, and the cargo receiver encounters a damage, the carrier will in such cases have a liability as if goods were short-shipped or damaged but, as mentioned, there may be cases where a more far-reaching liability may be imposed on him for wrongful statements. The use of so-called "back letters", such as letters of indemnity, has already been mentioned (see section 6.5.3.3).

The procedure looks very different when loading containers and trailers, but, as it is less relevant to chartering matters, no extensive reference will be made to that.

6.6.9 Date of bill of lading

The bill of lading is a receipt for the goods that have been received for shipment or loaded on board. In either case the correct method of dating the bill of lading is to insert the date when the last parcel of the particular cargo lot was received (in the former case) or when the last parcel of the lot was taken on board (in the latter case). This means that every lot must be regarded separately.

Sometimes, in bulk shipping the shippers wish to have the bills of lading dated differently for various reasons. For example, there may be customs duties introduced on a certain date, and in order to avoid the consequences of such new tariffs the shipper may request the ante-dating of the bill of lading. The master and/or the carrier should not accept such a procedure as this may constitute fraud and, if discovered, may cause serious difficulties with receivers, bankers, authorities etc. The carrier's liability for incorrect dating of bills of lading is usually not covered by P&I insurance. However, in liner business post-dating does not seem to be uncommon, due to the volume of cargo handled, the diversity of shippers and the speed of operations. This may just mean that all bills of lading are dated and signed some time after all the goods have been received or loaded.

It is quite common to find in time charterparties (and for that matter also in voyage charterparties) a clause explicitly stating that the owner shall "sign bills of lading as presented" and also that the shipowner undertakes to deliver cargo even if bills of lading are not presented, provided however, that a guarantee is given by a charterer's parent or by a bank covering the risk of the carrier for possible damages to be paid for having delivered cargo to somebody not entitled to receive it. However, it needs to be stressed that "as presented" does *not* mean that the carrier shall have a duty to sign a bill of lading that is incorrect. Regarding the delivery of cargo without a bill of lading being presented, it is worth noting that a guarantee is not worth more than the guarantor's financial standing and integrity.

6.6.10 Basic features of Hamburg Rules

The Hamburg Rules of 1978 were intended to supersede the Hague/Hague-Visby Rules. Even though the Hamburg Rules have had limited practical application, their principles were adopted by the next convention; the Rotterdam Rules of 2008.

Comparing to the Hague/Hague-Visby Rules, except for the change in layout, the *Hamburg Rules* presented some major material changes, as follows:

- they apply to all contracts for carriage of goods by sea between two States, except when the contract is a charterparty;
- the "error in navigation" exception has been abolished and the "fire" exception narrowed;
- the performing and contractual carrier will be jointly and severally liable against the cargo owners;
- the bill of lading will be conclusive evidence of the contract of carriage against the carrier if the bill of lading has been transferred to a third party who acts in good faith; and
- the limitation amounts have been increased.

The Hamburg Rules won little acceptance and did not eventually manage to replace the older rules on an international scale. Whether the latest convention (Rotterdam Rules) will finally come into force as a binding statutory regime of international sea transport is an open question, since only a few countries have proceeded to its ratification. This convention has, among other changes, reintroduced the catalogue of liability exceptions.

6.7 Insurance matters

Shipping and transportation involves substantial risks on the part of the carrier (shipowner) as well as the cargo owner. The various risks involved have since long been covered by different insurances. From the shipowner's point of view, there is a risk of damage to or loss of the vessel, which has to be covered. This is done through the so-called "hull and machinery" insurance. Furthermore, the shipowner may risk loss of income in case the ship, due to damage, is lying idle while being repaired. Such risk may be covered through a particular "loss of income" insurance. But the shipowner in the capacity of carrier also has a risk for damage occurring to cargo, people on board the vessel, passengers, persons ashore such as stevedores etc. Thus, the shipowner normally has the "protection & indemnity" (P&I) insurance which covers the shipowner's liability for damage of, loss of or delay of cargo in case he is liable. The shipowner may also be liable for oil pollution caused by the vessel. This major risk will also be covered by the P&I insurance and to some extent through the hull insurance. On the other hand, the cargo owner faces a risk of loss of or damage to the goods or delay of their delivery, therefore he will generally carry a cargo insurance policy covering these particular risks. There are a number of risks involved in the sea transport of goods and the different parties may cover them by various insurances. The cargo owner will typically have his risks covered by cargo insurance at the same time as the carrier will cover his liability risk through the P&I insurance.

6.7.1 Liability against third parties

Occasionally, there are claims from a third party other than cargo claims. For instance, claims from stevedores injured during loading or discharging, from passengers, claims for pollution of the sea, or claims as a result of collision with other vessels, tugs, pilot boats, piers etc.

In most cases the owner is primarily liable against a third party for such damages. But, sometimes the primary liability also rests on the charterers. As an example, time charterers in some countries have been held liable for damages caused by oil spillage and for accidents in which passengers were injured. When the primary liability rests with the owner, he may sometimes have a chance to claim recovery from charterers. This is especially so in time chartering when stevedores, tugs, pilots, etc. are employed by the time charterers. On the other hand, when primary liability rests on the charterer, he can also have the opportunity to seek recovery from the owner.

Owners' liabilities against cargo owners, passengers and stevedores are covered by P&I insurance, which typically covers all owners' liabilities against third parties. An important and ever-growing issue regarding third party liability of shipowners concerns oil pollution. Liability rules in this respect have become more and more extensive. In this field, the USA has played a predominant role by establishing the *Oil Pollution Act of 1990* (*OPA '90*). In view of the very high claim amounts at stake, such liability rules strain significantly the P&I Clubs.

As regards oil pollution, TOVALOP and CRISTAL should also be mentioned. *TOVALOP (Tanker Owners Voluntary Liability for Oil Pollution)* is a private tanker owners' organisation guaranteeing cover for pollution liability exceeding what is covered by the P&I Clubs. TOVALOP clauses are found especially in tanker time charterparties and the intention in that context is to guarantee that any liability should be on the owners and not on the time-charterers, as well as that owners have the extra cover given by TOVALOP. *CRISTAL (Contract Regarding an Interim Supplement to Tanker Liability for Oil Pollution)* is a cargo owners' plan which is supplementary to TOVALOP, providing compensation in connection with cargoes carried in vessels covered by the TOVALOP scheme.

Although claims from third parties can be considerable, their thorough examination goes beyond the scope of this book. Owners typically seek valuable advice and guidance from their P&I clubs and hull underwriters when such cases arise.

6.7.2 Cargo insurance and P&I cover

From the above it is evident that there is a risk and liability distribution between the seller and the buyer under the sales contract often following an Incoterms® clause. A traditional CIF purchase puts on the seller a duty to insure the goods only on minimum cover. Should the buyer wish to have extra insurance protection, this should be agreed as quickly and explicitly as possible with the seller, or the buyer should make his own extra insurance arrangements. Therefore, actual cargo insurance may be on different terms and conditions and against different risks than those provided by the Incoterms® rules. For example, "all risks" may be agreed to get covered or large manufacturing or trading companies may carry their own insurances on an annual basis. As it has been seen, in relation to the cargo interest the carrier has a certain minimum liability, depending on the applicable regime of each case, there is thus another risk distribution. The ocean carrier normally covers this liability by being a member of a protection and indemnity (P&I) Club. These Clubs cover the members' liability for cargo damage, personal injury, oil pollution and certain other risks. The rules of the P&I Clubs are more or less standardised. This means that, if a buyer of the cargo under a sales/purchase agreement encounters a loss related to the goods purchased, he would normally turn to the cargo insurer for compensation. The cargo insurer would then turn to the carrier for compensation in accordance with the liability rules applicable, and the carrier would subsequently be reimbursed by his P&I Club. However, it must be emphasised that under P&I insurance the carrier is not reimbursed for damage occurring due to a clean bill of lading having been issued, which should have been marked, or due to cargo having been wrongfully delivered without the surrender of an original bill of lading.

CHAPTER 7

Charter forms

This is the "backbone" of this book, forming the transition towards the core subjects of shipbroking and chartering practice. The charter types influence considerably the revenue side, the cost structure, the risks undertaken, thus the profitability of a shipping company. Understanding the mechanisms behind the vessels' charter types is a key aspect in the commercial management of ships and for ship management in general. This chapter aims to present the most important types of charter and explain how they function. Emphasis is placed on the most popular types of vessels' charter, namely the voyage charter, the time charter, the bareboat charter and the contract of affreightment. The text deals with the following: first, fundamental differences between bulk and liner shipping are examined as far as chartering matters are concerned; second, basic chartering principles and charter types are generally discussed forming the basis for a detailed analysis of chartering practice in the following chapters. Obligations, duties, liabilities and rights of the involved parties are briefly discussed per type of charter; third, standard forms of charterparties per type of charter are introduced; and finally, cost and risk allocation per type of charter is examined.

7.1 General remarks about chartering

A shipowner may enter into a vessel charter with a cargo owner or an entity in need of tonnage in its business. The shipowner and the charterer are the contracting parties (see section 9.3) in the relevant charter document, namely the *charterparty*. The parties generally agree to use a certain standard type of charter form and then add or delete clauses to reflect the circumstances of each individual fixture. The charter form selected depends on several factors, such as the purpose of the vessel's use, the vessel's type and particulars, the trading options and limitations, the cargoes to be carried and the parties involved. Some of these factors have been discussed above, while others will be examined further below.

A *vessel's charter* means that the owner (or the disponent owner[1]) of a vessel in one way or another promises to put a vessel at the disposal of the charterer for a particular voyage or for a certain period. The charterer, in his turn, promises to pay the agreed freight or hire. The management of a ship involves a number of costs. There are *fixed capital costs* (e.g. for debt amortisation and servicing), *fixed operating costs* for the daily management of the vessel (including manning,

---

1 Disponent owner is a person or company which has commercial control over a vessel's operation without owning the ship (e.g. the "charterer" in a bareboat charter who becomes "owner" in a subsequent time or voyage charter is a disponent owner for the second charter).

repairs, maintenance, insurance etc.) and *variable voyage costs* depending on the vessel's employment (e.g. bunkers, port expenses etc.). Shipping business is also connected with different risks, which are not the same when the ship is in port or at sea. In a charterparty, the costs and risks are divided between the contracting parties, namely the *shipowner* and the *charterer*, in various ways (see section 7.6). Judgment of the market expectations and allocation of the risks involved with regard to various factors influence the choice of the type of charter and the level of the freight or hire rate.

Apart from the individuals who own ocean tonnage, nowadays many ship-owners engaged in ocean transportation are companies or partnerships of various kinds, sometimes large multi-national companies. It has also become increasingly common for shipowners to co-operate in many ways. As an example, they may have entered into an agreement to have a common technical management of their vessels. This may not be an extensive form of co-operation, but there are also several other examples of much more important and wide common services provided, such as joint ventures or pool agreements etc. (see also sections 4.1 and 7.2). Another important modern feature is the segregation among ownership, management, operation and trading of vessels, which all are different functions related with the shipping business. One may choose to describe ocean shipping from several angles, but, as far as chartering and shipbroking practice is concerned, the most important distinction is between *liner service* and *chartering vessels in the open market*, since these reflect basically different business ideas and types of vessel employment (see also section 1.1.3).

Over a long period, the structure of shipowning has changed considerably. Traditionally, a shipowner (shipping company) was involved in most or all the functions related to shipping business. They were shipowners arranging for financing, selection and employment of personnel (officers and crew), insurance, bunkers, maintenance (repairs, spares etc.), as well as for finding employment for the ship (chartering). Now, these functions are often split up between various entities, not seldom having their places of business in different countries (see chapter 4).

7.2 Liner and bulk shipping from chartering perspective

In liner shipping the shipowner (carrier, operator) runs a regular service between more or less fixed ports and usually on a fixed time schedule. The liner operator acts as a common carrier, accepting all general cargo shipped between the ports covered by his service. Due to high operating and administrative costs, liner companies have formed few and strong alliances to offer their services worldwide. It should always be remembered that all forms of co-operation in the ocean transportation are subject to strict anti-trust laws, not only from the USA but also from the EU competition authorities. Those involved in international carriage of cargo by sea should be aware of the EU competition law framework, particularly when it comes to pool and co-operation arrangements. A shipper who wants to book cargo space on board a vessel (typically a containership) contacts the agent of a particular line, who then often confirms the sea transport by a so-called *"booking note"* (*B/N*). When the goods have been received for shipment or shipped on board, a bill of lading will be issued on behalf of the carrier.

In bulk/tramp shipping, the vessel is plying between different ports depending on where it finds suitable cargoes. This is at least how traditional bulk/tramp shipping is often described. The basic idea still holds true, but the situation within this sector is rather varied. The basic document here is the *charterparty* (*C/P*) and all terms and conditions are negotiated individually, often based on a previous charter. As in liner shipping, bills of lading are issued upon receipt or upon shipment of the goods. Thus, there may be a conflict between the terms of the bill of lading and the charterparty provisions.

A feature of the liner operator's business philosophy is that he will try to remain in his particular trade network and develop his tonnage, so as to serve clients and sustain profitability. Sale and purchase of vessels is therefore rather a consequence of a new investment or a disinvestment decision with respect to the liner service provided. In bulk shipping, by contrast, the sale and purchase of ships plays a much more central role. An owner calculates and decides whether to ride on a favourable high freight level wave or instead sell a vessel at peak price. The second-hand market and the freight market are normally closely related.

Liner pricing schemes used lead to a low volatility of freight rates, comparing to those of the bulk markets (see sections 2.1 and 2.2). On the other hand, in chartering business of the open market the freight is negotiated on an individual basis, but the general freight market level plays a decisive role and sets a framework (see sections 2.1 and 2.3). Whereas in bulk shipping changes in freight levels are often both very fast and violent, changes are slower in liner business. Liner operators are normally hit at a later stage during a recession than the bulk operators. Correspondingly, the effects of a boom will reach the liner operator later than the bulk operator.

There are no watertight walls between the liner and the bulk sector. However, in the modern era of shipping, the ever-increasing degree of vessels' specialisation has restricted the exchange of tonnage between the sectors. Thereby, the freight levels in the open market are generally not affected by fluctuations of rates in the liner market, and vice versa.

7.3 Types of charter

Chartering or similar sea transport engagements, including booking transportation of cargoes with liner ships (even that is not considered a chartering business form in the strict sense), can be based on different methods and principles, as follows:

- *Chartering vessels in the open market on a charterparty basis versus liner services provided on a booking note basis*

A crucial distinction is that made between liner business and bulk/tramp ship operations as explained in section 7.2. In *liner shipping* the liner operator generally acts

219

as a common carrier, accepting all general cargo shipped between the ports covered by his service. Terms and conditions of the cargo transport (mostly containers) are agreed on the "booking note", while the contract of carriage is usually the "bill of lading". On the contrary, in non-regular, *bulk/tramp shipping*, the shipowners continuously seek the best employment for their vessel considering its type, present position, state and expected development of the freight market etc. Terms and conditions of vessel employment are depicted on a "charterparty".

- *Fixed sum versus payment for time spent*

In liner business owners' remuneration is normally fixed, but often including cost variation clauses (see further section 11.2). Charter agreements may be divided into two wide groups. On the one hand, *project-based agreements*, where the owners are paid a *fixed sum* for doing a specified job, and on the other hand *time-based agreements*, where the owners are paid on the basis of the *time spent* by the charterers for the use of the vessel or part of it. Fixed sum is also called *lumpsum*. A lumpsum agreement can be either a total fixed sum like "*USD 350,000*" or a calculated fixed sum like "*USD 40 per vessel's cubic metre cargo space available*". Project-based/fixed sum types of charter, such as *voyage charters* and *liner services*, will be dealt with in chapter 11, the time-based types of charter, such as *time charters and bareboat charters*, will be handled in chapters 12 and 13, while contracts of affreightment as the most important of the hybrid charter forms which cannot easily be sorted under any of the above-mentioned types of charter will be discussed in chapter 13.

- *Use of the ship from a capacity point of view*

An important basis for distinguishing different types of charter agreements is the use of the ship from a capacity point of view. The charterer may have chartered the whole vessel, that is, all the space of it. Then, the charterparty spells out that the charterer shall deliver "*a full and complete cargo*" to be loaded within the limits of the ship's capacity. If the owner cannot find a charterer for the whole vessel, he may divide the vessel's cargo space between several charterers who may each use, for example, certain portions of the vessel or certain cargo holds. This is known as *space* or *slot charter*. Space charter is not the same thing as when several charterers together charter the vessel. In the latter case, the individual charterers will not have separate rights of control, but will have to act jointly or by authority. In the open market, the most common charter types are those concerning the chartering of the whole vessel. On the other hand, in liner business, the owner (carrier) normally promises to carry a specified cargo (e.g. 10 boxes of machinery, 100 bags of coffee etc.), among many other cargoes carried at the same time, typically in containers. This is known as the carriage of *general cargo*.

- *Use of the ship from a functional point of view*

From a functional point of view, the most important distinction of charter types is made among a voyage charter, a time charter, a bareboat charter and some hybrid forms.

The charterer and the owner often agree that the ship will carry a certain cargo from point A to point B (or will make several consecutive voyages between specific points). The freight to be paid is calculated for the voyage or the voyages to be performed. This charter is known as *voyage charter*, while *consecutive voyages* charter forms rather a variation of a voyage charter.

Another charter type is the *contract of affreightment* (*CoA*), where a shipowner may agree with a charterer to carry for him a large quantity of goods, on specific voyages between certain ports and within a specified period (e.g. one year). One problem with the term "contract of affreightment" is that it is sometimes used to describe a freight contract in general, rather than the above-mentioned specific charter type. Depending on the circumstances, synonym concepts of *quantity contract* or *transport contract* or *volume contract* may be used also to describe a CoA. In order to perform his obligations under a contract of affreightment, the shipowner may employ several of his vessels on an almost continuous basis which in its regularity is similar to liner trading. By using efficiently the contracts of affreightment, the shipowner may fill up his tonnage capacity and make a profit on additional, marginal or return cargoes. Contracts of affreightment may imply an efficiently operated, advanced transportation system with a regular flow of cargo to be served.

There may be particular circumstances where a large business enterprise may be both a cargo owner and a shipowner/ship operator, this is the so-called *"industrial carriage"* case. For example, this appears in the oil sector where the large oil companies may own their own tonnage, but acting in parallel as important charterers of vessels in the open market.

The owner often puts the ship at the disposal of the charterer for a certain period of time, during which the charterer, within the limits of the agreement, controls the commercial employment (not the operation) of the vessel. In such cases, the price paid to the owner is not called "freight", but "hire", determined per time unit (for example per day) and paid regularly in advance. This type of charter is known as *time charter*.

Bareboat charter (or *demise charter*) is another form of a period charter, where the vessel is put at the disposal of the charterer for a certain period of time, but here the charterer takes over the possession and full control of the vessel (i.e. the entire responsibility for the operational and commercial function of the ship). All the costs and expenses except the capital costs are borne by the charterer. The capital costs are the only remaining to the shipowner.

Sometimes, the picture is often much more complex, since mixed charter forms have evolved and a charter agreement may sometimes have features of a joint venture, where the co-operation and profit/loss sharing idea comes more to the fore than it does in traditional charter forms. Today, it is not uncommon for a second-hand purchase or a newbuilding contract of a vessel to be connected with a joint venture scheme or a charter contract. It often occurs a sale and purchase agreement to be related with a "charter-back" arrangement (e.g. a sale and time or bareboat charter back agreement). Furthermore, a bareboat charter or a second-hand purchase may often be combined with a specific ship management agreement.

The different forms of charter will be more closely described below, although still in general terms (for a more detailed description, see chapters 11–13).

7.3.1 Voyage charter

Under this type of charter a vessel is employed for a single voyage. The person who charters the ship is known as a voyage charterer, the payment is called freight and the contract a voyage charterparty. This form of charter is typical within bulk/tramp trading (open charter market). The "charterer" may be the person owning the cargo or may charter the vessel for someone else's account. The "shipowner" of a voyage charterparty, from whom the actual voyage charterer charters the ship, may himself be a time charterer or even a voyage charterer who sub-charters (sub-lets) the ship. In case the shipowner of the charterparty is not the registered owner of the ship, he is normally described as "*time chartered owner*" or "*disponent owner*". Thus, there may be a chain of charterparties which must all be regarded as separate and distinct from one another.

From a practical point of view, a voyage charter means that the owner promises to carry on board a specific ship a particular cargo from one port to another. The vessel shall arrive at the first loading port and be ready to receive the cargo on a certain day or within a certain period of time.

Under a voyage charter the owner retains the operational control and the commercial management of the vessel, being responsible for all the (variable) voyage expenses, such as bunkers, port charges, canal dues, extra insurances, etc., further to the (fixed) daily running costs of the vessel. The charterer's costs are usually expenses and charges relating to the cargo. Loading and discharging costs are divided between the owner and the charterer in accordance with the agreement from case to case. For example, in FIO (free in and out) terms, the charterer bears the costs involved in connection with loading and discharging of cargo. When the charterer controls the cargo-handling operations, he also has the responsibility for the efficiency of the loading and discharging, as well as for the time the vessel spends at ports. Often, but not always, he may have a liability with respect to damage occurring to the goods during loading and discharge.

The relationship between the parties is determined in the voyage charterparty. The names of the parties and the ship are stated, as well as the size of the vessel, the cargo to be carried, places of loading and discharge etc. There will be a clause on the freight to be paid (amount to be paid, time of payment and method of payment) as well as on laytime and demurrage (see chapters 11 and 15). The costs and risks are distributed between the parties. Since the owner bears the operational and commercial costs, the terms dealing with costs and expenses will only mention explicitly a limited number of items, such as expenses with regard to the cargo, perhaps costs for loading and discharging, sometimes certain extra insurance costs, etc. and not least the costs due to liability for damage to the cargo and damage to the vessel. The charterparty may also regulate the allocation of costs and risks for unforeseen events.

The discharging port need not be nominated in the voyage charterparty, and if such is the case, the charterer must have the right later to direct the ship within a certain range to a specific port of discharge. A basic feature of the charter is that the nominated vessel shall be put at the disposal of the charterer. However, it is not uncommon for the actual ship not to be nominated at the time when the charter is concluded, but that only the type of ship is described, with the actual ship to be nominated later. Furthermore, the owner often reserves the right to substitute a vessel or sometimes there is even a duty to substitute a vessel.

The ship must be in the geographical position which the owner specified when the charter was concluded. The vessel must, without undue delay, be directed to the port of loading. A cancelling day is often determined for the latest allowed arrival of the ship at the port of loading and, if she has not arrived at that time, the charterer may cancel the charter. The charterer may also be entitled to claim damages when the arrival of the vessel at loading port is delayed, if the delay is due to owner's negligence. However, the forthcoming voyage will often take place at a later stage. Finally, the owner has then a duty to carry out the agreed voyage or voyages without unnecessary delay and without deviating from the agreed or customary route.

A divergence from the voyage *route* is called *deviation*. In case deviation is not allowed (by agreement, by custom or by law), the laws of most countries put on the owner a far-reaching liability for damage to the goods. In the port of loading the vessel must proceed to the berth assigned by the charterer provided that this berth is safe. If the master does not receive any order to proceed to a certain berth, he has to make the choice himself and, if possible, select and proceed to a customary and safe berth.

In the port of loading the charterer must procure the agreed cargo. Unless otherwise agreed, the cargo must not be of a dangerous nature. In voyage charter the type of cargo is specified and, in the majority of cases, once such a cargo has been accepted for carriage by the owner, he cannot at a later stage claim that it is dangerous. However, there may be situations where circumstances will turn the cargo into dangerous goods. Problems related to dangerous cargoes are more common in liner services and time chartering.

The cargo must be brought alongside the ship at the loading port by the charterer and must be collected from the ship's side at the port of discharge by the charterer or the recipient (consignee) who will be the legal holder of the bill of lading. Particularly with bulk cargoes, the charterer often undertakes to pay for loading and discharge. In this respect, one often meets in the voyage charterparty an *FIO* (*free in and out*) clause, or similar, such as FIOS (free in, out and stowed) or FIOST (free in, out, stowed and trimmed). The FIO clause puts on the charterer an obligation to pay for loading and discharging operations. The basis is also that the charterer will be liable for damages to the cargo occurring during loading and discharging. Since the master has a duty to supervise the orderly loading and discharge (particularly from a vessel's seaworthiness point of view), the owner under an FIO clause may also, in certain circumstances, be liable for damage to the cargo. On the contrary, the phrase *liner terms* is used to mean that the owner shall bear the same cargo-handling costs, as he would in liner service. The concept of "liner terms" is not very precise and cannot be recommended for use in the bulk trades, except in individual cases when the parties know the exact consequences of such cost and risk distribution. Moreover, specific reference should also be made to a concept of the same meaning that may be seen in bulk shipping, the *gross terms*, which formed an alternative to FIO option of cargo-handling cost allocation in the *Gencon '76 (part II, clause 5(a) "loading/ discharging costs – gross terms"*), providing that loading, stowage and discharging was to be carried out by the owners, with charterers being responsible for bringing and receiving the cargo alongside. Under *Gencon '94*, the gross terms alternative has been removed, reflecting the practice that fixtures on the Gencon form are normally on FIO terms or similar[2] (see appendix 1, *Gencon '94, part II, clause 5(a) "loading/discharging – costs/risks"*, and see further section 11.6).

Where the charterer carries out the loading and/or discharging, the parties generally agree that he will have a certain period of time at his disposal for the loading and discharge of the vessel, the so-called *laytime*. The laytime is a reflection of the basic idea of voyage charter, that the owner, who is operating the ship, will be liable for all delay in relation to the transit, whereas the charterer may be liable (or partly liable) for delay in loading and discharge. If the charterer fails to load and/or discharge the vessel within the laytime specified, he has to pay compensation for the surplus time used, the so-called *demurrage*. To a certain extent, the charterer may also be liable for loss of time if there is no berth available for the vessel in the port of loading and also for certain other losses of time that may occur as a consequence of the charterer's acts or omissions. On the other hand, if the charterer saves time for the ship by carrying out his undertakings more quickly than agreed, he may be entitled to claim compensation, the so-called *despatch or dispatch money*, but generally only if an agreement has been reached to this effect.

A charterer of a whole vessel usually has a duty to deliver a full cargo within the ship's capacity. For that purpose a clause of the type "*a full and complete cargo*" of the agreed goods to be delivered and loaded is used, and correspondingly, the owner has a duty to receive the goods and carry them.

Unless a *lumpsum freight* is paid, a form of freight compensation, the so-called *deadfreight*, may be claimed by the owner if too little cargo is delivered or the cargo is delivered in such a state that the ship's full capacity cannot be utilised. This compensation is based on the difference between the full freight to which the owner would have been entitled if all cargo were delivered and the freight to be paid according to the intaken quantity, less any expenses saved for short-delivered cargo. On the other hand, if the vessel cannot load the agreed quantity – she may have been described wrongly or may have taken on board too large a

---

2 Cooke, J., Young, T., Ashcroft, M., Taylor, A., Kimball, J., Martowski, D., Lambert, L.R. and Sturley, M. (2014) *Voyage Charters* (4th edition, Informa Law from Routledge, p. 776).

quantity of bunkers – a corresponding freight reduction will be made. Difficult questions of evidence may arise under such circumstances.

The charterer has a duty to deliver cargo and to perform his undertakings and may not, unless there is an express agreement to the contrary, allege that it is difficult to find cargo or to have it made available to the vessel. However, some charterparties contain exemption clauses to this effect. These clauses are normally understood to mean that the charterer is only exempted from his duty to procure cargo if the hindrance has had an effect on the loading or discharging work, but in some charterparties the exemption clauses are more far-reaching.

The freight is normally paid on delivery of cargo unless something else has been agreed. However, prepayment clauses are common, but freight will be settled and paid only for the cargo discharged after the voyage. If the ship is lost or does not reach its destination, the Anglo-American principle is that no freight will be paid at all. In some legal systems the owner may be entitled to a proportionate freight in such circumstances, if the cargo has been moved toward its destination. In order to protect the owner's right to freight, the freight prepaid clause is often amended with the following wording: *"freight shall be considered as fully earned upon shipment and non-returnable in any event whether or not the voyage shall be performed and whether or not the vessel and/or cargo shall be lost or not lost"*.

Unless the freight is earned and has actually been paid upon loading, the owner may need some security for the due freight payment. When the goods have been loaded on board, the owner has thus physically taken into charge property belonging to the charterer (if the charterer is the owner of the goods). At least, in this case, the general principle seems to be that the owner has a right for lien on the goods. If he has such a lien there may also be justification for the charterer to remain responsible for payment, since the owner may, at the destination, refuse to discharge and deliver the cargo unless the receiver pays what is owed (see further section 11.9 about *lien* and *cesser*).

The voyage charter is further analysed in chapter 11.

7.3.2 Time charter

Under a time charter the crew is employed by the owner, who is also responsible for the nautical operation and maintenance of the vessel and the supervision of the cargo – at least from a vessel's seaworthiness point of view. Within the framework of the contract, the charterer decides the voyages to be made and the cargoes to be carried. It is often said that the charterer is responsible for the commercial employment of the ship, whereas the owner remains responsible for the nautical operation. This distribution of functions puts the master of the vessel in a kind of a demanding position between the owner – his employer and main principal – and the time charterer, having to take both into consideration.

The time charterer may be a shipowner who for a time needs to enlarge his fleet, or a cargo owner (seller or buyer of goods) with a continuous need of transport, who does not want to invest money in a ship but wants to have the control of the commercial employment of the vessel. Sometimes a shipbroker or an agent is engaged in time chartering a vessel in order to speculate on the freight market.

The time charter determines a time and place for the delivery of the vessel from the owner to the charterer and redelivery from the charterer to the owner. Depending on the place of delivery/redelivery, the length of the charter period, the scope and the particulars of the charter, one may distinguish some variations of the time charter; namely a *trip time charter*, a *round voyage time charter* and a *period time charter*. A trip time charter will take the vessel from one place to another exactly as under a voyage charter, but here charterer is paying hire per day, instead of freight per ton of cargo carried. When there is a time charter on a round-trip basis the delivery and redelivery of the ship will take place in approximately the same geographical area. In a period time charter the place of delivery and redelivery of the ship will often be agreed separately, but often within a certain range of ports. Apparently, the two hybrid time charters (trip time and round voyage) are different from the traditional period time charter. When the ship is engaged for a period, she will be employed within an agreed geographical area or on a worldwide basis but typically within internationally acceptable trading/navigating limits. Delivery/redelivery will be normally agreed to take place somewhere within an agreed geographical area, e.g. *"US East Coast, Jacksonville–Boston range"*. The time charter period may last from a number of days to a number of years. As will be discussed further, it is not an easy task to set out precisely when the vessel shall be redelivered, and therefore, the parties may have to use different contractual methods to solve this particular problem. The types of cargo allowed for carriage will normally be agreed specifically in the time charterparty.

It is not uncommon that the parties agree on an option, that is, the charterer and/or the owner will be entitled to demand a prolongation (extension) of the charter for a certain time on the same or revised terms and conditions or on terms and conditions to be mutually agreed. The charterparty then spells out when the owner/charterer shall inform his counter-party that he wishes to use his option (option declaration). This is particularly the situation in cases of time charters over at least one year, and the charterparty may then stipulate for example: *"charter period 2 years, 2 months more or less in charterer's option, such option to be declared on. . ."*. A slight hire adjustment may be agreed for the optional period.

The hire is payable in advance for 15 days or a month or other agreed period. If the hire is not paid promptly, the owner may be entitled to cancel the charter. This right to cancel, which may also be exercised due to a minor delay in payment, stems from the inadequate legal security the owner enjoys should the hire not be paid. Certain limits may be inserted in the time charterparty to prevent the owner from exercising his right of cancellation, at least when caused by technicalities (see anti-technicality clauses and section 12.6.3).

The chartered vessel has to be in conformity with the charterparty with respect to the cargo carrying capacity, speed, bunker consumption and other agreed terms and conditions. The cargo-carrying capacity is particularly important to the charterer. If he is planning to transport heavy goods (deadweight cargo), the vessel's deadweight or the weight the vessel can load, namely *deadweight cargo capacity* or *dwcc* is important to him. If he is planning to transport light and bulky goods (cubic cargo), the volume of the ship is more important. Special demands are often made on specialised vessels as to particular gear and equipment needed. For example, with respect to oil tankers the capacity of the pumps is important. Similarly, reefer vessels must meet certain requirements in respect to refrigerating capacity. Typically, the shipowner has by contract a duty to keep the vessel seaworthy during the charter period. In Anglo-American law the owner has a strict liability for the vessel's seaworthiness and fitness for service at the time of the delivery of the vessel to the time charterer, a liability from which the owner may exempt himself by agreement, at least to a certain extent. On the other hand, it is quite common that the charterparty defines that the vessel is "*to be maintained throughout the currency of the charter*".

As under a voyage charterparty, the ship must be delivered to the time charterer not later than a certain date. Any delay beyond the *cancelling date* entitles the charterer to cancel the charter. The voyages under a time charter also have to be carried out without delay. If the vessel is delayed due to a breakdown of machinery or for other specified reasons, she may be *off-hire*, and then a reduction of the time may be made so that no hire will be paid during the off-hire period. But under a time charter, the owner cannot be basically blamed for delay not caused by the ship. Time lost as a result of adverse weather is thus the responsibility of the charterer. This is also in accordance with the basic risk distribution between the charterer and owner in a time charter. Modern tanker time charterparties may state that the owner is entitled to full hire based on an agreed speed from pilot station to pilot station, thus the owner then carries more of the time risk than he would have according to the time risk distribution under more traditional time charterparties.

Under a time charter the owner's principal duties are thus aimed at faultless manning, as well as technical and operational ship management. In that respect, the charterparty puts on him a basic responsibility for the correct performance of the voyages.

The liability for the cargo may be determined in different ways and may rest with the shipowner or with the charterer or may be divided between them in one way or another. The charterer often has a right to give certain instructions about the signing of bills of lading, whether these are signed by the master or by the agent or the shipowner or the charterer.

When giving employment orders to the vessel, the charterer must keep within the trading limits prescribed by the contract, with respect to geographical areas as well as cargoes to be carried (*trading limits* and *cargo exclusions*). Unless the parties have reached an agreement to the contrary, the charterer may only order the vessel to safe ports and berths. The charterer must follow the terms and conditions of the charterparty as to excepted cargoes and, as in a voyage charter, he must not ordinarily have goods carried which may cause damage to the ship, the personnel or other cargo.

The charterer is liable for costs directly connected with the commercial use of the vessel, for example bunker costs, port charges, as well as expenses for the loading and discharge of cargo. Furthermore, the charterer may be liable for damage (normal wear and tear excepted) caused to the ship in connection with her use. If the charterer fails to employ the ship, he must still pay hire since he is principally liable for the commercial use of the vessel.

At the end of the charter period the charterer has to redeliver the vessel to the owner at the place or area agreed. It would often be hard for the charterer to use the ship effectively during the last part of the charter period if he had to redeliver her on a particular day. Therefore, the charterparty usually contains provisions on *overlap*, entitling the charterer to use the vessel for a reasonable time after the expiration of the charter against an agreed hire, or on *underlap*, entitling the charterer to redeliver her somewhat earlier than the basic charter provides.

The time charter is further analysed in chapter 12.

7.3.3 Bareboat charter

A bareboat or demise charter is a quite different form. This contract resembles a lease of the ship from the owner to the charterer. The bareboat charter usually means that the vessel is put at the disposal of the charterer without any crew. The charterer will thus take over almost all of the owner's operational and managerial functions, except for the payment of capital costs. This means that the charterer will have the commercial as well as the operational responsibility for the vessel, paying for crewing, maintenance and repair, insurance etc.

The bareboat charter had been traditionally a rather unusual type of charter, but with changing trading and investment patterns it has become more common in the last decades. Sometimes, a second-hand sale has been disguised as a bareboat charter with an option to buy in order that taxation can be avoided. Bareboat charter usually covers a certain period of time, typically a long one. Furthermore, the charter is often hinged to a ship management agreement. As mentioned, the bareboat charter may be connected with a purchase option, either at expiration of the charter or during the charter period.

Bareboat chartering may often be described as a kind of ship financing rather than as a genuine charter agreement, one of the reasons being that the owner has surplus capital to invest, whereas the charterer, lacking such capital, needs the vessel commercially. Such a type of a bareboat charter is a form of "financial leasing", a modern type of financing based on a three-party relation, where the current owner of the vessel is the seller of the ship and the "shipowner" of the bareboat charter, the financier is a mortgagee (bank) which consents to the bareboat/sale transaction, while the "charterer" of the bareboat charter is the buyer of the ship who initially pays the bareboat hire for a certain period and then becomes the actual owner by exercising the "option to buy" and paying an agreed amount at the end of the bareboat charter.

Various factors, such as maritime policies applied, may lead to a growing use of bareboat in spite of several different problems that may arise with respect to the nationality of the ship, manning rules etc.

The bareboat charter is further analysed in chapter 13.

7.3.4 Consecutive voyage charter

Consecutive voyage charters are special variations of voyage charters in which the vessel is contracted for several voyages which follow consecutively upon one another. Sometimes, the charterparty states that the ship will make a certain number of consecutive voyages and sometimes that she will make as many voyages as she may perform during a certain period of time. In the latter case, the parties have agreed, as in time charter or a CoA, that the vessel will be at the disposal of the charterer for a certain period of time. Therefore, as a consecutive voyage charter contains both voyage and time charter elements, it is considered a hybrid charter form.

In a typical consecutive voyage charter a named ship is chartered usually on one charterparty, to proceed loaded from loading port to discharging port, to return in ballast and repeat the voyage consecutively until all the agreed cargo has been transported. The individual voyages are made on voyage charter terms and conditions, with the freight typically being paid per voyage in USD per ton of cargo carried, a laytime calculation in ports of loading and discharge respectively, etc. This means that the risk and cost distribution of a charterer in a consecutive voyage charter is very different from that of a time or a CoA charterer (see section 7.6). Basically, the problems arising under agreements for consecutive voyages are those of voyage charters, but the time factor causes certain structural differences, both related to costs and income aspects. Consecutive voyage charterparties often contain provisions protecting the owners' interests, such as bunker clauses, escalation clauses, currency clauses or certain other clauses related to long-term cost variations (see section 13.2.2.3).

This charter type is common where large volumes of cargo are concerned, but while this method lacks the flexibility of the CoA (where not a named ship but any ship of agreed specifications may execute the voyages), the freight rates may be possibly higher here to take into account the ballast, non-earning, return voyage from discharge port to load port. The consecutive voyages may be for a specific number of round-voyages, usually of a rather short distance. Long term such charters may also be found, then having similarities with time charters, but without keeping some of the disadvantages to the charterers of a time charter. For example, in a time charter the charterer is obliged to pay hire for a period of time even though the open market rates have declined in the meanwhile.[3] On the contrary, in a consecutive voyage charter the charterer may have a greater flexibility, as he may have agreed to pay freight per voyage in accordance with the prevailing open market rates of each voyage.

In this hybrid charter type, the owner and the charterer should exercise great caution when it comes to determine rates of *freight* and *demurrage*, since charter rates which diverge from the prevailing market rates may induce the charterer to abuse the charterparty. For example, if the freight rate is high and the demurrage rate low, the charterer may be tempted to keep the ship lying idle on demurrage instead of making a new voyage.

---

3 www.shipinspection.eu (accessed 1 May 2017).

7.3.5 Contract of affreightment

A contract of affreightment (CoA) is also a hybrid charter borrowing characteristics from a voyage and a time charter. It is often called *quantity contract* or *volume contract*, because under a CoA the owner promises to satisfy the charterer's need for transport capacity over a certain period of time, often one year or even several years. It is not unusual that quantity contracts are made up within the framework of liner operations. Under a quantity contract the individual vessel has less importance for the charterer, but the important aspect is that the owner shall perform his duty to carry with an agreed type of tonnage, namely a vessel of agreed specifications which may very well be a chartered vessel from another owner or operator. A similar contract form is the so-called *requirement contract* or *service contract*. Under such agreements, the quantity of cargo to be carried is not guaranteed by the charterers or the shippers and the owners will place tonnage as and when required according to a notice and nomination system.

Shipping companies without owned ships may undertake as operators to carry out such transportation services, therefore they charter-in tonnage to fulfil the individual voyages. The voyages of a CoA may then be carried out with tonnage of the owner's choice but within the framework of the contract. The terms and conditions under this contract will not affect the shipowning position of the head owner, since he is only bound by the transport agreement with his charterer.

The contract of affreightment is further analysed in chapter 13.

7.3.6 Space (slot) charter

This is not a form of vessel charter in the typical sense. In liner shipping it is common for a shipper or a forwarding agent to hire a specified part of a vessel's capacity or get the first option to use a certain part of a vessel's capacity. With such agreements as a base, a liner operator can provide a liner service without employing any of its owned or time-chartered vessels.

In 1993 BIMCO first issued a standard document with the code name Slothire, based on the idea that the charterer hires a specified number of "slots" from the owner. A "slot" was defined as "the space on board the vessel necessary to accommodate one TEU". The document was evidently intended for the container vessels.

This type of charter, also known as "space charter", was in use before Slothire was issued. The idea is that the owner lets to the charterer a certain part of the vessel (e.g. one specified deck) or a certain part of the vessel's capacity (e.g. specified in slots, area, volume, weight, metres of rail etc.).

The remuneration to the owner can be based on capacity booked or capacity used and it can be calculated per voyage or per time unit as the parties agree. In Slothire the remuneration is based on "hire per voyage" for capacity booked irrespective of the capacity actually used.

An important question is whether the owner or the charterer shall be liable as the carrier against the cargo owners. The answer to this depends on the construction of the charter contract. The normal routine is that the charterer, in his capacity as "disponent owner", books the cargo carriage in his own name and thus acts as "contracting carrier" (see chapter 6). Moreover, the bills of lading are normally issued by the charterer in his own name and by using his own forms. The bill of lading forms vary in respect with the "identity of carrier clause" and each case must therefore be assessed on an individual basis as to whether the charterer or the owner or both are liable against the cargo owner. As regards the relation between the charterer and the owner, the solution in Slothire is that owners are liable in accordance with the Hague-Visby Rules, but there is no other liability-sharing clause.

Since the owner has very limited information about the cargo, it is essential that the contract specifies what kind of cargo is acceptable to the owner. In Slothire the owner has the right to be informed about the cargo and, if necessary, open the containers.

Charterers in some cases handle loading and discharging in the same way as in time chartering but, as several charterers are often involved, it is also common for the cargo to be delivered to a terminal and for the owners (liner operators) to handle the loading and discharging.

Space charter is used not only in liner trades, but also as a supplement to the regular transport needs of the industrial carriers, for example the big forest companies. If an industrial company has vessels on time charter but not sufficient cargo to fill the chartered vessel, they can agree with a forwarding agent that he space charters the vessel's free capacity and acts as disponent owner or similar against the cargo owners.

7.4 Chartering documents

The most important documents governing the commercial and legal relationships between the parties are *charterparties* and *bills of lading*, but other documents such as *booking notes*, *delivery orders* and *mate's receipts* also play an important role (see section 6.5.3). On top of these, there are documents such as *cargo manifests, invoices, customs declarations* etc., which are required by various authorities. In some cases numerous copies of the original documents are issued further to the originals. For example, the bill of lading is normally issued in three originals and several copies. An export transaction normally embraces extensive paperwork, although efforts have been made to simplify the documentation and the document routines, for example by the use of computers.

As a matter of principle oral agreements are generally binding, but particularly in international charter transactions, due to the necessity of evidence the parties make out a written document, namely the charterparty.

Figure 7.1 shows the place of the principal documents in the chartering and shipping process, while briefly discussing how the different documents are inter-related.

Under charterparty (C/P) terms the master will sign the bill of lading (B/L) when he has ascertained that all cargo has been loaded on board (and the owners have collected the freight if *freight prepaid* has been agreed).

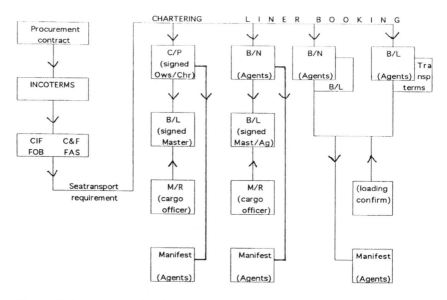

Figure 7.1 Documents in the Chartering – Freighting – Loading Process

In liner trades, where the booking note (B/N) is the basic sea transport agreement, the bill of lading will be signed by the master or the liner agent as per the standing authority. Verification of information related to the cargo is based on the corresponding mates' receipts (M/R) which may contain *remarks* about cargo condition or quantity at the time of loading.

The cargo manifest is a cargo list compiled and issued by the loading agents for use by the owners' various departments and externally by authorities, agents and port services. Some copies of the manifests may be for internal use solely by the owners. It is a shipping document that summarises all bills of lading that have been issued by the carrier or its representative for a particular shipment. For example, a cargo manifest may show the shipment's consigner and consignee, as well as listing product details such as number, value, origin and destination.

It must be noted that the mutual agreement for sea transport between the charterers or shippers (paying freight) on one side and the owners or the line (receiving freight) on the other side is the *charterparty* (in bulk shipping) or the *booking note* (in liner shipping). The *bill of lading* is the document representing the cargo, with the purpose to verify the owner of the goods, to be a receipt for cargo received for loading onboard (or that the cargo has been shipped), as well as to be evidence that there exists an agreement for sea transport (C/P or B/N).

7.4.1 Approved and private chartering document forms

Charterparties and bills of lading are almost always made out on standard forms. BIMCO (see section 3.2.2) plays an important role in the drafting of standard forms of shipping documents (particularly charterparties and bills of lading) and has produced a large number of so-called *approved documents*. Among these, a distinction is made between *agreed, adopted* and *recommended forms.* Figure 7.2 below presents a classic explanation of BIMCO-approved documents.

"Agreed" – "Adopted" – "Recommended" Documents

The application in practice of the various expressions mentioned above may be explained as follows:

"**Agreed**". The charter has been agreed between BIMCO (or the Chamber of Shipping of the United Kingdom*) or Comité Central des Armateurs de France or other associations of shipowners) with one or more groups of charterers or other institutions (for instance, the Polish Coal Charter Committee, the Timber Trade Federation of the United Kingdom, the Syndicat National du Commerce Exterieur de Cereales, Paris or CMEA, Moscow).

The printed conditions of an "Agreed" charter must not be altered or deleted without the express approval of all the organisations who have agreed the charter. An "Agreed" document is compulsory for the trade for which it is intended.

"**Adopted**". If a charter "Agreed" in that way following negotiations between, for instance, BIMCO and one or more groups representing charterers is officially supported by another association of shipowners, for instance, the Chamber of Shipping of the United Kingdom, it is stated that the Chamber of Shipping of the U.K. has "Adopted" the charter; or, on the other hand, if BIMCO wants to support one or the other charter negotiated and "Agreed" between the Chamber of Shipping of the U.K. and one or more groups of charterers, then it is stated that the charter has been "Adopted" by BIMCO.

Moreover, a document issued by an organisation of shipowners, for instance, INTERTANKO, for use in a special trade without having actually been "Agreed" with any particular group of charterers, may be "Adopted" by BIMCO.

An "Adopted" document is compulsory for the members of the organisation who have adopted it if it is an "Agreed" document.

"**Recommended**". When there has been no proper group or groups of charterers with whom to negotiate a particular charter, for instance, the "Gencon" Charter, it is issued as a "Recommended" charter.

The same is the case if the parties with whom a certain charter has been negotiated will not be able to bind their members to use the charter as a clean document. This is the position, for instance, for the "Norgrain" Charter and the "Nuvoy" Charter.

Whereas BIMCO naturally wishes the printed text of a "Recommended" charter to be followed by charterers and shipowners, there is no compulsion in this respect.

"**Approved**". This is the expression used for charters – whether "Agreed", "Adopted" or "Recommended".

"**Issued**". A form of charterparty for the establishment of which it might be said that BIMCO is responsible, is referred to as "Issued" by BIMCO.

"**Copyright**". In several charterparties printed during recent years it has been shown that the copyright is held by "X", usually the party which has issued the document. This has been done in order to discourage sundry parties from printing copies without having proper authority and possibly in such copies deviating from the "official" wording.

*) (From 1975 the General Council of British Shipping)

BIMCO issue several "approved documents". These are classified in accordance with the above explanation. A booklet with a complete set of the approved documents can be bought from BIMCO.

Figure 7.2 BIMCO "Approved Documents"

Both shipowners and cargo interests (charterers) are well represented in BIMCO; thus their documents are considered to be fair, balanced, up to date and accepted from all shipping practitioners.

On the other hand, large shipping or industrial companies or major shippers often design their own charterparties (*private forms*), which they normally use as a basis for chartering negotiations and their cargo transportation. This is the exact case in tanker chartering, where oil majors issue and follow their own charter forms (see also section 7.4.2).

7.4.2 Charterparties

Legal problems may arise if additional terms and conditions are inserted into the standard charterparty forms, since this may require deletions and adjustments in the printed text, as well as further additions. It should be mentioned that the parties very seldom use a charterparty form without making any amendments. Even the private types are often based on a standard form which has been amended by individual clauses.

The purpose of standard charterparties is to standardise a number of clauses frequently used by different parties in different trades, helping the parties eliminate their workload, since it will only be necessary to fill in certain items, such as the names of the involved companies and details about the vessels, ports, cargoes, laytime and demurrage, notice time, freight or hire etc. Amendments and modifications in a standard charterparty necessitate careful adjustments in the printed text. This is often forgotten and in such case the charterparty may become ambiguous and the object of a dispute. Furthermore, there are some *agreed charterparties* (e.g. the *Scancon*) which are intended to be used as is, without any changes or amendments. These particular charterparties seem to have restricted application.

Brokers often have a routine to draft a charterparty; among two parties a specific pattern may have evolved to treat certain items in a particular way. Where two parties have already concluded a charter on certain terms and conditions in the past, it may often be hard to convince the counter-party (or in practice his broker) that a clause should be drafted differently in a new deal between the parties. However, depending on past legal cases, changed customs and practices etc., the parties often have to adjust an old charterparty form. New commercial techniques, legislation, practices and circumstances may be a good ground for the parties to make considerable "riders" and amendments to the standard form. The market situation and the negotiating skills of respective parties or groups of interests may lead to different solutions, which gradually result in the update of the standard forms and the publication of new versions.

In the chartering negotiations there may be certain difficulties in establishing the borderline between "main terms" and "details" of the charterparty. Thus, the end product of the charter negotiations, namely the final charterparty, does not reflect only the commercial realities of each case, but also the level of knowledge and the availability of time among brokers, charterers and owners.

The contents and layout of voyage charterparties differ from those of time charterparties, where the former cover charters related to one voyage, while the latter are related to charters about the commercial use of a ship over a period of time. The voyage charter standard forms are numerous, since in voyage charter the trades and the goods show such considerable variations and may require separate solutions. Within time charter the variation is much less and the number of standard forms used is comparatively small.

The charterparty forms usually have code names which are often connected with the intended use of the form. This is a typical situation in respect to BIMCO contracts. For instance, *Polcoalvoy* is a voyage charterparty (VOY) intended for coal trades (COAL) and drafted in co-operation with Polish shipping interests (POL). Among the several *voyage charterparty forms* produced by BIMCO, some names may be mentioned such as *Baltcon*, *Sovcoalvoy*, *Scancon* and *Nuvoy*. Among the BIMCO forms, the *Gencon* charterparty (see appendix 1 for *Gencon '94*) merits particular mention since it is intended to be used when there is no suitable special voyage charter form available. The Gencon charterparty contains comparatively few standard clauses, since it should be possible to use it as the basis for all trades. The Gencon form seems to have gained gradually more use, but normally it requires several amendments and riders with respect to the individual business. The standard forms are often gradually revised and amended by the issuing organisations, thus it is important that the negotiating parties clearly agree on the particular edition to be used.

With respect to the *tanker voyage charterparties*, the forms are dominated by the large oil companies, which have all drafted their own types, all of which being regularly revised. For example, Shell issues and updates a voyage charter form called *Shellvoy* (see *Shellvoy 6* in appendix 2), while BP issues the respective *BPvoy*. These forms are fairly similar and more or less of a "take-it-or-leave-it" type. Intertanko, the international association of independent tanker owners (see section 3.2.4), has adopted the *Tankervoy '87*, a charter form used occasionally. This document has been influenced by the charterparty forms introduced by the oil companies. Additionally, *Asbatankvoy* is a tanker charter form corresponding to the previous *Exxonvoy*, but also with limited application.

BIMCO has also published some important standard *time charterparties*; *Baltime*, *Linertime* and *Gentime*. This latter form has been designed as a form that should be adaptable to various individual requirements. The first form is basically an old charterparty form which was revised in 2001 to meet modern requirements, whereas Linertime was lately updated in 2015 to reflect current time charter practices where liner operation is involved. The Gentime is a later form first published in 1999. Further to that, the most widely used standard time charterparty for the dry cargo sector remains the *New York Produce Exchange* (*NYPE*). It was first drafted by American broker interests in 1913. Its latest revision of 2015 is the sixth one, reflecting current developments. *NYPE 2015* (see appendix 6), though published by ASBA (Association of Shipbrokers and Agents, USA), it was jointly authored by ASBA, BIMCO and SMF (Singapore Maritime Foundation). NYPE 2015 is a modernisation and substantial enlargement compared with previous major versions: *NYPE '46, Asbatime 1981* and *NYPE '93*. NYPE 2015 contains 57 clauses and one appendix. Despite the numerous updates, it must be mentioned that the NYPE '46 edition is still very commonly used in the market. In addition, during the 1970s, the International Shipbrokers Federation introduced the *Fonasbatime*, a time charter form not frequently used. In general, Baltime is traditionally regarded as the time charterparty most favourable to the owner, while NYPE is considered to be more favourable to the charterer. However, NYPE '93 seems to be regarded as a reasonably balanced document acceptable to both owners' and charterers' interests. It is obviously too early, however, to say whether the new NYPE 2015 will manage to replace NYPE '93 or even NYPE '46, as in shipping, old, officially replaced standard forms have a tendency to survive many years after the official replacement by the new version. For the *tanker time charterparties*, the oil companies have drafted their own forms, such as *BP-time, Mobil-time, Shelltime* (see *Shelltime 4* in appendix 5) etc., having them regularly revised. Intertanko has drafted *Intertanktime* in the past; however the document found limited practical use. For the more specialised vessel types, particular private forms may be used in practice (e.g. in reefers).

Concerning *bareboat charterparties*, the prevailing standard form is published by BIMCO and is called *Barecon* (see appendix 8, *Barecon 2001*). Regarding *contracts of affreightment*, there are a few standard forms used for this type of maritime business, the most popular being the *Gencoa* (a modern, general purpose contract for dry bulk cargoes, published by BIMCO in 2004, see a sample in appendix 9), the *Volcoa* (an older document for dry bulk cargoes, published by BIMCO in 1982) and the *Intercoa* (an older form for the carriage of oil products, drafted by Intertanko but not well established in the market).

It needs to be re-emphasised that there may not be much left of the printed text when it comes to an individual charter transaction. There are frequent deletions and amendments in the printed text, while on top of that, a large number of clauses may be added. It goes without saying that the result is often not a very well-thought and structured legal document, where all the pieces have been carefully put together.

A comprehensive list of the most known standard forms of charterparties may be found in appendix 10.

7.4.3 Transport documents

The transport documents (mainly bills of lading and sea waybills) and their relations to the charter documents and sales agreements were analytically dealt with in chapter 6.

Before proceeding to the following section, a summary of the most important chartering modes mentioned above, together with respective notes and remarks on principal procedures and documentation, may be found in Figure 7.3.

VOYAGE CHARTER

SPOT				
Single voyage port to port	Full cargo	F. i. o. (Liner terms)	C/P	Terms negotiated
Single voyage port to port	Part-cargo	F. i. o. or Liner terms	C/P or B/N	Terms negotiated
Single voyage port to port	Liner booking	Liner terms	B/N (Spec. doc.)	Terms as per tariff

CONTRACT				
Consecutive voyages	Full cargoes	F. i. o.	C/P basis	Terms negotiated

NOTE: Same named ship for total contract, to return immediately after each discharge to lift next cargo until total quantity carried.

Contract of Affreightment	Full or part cargoes	F. i. o. or Liner terms	Basis C/P or B/N	Terms negotiated

NOTE: Mutual agreement on total quantity, shipping schedule, freight and terms. Owners to nominate suitable ships as per agreed schedule.

Requirement or service contr.	Cargoes/Quant to be nominat.	F. i. o. or Liner terms	Basis C/P or B/N	Terms negotiated

NOTE: Mutual agreement on freight and other terms, except Charterers or Shippers option to call for transport as per contract as and when cargo is available. Owners will then endeavour to nominate suitable ship or ships voyage by voyage.

TIME CHARTER

TRIP				
Single trip out port to port	Duration delivery to redelivery	Time chartering conditions	C/P	Terms negotiated
Round voyage from port out to port/s and return	Duration delivery to redelivery	Time chartering conditions	C/P	Terms negotiated

NOTE: A ship may be chartered for trip out with Charterers option round.

PERIOD				
Ship at Chart. disposal for agreed durat.	Time specified (days/months or years)	Time chartering conditions	C/P	Terms negotiated

NOTE: A ship may be chartered for one period with Charterers option further period/s in direct continuation.
A ship may be chartered for period/s in combination with sale to Charterers (Sale with charter back or a hire-purchase agreement).

BAREBOAT CHARTER

PERIOD				
Ship at Chart. disposal and management for agreed duration	Time specified (years)	Bareboat chartering conditions	Bb C/P	Terms negotiated

NOTE: A ship may be bareboat chartered for a period with Charterers option purchase and take-over at the end of the period.

Figure 7.3 Charter Types and Documents

7.5 Management agreements

Instead of operating ships with owned or chartered vessels, a shipping company may try to sell or buy "know-how" and services by particular ship management agreements. This is a type of agreement that has become much more common with the increasing functional split-up of the shipowner's duties. It is reminded that chapter 4 has dealt with ship management aspects and their relation to chartering business. Moreover, the most widely used standard ship management agreement form is that published by BIMCO and called *Shipman* (see appendix 15 for *Shipman 2009*).

The management agreement is not a chartering agreement in its traditional, absolute sense, but rather a shipping know-how and service agreement, arising from an outsourcing ship management model, where the manager in one way or another puts his particular knowledge at the disposal of the principal (shipowner). The owner will thus entrust to another person (the manager) one or several of his functions. A ship management agreement may be either more restrictive covering only some services (e.g. manning, insurances, accounting etc.), or it may be more comprehensive covering several functions (e.g. crewing and technical management) or even the whole management of the vessel including the commercial management (chartering). Therefore, though not a chartering agreement in itself, a management agreement may considerably influence the commercial employment of a vessel.

When commercial management is undertaken by a ship manager, the latter concludes agreements with respect to the vessel in the name of the owner and for the owner's account. The owner in turn covers the manager for all his expenses and also pays to him a compensation, which may be determined in various ways, typically having the form of a management fee per vessel per day or per month. The idea behind this type of agreement is that the principal shall bear the commercial risk, even though the manager shall decide about the vessel's commercial operation and employment. Obviously, there must be a basis of confidence between the parties.

The ship management agreement has come to play a role of ever-growing practical importance for several reasons. In periods of shipping recession some owners go bankrupt and the receivers in bankruptcy or banks, normally without knowledge of shipping, entrust the commercial activity to a manager for a period of time. Similarly, several shipyards act in the same way, when buyers under shipbuilding contracts are unable or refuse to take delivery of the vessel under construction. Furthermore, in the phase of the upward shipping cycle, investors tend to buy newbuildings or second-hand tonnage without having sufficient knowledge of the shipping business, thus for a period they may entrust the ship to a manager until second-hand prices go up so that be able to sell at a profit. Besides, the management agreement may be used by an investor in shipping, lacking sufficient knowledge in the trade, but intending to get familiar and then become a ship operator in the longer term.

Therefore, the shipowner's motives for delegating or outsourcing management services, as well as the respective management models, may vary considerably.

At this point, having now examined the types of charter and how they work, it would be beneficial to redefine how commercial management of ships may be integrated within the whole management system of a shipping company, as this is illustrated by an example in Figure 7.4.

As it may be seen, in this example there are three major divisions/managerial units of a shipowning company contributing mutually to the commercial result which comes not only from vessels' trading and operation, but also from sale and purchase of ships. The first unit is concerned with the financial and corporate management of the company. The second unit is concerned with the operational and technical management of the fleet. The third unit is concerned with the commercial management of the fleet. In a fully integrated company all the above functions are found in one and the same house. However, it is known that shipping is a purely international business and many operations are multi-national, so in this example the financial management may be effected by a fund based in Switzerland, the operational/technical management in Singapore, the commercial operation in Stockholm, while the ships may be registered in and flying the flag of Panama. In such a hypothetical case, the financial relationships and the contractual chartering agreements between the off-shore departments or companies involved could be the

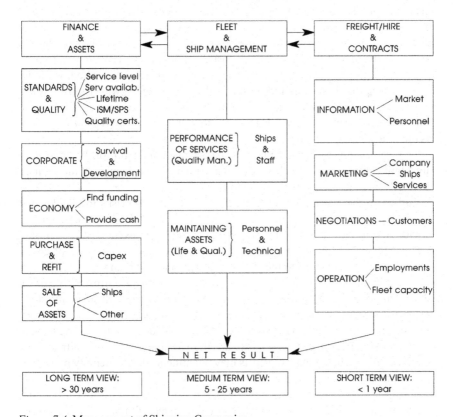

Figure 7.4 Management of Shipping Companies

following. The Panamanian shipowning company is funded by the Swiss fund. The ship is hired from the Panamanian shipowning company to the Singaporean operational manager under a bareboat charter. Then, the ship is let out on time charter from the Singaporean operational manager to the Swedish commercial manager, who in turn takes the earnings from the market, either in the form a voyage charter rate or from another time charter or by employing the vessel in a liner trade or from another kind of contractual employment. In this example, it is implied that all the involved entities – apart from the last one – belong to the same shipping group. One may imagine how complicated things may become when third party interests are involved in these transactions or numerous sub-charters take place.

7.6 Cost allocation per charter type

The commercial management of a ship always involves certain costs, undertakings, obligations, duties, risks and rights. The owners and the charterers have to determine all these different elements before distributing them among themselves, when considering the charter form to be used and the necessary amendments to be made.

As to the costs involved, first the ship's *capital costs* must be taken into account, that is, return and interest with respect to own and external capital (from a cash flow point of view the repayment of external capital must also be brought into the picture). Then, the ship's *operating or running costs* follow. The ship must be manned, this involving wages, social costs, sickness costs, travel costs, training costs, etc. The vessel has to be continuously maintained and repaired, while the owner has normally insured the vessel (hull and machinery, war risks) as well as his liability (P&I, MII). Finally, the ship's *voyage costs* are considered. Bunkers and other consumption materials (except lubricants which are typically regarded as operating expenses) have to be paid for. Port/canal charges and other fees have to be paid, loading and discharge must be arranged and paid for. Besides, there are administrative costs which are dependent on the extensiveness of the business generally and the engagement of the individual vessel.

Further to the distribution of these costs, there are also risks to be allocated. For instance, who will bear the risk for loss of time arising from weather hindrance during the transit or in port, strikes, or political events? Who will bear the risk for a bad freight market? When the calculation is made it is of course necessary to pay attention to the profit or loss allocation arising.

The ship costs may be divided into *fixed costs* which are irrespective of the ship's employment and *variable costs* which are directly influenced by the ship's trading. The corresponding standard classes of costs are then: the capital costs and the operating or running costs are generally considered as the fixed elements of ship costs, while the voyage costs are the variable element. Additionally, it should be remembered that ship costs may be influenced considerably by legislation applied in different countries.

Figure 7.5 and Table 7.1 show how costs, expenses and risks are allocated among the contracting parties (shipowner and charterer) under different types of charter.

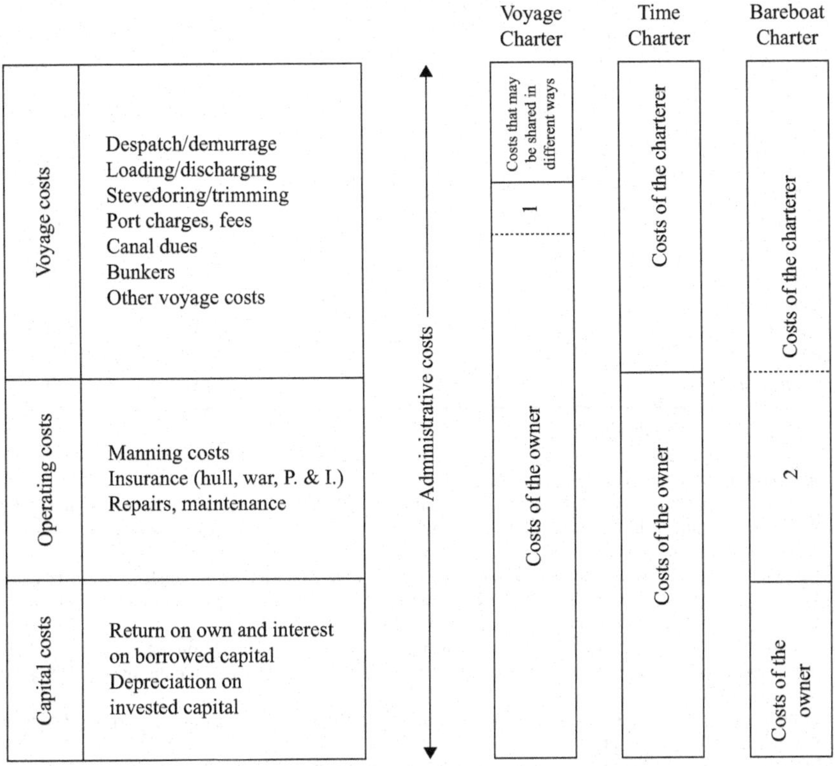

		Voyage Charter	Time Charter	Bareboat Charter
Voyage costs	Despatch/demurrage Loading/discharging Stevedoring/trimming Port charges, fees Canal dues Bunkers Other voyage costs	Costs that may be shared in different ways — 1	Costs of the charterer	Costs of the charterer
Operating costs	Manning costs Insurance (hull, war, P. & I.) Repairs, maintenance	Costs of the owner	Costs of the owner	2
Capital costs	Return on own and interest on borrowed capital Depreciation on invested capital			Costs of the owner

Administrative costs

(1) Certain costs arising in connection with port calls are to be paid by charterer.
(2) Costs for manning, insurance, repairs, maintenance, etc., are sometimes shared between the owner and charterer.
Both parties will have administrative costs.

Figure 7.5 Allocation of Costs and Risks per Charter Type

7.7 "Charter chains"

A vessel may be involved in several different charter contracts at the same time. The following example illustrates such a "charter chain" among various parties (persons and companies).

A is the *registered (real) owner* of the vessel. Since he is only interested in investing money in shipping, he has made a management agreement with B, whereby B will be responsible for different tasks in relation with the operation of the vessel, such as maintenance, repairs, manning, insurance, etc. B will also have a duty to operate the ship commercially, but the commercial risk is still vested with A, which means that a bad charter market will affect the income of A. Instead, if A and B make a bareboat charter, B will appear as the functional owner, and then the commercial risk will be vested with B. Under a management agreement between A and B, B will act as *agent* for A or

Table 7.1 Allocation of Costs and Risks per Charter Type

Cost/Risk Charter	Bareboat Charter	Time Charter	Voyage Charter	Liner Trade
Time risk in port	C	C	CO[1]	O
Loading/Unloading	C	C[2]	CO[3]	O
Port charges	C	C	O[4]	O
Bunkers	C	C	O	O
Time risk at sea	C	C[5]	O	O
Soliciting for cargo	C	C	O	O
Manning	C[6]	O	O	O
Repairs/Maintenance	CO[7]	O	O	O
Insurance	CO[7]	O[8]	O[8]	O
Capital costs	O	O	O	O

C = Charterer   O = Owner

[1] Under a voyage charter the risk of time in port is distributed through charterparty provisions dealing with laytime and demurrage (see chapters 11 and 15).

[2] Under time charter the costs of loading and discharge lie with the charterer. The work will normally be carried out under the supervision of the ship's officers and the ship will give so-called customary assistance with the vessel's crew.

[3] Liability and costs for loading and discharging under voyage charter will be distributed differently from case to case. Sometimes all costs will lie with the owner (liner or gross terms) and sometimes they will rest with the charterer (fio terms or similar).

[4] The owner will pay for normal port charges which rest with and are levied on the vessel, as well as tugs, moorings etc. Certain costs resting with the cargo will according to the main principle be paid by the charterer.

[5] Some charterparties (most of all those used in oil transportation) provide that some risks of time at sea will lie with the owner.

[6] Sometimes the master and even some of the senior officers are employed by the owner.

[7] As to repairs, maintenance and insurance, there are different solutions in the bareboat charterparties, but frequently these costs lie with the charterer.

[8] Even if hull & machinery, protection & indemnity, war risk and (possibly) mortgagee interest insurance are normally provided for and paid for by the owner, it is usual that the time charterer buys a limited P&I insurance, and also, under certain circumstances, he contributes to extra hull and war risk premiums. Under time charter and sometimes under voyage charter, the charterer may insure his liability towards the owner through a so-called *charterer's liability insurance*.

possibly as *correspondent owner*. In the case of a bareboat charter between A and B, the latter will instead act as a *disponent owner* or in some similar capacity.

B, in his turn, has time-chartered out or sublet the ship to C. In the relation B/C, B is acting as agent for the owner, thus he is a correspondent owner or a disponent owner, while C is the time-charterer. C in his turn has chartered the vessel to D under a voyage charter. In the relationship C/D, C is the *time chartered owner*, and D is the voyage charterer. From A's point of view, under a bareboat charter, B is the charterer and C and D are sub-charterers. A has then no direct relation with C or D. From B's point of view C is the charterer and D is the sub-charterer. Conversely, from D's point of view, C is the owner, etc. It is important to observe that those involved in a charter chain have a basic relationship with their contractual party only. That means that they may not even be able to identify the other links in the chain.

It is common that such charter chains exist in the market, and, even if a party is only contractually involved in his own relationship in the chain, it may be important that all parties involved are aware of their respective positions when something happens. The action of each party must be based on the contract in which he is involved. It is also important for a charterer negotiating a sub-charter to take carefully into consideration the framework set by his existing charter with the owner. In our example, when sub-chartering the vessel to D, C must take into consideration the terms and conditions of his charter with B. If he fails to maintain the balance, he may face greater risks and costs in the one relationship than he will be able to recover in the other. He may also face situations impossible to solve because charterparties may be contradictory. In other words, if C has time-chartered the vessel from B, and then sublets the vessel to D, ideally C would prefer to have terms and conditions of the second charter "back-to-back" with the first one.

From a practical point of view, an important factor which can lead to complications is the use of bills of lading. The bill of lading is an independent document which, depending on the circumstances, may involve one or several of the parties directly in relation to the cargo consignees.

CHAPTER 8

Chartering routines

*This chapter is concerned with a substantial subject of shipbroking and char-
tering practice; namely the chartering negotiations. Initially, it deals with an
analytical description of chartering negotiation procedure, comprising three
stages; investigation, negotiation and drawing up of the charterparty. This part
is enriched with real practical examples of orders, position lists and offers illustrating the cases and the differences among the various charter types. Furthermore, the main commercial guidelines of charterparty drawing-up are discussed.
Some examples of special chartering routines are mentioned, while finally, the
principles of chartering negotiations are introduced as guided by the Baltic Code
of Ethics and Market Practice. Throughout this chapter, great emphasis is placed
on the explanation of the chartering terminology and abbreviations. As this is
a value-adding tool for shipbroking and chartering practitioners, it is highly
recommended this section to be read in close connection with the glossary found
at the end of the book.*

8.1 Chartering negotiation procedure

A charterparty is a contract which is negotiated in a free market, subject only to
the laws of supply and demand.[1] While the relative bargaining strengths of the
parties will depend on the current state of the market, shipowners and charterers
are able to negotiate their own terms free from any statutory interference. However, they will invariably select a standard form of charterparty as the basis of
their agreement, to which they will probably attach additional clauses to suit their
own requirements.

The practice of negotiation in dry cargo and tanker chartering is similar, the
main difference being the speed with which the offers and counter-offers are
exchanged. The chartering negotiations in tanker market are speedier compared
to those in the dry market.

Comparing the chartering practice in bulk market and the booking procedure
in liner market there are many differences. Liner booking procedure is normally
much simpler as the traffic is performed in accordance with previously established terms, both as to the freight and as to other conditions found in the line's
pricing scheme. The sailing schedule gives dates for loading and discharging, a
description of the vessel, shipping documentation etc.

---

1 Wilson, J.F. (2010) *Carriage of Goods by Sea* (London, Pearson Education Ltd, 7th edition,
p. 3).

On the other hand, the chartering negotiation procedure in the open market can be divided into three stages, namely the *stage of investigation*, the *stage of negotiation* and the *follow-up stage*.

8.1.1 Stage of investigation

The investigation stage commences when a charterer directly or through a broker enters the market with an order (called a cargo order).

The *cargo order* presents the interest of the charterer for a specific type of charter, a specific type of trade and a specific type of vessel.[2] There is also the case where the investigation stage commences when a shipowner directly or through a broker enters the market with a position list.

The *position list* presents the interest of the shipowner for a specific type of charter and includes the particulars of the vessel as well as her geographical position.

Circumstances may vary somewhat, depending on whether the sale/purchase transaction of the cargo generating the transport is finally concluded or not. This should be evident from the wording of the order. The manner of expressing this may be varied, but a business is considered to be complete from the point of view of chartering technicalities only when the cargo sale is fully in order and signed, when the documentary letter of credit is obtained (if required), when shippers and receivers are prepared, respectively, to sell and buy the goods and when the cargo is ready and available for shipment or can be made available for loading at a certain specified time.

Before the charterer enters the market with the order, he has to decide if he is prepared to commence firm freight negotiations immediately with a shipowner or if he wishes primarily to collect suggestions for different opportunities and intends to start negotiations only after the material gathered has been evaluated. If the charterer is prepared to enter immediately into firm negotiations then the order may open with the following wording:

- FIRM . . .
- FIRM ORDER . . .
- CHARTERERS ARE NOW FIRM AS FOLLOWS . . .
- DEFINITE, FIRM AND READY TO GO . . .
- FIRM WITH LETTER OF CREDIT IN ORDER . . .

When the sale of goods has been concluded, but the charterer does not want to enter into immediately firm negotiations, this may be indicated by

---

2 Throughout this section, real examples of cargo orders are presented which have been compiled from the following sources (accessed 10 June 2016):
- www.shippingonline.cn/chartering/index.asp
- http://chartering.shipsworld.com/2014/01/open-cargo-offer.html
- www.ship.gr/shipbroker/cargoope.htm.

marking the order FIRM or DEFINITE but at the same time with the following words:

- INDICATIONS ONLY
- PLEASE INDICATE
- PLEASE PROPOSE

On the other hand, if the purchase negotiations have not yet been concluded, but the charterer nevertheless requires a freight quotation or at least an idea of the prevailing freight market level, this should be shown in the order by opening it with the words:

- PROSPECTIVE ORDER
- ORDER EXPECTED TO BECOME DEFINITE
- ORDER NOT YET DEFINITE

If the charterers do not have any definite plans, but only wish to make a general investigation of the shipping possibilities, this may be indicated by the phrases:

- POSSIBILITY ONLY
- CHARTERERS HAVE A POSSIBILITY TO WORK UP FOLLOWING BUSINESS

It is not unusual for charterers to put out an anonymous order and request the broker to keep the origin of the order secret until proposals of tonnage have been submitted from serious owners. The broker then denominates the origin and shows that the charterer is well known to him by "FIRST CLASS CHARTERERS (FCC)", "A1 CHARTERERS" or maybe "DIRECT FIRST CLASS CHARTERERS". These expressions cannot be used by other brokers who receive and further the order to their contacts in turn, since they do not know the identity of the charterer.

The contents of the order will then cover those items which the shipowner requires to make his calculations and evaluations. More specifically, the minimum of information that should be included at the cargo order of a voyage charter is the following:

- CHARTERER'S NAME AND DOMICILE
- CARGO QUANTITY AND DESCRIPTION OF THE COMMODITY
- LOADING AND DISCHARGING PORTS
- THE PERIOD WITHIN WHICH THE VESSEL IS TO BE PRESENTED FOR LOADING (LAY/CAN)
- LOADING AND DISCHARGING RATES AND TERMS
- ANY RESTRICTIONS REGARDING TYPE OR SIZE OF SHIP OR AGE OR FLAG
- C/P FORM ON WHICH THE CHARTERER WISHES TO BASE THE TERMS AND CONDITIONS
- COMMISSIONS TO BE PAID BY THE OWNER

This is the absolute minimum of information required to get an owner interested and to make calculations and evaluations. If one or more of the items above are not given by the charterer (shipper), his forwarder or broker, then the owners are left with something they have no means of calculating and evaluating, so that order will most likely be put aside or dropped completely. Apart from this, the presentation of a faulty or incomplete order gives a very unprofessional impression. In addition to items in the checklist above, the charterer may also mention the approximate freight level that he wants to have as a starting point for the discussion or the negotiation (the charterer's *freight idea*), but such information is often omitted from the original order for reasons of negotiation tactics.

An example of *a cargo order at a voyage charter* is the following:

FCC REQUESTS OWNER'S COMPETITIVE RATES FOR THE FOLLOWING FIRM ORDER:
35–40 000 MTS 5% MOLCO COAL IN BULK, SF ABOUT 1.3
POL AT ANCHORAGE AT NEVELSK, SAKHALIN ISLAND RUSSIA
POD AT BERTH TAICHUNG OR TAIPEI OR KAOHSIUNG, TAIWAN IN CHOPT
LAYCAN 10–15 JUNE 2015, TRY VESSEL'S DATES IN JUNE
LD/DIS RATE 3000 MTS WWD SSHEX UU / 6000 MTS WWD SHINC
LOADING AND DISCHARGING BY SHIP'S GEARS
FREIGHT INVITE OWNERS BEST FIOT
GENCON '94 CP
COMM 2.5%

This order concerns a first-class charterer's (FCC) interest for a geared vessel to execute a voyage charter carrying in bulk coal of about 35,000–40,000 mt (MTS), 5% more or less on charterers' option (MOLCO), with about 1.3 stowage factor (SF ABOUT 1.3), from an anchorage at Nevelsk in Russia, which would be the port of loading (POL AT ANCHORAGE AT NEVELSK, SAKHALIN ISLAND RUSSIA), to a berth at Taichung or Taipei or Kaohsiung in Taiwan, which would be the discharging port in charterers' option (POD AT BERTH TAICHUNG OR TAIPEI OR KAOHSIUNG, TAIWAN IN CHOPT). The vessel should be available at the port of loading on 10–15 of June 2015 (LAYCAN 10–15 JUNE 2015); after this date the charterer could opt to cancel the charterparty. The rate of loading would be 3,000 mt per weather working day, Saturdays, Sundays and holidays excluded from laytime[3] unless used; the rate of discharging would be 6,000 mt per weather working day Sundays and holidays included in laytime (LD/DIS RATE 3000 MTS WWD SSHEX UU / 6000 MTS WWD SHINC). The loading and discharging operations would be undertaken by the ship's gears (LOADING AND DISCHARGING BY SHIP'S GEARS). The charterer invited the owner to make a freight offer (FREIGHT INVITE OWNERS BEST) by taking into consideration that charterer would

---

3 See further analysis of voyage charter in chapter 11 and laytime calculation in chapter 15.

be willing to pay the cargo-handling expenses (FIOT stands for "Free, In, Out and Trimmed" terms). So, the freight would include the sea carriage but not the loading, discharging and trimming expenses. The preferred charterparty form was the Gencon '94 (GENCON '94 CP). The commission which should be paid by the shipowners is 2.5% (COMM 2.5%). Since the order was firm (FCC REQUESTS OWNER'S COMPETITIVE RATES FOR THE FOLLOW-ING FIRM CARGO), the charterer would be willing to enter immediately into firm negotiations.

Another example of *a cargo order at a voyage charter* is the following:

FCC REQUESTS OWNER'S PROPOSAL FOR:
BGE 500 MTS
L-DAESAN PORT, KR
D-KHH PORT, TAIWAN (W/#28 OR W/#30)
END JUNE 2015
L RATE: 80 MT/PH
D RATE: 80 MT/PH DISCHARGE SHINC REV
STAINLESS HULL REQUIRED
DWT: MIN 600 TO MAX 10000
IDEAL FREIGHT IS $57 USD/PER MT
PLS PPS C/P
COMM: 2.5%

This order concerns a first-class charterer's (FCC) interest for a chemical vessel to execute a voyage charter carrying chemical cargo butyl glycol ether (BGE) of about 500 mt (MTS), from the port of Daesan in Korea, which would be the port of loading (L-DAESAN PORT, KR) to the Kaohsiung port at TAIWAN (D-KHH PORT, TAIWAN), which would be the discharging port, at wharf 28 or wharf 30 (W/#28 OR W/#30). The vessel should be available at the port of loading at the end of June (END JUNE 2015); after this date the charterer could opt to cancel the charterparty. The rate of loading would be 80 mt per hour (L RATE: 80 MT/PH); the rate of discharging would be 80 mt per hour Sundays and holi-days included in laytime reversible[4] (D RATE: 80 MT/PH DISCHARGE SHINC REV). The charterer required a stainless chemical vessel of about 600–10,000 deadweight tons (STAINLESS HULL REQUIRED, DWT: MIN 600 TO MAX 10000). Furthermore, the charterer suggested a freight of USD 57 mt of chemical cargo shipped onboard the vessel (IDEAL FREIGHT IS $57 USD/PER MT). The charterer asked for the suggestion of the shipowners regarding the form of charterparty that would be used (PLS PPS C/P). The commission that should be paid by the shipowners is 2.5% (COMM: 2.5%). The charterer required from the shipowner a proposal (and not a firm offer), which means that the charterer was not willing to enter immediately into firm negotiations (FCC REQUESTS OWNER'S PROPOSAL).

---

4 See appendix 3 for a definition of reversible laytime.

An order concerning a time charter engagement is presented on the market in largely the same way as for voyage chartering, with the exception that details about cargo, ports, loading and discharging rates and terms are exchanged for details about the vessel, the intended trade, duration of time charter period and places for delivery and redelivery.

In the cargo order of a time charter, the minimum of information required to get an owner interested is the following:

- CHARTERER'S NAME AND DOMICILE
- PLACES OF DELIVERY AND REDELIVERY OF VESSEL
- THE TIME CHARTER PERIOD
- DETAILS ABOUT THE INTENDED TRADE
- ANY RESTRICTIONS OR PREFERENCES REGARDING THE TYPE OR SIZE OF SHIP
- C/P FORM ON WHICH THE CHARTERER WISHES TO BASE THE TERMS AND CONDITIONS
- COMMISSIONS TO BE PAID BY THE OWNER

An example of *a cargo order at a time charter* is the following:

ACCT "TRADEBUSINESS" OPEN FOR FOLL:
T/C PERIOD: 12 MONTHS, 15 DAYS –/+ CHOPT
SIDBC/TWEEN MPP – 14 UP TO 22000 DWAT – MAX 24 YEARS OLD – GOOD GEARED
DEL ANY MED AND OR BLACKSEA
REDL MEDSEA AND OR P.G CHOPT
LAYCAN: 26TH DEC 14
TRADING AREAS: MEDSEA, REDSEA, P.G. EXCL IRAQ BUT IRAN INCLUDED, W.E.C INDIA INCL COLOMBO, WEST AND EAST AFRICA
CGO: MAINLY STEEL, BULK AND OR BGD MINERALS, BGD CGOES, FOOD STUFF, ANIMAL FEED BULK FERTS, TIMBER, IRON ORE, GENERALS, LAWFUL CGO NON DANGEROUS
HIRE DEPENDS ON VESSEL'S CONSUMPTION, SPEED
BUNKER CL TO BE MUTUALLY AGREED
2.5 PCT TTL HERE
OWISE NYPE

This cargo order concerns a charterer's interest (the name of the charterer is "Tradebusiness") for a good geared single deck bulk carrier (SIDBC) or tween deck multi-purpose (TWEEN MPP) of 14,000 up to 22,000 deadweight all told tonnage (14 UP TO 22000 DWAT) and of maximum 24 years old to charter for a one-year time charter period. The vessel would be redelivered to the ship-owner about 15 days before or after the expiration of the one-year flat period at charterer's option (T/C PERIOD: 12 MONTHS, 15 DAYS –/+ CHOPT).

The vessel would be delivered to the charterer in any geographical area in the Mediterranean Sea or in the Black Sea (DEL ANY MED OR BLACKSEA) and it would be redelivered to the shipowner in any geographical area in the Mediterranean Sea or in the Persian Gulf at charterer's option (REDL MEDSEA AND OR P.G CHOPT). The vessel should be delivered until 26 December 2014 (LAYCAN: 26TH DECEMBER 2014); after this date the charterer can opt to cancel the charterparty. The trading areas where the vessel would be employed include the Mediterranean Sea, the Red Sea, the Persian Gulf excluding Iraq and including Iran, the West and East Coast of India including Colombo and the West and East Africa (TRADING AREAS: MEDSEA, REDSEA, P.G. EXCL IRAQ BUT IRAN INCLUDED, W.E.C INDIA INCL. COLOMBO, WEST AND EAST AFRICA). The charterer had the intention to ship mainly steel, bulk and/or bagged minerals, bagged cargoes, food stuff, animal feed, bulk fertilisers, timber, iron ore, generals and any lawful cargo; he had no intention to ship dangerous goods (CGO: MAINLY STEEL, BULK AND OR BGD MINERALS, BGD CGOES, FOOD STUFF, ANIMAL FEED, BULK FERTS, TIMBER, IRON ORE, GENERALS, LAWFUL CGO NON DANGEROUS). The charterer stated that the amount of hire will be determined in accordance with the vessel's fuel consumption and the ship's speed (HIRE DEPENDS ON VESSEL'S CONSUMPTION, SPEED). The bunker clause at the charterparty would be agreed mutually among the shipowner and the charterer (BUNKER CL TO BE MUTUALLY AGREED). The commission which should be paid by the shipowner is 2.5% total (COMM 2.5 PCT TTL HERE). The preferred charterparty form was the NYPE except the case where another charterparty form would be suggested by the shipowner (OWISE NYPE). The charterer was willing to enter immediately into firm negotiations (PLS OFFER OPEN TONNAGE SUITABLE FOR).

Another example of *a cargo order at a round voyage time charter* is the following:

FCC KINDLY REQUESTS OFFER OF SUITABLE VSL FOR BELOW ORDER:
NEED SUPRAMAX
TC ROUND DEL BANDAR ABBAS, REDL BANDAR ABBAS
CARGO: IRON ORE
QUANTITY: ABOUT 55000 MT
LOAD PORT: BANDAR ABBAS – IRAN
DISCHARGE PORT: MAIN PORT OF CHINA
LAYCAN: 10TH OF MAY 2014
LOAD/DISCH RATE: 7000/15000
COMM 1.25% ADCOM 1.25%
OWISE NYPE

This cargo order concerns a first-class charterer's (FCC) interest for a supramax vessel (NEED SUPRAMAX) to charter for a round voyage time charter (TC

ROUND). The vessel would be delivered and redelivered at Bandar Abbas in Iran (DEL BANDAR ABBAS, REDL BANDAR ABBAS). The latest date of delivery is 10 May 2014 (LAYCAN: 10TH MAY 2014); after this date the charterer can opt to cancel the charterparty. The vessel would be used for the carriage of 55,000 mt iron ore from Bandar Abbas (the loading port), to a main port in China (the discharging port). The rate of loading will be 7,000 mt and the rate of discharging will be 15,000 mt (LOAD/DISCH RATE: 7000/15000). The brokerage commission which should be paid by the shipowner is 1.25% as well as an address commission of 1.25% is payable (COMM 1.25% ADCOM 1.25%). The preferred charterparty form was the NYPE except the case where another charterparty form would be suggested by the shipowners (OWISE NYPE). The charterer asked from the shipowner his offer for a vessel suitable for his cargo order (KINDLY REQUESTS OFFER OF SUITABLE VSL FOR BELOW ORDER), which means that the charterer was willing to enter immediately into firm negotiations.

The minimum of information that should be included in the cargo order of a COA charter is the following:

- CHARTERER'S NAME AND DOMICILE
- CARGO QUANTITY (IN TOTAL AND PER SHIPMENT) AND DESCRIPTION OF THE COMMODITY
- LOADING AND DISCHARGING PORTS
- THE PERIODS WITHIN WHICH THE VESSEL IS TO BE PRESENTED FOR LOADING
- LOADING AND DISCHARGING RATES AND TERMS
- C/P FORM ON WHICH THE CHARTERER WISHES TO BASE THE TERMS AND CONDITIONS
- COMMISSIONS TO BE PAID BY THE OWNER

An example of *a cargo order at a CoA charter* is the following:

FCC REQUESTS OFFER FIRM FOR:
500000 MT OF AGGREGATE LIMESTONE (SF 1.4–1.8)
UAE/BAHRAIN
20,000–30,000 MT PER SHIPMENT
LAYCAN 20–25 NOVEMBER 2014
GENCOA C/P
ADDCOM 1.25% + COMM 1.25%

This order concerns a first-class charterer's (FCC) interest for a vessel to execute a CoA charter carrying an aggregate limestone quantity of 500,000 mt (MT) with 1.4–1.8 stowage factor (SF 1.4–1.8). The loading port or ports would be a port or ports in United Arab Emirates (UAE) and the discharging port or ports would be a port or ports in Bahrain. The charterer asked for consecutive shipments of

20,000–30,000 mt each. The vessel should be initially available at the port of loading on 20–25 November 2014 (LAYCAN 20–25 NOVEMBER 2014); after this date the charterer could opt to cancel the charterparty. The preferred charter-party form was the Gencoa (GENCOA C/P). The shipowner would be responsible for the payment of 1.25% commission (COMM 1.25%) and 1.25% address commission (ADDCOM 1.25%). The charterer was willing to enter immediately into firm negotiations (FCC REQUESTS OFFER FIRM).

Another (more analytical) example of *a cargo order at a CoA charter* is the following:

FCC REQUESTS OFFER FIRM FOR:
COA FOR 1YEAR FROM 1ST JANUARY 2009
LOOKING FOR TANKER FOR LOADING CRUDE PALM OIL IN BULK
CARGO/QTY: 25000 +/– 5% OWNERS OPTION, 1–3 GRADES CRUDE PALM
OIL (SP. GR 0.85–0.89 APPROX, HEATED, 55, DEG C) PRODUCTS (EXCEPT
PALM FATTY ACID)
OWNERS MAY NOMINATE OTHER TONNAGES FROM THEIR FLEET AT
A LATER STAGE BUT SUCH VESSELS SHOULD BE OF SIMILAR OR BETTER
CONDITION IN ALL RESPECTS.
SHIPMENT: 1 SHIPMENT CONSECUTIVELY PER MONTH OF 25000 MTS
WITH 5PCT MOLOO SHIPMENT
LOADPORTS: 1 OR 2 SP/SB DUMAI/BELAWAN/LUMUT/PASIR
GUDANG/BUTTERWORTH/PORT KLANG
DISPORTS: 1/2 SB HOUSTON PORT – TEXAS, USA
LAYTIME: 165 MTPH FOR LOAD PORT, 165 MTPH FOR DIS PORT
L/D SHINC REVERSIBLE
FRT IDEA OFFER: USD 68 PMT (TO BE SAME RATES EVERY VOYAGE)
NO DEADFREIGHT ON CHRTRS ACCOUNT PROVIDED MINM QTY
SUPPLIED.
INTERCOA C/P
COMM 2.5% BROKERAGE

This order concerns a first-class charterer's (FCC) interest for a tanker vessel to execute a year CoA charter starting on 1 January 2009 (COA FOR 1YEAR FROM 1ST JANUARY 2009). The tanker would carry in bulk crude palm oil products (except palm fatty acid) of 1–3 grades, of specific gravity 0.85–0.89 and heated at 55 degrees Celsius (SP. GR 0.85–0.89 APPROX, HEATED, 55, DEG C). The shipowner might nominate and use other tankers (from his fleet) at a later stage but such vessels should be appropriate for the execution of the CoA charter (OWNERS MAY NOMINATE OTHER TONNAGES FROM THEIR FLEET AT A LATER STAGE BUT SUCH VESSELS SHOULD BE OF SIMILAR OR BETTER CONDITION IN ALL RESPECTS). The charter concerned consecutive monthly shipments of 25,000 mt with 5% more or less on shipowners option (SHIPMENT: 1 SHIPMENT CONSECUTIVELY PER MONTH OF 25000 MTS

WITH 5PCT MOLOO SHIPMENT). The loading ports would be one or two safe ports or berths (LOADPORTS: 1 OR 2 SP/SB) in Dumai, Belawan, Lumut, Pasir, Gudang, Butterworth, Port Klang. The discharging ports would be one or two safe berths at Houston Port in Texas (DISPORTS: 1/2 SB HOUSTON PORT – TEXAS, USA). The rate of loading and discharging would be 165 mt per hour, Sundays and holidays included in laytime; the laytime would be reversible (LAYTIME: 165 MTPH FOR LOAD PORT, 165 MTPH FOR DIS PORT, L/D SHINC REVERSIBLE). The freight rate suggested by the charterers was USD 68 per mt of cargo shipped onboard the tanker. This rate should be the same during the execution of all voyages of the CoA charter (FRT IDEA OFFER: USD 68 PMT, TO BE SAME RATES EVERY VOYAGE CONTRACT). The charterer was not willing to pay deadfreight in case where no full and complete cargo was loaded onboard provided he has shipped the minimum agreed quantity of cargo (NO DEADFREIGHT ON CHRTRS ACCOUNT PROVIDED MINM QTY SUPPLIED). The vessel should be available at the port of loading on 1 January 2009; after this date the charterer could opt to cancel the charterparty. The preferred charterparty form was the INTERCOA (INTERCOA C/P). The commission which should be paid by the shipowner was 2.5% (COMM 2.5% BROKERAGE). The charterer was willing to enter immediately into firm negotiations (FCC REQUESTS OFFER FIRM).

Moreover, the minimum of information that should be included in the cargo order of a bareboat charter is the following:

- CHARTERER'S NAME AND DOMICILE
- PLACES OF DELIVERY AND REDELIVERY OF VESSEL
- THE CHARTER PERIOD
- DETAILS ABOUT THE INTENDED TRADE
- ANY RESTRICTIONS OR PREFERENCES REGARDING THE TYPE, SIZE, AGE OR FLAG OF SHIP
- C/P FORM ON WHICH THE CHARTERER WISHES TO BASE THE TERMS AND CONDITIONS
- COMMISSIONS TO BE PAID BY THE OWNER

An example of *a cargo order at a bareboat charter* is the following:

FCC REQUESTS OFFER FIRM FOR:
MPP VESSEL, NON OVERAGED
FOR B/B PERIOD 2 YEARS + 1 YEAR AT CHOPT
DELY ANY MED TRY BLACK SEA
LAYCAN 20–30 JUNE 2015
REDEL WITHIN TRADING LIMITS
TRADING WORLDWIDE
INTENTION NON DANGEROUS GENERALS
BARECON C/P
COMS 5% TTL HERE

This order concerns a first-class charterer's (FCC) interest for hiring under a bareboat charter a non-overaged multi-purpose vessel (MPP VESSEL). The bareboat charter period would last two years with a possibility of charter's renewal for one year more at charterer's option (FOR B/B PERIOD 2 YEARS + 1 YEAR AT CHOPT). The vessel would be delivered at any geographical area in the Mediterranean Sea or preferably in the Black Sea (DELY ANY MED TRY BLACK SEA) and redelivered at any geographical area within the trading limits of ship's employment (REDEL WITHIN TRADING LIM-ITS). The vessel should be delivered on 20–30 June 2015 (LAYCAN 20–30 JUNE 2015); after this date the charterer could opt to cancel the charterparty. The ship would be employed worldwide. Furthermore, the intention of the charterer was to not ship dangerous general cargoes. The preferred charterparty form was the BARECON (BARECON C/P). The commission which should be paid by the shipowner was 5% (COMM 5% TTL HERE). The charterer was willing to enter immediately into firm negotiations (FCC REQUESTS OFFER FIRM).

As it has been mentioned, sometimes the investigation stage commences when a shipowner directly or through a broker enters the market with a position list. The contents of the position list cover the following items:

- SHIPOWNER'S NAME AND DOMICILE
- DESCRIPTION OF THE VESSEL
- THE PERIOD WITHIN WHICH THE VESSEL IS AVAILABLE
- TYPE OF CHARTERING (VOYAGE, CONSECUTIVE VOYAGES, TIME, BAREBOAT, COA)
- LOADING AND DISCHARGING RATES AND TERMS
- ANY RESTRICTIONS OR PREFERENCES REGARDING TYPE OF CARGO
- C/P FORM ON WHICH THE SHIPOWNER WISHES TO BASE THE TERMS AND CONDITIONS OF CARRIAGE
- COMMISSIONS TO BE PAID BY THE OWNER

An example of *a position list* is the following:

OWNER REQUESTS CHARTERER'S PROPOSAL FOR THE BELOW VSL FOR V/C
OPEN AT NORTH KOREA ON 6 JUNE 2015
BULK CARRIER
3960 DWT, FLAG: CAM, BUILT NORWAY 2008
GRT/NRT: 2355/1318, LOA/D/BM: 89.50/13.8/6.4M 2H / 2H
G/B CAPACITY: 4800CBM, HATCH SIZE: NO 1: 25.8M*10.20M NO.2: 25.2* 10.20M
HOLD SIZE: NO.1: 30.6M*10.2M NO.2: 25.2M*10.2M
TRADING AT CHINA/JAPAN/S.KOREA/N.KOREA/RUSSIA/FAR EAST
NOT SHIP DANGEROUS GOODS

This position list presents a shipowner's interest for voyage chartering his small bulk carrier (THE BELOW VSL FOR V/C), open at North Korea on 6 June 2015. The vessel was built in Norway in 2008 (BUILT NORWAY 2008) and has the dimensions of length overall, draught and beam as described in the position list. Besides, it has two holds and two hatches (LOA/D/BM: 89.50/13.8/6.4M 2H / 2H). Her deadweight tonnage is 3,960 tons, her gross registered tonnage is 2,355 tons and her net registered tonnage is 1,318 tons (GRT/NRT: 2355/1318). The size of the first hold is 30.6 metres × 10.2 metres and the size of the second hold is 25.2 metres × 10.2 metres. The size of the first hatch cover is 25.8 metres × 10.2 metres and the size of the second hatch cover is 25.2 metres × 10.2 metres. The total grain and bale capacity of the ship is 4,800 cubic metres (G/B CAPACITY: 4800CBM). The intention of the shipowner was for the vessel to be employed in trading areas such as China, Japan, South Korea, North Korea, Russia and the Far East. Furthermore, the shipowner was not willing to ship dangerous goods on his vessel.

8.1.2 Stage of negotiation

When the owner deems the received order to be worth considering, he reverts to the broker or, in case the order was received direct, to the charterer. The owner will normally contact the broker who first brought the order. If a number of brokers have presented the order at about the same time, the one who is "closest" to the charterer is contacted or, in any case, the one who is supposed to be in the best position to negotiate with the charterer in question for the owner's account. The latter can express his interest in various ways. More often, the owner presents his ship and his abilities to meet with the intentions according to the order and submits a *freight indication*. He is still uncommitted with regard to the figures and terms mentioned, but such an indication will advise the charterer of the owner's starting point for a possible negotiation.

Furthermore, the charterer can compare the freight quoted with his own opinion about the proper freight level and can also compare it with suggestions made by other owners. An indication is often given without any time limit since it will not commit the parties. Still the owner is supposed to present – if and when submitting a firm offer later on – freight and terms that are no worse for the charterer than those initially indicated by him. Alternatively, the owner can give the charterer a fairly rough suggestion just in order to sound out the basis for a possible negotiation and let this proposal be accompanied by a so-called *freight idea*. This will certainly indicate a freight level which the owner considers to be suitable as a basis for further discussions, but which may be adjusted upwards or downwards in an eventual offer, when the owner has made more careful calculations.

A proposal, a freight idea or an indication form part of the negotiation stage and form a basis for the charterer's calculations and evaluations of chartering possibilities. The charterer may go on discussing with a number of owners their own

proposals, ideas and indications until he finds a suitable counterpart for negotiations. The charterer will then revert to this owner asking for a firm offer on
the basis of the conditions given in the order or in accordance with the previous
discussions. It may happen that the charterer will reply to the owner's indication
with a firm offer.

If the cargo order of the charterer is firm, the owner may choose to make a firm
offer right away. This can be done when the trade is well known and the freight
level is more or less established and when the ship's size and position fits in well
with the conditions given in the order. A firm offer may also be the most suitable when the owner expects keen competition, especially in a declining freight
market.

The first official offer in chartering negotiations is usually made by the shipowner and is called the *firm offer*. This is not an unbreakable rule and, as it has
been mentioned, there is nothing to stop a charterer opening the proceedings. The
stage of chartering negotiation procedure starts when the first firm offer is structured. Then offers and counter-offers from each side will follow until everything
has been agreed. There is a distinction between offers and counter-offers. When
the recipient of an offer accepts it in its entirety then a contract has been concluded. If, however, the recipient replies rejecting the offer entirely but making a
proposal to the other party, then that also is an offer. If the recipient replies to the
offer accepting some parts of the proposal, but rejecting or amending other parts
of it, then that is a *counter-offer*.

The two sides usually come together through respective brokers of the open
market which are called "*competitive brokers*", although many shipowners
and charterers have specialised chartering departments in their own companies
staffed with so called "*in-house brokers*". Negotiations must be conducted with
care and accuracy.

The negotiation stage can be divided into two parts (phases). The first part concerns the *negotiation of the main terms*. During this part, the charterer's broker
will give to the owner's broker the charterparty on which the charterer wishes to
base the negotiations and it will then be the job of the owner's broker to study
the charterparty and discuss it with his owner. The second part concerns further
negotiations about the details and the wording of the clauses which have not
been taken up during the first part. There has to be complete agreement on all of
the terms and details between the two principals for an enforceable contract to
come into being.

8.1.2.1 Negotiation of main terms

A "firm offer" should be limited as to time and definite as to terms. Opening "firm
offers" are normally based on the main terms and such offers are made subject
to agreement of further terms and conditions of charter. In many cases there is a
variety of "subjects" to be lifted before a charter is concluded.

The firm offer in voyage charter should indicatively contain the following
information:

- THE SHIP'S NAME AND PARTICULARS (DESCRIPTION)
- NAME OF THE SHIPOWNERS
- CARGO QUANTITY AND DESCRIPTION OF THE COMMODITY
- LOADING AND DISCHARGING PORTS AND BERTHS
- LAYDAYS/CANCELING DAY (LOADING NOT TO COMMENCE BEFORE THE FIRST DATE AND THE CHARTERERS HAVING THE OPTION TO CANCEL THE CHARTER IF THE SHIP DOES NOT PRESENT ITSELF BEFORE THE SECOND DATE)
- LOADING AND DISCHARGING RATES AND TERMS (THE RATES OF LOADING AND DISCHARGING, INCLUDING A REFERENCE AS TO HOW TIME WILL COUNT, E.G. 12000/9000 SHEX).
- DEMURRAGE AND DESPATCH RATES
- FREIGHT AMOUNT AND CONDITIONS FOR PAYMENT OF FREIGHT
- CLAUSES GOVERNING TIME COUNTING AND COMMENCEMENT OF LAYTIME, BUNKER CLAUSE, CLAUSES GOVERNING EXTRA INSURANCE PREMIUMS, TAXES, DUES, ETC., WHICH THE OWNER CONSIDERS TO BE OF PRIME IMPORTANCE
- CHARTERPARTY FORM TO BE USED
- TOTAL COMMISSIONS
- REPLY TIME

There are certain differences from the details enumerated above when tanker chartering on voyage basis is concerned, where the most important are:

- loading and discharging rates are not given separately but as a number of total days (hours) for loading and discharge ("*laytime allowance all purposes*"); and
- the freight rate is normally given by reference to Worldscale (see sections 14.3.1, 14.3.2).

It has for many years been the custom for brokers to record the progress and details of negotiations in a "day book".[5] This can provide a checklist as to the agreed position and outstanding issues and can later, in the event of a dispute, be used to safeguard their own and their principal's position. However, in the modern office environment there is less reliance on paper documents and copies of e-mails, instant messaging exchanges and the like may represent an equivalent of a day book. It is essential that such correspondence is recorded and retained for a reasonable period of time, at least until the charterparty has ended and all matters have been finalised. An *offer check list of a voyage charter* follows. It includes *alternative wordings* that may be used in negotiations. Voyage charter terms, calculations and practice are discussed in chapters 11, 14 and 15.

---

5 The Baltic Exchange (2014) *The Baltic Code 2014* (p. 18).

Checklist 1: Offer / Indication (Main Terms)
VOYAGE CHARTER

Off/Ind from	We/Account...indicate/offer firm as follows:
Off/Ind to	Account ....Charterers/Owners
	whom please name in full on replying, for Owners/Charterers
	approval,...
Ship	Vessel/s "..." or Owners option
	substitute, "as described", with all details "about", viz.: Year built............................
	Flag..............., Dwat..................., Cubic cap grain/bale........./........., Gear...........,
	Holds/Hatches.............. /..................., Other details...................................
Vessel subjects	Subject Rearranging schedules/Availability of bunkers /........................
Cargo	For a full/part cargo about Min/Max....................ltons/mtons with 5 / 10 % moloo,
	commodity..............................., with stowfactor..
Loading	Loading 1/2 good and safe berth/s, 1/2 good and safe port/s..................................
	in rotation..
Discharge	Discharging 1/2 good and safe berth/s, 1/2 good and safe port/s...........................
	in rotation...
Conditions	Ports/berths to be always accessible and vessel to remain always safely afloat.............
Laydays	Lay/can..
L/D terms	Rate of load/discharge................. /.......................ltons/mtons daily/per wh/per day
	of 24 running hours, SHEX/FHEX/SHINC/FHINC/Scale load.......... uu/eiu...........
	wp, non-reversible/reversible,......... Any time lost in waiting for berth at or off the port,
	whether in berth/port or not, to count as loading/discharging time without exceptions.
	All costs for shifting between berths to be for Charterers/Ows account, any time
	used to count/not to count, as load/discharge time,..
Freight	Freight rate................., per lton/mton/lumpsum/cbm fios/fiot/liner terms...............,
	gross/net intaken/BL weight/cubic.
	Freight additional/s................................... Bunker/Freight scale/clause...................
Payment	Freight to be.................. % prepaid on signing/releasing BL/after.............. days of
	issuing BL, and balance upon...............................
Taxes/dues	All taxes and/or dues on cargo and/or freight .... freight
	tax, to be for Charterers/Owners account ....
Dem/Desp	Demurrage.............................. per day or pro rata with free/half despatch, working
	time/all time saved both ends...
Agents	Owners/charterers agents both ends..
Spec. clauses	War risk clauses.................... /..................... clauses to apply in full
C/P form	.... C/P........................ subject to all further details
Commission	.... % total commission your end, including..............% address
Subjects	Subject to..
Reply	This is firm for reply here.. hours our time,
	Date...

END OFFER

NOTES: Brokers/Owners/Charterers comments are...............................

....

....

....

....

The firm offer in a time charter should indicatively contain the following information:

- THE SHIP'S NAME AND OTHER IDENTIFYING DETAILS
- OTHER DETAILS OF THE SHIP SUCH AS TOTAL DEADWEIGHT; GRAIN AND BALE CUBIC CAPACITIES; NUMBER OF DECKS; NUMBER OF HOLDS AND HATCHES; NUMBER AND CAPACITIES OF DERRICKS OR CRANES, THE SHIP'S SPEED AND DAILY FUEL CONSUMPTION EXPRESSED AS SO MANY KNOTS ON SO MANY TONS OF WHATEVER TYPE OF FUEL THE SHIP USES
- NAME OF THE SHIPOWNERS
- DESCRIPTION OF THE TIME CHARTER ENGAGEMENT
- PLACE OF DELIVERY OF THE VESSEL TO THE CHARTERER (OFTEN AN EXACT PLACE) AND PLACE OF REDELIVERY TO THE SHIPOWNER (OFTEN A RANGE OF PORTS)
- LAYDAYS/CANCELING DAY FOR THE DELIVERY (DELIVERY OF VESSEL NOT BEFORE A CERTAIN DATE AND THE CHARTERERS' OPTION TO CANCEL IF VESSEL DELIVERED LATER THAN A CERTAIN DATE)
- INTENDED TRADE WITH GEOGRAPHICAL & TRADING LIMITS FROM THE OWNER'S SIDE
- QUANTITY AND PRICE OF BUNKERS ON BOARD ON DELIVERY & REDELIVERY OF THE SHIP
- HIRE AND CONDITIONS FOR HIRE PAYMENT (STATING WHETHER IT IS TO BE PAID MONTHLY OR SEMI-MONTHLY AND ALWAYS IN ADVANCE)
- OTHER CLAUSES WHICH THE OWNER WISHES TO NEGOTIATE AS MAIN TERMS
- CHARTERPARTY FORM TO BE USED
- TOTAL COMMISSIONS
- REPLY TIME

An *offer checklist of a time charter* follows. It includes *alternative wordings* that may be used in negotiating the chartering terms. Time charter terms, calculations and practice are analytically explained in chapters 12 and 14.

Checklist 2: Offer/Indication (Main Terms)

TIME CHARTER

Off/Ind from	We/Account... indicate/offer firm as follows:
Off/Ind to	Account... Charterers/Owners, whom please name in full on replying, for Owners/Charterers approval
Ship	Vessel/s "... " or Owners option substitute, "as described", with all details "about", viz.: Year built........, Flag......, Dwt....... SF/SW ..., Cubic cap. grain/bale......... /........, Gear......., Holds/Hatches....... /......., Speed........ Consumption FO/DO/grades...... /...... /......
Employment	For one T/C-trip R/V T/C-period.................................... via port/s....................................
Trading	Intended cargo/trade ....
Duration	.... days without guarantee/period with +/– days.......................... in Charterers'/Owners' option
Limits/Excl	Always with INL, trading exclusions................., cargo exclusions.......................
Vessel limit	Vessel is sailing under ITF agreement or equivalent, not blacklisted, ISM,..............
Delivery	Delivery any time day/night SHINC at/tip..
Redelivery	Redelivery............../dop..............., within .... range
Laydays	Lay/can...
Hire	Rate of hire.................... per day/monthly .... per Dwt/cft, incl/excl over-time ....monthly or pro rata in advance ....
Bunkers	Bunkers on delivery/redelivery FO/DO......... /........ tons, at................................ / ...., same quantities/prices..
Spec. clauses	Clauses... to apply in full.............................
C/P form	C/P... subject all further details
Commission	.... % total commission your end including .... % address
Subjects	Subject to Charterers approval of plan/inspection/ ....
Reply	This is firm for reply here.. hours our time, date..

END OFFER

NOTES:	Brokers/Owners/Charterers comments are..

....

....

....

....

....

The firm offer in a bareboat charter should indicatively contain the following information:

- THE SHIP'S NAME AND PARTICULARS (DESCRIPTION)
- NAME OF THE CHARTERERS
- DESCRIPTION OF THE BAREBOAT CHARTER ENGAGEMENT
- PLACE OF DELIVERY OF THE VESSEL TO THE CHARTERER (OFTEN AN EXACT PLACE) AND PLACE OF REDELIVERY TO THE SHIPOWNER (OFTEN A RANGE OF PORTS)
- LAYDAYS/CANCELING DAY FOR THE DELIVERY (DELIVERY DATE OF VESSEL NOT BEFORE A CERTAIN DATE AND THE CHARTERERS OPTION TO CANCEL IF VESSEL DELIVERED LATER THAN A CERTAIN DATE)
- INTENDED TRADE WITH GEOGRAPHICAL LIMITS AND OTHER TRADING LIMITS FROM THE OWNER'S SIDE
- HIRE AND CONDITIONS FOR HIRE PAYMENT (STATING WHETHER IT IS TO BE PAID MONTHLY OR SEMI-MONTHLY AND ALWAYS IN ADVANCE)
- CLAUSES NEGOTIATED AS MAIN TERMS
- CHARTERPARTY FORM TO BE USED
- TOTAL COMMISSIONS
- INSURANCE CLAUSE
- REPLY TIME

An *offer checklist at a bareboat charter* follows. It includes *alternative wordings* that may be used in negotiating the charter terms. Bareboat charter terms are discussed in chapter 13.

Checklist 3: Offer/Indication (Main Terms)
BAREBOAT CHARTER

Firm for reply by...

For account of [name and domicile].. as charterers

Name of vessel:..

Description of vessel:..

Delivery port/area:..

Redelivery port/area: ....

Laydays/Cancelling date: ....

Position and expected date of readiness to deliver: ....

Duration of bareboat charter: ....

Trading limits permitted: ....

Cargo exclusions/permitted cargoes: ....

Rate of hire (per day): ....

When/how payable: ....

Bunker quantities/prices on delivery/redelivery: ....

Form of charterparty: BARECON ....

Commission   .... % total commission your end including .... % address

Subjects   Subject to Charterers approval of plan/inspection/..

Reply   This is firm for reply here... hours our time,

             date...

END OFFER

NOTES: Brokers/Owners/Charterers comments are...

....

....

....

....

The firm offer in a COA charter should indicatively contain the following information:

- NAME OF THE CHARTERERS
- CARGO QUANTITY AND DESCRIPTION OF THE COMMODITY
- LOADING AND DISCHARGING PORTS AND BERTHS
- LAYDAYS/CANCELING DAY (LOADING NOT TO COMMENCE BEFORE THE FIRST DATE AND THE CHARTERERS HAVING THE OPTION TO CANCEL THE CHARTER IF THE SHIP DOES NOT PRESENT ITSELF BEFORE THE SECOND DATE)
- LOADING AND DISCHARGING RATES AND TERMS
- DEMURRAGE AND DESPATCH RATES
- FREIGHT AMOUNT AND CONDITIONS FOR PAYMENT OF FREIGHT
- CLAUSES GOVERNING TIME COUNTING AND COMMENCEMENT OF LAYTIME, BUNKER CLAUSE, CLAUSES GOVERNING EXTRA INSURANCE PREMIUMS, TAXES, DUES, ETC., WHICH THE OWNER CONSIDERS TO BE OF PRIME IMPORTANCE
- CHARTERPARTY FORM TO BE USED
- TOTAL COMMISSIONS
- REPLY TIME

An *offer checklist at a CoA charter* follows. It includes *alternative wordings* that may be used when negotiating a CoA (see the terms and practice of a CoA explained in chapter 13).

Checklist 4: Offer/Indication (Main Terms)

COA CHARTER

For reply by...

For account of [name and domicile].. as charterers

Type of ship and vessel particulars (specifications): ....

Cargo quantity:...

Cargo description:..

Rate of freight:... Where and how paid:..

FIOS/FIOT/FIO SPOUT TRIMMED:..

Loading port(s)..................................... Discharging port(s):...

Laydays/Cancelling:...

Position and expected date of readiness to load:...

Loading rate/Discharging rate or days permitted: ....

Demurrage/Despatch: ....

Dues/taxes (for account of): ....

Owners/Charterers to appoint/nominate agents both ends:...................................

Extra Insurance (for account of): ....

Total commission including address: ....

Form of charterparty: GENCOA etc... subject to all further details

Commission   .... % total commission your end, including........................ % address

Subjects   Subject to...

Reply   This is firm for reply here............................... hours our time,

                     Date...

END OFFER

NOTES: Brokers/Owners/Charterers comments are...

....

....

....

....

When negotiating the main terms of a charter, the details that are typically included in the description of vessel's particulars may be the following:

- vessel's name;
- year built;
- flag;
- classification society;
- deadweight (may be given in different ways, e.g. DWCC, DWAT, Summer Deadweight etc.);
- cargo space cubic (in most cases both grain and bale cubic);
- number of hatches and holds;
- cargo gear;
- speed;
- bunker consumption (FO and DO – only applicable on time charter engagement);
- other details of importance for the intended cargo and trade.

264

In practice, the vessel particulars cannot be given with great exactness and it is customary that the description of the ship is followed by the words "ALL DETAILS ABOUT". The shipowner's official description of a ship in tonnage lists, pamphlets and their website is often concluded by the sentence "ALL DETAILS GIVEN WITHOUT GUARANTEE BUT GIVEN IN GOOD FAITH AND BELIEVED TO BE CORRECT" and that is exactly the meaning of the word "ABOUT" in the particulars of the ship given when submitting the offer. It may be emphasised that the precise legal effect of these words is not always easy to foresee, but the individual circumstances may differ and thereby also the legal consequences.

Every offer and counter-offer should state the reply time, date and place for the reply. The reply time will normally be a few hours, but in any case good sense will ensure that there will be enough time for the broker to pass the offer to his principal and to leave a reasonable period for it to be considered. The time limit must be clear and unambiguous. Therefore, although the words "*immediate reply*" or "*prompt reply*" are in common usage, it is advisable not to use such terms because they are inexact. An offer or counter-offer is valid only in the case where the reply is given within the time limit.

One of the most important tasks that should be discussed between the parties is the determination of the freight level in a charter. The factors that are taken into serious consideration from the negotiating parties for the *determination of the fixture rate* may be the following[6] (see also section 2.3):

- type, age and condition of the vessel;
- current state of the freight market for the chartered tonnage;
- expectations of the parties for the freight market;
- charter period (the freight levels of voyage charters are more volatile comparing with the freight levels of time charters);
- overall cost of providing the vessel;
- negotiating power of the parties;
- vessel's position;
- chartering policy or marketing strategy aspects (see chapter 5).

In practice, it never happens that one party replies to a first offer by a "*clean accept*", but instead the reply will normally be one of the following:

- "*Accept your last offer, except . . .*" followed by the terms it is proposed to change. This is a counter-offer, where the recipient is agreeing certain parts of the offer previously received and this is covered by the word "accept", but desires certain amendments, deletions and additions which are listed and covered by the word "except".

---

6 Giziakis, K., Papadopoulos, A. and Plomaritou, E. (2010) *Chartering* (Athens, Stamoulis Publications, 3rd edition, in Greek, pp. 481–482).

- *"Decline your last offer and offer firm as follows . . ."*. This is a complete rejection of the last offer received (possibly because it is in the wrong format and/or on the wrong terms), but an alternative detailed offer is made by the offeree to the offerer.
- *"Decline your last offer without counter"*. The offer is declined by the recipient. Both the parties are then free to work the cargo or vessel elsewhere.
- *"Repeat our last offer, except. . ."* followed by the terms it is proposed to change. This is a complete rejection of the last offer received. The last recipient rejects the offer of the last offerer. Instead, he insists on his last offer proposing an amendment to that.

An offer and a counter-offer frequently have a reservation, or "subject" in other words, which must be cleared before the chartering contract is considered binding[7] (the legal aspects of subjects are presented in section 9.7.3). The most common types of *"subjects"* are the following:

- *Subject Stem (=subject to enough merchandise)*: The charterer has to verify that cargo is or will be available at the loading port. In other words, the fixture is closed subject to the availability of cargo on the date or dates on which a ship is offering to load.
- *Subject Sale*: The charterer has to verify that the sale of goods is fulfilled.
- *Subject Details*: The parties have agreed on main terms, but secondary aspects need to be clarified, for example whether the vessel can obtain certain necessary certificates for the specific trade. Fixture of the charter will be finalised in a later stage when parties agree on details, i.e. on terms and conditions which, although important, do not have a significant effect upon the financial aspects of the charter.
- *Subject Survey*: In the case of a time or bareboat charter, the charterer wants to check the condition of the vessel before the fixture of the charter is finalised.
- *Subject Free* or *Subject Open* or *Subject Unfixed*: Term used in a shipowner's offer. The shipowner informs the charterer that he negotiates with other parties too. A possible acceptance of the offer by the charterer will result in a fixture, only if the vessel has not been fixed to another interested party.
- *Subject Shippers'* or *Subject Receivers' Approval*: The charterer must check with the shipper or receiver or the cargo buyer that the vessel, its expected arrival date and cargo size are acceptable at the receivers' discharge terminal. Shippers' or receivers' approval of the ship is a condition precedent of the fixture.
- *Subject to Management Approval*: Many charterers keep records of vessels' performance and may wish to check that there is nothing against

---

7 Collins, N. (2000) *The Essential Guide to Chartering and the Dry Freight Market* (London, Clarkson Research Studies, pp. 148–150); Coulson, E.C. (1995) *A Guide for Tanker Brokers* (London, Clarkson Research Studies, pp. 10–11); The Baltic Exchange (2014) *The Baltic Code 2014*.

the vessel in their records. Fixture will be final if charterer approves the vessel's and shipowner's track record.

- *Subject to Approval of Charterers by Owners*: Many shipowners keep records of charterers and may wish to check that there is nothing against the company in their records.
- *Subject Head Charterer's Approval*: This subject will normally indicate that the cargo in question is a relet or sublet and charterers have to get approval of the vessel from their head charterers.
- *Subject Board Approval*: This subject is used when the Board of Directors of either principal has to approve the final fixture, but this should be viewed with some caution as such approval can be refused without a specific reason being given.
- *Subject Charterer's Reconfirmation*: This subject is now commonplace and can be used by charterers to hold a vessel while waiting to judge the market direction and sometimes to see if cheaper tonnage becomes available. This is a very onerous subject for an owner as the charterer simply does not need to give any explanation as to why a business is failed. It is recommended that any subject should be more specific in nature to reflect the actual situation.

The negotiations will continue in this way by "taking and giving" offers and counter-offers from both sides until the parties have reached an agreement upon the main terms. This agreement on "main terms", always *"subject to details"* (and other subjects), is concluded by a *"confirm"*. The last reply from the owner's or charterer's side can be concluded by a confirmation, such as one stating: "CONFIRMS HEREBY THE FIXTURE SUBJECT TO DETAILS". Then, the party who has received a "confirmation" has to respond by making a *"reconfirmation"*.

At this stage the charterers or their brokers will immediately compile a full recapitulation of all terms and details so far agreed. This *"recap"* is given to the owner or to the broker representing the owner in the negotiations and this recap should be carefully checked and confirmed by both parties without delay. Because the parties are working within narrow time limits, the offers and counters are given for reply within a number of hours down to immediate reply ("THIS IS FIRM FOR REPLY HERE XX HOURS OUR TIME TODAY/THIS IS FIRM FOR IMMEDIATE REPLY"), and the time allowance tends to become shorter as the parties are coming closer to a "confirm". It is not unusual that the last round takes place with the owners' and charterers' brokers in direct telephone contact with each other, and both brokers also in direct contact with their respective principals over another line.

It must also be stressed how important it is for the parties participating in negotiations to make careful notes and to keep all the paperwork in good chronological order, keeping records of all notes, e-mails and other documents used in any way during the discussions and the firm negotiations from the very beginning until the end. The negotiations may have been a mixture of "Accept . . .

except" and "Repeat last . . ." and may have been carried out both over telephone and via e-mail. In other words, it must be a prerequisite that the documentation should clearly show what has been said and agreed. It is an advantage if at least the first full round is fully and completely documented on e-mail and recapitulation is practically always submitted immediately after the parties are "fixed sub details". A day book together with some kind of a firm offer checklist, which can be amended as negotiations proceed, should always be used by brokers to record important elements of negotiations and safeguard their position.

Figure 8.1 presents the normal routines for negotiations of main terms. Obviously the duration of the talks, the number of terms to be dealt with, the chain of brokers etc., will be different from business to business.

8.1.2.2 Negotiation of details

When the main terms are settled, the negotiating parties must agree the charterparty details. The second phase of the negotiation stage concerns the discussion of these details. In other words, this stage is about all the additional terms which have to be fully clarified before the charter (fixture) is considered complete.

As a matter of principle, those conditions that are of vital importance for the charter engagement should have already been agreed as main terms. On some occasions the negotiations may be cut off if the parties cannot agree on one or more of the details that are of importance. However, one should not use details of the charterparty as an excuse to break off the negotiations if the real reason is something else.

During the negotiations about the main terms it is sufficient to refer to a charterparty form, which can be one of the following kinds: a standard form adopted or approved by BIMCO or another organisation (e.g. ASBA, Intertanko etc.); some other well-known standard form recognised by both parties or the charterers; or the charterers' or owners' own standard form of charterparty. Throughout the main terms negotiations, the reservation "*subject to details*" is maintained by both parties.

The discussions of the second part (phase) of the chartering negotiation stage might be long-lasting. This phase does not usually include offers and counter-offers, but the suggestions of the parties. Therefore, no time limits exist and the parties use phrases like "CHARTERERS SUGGEST THE FOLLOWING AMENDMENTS TO . . .". The charterers now have to present all suggestions on amendments, deletions and additions to the printed text. These may be numerous due to the fact that even the most recently devised standard charterparty forms usually undergo many deletions and additions to the printed text. Some pages of typed additional clauses ("*rider*") are often required to cover the specific intentions of the parties. If the additional clauses and amendments are numerous, the owners will receive the AMENDMENTS TO PRINTED FORM or *PROFORMA*[8] by fax, e-mail or another modern way of communication. Each party is at liberty

---

8 A document containing all the terms and conditions of a contract between a shipowner and a charterer but which is unsigned and therefore is not the contract itself.

to change its mind or introduce new items into the negotiations at any time until the contract is agreed in its final form. However, the brokers and chartering staff should try to avoid doing this as it does not give an impression of trust, competence and professionalism on the side of the party changing the terms.

When both parties have agreed on every detail, there will follow a *confirmation* of the deal, stating that: "HEREBY CONFIRM/RECONFIRM THE FIXTURE". After the agreement of the details, all subjects have to be declared clearly and in order by the charterers before the vessel can be considered fixed. If agreement is reached, a *recapitulation (recap)* message should be exchanged between all parties summarising the final agreement. The recap will set out in full all the

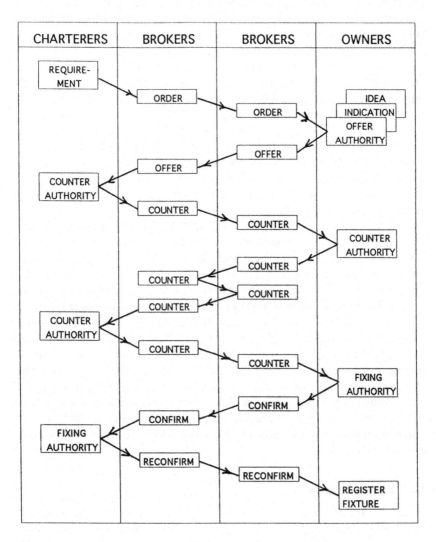

Figure 8.1 Negotiations Procedure

details of the fixture and the wording of the various clauses agreed. This "recap" is drawn up by the charterer's broker and given to the owner or to the broker representing the owner in the negotiations for commentary. The recap should be carefully checked by both parties without delay. The ship can immediately start loading where a prompt spot position is concerned and the fact that the parties have not yet had time to sign or even type the formal document – the original charterparty – has no practical influence on the charter agreement at this stage, provided that a recap has been fully agreed.

Sometimes a FIXTURE CONFIRMATION is required before, for example, a SUBJECT regarding STEM can be lifted or RECEIVERS' APPROVAL can be obtained. The owners may then protect themselves during the negotiations by requesting SUBJECT TO STEM/RECEIVERS' APPROVAL TO BE LIFTED WITHIN XX HOURS AFTER CONFIRMATION OF FIXTURE. Under such conditions, the fixture is still not clean and may fall. The charterers may not succeed in calling forward the cargo for the agreed time of loading or the receivers may refuse to approve the ship or the chartering terms. Should the party who has introduced a subject fail to lift it within an agreed time limit, the counterpart is no longer committed to the business.

In all cases of time limits, whether it is a question of time limits for a counter, for declaring STEM/RECEIVERS' APPROVAL IN ORDER or for waiving other subjects, it is possible for the parties to make a mutual agreement for a new and extended time limit. The date of the charterparty will be the last day on which the parties reach a clean fixture, which means the date when the last remaining subject is lifted.

At this point of analysis, it should be mentioned that there is a fundamental difference between British and American law on the matter of "subject details". Under British law, if the details can not be agreed upon, then there is no contract. Under American law, if a party accepts the offer made "subject to details", then there is a binding contract and the parties are obliged to continue to work out the details. However, there is always the doubt about what the "details" are and what the "main terms" are. Any term which could involve a monetary gain or loss should be comprised in the main term negotiations, e.g. crew war bonuses etc. A general principle is that those conditions which are of vital importance for the charter engagement should be considered as main terms. For the avoidance of doubt, instead of "sub details", the words *subject mutual agreement of all outstanding charterparty terms* will be clearer. This will also help avoid any potential problem due to differences in interpretation of English and American law, as the parties have clearly agreed that all outstanding terms have to be agreed before there is a fixture.

8.1.3 Follow-up stage

During the follow-up stage (when the fixture is finalised), the main task is the drawing up of the charterparty. The charterer's broker draws up the charterparty for the owner's broker to check. The typewritten charterparty is constituted of the *printed form* appropriately amended and filled in with the additional *rider* clauses attached. Any mistakes are dealt with in one of two ways. If no party has signed the charterparty, the brokers could alter the incorrect terms to accord with the negotiation. But, if the charterparty has already been signed by a party (or his broker on his behalf), the brokers should not alter anything without the agreement of the other party. In any case, the charterer's broker has to copy and distribute the correct charterparty and then ensure that all the relevant documents are duly signed.

Due to the fact that there is some delay in preparing the original signed charterparty – especially if the principals want to sign the charterparty themselves and not their broker on their behalf *"as agents only"* (see section 3.5.1) – the owner asks his broker to prepare a working copy of the charterparty (*proforma copy*) and send it directly to the master for guidance. Afterwards, the owner's broker should keep the charterer closely informed of the vessel's position and expected time of arrival at the first port of the charter.

If during the execution of the charter the parties agree to change a term in the charterparty, an *addendum* will be issued, detailing the relevant change(s). The addendum must be signed by both parties and attached to the original charterparty. The same procedure must be followed if there is more than one change in the charterparty terms but at different times. In this case the addenda must be numbered consecutively and dated for the day when the new terms were mutually agreed.

Figure 8.2 depicts how a typical set of charterparty documents is structured, as described above.

BIMCO provides commercial guidelines for the business of chartering and recommends some classic rules of charterparty drawing up. More specifically[9]:

- Use proper and well-established contract forms for the particular business.
- Stick to tested clauses. Hastily drafted clauses are costly "dispute-breeders".
- Remember that clauses which seem unimportant while things run smoothly can be all-important when something goes wrong.
- Make it a habit to compare parallel clauses in different contract forms to see their advantages/disadvantages.
- Display prudence by asking yourself "why?" and "in whose favour?" when alterations to printed text are proposed.
- Benefit from expertise of shipbrokers skilled in the chartering profession.
- The art of avoiding mistakes is the essence of experience.
- Combine routine with imagination. They need each other.

---

9 BIMCO (1992) *Check Before Fixing* (BIMCO Publications, p. 225).

- Be constantly aware of the difference between "just shipping papers", like timesheets, etc. and a bill of lading which is a document of title to value, namely goods.
- In international shipping, mutual trust is fundamental – assist in preserving it.
- "Fraud prevention" is not an empty phrase. Awareness of the dangers is the keyword.
- The integrity of the partner to the contract is more important than the attractive terms offered.

The legal aspects of charterparty construction and interpretation are discussed in chapter 9.

Almost all charterparties, as well as many other contracts agreed in international trade, are concluded under English law (sometimes more precisely expressed as "*the Laws of England and Wales*"). There may also be a specific statement that disputes will be referred to the English courts, without which other courts may hear cases albeit applying English law. Specific legal advice can only come from practising lawyers.

Generally, the parties to a charterparty have freedom to contract on such terms as they may agree during negotiations. The aim should be clarity of expression and the avoidance of ambiguity and inconsistency of clauses. If disputes arise, which eventually come before the court or an arbitral tribunal for determination, the judgment or award will normally reflect the presumed intent of the parties. The *case law* thus made (unwritten law in the sense that it is not an Act made by Parliament) represents the *common law* which

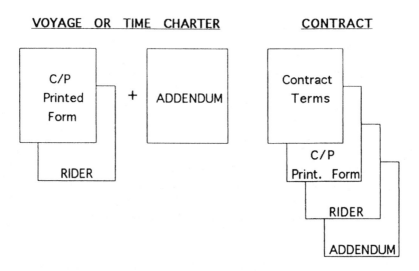

Figure 8.2 Constructing the Charterparty Document

develops according to the changing needs of commerce.[10] A term of a contract may be[11]:

- a *condition*, the breach of which entitling an aggrieved party to elect to be released from further performance and claim damages for any loss suffered, or maintain the contract and sue for damages;
- a *warranty*, the breach of which carrying only the entitlement to sue for damages; or,
- an *innominate* term. Whether the term amounts to a condition or a warranty is a matter of construction and interpretation of the contract, depending on the intention of the parties and the whole of the circumstances.

8.2 Special chartering routines

Tender business is negotiated somewhat differently from normal chartering routines as described above. In the terminology of chartering, there are two forms of a tender.

In one case there are no real negotiations, but charterers, who are very often a governmental or semi-governmental organisation, enter the market with an order in the normal way, but with all terms and conditions on a "take it or leave it" basis. The order is marked "*tender*" or "*tender business*" and states the latest date and time at which offers should be in the hands of the charterers. Respectively, a time limit will be determined up to which the charterers should reply. The owner who wishes to submit offers has to state his lowest freight quotation and declare agreement to all terms and conditions stipulated by the charterers (often given in the order by referring to a familiar official pro forma charterparty).

When the time limit for tendering is reached, the charterers will compare the offers received and they will pick out the owner who, in addition to accepting the terms, has also submitted the most favourable (lowest) freight quotation. This owner will be advised that he has won the tender and thereby the fixture is concluded. The charterparty terms for a business done in this way, sometimes called a "*freight tender*", are often hard and costly as seen from the owner's point of view and sometimes the owner may succeed in compensating himself by quoting somewhat higher freights than would otherwise exist in the market.

The other case of tenders concerns a "*cargo tender*". In this case it is the exporter or supplier or seller of goods who has to offer on a tender for sale and transport of goods requested by a cargo buyer. The exporter will then act as charterer and has to include complete and fixed chartering conditions in his sales offer. The exporter/charterer then enters the market with an order in the usual

---

10 The Baltic Exchange (2014) *The Baltic Code 2014.*

11 Plomaritou, E. (2015) *Charterparty Contract* (London, Lloyd's Maritime Academy, Module 4 of Distance Learning Course "Postgraduate Diploma in Maritime Law"); Plomaritou, E. (2014) "A Review of Shipowner's & Charterer's Obligations in Various Types of Charter" *Journal of Shipping & Ocean Engineering* Vol. 4, Issue 11–12, pp. 307–321.

way and, in this case, it must be mentioned in the order what type of business is concerned. Thereafter, normal routine chartering negotiations will be carried out with the exception that the charterer will maintain a reservation like *"subject to tender being awarded"*. If the charterer wins this tender, then the shipowner will automatically get the charter in accordance with the terms agreed.

Offers on such a cargo tender are usually submitted by a number of different charterers/exporters. There is nothing preventing an owner from concluding fixtures with more than one of the exporters since only one of them will obtain the business.

8.3 Rules of chartering negotiation: the Baltic Code of Ethics

The motto of the Baltic Exchange – *"Our Word Our Bond"* – captures the importance of ethics in shipping. Baltic members need to rely on each other and, in turn, on their principals, for contracts verbally expressed and only subsequently confirmed in writing. The terms of a contract, whether oral or written, are therefore considered sacrosanct and ethical business practice is an essential commitment of Baltic members. In addition, the Baltic Exchange have highlighted certain matters which are worthy of close attention from their members and generally speaking from all market practitioners, having given the following guidance on required standards. These include, but are not limited to, the following basic *principles*[12]:

- All shipping market practitioners are required to honour their contractual obligations in a timely manner.
- In the conduct of their profession, shipping market practitioners must exercise reasonable care to avoid misrepresentation and shall be guided by the principles of honesty and fair dealing.
- A broker must only offer or bid a ship or cargo when duly authorised by a principal or by a broker acting on the instructions of, and with the authority of, the principal. A broker must not purport to hold or make use of authority where that authority is not in fact held, nor may a broker alter the substance of any authority without the approval of the principal concerned.
- An owner or owner's broker may only offer a vessel firm for one cargo at a time. Similarly, a charterer or charterer's broker may only offer a cargo firm to one vessel at a time.
- A principal may receive multiple firm offers for a vessel or cargo but must always make it clear at the time if he is already out firm elsewhere.
- An unsolicited offer or proposal does not necessarily establish the channel of negotiation.
- Prior to quoting business from a principal previously unknown to him, a broker should take reasonable steps to obtain the background and reputation of the principal concerned. However, where this has not been possible, the situation should be clearly communicated to any counter-party.

---

12 The Baltic Exchange (2014) *The Baltic Code 2014.*

- All parties must ensure there is absolute clarity regarding the payment of broker commissions. In the event it is anticipated that commissions will be deducted from hire and paid to the broker by the charterer, then this must be expressly stated in both the recap and the charterparty. Any subsequent change must be similarly documented.
- Brokers who act as Baltic panellists are required to pay careful attention to the instructions offered by the Baltic Guide about the specification, production and management of benchmarks. Impeccable standards of honesty and integrity are critical to this role.

Unacceptable practices include, but are not limited to, the following:

- It is unacceptable for brokers to offer named tonnage against tenders without the authority of owners or disponent owners.
- Brokers must not imply that they hold a ship or cargo firm or exclusively when they do not, in order to secure a response from another party.
- A vessel must not be held on "subjects" for the purpose of determining market direction. Failing a vessel on "subjects" for such spurious reasons is unacceptable.
- It is never acceptable to attempt to manipulate prices in the FFA (freight derivatives) market through the abuse of "subjects" in the physical market.
- Except where expressly contemplated in the charterparty, the offsetting of other claims against hire or freight payments is unacceptable.
- Where a principal operates a company (wholly, partially or separately owned), great care must be taken in considering the company name. Where the name is similar to that of the parent company, market participants are likely to associate the goodwill of the parent with the subsidiary or separate company. In these circumstances, whatever the precise legal position, it is unacceptable if the "subsidiary" fails to meet its obligations while the parent is in a position to meet those obligations or pay appropriate damages. For this reason, it is not uncommon in charter engagements that a *performance guarantee* is sought from the parent company.
- It is unacceptable to withhold payment of undisputed sums, including commission to brokers.
- It is not acceptable for a charterer to fix two vessels or more for one cargo and then hold the vessels over a period of time on "subjects".
- It is unacceptable to distribute route or index rates, produced by the Baltic Exchange from its panel reporting companies, for the purpose of pricing charters or contracts, without an appropriate commission to a Baltic broker.
- Redelivery of a vessel from the time charterer at any time prior to the expiration of the minimum period, unless mutually agreed in advance with the owner, is unacceptable.

- Failure to nominate cargoes or vessels when required under the terms of a contract of affreightment, is unacceptable.

A member of the Baltic Exchange who fails to comply with any of the above terms or practices of the Baltic Code may be disciplined under the Rules. The Directors have power to censure, suspend or expel an individual member and/or a company from the Exchange.

CHAPTER 9

Basic legal knowledge on charterparties

This chapter attempts to introduce the legal perspective of the charterparties. Some of the fundamental legal principles applying to charterparties are presented in the first part, where the reader is familiarised with the contracting parties, the applicable law and the legislation of the charter documents. Then, dispute settlement procedures are discussed, the pros and cons of arbitration are weighed against those of court proceedings, and relevant charterparty clauses are commented upon. Additionally, a section is devoted to highlighting the utmost importance to be given on the evidence of the facts and the burden of proof when a dispute arises, while the complexity of respective legal principles is also emphasised. Furthermore, critical rules and practices are examined in respect to the construction and interpretation of the charterparties. This includes various topics of interest, such as the design of a document, the importance of the implied terms and the most common rules applying to charterparty interpretation when wording is ambiguous. Above all, this section deals with the overwhelming application of English common law on charterparties, its differences against US law or other legal systems and, finally, focus is given to the legal aspects and implications of a very common, significant and controversial feature of charter agreements, namely the "subject" provisions.

9.1 General legal remarks

Every country has its own legal system, which differs to a greater or a lesser extent from that of another country. In certain legal fields the differences may be much smaller than in other fields. In parts of the commercial law, such as contracts of sale and purchase of goods, chartering matters, charterparties and bills of lading etc., there is a higher degree of international harmonisation than there is in many other fields of law, but the governing law is still basically national. In this context, it is important to spell out that there are certain groups of legal systems linked to each other. Very broadly, one may distinguish a number of legal families, such as the Anglo-American common law system, the European continental civil law system, or a system based on Chinese law, Indian law etc. The most important legal families, such as those examples already mentioned, have had great impact on the development of legal systems on national level in several countries.

Common law is generally uncodified. This means that there is no comprehensive compilation of legal rules and statutes. While common law does rely on some scattered statutes, which are legislative decisions, it is largely based on precedent, meaning the judicial decisions that have already been made in similar cases. These precedents are maintained over time through the records of the courts. The precedents to be applied in the decision of each new case are determined by the presiding judge. Common law functions as an adversarial system where there is a contest between two opposing parties before a judge who moderates. In contrast, *civil law* is codified. Countries with civil law systems have comprehensive, continuously updated legal codes that specify all matters capable of being brought before a court, the applicable procedure and the appropriate punishment for each offence. In a civil law system, the judge's role is to establish the facts of the case and to apply the provisions of the applicable code. The judge's decision is consequently less crucial in shaping civil law than the decisions of legislators who draft and interpret the codes.[1]

With regard to chartering, the two most important legal systems are *the Anglo-American common law system which is based on case law* and *the European continental civil law system which is basically codified.* Nowadays, these basics are no longer very true in practice, since there is much legislation in common law systems and much case law in "civil law" systems.

French and German law have a maritime codification covering, inter alia, chartering through non-mandatory regulation. That means that the code will prevail only if the parties have not specifically contracted on a particular point or there is not a custom to another effect. On the other hand, in English or US law there is no codification with respect to chartering, but case law prevails. In essence, common law is made by judges sitting in courts applying statute and legal precedent from previous cases. The standard charterparties used, although differently designed, have contributed to a harmonisation of the laws of international carriage of goods by sea. Furthermore, *charterparties in their vast majority make English law applicable*, thus in that respect English law itself has had a major harmonising effect. Typically, charterparties refer to a particular legal system which shall apply to a possible dispute arising from a charterparty (*choice of law clause*), while also there will often be a reference to a particular court or to an arbitration panel which shall consider the dispute and render judgment (*jurisdiction clause*).

As to the bills of lading, the situation is very different, insofar as legislation (to a certain extent based on one of the international cargo conventions) has been introduced with respect both to the carrier's liability for damage to goods carried and to the particular characteristics of the bill of lading. Nevertheless, bills of lading very often contain also both a choice of law clause and a jurisdiction clause, which, however, may be set aside by a court in a number of countries.

It is also important to keep in mind that the outcome of a dispute may vary depending on the law that will apply or even on the application of the law by a particular court or arbitration panel. Although there are several similarities depending on the globally accepted trade practices and the adopted international

---

1 www.law.berkeley.edu/library/robbins/CommonLawCivilLawTraditions.html (accessed 15 June 2017).

conventions, there may be considerable differences in the outcome of a charter dispute.

9.2 Contract law principles applying to charterparties

The negotiation and contracting procedure of a charterparty was described in chapter 8. At this point, some critical issues of general contract law nature will be examined. The reason for this is that contracting in shipping does not substantially differ from general contract law, though there are of course specific problems occurring in view of the particularities in the field of commercial trade. In this perspective, it is necessary to keep in mind that there are many similarities among most of the legal systems with respect to contract law considerations, but English law is characterised by some specific features. Law is in many respects national in character, but as has been discussed above, there are some international elements, such as those governed by the international cargo conventions, the international trade practices and the internationally used standard charter contracts or transport documents which all have major importance from a chartering view. It seems that charterparties are often subject to English law; therefore some consideration will be given below to English contract law aspects apart from the more general aspects applying. Even if several contract law principles are generally common in most legal systems, there are certain differences which may have an impact on individual disputes. There are two important factors in this context. First, when there shall be a binding contract? Second, if there is a dispute between the parties with respect to the understanding of the contract, which principles of interpretation shall prevail and how they will be applied?

A generally accepted principle seems to be that oral agreements are binding and enforceable. A problem may then arise when the parties have different views, to investigate whether they had made an agreement or they were just negotiating. Some agreements must be in writing in order to be effective and this requirement may vary from one legal system to another. However, it is not unusual that parties specifically agree that a contract shall be binding only when it is in written form and only when it has been signed by the parties. Though not in all legal systems and not under all circumstances, a basis is that an oral offer is binding upon the offeror for a certain period, unless it is expressly stated or evident that the offer shall not be binding. How long an offer is binding depends on the circumstances, particularly if this is expressly spelt out in the offer, for example by stating that "*this offer is binding until the closing of business on November 25*".

In practice, it may be very hard to determine exactly when an agreement has been concluded, since negotiations may be both lengthy and complex. Under such circumstances, it is not always easy to determine the exact moment when the parties have come to the final and all-embracing agreement, unless there is a requirement that the agreement shall only be binding when it has been signed. A dispute may arise over various subtle matters, for example on whether a full agreement has been concluded or whether it was just a common understanding of the parties (which does not amount to a legally binding agreement), or even on whether certain points have been agreed on or have been deliberately left open, etc. However, as it has been explained in section 8.1.2.1, it is fairly common that some points have been left open deliberately when "subject" terms are used in chartering negotiations. In such cases, the agreement will be considered completed when a certain condition is fulfilled, for instance the approval of board of directors, the approval of the central bank, the details of the charter being agreed etc.

The reason why commercial contracts are typically made in writing is explained from the need for evidence between the parties, as well as from the administrative need for documentation in large organisations. Since there is no legal requirement that a charter agreement has to be made in writing, an agreement will be binding when the parties are in agreement irrespective of the form. Therefore, it depends on what the parties have agreed, whether a binding charter comes into force only when the charterparty has been signed or whether the charterparty is seen only as a confirmation of a charter already agreed upon. Charter agreements are probably very seldom oral, while bills of lading, being documents of title, are always written. When a written contract is used, for practical purposes, the agreement is often regarded as concluded only upon the signing of the contract. Legally, the agreement may very well be binding at an earlier stage, which means when the parties are deemed to be in agreement. However, in business contracts it is often expressly stated (or at least commonly understood) that the agreement shall be binding on the parties only upon signing. This seems to be less common in charterparties than in other business contracts, as long as in charter agreements a number of "subjects" may exist and shall have to be lifted before there shall be a finally binding agreement.

Charter negotiations are mainly carried out by telephone and e-mail. Nowadays, the telex is largely outdated in most markets and negotiations are mostly carried out to an increasing extent over the telephone and by e-mail or other electronic means (e.g. teleconferences). The agreement is legally binding when the parties have reached an agreement after negotiation. As mentioned above, charter negotiations are often carried out step by step. The "main terms" may first be agreed between the parties but "subject details", which means that the parties have agreed that minor details remain outstanding before there shall be a finally binding agreement. Often, the negotiations are also brought up to a point where the charter agreement will be concluded as soon as the specified "subjects" are lifted or waived (see sections 8.1.2.2 and 9.7.3).

Normally, a "recap" (recapitulation of the terms and conditions agreed) will be made out to be accepted by the parties at the end of the negotiations and before the original charterparty is drafted. *The accepted recap may then be the legally binding agreement, even if the charterparty is only signed later.* As also noted above, charter agreements are almost always concluded in written form. However, sometimes time is too short to fix the terms and conditions in a written document or sometimes a charterparty is not signed as a result of a mistake or because of the refusal of one of the parties, etc. Despite the failure to agree on all terms and/or to have a finally signed charterparty, a charter may be executed and a voyage may still be performed. In such cases, problems of different types may arise.

It goes without saying that a dispute arising after a voyage has been performed, without a charter having been signed and without a recap having been properly transmitted, may be very hard to resolve. A situation may then occur where the parties are in disagreement as to cargo quantities, laytime, demurrage or even the freight level. It may also be a problem to determine whether a dispute should be referred to arbitration in accordance with an intended charterparty or whether it should be brought before a competent court – this in itself may be a very costly and lengthy point of dispute.

Since parties typically use a standard form of charterparty and then make deletions, modifications and amendments (*note:* the actual charterparty will often contain more rider clauses and amendments than the printed base text), several ambiguities may appear unless the parties are very careful when making the amendments. Since charter negotiations are carried out under pressure of time, a final charterparty may often be easily criticised from a formal legal viewpoint.

If a dispute arises between the parties concerning the interpretation of the charterparty or the way in which it has been performed, the matter will be decided either by arbitrators or by a court of law. In most cases the parties choose to settle their disputes by arbitration rather than by court proceedings. In either case, however, certain rules and principles of law will be applied to decide the particular matter in dispute, although it must be said that it is often difficult to predict the result with any degree of certainty.

9.3 Contracting parties

As has been discussed, the sales contract is to a large extent the trigger for the charter agreement, while it also has an impact on the bill of lading. The seller and the buyer of cargo thereby play a central role in forming the contents of the charter agreement. Depending on the transport clause agreed in the contract of sale, either the seller or the buyer of the goods will be the counter-party of the carrier in a bill of lading or the counter-party of the shipowner in the charterparty, as the case may be. Thus, either the seller or the buyer of the merchandise may usually appear as the named charterer in the charterparty. It may be said that the seller is often the shipper and the buyer is the consignee of the goods, however this is not an absolute rule. Furthermore, depending on the circumstances, the carrier in a bill of lading may be a shipowner, or a time-chartered "owner", or even a bareboat charterer/disponent owner. Generally, where there is a voyage or time charterparty, the bills of lading are signed by the master on behalf of the shipowner. In these circumstances the shipowner would be deemed the carrier who enters into the contract of carriage with the shipper. There may be situations where the charterer issued the bill of lading in his own name. Here, the charterer will be regarded as the principal, hence liable on the contract of carriage. However, bills of lading issued in the charterer's name may contain a demise clause which seeks to transfer contractual liability to the shipowner.[2]

Basically, only the person who makes an agreement is bound by it. Charterparties are usually negotiated through the assistance of brokers, working on owners' or charterers' account, or as plain intermediaries between them. In practice the charterparty may often be signed by a broker as agent (*"for the owner"*, *"for the charterer"* or *"as agent only"*). The owner and the charterer are naturally bound by the measures taken by, and the signature of, their agent if these are made within the limits of his authority. If the broker does not disclose his principal he may himself be bound by the contract. These problems have been illustrated above in section 3.5.1.

It should be added here that the concept of *"agent"* has two meanings. It may involve a practical function as well as a legal power. There are various types of agent in the maritime sphere (such as the ship's agent) and shipbrokers could also be seen as one of them. Some functionaries are clothed with a certain power to represent and bind a principal. Thus, a shipbroker is seldom authorised to sign for and bind his principal without having obtained a particular power of attorney.

The following is an illustration of the practical problems that may arise. It may happen that a brokerage firm or a ship agency office in London or New York is owned by a person who is also the owner of one or several single-ship owning companies, often registered in Panama, Liberia, the Marshall Islands, etc. In accordance with general legal principles, *only the principal is bound by the agreement entered into for his account by his agent.* Furthermore, a company is a legal entity and liable only for its own debts. Therefore, if the broker or agent mentioned above signs a charterparty *"as agent"* for the owner, only the shipping company (at least as a general principle) is bound by the contract, even if the same person owns the agency and the shipping company and is also personally rich. This is based on the *principle of independence of each legal entity.* However, there are certain limitations to this principle which in some cases have been developed in English and maybe more particularly in American law under the heading *"piercing the corporate veil"*. This means the legal effort to prove that various companies are owned by the same person, thus liability may be spread over the companies of the same group or their assets (e.g. ships) or even to the person itself. Similar considerations have taken place in various legal systems, sometimes through particular legislation. Nevertheless, it must be said that breaking the "corporate veil" remains rather difficult in most legal jurisdictions worldwide.

9.4 Applicable law and legislation

It is sometimes difficult to decide which law should apply to a dispute, but normally the charterparty stipulates the particular law to apply, either through a printed clause or a particularly negotiated clause added in the rider. In such case,

---

2 Carr, I. and Stone, P. (2014) *International Trade Law* (Routledge, 5th edition, p. 8).

the agreement of the parties will normally prevail. If they have not made any agreement on the point, there may be certain difficulties in establishing the law applicable, but in law particular methods have been developed. The choice of the applicable law may then depend on several individual factors: the nationality of the parties; the place where the contract has been concluded; the place of the contractual performance; the language of the agreement, etc. This choice is important since legal principles may vary considerably between different legal systems. For instance, it will be extremely difficult to determine the law applicable in a case where the shipowner is Swedish, the time charterer ("time-chartered owner") is Greek or French, the subsequent sub-charterer or voyage charterer is English, the shipper Dutch and the cargo consignee American, as in such an example major differences would exist in the legal systems of the respective countries. These several relationships would probably be governed by different agreements, and different laws might be applicable under the relevant contracts.

As mentioned, a charterparty normally contains a choice of law clause and a jurisdiction clause, explicitly referring a dispute to be decided by a specific procedure (e.g. arbitration or legal course), in a specific country or city and in accordance with a specific law. In ocean charterparties, disputes are commonly referred to arbitration or legal procedure in London or New York, with English or USA law to apply respectively. Several BIMCO documents set out a relevant choice of applicable law for the parties (see for example *Gencon '94, part II, clause 19 "law and arbitration"* in appendix 1). In relation to the great number of charter transactions taking place globally, very few disputes reach the point of arbitration proceedings and even fewer are cleared in the legal courts, while most are settled, more or less amicably, between the parties.

9.5 Court proceedings and arbitration

9.5.1 Court proceedings

When a dispute arises between the parties, which needs to be referred to court proceedings, the first problem may thus be to find out whether the court is competent to judge. The procedural rules vary from country to country. The most frequent pattern is that court proceedings may be channelled through three basic layers of courts. For example, under English law a judgment at first level may be appealed to a Court of Appeal and then to the Supreme Court (which has replaced the House of Lords). The possibilities to appeal a judgment may vary considerably in different legal systems. Court proceedings are public and may normally take a long time due to appeals.

The costs of a legal action may be considerable, covering certain court charges, counsel's fees, interest losses, losses due to inflation, costs for and in connection with witnesses, etc. The winning party may often be awarded counsel's fees, or part thereof, from the losing party. In some countries the winning party may be awarded interest (at varying rates) and possibly compensation for loss due to currency exchange rate changes, etc. In the United States the prospects of a winning party being compensated for counsel's fees are relatively limited. English rules allow cost compensation to the winning party, but they are rather restrictive as to interest awarded, since the discretion allowed to the courts is used somewhat cautiously.

9.5.2 Arbitration

Unless the charterparty expressly states that a dispute under the agreement shall be settled by arbitration, it will be referred to court proceedings. It is thus absolutely necessary that the parties agree on arbitration as the means of resolving a dispute. National legal systems often contain legislation with provisions for the appointment of arbitrators, for conducting an arbitration proceeding and for the enforcement of an arbitration award, etc. Such legislation may also contain rules on the possibility of appealing to a general court after an arbitration award. A common principle seems to be that each party nominates one arbitrator, and the nominated arbitrators in their turn jointly appoint an *umpire*. If the arbitrators cannot agree on a solution, the umpire will have the casting vote. In some arbitration schemes it will be the duty of a certain body either to appoint the arbitration panel or to appoint the umpire. A losing party may not normally appeal from the award. In many countries an arbitration award may be appealed only on formal and serious grounds, for example, if the arbitrators have wrongfully refused to hear a witness, or if they have been bribed, etc.

Since England has historically had a certain importance in maritime arbitration, some words should be mentioned here concerning the particularities of the UK arbitration system. Prior to the Arbitration Act 1979, English courts maintained their power to guide the development of the legal system and thus, even under arbitration proceedings, one party could demand that a legal question be referred to court procedure before the arbitration was finished ("*to state a special case*"). The advantage of a relatively faster proceeding was thereby lost. This unsatisfactory situation was remedied to some extent by the Arbitration Act 1979 which now allows judicial review only in certain arbitration cases. In order to solve other problems, a new *Arbitration Act* was introduced in 1996, which seems to have served its purpose reasonably well.

BIMCO has drafted a set of standard arbitration clauses, which are usually included in various BIMCO documents (charterparties, bills of lading etc.). Typically, one option offered is based on English law with London arbitration and one on US law with New York arbitration. It must be noted that the full wording of the *BIMCO standard dispute resolution clause/law and arbitration clause 1998*, contains, apart from the arbitration option, provisions stating that the parties may agree to refer to *mediation*[3] any disagreement or dispute arising from the charterparty. Furthermore, after the introduction of the Intermediate Claims Procedure

---

3 Mediation essentially involves the appointment of an individual to go between the parties and see if they can find common ground or tease out settlement terms that would be acceptable to both sides (www.theshippinglawblog.com, accessed 1 September 2017).

by the London Maritime Arbitrators Association (LMAA) in 2009, which was to deal with claims amounting between USD 100,000 and 400,000, both BIMCO and LMAA co-operated to jointly produce a relevant additional wording to the standard BIMCO clause.

It is worth adding that the International Chamber of Commerce has drawn up a special procedure for the appointment of arbitrators which, however, is rather circumstantial and not generally favoured in shipping business today. The Comité Maritime International (CMI) has suggested an arbitration system in which the parties choose arbitrators from a CMI list covering a number of well-qualified persons. This system should be completed with an agreement on the law to be applied and the place where the arbitrators should meet. In a number of countries there are also particular arbitration centres which have been developed to attract dispute settlements.

9.5.3 Arbitration or litigation (legal action)?

It is not possible to state in general terms whether arbitration or court procedure is preferable. In commercial contracts arbitration is often preferred owing to aspects of cost burden, the time aspect and secrecy. By tradition, arbitration procedure has been regarded as quicker and less expensive than court procedure, while the parties, for different reasons, generally prefer that the procedure is not public. In countries where the courts have little commercial experience, the parties may also prefer to have a dispute decided by persons who, in their view, have such knowledge and expertise.

On the other hand, the most popular arbitrators are frequently very busy and it should be underlined that a long time may elapse before three busy arbitrators and two busy counsellors find sufficient time available for common meetings. Certain parties may also consider it an advantage to have a dispute decided by ordinary courts. Another feature to take into consideration is the high fees charged by arbitrators for which the disputing parties are responsible jointly and severally.

Arbitration awards may have another advantage due to an international convention (the so-called *New York Convention*[4]) on the enforcement of arbitration awards, whereby arbitration awards given in one convention country are recognised in another country which is a party to the convention. In spite of that convention, it may nevertheless appear to be somewhat cumbersome to have an arbitration award given in one country exercised in another one. Without the convention such problems might, however, be difficult to overcome, because the authorities of a country may request a new trial or at least an affirmation of the decision before it can be enforced. Several of the largest trading nations are parties to the New York Convention. With respect to court proceedings and judicial judgments, there is no clearly equivalent solution as that applying to the arbitration awards, but within the EU there are particular rules to similar effect.

---

4 See www.newyorkconvention.org (accessed 15 June 2017).

It should also be mentioned that, in practice, a winning party may find that a favourable decision will not bring him any money since there is no money had by the counter-party. When a party has reasons to suspect that the other party has no money, he will try to arrest some property belonging to the latter to be used to cover the amount to which he may be entitled. The *arrest provisions* differ considerably between the various legal systems and jurisdictions, also depending heavily on the property to be arrested.

Both New York and London are popular centres for arbitration in charterparty disputes, but, depending on the parties involved, arbitration proceedings may also be conducted in Moscow, Paris, Hamburg, Beijing, Singapore (see appendix 6, *NYPE 2015, clause 54 "law and arbitration"*) etc. It should be noted that a dispute may be determined differently by English arbitrators than by American arbitrators, while differences may also come up if the arbitrators are "commercial men" rather than lawyers. Particularly where American charterers are involved, there are charterparties stating a maximum fee for the arbitrators when the disputed amounts are limited.

It is important to bear in mind that a charterer, having in a charterparty an arbitration clause referring a dispute to arbitration in London and according to English law, when chartering the vessel out (thus having a charter chain or sub-charter or sub-let), he should ensure that an equivalent clause is included in the subsequent charterparty. This is to avoid, as far as possible, the situation where arbitrators under one charterparty will come to one conclusion and arbitrators under the other charterparty will come to another. It may also be an advantage to refer general average proceedings and a charterparty arbitration to the same place, governed by the same law.

Furthermore, it is quite common for the parties, instead of a traditional arbitration clause, to make a special agreement to refer a certain question of principle or the whole dispute to BIMCO or to a qualified and neutral person, for example a reputable law firm, a university or a fellow member of a relevant business association.

9.6 Evidence

It does not matter how the material rules governing a relationship are designed, if the party invoking the rules cannot convince the arbitrators or the court that his version of the facts and his suggestions concerning the legal merits of the case are correct. Therefore, it is of utmost importance that the party who relies on a certain provision produces evidence of the facts supporting his view. For example, a fairly common basic legal idea seems to be that the injured party will have to prove that he has suffered damage, recognise the "person" who has caused this damage, justify the extent of the damage and, in many legal systems, he may also have to prove that the counterpart has been negligent. In a contract, the parties will normally be bound by their contractual undertakings. For instance, under English law, that party who has promised something will be bound by his promise irrespective of possible negligence. In some cases, the burden of proof will change from one party to the other. In other cases, the court or the arbitrators may prefer to have an overall picture of the facts brought in so as to judge. Sometimes, there will be a defined presumption which a wrongdoer has to overcome in order to avoid liability. If, for example, the question of liability for damage to the cargo is raised under the cargo conventions (e.g. the Hague Rules or Hague-Visby Rules), the cargo interests will have to prove that there is a case of cargo damage and that this damage occurred during the custody period of the carrier, whereas it will then be on the carrier to prove that the damage was not caused by his negligence or that of his employees or servants.

Legal principles concerning evidence and the burden of proof are highly complex. It is impossible to give a broad outline covering all possibilities, but suffice it here to mention that these principles exist and the parties, in their contracting, may count on or dispose of them to some extent, depending on their intentions. For example, a certain clause may prescribe that the burden of proof shall rest with one of the parties. Another example concerns the agreement of the parties to appoint a common independent surveyor when a damage occurs, etc. However, for practical purposes, it may be of considerable benefit for the parties to have a basic knowledge of the material legal rules applying, in order that they can obtain relevant evidence according to the circumstances. In other words, when something occurs, people may be able to get a written statement from a reliable and well-reputed person, find witnesses, make careful notes and observations about the facts, etc.

9.7 Construction and interpretation of charter agreements

9.7.1 Design of the charterparty

A charter relationship will normally be covered by a charterparty. The basis will typically be a standard form of charterparty, modified and amended by riders and addenda in accordance with the individual agreements. A charterparty must be correct as to its material contents and should reflect precisely what the parties have agreed. Its language should be unambiguous so that it expresses the intention of the parties. English law is known for applying more strict interpretation rules than many other legal systems. This means that English courts/arbitrators will generally follow closely and apply the wording of a document. Furthermore, it must be stressed that English law does not recognise general good faith obligations. That being said, it should be underlined that English law seems to apply a common business sense approach in the interpretation of charter documents, although the wording of them will always remain the basic point of deviation from this principle.

Through time, English court decisions have had an important impact on the meaning given to certain expressions and contractual clauses used in chartering. The effect of court decisions which change or modify a well-established understanding of a principle may initially cause some confusion in the market and result in certain counter-measures or actions being taken by critical shipping bodies such as BIMCO or International Chamber of Shipping (ICS), or other organisations such as Nordisk Defence Club (known also as Nordisk[5] or Nordisk Skibsrederforening) and various P&I Clubs. New clauses and/or wordings will probably be introduced to meet the new limits set by court decisions or to avoid or restrict the effects of the court decisions, adjusting the market practice accordingly. Thus, for all the practitioners involved in the chartering and shipbroking profession, it is extremely important to follow closely new court decisions in order to have an up-to-date knowledge of the meaning of certain expressions and clauses.

When comparing charterparties, one will find that they differ considerably with regard to their material contents as well as to their layout. Such differences depend on varying customs, demands and practices resulting from different sectors and trades. Documents are therefore constantly revised in order to meet such requirements. It is common that charterparties have a code name, often printed at the top of the form. The clauses are numbered and sometimes every line of the document is numbered as well (see for example *Gencon '94*, appendix 1). In the margin of the form there is often a heading giving a general idea of the contents of each paragraph or clause. BIMCO seems to have widely adopted such a system with a *box layout*, meaning that individual particulars of the document are entered into the boxes provided on the first page, while the general clauses are described on a separate sheet (see *Gencon '94* in appendix 1). However, this is by no means a generally accepted method. Tanker charterparties, all versions of the NYPE form and many other documents do not follow this "box layout" design (see for example *Shellvoy 6* in appendix 2 and *NYPE 2015* in appendix 6).

9.7.2 Offers and acceptance, written or no particular charter form

Reverting back to what has been discussed in chapter 8 about chartering negotiations, these matters will now be dealt with having a little more of a legal perspective in mind. When a shipowner is informed that a charterer needs tonnage of a type that the owner is able to provide, he first makes calculations based on the actual vessel and the specific requirements of the charter. If these freight calculations seem reasonable (see analysis in chapter 14), the owner may make an offer in accordance with the considerations described above in the chartering negotiation procedure.

Although the agreement is binding as soon as the parties have agreed on all terms and conditions, a charterparty is usually made out in order that the provisions shall be precisely fixed. Basically, one may say that the charterparty is decisive to show what has been contracted between the parties unless one of them proves that something else has been agreed. English law, more than many other legal systems, applies the so-called *parol evidence rule*. This rule basically means that only matters which are found to be expressly dealt with in the contract will be allowed by the court/arbitrators in the interpretation of the contract. The supporting rationale for this rule is that since the contracting parties have

---

5 See www.nordisk.no (accessed 15 June 2017).

reduced their agreement to a single and final writing, extrinsic evidence of past agreements or terms should not be considered when interpreting that writing, as the parties had decided to ultimately leave them out of the contract. In other words, one may not use evidence made prior to the written contract to contradict the writing. English courts, as well as US courts possibly to somewhat lesser extent, are thus less inclined to allow evidence other than that found *in* the contract than are, for example, German or Scandinavian courts. However, it must be emphasised that there are many instances where English courts and arbitrators consider terms and conditions to be *implied*, even covering fundamental principles on the laws of the carriage of goods by sea, such as seaworthiness, no deviation from the agreed route, reasonable despatch etc. It should also be mentioned that international commercial contracts (including contracts related to shipping matters) often contain a so-called *"merger clause"* specifically setting out that only what is specifically in the contract will be taken into consideration. On top of such clauses, commercial contracts will also often contain *"no oral amendment clauses"*, which mean that amendments shall be binding only when made in writing.

Figure 8.1 has described schematically how the charter negotiations may be carried out. The general contract principle is that an offer is binding, even though English law is somewhat different on this point due to the doctrine of consideration (see below at this section). Then, a counter-offer will be regarded as a rejection of the original offer in conjunction with a new offer binding upon the person who has given the counter-offer. In order that there shall be a binding agreement, any offer (or counter-offer) and the respective acceptance must be identical. Then, both parties will be bound.

An offer is not binding for any length of time. If the offer prescribes a certain time before which it must be accepted, the expiration of this time means that the offeror is no longer bound. If no time has been expressly stated, the basis is that the offeree shall have reasonable or customary time at his disposal to reply. This time is determined with regard to the importance of the business, the circumstances in which the offer has been given, the speed of the transactions in the trade, the prompt manner of the charter, etc. In any case, the parties should explicitly prescribe the terms and conditions in connection with the offer and acceptance.

The basic general principles of contract law have been described above. At this point, however, it is worth emphasising that legal handling of the details of a charter differs considerably among various legal systems. In English law the *doctrine of consideration* prevails, which means that the offeror is not bound by his offer unless the offeree has given some value, namely consideration. Indeed, this doctrine indicates that there is no binding contract unless consideration has been given. English law and US law, though the latter to a lesser extent, thereby differ from the general basic pattern that an offer is binding. It is hard today to foresee whether an English court would really apply this doctrine of consideration to an international charter contract, but it is clear that many business transactions are made without regard being given to this doctrine. It is apparent that, when these principles are applied, practical problems may arise when trying to determine if and when an agreement is binding, if a certain offer is binding, etc. In particular, various "subjects" used during the negotiations may deteriorate the understanding of the parties and the clarity of the agreement, thus causing additional and severe problems of interpretation.

9.7.3 "Subject" provisions

Having explained the meaning of the most important "subject" terms in section 8.1.2.1, their respective legal aspects will be examined here.

A "subject" provision in a charter agreement may give rise to various legal problems. Apparently, a *"subject to government approval"* term gives to the parties a much narrower frame to act than an agreement made *"subject to the board's approval"* or *"subject details"*. Unless the parties have agreed on the specific reason why the board's approval has to be obtained, any refusal by the board to accept the contract may be invoked to avoid the binding force of the contract.

"Subject" provisions are very common when contracting in shipping. The "subjects" involved vary largely: *"subject stem"*; *"subject board's approval"*; *"subject approval of relevant authority"*; *"subject financing"*; *"subject details"* are some typical expressions. A "subject" may sometimes be regarded as a *"condition precedent"*, sometimes not. To some extent, at the least, this is a question depending on the quality of the "subject": does it have any substance or only a minor importance?

Naturally, the general idea of a "subject" provision is that it shall be used in a loyal and ethical way in relation to the counter-party. For reasons of evidence it may be hard to establish a case of disloyalty and whether such disloyalty has caused any damage or loss having any legal effects. If a party has conceded by accepting a wide "subject" provision, such as *"subject board's approval"*, he has given a wide discretion to his counter-party to get out of a "subject deal" by claiming that the board has not accepted the deal. It will be hard, particularly in English law, to establish that the subject provision has been used contravening the *"good faith"*. A party may possibly found a claim in damages if he can establish that the counter-party made a "conditional" contract with him (e.g. "subject board's approval") with the sole purpose of preventing him from making a contract with somebody else. Thus, under very particular circumstances, there may be a situation where one of the parties could apply arguments based on "good faith" abuse by the counter-party.

Another question may be raised with regard to the *"subject details"* stipulation. There are some critical queries to be answered: Where do the parties stand in the negotiation and the contracting process when they have agreed on the "main terms" but "subject details"? Are they bound at all at this time? How does each party perceive his commitment at this point? Could either of them use disagreement on any minor detail to correctly allege that he is not bound? In which instances could there be a claim for damages?

The basic rules of contract law will typically apply, but regard must always be given to the peculiar practices of shipping. In English as well as in US law – as a general remark this should be true for most legal systems – the basic idea is that there can be no contract until the parties have reached clear agreement on at least all essential terms, and in English law basically on all terms.

As it has been seen, chartering negotiations are carried out in two steps: that part where the *"main terms"* are covered and that where the *"details"* are determined. When the parties have fixed the "main terms", they have made a fixture *"sub details"*, but as mentioned, several other "subjects" may also be involved. The practice of chartering negotiations may bring some legal problems. The basic legal questions are: Is a "sub" a condition precedent? Is "sub details" always or sometimes a condition precedent, when the parties have fixed the main terms? If fixing the main terms would imply the conclusion of a contract, what happens if the parties cannot agree on the details?

Different types of "subject" may have different implications, but the individual circumstances of the negotiations and the individual design of the "subject" will have a decisive role on the effects. There are basically three possibilities when "subjects" are used; either there is no binding contract at all, or there is a contract that will not bind fully until the subject has been waived/lifted, or there is a contract which binds immediately but will cease to do so if the subject is not waived/lifted. As mentioned, in English law the term *"subject to contract"* has been held to show an intention not to be bound until a formal contract is subsequently entered into. Generally, the expression "subject to contract" seems to indicate clearly that there is not yet any binding contract and presumably most legal systems would come to the same conclusion in similar circumstances. In certain circumstances damages may also be awarded in case of negotiations taking place in bad faith.

There is a clear difference between English and US law when it comes to the question of *"subject detail provisions"*, where English law will hardly ever be inclined to allow a contract to come up if a subject set out in a particular provision has not been lifted/waived.

In the US case *A/S Custodia v Lessin International, Inc, 503 F.2d. 318 (2d Cir. 1974)*[6] the issue was whether there was a binding charterparty. The court held, inter alia: *"The critical issue is not whether the charterparty was signed by the party sought to be charged, but whether there was a meeting of the minds of the parties as to the essential terms of the agreement, even though unsigned by one party"*.

When considering the phrase "sub details" it must not be overlooked that the parties may to some extent themselves characterise what are "main terms" and "details", respectively. By agreeing on a fixture "sub details", the parties have actually made an agreement at least to some degree, while they may also have initially agreed to come to terms with respect to the details. On the other hand, it may be maintained that the parties have only come to a conclusion regarding the

---

6 http://law.justia.com/cases/federal/appellate-courts (accessed 25 June 2017).

main terms and that the details remain to be agreed on. The details would then be regarded as conditions precedent for the final agreement and the contract.

A number of US cases have determined the question. Taking into consideration a number of such cases, the courts have found that *"a binding fixture occurs when there is an agreement on all essential ("main") terms. The "subject details" does not create a condition precedent . . . Thus, a party is not entitled to renege on a main term just because pro forma details still remain open"*.

Therefore, some difficult problems may arise. First of all, the borderline between "main terms" and "details" must be determined and this is not always a very easy task. Then, to what extent are the terms defined by custom and trade practice? How are these terms related with ship and cargo operations in various trades? To what degree may the parties dispose of the significance of the main terms and details?

Undoubtedly, the parties have the absolute will and intention to determine what is included in "main terms" and "details". If they have explicitly characterised as a "main term" an item that would normally be referred to as a "detail", then this must be recognised as a "main term". There may also be a distinction between the understanding of "main terms" and "details" in various trades. However, it is impossible to determine with any degree of accuracy an exact overall significance of specific "main terms" and "details" applying to every situation. Thus, it may very well be that a certain detail may have more significance in one trade than in another.

In addition, it goes without saying that the outcome of a case may probably be different if English or US law is applied.

The following general principles could be extracted and summed-up, although any conclusions can be made only with great caution. If the parties have agreed on most main terms, but there are still some outstanding points, at least a US court may find that there is already a binding contract if the outstanding items do not have major significance. However, it seems to be always in the court's discretion to decide whether or not an item should be characterised as "main".

On the other hand, an English court or arbitration panel would rather be more cautious in allowing a contract binding force in spite of outstanding points, unless these could be regarded as having only minor importance. In any case, the basic understanding of the shipping industry seems to be that there is normally no contract until all terms have been fixed, or at least the great bulk of them. Nevertheless, the individual situation and the circumstances may undoubtedly have a major impact on that.

It is felt that US courts in some cases have gone far in establishing that there is a binding contract if the parties have made a fixture "sub details". The impression one gets is that US courts may hold that the parties "fixing sub details" have thereby declared that there is a meeting of minds between them and that the details will not mean any change to this. However, one may ask why the parties are then fixing "sub details". By that, did they intend to leave to the court or arbitration panel to fill in what they cannot themselves agree on? Some cases seem to indicate that a particular item may very well be regarded by a US court as a "detail" in one case and a "main term" in another one. This is certainly an unforunate situation which may cause controversy and dispute.

9.7.4 Construction and interpretation rules for charter documents

Charterparties are the result of negotiations. It is important to keep this fact in mind when a charterparty is constructed or interpreted. A charterparty is ordinarily based on the fixture made by brokers covering what the parties have agreed. If it is alleged that a clause does not express the parties' will, the oral agreement behind it may be regarded as decisive if its content can be established. If legislation is applicable, it may give some guidance. Sometimes, the exchange of messages during the preceding negotiations may be used to cast some light on the meaning of a clause to which the parties dispute. Even circumstances which have been used in previous negotiations and agreements between the parties or otherwise may be taken into consideration in interpretation. In general, however, the written provisions in the charterparty will be given priority. Sometimes, reference is made to the discussions during the negotiations in order that the meaning of a certain phrase can be explained. Basically, the clauses used should be interpreted as they are worded in the charterparty. Courts and arbitrators may apply various principles or methods in their interpretation and, as mentioned, the basic idea under English law has been that the court has to find the meaning of the contract in the contract. This principle seems to be applied less rigidly nowadays than before.

It is always necessary to bear in mind that several of the charterparty clauses have not been individually negotiated between the parties, but were drafted collectively and were imprinted in the standard text of the charterparty. The parties may not even have been aware of many clauses or the deeper meaning of them; thus it is then almost impossible to trace any individual intentions.

Particularly in voyage chartering, it is typical that the freight agreements are negotiated under great pressure of time. The parties have no time to weigh and balance their words carefully. Separate clauses are sometimes hinged to or stamped on the contract without regard being given to the printed wording. New provisions are typed and brought into the printed form between the narrow lines without regard being given to their effects on the charterparty as a whole. One interpretation principle is generally considered to be that clauses hinged to, stamped on or added into the charterparty will apply before the printed original text.

However, the riders are often less well phrased than the original provisions of the form. It is not unusual that they are intended for situations other than those actually regulated in the charterparty; therefore it may then be difficult to give them an unambiguous meaning. Another principle that may be applied is that imprecise and ambiguous wording will be construed against the party who furnished the provision (*contra proferentem rule*). When interpreting a charter-party, it may be necessary to disregard details and try to determine the intentions of the parties. If no intention can then be unambiguously determined, it may be necessary to reconstrue the charterparty to give it a sensible meaning. As it has been emphasised, "subject details" provision may cause certain difficulties, since it is not always very clear to distinguish a "main term" from a "detail". One cannot always rely on a minor detail to avoid a contract. Moreover, a detail may sometimes be construed as a main term having finally a major impact on the contract.

As mentioned above, standard charterparties often contain a provision that a dispute shall be decided at a certain place in accordance with the laws there governing. Several standard charterparties set out that a dispute shall be decided by arbitrators in London, whereas others refer disputes to be settled by arbitration in New York. The parties may agree on another solution and may also decide on which law to apply in case a dispute arises.

As it has been also pointed out, English or US law dominates in ocean charter practice. In English or US law there is no particular legislation specifically dealing with charterparties. If the parties disagree on the understanding of the contract, the dispute will be decided in the light of previous court judgments. Courts and arbitrators will then fall back on the general law of contract. The pre-eminence of English and US law in ocean chartering has led to a significant role and great interest being attached to English and US court and arbitration decisions. Even very old decisions may thus still have great fundamental importance, if no later case has changed ("*reversed*") their effect. The growth of the number of decisions has caused charterparties to become more and more extensive, since the parties may wish to clarify certain principles or avoid the effects of a legal dispute. Through the passage of time, additional clauses are introduced which govern new problems arising through commercial shipping practice.

Certain general principles may be discussed about the construction and interpretation of charterparties. English courts or arbitrators use as a basis to determine the applicable legal principles and make their decisions the following: first, the *wording of the charterparty*; second, *previous decisions*; and third; *commercial customs*. There is no common principle preventing the parties from trying by agreement to avoid the effect of court decisions. Generally, English courts still seem to feel more or less bound by a past decision given by a higher court.

Even if the parties are supposed to have comprehensively regulated their relationship in the charterparty, there are circumstances which may not have been clearly expressed but are implied, for example, reference to commercial customs or the conduct of the parties. Such *implied terms* have the same effect as express provisions and may be used by the courts to explain the intention of the parties and determine the meaning of certain legal principles.

The construction and interpretation of a charterparty cannot be conducted solely on the basis of the ordinary English meaning of the words which the parties have used in their contract. The most important *rules of charterparty construction and interpretation* may be summarised as follows[7]:

- The primary consideration in construing any contract is the *intention of the contracting parties*. Thus, a charterparty must be construed in the light of the particular undertaking with which it is concerned.
- Where there is a *conflict between the printed and written parts of the contract* owing to an error or to inadvertence, the intention expressed by the written part should, as a general rule, be preferred to that expressed by the printed part. It is therefore unnecessary, and indeed often impossible, to give full effect to every printed clause.
- The *"contra proferentem"* rule usually applies, meaning that any ambiguous term of the contract is to be construed most strongly against the party for whose benefit it is intended.
- The *"ejusdem generis"* rule is often applied too. According to that, general words which are tacked on to specific words are to be construed as referring only to things or circumstances of the same kind as those described by the specific words. This may be understood from the case *Tillmans & Co. v SS Knutsford Ltd* [1908] AC 406, where the respective charter term was stating *"war, disturbance, or any other cause"*. The court decided that ice was not covered by the wording, although the term *"any other cause"* was entirely generic and could cover anything. Ice was not covered as having no connection with war or warlike disturbances. In some cases, however, the general words are the governing words and the specific words are subordinate. But doubt has been expressed as to whether the ejusdem generis rule or the discussion of it in relation to different words is really of much assistance where the clause to be construed contains the words "such as". The ejusdem generis rule may be excluded by apt words in the document.
- It is not clearly settled whether the court is entitled to *refer to a clause which has been deleted* from the document. It depends on the case.
- The *grammatical construction* should be adopted except where there is a clear intention to the contrary.
- The *whole of the document* must be looked at.
- *The words must be construed in their ordinary meaning*. Thus, the word "reachable" in the phrase "reachable on her arrival" means "able to be reached". It is not limited to a case where a failure of a vessel to reach the place concerned is due to physical causes. But, technical words must be given their technical meaning.
- The *meaning must be limited by the context* in which the words are used.

---

7 Giziakis, K., Papadopoulos, A. and Plomaritou, E. (2010) *Chartering* (Athens, Stamoulis Publications, 3rd edition, in Greek, pp. 478–480); Ivamy, H. (1989) *Payne and Ivamy's Carriage of Goods by Sea* (London, Butterworths, 13th edition, pp. 130–135); Mocatta, A., Mustill, M. and Boyd, S. (1984) *Scrutton on Charter Parties and Bills of Lading* (London, Sweet & Maxwell Ltd., 19th edition, pp. 1–22).

- The words of the document must, where possible, be construed *liberally*, so as to give effect to the intention of the parties.
- Where the *words are capable of two ways of syntax, the reasonable construction is to be preferred* as representing the presumed intention of the parties.
- An *express term in a document overrides any implied term* which is inconsistent with it.
- The *same words or phrases in a document should where possible be given the same meaning*, but this rule must always comply with the particular context.

CHAPTER 10

Common charterparty clauses and concepts

Before discussing in depth the typical clauses of each charter type, this chapter will focus on general questions, concepts and clauses commonly applying to all different charter types and shipping contracts. Various topics of considerable interest are examined, such as the standard elements and the layout of a charterparty, the identity of the contracting parties and the possibility of their substitution in a contract, the importance of an exact vessel's description together with the crucial concept of vessel's "seaworthiness", as well as the different meaning of a "lay/can" term in a voyage charter comparing to a time charter. Moreover, critical shipping, chartering and legal concepts are further presented, together with a commentary on respective charterparty clauses. This analysis comprises cargo liability allocation and the "paramount clause", the "war clauses", terms concerning the effect of cost variations on the contractual relationship (e.g. "hardship clauses", "bunker clauses", "currency clauses", "escalation clauses" etc.), the "doctrine of frustration" of the contract, "arbitration clauses", time limits, "exception clauses" and the "force majeure clause", liens and arrests, the concept of general average and the "New Jason clause", the vessel collision rules and the "both-to-blame clause", the "ISM clause" and finally the most recent "piracy clause".

10.1 Preamble of a charter contract

Written contracts often start with a preamble, in which the parties and the main contents of the agreement are presented. For example, a preamble of a voyage charterparty can be formulated in the following way (*Gencon '94, part II, clause 1*):

> "*It is agreed between the party mentioned in Box 3 as Owners of the steamer or motor-vessel named in Box 5, of the GT/NT indicated in Box 6 and carrying about the number of tons of deadweight cargo stated in Box 7, now in position as stated in Box 8 and expected ready to load under this Charter Party about the date indicated in Box 9, and the party mentioned as Charterers in Box 4 that:*
> *The said vessel shall, as soon as her prior commitments have been completed, proceed to the loading port(s) or place(s) stated in Box 10 or so near thereto as she may safely get and lie always afloat, and there load a full and complete cargo (if shipment of deck cargo agreed same to be at the Charterers' risk and responsibility) as stated in Box 12, which the Charterers bind themselves to ship, and being so loaded the vessel shall proceed to the discharging port(s) or place(s) stated in Box 11 as ordered on signing Bills of Lading, or so near thereto as she may safely get and lie always afloat and there deliver the cargo*".

1. Shipbroker	RECOMMENDED THE BALTIC AND INTERNATIONAL MARITIME COUNCIL UNIFORM GENERAL CHARTER (AS REVISED 1922, 1976 and 1994) (To be used for trades for which no specially approved form is in force) CODE NAME: "GENCON" Part I	
	2. Place and date	
3. Owners/Place of business (Cl. 1)	4. Charterers/Place of business (Cl. 1)	
5. Vessel's name (Cl. 1)	6. GT/NT (Cl. 1)	
7. DWT all told on summer load line in metric tons (abt.) (Cl. 1)	8. Present position (Cl. 1)	
9. Expected ready to load (abt.) (Cl. 1)		
10. Loading port or place (Cl. 1)	11. Discharging port or place (Cl. 1)	
12. Cargo (also state quantity and margin in Owners' option, if agreed; if full and complete cargo not agreed state "part cargo" (Cl. 1)		

Figure 10.1 Section of Gencon's Box Layout

In a preamble of this design the various parts of the agreement are tied up with each other. In the Gencon form and in many other modern charter-party forms often issued by BIMCO, the *box layout* system is used, which means that the written agreement is divided into two main parts with cross-references between them. The first is the *box part* with all specifications for the relevant vessel and voyage, while the second one is the *text part* with all the printed clauses. A typical such example of a box layout design may be seen in *Gencon '94, part I* as presented in Figure 10.1 above. On the contrary, there are some other, commonly used charterparties, such as the standard tanker forms or NYPE, which do not adopt this box design, but their preamble is typically structured with free text and blank spaces to be filled by the parties. A typi-cal example of a tanker charterparty layout design may be seen in appendix 2 (*Shellvoy 6*).

In most cases the charterparty also has a third part, the *rider*, where additional, photocopied standard clauses or typewritten, individually negotiated, clauses are inserted. This rider is often much longer than the printed form used and in many cases so many changes have been made in the basic standard document that one may question whether it is still a standard form.

10.2 Parties to the contract

The charterer, the shipowner and other persons and parties involved in a charter agreement have been mentioned above. In this section, some questions about the identity of the parties will be discussed.

10.2.1 Identity of the parties

Both the shipowner and the charterer should be able to form an opinion about the other party before they are bound to the agreement. Both during and after the charter period each party must have the opportunity to force the other party to fulfil his obligations, if needed. Therefore, it is essential in the first place to know the identity, the full style and contact details of the other party. It is not unusual for the charterer to be represented by an agent and known to the other party only by expressions, such as *"Messrs NN as agents for charterers"*. It is important not to make any commitments and always to have a chance to terminate the negotiations if the other party turns out to be unacceptable owing to insolvency, bad reputation, etc. As various kinds of notices must be given to shippers, receivers or other entities, it is always important to know the identity and full contact details of those persons (companies).

10.2.2 Substitution of owner or charterer

Sometimes, during a charter, the owners or the charterers wish to replace themselves with other owners or charterers respectively. For instance, it is not unusual that the owner in a long period time charter agreement wishes to sell his vessel and let the new owner of the vessel enter as owner into the time charterparty. It also may happen that the charterer wishes to sub-charter the vessel to another charterer. There is a legal distinction between these cases, since in the first case the original owner will no longer be a party to the contract after the transaction, but in the second case the original charterer will still be primarily liable to the owner. Basically, the owner can not sell the vessel during the time charter period and let the new owner enter into his place as party to the charter unless a particular agreement has been made to such effect. The legal instrument that formalises an arrangement to substitute one party for another in a contract is called *"novation agreement"*. If the owner who is selling is solvent and reliable, a practical solution and compromise may be that the charterer accepts the new owner as party to the charter in combination with a guarantee from the selling owner for the fulfilment of the obligations of the new owner. Sometimes, it may be an advantage for the charterer to have a new, financially stronger, owner, but he may nevertheless refuse to accept the proposal. In such a situation the shareholders of the owner may instead choose to sell the shipowning shares to the new "owner". The situation might be correspondingly the same on the charterer's side.

The charterer's right to *sub-let* (sub-charter) the vessel is usually confirmed in the charterparty. This can be done in the following way in a time charterparty (*Gentime, part II, clause 15(i) "sub-letting"*):

> *"The Charterers shall have the right to sub-let all or part of the Vessel whilst remaining responsible to the Owners for the performance of this Charter Party".*

In other words, the agreement is that the time charterer remains responsible to the owner although he has handed over his rights to "order and direct" the vessel to another time charterer. Unless it is expressly agreed in the charterparty, the time charterer cannot transfer his obligations against the owner to another time charterer.

10.3 Signing of the agreement

A charterparty can be signed either by the contracting parties or by someone authorised by them, usually a shipbroker (about the identity and role of the parties, see sections 10.2 and 3.5). By whom and where the charterparty is signed can be important in some situations, such as in the case of applicable law (see section 9.4).

It is important to check that the final charterparty text is in accordance with the fixture and the "recap" made at the time of the fixture. If an incorrect charterparty is signed and sent to the other party, or if a party fails to protest when he gets an incorrect charterparty signed by a broker, the incorrect charterparty may be binding for the parties. The chances of rectifying afterwards are limited under English law, unless a protest is made "within reasonable time" and provided that the parties are in agreement about the rectification.

Under English Law, there is no requirement that a charterparty should be made in a particular manner. As long as the parties have reached complete agreement, a charterparty signed by or on behalf of the parties is unnecessary (i.e. not compulsory).[1] The parties instead can base their relationship on a "recap" following an e-mail exchange, perhaps with an additional reference like *"otherwise as per Gencon form"*, *"otherwise as per C/P dated . . . for M/V XYZ"* or similar. Such methods, however, easily give rise to confusion and dispute. Thus, if the parties use to charter vessels to and from each other frequently, they should avoid doing that only on an e-mail exchange and a "recap" basis, but instead they should work out with a *pro forma charterparty* and a *fixture note form*, which can be issued for each individual fixture.

10.4 Vessel

10.4.1 Nomination, identity and substitution

Depending on the type of charter contract, the ship may have a more or less central position in the charter agreement. The basic idea in shipping has been that it is important for the client (shipper/charterer) to know exactly which vessel is to be used for the carriage. It is also important for him that a particular vessel is nominated at an early stage. This basic concept nowadays seems to be less predominant, but it applies with varying force depending on the circumstances.

In conventional liner shipping (as well as in tramp shipping) the bill of lading is normally of the type known as a *shipped bill of lading*, that is, the bill of lading

---

1 Kimball, J., Cooke, J., Martowski, D., Lambert, L., Taylor, A., Young, T., Ashcroft, M. and Sturley, M. (2014) *Voyage Charters* (Informa Law from Routledge, 4th edition, p. 4).

is issued when the goods have been loaded on board the vessel. Obviously, this particular vessel then plays a central role. In modern liner business, where the *received for shipment bill of lading* plays a much more dominant role, the particular vessel has less importance, but the customer trusts the carrier to perform well, irrespective of which vessel is going to be used.

In time charter and bareboat agreements, which can both be classified as a kind of vessel hiring agreement, the vessel is a central factor. In the voyage charter agreement, which can be classified as a transportation agreement for a certain cargo between certain ports, the description of the vessel itself does not have the same central position as in the period charters. For instance, it is not unusual that voyage charter agreements are concluded before it is known which ship will be used. In such cases the ship in the charterparty is mentioned as "*vessel to be nominated*" or similar. The owner has in such a case an obligation to nominate a vessel suitable for the intended cargo, ports, etc. In quantity contracts (see chapter 13) where the basic task under the contract is to move certain quantities of goods within a certain time period, the normal procedure is that the ship is not named in the agreement. In those cases where the vessel is not nominated at the time of the fixture, it is advisable to agree as to when the owner shall make his nomination. If the nomination is made too close to the loading, the shippers may have difficulties in supplying the merchandise, preparing the shipping documents, etc.

When a named vessel is fixed for a charter, the existence of the agreement is also dependent on the existence of the vessel. If the vessel is lost or declared a "constructive total loss" (CTL), the charter agreement is "*frustrated*", which means that it is terminated automatically and no longer exists. The charter agreement can be also frustrated for other reasons, for instance if the ship is delayed for an extensively long period. The English "*doctrine of frustration*" is sometimes referred to by charterers or owners when they wish to cancel a charter agreement for economic reasons (see further in section 10.8.5).

In voyage chartering, especially, it is often agreed that the vessel may be replaced by another vessel. Sometimes, the charterparty may prescribe for example "*MS Eugen or substitute*", or an alternative wording may be "*MS Eugen, owner's option to substitute vessel of same class and similar size and position*". It is essential to specify how far this right to substitute goes. Is there only a right for the owner to nominate another ship, or is there also an obligation for him to nominate another ship if the one already nominated is lost, or not available? Can the vessel be replaced several times? Should the right to substitute cease a certain number of days before the planned commencement of loading? Should it be possible to substitute only with certain named vessels or types of vessels or should it be possible to substitute with any vessel that can carry the cargo?

Not only the name, but also the nationality, call sign, IMO-number, year of build, type (e.g. motor tanker, reefer, etc.) are usually specified in the charter agreement. The owner cannot, without the permission of the charterer, alter any of the vessel's essential characteristics as they have been described in the charterparty. For instance, if the owner wishes to change the nationality of the vessel (i.e. the flag), he has to get permission from the charterer as the nationality of the vessel is in many cases essential to the charterer for various reasons. The vessel's description is of utmost importance in chartering matters and will be dealt with separately in connection with the voyage charterparty and the time charterparty (see chapters 11 and 12). At this point, however, it should be mentioned that oil companies often have far-reaching demands on the quality of the vessel in their charterparties. This quality aspect is safeguarded by thorough *vetting* processes and extensive *questionnaires* which have to be successfully passed by tanker vessels, so that to get accepted by their charterers. *Shellvoy 6* may be used as an example of a vessel's description clause which is far-reaching (see appendix 2, *part I, clause (A) "description of vessel"*).

10.4.2 Trading limits

The hull underwriters maintain geographical trading limitations in connection with the vessels they insure. The limits may be slightly different between various underwriters. Some trading areas are always accepted, others are always excluded (mainly the Arctic areas) and others are accepted only between certain dates and excluded for the remaining part of the year. The common rules about the vessels' trading limits are the so-called *"International Navigating Limits"* *(INL)* which are issued by the Institute of Chartered Underwriters in London and on 1 November 2003 replaced the previous *"Institute Warranty Limits"* *(IWL)*.[2] The INL define the geographical limits within which ships are able to operate without incurring additional insurance premium from hull and machinery and other relevant underwriters. Operating outside the INL, in areas which can include significant hazards such as ice, could lead to damage to the ship and delay necessitated by repairs.

The hull underwriters' rules concerning accepted and excluded trading areas are based on the average ice and weather conditions and, therefore, these rules remain normally unchanged year after year. The restrictions drawn up in connection with war insurance for the vessel are based on the risk of damage caused by war, hostilities, terrorism, strikes etc. As these risks vary greatly, the underwriters often issue on a regular basis new rules and updates about restricted areas and additional war premiums.

The ship's trading limits are dependent on the manning and construction of the vessel, as well as on the technical equipment on board. For instance, it may be that a ship to be used in worldwide ocean trading must have more officers and crew members than if the same vessel is used for coastal service only. In some countries, or for the transition through some canals and seaways, it is necessary for the vessels to have special technical equipment. For example, such equipment is required when passing through the Suez Canal and the St. Lawrence Seaway.

---

2 Reay, J. and Rees, C. (2016) *International Navigating Limits* (The Standard Club Ltd, www. standard-club.com).

It is noted that only the vessel's trading limits are mentioned here. Additional restrictions, mainly based on political relations between various countries, are often expressly inserted into the charterparty. This will be explained further in sections 12.3.1 and 13.2.2.

10.4.3 Seaworthiness

It is usually stated in the charterparty that the owner shall keep the vessel in a seaworthy condition. Also, when no such clauses are inserted, the owners have an obligation usually *by law* or by an *implied warranty* to keep the vessel in a sea-worthy condition. Even if it is possible for the owners to insert a valid exception clause concerning the liability for seaworthiness, in specific cases the clause may not be valid. The most obvious example is perhaps when owners try to exempt themselves from liability under the Carriage of Goods by Sea Act (COGSA) and other laws based on the Hague/Hague-Visby Rules or similar.

The concept of seaworthiness can be described as having three aspects:

- seaworthiness from the technical point of view;
- cargoworthiness; and
- seaworthiness for the intended voyage.

Technical seaworthiness includes the ship's design and condition in hull and machinery, as well as her stability. *Cargoworthiness* means that the vessel shall be suitable for the intended cargo and properly cleaned, while *seaworthiness for the intended voyage* means that she will be satisfactorily equipped, manned, bun-kered etc. for the intended voyage.

When judging whether the vessel is seaworthy or not, the circumstances at each stage of a voyage and in each situation must be considered (*seaworthiness by stages*). A ship that is seaworthy for trading on the River Thames may not be seaworthy for a voyage from England to New York, while further a ship that is seaworthy during loading may not be seaworthy for the intended voyage unless additional fuel, charts etc. are taken on board.

A special question related with seaworthiness for the intended voyage is to what extent the vessel must be technically equipped and furnished with certif-icates necessary for her to be able to call at a certain port or a certain country without risk of delay.

So far as the usual certificates and documents are concerned, the owner and the master must keep all necessary certificates up to date, both in time and voyage chartering. An exception may be the situation when the vessel is, for instance, on time charter trading worldwide. If in such a case the ship's schedule is changed at very short notice and the vessel is destined for a port or country normally not called at by the charterer, the owner should be entitled to some extra time to get the necessary documents.

Concerning documents requested by persons or bodies other than national authorities, for instance by the ITF (International Transport Workers' Federation), the situation is not clear. In those cases where it is generally known that labour unions claim a certain document or certificate, the owner, most probably, has an obligation to keep such documents or certificates on board, but when the request from a union or other body could hardly be expected, the situation is more difficult. Quite often, special clauses dealing with this problem may be found in the charterparties. As regards restrictions and rules issued by authorities at very short notice, the problem must be solved from case to case. A general trend in shipping seems to be an increasing demand for a careful description of the ship and the certificates to be on board or available and a more extensive liability on the shipowner as to his warranty in this respect.

A particular aspect of making the ship seaworthy, in the sense of being fit for the reception of cargo, is the cleaning of holds. This goes for all vessel types, but the extent of cleaning depends on the trade. As to dry cargo trades, it goes without saying that a cargo of grain cannot follow upon certain types of cargo without very careful cleaning of holds. Furthermore, a tanker regularly lifting crude oil (dirty cargo) cannot carry a clean cargo without a thorough cleaning. Tanks, pipelines and pumps must be cleaned between each voyage. Several types of cleaning devices have been developed in tanker trades, such as the Butterworth and Gunclean systems.[3]

Frequently, one finds in charterparties provisions such as *"cleaned to the charterer's inspector's satisfaction"*. Such a clause can be risky, burdensome or harmful for the owner. In certain trades the cleaning has to be to the satisfaction of a certain authority and this clause is usually less risky from the owner's point of view.

10.5 Lay/Can

Both in voyage charter and time charter it must be agreed when the vessel should be ready to load at the first port or delivered to the charterer, respectively. The owner and the master have an obligation to do their utmost to ensure that the vessel reaches the first loading port (in voyage charter) or the place of delivery (in period charter) at or before the day stated for the expected or estimated readiness for loading. If the owner or master intentionally or by negligence delays the vessel and causes her to be late, the owner may be liable in damages for breach of contract. A so-called *"lay/can"* clause is usually agreed, for instance *"lay/can March 1–15"*. The importance of notices given by the ship before arriving at the first loading port of a voyage charter is dealt with in section 11.8.1.

10.5.1 "Lay"

"Lay" is a short form of *"laytime not to commence before"*. Under a voyage charterparty, if a ship is ready at the first loading port before the agreed *"layday"*, the owner cannot claim that the charterer should start to load the vessel or that

---

3 www.butterworth.com (accessed 1 June 2017).

the time should commence to count. This situation will be discussed further in section 11.7 and chapter 15.

If a vessel chartered under a time charterparty arrives at the port or place of delivery before the agreed layday as defined by this term, the charterers have no obligation to take delivery of her and, unless the charterers agree to an earlier delivery, the ship has to wait without earning anything for the owners. Sometimes, the charterers wish to commence the loading of the vessel before the first layday but without taking delivery of her, thus without paying for her. The owner has no obligation to accept such a procedure; therefore if the charterers wish to commence the loading before the first layday, the parties must be in clear agreement concerning the payment of hire, allocation of risks etc. during the period up to the agreed layday.

The layday is not always exactly stated. For instance, in the preamble to the *Gencon '94 form* (see appendix 1, *part II, clause 1*), the expression "*expected ready to load under this Charter Party about the date indicated in Box 9*" is used. To find out the meaning of the word "*about*", the circumstances in the relevant case must be taken into consideration. The longer the period between the fixture and the first layday, the longer the period covered by the expression "about".

10.5.2 "Can"

If the vessel has not promptly arrived at the loading port of a voyage charter, or port or place of delivery of a period charter, then on the cancelling day most charterparties give the charterer an absolute right to cancel the charter agreement. In other words, the ordinary cancelling clauses, as for instance in *Gencon* or *Baltime*, are applicable when the ship has been delayed for reasons which cannot be controlled by the owner and when the owner and the master have done their utmost to speed up the vessel.

When it is obvious to the owner that the vessel has no chance of arriving at the first loading port or place of delivery before the cancelling date, it is important for him to get the charterer's declaration whether or not he will cancel. Under English law, the charterer is not obliged to give such a declaration unless this is expressly stated in the charterparty.

The relevant problems and the way they can be handled are indicatively illustrated in the following clause (*Gentime, part II, clause 1(d) "period and delivery/cancellation"*):

> "*Should the Vessel not be delivered by the date/time stated in Box 10 the Charterers shall have the option to cancel the Charter Party without prejudice to any claims the Charterers may otherwise have on the Owners under the Charter Party. If the Owners anticipate that, despite their exercise of due diligence, the Vessel will not be ready for delivery by the date/time stated in Box 10, they may notify the Charterers in writing, stating the anticipated new date of readiness for delivery, proposing a new cancelling date/time and requiring the Charterers to declare whether they will cancel or will take delivery of the Vessel. Should the Charterers elect not to cancel or should they fail to reply within two (2) working days (as applying at the Charterers'*

place of business) of receipt of such notification, then unless otherwise agreed, the proposed new cancelling date/time will replace the date/time stated in Box 10. This provision shall operate only once and should the Vessel not be ready for delivery at the new cancelling date/time the Charterers shall have the option of cancelling this Charter Party".

The intention of this wording is not only to give the charterers the right to cancel if the vessel is late. The clause also protects the owners by giving them the right to fix a new cancelling day if the charterers fail to declare whether they will cancel or not. This practice is similarly followed by the *Gencon '94* voyage charter form (see appendix 1, *part II, clause 9 "cancelling clause"*) which provides that the charterers shall have to declare their option of cancelling the charterparty *"within 48 running hours after the receipt of the owners' notice"* of a (new) delayed arrival of the vessel at the loading port. If the charterers do not exercise their option to cancel the charter, then the seventh day after the new readiness date of the vessel will be automatically deemed as the new cancelling date. This is interesting to be examined in contrast with the *Gencon '76* form, where the respective term provides that the charterers must on demand declare their option to cancel the charter at least 48 hours before the vessel's expected arrival at the port of loading. This means that where the owner, a couple of weeks before the cancelling date, knows that the ship has no chance of arriving before the cancelling date, he has no right to demand the charterer's declaration and, if the charterer is not co-operative, the owner may have to start the ballast voyage towards the first loading port, in order to avoid a claim for breach of contract from the charterer.

10.6 Cargo liability and "paramount clause"

Regarding the relation between shipowner and charterer under charterparties, there are no compulsory (mandatory) rules concerning cargo liability. Some charterparties tend to relieve the owner from much of his cargo liability, whereas others have provisions more or less in line with the mandatory cargo liability regime (see section 6.6.2). Although the parties in charterparties are thus basically free to determine the extent of the owner's cargo liability, it is not uncommon to find a separate provision, a so-called *"paramount clause"*, concerning the liability for damage to or loss of the goods. A paramount clause may be drafted in different ways; but the basic idea is that the Hague Rules or Hague-Visby Rules or national legislation based on these international conventions shall be applicable in case of cargo damage/cargo liability.

A paramount clause of a charterparty may prescribe that *a standard wording shall be inserted into all bills of lading issued under the charterparty*, or the clause shall cover only the *cargo liability* framework under the charterparty, or finally the clause may apply to the charterparty on its entirety. In the latter case, various legal problems may arise, since the Hague Rules or the similar subsequent conventions are geared to cargo liability allocation and not to chartering business and practice.

A paramount clause is one of the "protective clauses" that may be typically found in various charterparties or bills of lading. Indicative wordings of the term may be seen in appendix 2, *Shellvoy 6, part II, clause 37 "clause paramount"*, as well as in appendix 6, *NYPE 2015, clause 33(a) "protective clauses – general clause paramount"*.

10.7 War clauses

In time of war, revolution or other similar disturbances, the crew, the vessel and the cargo may be exposed to certain risks. The personnel on board may be injured or killed, while cargo and ship can be damaged or lost. Furthermore, there is a risk of delay and extra costs, for instance extra insurance premiums for cargo and vessel or additional wages of the crew. In order to make sure of the rights, the obligations and the liabilities of the parties when crew, ship and cargo are exposed to such risks, a special war clause is usually agreed in the charterparty. War clauses can be divided into two groups; *war cancellation clauses* and *war risk clauses*.

10.7.1 War cancellation clauses

BIMCO has published a standard war cancellation clause. Its latest edition was issued in 2004. The intention of such a clause is normally to give both contracting parties a chance to cancel the charter agreement when the freight market has totally changed as a result of war between certain countries, or when further trading with the vessel is prevented as a result of requisition or similar action from the vessel's home country. The war cancellation clauses may be typically found in long-term period charterparties and contracts of affreightment, but they are to a growing extent also found in shorter time charterparties or even in voyage charterparties. It must be noted that the latest edition of NYPE has removed such a war cancellation provision, which instead is included in the previous *NYPE '93* (*clause 32 "war cancellation"*).

BIMCO standard war cancellation clause 2004 is aligned with the respective clause found in Barecon 2001, which has the following wording (see appendix 8, *Barecon 2001, part II, clause 26(f) "war"*):

"*In the event of the outbreak of war (whether there be a declaration of war or not): (i) between any two or more of the following countries: the United States of America; Russia; the United Kingdom; France; and the People's Republic of China (ii) between any two or more of the countries stated in Box 36, both the Owners and the Charterers shall have the right to cancel this Charter, whereupon the Charterers shall redeliver the Vessel to the Owners in accordance with Clause 15, if the Vessel has cargo on board after discharge thereof at destination, or if debarred under this Clause from reaching or entering it at a near, open and safe port as directed by the Owners, or if the Vessel has no cargo on board, at the port at which she then is or if at sea at a near, open and safe port as directed by the Owners. In all cases hire shall continue to be paid in accordance with Clause 11 and except as aforesaid all other provisions of this Charter shall apply until redelivery*".

10.7.2 War risk clauses

While the war cancellation clauses at first hand are found in long-term period charter agreements or contracts of affreightment, the war risk clauses should be found in all charter agreements.

BIMCO has historically published the "Conwartime" and the "Voywar" war risks clauses, respectively for time and voyage charterparties. Attempting to reflect views recently expressed by the courts, changes in trading practices and insurance matters, their last revision was completed in 2013, replacing the previous versions of 1993 and 2004. These standard clauses were updated and are to be incorporated into all new and revised BIMCO standard charterparties and other documents.[4]

A war risk clause must always have a definition of "*war risk*". The following example is from BIMCO's clause *Voywar 1993*, as found in *Gencon '94* (see appendix 1, *part II, clause 17(1)(b) "war risks"*):

> "*'War Risks' shall include any war (whether actual or threatened), act of war, civil war, hostilities, revolution, rebellion, civil commotion, warlike operations, the laying of mines (whether actual or reported), acts of piracy, acts of terrorists, acts of hostility or malicious damage, blockades (whether imposed against all vessels or imposed selectively against vessels of certain flags or ownership, or against certain cargoes or crews or otherwise howsoever), by any person, body, terrorist or political group, or the Government of any state whatsoever, which, in the reasonable judgement of the Master and/or the Owners, may be dangerous or are likely to be or to become dangerous to the Vessel, her cargo, crew or other persons on board the Vessel*".

In the latest version of the clause, *Voywar 2013*, war risks include not only the actual or threatened war and warlike operations, but also the "reported" ones. Besides, piracy now includes "*violent robbery and/or capture/seizure*" to ensure consistency with the BIMCO piracy clause. Attacks of this type often occur nowadays and, while not technically regarded as piracy under international law, they are treated as such for insurance purposes.[5]

In many war risk clauses the definition is narrower. For instance, the war risk clause may be applicable only when the port is "*declared blockaded by reason of war*" or similar. Sometimes, the war risk clauses may also state that the decision as to whether a war risk exists or not lies exclusively with the owner.

The purpose of a war risk clause is to establish the respective parties' rights and obligations when crew, vessel and cargo are exposed to a war risk. Critical questions to be addressed are: Can the owner only, or both the charterer and the owner, cancel the charter agreement without compensation or is it an obligation on the charterer to arrange other cargo or to pay deadfreight (see glossary)? Is the owner obliged to go to another port or another area where the war risk does not exist? Who will pay for delay when the loading, the sea voyage or the discharging

---

4 BIMCO *War Risks Clause for Voyage Chartering (VOYWAR 2013), Explanatory Notes* (www. bimco.org, accessed 14 April 2017).

5 BIMCO *War Risks Clause for Time Chartering (CONWARTIME 2013), Explanatory Notes* (www.bimco.org, accessed 14 April 2017).

is hindered and who will pay for the extra insurance and extra wages for the crew?

Sometimes, the hull and war risk underwriters or the authorities (e.g. flag, classification society, port, etc.) give instructions to the ship that certain areas, owing to war risks, must be avoided. A war risk clause must state clearly that the owners are entitled to follow such instructions.

10.7.3 War risk clauses in voyage charters and time charters

Typically, the standard charterparty forms have a printed war risk clause. In time charters, various editions of the BIMCO Conwartime clause are often used (see appendix 6, *NYPE 2015, clause 34 "BIMCO war risks clause Conwartime 2013"* or appendix 4, *Gentime, part II, clause 21 "war risks (Conwartime 1993)"*). In voyage charters, respective editions of the BIMCO Voywar clause are included in the charter documents. As both the clauses are lengthy, for their full text the reader may refer to BIMCO. Comparing the concept and application of the clauses, it is important to know that in Conwartime a war risk may exist before or after a charterparty has been concluded, whereas Voywar focuses on the position before loading or after the voyage has commenced.[6]

Other war risk clauses, apart from those published by BIMCO, can also be used in chartering negotiations. These clauses may not be sufficient to cover the needs of a modern charter agreement, thus leading to disputes. Such controversial or outdated clauses should be avoided, in particular as far as period charterparties (time or bareboat charters) are concerned.

A ship operator should align war risk clauses designed for voyage chartering with those designed for time chartering. For example, when acting as "time chartered owner", "disponent owner" or similar, he must be careful to include in the *charter-out* a war risk clause that is no less favourable to him than the one included in his *charter-in*. If Conwartime 1993 is used when chartering-in a vessel on a time charter basis, Voywar 1993 should be used if the ship is chartered-out on a spot basis. If Conwartime 2013 is used for a time chartered vessel, Voywar 2013 shall be used for voyage agreements of the same vessel. Additionaly, the bill of lading war clauses must be drafted accordingly to give sufficient protection, equivalent to that of the respective charterparty.

10.8 Effect of cost variations on the contractual relationship

The basic idea here is that the parties are bound by their charter agreement, irrespective of any later economic developments. This idea is sometimes stressed by a so-called *"come hell or high water clause"*, whereby the parties agree that they will be bound by their contractual rights and obligations, whatever the future circumstances. Should there be an unforeseen cost increase, this will normally

---

6 BIMCO *War Risks Clause for Voyage Chartering (VOYWAR 2013), Explanatory Notes* (www. bimco.org, accessed 14 April 2017).

not affect the obligations of the party having to pay unless that amounts to "frustration" of the contract (see section 10.8.5), which is not often the case. Thus, the parties will have to regulate contractually the respective questions if they want the economic development to have any effect on their rights and duties. In such cases, specific clauses are sometimes found, particularly in charter contracts covering a long period of time. They may be described or titled as "*hardship clauses*", "*bunker clauses*", "*currency clauses*", "*escalation clauses*" etc. Their aim and construction vary widely.

A "*hardship clause*" may aim at the renegotiation of the contract if the economic conditions change substantially, and if the parties cannot agree during renegotiation, the suffering party may then be forced to cancel the agreement. Such clauses may be drafted in many different ways. Depending on the drafting, they may or may not give the intended protection. "*Bunker clauses*" may be of a type whereby the owner will be compensated when bunker prices are increased or where he is relieved from his obligations in case of bunker shortage. "*Currency clauses*" and "*escalation clauses*" are generally designed as "compensation clauses" only.

When the charter agreement covers a long period (particularly a bareboat, time chartering, a contract of affreightment or consecutive voyages), the parties must also consider the risks arising from changed economic conditions, especially rising costs and variations in the currency exchange rates. It is often hard to draft a currency clause, an escalation clause or a bunker cost clause, which will cover all occurrences. Therefore, such clauses may in some cases appear to have an adverse effect to what was intended. It may be advisable to consult both financial experts and lawyers when it comes to the drafting of such a clause. Standard clauses drafted by BIMCO may be used as a base, but as in every case when a standard clause is used, the circumstances in connection with the specific agreement should be taken into consideration. A few relevant examples will be given below to explain the situation and the difficulties.

10.8.1 Currency clauses

The following examples explain the problems that may arise due to variations in the relative currency exchange rate.

A shipowner who has all his costs in pounds sterling estimates the costs for a certain voyage at GBP 24,500. The freight is fixed at USD 25,000 which, with an exchange rate at USD 1 = GBP 1, gives an equivalent income of GBP 25,000 when translated at home currency. The surplus is consequently calculated at GBP 500. If, before the payment of the freight, the currency rate is changed at USD 1.20 = GBP 1 (a 20% weakening of the US Dollar), the owner's compensation translated at home currency will be limited to about GBP 20,800, which means that instead of a surplus of GBP 500 he will have a deficit of about GBP 3,700. If there was a currency clause in the charterparty stating that the freight should be based on an agreed exchange rate of USD/GBP = 1 and that possible changes in this rate would be adjusted accordingly, the owner would have been entitled to a freight payment of

USD 30,000 [i.e. USD 25,000 × (1+20%)]. In such a way, the surplus, when translated at home currency, would have been unchanged at GBP 500 [i.e. (USD 30,000 ÷ 1.20) – GBP 24,500], being again sufficient to cover costs.

When drafting such a clause several problems have to be considered. First, the parties have to decide whether a currency clause shall be inserted or not. If they so decide, they have to draft the clause. This is not always easy. The parties have to decide on various matters, such as whether the clause should work two ways or it will protect only one of them, whether the rate variations have to reach a certain level before the clause is applied, etc.

In liner business the pricing mechanisms are often based on a certain *Currency Adjustment Factor (CAF)*. This is a fee placed on top of standard freighting charges for liner carrier companies. The charge was developed to account for constantly changing exchange rates between the US Dollar and other currencies. Thus, its goal is to offset any losses arising from constantly fluctuating exchange rates for carriers. Calculation basis and methodology might vary from company to company. As a rule of thumb, the CAF increases as the US Dollar decreases in most circumstances. The surcharge is applied as a percentage on top of the base exchange rate agreed. Due to this added, unpredictable charge, shippers tend to prefer entering into "all inclusive" contracts at one price, that account for all applicable charges, so as to limit the CAF effect.

The following example of a *parity clause* is a typical one giving a two-way protection:

> "*The freight and the demurrage rate in this charterparty is based on a rate of exchange where USD 1 is equal to EUR . . . (the contractual rate of exchange). If at the date of actual payment, the fixing rate for US Dollars quoted by . . . Bank, differs from the contractual rate of exchange, the US Dollar shall be adjusted to realise the same amount of EUR as if the contractual rate of exchange was used*".

10.8.2 Escalation clauses

The object of an escalation clause is to protect the party suffering from cost increases, or rather to compensate him wholly or partly for his cost increases. The idea may then be that the freight shall continuously, or at certain intervals, be adjusted in accordance with the cost changes. The costs of particular importance in this perspective are those for manning, maintenance & repair and insurance of the vessel.

The basic problem with escalation clauses is to find a base or a formula for the recalculation of the freight. Sometimes, a particular cost factor will be used, sometimes an index (of one kind or another) will be applied and in other cases the actual cost changes will be used. Thus, if for instance the owner's costs have increased by 11% over a certain period, he may be entitled to a respective 11% freight increase when an escalation clause provides for an equal adjustment of freight to the increase of costs. However, such clauses may be thought to minimise the owner's cost management incentive. Another way is that the parties agree beforehand that the freight will be increased by an agreed percentage at certain intervals or dates.

An *example of an escalation clause* applying to a period charter is the following:

> *"The rate of hire agreed in this charter is based upon the level of owners' monthly operating expenses ruling at the date of this charter as shown in the statement for future comparison attached hereto, including provisions, stores, master's and crew's wages, war bonus and other remuneration, maintenance and usual insurance premiums.*
>
> *By the end of every year of the charter period the average monthly expenses for the preceding year shall be compared with the basic statement attached hereto. Any difference exceeding 5 per cent, to be multiplied by 12 and regulated in relation with the next hire payment. The same principle to apply pro rata at the termination of the charter for any part of a year"*.

10.8.3 Bunkers clauses

Currency clauses and escalation clauses are used mainly in agreements covering a long period of time. However, it may be advisable to insert into short-term charter agreements other clauses covering cost element fluctuations which may vary rapidly, particularly where neither of the parties may affect the cost. A typical example concerns bunkers' cost element. If bunker prices increase considerably during the period between the fixture of a spot charter and the commencement of the voyage, the owner's calculation may turn out to be totally wrong. A particular bunker clause may be entered in the charterparty specifying that the freight payable is based on a bunker price at USD X per ton and that any change in the bunker prices shall entitle the owner to a corresponding freight compensation or adjustment.

Liner shipping pricing schemes are normally including a *Bunker Adjustment Factor (BAF)*. This is a floating part of the sea freight charge, which represents additions to the freight paid, arising from changes to oil prices. In the past, BAF charges were collectively determined by liner conferences to be applicable for a certain period on a certain trade route. As from October 2008, the European Commission has banned carrier conferences, following anti-trust policies, thus shipping lines now set their own independent BAF rates which are closely monitored by the EU to ensure that no collusion occurs in price setting.

10.8.4 Other clauses dealing with cost allocation

Certain other costs which are unknown or difficult to estimate beforehand may be dealt with in special clauses.

For instance, the following clause concerns insurance charges and is often found in voyage charterparties:

> *"Any additional insurance on vessel and/or cargo levied by reason of the vessel's age, flag, ownership, management, class or condition to be for owner's account"*.

Another example concerns freight tax payment, which may burden the charterers or the owners, according to the agreement. The wording may be as follows:

> *"Freight tax, if any, to be for Charterers' (or Owners') account"*.

Many countries levy freight taxes. In other words, taxes are imposed on income generated from carriage of goods by sea, usually on export cargoes. In some cases, time charter and bareboat hire is also considered to be taxable income. Shipowners and ship managers can be affected, especially those who are not resident in those countries levying the tax. This may be of crucial importance for shipping groups listed in the US stock exchanges. Sometimes, the agency fees contain a component that turns out to be a freight tax, but the owner had little or no warning of such taxes before fixing the ship. BIMCO's role has been critical on this subject, as it used to issue an annually revised booklet, called *"Freight Taxes"*, which provided valuable information about taxes exercised in various countries, while this service is currently provided on-line to BIMCO members. Shipowners can improve the accuracy of their voyage estimations by using this service, as it contains concise and up-to-date information on countries that impose taxation on foreign ships using their ports.

A number of clauses are used to allocate freight taxes between the contracting parties. For time charterparties, the following provision is typical[7]:

> *"All taxes and dues on the Vessel and/or cargo and on charter hire and freight arising out of cargoes carried or ports visited under this Charterparty shall be for the Charterer's account".*

For voyage charterparties, the following wording is indicative:

> *"Dues and other charges levied against the Vessel shall be paid by the Owners, and dues and other charges levied against the cargo shall be paid by Charterers. Without prejudice to the foregoing, . . . the Vessel will be free of any wharfage, dock dues, quay dues, . . . or other taxes, assessment or charges calculated on the basis of the quantity of the cargo loaded or discharged and free also of . . . taxes on freight and any unusual taxes, assessment or government charges in force at the date of this Charterparty or becoming effective prior to its completion, either on the Vessel or on the freight, or whether or not measured by the quantity or volume of the cargo".*

The general principles for allocation of costs between charterers and owners will be explained in more detail in chapters 11–13, where types of charter are analysed in depth.

10.8.5 Frustration of charter contract

As mentioned in section 10.4.1, the English *"doctrine of frustration"* may sometimes be invoked by charterers or owners when they wish to cancel a charter agreement for economic reasons. All the difficult questions in connection with the doctrine cannot be explained at this point. However, it should be noted that it is usually very difficult to judge in advance whether the court or the arbitrators will consider an agreement frustrated or not. One should therefore be careful and

---

7 www.shipinspection.eu (accessed 15 April 2017).

always take legal advice before informing the counter-party that the agreement is considered to be terminated on the grounds of the "doctrine of frustration".

10.9 Arbitration clauses

Questions about the choice of law, the arbitration procedure or the legal action have to some extent been discussed in chapter 9. To avoid disputes about which law is applicable to the charter agreement, all charterparty forms should contain a clause dealing with the law applicable to and the procedure for the handling of disputes between the parties. The charterparties usually have reference to arbitration, while bills of lading more often refer to court procedures. An arbitration clause should not only have a reference to the applicable law, but also rules about the procedure when arbitrators are to be nominated. When English law is applicable, the arbitration clause sometimes has a reference to an *Arbitration Act* which deals with the procedure; specific reference should be made to the Arbitration Acts of 1950, 1979 or 1996.[8]

Modern charter contracts often contain a "split" arbitration clause where the parties choose whether an arbitration shall be referred to London, New York or any other place (see for example appendix 4, *Gentime, part II, clause 22 "law and arbitration"* or appendix 6, *NYPE 2015, clause 54 "law and arbitration"*). These clauses normally state that the contract shall be governed and construed in accordance with the law of the place chosen for arbitration. It may happen that the parties, who according to the arbitration clause shall choose the place for arbitration, fail to agree to that. The charterparties therefore may provide for a "default solution", like in *Gentime, part II, clause 22(d) "law and arbitration"*. Finally, it is common for the arbitration clauses to make special reference to "small amounts disputes".

10.10 Time limits

Most countries have general time limits for claims and usually the charterparties also have such limitations. The one-year limit in connection with cargo claims under the bill of lading conventions is one example already mentioned. As regards time limitations in charterparties, a general recommendation is to avoid limits shorter than a year.

The time limits under the general contract law differ from country to country and both parties in the charter agreement must find out what limitations for bringing suit are applicable in the relevant case. Under English Law, the key limitation period for the purposes of commercial litigation or arbitration is six years for actions arising out of charterparties. Other countries have shorter limits, for example France has a one-year limit and Spain has a six-month limit. It must also be noted that, even if the charter agreement is governed by English law and accordingly the limitation is six years, the laws and the rules of the country where

---

8 www.legislation.gov.uk/ukpga/1996/23/contents (accessed 15 April 2017).

the defendant has his place of business may be relevant. For example, if the charterers are Spanish, the owners must be aware of the Spanish six-month limit and not rely on the English six-year limit which is applicable to the charterparty if that is governed by English law. It is also important to find out from what day or from what event the time limit should count. Sometimes, time in this respect starts to run from the time of final discharge of cargo, whereas sometimes it starts to run from different points of time or certain facts.

10.11 Exception clauses

Charterparties usually contain clauses which exempt the owners or both owners and charterers from liabilities. These clauses are sometimes related only to specified loss or damage (e.g. loss or damage to cargo), but sometimes they are of a more general nature. The bill of lading conventions exempt in some cases owners from loss or damage to cargo, as it has already been discussed in section 6.6. Another example is the *cesser clause*, where in a voyage charterparty the charterer's liability ceases on shipment of the cargo. In such a case, the charterer intends to transfer to a shipper his right to have goods carried. The clause is usually related with the shipowner's right to have a lien over the shipper's goods for the freight, deadfreight and demurrage payable under the charterparty. Thus, the charterer is only released from liabilities that have been replaced by a lien given to the shipowner.

The following two examples concern *exception clauses* of a general nature (the first is about a voyage charterparty, while the second one is for a time charterparty):

Gencon '94, part II, clause 2 "owners' responsibility clause"

"The Owners are to be responsible for loss of or damage to the goods or for delay in delivery of the goods only in case the loss, damage or delay has been caused by personal want of due diligence on the part of the Owners or their Manager to make the vessel in all respects seaworthy and to secure that she is properly manned, equipped and supplied or by the personal act or default of the Owners or their Manager.
And the Owners are not responsible for loss, damage or delay arising from any other cause whatsoever, even from the neglect or default of the Master or crew or some other person employed by the Owners on board or ashore for whose acts they would, but for this Clause, be responsible, or from unseaworthiness of the Vessel on loading or commencement of the voyage or at any time whatsoever".

Baltime 1939, edition 2001, part II, clause 12 "responsibility and exemption"

"The Owners only shall be responsible for delay in delivery of the Vessel or for delay during the currency of the Charter and for loss or damage to goods onboard, if such delay or loss has been caused by want of due diligence on the part of the Owners or their Manager in making the Vessel seaworthy and fitted for the voyage or any other personal act or omission or default of the Owners or their Manager. The Owners shall not be responsible in any other case nor for damage or delay whatsoever and howsoever caused even if caused by the neglect or default of their servants. The Owners shall not be liable for loss or damage arising or resulting from

strikes, lock-outs or stoppage or restraint of labour (including the Master, Officers or Crew) whether partial or general. The Charterers shall be responsible for loss or damage caused to the Vessel or to the Owners by goods being loaded contrary to the terms of the Charter or by improper or careless bunkering or loading, stowing or discharging of goods or any other improper or negligent act on their part or that of their servants".

Both the Gencon and the Baltime clauses seem to be very favourable to the owner. It should be noted, however, that courts and arbitrators are restrictive in their interpretation of such clauses and the owner cannot therefore rely fully on similar text.

Another kind of exception clause may be the *"force majeure"* wording which refers to mutual relief of the parties, as follows:

"Charterers and Owners exempt each other from responsibility for non-performance of this agreement when same is caused by Acts of God, Governmental, Institutional Restrictions or any other cause beyond control of either party".

This clause can be referred to both by charterers and owners, which is not the case with the above-cited Gencon and Baltime clauses.

Sometimes, a *"limitation of liability"* provision may be agreed and drafted as per below (*Gencon '76, part II, clause 12 "indemnity"*):

"Indemnity for non-performance of this Charterparty, proved damages, not exceeding estimated amount of freight".

It should be pointed out that this clause is not included in *Gencon '94*.

As indicated, many different kinds of exception clauses are found in the charterparties and it is often difficult to find out to what extent they are applicable to a relevant situation. The main problem with the exception clauses is that they are very often disregarded during the negotiations. The printed clauses in standard forms easily "slip in" more or less unnoticed by the parties. The probable explanation is that they are not often referred to by the parties and therefore are considered to be harmless. This is not at all correct. The existence and wording of an exception clause may be decisive and, particularly when large amounts of money are involved in a dispute, the parties refer to the exception clause to try to win the case. The parties are recommended to read carefully all the exception clauses and consider their contents before accepting them. This is, of course, a general recommendation applying also to all other clauses in the charterparty.

10.12 Maritime liens

A shipowner may exercise a lien on goods carried on board the vessel for charges like freight, deadfreight, demurrage, expenses for the cargo, general average contribution, etc. Liens on goods can be based on the applicable general law, on express agreement in the charterparty or bill of lading, or on both the general law and express agreement. On the contrary, sometimes a claim against the owner will be connected with a lien on the vessel. Such a lien may remain on the ship even if that is sold to another shipowner. In time and bareboat chartering, owners, by agreement, often have a right for lien on the freight due to the charterers under any underlying bill of lading or sub-charterparty. In order to find out the chances of exercising a lien in a relevant situation, not only the contracts (charterparty and bill of lading), but also the applicable laws (the law of the contract and the law in the relevant country where the lien will be exercised), must be considered. Liens are further discussed in various sections throughout the book (see index under the word "lien").

10.13 Arrest of vessels

Persons or companies who have claims against a shipowner sometimes may proceed in arresting one of the shipowner's vessels in order to get payment or security for payment. The rules applying to an arrest of a vessel vary considerably, depending mostly on the applicable law, namely the legal jurisdiction in the country where the arrestor intends to arrest the vessel. It is therefore essential both for the arrestor and the shipowner to appoint a local lawyer able to provide legal advice, evaluate the circumstances of the case and handle the formalities.

As an example of the variations between different countries, a ship in some countries can be arrested only for claims secured by a maritime lien or a mortgage on the vessel, whereas in other countries the ship can be arrested for any type of monetary claim irrespective of being secured or not. Sometimes the arrestor must produce evidence and security for his claim and in other cases a vessel can be arrested on very loose grounds and without security. Considering this, it goes without saying that detailed recommendations cannot be given to the parties in this respect. Generally speaking, it is recommended that a shipowner should act immediately when there is a risk of arrest. He should consult his legal advisors, the P&I Club, his bankers, etc., preparing defences, arguments and securities to avoid delay to the vessel. The person or company who intends to arrest a vessel should also note that, even if it is sometimes very easy to do so and thereby get security, they risk receiving a counter-claim for the delay of the vessel if the arrest is proved to have been made without justification.

10.14 General average

The definition of general average is contained in section 66(2) of the UK Marine Insurance Act 1906 as follows[9]:

> *"There is a general average act, where any extraordinary sacrifice or expenditure is voluntarily and reasonably made or incurred in time of peril for the purpose of preserving the property imperilled in the common adventure".*

---

9 Hudson, N.G. and Harvey, M.D. (2010) *The York-Antwerp Rules: The Principles and Practice of General Average Adjustment* (Informa Law from Routledge, 3rd edition, p. 31).

Therefore, there is a general average act when, and only when, any extraordinary sacrifice or expenditure is intentionally or reasonably made or incurred for the common safety and for the purpose of preserving from peril the properties involved in a common maritime adventure. An inherent element of the general average is that sacrifices and expenditures are proportionally borne and shared by the different contributing interests of the maritime adventure. The subject matter of general average includes all the interests of the common adventure which are at risk. Such interests are physical, namely the ship, the cargo, the bunkers, stores, personal effects; but, there are also those interests which are dependent on the safety of the physical property, such as the freight, time charter hire (which are earned upon the safe carriage of the cargo) and any other property involved which is at risk during a maritime common adventure.[10]

A typical, but rather old-fashioned, example of general average concerns the situation where a deck cargo is jettisoned in order to balance a listing vessel and thereby save her, her other cargo and freight. Another up-to-date example is when a vessel in distress is saved.

Nearly all general averages are adjusted in accordance with the so-called *"York-Antwerp Rules (YAR)"*. This is a set of rules which outlines the international framework of general average settlements. The rules were first established in 1890 and have been amended several times since then. The last revisions are those of 1994, 2004 and the most recent of 2016. It is common that charterparties, contracts of affreightment, bills of lading, waybills and marine insurance policies have a reference to one version of these rules. Under the rules, a danger must be imminent, there must be a voluntary jettison of a portion of the ship's cargo in order to save the whole and the attempt to avoid the danger must be successful. If these conditions are true, then all parties involved in the maritime adventure must share proportionately the financial burden of the losses incurred to the owner(s) of any cargo that was jettisoned to save the vessel, the cargo and the other property.[11] Before the cargo is discharged from a vessel when general average is declared, the cargo owners, other interests or their underwriters usually have to give "bonds", which guarantee their contribution to the forthcoming general average adjustment.

YAR 2016 was approved by CMI (Comité Maritime International)[12] in May 2016, after a long drafting process which began in 2012. All industry partners such as BIMCO (representing shipowners), ICS (International Chamber of Shipping) and IUMI (International Union of Marine Insurance) have agreed to support the 2016 revision. These rules have a good prospect of being widely adopted in place of the York-Antwerp Rules 1994, the set of rules which is at present most commonly incorporated by reference into charterparties and bills of lading. Thus, the York-Antwerp Rules 2016 are expected to fill the gap created

---

10 www.lloydslistintelligence.com (accessed 17 April 2017).

11 www.investopedia.com (accessed 17 April 2017).

12 Both the YAR 2016 and the respective CMI Guidelines may be found at www.comitemaritime.org.

by the failure of the 2004 Rules which, whilst promoted by cargo interests, never found acceptance in the shipowning community as they were less favourable for the owners.[13]

The complicated questions which arise in connection with a general average situation extend beyond the scope of this book. However, attention must be drawn to the *"Jason Clause"* or *"New Jason Clause"* or *"Amended Jason Clause"*, which are alternatives often found in the charterparties or other contracts of carriage. This clause was initially drafted to avoid the consequences of a court case in the United States which held that a shipowner could not recover the cargo's proportion of general average arising out of negligent navigation or errors in ship management. Nevertheless, it is doubtful to what extent a Jason clause or similar is valid.

The *"BIMCO New Jason clause"* has the following wording[14]:

> *"In the event of accident, danger, damage or disaster before or after the commencement of the voyage, resulting from any cause whatsoever, whether due to negligence or not, for which, or for the consequence of which, the Carrier is not responsible, by statute, contract or otherwise, the goods, Shippers, Consignees or owners of the goods shall contribute with the Carrier in general average to the payment of any sacrifices, losses or expenses of a general average nature that may be made or incurred and shall pay salvage and special charges incurred in respect of the goods.*
>
> *If a salving ship is owned or operated by the Carrier, salvage shall be paid for as fully as if the said salving ship or ships belonged to strangers. Such deposit as the Carrier or his agents may deem sufficient to cover the estimated contribution of the goods and any salvage and special charges thereon shall, if required, be made by the goods, Shippers, Consignees or owners of the goods to the Carrier before delivery".*

A general average clause is one of the "protective clauses" typically found in a dry cargo voyage charterparty (see appendix 1, *Gencon '94, part II, clause 12 "general average and new Jason clause"*), in a tanker voyage charterparty (see appendix 2, *Shellvoy 6, part II, clause 36 "general average/new Jason clause"*), as well as in a time charterparty (see appendix 6, *NYPE 2015, clause 33c "protective clauses – new Jason clause"*).

10.15 Collision

Collision between ships or between, for example, a vessel and a quay, a dolphin, a shore crane or a similar object can give rise to considerable loss or damage to the vessel, goods or other property. Delay is very often caused and in some cases people are injured or even killed. The governing rules about liability in respect with collisions are complicated and cannot be fully discussed in this

---

13 BIMCO *BIMCO to Refer to New York-Antwerp Rules 2016 in Future Documents* (www.bimco. org, accessed 17 April 2017); Sarll, R. and Kemp, A. (2016) *York-Antwerp Rules 2016: A Summary* (Shipping & Trade Law, Informa plc., 15 July 2016); Norwegian Hull Club (2016) *York Antwerp Rules 2016 Finally Approved* (www.norclub.no, accessed 12 May 2016).

14 BIMCO *New Jason Clause* (www.bimco.org, accessed 17 April 2017).

book. However, as many contracts of carriage contain a so-called "*both-to-blame collision clause*", some basic elements will only be explained here.

The "Brussels Collision Convention" or "Collision Convention 1910" or formally "the Convention for the Unification of Certain Rules of Law with respect to Collisions between Vessels" is a 1910 multi-lateral treaty that established the rules of legal liability that result from collisions between ships at sea. According to the Convention, three general rules are applying:

1. If a collision occurs that is accidental or of uncertain cause, the damages are borne by the party that suffers them.
2. If a collision occurs that is the fault of a party, the party at fault is liable for the damages that were caused.
3. If a collision occurs that is the fault of more than one party, the parties at fault are liable in proportion to the faults respectively committed. If it is not possible to determine the proportional fault, the liability is apportioned equally between the parties at fault.

Therefore, from the Collision Convention 1910 it is inferred that, when two ships are to blame for a collision, the cargo in vessel A can recover its loss from vessel B in the same proportion as if B was to blame for the collision. But, if the contract of carriage exempts the owner of vessel A from liability for loss or damage to cargo when the loss or damage is caused by error in navigation (see section 6.6.5), the owner of cargo on board vessel A cannot get the remaining part from owner A. Furthermore, the Collision Convention 1910 has not been ratified by the United States and according to US law the cargo in vessel A can recover the whole of its loss from vessel B, which in turn can get 50% of this loss back from vessel A, notwithstanding the fact that vessel A is exempted from liability for damage caused by nautical error.

The "both-to-blame collision" clause was designed with the intention of achieving the same result under US law as under international law as described by the Collision Convention 1910. However, the clause has been held by the US Supreme Court to be void and cannot be enforced in the USA. The clause can therefore only be invoked under very special circumstances outside the USA.

To sum up, according to the Hague-Visby Rules, if the carrier has exercised due diligence to provide a seaworthy ship, he is not liable for cargo claims resulting from a collision partly or wholly caused by negligent navigation (*Hague-Visby Rules, art. IV, par. 2a*). Since it is common that both vessels are partly to blame for a collision, cargo interests may then present their claims in tort against the non-carrying vessel. Under US law, claimants could recover their claims in full from the owners of the other vessel, who could then recover one half from the carriers. But, this circumvents the navigational error defence, creating also the anomaly that cargo interests cannot recover if the carrying vessel is wholly to blame. Therefore, the both-to-blame clause is designed to preserve the protection which the carrier has under the Hague-Visby Rules by giving a contractual indemnity against the cargo interests. Further to that, charterparties usually contain a clause requiring that all bills of lading issued must also contain the both-to-blame clause, providing an indemnity if not incorporated.[15]

The *"both-to-blame collision"* clause is one of the "protective clauses" typically found in a dry cargo voyage charterparty (see appendix 1, *Gencon '94, part II, clause 11 "both-to-blame collision clause"*), in a tanker voyage charterparty (see appendix 2, *Shellvoy 6, part II, clause 35 "both to blame clause"*), as well as in a time charterparty (see appendix 6, *NYPE 2015, clause 33(b) "protective clauses – both-to-blame collision clause"*).

The *"BIMCO both-to-blame collision clause"* has the following wording[16]:

> "If the Vessel comes into collision with another ship as a result of the negligence of the other ship and any act, neglect or default of the Master, Mariner, Pilot or the servants of the Carrier in the navigation or in the management of the Vessel, the owners of the cargo carried hereunder will indemnify the Carrier against all loss or liability to the other or non-carrying ship or her Owners in so far as such loss or liability represents loss of, or damage to, or any claim whatsoever of the owners of said cargo, paid or payable by the other or non-carrying ship or her Owners to the owners of said cargo and set-off, recouped or recovered by the other or non-carrying ship or her Owners as part of their claim against the carrying Vessel or Carrier. The foregoing provisions shall also apply where the Owners, operators or those in charge of any ship or ships or objects other than, or in addition to, the colliding ships or objects are at fault in respect of a collision or contact".

10.16 International Safety Management Code (ISM)

The International Safety Management (ISM) Code applies compulsorily under international law to all cargo vessels and mobile offshore drilling units of 500 gross tonnage and upwards. The Code has been implemented to all passenger ships (including high-speed craft), oil tankers, chemical tankers, gas carriers, bulk carriers and cargo high-speed craft since 1 July 1998, while other cargo ships, such as containerships and mobile offshore drilling units have been obliged to comply with the Code since 1 July 2002.

As it was self-explanatorily stated by BIMCO[17]:

> "The ISM Code represents only one part of the substantial volume of regulations to which shipowners are bound under the law of the Flag State. As part of the SOLAS Convention 1974, as amended, implementation of the ISM Code is mandatory for all Contracting States under international law. Most standard charterparties contain fairly all-embracing provisions requiring the owner to ensure that the vessel is in full compliance with all relevant international rules and regulations, and possesses the necessary certificates, to permit the vessel to trade within the agreed trading limits. Therefore, from a strictly legal point of view, BIMCO considers that there is no readily identifiable contractual need to make a specific reference to the ISM Code in a voyage or time charter.

---

15 Skuld (2009) *Both-To-Blame Collision Clause* (www.skuld.com, accessed 4 September 2009).

16 BIMCO *Both-to-Blame Collision Clause* (www.bimco.org, accessed 17 April 2017).

17 BIMCO *BIMCO Standard ISM Clause for Voyage and Time Charterparties* (BIMCO Special Circular No. 1, 4 February 1998).

Nevertheless, in response to the demand of Members and for those who may feel more comfortable incorporating a specific reference to the ISM Code in their charterparties, BIMCO has devised a broad and neutrally worded ISM Clause".

BIMCO has introduced the following standard *ISM Clause* for voyage and time charterparties:

"From the date of coming into force of the International Safety Management (ISM) Code in relation to the Vessel and thereafter during the currency of this Charterparty, the Owners shall procure that both the Vessel and 'the Company' (as defined by the ISM Code) shall comply with the requirements of the ISM Code. Upon request Owners shall provide a copy of the relevant Document of Compliance (DOC) and Safety Management Certificate (SMC) to the Charterers.
Except as otherwise provided in this Charterparty, loss, damage, expense or delay caused by failure on the part of the Owners or 'the Company' to comply with the ISM Code shall be for the Owners' account".

10.17 Piracy

Piracy clauses setting out party rights and obligations in response to increasing piracy risks were first issued in 2009. BIMCO initially drafted three provisions respectively for time charterparties, consecutive voyage charters/COAs and single voyage charters. However, following a recent court case, changing trade practices, the need for clarifying charterers' liabilities after a vessel is released following seizure, as well as insurance matters, a review was made by BIMCO to all three clauses in 2013 to ensure that the provisions remain in line with commercial requirements. BIMCO strongly recommends that the latest versions of the piracy clauses should always be used.[18] The specific wording of "*BIMCO piracy clause for time charter parties 2013*" may be seen in appendix 6, *NYPE 2015, clause 39*. The relevant provisions about single voyage charters and consecutive voyage charters/COAs may be sourced by BIMCO.

---

18 BIMCO *BIMCO Revised Piracy Clauses* (BIMCO Special Circular No. 7, 19 July 2013).

CHAPTER 11

Voyage charter

This chapter examines in detail typical clauses found and critical matters accruing from a voyage charter. Initially, the importance of an accurate vessel's description, the nomination of safe ports and berths, the execution of the voyage with utmost despatch and with no deviation, as well as problems related to the quantity or the quality of the cargo, are highlighted. Then, various freight matters are commented, comprising the fixing, the risk, the payment and the security of freight, the deadfreight and the brokerage commission. In addition, the crucial allocation of costs is discussed concerning loading/discharging and other cargo-handling costs, harbour costs, freight taxes, delays from strikes and agency expenses. Analysis goes further to deal with other specialised voyage charter subjects, as the lien, the cargo liability and the damage to the vessel. The content of the chapter is enriched with examples from real clauses sourced from standard forms of voyage charterparties; both dry and tanker. Finally, due to the extent of analysis and the weight of importance, the key voyage charter issue of laytime and demurrage is referred to chapter 15. Thus, it is recommended that the reader should study this chapter together with chapter 15, consulting also the glossary and appendix at the end of the book, where necessary.

11.1 Definition

Types of charter have been presented in section 7.3. In particular, voyage charter was covered in section 7.3.1. At this point, only a short definition of the voyage charter will be provided.

A *voyage or spot charter* concerns the case where a vessel is chartered for a single voyage between certain ports. Practically, the owner promises to load on board his (named) ship an agreed quantity of cargo which has to be transported from specific loading port(s) to specific discharging port(s). The voyage charterer pays freight per ton of cargo carried. The charter agreement is governed by a voyage charterparty. This form of charter is typical and common within bulk/tramp trading (open charter market), but almost impossible to find in the liner market since at this type of business liner carriers themselves are those who undertake to carry out the scheduled voyages with owned or period-chartered vessels chartered from individual shipowners. In a voyage charter, the owner retains the operational control and the commercial management of the vessel, being responsible for all the (variable) voyage expenses, such as bunkers, port charges, canal dues, extra insurances, etc., further to the (fixed) daily running costs of the vessel, such as manning, maintenance and repair, insurance, etc. The charterer's costs are usually only expenses and charges relating to the cargo.

The most significant subjects of a voyage charterparty are the description of the voyage, the cargo and the vessel, the allocation of duties and costs in connection with loading and discharging of cargo, the specification and payment of the freight, the laytime and demurrage rules, the allocation of the liability for the cargo and the allocation of other costs and risks. Depending on the circumstances, other questions and clauses can also be very important in the negotiations between the owners and the charterers. The most critical parts of a voyage charter are discussed below.

11.2 Vessel

11.2.1 Description of vessel

In most cases a specific ship is nominated. Thus, the vessel's name, IMO identification number and call sign, year of build, nationality, deadweight, gross and net tonnage and sometimes speed are stated in the charterparty. The need for the description of the vessel in the voyage charterparty very much depends on the circumstances. The type of cargo and the intended ports and seaways especially determine what details about the ship must be mentioned during the negotiations and in the charterparty.

The ship's draught, length, breadth and sometimes also the height over the waterline (air draught) can be very important in narrow seaways and ports and in passage under bridges and hanging power-lines. Also, the equipment for cargo handling (winches, cranes, pumps, etc.) and the design and condition of the cargo compartments are often important for the vessel's fitness for the intended cargo. The number of hatches, type of hatch covering, as well as the length and the breadth of hatch openings and ramps are important details when the charterers and the owners estimate the speed and cost for loading and discharging of cargo. Some cargoes may need special equipment, such as reefer plant and CO-equipment. In oil transportation the pumping capacity of the vessel has particular importance.

Both the owners and the charterers must, as far as possible, try to specify all those details about the cargo and the vessel that are necessary for economic calculation and practical planning of the loading, carrying and discharging of a cargo. If the cargo or the ship have some unusual or unexpected qualities, the other party should be made aware of these.

11.2.2 Specification of vessel's cargo carrying capacity

The specification of the vessel's cargo capacity is important. It can be described in several ways, with the deadweight capacity and the cubic capacity being the most common ones.

The *deadweight capacity* is the ship's weight-carrying capacity, usually specified in metric tons (or tonnes), but sometimes still in long tons (see analytically appendix 16 about measurements). The deadweight capacity normally includes the vessel's capacity, not only for cargo but also for fuel, fresh water and stores. To avoid mistakes and to make clear that fuel etc. is also included, it is common to add the words "*all told*" to the deadweight capacity figure. Instead of "*deadweight all told*" (*DWAT*), the "*deadweight cargo-carrying capacity*" (*DWCC*) is sometimes used (see *DWAT* and *DWCC* in glossary). For instance, *Gencon '94* uses the "dwt all told" expression (see appendix 1, *part I, box 7 and part II, clause 1*), while *Gencon '76* (*part I, box 7 and part II, clause 1*) uses the "dwt cargo carrying capacity" term. The difference between deadweight capacity and the deadweight cargo-carrying capacity is that the cargo-carrying capacity does not include the capacity necessary for fuel, freshwater, stores or other extras. It must be noted that when the deadweight capacity is stated in the charterparty, the owners are not free to bunker the vessel as they wish. Bunker quantity, as well as freshwater, stores etc., must be adjusted to the intended voyage (including, of course, the necessary safety surplus of bunkers). If the vessel has unjustified high quantities of bunkers on board and the charterers thereby cannot use the ship as intended, the owners may be held liable for damages against the charterers. These damages may include both reduction of freight and compensation for the charterers' extra costs to ship the cargo in another vessel. If the cargo is perishable, e.g. bananas, the owners also risk liability for damage to the cargo as a result of short shipment. Both the deadweight capacity (dwat) and the cargo-carrying capacity (dwcc) must be related to certain vessel's marks (e.g. concerning loadlines, draught, freeboard etc.).

The vessel's *cubic capacity* is typically used for dry cargo vessels and stated both in grain and in bale. The *bale capacity* is the volume available for boxes, cartons or other general cargo, etc. The *grain capacity*, which almost always is higher than the bale capacity, also includes those parts of the cargo holds that can be filled with "floating", homogeneous, dry bulk cargo, such as grain, phosphates, etc. (see terms *BL*, *Cargo Capacity*, *GR* and *SF* in glossary).

Both the deadweight capacity (or dwt cargo-carrying capacity) and the cubic capacity are usually stated in connection with the word "*about*". This word does not relieve the owners from their obligation to state the capacity as accurately as possible.

The specification of vessel's cargo carrying capacity is crucial as far as voyage estimation is concerned. Voyage estimation principles are analysed in section 14.1, while, more specifically, measurement of cargo is covered in section 14.1.2.2.

11.3 Voyage

11.3.1 Nomination of ports – rotation

The place for loading or discharging of cargo can be agreed in several ways, for instance:

- a fixed berth, for example "*berth 2 at Lagos*";
- a fixed port, for example "*1 safe berth Sydney*";
- a fixed area, for example "*1 safe port / 1 safe berth Japan*";

- a port or an area for order, for example "*US Gulf for order*"; or
- several berths and/or ports, for example "*berth 2 at Lagos and 1 safe berth Casablanca*".

If a port is to be nominated later, thus not being fixed in the charterparty, then it is advisable to state the latest time at which the charterers can nominate the port. For example, such a clause may have the following wording:

"*Loading ports to be nominated by Charterers latest when the vessel is passing Gibraltar*",

or

"*Discharging port to be nominated by Charterers latest at commencement of loading*".

When no such clause is inserted into the charterparty, the charterers should nominate the port or ports well in advance so that no extra cost for waiting time and deviation is caused to the vessel. When the charter agreement contains several loading ports or discharging ports, it is common that the owners try to introduce a clause providing that the ports shall be called "*in geographical rotation*". The intention is to avoid extra steaming time.

Unless otherwise expressly agreed or customary, the charterers are entitled and have a duty to appoint a berth for the vessel. The charterers cannot nominate any port or berth and the owners are not strictly obliged to follow any directions from the charterers. Most voyage charterparties state that ports and berths shall be safe. The voyage charterparties usually also contain an ice clause and a near clause. These critical aspects are presented below.

11.3.2 Safe port, safe berth, always afloat

Most charterparties state that the ports and berths nominated by the charterers shall be safe. The word "safe" in this context refers not only to factors such as high winds, heavy swell, insufficient or bad construction of quays, dolphins, etc., but also to other factors such as warlike operations and political disturbances (these last-mentioned factors are often dealt with in special war clauses as seen in section 10.7).

In the majority of charters this implied obligation is reinforced by an express term to the same effect. A classic definition of a safe port was provided by Sellers LJ in the *Eastern City [1958] 2 Lloyd's Rep. 127*:

"*. . . a port will not be safe unless, in the relevant period of time the particular ship can reach it, use it and return from it without, in the absence of some abnormal occurrence, being exposed to danger which cannot be avoided by good navigation and seamanship*".[1]

---

1 Wilson, J.F. (2008) *Carriage of Goods by Sea* (London, Pearson Longman, 6th edition, p. 25).

A stipulation in the charterparty that charterers shall nominate safe ports and safe berths does not mean that the owners and the master can refrain from investigating the safety of the port and the berth. Neither are the charterers strictly liable for their safety. It is difficult to find the borderline between the respective parties' liability and the obligation to investigate, and it is in most questionable cases impossible to establish beforehand whether a certain port or berth from a legal point of view is safe or not.

As a general rule, it can be said that the earlier the owners and the master are informed about intended ports and berths, the more liability rests on them as regards investigation of the safety. Consequently, when during the negotiations and in the charterparty agreement have accepted a certain port or a certain berth, they have little chance of getting damages from the charterers if the port or the berth turns out to be unsafe. On the other hand, the charterers have little chance of escaping liability for damage to the ship when the finally unsafe port or berth has been nominated after the negotiations and the fixture. In the latter case, the owners and the master have had little or no chance to influence the choice of port or berth.

Another general rule is that, where the master has agreed to call at a certain port or to moor at a certain berth, it does not mean that the owners' right to claim damages from the charterers has been waived. The charterers' liability for safety remains even when the master has made an excusable wrong decision and called at a port which later turned out to be unsafe.

Disputes about safe ports and safe berths are very complicated, especially as regards production of evidence. The outcome of a dispute very much depends on the law which governs the charter agreement. Apart from safety, it is also common that the charterparties contain a special statement stipulating that the ship shall always "*lie afloat*". However, it may be agreed that charterers are entitled to nominate a berth where the vessel can "*lie safely aground*" (see terms *AA, AAAA* and *NAABSA* in glossary).

11.3.3 Near clause

There is an obligation on the owners to take the vessel to the agreed loading or discharging place. In order to protect the owners against unforeseeable difficulties, a so-called "*near clause*" is often inserted in the voyage charterparty. In *Gencon '94* (see appendix 1 *part II, clause 1 "preamble"*), the relevant provision reads (inter alia):

> "*The said Vessel shall, as soon as her prior commitments have been completed, proceed to the loading port(s) or place(s) stated in Box 10 or so near thereto as she may safely get and lie always afloat . . .*".

There is a similar clause for the discharging port. The intention of the clause is to protect the owners against such hindrances that arise after the negotiation and the fixture. When such a hindrance arises, the owners are not obliged to take the ship closer to the agreed place or port than she can safely get and lie always afloat. When judging whether a port is safe or unsafe, there is a difference between those cases where the vessel – according to the charterparty – is ordered to a certain berth or port and those cases where the vessel is ordered to a certain range of ports. In the first case, there is an obligation on the owner to find out beforehand whether the ship can safely go to the nominated port or the berth. In the latter case, it is the charterers' duty to make sure that they nominate ports and berths suitable for the vessel.

When the normal route is hindered, the owners cannot usually rely on the near clause where there is a possibility of reaching the port or the berth via another route, even if this means extra costs for the owners (see also the comment about frustration in sections 10.4.1 and 10.8.5). Neither can the owners rely on the near clause when the obstacle is temporary.

11.3.4 Ice clause

In some trades and at times of the year where there is risk of ice, the charterparty must contain a so-called "*ice clause*".

In section 10.4.2 regarding a vessel's trading limits, it was mentioned that hull underwriters define special trading limits for all vessels, based on ice and weather conditions in certain areas. It goes without saying that the owners cannot accept ports or trading areas outside these limits and, when there is a possibility of breaking the trading limits against extra insurance, the owners should be very cautious. Under all circumstances, the owners must insist on having a sufficient ice clause when there is any risk of ice on the intended voyage. The near clause gives the owners some – but far from sufficient – protection in this respect.

Indicative questions that must be dealt with in the ice clause are:

- Is there an obligation on the owners to let the vessel break ice or follow an ice-breaker?
- What possibilities have the owners to refuse a certain port or area, or to order the ship to leave before loading or discharging is completed, when there is a risk of the vessel being frozen in?
- Are the owners entitled to full, or only reduced, freight when the vessel has to leave the loading port with only a part cargo?
- Who shall decide what to do with the cargo on board when it is impossible to reach the originally intended discharging port?
- Who shall pay for delay caused to the ship as a result of ice or ice risk at the loading port, sea voyage or discharging port?
- Who shall pay for extra insurance on the vessel and damage caused to the ship by ice?

All the above and other similar questions are important when there is a risk of ice. It should also be noted that delay of the ship by reason of cold weather can be dealt with in the laytime clauses (see chapter 15) and the contracting parties to the charterparty must ensure that these clauses are not contradictory to the ice clause.

In *Gencon '94* (see appendix 1, *part II, clause 18 "general ice clause"*) there is a printed ice clause. The provision has one section for the "port of loading" and one for the "port of discharge". Each section is divided into three sub-sections; the first dealing with ice problems or risks in the port before the vessel's arrival, the second dealing with ice problems or risks in the port after the vessel's arrival and the third dealing with other problems/questions. The rather odd phrase of *Gencon '76* stating that the ice clause was not applicable in the spring has been deleted in *Gencon '94*.

When *"ice-class vessels"* (i.e. specially designed and constructed vessels for trading in ice) are chartered for a voyage where ice can be expected, the traditional ice clauses are usually avoided from the charterparty. Instead, special "tailor-made" clauses may be drafted.

BIMCO last revised its ice clauses in 2005 and created a standard clause for voyage charters, the so-called *"BIMCO Ice Clause for Voyage Charter Parties"*. The relevant amendments were made because the previous ice clauses were silent on the issues of forcing ice and following ice breakers. Besides, provisions were needed to protect the owners against the risk of ice being experienced on the approach voyage. Consequently, in the revised clause a provision was added that makes it clear that the vessel should not be obliged to force ice, but may reasonably be expected to follow ice breakers where other vessels of the same size, class and construction are doing so.[2]

11.3.5 Sea voyage

Sometimes the charterparty expressly states what route the vessel shall take, for instance *"Sydney to Lisbon via Cape of Good Hope"*. With such a clause the owners or the master cannot direct the vessel via the Suez Canal. Without such or a similar clause concerning the route, the master will choose the usual route or one of the usual routes. In any case the master has the right to make such alterations of route or necessary deviations as he deems advisable for the safety of the crew, vessel and cargo. As a general rule it can be said – and this is also an implied term of the contract – that the master shall carry out the voyage with the *utmost despatch*.

11.3.6 Deviation

The word "deviation" basically embraces only the geographical deviation of the vessel from the appropriate route. However, it must be remembered that the concept of deviation also contains deviation other than geographical. As examples of non-geographical deviation stoppage, slow-steaming (i.e. steaming with reduced speed) and unusual handling of the cargo may be mentioned. It is difficult to give a precise definition of deviation.

---

2 BIMCO *BIMCO Ice Clauses* (BIMCO Special Circular No. 1, 24 February 2005).

As mentioned in regard to the Hague-Visby Rules (see section 6.6.5), the distinction between lawful deviation and unlawful deviation is critical. The borderline between these two concepts is not always so easy to find. Generally, it can be said that deviation for the purpose of avoiding danger to crew, vessel and cargo and deviation for the purpose of saving life or property at sea are lawful deviations. Naturally, the deviation must be reasonable and, when judging whether the deviation is reasonable, not only the interests of the owners but also the interests of the charterers must be considered.

Most voyage charterparty forms contain a printed deviation clause. Sometimes this is called "*scope of voyage*" clause which is also the frequent expression used in bills of lading. The *deviation clause* in *Gencon '94* (see appendix 1, *part II, clause 3 "deviation clause"*) has the same wording as that of *Gencon '76*, which is the following:

> "*The vessel has liberty to call at any port or ports in any order, for any purpose, to sail without pilots, to tow and/or assist vessels in all situations, and also to deviate for the purpose of saving life and/or property*".

The deviation clauses are usually *worded* to the benefit of the owners, but *interpreted* to the benefit of the charterers (or cargo owners) and if an owner really wishes to safeguard his rights to deviate for a certain reason he must specify this, as clearly as possible, during the negotiations and in the charter agreement. When bunker prices have risen and when for some time it has been difficult to get bunkers, special bunker deviation clauses become common. These clauses not only give owners the right to deviate for the purpose of getting bunkers, but also they usually state expressly that the owners have the right to order the ship to proceed at reduced speed so as to get a lower bunker consumption. It should also be stressed that re-routeing for the changing of crew is often regarded as unlawful deviation.

Unlawful deviation is a breach of contract and in some cases the charterers may be entitled to damages as well as to cancel the charter agreement. Under the typical terms of the bills of lading and according to common P&I rules, any unlawful deviation of the vessel is not permitted. It must be emphasised that even if the charterparty includes a "*liberty clause*" giving permission to the vessel to deviate for bunkering, this liberty to deviate depends in fact on the wording of the bill of lading. It is the cargo owner (namely the holder, at any time, of the bill of lading) that provides permission to deviate. Without bill of lading permission, there is no right to deviate, and therefore P&I cover is frustrated and deviation insurance is required.[3]

11.4 Cargo

11.4.1 Type, specification and condition of cargo

The description of the cargo is important for several reasons. Owners who, during the negotiations and in the fixture, accepted a certain cargo are also obliged

---

3 *Swedish Club Deviation Insurance* (www.swedishclub.com, accessed 25 April 2017).

to carry out the transportation of this cargo. This means that the owners have to get all necessary details of the cargo from the charterers or from someone else (e.g. shippers), in order to be able to find out whether the cargo is suitable for the vessel and estimate the costs of cargo handling and transportation.

What exact details about the cargo need to be specified during the negotiations and in the written agreement depends on the type of cargo. Some commodities are so well known to the parties that only a very short specification has to be given. In other cases it may be necessary to give a detailed declaration about the physical and chemical specifications of the cargo, followed by specified instructions for its handling and transportation.

If the cargo delivered to the vessel is not in accordance with its description, the owners may be entitled to compensation. In some cases, when the cargo delivered differs on essential points from the given description, the owners may also be entitled to cancel the agreement and claim compensation for loss of freight.

When the cargo is described as "general cargo", it is necessary to insert special clauses about the carriage of dangerous goods. In such a "dangerous cargo clause" the owners usually limit their obligation to carry dangerous cargo, while the charterers are under an obligation to give all essential details of the cargo to the owners well in advance of loading.

In transportation of oil products, the carrier must always be aware of the difficulties or peculiarities related with cargo handling, problems occurring in loading/discharging, while he must also be familiar with caution needed to prevent from fire and explosion, as well as from damage to tanks, coatings, and pipelines. This may be particularly complicated with regard to oil products or chemicals, but also to some extent in relation to the crude oil cargoes. Crude oil may be dangerous when it is *spiked* with naphtha to ease the flow. Some kinds of crude oil cargoes are sulphurous and corrosive, while others have a waxy deposit. In low ambient temperatures the question may be whether the *heating coils* in the tanks are effective enough and whether a considerable amount of bunker fuel will have to be spent in maintaining or increasing the temperature. This may create problems for both the ongoing voyage and subsequent trading of the vessel.

A particular problem relates to the *heating of cargo*, i.e. whether the owner has an obligation to raise the cargo temperature. *Shellvoy 6* (see appendix 2, *part II, clause 27 "heating of cargo"*) is based on owners' "best endeavours" principle to comply with a charterers' request to change the cargo temperature, while charterers shall pay for any additional bunkers consumed, and any consequential delay to the vessel shall count against laytime. Suffice it here to point out that the parties should be aware of the problems that may occur in such cases, particularly regarding cost and time.

11.4.2 Cargo quantity

It is important both for the charterers and for the owners that the cargo quantity is clearly specified. The freight is often calculated on the quantity of cargo carried and the owners must therefore make certain that at least a minimum quantity is stated in the charterparty. For the charterers, the specification of the cargo quantity in the charterparty is critical as the owners' acceptance of the quantity also means that the charterers have a chance to claim damages if the owners fail to load the accepted quantity.

The cargo quantity can be fixed in several ways. Many charter agreements state that the charterers shall furnish the ship with "*a full and complete cargo*". This means that the charterers are obliged to load as much cargo as the vessel can carry, that is, the vessel's deadweight capacity is fully used when it is a heavy cargo and the cubic capacity is fully utilised when it is a light cargo.

There are various other ways to state the cargo quantity, such as "*x tons*", "*about x tons*", "*between x and y tons*", "*between about x and about y tons*", "*not less than x tons*", etc. The word "*about*" gives a flexibility that varies depending on the type and quantity of the cargo and the trade (5% is often regarded as a recognised variation figure). If the charterparty prescribes a specific variation from the agreed quantity, it should also state in whose discretion there is such flexibility, for instance "*in owners' option*", "*in master's option*" or "*in charterers' option*". If, for some reason, it is important that certain quantity limits must not be exceeded or underdrawn, this should be clearly stated at the charterparty and a special note should be served to the master and to the agents.

When quantities are expressed during the negotiations, in the charter agreement and in the voyage instructions, the *type of ton* referred to should always be explicitly mentioned. It is thus not sufficient to say, for instance, 5,000 tons. It must also be stated what kind of tons are meant, namely metric tonnes (or metric tons) or long tons. This can also be important when the *stowage factor* (i.e. the number of cubic feet a ton will occupy in stowage) is used, as the stowage factor is sometimes based on long tons and sometimes on metric tonnes (see appendix 16 for measurements and stowage factor, as well as term *SF* in glossary).

11.5 Freight

In the respected legal text *Scrutton on Charterparties and Bills of Lading*,[4] freight is described in the following way:

> "*Freight is the reward payable to the carrier for the carriage and arrival of the goods in a merchantable condition, ready to be delivered to the merchant*".

11.5.1 Fixing of the freight

The freight can be fixed in several different ways. One way is to base it on the cargo quantity, for instance "*X $ per metric tonne*" or "*X $ per ctn*" (ctn = carton). Another way is to fix the freight at a certain amount independent of the cargo quantity. This is usually called "*lump sum freight*". A variation on the

---

4 Scrutton, T.E., Boyd, S.C., Burrows, A.S. and Foxton, D. (1996) *Scrutton on Charterparties and Bills of Lading* (London, Sweet & Maxwell, 20th edition, p. 323).

lump sum freight is to base the freight on the size of the vessel, for instance "*X $ per deadweight ton*". This solution is used especially in quantity contracts (see chapter 13) where the voyages are performed by different ships often not known when the contract is fixed. In oil transportation (crude and products) spot freight rates are typically determined in accordance with the so-called "*Worldscale system*" which is presented and analysed with practical examples in section 14.3. Nevertheless, within the broader tanker family, the freight rates for gas carriers and chemical tankers are not expressed by Worldscale rates, but the former is typically reported in "*$ per cubic metre*" and the latter in "*$ per ton*".

When the freight is based on a certain amount "per ton" it is again important to make clear what kind of ton is meant (metric tonne or long ton).

Sometimes disputes may arise from the question whether the freight should be based on intake or delivered quantity or if it should be based on the gross or the net weight of a cargo. Concerning the latter problem, it is usually said that the freight will be based on the gross weight unless otherwise agreed or customary in the trade. As regards the first question, the basic rule under English law is that the freight is payable only on so much cargo as has been shipped, carried and delivered and this means that the smallest of the two quantities (i.e. received or delivered) is the base for the calculation of freight. Both these questions are often expressly dealt with in the charterparties. On this point, reference should be made to cargo retention clauses (see section 11.10.3 below).

11.5.2 Freight risk – when is the freight earned and payable?

The principal rule is that the freight is earned when the owners have fulfilled their obligation to carry the cargo and are ready to deliver it to the receiver. Thus, the master should, figuratively speaking, deliver the cargo with one hand at the same time as he collects the freight with the other. This means that if, for some reason, the owners cannot deliver the cargo, they are not entitled to freight. The *freight risk*, that is, the risk that the owners, fully or partly, fail to fulfil their obligation to carry the cargo and thereby lose their right to collect freight, thus lies with the owners. Should the vessel sink and, together with the cargo, be a total loss, the owner is not entitled to freight even if the vessel has almost reached her destination.

According to this rule, if only part of the cargo is delivered at the port of destination (*short delivery, shortage*), the owners are entitled only to proportionate freight for the cargo actually delivered. If the cargo reaches the port or place of destination in a damaged condition, the owners are entitled to freight only if the cargo is "in a merchantable condition" and if it is still the same kind of cargo. In connection with a shipment of cars, for instance, the owners are entitled to freight for damaged cars only if the cars can still be considered as cars, and not as scrap metal, and if the damaged cars have some value.

The owners' right to collect freight must not be confused with their obligation to pay compensation for the damaged cargo. It is worth noting also that the charterers have basically no right to deduct counterclaims for damaged cargo or other counterclaims from the freight. According to English law, freight is normally payable in full even if the charterers have a justified counterclaim against the owner. However, tanker voyage charterparties, however, often allow for deductions against the freight and in practice these questions are solved through particular clauses.

If a lump sum freight is agreed, the owners are entitled to full freight even if only some part of the cargo reaches the port or place of destination. But if all cargo is lost, the owners are not entitled to freight, according to the above-described principle. If the cargo is delivered at the wrong place, the owners are not entitled to freight according to English law. However, in some legal systems the owner will under such circumstances be entitled to a so-called *distance freight*, proportionate to the distance actually carried as compared with the total distance. In order to collect freight, the owners must arrange transportation from the discharging port to the correct port or place of destination agreed.

The rules about when the freight is earned and payable are often modified in charter agreements. Clauses like *"freight earned and payable upon shipment, ship and/or cargo lost or not lost"* are frequently found in voyage charter-parties and mean that the owners are entitled to freight at the loading port and the freight is not refundable if part or the whole cargo and the vessel do not reach the destination.

When the freight risk lies with the owners, they can take out a special freight risk insurance which covers the situation where the cargo is lost during the transportation. This is the so-called "loss of earnings"[5] vessel's insurance cover which protects the owner from loss of income arising from physical damage to the vessel in a wide range of situations. This insurance does not protect the owners against insolvent charterers.

The payment of freight may also be secured by other measures which are presented below in section 11.5.5.

11.5.3 Deadfreight

When the charterers fail to deliver the agreed quantity of cargo to the vessel, the owners will normally be entitled to compensation for their loss of freight. This compensation is called *"deadfreight"* and the respective amount is calculated by deducting what is saved in owners' costs from the freight that should be paid for that part of the cargo which has not been delivered.

In order to secure the payment for the deadfreight claim the owners (or the master) must arrange the following:

- They must get a declaration from the charterers that no further cargo will be delivered to the vessel. It is not sufficient to get this declaration from the shippers only, as the charterers may assert later that they could have arranged additional cargo if they had been contacted before the vessel sailed.

---

5 The Gard Group *Loss of Hire Cover* (www.gard.no, accessed 25 April 2017).

- The vessel's additional capacity, both in cubic and in deadweight, must be established before commencement of loading. This can be done, for instance, by an independent surveyor.
- In order to safeguard the possibility of exercising a lien over the cargo against the receiver, a remark concerning the short shipment which establishes the owners' claim for deadfreight should be inserted into the bills of lading (see section 11.5.5 below).

Another difficult question is to find out when the owners are entitled to let the vessel sail from the loading port if they fail to get a declaration from the charterers that no more cargo is available, or when the charterers say that additional cargo will come but nothing happens. As long as the owners get sufficient compensation in the form of an acceptable demurrage paid day by day, week by week or on a similar basis, the problem is perhaps not so bad. The situation is worse when the demurrage rate is low or not payable until after the voyage and when owners fear that the charterers are insolvent or unwilling to pay. Questions and problems arising from such situations are difficult to solve, therefore, the owners should be careful and take legal advice before they order the vessel to leave the port.

11.5.4 Payment of freight

Payment of the freight may not necessarily take place at the same stage as when the freight is considered earned. It is thus possible and not unusual that the voyage charterparties contain a clause stating that "*freight is earned upon shipment . . .*" in combination with a provision dictating that "*freight is payable before commencement of discharging*" (or "*before breaking bulk*"). Sometimes the charterers and the shippers wish to have the bills of lading marked "*freight prepaid*". In such cases the owners should insist that the freight is payable and that they get the payment before the bills of lading are issued and delivered to the shippers.

The payment process should be specified in the charterparty. Currency (see section 10.8.1), mode and place of payment, name of bank and number of bank account, etc., are usually stated in the payment clause. As the costs of transferring the freight are sometimes quite high, they should also be allocated in the charterparty. An example of a freight payment clause is presented in *Shellvoy 6* (see appendix 2, *part II, clause 5 "freight"*). This should be connected with *clause 10* titled "*charterers' failure to give orders*" of *Shellvoy 6*, where the owners' right to terminate the charterparty if charterers fail to make payments is described as follows: "*. . .Charterers shall pay the full amount due within 14 days after receipt of Owners' demand. Should Charterers fail to make any such payments Owners shall have the right to terminate this Charter by giving written notice to Charterers or their agents. . .*".

Serious trouble may be caused when some countries have restrictions on money transfers abroad. In some countries, particularly in connection with demurrage, it is practically impossible to arrange a remittance to another country and a careful owner should investigate these matters before he finally accepts the fixture.

In tanker charterparties regard should also be given to oil residues and possible freight payable in that connection. For example, *Shellvoy 6* (see appendix 2, *part II, clause 40(4) "oil pollution prevention/ballast management"*) contains some reference to this point.

11.5.5 Security for payment of freight

As mentioned in section 10.12 which discussed maritime liens, the owners usually have a legal and/or a contractual lien over the cargo as security for the payment of freight. As regards such claims and such freights which are due for payment but not paid before the bills of lading are issued, the owners and the master must ensure that a remark concerning a claim for non-paid freight is made in the bills of lading. Without such a remark the owners have no possibility of exercising a lien over the cargo as security for claims and payments accruing or due for payment before the issuing of bills of lading. Sometimes, the owner succeeds in securing freight payment by way of an irrevocable letter of credit (see section 6.4), which often gives the owner a fair security but at the same time complicates the negotiations.

11.5.6 Brokerage

The role of shipbrokers has been analytically described in section 3.5.1. When brokers have been involved in chartering negotiations, they are entitled to *commission*. The so-called *"brokerage"* is usually a certain percentage of the freight. Brokers are not entitled to commission on demurrage and damages for detention unless this is expressly stated in the charterparty or otherwise agreed. However, the brokers commonly try and achieve to get commission on demurrage and damages for detention. Moreover, the printed charterparty forms often entitle the brokers to some compensation if the charter agreement is cancelled or otherwise terminated beforehand. An example of a brokerage clause can be seen in *Gencon '94* (appendix 1, *part II, clause 15 "brokerage"*).

At a specific point the clause is difficult to understand, causing some ambiguity. The standard clause provides that:

> *"In case of non-execution (of the charter) at least 1/3 of the brokerage on the estimated amount of freight to be paid by the party responsible for such non-execution to the Brokers as indemnity for the latter's expenses and work".*

It may not be clear enough to define who is for instance *"the party responsible for such non-execution"* when the owner and the charterer, after a dispute, compromise and agree to cancel the contract. Another problem may arise from the fact that the broker under English law is not considered as a party to that contract and therefore he cannot sue on the basis of the charterparty.

11.6 Loading and discharging

The task of arranging and the respective costs for loading and discharging the cargo may be allocated between the contracting parties in different ways. The stipulation used in *Gencon '94* (see appendix 1, *part II, clause 5(a) "loading/ discharging – costs/risks"*) is the so-called *"f.i.o.s.t term"*, where the charterers are those who arrange and pay for all cargo-handling expenses. The provision reads as follows:

> *"The cargo shall be brought into the holds, loaded, stowed and/or trimmed, tallied, lashed and/or secured and taken from the holds and discharged by the Charterers, free of any risk, liability and expense whatsoever to the Owners. The Charterers shall provide and lay all dunnage material as required for the proper stowage and protection of the cargo on board, the Owners allowing the use of all dunnage available on board. The Charterers shall be responsible for and pay the cost of removing their dunnage after discharge of the cargo under this Charter Party and time to count until dunnage has been removed".*

The *"gross terms"* alternative included in *Gencon '76* has been deleted from *Gencon '94* with the explanation that it is no longer commonly in use. However, when gross terms are agreed in a charterparty, the wording may be as follows (*Gencon '76, part II, clause 5(a) "loading/discharging costs – gross terms"*):

> *"The cargo shall be brought alongside in such a manner as to enable vessel to take the goods with her own tackle. Charterers to procure and pay the necessary men on shore or on board the lighters to do the work there, vessel heaving the cargo on board".*

According to the "gross terms" alternative, the borderline at loading is when the cargo is delivered from the charterers/shippers alongside the vessel at a place where the vessel can reach the goods with her own tackle. At discharging, the borderline is when the vessel delivers the cargo alongside to the recipients but not beyond the reach of her tackle. This alternative can also be described as *"from hook to hook"* and the intention is that the owners shall arrange and pay for all work within the "hook to hook" period.

The gross terms alternative is the one commonly stated in the liner bills of lading and thus it is also called *"liner terms"*. However, the expression "liner terms" is not very precise and should be avoided. The true definition of "liner terms" originally was that the cargo should be loaded and discharged on the same terms and conditions as were used by liner vessels for the same kind of cargo in the same ports and berths. As the terms and conditions used by the liner vessels can be difficult to find out and define, and as they can also vary within one port, both parties must be sure that they know what the expression means for the intended voyage before they use it in negotiations and in a charterparty.

When FIO terms have been agreed, the main part of the planning and the costs of cargo handling lies on the charterers. They should not only deliver the cargo to the vessel, but also load and discharge it. When similar alternatives apply, such

as FIOS, FIOSPT, FIOST, FIOT, etc., the charterers are further obliged to undertake other relevant operations such as stowage, trimming etc. (see glossary for
the following terms: *FIO, FIOS, FIOSPT, FIOST, FIOT* and compare them with
FI, FILO, FILTD, FO, Gross Terms, Liner Terms, LIFO). It is also said that the
owners shall provide winchmen, but as this is quite unusual nowadays that part
of the clause is often deleted.

As the costs for handling the cargo at loading and discharging ports are often
an important part of the total costs for the voyage, both parties should, during the
negotiations, carefully investigate what costs will be involved in the intended voyage. It is of utmost importance that the clauses dealing with loading and discharging of cargo make sufficiently clear the allocation of costs, duties and liabilities.

The way the stowing, lashing and securing of the cargo is performed is also
significant for the safe carrying of the cargo and for the vessel's seaworthiness.
The owners usually have some responsibility for the cargo and they are always
to a certain degree liable for the seaworthiness of the vessel. Even in those cases
where the charterers, according to the charterparty, should arrange for and pay
everything in connection with loading, stowing, trimming, lashing, securing
and discharging of the cargo, the master must ensure that the cargo is properly
handled and that the loading, securing etc. are performed in a way that does not
endanger the crew, the vessel and the cargo during the voyage. The master has
not only a right, but also an obligation, to intervene when the cargo is loaded,
stowed, secured, etc. in an unacceptable way with regard to the safety of the crew,
vessel and cargo.

The cargo-handling matters are fields of high interest and common dispute. It
is recommended to be studied together with section 6.6 about owners'/carriers'
liability for cargo and chapter 15 about laytime.

11.7 Laytime

According to "Laytime Definitions for Charter Parties 2013" (see appendix 3):

- *Laytime* is defined as "*the period of time agreed between the (contracting) parties during which the owner will make and keep the vessel
  available for loading or discharging without payment additional to the
  freight*".
- *Demurrage* is defined as "*an agreed amount payable to the owner in
  respect of delay to the vessel once the laytime has expired, for which the
  owner is not responsible. Demurrage shall not be subject to exceptions
  which apply to laytime unless specifically stated in the charter party*".
- *Despatch* is defined as "*an agreed amount payable by the owner if the
  vessel completes loading or discharging before the laytime has expired*".

Laytime and demurrage are considered matters of crucial importance and fields
of intense disputes in voyage charters. Therefore, drafting of laytime clauses and
counting of laytime in theory and practice are addressed separately in chapter 15.

11.8 Routines and allocation of costs

11.8.1 ETA notices

The voyage charterparty usually has clauses according to which the owners shall keep charterers, shippers and receivers informed about the vessel's position and the *estimated time of arrival (ETA)* at respective ports. The purpose of these clauses is to give charterers and/or shippers and/or receivers a chance to pre-pare documents, provide or receive the cargo and plan the loading or discharging procedure.

A *notice clause* may have the following wording:

> "*Master to give telegraphic ETA-notice to Messrs. 'X' 96, 48 and 24 hours before vessel's estimated arrival to loading port*".

Unless this is expressly agreed, owners are not strictly liable for the conse-quences if the vessel arrives later than indicated in the notices. For instance, if the shippers or the receivers have to pay waiting costs for stevedores when the ship arrives late due to bad weather or other hindrances outside the owners' control, the owners are not liable for these extra costs. Only if the ETA notices have been unrealistic when given, or if the master or the owners have intention-ally delayed the ship or failed to inform about delay in relation to given ETA notices, can charterers, shippers or receivers have a chance to get compensation from the owners.

11.8.2 Allocation of costs

11.8.2.1 Harbour dues

A vessel's call at port gives rise to several costs, for example costs for pilots, tugs, mooring, lights, watchmen and dues for quay and cargo. The principal rule is that dues which fall on the vessel and are calculated on the basis of the ship's size shall be paid by the owners and dues which fall on the cargo and are calculated on the basis of the type and quantity of the cargo shall be paid by the charterers (or shippers/receivers).

It is possible for local rules to demand payment by the owners of dues that are traditionally connected with the cargo or the cargo handling ashore. In the relationship of port authority/shipowner, the latter usually has no other choice than to pay, but this does not mean that the shipowner is also responsible for the cost under the charterparty. If the owners, under the rules of the port, have been forced to pay for something which under the charterparty falls on the charterers, the owners are entitled to recover from the charterers. To avoid disputes, the fol-lowing clause may be inserted in the voyage charterparty:

> "*If one of the parties to this Charterparty has been forced to pay dues in connection with calls at any port which, as between the parties, would have been the responsi-bility of the other party under the terms of this Charterparty, the latter shall compen-sate the former for such payment*".

11.8.2.2 Freight taxes

In many countries the tax system includes special taxes on freight and other taxes connected with the loading or discharging of ships in the country. The parties must agree on whose account such taxes shall be. The best way is to find out exactly what taxes will be debited for the intended voyage. BIMCO has been a valuable source of information concerning freight taxes imposed per country. Taxes known beforehand can be dealt with directly in the charterparty but, as new tax laws may be introduced with very short notice, it is also advisable to have a clause dealing with the question in a more general way, as for instance:

> "*Taxes on freight or cargo to be for Charterers' account and taxes on vessel to be for Owners' account*".

11.8.3 Strike clauses

Considerable delays and costs may be the result of strikes in loading or discharging ports or in seaways through which the vessel has to pass on her voyage. Therefore, voyage charterparties usually contain a strike clause dealing with the various problems and costs resulting from strikes. Such clauses are often complicated to construe. The general strike clause was amended by BIMCO in *Gencon '94* in order to become less ambiguous than the *Gencon '76* respective clause.

Since strike clauses are complicated, only some questions and problems arising when such clauses are drafted will be spotted below:

- To what extent are owners entitled to compensation from charterers for delay of the ship due to strike and how shall the compensation be calculated (demurrage rate, daily cost for vessel, market rate or other)?
- Liability for consequential losses?
- The parties' rights to cancel?
- What is the situation where a part cargo is already on board when a strike starts and prevents further loading?
- The owner's rights to complete with other cargo in the same or other ports when a strike bursts out?
- The charterers' right to order the vessel to other ports?

Additional questions and examples on how such problems can be solved may be found in the general strike clause in *Gencon '94* (see appendix 1, *part II, clause 16 "general strike clause"*).

11.8.4 Agents

Normal practice in voyage chartering dictates that agents are paid by the owners. Notwithstanding this, it is not unusual that the agents are nominated by the charterers, a situation that may sometimes be very difficult for the owner. When agents are nominated by charterers, the owners sometimes appoint their own agent – usually called a "*husbandry agent*" – to take care of owners' matters, such as repatriation of crew members, contact with shipyards, or generally representing the owners' interests against the charterers, shippers or receivers.

If the agents are reputable and established, it may not be necessary for the owners to have their own husbandry agents, but as it still happens too often that port agents who are closely connected with shippers or receivers disregard their obligations to the owners and take care of shippers' or receivers' interests, the owners should always be careful when the port agents are not known to them.

In some countries and ports only one firm may be available as a port agent and this firm often also acts as a representative for shippers or receivers as well as a representative for P&I Clubs, hull underwriters, cargo underwriters, etc. It goes without saying that it is difficult for one firm with all these functions to act in a balanced way when there are conflicts between the various interests it represents.

11.9 Cesser and lien

11.9.1 Introduction

In voyage chartering it is not unusual for the charterparty to contain a clause relieving the charterers from liability. The liability usually ceases from the moment the vessel has been loaded. Such a clause, often given the heading "*cesser clause*", may have the following wording:

> "*Charterers' liability to cease when cargo is shipped and Bills of Lading signed, except as regards payment of freight, deadfreight and demurrage (if any) at loading port*".

The intention is that the owners shall turn to the cargo owners with any additional claims as for instance demurrage at the discharging port, or to the shippers for demurrage at the loading port. The cesser clause is usually combined with a "*lien clause*" according to which owners, as security for their claims, have a lien on the cargo (see section 10.12). A lien clause may have the following wording:

> "*It is also agreed that the Owners of the said vessel shall reserve to themselves the right of lien upon the cargo laden on board for the recovery and payment of all freight, deadfreight and demurrage (if any)*".

It may occur that the cesser and lien clauses are combined. This was the case in the *Gencon '76* form (*part II, clause 8*), which had the heading "lien clause". The cesser clause was "hidden" at the end of the clause, as follows:

> "*Owners shall have a lien on the cargo for freight, dead-freight, demurrage and damages for detention. Charterers shall remain responsible for dead-freight and demurrage (including damages for detention) incurred at port of loading. Charterers shall also remain responsible for freight and demurrage (including damages for detention) incurred at port of discharge, but only to such extent as the Owners have been unable to obtain payment thereof by exercising the lien on the cargo*".

In the *Gencon '94* form (see appendix 1, *part II, clause 8 "lien clause"*), the "cesser-part" of the lien clause (*"but only . . . on the cargo"*) has been deleted and the provision has been amended considerably, as follows:

> *"The Owners shall have a lien on the cargo and on all sub-freights payable in respect of the cargo, for freight, deadfreight, demurrage and claims for damages and for all other amounts due under this Charter Party including costs of recovering the same".*

11.9.2 Is the cesser clause justified and valid?

The cesser clause is rather out of date and out of current market practice, thus it should not be proposed by charterers or accepted by owners. Notwithstanding this, it may be found even in modern charterparties. One of the reasons for this may be that the clause is often "hidden", as in the above-cited older *Gencon '76* clause (see 11.9.1). Another reason may be that the parties are sometimes unaware of the seriousness of the clause. Even if the charterers and owners have smoothly made several shipments with a cesser clause included in the charterparty, the owners should not take it for granted that the charterers will continue to disregard the clause. Charterers may encounter economic problems or be in dispute with the receivers and then, in order to protect their own interests, they may perhaps read the charterparty more carefully and find that legally they have an opportunity to avoid some expenses they originally thought they had to bear.

As regards the validity of the cesser clause, under English law it seems to be an established rule that the cesser clause is valid only if it is combined with a lien clause giving a legally valid right to lien which also is practically possible to exercise in the relevant case (*"cesser is co-extensive with lien"*). The charterer's liability shall cease if, and to the extent that, the owners have an alternative remedy by way of lien on the cargo.[6]

11.9.3 Exercising the lien

Before the owners place a lien on the cargo, they must find out the legal and practical possibilities and difficulties in the actual country and port. In some countries it is not legally possible to exercise a lien over cargo. Moreover, even if the owners are legally entitled to exercise a lien over the cargo, it may nevertheless be impossible for practical reasons. For instance, it may be that the only place, shed, tank etc. where the cargo can be stored ashore is controlled by the same person or company against whom the owners have a claim.

It is often legally doubtful whether the owners are entitled to exercise a lien by keeping the cargo in the vessel, since in all circumstances they will, by such an action, delay the vessel, causing additional costs and legal difficulties. In some countries where legal security is less developed, although the owners may exercise a lien in a correct way, they can be involved in various difficulties which delay the ship and thereby cause extra costs.

---

6 Wilson, J.F. (2008) *Carriage of Goods by Sea* (London, Pearson Longman, 6th edition, p. 303).

In view of all these possibilities, owners should always take legal advice and, if they have reason to fear difficulties or hindrances, they should take care well in advance of the ship's arrival at the discharging port.

11.9.4 Owners collecting from receivers or shippers

When the owners, by a clause in the charterparty, have the right to collect demurrage from the receivers or shippers (see chapter 15 for the analysis of laytime and demurrage), it should be clearly stated in the contract that the charterers remain ultimately responsible. In addition, it should be stated after how long a time the owners may claim payment from the charterers if they are not paid by the receivers, shippers, etc. A clause which may be considered as reasonable and could be accepted by owners is the following:

> "Demurrage at discharging port to be settled directly between Owners and Receivers, but Charterers to remain ultimately responsible and in case payment from Receivers is not effected within x days after discharging (or: after invoice date) Charterers to pay demurrage to Owners".

It goes without saying that the owners should accept such a clause only if the charterers are reliable and solvent, as the owners in this situation have no way of using the cargo as security for their claim against the charterers.

11.10 Cargo liability

The background knowledge of this entity has been presented in chapter 6 and more specifically in sections 6.5 and 6.6, where the international statutory framework of the bills of lading together with the basic principles about carrier's liability against cargo were covered.

In a voyage charterparty, the liability for the cargo shall be allocated as the owners and charterers may agree. There is no compulsory minimum liability for owners according to the contract law, as it is imposed by the international cargo conventions (e.g. Hague Rules, Hague-Visby Rules, Hamburg Rules, Rotterdam Rules).

Some charterparty forms more or less free owners from liability for the cargo, while others put a far-reaching liability on owners in this respect. Sometimes, the charterparty contains a *paramount clause* (see also sections 6.6.2, 6.6.3 and 10.6) which makes the Hague Rules or Hague-Visby Rules applicable only to the carrier's (owner's) liability for cargo under the charterparty, or to the whole charterparty, or to the bills of lading issued under the charterparty, as the case may be.

11.10.1 Owners' liability when voyage charterparty and bill of lading are involved

Under many standard charterparties, as for instance the Gencon form, owners' liability against cargo is very limited. But, as in most cases the master issues a bill of lading with a more extensive liability for the owners, the arising question is whether the charterparty or the bill of lading shall be decisive for the owners' liability. The problem may be divided into two questions. The first is to what extent the owners are liable against the receivers/bill of lading holders? The second is to what extent the owners can recover from the charterers if they are forced to pay something to the receivers/bill of lading holders for which they are not liable under the charterparty?

11.10.2 Liability against cargo owners

The bills of lading usually contain a paramount clause, a jurisdiction clause and some other clauses which may be contradictory to the clauses contained in the voyage charterparty. To make clear that the charterparty – not the bill of lading – is the governing agreement for the shipment, owners often insist on having a clause inserted in the bill of lading with reference to the terms of the charterparty. For instance, such an *incorporation clause* may have the following wording:

> *"All the terms, conditions, clauses and exceptions contained in Charter Party dated. . . . . between. . . . ., including the Jurisdiction clause, are hereby expressly included in this Bill of Lading and are deemed to be incorporated herein. All the terms conditions, clauses and exceptions contained in this Bill of Lading – including the Paramount clause – are null and void to such extent as they are contrary to any provisions in the said Charter Party but no further".*

It is doubtful up to what extent owners can rely on such a clause as regards liability for cargo in relation to the consignee (who is not the charterer), as that is contradictory to the rules contained in the Hague/Hague-Visby Rules or similar, prescribing a minimum liability for the carrier. However, the clause may be of some value for other reasons, for instance in connection with demurrage claims or when countries are involved which have not signed the bill of lading conventions.

To avoid difficulties with bankers when the payment for the cargo is made by way of a letter of credit, owners should state in the charterparty that bills of lading shall contain a clause referring to the charterparty. Unless the bankers are instructed that such an incorporation clause is acceptable, they will not accept the bill of lading.

When the receivers are also the charterers, the bill of lading will not have the same effect as usual and the receivers/charterers cannot claim against the owners under the bill of lading as the charterparty is the main contract between them. However, owners must always be aware that receivers/charterers may transfer the bill of lading to someone else who is not bound by the charterparty and therefore not prevented from claiming under the bill of lading.

11.10.3 Cargo retention clauses

In tanker voyage charters cargo claims often are caused from the peculiarities of cargoes carried. Some shortage of cargo always occurs due to evaporation and sedimentation. The allowance for such losses should be determined by the custom of the trade. In oil cargoes an allowance of 0.5–0.75% to cover evaporation and unpumpable sediment is considered acceptable. When there is a global environment of increasing oil prices, charterers seek to insert the so-called "*cargo retention clauses*" to the charterparty, which often have the effect of letting the owners bear all such risks and payment of freight is based on the *delivered weight of cargo carried.*

Some of the printed tanker charterparty forms do not include a clause of cargo retention, but in most deals the contract will contain such a provision as a rider. It is particularly important for an owner to ensure that a charterer's right of deduction from freight is without prejudice to defences available to the owner. From the charterer's viewpoint, it is important to ensure that the cargo quantity remaining on board (ROB) should be "determined" or "established" by an independent surveyor before any deduction from freight is made. The principles embodied in *Shellvoy 6* (see appendix 2, *part II, clause 48 "cargo retention"*) seem to protect all legitimate interests of both parties.

11.10.4 Redress

If owners have to make payments for cargo claims under the bill of lading to a greater extent than according to their liability under the charterparty, it seems clear that under English law they are entitled to compensation from the charterers. However, this is more a "legal right" than a "real right", as charterers rarely and very reluctantly will agree to such compensation. If the owners intend to seek recourse against the charterers, they should make the charterers aware of this from the beginning by inserting a redress clause into the charterparty. As an example, the typical *redress clause 1968* has the following wording:

> "*If one of the parties to this Charterparty has been obliged to make payment or institute defence in respect of a claim by a third party, under a Bill of Lading or otherwise, of a nature which, as between the parties, would have been the responsibility of the other party under the terms of this Charterparty, the latter shall indemnify the former for all loss, damage or expenses resulting therefrom. However, the indemnity payable under this Clause in respect of discharge of such claims shall be reduced to the extent the party in question could have limited his liability if he had been held liable directly to the claimant in the jurisdiction in which the claimant proceeded against the other party*".

In *Gencon '94* (see appendix 1, *part II, part of clause 10 "bills of lading"*) this problem is handled as follows:

> "*The Charterers shall indemnify the Owners against all consequences or liabilities that may arise from the signing of bills of lading as presented to the extent that the terms or contents of such bills of lading impose or result in the imposition of more onerous liabilities upon the Owners than those assumed by the Owners under this Charter Party*".

11.11 Damage to the vessel

If the vessel is damaged as a result of bad weather, error in navigation or cargo handling, collision with other ships, buoys etc., the owners will have little chance of securing compensation from the charterers. Only if agreed, or in some cases if the charterers are in breach of contract, or if they have acted negligently or fraudulently, may the owners have a possibility of recovering financial compensation from the voyage charterers for such damage. The most common case of owners' financial recovery is when the damage has been caused by an unsafe port or berth, or by stevedores, or when the cargo has been injurious. The concept of safe and unsafe ports and berths has been discussed above in section 11.3.2.

In cases of damage to the ship caused by the cargo, charterers' description of the cargo during the negotiations and in the charterparty is important. This question has also been dealt with above in section 11.4. From the owners' point of view, it is important to have a satisfactory description of the cargo in the charterparty and, as it is often difficult to judge beforehand whether the cargo will be injurious or not, it is to the benefit of the owners having a general statement in the charterparty to the effect that the cargo shall be non-injurious to the vessel.

When the damage is caused by stevedores, it is essential from the viewpoint of liability to ascertain whether the charterparty provides that the owners or the charterers should arrange and pay for the loading and/or discharging of the vessel (see section 11.6). However, the fact that the charterers, according to the charterparty, must be responsible to arrange and pay for the loading and/or discharging of the ship does not automatically mean that the charterers are also liable for damage caused by stevedores. The mere fact that the damage has been caused by charterers, or someone employed by charterers, is in many countries not itself sufficient ground for liability. Very often, negligence must also be proved. Another complication is that damage to the vessel in connection with loading or discharging may not be discovered until a long time after the damage has occurred and in those cases it may be difficult for the owners to prove on which voyage the damage occurred.

When the damage has been caused totally or partly by bad stowage, the owners face additional difficulties as the master has an obligation to supervise the loading. Concerning stevedore damages, *Gencon '94* introduced a new important provision, not found in the previous version of *Gencon '76*. This has the following wording (see appendix 1, *Gencon '94, part II, clause 5(c) "loading/ discharging – stevedore damage"*):

> *"The Charterers shall be responsible for damage (beyond ordinary wear and tear) to any part of the Vessel caused by Stevedores. Such damage shall be notified as soon as reasonably possible by the Master to the Charterers or their agents and to their Stevedores, failing which the Charterers shall not be held responsible. The Master shall endeavour to obtain the Stevedores' written acknowledgement of liability.*
> *The Charterers are obliged to repair any stevedore damage prior to completion of the voyage, but must repair stevedore damage affecting the Vessel's seaworthiness or class before the Vessel sails from the port where such damage was caused or found. All additional expenses incurred shall be for the account of the Charterers and any*

time lost shall be for the account of and shall be paid to the Owners by the Charterers at the demurrage rate".

Similar problems may arise under time chartering and the reader can compare with section 12.11.

11.12 Consecutive voyage charter

A consecutive voyage charter is a variation of a voyage charter in which a named vessel is contracted for several voyages which follow consecutively upon one another. It is a hybrid charter form as it contains both voyage and time charter elements. This type of charter was discussed in section 7.3.4.

11.13 Voyage charter and liner business

Throughout this book it has been made clear that bulk and liner markets differ widely and structurally. From a chartering and shipbroking perspective, bulk shipping is by far more significant than liner market. With respect to liner business, emphasis has been given to various aspects relevant to chartering matters or similar. More specifically, structural differences between the two crucial sides of ocean shipping were highlighted in section 1.1.3, the liner pricing aspects in section 2.2, the liner information network and people in sections 3.3, 3.4 and 3.5, the shippers' and carriers' chartering policy and marketing strategy were discussed in sections 5.1, 5.2 and 5.5, a distinction was made between liner and bulk shipping from a chartering perspective in section 7.2, while the contracts of carriage were examined in 7.4 and the cost allocation in 7.6. Thus, at this point, only the overlap of the liner market with voyage chartering will be examined briefly.

Liner service might be regarded as a special form of a voyage charter agreed on "liner terms", i.e. where owners arrange and pay for loading and discharging of the vessel. In fact, those two alternatives of a vessel's trading are not so close as it initially seems, having crucial differences which arise from the structural divergence between bulk and liner markets.

A significant difference between a liner service and a voyage (spot) charter on liner terms is that in voyage chartering the owner usually have one charterer per vessel's voyage, while in liner service the owners (called "carriers") normally have numerous "clients" per voyage which may be called "shippers" or "merchants" or "cargo owners".

Therefore, in voyage chartering a shipowner and a charterer agree, via their shipbrokers, to employ a vessel for a specific voyage in order to carry a specific cargo, and this agreement is commonly manifested in a voyage charterparty which forms the contract of cargo carriage. The shipping service is tailor-made, executed on a "one ship – one cargo" basis and the charterer pays freight calculated in USD per ton of cargo carried. On the contrary, in liner service the shipowner (carrier, operator) runs a regular shipping transport service between more or less fixed ports and usually on a fixed time schedule. The liner operator generally acts as a "common carrier", accepting all general cargo (containers) shipped between the ports covered by his service. Many shippers book the transport of their cargoes with a specific vessel which executes the regular shipping transport services. The freight is commonly paid in USD per TEU or FEU. The arrangement for the carriage of cargo is made via the agents of a particular shipping line and is manifested in a document called booking note (see appendix 11), not in a charterparty. Both in liner and bulk shipping services, various forms of bills of lading are issued and signed when the goods are received for shipment or shipped on board. However, in liner market they are commonly called "sea waybills" and are non-negotiable (see sections 6.5.3 and 7.4).

Summing-up, voyage charters as known in the open bulk market may be rarely seen in the liner market, because the liner service itself, though executed on a voyage-by-voyage basis, is founded on a completely different shipping transport philosophy. Thus, it may be said that voyage charters are almost non-applicable to the liner market, particularly as far as the fully cellular containerships are concerned.

CHAPTER 12

Time charter

In this chapter, the most common type of period charter contract is examined; the time charter. Typical clauses and critical matters are discussed. First, it is empha-sised that the description of the vessel is more important, detailed and precise in the time charter than in a voyage charter. Then, the importance of trading limitations is highlighted, combined with an explanation of the "trip time charter" and "ballast bonus" terms. Cargo aspects follow, together with a thorough discussion about the period of the contract, the time, the place and the allocation of costs on vessel's delivery and redelivery, as well as the vessel's last voyage and the overlapping/ underlapping situations. A subject of considerable importance and dispute is then analysed; hire and off-hire. In addition, the crucial allocation of costs is commented upon, as well as the key position of the master under a time charter. Analysis goes further to deal with cargo liability allocation between owners and charterers, another subject of major confrontation. Finally, the matter of a possible vessel's damage is addressed. The text is enriched with examples of clauses sourced from standard forms of time charterparties; both dry and tanker. The reader may seek to consult the glossary and the appendix at the end of the book, where necessary.

12.1 Definition

Time charter was initially described in section 7.3.2. In this part, only a short definition of the time charter will be provided, before specific clauses and prob-lems are further examined.

A *time charter* may be classified as one for hire of a certain vessel. In this respect, the time charter differs considerably from the voyage charter, which is an agreement for carriage of a certain cargo, with a certain vessel and for a certain voyage. The character of a time charterparty as a hire agreement can be noticed in several ways. The time charter is the most common form of a period charter. In this type, the commercial use of the ship passes to the charterer for an agreed period of time, which may be short, medium or long-term. The owner keeps the commercial operation of the vessel (crewing, insurance, repair and maintenance, supplies, stores and lubricants), whilst the charterer undertakes the commercial employment of the vessel, for instance the nomination of ports and the decision-making about the vessel's trading, as well as the payment of voyage and cargo-handling costs, such as bunkers, port charges, canal dues, extra insurances, ste-vedore expenses etc. It is worth emphasising, however, that navigation decisions remain on the owner and the master. The charterer is obliged to pay the agreed daily "hire" per time unit (instead of freight per ton of cargo as in the voyage charter). The hire is paid at regular intervals, for example in USD per day, payable every 15 days or monthly in advance. Instead of a certain voyage and a certain cargo as per spot charter, a trading area and specific cargo types allowed to be carried with the ship will be agreed in the time charter. Neither is the owners' position against a third party the same in time chartering as in voyage chartering. It is the time charterer who operates the ship commercially and thus he has the closest contact with shippers, receivers etc. The time charter agreement is typically governed by a time charterparty. The standard documents are much less in number than the respective voyage charter forms. This type of charter is common both in bulk/tramp trading (open charter market) and in the liner market.

For a discussion of various questions about time charters and an illustration on different ways of approaching the respective answers, reference is made throughout this chapter and in the appendix to a well-known tanker time charterparty (*Shelltime 4* in appendix 5), as well as to two reputable general purpose and dry cargo time charterparties (*Gentime* in appendix 4 and *NYPE 2015* in appendix 6).

It must be also highlighted that FONASBA (The Federation of National Associations of Ship Brokers and Agents) has issued the *Time Charter Interpretation Code 2000*, which is "an endeavour to interpret existing time charterparty clauses, as well as to assist disputing parties where charterparties are silent or non-determining". This is a rather self-explanatory text, illuminating critical aspects of time charters and included in appendix 7.

12.2 Vessel

12.2.1 Description of vessel

Generally, the description of the vessel is more important, detailed and precise in the time charter agreement than in the voyage charter agreement. All details about the ship (carrying capacity, cargo-handling equipment, construction, speed, fuel consumption, nationality etc.) must be known by the charterers during the negotiations with the owners. Charterers should form an accurate opinion about the commercial value of the vessel and it is, therefore, important for them that they have correct and sufficient information about her.

The normal situation in voyage chartering is that both cargo and ports are known beforehand, thus owners and charterers can therefore pick out only those details about the vessel that are relevant. In time chartering, the charterers may sometimes know beforehand what cargo they will carry and what ports will be used for loading and discharging, but more often they do not know beforehand either the cargo to be carried with the ship or the trading areas and ports of call. Therefore, the charterers cannot be happy only by receiving a few main details about the vessel, as it is the case in voyage chartering.

In addition to the general data about the vessel (name, call sign, year of build, nationality, IMO-number, GT and NT, draught, length and depth, number of holds/hatches etc.), charterers, especially when the ship will be chartered for a long period, require a more detailed description. Therefore, they usually get copies of the *General Arrangement plan (GA-plan)* or other ship documents providing information about the ship and her construction. It is also important to know about the vessel's ice class and other special certificates.

An example of a diagrammatic description of a handysize bulk carrier may be seen in Figure 12.1.

WORLD UNIVERSITY TYPE

(FOR CHARTER PARTY PURPOSES, ALL DETAILS "ABOUT")

Principal particulars of »Trader« class bulk-carriers

Type	»Trader«
Length overall . . . . . . .m	178.70
Length b. pp. . . . . .m	170.00
Beam mld. . . . . .m	28.00
Depth mld. . . . . .m	14.00
Draft, design . . . . . . .m	9.50
Deadweight . . . . .t	29,300
Draft scantling . . . . . .m	9.70
Deadweight . . . . .t	30,000
Gross tonnage . . . . . .GT	20,000
Cargo hold volume . .cbm	40,000
Main engine	MAN B&W
Type	6 S 42 MC
Power . . . . .kW	6,480
Speed . . . . .rpm	136
Ship speed . . . . .kn	14.3
Endurance . . . . .sm	15,500
Classification	ABS

Loading cap. per inch on full DWT — **90 LT**

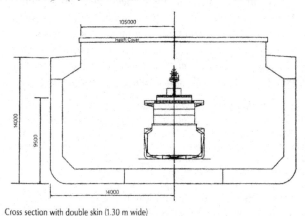

Cross section with double skin (1.30 m wide)

ALL PARTICULARS/DETAILS BELIEVED TO BE CORRECT BUT NOT GUARANTEED

This example of a ship's particulars is theoretical and for educational purposes only.

Figure 12.1 Diagrammatic Description of Vessel

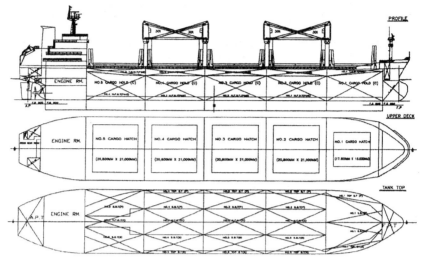

Profile and deck views of "Trader" class double bulk-carrier

Figure 12.1 (Continued)

12.2.2 Vessel's cargo capacity

The ship's cargo capacity is described in the same way as in the voyage charterparty (see section 11.2.2), that is, in most cases by deadweight and/or cubic capacity. However, in many circumstances it may be necessary to have additional information about the vessel's cargo capacity, for instance how many containers and how many reefer containers a containership can take on deck and under deck.

The time charterers have at their disposal all compartments which can be used for cargo. For example, in the *Shelltime 4* form this is expressed in the following way (see appendix 5, *clause 10 "space available to charterers"*):

> *"The whole reach, burthen and decks on the vessel and any passenger accommodation (including Owners' suite) shall be at Charterers' disposal, reserving only proper and sufficient space for the vessel's master, officers, crew, tackle, apparel, furniture, provisions and stores, provided that the weight of stores on board shall not, unless specifically agreed, exceed (to be filled) tonnes at any time during the charter period".*

When the ship has accommodation for passengers, it is usually also stated whether or not the charterers have the right to use this space and what extra payment per passenger per day the owners are entitled to.

As information about the vessel's cargo-carrying capacity is very important for the time charterers, the owners must declare these details as correctly as possible. Incorrect information about the cargo-carrying capacity may lead to deduction of the hire or, when the difference is considerable, the charterers may also be entitled to cancel the agreement on grounds of *"misrepresentation"* and claim for damages.

12.2.3 *Vessel's speed and bunker consumption*

This is a field of great dispute on time charters. As the charterers pay hire per time unit, the vessel's speed capability and bunker consumption are essential for judging the operating and chartering potential of the vessel. The speed and bunker consumption statements in the time charterparties are usually connected to certain weather conditions and ship's draught. In *Gentime* (see appendix 4, *part I, box 5 "vessel's description"*), the base for the vessel's speed capability is described as follows:

> *"Speed and Consumption on Summer dwt in good weather, max. windspeed 4 Bft".*

The type of fuel is also important. In *Gentime*, specification of fuel oil is given in *part I, box 23 "fuel specifications"* and *part II, clause 6(d) "bunkers – bunkering"* (see appendix 4). In view of the fact that vessels are often ordered to proceed with *"economical speed"* or *"low speed"*, it is recommended that not only consumption on full speed is stated in the charterparty; consumption on "economical speed" and "low speed" should also be agreed.

In accordance with English law, a speed clause is generally not understood to be a *continuing warranty* of the ship's speed capability and bunker consumption during the whole time charter period, unless that is clearly stated in the contract. In accordance with established principles (as set out in *The Apollonius [1978] 1 LLR 53* and re-confirmed in later decisions), it seems that the speed warranty applies – in the absence of an express stipulation that the warranty is to apply throughout the duration of the charter – no later than the time of delivery of the vessel under the charter. To impose a continuing warranty as to the vessel's performance, an express provision is required. In the absence of that, the performance warranty applies only at the time of delivery into the charter service. This may be reinforced even by specific wording of some charter documents, where it is agreed that only during the negotiations or at the time of the fixture or at the time the vessel enters into service under the charterparty, she is capable of steaming at the stated speed on the stated consumption.

On the contrary, as the matter of the continuity of performance warranty is rather controversial and historically a ground for dispute, it must be said that most standard time charter forms impose on the owner a duty to maintain the ship throughout the charter period and the master has a duty to prosecute his *voyages* with utmost despatch (for example, see *NYPE 2015, clause 6(a) "owners to provide"* and *clause 8(a) "performance of voyages"* in appendix 6). These clauses imply that the ship has to maintain her warranted performance, during good weather periods, throughout the charter period and this is now a generally accepted principle in London proceedings as a matter of English law.[1]

This view is not only supported by the FONASBA *Time Charter Interpretation Code 2000* which states that the speed warranty shall apply for the duration of

---

1 Furmston, O. and Hosking, B. (2015) *Speed and Performance Claims* (The Standard Club, March 2015, www.standard-club.com).

the time charter irrespective of the vessel being fully or partly loaded or in ballast (see appendix 7), but also by the relevant provision of the recently published *NYPE 2015* (see appendix 6, *clause 12(a) "speed and consumption"*) which stipulates as follows:

> *"Upon delivery and throughout the duration of this Charter Party the Vessel shall be capable of speed and daily consumption rates as stated in Appendix A in good weather on all sea passages with wind up to and including Force four (4) as per the Beaufort Scale and sea state up to and including Sea State three (3) as per the Douglas Sea Scale (unless otherwise specified in Appendix A). Any period during which the Vessel's speed is deliberately reduced to comply with the Charterers' orders/requirements (unless slow steaming or eco speed warranties have been given in Appendix A) or for reasons of safety or while navigating within narrow or restricted waters or when assisting a vessel in distress or when saving or attempting to save life or property at sea, shall be excluded from performance calculations".*

In general, as the vessel's good performance is important for the time charterers during the entire charter period, they often try to get the speed described as *"average service speed"* or similar in the charterparty. Furthermore, in the modern tanker time charterparty forms, the technique in construing the speed clause is usually more like the one used in a voyage charterparty. Here, the weather risk at sea is put on the owners and the speed/consumption factor is described in great detail, as for example in *Shelltime 4* (see appendix 5, *clause 24 "detailed description and performance"*).

Speed capability should always be connected with bunker consumption and, when the charterers scrutinise the log abstract to find out the vessel's performance, they must look at both speed and consumption. *Speed claims*, that is, claims based on low speed/high bunker consumption, are often complicated and difficult to negotiate. In most cases considerable amounts are involved and the parties should therefore be careful when they draw up the charterparty clauses.

A particular problem regarding speed and bunker consumption is bottom growth on the vessel. When the vessel has been idle for a long period in tropical areas, the speed capability will be reduced considerably. Some charterparties have special clauses dealing with this problem. In the new time charter form *NYPE 2015*, this is developed in *clause 30 "BIMCO hull fouling clause for time charter parties"* (see appendix 6).

12.2.4 Vessel's seaworthiness and maintenance

The shipowners' obligations as regards the vessel's seaworthiness have been dealt with before in different contexts (for example see section 10.4.3).

In the time charter agreements it is often expressly said that the owners shall deliver the ship to the charterers in a seaworthy condition. For instance, in the *Gentime* form (see appendix 4, *part II, clause 11 "owner's obligations"*) it is said that: *"the Owners shall deliver the Vessel . . . in a thoroughly efficient state of hull and machinery and shall exercise due diligence to maintain the Vessel . . . in every way fit for the service throughout the period of the Charter Party"*.

Therefore, for both the charterers and the owners it is important not only that the vessel is delivered in accordance with the agreement and in a seaworthy condition, but also that it should be kept in the same good order and condition during the charter period. When the charter agreement covers long periods, it might be advisable to make this clause a little more specific. In this connection, clauses dealing with liability for damage to the vessel or other clauses concerning liabilities and exceptions from liabilities must also be considered.

Even without an express agreement to that effect, the shipowner will have a duty with respect to seaworthiness and maintenance. In English law, the owners' warranty of seaworthiness is *implied*, unless anything to the contrary is stated in the charterparty.

12.3 Trade

12.3.1 Geographical limits

It has already been mentioned that the hull and war risk underwriters dictate certain limits for the vessel. Time charterparties usually contain additional limits for the trading. Basically, it is the time charterers who direct the vessel. In the *Gentime* form (see appendix 4, *part II, clause 13 "charterers' obligations"*), this is expressed, among other terms, in the following way:

"*The Charterers shall furnish the Master with full and timely instructions*".

Instructions must be given subject to the limits of the charter. The "limit of the charter" usually includes several kinds of limitation. The owners must, in the first place, ensure that those limits stipulated by the underwriters are also included in the time charterparty. This is usually done by using the wording "*. . . but always within hull underwriters' trading limits*" or similar. It must be noted that a reference to Institute Navigating Limits (INL) is not always sufficient as other limits may be used by the underwriters.

In the war risk clause it is also often stated that the owners and the master "*have liberty to comply with any orders . . . given by any committee or person having under the terms of the war risk insurance on the vessel the right to give any such orders or directions*".

Additional limitations contained in the concept "limits of the charter" are for various reasons usually inserted. One reason may be that the owners do not want to have the ship trading too far from the home country, as this will cause extra costs for the crew. When the trading limits cover a large area, for instance "*worldwide trading always within INL and excluding following countries . . .*", the owners sometimes wish, for financial reasons, to have a written undertaking from the charterers' side that the ship will visit its home country or countries near its home country once or twice a year for changing of crew, drydocking, etc. Such a clause may have the following wording: "*Vessel to call Europe twice a year evenly spread*".

Very often there are also political reasons for trading limitation. Some countries do not accept vessels which have earlier traded with other countries or are owned or controlled by persons or companies from certain other countries. To avoid difficulties, trading exclusions may be agreed in the charterparty.

A general recommendation, as far as geographical concepts are concerned, is that wordings like *"southern Europe"* or *"Baltic in season"* should be avoided, as it is difficult to find out what areas they really cover. It is better to mention the various countries included or excluded or to give specific geographical limits. When the wording *"in season"* is used, the season should be specified.

It is worth pointing out that geographical descriptions, often abbreviated, are forming a crucial part of chartering communications. The reader may find many of the internationally established geographical abbreviations in the glossary, for example *"ARA: Amsterdam – Rotterdam – Antwerp: (geography) Selection of European ports of call"* or *"Continent: (geography) It includes ports or places in the European continent from Bordeaux in south to Hamburg in north, including both of them and Rouen"*.

12.3.2 Non-geographical limits

For those trades, countries and ports which are within the geographical limits, there are usually further trading limitations of a non-geographical nature. The following clause is from *Gentime* (see appendix 4, *part II, clause 2(a) "trading areas – trading limits"*):

> *"The vessel shall be employed in lawful trades within Institute Warranty Limits (IWL) and within the trading limits as stated in Box 13 between safe ports or safe places where she can safely enter, lie always afloat, and depart"*.

According to this clause, the vessel shall be used only for lawful cargo in lawful trades. This means that the trade and the cargo must be lawful, not only by the law of the countries where the loading and discharging take place, but also in the country where the ship is registered and by the law governing the charterparty.

Ports shall be safe (see above, section 11.3) and the ship shall, as agreed by the parties, either *"lie always afloat"* or *"always afloat or safely aground where it is customary for vessels of similar size or draught to be safely aground"*. *NYPE 2015* (see appendix 6, *clause 1(d) "duration/trip description"*) gives an option to the charterers to order the vessel to load or discharge at a place where she *"may lie safely aground"*. The clause is not applicable if the space intended to fill in ports or areas is left blank.

Further to this provision, there is usually a clause dealing with ice and other difficulties or dangerous situations. Such a clause, often found under the title *"excluded ports"* or similar, can have the following wording (*Linertime 2015, clause 17 "excluded ports"*):

> *"The Vessel not to be ordered to nor bound to enter:*
> (a) *any place where fever or epidemics are prevalent or to which the Master, Officers and Crew by law are not bound to follow the Vessel;*
> (b) *any ice-bound place or any place where lights, lightships, marks and buoys are or are likely to be withdrawn by reason of ice on the Vessel's arrival or where*

there is risk that ordinarily the Vessel will not be able on account of ice to reach the place or to get out after having completed loading or discharging. The Vessel not to be obliged to force ice, nor to follow ice-breakers when inwards bound. If on account of ice the Master considers it dangerous to remain at the loading or discharging place for fear of the Vessel being frozen in and/or damaged, he has liberty to sail to a convenient open place and await the Charterers' fresh instructions. Detention through any of above causes to be for the Charterers' account".

The intention behind the first section of the clause is to protect the crew against fevers and epidemics. The next section is the ice clause which is self-explanatory (see discussion of ice clauses in section 11.3.4). The war clause also sometimes limits the charterers' rights to use commercially the vessel (see discussion of war clauses in section 10.7).

12.3.3 Breaking of trading limits

If the time charterers wish to direct the vessel to ports or places outside the trading limits of the charterparty, they must firstly get permission from the owners, who should sometimes seek permission from the insurance underwriters.

A wording stating that *"the charterers have the right to break vessel's trading limits provided they pay the extra insurance premiums"* can be found in the time charterparties. Such a provision is not acceptable from the owners' point of view, as they cannot provide in advance an "open" permission to the charterers to break the trading limits. Each time the question arises, the underwriters must be consulted and a special agreement between the charterers and owners should be drawn up. In such agreements, not only the costs for extra insurance premiums should be considered, but also the risk of delay and physical damage to the vessel.

12.3.4 Requirements of the trade

As it is important for the charterers that they can use the vessel within the trading limits and without disturbances, they often insist on clauses such as:

"Owners to ensure both that the Vessel is provided with such technical equipment and certificates, and that the terms and conditions on which the Master, Officers and Crew are engaged are such, as are necessary to avoid any delay or hindrance with respect to the use of the Vessel within the trading limits".

Clauses like this may create difficulties for the owners, especially when new regulations are introduced. Therefore, a solution may be that owners and charterers agree that owners' obligations in this respect are limited to rules and regulations in force when the charterparty is agreed.

12.3.5 Trip time charter

When the ship is chartered on time basis, but for a specified trip, this hybrid type of charter is called *"trip time charter"* or *"time charter trip"*, as it combines elements of voyage and time chartering. In a time charterparty, a clause as the following is sometimes used instead of usual trading limits, to transform a typical time charter in a time charter trip:

> "One time charter voyage with loading 1 or 2 ports in Sweden and discharging 1 or 2 ports in Brazil. Redelivery on dropping outward pilot[2] at last discharging port. Total period estimated to 30 days".

NYPE 2015 (see appendix 6, *clause 1(a) "duration/trip description"*) reflects the parties' possibilities to choose whether the agreement will be for a specific period or for a specific trip.

As always, when the basic principles are set aside, the parties must look through the other clauses of the charterparty and make necessary amendments in order to keep a solid charter contract. Most standard time charterparty forms have a clause giving the owners an opportunity to claim additional hire for the last voyage under the charterparty, if the vessel is not redelivered in due time. The wording of these clauses is not suitable for trip time chartering and should thus be amended, for example by stating that the charter hire is applicable only for 30 days (in the above-mentioned example) and that the owners are entitled thereafter to the market rate if higher than the charter rate.

Sometimes, the charterparty contains both ordinary trading limits and a description of a time charter trip, for instance:

> "World-wide trading within INL[3]",

combined with

> "One time charter trip from UK to one or two ports Spanish Mediterranean coast".

In such a case, are the charterers then entitled to send the vessel from the UK via Norway to the Spanish Mediterranean coast? The answer is difficult to find and such confusing combinations of clauses should be avoided. In this example, if the intention is to send the vessel directly from the UK to Spain, the words "*worldwide trading*" should not be inserted. On the other hand, if the intention is that the charterers should have a possibility of sending the ship to other places, the trip UK/Spain should not be mentioned at all in the charterparty, or only be mentioned as a non-binding intended voyage.

12.3.6 Ballast bonus

It goes without saying that it is advantageous for the time charterers if the vessel is delivered at a place where it can be loaded immediately. Similarly, it is to the advantage of the owners if the vessel is redelivered at a place where it can easily

---

2 See *DOP* in the glossary.
3 See *INL* in the glossary.

get a new cargo or a new charter at a good rate. As a consequence of this, the delivery and redelivery ports or places are often reflected in the economic calculation and in the hire.

Instead of having the hire influenced by delivery and redelivery positions, the parties sometimes agree about a ballast bonus to be paid. For instance, if a vessel is planned to be finally discharged under the time charter at port X, the time charterer most probably also wishes to redeliver her at port X. Presuming it is impossible to find a new cargo at port X and the nearest port where cargo is available is town Y, ten days' steaming from port X, the owner must consider the ten days' steaming time and the relevant bunker consumption from port X to town Y in his calculation for the time charter. This can be done in several ways. One alternative is that the vessel continues on charter and is not redelivered until her arrival at town Y. However, the parties may agree instead that the vessel shall be redelivered at port X and that the owners shall get a lump sum compensation – a "*ballast bonus*"[4] – for the theoretical steaming time and the bunker consumption cost from port X to town Y. Such a ballast bonus may also be converted to hire and added to the hire for the actual charter period.

The advantage of ballast bonus, either paid as a lump sum compensation or added to the ordinary hire, is that the parties are discharged from their obligations and liabilities during the ballast bonus-covered period and voyage. This means, for instance, that the charterers are not liable for the safety of ports and channels and bear no financial risk for the delay of the vessel by bad weather, strikes of pilots or similar occurrences. The owners are free to do what they wish with the vessel and, in this specific example, they are not obliged to direct her to town Y. Depending on the circumstances, ballast bonuses can be paid by the owners to the charterers or vice versa, at delivery and/or at redelivery of the vessel.

12.4 Cargo

12.4.1 Type and specification of cargo

Apart from the trading limits, the most important restriction as regards the time charterers' freedom to use and direct the ship is the restriction on cargoes to be carried by the vessel. In the first place, the type of vessel is decisive for the kind of cargo to be carried. Some vessels are specially built and equipped for one kind of cargo only and in such a case this should be stated in the charterparty. Other ships can take a limited number of cargo types and also in this case the best way is to specify them in the charterparty. However, many ships are intended and suitable for many kinds of cargo and in those cases time charterparties usually describe the accepted cargo as, for instance, "*lawful merchandise non-injurious to the vessel*", or "*ordinary dry cargo non-injurious to the vessel*" or similar. It is worth noting the difference compared with the voyage charterparty, where the description and specification of the cargo have a more central position.

---

4 See also *BB* in the glossary.

12.4.2 Excluded cargo

Sometimes, the general description of cargo accepted for the vessel will, by itself, exclude some cargoes. For instance, if the general cargo description is "*lawful merchandise non-injurious to the vessel*", then all unlawful and injurious cargoes are not allowed. In addition, the printed charterparty forms usually also contain a specification of cargo that is excluded from carriage. As an example, see appendix 4, *Gentime, part II, clause 3 "cargo – restrictions and exclusions"*.

12.5 Period

12.5.1 Length of period

Time charterparties regularly contain a clause stating the length of the charter period. The basic period agreed is called "*flat period*". The traditional way to describe the charter duration is to fix a certain period. For instance, the first line of clause 1 in *Gentime* form reads "*the Owners let and the Charterers hire the Vessel for the period/trip(s) stated in Box 6*", where box 6 refers to the "*period of charter*".

Another alternative is to agree that the vessel shall perform one or several fixed voyages, as described in section 12.3.5 regarding trip time chartering.

As it is difficult to determine exactly beforehand when the ship will be redelivered to the owners, the charterparties usually have a certain built-in flexibility. Both the flat period and the redelivery date are often described together with the word "*about*". It is also possible to state a certain flat period or a certain redelivery date with the addition "± *15 days in charterers' option*" or similar. Combinations of these two methods or other stipulations are also found. When establishing the meaning of "*about*", several factors will be considered, but particularly decisive will be the length of the "flat period", or the length of the voyages embraced by the charter period. When the charterers have an optional right to prolong the charter period, such options are normally for the benefit solely of the charterers. If the market rate goes down during the charter period, the charterers will probably not use their option and the owners will have to find new employment for the vessel. The charterers may choose another ship, or perhaps the same ship, at a lower hire rate than in the old charter. If the market rate has gone up, the charterers will probably use their option as, in that way, they get the vessel at a rate lower than the prevailing market rate.

Especially when there is a big gap between the market hire and the charterparty hire, disputes easily arise concerning the length of the period. If the charterparty hire is higher than the market hire, the charterers try to redeliver the ship as soon as possible, whereas if the charter hire is lower than the market hire, they try instead to keep her for as long as possible.

12.5.2 Overlap/underlap – last voyage

The vessel is sometimes redelivered to the owners before and sometimes after the agreed redelivery date or period. In the first case there is an *underlap* situation and in the latter an *overlap*.

The owners cannot refuse to take the ship if the charterers redeliver her earlier than they are entitled to, in spite of this being a breach of contract on the charterers' side. The owners have an obligation to try to minimise their loss by seeking alternative employment for the vessel, but if they fail or if they get lower revenue compared with the previous charter, they are entitled to compensation from the charterers. Nevertheless, it is not always clear how this compensation should be calculated.

When the charterers are planning the *last voyage* for the ship under the time charter, they must take into consideration that she has to be redelivered in accordance with the agreement in the charterparty. As it is often difficult to plan or estimate exactly when the vessel will be redelivered, the charterparty forms usually have a special clause about the last voyage. In the *Gentime* form (see appendix 4, *part II, clause 4(d) "redelivery – last voyage"*), this is dealt with as follows:

> "*The Charterers warrant that they will not order the Vessel to commence a voyage (including any preceding ballast voyage) which cannot reasonably be expected to be completed in time to allow redelivery of the Vessel within the period agreed and declared as per clause 1(a). If nevertheless such an order is given the Owners shall have the option; (i) to refuse the order and require a substitute order allowing timely redelivery; or (ii) to perform the order without prejudice to their rights to claim damages for breach of charter in case of late redelivery. In any event, for the number of days by which the period agreed and declared as per clause 1(a) is exceeded, the Charterers shall pay the market rate if this is higher than the rate stated in Box 24*".

According to this clause, the owners are entitled to the market rate for the overlap period if the market rate is higher than the rate stipulated in the charterparty. If the market rate is lower than the charterparty rate, the latter rate will apply also for the overlap period. It is noted that this clause does not mean that charterers are free to prolong the charter period. This is also a question that has to be taken into consideration in connection with time charter trips.

12.5.3 Extension of flat period due to off-hire periods

Charterers are not entitled to an extension of the flat period because of off-hire periods which occurred during the charter, unless this is expressly stated in the charter agreement. If such a clause is inserted, it is advisable to state also the latest time by which the charterers must notify the owners that they intend to exercise their option to extend the charter period. Furthermore, the hire for the additional period should be determined, as well as the question of whether possible off-hire during the extension period will give the charterer a right to additional extension.

12.5.4 Delivery and redelivery of vessel

A charter period is demarcated by the delivery to and redelivery from the time charterers. In respect to delivery and redelivery, several questions arise which must be dealt with in the charterparty.

In *Gentime* (see appendix 4, *part II, clause 1(b) & 1(c) "period and delivery – delivery place & delivery time"*) the vessel's delivery is described as follows:

"...

    (b)   *Delivery Place: The Owners shall deliver the Vessel to the Charterers at the port or place stated in Box 8 or a port or place within the range stated in Box 8.*

    (c)   *Delivery Time: Delivery shall take place no earlier than the date/time stated in Box 9 and no later than the date/time stated in Box 10. Delivery shall be effected at any time day or night, Saturdays, Sundays and holidays included".*

In addition, *Gentime* outlines the vessel's redelivery to the owners by the following clause (see appendix 4, *part II, clause 4(a), 4(b) & 4(c) "redelivery – redelivery place – acceptance of redelivery – notice"*):

    "*(a)   Redelivery Place: The Charterers shall redeliver the Vessel to the Owners at the port or place stated in Box 17 or a port or place within the range stated in Box 17, in the same order and condition as when the Vessel was delivered, fair wear and tear excepted.*

    (b)   *Acceptance of Redelivery: Acceptance of redelivery of the Vessel by the Owners shall not prejudice their rights against the Charterers under this Charter Party.*

    (c)   *Notice: The Charterers shall give the Owners not less than the number of days notice stated in Box 18 indicating the port or place of redelivery and the expected date on which the Vessel is to be ready for redelivery".*

There are also other clauses connected with the delivery of the vessel, as for example the following (*Gentime*, see appendix 4, *part II, clause 1(d) "period and delivery – cancellation"*):

"Cancellation: Should the Vessel not be delivered by the date/time stated in Box 10 the Charterers shall have the option to cancel the Charter Party without prejudice to any claims the Charterers may otherwise have on the Owners under the Charter Party. If the Owners anticipate that, despite their exercise of due diligence, the Vessel will not be ready for delivery by the date/time stated in Box 10, they may notify the Charterers in writing, stating the anticipated new date of readiness for delivery, proposing a new cancelling date/time and requiring the Charterers to declare whether they will cancel or will take delivery of the Vessel. Should the Charterers elect not to cancel or should they fail to reply within two (2) working days (as applying at the Charterers' place of business) of receipt of such notification, then unless otherwise agreed, the proposed new cancelling date/time will replace the date/time stated in Box 10. This provision shall operate only once and should the Vessel not be ready for delivery at the new cancelling date/time the Charterers shall have the option of cancelling this Charter Party".

12.5.5 When shall the vessel be delivered and redelivered?

The matter of the time of vessel's delivery and redelivery has been discussed above in section 12.5 as well as in section 10.5 relating to lay/can. It has been mentioned that if the vessel arrives too early at the delivery port, the charterers are not obliged to take delivery before the layday, whereas if it arrives too late, the charterers are entitled to cancel the agreement. In some situations the charterers are also entitled to damages. Besides, it was mentioned that time charterparties usually accept a certain flexibility as regards the time for redelivery. If the charterers redeliver the ship too late, the owners may be entitled to damages from the charterers. The terms in the charterparty, the governing law and the reason for the late redelivery must be considered. If it becomes evident that at the time the vessel was ordered on its last voyage the charterers realised, or should have realised, that it would not be possible for them to redeliver the vessel in accordance with the contract, the owners usually stand a good chance of getting damages for their loss, if any. The situation is more difficult when the redelivery has been delayed by a reason outside the charterers' control, provided that the charterers were not negligent.

Many charterparties state that the vessel can only be delivered and redelivered during weekdays and during office hours. It is recommended to clarify whether Universal Time Coordinated (UTC) or local times should be applied when the exact time for delivery and redelivery is established.

12.5.6 Where shall the vessel be delivered and redelivered?

The port or place of delivery and redelivery can be more or less specified. Sometimes a certain port is agreed and sometimes a certain area or range, for example *"vessel to be delivered and redelivered in the Mediterranean"*. When only an area or range is determined, it is usually the owners who choose the place of delivery and the charterers who decide the port of redelivery.

Delivery and redelivery may not necessarily take place when the ship is in port. It is not unusual that the charterparties contain a delivery or a redelivery clause of the following type:

> *"Vessel to be delivered (redelivered) on dropping outward pilot[5] at x-town"*.

It should be noted that such a clause can cause difficulties in situations where, for instance, both port pilots and river pilots are available.

12.5.7 In what condition shall the vessel be delivered and redelivered?

On delivery to the charterers, the vessel shall be seaworthy and conform to the requirements of the contract. For example, this is depicted by a wording of the following manner:

> *". . . she being in every way fitted for ordinary dry cargo service with cargo holds well swept, cleaned and ready to receive cargo before delivery under this charter"*.

---

5 See *DOP* and compare with *TIP* and *APS* terms in the glossary.

As regards redelivery, the following or similar clauses are used:

"*. . . the vessel to be redelivered on the expiration of the charter in the same good order as when delivered to the charterers (fair wear and tear excepted). . .*".

If problems connected with damage to the vessel are disregarded, the meaning of these provisions is that upon delivery the charterers can require the ship to be in the condition specified in the contract and ready to commence commercial trading for them, while they are also obliged to redeliver the vessel in a similar condition, enabling the owners to start immediate commercial trading for their own account (or for another time charterer).

A question which quite often causes problems is the cleaning of the cargo holds before redelivery. The charterers sometimes wish to have clauses of the following type inserted into the charterparty (*NYPE 2015*, see appendix 6, *part of clause 10(a) "rate of hire; hold cleaning; communications; victualing and expenses"*):

"*Unless otherwise mutually agreed, the Charterers shall have the option to redeliver the Vessel with unclean/unswept holds against a lumpsum payment of . . . in lieu of hold cleaning, to the Owners (unless Vessel lost)*".

This and similar clauses can be very burdensome to the owners. Since they cannot estimate beforehand how many men/hours they will need to clean the ship, they may be in a position to not have sufficient time on a ballast voyage before the next charter, thus losing "expensive" time during which the ship cannot be used commercially. From the owners' point of view, it is better to discuss such lump sum compensation when the vessel is at the redelivery port and when it is known what the next employment will be.

12.5.8 Allocation of costs at delivery and redelivery

When the vessel is delivered under a time charter, liability for certain costs, for example the variable costs for bunkers, harbour dues, agency fees etc., goes over from the owners to the charterers. In the opposite way, liability for these costs passes over to the owners at redelivery.

In order to get a basis for the allocation of costs, *special survey reports* (on-hire or off-hire) are usually issued in connection with the delivery and the redelivery. In these reports the exact time for delivery and redelivery, together with quantities of fuel and diesel on board are stated. Damage to the vessel and her general condition are also mentioned. Such *damage reports* often have an important function in discussions about liability for damages which sometimes arise during and after the charter period.

Charterers and owners can make separate surveys, but it is common that they agree to have a joint survey by an independent surveyor. The parties must agree not only for whose account the survey is, but also in whose time. The following clauses show alternative solutions:

"Unless otherwise mutually agreed the Owners and Charterers shall each appoint surveyors for the purpose of determining the condition of the Vessel at the time of delivery and redelivery hereunder. Surveys whenever possible to be done during service, but if impossible any time lost for on-hire survey to be for Owners' account and any time lost for off-hire survey to be for Charterers' account", or
"A joint survey at delivery to be arranged by Owners and effected in their time. A joint survey on redelivery to be arranged by Charterers and effected in their time. Costs for both surveys to be shared equally".

As regards fuel, the charterparty should state the prices to be applied at delivery and redelivery. The following example is from *NYPE 2015* (see appendix 6, *part of clause 9(a) "bunkers – bunker quantities and prices"*):

"The Charterers on delivery, and the Owners on redelivery or any termination of this Charter Party, shall take over and pay for all bunkers remaining on board the Vessel as hereunder. The Vessel's bunker tank capacities shall be at the Charterers' disposal. Bunker quantities and prices on delivery/redelivery to be (agreed prices to be inserted)".

It is very difficult to draft a clear fuel price clause, but an alternative, may be the following (also taken from *clause 9(a)* of *NYPE 2015*):

"The Charterers shall not take over and pay for bunkers Remaining On Board at delivery but shall redeliver the Vessel with about the same quantities and grades of bunkers as on delivery. Any difference between the delivery quantity and the redelivery quantity shall be paid by the Charterers or the Owners as the case may be. The price of the bunkers shall be the net contract price paid by the receiving party, as evidenced by suppliers' invoice or other supporting documents".

When the vessel is delivered or redelivered at the quay, the liability for harbour dues changes from one party to the other during the ship's call at port, thus it may be difficult to find out how the harbour dues should be shared between them. To avoid this problem, the charterparties usually contain a clause dealing with this question. The *Linertime* form and the *Baltime* form have the following solution (see *Linertime 2015, part II, clause 5 "charterers to provide")*:

"The Charterers to pay all dock, harbour, light and tonnage dues at the ports of delivery and re-delivery (unless incurred through cargo carried before delivery or after re-delivery). . .".

12.6 Hire

The hire is the financial payment to the owners for chartering the manned and equipped vessel to the time charterers. The basic rule is that hire shall be paid from the moment when the ship is delivered to the charterers until she is again redelivered to the owners at the termination of the charter period. Under some circumstances, mainly defined in the *"off-hire"* or *"suspension of hire"* clauses (see section 12.7), the time charterers are relieved from their obligation to pay hire to the owners.

12.6.1 Fixing of hire

The hire can be expressed in various ways, for instance "*X US Dollars per 30 days*", "*X US Dollars per day*", "*X Euros per 30 days and deadweight ton*", etc. The choice depends mainly on the type of vessel and the trade.

Hire "*per month*" should be avoided as this expression is understood as a calendar month, for instance from and including 9 February to and including 8 March. The number of days during such a period will vary between 28 and 31 days and this means that the hire per day will be different from month to month, which may cause difficulties when off-hire is calculated. It may then be better to express the hire in such a way that the daily hire will be the same throughout the charter period, therefore, when monthly payment is agreed, it is common that the hire is calculated and payable "*per month of 30 days*".

12.6.2 Payment of hire

The procedure for payment of hire is dealt with in *Gentime* form in the following way (see appendix 4, *part II, clause 8(b) "hire – payment"*):

> "*Payment of hire shall be made in advance in full, without discount every 15 days to the Owners' bank account designated in Box 25 or to such other account as the Owners may from time to time designate in writing, in funds available to the Owners on the due date*".

In time chartering the financial payment to the owners – the *hire* – is paid in advance. The difference from voyage chartering is worth to be highlighted, where the principal rule is that the owners get their payment – the *freight* – when the sea voyage has been terminated and they are ready to deliver the cargo at the port of destination (see and compare with section 11.5). The reason why the owners are paid *in advance* in time chartering is that they do not have the same possibility as in voyage chartering of securing their payment by exercising a lien over the cargo (see further below in this section about late payment and owners' security).

Payment periods of 15 or 30 days are commonly used, but other routines also exist. For instance, *NYPE 2015* (see appendix 6, *clause 11(a) "hire payment – payment"*) provides that the payment shall be made "*15 days in advance*". This is also quite common in short time charters.

Periods of hire and time of payments must not be mixed. If the hire is to be paid for 30-day periods in advance, the monthly date of payment will differ from period to period. However, the amount paid will be the same (if deductions for off-hire and similar reasons are disregarded). On the other hand, if the hire is to be paid "*monthly in advance*" and is fixed at "*X US Dollars per day*" or with a similar method where the daily hire is the same all the time, the monthly date for payment will be the same from one period to another. However, the amount paid will be different as the number of days in the period will vary from 28 to 31.

12.6.3 Late payment of hire and owners' security

As mentioned above, the hire is payable in advance. If the charterers are in default with payment by paying either too late or too little, the owners are entitled, under English law and according to most time charterparty forms, to cancel the charter agreement. In the *Gentime* form this is expressed in the following way (see appendix 4, *part II, part of clause 8(c) "hire – default"*):

> "*In default of punctual and regular payment of the hire the Owners shall have the right to withdraw the Vessel without prejudice to any other claim the Owners may have against the Charterers under this Charter Party*".

According to the wording of the *Gentime* clause and similar clauses in other forms, even a small default in payment gives the owners a right to cancel the whole agreement. The explanation for this clause, which must be considered rigorous, is that the right to cancel is one of the few possibilities owners have to protect themselves against insolvent charterers and charterers who are not willing to pay. Unfortunately, these clauses very often do not give owners the protection intended when it comes to the practical situation, at least not when cargo has been taken on board. For, as soon as a bill of lading has been issued, the owner will have a duty to the bill of lading holder to perform the transport. Unless the owner can get a lien over the freight payable to the time charterer under the sub-charter, he may have to deliver the cargo at the bill of lading destination without getting anything from the time charterer.

Over the years there have been several disputes about the owners' right to cancel on the ground of default in payment of hire. It is difficult to extract the principles from these cases, but it can be noted that the owners may lose their right to cancel if they have previously, without protest, accepted late payments. Besides, the owners may not be entitled to cancel for only a small default in payment, if charterers have previously made correct payments. From this, it is inferred that it is important for owners to always *protest* when the hire payment is late or when the charterers have made unauthorised deductions from the hire. If the owners fail to protest, it may become considered as an accepted procedure for future payments.

Payments of hire are commonly made via banks and in most cases payment is not considered as effected until the money reaches the owners' bank. As the remittance is frequently delayed in the banks, it is not unusual for the time charterparties to have a "*non-technicality clause*" or "*anti-technicality clause*" in order to prevent the owner from cancelling due to technical delays in the payment. Such a clause should contain an undertaking by the owners to notify the charterers if and when the payment is late, or if the owners (for other reasons) do not accept the amount. Furthermore, the clause should also allow the charterers some additional time before the owners are entitled to cancel the charter agreement. A typical example is given by the following provision (see appendix 4, *Gentime, part II, part of clause 8(c) "hire – default"*):

> "*Where there is a failure to make punctual and regular payment of hire due to oversight, negligence, errors or omissions on the part of the Charterers or their bankers,*

> *the Owners shall give the Charterers written notice of the number of clear banking days stated in Box 26 (as recognized at the agreed place of payment) in which to rectify the failure, and when so rectified within such number of days following the Owners' notice, the payment shall stand as regular and punctual. Failure by the Charterers to pay hire within the number of days stated in Box 26 of their receiving the Owners' notice as provided herein, shall entitle the Owners to withdraw the Vessel without further notice and without prejudice to any other claim they may have against the Charterers.*
>
> *Further, at any time after the period stated in Box 26, as long as hire remains unpaid the Owners shall, without prejudice to their right to withdraw, be entitled to suspend the performance of any and all of their obligations hereunder and shall have no responsibility whatsoever for any consequences thereof in respect of which the Charterers hereby agree to indemnify the Owners. Notwithstanding the provisions of Clause 9(a)(ii), hire shall continue to accrue and any extra expenses resulting from such suspension shall be for the Charterers' account".*

It is clear from the text above that both the charterers and the owners must be very careful. Charterers must ensure that remittances of hire are made well in advance before the hire is due, as there is always a risk that the owners will take the opportunity to cancel the charter agreement if they can get better terms from another time charterer. On the other hand, it is important that the owner is cautious and takes legal advice before cancelling on the grounds of defaulted payment, as an unjustified cancellation may entitle the charterers to claim damages from the owners.

In addition, the time charterparties usually have a *"lien clause"* which can have the following wording (see appendix 5, *Shelltime 4, clause 26 "lien"*):

> *"Owners shall have a lien upon all cargoes and all freights, sub-freights and demurrage for any amounts due under this charter; and Charterers shall have a lien on the vessel for all monies paid in advance and not earned, and for all claims for damages arising from any breach by Owners of this charter".*

The intention of this clause is to protect the owners against insolvent charterers, but it looks more helpful than it actually is in practice. The cargo on board the vessel usually belongs to someone other than the time charterers. The owners have, according to the bill of lading, an obligation to deliver the cargo to the bill of lading holders. As the owners are bound by their obligations to the cargo owners from the moment they have started loading the cargo, in most cases they have to execute the cargo voyage and fulfil their obligations to the cargo owners even if the time charterers fail to pay the hire.

Regarding *"sub-freights belonging to the time charterers and bill of lading freights"*, it is often difficult for the owners to get the information they need in order to notify the bill of lading freight payer that they have a (right for) lien over the sub-freight which he is bound to pay. In many cases the sub-freight (bill of lading freight) is prepaid, which means that the owners have no security at all.

The subject of late payment or non-payment of hire and the owners' right to withdraw the vessel is one of those major time charter subjects interpreted in *FONASBA Time Charter Interpretation Code 2000* (see appendix 7).

12.6.4 Deductions from hire

When the advance payment of hire is to be made, the charterers often wish to make deductions for off-hire having taken place during previous periods, for cash paid by agents to the master, for disbursements on owners' account, for planned off-hire (e.g. drydocking) and for other monetary claims that the charterers may have against the owners. As default in payment may give the owners a right to cancel the charter (see section 12.6.3 above), it is important for charterers either to rely on a clause which gives them a right to make such deductions, or to get the owners' approval before the deduction is made. It is not clear to what extent the charterers are allowed to make deductions without permission from owners and without provisions in the charterparty to such effect.

12.6.5 Payment of last instalment of hire

As the last period of hire in most cases is not as long as the normal full hire payment period, and as the charterers will usually have a claim against the owners for bunkers remaining on board at redelivery, the time charterparty forms frequently contain a *"last hire payment clause"* which may have the following wording (see appendix 4, *Gentime, part II, clause 8(e) "hire – redelivery adjustment"*):

> *"Should the Vessel be on her voyage towards the port or place of redelivery at the time payment of hire becomes due, said payment shall be made for the estimated time necessary to complete the voyage, less the estimated value of the fuels remaining on board at redelivery. When the Vessel is redelivered to the Owners any difference shall be refunded to or paid by the Charterers as appropriate, but not later than thirty days after redelivery of the Vessel".*

12.7 Off-hire

12.7.1 Importance

As already mentioned, the principal rule is that the charterers must pay hire from the time the vessel is delivered to the charterers until the time she is redelivered to the owners at the end of the agreed charter period. The financial risk for delay of the vessel due to bad weather, strikes of pilots or stevedores etc., during the charter period, normally rests on the charterers. However, when the vessel is delayed under certain conditions agreed in the charterparty and usually attributable to the crew or connected with the vessel, the charterers may be entitled to compensation in accordance with a special stipulation called an *"off-hire clause"*, a *"suspension of hire clause"* or similar. Examples of such clauses may be seen in *Gentime* (see appendix 4, *part II, clause 9 "off-hire"*), in *Shelltime 4* (see appendix 5, *clause 21 "off-hire"*) and *NYPE 2015* (see appendix 6, *clause 17 "off-hire"*).

Charterers are entitled to off-hire only if the ship is delayed for a reason which in accordance with the off-hire clause (or in accordance with the applicable law) is recognised as a ground for off-hire. Off-hire can be compared with other *liquidated damages* (e.g. demurrage) which means that it is a compensation agreed beforehand between the parties. The compensation to charterers is based on the charter hire and charterers do not have to prove their loss. Even if they can prove that their loss is higher than the agreed charter hire, they are not entitled to more than what is agreed beforehand. On the other hand, they still get compensation based on the charter hire if their actual loss is less. A characteristic of off-hire is that the charterer may be entitled to make the deduction from hire, notwithstanding the absence of any breach of contract or negligence by the owners. However, if the owners are in breach of contract or if they or the people on board have been negligent, the charterers may be entitled to damages or off-hire or both, at their own choice.

Off-hire clauses sometimes have a special section about "*detention for charterers' account*". For instance, the relevant clause in *Linertime 2015 (part II, clause 14(B) "suspension of hire etc. – detention for charterers' account")* has the following wording:

> "*In the event of the Vessel being driven into port or to anchorage through stress of weather, trading to shallow harbours or to rivers or ports with bars or suffering an accident to her cargo, any detention of the Vessel and/or expenses resulting from such detention to be for the Charterers' account even if such detention and/or expenses, or the cause by reason of which either is incurred, be due to, or be contributed to by, the negligence of the Owners' servants*".

This provision does not deal with situations where the vessel's operations are hindered or prevented by charterers' breach of contract. If charterers are in breach of the contract, owners shall not suffer. The situation can be handled in different ways. One possibility is that the vessel continues on-hire and another possibility is that the vessel is considered off-hire and the owners are compensated by way of damages. The difference can be important if, for instance, charterers have an insurance for charterers' liability for damage to hull. Such an insurance may compensate charterers for payments of damages, but not for hire costs payable during a period when the vessel is hindered or prevented in accordance with the "detention for charterers' account" clause.

12.7.2 Off-hire claim

To find out whether a vessel is off-hire or not and to prepare the off-hire claim, the following questions should be answered:

- Is the reason for the delay included in the list of grounds for off-hire in the off-hire clause or by applicable law?
- Is there any "threshold rule" (see section 12.7.4 below) and, if so, will this rule be applicable in the relevant situation?
- What is the loss of time?
- What is the loss of money?
- What is the deduction of off-hire?

Before dealing with these questions separately, it must be pointed out that if the charterers have caused the delay to the ship, they cannot normally get off-hire compensation from the owners even if the delay is covered by the off-hire clause (for example see the *Linertime 2015 clause 14(B)* above).

12.7.3 Grounds for off-hire

The first step is to find out whether the reason for the delay is covered by the off-hire clause in the relevant charterparty. Some contracts are more and others less extensive in this respect. When the charterparty is governed by English law, it seems that the clause is generally interpreted restrictively. Under other legal systems, for example the Scandinavian law, the clause is regarded more as a description of a principle and it is supplemented by the provisions of the maritime code. Thus, it can generally be said that the charterers have less chance to get off-hire compensation when the charterparty is governed by English law compared with other cases, as for instance under Scandinavian law.

12.7.4 Threshold rule

If it is found that the reason for the delay is covered by the off-hire clause, the next step will be to find out whether there is a *threshold* in the off-hire clause and, if so, whether it is applicable.

Many standard time charterparty forms have thresholds, where it is stated that the charterers are entitled to off-hire only if the vessel is hindered or prevented for more than an agreed number of hours (usually 12 or 24 hours). *Baltime 1939 (revision 2001, part II, clause 11 "suspension of hire etc.")* has such a threshold of *"twenty-four consecutive hours"*, but in *NYPE 2015* no such favour is given to the owners. As the threshold rule is worded in Baltime, the hindrance – not the loss of time – must continue for a certain number of consecutive hours. This means that, if the ship has problems with her main engine and steams at half speed for 30 hours, a threshold of 24 hours does not prevent off-hire, although the time loss is only 15 hours.

It should be noted that the rule, as construed in Baltime, is a "threshold" and not a "deduction" or "deductible". For example, if the vessel has to stop for 35 hours due to engine breakdown, the off-hire deduction will be for 35 hours, not for 35 less 24 hours. Some charterparty forms have thresholds for some kinds of delays, but no threshold for other delays. For instance, even though *Linertime 2015 (part II, clause 14(A) "suspension of hire etc.")* has an off-hire threshold of a number of consecutive hours that has to be agreed beforehand between the parties in box 31, no threshold rule is applicable when the reason for the delay is a breakdown of winches, as per the relative *Linertime 2015* provision below (*part II, clause 14(A) "suspension of hire etc. – winch breakdown"*):

> "*In the event of a breakdown of a winch or winches, not caused by carelessness of shore labourers, the time lost to be calculated pro rata for the period of such inefficiency in relation to the number of winches required for work. If the Charterers elect to continue work, the Owners are to pay for shore appliances in lieu of the winches, but in such cases the Charterers to pay full hire. Any hire paid in advance to be adjusted accordingly*".

The threshold rule causes many disputes and it is arguable whether it is at all justified. After all, the charterers pay hire to the owners in return for the use of the vessel. Thus, it is difficult to understand why the charterers should also pay for periods when they are unable to use it, due to breakdown or other hindrances on the vessel's/owners' side.

12.7.5 Loss of time

The next step is to calculate the loss of time. Charterers are not always entitled to off-hire for all time actually lost. For instance, according to *Gentime* (see appendix 4, *part II, clause 9(a) "off-hire – inability to perform services"*), the ship is off-hire only if it is "*unable to comply with instructions of the Charterers*". Therefore, if the instruction is to "*await orders*", the vessel may be *able* even if the main engine is temporarily out of order. However, charterers may in such situations argue that the vessel shall be ready for immediate departure even when waiting for orders and therefore it should be considered off-hire as long as the main engine is not in working order.

Another critical example concerns the case where the vessel, after an engine breakdown in the North Sea, is towed to Hamburg for repairs. Will she be on hire again when the main engine is repaired in Hamburg or is the charterer entitled to off-hire for the time the vessel needs to get back into the position she had when she went off-hire? To handle this question, charterers often wish to insert a "*put back*" clause like the following (see appendix 6, *NYPE 2015, part of clause 17 "off-hire"*):

> "*Should the Vessel deviate or put back during a voyage, contrary to the orders or directions of the Charterers, for any reason other than accident to the cargo or where permitted in Clause 22 (Liberties) hereunder, the hire to be suspended from the time of her deviating or putting back until she is again in the same or equidistant position from the destination and the voyage resumed therefrom*".

It is doubtful to what extent consequential loss of time will be considered as off-hire. An example illustrating such off-hire problems concerns the situation where the vessel has been off-hire in port awaiting crew members (deficiency of men) and then, when the crew members are on board, has to postpone its departure due to a tug strike which started while the vessel was off-hire awaiting the crew members. To find out whether such a consequential delay will entitle the charterers to an off-hire deduction, the wording of the off-hire clause in the relevant charterparty and the applicable law must be checked.

NYPE 2015 (see appendix 6, *clause 38 "slow steaming"*) deals also with the situation where the vessel is steaming with reduced speed. Moreover, as stipulated in *NYPE 2015* (*last part of clause 17 "off-hire"*) when time is lost as a result of slow steaming caused by defect in the vessel, breakdown etc., the time lost shall be deducted from the hire. Besides, *bunkers used by the vessel while off-hire* and the cost of replacing same shall be for the owners' account and therefore deducted from hire.

12.7.6 Loss of money; deduction of off-hire

When the loss of time is established, it must be converted into money. This is not very hard when the hire is counted per day, per 30 days or similar. When the hire is counted "per month" the situation may be somewhat more complicated, since the hire per day, which may vary during the off-hire period, has first to be established.

As mentioned above in section 12.6.3 default in payment of hire may give the owners a right to cancel the charter agreement. Therefore, the charterers must be very careful to investigate their legal position before any off-hire is deducted.

12.7.7 Other obligations during off-hire periods

Especially when the ship is off-hire for a long period, a question arises as to what extent the charterers' other obligations under the charter agreement remain during the off-hire periods. For instance, do the charterers have to pay for bunkers consumed and harbour dues incurred during the off-hire period? Legally, it seems to be clear, at least under English and US law, that unless express provision has been made to the contrary, the charterers' other obligations remain during off-hire periods. For some reason the development in practical life has been to the contrary, i.e. charterers usually do not pay for fuel during off-hire periods. In order to establish this contractually, the words "*whilst on hire*" are often inserted at the beginning of the clause entitled "*charterers to provide*" or similar (see for example appendix 4, *Gentime, part II, clause 13 "charterers' obligations"*).

12.7.8 Insurance for loss of hire

Long periods of off-hire can be disastrous, particularly for shipowners operating only one or a few vessels. These shipowners should therefore consider arranging a "*loss of hire*" or "*loss of earnings*" insurance which gives protection when the vessel, as a result of a breakdown or similar emergency, is off-hire. The traditional "loss of hire" insurance is based on loss of time resulting from the same kind of casualties as are covered in the vessel's hull insurance. This means that loss of time resulting from strikes is not covered, but shipowners have the possibility of additionally arranging a strike insurance.

12.8 Damages and pre-termination of charter

A difficult situation for the time charterer is when the chartered vessel turns out to be of an unacceptable standard. If the ship runs into various kinds of technical difficulties and breakdowns, or for other reasons is often hindered during its service, the charterer can, to a certain degree, seek compensation under the off-hire clause, but consequential damages and costs are usually not covered. If the vessel is in an unusually bad condition, it may be difficult or even impossible for the time charterer to appropriately use it in his service.

A good way for time charterers to protect themselves in this respect is to request for a *performance guarantee* from the owners' side in the charterparty. However, it can be difficult to draft such a security, as a good performance of the vessel includes not only the various technical aspects, but also the maintenance and manning aspects, as well as the owners', master's, officers' and crew's capability and willingness to offer the best possible service.

Nevertheless, the main problem with the performance guarantees is that the owners would try not to accept such an obligation. A performance guarantee gives the charterers sufficient protection, while at the same time provides them with an option to cancel the charterparty if the vessel turns out to be below the agreed operating standard. Such option to cancel is not acceptable by owners and their bankers.

Considering the matter of vessel's bad performance, the questions and problems which arise for time charterers when they intend to claim damages (not only off-hire) and when they wish to terminate the charter before the flat period expires, are too complex to discuss in detail in this book. Only a few of the different legal bases that may be used as charterers' arguments of asserting vessel's bad performance will be mentioned below:

- Misdescription of the ship (i.e. the vessel is not in accordance with the description given by the owners during negotiations and in the charterparty).
- The vessel is not kept and maintained in accordance with the initial description.
- The ship is not delivered and maintained in a seaworthy condition as stated or implied in the charterparty.
- The vessel is not manned with master, officers and crew formally and practically competent to handle her, the equipment on board and the cargo.

12.9 Routines and allocation of costs

The charterers' and the owners' respective tasks and costs under a time charter agreement have been discussed in various parts above (see, for example, sections 7.3.2 and 7.6). In this section a greater emphasis will be given to some of the relevant charterparty clauses.

12.9.1 Directions and instructions to the vessel

All time charterparties have "*employment clauses*" of the following type (see appendix 6, *NYPE 2015, clause 8 "performance of voyages"*):

> "*(a) Subject to Clause 38 (Slow Steaming) the Master shall perform the voyages with due despatch and shall render all customary assistance with the Vessel's crew. The Master shall be conversant with the English*

> *language and (although appointed by the Owners) shall be under the orders and directions of the Charterers as regards employment and agency; and the Charterers shall perform all cargo handling, including but not limited to loading, stowing, trimming, lashing, securing, dunnaging, unlashing, discharging, and tallying, at their risk and expense, under the supervision of the Master.*
>
> (b) *If the Charterers shall have reasonable cause to be dissatisfied with the conduct of the Master or officers, the Owners shall, on receiving particulars of the complaint, investigate the same, and, if necessary, make a change in appointments".*

Since it is the time charterers who use the vessel commercially, the master will receive all his instructions and directions concerning the vessel's *employment* from them and not from the owners. The master should keep full and correct *logs* of the voyages, as requested by the time charterers or their agents. The master should furnish charterers, when required to do so, with copies of log-books, port sheets, weather reports and reports about the ship's speed and bunker consumption, etc. All these documents are important for the time charterers, both for their relationship with sub-charterers, shippers and receivers, as well as for their relationship with the owners.

12.9.2 Master's position

The master has a key position under a time charter, since he has to follow the instructions of both the owner and the time charterer. He represents two opposite parties and has to look after the interests of both of them.

Although the master receives ship's employment instructions from the time charterers and should comply with them, he need not necessarily follow the orders and instructions in every situation. The master has a responsibility for the safety of the crew and the vessel, while he also has responsibilities with regard to the cargo owners and other third parties. If, according to the master's well-founded opinion, the time charterers' orders and instructions jeopardise the crew, the ship, the cargo or other persons or property, the master has not only a right, but also an obligation, not to obey the orders. In such a difficult situation, the master must contact not only the time charterers but also the owners, and try to resolve the problem without causing dispute to the involved parties.

If the master does not get clear and acceptable orders from the time charterers and the cargo owners, he should follow the orders from his own owners provided that these are acceptable considering the safety of the crew, vessel, etc. Many time charterparty forms have a special clause about the situation where the time charterers are not satisfied with the master, officers or crew. For instance, such clauses may have a wording as in the one cited above (see *NYPE 2015, clause 8(b) "performance of voyages"*). In other time charterparty forms the corresponding clause is more severe for the owners, obliging them to make changes in the master appointments.

Whether it is expressly stated in the charterparty or not (*express* or *implied* term), the master must prosecute the voyage with the *utmost despatch*. The time charterers pay per time unit and any delay of the vessel usually means less revenue for them. During the sea voyage the master must choose the fastest route without jeopardising the safety of the ship. Before arrival at the port, all documents must be prepared to avoid delay with formalities, while the *master must supervise loading and discharging* in order to get the quickest possible despatch. He should also co-operate with the time charterers and their agents, providing them with all necessary information and assistance.

12.9.3 Customary assistance and overtime

Most time charterparty forms state that the master must give the charterers customary assistance with the vessel's crew. The concept of "*customary assistance*" is often discussed and argued about between charterers and owners.

The general definition of the customary assistance concept is that the master and the crew should give the same assistance to the time charterers as they would give the owners if they were trading for their account. This means that the crew, without extra charge to the time charterers, should carry out the usual cleaning of cargo holds after discharging. They should also undertake the necessary rigging, opening and closing of hatches before, during and after loading and discharging. The master's and owners' obligation to give customary assistance is not limited to such assistance as can be given without overtime compensation for the crew, but the charterers must accept that cleaning, rigging, etc. cannot always be done without delaying the vessel. If the charterers wish to avoid delay by employing extra men from ashore, the cost of doing so will usually be for the charterers' account. In addition, when local rules or customs do not allow the crew to carry out those duties, the cost of stevedores or extra labour will be for the charterers' account.

During the voyage the master and the crew should, without extra cost to the charterers, keep control over the cargo and, if necessary, make additional lashing or securing. However, the charterers cannot normally claim that the crew, without additional payment, should arrange for the shifting and restowing of large quantities of cargo.

In time chartering, for practical reasons, owners and charterers sometimes make more detailed agreements about the cleaning of holds, specifying for instance that all cleaning of holds should be for charterers' account and carried out by extra men from ashore if the ballast voyage is shorter than X days. On longer ballast voyages the cleaning should be performed by the crew.

Concerning overtime for officers and crew, various methods are used. Sometimes it is stated that the hire includes overtime to officers and crew, whereas other times the charterers may pay an extra lump sum per month for overtime. Both these ways are, for practical reasons, probably better than the alternative method of keeping a special book for recording overtime for time charterers' account, as this will create additional work both for the people on board and for the owners and time charterers in the offices.

12.9.4 Allocation of costs

The owners must place the vessel at the time charterers' disposal and during the charter period provide and pay for manning, insurance, maintenance and other costs relating to the *operational use* of the vessel. On the other hand, the charterers provide and pay for bunkers (*excepting lubricating oil which is typically for the owners' account*), harbour dues, pilotage, costs for cargo handling (loading/discharging) and other costs relating to the *commercial use* of the vessel.

Time charterparties normally contain clauses in which the parties' respective obligations are split. These clauses, often with headings including the words *obligations* and *requirements*, are rather extensive in modern charterparties, compared with similar clauses in old charter forms. It is not possible to comprise in a charterparty all the costs that may arise during the charter period. Therefore, discussions and disputes concerning the responsibility for various expenses are common in time chartering. As regards costs not expressly mentioned in the charterparty, it may, be said as a general rule that all costs which are compulsory in a port are for charterers' account, as they are a direct consequence of charterers instructing the vessel to proceed to the port and the owners cannot avoid them. Concerning other costs which are not compulsory and not clearly related to one of the parties, the question must be discussed case by case. For further reading and comparison among relevant time charterparty clauses, one may refer to *Gentime* (see appendix 4, *part II, extensive clauses 11–16), NYPE 2015* (see appendix 6, *rather short clauses 6–7)* and *Shelltime 4* (see appendix 5, *rather short clauses 6–7)*. In many other forms the corresponding stipulations about obligations and requirements are more spread in the text.

As an example of costs which often lead to disputes, the cost of watchmen and garbage disposal can be mentioned. Agency fees can also quite often give rise to disputes (the principal rule is that they are for the time charterers' account). Most charterers accept that they have to provide owners with a certain basic service from agents without extra cost to the owners. However, if the agency fees can be directly related to something which is for the owners' account, such as manning or maintenance, the charterers are not willing to pay to the same degree. To avoid this problem, the charterers sometimes wish to insert a remark by way of clarification, such as:

> "*Whilst on hire the Charterers to pay for . . . agencies (unless attributable to maintenance and manning of the Vessel or otherwise for the benefit solely of the Vessel, Master, Crew or the Owners). . .*".

12.9.5 Information

In order to achieve better co-operation and planning, the parties in most cases have an obligation to keep each other informed about future schedules for the vessel. The owners need a schedule for the ship in order to be able to better plan the exchange of crew members, the supplying of spare parts etc., while the charterers need for the planning of their operations an owners' schedule for drydocking and other necessary maintenance for the vessel.

12.10 Cargo liability

The question of liability for the cargo has been dealt with in chapter 6.

In time chartering, as in voyage chartering, the charterers and owners can allocate the liability for cargo as they wish, but as liability under a bill of lading is also involved, the situation is sometimes complex from a legal standpoint. Cargo owners usually claim under the bill of lading and the first question is whether the owners, the time charterers, or both, are liable to the cargo owners. A second question is how the liability should ultimately be allocated between the time charterers and the owners.

12.10.1 Liability to cargo owners

Cargo liability is a charterer's major area of risk in time charters. In respect of liability for loss of or damage to cargo, charterer may, depending on the contract terms and the applicable laws, be considered as the legal "carrier" of the cargo. The charterer faces liability against cargo interest in two distinct ways. First, he may be found directly liable to the cargo owner, because he has issued his own bill of lading, or because under the relevant law (which will depend on where the accident occurred, or where the vessel trades, or the bill of lading terms), he may be determined by the courts to be the "carrier" under the bill of lading. Secondly, the charterer may be indirectly liable for damage to cargo, because he shall have to indemnify the shipowner or the disponent owner or his sub-charterer under either a charter contract or a booking note. Typically, time charterers may be called to indemnify owners under the charter for cargo damage caused by bad stowage or defective lashing or securing carried out by the charterer's stevedores (note also that voyage charterers bear a similar risk when they charter on FIOS terms). On the other hand, even if a charterer has a complete right of indemnity in respect of cargo damage, either against the shipowner or the disponent owner or the sub-charterer, he remains exposed if he cannot make a recovery because of insolvency of the other party, or inability to enforce his claim.[6]

In general, if charterers issue their own bill of lading forms, the contract of carriage will normally be between the charterers and the shipper. In that case, it must be ensured that the terms printed on the bill of lading make clear who the carrier is. On the contrary, if a time-chartered ship issues a bill of lading by using her owners' own bill of lading form, particularly when not mentioned that the vessel is time-chartered, then the contract of carriage may be deemed to be between the owners and the shipper.

Some older bill of lading forms used to contain an "*identity of carrier*" or a "*demise*" clause seeking to identify the shipowner as the carrier in the bill of lading.

---

6 West of England *Charterer's Risks and Liabilities* (www.westpandi.com, accessed 25 May 2017).

An identity of carrier provision may have the following or similar wording (*Conlinebill 1978, clause 17 "identity of carrier"*):

> *"The Contract evidenced by this Bill of Lading is between the Merchant and the Owner of the vessel named herein (or substitute) and it is therefore agreed that said Shipowner only shall be liable for any damage or loss due to any breach or non-performance of any obligation arising out of the contract of carriage, whether or not relating to the vessel's seaworthiness. If, despite the foregoing, it is adjudged that any other is the Carrier and/or bailee of the goods shipped hereunder, all limitations of, and exonerations from, liability provided for by law or by this Bill of Lading shall be available to such other.*
>
> *It is further understood and agreed that as the Line, Company or Agent who has executed this Bill of Lading for and on behalf of the Master is not a principal in the transaction, said Line, Company or Agent shall not be under any liability arising out of the contract of carriage, nor as Carrier nor bailee of the goods".*

Furthermore, demise clauses state that if the legal "carrier" of the bill of lading is not the actual owner or the demise charterer of the vessel, he merely acts as agent for the vessel owner and has no liability at all as a carrier, though he may have issued the bill of lading. A *demise clause* follows this wording or similar:

> *"If the ship is not owned or chartered by demise to the company or line by whom this bill of lading is issued, the bill of lading shall take effect as a contract with the owner or demise charterer as the case may be as principal made through the agency of the said company or line who act as agents only and shall be under no personal liability whatsoever in respect thereof".*

According to such clauses, the liability for cargo under the bill of lading rests on the owners of the vessel (the *performing carrier*) and not on the time charterers (the *contractual carrier*). It must be said that such clauses have been considered invalid under many legal jurisdictions (e.g. Canada, Germany), thus the charterer may be finally found liable. However, under English law the clauses are basically considered enforceable. Besides, under the Hague/Hague-Visby Rules it has been argued that these clauses are unenforceable constituting non-responsibility clauses, which are outlawed by the Rules. Under the Hamburg Rules, both the contracting carrier and actual (performing) carrier have responsibility under the Rules. Demise and identity of carrier clauses may therefore be expressly in derogation of the Hamburg Rules system and thus being unenforceable. Moreover, since 1994 UCP 500 (art. 23(a)) has established a requirement that the apparent carrier must be clearly identified on the face of a bill of lading, so by accepting a demise or identity of carrier clause, a shipper could in some circumstances end up in breach of letter of credit requirements. This is a further reason for seeking to avoid the inclusion of such clauses. However, a "contractual carrier" who seeks to include such clauses in bill of lading terms may be best avoided altogether, as this may indicate an attempt to secure nil liability for any of its actions.[7]

---

7 Freight Transport Association *Demise and Identity of Carrier Clauses* (www.fta.co.uk, accessed 25 May 2017).

Although the time charterers may legally be able to reject liability for cargo claims under the bill of lading by reference to the identity of carrier or the demise clause, they quite often handle the claims as if they were liable to the cargo owners. Especially when the time charterers are large operators and use their own bill of lading forms (e.g. in the liner business), they want to maintain good relations with the cargo owners and excellent reputation within the market, therefore they settle cargo claims as if the time chartered ship was their own.

These clauses are nowadays considered rather outdated, confusing and controversial. Therefore, most reputable liner operators have ceased including them in their bill of lading terms. Modern standard bills of lading are also aligned to this direction, thus, for example, construction of *Conlinebill 2000* and *Conlinebill 2016* (see appendix 14) is now based on the principle that the carriers' name and principal place of business shall only be inserted in a specific box on the first page of the document, denoting clearly who the carrier is without causing misinterpretation.

It has become clear that liability against cargo depends mostly on who the carrier is. To conclude, therefore, it would be helpful if we investigated how this matter is defined by the international cargo conventions, according to an enlightening analysis by Hill Dickinson.[8] As per the *Hague/Hague-Visby Rules (art. I(a))*, the carrier is the *"owner or charterer who enters into contract of carriage with a shipper"*. The *Hamburg Rules (art. 1.1, 10 and 11)* determine that the carrier is *"any person by whom or in whose name a contract of carriage has been concluded with a shipper, covering both the 'actual' and the 'contractual' carrier"*. Finally, in the *Rotterdam Rules (art. 1)* the carrier is *"a person that enters into a contract of carriage with a shipper, but obligations extend to 'performing parties' acting at the carrier's request or under the carrier's supervision or control"*.

12.10.2 *Allocation of cargo liability between owners and charterers*

As already mentioned, charterers and owners are free to make what allocation of cargo liability they wish under the charterparty. Some printed charter forms, such as for instance the Baltime, relieve more or less owners of liability. According to *Baltime 1939 (revision 2001, part of clause 12 "responsibility and exemption")*, the owners are liable for loss or damage to cargo on board only if the loss or damage *"has been caused by want of due diligence on the part of the owners or their manager in making the vessel seaworthy and fitted for the voyage or any other personal act or omission or default of the owners or their manager"*.

Sometimes the charterparties contain a *paramount clause* which brings the application of the Hague Rules or the Hague-Visby Rules in the charter (see sections 6.6.2, 6.6.3 and 10.6). This issue is made even more complicated when the paramount clause is inserted in a time charterparty.

In order to avoid costly and protracted litigation between owners and charterers in finding fault for cargo claims, several P&I Clubs forming the *International*

---

8 Hill Dickinson *Cargo Conventions: Comparing Hague, Hague-Visby, Hamburg and Rotterdam Rules* (p. 5).

Group of P&I Clubs (IG) have agreed a special procedure for the simple and fair apportionment of liability for cargo under *NYPE* or *Asbatime* time charterparties. The current version of the agreement is officially named *"The Inter-Club NYPE 1996 Agreement (as amended 1 September 2011)"*, but in short it is usually called *"The Inter-Club Agreement (ICA)"* or *"The Produce Formula"*. The Inter-Club Agreement first came into force in 1970, then it was subsequently revised in 1984, 1996 and 2011. The "Produce Formula" contains the following allocation of cargo liability under a time charterparty or contracts of carriage authorised under such charterparty, as seen in Table 12.1.[9]

Unless the standard *clause 27* of *NYPE 2015* is amended (see appendix 6, *NYPE 2015, clause 27 "cargo claims"*), the latest (2011) version of the ICA

Table 12.1 Allocation of Cargo Liability under Inter-Club NYPE Agreement 1996 (as amended September 2011)

ICA Clause	Cause of Cargo Claim	Apportionment
8(a)	Claims in fact arising out of seaworthiness and/or error or fault in navigation or management of the vessel	100% Owners
	save where the Owner proves that the unseaworthiness was caused by the loading, stowage, lashing, discharge or other handling of the cargo, in which case the claim shall be apportioned under sub-clause (b).	
8(b)	Claims in fact arising out of the loading, stowage, lashing, discharge, storage or other handling of cargo	100% Charterers
	unless the words *"and responsibility"* are added in clause 8(a) of NYPE '93 / NYPE 2015 (see appendix 6) or there is a similar amendment making the Master responsible for cargo handling in which case	50% Charterers / 50% Owners
	save where the Charterer proves that the failure properly to load, stow, lash, discharge or handle the cargo was caused by the unseaworthiness of the vessel in which case	100% Owners
8(c)	Subject to (a) and (b) above, claims for shortage or overcarriage	50% Charterers / 50% Owners
	unless there is clear and irrefutable evidence that the claim arose out of pilferage or act or neglect by one or the other (including their servants or sub-contractors) in which case	100% to the party whose act or neglect gave rise to the claim
8(d)	All other cargo claims whatsoever (including claims for delay to cargo)	50% Charterers / 50% Owners
	unless there is clear and irrefutable evidence that the claim arose out of the act or neglect of the one or the other (including their servants or sub-contractors) in which case	100% to the party whose act or neglect gave rise to the claim

9 UK P&I Club (2011) *Inter-Club Agreement (as amended 1 September 2011)* (www.ukpandi. com, accessed 25 August 2011); Hosking, B. and Furmston, O. (2016) *The Inter-Club Agreement* (The Standard Club Ltd, www.standard-club.com).

will be automatically incorporated into the *NYPE 2015* form, without the need for any additional or adjusted wording.[10] However, the ICA is not limited to just the NYPE and Asbatime forms, but it can be incorporated into any other time charterparty form (for example, the Produce Formula is often used between the parties when a paramount clause has been inserted in the Baltime form). Indeed, parties are free to incorporate the ICA into any contract, but care should be taken when doing, so as there may be a greater chance of inconsistencies between the ICA provisions and the subject charterparty wording. The ICA can also be incorporated in part. However, this is not recommended as best practice. If attempts are made to incorporate the ICA, clear wording should be used as to the exact extent of the incorporation. The apportionment of liability for cargo is important and, especially when the time charter agreement is for a long period, the shipowners should be sure to take legal advice from their P&I Clubs.

12.11 Damage to the vessel

During the charter period, the vessel is exposed to *wear and tear* and certain *risks of damage*. Both wear and tear and damage may cause considerable maintenance and repair expenditure. Therefore, it is important to make the allocation of liability in this respect as clear as possible. It has already been mentioned that the owners should insure the ship and maintain her in a thoroughly efficient state in hull and machinery during the charter period. In the redelivery clause it is usually stated that the charterers have to redeliver the ship "*in the same good order and condition as when delivered under the charter (fair wear and tear excepted)*". Sometimes, the charterparty contains also a clause expressly stipulating under what conditions the charterers shall be liable for damage to the ship, but in most cases the answer must be found in other clauses and by reference to the applicable law.

12.11.1 Vessel's damage from bad weather, collision and grounding

Shipowners normally have little chance of obtaining compensation from the charterers for damage caused to the vessel by bad weather, collision, grounding or similar. Only if the shipowners can prove that the charterers' breach of contract or negligence has caused the damage, may they have a chance of receiving compensation. Such a practical example is where time charterers have directed the vessel to an unsafe place or port and this has caused severe problems to the vessel.

12.11.2 Vessel's damage from fuel oil

Considerable disputes may arise from the fact that bunkering cost is borne by the charterers in a time charter, whereas owners are responsible for keeping the operating performance of the vessel on the agreed and acceptable standards.

---

10 Hosking, B. and Furmston, O. (2016) *The Inter-Club Agreement* (The Standard Club Ltd, www.standard-club.com).

Past increases in fuel oil prices have created a side market for fuel oil of poorer quality. Traditionally, charterparties used to describe with only a few words what kind of fuel oil should be supplied to the vessel. As a result of cases with bad quality fuel oil, many charterparties today have a more precise description of the fuel oil to be used. For instance, reference may be made to *Gentime* (see appendix 4, *part II, clause 6 "bunkers" and clause 13(b) "charterers' obligations – bunker fuel"*) or *NYPE* 2015 (see appendix 6, meticulous and extensive *clause 9 "bunkers"*). A specific quote about bunker quality and charterers' liability for loss or damage caused by supply of unsuitable fuel is dealt with in *NYPE 2015, clause 9(d) "bunker quality and liability"*, reading as follows:

> *"(i) The Charterers shall supply bunkers of the agreed specifications and grades: (text to be entered). The bunkers shall be of a stable and homogeneous nature and suitable for burning in the Vessel's engines and/or auxiliaries and, unless otherwise agreed in writing, shall comply with the International Organization for Standardization (ISO) standard 8217:2012 or any subsequent amendments thereof. If ISO 8217:2012 is not available then the Charterers shall supply bunkers which comply with the latest ISO 8217 standard available at the port or place of bunkering.*
>
> *(ii) The Charterers shall be liable for any loss or damage to the Owners or the Vessel caused by the supply of unsuitable fuels and/or fuels which do not comply with the specifications and/or grades set out in Sub-clause (d)(i) above, including the off-loading of unsuitable fuels and the supply of fresh fuels to the Vessel. The Owners shall not be held liable for any reduction in the Vessel's speed performance and/or increased bunker consumption nor for any time lost and any other consequences arising as a result of such supply".*

12.11.3 Vessel's damage from cargo

If the ship has been damaged by the cargo, the owners can seek compensation from the charterers in two ways. First, the charterers may be held responsible if they have shipped a cargo which is generally *"dangerous"* or which is not permitted under the charter agreement. As mentioned above (section 12.4), time charterparties usually have a clause excluding a number of specified cargo types and all cargoes likely to be injurious to the ship. Secondly, the owner may seek compensation from charterers when the cargo has been loaded, stowed or secured insufficiently and the vessel is damaged thereby. This situation is usually more complicated, as the master and officers normally supervise the loading and securing of the cargo. It is difficult to find the borderline between the charterers' and owners' liability in this respect. However, the tendency seems to be for charterers to be held liable, unless there is obvious negligence on the part of the master or officers.

12.11.4 Vessel's damage from other causes

The most common type of other damage to the ship is that caused by stevedores. In this respect, the extent of the charterers' liability should be defined in the charterparty, while the applicable law will provide additional rules. Time charterparties quite often contain special clauses stating under what circumstances the charterers are liable for vessel's damage caused by stevedores and these provisions are usually very harsh for owners. For instance, it is not unusual to find clauses which dictate that the charterers will be liable for stevedore damages, only if the master protests by informing the charterers immediately when the damage occurs, while obtaining also from the stevedores a written statement that they accept liability for the damage. A *stevedore damage* may be discovered weeks or perhaps months after it occurred and, as it is more or less impossible to get an acceptance of responsibility from stevedoring companies, such a clause is hard for the owners to accept.

Nevertheless, the master must assist the charterers in collecting evidence to support their claim against the stevedores. Such a requirement for some kind of action and contribution on the part of the master should be included in the charterparty. The following wording is sourced from *NYPE 2015, part of clause 37 "stevedore damage"* (see appendix 6):

> "*Notwithstanding anything contained herein to the contrary, the Charterers shall pay for any and all damage to the Vessel caused by stevedores provided the Master has notified the Charterers and/or their agents in writing within twenty-four (24) hours of the occurrence but in case of hidden damage latest when the damage could have been discovered by the exercise of due diligence. Such notice to describe the damage and to invite Charterers to appoint a surveyor to assess the extent of such damage*".

The master and the officers on board must supervise the loading, stowing, trimming and discharging, in order to ensure that any damaging material or method is avoided. If the stevedores do not follow the instructions they get from the master or the officers, both the owners and the time charterers should be informed immediately. In many cases, the local representatives for underwriters and P&I Clubs can be of assistance.

The vessel may also be damaged by pilots, tugs etc. during the vessel's approach to, or departure from, the port. Although pilots and tugs are employed and paid for by the charterers, such damages will only under special circumstances be considered the charterers' responsibility.

12.11.5 Repair of vessel's damage

As mentioned above (sections 12.2.4 and 12.5.7), under many time charterparty forms it is agreed that the vessel should be redelivered in the same good order and condition as when delivered. This does not mean that the charterers are prevented from redelivering her before any damage has been repaired for their account. In normal conditions the owners cannot refuse to take redelivery of a damaged vessel. However, if the charterers are liable for the damage and the repairs delay the ship, the owners can instead submit a claim for that cost and loss of time against the charterers.

12.12 Protective clauses

Modern time charterparties often include various protective clauses. For example, *Gentime* (see appendix 4, *part II, clause 17(b) "protective clauses"*) provides that:

> *"The Charterers warrant that Contracts of Carriage issued in respect of cargo under this Charter Party shall incorporate the clauses set out in Appendix A".*

The protective clauses listed in Appendix A of Gentime are the war risk clause *"Voywar 1993"*, the *"Paramount Clause"*, the *"General Average"* clause, the *"Himalaya Clause"*, the *"New Jason Clause"* and the *"Both-to-Blame Collision Clause"* (see also chapter 10 for analysis of these clauses).

The intention with the "protective clauses" is to protect the owners by obliging charterers to insert certain clauses in underlying charterparties, bills of lading, sea waybills or similar types of contracts. In practice, the charterers seldom check that these clauses are included in the underlying documents. Neither are owners or their masters normally concerned about the printed texts of these contracts. However, if the owners suffer as a result of charterers' failure to insert any of the stipulated clauses, the charterers can be forced to compensate the owners for any economic loss resulting from the failure.

CHAPTER 13

Bareboat charter and contract of affreightment

This chapter looks at two forms of chartering, not commonly found in the market as voyage and time charters do, but nevertheless very challenging alternatives; the bareboat charter and the contract of affreightment (CoA). Bareboat – a form of period charter – is an option of high risk to the shipowner, as the vessel is put at the disposal of the charterer who takes over the possession and the complete control of it. The crucial role of the vessel under a bareboat is spotted and the allocation of duties, obligations, rights and costs is examined in respect with critical topics, e.g. vessel's commercial operation, navigation, delivery and redelivery, manning, insurances, maintenance and repair, cargo handling, cargo liability, hire payment, lien and indemnity, claims against third parties, etc. A CoA, on the other hand, is the most noteworthy of hybrid charters (combining elements of voyage and time charter), where the cargo and the time – but not a specific vessel – play the foremost role. Analysis follows a similar pattern, focusing on the structure and benefits of such a contract, as well as on critical subjects, peculiarities and charterparty clauses about the period, the cargo, the vessels, the shipments, the nominations, the charterparty construction and the role of shipbrokers.

13.1 Bareboat charter

13.1.1 Definition

This form of chartering is rarely encountered in the market compared with voyage or time charters. A *bareboat or demise charter*[1] is a type of period charter, where the shipowner charters his ship unmanned and without supplies to the charterer for a long time (even lasting for the entire economic life of the ship). In return, the shipowner receives the agreed daily hire from the charterer. On the other side, the charterer plays more the role of the shipowner during the charter period than that of the typical charterer as has been described so far.

This type of contract is not technically a contract of carriage, but it rather resembles to a long-term lease of the ship from the owner to the charterer, as long as it passes to the charterer the possession of the ship – but not the ownership – together with the management, the operation, the control, the manning, the insurance, the maintenance, the employment and the navigation of the ship.

---

1 Giziakis, K., Papadopoulos, A. and Plomaritou, E. (2010) *Chartering* (Athens, Stamoulis Publications, 3rd edition, in Greek, pp. 595–609); Plomaritou, E. (2014) "A Review of Shipowner's & Charterer's Obligations in Various Types of Charter" *Journal of Shipping & Ocean Engineering* Vol. 4, Issue 11–12, pp. 307–321.

While in the typical time charter the shipowner retains control over the operation of his ship, the bareboat charterer replaces the shipowner and for the duration of the charter he takes full control of the ship. For this reason, "bareboat charterer" is also called "*disponent owner*" or "*quasi-owner*". Thus, the vessel is put at the disposal of the charterer who takes over almost all of the owner's functions (i.e. commercial, operational and technical responsibility), except for the payment of capital costs. The relevant term of the charterparty states that "*the Vessel shall be in the full possession and at the absolute disposal for all purposes of the Charterers and under their complete control in every respect*" (see appendix 8, *Barecon 2001, part II, clause 10(a)(i) "maintenance and operation – maintenance and repairs"*).

The bareboat charter had earlier been a comparatively unusual type of charter, but with changing trading and investment patterns in the last decades, it has become more common nowadays. In modern forms of bareboat, the "owner" of the charter undertakes to find bank financing for a newbuilding or a second-hand ship. At the same time, it secures a bareboat charter with a "charterer" (ship manager), assuming that he will be able to repay the bank loan from the collected hire of the bareboat charter. On the other hand, the charterer is usually a large and experienced shipping company (e.g. a liner operator or an oil company), which does not wish to bear the cost and the risk of investment or burden its balance sheet with assets and debt, while at the same time it needs additional tonnage for a certain period and under its full control to meet its transport needs. It is possible to agree that at the end of the charter the ship will return to the full control of the shipowner or will be bought at an agreed price by the charterer *(hire – purchase agreement)*. Sometimes, a second-hand sale has been disguised as a bareboat charter with an "*option to buy*" in order that taxation can be avoided.

Bareboat charter usually covers a certain period of time, sometimes a very long one. It is often hinged to a ship management agreement. In respect to bareboat charterparties, the most popular one is BIMCO's standard form *Barecon 2001* (see appendix 8). It is built up by five parts, numbered I to V whereof:

- Part I is the box-part,
- Part II includes the basic clauses,
- Part III is optional and comprises provisions to apply for newbuilding vessels only,
- Part IV is optional and comprises provisions to apply for a hire/purchase agreement only, and
- Part V is optional and comprises provisions to apply for vessels registered in a bareboat charter registry.

Various factors, such as maritime policies applied, may lead to a growing use of bareboat in spite of several different problems that may arise with respect to the nationality of the ship, manning rules, etc.

Clauses of great significance are those about the description of the vessel, handling of the hire period, delivery and redelivery of the vessel, hire amount, payment and security, handling of ship's maintenance.

Payment of the hire shall be made in advance and the principal rule is – though exceptions always exist – that the owners shall be entitled to withdraw the vessel from the service and terminate the charter if the charterers fail to pay in accordance with the charter agreement.

The charterers shall during the charter period maintain the vessel in good condition and keep the vessels' class and certifications updated. At redelivery, the vessel shall be in the same good condition as on delivery, fair wear and tear (not affecting class) excepted. During the main part of a long-term bareboat charter this is normally not a problem, as it is in both parties' interest that the vessel is kept in good condition. But, at the end of a charter period, in an agreement not giving the charterers a right to purchase the vessel, or to take benefit of the vessel's overvalue, the charterers may be tempted to stop or reduce the maintenance in order to save costs. Bareboat charter forms usually have provisions giving the owners full access to all documents relevant for the maintenance of the vessel, also permitting owners to inspect the vessel at any time without hindering the commercial use of the vessel.

Bareboat charter forms usually provide two alternatives for the insurance and repairs of the vessel. In *Barecon 2001* (see appendix 8, *part II, clause 13 "insurance and repairs" and clause 14 "insurance, repairs and classification"*), there are two mutually excluded options; the first (*clause 13*) states that insurance and repairs shall be arranged and paid by the charterers, whereas the second one (*clause 14*) puts the insurance responsibility on the owners (while the repairs remain to the charterer).

With the brief description so far, it is clear that the benefit of a bareboat charter is reciprocal. On the one hand, the shipowners can be individuals, with or without experience in shipping, who are able to invest in a ship without assuming responsibility for the organisation and management of day-to-day operations. On the other hand, the charterers are experienced shipping operators or large organisations that take over the ship management without being forced to invest considerable amounts of capital.

Finally, it should be noted that the bareboat charterer is regarded as the carrier for the purpose of the "Hague-Visby Rules", he becomes liable against a possible damage to the cargo for bills of lading signed by the master, while he is entitled to the benefits of possible salvage earnings. On the contrary, the shipowner cannot normally exercise a right for lien on the cargo, since he does not have the vessel's possession, unless this has been expressly agreed in the charterparty.

13.1.2 Vessel

13.1.2.1 Vessel's description
During the charter negotiations of a bareboat, the shipowner is obliged to give accurate information about his ship to the charterer, so that the latter can have a clear picture of the commercial value of the ship. Sometimes, an inspection of the ship, its certificates, logbooks and other documents takes place by the charterer.

In this charter, the description of the ship is of greater importance compared to a voyage or time charter. This is due to the fact that in a bareboat charter the ship remains at charterer's disposal for a long time (usually many years), so that the charterer does not know in advance what cargoes will be carried or which ports will be approached during the charter. Thus, the shipowner is required to provide the charterer with details about the ship's cargo carrying capacity, the vessel's class, insurance, speed, fuel consumption, etc.

In case of provision of inaccurate information, the cause of the "misrepresentation" and the shipowner's intention should be sought. Intentional "misrepresentation" gives the right to the charterer to cancel the charterparty, while a non-deliberate wrong description of the ship entitles the charterer to claim damages.

13.1.2.2 Vessel's delivery

The shipowner is under an obligation to deliver a seaworthy vessel, in accordance with the charterparty requirements, at the agreed place of delivery and at the specified time. Once the ship is delivered to the charterer, the latter becomes the "disponent owner" of the ship and acquires its commercial, operational and technical responsibility.

If the ship arrives at delivery port before the specified time of the charterparty, the charterer is not obliged to take it sooner. If the ship is delivered later than the specified time or delivered to a port other than the agreed one, then the charterer has the right to cancel the contract.

In the case of a *latent defect* which comes up during the period between the date of vessel's delivery and 12 months thereafter, the shipowner is held responsible for the repair of the damage (see appendix 8, *Barecon 2001, part II, part of clause 3(c) "delivery"*). Problems arise in the event that the defect appears after the expiration of the 12-month period, when the charterer is required to repair the damage, even if he proves that the vessel's defect was latent at the date of delivery. The term "latent defect" means "an inherent defect of the ship which is not, or should not have been, known to the shipowner at delivery".

Extensive ship inspections take place on the date of delivery. Inspections are carried out by surveyors jointly appointed by the parties (joint on-hire surveys). Their extent is greater than that of ships' inspections during time charters.

13.1.2.3 Vessel's seaworthiness and condition

The shipowner is required to deliver the ship to the charterer in a seaworthy condition and in accordance with the charterparty agreement. If the ship is unseaworthy, that is, it has a feature which endangers the ship, the crew or the cargo, causes delays on the ship or makes it practically impossible to navigate, load or unload, then the charterer is entitled to claim damages. The shipowner's obligation to provide a seaworthy vessel at delivery is not absolute under a bareboat charter. It is sufficient for the shipowner to show reasonable care to deliver a seaworthy ship.

The vessel's condition at delivery, during the charter and on redelivery is of great importance in a bareboat charter. Although the charterer is responsible for the ship's maintenance during the charter, the shipowner is entitled to inspect the condition of the ship at any time, after a reasonable and timely notice.[2] Under a relative charterparty term (see appendix 8, *Barecon 2001, part II, clause 8 "inspection"*), the charterer has the right to request an inspection of the ship:

- In order to verify its condition, as well as its state of maintenance and repair by the charterer. The shipowner shall bear the cost of the drydock, unless it is proved that necessary repairs or maintenance are required to bring the ship back to the appropriate condition.
- If the charterer has not made drydocks of the ship at regular intervals, as stipulated in the charter contract. Here, the charterer carries the cost of the docking.
- For commercial purposes, provided that the current commercial employment of the ship is not hindered. The costs are borne by the shipowner in this case.

Under any circumstances, the time for inspection and repair is usually borne by the charterer, i.e. the ship remains "on hire".

13.1.2.4 Vessel's redelivery

Under a bareboat charterparty, it is the charterer's obligation to redeliver the ship to the owner at the agreed time, at the specified place and in the same good order and condition as when received, wear and tear excepted.

In case of a delayed vessel's redelivery, the reason of the delay will be sought. If no liability may be attributed to any of the parties, then the charterer is relieved of his responsibility and shall pay hire in accordance with the charterparty up to the time of vessel's redelivery. If the reasons for the delay are due to the charterer, then he is obliged to pay hire in accordance with the prevailing market rate (provided this is higher than the agreed charterparty hire rate) up to the time of vessel's redelivery.

If the ship is redelivered at a place different than that stipulated in the charterparty, the shipowner is entitled to claim for compensation. In addition, if the ship turns out to be damaged on redelivery, the shipowner is entitled to claim the cost of repairs and any possible loss of profit during repairs.

13.1.3 Commercial operation and management of vessel

The commercial employment, the commercial operation and the management of the ship are at charterer's hands in a bareboat charter. The charterer is responsible for the planning, organisation and control of the voyages to be executed by the ship. It is also the responsibility of the charterer to choose the cargoes to be carried, as well as the trading areas and the ports of call.

---

2 Todd, P. (2015) *Principles of the Carriage of Goods by Sea* (New York, Routledge, p. 153).

13.1.4 Navigation

The charterer is responsible for the safe navigation of the ship. In a bareboat charter, the navigation instructions are given by the charterer, and the master is required to comply. In addition, the charterer is responsible for the actions or omissions of the master and the crew against the shippers, recipients or any other third parties.

In case that a bareboat vessel causes a collision, the charterer becomes liable. Moreover, the charterer is always under an obligation to nominate safe ports of call for the ship, otherwise he will be responsible for repairing any damage caused from the ship's approach to unsafe ports.

13.1.5 Manning

In the bareboat charter, the crew is designated and paid by the charterer. The master and the crew are obliged to comply with the charterers' instructions regarding vessel's navigation, employment and agency. The manning of the ship depends on the requirements and rules of the flag the ship carries. The contracting party that recruits and employs the master and the crew on its behalf is the crucial differentiating "test" between a time charter and a bareboat charter. To judge that a charterparty is a "demise charterparty", the responsible party for the manning of the vessel should be the charterer (*Baumwoll Manufactur Von Carl Scheibler v Furness [1893] AC 8*).[3] As a result, under a bareboat charter the master always acts as the agent or servant of the charterer (see appendix 8, *Barecon 2001, part II, clause 10(b) "maintenance and operation – operation of the vessel"*).

13.1.6 Equipment and provisions

Throughout the bareboat charter, the charterer is responsible for providing all necessary equipment and supplies to the ship, so that the ship remains seaworthy and meets the transport requirements. Thus, the costs and the responsibility for supplying the vessel with bunkers, lubricants, water, food and other supplies are borne by the charterer. Moreover, it is a charterer's obligation to replace the ship's damaged or worn equipment (see appendix 8, *Barecon 2001, part II, clause 10(b) "maintenance and operation – operation of the vessel" and clause 10(f) "maintenance and operation – use of the vessel's outfit, equipment and appliances"*).

13.1.7 Insurances

Ship insurance is a matter of great importance in bareboat charter negotiations. Once the ship's insured value is first determined, the charterer usually bears the cost and liability of the insurance, protecting not only his own interests, but also those of the shipowner and the ship mortgagee (bank).[4]

---

3 Todd, P., Gaskell, N., Clarke, M., Glass, D. and Hughes, A. (1993) *Contracts for the Carriage of Goods* (London, Lloyd's of London Press Ltd., Part A, p. 279).

4 The bareboat charterer normally undertakes the cost of mortgagee's (bank's) insurance, with a special type of insurance called "Mortgagee Interest Insurance (MII)".

In particular, the charterer ought to undertake the following obligations[5]:

- Ensure proper entry and insurance of the ship at a protection & indemnity club (P&I insurance).
- Insure the ship for hull & machinery insurance (H&M), as well as for war risk insurance.
- Pay for premiums and calls.
- Monitor whether all insurance claims of the ship are paid by the insurance companies.
- Care for the renewal of all required insurances.

Bareboat charter forms usually provide two alternatives for the insurance and repairs of the vessel. For example, in *Barecon 2001* (see appendix 8, *part II, clause 13 "insurance and repairs" and clause 14 "insurance, repairs and classification"*), there are two mutually excluded options: the first (*clause 13*) states that insurance and repairs shall be arranged and paid by the charterers, whereas the second (*clause 14*) puts the insurance responsibility on the owners (while the repairs remain to the charterers).

According to the *Barecon 2001* (see appendix 8, *part II, clause 13 "insurance and repairs"*), the following important issues of ship insurance are identified:

- Insurance policies will cover the parties according to the distribution of their interests.
- It is essential that the charterer sends copies of the insurance policies to the shipowner and obtains the shipowner's written permission for these documents, so that the shipowner is always kept up to date and later misconceptions be avoided.
- The charterer or the shipowner, as the case may be, is required to show all the reasonable care in order for the ship to be insured on a complementary basis against various risks, e.g. delays from time-consuming repairs, etc.
- The charterer assumes the responsibility and the cost of repairs for any insured damage, while he is also the person who receives the insurers' compensation against such expenses. However, in the event of total loss of the ship, the compensation is paid by the insurance company to the shipowner, who in turn is obliged to distribute the amount between the charterer and himself according to the distribution of their interests.[6]

Barecon 2001 (see appendix 8, *part II, clause 14 "insurance, repairs and classification"*) provides the shipowner with an alternative option to undertake the

---

5 Bonnick, S. (1988) *Gram on Chartering Documents* (London, Lloyd's of London Press Ltd., 2nd edition, p. 83); Chitty, J.W. (2008) "Bareboat Charters: Can a Shipowner Limit Liability to Third Parties?" *Georgia State University Law Review* Vol. 25, Issue 2, Article 2, p. 498.

6 Todd, P. (2015) *Principles of the Carriage of Goods by Sea* (New York, Routledge, p. 154).

ship's hull & machinery and the war risk insurance (but not P&I insurance). In this case, the hire rate should be adjusted to reflect the additional cost of the shipowner and the cost saving of the charterer. When this alternative is agreed, the shipowner bears the cost and the responsibility of the vessel's insurance, whereas the obligation to carry out repairs always remains with the charterer.

13.1.8 Maintenance and repair

The bareboat charter agreement requires the ship to be properly maintained, to be kept in good condition and achieve the best possible operational performance. In case of defects, deficiencies or damage to the ship, the charterer is obliged to carry out all repairs at his own expense. Further to that, the charterer must always keep the ship in class. If the classification society or any legislation requires modifications or improvements to the ship or its equipment, the cost of which amounting to a percentage of the insured value of the ship (typically 5% of the insured value if the parties do not specify otherwise), then it is agreed that the terms of the charterparty should be renegotiated in arbitration, so that the allocation of these costs to be decided between the contracting parties and a new hire rate amount to be agreed up to the end of the charter (see appendix 8, *Barecon 2001, part II, clause 10(a)(ii) "maintenance and operation – new class and other safety requirements"*).

Shipowners shall have the right, during the charter, to carry out inspections of the ship or its logbooks to check its condition. From a practical point of view, it is not easy for the shipowners to carry out inspections if the ship is not in drydock. However, the charterparties normally provide that the charterer should place the ship in drydock whenever that is requested by the shipowner.

Last but not least, it is to be noted that the shipowner has the right to withdraw the ship from the charter, if the charterer fails to perform the required ship repairs within a reasonable time.

13.1.9 Assignment of charter or sub-demise or sale

Unlike voyage or time charter, a bareboat agreement does not allow the charterer to assign the charter or sub-charter the vessel in a new bareboat charter (*sub-demise*), without the prior written consent of the shipowner. In addition, the shipowner is not permitted to sell the ship during the bareboat charter without the charterer's written consent and subject that the ship's buyer accepts the assignment and continuation of the charter (see appendix 8, *Barecon 2001, part II, clause 22 "assignment, sub-charter and sale"*).

13.1.10 Loading and discharging operation

The charterer is obliged to carry out the loading, stowage and unloading of the cargo at his own expense, under his own and the master's supervision. Loading and stowage must take place in such a way that the cargo does not suffer damages and the ship does not lose its stability. In case of damage, during loading/unloading or stowage, the charterer is responsible for the repair and restoration. The completion of loading procedure requires a smooth co-operation of the charterer and master with agents, stevedores, customs authorities etc. The signing of the bill of lading by the master shall bind the charterer as a carrier in accordance with the Hague-Visby Rules.

In bareboat charter, as well as in all other types of charter, the charterer must ship on board and carry goods that are legal and not dangerous, i.e. do not jeopardise the safety of the ship, the crew and the workers, or do not result in the ship's detention at port.

13.1.11 Delivery of cargo

As already mentioned, in all cases under a bareboat charter the bills of lading are issued on behalf of the charterer, who undertakes the role of the "carrier". The duties of the carrier in any form of charter include the exact description of the cargo loaded on board, the safe transport of goods and the responsibility of delivering them in good condition to the correct consignee against presentation of the bill of lading.

The general rule dictates that the carrier must deliver the cargo to the consignee (the holder of the bill of lading or a consignee's representative) at the agreed port of destination and in the same good condition as received. Under a bareboat charter, in case of damage or loss (partial or total) of the cargo, occurring during the course of individual voyages, the consignee is entitled to claim compensation from the bareboat charterer ("disponent owner" of the vessel).

In the event of a delayed bill of lading at the port of destination, the carrier (bareboat charterer) will be in a difficult position since, if he decides to deliver the goods without the bill of lading being presented, he will be asked for damages when the delivery proves to be wrong.

In case of damage, loss or non-delivery of the cargo, the bareboat charterer is required to prove that he is not liable, or otherwise the consignee of the cargo is entitled to claim damages. In addition, the charterer may be relieved of liability if he proves that the cause of the problem was an exempted risk of the bill of lading or the law governing the cargo transport agreement.

13.1.12 Hire

In a bareboat charter, the parties have absolute freedom to negotiate the hire amount, as well as the method and time of its payment. The hire is usually paid every month in advance, from the time of ship's delivery up to the time of redelivery. *Barecon 2001* (see appendix 8, *part II, clause 11 "hire"*) contains conditions relating to special cases of payment of the hire, such as loss of the ship, the charterer's inability to pay the hire, etc. Under this clause, it is provided that:

- In the event of loss of the ship, the shipowner shall not be entitled to hire payment *"from the date and time when she was lost or last heard of"* and thereafter.

- For any delay in the payment of hire, the shipowner is entitled to claim interest on the hire amount at an annual interest rate agreed in the charterparty.

Further to clause 11, *Barecon 2001* deals with the matter of vessel's withdrawal due to a failure of hire payment in *clause 28(a) "termination – charterers' default"*, providing that:

> "*The Owners shall be entitled to withdraw the Vessel from the service of Charterers and terminate the Charter with immediate effect by written notice to the Charterers if the Charterers fail to pay hire in accordance with Clause 11. However, where there is a failure to make punctual payment of hire due to oversight, negligence, errors or omissions on the part of the Charterers or their bankers, the Owners shall give the Charterers written notice of the number of clear banking days stated in Box 34 (as recognised at the agreed place of payment) in which to rectify the failure, and when so rectified within such number of days following the Owners' notice, the payment shall stand as regular and punctual. Failure by the Charterers to pay hire within the number of days stated in Box 34 of their receiving the Owners' notice as provided herein, shall entitle the Owners to withdraw the Vessel from the service of the Charterers and terminate the Charter without further notice*".

The contrast should be noted against the previous version of the charterparty (*Barecon 89, part II, clause 10(e) "hire"*) which stipulates that:

> "*. . . in default of payment beyond a period of seven running days, the Owners shall have the right to withdraw the Vessel from the service of the Charterers without noting any protest and without interference by any court or any formality whatsoever, and shall, without prejudice to any other claim the Owners may otherwise have against the Charterers under the Charter, be entitled to damages in respect of all costs and losses incurred as a result of the Charterers' default and the ensuing withdrawal of the vessel*".

13.1.13 Lien and indemnity

English common law does not grant to any contracting party the right for lien on the vessel, so that to enforce the other party to perform his duties. However, a specific charterparty clause may grant the charterer such a right for lien on the vessel for amounts paid in advance and not earned from the use of the ship, e.g. as per *Barecon 2001* (see appendix 8, *part II, part of clause 18 "lien"*): "*Charterers to have a lien on the Vessel for all moneys paid in advance and not earned*".

Another term of the bareboat charterparty usually provides that, during the period of the charter, the charterer should not burden the vessel with any additional lien or encumbrance, which would prejudice and take precedence over the shipowner's interests, e.g. "*Charterers will not suffer, nor permit to be continued, any lien or encumbrance incurred by them or their agents, which might have priority over the title and interest of the Owners in the vessel*" (see appendix 8, *Barecon 2001, part II, part of clause 16 "non-lien"*).

The next clause of this charterparty (see appendix 8, *Barecon 2001, part II, part of clause 17 "indemnity"*) stipulates that the charterer must compensate the shipowner "*against any loss, damage or expense incurred by the Owners arising out of or in relation to the operation of the vessel by the Charterers*", or "*against any lien of whatsoever nature arising out of an event occuring during the Charter Period*", as well as "*against all consequences or liabilities arising from signing Bills of Lading or other documents*". Furthermore, if the vessel is *arrested* or *detained* as a consequence of the ship's management by the charterer, the latter is obliged to assume the responsibility and the cost of the ship's release within a reasonable time. On the contrary, if the arrest is due to claims against the shipowner, then he is the one who should act accordingly to release the vessel, assume the responsibility and cost, as well as proceed in compensating the charterer.

In bareboat charter, the master and the crew become *servants* of the charterer and through them the charterer acquires the *ship's possession*. Due to the fact that ship's possession passes to the charterer, English common law does not confer on the shipowner a right for lien on the cargo if bareboat hire is due. However, an express charterparty term may provide that the shipowner is entitled to a right for lien on the cargo or sub-hire or sub-freight of the bareboat charterer, e.g. *"The Owners to have a lien upon all cargoes, sub-hires and sub-freights belonging or due to the Charterers or any sub-charterers and any Bill of Lading freight for all claims under this Charter"* (see appendix 8, Barecon 2001, part II, part of clause 18 *"lien"*).

13.1.14 Claims against third parties

Special reference should be made to the charterer's liability against third parties, for acts or omissions of himself or his servants. The charterer is responsible to restore any damage caused to third parties, as for example to ports, terminals or berths, cargo interests, pollution of the marine environment, personal injury or death, shipwrecks, delays, deviations or collisions caused from ship's negligence, etc. The charterer, under certain circumstances, may be relieved of his liability if the charter agreement includes such relevant exemption clauses.

13.1.15 Salvage and towage

Unlike time charter where the benefit from salvage is shared by both parties, in bareboat chartering the salvage and towage earnings belong solely to the charterer. In addition, the charterer will bear any costs for the recovery of potential damages arising from the vessel's effort to save life or property at sea. However, the shipowner should always be informed accordingly by the charterer.

13.1.16 Cost allocation

As far as ship's cost allocation is concerned in a bareboat charter, the shipowner typically bears the following expenses:

- *Capital costs:* This includes all capital expenditure, such as for example the equity part of the initial investment or the debt servicing (capital repayment and interest payment of loans). The amount of these costs depends on the type of debt financing and on the amount of equity put by the shipowner in the initial investment.

- *Inspection and drydocking costs:* As mentioned (see section 13.1.2.3), during a bareboat charter shipowners have the right to carry out inspections of the vessel and its logbooks, in order to monitor its condition. In that case, the cost of drydocks, surveys or inspections and the possible delays therefrom shall be typically borne by the shipowner. However, the time required "*in respect of inspection, survey or repairs shall be for the Charterers'account and form part of the Charter Period*" (see appendix 8, *Barecon 2001, part II, part of clause 8 "inspection"*), thus it shall count as time "*on hire*". On the other hand, if it is deemed necessary for repairs to take place in order to keep the vessel seaworthy, then the repair and drydock costs will be borne by the charterer. But, if a latent defect is manifested itself on board the ship within an agreed period from the date of vessel's delivery, then the shipowner shall be liable for the cost – but not the time – of repairs of the damage. In *Barecon 2001*, this period is determined to 12 months, unless otherwise agreed by the parties (see appendix 8, *2001, part II, part of clause 3 "delivery"* and *part I, box 32 "latent defects"*).
- Sometimes, it may be agreed that the shipowner will assume the obligation and cost of the *ship's insurance* or will have the right to approve the appointment of the ship's master and officers.

Furthermore, the costs borne by the charterer in a bareboat charter are as follows:

- *Operating or running costs:* All fixed operating costs of the ship are included, such as manning (crewing) costs comprising wages, social welfare, sickness, travel etc., costs for supplies, stores and spares, lubricants and provisions, insurance costs, maintenance and repair costs and administrative expenses.
- *Voyage costs:* This includes all variable costs related with the individual voyages executed under a bareboat charter, such as bunkers cost, port charges, light dues, pilotage dues, anchorage/mooring dues etc.
- *Cargo-handling costs:* All such costs as those related with loading, stowage, trimming, discharging etc. are included in this category.

13.2 Contract of affreightment (CoA)

13.2.1 Definition

As has been already defined in sections 1.1.1 and 7.3.5, a *contract of affreightment (CoA)* is a medium to long-term, hybrid type of charter. The shipowner undertakes to serve charterer's needs by carrying specific quantities of homogeneous cargo, at specific dates of shipments and within an agreed period of time (e.g. four shiploads of iron ore per year), in specific voyages, with no named ship.[7] The charterer usually pays the freight in USD per mt of cargo carried in each executed voyage. CoA is considered a *"hybrid"* form of charter, as combining voyage and time charter elements.

13.2.1.1 Need

It has been explained so far that the traditional voyage charter agreement is designed to serve the situation where one charter agreement refers only to one voyage of the chartered vessel. However, there is often a need for a charter contract which covers several shipments. This may sometimes be arranged by time chartering or alternatively by voyage chartering for consecutive voyages. In both cases the voyages are normally performed with the same vessel and in direct continuation. A somewhat different method is the use of a so-called contract of affreightment (CoA), or sometimes referred to as volume contract. Agreements covering more than one cargo shipment or one vessel's voyage give rise to several questions in addition to those arising from contracts covering one voyage only. Up to this point, the analysis has dealt with three basic "pure" charter types, i.e. voyage charters (see chapter 11), time charters (see chapter 12) and bareboat charters (see section 13.1), as well as with two "hybrid" charter forms, namely consecutive voyage charters (see sections 7.3.4 and 11.12) and trip time charters (see section 12.3.5). Below, focus will be given to the most common and complex of the hybrid charter types; the contract of affreightment. Since the abbreviated term CoA seems to be generally used and recognised worldwide, it will be used throughout the following text.

13.2.1.2 Scope and benefit

The CoA is often a medium to long-term practical solution for both the shipowner and the charterer. It allows greater flexibility for both parties in various respects. When choosing a CoA, the time spent on negotiations for the individual shipments is limited, while the persons and companies involved have a better possibility of co-operating and improving the practical details about loading, carriage and discharging. The necessary administration and planning may also be easier to handle if the same persons and companies are well acquainted with each other. Disturbances and difficulties arising during the first shipment may be fine-tuned in the course of the contract by smooth and efficient co-operation between the parties. Mutual amendments to the written contract may then follow. Personal knowledge between owners' and charterers' respective staffs usually makes it easier to anticipate, prevent and resolve problems. It has to be mentioned that changing market conditions may tempt one of the parties to avoid his contractual duties in a CoA. Nevertheless, this has nothing specific to do with CoAs, as it may happen in any other charter form too.

From a charterer's point of view, a CoA has some valuable advantages, as further presented.

---

7 Gorton, L. and Ihre, R. (1990) *A Practical Guide to Contracts of Affreightment and Hybrid Contracts* (London, Lloyd's of London Press Limited, pp. 3, 4).

For many commodities, transportation and handling costs are a considerable part of their final cost. Transportation may also indirectly be of great importance, as difficulties in carriage may cause shortfalls in necessary components and thereby serious delays in production. For a seller or a buyer of a commodity, problems in transportation can easily cause considerable extra expense in the form of extra storage, extra handling, etc. Furthermore, the cargo owner often calculates and compares transportation costs, including interest for keeping large stocks. From such a logistics point of view, to find a reliable shipowner as counter-party is of primary importance for the charterer, since the steady supply of the raw materials and goods may be particularly important. Depending on the contractual solution chosen, the party responsible for transportation may be held liable even for consequential damages if he fails to arrange transportation as agreed. Considering this, it is advantageous for a charterer, whether he is a seller or a buyer of cargo or someone else who is responsible for transportation, to make sure beforehand that tonnage will be available for the necessary sea transport of the cargo when needed. Among the various ways indicated for a shipper or receiver to arrange sea transportation, a practical and convenient method is to enter into a CoA with a reliable shipowner or ship operator. Particularly for large international industries and trading companies, logistics considerations in the calculation of storage and transport costs have become crucial. Sophisticated planning in production and delivery may reduce the storage costs, but this necessitates timely deliveries by the carrier. The concept of "just in time" in production systems has become increasingly important in the last few decades, thus the reliability of the shipowner is considered fundamental.

Another factor which may be important for a seller or a buyer of cargo is that, by using a CoA, he can avoid fluctuations occurring in the freight market. Therefore, he is able to make more accurate calculations and avoid disastrous cost differences. The same end may be reached via a time charter, but the charterer will then also take on the commercial employment of the vessel, something he may wish to avoid. The risk of strikes and port congestion are two additional parameters considered when selecting the particular charter type and contract.

On the other hand, a CoA offers also considerable advantages to the shipowner, as follows.

A CoA provides economic stability and visibility for the owner. A large fleet operator often selects to enter into a long-term CoA, where his available tonnage may be employed. If the spot market collapses in the future, he will still secure an agreed income, at least as long as the charterer is able to pay. On the contrary, however, where the owner enters into a CoA in a period of low freight rates and the freight market then increases, the result may be economically disastrous for him, since he might then at a later time have been able to find economically better employment for his vessels. Another advantage is that long-term CoAs (like for that matter time charters) will enable the shipowner to obtain better opportunities to finance the acquisition of vessels. It is not unusual that vessels are designed, built and financed against a certain CoA. It is worth noting that the owner (or operator) also has similar advantages to gain when his vessel is employed on a long-term time charter, but with such an arrangement he is less flexible than when his vessels are covered by a CoA.

13.2.1.3 Terminology
Since the most important characteristic of a CoA, compared with other charter forms, is that it is linked more to the cargo volume to be carried and less to the individual vessel, some synonym terms may be found in shipping practice, such as *"cargo contract of affreightment"*, *"cargo contract"*, *"quantity contract"*, *"volume contract"*, etc. The terminology does not seem absolutely clear under English law, where a *"contract of affreightment"*, apart from a specific hybrid charter type, may also be interpreted as meaning a voyage charter or any contract of cargo carriage or any charterparty in general. Similar questions or grey areas may appear in other legal systems too. In general, a distinction is typically upheld between "contracts of carriage" and "contracts of affreightment" in international shipping bibliography. What must be emphasised here is that parties should clarify what exactly they are intending to do when using a particular terminology in the charter contract. For that reason, *"volume contract"* or *"quantity contract"* may sometimes be the preferred terms in chartering and shipbroking practice to describe a CoA charter.

13.2.1.4 Characteristics, terms and examples
The main parameters in a CoA are related to the total cargo quantity covered by the contract, as well as the cargo quantity per voyage/shipment, the programme of shipments, the agreed freight rate in relation to possible fluctuations of the freight market, the vessels (or type of vessels) and the contract period.

In some cases it is possible to set out precisely the respective obligations of the parties by specific figures, such as *"the sale of 102,000 tonnes of wheat"* or *"the carriage of 55,000 MT plus/minus 5 per cent"*. Instead, the parties may often use a less specific language, for example *"not less than 60,000 MT"*, or *"30,000–60,000 MT in buyer's option"*.

A CoA can have different bases to get structured. The following examples illustrate some alternatives:

- an owner undertakes to carry Q tons of grain in total, between port X and port Y, during 2018;
- an owner undertakes to carry all cargo shipped by the charterer from loading port A to the destination B during the period 2018–2022;
- an owner to have the right to carry all crude oil imported by the charterer during 2018 and 2019;
- an owner to have the obligation to carry all vehicles exported by the charterer during the period 2018–2022, while the charterer to guarantee that he will have at least five shipments per year, each consisting of minimum X (quantity) of Y (type) vehicles.

There are obviously several different ways of describing the duties and rights of the parties in a CoA. Volume contracts differ from other charter types insofar as they contain, separately, both a time element and a voyage element. This means a difference as compared with consecutive voyages in that the time factor is determined separately from the voyage element in a CoA, whereas in a consecutive voyage charter a number of voyages take place in direct continuation, one after the other.

The generic nature of the CoA is that there may be a flexibility with respect to the vessels to be used, the ports involved and the cargoes to be carried.[8] It is especially important that both parties do their utmost in order to find the optimal solution (see further section 13.2.5). In a CoA, the time element and the cargo quantity element thus both play a role, but the quantity will have to be weighed against the period involved. The idea is that the charterer and the owner agree that a vessel of specified particulars shall, during a certain period (e.g. six months, 12 months, three years), but not on a consecutive basis, perform a number of voyages with respect to the carriage of a certain quantity (minimum/maximum) of goods of specified nature or goods of specified types, between a number of agreed ports. The voyages should be performed on a *"fairly evenly spread basis"* or words to similar effect, which means that the charterer, unless otherwise agreed, is not entitled to require the owner to carry most of the cargo during a short period of time, e.g. in the beginning or the end of the defined period. This reflects the particularly co-operative nature of this type of contract.

The CoA is usually a contract:

- for the carriage of a specified type and quantity of cargo by vessels of specified characteristics;
- covering at least two but often several shipments;
- running over a certain period (sometimes over several years).

For example, a typical CoA may concern the regular carriage of iron ore from Brazil or Australia to China.

In the CoA it is the cargo rather than the ship which is in focus. The CoA is thereby different from other contracts of carriage, which have their basis in the use of a particular named ship. This difference is important, as a traditional voyage or time charterparty is usually abandoned if the vessel is lost, while a CoA still normally remains in force if the ship intended for the voyage is lost or is otherwise not available for the shipment. This does not mean that the identity and characteristics of the ship are unimportant – they may be important parts of the CoA – but the main obligation on the owner is still to carry the cargo and he is not normally relieved of this obligation if the vessel is lost. The explanation for this is that the owner is usually free to choose the tonnage to execute the CoA, therefore he can rarely claim that he is exempted from his duty to nominate a ship owing to difficulties in arranging tonnage. Even if the vessel which the owner has intended to use for the voyage has become a loss, he still has the opportunity and

---

8 Gorton, L. and Ihre, R. (1990) *A Practical Guide to Contracts of Affreightment and Hybrid Contracts* (London, Lloyd's of London Press Limited, p. 55).

obligation to arrange for another ship of similar type. When the vessel already nominated for the particular voyage is lost, the owner is under an obligation to nominate another vessel.

The number of voyages is another important feature. Although a CoA may theoretically be fixed for one voyage only, one would hardly recognise such contract as a CoA. As a general rule, a CoA covers at least two shipments. On the other hand, a contract can cover several shipments without actually being a CoA. This is the situation when a voyage charterparty is drawn up for consecutive voyages. Such a contract differs from the CoA in three ways. First, the contract for consecutive voyages is linked to a certain vessel, with or without the right or obligation of the owner to substitute. Secondly, the voyages covered by a contract for consecutive voyages are *consecutive*, that is, sequential, one coming immediately after another. This implies that the consecutive voyages will involve the same types of cargo. Thirdly, a contract for consecutive voyages, but not necessarily a CoA, is based on voyage charter terms and conditions (i.e. under a CoA the individual voyages are usually – but not always – covered by a voyage charterparty).

Another characteristic is that the CoA usually runs over a long period. This is not per se an important feature, as the period covered by a CoA is not necessarily longer than other contracts of carriage.

13.2.1.5 Documents

As mentioned (see section 7.4.2 and appendix 10), a number of standard charterparty documents with respect to voyage chartering and time chartering exists. The situation is not the same for contracts of affreightment. The probable explanation is that in most cases a CoA needs a design which is tailor-made and adapted to the specific circumstances. The CoA must also include a number of clauses dealing with questions that are specific to the individual contract.

The parties should be careful to analyse and specially design each component in the CoA. The result will be a document which contains parts from traditional voyage chartering and other parts from traditional time chartering. It is incorrect to say that a CoA is a special form of voyage chartering. A CoA is basically a contract which cannot be classified either as a voyage charter or a time charter. This may cause difficulties, as shipping people, when dealing with a "hybrid contract", may try to use as a point of departure a time or a voyage charterparty, instead of pinpointing the particular solutions needed in the individual case. As a consequence, contractual solutions are sometimes agreed which do not match with the actual needs of the case. It is thus important that the parties make sure that they conclude an agreement which reflects their intentions and ensure that the contract is properly worded.

It will be obvious from the below discussion that the characteristics of a CoA are often set out in an overriding frame charter agreement (CoA charterparty) containing the general main contract provisions, whereas the individual voyages are covered separately by voyage charters and respective charterparties. However, in practice there are different solutions to be followed depending on the choice of the parties.

Quite often the parties use a standard CoA form, as an overriding frame agreement dealing with fundamental CoA aspects, such as cargo quantities, shipments, periods, owner's remuneration, type of vessel, etc. Attached to this, they use an ordinary standard voyage charterparty for the individual voyages and the daily operation. Another solution is to have a standard voyage charterparty with additional clauses (rider) dealing with the specific CoA questions. A third possibility is to use a tailor-made contract, where all provisions are negotiated and designed solely for the parties, the cargo and the carriage involved. The circumstances with respect to the specific negotiation must be foremost in the choice of documentary construction.

Sometimes, the individual vessels are just nominated by a simple fax or e-mail or similar method, but in other cases the parties prefer to draw up a formal *fixture note* for each nominating vessel. Such a fixture note gives necessary details about the specific vessel to execute a voyage. It should be mentioned that fixture notes may also be used in spot chartering. The system here is that the fixture note covers the facts applying to a planned individual voyage, while other terms have been included in the agreement by a reference to a standard charter form (for instance "*otherwise as per Gencon charterparty dated . . .*" or "*otherwise as per Gencoa charterparty dated . . .*").

There are three main standard CoA forms in practical use, namely the *Intercoa 80*; the *Volcoa*; and the *Gencoa*. *Intercoa 80* is an old, standard document published by Intertanko in 1980, intended to be an overruling, steering contract of affreightment for shipments of oil products. It was designed to be used together with *Intertankvoy 76* as underlying document. However, it is also possible to amend the contract for use in combination with other voyage forms. Another standard CoA is the *Volcoa*, an old, outdated document published by BIMCO in 1982 and intended for dry bulk cargo trading. Volcoa was the forerunner to the most popular and modern contract, the general-purpose CoA under the title *Gencoa* (see appendix 9), published by BIMCO in 2004 and designed as a steering form to be used with any dry cargo charterparty as underlying document.

13.2.2 Period

It goes without saying that the longer the contract period and the more complex the voyage schedules, the greater is the need for a contract in which all parts are specially negotiated and worded. In a contract covering a single voyage it is easier for the parties to accept a standard document containing solutions which may not be perfect than it is in a long-term contract covering several shipments. In the latter case each and every cost, risk, function etc. must be thoroughly considered and all clauses in the written contract be properly worded.

There are no limits as regards the length of the contract period in a CoA. However, the maximum and minimum periods are governed by practical considerations. If it is possible to make a CoA for one trip only, the parties will hardly recognise such a contract as a CoA. Nevertheless, if the owners have both the right and the obligation to substitute a vessel, the charterparty is legally more like a CoA than an ordinary voyage or time charterparty.

Practical considerations will limit the contract period to a certain extent. It is difficult for both parties to foresee changes in the market, costs or in technical developments. Besides, the global geo-political situation is also difficult to foresee and, as all these factors are critical for long-term contracts, it is not common to find contracts covering periods longer than 4–5 years. In such long durations, the parts of the contract dealing with the owner's remuneration and currency matters are also difficult to handle. Thus, the parties often choose to fix for a shorter, medium term and indicate that they intend to prolong the contract in the future, having such an option for that, instead of drafting beforehand a firm contract covering a very long period.

13.2.2.1 Alternative ways to define period

The contract period can be established in many ways, for instance:

- a fixed period which terminates automatically, i.e. without notice from any of the parties;
- a fixed period which is automatically prolonged with another fixed period, unless one of the parties gives notice of termination;
- a fixed period with an option for one of the parties (or both) to get prolongation with another fixed period;
- a period which is not fixed in length, but terminates after a fixed period from the time when a notice of termination is given by one of the parties.

It is also possible to agree on other solutions, combinations or variations of the different methods. For example, in the fourth case above it is not unusual to have a minimum fixed or guaranteed period, that is, a period from the commencement of the contract up to a certain date or for a certain duration, during which a notice of termination cannot be given by any of the parties.

When the option with a notice of termination is followed, the length of the period from the notice until the actual termination must also be agreed in the contract. The length of this notice period is sometimes short and in other cases fairly long, depending on the intentions of the parties. Especially in long-term contracts, the contract period is sometimes divided into part periods with individual terms. In addition, it is often the clauses about the owner's remuneration that vary from part period to part period.

13.2.2.2 Commencement and termination of period: borderline between part periods

It is usually insufficient to only describe the contract period with a term denoting just the commencement and the end of the overall period, for instance "*2018–01–01 to 2021–12–31*". Each voyage covers a period of time. Thus, it should be established in a more precise way what event should trigger the beginning or the end of a period, or at what stage a voyage (or part of it) will be covered by the terms of a specific period (a similar problem may arise in consecutive voyages). The parties should consider in advance how to decide whether a particular voyage, or part of a voyage, belongs to one stage or another of the contract. One way to do this in order to describe more specifically the contract period is to add: "*the first vessel to be load ready at the loading port in the period January 1–15, 2018, and the last vessel under the contract to be ready to load at the loading port not later than December 1, 2021*", or a similar clause.

When the period is divided into part periods, it is important that the contract establishes to which part period a certain voyage belongs. If uncertainty arises in this respect, the parties may have problems in establishing whether the freight rate for the previous or the next part period shall apply for a certain voyage, whether the quantity on the voyage shall be referred to the previous or the next part period, etc.

13.2.2.3 Early termination of contract and interruption of operations

Even if the basic legal idea puts on a promisor a duty to perform according to his promise, there are a number of limitations to this. Another facet is that non- or malperformance from one of the parties may result in a breach of the contract. A breach may give the other party a right of various remedies. If the suffering party encounters a loss or expense, he may demand damages. A breach of one's contractual duties may even lead to a right for the other party to terminate the contract. Thus, as elsewhere in contract laws, there are critical events that depend upon one or both of the parties and events which have developed through circumstances beyond the control of either party. There are certain nuances between law systems with respect to the evaluation of a breach and the respective remedies. Further to that, the parties are able to predetermine certain breach events in the contract, which, if they occur, will or may be regarded as events of default leading to termination of the contract or to another remedy.

It is quite common in long-term contracts to find clauses whereby the parties have agreed to relieve, under certain fulfilled conditions, one or both of them from all or some duties, or entitling both or either of them to terminate the contract. For instance, one may find general *force majeure* clauses, or particular *war risk* and *war cancellation clauses*, *weather hindrance clauses* (such as *ice clauses*, etc.). Furthermore, the parties may have introduced particular *hardship*, *crisis* or *catastrophe* clauses, or some other kind of *renegotiation*, *escalation* clauses or similar (see further sections 10.7 and 10.8). The reason is that contracts covering long-term periods include risks that may cause minor or major disturbances, making it difficult or even impossible for one or both of the parties to fulfil their obligations. Such events may cause interruption in the CoA operations or even early termination of the contract.

Few examples will be further mentioned to illustrate various situations of disruption that may arise in a CoA. A vessel may not arrive at the port of loading at all, or it may arrive late. In some cases the ship may not be in a contractual condition, while in other cases the vessel or the owner may fail to perform the voyage. The owner may, for various reasons, fail to nominate a vessel, or the intended vessel may suffer an engine breakdown. The charterer may not deliver cargo to the vessel, or may deliver cargo too late or deliver a non-contractual type or quality of cargo. It may also happen that charterers fail to pay freight or other costs in accordance with the contract.

Thus, the situations may vary greatly and the consequences may differ depending on the circumstances and the contract terms. Some of the key factors that have to be considered when a problem occurs are presented below:

- Does the contract contain any clause which directly or indirectly deals with the relevant problem, or is it silent?
- Has the problem been caused by circumstances totally beyond the control of the parties or has it been caused by an act or omission of one of the parties? If caused by one of the parties, is the problem due to negligence of or breach of contract by that party or similar?
- Has it been possible for any of the parties to prevent or mitigate the loss and have such steps been taken?
- Is it a single and isolated problem or is it a question of repeated events?

If the contract contains an express stipulation with respect to situations that may cause breach, hardship or impossibility in the performance of the contractual obligations, such provision will govern, unless there is a contravening mandatory law applying, or otherwise this provision has not been accepted by a court or arbitration decision. If the situation or the consequences thereof are not covered by a clause, the starting point will be the applicable general law (legislation or case law). These are highly complex legal issues and beyond the scope of this book.

The result of an interruption or an early termination of the contract can be that each party will simply have to bear its own losses which can include costs, loss of profit and also liability for damage against a third party. In many cases one of the parties, or perhaps both, has the right to claim damages from the other party. A failure by one party can also give the other party the right to interrupt the operation or cancel one or several voyages or the entire CoA.

A sanction that is quite often found in a CoA is that the failing party shall compensate the other by extension of the contract for a period or a quantity equal to the lost period or quantity. Both *Intercoa 80* and *Volcoa* have clauses dealing with this situation.

Contracts of affreightment use various wordings to deal with circumstances where the operation is interrupted. Many of these clauses refer to *force majeure* situations. For instance, *Gencoa* (see appendix 9, *part II, clause 15 "interruption of performance"*) comprises a typical *force majeure* clause, dealing also with the damage by stating that neither of the parties shall be liable for the consequences of the interruption and quantities not carried cannot be demanded to be shipped in retrospect. The clause reads as follows:

> *"Neither the Owners nor the Charterers shall, except as otherwise provided in the attached charter party, be responsible for any loss, damage, delay or failure in performance hereunder arising or resulting from act of God, act of war, act of terrorism,*

seizure under legal process; quarantine restrictions; strikes; boycotts; lockouts; riots, civil commotions and arrest or restraint of princes, rulers or people. Quantities not carried as a result cannot be demanded to be shipped".

Another similar wording is used in *Volcoa (part II, part of clause 19.1 "interruption of performance")* where it is stated that:

"If the performance of this Contract or part of it is interrupted through any event whatsoever which cannot be avoided or guarded against by either party, the performance affected shall be suspended until the hindrance ceases to have effect".

If the operation is interrupted, or if any of the parties fails to fulfil any of his obligations, without any reference existing to a relevant clause in the contract, then the failing party will in most cases be liable for damages suffered by the other party.

Intercoa 80 (clause I(c) "late payment of freight and demurrage – suspension") deals with the situation where a breach – but not an interruption – from one of the parties gives the other party the right to suspend the operation. More specifically, if the charterers fail to pay freight or demurrage, the owners have the right to suspend the operation by refusing (i) to nominate further tonnage, (ii) to let the vessel proceed to loading or discharging port, (iii) to load or receive cargo for shipment, (iv) to issue bills of lading for any cargo received or loaded, or finally (v) to discharge or deliver cargo. It is further stated that the time lost shall count as laytime or as time on demurrage and that the charterers shall hold the owners harmless in respect of any third-party claims arising from the suspension. On top of this, the owners may have the right to claim damages if they have suffered additional loss.

It is essential to distinguish between a situation where it is impossible to continue the operation and a situation where it is difficult and expensive to continue the operation. In the latter case, the suffering party will normally have to continue. Situations like these are often covered by escalation clauses (see section 10.8).

13.2.3 Cargo

13.2.3.1 Type of cargo

As long as the contract of affreightment adopts chartering principles stemming from voyage and time charter, the problems and questions concerned with the type of cargo in a CoA are essentially the same as those found in the fundamental types of charter (see section 11.4 about voyage charter and section 12.4 about time charter). The type of cargo to be carried is usually defined in the CoA, notably when the contract is based more on time charter principles. Sometimes, only one commodity is going to be transported under the CoA, or alternatively there may be a basic cargo to be carried and other commodities to be additionally stipulated either as planned options or as possible completion cargoes.

13.2.3.2 Total quantity of cargo

It is not enough to state the contractual number of tons or other cargo units. The respective obligations of the parties in respect with cargo quantities are also important. When the cargo quantity is evaluated during the chartering negotiations, it is therefore necessary to analyse the contract from several aspects.

Under any CoA, the following three fundamental questions must be answered:

- Is the cargo quantity fixed or not fixed?
- Is there an obligation on charterer's side to offer cargo to the owner or not?
- Is there an obligation on owner's side to carry cargo offered by the charterer or not?

Concerning the first question, the quantity covered by the contract is sometimes fixed in a very precise way, such as "*X metric tons*", "*Y units*" etc. The quantity may also be fixed by a minimum and maximum, like "*minimum X and maximum Y mt*" or "*between X and Y units*". In both cases the word "*about*" or expressions like "*X per cent more or less*" or "*X per cent more or less in Owners' (Charterers') option*" or similar are often used to give more flexibility.

The cargo quantity may also be described by reference to charterers' production during a certain period, like "*All Charterers' export on CIF basis for 2020*". Otherwise, it may be based on charterers' specific requirement. Such requirement can be more or less known beforehand, depending on the type of commodity, the nature of the charterers' sales contracts, etc. *Requirement contracts* can be combined with minimum or maximum quantity figures, or sometimes both minimum and maximum figures, e.g. "*Charterers' production during 2020 up to X mt*" or "*Charterers' production 2020 not less than Y mt*".

It is not always easy to find out whether the cargo quantity is fixed or not. For instance, when the quantity of cargo is described as "*all Charterers' production of potato during the contract period*", the quantity is in a way fixed but in another way is not. It is fixed to the quantity actually produced during the contract period, but as this quantity is not known beforehand when the contract is negotiated and concluded, it is not fixed for calculation purposes. This means that the owner may face a loss if no or little cargo is delivered, but this is a loss which he will have to carry. The important thing during the negotiation is to ask how much cargo (maximum, minimum, expected quantity) is to be carried under the contract and then evaluate the answer together with other components of the contract.

Concerning the second question, the charterer has sometimes only the *option* to carry his cargo by the vessels of a particular owner. In other cases, it is the charterer's *obligation* to deliver cargo for shipment under the CoA. The charterparty construction commonly refers that the charterer has an obligation to deliver a certain quantity and an option to deliver additional quantities. The expression "*first refusal*" may often be used, as for instance "*Charterers to give owners first refusal on all his shipments of potato from the Canadian Atlantic coast during 2019*". Such an expression does not imply a commitment on the charterer's side, other than to give the owner the right of first choice for each cargo shipment. This term has little value for the owner, unless it is combined with a CoA containing at least the main terms, such as minimum cargo quantities, freight, allocation of costs, functions, etc.

Concerning the third question, it is further critical to find out whether the owner has an obligation to carry all cargo offered, or whether it is just a right for him to transport the provided cargo if he so wishes.

13.2.3.3 Overlifting and shortlifting

Apparently the charterer is liable in damages if he does not deliver the cargo agreed. Under the individual voyages, there may in such situations be a case of claim for deadfreight (see glossary). If the charterer has promised certain yearly quantities, he may face difficulties in three stages: the individual voyage; the yearly quantity; and the total quantity.

Intercoa 80 (clause C "overlifting"and clause D "shortlifting") deals with the problems where under a contract year the vessels have shipped greater or lesser quantities, respectively, than provided for in the contract. *Clause C* about over-lifting reads as follows:

> *"If in the course of a contract year more cargo has been lifted than is provided for in the Preamble, such overlifting shall have no bearing upon the quantities to be carried under this Contract".*

Clause D about shortlifting reads:

> *"If it appears that by the end of a contract year less cargo will have been lifted than agreed to, the party not responsible for the shortlifting shall, until the year is out, have the option to add the cargo not so lifted to the quantity agreed for the next year. Such option must be exercised by written notice. In respect of shortlifting in the final contract year, the option can only be exercised for loading within the quantity limits provided in Clause (A) above (i.e. 'shipments'), and only for shipment within the first . . . months after the end of the final year.*
> *Whether or not any such option is exercised, no claim which the parties may, for any reason, have against each other shall be prejudiced thereby".*

The solution proposed when more cargo has been lifted is that the extra quan-tity shall not have any effect on the quantities originally intended for the follow-ing contract years. The parties can of course agree to the opposite, that the extra quantity carried under one contract year shall result in a corresponding reduction of quantities for the remaining part of the contract period. If the parties choose to offset the overlifted quantity against the remaining total quantity, they must – especially if the overlifted quantity is large – consider the effects on the remain-ing shipping programme, size of vessels, etc. If several part periods remain, the parties must also agree on the method to be followed for the reduction of the remaining total quantity shared between the remaining part periods. A last but not inferior solution is perhaps not to have any clause about overlifting. If the situa-tion arises, the case can then be discussed in the light of the facts and estimates of the time for shipment.

13.2.3.4 Final shipment

Even if the parties have agreed on an *"about quantity"* per voyage, there may be a residual balance for the last voyage. The owner, who has taken on an obligation to carry goods, namely a certain total quantity from one place to another, has not carried out his undertaking until the whole quantity has been transported. Therefore, there are good reasons to presume that the owner has an obligation to carry a residual quantity even if this would not give him a full cargo. In order to protect himself against expensive surprises, the owner should insert a provision regarding the quantity of cargo that he has to take on the last voyage. For example, *Gencoa (part II, clause 5 "final shipment"* and *part I, box 11 "final shipment")* contains provisions whereby the parties, by filling a specific box in part I of the contract, can agree on a minimum quantity to be carried for the final shipment. If the size of the vessel has been specified in the contract, it is further possible to solve the problem with a clause stating that the vessel shall be furnished with a *"full and complete"* cargo.

13.2.4 Vessels

As the CoA is structured around the transportation of the cargo, however not by a certain vessel, the individual ship or ships may not be mentioned at all in the CoA. The owner shall ensure that the vessels used for transportation under the CoA are suitable for the cargoes, the trading areas, the ports of call and the seaways. However, the name and/or type and/or category and/or size of ships may be specified directly or indirectly in the CoA. This can be done in several ways, for instance *"Owners to nominate only vessels suitable for handling of palletised cargo"* or *"Owners to nominate only vessels of X-type"* or *"Owners to nominate only vessels flying British flag"*, etc.

In contracts of affreightment the starting point is often what may be called a generic obligation, which means that there is a fleet of tonnage available, whereof one vessel will in the end be nominated for the particular voyage. This question is of great importance, since there is a difference between the situation in which the owner has nominated a vessel and the situation in which the vessel has not yet been nominated. Furthermore, another critical question has to do with the consequences of the owner failing to nominate the vessel in time.

It is crucial that interest is gradually concentrated on a named vessel. The owner has initially an *"abstract" or "generic" obligation*, even if there may be a number of restrictions. From the outset, there is the possibility of choice, but at some stage the owner has to make his decision, perhaps still with a legal and practical possibility of changing his mind. As the time of actual performance (tendering of notice) approaches, his freedom becomes – at least commercially – more or less limited. At a certain stage he must also be regarded as legally bound *vis-à-vis* the charterer. He no longer has the right to use another vessel even if he would prefer to do so. But instead, there may exist a duty to do precisely this, if something happens to the original named vessel. To sum up, the abstract obligation is gradually concentrated to a specific vessel. To put it differently, the abstract obligation to have a certain lot of cargo shipped at about a given date on a vessel of a specific type is gradually transformed into a *specific obligation* where a certain lot of cargo shall be shipped at a specific date on a named vessel.

13.2.5 Programme of shipments and nomination procedure

Under a CoA covering several shipments, it is sometimes agreed from the beginning when the different loadings will take place and how much cargo each vessel under the contract will load. However, the parties are usually flexible enough, to adjust their plan either in respect to time for shipments or the quantities lifted for each shipment. It is significant that both parties are as flexible as possible. For instance, if one of the parties insists on a certain loading date, a certain quantity of cargo or something else which he can request according to the contract, the cost for the other party may increase even without corresponding savings for the one who insists. This will have a negative influence on the total economy of the venture.

In long-term contracts it is very difficult to agree beforehand exactly when the different shipments shall take place and what quantities will be lifted for each shipment. Therefore, the parties usually choose to agree only on the framework and the general procedure, not on a more detailed planning. This is sometimes done by using expressions such as:

> "*The shipments under this contract shall be evenly (*or *'fairly'* or *'fairly evenly')* spread over the contract period*", or

> "*The 20 shipments under this contract shall be allocated as follows: 5 vessels to be presented loadready at loading port during the period January–March, 10 vessels during the period April–June and the remaining 5 vessels during the period July–December. All shipments to be evenly spread within each period*".

The parties also have to agree about the procedure for fixing a more detailed schedule. For instance, this can be done by a clause providing that the owner (or the charterer) at a certain date shall present a schedule including dates for loading and names of the ships intended. Sometimes the schedule is finally fixed in this way and sometimes the schedule is merely a base for a more detailed discussion between the parties.

When the final schedule is established, a system of notices often takes over. A clause dealing with such notices can have the following wording: "*The owners or the vessel to give ETA-notices 30, 15, 5 and 2 days prior to estimated time of loadreadiness at first port of loading. The owners to keep charterers informed about all changes in vessel's expected loadreadiness*". Such notices often have different values. Expressions such as "*preliminary notices*" or "*definite notices*" are used without a clear understanding of what the different kinds of notices mean. To avoid misunderstanding, it should be established to what extent the owner has the right to change the vessel's ETA and to what extent he is bound by a notice once given.

One may say that the programme, namely the scheduling of shipments, is the gist of the whole idea in the CoA. This is where the co-operation of the parties should be made clear. The owner and the charterer have to co-operate smoothly in order to achieve the optimum from the whole project. Both the parties should keep each other well informed of the key events, the position of vessels, the availability of cargoes, etc. This is what actually happens in most cases, taking into account that the parties normally wish to continue their co-operation in the long term.

Difficulties may arise particularly when the market changes substantially from the expectations at the time of fixing the contract, be it from the owner's or from the charterer's point of view. In a strongly growing freight market, a situation may thus arise where the owner feels tempted to employ the vessels in the open market to obtain better freight rates, rather than to keep on performing the CoA with the charterer. On the contrary, in a decreasing spot market climate, the situation may be the other way round, as the charterer may be inclined to escape from his obligations under a CoA and seek tonnage in the open market at a lower freight rate, rather than fulfilling his commitment under the CoA.

A well-written contract may not prevent difficulties from occurring, but it will certainly form a reasonable and necessary basis for discussion and problem solving.

13.2.6 Individual clauses

Notwithstanding the need for individual consideration of each component of a CoA, it is often possible to use standard charterparty forms or standard clauses as part of the CoA agreement. However, in "hybrid contracts" one must be very careful to avoid an inappropriate combination of clauses or using established shipping terms and concepts for purposes other than they are intended for.

Some clauses are of special importance in long-term contracts. It has already been mentioned that clauses dealing with the nomination of the vessel and the cargo are more complicated in a CoA than in voyage charterparties, while other important provisions are the currency clauses, escalation clauses and clauses of a *force majeure* nature (see sections 10.7, 10.8 and 13.2.2.3).

Finally, it should be mentioned that the parties in a CoA sometimes agree to *average* the effect of certain circumstances or clauses. For example, it is not unusual that laytime calculations are seen as a whole for the contract period or for a specific part of the contract period. Demurrage or despatch is calculated per voyage, but the final settlement is not done until the average result of all voyages is known (see chapter 15 for analysis of laytime).

13.2.7 Shipbrokers' role

The shipbroker's role is not the same in long-term contracts as in contracts covering only one voyage. In long-term contracts the parties may prefer to have a direct contact with one another as regards daily operational questions. This may lead to a situation where the broker, who once brought the owner and the charterer in contact, does not take any part in the daily exchange of information and perhaps is not even needed in negotiations concerning prolongation, amendments, etc. of the contract.

Sooner or later this will probably result in a situation where the payment to the broker – the commission – will be questioned. Legally and contractually, it is best for the parties and the broker or brokers to discuss and agree about commission at the beginning. Shall the commission be limited to a certain part of the contract period, shall the broker be entitled to commission on prolonged contracts or contracts that later come into force instead of the original contract and shall the broker be entitled to commission on other similar contracts between the parties? If these matters are not solved beforehand, the parties and the broker will certainly have difficulties when the questions arise, as this is a partly grey area in international maritime law.

On the other hand, it is a somewhat delicate situation for a charterer or an owner to discuss limitations of broker's commission at the same time as they try, through the broker, to solve all the important questions of a long-term CoA. Therefore, the contracts are often silent as regards the broker's right to gain commission on prolonged contracts or other contracts between the parties. The laws relating to intermediaries vary greatly between different countries and there is no general idea that a broker will automatically be entitled to brokerage in case of charter prolongation. This will depend on the applicable law, the circumstances of the case, the custom, the practice, etc.

CHAPTER 14

Freight calculations

This chapter deals with practical aspects of chartering calculations concerning different charter forms and vessel types. Initially, the voyage estimation principles and stages are examined. Then, focus is given to various important terms, but above all on the explanation of the Time Charter Equivalent (TCE). Tanker chartering calculation particularities are finally highlighted by providing a thorough analysis of Worldscale. Practical examples are presented throughout the chapter to enlighten the commercial aspects of chartering and shipbroking business. The most critical case studies concern an analytical voyage estimate of a dry bulk vessel, some brief tanker examples in respect to the application of Worldscale and, finally, the methodology of converting a time charter hire rate to a Worldscale spot tanker rate, and vice versa.

14.1 Voyage estimation

A number of calculations must be worked out by the shipowner in order to determine the most advantageous fixture for his vessel. The best fixture may be considered the employment of the ship that will give the best revenue per day for as many days as possible, paid by a solvent charterer. Therefore, a voyage estimation consists broadly of income minus expenditure, like any profit and loss account. In other words, a voyage estimation calculates the cost for the carriage of a specific cargo from one port to another and examines whether the rate of freight will cover the shipowner's expenses and a reasonable profit will be earned. Although it might seem an easy matter to make the above-mentioned calculations, these estimations can, in fact, turn out to be somewhat complex. It is not sufficient for a shipowner to quote just "what is needed and a little bit more" during chartering negotiations. If the prevailing market is low, this owner will be unable to find employment, whereas if it is a high market situation, he will certainly find employment but at an under-marketed rate. Since the periods of low market conditions normally last considerably longer than periods with a high freight market, the shipowner applying such a principle when operating in the open market would soon find himself out of business.

Owners examine a number of different alternatives when calculating on each individual open-ship position. Although it is easier to calculate which ship employment will give the best revenue per day, it is quite difficult to estimate whether this is a voyage which puts the ship in the best position for her next employment. If a number of alternative voyage calculations for one ship show the same result per day, consideration must also be given to the duration of the voyage or time charter engagement for each specific case. The freight market may change during the time of the ship's employment and, if the market goes up, the owner will wish to negotiate and start the next employment (which, he hopes, will give a better result) as soon as possible. It is also anticipated that the owner will aim at fixing on a level which reflects the upward trend and gives a well-balanced result of the charter. Obviously, if falling freight market conditions are anticipated, the owner would try to secure longer employments at rate levels reflecting the spot-market conditions ruling on the date of fixing, in other words he would try to fix the vessel before the market actually falls.

The above-mentioned work is made by the shipowner under pressure of time, since ships cannot be allowed to remain idle in the hope that a more advantageous offer of employment will be forthcoming. Time is money and there is no ample time to make thorough investigations and assessments of every item. Unfortunately, it also happens that there is usually insufficient time to analyse the counterpart's financial standing. The final voyage result will also be influenced by a number of external circumstances, which, even the foreseeable ones, can only be put into figures by rough estimation at the time when the calculation is made. It is also a question of trying to translate various terms and clauses in the charterparty form or the *pro forma* contract suggested by the charterers, into figures and costs for the owner's account, and vice versa. Thereby, the owner may, if he is successful in his estimations, reach a satisfactory mix of charter terms and conditions.

The tools used in the calculation work comprise easily accessible and complete details of the ships, together with port agents' advice about port dues and charges, stevedoring tariffs, productivity of various ports in handling different commodities, information about draught restrictions and other limitations, etc. It is always crucial to have reliable and efficient port agents all over the world who can assist in supplying necessary information.

Owners are also used to keep a library of handbooks on cargo handling and other matters. Furthermore, at the stage of pre-calculation, it is always necessary to work closely with those persons who supervise the running of the ship, arrange for bunkering, give instructions to the Master and who are generally responsible for the ship's performance in fulfilling the contractual undertakings stemming from the current charterparty. This operational staff, which has accumulated great experience of ports, ships and cargoes, may provide useful information, foresee the practical consequences and estimate the costs for most of the chartering alternatives or charterparty clauses.

For commercial reasons, a comparison of the final "voyage estimation" with the "eventual results" of a realised voyage is recommended, so that any future errors may be avoided.

There are only a few differences between voyage estimates for dry cargo ships and tankers. For those charters based upon Worldscale,[1] the laytime calculation

---

1 www.worldscale.co.uk (accessed 18 August 2015).

(time allowed for cargo handling in ports) is easier as the scale typically allows for 72 running hours in aggregate for loading and discharging or "*all purposes*" (see *Worldscale 2015, preamble, part B, term 2*) and 96 hours total in ports (see *Worldscale 2015, preamble, part A, term 4b*).[2] An expense in tankers which does not occur in dry cargo involves the consumption of bunkers for ancillary purposes, such as cargo heating, pumping cargo and tank cleaning. It is extremely difficult to assess bunker consumption for heating cargo, depending on the temperature at which the cargo is loaded, whether in wing or centre tanks and on the ambient temperature of the sea and air during the voyage. Only the technical department of the managing company can give an accurate assessment for this purpose. Pumping and tank cleaning are easier tasks to be calculated, although again the technical managers must be asked for an average bunker consumption based on past experience.

14.1.1 *Voyage estimate form*

The use of standard "estimate forms" helps the shipowner in producing consistent estimates of chartering alternatives. Figure 14.1 provides a classic sample of a voyage estimate form which includes all the necessary elements for making proper calculations, although nowadays the majority of shipowners use voyage estimating software programmes. Figure 14.2 presents an example of a completed calculation form that can be used for both voyage and time charter estimations (see section 14.2.2). Some shipping companies also have their own printed calculation forms in order to simplify the work and to facilitate the evaluation of calculation results. For voyage estimating, it is essential that the estimator has knowledge of various shipping matters, such as maritime geography, ship's measurements, stowage factors, conversion factors etc. (see appendix 16). The practical layout of a voyage estimation, as well as the presentation of the result may vary.

A *voyage estimate form includes* mainly the following items:

- *The ship's name and main particulars*

This defines the individual *vessel* or *special class of ships* of interest in the calculation and thereby specifies the *cargo capacity, speed* and *bunker consumption* on which the calculation is based. Generally, this outlines at the same time the average type and size of ship for which the result of the calculation will be applicable on a similar voyage under the same market conditions.

- *Period of time*

The period of time for which the figures used in the calculation are valid has to be noted, since the freight market level and the cost levels vary continuously.

---

2 See section 14.3.1 for Worldscale and chapter 15 for laytime calculations.

- *Intended voyage*

The intended voyage is specified via the loading and discharging ports and up to the position where the ship is expected to start her next employment. Therefore, a possible passage in ballast should also be included in the estimate. The *voyage plan* for calculation purposes has to be determined from case to case. For trades and engagements that invariably cover a *"ballast leg"* it may be made a rule always to begin, or alternatively end, the voyage with the ballast leg. Passages through *canals* and other *fairways*, which prolong the duration of the voyage and incur special extra costs, also have to be included in the calculation.

- *Cargo*

The type and description of the *commodity* is entered, together with the *stowage factor* (if applicable) used for calculation on *cargo intake* (quantity to be loaded). The cargo quantity is noted by volume or weight measurement, depending on the measurement on which the freight is calculated. The quantity of cargo that can be loaded onboard the vessel depends on a number of limiting factors, such as the *stowage factor* (see section 1.2.4 and appendix 16), the *ratio of the deadweight all told (DWAT) with the deadweight cargo capacity (DWCC)*, the *loadline zones* of the vessel in relation to the voyage, the *season*, the *salinity of water* in the ports and finally the *maximum draught of the vessel* in relation to the voyage. Moreover, the calculation form always indicates the relevant term of the charterparty which determines the *"laytime"* for the loading and unloading operation of the cargo (see chapter 15).

- *Freight*

Generally, the *freight* is commonly expressed in USD per metric tonne or tonne (or metric ton in the US language[3]) of 1,000 kgs, or per English or long ton of 1,016 kgs. Most of the dry bulk fixtures concern homogeneous heavy cargoes where the available deadweight cargo capacity (instead of the available volume of the ship) is the limiting factor. However, for especially bulky cargoes, for general cargoes or often for chemical and gas cargoes, there are a number of alternatives for the assessment and expression of freight, for example expressed in USD per m^3 (cbm) or per ft^3 (cb.ft.) of cargo carried. The freight rate may also be quoted either per unit of weight or per unit of volume (W/M). This acronym stands for *"Weight or Measurement"* and means that the basic unit for assessment of freight in this case is the one that gives the highest total freight amount for the parcel or the commodity in question. Light cargo is typically charged based on measurement (volume), while heavy cargo based on weight. This manner of calculation is commonly used in liner trades and is then referred to as *"freight per revenue ton (R/T)"*. Revenue ton determines

---

3 As a simplified form, the term "metric ton" is often preferred (instead of "metric tonne" or "tonne") in daily chartering communications or shipping publications worldwide.

the freight rate paid for the container carriage and may also form the basis for surcharges, such as the Bunker Adjustment Factor (BAF) or Currency Adjustment Factor (CAF). The liner pricing is charged based on the "W/M" system, as explained before. In modern days, where the metric units are most commonly used, one revenue ton is either 1 metric ton ("tonne") or 1 cubic metre, whichever gives the higher revenue to the carrier. The carrier usually retains the discretion to determine which measurement unit to use.[4] Freight may also be quoted on a *lump sum* basis, which in fact means that the owner puts a specified tonnage/cargo space at the charterer's disposal. This space may then be filled in the best possible way in return for payment of the agreed lump sum freight amount.

- *Costs*

This includes the vessel's voyage expenses in respect to a specific voyage. The most important item of voyage expenses is the *bunkers* cost. On the costs side in the voyage calculation, a lump sum covering *port costs* and *cargo-handling* expenses is usually noted. For every port these two cost items constitute the largest part of the disbursements account, which the port agent will present to the owner after the call. The port costs might be very difficult to determine in advance, even if there is sufficient time to get an estimate (*pro-forma account*) from the agents. In addition, *commissions, additional insurance premium* and *other extra costs* are included in this category.

- *Rate of exchange*

This item includes the *currency* and the *rate of exchange* in which the freight will be paid. In order to perform the voyage estimates, all revenues and costs must be converted to a common currency, which normally is *US Dollars*.

- *Final result*

The calculation form includes a final section, which specifies the financial results of the voyage estimations. The main elements of the calculation are: the *Gross Freight*, the *Net Freight* resulting after the deduction of brokerage/commissions, the *Gross Voyage Result*, the *Gross Daily Result*, the *Net Daily Result* and the *Time Charter Equivalent (TCE)*. The final result of a voyage estimate is given through the following main steps of calculations:

- Add the totals of brokerage and commissions, bunkers, port expenses, cargo handling, additional insurance and other extra costs. This sum is then subtracted from the adjusted amount of gross freight revenue and the result is the amount which represents the income of the voyage after payment of the variable costs for performance of this voyage.

---

4 www.shipinspection.eu (accessed 18 August 2015).

- Divide this amount by the number of voyage days to get the result per day, earned by the ship in question, during the duration of the intended voyage.
- The daily revenue is a figure used for comparison, showing:
  - whether the voyage is profitable in absolute numbers when compared with the vessel's fixed costs element (operating and capital expenses),
  - whether the voyage gives a better revenue than alternative employments available at the same time,
  - whether the revenue per day ("the time charter equivalent") conforms with the current spot market level.

As mentioned previously, the judgment must include considerations of the expected freight market development throughout the duration of the voyage. It is also of importance to consider whether the ship will be open again, after the performance of the voyage, in a good or bad position, with regard to the then expected possibilities of getting a new employment.

Profitability in the short perspective may be deemed obtained if the revenue per day covers the daily operating costs for the ship, for example costs for manning and personnel, repair and maintenance of the vessel, provisions and spare parts, insurance and administration. In order to be profitable in the long run, however, the daily revenue must also cover the capital costs (interest, depreciation and loan amortisation).

14.1.2 Stages of voyage estimation

This section describes analytically the stages of voyage estimation, as follows.

14.1.2.1 First stage: voyage plan
During this stage the estimator must consider what route should be taken and what bunkering arrangements should be made. The voyage should commence from the time and the place where the ship completes discharge of the cargo of the previous charter (sailing from the pilot station of the discharge port of the previous voyage). In this manner, the first part of the voyage will be a ballast leg, unless the vessel finds a cargo out of the port in which she has just discharged. This is a more logical method than that of starting the estimation from a loading port.[5] In the latter case, the estimator commences the voyage at the loading port and the laden passage is followed with a theoretical ballast leg back to the loading port again. However, while this might sometimes be realistic for tankers, bulk carriers rarely proceed on the same voyage twice, so the most realistic alternative of "*discharge port to discharge port*" is most commonly used.

The voyage plan is specified via loading and discharging ports up to the position where the ship is expected to start her next employment, i.e. so that

---

5 Packard, W. (1996) *Voyage Estimating* (Surrey, Fairplay Publications).

VOYAGE CALCULATION FORM

Ship:				Open date:	Laycan:	Voy. Nr:
Voyage/TC-employment:						

Currency:	Exch. Rate:					
Cargo/Employm.	Quantity/Time	Rate		Income	Comm. %	Adj. Income
Desp. / Demurr.:					- / + :	
					INC. TTL: *	

Port	Port charges	Port/Can days	C/P-Terms	Load/Disch. costs
1.				
2.				
3.				
4.				
Waiting:				
Canal:				

Distance:	Speed:	Sea days:	Days on TC:	Port days:	Total voy. days:

Fuel/day (M.E.):	Quantity:	Price:	Cost:	TOTALS:	
				Bunkers	
Diesel/day (A.E.):	Quantity: (+)	Price:	Cost:	Port	
				L/D	
				Comm.	
Notes:				Ex.ins.	
				Miscell.	
				COST TTL: *	
				GR.REV: */*	
				REV/DAY:	
(+) If shaft generator, calculate on port time only				Date:	Sign:

Figure 14.1 Voyage Calculation Form

a possible passage in ballast should be included in the voyage estimation. The proper route should be selected. In other words, each leg of the proposed voyage should be clearly determined. In order for the estimator to select the *proper route*, he has to take into consideration *critical factors* such as distance tables, weather

Ship: WORLD ACADEMY		Period: Jan-Feb	Year: 2009	Voy. Nr: 1 A-09
Voyage/(TC-employment): Alex – Odessa – Suez – Shanghai				

Currency: $	Exch. rate:				
Cargo/Employment	Quantity/Time	Rate	Income	Comm. %	Adj. Income
Blk urea	27000	43	1161000	6.25	
Despatch/Demurrage:				–/+:	0
				INC. TTL: *	1161000

Ports	Port charges	Port days	C/P-Terms	L/D price	Load/Discharge costs
Odessa	75000	7 + 1.5 + 1	4000 SHEX		
Suez	160000		-		
Shanghai	30000	13.5 + 3 + 1	2000 SHEX		

Distance:	Speed:	Sea days:	(Days on TC)	Port days:	Total days:
10000	14	31.25	1	27	59.25

Fuel/day (ME): 22	Quantity: 710	Price: 210	Cost: 149100	TOTALS:	
				Bunkers	220500
Diesel/day (AE): 2	Quantity: 119	Price: 600	Cost: 71400	Port	265000
				L/D.	0
Notes:				Comm.	72563
	Freight +/–1 $ = $ 427 per day			Ex.ins.	
				Extras	10000
				COST TTL:	568063
				GR. REV:	592938
				REV/DAY:	10007
					10007
				Date 20/01/2009	Sign. JAS

Figure 14.2 Voyage Calculation Form for Voyage & Time Charter

conditions, bunker consumption, speed, canal dues, bunkering ports etc. More specifically[6]:

- *Bunkering ports.* The bunkering port used in a voyage can have an important influence on the voyage profit. Bunkering may take place at

6 Giziakis, K., Papadopoulos, A. and Plomaritou, E. (2010) *Chartering* (Athens, Stamoulis Publications, 3rd edition, in Greek, pp. 930–937).

the last port of discharge; at the loading port; or at a specific bunkering port en route. It must be appreciated that if bunkering takes place between the port of loading and the port of discharge, a smaller quantity of fuel can be carried and more cargo may be lifted.[7] It is sometimes profitable to bunker at more than one port on the loaded passage, but the revenue from extra cargo carried might be offset to some extent by the additional cost of calling at the bunkering port. Again, if the cargo is volume-constrained rather than weight-constrained, the deadweight taken up by fuel may be of little consequence. The price of fuel at alternative bunkering ports should also be taken into account. It is sometimes cheaper to carry "more fuel and shut out cargo" if the fuel price differential is greater than the freight rate for cargo. The estimator must develop a network of reliable bunkering agents, so as always to be in a position to get informed accurately in respect of the prevailing bunker prices worldwide.

- *Maritime Atlas (e.g. Lloyd's Maritime Atlas) and Distance Tables.* The atlas and the distance table are necessary instruments for displaying different possible routes. The estimator may have to consider carefully various alternative passages for each leg. For example, is it a shorter distance, from New Orleans to Singapore via Gibraltar and the Suez Canal, or via the Cape of Good Hope? Since the route via Gibraltar and the Suez Canal is shorter, it is the most appropriate if the time is of essence. However, the disadvantages of this route are the costs of canal tolls and allowances for canal transit delays. The route via the Cape of Good Hope is the cheaper route, but the longer as well. There are various distance tables and internet sites commercially available which can be used, but estimators should also have a fairly accurate idea of the major world distances.[8] A useful method is to divide the world into areas (this mainly falls into oceans) and then learn a number of strategic mileages across each area. Alternatively, instead of actual distances one can think in terms of days steamed. As a "rule of thumb", a speed of 14 knots works out at almost exactly three days per 1,000 nautical miles.

- *Ocean currents and weather systems* may also be important in deciding on a particular route. The estimator has to consider if it is necessary to allow extra time at sea for anticipated stormy weather, or to calculate extra mileage for an alternative route as may be recommended by a weather routing company contracted by the shipowning company. Figure 14.3 presents a world weather chart and Figure 14.4 presents a chart of ocean currents.

---

7 Evans, J.J. and Marlow, P.B. (1990) *Quantitative Methods in Maritime Economics* (London, Fairplay Publications, 2nd edition, pp. 96–98).

8 See appendix 16 for a basic global distance table and www.sea-distances.org.

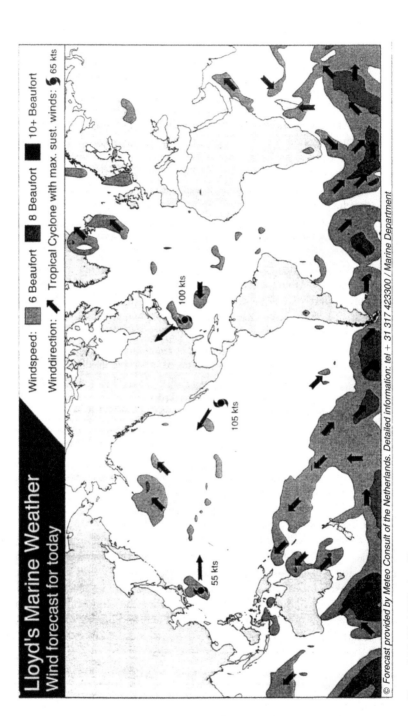

Figure 14.3 World Weather Chart

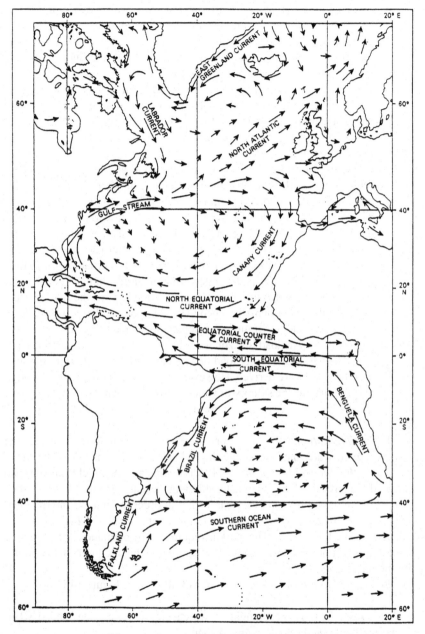

Mean surface current circulation for the Atlantic Ocean

Figure 14.4 Ocean Currents: Atlantic

- Passages through *canals* and other *fairways*, which either prolong or shorten the duration of the voyage and incur extra costs, also have to be taken into consideration in determining the proper route. The most prominent such examples are: the Panama Canal, the Suez Canal, the Great Lakes, St. Lawrence Seaway, etc.
- *Vessel's speed and fuel consumption* at different speeds. In some cases it is better to proceed more slowly and economise on bunkers. In other cases, it is more advantageous to proceed at full speed if an early arrival at loading port means that, according to the charterparty, the owner can benefit from that.
- *A map of load line zones.* For environmental and navigational safety reasons, the world's oceans are divided into a number of different zones which indicate the load line up to which a ship may be legally loaded. The maximum weight of cargo that a vessel can carry (i.e. the ship's deadweight capacity) is determined by its load lines and this varies slightly because each ship has a maximum depth (draught) to which it is permitted to be loaded in accordance with international maritime rules. Vessels' load lines differ according to ship's dimensions, the part of the world in which the ship is loading or navigating, the season of the year and the water densities encountered in ports and at sea (salt, fresh or brackish water). All these are depicted in a load line zone map (see Figure 14.5). The load line zones are basically winter, summer and tropical. The vessel's summer load line is the primary load line from which all other marks are derived. However, taking into consideration all other factors, such as the salinity of water, the world is finally divided up into the six load line zones which are shown and explained below.

A ship's "*international load line*" or "*load line*" is the mark on her hull that shows where the waterline is when the ship is loaded at full capacity. In the past it was called "*the Plimsoll line or mark*". It was named after Samuel Plimsoll, who instigated the passage of the Merchant Shipping Act of 1875, which established the marking of a load line on every cargo ship in order to improve international navigation. The distance between the deck line and the mark to which the vessel is loaded is called *freeboard*. The mark is required to be permanently fixed to the vessel amidships on both sides of the hull and painted in a colour that contrasts with the hull colour.

There are *six load lines for each vessel*, as follows (see Figure 14.6):

F – Fresh: This is the draught to which the vessel can be loaded when navigating in the Fresh designated zone.

TF – Tropical Fresh: This is the draught to which the vessel can be loaded when navigating in the Tropical Fresh designated zone.

T – Tropical: This is the draught to which the vessel can be loaded when navigating in the Tropical designated zone.

International Load Line Zones and Areas 15th Edition

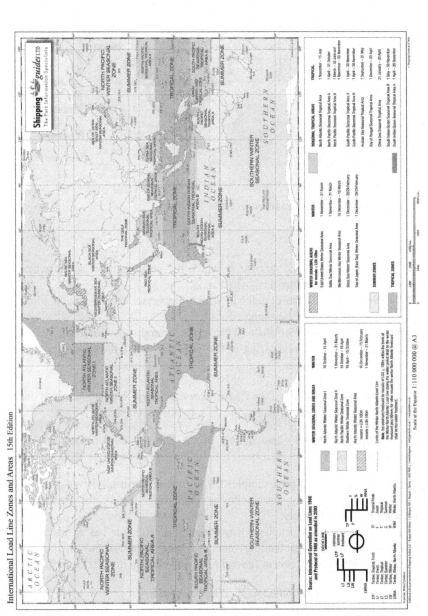

Figure 14.5 Load Line Zones Map and Areas

Published with kind permission of Shipping Guides Ltd. Reigate Hill House, 28 Reigate Hill, Reigate, Surrey, RH2 9NG, United Kingdom. See www.portinfo.co.uk.

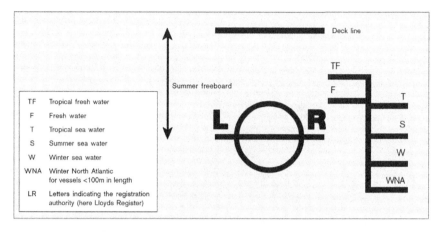

Figure 14.6 Load Lines

Source: www.ukpandi.com (accessed 20 August 2015).

S – Summer: This is the draught to which the vessel can be loaded when navigating in the Summer designated zone.

W – Winter: This is the draught to which the vessel can be loaded when navigating in the Winter designated zone.

WNA – Winter North Atlantic: This is the draught to which the vessel can be loaded when navigating in the Winter North Atlantic designated zone.

Please note that the initials of the *Classification Society,* that has surveyed the vessel's load line, are also marked on the hull. In our example:

LR – Lloyd's Register: The initials of the Classification Society which assigns the marks.

Other possible initials are for example: BV – Bureau Veritas, AB – American Bureau of Shipping, etc. The circle with the line through it indicates whether or not the cargo is loaded evenly.

After the determination of the *voyage legs,* the estimator has to calculate the *duration* of the voyage (sailing time and time in ports) and the *bunker consumption* (fuel consumption at sea and fuel consumption in ports), as follows:

DURATION OF THE VOYAGE =

Steaming time (sailing time at sea) + Time in ports (it depends on laytime)

BUNKER CONSUMPTION =

Bunker consumption at sea (FO) + Bunker consumption in ports (FO & DO)

The number of *days at sea* (*sailing time*) may be calculated by dividing the miles of the voyage (the sum of miles of voyage legs) by the ship's speed. The estimator has to add some possible delays caused by canal transits, bunkering calls, bad weather etc. It is common knowledge that delays can be anticipated due to passages through canals or other fairways and their effect should be taken into account. It may be safer to allow two days for each passage through the Suez and Panama Canals because time can be lost waiting, as well as during the transit itself. Delays may also sometimes be experienced either at sea or in port due to bad weather conditions. It is not normal to allow additional steaming time for possible bad weather, unless it is certain from the nature of the trade/voyage that delay will be experienced. Bunkering calls also may be lengthy and provoke half an extra day delay to the vessel. Furthermore, where a ship has to call at multiple loading and/or discharging ports, extra time should be added to the sailing time for delays caused by entering and leaving each port. For estimating purposes, it may be sufficient to allocate one day for each call.

The multiplication of the number of sailing days by the ship's daily bunker consumption leads to the calculation of the *bunker consumption at sea* (in fuel oil).

Then, the estimator has to calculate the *time spent in ports*. Sometimes, the charterparty includes terms which define a number of days allowed for loading and a number of days allowed for discharging (*definite laytime*, see chapter 15). In this case the estimator has only to add time for likely holiday periods[9] and an allowance for possible bad weather delays, in order to calculate the total expected time in each port. He can further estimate the *port bunker consumption* by multiplying the number of days in ports by the ship's daily bunker consumption at ports (in fuel oil and in diesel oil).

The calculation of the time spent in loading and discharging ports is more complicated if the charterparty includes terms which stipulate a loading or discharging rate of so many tons per day (*calculable laytime*). In this case, the estimator has first to calculate the total cargo to be loaded (2nd stage of voyage estimation) and then return to finalise the calculation of time and bunker consumption in ports. The above-mentioned difficulty does not exist in the tanker trades, where a standard 72 hours "all purposes" laytime (i.e. overall time for loading and discharging) is usually agreed at the charterparty, by adopting what is defined in Worldscale terms and conditions.

14.1.2.2 Second stage: measurement of cargo

It is necessary to calculate how much cargo can be loaded by weight, but at the same time the estimator must ensure that the cubic capacity of the ship is sufficient to hold that quantity. A vessel may not be able to carry the maximum weight of cargo if the volume of that maximum weight of cargo is too big for the holds. At this point of analysis, it is worthwhile to mention some useful *definitions*. More specifically:

The *capacity of a vessel* may be calculated in two ways:

---

9 BIMCO provides regular information about working hours, holidays, etc. in ports located all over the world.

- The calculation of vessel's *tonnage capacity* (this means the vessel's carrying capacity measured in terms of deadweight tonnage).
- The calculation of vessel's *volume capacity* (this means the vessel's registered tonnage or the vessel's cubic capacity measured in cubic metres or cubic feet).

The calculation of *deadweight tonnage capacity* comprises:

- *Deadweight All Told (DWAT)*: This represents the total weight a vessel can carry and includes cargo, fuel, stores, fresh water and other constants.
- *Deadweight Cargo Capacity (DWCC)*: This represents the total weight of cargo only that a vessel can carry.

The calculation of *registered tonnage* concerns:

- *Gross Registered Tonnage (GRT)*: This represents the calculation of the total enclosed space in the ship calculated in registered tons (1 registered ton = 100 cubic feet).
- *Net Registered Tonnage (NRT)*: This represents the calculation of the total enclosed space in the ship used for cargo carriage. Therefore, the NRT is the total enclosed space in the ship (GRT) less that for machinery and accommodation.

The calculation of *cubic capacity* concerns[10]:

- *Grain Capacity*: This represents the underdeck capacity of a vessel for the carriage of bulk cargo. It is the total cubic capacity of a ship's holds (measured in cubic metres or cubic feet) available for the carriage of grain or any other free-flowing bulk cargo which is capable of filling the space between the ship's frames, thus it includes the broken stowage.[11]
- *Bale Capacity*: This represents the underdeck capacity of a vessel for the carriage of general cargo. It is the total cubic capacity of a ship's holds (expressed in cubic metres or cubic feet) available for the carriage of solid cargo which is not capable of filling the spaces between the ship's frames. More specifically, bale capacity includes hatchways but excludes void spaces behind cargo battens and beams. In other words, bale capacity does not include the broken stowage.

The estimator has to examine various parameters aiming at the maximisation of the cargo intake, since revenue is earned normally per ton of cargo carried. Initially, he has to find out whether any of the ports on the proposed voyage

---

10 www.bbc-chartering.com (accessed 14 August 2015); Stephens, K. (2014) *Glossary: Chartering & Shipping Terms* (www.rickmers-linie.com).

11 *Broken Stowage*: The unavoidably unused cargo space in a ship or a hold when stowing cargo. The lost space depends upon the kind and shape of cargo, the shape of holds, the packing and stowing method, etc. For example, the space taken up by a bundle of bars of irregular length would be calculated on the basis of the longest length, as if all the bars were of that length. The wasted space is broken stowage.

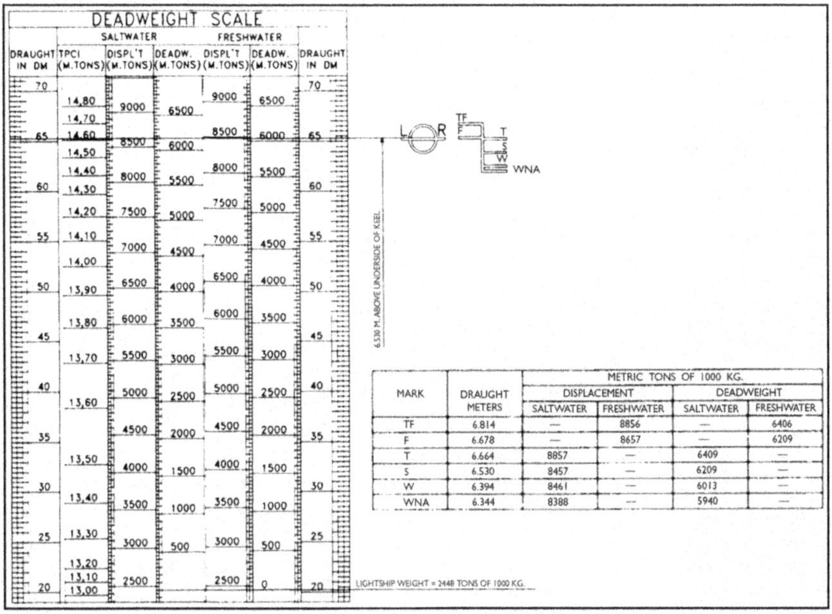

DEADWEIGHT SCALE

MARK	DRAUGHT METERS	DISPLACEMENT		DEADWEIGHT	
		SALTWATER	FRESHWATER	SALTWATER	FRESHWATER
TF	6.814	—	8856	—	6406
F	6.678	—	8657	—	6209
T	6.664	8857	—	6409	—
S	6.530	8457	—	6209	—
W	6.394	8461	—	6013	—
WNA	6.344	8388	—	5940	—

LIGHTSHIP WEIGHT = 2448 TONS OF 1000 KG.

Figure 14.7 Deadweight Scale

have draught restrictions. If not, he still needs to confirm that the cargo-handling berths (at which the vessel will call) are similarly free of any restrictions, not only alongside, but throughout the port route between the sea and the berth. If there is sufficient draught at all ports and berths, he must then consider the question of load line zones on the proposed voyage, since on this basis he will make his bunkering plans. Knowledge of load line zones is essential. All zones transited between loading and discharging ports must be considered.

Further on, the estimator has to calculate the cargo lifting and the bunker replenishment, bearing load line zones in mind.[12] To discover the ship's allowed draughts on the basis of various zones and to find deadweight allowances against these draughts, the estimator must rely on close examination of the vessel's *Capacity Plan*, which has such information displayed together with the *Deadweight Scale* and the *General Arrangement* of the vessel (see Figures 14.7 and 14.8). The scale will be of vital use in cases where calls are necessary to draught-restricted ports on the proposed voyage. Besides, the Deadweight Scale provides also a method for estimating the additional draught or for determining the extra load that could be taken onboard when a vessel is being loaded in water of density less than that of salt water, namely fresh or brackish water found in river estuaries etc.[13] The

---

12 Packard, W. (1996) *Voyage Estimating* (Surrey, Fairplay Publications, pp. 9–10).

13 Kemp, J.F., Barrass, C.B. and Young, P. (2001) *Ship Stability. Notes & Examples* (Oxford, Butterworth-Heinmann, 3rd edition, p. 382).

431

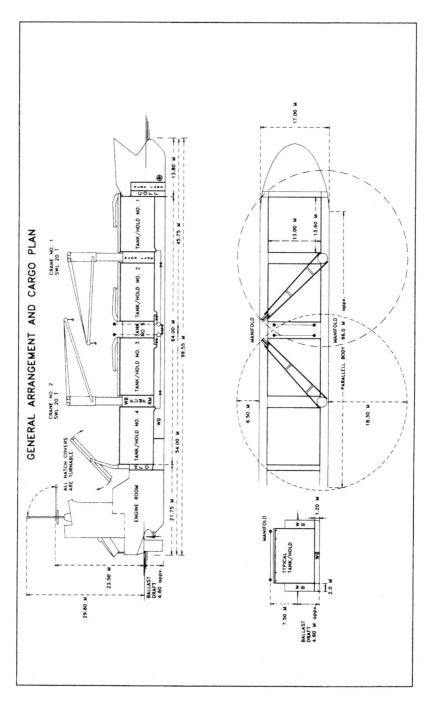

Figure 14.8 General Arrangement and Cargo Plan

Deadweight Scale shows against a particular draught the ship's deadweight and its displacement in both salt and fresh water. *Displacement Tonnage* is the actual weight of the vessel and it is based on the Archimedes Law. According to the Archimedes Law, the weight of the body is equal to the weight of water it displaces. *Loaded Displacement* is the total weight of the ship and all that it is carrying. *Light Displacement Tonnage (LDT)* is the actual weight of the empty ship. Consequently:

LOADED DISPLACEMENT =

LIGHT DISPLACEMENT TONNAGE (LDT) + DEADWEIGHT
TONNAGE (DWT)

The Deadweight Scale displays columns of scale for freeboard (f), deadweight (dwt) in salt water and in fresh water, draught of ship (mean), displacement in tons in salt water and in fresh water, *tonnes per centimetre immersion (TPC[14])* in salt water and in fresh water and *moment to change trim 1 cm (MCTC or MTCTC[15])*. Furthermore, the Deadweight Scale shows against a particular draught the ship's decrease/increase in tonnage for every decrease/increase in draught. By placing his ruler against the particular draught in question and looking along the line made by the ruler across the scale, the estimator can discover the ship's deadweight in either salt or fresh water conditions. A relevant term is called *"Fresh Water Allowance" (FWA)* and is important when the ship is to navigate in fresh water conditions. Each cubic metre of fresh water has a weight of 1,000 kgs (1 tonne), instead of 1,025 kgs (1.025 tonne) in the case of salt water.

The hull must displace sufficient cubic metres of water to balance the weight of the vessel exactly. If the vessel moves from sea water to fresh water conditions, it will need to displace more cubic metres of fresh water to balance its weight. In sea water, the vessel will not sink as far as it will in fresh water, thus the draught in sea water will be less than in fresh water. The difference between the two draughts is called Fresh Water Allowance. FWA is measured as the distance between the top of the Summer (S) load line and the top of the Fresh (F) load line of the ship (see Figure 14.6). It is important to take advantage of the FWA, because there will be a loss of cargo carried and therefore a loss of revenue, if the vessel only loads up to

14 *TPC (Tonnes per Centimetre immersion)*: A quantity, for example of cargo or fuel, needed to immerse a ship one further centimetre. This quantity varies not only ship by ship but also according to the quantity already on board. *TPI (Tons per Inch immersion)*: Similar term which shows the quantity of cargo or fuel needed to immerse a ship one further inch (source: www.bbc-chartering.com).

15 *Trim* represents the longitudinal inclination of the ship and it is given as a difference between the forward and aft draughts. When aft draught is greater than forward draught (usual situation), the trim is positive or *"trimmed by the stern"*. When forward draught is greater, the trim is negative or *"trimmed by the head"*. For example, a ship with a forward draught of 5 m. and an aft draught of 5.75 m. will have a positive trim of 75 cm. Shifting, loading and unloading of a mass (e.g. cargo or fuel) will affect a ship's trim. The change in trim when handling masses is measured using the concept of MCTC and MCTI. *MCTC* is the Moment to Change Trim 1 centimetre. *MCTI* is the Moment to Change Trim 1 inch. All the values for the above terms for a ship can be found in the ship's stability book (source: www.tc.gc.ca/eng/marinesafety/tp-tp14609-3-stability-180.htm, accessed 2 September 2017).

the summer load line level in freshwater. In that way, when the vessel reaches sea water it will sink up to the summer load line level again.

Furthermore, when a vessel loads in a harbour with brackish water, the specific gravity of the dock water ranges between that of the salt water (1,025 kgs/cbm) and that of the fresh water (1,000 kgs/cbm). This important information must be exactly obtained by the port agent or the water must be tested with a hydrometer. The quantity that the summer load line can be further immersed is then calculated as a percentage of the FWA and is called *"Brackish Water Allowance" (BWA)*.[16] For example, if a vessel with a FWA of 50cm loads in dock waters with a specific gravity (SG) of 1,005 kg/cbm, it may be said that this water is only four fifths fresh, so the vessel can use 40 cm of its 50cm FWA, if it must float at the summer load line out at sea.

When the applicable deadweight figure is determined, the estimator has to deduct from that the bunkers expected to be on board at this stage of the voyage, and make an allowance for constant weights (which consist of stores, fresh water, lubricants, spares and the weight of the crew). For each leg of a proposed voyage it is essential that allowance is made for the ship to carry a good safety surplus of bunkers (around 15–25% as a rule of thumb) in addition to the actual bunkers required for normal consumption for that leg. After the above-mentioned deduction, the remaining figure is the maximum cargo weight the ship can carry or the *Deadweight Cargo Capacity (DWCC)*.

$$DWCC = DWAT \text{ (from scale)} - [BUNKERS + CONSTANTS]$$

At this point, the estimator has to examine if the vessel has the space to carry the particular tonnage of cargo. The weight of the cargo multiplied by the stowage factor gives the volume or space which this cargo would normally occupy in the ship's holds (including the broken stowage, i.e. the space not occupied by cargo in a ship's hold due to the non-uniform shape of the general cargo or due to fittings in the ship). This figure must be less than the actual available space onboard. To sum up:

$$DWCC = CUBIC\ CAPACITY\ (GRAIN\ OR\ BALE^{17}) \div STOWAGE$$
$$FACTOR\ or$$
$$CUBIC\ CAPACITY\ (GRAIN\ OR\ BALE) = DWCC \times STOWAGE\ FACTOR$$

In general, cargoes with stowage factors of less than one cubic metre per tonne (or 40 cb. ft. per long ton of 2,240 lb.) are limited by weight; those with stowage factors of more than one cubic metre per tonne (or 40 cb. ft. per long ton of 2,240 lb.) are limited by volume.[18] For cargoes other than bulk commodities – and especially cargoes with a large volume in relation to their weight – it may happen that the margin for broken stowage included in the stowage factor given by the charterers or shippers is too narrow. Furthermore, the volume given may be *"net*

---

16 See also *BWAD, FWAD* and *SWAD* terms in the glossary.

17 Normally grain capacity is meant in bulk cargoes and bale capacity for general cargoes, but during calculations this should have been made clear.

18 See appendix 16 regarding stowage factors of indicative cargoes.

on quay" and in such a case the owners have to determine what has to be added to cover broken stowage in the ship's holds.

Once the cargo quantity and the loading/discharging rates per day are known, the time spent in ports as well as the bunker consumption in ports may be estimated at this stage of calculations. Various delays may cause necessary adjustments to the expected port time.

14.1.2.3 Third stage: calculation of costs

This stage includes the estimation of voyage costs. The voyage expenses are defined as the variable costs incurred for the execution of a voyage and include the bunkers cost, port charges, canal dues and other transit costs, cargo-handling expenses, extra insurance premiums etc. (see Figure 14.9).

As it is known, the most important item of voyage expenses is the *bunkers cost*. The quantity of fuel actually consumed by a ship depends on its hull condition and the speed at which it is operated. The vessel's speed is in turn influenced by two critical factors, bunkers price and freight rates. Slow steaming is a tactic followed by the shipowners during periods of depressed freight rates and high bunkers cost. Typically, the main engines in modern ships use fuel oil of a heavier grade than the auxiliary engines, which require light and more expensive fuel. Therefore, the costs for fuel oil (FO) – which is related to the sailing distance – and the costs for diesel oil (DO) – which is consumed each day of the voyage whether at sea or in port – are calculated separately. For voyage calculation purposes, DO consumption is usually considered only for the time in port for ships having shaft generators.[19] It must also be noted that the main engines of modern ships have considerably lower fuel consumption than engines of their older sisters. Furthermore, it must be mentioned that in periods of depressed freight rates combined with high oil prices, such as that occurred from 2009–2014 in all freight markets, shipbuilders find ways to promote new ship designs and attract the commercial interest. The so-called "eco-ships" were marketed during these years by the shipyards as the solution for shipowners to survive in a prolonged environment of high oil prices and low freight rates. However, this trend somewhat slowed down in 2015–16, as the oil prices decreased significantly.

In the "ship's particulars" or the vessel description in the charterparty, the performance speed is given. Not only this is the average speed with which the ship has been designed and built, but also the speed that the vessel is able to maintain during normal weather conditions. This speed is used in the voyage calculation as a basic figure. For any given speed, fuel consumption depends on hull design and hull smoothness. Between dry-dockings, marine growth on the hull of the ship increases its water resistance, reducing the achievable speed by 2 or 3 knots in extreme cases.[20] Operation of the vessel at lower speeds results in fuel savings due

---

19 ABB (2014) *Shaft Generator Drive for Marine: Decreasing Emissions, Improving Safety* (www.abb.com/marine).

20 Stopford, M. (1997) *Maritime Economics* (London, Routledge Publications, 2nd edition, p. 169).

VOYAGE COSTS:

BUNKERS
PORT DUES & CHARGES
COMMISSIONS/BROKERAGE
LOAD/DISCHARGE
EXTRA INSURANCE
MISCELLANEOUS

THE VARIABLE COSTS ELEMENT

OPERATING OR RUNNING COSTS:

ADMINISTRATION (SHORE)
CREWING OR MANNING
MAINTENANCE & MATERIALS
REPAIR & SPARE PARTS
DRYDOCKING/SPECIAL SURVEY
CLASS & CERTIFICATES
INSURANCE & CLAIMS
LUBOIL & FRESHWATER

THE FIXED COSTS ELEMENT

CAPITAL COSTS:

LOAN CAPITAL & INTEREST
DEPRECIATION

NOTE: THE TIME CHARTER EQUIVALENT (TCE) IN THE VOYAGE CAL-CULATION IS THE REVENUE PER DAY AFTER DEDUCTING THE VOYAGE COSTS FROM THE TOTAL VOYAGE INCOME AND DIVIDING RESULT BY NUMBER OF VOYAGE DAYS (Days at sea plus days in Port plus ballast days). Sometimes the FIXED COSTS ELEMENT is referred to as the T/C-EQUIVALENT. THE COMPARISON FACTOR in the Owners' daily consideration for scheduling ships is the REVENUE PER DAY to be compared with:
• *Total vessel's costs*
• *Current market level/development*
• *Alternative employments/markets*
• *Lay-up or sale conditions*

Figure 14.9 Vessel's Costs

to the reduced water resistance. It has to be noted that even a small change in the average speed will cause a considerable difference in fuel consumption during the voyage. In certain conditions it may be economic to reduce the speed and prolong the duration of the voyage for a number of days in order to reduce the bunkers costs (vessel's slow steaming tactics). In addition, the fuel consumption when the vessel is fully laden is far larger than when she is proceeding in ballast at the same speed.

Consequently, there may be considerable variations in the fuel consumption of vessels of a similar size and speed. Furthermore, no two voyages of one ship are likely to be exactly the same in terms of bunkers cost, due to:

- Draught considerations and load line zones en route.
- Fuel price fluctuations due to geopolitical, commercial and economic reasons.
- Difference of fuel prices from bunkering port to bunkering port. Sometimes, it may be advantageous to call frequently at bunkering ports to shorten bunker quantity requirements, thereby maximising cargo intake. In this case, however, the extra time, risk and expense involved should be taken into consideration.
- Difference between fuels' prices obtainable from the supplier's installation and those for bunkers delivered onboard by barge or tanker lorry. For example, the cost of putting the vessel alongside the installation which may involve tugs could be prohibitive.[21]
- Balance of fuel prices against freight income. Sometimes, the difference in price for bunkers is so great during a voyage that it becomes more advantageous for the shipowner to carry extra bunkers rather than maximise his cargo lifting.

The manner of simply adding a standard percentage, for example 5%, to all tabular distances, to cover for *adverse weather conditions and currents*, is a very rough tool during the estimations, especially considering the large amounts of money involved in bunker payments. Anticipated wind and weather conditions for the intended ocean passage are fairly predictable and the ship's actual progress can be monitored by employing a weather routing system. The surface currents of the oceans are also very well charted and may thus be forecasted and pre-calculated.

Figures 14.3 and 14.4 show on one side a typical world weather situation on a certain date as given in *Lloyd's List*. One can see, for the different geographical areas around the globe, the wind situation to be expected as caused by the normal frontal and seasonal systems, together with no less than three tropical revolving storms in progress. On the other side, one may have an example of the surface current systems in the Atlantic Ocean (HM Meteorological Office). Similar charts are available for the Indian Ocean, the Pacific Ocean and other special areas. For instance, under the certain weather conditions seen in Figure 14.4, a ship of any kind or size or draught on a passage from Gibraltar to Venezuela would benefit from currents throughout the voyage and that could add an extra knot or two to the vessel's logged performance speed through the water. The reverse situation

---

21 Packard, W. (1996) *Voyage Estimating* (Surrey, Fairplay Publications, p. 14).

would of course affect a vessel proceeding in the opposite direction. These matters are also of importance when dealing with *speed claims*.

In voyage estimations, the theoretical distance covered during a cargo voyage (including connecting ballast legs) or the respective calculated time may be increased by the use of certain rules of thumb. For example, this may be done by consistently increasing the total estimated distance by a fixed percentage, or by adding one day per each canal transit, etc. This is a conservative approach in order to allow for unpredictable adverse developments, such as bad weather conditions, strong streams and currents, passages requiring speed reductions, etc. It is the *sea voyage time* pre-calculated in this way that determines the *FO consumption,* thereby the cost calculated for fuel oil during the intended voyage.

The *diesel oil (DO) consumption* varies from day to day within certain limits, depending on which auxiliary engines are running. Nevertheless, for calculation purposes and in the vessel's official particulars, an average figure is used for the consumption per day which is determined from statistics of previous voyages of the ship in question.

The sum of port days and days at sea gives the *total voyage time* which is used for calculating the *DO consumption (except for vessels with shaft generator where DO consumption is calculated only for the time in port)*. This number of total voyage days is the same number that will be used when arriving at the final calculation for finding the voyage revenue per day.

The *bunker prices* for FO and for DO vary considerably both from time to time and among the different places for bunker replenishment. All ports do not have bunkering facilities and some ports that may supply bunkers might not be able to supply all the different grades.

The estimator has to take into consideration the above-mentioned factors during the calculation of bunkers cost. If the fuels remaining onboard the vessel at the commencement of the voyage are insufficient for the execution of the charter, then the estimator has to calculate the quantity of extra bunkers required (in accordance with the ship's bunker consumption already estimated at the first stage of calculations). More specifically, the *total bunkers cost* is equal to:

TOTAL BUNKERS COST =
BUNKERS REMAINED ONBOARD (ROB) × FUEL PRICE
ON THE DATE OF PURCHASE
+
EXTRA BUNKERS REQUIRED AT SEA × PRESENT FUEL PRICE
+
EXTRA BUNKERS REQUIRED IN PORTS × PRESENT FUEL PRICE

Another major item of voyage costs concerns the *port expenses*. Port charges include various fees levied against the vessel and/or cargo for the use of the facilities and services provided by the port. All the different costs that the ship

438

will incur from arriving at the pilot station (APS) or from taking her inward pilot (TIP) until dropping her outward pilot (DOP)[22] have to be estimated and pre-calculated in the best possible way. The actual port charges may be calculated in four different ways, based on: the volume of cargo; the weight of cargo; the gross registered tonnage of vessel; or the net registered tonnage of vessel. The actual level of port costs depends on the pricing policy of the port authority, the size of the vessel, the type of cargo loaded/discharged and the time spent in port. It is difficult to estimate with any degree of accuracy the duration of time the vessel will spend in ports and furthermore the respective port charges.

International organisations, such as BIMCO and INTERTANKO, provide information on port charges. However, such charges are difficult to be assessed beforehand even when they come from official sources.

The best way of estimating port expenses is by experience or the requested advice from *port agents* who have local knowledge. In order to make accurate estimations, the agent needs to take from the shipowner the vessel's particulars, such as net or gross tonnage, length, draught, special features etc. The agent also needs to know the vessel's business in the port, so he can discover to which berth the ship would have to go, a critical factor in estimating the expenses involved. After making all the necessary calculations, the port agent sends the shipowner a *pro-forma disbursement account*, which includes all the expenses (voyage and running costs) incurred in a port. The pro-forma disbursement account is intended to be an estimate of the actual disbursement account and is for guidance purposes only. Whilst the agent does take every care to ensure that the figures and information contained in the pro-forma disbursement account are as accurate as possible,[23] the actual disbursement account may, for various reasons, differ from the pro-forma disbursement account (see Figure 14.10). At this point, it should be mentioned that the estimator must not confuse the voyage expenses with the running (operating) costs which are also included in the disbursement account. *Only the voyage expenses should be included in the "port expenses" item of the voyage estimate.*

Canal transit expenses are similar to port disbursements and must also be undertaken into serious consideration by the estimator. Mere calculation of the canal dues payable will not be enough, as extras typically mount up the bill, for such items as agency and towage – actual or for escort purposes. It is needless to say that the estimator should consult experienced local agents before proceeding in calculations involving such canal or fairway transits. For example, the toll structure of the Suez Canal is extremely complicated, as tariffs are expressed in SDRs per SCNT. Special Drawing Rights (SDRs) were chosen as currency units to avoid losses from fluctuations in exchange rates, whilst Suez Canal Net Tonnage (SCNT) is a special ship measurement based on late 19th century rules.

---

22 See *APS*, *DOP* and *TIP* terms in the glossary.
23 Plomaritou, E. (2015) *What Agents Need to Know about Chartering* (London, Lloyd's Maritime Academy, Module 6 of Distance Learning Course "Diploma for Ship and Port Agents").

STANDARD DISBURSEMENTS ACCOUNT

Shipagent		Owners/Chartered Owners/Disponent Owners

Port:	Date:	Vessel:	Voy. No.
Arrived from:	Date/Hour:	NRT	GRT
Sailed for:	Date/Hour:	TDW	LOA
Cargo loaded:	Cargo discharged:	☐ Repairs ☐ Other	☐ Bunkers

Voucher No.				
	PORT CHARGES	Harbour Dues		
		Light Dues		
		Pilotage		
		Towage		
		Mooring/Unmooring		
		Shifting		
		Customs Charges		
		Launch/Car Hire		
		Agency Remuneration		
		Telex, Postage, Telegrams		
			Total	
	CARGO CHARGES	Stevedoring Expenses		
		Winchmen/Cranage		
		Tally		
		Overtime		
			Total	
	SHIP CHARGES	Cash to Master		
		Water		
		Stores/Provisions		
		Crew Expenses		
		Repairs		
			Total	
	STATEMENT	Credit to Owners' Account	TOTAL	
		Balance due us/you		

Printed by The BIMCO Charter Party Editor

Figure 14.10 Standard Disbursements Account

Source: www.bimco.org (accessed 20 August 2015).

RECOMMENDED BY THE BALTIC AND INTERNATIONAL MARITIME CONFERENCE (BIMCO) AND THE FEDERATION OF NATIONAL ASSOCIATIONS OF SHIP BROKERS AND AGENTS (FONASBA)

SCNT broadly corresponds to the cargo carrying space below deck, though not directly comparable to more normal and modern ways of measurement of cargo capacity. The relevant SCNT certificate is issued from a classification society. The final cost for passing the Suez Canal depends on a series of factors, such as the type of vessel, the SCNT, the GRT, the draught and beam, whether it will be laden or in ballast, whether it will sail northbound or southbound, etc. For the Panama Canal transit, pricing aspects are somewhat simpler, as the tolls are commonly paid in US Dollars; however the charges are also based on a respective ship measurement called Panama Canal Net Tonnage (PCNT).

The estimator has to calculate also the *cargo-handling expenses*, such as loading, trimming, stowage and discharging costs. Other extra cargo-handling cost items may be incurred, the cost of hold cleaning being the most frequent one, whilst considerable amounts may be faced for dunnaging, lashing and securing the cargo. These costs depend on the cargo type and the terms of the charterparty. The wording of the original cargo order must be such, that it is clearly understood how the costs for cargo handling are intended to be distributed between the parties. As for the estimation of total port costs, these cargo-handling expenses are difficult to be pre-calculated or allocated between the ports of call, thus very often the first calculation will have to be made on a rough estimate only.

The charterer is obliged to arrange and pay for the cargo-handling expenses if there are *"FIO terms" (Free In Out)*[24] or similar at the charterparty. Alternatively, the charterparty may stipulate *"gross terms"* or *"liner terms"*[25] when the loading and discharging arrangements and costs are to be undertaken by the shipowner. In the latter case, the estimator will need to check carefully with the local port agent the exact extent of the owner's liabilities, as well as how much time and

---

24 *FIO (Free In and Out)*: Voyage charterparty term commonly used in bulk shipping qualifying a freight rate which excludes the arrangement and cost of loading and discharging from the shipowner. Loading and discharging expenses are for charterers' account. Since the shipowner has no control over loading and discharging, it is common that suitable clauses for laytime and demurrage are agreed to allow for delays at the loading and discharging ports. If the intention is to expand the application of the term in other cargo-handling processes, such as stowing, dunnaging, lashing and securing or trimming, this should be clearly stated in the provision (see below). Similar terms are considered the following:

FIOS (Free In Out Stowed): Equivalent to FIO, specifying also that stowage is for charterers' or shippers' account. It is commonly used in carriage of general cargo.

FIOT (Free In Out Trimmed): Equivalent to FIO, specifying also that trimming is for charterers' or shippers' account. It is typically used in carriage of bulk cargo.

FIOST (Free In Out Stowed Trimmed): Equivalent to FIO, but concerning also both stowing and trimming.

FIOSPT (Free In Out Spout-Trimmed): Equivalent to FIO, but concerning also spout-trimming. It is typically used in carriage of dry bulk cargoes (e.g. grain) which are loaded by spouts or chutes or conveyors or elevators that ensure even loading of cargo in holds.

FIOLSD (Free In Out Lashed, Secured and Dunnaged): Equivalent to FIO, but concerning also lashing, securing and dunnaging of cargo. It is typically used in carriage of containers and general cargoes (source: www.bbc-chartering.com/toolbar/tools/abbreviations.html, accessed 2 September 2017).

25 *Gross Terms (GT)*: Voyage charter term in which the shipowner arranges and pays for loading and discharging.

Liner Terms (LT): Freight consists of the ocean carriage and the cost of cargo-handling at loading and discharging ports according to the custom of those ports. This varies widely from country to country and from port to port (source: BBC Chartering, "Chartering Terms").

expense can be expected. Other terms[26] that are more difficult to translate into cost figures may also be used, like *"berth terms"*, or any combination of terms like *"li/fo"* (*"liner in/free out"*), *"fi/lo"* (*"free in/liner out"*). All these terms imply that the owner will have to accept responsibilities and costs – to a greater or lesser extent – for loading and discharging. The extent of such undertakings has to be negotiated and the terms must be as exactly as possible specified in the charterparty.

At the time of pre-calculation one should also rely on information from agents at the intended ports of call and on one's own previous experience about slow or quick despatch (i.e. completion of ship's work in a port), so that to conclude about the expected *despatch time in ports* to be calculated. In any trading except liner traffic it is customary (in order to maintain a safety margin) to calculate cargo work during ordinary hours only (straight time). This is normally followed in practice, even if it is known that work is performed regularly in the port in question during a second shift or even around the clock. When giving FIO or similar terms in the order, the charterers must at the same time state the cargo-handling productivity they are willing to guarantee (the load and discharge rates of cargo are also a critical subject of freight negotiations). The owners for their part have to judge – on the basis of information obtained from agents and on the basis of their own previous experience – whether the figures given are in accordance with actual conditions or not. The *load/discharge rates* are described in the *"laytime clause"* of the charterparty and quantities are usually specified by mt per day, or by a number of days for loading and discharging respectively, or they may also be expressed as total number of days to be used for both loading and discharging (*"total days all purposes"* or *"reversible laytime"*). Sometimes, vague and ambiguous terms may be agreed, known as *"fast as can (fac)"* or *"custom of the port (cop)"* or *"customary quick despatch (cqd)"* terms. These are difficult to interpret and apply in practice, often causing disputes and claims (see analytically chapter 15 for laytime calculation).

Together with the statements of cargo-handling productivity, it must also be noted whether work-free holidays are agreed in the laytime clause or not (*SHEX* or *SHINC* term respectively). If a "SHEX" term has been agreed, Sundays and

---

26 *Berth terms*: Outdated and ambiguous voyage charterparty term, interpreted as:
  – Synonym to "liner" or "gross terms" where cargo-handling arrangements and expenses are for the owners' account.
  – Expression signifying that the contract of carriage and the cargo-handling processes are subject to the customs and conditions of the ports of loading and discharging.
LI/FO (Liner In / Free Out): Voyage charterparty term where cargo loading arrangements and expenses are for the owners' account. Freight is inclusive of sea carriage and cost of loading. Discharging expenses are for the charterers' or shippers' or receivers' account. There may be a laytime and demurrage provision for the port of discharging since the carrier has no control over discharging (source: BBC Chartering, "Chartering Terms").
FI/LO (Free In / Liner Out) or FI/LTD (Free In / Liner Term Discharge): Similar term, but here freight is inclusive of sea carriage and cost of discharging. Cargo loading arrangements and expenses are for the charterers' or shippers' account. There may be a laytime and demurrage provision for the port of loading since the carrier has no control over loading (source: BBC Chartering, "Chartering Terms").

Holidays are excluded from counting as laytime, thus in the voyage calculation the time to be used for loading/discharging must be prolonged by one or two days per each seven-day period per call.

If the owners judge that the statements about loading and discharging given in mt per day by the charterers compare reasonably well with the actual conditions, the *effective net port time* may be calculated by dividing the total cargo quantity to be handled at every port of call by the actual rate of loading/discharging for the respective port.

There are additional time factors which may prolong the stay at a port, for example, the time elapsing from the notice of readiness to receive or deliver cargo having been given until the laytime commences to count against the charterers. Owners normally cover such *"notice days"* or *"turn time"* by increasing the port time in voyage calculation by one day per port of call. This may be applicable for all FIO or similar charters as a rule of thumb, but always evaluated on a case-by-case basis.[27] The ship may also encounter delays in *waiting*, for example if it is impossible to obtain cargo stem (i.e the cargo is not delivered promptly for loading), or laydays for loading the cargo do not fit in exactly with the current ship's position and the ship arrives too early in the loading port. Finally, delays may be caused by *shifting* between berths, thus the ship may be kept waiting for a berth for a number of unforeseeable reasons and for any length of time.

If the loading/discharge rate which the charterers agree to in the charterparty is lower than the actual rate, then the ship will get a turn-round time in port which is shorter than the duration of time corresponding to agreed charterparty terms. In this event, the charterers may profit by reimbursement (*despatch money*) from the owners for the time saved (see appendix 3: "Laytime Definitions for Charter Parties 2013"). It is common in these cases to talk about "despatch cargoes" and there are charterers and groups of shippers who systematically wish to have such charterparty terms, so that they will earn such despatch money from the owners. On the contrary, ships may be kept in port for a longer duration than provided for in the charterparty. This occurs more often comparing to "despatch" cases. In such circumstances, the charterers will normally reimburse the owners for the extra costs incurred by paying *demurrage* (see also appendix 3). Both despatch and demurrage terms have to be considered when negotiating FIO terms. Very often, in dry bulk trades the amount of despatch money to be paid per day is fixed at half the demurrage amount (*"demurrage/half despatch"*). It is important that the calculation conforms as closely as possible with actual circumstances where the number of days in port is concerned. But, it is also important for the owners to fix a demurrage amount which covers all costs and extras that may be incurred. The *demurrage* or *despatch* amounts are entered into the voyage calculation by notation, for example, on the income side as a

---

27 When "gross terms", "liner terms" or similar are agreed, no laytime exists. However, even in this case specific terms can be agreed for a speedy and timely loading and discharging to cover the shipowners' interests. Under circumstances where the cargo handling is slower than it should have been, the owner can claim "damages for detention", instead of "demurrage" (De Zwarte, E. (2007) *There is so Much More in Laytime*, Arklow Co. Wicklow, Ireland, p. 66).

plus or minus item. It must be stressed that in tanker voyage charters no despatch amount is usually agreed.

Finally, there are two particular expenses that are often incurred, each of which can reach a considerable amount of money: *extra insurance premiums* and *taxes*. The estimator has to take into consideration the extra insurance expenses incurred due to:

- Breach of geographical limitations imposed by vessel's hull underwriters.
- Breach of geographical warranties imposed by the ship's war-risk insurers.
- Classification of particular vessels as "over-age" by cargo underwriters.

There are a number of various other insurance cost items that also may have to be considered with respect to the intended voyage, for example cargo carried on deck at owners' risk, etc. These are not normally included in the ship's regular insurance cover. There may also be a question of war risk bonuses or other occasional additions to the regular costs for the ship's crew depending on the intended trading. Political and labour unions' regulations in certain ports may cause considerable extra costs for the shipowners.

At this point, it should be mentioned that if the freight market is in the owner's favour, he may get the charterers to pay for the extra insurance premium that will be charged, for example from a call at a port situated in a war zone. Being in a less favourable position, the shipowner may have to absorb this cost.

In addition, the estimator has to be aware of taxes that may be applicable to certain trades. It has become common for the exporting or the importing country to require a freight tax, calculated on the gross freight amount, to be paid by the owners. BIMCO produces accurate information about worldwide taxes, regularly updated.

14.1.2.4 Fourth stage: calculation of income

Initially, the estimator has to calculate the gross freight which represents the gross sum to be paid to the owner for the carriage of cargo in his ship.[28] The cargo quantity intake has been already calculated during the second stage of the voyage estimations. *Gross freight* is determined by multiplying the agreed cargo quantity by the freight rate per mt.

GROSS FREIGHT =
AGREED QUANTITY OF CARGO × FREIGHT RATE PER
MT OF CARGO

---

28 Plomaritou, E. (2015) *Earning Revenue from Ships* (London, Lloyd's Maritime Academy, Module 5 of Distance Learning Course "Diploma in Shipping Commercial Management").

Sometimes, the shipowner is to be paid a *lump sum* freight instead of a freight rate per mt. In this case the lump sum freight figure automatically becomes the gross freight. There are rare occasions, however, where the owner expects to spend a lot of time at either the loading or the discharging port, waiting for cargo to be loaded or discharged. Time spent in addition to laytime will give rise to the agreed compensation called *demurrage* and payable to the shipowner. On the other hand, *despatch* money will be payable by the shipowner to the charterer if cargo handling is completed before laytime expires. Demurrage is usually agreed in the charterparty to be payable at a certain lump sum rate per day, or pro rata for part of a day. Despatch is normally agreed to be paid at half the demurrage rate. In some extent the estimator may be able to foresee such payments and, if so, they will form adjustments to the freight revenue.[29] Gross freight will be subject to a deduction due to a despatch or to an addition due to a demurrage. In the case where the charterer is not able to load a full and complete cargo onboard the vessel, he is liable to compensate the shipowner for loss of freight equal to the cargo unavailable. This compensation is called *deadfreight* and is added to the gross freight.

Furthermore, the estimator always has to deduct any *commission* and *brokerage* from gross freight. Although the gross freight figure comprises both freight and any demurrage, it is subject to the same deductions of commission and brokerage.

Shipowners should also be aware that in some countries taxes are payable on revenue earned. The estimator has to deduct any *freight tax* at this stage.

After the above-mentioned calculations, the resultant figure is the *net freight*.

$$\text{NET FREIGHT} =$$
$$[\text{GROSS FREIGHT} + (\text{DEMURRAGE} + \text{DEAD FREIGHT} +$$
$$\text{OVER FREIGHT} + \text{BALLAST BONUS} - \text{DESPATCH})] -$$
$$\text{COMMISSION} - \text{BROKERAGE}$$

14.1.2.5 Fifth stage: final result

The estimator, in order to calculate the *gross voyage result* (in other words the voyage profit or loss), has to deduct the total voyage expenses from the net freight figure.

$$\text{GROSS VOYAGE RESULT} = \text{NET FREIGHT} -$$
$$\text{TOTAL VOYAGE EXPENSES}$$

By taking into account the total number of days spent to perform the voyage, the gross daily result can be calculated. The *gross daily result* comes from the division of gross voyage result by the voyage duration and gives the estimator an easily comparable figure for any selection of different voyages. This figure may be regarded as a basic tool of the shipowner for making appropriate chartering decisions as concern as the employment of his vessels. The gross daily

---

29 Plomaritou, E. (2015) *Demurrage, Damages for Detention, Despatch* (London, Lloyd's Maritime Academy, Module 4 of Distance Learning Course "Certificate in Laytime and Demurrage").

result is almost equal to the *time charter equivalent* or *TCE* (see below the TCE formulas).

GROSS DAILY RESULT = GROSS VOYAGE RESULT ÷
DAYS OF THE VOYAGE

To calculate the net daily result, it will be necessary to incorporate the daily running costs. So, from the gross daily result, the vessel's daily running costs should be deducted, leaving the net daily result.

NET DAILY RESULT = GROSS DAILY RESULT – DAILY RUNNING COSTS

It is up to the shipowner to decide whether or not the capital costs should be included in this figure (apart from the operating expenses), but, whether included or not, it is vital to have a consistent method.

If a number of alternative voyage calculations for one ship were to show the same result per day, consideration would further need to be taken of the duration of the voyages or the alternative time charter engagements. Where options yield similar daily gross surpluses, the shipowner is likely to fix the one of shorter duration in a rising market and that of longer duration in a falling market. Moreover, the freight market may change during this time and, if the market goes up, the owner will wish to negotiate and start the next employment as soon as possible. But, under anticipated falling market conditions, the owner would try to secure longer employments at rate levels reflecting the spot market conditions prevailing on the date of fixing.

In the shipowner's daily considerations for chartering a ship, the critical factor is the ship's *revenue per day*, as compared with:

- Vessel's *total costs per day* (daily voyage, operating and capital expenses);
- *Current and forecasted market level;*
- *Alternative chartering employments/market opportunities;*
- *Lay-up* or *sale* conditions.

The shipowner wants to know the time charter equivalent of a particular voyage he is evaluating, which will give him a comparison with alternative time charter business that are available in the market. The *Time Charter Equivalent (TCE)* in a voyage calculation is given by the revenue per day after deducting the voyage costs per day, or alternatively by deducting the voyage costs from the total voyage income and dividing the result by the total number of voyage days (i.e. loaded days at sea plus ballast days at sea plus days in ports). The Time Charter Equivalent may therefore be calculated as follows:

TIME CHARTER EQUIVALENT =
$$\frac{\text{GROSS FREIGHT (OR TOTAL VOYAGE INCOME)} - \text{VOYAGE COST}}{\text{VOYAGE DURATION}}$$

446

or

TIME CHARTER EQUIVALENT =
GROSS DAILY RESULT + % OF COMMISSIONS

or

TIME CHARTER EQUIVALENT =
TOTAL VOYAGE REVENUE PER DAY – VOYAGE COST PER DAY

14.1.3 Voyage estimation example

The ability to carry out an accurate voyage calculation is an important skill for a shipbroker. Voyage estimates allow comparison between one piece of voyage business with another, as well as with ship's employment under time charter. In this way, the broker can advise his principal of charter market alternatives. There are many formats for a voyage calculation, including software packages. Figure 14.11 reproduces a dry cargo voyage estimation example as given by the Baltic Exchange in the latest Baltic Code,[30] so as an official case to be used as the basis of knowledge. Authors' commentary on the case intends to familiarise the reader with basic elements of voyage calculations.

The respective voyage charter is based on Free In Free Out (FIO) terms, while full definite laytime is used for both loading and discharging ports for simplification purposes. It is noted that a similar type of voyage calculation may be used for both dry cargo and tanker business. Greater emphasis should be placed on the logic, methodology and practicality of the calculations rather than on the precise figures, which vary constantly, depending on the ever-changing market conditions.

VOYAGE DETAILS

- Vessel's name: BPI
- Current vessel's position: Rotterdam (Netherlands)
- Loading port: Santos (Brazil)
- Bunkering port: Singapore (Singapore)
- Discharging port: Qingdao (China)
- Cargo: 65,000 mt grain (Santos – Qingdao is a typical grain trade)
- Gross Freight Rate: $40.00 / mt f.i.o. (free in & out), i.e. the arrangement and cost of loading and unloading is undertaken by the charterer and is not included in the freight
- Commission: 5%

---

30 The example has been sourced from the Baltic Code 2014. It is reproduced with the kind permission of the Baltic Exchange and is annotated by the authors.

Vessel's name	BPI	Ballast speed	14	Draft restriction
Year of build		IFO consumption	34	n/a
Deadweight	76,600	Laden speed	14	Winter allowance
Draft	14.14	IFO consumption	36	n/a
TPC	66	MDO at sea	0	Cargo lift
Grain cubic	90,700	MDO in port	0.1	65,000
Bunkers/Constants	2,000	IFO in port	3	
IFO price	609	Speed allowance (B)	0.98	7 % sea margin
MDO price	911	Speed allowance (L)	0.98	7 % sea margin

	Distance	Sea days	Port days	Port costs
Rotterdam				
Santos	5,412	17.32	9.625	65,000
Singapore (bunkers)	8,956	28.66	0.5	3,500
Qingdao	2,458	7.87	9.63	60,000
Totals	16,826	53.85	19.75	128,500

Ballast days	17.32
Laden days	36.53
Port days	19.75
Total days	73.60
IFO at Sea	1,159,439
MDO at Sea	0
IFO in Port	36,083
MDO in Port	1,799
Port costs	128,500
Misc	15,000
Total Expenses	1,340,821

Cargo lift	Gross freight pmt	Commission	Total net freight	Equivalent net t/c
65,000	40.00	5%	2,470,000	15343

Result is a net Timecharter of $15,343 per day over 73.60 days

Source: Baltic Exchange (2014) *The Baltic Code 2014* (p. 22).

Figure 14.11 Dry Cargo Voyage Estimation Example

The ship is currently at Rotterdam and should proceed to Santos in order to load a grain quantity of 65,000 mt. She will perform a carrying voyage to the port of Qingdao, where she will discharge the cargo. During the trip and without deviating from the normal route the ship will stop in Singapore for bunkering.

For the voyage calculations, the following information is considered necessary:

- DWT (summer): 76,600 mt (no winter allowance applicable)
- Draught: 14.14 m. (no draught restrictions applicable)

- Tonnes per Centimetre Immersion (TPC): 66 mt
- Grain cubic capacity (hold capacity): 90,700 cu.m.
- Speed (ballast): 14.0 knots
- Speed (laden): 14.0 knots
- Speed allowance[31]: 0.98 knots or 7% sea margin (ballast and laden)
- Bunkers/Constants ROB (Remaining on Board): 2,000 mt
- IFO Consumption (ballast): 34 mt/day
- IFO Consumption (laden): 36 mt/day
- MDO (at sea): 0
- IFO Consumption (in ports): 3 mt/day
- MDO Consumption (in ports): 0.1 mt/day
- IFO price: $609 / mt
- MDO price: $911 / mt
- Port disbursements: Santos $65,000 / Singapore $3,500 / Qingdao $60,000
- Distances in miles:

Rotterdam–Santos	5,412 miles
Santos–Singapore	8,956 miles (via Cape of Good Hope)
Singapore–Qingdao	2,458 miles

- Canal dues: Not applicable

VOYAGE PLAN (DISTANCES, TIME, CONSUMPTION)

First, the number of days required to run each leg of the journey is calculated, i.e. from Rotterdam (the port in which the ship is according to the last charter) to Santos (port of loading) then to Singapore (bunkering port) and finally to Qingdao (discharge port). Second, based on the voyage days and the daily bunker consumption of the ship, it is calculated the total quantity of bunkers. Thus, for the leg Rotterdam–Santos, the distance is 5,412 miles and the ship takes 17.32 days to perform at a speed of 13.02 knots (ballast speed 14.00 knots less speed allowance 0.98 knots). As for bunkers consumption, the vessel consumes 34 mt of fuel oil per day in ballast and no diesel oil. Therefore, to execute the leg Rotterdam–Santos they are required 589 mt of fuel oil (17.32 days × 34 mt/day). Similarly, the fuel consumptions for the remaining legs of the voyage are calculated, as follows.

---

31 If the weather is bad, the ship's resistance may increase compared to operating in calm weather conditions. It is common ground between the parties that the vessel is given an allowance to perform at a minimum speed which is less than the service speed specified in the charterparty. This is typically described by the word "about" which may accompany the vessel's service speed in relevant charterparty clauses. Here, in this example, the vessel is allowed a 7% sea margin or a reduced speed by 0.98 knots to sail in adverse sea conditions.

Voyage Plan				
	Distance (miles)	Days	IFO (mt)	MDO (mt)
Rotterdam	–	–	–	–
Santos	5,412	17.32	589	–
Singapore	8,956	28.66	1,032	–
Qingdao	2,458	7.87	283	–
Total	16,826	53.85 (ballast 17.32 + laden 36.53)	1,904	–

PORT DETAILS

For simplification purposes, estimation of time in ports is made for a full definite laytime used for both loading and discharging ports in this example. So, total laytime is almost divided by two, half spent in Santos and half in Qingdao. Besides, half a day is estimated for the bunkering call in Singapore. However, in real-life cases, the estimator should thoroughly check the laytime clause in order to see if definite or calculable laytime has been agreed, whether SHEX (Sundays Holidays Excluded) or SHINC (Sundays Holidays Included) terms apply, if there is "notice time" before laytime starts to count etc., so as to foresee how much time is going to be spent in port calls. In this case, the laden voyage will be via the Cape of Good Hope, so no passage from any canal is forecasted. Then, on the basis of estimated days in ports and the daily bunker consumption at ports, the total quantity of bunkers consumed in the ports is calculated. For example, in Santos the ship is expected to consume about 29 mt of fuel oil (9.625 days × 3mt/day) and about 1 mt of diesel oil (9.625 days × 0.1mt/day). The results of all these calculations are shown in the following table.

Port Details				
	Days	IFO (mt)	MDO (mt)	Port Costs ($)
Rotterdam	–	–	–	–
Santos	9.625	28.88	0.963	65,000
Singapore	0.5	1.5	0.05	3,500
Qingdao	9.63	28.88	0.963	60,000
Total	19.75	59.26	1.98	128,500

BUNKERS COST

The estimator should thoroughly check bunkers remaining on board from previous trips, the cost of which is estimated based on the purchase price during previous voyages, as well as the bunkers that should always remain as safety margin, the bunkering ports and the bunker prices worldwide and in relation with the voyage, the cargo quantities in relation to the bunkers, the load line zones during the voyage, etc. For simplification purposes in this example, there will be one stop for bunkering in Singapore and all bunker prices are considered fixed (i.e. IFO price at $609 / mt and MDO price at $911 / mt) for all quantities, both those remaining on board and those required for the voyage. Thus, the total cost of bunkers will be calculated as follows.

	Bunkers Cost in ports				
	IFO (mt)	Total IFO Cost ($)	MDO (mt)	Total MDO Cost ($)	Total Bunkers Cost in Ports ($)
Rotterdam	–	–	–	–	–
Santos	28.88	17,585	0.963	877	18,462
Singapore	1.5	913	0.05	45	958
Qingdao	28.88	17,585	0.963	877	18,462
Total	59.26	36,083	1.98	1,799	37,882

	Bunkers Cost at sea				
	IFO (mt)	Total IFO Cost ($)	MDO (mt)	Total MDO Cost ($)	Total Bunkers Cost in Ports ($)
Rotterdam	–	–	–	–	–
Santos	589	358,669	–	–	358,669
Singapore	1,032	628,455	–	–	628,455
Qingdao	283	172,315	–	–	172,315
Total	1,904	1,159,439	–	–	1,159,439

CARGO DETAILS

The estimator should then calculate the total cargo quantity that can be loaded and transported by the ship.

First, possible restrictions by the dwt capacity (weight) of the ship will be examined. *The critical point for finding the available deadweight cargo capacity of the ship is when the ship will carry the greatest amount of fuel while being already loaded.* To find the available deadweight cargo capacity, one should deduct from the summer deadweight of the ship, the stores, water and constants, the bunkers for the voyage and the bunkers' safety margin. The result is the available deadweight cargo capacity when the ship is in the summer load line zone. However, if the critical point is for example a loading port situated in the tropical load line zone, the ship could have been even more immersed in the water when sailing from this port until she reaches the summer zone. Thus, the quantity of fuel consumed until then, may be offset by a corresponding quantity of additional cargo. By following this process, the maximum amount of cargo intake has been calculated and it must be checked if it is within the cargo quantity limits described in the charterparty. For simplification purposes in this example, cargo lift is defined at 65,000 mt which may be comfortably loaded by a 76,000 dwt bulker.

Second, possible limitations due to the volume of the cargo load will be considered. The grain cargo has stowage factors ranging between about 1.3–1.73 cubic metres/mt and the grain cubic capacity of the holds of the ship is 90,700 cubic metres. Therefore, by dividing 90,700 with 1.73 (wheat or oats) it comes that the available cargo space would be enough to load only 52,400 mt of the consignment. However, Santos is an exporting port of soya beans which have a stowage factor of about 1.3 cbm/mt, thus by dividing 90,700 with 1.3, it comes that the available cargo space would be enough to load about 69,700 mt of cargo. Consequently, as long as the example is simplified, it seems very possible that no restriction arises either on the volume of cargo intake.

VOYAGE COSTS, GROSS FREIGHT, NET FREIGHT, GROSS VOYAGE SURPLUS

The next step is to estimate the overall costs and revenues of the voyage. The bunkers cost and the port expenses are obtained from the previous calculating tables. The cargo-handling cost is not borne by the shipowner (FIO terms in the charterparty). To calculate the total gross freight, the cargo lift quantity is taken into account multiplied by the gross freight per mt. After the deduction of commissions from the total gross freight, the total net freight results and after deducting the voyage costs (variable cost), the gross voyage surplus comes. These are illustrated in the following tables.

Voyage Costs ($)	
BUNKERS	1,197,321
– At sea $1,159,439	
– In ports $37,882	
PORTS	128,500
MISCELLANEOUS	15,000
CARGO HANDLING	–
CANALS	–
TAXES	–
TOTAL	1,340,821

Voyage Revenues ($)	
GROSS FREIGHT	2,600,000
– 65,000 mt × $40 / mt	
(-) COMMISSION (5%)	130,000
NET FREIGHT	2,470,000
(-) VOYAGE COSTS	1,340,821
GROSS VOYAGE SURPLUS	1,129,179

FINAL RESULT OF THE VOYAGE

The final result of the voyage estimation is summarised in the next table.

Final Result

TOTAL DAYS OF THE VOYAGE = DAYS AT SEA + DAYS IN PORTS = 53.85 + 19.75 = 73.60

GROSS VOYAGE SURPLUS OR PROFIT = $1,129,179

GROSS DAILY SURPLUS OR PROFIT = $1,129,179 ÷ 73.60 DAYS = $15,343 / DAY = **NET TIME CHARTER EQUIVALENT**

NET DAILY SURPLUS OR PROFIT = GROSS DAILY SURPLUS – DAILY RUNNING COSTS[32]

TIME CHARTER EQUIVALENT = GROSS DAILY SURPLUS + ALLOWANCE FOR T/C COMMISSION (5%) = $15,343 + $767 = $16,110 / DAY

14.2 Special estimations

14.2.1 Consecutive voyages, CoA and marginal estimations

The same principles of calculation are applicable to *consecutive voyages* or to *contracts of affreightment (CoA)*. Such engagements often last for a longer period of time and it may be difficult to estimate the evolution of cost elements during the charter period. In addition, it is crucial at the stage of pre-calculation to determine how the ship should be optimally traded in order to minimise the time in ballast. For example, will cargoes to be carried under a CoA be used as return voyages in an established trade, where the owners expect well-paying cargoes in the opposite direction or where a similar contractual engagement has already been secured? Is the intention to execute the contract shipments as round voyages with the return leg in ballast? Or are the contract voyages to be carried out as intermediary voyages filling a gap between two other charter engagements?

There are instances where calculations do not cover complete voyages, but it seems more appropriate to make what is called a *marginal calculation*. For example, this can occur when a ship is negotiating to be fixed for a specific cargo voyage, whilst steaming either in ballast or with only a part of the cargo space occupied. There may also be a cargo which requires some deviation in time and distance from the immediately intended route, but which nevertheless would take the ship in the right direction. It is characteristic for such a "*way-cargo*" that the freight revenue from this cargo alone does not justify fixing the ship for this voyage. However, the fact that the ship will be directed along largely the same route anyway, makes the freight for the way-cargo a positive supplement to the overall

---

32 A panamax bulker may typically have OPEX of about $6–7,000 / day as per 2017, depending mostly on the age and the operational standards of the vessel. The daily capital costs may range widely, depending on how and when the vessel was financed. Besides, it is a matter of the owners' decision whether to include and how to present CAPEX in this calculation.

voyage result, or at least helps in reducing the loss in the case of a ballast trip. In such marginal calculations, only the bunker costs for the extra distance (deviation) and the additional costs related to the prolongation of the voyage time are considered. The expected costs for extra ports of call, cargo handling etc., caused by the shipment of the way-cargo, have also to be taken into account. The extra freight revenue, minus all extra costs related to the way-cargo, is the supplementary net freight for making the deviation. When dividing this supplement by the number of extra days, a surplus per day is obtained. This result can be compared with the general required trading revenue per day for the ship during the period in question. This comparison will show whether or not it is profitable to take the cargo. The final decision may also be influenced by other factors, such as positioning of the vessel, marketing purposes (customer relationships), etc.

14.2.2 Time charter estimations

In the case of a time charter, the calculations are simple. The time charterer is obliged to pay the owners an agreed rate of hire ($ per day) which is usually paid in advance every 15 days, 30 days, or monthly. The hire normally includes everything except what has to be paid for bunkers on board, which are for charterers' account on delivery of vessel and for owners' account on ship's redelivery to the owner. However, in some cases the owners have to take into account that the intended trading (charterer's decision and responsibility) may incur higher daily operating costs than normal, for example because of overtime work for the crew, expensive travelling when crews are exchanged, higher average costs for maintenance and spare parts, extra insurance premiums, or possible costs for certain cargo-handling material and equipment. The ballast leg from the previous charter to the point of delivery and from the point of redelivery to a new employment area is normally for the owners' account. Naturally, this is a cost which the owner will try to cover by adjustment of the hire level of the time charter. He may also succeed in negotiating a special ballast bonus.

It is useful to note some different ways of stating the time charter hire. The time charter hire may be defined as the gross hire.

GROSS HIRE = TIME CHARTER HIRE PER DAY

The brokerage and the address commission[33] are calculated in the same way as for ordinary voyage freight to determine the net hire.

---

33 *Brokerage:* Fee or commission payable by a shipowner to a shipbroker for successful negotiation of a charter. It is normally expressed as a percentage of the freight and demurrage or hire or other forms of revenue (e.g. deadfreight, ballast bonus etc.). Brokerage may or may not be payable, according to the terms of the charterparty, should the voyage or period of the charter not be completed (source: www.bbc-chartering.com).

Address Commission (adcom): Commission payable by the shipowner to the charterer. The reason for this system is sometimes said to be that the charterer's shipping department for book-keeping purposes must show some kind of income from their activities. State trading countries regularly include a 5% address commission in their orders (source: www.bbc-chartering.com).

NET HIRE = GROSS HIRE – COMMISSION/BROKERAGE

Furthermore, the estimator has to deduct the daily running (operating and possibly capital) cost from the hire earned per day to achieve the daily profit.

DAILY PROFIT = HIRE PER DAY – DAILY RUNNING COST

If there is any difference between the agreed charterparty price of bunkers paid by charterers on delivery and the actual bunkers price paid by the owners, this should be taken into consideration by the estimator.

In the dry cargo market it is common to agree a daily hire rate, for example "*$8,750 per day*". For longer periods and with regard mainly to the largest vessel sizes (e.g. capesizes), the hire is sometimes expressed as a certain amount per deadweight ton per month, for example, "*$4.75 per dwt per 30 days*". In reefer trading, however, it is common practice to fix the hire at a certain amount per cubic foot bale, for example, "*75 cents per ft³ per 30 days*". Sometimes, the hire is expressed on the basis of a rate per summer load line deadweight capacity, irrespective of where (load line zone) the ship is to be used. In this case, the rate per summer deadweight ton can be calculated as follows[34]:

TIME CHARTER RATE PER SUMMER DWT PER MONTH ($) =
GROSS DAILY HIRE ($ PER DAY) × 30.4375 DAYS (PER CALENDAR MONTH
WHICH ALLOWS FOR THE EXTRA DAY EVERY FOURTH YEAR) ÷
SHIP'S SUMMER DWT

The estimator, in order to find the gross daily hire equivalent to a rate per summer deadweight ton, has to reverse the above equation as follows:

GROSS DAILY HIRE ($ PER DAY) =
TIME CHARTER RATE PER SUMMER DWT PER MONTH ($) × SHIP'S SUMMER
DWT ÷ 30.4375 DAYS (PER CALENDAR MONTH WHICH ALLOWS FOR THE
EXTRA DAY EVERY FOURTH YEAR)

By the simple calculations described above, the estimator may examine if the time charter is financially attractive in relation to some voyage alternatives.

14.2.3 Reefer estimations

In reefer trades the calculations are mainly the same as those in the dry cargo trades, while marginal calculations are very common and similar to those in liner business. It is also characteristic that reefer ships may have open space on the ballast voyages, but nevertheless, because of tight scheduling for their contractual undertakings, they may not have time left even for a short deviation. However, there are trades both in the Atlantic and the Pacific, where reefer owners combine a conventional

---

34 Packard, W. (1996) *Voyage Estimating* (Surrey, Fairplay Publications, p. 45).

reefer transport in one direction with a liner-like service in the back-haul direction. The latter case appears as a semi-container dry cargo operation, for which service the calculation will be about the same as given below for the regular lines.

14.2.4 Liner estimations

In liner business there is often a need to make marginal calculations for transports within or in the vicinities of the ordinary trading area or route which, for various reasons, cannot be regarded as regular cargo bookings. Frequently, the additional cargo may involve loading or discharging at a port not regarded as a basic port according to the trade lane, but which may be reached through a minor deviation. It may also be a question of loading and discharging at ports along the normal route, but in addition to the normally scheduled stops. If a liner vessel has got the time within the framework of the schedule and has also open space which is not intended to be filled by ordinary bookings, then it may be possible for the owners to calculate a freight for a way-cargo. In principle, this revenue should cover the costs of the extra port calls, extra bunkers, cargo handling and possibly extra material, resulting finally in a decent profit.

If the prevailing freight level is high, the owners may, by fixing at market level, get a substantial addition to the voyage net result. But during low market conditions, the owners may well have to abstain from taking the cargo. If the ship's schedule is tight, under all market conditions the calculation has to consider not only the required daily operating surplus, but also a possible extra cost borne by the liner operator for chartering-in extra tonnage to fill the gap in schedule caused by the deviation made by the ordinary scheduled ship. Conversely, in a low market environment, even if the vessel has not got any free space for the way-cargo, the owners might check out whether the marginal calculation shows an interesting surplus should the ordinary (but low-paying) parcel be replaced by the way-cargo offered. Although the marginal calculation may show a surplus, it could nevertheless be impossible for the owner to accept the extra cargo because of his relationship with regular customers or due to other market implications.

14.3 Tanker estimations

A complete voyage calculation concerning tanker trading should follow the same methodology and contain largely the same items as already discussed. However, the peculiarities in cargo handling, the practical manner of calculating the time counting parameters and, above all, the freight fixing system differ to a great extent. For time-counting purposes and the related inputs in the voyage calculation, normally no despatch is agreed in tanker charterparties and the total time allowed for loading and unloading a tanker (other than the smallest sizes) is 72 hours altogether.

In respect of the expression of voyage freight rates, most tanker fixtures (except for shipping quantities below about 10,000 dwt, chemical parcels and gas cargoes) are quoted with reference to an international freight scale system called "*New Worldwide Tanker Nominal Freight Scale*" or "*Worldscale*" *(WS)* for short. As it is virtually impossible to trade tankers without having access to this information, special mention to Worldscale will be made in the next section. Through that, particular aspects of tanker chartering will be examined.

14.3.1 Worldscale[35]

14.3.1.1 Historical background[36]

The concept of freight rate schedules originates from World War II. During the war, first the British Government and later the US Government requisitioned shipping and owners were receiving compensation on the basis of a daily hire rate. From time to time, the Governments were able to make requisitioned tankers available on a voyage basis to the major oil companies. On such occasions, the oil companies paid freight to the government concerned and the rate of freight, which was dependent upon the voyage performed, was determined in accordance with a scale or schedule of rates laid down by that government. The freight rates were calculated so that, after allowing for port costs, bunker costs and canal expenses, the net daily revenue was the same for all voyages.

That was the genesis of the principle for tanker rate schedules or scales, namely the owners should receive the same net daily revenue irrespective of the voyage performed. Government control of shipping continued until 1948 and by that time the tanker market had come to recognise the advantages of freight rate schedules. Between 1952 and 1962, a number of different schedules were issued as a service to the tanker trade by non-governmental bodies; "*Scales Nos. 1, 2 and 3*" and then "*Intascale*" in London, "*ATRS*" in New York.

In 1969, a joint London/New York effort to replace both Intascale and ATRS was initiated. The production was called "*Worldwide Tanker Nominal Freight Scale*", more usually known under its code name "*Worldscale*". The word "nominal" was initially used to emphasise that it was only during the period of government control that the schedule rates were intended to be used as actual rates. Subsequently, the word "nominal" reflects the situation where actual tanker charter rates are freely negotiated as percentage adjustments to the published freight scale rates of a theoretical non-existing vessel (see further below).

With the introduction of Worldscale, it became a customary practice to express tanker spot freight rates in terms of a direct percentage of the scale rates, instead of a plus or minus percentage. This method is known as "*points of scale*" and thus Worldscale 100 means 100 points or 100% of the published rate or "*Worldscale flat*", while Worldscale 250 means 250 points or 250% of the published rate and Worldscale 30 means 30 points or 30% of the published rate. Under the older methods, these would have been referred to as "plus 150%" and "minus 70%" respectively.

"*New Worldscale*" was introduced in 1989 and is currently still in force.

---

35 Worldscale methodology and practical examples are presented in this section with the kind permission of Worldscale Association (London) Limited. Information is provided according to 2015 figures. For a current update, interested parties should always consult the latest version of Worldscale.
36 www.worldscale.co.uk (accessed 20 August 2015).

14.3.1.2 Description, rationale and use

Worldscale may be defined as a nominal freight scale applying to the carriage of crude oil and oil products in bulk by sea. It is an internationally widespread freight index system for tankers which provides a method of calculating the applicable freight to oil transport. The "*New Worldscale*" was introduced with effect from 1 January 1989 and the word "new" was then added to differ from the previous freight systems. Nowadays, it is generally understood that "Worldscale" refers to the new scale.

Worldscale is a set of *predefined reference tables* that determine (estimate) the *freight rate levels* for a *notional*[37] *standard vessel* for each of about 320,000 *sea routes*[38] (*round trip voyages*), which can be made worldwide.

According to the scale *assumptions*, the fictional standard tanker has specific features in respect of its tonnage, speed, fuel consumption, etc. The model-tanker is considered to have a deadweight capacity of 75,000 mt, an average speed of 14.5 knots, a consumption of 55 mt fuel oil per day at sea and a fictional daily fixed cost element of USD 12,000.[39] It must be stressed that the assumed daily cost used for the calculations is only a theoretical figure which does not take into account, for example, the varying cost levels between the different countries.

Besides, there are also some fundamental operating and trading assumptions applying to the standard vessel for all possible trades in respect of the freight scale calculations. For example:

(1) the distances of all trade routes are clearly defined, expressed and published in the scale,
(2) the calculations are based on a fixed port time of four days (72 hours) in total for loading and discharging for all trades,
(3) voyage time is determined by the ship's speed and distance routes which are both clearly specified,
(4) bunker prices are calculated on a monthly basis average for the period running from 1 October to 30 September of previous year,
(5) port costs, canal transits and other direct costs are taken into account and continually monitored for each new publication, and
(6) amendments to published rates can be made during the year if considered by the Associations to have crucial effect.

The freight rate determined for the standard vessel on each sea route is defined as the *WS100* or *W100* of that route, called "*flat rate*" or "*WS flat*", always calculated in US Dollars per mt. This is the benchmark for assessing, quoting, negotiating and fixing the level of freight rates in real-life tanker charters for each particular route. Market levels of tanker spot freight rates or individual tanker fixtures are expressed in terms of a percentage or a Worldscale equivalent of the

---

37 The ship is non-existing in real life, but it is described in accordance with exact, up-to-date specifications and theoretically operated on the basis of specific, current market assumptions.
38 www.worldscale.co.uk (accessed 20 August 2015).
39 www.worldscale.co.uk (accessed 20 August 2015).

nominal freight rate (flat rate). A fixture rate of WS100 would mean the actual ship in question was fixed at the same freight level as the flat rate was calculated and issued in the tables for the standard ship. It must be clarified that *each WS100 is a freight rate expressed in US Dollars per metric tonne of cargo, which is equivalent with the unit cost*[40] *of the standard ship for a specific round trip voyage.* In other words, the *flat rate is the freight rate per metric tonne of cargo carried that should be earned from the standard ship, so that its total voyage revenue equals its total voyage costs. WS 100 is effectively the break-even point of the standard vessel for each route,* in accordance with the basis of calculation. In practice, this does not apply to any other vessel size except that of the standard vessel. For smaller vessels (than the size of the standard ship) actual break-even figures will tend to be higher than the flat rate, whilst for larger sizes actual break-even figures will be lower than the flat rates.[41] This occurs due to economies of scale.

A simple example may illustrate the use of Worldscale. Assuming that the tables show a "flat rate" of US$ 18.00 per mt for transportation of crude oil from the Arabian Gulf to Western Europe and one tanker is fixed to carry 150,000 mt at WS60 for this voyage, this means that the actual freight rate earned is 60% of US$ 18.00 of the scale, i.e. the ship was chartered by US$ 10.80 per mt. Since the Worldscale principle is to provide at WS100 the same net return per day irrespective of voyage performed by the standard vessel, its greatest utility as a chartering tool lies in the easiness, consistency and flexibility with which the owner can compare potential returns from alternative charters. Market levels for differing vessel sizes and trade routes can be assessed and compared. However, one cannot surely state that if a shipowner fixes a cargo at WS75 and another owner fixes a cargo of the same size at the same time in another trade at WS80, then the latter has obtained a higher freight earning, since the various cost elements (bunkers, port costs and daily running costs) in practice have a different impact on the different voyages and ships. In any case, as the WS rates may be translated into daily results, the tanker owners can produce a series of voyage calculations for their different sizes of ships and their most frequent trades, tabulating the results. Then, they have available a number of different WS rates for each trade and can judge and evaluate the various alternative employments offered.

It is worth pointing out that, while the voyage fixtures and respective freight rates for crude and product tankers are commonly reported in Worldscale terms, spot rates for gas carriers and chemical tankers are typically expressed in US Dollars per mt or per cubic metre or per cubic foot.

Worldscale publication is annually revised on 1 January each year, so that the flat rates correspond to changes of tankers' operating and trading costs, namely using updated bunker prices, port costs and currency exchange rates. Information is provided on a subscription basis and subscribers include tanker owners/managers, oil companies, shipbrokers, shippers and traders.

---

40 Unit cost means here the ship's total cost from the voyage, per metric tonne of cargo carried.
41 www.worldscale.co.uk (accessed 20 August 2015).

Worldscale is a non-profit-making organisation. It was set up corporately in 1962, changed name in 1969 and now exists, having adopted the current standard vessel size, since 1989. *Worldscale Association (London) Limited* from London and *Worldscale Association (NYC) Inc.* from New York are the joint sponsors and publishers of the scale. The corporation is managed by shipping professionals and directors from prominent shipbroking companies in London and New York, as follows[42]:

Members – London	*Members – New York*
H Clarkson & Company Ltd	McQuilling Brokerage Partners Inc
Galbraith's Ltd	Mallory Jones Lynch Flynn & Associates
E A Gibson Shipbrokers Ltd	Odin Marine
Simpson, Spence and Young	Poten & Partners Inc
Braemar ACM Shipbroking	Charles R Weber Company
	Dietze & Associates Inc

14.3.1.3 Practical tips
Apart from the fundamental assumptions described above, some more details may be further presented in respect of the Worldscale calculations and use in practice:

- Published flat rates are based upon specific load and discharge ports (round voyages) rather than ranges of ports. Flat rates for any combinations of ports or transhipment areas can be calculated with up to five load ports and ten discharge ports. More complex voyages are available on request.
- The cheapest route is calculated and published for each trade, taking into consideration distance, canal and pilotage fees. The shortest route may not necessarily produce the lowest rate. The following route indicators are used both in the Schedule and when quoting rates:

  C: via Cape of Good Hope, laden and in ballast
  CS: via Cape of Good Hope laden, Suez Canal in ballast
  S: via Suez Canal, laden and in ballast
  P: via Panama Canal, laden and in ballast
  CP: via Cape of Good Hope laden, Panama Canal in ballast
  H: via Cape Horn, laden and in ballast
  CH: via Cape of Good Hope laden and in ballast, or Cape Horn laden and in ballast

- In the published tables, voyages are listed in alphabetical order by discharge port. Users need to find the discharge ports shown in bold capital

---

42 www.worldscale.co.uk (accessed 20 August 2015).

letters and then (under that discharge port) find the load port listed beneath and read the USD/mt and distance miles for the rate.

- Important information is given by the book notes which can be found against the discharge and load ports. Book notes will identify "*additions*" that will need to be applied and "*differentials*" that will need to be considered along with the rate provided in the rates pages (see further below).

- *Additions* relate to voyages loading within the Arabian Gulf (alternative definitions: Persian Gulf or Middle East Gulf), Black Sea and Lake Maracaibo. The rates of the additions are published in a separate part of the book (blue pages). Additions are used for geographical simplification and reduction of the number of possible rates requiring calculation. A transit point (*waypoint*) on the entry/exit to these areas is used. In the case of the Black Sea, rate is calculated from any port in Black Sea to Uskudar (Turkey). The remainder of the voyage is calculated from Uskudar onwards. For example, to find a rate for loading Constanza and discharging Genoa in the Worldscale book, one finds "GENOA" in the rates section of the book, then under that, looks for Uskudar for part of the rate. The addition is for the Constanza to Uskudar route. These two rates and mileages should then be added together for the complete rate. The agreed percentage or Worldscale equivalent of the fixture should be applied also to the rate addition.

- *Differentials* are published in a separate section of the book (pink section) and numbered sequentially D-1, D-2 etc. Book notes identify the page on which the differential is listed. Differentials are used to cover costs that do not fit in the Worldscale flat rate or their application may be dependent on particular factors. Where costs are dependent on factors such as cargo type or loading/discharging quantities, then differentials may be applied. Differentials fall into two categories, as follows:

  ○ *Fixed Differentials*
  Typical examples of fixed differentials are the canal dues differentials for Panama and Suez. These can be paid separately by the charterer directly to the canal authorities or included in the freight payment as fixed differentials. *The percentage or Worldscale equivalent agreed in a fixture should not be applied to a fixed differential.* Many fixed differentials are applied per tonne of cargo and should be paid in accordance with the actual cargo size in question, not that of the standard vessel. For example, in Rotterdam the differential varies with vessel, cargo size and crude or products loaded/discharged. This reflects the prevailing port tariff.

  ○ *Variable Differentials*
  Variable differentials are often used where various terminal costs differ within the same port. The addition or deduction in USD, stemming from a variable differential, is made to the flat rate. Since the terminal costs are included in the rate applying to a stated terminal, the differential is used to take into account different costs applying to different terminals of the same port. *The percentage or Worldscale*

equivalent agreed in a fixture is applied to the variable differential. These are commonly used for ports also providing a single buoy mooring (SBM[43]), where cost differs from other berths/terminals.

- Annual bunker prices and consumption rates concern standard 380 cst fuel. Where low sulphur fuels are required by local legislation covering part of the voyage passage, then additional allowances are incorporated into Worldscale rates as fixed differentials applied by voyage mile steamed. Where low sulphur fuels are required for in-port consumption, then an allowance is included within the flat rate for the voyage in question.

- The voyage time and port time are calculated and multiplied by the fixed daily hire element ($12,000/day). This allowance is included in the published rate calculation. In fact, this is a theoretical, arbitrary and somewhat vague assumption, nominally representing the standard ship's fixed costs, namely the operating costs and the capital costs (if any). In practice, an owner's knowledge of the costs of his own ship, including capital expenses, yields the relative vessel competitiveness and profitability at any given index (scale) level. As an actual panamax tanker of 75,000 dwt (like the standard vessel) may have about US$ 8,000–10,000 as a real figure of daily OPEX in 2017, then it remains to the owner to make the adjusting calculations, by adding the capital costs of his vessel and the desired profit to the WS equivalent computed on an operating basis, to arrive at the all-inclusive required WS rate level for his ship or fleet. It goes without saying that a fully amortised older tanker will have lower actual total cost of transporting a tonne of oil in a specific route (thus lower break-even point) than a new tanker paying down principal and interest in addition to its operating costs.[44]

- Port costs in relation to the standard vessel are assessed and treated within the Worldscale system, dependent upon where and how they are charged, as either:

  ○ Normal costs for which an allowance is provided in the flat rate.
  ○ Voyage Costs normally relating to routing options. These will be included in the flat rate calculations. Panama and Suez canal tolls are differentials due to their significance and complexity.
  ○ Charterers' account.
  ○ Fixed or variable differentials.
  ○ Not included at all.

The objective is to include in the rate calculations realistic allowances for all of those port cost items which are levied against the vessel (i.e. are

---

43 *Single Buoy Mooring (SBM)*: A loading buoy anchored offshore, that serves as a mooring point and interconnect for tankers loading or offloading liquid or gas products.
44 Uttmark, G. *Worldscale and the Zen of Tanker Forecasting* (www.marinemoneyoffshore.com, accessed 25 February 2017).

for owners' account), even when they are assessed on the quantity of cargo loaded or discharged, or by reference to the time spent in port/ alongside a berth. Allowances are made for vessel's items such as: light dues; pilotage (in and out); towage (in and out); terminal fees/charges; mooring and unmooring; stand-by tugs and/or stand-by launches; watchmen; conservancy dues; harbour dues; port dues; quay dues; berth hire; tonnage dues; wharfage/dockage/berthage; launches; port clearance; quarantine/free pratique fees; customs surveillance/attendance; customs overtime; sundries and petties; agency; ISPS costs.

- Charterers' account items are listed by country and may be relevant to particular voyages. Items levied upon or against a vessel may be "for charterers' account" with no allowance included in the flat rate. Owners are entitled to obtain reimbursement from the charterers for such costs involved. Charterers' account items include, for example, tugs and harbour dues, which cannot be included in the flat rate.
- The Worldscale system is based on the standard vessel of 75,000 dwt as this is still considered to be near the "average" type of tanker vessel, in terms of size, number and performance. This is periodically checked against fleet statistics. No allowance is made for any costs that would not be incurred by a vessel of the size of the standard vessel. It is the responsibility of the contracting parties to agree between themselves a method of settlement in respect of any of these expenses that may be actually incurred.
- The *calculation of freight* is thus made as follows:

Worldscale flat rate (including any additions) × Worldscale Equivalent × Cargo Quantity
Plus where applicable:
Variable Differentials × Worldscale Equivalent × Cargo Quantity
Fixed Differential (dependent on wording of each differential in the current Worldscale)
Add any items related to each case by supplementary Worldscale messages

- No allowance is made for any tax on freight or income tax, nor is there any provision as to whether such taxes are for owners' or for charterers' account. No allowance is made for any additional marine insurance incurred when trading in certain areas. No allowance is made for any deviation for any purpose. No allowance is made for any deballasting expenses, nor is there any provision as to whether such costs are for owners' or for charterers' account.

14.3.1.4 Contents and structure[45]

All subscribers are supplied with a Worldscale book each year, which has the following structure and contents:

---

45 www.worldscale.co.uk (accessed 20 August 2015).

- *Preamble Part A: Explanatory Notes*
  It includes: definitions; general explanation; basis of calculations; route policy/distances; assessment of port costs; revision policy; transshipment areas.
- *Preamble Part B: Terms and Conditions*
  It includes: effective date of scale; laytime allowance; port and terminal combinations; charterers' account items.
- *Preamble Part C: Table of Demurrage Rates*
- *Preamble Part D: List of Ports*
  It includes: ports and trans-shipment areas alphabetically ordered by port, country and geographical area.
- *Schedule of Flat Rates (WS100)*
  It includes the basic part of the calculated rates.
- *Fixed Rate Differentials (Worldscale percentage does not apply)*
  It includes: canal transit dues; high cost items based on vessel/cargo size.
- *Variable Rate Differentials (Worldscale percentage applies)*
  It allows for different cost of various berths in the same port.
- *Additions*
  For three major loading areas (Arabian Gulf, Black Sea and Lake Maracaibo) a *waypoint* is defined within each area to allow combinations of routes and therefore alternative chartering options.

14.3.1.5 WSHTC or WHTC (Worldscale Hours Terms and Conditions)
This term or abbreviation is usually incorporated in a tanker charterparty to denote that the currently prevailing Worldscale terms have been adopted to the charter.

14.3.1.6 Laytime, demurrage, despatch, lay/can[46]
Worldscale encompasses demurrage and various other costs. Ships of different size ranges have differing demurrage rates. These are adjusted in line with the negotiated Worldscale freight rates, but today owners and charterers are tending to prefer trading on daily lump sum US Dollar demurrage rates. Demurrage commences on the expiry of 72 hours total laytime SHINC (Sundays Holidays included) which is allowed for loading and discharging purposes according to WS terms, but despatch money is not paid in the tanker industry whatsoever.[47] Laydays and cancelling dates are generally very narrow, being probably no more than two or three days in tanker trades, but many principals are now insisting on a ship arriving at load port with only a 24-hour spread due to the limited availability of stems. Where a full cargo may not be secured, charterers often guarantee to provide a minimum quantity to be loaded, having the option to lift up further

---

46 The Baltic Exchange (2014) *The Baltic Code 2014* (pp. 30–31).
47 The laytime practice is analysed in chapter 15.

quantities up to the full cargo. This amount of cargo carried over and above the minimum quantity stated in the charterparty is classified as *"overage"* cargo and freight for that tends to be paid at 50% of the charterparty rate. Freight on voyage charters is typically payable upon completion of discharge, although charterers with an unproven track record would probably have to concede a freight remittance before breaking bulk (=discharging) or even arrange a bank guarantee, which is little different from the dry cargo case.

14.3.1.7 Time charter[48]

Worldscale is a useful chartering tool for voyage charters, consecutive voyages charter and contracts of affreightment. However, time charter for tankers is similar to dry cargo, either for a period of time or for specific trips. Period charters can be used by oil companies/traders to hedge their long term needs and contracts in what can sometimes be a very volatile market. As it occurs with voyage charters, most of the major oil companies have their own standard time charterparties, such as Shelltime, BPtime etc., while the hire is usually agreed at a daily rate expressed in US Dollars, the same as in dry cargo markets. Worldscale is not commonly used in time charters, except when the time charter rate is directly linked to the spot market freight indices or routes, e.g. the Baltic Dirty Tanker Index (BDTI) or route TC2 in the Baltic Clean Tanker Index (BCTI), etc.

14.3.2 Worldscale practical examples[49]

This section deals with useful practical examples intending to familiarise the reader with functional modes of Worldscale, as well as with day-to-day commercial aspects of tanker chartering. As the tanker market is dynamic and constantly changing, numbers and figures of the examples are approximations of real figures used for illustrating purposes only. This has been made intentionally, as long as this text does not wish to substitute the primary and original source of market information, such as the Worldscale organisation itself or Intertanko or the specialised tanker brokers, etc. Instead, the following cases are given just for educational purposes to enlighten the rationale of tanker market freight calculations and Worldscale methodology. It should be noted therefore that flat rates of the examples are not the published ones from official Worldscale tables. Further to that, costs and other practical matters presented (e.g. bunkers prices, port and canal dues, vessels' speeds, bunkers' consumptions, Worldscale terms and conditions,

---

48 The Baltic Exchange (2014) *The Baltic Code 2014.*
49 Giziakis, K., Papadopoulos, A. and Plomaritou, E. (2010) *Chartering* (Athens, Stamoulis Publications, 3rd edition, in Greek, pp. 317–326); Evans, J.J. and Marlow, P.B. (1990) *Quantitative Methods in Maritime Economics* (London, Fairplay Publications, 2nd edition, pp. 102–103); Coulson, E.C. (1995) *A Guide for Tanker Brokers* (London, Clarkson Research Studies, pp. 26–27); Wood, P. (2000) *Tanker Chartering* (London, Witherby & Co Ltd., p. 76).

etc.) may not be fully up to date, as long as they vary widely according to market practices and conditions.

Example 1: Hypothetical calculation of the WS 100 (flat rate) of "Worldscale", for a round voyage from the loading port Mina Al Ahmadi (Kuwait) to the discharging port Milford Haven (United Kingdom), based on a laden trip through Cape of Good Hope and ballast trip through Suez Canal.

According to the Worldscale, the asked flat rate is indicated "CS" and it should be emphasised that the tables calculate separate flat rates for round trips via Cape of Good Hope ("C") and round trips through Suez Canal ("S"), both of each laden and in ballast respectively. In practice, the flat rate requested must be assessed in relation to a transit point (waypoint) defined in the Arabian Gulf (Quoin Island), i.e. a voyage Milford Haven–Quoin Island and an "addition" Quoin Island–Mina Al Ahmadi. These two rates and mileages should then be added for the correct flat rate. For reasons of simplification, the example will not include the waypoint.

DISTANCES

Laden: Mina Al Ahmadi–Milford Haven via Cape	11,115 miles
Ballast: Milford Haven–Mina Al Ahmadi via Suez	6,257 miles
Total distance of round voyage	17,372 miles

VOYAGE TIME

Worldscale (*preamble part A, par. 4 "basis of calculation"*) provides for the following assumptions:

- Service speed of 14.5 knots (miles/hour) for the standard vessel. Hence, the ship sails 348 miles/day (14.5 × 24 hours) and will take about 50 days to make the round voyage (17,372 ÷ 348).
- A total time of 4 days at the two ports of call. Additional 12 hours allowed for each extra port involved.
- Time allowed for each transit of Suez Canal is 30 hours (1.25 days).

Thus:

Time at Sea	50.00 days
Time in Ports	4.00 days
Time in Suez	1.25 days
Total Time	55.25 days

BUNKER CONSUMPTION

Worldscale (*preamble part A, par. 4 "basis of calculation"*) provides for fuel oil consumption of 55 mt/day at sea (steaming), 5 mt for each port involved in the voyage and 100 mt per round trip for various other reasons.

466

Thus:

Consumption at Sea	2,750 mt (55 mt/day × 50 days)
Consumption in Ports	10 mt (5 mt/port × 2 ports)
Additional	100 mt
Total Consumption	2,860 mt

TOTAL VOYAGE COST

Worldscale (*preamble part A, par. 4 "basis of calculation" & par. 7 "port costs"*) provides for a fixed hire element (fixed cost of the standard vessel), an average worldwide bunker price for fuel oil (380cst) and the port costs for the specific two ports. Assuming that the average fuel price is set at USD 614.18 / mt and the total cost of two ports of call is USD 100,000, the total voyage cost comes.

Thus:

Fixed Cost	$ 663,000 ($12,000 / day × 55.25 days)
Fuel Costs	$1,756,555 (2,860 mt × $ 614.18 / mt)
Port Costs	$ 100,000
Total Voyage Cost	$2,519,555

CARGO

Worldscale (*preamble part A, par. 4 "basis of calculation" & par. 5 "notes on calculation"*) provides that the standard vessel has a total deadweight capacity of 75,000 mt. This capacity includes the quantities of bunkers, supplies, fresh water, etc. which must be deducted in calculating the net quantity of cargo to be carried. It is also assumed for calculating purposes that the ship will acquire 50% of the total bunkers required for the round voyage at the loading port.

Thus:

Ship's DWT	75,000 mt	
(-) Supplies and Bunkers Reserve		500 mt
(-) Voyage Bunkers		1,430 mt (2,860 mt × 50%)
(-) Fresh Water etc.		80 mt
(-) Total Deductible Quantity	2,010 mt	
Cargo	72,990 mt	

FLAT RATE

Flat rate for the voyage would be calculated as:

WS 100 = Total Voyage Cost ÷ Cargo Quantity = $2,519,555 ÷ 72,990 mt = $34.52 / mt of cargo[50]

---

50 It is stressed again that this is not the actual published Worldscale flat rate for the specific round voyage. All examples are presented only for illustrative purposes.

Suez Canal dues are not incorporated in the calculation of the "flat rate". Fixed rate differentials can be paid separately by the charterers (e.g. in this example to the Suez Canal authority) or added as a lump sum amount in the freight payment to the owner. For example, a ship of 140,000 dwt with net tonnage crossing the canal (Suez Canal Net Tonnage or SCNT) of 70,000 mt, on the ballast leg would pay extra:

$ 221,900	($3.17 / SCNT × 70,000 SCNT)
$ 174,100	(lump sum amount for the passage)
$ 8,580	(towage cost)
$ 404,580	

Hence, the amount of $404,580 would be paid by the charterer as "fixed differential".

Example 2: (a) Hypothetical calculation of the WS 100 (flat rate) of "World-scale", for a round voyage from the loading port Jebel Ali (United Arab Emirates) to the discharging port Swansea (United Kingdom) and (b) Calculation of WS 65

To find the "flat rate" of a round trip, first the port of unloading is sought from the top of the WS tables and then the loading port at the bottom of the tables. The combination gives the mileage distance between the two ports and the "flat rate" of the route. Distance always refers to a round voyage, thus to obtain the actual distance between the ports, the total mileage of the route should be divided by two. In this example, the calculation of the distance and the flat rate is made by using the transit point and the addition about the Arabian (Persian or Middle East) Gulf. The focal point of the Gulf is Quoin Island. The distances and flat rates of the transit points are included in separate pages of the tables, from where relevant freight rates are taken sequentially corresponding to part trips, namely Jebel Ali-Quoin Island and Quoin Island–Swansea. The sum of the two individual rates gives the overall flat rate for the route Jebel Ali–Swansea.

Assuming that[51]:

- Flat rate of Swansea/Quoin Island is $15.00/mt
- Flat rate of Quoin Island/Jebel Ali is $2.00/mt

Then, WS 100 in the route Swansea–Jebel Ali would be $17.00/mt.

Thus:
WS 100 = Flat Rate $17.00/mt
WS 65 = $17.00 × 65% = $11.05/mt

---

51 Discharging ports are always set out first for all round voyages in the published tables.

It should be noted that Worldscale gives three alternative flat rates and distances for this route. The first route via Cape of Good Hope (C) laden and in ballast, the second through Suez Canal (S) laden and in ballast, while the third option is about a laden journey via Cape of Good Hope and a ballast via Suez (CS). However, this example focuses on the rationale of calculating a flat rate by using a transit point ("waypoint") and an "addition" route when loading in one of the three specific areas of the tables. The percentage variation or WS equivalent of the fixture should be applied to the rate addition.

Example 3: Hypothetical calculation of the WS 100 (flat rate) of "Worldscale", for a round voyage from the loading port Veracruz (Mexico) to the discharging port Tarragona (Spain) when discharging in "Repsol Sea Buoy" anchorage.

Assuming that:

- Flat rate of Tarragona/Veracruz is $10.00/mt
- For discharging in "Repsol Sea Buoy" anchorage a variable differential of $0.20/mt is added

Thus:

Tarragona–Veracruz	$10.00/mt
(+) Variable differential	$ 0.20/mt
WS 100 =	$10.20/mt

Variable differentials are often used where terminal costs differ within the same port. The additions (as in this example) or deductions in USD per mt are made directly to the flat rate.

Example 4: (a) Hypothetical calculation of the WS 100 (flat rate) of "Worldscale", for a round voyage from the loading port Oguendjo Terminal (Gabon) to the discharging port Lisbon (Portugal) and (b) Calculation of the gross freight received by the shipowner to transport 70,000 mt of crude oil on this route, in WS 150.

Assuming that:

- Flat rate of Lisbon–Oguendjo Terminal is $8.00/mt
- For loading in Oguendjo Terminal a fixed differential $1.00/mt is added

Thus:
Lisbon–Oguendjo Terminal flat rate = $8.00/mt
WS 150 = 70,000 mt × ($8.00/mt × 150%) = $840,000
Fixed Differential = 70,000 mt × $1.00/mt = $70,000
Gross Freight Payable = $840,000 + $70,000 = $910,000
Fixed differential is never incorporated in the flat rate.

Example 5: (a) Hypothetical calculation of the WS 100 (flat rate) of "Worldscale", for a round voyage from the loading port Aruba (Netherlands Antilles–Caribbean Sea) to the discharging port Philadelphia (US East Coast); and (b) Calculation of WS 50; and (c) Gross freight received by the shipowner to transport 80,000 mt of crude oil on this route, in WS 50; and (d) Daily gross freight in WS 50, supposing that total round voyage time is 15 days (including fourdays in ports).

Assuming that:

- Flat rate of Philadelphia–Aruba is $6.00/mt

Thus:
WS 100 = Flat Rate $6.00/mt
WS 50 = $6.00/mt × 50% = $3.00/mt
Gross Freight Payable in WS 50 = 80,000 mt × $3.00/mt = $240,000
Daily Gross Freight = $240,000 ÷ 15 days = $16,000/day

Example 6: Further to the previous example, if the owner has the option to discharge the 80,000 shipload in Hamburg (Germany) instead of Philadelphia (USA), what is the WS rate to be asked for the Aruba–Hamburg round voyage, so that to be equivalent with the WS 50 rate in the Aruba–Philadelphia round voyage, supposing that total round voyage time is 32 days (including four days in ports) for the the Aruba–Hamburg trip?

In order both round voyages to be considered equivalent, they should earn the same daily gross revenue for the shipowner. To calculate the equivalent WS rate, a reverse process should be followed.

The owner should earn from the Aruba–Hamburg voyage a daily gross freight of $16,000 (as in the Aruba–Philadelphia trip).

Thus, total gross freight for the Aruba–Hamburg voyage is:

Gross Freight = $16,000 / day × 32 days = $512,000
Supposing that from the tables it is sourced a "flat rate" (WS 100) at $14.00/mt for Aruba–Hamburg.

To calculate the requested equivalent WS rate, the following relationship is formed:

80,000 mt ($14.00/mt × WS?) = $512,000 ⇒
$14.00/mt × WS? = $6.40/mt ⇒ WS ? = 6.40 ÷ 14.00 = 0.45 or WS 45

Thus, to earn the same daily revenue, the owner may accept either WS 50 for the Aruba–Philadelphia trade or WS 45 for the Aruba–Hamburg trade.

It is therefore confirmed that, the longer a round voyage the lower equivalent WS is required to bring about the same financial result.

Example 7: The owner of a 200,000 dwt tanker estimates that he has to request a freight rate of $12.80/mt to break-even the total cost of his ship in a specific round voyage. Suppose that for the same trip the flat rate (WS 100) is $16.20/mt. How can the break-even WS rate be calculated for each trip of this ship?

The break-even point of this ship as a WS percentage is calculated as follows:

($12.80/mt ÷ $16.20/mt) × 100 = 79 = WS 79

Thus, for every round voyage of this ship it is required a minimum WS 79, so as vessel's trading to be profitable.

Example 8: An owner has estimated that he wishes to fix his 105,000 dwt afra-max tanker with a full cargo requesting a freight rate of WS 60. What is the equivalent WS percentage to be requested if the vessel is to load only 90,000 mt of cargo?

105,000 mt × WS 60 = 90,000 mt × WS ? ⇒
WS ? = 105,000 × 60% ÷ 90,000 = 0.7 = 70%

Thus, the equivalent rate is WS 70.

Example 9: Conversion of time charter hire to equivalent voyage cost expressed as a Worldscale rate (i.e. tanker voyage/spot rate), for transporting oil from the loading port Ras Tanura (Saudi Arabia) to the discharge port Rotterdam (Netherlands) and return to Ras Tanura. The two voyage legs of the round trip will be executed via the Cape of Good Hope and the total distance will be 22,930 miles. The ship is expected to remain four days at ports. Total ship's capacity is 280,315 dwt. Its average service speed is 14 knots, fuel consumption 150 mt per day at sea and 200 mt during the total stay of the ship in ports. Water, supplies and other constants are estimated at 400 mt. The fuel cost is $185/mt. The total port expenses are estimated at $170,000. The proposed time charter hire rate is $2.20 per dwt per month.[52]

VOYAGE DURATION
Steaming time =
Total mileage of round voyage Ras Tanura/Rotterdam/Ras Tanura via Cape of Good Hope ÷ (Vessel's speed × 24 hours)

$$= \frac{22,930 \text{ miles}}{14 \text{ knots (miles/hour)} \times 24 \text{ hours}} = \frac{22,930 \text{ miles}}{336 \text{ miles per day}} = 68.24 \text{ days}$$

Voyage duration = Steaming time + Port time = 68.24 + 4 = 72.24 days

---

52 Coulson, E.C. (1995) *A Guide for Tanker Brokers* (London, Clarkson Research Studies, pp. 30–33). The example is based on this publication. It has been slightly adjusted by the authors and is reproduced with the kind permission of Clarksons Research. Emphasis should be put on the structure of thinking and on the commercial principles of the exercise. For a current update of the data, the reader should always seek advice from market experts, e.g. shipping research providers, shipbrokers, ship managers, etc.

DAILY AND TOTAL HIRE

Daily hire = (DWT × Hire rate per dwt per month × 12 months) ÷ 365 days =
= (280,315 dwt × $2.20 × 12 months) ÷ 365 days = $20,275 daily hire
Total Hire or Fixed Cost of the Voyage = Daily Hire $20,275 × Total Voyage
Time 72.24 days = $1,464,666

TOTAL COST OF THE VOYAGE

Fuel Consumption at sea = 150 mt per day × 68.24 days steaming = 10,236 mt
Fuel Consumption in ports = 200 mt
Total Fuel Cosumption = 10,236 + 200 = 10,436 mt
Total Fuel Costs = 10,436 mt × $185/mt = $1,930,660
Total Cost of Voyage = Total Hire or Fixed Cost of the Voyage + Total
Fuel Costs + Total Port Costs and other Variable Costs of the Voyage =
$1,464,666 + $1,930,660 + $170,000 = $3,565,326

CARGO QUANTITY

Cargo Capacity = Total DWT − (Bunkers + Supplies + Water + Constants +
Bunkers Reserve) = 280,315 dwt − (10,436 mt of bunkers for the voyage + 750
mt safety bunkers reserve for 5 days + 400 mt of supplies, water, constants +
1,130 mt due to sagging[53]) = 267,599 mt of cargo to be carried

COST PER MT OF CARGO CARRIED AND EQUIVALENT VOYAGE RATE IN WS TERMS

Cost per mt of cargo carried = Total Cost of Voyage ÷ Cargo Quantity =
$3,565,326 ÷ 267,599 mt = $13.32/mt of cargo
Equivalent Worldscale Rate = Cost per mt of cargo carried ÷ WS 100 for round
voyage Ras Tanura–Rotterdam–Ras Tanura via Cape of Good Hope

Assuming that it is sourced from the prevailing tables a reference WS flat rate
(WS 100) for the specific route which is $18.50/mt.
Thus, this ratio is formed:

$13.32/mt ÷ $18.50/mt = 0.72 = WS 72

Therefore, for the specific VLCC of this example, a time charter hire rate of
$2.20 per dwt per month is equivalent with cost or freight rate of $13.32 per mt
of cargo carried or WS 72 for the round voyage Ras Tanura–Rotterdam via Cape
of Good Hope.

Example 10: Conversion of worldscale rate (i.e. tanker voyage/spot rate) to time
charter equivalent hire (TCE). By following a reverse process to that of the previous

---

53 *Sagging:* Large vessels loaded to capacity can be deeper at some point in the keel length than
the bow and stern areas, thus a factor for reduced cargo quantity is calculated which would keep
the vessel within loadline regulations (Coulson, E.C. (1995) *A Guide for Tanker Brokers*, London,
Clarkson Research Studies, p. 33).

example, a percentage rate WS 72 for the round voyage Ras Tanura–Rotterdam–
Ras Tanura via the Cape of Good Hope to be converted in time charter equivalent
hire (TCE). Total distance of round voyage is 22,930 miles. The ship is expected to
remain at ports four days. Total ship's capacity is 280,315 dwt. Its average service
speed is 14 knots, fuel consumption 150 mt per day at sea and 200 mt during the total
stay of the ship in ports. Water, supplies and other constants are estimated at 400 mt.
The fuel cost is $185/mt. The total port expenses are estimated at $170,000.[54]

VOYAGE DURATION
Steaming time =
Total mileage of round voyage Ras Tanura–Rotterdam–Ras Tanura via Cape of
Good Hope ÷ (Vessel's speed × 24 hours)

$$= \frac{22{,}930 \text{ miles}}{14 \text{ knots (miles/hour)} \times 24 \text{ hours}} = \frac{22{,}930 \text{ miles}}{336 \text{ miles per day}} = 68.24 \text{ days}$$

Voyage duration = Steaming time + Port time = 68.24 + 4 = 72.24 days

CARGO QUANTITY
Cargo Capacity = Total DWT − (Bunkers + Supplies + Water + Constants +
Bunkers Safety Reserve) = 280,315 dwt − (10,436 mt of bunkers for the voyage
+ 750 mt bunkers safety reserve for 5 days + 400 mt of supplies, water, constants
+ 1,130 mt due to sagging) = 267,599 mt of cargo to be carried

FREIGHT REVENUE
Assuming that it is sourced from the prevailing tables a reference WS flat rate
(WS 100) for the specific route which is $18.50/mt.
Thus, this ratio is formed:

$13.32/mt ÷ $18.50/mt = 0.72 = WS 72

Total Freight of the Voyage = Cargo Quantity × WS 100 × WS percentage of the
voyage charter = 267,599 mt × $18.50/mt × WS 72 (72%) = $3,564,419

VOYAGE COSTS
Fuel Consumption at sea = 150 mt per day × 68.24 days steaming = 10,236 mt
Fuel Consumption in ports = 200 mt
Total Fuel Cosumption = 10,236 + 200 = 10,436 mt
Total Fuel Costs = 10,436 mt × $185/mt = $1,930,660
Voyage Costs (Variable Cost of the Voyage) = Total Fuel Costs + Total Port Costs
and other Variable Costs of the Voyage = $1,930,660 + $170,000 = $2,100,660

---

54 Coulson, E.C. (1995) *A Guide for Tanker Brokers* (London, Clarkson Research Studies, pp. 31, 34–35). The example has been based on this publication. It has been slightly adjusted by the authors and is reproduced for illustrative purposes with the kind permission of Clarksons Research. Emphasis should be given to methodology, not on the accuracy of the market data.

GROSS VOYAGE SURPLUS

Gross Voyage Surplus = Total Freight of Voyage – Voyage Costs (Variable Cost of the Voyage) = $3,564,419 – $2,100,660 = $1,463,759

TIME CHARTER EQUIVALENT HIRE (TCE)

Time Charter Equivalent Daily Hire (TCE) = Gross Voyage Surplus ÷ Voyage duration =

$1,463,759 ÷ 72.24 days = $20,262 / day

Time Charter Equivalent Hire per dwt per month =

(Daily Hire × 365 days) ÷ (Ship's DWT × 12 months) =

= ($20,262 / day × 365 days) ÷ (280,315 dwt × 12 months) = $2.20 per dwt per month

Therefore, for the specific VLCC of this example, a spot rate of $13.32 per mt of cargo carried or WS 72 for the round voyage Ras Tanura–Rotterdam via Cape of Good Hope is equivalent with a time charter hire rate (TCE) of $20,262 per day or $2.20 per dwt per month.

CHAPTER 15

Laytime calculations

The final chapter addresses the commercial and practical aspects of laytime calculations; a field of great challenge among chartering and shipbroking matters in a voyage charter. The rules and principles of handling time risks are initially presented. Then, emphasis is given to the explanation of terminology, methodology and calculations of laytime, based on the official "Laytime Definitions 2013". The documents needed during the calculations, as well as the peculiarities faced on dry and liquid cargo laytime, are thoroughly examined. A comparative analysis of the latest "Laytime Definitions 2013" against the previous "Voylayrules 1993" follows. Finally, at the end of the chapter, some practical examples are presented to analytically explain and enlighten the laytime subjects. In general, it may be said that laytime is to a great extent a combination of commercial practice, agreement of the parties and interpretation of the charterparty wording. Therefore, clear intention of the parties and unambiguous charterparty wording is always the key to avoid lengthy and costly disputes.

15.1 Introduction

Laytime is defined as the period of time agreed between the shipowner and the charterer at the voyage charter, in which the charterer undertakes to load and discharge the vessel, without payment additional to the freight. Since *"time is money"* for all shipping practitioners, the time allowed to the charterer is not unlimited. Many disputes on voyage charter agreements are connected with the calculation of laytime. It is certain that some of the problems might have been avoided if the laytime clauses were worded more distinctly. Unfortunately, the printed clauses in the standard forms of charterparties are sometimes worded in a hazy way and therefore the well-known printed standard forms must often be amended to get a clear picture of how laytime should be calculated. A recommendation is to include in the charterparty any of the interpretation rules that maritime organisations have published during the years. *"Voyage Charterparty Laytime Interpretation Rules 1993"*, widely known as *"Voylayrules '93"*, and *"Laytime Definitions for Charter Parties 2013"*, known in short as *"Laytime Definitions 2013"*, will be mentioned and analysed below.[1] Full text of Laytime Definitions 2013 is reproduced with the kind permission of BIMCO in appendix 3.

---

1 Laytime is a matter of considerable importance, free expression, negotiation and agreement of the parties, application of law, trade practice and a common field of dispute in voyage chartering. Thus, laytime aspects may have a wide interpretation, application and impact in commercial practice. This

The *purposes of laytime calculation* are:

- To calculate the time allowed by the shipowner to the voyage charterer in which the latter should load and/or discharge the cargo.
- To calculate the so-called "*demurrage*" or "*despatch*", namely an agreed compensation paid to the owner if time is lost from cargo-handling operations (i.e. demurrage is paid when actual loading/discharging time exceeds laytime), or respectively, an agreed compensation paid to the charterer if time is saved from cargo-handling operations (i.e. despatch is paid when actual loading/discharging time falls short of laytime). See further section 15.11.
- To provide evidence in the case of a dispute which ends up to arbitration or to a court for resolution.

15.2 Time risk during sea voyage

In voyage chartering the time risk during the sea voyage rests solely with the owners. Sometimes, this principal rule is set aside by clauses in the charterparty. One such example may be found in *ExxonMobilvoy 2012 (part II, clause 21(a) "ice during voyage")*, stipulating that the charterer may be obliged to compensate owners for additional steaming and bunker costs caused by ice during the sea voyage, preventing the vessel to reach at the agreed port. Ice clauses are designed for ice problems occurring in or near the loading and discharging ports.

15.3 Vessels' ETA (Estimated Time of Arrival) notices

General comments about ETA notices have been presented in section 11.8.1. If ETA notices are not given as agreed, the owner may, depending on the circumstances, be liable for charterer's economic loss caused by the delayed or missing ETA notice. Sometimes, it is expressly agreed that such compensation to the charterers shall be an additional time allowed for loading and/or discharging (laytime), e.g. as per *ExxonMobilvoy 2012, part II, clause 10(d) "estimated time of arrival (ETA)"*.

15.4 Vessels' arrival at the agreed destination

As the risk of delay during the sea voyage rests with the owners, while the risk of delay when the vessel is at a port is shared between the owners and charterers, it

---

analysis has been based on the latest official laytime rules applying to the market, namely "Laytime Definitions 2013", which were jointly published in September 2013 by BIMCO, FONASBA, CMI and the Baltic Exchange as the sponsoring bodies. Laytime terminology of this chapter follows the interpretation given by these rules. Further to that, the respective, official commentary of the sponsoring organisations on these rules is presented to the text, where considered necessary, to enlighten the way of thinking behind the rules (for a full text of the official commentary please refer to BIMCO, Special Circular No. 8 "Laytime Definitions for Charter Parties 2013", 10 September 2013).

is important to establish when the sea voyage reaches at the end and the system of rules applying to the ship's stay in port takes over.

The vessel must reach at the agreed destination before she can be considered as an "arrived ship". Consequently, the more precisely the destination is described at the charterparty, the more is needed before the vessel has arrived at destination.

Voyage charters are of three types, depending on whether the loading or discharging point is specified to be a berth, a dock or a port. In accordance with that discrimination, the charterparties are classified as follows:

- *"berth" charterparties*;
- *"dock" charterparties*;
- *"port" charterparties*.

According to Laytime Definitions 2013 (term 1), *"port shall mean any area where vessels load or discharge cargo and shall include, but not be limited to, berths, wharves, anchorages, buoys and offshore facilities as well as places outside the legal, fiscal or administrative area where vessels are ordered to wait for their turn no matter the distance from that area"*. Furthermore, as per Laytime Definitions 2013 (term 2), *"berth shall mean the specific place where the vessel is to load or discharge and shall include, but not be limited to, any wharf, anchorage, offshore facility or other location used"*.

According to the official commentary (2013),[2] if comparing to "Voylayrules '93", the term "port" was amended to reflect the wider concept of port area explained in *The "Johanna Oldendorff" [1971] 2 Lloyd's Rep. 96; [1972] 2 Lloyd's Rep. 292; [1973] 2 Lloyd's Rep. 285* with reference now made to *"places outside the legal, fiscal or administrative area"* of the port. The term *"offshore facilities"* was also added. Furthermore, concerning *"berth"*, the restrictive reference to *"place within a port"* (as per Voylayrules '93) has been replaced by an open-ended list of cargo-handling locations.

The charterer shall nominate a safe port (see also section 11.3.2) where, at an agreed time in the charterparty, the ship can reach, enter, remain at, and depart from, without being exposed to danger which cannot be avoided by good navigation and seamanship.

Some abnormal or unforeseeable occurrence may remove any liability from the charterer in respect of his responsibility to order the ship at a safe port, in case the vessel is finally harmed due to that cause. However, the charterer remains responsible to make a fresh order to direct the ship in a safe port.

A safe anchorage or a safe berth is an anchorage or a berth correspondingly, where the ship can reach, remain at and depart from without being exposed to danger which cannot be avoided by good navigation and seamanship. The meaning of "safety" is similar to that described above for a "safe port".

---

2 BIMCO *Laytime Definitions for Charter Parties 2013* (Special Circular No. 8, 10 September 2013). For the avoidance of repetition, it is noted here that commentary of the "Laytime Definitions 2013" refers to this source, wherever it is mentioned in the text.

With regard to berth and dock charters, the position is relatively straight-forward, as the vessel becomes an "arrived ship" when it enters the specified berth or dock respectively. In both cases the risk of delay in reaching the specified berth or dock must be borne by the shipowner. It should be noted that berth charterparties are rare in tanker trades.

In case of a port charterparty, it is more difficult to define the test for an "arrived ship", due to the larger area involved and the variety of definitions for a port, dependent on whether it is regarded from a geographical, administrative or commercial standpoint. According to common law (The "Johanna Oldendorff" [1971] 2 Lloyd's Rep. 96; [1972] 2 Lloyd's Rep. 292; [1973] 2 Lloyd's Rep. 285), the practical test for an "arrived ship" in port charterparties is based on the following propositions[3]:

- The vessel must be within the geographical and legal area of the port in the sense commonly understood by its users.
- The vessel must be immediately and effectively at the disposal of the charterer in the sense that it can reach the berth quickly when informed that one is vacant.
- The vessel must be anchored at a place where ships of similar type and size usually lie while waiting for a berth at that port.

In general, all charterparties should clearly define the precise point at which the risk and cost of time lost is transferred from shipowner to charterer.

15.4.1 "Waiting for berth"

The best way for the owners to protect themselves is to insert a special "waiting for berth" clause or to have the words "whether in berth/port or not" (WIBPON) inserted in the laytime clause, so that to make clear that the laytime can count when the vessel is at the customary or indicated waiting place. Such clauses may also allow time to count as laytime when the ship is not an arrived ship with relation to the destination as described in the charterparty.

The question about whether a berth is reachable on vessel's arrival has been much discussed particularly in connection with voyage tanker charters for a number of years. Unfortunately, as a result of contradictory cases, the situation here is very often unclear.

15.4.2 "Reachable on arrival" or "always accessible"

"Reachable on arrival shall mean that the charterer undertakes that an available loading or discharging berth be provided to the vessel on arrival at the port which the vessel can reach safely without delay". (Laytime Definitions 2013, term 3).

---

3 Wilson, J.F. (2010) Carriage of Goods by Sea (London, Pearson Education Ltd, 7th edition, p. 54).

"Always accessible shall mean that the charterer undertakes that an available load-ing or discharging berth be provided to the vessel on arrival at the port which the vessel can reach safely without delay. The charterer additionally undertakes that the vessel will be able to depart safely from the berth and without delay at any time before, during or on completion of loading or discharging". (Laytime Definitions 2013, term 4)

According to the official commentary (2013), the term *"reachable on arrival"* has been the subject of considerable litigation over the years. The revised text of 2013 definitions was based on the current legal position that delay due to bad weather or congestion or both is a breach of charterers' obligations. The poten-tially disputatious qualification *"in the absence of an abnormal occurrence"*, included in Voylayrules '93, was deleted. Moreover, the provision *"always accessible"* has been treated by the authorities as synonymous with *"reachable on arrival"* in the context of getting into a berth, but the position on departure has been less clear. The term has therefore been set out separately with the second sentence covering the position on departure requiring charterers to enable the vessel to leave safely and without delay.

Many charterparties require the charterer to nominate *"a reachable berth"* on the vessel's arrival at destination. Such a clause transfers the risk of delay to the charterer if he cannot nominate a vacant berth because of congestion in the port (*The "Angelos Lusis" [1964] 2 Lloyd's Rep. 28*). The application of the clause is not restricted to cases of physical obstruction, but also covers situations where a berth is available but not "reachable" due to bad weather conditions or fog. The vessel does not need to be an "arrived ship"; all that is required is that it must have reached a point either inside or outside the port, where it would wait in the absence of the nomination of a berth. From that point, the charterer will have to bear the risk of any delay, in that he will be liable for damages for breach of contract in failing to nominate a reachable berth. However, if the vessel is also considered to be an "arrived ship" at that point, resulting in commencement of laytime, then the charterer cannot be required to pay twice for the same time lost. That means, once laytime has begun, the charterer can trade off any time saved in loading against the initial time lost while he was prevented from nominating a "reachable berth". On the other hand, if the vessel is not an "arrived ship" at that point, then the two periods run independently. That means any time saved in loading cannot be set off against time lost while waiting for a reachable berth to be nominated (*The "Delian Spirit" [1971] 1 Lloyd's Rep. 64; [1971] 1 Lloyd's Rep. 506*).

15.4.3 Clauses designed for specific ports

In case of frequently congested ports, where the normal waiting place is outside port limits, standard clauses usually provide that laytime is to run from the time when a vessel reaches a specific point but is unable to proceed further because of a shortage of berths or other obstruction. Such a clause will be effective even though the vessel does not become an "arrived ship" at that point.

15.5 Vessels' readiness

15.5.1 Principal rule

The principal rule in the wide sense is ". . . *before a ship can be said to be truly ready to load and discharge, she must have complied with customs, quarantine and other requirements imposed upon her by the local authorities (administrative readiness)*".[4] Readiness includes *physical, legal* and *administrative readiness*. Physical readiness means that the vessel shall be clean and ready to take on board the intended cargo (cargoworthy ship) or to discharge the cargo. Legal and administrative readiness means that the ship shall be clear of the formalities (customs clearance, documentation etc.) and also be in accordance with the commercial agreements ready for the commencement of loading or discharging.

15.5.2 General exceptions from the principal rule

The vessel need not necessarily be in all respects legally and physically ready to be able to give a valid notice of readiness (see section 15.6). Depending on the circumstances, the charterers must accept that the vessel can be considered ready although some preparations on board remain to be done (for instance, the uncovering of hatches) or some formalities remain to be dealt with (for instance, customs clearance and "free pratique" permission as required by the health authorities). Such exceptions from the principal rule are especially justified in ports where the physical or formal measures cannot, or will not, due to local rules or routines, be taken until the vessel is moored.

15.5.3 Agreed exceptions from the principal rule

It is also common that the charterparty has clauses waiving requirements imposed by the principal rules. For example, Voylayrules '93 have a definition (term 23) which modifies the principal rule about readiness. According to that term, the coming completion of the ship's formalities, *free pratique* and *custom clearance*, shall not mean that the ship is not ready and thereby hinder the tendering of notice of readiness. However, any time actually lost by reason of delay in the vessel's completion of either of these formalities shall not count as laytime or time on demurrage.

In Laytime Definitions 2013, the *free pratique* is said to "*mean that the vessel complies with the health requirements*". As per official commentary, "*the provision now relates only to compliance with port health requirements*" which means that the definition has no direct influence on the concept of vessel's readiness. It is further explained that the new definitions refrain from clarifications of *free pratique* and *custom formalities*, as these vary considerably from one state to another.

The above-mentioned clauses and definitions mainly apply when a berth is not available in a berth charter. When there is a berth charter, notice of readiness

---

4 Tiberg, H. (2013) *Law of Demurrage* (London, Sweet & Maxwell, 5th edition, p. 302).

(NoR) is normally given when the ship has arrived at berth. However, if the berth is unavailable, under such clauses the vessel may give NoR *"whether in free pratique or not"* (WIFPON) and/or *"whether customs cleared or not"* (WCCON). In other words, such formalities become irrelevant to the tendering of a valid notice of readiness, whilst a berth is unavailable. In general, with a WIFPON or WCCON qualification to the tendering of NoR, formalities may not affect the vessel's readiness and the commencement of laytime, which will start to count in accordance to the charterparty, even though – and as long as – a berth remains unavailable.

In tanker voyage charters, if tanks are to be inspected by or on behalf of charterers for cleanliness, there is a need for provisions related to consequences of such time lost (e.g. see appendix 2, *Shellvoy 6, part II, clause 2 "cleanliness of tanks"*).

15.6 Notice of vessels' arrival and readiness

When the vessel is arrived and ready to load or discharge, the master usually gives a *Notice of Readiness* (NoR) stating that the vessel is now ready to load. Quite often the charterers are entitled to a *notice time (free time, grace time)* before the laytime starts to run (see section 15.7).

15.6.1 Written notice

Unless otherwise expressly agreed, the notice may be delivered orally or by a written message. In order to avoid misconceptions and disputes about whether NoR has been validly given or not, oral notices should be avoided. Voylayrules '93, term 20, seems to be generally accepted, but it is not repeated in Laytime Definitions 2013. This rule dictates that *"in writing shall mean any visibly expressed form of reproducing words; the medium of transmission shall include electronic communications such as radio communications and telecommunications"*.

15.6.2 Time of NoR provision

The NoR shall be delivered as soon as the ship is ready to commence loading or discharging. This means that if the vessel is ordered to wait outside the berth or port in a "berth" or "port" charterparty respectively, the notice should be delivered. If the charterparty states that the notice must be given within office hours, a notice given after office hours will not be valid and will not come into force until the next period of office hours. Office hours are generally understood to mean ordinary office hours in the relevant port and the charterers cannot, by earlier closing their office, postpone the notice time and thereby the counting of the laytime.

The notices of readiness and the statements of facts (see section 15.12) are those documents which state both when a notice has been delivered and when it has been accepted. It should be noted that if the notice of readiness is correct, the charterers cannot postpone the running of notice time and laytime by refusing to accept the NoR.

15.6.3 Sea notice

It happens sometimes that notice of readiness is given before the vessel actually arrives at the agreed destination, for example, when the pilot is on board. Such notices given in advance are called s*ea notices* or *premature notices* and will not, unless otherwise agreed, come into force until eventually the vessel is in fact arrived and ready. As such notices can be considered totally invalid, the ship's master shall give a fresh NoR when the ship in fact is arrived and ready. If the ship's master maintains that the sea notice given earlier was valid, the new NoR should be marked "*without prejudice to the NoR given at . . .* (insert earlier time and day of first NoR)".

The "validity" of the notice depends on whether the vessel has arrived at the contractual destination and whether it is then physically and legally ready to commence cargo operations.[5] If the document is given, but it is not valid as a "notice of readiness"; it is said to be a "nullity". An invalid notice may be the cause of laytime not commencing and if cargo operations are in fact carried out, this could be to the advantage of the charterer. The validity of the notice of readiness depends on the clauses of the charterparty and the concept of the "arrived ship". One element of "validity" is the vessel's "arrival". Another essential element is its "readiness" to load or to discharge. This may be referred to as being "*ready in all respects*". This means that the vessel must be physically ready and also legally ready (permitted) to load or discharge the cargo. If it is not so ready, the document given (NoR) may be considered to be "premature" and can be rejected. Delay caused by the vessel not being arrived and ready to load or delay sustained by not giving a valid NoR is at the shipowner's risk.

The "correctness" of a notice of readiness depends on "how" and "where" it is given and the time when it is given and accepted. An incorrect notice is one that may not have been given in the prescribed manner and thus have little effect.[6] The notice of readiness not only must be given during prescribed "office hours", but also, if the original document is invalid as a "notice of readiness", fresh documents may have to be given by the master at regular intervals. "Office hours" usually includes only business-office working hours and not port or stevedore working hours. However, if the charterparty clearly permits notices to be given on Saturdays (for example, from 0900 to 1200 hours), a "correct" notice of readiness may be given by e-mail, fax etc., even though the offices of the addressees of the messages are closed. If the charterparty requires the notice of readiness to be given in office hours and this is done outside such a period, the notice will be effective only at the start of office hours on the next working day.

---

5 Lopez, J.N. (1992) *Bes'Chartering and Shipping Terms* (London, Barker & Howard Ltd., 11th edition, pp. 192–196).

6 Lopez, J.N. (1992) *Bes'Chartering and Shipping Terms* (London, Barker & Howard Ltd., 11th edition, pp. 192–196).

15.6.4 Lay/can

The time when a notice of readiness can be given is also prescribed in the "lay-days and cancelling" (lay/can) clause, in which it may be stipulated that laytime should not commence before a certain day (lay), whereas if the vessel's notice of readiness is not given before a subsequent certain day (can), the charterers have the option to cancel the charter. For example, the clause may take the form "*Laydays 1st September/Cancelling date 15th September*" (see also section 10.5). There is usually no prohibition on the master's giving a correct notice of readiness and "consume" the notice time before the laydays are agreed to begin. However, the laytime will not commence until the agreed earliest time of the lay/can clause.

15.6.5 NoR in each port?

It is not always clear from the charter agreements whether NoR must be given in each port or if it is sufficient to give it only in the first loading and/or discharging port. According to the English Common Law, a notice of readiness is not necessary to be given in the discharging port. However, the recommendation is to tender NoR in every port where laytime counting shall take place, in order to avoid disputes. Nevertheless, this does not mean that the owners should provide the charterers with a notice time simply because a notice of readiness has been given, if this has not been agreed in the charterparty.

15.7 Notice time

15.7.1 Length of notice time

Many voyage charterparties give the charterers extra time after a valid notice of readiness has been given. The original intention with the so-called "*notice time*" was that the charterer, or the shipper/receiver, after they had been made aware of the ship's arrival and readiness, should be allowed a certain time to arrange for loading or discharging. In modern times, when ships are equipped with fax and e-mail, with the owners being in most cases in constant contact with the charterers, there is no practical reason for such notice time. However, most printed voyage charterparty forms still entitle the charterers to notice time. For example, in *Gencon '94* (see appendix 1, *part II, part of clause 6(c) "laytime – commencement of laytime (loading and discharging)"*) the clause is worded as follows:

> "*Laytime for loading and discharging shall commence at 13.00 hours, if notice of readiness is given up to and including 12.00 hours, and at 06.00 hours next working day if notice is given during office hours after 12.00 hours. Notice of readiness at loading port to be given to the Shippers named in Box 17 or if not named to the Charterers or their agents named in Box 18. Notice of readiness at the discharging port to be given to the Receivers or, if not known, to the Charterers or their agents named in Box 19*".

483

Another way to state notice time is that followed in a tanker voyage charter-party (see appendix 2, *Shellvoy 6, part II, part of clause 13 "notice of readiness/ running time"*):

> *"Time at each loading or discharging port shall commence to run 6 hours after the vessel is in all respects ready to load or discharge and written notice thereof has been tendered . . .".*

Although the system providing for notice time is somewhat obsolete today, there is a situation in which it may be justified. If the vessel arrives during a holiday period or at night, the charterers perhaps have no practical chance of commencing the loading or the discharging at once. Thus, there is a risk that she will be idle from the time of arrival until the commencement of ordinary working hours in the relevant port. If the parties agree that this risk shall rest with the owners, they can insert in the charterparty a clause of the following type:

> *"Laytime to commence at the beginning of next ordinary working shift after vessel's arrival".*

Once the notice time has started to run, it runs, unless otherwise expressly agreed, notwithstanding any exceptions in the laytime clause. Therefore, the notice time can be counted during a Sunday or a holiday, even though these days may be excluded from laytime under the laytime clause. In many cases, the relevant clause will take this problem into consideration.

15.7.2 Notice time before the first layday

Unless otherwise agreed, NoR can be given and notice time counted before the first agreed layday.

15.7.3 Laytime counting during notice time

According to English law, when the loading or the discharging commences before the notice time expires, the owners are not entitled to count time unless this has been expressly agreed in the charterparty. Such a clause can have the following typical wording:

> *"Time actually used before commencement of laytime shall count".*

It is noted that the clause only refers to *the time actually* used, impliedly for cargo handling. This means that breaks (e.g. for meals) do not count as laytime, as long as the notice time has not elapsed.

15.8 Commencement of time counting

Laytime will commence after:

- the vessel arrives at the agreed destination (port, berth, etc.),
- the vessel becomes physically and legally ready to load or discharge cargo,
- the notice of readiness is correctly tendered by the master or agent of the owner.

If a notice time has been agreed in the charterparty, the principal rule is that the laytime starts to count when the notice time has elapsed. However, as mentioned in section 15.7.3, counting of laytime can start even before the notice time has elapsed.

During the years, a number of clauses have been developed for handling the situations where the vessels for some reasons cannot go straight into the berth or place for loading or discharging. These cases are complicated enough and many times they have been settled in courts and arbitrations. For better understanding of relevant provisions, the reader may refer back to the terms *"reachable on arrival"* and *"always accessible"* as analysed in section 15.4.2, as well as finding some more expressions below.

According to Laytime Definitions 2013, term 26, the typical phrase *"time lost waiting for berth to count as loading or discharging time"* or *"as laytime"* shall mean that: *"if no loading or discharging berth is available and the vessel is unable to tender notice of readiness at the waiting-place then any time lost to the vessel shall count as if laytime were running, or as time on demurrage if laytime has expired. Such time ceases to count once the berth becomes available. When the vessel reaches a place where she is able to tender Notice of Readiness, laytime or time on demurrage resumes after such tender and, in respect of laytime, on expiry of any notice time provided in the charterparty"*.

The most common such clause designed to shift the risk of delay is the *Gencon '94* provision [see appendix 1, *part II, part of clause 6(c) "laytime – commencement of laytime (loading and discharging)"*] which stipulates that time lost in waiting for berth is to count as loading (or discharging) time. The objective of this clause is to shift the risk before the vessel becomes an arrived ship, i.e. from time when ship could have entered a berth had one been available. In case of a berth charter, it covers the period while the vessel is waiting in port until a berth is available. In case of a port charter, it applies while the vessel is waiting outside the port or even while it is waiting inside the port but not "immediately and effectively" at the disposal of charterer. The crucial question is whether the basic reason for the delay is the unavailability of a berth. The clause was initially a berth charter clause, which later was included in port charters due to its popularity. This extension of use has led to some confusion in its interpretation in port charters, as there is a possibility of overlapping between waiting time and laytime provisions. Nowadays, it is clear that, even when the clause states that *"all time lost waiting for a berth to count as laytime"*, all such time lost is to be treated as laytime as if the vessel had become an "arrived ship" (*The "Darrah" [1967] 1 Lloyd's Rep. 285; [1976] 2 Lloyd's Rep. 359*).

If such a term is agreed in the charterparty, in respect of laytime calculation it must be noted that:

- Laytime is to start from the time the notice of readiness (NoR) is presented by the master to the charterers' agent, even though the vessel is held up because no berth is available.
- Time lost in waiting for an available berth shall count as laytime, until laytime expires or an available berth is found (whichever occurs first). If laytime expires first, whilst the vessel is still waiting, thereon the vessel is "on demurrage" even if she may still be waiting.
- If, whilst the vessel is waiting for a berth, laytime has not expired yet, all laytime exceptions shall apply as if the vessel would actually load/discharge.
- If, whilst the vessel is waiting for a berth, laytime expires and the vessel is "on demurrage", all laytime exceptions shall not apply ("*once on demurrage always on demurrage*").
- Waiting time, whilst the vessel is either "on laytime" or "on demurrage", shall cease to count once the berth becomes available.
- When a berth becomes available and the vessel reaches a place where she is able to tender fresh NoR in accordance with the charterparty, laytime or time on demurrage shall resume after such tender. In respect of laytime, time shall be resumed on expiry of any notice time provided by the charterparty to the charterers, so as they can get ready to load or discharge the cargo. But, in respect of demurrage, time shall be immediately resumed after tender of NoR, even though a notice time may have been provided in the charterparty.
- The main purpose of the clause is to transfer the burden and risk of the time lost because a berth is unavailable, from the shipowner to the charterer.
- The effect of the provision is the same whether the charter is a "berth charter" or a "port charter". In a "berth charter", the vessel will not become an "arrived ship" until the contractual destination (berth) is reached. NoR is not valid until the vessel becomes an "arrived ship". In this situation, the "time lost" provision can certainly help the shipowner if the vessel has to wait for the berth. However, even in a "port charter", the "time lost" provision may protect the shipowner, when the vessel may have to wait outside the port limits and this may not be the "*place where waiting ships usually lie*". In such cases, the vessel cannot be an "arrived ship", but the clause may shift the burden.

Furthermore, Laytime Definitions 2013, term 27, includes another similar wording:

> "*Whether in Berth or Not*" *(WIBON)* or "*berth or no berth*" shall mean that "*if the designated loading or discharging berth is not available on arrival, the vessel on*

reaching any usual waiting place at the port, shall be entitled to tender Notice of Readiness from it and laytime shall commence in accordance with the charterparty".

The official commentary (2013) explains that the term relates to delays due to congestion (but not on account of weather). Besides, a major change has been made. Under Voylayrules '93, laytime or demurrage ceased once a berth became available and would not resume until the vessel was at the berth. This meant that the owner would have to bear the risk of any intervening delay, even if not otherwise contractually responsible. An adjustment has therefore been made, so that time will always run in accordance with the underlying charterparty provisions.

The so-called "WIBON" clause has a similar effect to the "time lost" clause. However, it applies only in berth charterparties, when a ship arrives at her destination and finds no berth available. The effect of the clause is to convert a berth charterparty into a port charterparty, so the vessel becomes an "arrived ship" and the laytime clock starts earlier. The clause enables the shipowner to give a valid NoR to load as soon as the vessel arrives in port, provided that other conditions for a valid NoR are satisfied. The clause is interpreted as applying only to cases where a berth is not available due to port congestion, not to cases where a berth is available but unreachable due to bad weather, tide etc. In respect of laytime calculation, the clause has similar effect and use to that of a "time lost" clause.

Laytime Definitions 2013, term 28, makes also reference to the following wording:

> *"Whether in port or not" (WIPON)* shall mean that *"if the designated loading or discharging berth and the usual waiting place at the port are not available on arrival, the vessel shall be entitled to tender Notice of Readiness from any recognised waiting place off the port and laytime shall commence in accordance with the charterparty"*.

As per official commentary (2013), this is a new term enabling an owner to give notice of readiness from any recognised waiting place "off the port" if unable to proceed to the usual waiting place.

This has similar meaning and effect to that of a WIBON clause. According to that term, it is not necessary for a vessel to be within port limits for laytime to start counting. The shipowner is enabled to give a valid NoR to load, as soon as the vessel arrives outside the port, but anchored at a place where ships of similar type and size usually lie while waiting for a berth at that specific port. As WIBON, it applies only to cases where a berth is not available due to port congestion.

15.9 Laytime allowance

Laytime is usually *fixed* between the parties in the charterparty, either by a number of days or hours or by a cargo handling rate per day (for example *"ten days"* or *"72 hours"* or *"loading 3,000 mt per day"*), whether for loading or for discharging or for both activities (the last case known as *"for all purposes"*). Instead, there are two wide alternatives where *time allowed is not fixed*. First, laytime may be *calculable*. This means that in order to define the allowed period of laytime, calculations must first be carried out, based on the terms of charterparty and on the events described at the statement of facts. Second, an owner will occasionally agree for his ship to be loaded or discharged as per *"custom of the port"* (COP) or on *"as fast as can"* (FAC) terms, in which case the laytime is regarded as *indefinite* causing several problems in calculations.

The laytime may be commonly determined in various ways, as the following:

- As a fixed number of days, for instance:
  "Five running days allowed for loading".
- As a daily loading/discharging rate, for example:
  "Loading at a rate of 5,000 mt per day".
- As a loading/discharging rate per hatch per day, like:
  "Loading at a rate of 200 mt per hatch per day".
- By using the vessels loading capacity as base, like:
  "Five running days allowed for loading based on vessel's cubic capacity of 500,000 cb. ft. Time allowed to be adjusted pro rata for larger or smaller vessels".

In connection with the cargo-handling rate per day and hatch, various phrases are used. *"Workable hatch"* and *"available hatch"* indicate that only the hatches actually used shall count and the total time allowed is usually calculated by dividing the quantity in the largest hatch with the daily rate per workable or available hatch. This method is less favourable to the owners than the method when only the word *"hatch"*, not connected with the words "available" or "workable", is used. In the latter case, the total time allowed is calculated by dividing the total quantity loaded on board a vessel with the product of the number of hatches and the daily cargo-handling rate.

In the tanker trades, the laytime is often counted until the disconnection of hoses, or until the delivery of the necessary transport documents.

It is not unusual, especially in contracts of affreightment, that the time allowed is related to a fixed cargo-handling capacity figure for a specific size of vessel and that the time allowed varies with larger or smaller ships, for example *"liner terms with customary quick despatch"* or *"as fast as the vessel can receive/deliver (FAC)"*. These clauses are not beneficial to the owners. It is difficult to prove that the charterers have loaded or discharged the ship so slowly, that the owners are finally entitled to demurrage. For the owners, it is important to have the FAC clause basically connected with the cargo-handling capability of the vessel. If the clause is not connected with the capability of the vessel, the owners have very little chance to get compensation for delay beyond the control of the charterers (for instance, due to lack of wagons or traffic problems ashore). For such cases, some charterparties also contain the so-called *force majeure* clauses.[7] Another problem

---

7 *Force majeure:* Meaning "superior force", it is a common clause in contracts that essentially frees both parties from liability or obligation when an extraordinary event or circumstance beyond the

for the owners is the fact that the charterers (and/or shippers and/or receivers) who have entered into a charter agreement with a FAC clause normally do not calculate or expect that the owners will claim demurrage. This "psychological difficulty", together with the judicial difficulties, make it tough for the owners to claim and collect the demurrage they are entitled to.

Unless otherwise agreed, the calculations for demurrage/despatch are drawn up separately for loading and discharging (see analytically section 15.11 about the laytime result and section 15.17 for practical examples). If more than one loading ports or discharging ports are involved, only one calculation is being made for the loading ports together and one for the discharging ports together. The main principle of separate calculations for loading and discharging is often set aside by a special agreement in the charterparty. This can be done by using, for instance, the wording "*time allowed for loading and discharging, eight days altogether*" or "*time allowed, eight days all purposes*".

Sometimes, the words "*reversible*" or "*average*" are used, as for instance "*three days for loading and five for discharging, loading and discharging times to be reversible*" or "*three days for loading, five for discharging, charterers having the right to average loading and discharging times*". In the case of reversible laytime, the times are added to a total time for loading and discharging. What is left from the total time used for the loading will be the "allowed time" for discharging. If all the time is used for loading, the vessel is on demurrage on arrival at the discharging port and the time will then count immediately (it should be noted that in this case notice of readiness should be delivered in order to avoid disputes, although a notice of readiness is typically not necessary in the discharging port). In the case of the average laytime, the loading and discharging calculations are drawn up separately. Thereafter, the demurrage and despatch times are added or set off (averaged) against each other and finally the demurrage or despatch amount is calculated on the result.

According to Laytime Definitions 2013 (term 23), "*average laytime*" or "*to average laytime*" means that "*separate calculations are to be made for loading and discharging and that any time saved in one operation is to be set off against any excess time used in the other. Average laytime arises where separate calculations are performed for the loading and discharging ports, with the final results being combined in order to assess what is finally due (for example time saved at one port is deducted from demurrage time at the other)*".

Furthermore, Laytime Definitions 2013 (term 24) define "*reversible laytime*" as "*the option given to the charterer to add together the time allowed for loading and discharging. Where the option is exercised the effect is the same as a total time being specified to cover both operations*".

Contrary to the "average laytime" where separate calculations are made for loading and discharging, in "reversible laytime" one unique calculation is made

---

control of the parties, such as a war, strike, riot, crime, or an event described by the legal term "act of God" (such as hurricane, flooding, earthquake, volcanic eruption etc.), prevents one or both parties from fulfilling their obligations under the contract.

for both operations which are considered to be one for the purposes of laytime calculation. From the total laytime allowance for both cargo operations, total loading and discharging time is deducted and the resultant demurrage or despatch amount is calculated. Where there is more than one loading ports during a voyage charter, a "reversible laytime" calculation may be agreed to apply only to the loading ports.

The result will often be the same whether the reversible time system or the average system is used. However, as the rule "*once on demurrage, always on demurrage*" (see sections 15.10, 15.11) may cause considerable financial difference between the two systems, it is important to be aware of that. The clauses are often constructed as optional in the charterers' choice, for instance "*laytime for loading and for discharging to be reversible in charterers' option*". In such cases, the owners will always lose as the charterers will calculate both separately for loading and discharging and also as one calculation under the reversible time methodology. Thereafter, they will follow the calculation which gives the best outcome for themselves. The application of these terms is illustrated by practical examples provided in section 15.17.

15.9.1 Definite laytime

As it has been mentioned in the previous section, the definite laytime specifies how many days/hours are allowed to the charterer, whether for loading or for discharging, or for both activities, the latter sometimes being known as for "*all purposes*". Typically, in this case laytime is exactly defined as a number of days or hours. However, there is a variety of expressions used to determine laytime. The most important definitions and abbreviations in respect of the "*laydays*" are briefly described and commented below (see also appendix 3):

- "*Day shall mean a period of twenty-four (24) consecutive hours. Any part of a day shall be counted pro rata*" (Laytime Definitions 2013, term 8). As per official commentary (2013), in contrast to a "calendar day" (definition no. 9, see below) and a "conventional day" (definition no. 10, see below), an unqualified "day" is now described as a period of 24 consecutive hours.
  From the owners' point of view, this is the most favourable description of a "layday", as it comprises Sundays and holidays in the laytime.
- "*Calendar day shall mean a period of twenty-four (24) consecutive hours running from 0000 hours to 2400 hours. Any part of a day shall be counted pro rata*" (Laytime Definitions 2013, term 9). According to the official commentary (2013), it is a new term which covers a period of 24 consecutive hours running from 0000 to 2400 hours.
- "*Conventional day shall mean a period of twenty-four (24) consecutive hours running from any identified time. Any part of a conventional day shall be counted pro rata*" (Laytime Definitions 2013, term 10). According to the official commentary (2013), it is a new term also which has

been included in recognition of the fact that a period of 24 hours in relation to laytime counting is likely to start at any point during a calendar day.

- *"Working Day* (abbrev. WD)[8] *shall mean a day when by local law or practice work is normally carried out"* (Laytime Definitions 2013, term 11). As per official commentary (2013), the meaning has been brought into line with prevailing English law.

  When such a term is agreed, the parties are recommended to definitely determine in the charterparty which days are considered to be "working days" and which are regarded as "holidays" in a specific port. To avoid confusion, parties should be fully aware of the local law and practice at each port of call. Moreover, if days are to be excluded from laytime, that should be stated explicitly in the charterparty. Most commonly, when "working days" have been agreed to in the charterparty, Sundays and holidays are further explicitly excepted from laytime (*"SHEX term"*). A working day is a period of 24 consecutive hours running from 0000 hours to 2400 hours.

- *"Running days* (abbrev. RD) *or Consecutive days* (abbrev. CD) *shall mean days which follow one immediately after the other"* (Laytime Definitions 2013, term 12). The official commentary (2013) explains that the provision remained unchanged compared to the 1993 edition.

  This definition has no material difference to the term "days". Running days are consecutive days of 24 hours including weekends and holidays. The term emphasises the continuous manner of laytime. There must be other written expressions in the charterparty (e.g. SHEX term) if laytime is to be interrupted.

- *"Running hours or Consecutive hours shall mean hours which follow one immediately after the other"* (Laytime Definitions 2013, term 13). According to the commentary (2013), it is a new term reflecting practical usage, particularly in tanker charterparties.

- *"Holiday shall mean a day other than the normal weekly day(s) of rest, or part thereof, when by local law or practice work during what would otherwise be ordinary working hours is not normally carried out"* (Laytime Definitions 2013, term 14). As per the official commentary (2013), this is the unchanged mirror image of working day (definition no. 11, above).

- *"Weather working day* (abbrev. WWD) *shall mean a working day or part of a working day during which it is or, if the vessel is still waiting for her turn, it would be possible to load/discharge the cargo without interruption due to the weather. If such interruption occurs (or would have occurred if work had been in progress), there shall be excluded*

---

8 Abbreviations of the terms have been inserted by the authors to help the reader relate the theory, as presented by the official laytime definitions, with the chartering practice, which commonly uses abbreviated terms in the daily exchange of information.

from the laytime a period calculated by reference to the ratio which the duration of the interruption bears to the time which would have or could have been worked but for the interruption" (Laytime Definitions 2013, term 15). The official commentary (2013) explains that *"deductions for bad weather are calculated by reference to the length an interruption during a vessel's normal (or notional if waiting on turn) working hours bears to a period of 24 hours. Thus, a two hour stoppage during an eight hour working day is pro-rated to six hours (or four hours in the case of a twelve hour working day) and the time then added to the end of laytime. No deductions are made for rain occurring outside normal working hours"*.

- *"Weather Working Day of 24 Consecutive Hours shall mean a working day or part of a working day of 24 consecutive hours during which it is or, if the vessel is still waiting for her turn, it would be possible to load/discharge the cargo without interruption due to the weather. If such interruption occurs (or would have occurred if work had been in progress) there shall be excluded from the laytime the period during which the weather interrupted or would have interrupted work"* (Laytime Definitions 2013, term 16). According to the official commentary (2013), it is clarified that *"the actual duration of an interruption for bad weather at any time on a working day during or outside normal working hours and including periods on turn, is added to the end of laytime"*.

- *"Weather working day of 24 hours shall mean a period of 24 hours made up of one or more working days during which it is or, if the vessel is still waiting for her turn, it would be possible to load/discharge the cargo without interruption due to the weather. If such interruption occurs (or would have occurred if work had been in progress), there shall be excluded from laytime the actual period of such interruption"* (Laytime Definitions 2013, term 17). Official commentary states (2013) that *"this is an artificial day made up of twenty-four working hours. An eight hour working day is equal to three calendar days' laytime but with laytime suspended for stoppages due to bad weather in working hours or in working hours when work was contemplated"*.

- *"(Working Day) Weather Permitting shall have the same meaning as Weather Working Day of 24 Consecutive Hours (term 16)"* (Laytime Definitions 2013, term 18). According to the official commentary (2013), *"this has the same meaning and interpretation as Weather Working Day of 24 Consecutive Hours (definition no 16)"*.

Laytime Definitions 2013 provide four separate meanings for weather working days (definition 15–18 as analysed above) in an attempt to be in line with English law decisions. This is in contrast to the single provision in Voylayrules '93 which was covering three alternative forms of Weather Working terms. This is the most important differentiation of the latest definitions comparing to the previous edition.

For the sake of comparison and in order to understand the importance of this difference, the full wording of respective weather working terms, as per "*Voylayrules '93*", is presented below:

○ "*Weather working day (WWD) or weather working day of 24 hours or weather working day of 24 consecutive hours shall mean a working day of 24 consecutive hours except for any time when weather prevents the loading or discharging of the vessel or would have prevented it, had work been in progress*" (Voylayrules '93, term 12).

According to Voylayrules '93, this is a day on which work is normally carried out at a port (working day), which counts as laytime unless loading or discharging would have ceased because of bad weather. Time on which operations are interrupted or would have been interrupted if they were in progress does not count as laytime. For example, under this term when a vessel is waiting for an available berth, but bad weather conditions would have prevented her from loading/discharging if such work had been in progress, this time of interruption due to bad weather does not count as laytime. This term should be compared with "Weather Permitting" under Voylayrules '93 (see below). From the owner's point of view, a "Weather Working Day" is less favourable than a "Weather Permitting" term.

○ "*Weather permitting (WP) shall mean that any time when weather prevents the loading or discharging of the vessel shall not count as laytime*" (Voylayrules '93, term 13).

Under Voylayrules '93, this is a provision stipulating that laytime does not count when loading or discharging operations are actually interrupted by bad weather conditions. For example, under this term when a vessel is waiting for an available berth, but bad weather conditions would have prevented her from loading/discharging if such work had been in progress, this time of interruption due to bad weather counts as laytime. This is the significant difference comparing with a "Weather Working Day". From the owner's point of view, a "Weather Permitting" term is more favourable than a "Weather Working Day".

Two more definitions containing the word "*days*" are worth to be mentioned, even not included in Laytime Definitions 2013:

• "*Clear days shall mean consecutive days commencing at 0000 hours on the day following that on which a notice is given and ending at 2400 hours on the last of the number of days stipulated*" (Voylayrules '93, term 9).

This term has been removed from the revised edition of 2013. Clear days usually determine a "notice time". The first and last days are excluded from the calculation. For example, on 15 September the vessel gives a "*7 clear days' notice of expected date of readiness at port of loading*", so the charterer can get ready to deliver the cargo. Then, the date of owner's notice and the date of delivery of cargo are excluded from the calculation of seven clear days. In other words, such seven clear days count from 16 September 0000 till 22 September 2400 and the cargo should be ready for loading on 23 September.

- "*Days All Purposes*" (abbrev. DAP): It may be seen as a synonym to "reversible laytime" (see section 15.9 above and second example in section 15.17). Another wording with similar meaning may be "*time allowed for loading and discharging X days altogether*".

The two well-known expressions *Weather Working (WW)* and *Weather Permitting (WP)* have during the years caused many discussions and disputes. Many variations and opinions about the correct understandings of *WW* and *WP* exist. A comparatively new study[9] indicates that no well-established internationally accepted understanding exists. More discussions and disputes can be expected.

Expressions like "*Time allowed for loading 3 days WP*" or "*Time allowed for loading 3 days WW*" are often seen in voyage charter agreements. A recommendation is that charterers and shipowners discuss more in details and try to draft clauses understandable and acceptable for both sides. Unfortunately, this is not an uncomplicated task. Another way is to refer to any of the existing standard definitions, for example the "*Laytime Definitions for Charter Parties 2013*" and the official comments to these definitions as analysed before. It must always be remembered that, according to the official commentary of the sponsoring organisations, Laytime Definitions 2013 are "*in line with English law decisions*".

However, some time after the definitions were published, new discussions and disputes are still expected for the future. In respect of the weather exceptions, the following three fundamental questions should mainly be considered and answered between the parties in every charter agreement:

1. Shall weather stoppages in the port hinder also time counting for vessels waiting for turn to load or discharge?
2. Shall weather stoppages outside the ports' ordinary working periods, when the vessels anyhow would not load or discharge, influence the time counting?
3. In which way shall the weather stoppages mathematically be handled in the time counting?

Following the latest Laytime Definitions 2013, it was explained above in the official comments of Laytime Definition No. 18 about "*(Working Day) Weather Permitting*" that this term "*has the same meaning and interpretation as Definition No. 16 for Weather Working Day of 24 Consecutive Hours*". It is therefore sufficient here to handle only Laytime Definitions No. 15 and No. 16 which both clearly state that they include situations when "*interruption occurs, or would have occurred if work had been in progress*".

---

9 Tiberg, H. (2013) *Law of Demurrage* (London, Sweet & Maxwell, 5th edition, sections 8–25).

Definition 15 for "*Weather Working Day*" states that interruptions in time counting shall be calculated "*by reference to the ratio which the duration of the interruption bears to the time which would have or could have been worked but for the interruption*". In the official commentary this definition is further explained to mean that "*. . . deductions for bad weather are calculated by reference to the length an interruption during a vessel's normal (or notional if waiting on turn) working hours bears to a period of 24 hours. Thus, a two hour stoppage during an eight hour working day is pro-rated to six hours (or four hours in the case of a twelve hour working day)*".

Thus, in figures, if two hours stoppage in an 8-hour working day occurs, then:
Ratio: 2/8 hours = ¼
Number of hours not counted as laytime: ¼ × 24 hours = 6 hours.

Result: 2 hours is the length of the weather stop, 8 hours is the length of the normal working period and 24 hours is the length of a full weather working day. Weather stoppages outside normal working period are not taken into account. Thus, 18 hours is counted as laytime.

Definition 16 for "*Weather Working Day of 24 Consecutive Hours*" states that "*the actual duration of an interruption for bad weather at any time on a working day during or outside normal working hours and including periods on turn, is added to the end of laytime*". Weather stoppage both within and outside normal working periods are taken into account and the sum of these shall be deducted from the days of 24 consecutive hours.

Answering the first question above, for vessels waiting for turn to load or discharge both Definitions 15 and 16 provide that weather stoppages in port will cease the laytime counting.

Answering the second question above, in respect of weather stoppages occurring outside the ports' ordinary working hours (when the vessels are not loading or discharging), Definition No. 15 (weather working day) provides that no laytime deductions are made for weather stoppages (e.g. rain) occurring outside normal working hours. On the contrary, Definition No. 16 (weather working day of 24 consecutive hours) stipulates that an interruption for bad weather at any time of a working day, during or outside normal working hours, will cease the laytime clock, i.e. the respective time will be excluded from laytime.

Answering the third question above, Definitions No. 15 and No. 16 follow different methods to calculate the deduction for weather stoppages. According to Definition No. 16 (weather working day of 24 consecutive hours), the actual length of weather stoppages – any time during the day of 24 hours irrespective of vessel being berthed or not – is deducted from the day when time used is calculated. On the other hand, according to Definition No. 15 (weather working day), the proportion between the length of weather stoppages and the ordinary working period is inferred (converted) on a 24-hour basis to calculate how much of the 24-hour day shall be counted as laytime and which part will be deducted (excluded from laytime).

Examples of laytime calculation are given at the end of this chapter (see section 15.17), to enlighten the practical aspect of the above-mentioned terms. At this point, once again it should be stressed that the charterparty wording is always the base of laytime counting.

15.9.2 Calculable laytime

In this situation, periods of definite laytime can only be established once a calculation has first been carried out, based on clauses contained in the charterparty and on events described in the statement of facts (see section 15.12 about the role of the statement of facts). The duration of laytime may be ensued from tonnage calculations or from hatch calculations. More specifically:

- *Tonnage Calculations:* A charterparty will state that a vessel is to load and/or discharge at a set rate of tons per day/hour (e.g. for a vessel loading 30,000 mt of cargo at a rate of 10,000 mt/day, there will be three days laytime).
- *Hatch Calculations:* A charterparty will state that a vessel is to load and/or discharge at a set rate of tons per hatch and/or per day (e.g. a loading rate of 120 tons per hatch daily).

The most common definitions and abbreviations, in respect of calculable laytime, are briefly described below:

- *"Per hatch per day* (Laytime Definitions 2013, term 6) shall mean that *the laytime is to be calculated by dividing, the quantity of cargo, by the result of multiplying the agreed daily rate per hatch by the number of the vessel's hatches. Thus:*

$$Laytime = \frac{Quantity\ of\ cargo}{Daily\ rate\ per\ Hatch \times Number\ of\ Hatches} = Days$$

Each pair of parallel twin hatches shall count as one hatch. Nevertheless, a hatch that is capable of being worked by two gangs simultaneously shall be counted as two hatches".

- *"Per working hatch per day* (WHD) *or per workable hatch per day* (Laytime Definitions 2013, term 7) shall mean that *the laytime is to be calculated by dividing, the quantity of cargo in the hold with the largest quantity, by the result of multiplying the agreed daily rate per working or workable hatch by the number of hatches serving that hold. Thus:*

$$Laytime = \frac{Largest\ Quantity\ in\ one\ Hold}{Daily\ Rate\ of\ Loading\ or\ Discharging\ per\ Working\ or\ Workable\ Hatch \times Number\ of\ Hatches\ serving\ that\ Hold} = Days$$

Each pair of parallel twin hatches shall count as one hatch. Nevertheless, a hatch that is capable of being worked by two gangs simultaneously shall be counted as two hatches".

15.9.3 Indefinite laytime

In this case, laytime depends upon the custom of the port at which cargo operations are being performed, or upon the speed at which the ship can load or discharge, or on both. The shipowner may agree for his ship to be loaded or discharged as per *"custom of the port"* or on *"as fast as can"* terms. More specifically[10]:

- *"Customary Despatch (CD)"* or *"Customary Quick Despatch (CQD)"* or *"Custom of the Port (COP)"*: Charterers have the obligation to clear the ship (i.e. to finish loading or discharging) as quickly as possible in accordance with the customs of the port. Therefore, they have a wide scope, as they are excused from delays provided they have done their best under prevailing conditions of the port. In general, this is a vague term, usually not favourable to the shipowners, as there are no fixed criteria for how quick "customary despatch" should be. This term should be avoided because considerable uncertainty arises from its use. In the group of cases and wordings of indefinite laytime, owners may be put in the difficult situation of having to prove they are entitled to demurrage or damages for detention in case of serious delay.
- *"Fast As Can (FAC)"* or *"As Fast As the Vessel Can Receive/Deliver"*: This is another ambiguous wording of a non-fixed laytime. In such a case, laytime shall be calculated by reference to the maximum rate at which the ship in full working order is capable of loading or discharging the cargo. The final duration of laytime can be rather uncertain, depending on an opinion of the speed at which the vessel can in fact receive or deliver the cargo. Under a "fast as can" (FAC) term, the vessel's actual capability to load or discharge will be an obligation on the shipowner. On the other hand, charterers shall have the obligation to despatch the ship (i.e. to finish loading or discharging) as soon as is practical (= as soon as the vessel can . . .), without undue delay, and possibly in accordance with the custom of the port (COP) or "with customary quick despatch" (CQD). The "FAC" term may even be interpreted to denote the charterers' responsibility to ensure that cargo-handling facilities permit the ship to be loaded or discharged at a predetermined rate. At this point, comparing with a "customary despatch" (CD) or other similar term, it may be noted that the latter puts an obligation on the charterers' side to load/unload the cargo as fast as possible in accordance with custom of the port, no obligation to the owners' side. In any case, "fast as can" (FAC) terms or similar should be avoided, as long as they do not clearly describe the allocation of liabilities between the negotiating parties.

---

10 Lopez, J.N. (1992) *Bes' Chartering and Shipping Terms* (London, Barker & Howard Ltd., 11th edition, pp. 44, 63, 168).

15.10 Laytime counting and exceptions

After commencement of laytime, the time allowed to the charterer for loading/ discharging begins to run continuously and get reduced (this is referred to as the "*counting of laytime*") unless the charterparty contains applicable "*exception clauses*", during which the reduction of charterer's stock of time is interrupted. The parties to a voyage charter may agree that certain events may interrupt the counting of laytime. These will operate as a protection for the charterer. For example, Sundays, holidays, bad weather, strikes, ballasting, shifting of berth etc., are various events which may interrupt the counting (down) of charterer's laytime.

It is obvious that shipowners and charterers will attempt to calculate laytime most advantageously to themselves. Thus, the wording of laytime clauses must be as clear as possible to express the intentions of the contracting parties. Laytime has always been a field of hard negotiation and often of intense dispute between owners and charterers.

Having established the commencement and duration of laytime, the calculator must next make allowance for interruptions that have occurred during the laytime period. The most common causes of delay in loading/discharging operations, thus the respective most common laytime exceptions, may indicatively concern Sundays, holidays or other non-working days or periods in accordance with the customs of the ports, congestions in ports, bad weather conditions, strikes, political unrest, or even "*any other cause beyond the control of charterers*". In all the above-mentioned aspects of delay, if there is no express charterparty statement to the contrary, such events will not interrupt laytime which, once commenced, will continue uninterrupted until its expiration or until the completion of cargo operations.

The most common *definitions and expressions* in respect of the *exceptions of laytime* are briefly described below:

- "*Excepted*" or "*excluded*" shall mean that "*the days specified do not count as laytime even if loading or discharging is carried out on them*" (Laytime Definitions 2013, term 19).
- "*Unless sooner commenced*" shall mean that "*if turn-time*[11] *has not expired but loading or discharging is carried out, laytime shall commence*" (Laytime Definitions 2013, term 20). In respect to the above two terms, the official commentary (2013) states that Definition No. 19 remained unchanged, whilst No. 20 now has the effect of bringing forward the commencement of laytime if work begins prior to the contractual start of laytime.
- "*Unless sooner commenced in which case actual time used to count*" shall mean that "*actual time used during turn-time shall count as laytime*" (Laytime Definitions 2013, term 21). Similarly, the commentary (2013) states that the commencement of laytime remains in accordance with charterparty provisions, but time actually used in any prior period will count against laytime.

---

11 *Turn Time (TT)*: Time allowed in the charterparty, after NoR tendered and before laytime commences. It is usually quoted in hours (www.worldcoal.org). Synonym to "notice time".

- *"Unless Used" ("UU")* shall mean that *"if laytime has commenced but loading or discharging is carried out during excepted periods, actual time used shall count as laytime"* (Laytime Definitions 2013, term 22). According to the official commentary (2013), *"time used during excepted periods is set against laytime"*.
- *"Strike shall mean a concerted industrial action by workmen causing a complete stoppage of their work which directly interferes with the working of the vessel. Refusal to work overtime, go-slow or working to rule and comparable actions not causing a complete stoppage shall not be considered a strike. A strike shall be understood to exclude its consequences when it has ended, such as congestion in the port or effects upon the means of transportation bringing or taking the cargo to or from the port"* (Voylayrules '93, term 28). This term has been removed from the Laytime Definitions 2013.
- *"Weather Working Day"* or *"Weather Working Day of 24 Hours"* or *"Weather Working Day of 24 Consecutive Hours"* or *"Weather Permitting"* (Laytime Definitions, terms 15, 16, 17, 18): As explained in section 15.9.1.

Some of the most common *abbreviations* in respect of the *exceptions of laytime* are briefly explained below in alphabetical order:

- *ATUTC: All Time Used to Count:* Synonym to the term *"unless used"*.
- *EIU: Even If Used:* Time spent for loading or discharging on excepted periods (e.g. on Sundays or holidays) shall not count as laytime even though it was actually used.
- *FHEX: Fridays Holidays Excluded:* Fridays and holidays do not count as laytime.
- *FHINC: Fridays Holidays Included:* Fridays and holidays count as laytime.
- *SATPMSHEX: Saturdays Post Meridiem Sundays Holidays Excluded:* Saturdays after noon (1200), Sundays and holidays do not count as laytime.
- *SHEX: Sundays Holidays Excluded:* Sundays and holidays do not count as laytime.
- *SHINC: Sundays Holidays Included:* Sundays and holidays count as laytime.

15.11 Final analysis and result of laytime

The termination of cargo operations, namely the completion of loading or discharging, is considered to be the critical point which determines the result of laytime calculation. Ocassionally, special cargo-handling works, such as trimming, lashing, or securing may be necessary, the time for which would reasonably be counted as laytime. Moreover, the charter contract specifies whether time devoted to ascertaining a vessel's draught should count as laytime or not.

The final analysis will show if the shipowner or the charterer has to pay. If the cargo takes longer than the allowed time to load or discharge, the charterer must compensate the owner for the time so lost. This compensation can be *"damages for detention"* or *"demurrage"*. The main difference between these terms is that the former is *"unliquidated damages"*, that is the rate of compensation is not agreed in advance by the parties and may be determined by an arbitrator or judge, while the latter is *"liquidated damages"* agreed in advance at the charterparty. The first method of compensation is a lengthy and costly legal exercise. Consequently, the contracting parties avoid the problem by usually negotiating a rate of "demurrage" inserted in the charterparty.[12] However, even in that case, extensive delays may occur and damages for detention may be claimed by the owner beyond the agreed demurrage rate of the contract. Such damages may be assessed at the vessel's demurrage rate or at a higher rate relevant to the opportunity cost for lost freight revenue plus operating costs.[13]

According to Laytime Definitions 2013 (term 30), *"demurrage is the agreed amount payable to the owner in respect of delay to the vessel once the laytime has expired, for which the owner is not responsible. Demurrage shall not be subject to exceptions which apply to laytime unless specifically stated in the charterparty"*.

The last sentence is equally attributed with the classic phrase *"once on demurrage, always on demurrage"*. The amount of demurrage is negotiated with the contract and is usually expressed in US Dollars per day or pro rata for part of a day. Typically, address commissions and brokerages are deductible from demurrage payments, but this has to be clearly stated in the commission/brokerage clause. It must be noted that over time both English law and US law have liberalised their previous strict adherence to the above-mentioned phrase. Nowadays, every situation is distinguishable by the unique circumstances surrounding each event.[14]

On the contrary, if a vessel completes cargo operations within the available laytime, the charterer will be rewarded by the collection of despatch (or dispatch) money, which is normally set at half the daily rate of demurrage.

According to Laytime Definitions 2013 (term 31), *"despatch money or dispatch is the agreed amount payable by the owner if the vessel completes loading or discharging before the laytime has expired"*. Few charterers are powerful enough to negotiate that daily despatch rate should be the same as daily demurrage. For vessels that normally expect a fast turn-round in port (e.g. Ro/Ro ships, car carriers or coasters) it is not unusual for the contract to specify *"free despatch"* – no despatch at all. Typically, despatch does not apply to tanker voyage charters.

---

12 Lopez, J.N. (1992) *Bes'Chartering and Shipping Terms* (London, Barker & Howard Ltd., 11th edition, p. 166).

13 Haugen Consulting *What is Demurrage?* (www.haugenconsulting.com, accessed 15 June 2017).

14 Haugen Consulting *What is Demurrage?* (www.haugenconsulting.com, accessed 15 June 2017).

In respect of *"despatch"* the following *definitions and expressions* are worthy of mention:

- *"Despatch on all working time saved"* (abbrev. "WTS") or *"on all laytime saved"* shall mean that *"despatch money shall be payable for the time from the completion of loading or discharging until the expiry of the laytime excluding any periods excepted from the laytime"* (Laytime Definitions 2013, term 32).
- *"Despatch on all time saved"* (abbrev. "ATS") shall mean that *"despatch money shall be payable for the time from the completion of loading or discharging to the expiry of the laytime including periods excepted from the laytime"* (Laytime Definitions, term 33).

In respect of *"demurrage"* and *"despatch"*, the following group of *abbreviations* should be mentioned:

- *DFD: Demurrage/Free Despatch:* Owner has the right to receive demurrage, but charterer has no right to receive despatch, when such term is agreed. This is a common practice in short sea shipping, when the vessel's turn-around time is usually short (e.g. Ro/Ro vessels).
- *DHD or D½D: Demurrage/Half Despatch:* A common term for ocean-going dry cargo vessels, which defines that daily rate of despatch (if it arises) should be paid at half the agreed daily rate of demurrage.
- *DDO: Despatch Discharge Only:* Despatch is paid only in discharging port (if it arises).
- *DLO: Despatch Loading Only:* Despatch is paid only in loading port (if it arises).
- *FD: Free of Despatch:* No despatch amount is agreed between contracting parties.

Furthermore, a *comparison of important despatch terms and abbreviations* follows:

- *ATSBENDS or ATSBE: All Time Saved Both Ends:* Term used to describe how despatch money is paid. Synonym to the term *"DBEATS"* (see below). Despatch amount is payable:
  - ◦ at both ends, i.e. for loading and discharging operation;
  - ◦ for all time saved from both operations, in total.
  Therefore, the despatch amount is calculable for all the actual time saved from earlier completion of both operations till expiry of total laytime allowed for both operations, thus including periods excepted from laytime. Compare with *"AWTSBENDS"* below.
- *ATSDO: All Time Saved Discharging Only:* Despatch money is to be paid for all time saved, only for discharging operation. It is estimated for all

actual time saved from completion of discharging to expiry of laytime allowed for discharging, thus including periods excepted from laytime.

- *ATSLO: All Time Saved Loading Only:* Despatch money is to be paid for all time saved, only for loading operation. It is estimated for all actual time saved from completion of loading to expiry of laytime allowed for loading, thus including periods excepted from laytime.
- *AWTSBENDS* or *AWTSBE* or *ALTSBENDS* or *ALTSBE: All Working Time Saved Both Ends* or *All Laytime Saved Both Ends:* Term used to describe how despatch money is paid. Synonym to the term *"DBELTS"* (see below). Despatch amount is payable:

  ○ at both ends, i.e. for loading and discharging operation;
  ○ only for working time saved from both operations, in total.

  Therefore, the despatch amount is calculable for all working time saved from earlier completion of both operations till expiry of total laytime allowed for both operations, thus excluding periods excepted from laytime. Compare with *"ATSBENDS"* above.

- *AWTSDO* or *ALTSDO: All Working Time Saved Discharging Only* or *All Laytime Saved Discharging Only:* Despatch money is to be paid for working time saved, only for the discharging operation. It is estimated for all working time saved from completion of discharging to expiry of laytime allowed for discharging, thus excluding periods excepted from laytime.
- *AWTSLO* or *ALTSLO: All Working Time Saved Loading Only* or *All Laytime Saved Loading Only:* Despatch money is to be paid for working time saved, only for the loading operation. It is estimated for all working time saved from completion of loading to expiry of laytime allowed for loading, thus excluding periods excepted from laytime.
- *DBEATS: Despatch payable at Both Ends on All Time Saved:* Synonym to the term *"ATSBENDS"*. Despatch amount is payable at both ends, i.e. for loading and discharging operations, for all time saved from both operations, in total.
- *DBELTS: Despatch payable at Both Ends on Laytime Saved:* Synonym to the term *"AWTSBENDS"*. Despatch is payable at both ends, i.e. for loading and discharging operation, for all working time saved from both operations, in total.

15.11.1 Demurrage and damages for detention

The well-known expression *"once on demurrage, always on demurrage"* means that exception clauses (see section 15.10 above) do not apply to demurrage, unless they are clearly worded so as to have that effect. In most cases this means that when the laytime expires and the vessel is on demurrage, all the time thereafter (24 hours per day, seven days per week) shall count notwithstanding weather hindrances, holidays, strikes etc. However, time counting may be interrupted where such interruption is caused by the owner or the owner's servants or by a fault on the vessel's side. It is not clear whether "fault" in this respect means negligence, unseaworthiness or suchlike, or if it is the same as an inability from the ship's side to provide power to winches. In other words, when the ship is on demurrage, it is not straightforward whether the owners are strictly liable for any hindrance on the vessel's side or they are liable only for hindrances caused by negligence from the owners', master's or crew's side. In tanker charterparties, it is frequent that specific exclusions are foreseen to apply on demurrage. This is drafted through a wording where it is agreed that specific events, if they occur, "... *shall not count for laytime or as time on demurrage*".

The demurrage rate is the compensation that owners are entitled to, when loading and/or discharging is not completed before the allowed time expires. The demurrage rate is usually agreed to a certain amount per 24 hours or pro rata. Since demurrage is a kind of liquidated damages agreed beforehand between the parties, the owners do not have to prove their loss. Moreover, if they can prove that their loss is higher than the demurrage compensation, they are nevertheless not entitled to more than the agreed rate. On the other hand, they get full demurrage even if their actual loss is lower than the agreed rate.

Sometimes, the demurrage time may be capped. For instance, such a limitation is printed in *Gencon '76* (*part II, clause 7 "demurrage"*) as follows: "*Ten running days on demurrage at the rate stated in Box 18 per day or pro rata for any part of a day, payable day by day, to be allowed for Merchants altogether at ports of loading and discharging*". In the *Gencon '94* form, the limitation to ten days has been deleted.

When demurrage time is limited by agreement and allowed demurrage time is used, the owners are further entitled to "*damages for detention*". When owners claim damages for detention, they have to prove their loss. The demurrage rate is sometimes considered as prima facie evidence in this respect and quite often neither of the parties thinks about to change the situation when the allowed demurrage time has expired. However, it is important to be aware of the difference between damages for detention and demurrage, as the economic result can vary considerably. The main difference between these terms is that the former are "unliquidated damages", that is the rate of compensation is not agreed beforehand and the loss may be judged to get compensated, while the latter are "liquidated damages" agreed in advance at the charterparty. The first method is costly and lengthy, thus the contracting parties usually prefer to agree a rate of "demurrage" in the charter contract.

Furthermore, instead of limited demurrage time and damages for detention, the parties sometimes agree to have an escalating demurrage rate, for instance: "*demurrage for the first 10 days is agreed to be US$7,000 per 24 hours, thereafter US$9,000 per 24 hours*".

Clauses limiting the demurrage time do not solve the difficult question which arises when the shippers fail to deliver the agreed quantity of cargo and the charterers do not declare that they cannot get more cargo. In this situation, it is difficult for the owners to decide whether they should order the vessel to sail or wait for the remaining cargo. As long as the demurrage rate is sufficient and as long as the charterers pay the demurrage, in some cases the owners may not suffer, but if the rate is low and/or if the charterers do not pay and/or if the owners have other deployment commitments for the vessel, they should take legal advice in order to find out how to act.

In most cases, the calculation and payment of demurrage is made after final discharge and delivery of the cargo. If the owners wish to have a chance to exercise a lien over the cargo against their claim for demurrage, they should ensure that it is clearly stated in the charterparty that the "*demurrage is payable day by day*". Without such a clause, it is not clear when demurrage is payable and it may therefore be difficult for the owners to use the cargo as security by exercising a lien. *Gencon '76* (*part II, clause 7 "demurrage"*, see above) is stating that the demurrage is payable "*day by day*". In *Gencon '94* (see appendix 1, *part II, part of clause 7 "demurrage"*) the clause has been further developed as follows:

> "*Demurrage at the loading and discharging port is payable by the Charterers at the rate stated in Box 20 in the manner stated in Box 20 per day or pro rata for any part of a day. Demurrage shall fall due day by day and shall be payable upon receipt of the Owner's invoice*".

In the event the demurrage is not paid in accordance with the above, the owners may typically give the charterers a written notice to rectify the failure within 96 running hours. If the demurrage is not paid at the expiration of this time limit and if the vessel is at the loading port, the owners will be entitled at any time to terminate the charterparty and claim damages for any losses caused thereby (see appendix 1, *Gencon '94, part II, part of clause 7 "demurrage"*).

15.11.2 Despatch

If cargo is loaded faster than the allowed laytime, the vessel is considered to have been released earlier to the owner's control. That is an advantage for the shipowner who may agree to refund an amount of money to the charterer. This compensation is called "*despatch*" or "*dispatch*" and it is usually agreed at the dry cargo charterparties to be half the demurrage rate ("*DHD*" term in abbreviation). In some cases, for example in tanker charters, no despatch is typically payable unless an additional clause ("rider clause") is agreed.

As discussed in section 15.11, despatch can be calculated in different ways. Sometimes, charterers are entitled to despatch for "*all time saved*" and sometimes only for "*all working time saved*". In the first case ("*all time saved*"), the charterers should have compensation for all time the owners actually saved, which means all the running time from the moment the ship was actually ready until the moment the allowed laytime should theoretically have expired had the vessel still been in port at that time, therefore all laytime exceptions do not apply to this despatch calculation. In the latter case, when despatch is counted in accordance with the "*all working time saved*" provision, the compensation to the charterers is counted only on the basis of the remaining laytime allowed after the ship was finally loaded and/or discharged, thus all laytime exceptions apply to this despatch calculation and the respective time of exceptions is deducted from the despatch payment.

Payment of despatch is often not specified in the charter agreements. In trades where despatch is agreed and expected, it is not unusual that charter agreements may stipulate that a percentage of the despatch amount (e.g. 10%) shall be paid when the time counting for the voyage is ready. Final settlement of despatch will then be set off against the remaining freight.

15.12 Stages and documents of laytime calculations

A standard method of laytime calculation is suggested to be regularly used, but the shipowner and the charterer may have methods and forms that suit each party and differ. If standard forms are used, some areas of dispute may be reduced. The *stages of laytime calculation* (tankers and dry cargo laytime) are the following:

- Assessment of *laytime commencement*;
- Determination of *laytime duration*;
- Estimation of *laytime interruptions*;
- Determination of *laytime cessation*;
- *Final analysis* and *calculation of the amount of demurrage or despatch* owed.

To make proper laytime calculations, the calculator needs the following *documents*:

- Copy of the *voyage charterparty* (see appendix 1, *Gencon '94*, for a sample copy of a dry cargo voyage charterparty and appendix 2, *Shellvoy 6*, for a sample copy of a tanker voyage charterparty): The calculator has to study carefully all charterparty clauses which describe exactly how much time is available for loading or discharging and when laytime commences, it is interrupted or it ceases. Furthermore, the calculator has to take into consideration clauses related to the definition of "laytime", determination of the "arrived ship" and "notice of readiness" (if, how, where and when it should be given).
- Copy of *Notice of Readiness* (*NoR*): This is a formal notification by the vessel that a state of readiness, either to load or discharge, exists at the time when it is given (see also sections 15.6, 15.7). Upon arrival at customary anchorage at the port of loading, the master or his agent shall give the charterer or his agent notice by letter, telegraph, wireless or telephone that the vessel is ready to load the cargo.[15] It should be noted that if the vessel is not on the berth, the NoR may be tendered by telex, fax or any other more modern means of communication expressly stated

---

15 Cooke, J., Young, T., Taylor, A., Kimball, J., Martowski, D. and Lambert, L. (1993) *Voyage Charters* (London, Lloyd's of London Press, p. 275).

in the charterparty (e.g. e-mail), or even by the agent on the vessel's behalf. A hard copy will be prepared and signed later when the vessel reaches the berth. The onus is on the master, or possibly on port agents, to ensure correct delivery of the NoR. It is not necessary for a vessel to have been inspected, purged or granted free pratique to be able to tender a valid NoR. If, however, the vessel subsequently fails an inspection, NoR may become invalid. On passing the subsequent inspection, the vessel should tender her notice again. The notice of readiness is important because it informs the charterer for the readiness of the vessel in order to make all the necessary preparations of the cargo operations. As it has been mentioned, the giving and acceptance of the notice of readiness is also important because it is one of the triggers that cause laytime to commence. Laytime will commence after the vessel arrives, becomes physically and legally ready to load or discharge cargo, and the notice of readiness is correctly tendered by the master or agent of the owner.[16] The charterparty may prescribe that laytime commences after an agreed period has elapsed or from a certain time after the notice of readiness has been tendered and accepted. Normally, no notice of readiness is necessary at the discharging port, unless there is an express provision to the contrary in the charterparty.

- *Statement of Facts (SoF):* This is a document attached to the time sheet (see below). It is a record of events occurring during a ship's port visit that can affect the counting of laytime. The statement of facts is drawn up by the port agent and forwarded to the shipowner upon ship's departure. Shipowners and charterers may use their own forms of statement of facts and time sheets. Standard statement of facts forms have been drawn up by BIMCO and are recommended by FONASBA. The statement of facts form include information vital to the laytime calculator. Amongst other items, it comprises dates and times of tendering notice of readiness of the ship, commencement and completion of cargo operations and details of daily cargo working, together with reasons for interruption of cargo working. All parties concerned in the port operations of the ship are required to sign the form. Space is provided for the signatures of the agent drawing it up, the master of the vessel concerned, as well as a representative of the charterer and/or shipper and/or receiver.[17] Samples of statements of facts may be seen in the practical examples given at the end of the chapter.
- *Time Sheets:* Accurate records ought to be kept and consulted as a diary of activities, whether these are for cargo operations, or whether they concern exceptions to laytime or waiting periods. These records are called "time sheets" and show whether the allowed laytime has been exceeded or is not fully used.

16 Lopez, J.N. (1992) *Bes'Chartering and Shipping Terms* (London, Barker & Howard Ltd., 11th edition, p. 196).

17 Packard, W. (1993) *Laytime Calculating* (Surrey, Fairplay Publications, pp. 7–8).

A time sheet indicatively includes the following information (samples of time sheets may be seen in the practical examples at the end of the chapter):

- Date and hour of ship's arrival in the loading or discharging port.
- Date and hour of ship's arrival in the loading or discharging berth.
- Date and hour on which ship is physically and legally ready to start the loading or discharging operation.
- Date and hour on which notice of readiness was tendered.
- Date and hour on which notice of readiness was accepted by the charterers.
- Date and hour on which loading/discharging operation commenced.
- Days and hours on which loading/discharging operation took place.
- Date and hour on which laydays started.
- Loading and discharging speed according to the clauses of charterparty.
- Interruptions of laytime according to the terms of charterparty.
- The quantity of cargo loaded/discharged per day.
- The total quantity of cargo loaded/discharged.
- Statement of the time allowed for loading and discharging according to the laytime clause of the charterparty.
- Date and hour of loading/discharging completion.

The *accuracy of time sheets* depends on the following factors[18]:

- Definition of laytime: fixed, calculable or indefinite laytime.
- Category of laytime: separate calculations for loading and discharging ports, or options to the charterer for reversing or averaging laytime.
- Method of calculating laytime: the laytime clause of the charterparty will define how laytime is calculated, by using relevant wordings or exceptions, such as for example, *"per workable hatch per day"*, *"Sundays and holidays excepted, unless used"* etc.
- Commencement of laytime: the laytime clause of the charterparty will state the notice period (if any) after a valid notice of readiness is given.

Standard time sheet forms have been drawn up by BIMCO, but some shipping companies prefer to use their own designs.

15.13 Liquid and dry cargo laytime

The above sections attempted to explain the key aspects of laytime calculations, namely the definition, duration, commencement, interruption, analysis and result. The following two sections present the peculiarities faced in liquid and dry cargo laytime calculations.

---

18 Lopez, J.N. (1992) *Bes'Chartering and Shipping Terms* (London, Barker & Howard Ltd., 11th edition, p. 217).

15.13.1 Liquid cargo laytime calculations

The calculation of tanker laytime is relatively easy by comparison with dry cargo laytime calculation. The reasons for this difference are that within the dry cargo world, too many shipowners and charterers are activating, the ships are trading worldwide even calling at under-developed ports, while the full picture is completed with a considerable number of charterparty forms that include many alternative laytime wordings. On the other hand, in the tanker market, although tanker owners are fairly numerous, there are relatively few charterers, the ships are usually trading among fewer and more technologically advanced ports worldwide, while there are even fewer charterparty forms which have a marked similarity regarding laytime matters.

Tanker laytime is triggered by tendering a valid notice of readiness. Therefore, unless there is a clause in the charterparty to the contrary, the time that the NoR is accepted is not relevant. Under the majority of tanker charterparty forms, if the vessel anchors because the berth is occupied, time starts six hours after NoR is tendered, whereas if the vessel proceeds directly to the berth without any waiting time, time will start on berthing or on commencement of loading/ discharging, depending on the charterparty form. For instance, *BPvoy 4 (part 2, clause 7.3.2 "laytime/demurrage")* includes the following wording: *"Laytime, or if the vessel is on demurrage, demurrage shall commence, at each loading and each discharge port, upon the expiry of six (6) hours after a valid NoR has become effective as determined under Clause 6.3, berth or no berth, or when the vessel commences loading, or discharging, whichever first occurs"*. Clause 7 of BPvoy 4 has remained broadly the same, but numbered as *clause 11* in the recently published *BPvoy 5*.[19]

In a tanker charter, duration of laytime is usually stipulated by *"Worldscale Hours Terms and Conditions"* (abbrev. *WSHTC* or *WHTC*), as already discussed in section 14.3. When such terms have been agreed in a charterparty, laytime duration is determined by what the latest edition of Worldscale provides. It is reminded that Worldscale is the "commercial handbook" guiding on a subscription basis all tanker chartering practitioners worldwide. It is published annually by Worldscale Association (London) Limited and Worldscale Association (NYC) Inc. Currently, "Worldscale" provides that *"time allowed for loading and discharging shall be 72 hours and shall be subject to whatever qualifications, if any, that are stated in the applicable charterparty or contract"* (see *Worldscale 2015, preamble, part B.2 "laytime"*).[20]

However, it is not rare for a tanker charterparty to include terms which determine the total duration of laytime to be 96 instead of 72 hours. Sometimes, the duration of tanker laytime may even result from an agreed daily rate of cargo handling. This method may often be used in the vegetable oil trades, where different rates for loading and discharging may even be faced.

---

19 Eversheds Sutherland (2016) *Shipping: BPVOY5 to take effect on 21 March 2016* (United Kingdom, www.eversheds-sutherland.com).
20 www.worldscale.co.uk (accessed 18 August 2015).

In tanker charterparties, it is common practice that laytime continues not only until completion of loading/discharging (as in the case of dry cargo laytime), but until the cargo hoses have been disconnected. Some shipowners who suffered further delays after hoses were disconnected, waiting for documents to be delivered, submitted claims for detention. This resulted in some charterparty forms being amended, so that they may cover such eventualities with a clause stating that *"time will count if the vessel is delayed for charterers' purposes beyond a specified period, often 3 hours, after disconnection of hoses"*.[21]

Once a valid NoR has been tendered, whilst vessel is in port, all such time will count as laytime, except any delays caused by the vessel or unless there is an express exception in the charterparty. There are events, similar to the dry-cargo field, which suspend laytime in the tanker industry. Some typical examples of *"excepted periods" in tanker laytime practice* are[22]:

- *Breakdowns or inefficiencies of the vessel*, such as pumping difficulties at the discharge port or tanker's inefficient heating coils[23] in the cargo tanks. In case of pumping difficulties, charterers allege inadequate performance on the ship's part, while the owners counter by drawing attention to what they may consider was excessive back-pressure in the cargo lines. Additionally, in case of tanker's inefficient heating coils in the cargo tanks, owners defend charterers' allegations by drawing attention to a low air temperature affecting long cargo shore-lines.
- Any *delays attributable to the fault of the shipowner* for which charterer has no control. The same applies for any faults of subcontractors for whom owner is responsible.
- *Shifting* time from anchorage to berth, after giving NoR, suspends laytime.
- *Bad Weather* does not affect tankers in the same way as dry cargo trades. The few areas that do suffer bad weather delays, usually caused by swell, are well known to tanker charterers and operators. Where weather conditions (for example storm, fog etc.) do cause delays for tankers, however, that usually occurs in berthing, thus most of the printed charterparty forms and additional clauses address this issue.[24] Some clauses state specifically that delays due to bad weather will not count as laytime, while others make an oblique reference using terms such as *"delays beyond charterers' control shall not count"*. Some charterparties, as for example *Shellvoy 6* (see appendix 2, *part II, clause 13.1(a) "notice of readiness/ running time"*) do not exclude bad weather time, if it occurs after the vessel has berthed, but such time does not count if weather prevents berthing. Other charterparties, such as *Exxonvoy '90* and *BPvoy 4*, count all bad weather delays as halftime. The most widely used additional

---

21 Wood, P. (2000) *Tanker Chartering* (London, Witherby & Co Ltd., pp. 157–160).
22 Wood, P. (2000) *Tanker Chartering* (London, Witherby & Co Ltd., pp. 157–160).
23 Heating coils are generally used for heating the cargo in tanks.
24 Wood, P. (2000) *Tanker Chartering* (London, Witherby & Co Ltd., pp. 157–160).

tanker clause covering bad weather exceptions is the *"Conoco Weather Clause"*. It provides that *"delays in berthing for loading or discharging and any delays after berthing which are due to weather conditions shall count as one half laytime or as time on demurrage at one half demurrage rate"*.[25]

- Delays resulting from *conditions at the nominated ports not caused by charterer's fault or neglect or which could be avoided by the exercise of reasonable care on the part of the master*. At this point, special reference should be made to *strikes*. Whilst dry cargo charterparties comprise clauses in respect of strikes, this is not the case in tanker charterparties. This happens due to the fact that historically little time has been lost through strikes in the oil terminals, which if not privately owned by the major oil companies, they are usually operated by them under a contract with the terminal owner. The words *". . . strike, labour, dispute . . ."* are typically included in a general clause stating that any delays caused by a strike will count as half laytime or half the demurrage rate. Strike may be defined as a general concerted refusal by workmen to work in consequence of an alleged grievance about their working conditions. It is understood that this is extended to include stoppages in support of some other body of workers who have an alleged grievance.

- Delays resulting from *crude oil washing (COW)* and *disposal of residues*: Crude oil washing will normally be required in accordance with MARPOL requirements (International Convention for the prevention of pollution from ships, 1973 and its 1978 Protocol) and sometimes charterers will have further demands. The COW requirements may also have laytime effect. To comply with the requirements of MARPOL, oil residues must be retained on board and not discharged to the sea. All modern tanker charters contain clauses which, in broad terms, have the effect of giving the charterer the right to dispose of residues, compensating the owner for any loss of freight caused by their segregation and retention (see for example appendix 2, *Shellvoy 6, part II, clause 40 "oil pollution prevention/ballast management"*). Many charterers are willing to take delivery of residue oil, and to pay freight on it, but incompatible residues are sometimes refused by shore installations. Only *Asbatankvoy* always obliges the charterer to arrange for residues to be pumped ashore. A disposal of residue clause should take into consideration a number of points, such as how to deal with residues when there are two or more charterers, how to deal with the situation when the loading port does not have any facility, etc. From a laytime perspective, the importance is seen in *Shellvoy 6* (see appendix 2, *part II, clause 40(5) "oil pollution prevention/ballast management"*) where it is stated that: *"Whenever charterers require the collected washings to be discharged*

---

25 Intertanko (2011) *Shifting off a Berth due to Weather/Sea Conditions – Charterparty Provisions Compared* (3 October 2011, www.intertanko.com).

ashore pursuant to this clause, charterers shall provide and pay for the reception facilities, and the cost of any shifting therefore shall be for charterers' account. Any time lost discharging the collected washings and/or shifting therefore shall count against laytime or, if the vessel is on demurrage, for demurrage".

- *Force majeure* resulting in sudden or unforeseen interruption or prevention of loading or discharging.

In tanker chartering practice, if the cargo is loaded faster than the allowed laytime, the *shipowner does not typically pay despatch*, which is one crucial difference between dry cargo and tanker laytime calculation. If the laytime is exceeded, the charterer pays the owner *demurrage*, which may be expressed:

- As a daily rate. The most common way to see demurrage quoted in a charterparty is as a daily rate in US Dollars and will be negotiated reflecting the daily return that the owner expects to earn on the voyage.
- By reference to Worldscale. The Worldscale contains at preamble, part C, a table of demurrage rates covering every size of tanker.

15.13.2 Dry cargo laytime calculations

The calculation of dry cargo laytime is more complicated when compared to tankers, as long as dry cargo operations are affected by various factors not influencing tankers, such as the diversity in nature and handling requirements of cargo, the capability of the vessel and the port, as well as the recognition that loading procedures may last much longer than unloading or vice versa.

Dry cargo laytime commences either immediately or after a specified period (notice time) has elapsed or at a precise time after the notice of readiness has been given and has been accepted.

While the duration of tanker laytime is typically determined as a total period of 72 hours for loading and discharging altogether, the duration of dry cargo laytime may be expressed in the charterparty in a number of ways. It can be fixed, calculable or indefinite. If the laytime is fixed or calculable, this leads to considerable certainty in assessing the time used for the cargo operations. If laytime is indefinite then various problems arise. This subject was described in section 15.9. Here, a more in-depth analysis will follow in respect to the peculiarities of dry cargo laytime.

As it has been explained, laytime can be fixed by express words in the charterparty, such as a specific number of days, running days, working days, weather working days, days of 24 hours or 24 consecutive hours, etc. Normally, the charterer is that who will initially determine the laytime terms based on his experience with the cargo, ports, stevedores and equipment, while the owner will negotiate based on his experience with the vessel. Finally, the laytime wording of the charterparty will be also a result of the bargaining power between the parties involved.

Laytime can be calculable by reference to the rates of loading or discharging cargo. Since ships are loaded and discharged at different daily rates, during the course of a loading or discharging operation lasting several days, it is advisable for the charterparty to include the phrase *"average rate of"* when describing loading or discharging rates.[26] It is a common practice of discharging bulk cargo where, in the beginning the bulker is able to achieve very high discharging rates, "creaming" cargo from the top, but slowing down appreciably when remaining cargo is lying at the bottom and sides of the holds. The term *"average rate of"* serves the purpose of better describing the laytime duration and prevents any owner's claim if the cargo is discharged slower on some of the days.

Complications in laytime calculation can arise also when the duration of laytime is calculable by reference to the number of *"workable hatches"* or *"hatches"*, although this practice is followed in a limited extent and in some parts of the world. A cargo hatch is the opening on the deck through which cargo is loaded into and out of cargo holds. The expression *"per workable hatch per day"* is more in the charterers' favour than in the shipowners'. The word *"workable"* or *"working"* when qualifying a hatch means that the hatch can be worked because there is (or will be) cargo in the hold below it. If the cargo hold beneath the hatch in question is empty or is to remain empty, it is not a "workable hatch". Therefore the *"workability"* refers to the cargo in the hold and not to the fact that the vessel may have cranes or derricks above to serve the hatch in question.[27] On the other hand, the term *"per hatch per day"* may be used to calculate laytime with reference to the number of cargo hatches serving cargo compartments on the vessel. A hatchway could lie over a cargo compartment that may be empty. If there is no intention to work a particular cargo space through the hatchway that serves it, that hatch is still a *"hatch"* although it may not be in the legal category of a *"working hatch"*. The number of hatches and their category will influence the rate at which cargo is to be handled and therefore the rate of calculating laytime allowed for the cargo operations.[28] However, this does not take into consideration the fact that each hatchway (and cargo hold) may be worked at different rates. Nor does it take into consideration that the vessel's holds may be served by more than one hatch. The reasons for the different cargo-handling rates could be various, for example different sizes of cargo holds, different numbers of stevedore gangs, different cargo-handling equipment, a specific plan for the stability and safety of the vessel influencing the sequence of loading (or discharging), etc.

Finally, laytime may be indefinite by terms such as *"per custom of the port"* or *"as fast as can"*. When charterparties include the "fast as can" terms in the case of self-discharging or belt self-unloading bulkers, it is necessary for the charterer to guarantee a minimum take-away speed.[29]

---

26 Collins, N. (2000) *The Essential Guide to Chartering and the Dry Freight Market* (London, Clarkson Research Studies, pp. 203–208).

27 Lopez, J.N. (1992) *Bes' Chartering and Shipping Terms* (London, Barker & Howard Ltd., 11th edition, p. 199).

28 Lopez, J.N. (1992) *Bes' Chartering and Shipping Terms* (London, Barker & Howard Ltd., 11th edition, p. 199).

29 Collins, N. (2000) *The Essential Guide to Chartering and the Dry Freight Market* (London, Clarkson Research Studies, pp. 203–208).

The counting of dry cargo laytime is considerably affected and therefore interrupted by physical (for example rain and bad weather) and non-physical events (for example Sundays and holidays). Some typical examples of *"excepted periods" in dry cargo laytime practice* are:

- *Breakdowns or inefficiencies of the vessel*, such as breakdowns of vessel's gear (e.g. winches). It is reasonable that if a vessel's gear is being used and it breaks down, laytime should not continue during the period of breakdown.
- *Shifting* between berths. Time spent in shifting between berths is normally taken to be for owner's account, i.e. shifting time does not count as laytime. However, it may be a matter of negotiation and charterparty wording.
- *Weekends and holidays*. If cargo operations are performed during an excepted period (e.g. under a SHEX term), laytime will not count unless the charterparty allows it to, for example by using terms such as *"time not to count during weekends unless used"*.
- *Strikes:* A provision which can often have a very drastic influence on time is the strike clause. Some strike clauses deal expressly with the counting of laytime, whilst others are worded in less precise terms and it is sometimes difficult to find out whether they influence the time counting or not. In general, strike clauses are difficult to draw up and interpret. Typically, there should be a clause in the charterparty to the effect that delays due to shore strikes are not to count as laytime. For example, *Gencon '94* (see appendix 1, *part II, part of clause 16 "general strike clause"*) allows the owner to cancel the charter if there is a strike or lockout affecting or preventing the loading of cargo, unless the charterer agrees to *"reckon the laydays as if there was no strike or lockout"*. Moreover, the same provision further stipulates that if part of the cargo has been loaded before the strike, the owner must proceed with the cargo loaded, receiving freight for only such loaded cargo, but having the liberty to complete with other part-cargo. However, at a discharging port, if the strike has not been settled within 48 hours after vessel's arrival, the receiver may either order the vessel to another port or keep the vessel waiting by paying half demurrage after the expiration of the agreed laytime for discharging.
- Any delays attributable to the *fault of the shipowner* for which charterer has no control. The same applies for any *faults of subcontractors* for whom owner is responsible.
- *Bad Weather* affects considerably the loading and discharging operations of dry cargoes. As a consequence, bad weather typically causes the interruption of laytime counting. But, this is always a matter of negotiation and charterparty wording.
- *Force majeure*. It should be mentioned that interruptions of laytime are also caused by *force majeure* events which are completely unforeseeable and outside the control of either party. For instance, a failure of the charterers to provide cargo at the loading port, because of events beyond their control, is excepted from laytime under a *"force majeure"* clause.

In situations where cargo has been partially loaded and an event of laytime exception occurs, it is difficult to draft a clause which covers every eventuality and is fair and equitable to both parties. What is most usually agreed is that the vessel has the option either to stay until loading is completed or to sail and load a completion cargo en route.

If cargo takes longer than the agreed laytime to load or discharge, the charterer must compensate the owner for the time so lost. This compensation can be either "damages for detention" or "demurrage". In dry cargo practice, demurrage is usually expressed as *"US Dollars per day or pro rata"*. If cargo is loaded faster than the allowed laytime, then the reward of the charterer is the so-called "despatch" or "dispatch" which usually is agreed to be half the demurrage rate. It is found in almost all dry cargo charterparties except *Gencon '94*, but even then it is often inserted as a specific additional clause (rider).

15.14 More than one charterer for a specific voyage

Another situation which may raise questions about the counting of laytime is when more than one charterparty are in force for one specific voyage. Owners will face this situation if they have a voyage charter with two or more charterers, who each have only a part cargo for the vessel. Laytime calculations must be made out partially for each charterer. Provided the statement of facts is detailed and clearly states during which time and in which holds the various part cargoes have been loaded or discharged, the time counting for actual loading and discharging should not cause too many problems. However, time lost in waiting for berth and other idle periods will easily give rise to long discussions between owners and charterers. Thus, owners who intend to voyage charter to several charterers for the same voyage should, even during the negotiations, try to draw up precise clauses in order to act proactively and prevent from any problems in the future.

15.15 Importance of all charterparty provisions

The counting of laytime may also be influenced by other terms and circumstances than those mentioned in the basic laytime clauses. Both during the negotiations and when the laytime calculation is drawn up, other charterparty provisions which are of relevance with the laytime matters must be thoroughly considered.

15.16 Comparing "Laytime Definitions 2013" with "Voylayrules '93"

The most significant differences between those two sets of laytime principles are summarised in the respective BIMCO special circular dated September 2013. The highlights of this official report are worth being presented below[30]:

---

30 BIMCO *Laytime Definitions for Charter Parties 2013* (Special Circular No. 8, 10 September 2013).

- The "Laytime Definitions 2013" (see appendix 3) *"have been restored to the original 1980 concept and developed again as definitions"*, instead of "Voylayrules '93" which *"were issued as a self-standing code of rules and differed in a number of significant respects from generally accepted principles and practice such as the decision to combine three variations of 'Weather Working' day into a single Rule"*.
- *The sponsoring organisations* (BIMCO, FONASBA, CMI and Baltic Exchange) *agreed that the previous approach had been a factor contributing to the limited use of "Voylayrules" and that a fresh approach was required in the development of updated provisions which would be used in the markets. It was therefore agreed to revert to definitions, setting out statements of meaning, and that the content should reflect contemporary market needs based on the current state of English law.*
- *As a result, substantive and editorial amendments were made to a number of the Voylayrules provisions.*
- *Separate explanations were given once again to different forms of "Weather Working" day.*
- *New definitions were introduced including "Always Accessible" and "Whether in Port or Not".*
- *The term "Strike", which was introduced in Voylayrules, was deleted because the scope and effects are often given their own meaning in the underlying charterparty.*
- *The term "In Writing" was removed from the new edition as unnecessary, given that many, particularly BIMCO, charterparties include a clause covering the issue.*
- *The use of abbreviations has, for the most part, been avoided. In many cases, there is no generally accepted meaning and while parties may understand their own exchanges, abbreviations and acronyms can be capable of more than one interpretation. The "Laytime Definitions 2013" use abbreviations only in respect of Whether in Berth or Not (WIBON) and Whether in Port or Not (WIPON) which are widely understood.*

15.17 Practical examples

This section presents examples which are intended to better illustrate the laytime practice.

Example 1: Laytime calculation at 1st discharging port

A GENCON berth charterparty, with modifications and rider clauses, provides for: Cargo: Full cargo bulk corn subject to vessel's capacity; expect vessel to load about 25,250 mt and to discharge 10,000 mt at first discharging port with remainder at second discharging port.
Laytime for loading: 2,500 mt per Working Day Weather Permitting, SHEX, u.u.

Laytime for discharging: 2,500 mt per Working Day Weather Permitting, SHEX, u.u.

Laytime clause: *"Laytime for loading and discharging shall commence at 1 p.m. if Notice of Readiness is given before noon and at 8 a.m. next working day if notice given during office hours after noon. Time actually used before commencement of laytime shall count. Time lost in waiting for berth to count as loading or discharging time as the case may be".*

Demurrage and despatch clause: *"At loading and discharging ports demurrage at the rate of US$ 5,000 per day or pro rata for any part of a day to be paid by Charterers. Despatch at the rate of US$ 2,500 per day or pro rata for any part of a day to be paid by Owners for working time saved".*

Statement of Facts – First Discharging Port

Vessel arrived at Pilot station:	0900, Friday 9 August
Vessel berthed:	1240, Friday 9 August
Notice of Readiness tendered:	0900, Friday 9 August
Notice of Readiness accepted:	0900, Friday 9 August
Cargo weight/quantity:	10,000 mt
Discharging commenced:	1630, Friday 9 August
Winch breakdown; no discharging:	1445–1530, Monday 12 August
Discharging completed:	1615, Monday 12 August
Laytime allowed for discharging:	4d. 00h. 00m. (10,000 / 2,500)

Time Sheet

Date	Day	Time Used			Total Time Counted			Time Lost/ Saved			Remarks
		D	H	M	D	H	M	D	H	M	
9 Aug	Fri	0	11	00	0	11	00				0900: Vessel arrived; NoR tendered 1300: Laytime commenced 1630: Discharging commenced
10 Aug	Sat	1	00	00	1	11	00				Normal
11 Aug	Sun	0	00	00	1	11	00				No work; not counted
12 Aug	Mon	0	15	30	2	10	15	0	07	45	0000–1615: Discharged cargo 1445–1530: Winch breakdown; not counted 1615: Discharging completed; 7h. 45m. saved
13 Aug	Tue				3	10	15	1	00	00	1d. saved
14 Aug	Wed				4	00	00	0	13	45	13h. 45m. saved 1345: Laytime expires
Totals		2	02	30	4	00	00	1	21	30	Working time saved (despatch)

Despatch: 1d. 21h. 30m. @ $ 2,500 per day and pro rata = $ 4,740

Calculations/explanations/remarks

- Laytime allowed for discharging = 10,000 mt : 2,500 per Working Day Weather Permitting, SHEX, u.u. = 4 days.
- NoR was given during office hours before noon (9 August, 0900) and laytime for discharging commenced at 1300 same day (laytime clause), though discharging started a bit later, at 1630 of same day.
- Sunday does not count because no work took place (SHEX u.u.).
- Discharging was completed on 12 August at 1615, before expiry of available laytime.
- In order to calculate the despatch time, first it should be estimated when available laytime expires.
- Total laytime allowed for discharging is calculated 4d.
- On time of completion of discharge, actual total time used was only 2d. 02h. 30m.
- After the time of completion of discharge, only working time saved will be added in the column "Total Time Counted" (despatch payable on working time saved). As despatch time, only the working time remaining from the completion of discharge up to the end of available laytime (4d.) will be counted.
- Therefore, on 12 August:

  - Discharging took place for 16h. 15m. in total, except the time of winch breakdown (45m.). Those 45 minutes of winch breakdown do not count as laytime, whereas the remaining 15h. 30m. count and they are added in the column "Time Used".
  - The time after completion of discharge (7h. 45m.) is added in the column "Time Saved", because it is the working time saved of that day.
  - In the column "Total Time Counted" the 15h. 30m. of laytime and the 7h. 45m. of saved time are added. The time of winch breakdown is not counted.

- Up to midnight of 12 August, 2d. 10h. 15m. have been used from the total allowed time for discharging, which is 4d. From their difference, assuming that no laytime exception took place on 13 and 14 August, it arises that the stipulated time for discharging expires at 1345 of 14 August, when the available laytime runs out.
- Therefore, on 13 August, 1d. and on 14 August, 13h. 45m. are added in the column "Time Saved", because it is the working time saved of those days.
- Total time saved is 1d. 21h. 30m.
- Despatch amount to be paid to the charterer is calculated as follows:

  1 day   =   1.000000
  21 hours =   0.875 (see appendix 16)
  30 mins   =   0.020833 (see appendix 16)
                1.895833 days
                1.895833 days × 2,500 per day and pro rata = $ 4,739.58

- Another way to calculate despatch time "for working time saved" (see appendix 3, Laytime Definitions 2013, term 32) is to deduct total time used (2d. 02h.30m.) from the allowed four days. Note that this method cannot be used when time "for all time saved" (see appendix 3, Laytime Definitions 2013, term 33) is agreed. In the above example, the despatch amount would have been the same even if an "all time saved" term had been agreed.
- However, if we had assumed a rain stop occurring for five hours on 13 August, between 0900 and 1400, then:
  - Under a "working time saved" term, the laytime expiry would have been extended for five hours ending at 1845 on 14 August, but the despatch time and amount would have been unchanged comparing to the above example.
  - Under an "all time saved" term, the laytime expiry would have also been extended for five hours ending at 1845 on 14 August, but, comparing to the above example, five more hours would have been added as despatch time and the despatch amount would have been increased accordingly.
- The difference is clearly illustrated by Schofield[31]:

  > "If a charter allows ten working days for loading and the operation actually takes five working days ending on a Wednesday, a projection of when laytime would have expired if the full amount of time allowed had been taken would show that laytime would end the following Tuesday, i.e. a further five days excluding Sunday, a non-working day. The time therefore saved is six days on an 'all time saved' basis and five days on a 'working time saved' basis".

Another way of expressing the same thing would be to say that six actual days or five working days have been saved.

Example 2: *Comparison of normal, reversible and average laytime*

A charterparty, with modifications and rider clauses, provides for:
Laytime for loading: 6 days.
Laytime for discharging: 3 days.
Laytime clause: *"Laytime not counting from noon Saturday until midnight Sunday, even if used. . .".*
Demurrage and despatch clause: *"Demurrage payable at US$ 4,000.00 per day and pro rata. Despatch payable at half demurrage rate on all time saved."*

---

31 Schofield, J. (2016) *Laytime and Demurrage* (Informa Law from Routledge, 7th edition, p. 510).

Statement of Facts

Time at loading port to count from:	1200, Monday 25 November
Loading completed:	1200, Friday 29 November
Time at discharging port to count from:	1200, Thursday 12 December
Discharging completed:	2400, Thursday 19 December

Time Sheet – Normal Laytime

(1) Loading port

Date	Day	Time Allowed			Time Lost/ Saved			Remarks
		D	H	M	D	H	M	
25 Nov	Mon	0	12	00				1200: Laytime commenced
26 Nov	Tue	1	00	00				
27 Nov	Wed	1	00	00				
28 Nov	Thu	1	00	00				
29 Nov	Fri	1	00	00	0	12	00	1200: Completed loading 12h. saved (All time saved)
30 Nov	Sat	0	12	00	1	00	00	1d. saved (All time saved)
1 Dec	Sun	0	00	00	1	00	00	1d. saved (All time saved)
2 Dec	Mon	1	00	00	1	00	00	1d. saved (All time saved) 2400: Laytime expires
Totals		6	00	00	3	12	00	3d. 12h. Total time saved

(2) Discharging port

Date	Day	Time Allowed			Time Lost/ Saved			Remarks
12 Dec	Thu	0	12	00				1200: Laytime commenced
13 Dec	Fri	1	00	00				
14 Dec	Sat	0	12	00				Time not counted after 1200
15 Dec	Sun	0	00	00				Not counted
16 Dec	Mon	1	00	00				2400: Laytime expires
17 Dec	Tue	0	00	00	1	00	00	1d. lost
18 Dec	Wed	0	00	00	1	00	00	1d. lost
19 Dec	Thu	0	00	00	1	00	00	2400: Completed discharging (1d. lost)
Totals		3	00	00	3	00	00	3d. Total time lost

Despatch at loading port 3d. 12h. @ $ 2,000 per day or pro rata = $ 7,000
Demurrage at discharging port 3d. @ $ 4,000 per day or pro rata = $ 12,000
Net amount due to owners (demurrage) = $ 5,000

Time Sheet – Reversible Laytime							
Date	Day	Time Allowed			Time Lost/Saved		Remarks
		D	H	M	D	H	M	
25 Nov	Mon	0	12	00				1200: Laytime commenced
26 Nov	Tue	1	00	00				
27 Nov	Wed	1	00	00				
28 Nov	Thu	1	00	00				
29 Nov	Fri	0	12	00				1200: Completed loading
12 Dec	Thu	0	12	00				1200: Laytime resumed
13 Dec	Fri	1	00	00				
14 Dec	Sat	0	12	00				Time not counted after 1200
15 Dec	Sun	0	00	00				Not counted
16 Dec	Mon	1	00	00				
17 Dec	Tue	1	00	00				
18 Dec	Wed	1	00	00				2400 Laytime expires
19 Dec	Thu				1	00	00	1d. Time lost 2400: Completed discharging
Totals		9	00	00	1	00	00	1d. Total time lost

Demurrage 1d. @ $ 4,000 per day or pro rata = $ 4,000

Time Sheet – Average Laytime

On separate calculations:
Total time saved at loading port = 3d. 12h.
Total time lost at discharging port = 3d.
Net laytime saved = 12h.
Despatch: 12h. @ $ 2,000 per day or pro rata = $ 1,000

Calculations/Explanations/Remarks

- In "normal laytime", separate calculations are made for loading and discharging operations.
- Time allowed (laytime) for loading is six days. Laytime in loading port expires on Monday 2 December, 2400, as long as laytime does not count from noon Saturday until midnight Sunday, even if used (laytime clause).
- Loading is completed on Friday 29 November, 1200. It has been agreed in the charterparty that despatch is payable on all time saved (DATS). This means that despatch money is payable from the completion of loading (29 November, 1200) to the expiry of the laytime (2 December,

520

2400), including periods excepted from the laytime. Total time saved is 3d. 12h., counting as despatch in loading.

- Time allowed (laytime) for discharging is three days. Following the same calculation as in loading, it is found that laytime in discharging port expires on 16 December, 2400.
- Discharging is completed on 19 December, 2400. Therefore, demurrage is payable from the expiry of laytime (16 December, 2400) till the completion of discharge (19 December, 2400). Total time lost is 3d. counting as demurrage in discharging operation.
- From those two separate calculations, the result is that the net amount due to owners as demurrage is $5,000.
- In "reversible laytime", the charterer has an *option* to add together the time allowed for loading and discharging. Practically, it is as if a total time is specified to cover both operations and therefore one unique calculation is made.
- Total available time (laytime) for loading and discharging is nine days.
- Taking all laytime exceptions into account (in that case "*noon Saturday until midnight Sunday*"), laytime commences on 25 November, 1200, and is allowed for both operations altogether.
- At time of loading completion, on 29 November, 1200, laytime is paused. Up to that time, only four days have been used from the total available laytime (9 days). The remaining five days will be available for the discharging operation.
- Laytime is resumed when vessel is ready to discharge, on 12 December, 1200.
- Taking into account that "*noon Saturday until midnight Sunday*" is excepted from laytime, it is found that reversible laytime expires on 18 December, 2400, when the remaining five days allowed for discharging are run out.
- Finally, discharge is completed on 19 December, 2400. Therefore, vessel is "on demurrage" for one day.
- From this calculation, it comes that net amount due to owners as demurrage is $4,000. Probably, the charterer will exercise his option to "reverse" the laytime as this calculation gives a better outcome for himself, comparing to the normal laytime calculation where he should owe $5,000 as demurrage to the owners.
- In "average laytime", separate calculations are to be made for loading and discharging and any time saved in one operation is to be set off against any excess time used in the other.
- This calculation shows that net amount due to charterers as despatch is $1,000.

Conclusions

- In both "normal laytime" and "average laytime", separate calculations are made for loading and discharging operations.

- However, in "normal laytime" money is set off, whereas in "average laytime" time is set off.
- In "reversible laytime", the charterer has the option to use a total time allowance for both operations and therefore to make one unique laytime calculation if it is to his benefit.
- From our example it becomes very clear that, depending on the agreed terms of the charterparty, significant differences may arise in laytime calculations and therefore in the amounts to be paid or earned.
- The stipulation of charterparty terms is of paramount importance. Details do matter!

Example 3: *Comparison of "Weather Working Days of 24 Consecutive Hours" or "Working Days Weather Permitting" (Laytime Definitions 2013, synonym terms 16 and 18) against "Weather Working Days" (Laytime Definitions 2013, term 15)*

Statement of Facts	
Port ordinary working hours	From 0700 to 1900 (12 hrs)
Vessel arrived and anchored waiting for berth/ turn to load	0900, Monday
Notice of readiness was given	0900, Monday
Laytime begins (according to the notice time)	1400, Monday
Rain in port	From 1500 to 1700 hrs (2 hrs), Tuesday
Vessel shifted from roads to berth	1900 to 2100, Monday
Loading	Tuesday
Rain in port	From 0600 to 0800, Tuesday
Loading	Wednesday
Loading	Thursday

1st Case

Time allowed:
"3 Weather Working Days of 24 Consecutive Hours" or *"3 Working Days Weather Permitting"* (Laytime Definitions 2013, terms 16 and 18, respectively)

Time Sheet				
Day	Period	Time Used	Total Time Counted	Remarks
MON	0900–1400	–	–	At anchorage, notice time
	1400–1500	0d. 1h. 0m.	0d. 1h. 0m.	At anchorage, waiting for turn 1400 laytime begins
	1500–1700	0d. 0h. 0m.	–	Waiting for turn, rain stop ashore
	1700–1900	0d. 2h. 0m.	0d. 3h. 0m.	Waiting for turn

Time Sheet (contd.)				
Day	Period	Time Used	Total Time Counted	Remarks
	1900–2100	0d. 0h. 0m.	–	Shifting from roads to berth not to count according to charterparty clause
	2100–2400	0d. 3h. 0m.	0d. 6h. 0m.	Berthed
TUE	0000–0600	0d. 06h. 0m.	0d. 12h. 0m.	Berthed
	0600–0800	0d. 0h. 0m.	–	Rain stop
	0800–2400	0d. 16h. 0m.	1d. 4h. 0m.	Berthed, loading from 0800 to 1900
WED	0000–2400	1d. 0h. 0m.	2d. 4h. 0m.	Berthed, loading from 0700 to 1900
THU	0000–2000	0d. 20h. 0m.	3d. 0h. 0m.	Berthed, loading from 0700 to 1900
THU				Vessel on demurrage at 2000 hrs

2nd case

Time allowed:
"*3 Weather Working Days*" (Laytime Definitions 2013, term 15)

Time Sheet				
Day	Period	Time Used	Total Time Counted	Remarks
MON	0900–1400	–	–	At anchorage, notice time
MON	1400–1500			At anchorage, waiting for turn 1400 laytime begins
	1500–1700			Waiting for turn, rain stop ashore
	1700–1900	Note 1 0d. 4h. 48m.	0d. 4h. 48m.	Waiting for turn
	1900–2100			Shifting from roads to berth not to count according to charterparty clause
	2100–2400			Berthed
TUE	0000–0600	Note 2 0h. 22h. 0m.	1d. 2h. 48m.	Berthed
	0600–0800			Rain stop
	0800–2400			Berthed, loading from 0800 to 1900
WED	0000–2400	1d. 0h. 0m.	2d. 2h. 48m.	Berthed, loading from 0700 to 1900
THU	0000–2112	0d. 21h. 12m.	3d. 0h. 0m.	Berthed, loading from 0700 to 1900
THU				Vessel on demurrage at 2112 hrs

Note 1

MONDAY
Rain loss: 2h. (1500–1700)
Planned working: 5h. (1400–1900)
Loss ratio: 2/5
Loss: 2/5 × 8 = 3.2h.
Time used: 8h. – 3.2h. = 4.8h. = 0d. 4h. 48m.

Note that the eight hours in the loss ratio calculation is based on the assumption that time before arrival, the notice time and the shifting time shall not be included in the calculation of "loss". *"The time which would have or could have been worked but for the interruption"* is thus 1400–1900 plus 2100–2400 = 8 hours.

Note 2

TUESDAY
Rain: 2h. (0600–0800)
Rain loss: 1h. (0700–0800)
Planned working: 12h. (0700–1900)
Loss ratio: 1/12
Loss: 1/12 × 24 = 2h.
Time used: 22h.

Calculations/Explanations/Remarks
- According to Laytime Definitions, term 15, *"deductions for bad weather are calculated by reference to the length an interruption during a vessel's normal (or notional if waiting on turn) working hours bears to a period of 24 hours"*.
- According to a charterparty clause, shifting from anchorage to berth was not to count as laytime. So, the allowed time for loading on Monday was eight hours, from 1400 (begin of laytime) till 2400 excepting shifting time. From that time the weather stoppage proportion (according to the loss ratio) should be deducted, i.e. 3.2 hours. Thus, the time used as laytime on Monday was 4.8 hours or 4 h. 48m. According to the official commentary on Laytime Definitions, term 15 *"no deductions are made for rain occurring outside normal working hours"*. So, only one out of two hours of rain should be deducted from laytime and the calculation is proportional as per Note 2. Under Definition 16 or 18 the vessel is on demurrage on Thursday at 2000 hours, whilst under Definition 15 this happens on Thursday at 2112 hours.

GLOSSARY AND ABBREVIATIONS

Before signing a charterparty, negotiations usually take place quickly which often requires the use of specific terms and abbreviations. This section presents some of the most common terms and abbreviations that may be used during chartering negotiations and when drafting a charterparty. It must be emphasised that the use of the full terms is generally preferable to the abbreviated ones during the exchange of chartering messages, as long as in many cases there is no generally accepted meaning of the abbreviated terms, whilst acronyms can also be capable of more than one interpretation, leading to lack of clear communication and cultivating controversy. The aim of this section is not to define terms, interpret the law or set out a complete framework of chartering and shipbroking terminology, as a specialised dictionary or an advanced law book would do. Instead, the intention is to familiarise the reader with the most important wording as used and commonly interpreted in the daily chartering practice. In any case, all parties involved in chartering business should always be sure about the meaning of negotiated or contracted terms. The text below does not concern an exhaustive list of terms and the authors are not responsible for any errors or omissions in the interpretation.

- **AA or ASA: Always Afloat or Always Safely Afloat:** *(charterparty, port)* A charterparty term stipulating that the ship is to berth for loading or discharging without touching the bottom of the sea/river/lake etc. In some ports it is customary for ships to be driven ashore safely on the seabed in order to load or unload in low tide periods. By the term "always afloat" it is emphasised that the owner does not agree to put his ship in such a process. See also "sitting aground" or "safely aground" and "NAABSA".
- **AAAA: Always Accessible Always Afloat:** *(charterparty, port)* The ship should reach the berth of the port "always afloat". At the ship's call in a port, a berth should be available so the ship to start loading or unloading without delay.
- **ABS: American Bureau of Shipping:** *(general)* The American classification society.
- **ABT: About:** *(general)* A conditional term used in qualifying cargo, time, bunkers or speed. When discussing cargo, "about" usually covers

a margin of 5% more or less (e.g. *"about 50,000 mt"* means *"50,000 mt 5% more or less, at charterers' option"*). When referring to a period of time it may be usually interpreted as meaning 15 days more or less, although each case is considered on its own merit. Regarding speed, the tolerance is generally half knot.

- **ACCT: Account (for, of):** *(general)* On behalf of, responsible for, bill.
- **AD.VAL: Ad Valorem:** *(general)* Proportionately to the value of something (e.g. freight rate determined in accordance with the value of the cargo).
- **ADCOM: Address Commission:** *(charterparty, freight)* It is a commission on the freight or hire. It is due to the charterer by the shipowner and is deducted from the payable amount of freight or hire. It is a form of "rebate for the closing of business" granted by the owner to the charterer under a charter agreement. Unless agreed such a commission, the ship is *"free of address"*.
- **Advance Freight:** *(charterparty, freight, voyage charter)* In a voyage charter, unless it is otherwise agreed, it is an implied term that the freight for the cargo carriage is considered earned and payable at the place of destination, upon cargo delivery to the consignee. If the ship and/or cargo are/is lost before the ship reaches at her destination, the owner is not entitled to freight. Thus, in some cases it is explicitly agreed in the charterparty (express term) that a part or the whole of the freight is prepaid (payable in advance), to protect the right of the shipowner for freight earning even if the cargo is not delivered to the agreed destination. The freight prepaid or advance freight is not generally reimbursable to the charterer or shipper even if the cargo is lost.
- **AFMT: After Fixing Main Terms:** *(general)* After main terms of the charterparty have been fixed.
- **Aframax:** *(ship)* A tanker vessel typically ranging between 80,000–120,000 dwt.
- **AFSPS: Arrival First Sea Pilot Station:** *(charterparty, time charter)* Time charter term for the delivery of the ship to the charterer. The ship is deemed to have been delivered by the owner to the time charterer once it has reached the first pilot station at the delivery port.
- **AG: Arabian Gulf:** *(geography)* Synonym to "Persian Gulf" or "Middle East Gulf".
- **Agency Fee:** *(fees)* It is the remuneration of agents (normally ship or port agents) for their provision of various services to a ship during its port call. The amount of agency fees may vary depending on the size of vessel and the extent and nature of operations carried out, or it may be agreed on a lump sum basis.
- **AGW: All Going Well:** *(general)* If everything is in order and no unforeseen events or circumstances arise.
- **A/H: Antwerp to Hamburg:** *(geography)* European coastline from Antwerp to Hamburg.

526

- **Always Accessible:** *(laytime, voyage charter)* See appendix 3, "Laytime Definitions for Charter Parties 2013", term 4.
- **ANCH: Anchored:** *(ship, port)* The ship has been/is anchored.
- **AOH: After Office Hours:** *(general)* After the closing of standard working hours.
- **APS: Arrival Pilot Station:** *(charterparty, time charter)* Time charter term for the delivery of the ship to the charterer. The ship is deemed to have been delivered by the owner to the time charterer once it has reached the pilot station at the delivery port. Term disadvantageous for the charterers. See also "TIP" for comparison.
- **APT: Aft Peak Tank:** *(ship)* Fresh water or ballast water tank located in the stern (aft) of the vessel. It is considered important to the stability and seaworthiness of the ship.
- **ARA: Amsterdam – Rotterdam – Antwerp:** *(geography)* Selection of European ports of call.
- **AR or ARD: Arrived or ARVL: Arrival of the vessel** *(ship, port)* The ship has arrived at the port/berth.
- **ASAP: As Soon As Possible:** *(general)* Immediately, promptly.
- **ASBA: Association of Shipbrokers and Agents USA:** *(general)* Association representing shipbrokers and agents with offices located in the USA and Canada.
- **ATDNSHINC: Any Time Day or Night Sundays Holidays Included:** *(time charter)* Term usually relating to a time charter suggesting that the delivery or redelivery of the ship can be performed any time of day, including Sundays and public holidays.
- **ATSBENDS or ATSBE: All Time Saved Both Ends:** *(laytime, voyage charter)* Term related to despatch, synonymous with "DBEATS". The despatch amount is due at both ports (loading/unloading) for the total time saved from both operations. Therefore, the despatch amount is calculated for the whole time saved from the completion of loading and unloading up to expiry of total "laytime". The periods of laytime exceptions are included in the calculation (see comparison with "AWTSBENDS").
- **ATSDO: All Time Saved Discharging Only:** *(laytime, voyage charter)* Term related to despatch money. The despatch amount is due only at the discharging port for the total time saved in unloading operation. Therefore, the despatch amount is calculated for the whole time saved from the completion of unloading up to expiry of the "laytime", including laytime exceptions.
- **ATSLO: All Time Saved Loading Only:** *(laytime, voyage charter)* Term related to despatch money. The despatch amount is due only at the loading port for the total time saved in loading operation. Therefore, the despatch amount is calculated for the whole time saved from the completion of loading up to expiry of the "laytime", including laytime exceptions.

- **ATUTC: All Time Used To Count:** *(laytime, voyage charter)* Synonym to "unless used".
- **Austa: Australasia:** *(geography)* A region of Oceania, including Australia, New Zealand, the island of New Guinea and neighbouring islands in the Pacific Ocean.
- **Average Laytime:** *(laytime, voyage charter)* See appendix 3, "Laytime Definitions for Charter Parties 2013", term 23.
- **AWINL: Always Within International Navigating Limits:** *(ship, insurance, trading limits)* The ship should always be employed within the geographical limits imposed by the ship's insurance underwriters.
- **AWRI: Additional War Risk Insurance:** *(charterparty, ship, insurance)* It is an "extra" amount to be paid by the time charterer to the owner of a time chartered ship, if charterer wish to direct the ship in a port or area where military hostilities take place and the ship's insurers require an additional premium to cover the corresponding war risk. In a voyage charter it must be clearly agreed between the owner and the charterer who will be responsible to pay for this amount.
- **AWTSBENDS or AWTSBE or ALTSBENDS or ALTSBE: All Working Time Saved Both Ends or All Laytime Saved Both Ends:** *(laytime, voyage charter)* Term related to despatch, synonymous with "DBELTS". The despatch amount is due at both ports (loading/unloading) only for the working time of the laytime saved from both operations. Therefore, the despatch amount is calculated for the working time saved from the completion of loading and unloading up to expiry of total "laytime". The periods of laytime exceptions are excluded in the calculation (see comparison with "ATSBENDS").
- **AWTSDO or ALTSDO: All Working Time Saved Discharging Only or All Laytime Saved Discharging Only:** *(laytime, voyage charter)* Term related to despatch amount which is due only at the discharging port and only for the working time of the laytime saved in unloading. Therefore, the despatch amount is calculated for the working time saved from the completion of unloading up to expiry of "laytime". The periods of laytime exceptions are excluded from the calculation of despatch.
- **AWTSLO or ALTSLO: All Working Time Saved Loading Only or All Laytime Saved Loading Only:** *(laytime, voyage charter)* Term related to despatch amount which is due only at the loading port and only for the working time of the laytime saved in loading. Therefore, the despatch amount is calculated for the working time saved from the completion of loading up to expiry of "laytime". The periods of laytime exceptions are excluded from the calculation of despatch.
- **B4: Before:** *(general)* Previously than.
- **B4HAND: Beforehand:** *(general)* In advance.
- **B.A.: Buenos Aires:** *(geography)* Main port and capital of Argentina.
- **BAF: Bunker Adjustment Factor:** *(liner)* The liner freight is adjusted in accordance with fluctuations of the bunkers prices. Liner shipping

pricing schemes are normally including a floating part of the sea freight charge (BAF), which represents additions to the freight paid, arising from changes to oil prices.

- **Baltic:** *(geography)* It includes ports or places in the Baltic Sea.
- **Baltic Exchange:** *(general)* The most known shipping centre of the world, located in London.
- **BB: Ballast Bonus:** *(charterparty)* It is a lump sum amount paid to the owner as a "bonus" compensating him for the "ballast trip" (unladen journey) carried out by the ship from the last port of call or the last port of the previous charter to the port on which the new charter begins (e.g. the delivery port at a time charter). From a shipowner's point of view, the "ballast bonus" should represent at least the cost of bunkers and time spent to reach the ship at the port of the next charter. The "BB" practice is more prevalent in time charter, especially in periods of high rates.
- **BB: Below Bridges:** *(ship, port)* It is indicating that the vessel has to pass under bridges in a harbour to load or unload.
- **BB: Break Bulk:** *(cargo)* Cargo carried in the spaces of a ship in small quantities, packed in packages (parcels) or as individual items. It is generally considered as synonym to "general cargo". When the term is used as a verb (*"to break bulk"*), it means "to open the holds and start unloading".
- **BB: Bulbous Bow:** *(ship)* The front part of a vessel shaped in a bulbous form. It seeks to reduce the water resistance and increase the vessel's speed, in contrast to the V-shaped bow.
- **BBB: Before Breaking Bulk:** *(ship, freight)* It means "before start unloading". It is typically used to denote that voyage freight is payable after the ship's arrival at port of discharge, but prior to the start of unloading.
- **BBL: Barrel:** *(cargo, oil)* Unit of liquid cargo measurement, typically oil. A barrel equals to 34.97261 imperial gallons or 42 US gallons. Otherwise, 1 cubic metre of oil is equivalent to 6.29 barrels. If the specific weight of the oil is 0.8, a tonne of oil corresponds to about 7.9 barrels.
- **BC: Bulk Carrier:** *(ship)* A vessel carrying dry bulk cargo in its holds.
- **BCI: Baltic Capesize Index:** *(freight)* A "Baltic Exchange" index, measuring an indicative daily level of freight rates for "Capesize" bulk carriers (over 100,000 dwt).
- **BDI: Baltic Dry Index:** *(freight)* A "Baltic Exchange" index, measuring an indicative daily level of freight rates for all dry cargo vessels. It replaced "BFI" in 1999.
- **BDI: Both Days Included:** *(general)* Days mentioned are included (e.g. in a calculation or notice).
- **Berth:** *(laytime, voyage charter)* See appendix 3, "Laytime Definitions for Charter Parties 2013", term 2.
- **Berth terms:** *(charterparty, negotiation, voyage charter)* a. Synonym to "liner terms", but a wording rather outdated. The freight rate earned

by the shipowner includes the cost of sea transport, the cost of cargo handling in ports of loading and unloading and the stevedore expenses. The owner bears the responsibility, as well as the cost and the time of the sea voyage, loading, unloading and stowage of the cargo, or b. Voyage charterparty term, referring to the agreement about the speed of loading and unloading the ship, as well as the allocation of cargo-handling expenses. Such an agreement may be vague, stipulating for example that the ship should load or unload "*as fast as possible in accordance with the custom of the port*". Conversely, the term may be more specific, for example "*4000 t. gross / 2000 t. free*". Such a condition indicates that 4,000 tonnes of cargo should be loaded per day and the owner to pay for the cost of loading. Instead, 2,000 tonnes per day should be unloaded and the charterer to pay for the costs of discharge.

- **BFI: Baltic Freight Index:** *(freight)* It was one of the most important "Baltic Exchange" indices, expressing the daily level of freight rates for all dry cargo vessels from 1985 to 1999, when it was replaced by "BDI".
- **B/H: Bordeaux to Hamburg, inclusive:** *(geography)* European coastline from Bordeaux to Hamburg, including both of them.
- **BHF: Bulk Harmless Fertilisers:** *(cargo)* Dry cargo type.
- **BHSI, BHI, BHMI: Baltic Handysize Index, Baltic Handy Index, Baltic Handymax Index:** *(freight)* "Baltic Exchange" indices, measuring an indicative daily level of freight rates for "Handy" bulk carriers (20,000–50,000 dwt). The last two indices are not published anymore.
- **BIBI: Bye-bye:** *(general)* Informal way of closing a business message.
- **BIFFEX: Baltic International Freight Futures Exchange:** *(freight)* It was an exchange of future charter contracts (freight futures), which allowed shippers, shipowners and charterers to hedge their interests against unexpected and adverse changes in freight rates. Similarly, there was the "BIFFEX" index which was the measure of trading of these contracts. From April 2002 "Baltic Exchange" has ceased the trading of "BIFFEX" future contracts.
- **BIMCO: Baltic and International Maritime Council:** *(general)* International maritime organisation with multi-faceted contribution in shipping and chartering matters.
- **B/L: Bill of Lading:** *(international trade, shipping)* A document issued by a carrier which details a shipment of merchandise and gives title of that shipment to a specified party. Its role is crucial in the international trade.
- **BL: Bale Capacity:** *(ship, cargo stowage)* The cargo capacity of ship's holds, measured in cubic feet or cubic metres, excluding the "broken stowage", i.e. the empty spaces created in the holds due to the uneven shape of the general cargo or the shape of holds. "Bale capacity" is a key factor in calculating general cargo stowage. It is always smaller than the "grain capacity" of the ship (except in special cases, such as RO-RO, where the opposite may occur).

- **Bl Sea: Black Sea:** *(geography)* A sea located between Southeastern Europe and Western Asia.
- **Bona Fide:** *(general)* Legal term translated as "in good faith". It indicates that an action is taking place in good faith, with honesty and sincerity, without malice or bad intention.
- **Box:** *(cargo)* Container.
- **BPD or B/D: Barrels per Day:** *(cargo, oil)* See BBL above.
- **BPI: Baltic Panamax Index:** *(freight)* A "Baltic Exchange" index, measuring an indicative daily level of freight rates for "Panamax" bulk carriers (60,000–100,000 dwt).
- **BR: Brackish:** *(sea trading, port)* Mixture of salt and fresh water.
- **BRDTH: Breadth:** *(ship)* Ship's beam.
- **BRGDS: Best Regards:** *(general)* Greetings. Typical way of closing a business correspondence message.
- **Broken Stowage:** *(ship, cargo stowage)* The empty spaces that are inevitably generated in the holds of the ship while loading, due to the uneven shape of the parts of general cargo or the shape of the holds.
- **Brokerage or Commission:** *(charterparty, freight, hire)* It is the broker's remuneration for closing a "fixture" (charter). It is expressed as a percentage of the freight/hire earned by the owner. The term "brokerage" is preferable to the term "commission", as the latter is related more to "address commission", i.e. a commission paid back to the charterer or his brokers.
- **BSI: Baltic Supramax Index:** *(freight)* A "Baltic Exchange" index, measuring an indicative daily level of freight rates for "Supramax" bulk carriers (50,000–60,000 dwt).
- **BSS: Basis:** *(general)* The base, the foundation for an idea, an argument, a calculation or a process.
- **BST: Best:** *(general)* Most, optimal.
- **BV: Bureau Veritas:** *(general)* The French classification society.
- **BWAD: Brackish Water Arrival Draft:** *(sea trading, port, ship)* The maximum draft (or draught) of a ship on arrival at a port with "brackish water" (a mixture of sea water and fresh water). Such ports are commonly found in river estuaries. "Brackish water" has a density between that of "fresh water" (1,000 kgs/cubic metre) and "salt water" (1,025 kgs/cubic metre). The draught of the vessel to "brackish water" is higher than its draught to "salt water" (sea water) and less than its draught to "fresh water". See also "FWAD" and "SWAD".
- **C: Clean or Crane:** *(cargo, ship)* Depending on the context it may mean "clean" (e.g. clean products) or "crane" (e.g. ship's cranes).
- **C Am: Central America:** *(geography)* The southernmost, isthmian portion of the North American continent, which connects with South America on the southeast. It consists of seven countries: Belize, Costa Rica, El Salvador, Guatemala, Nicaragua, Honduras and Panama.
- **CAF: Currency Adjustment Factor:** *(liner)* The liner freight is adjusted in accordance with the currency exchange fluctuations. When

the liner cargo is payable in foreign currency and this currency is subject to major exchange rate fluctuations, the liner shipping company sometimes levies a currency surcharge (CAF) so as to compensate for those exchange rate risks. CAF is often charged on the basic sea freight as a percentage.

- **Calendar day:** *(laytime, voyage charter)* See appendix 3, "Laytime Definitions for Charter Parties 2013", term 9.
- **Capacity Plan:** *(ship)* It is the plan of the vessel, comprising the longitudinal and transverse profiles, diagrammes of ship's loadlines, as well as key particulars of the ship (e.g. GRT, NRT, DWT capacity, etc.).
- **Capesize:** *(ship)* A bulk carrier of over 100,000 dwt.
- **Car or Caribs: Caribbean Sea:** *(geography)* It includes ports located in the Caribbean Sea (Cayman Islands, Haiti, Jamaica, Puerto Rico, Barbados, etc.).
- **Cargo Capacity:** *(ship, cargo)* The quantity of cargo a ship can carry or else the space that a ship has available for cargo loading. There are two ways of measuring the cargo capacity of a ship, the first measuring the weight in deadweight tonnes (deadweight capacity), the second measuring the volume, so the calculation is made either in cubic feet or cubic metres (cubic capacity). Measurement in deadweight may be either "Deadweight All Told (DWAT)" which includes the ship's total deadweight in cargo, supplies, fuel, water, ballast, etc., or "Deadweight Cargo Capacity (DWCC)" which includes only the cargo deadweight. The measurement of the capacity by volume is respectively performed in two ways depending on the nature of the cargo. The "grain capacity" is used to measure the bulk tonnage and describes the available space of the ship's holds for loading, including the "broken stowage". Instead, the "bale capacity" is used to measure the capacity of the vessel for transportation of general cargo and does not include the "broken stowage". The "bale capacity" is therefore always less than "grain capacity".
- **Cargo Plan or Stowage Plan:** *(ship, cargo)* Ship's plan of cargo stowage.
- **C.B. & H.: Continent between Bordeaux and Hamburg:** *(geography)* It includes ports or places in the European continent from Bordeaux in south to Hamburg in north.
- **CBL: Cable:** *(general)* Telex.
- **CBT: Clean Ballast Tanks:** *(ship)* Specific cargo tanks dedicated to carry ballast water only.
- **CD or CQD: Customary Despatch or Customary Quick Despatch:** *(laytime, voyage charter, ship, cargo)* The charterer is obliged to load and/or unload the ship as fast as it is used and as fast as possible under the conditions prevailing at the time of loading or unloading at the port. It is an unclear term and usually aggravating for the shipowner.
- **CFR or C & F: Cost and Freight:** *(sale of goods)* Incoterms® 2010 rule, used only in sea transport. The seller delivers the goods on board

the vessel or procures the goods already so delivered. The risk of loss of or damage to the goods passes when the goods are on board the vessel. The seller must contract for and pay the costs and freight necessary to bring the goods to the named port of destination.

- **CFS: Container Freight Station:** *(ship, cargo)* Base of containers in a part of a port terminal. It is a place for the administration of containers, including spaces where goods are to be stored and stacked to be loaded in the "containers". It is usually under the management of freight forwarders (intermediaries) or container carriers.

- **C.H. & H.: Continent between Havre and Hamburg:** *(geography)* European coastline from Havre in south to Hamburg in north.

- **CHABE: Charterers Agents Both Ends:** *(general, voyage charter)* Charterers determine the agents in both ports (loading/unloading). Opposite: "OABE".

- **CHOP: Charterers' Option:** *(general)* By charterers' decision.

- **CIF: Cost Insurance Freight:** *(sale of goods)* Incoterms® 2010 rule, used only in sea transport. The seller delivers the goods on board the vessel or procures the goods already so delivered. The risk of loss of or damage to the goods passes when the goods are on board the vessel. The seller must contract for and pay the costs and freight necessary to bring the goods to the named port of destination. The seller also contracts for insurance cover against the buyer's risk of loss of or damage to the goods during the carriage. The buyer should note that under CIF the seller is required to obtain insurance only on minimum cover. Should the buyer wish to have more insurance protection, it will need either to agree as much expressly with the seller or to make its own extra insurance arrangements.

- **CIP: Carriage and Insurance Paid To:** *(sale of goods)* Incoterms® 2010 rule, used in all modes of transport. The seller delivers the goods to the carrier or another person nominated by the seller at an agreed place (if any such place is agreed between parties) and the seller must contract for and pay the costs of carriage necessary to bring the goods to the named place of destination. The seller also contracts for insurance cover against the buyer's risk of loss of or damage to the goods during the carriage. The buyer should note that under CIP the seller is required to obtain insurance only on minimum cover. Should the buyer wish to have more insurance protection, it will need either to agree as much expressly with the seller or to make its own extra insurance arrangements.

- **CLD: Cleared:** *(ship)* The ship has received certificate of pratique at port of loading or unloading. Clearance is commonly referred to as "free pratique".

- **Clear Day or Clear Days:** *(laytime, voyage charter)* They are net, continuous, calendar days that determine a period of time, e.g. a notice time. The word "clear" states that the first and last day of the notice period shall not be included in the calculation. In other words, if one party gives a notice, the other party has at its disposal a number of "clean" days to fulfil some obligation. For example, if the charterer is given "*7 clear days' notice of expected date of readiness at port of loading*" so as to prepare the cargo delivery, the date of sending the notice and the date of delivery of the cargo would not count on calculating seven clear days.

- **CMI: Comité Maritime International:** *(general)* Non-governmental, not-for-profit international organisation established in Antwerp in 1897, the object of which is to contribute by all appropriate means and activities to the unification of maritime law in all its aspects. It issues important publications related to shipping and chartering, e.g. it is one of the sponsoring organisations of "Laytime Definitions for Charter Parties 2013".
- **CNR: Charterer Not Reported:** *(general)* The name of the charterer has not been reported.
- **C/O: care of:** *(general)* Under care/responsibility of . . . It is used in business letters to denote that a letter or message is addressed to the person responsible for handling an issue.
- **COA: Contract of Affreigtment:** *(general)* Hybrid type of vessel's charter, combining elements of spot and time charter.
- **COB: Closing of Business:** *(general)* Fixing business or the end of working hours of a day.
- **COGSA: Carriage of Goods by Sea Act:** *(general)* National legislation aiming at the adoption and enforcement of international regulations for the transport of goods by sea under a bill of lading. For example, the "Carriage of Goods by Sea Act 1936" is the US enactment of the International Convention Regarding Bills of Lading, commonly known as the "Hague Rules". The "Carriage of Goods by Sea Act 1971" is UK legislation incorporating the "Hague-Visby Rules" into English Law. The "Carriage of Goods By Sea Act 1992" is a UK statute that repeals and replaces the "Bills of Lading Act 1855", making various provisions for the bills of lading and other documents of carriage.
- **COMPL: Completing:** *(general)* Finishing.
- **CONBULK: Container/Bulk:** *(ship, cargo)* A ship's capacity to carry both containers and dry bulk cargoes.
- **CONS: Consumption:** *(ship)* Ship's fuel consumption.
- **CONT: Container:** *(cargo)* A large metal box of a standard design and size used for the transport of goods by road, rail, sea, or air. The most important type of unitised cargo.
- **Continent:** *(geography)* It includes ports or places in the European continent from Bordeaux in south to Hamburg in north, including both of them and Rouen.
- **Conventional day:** *(laytime, voyage charter)* See appendix 3, "Laytime Definitions for Charter Parties 2013", term 10.
- **COP: Custom of the Port:** *(charterparty, voyage charter, cargo, port)* The cargo to be loaded or unloaded according to the custom of the port.

Therefore, no specific loading rate is stipulated in the voyage charter-party and the owner might require a higher freight rate to get covered against potential delays of the ship.

- **COW: Crude Oil Washing:** *(cargo, ship, tanker)* Technique of cleaning the cargo tanks of tankers. Cleaning is carried out by washing the walls of the tanks with the oil cargo itself during unloading.
- **C/P: Charterparty:** *(chartering, shipbroking)* It is the contract between the owner of a vessel and the charterer for the use of a vessel. The charterer takes over the vessel for either a certain amount of time (a period charter) or for a certain voyage (a voyage charter). The word "charterparty" comes from the Latin expression "charta partita" or "carta partita", meaning a legal paper or instrument, divided, i.e. written in duplicate so that each party retains half. It is the most crucial document in respect of chartering and shipbroking matters.
- **C.P.D.: Charterers Pay Dues:** *(charterparty, negotiation, voyage charter)* Charterparty term which specifies that charterers will pay for all dues charged for the ship. Opposite term: "V.P.D.".
- **CPP: Clean Petroleum Products:** *(cargo, oil)* Liquid products refined from crude oil, whose colour is less than or equal to 2.5 on the US National Petroleum Association scale. Clean products include naphtha, jet fuel, gasoline and diesel/gasoil.
- **CPT: Carriage Paid To:** *(sale of goods)* Incoterms® 2010 rule, similar to "CFR" but used in all modes of transport. The seller delivers the goods to the carrier or another person nominated by the seller at an agreed place (if any such place is agreed between parties) and the seller must contract for and pay the costs of carriage necessary to bring the goods to the named place of destination).
- **CR: Crane:** *(cargo, ship)* A tall metal structure with a long horizontal part, used for lifting and moving cargoes and heavy objects.
- **CSRS: Col/Snake: Columbia/Snake River system:** *(geography)* A container barging system facilitating the Pacific Northwest trade of USA with Asia and the rest of the world. Hub of the system is Oregon's port of Portland. Col/Snake system is a vital transportation link as long as it connects ports located in Columbia and Snake rivers with the Pacific Ocean. It forms a major commercial waterway of the Northwest coast, mostly in the trades of wheat, soybeans, wood, mineral bulks and automobiles.
- **CST: Centistokes:** *(cargo, oil)* Measurement unit of the viscosity of ship's bunkers. Viscosity depends on the density and clarity of bunkers.
- **CU.FT.: Cubic Foot:** *(cargo)* It is an imperial and US customary (non-metric) unit of volume, used in the US and the UK. It is defined as the volume of a cube with sides of 1 foot (0.3048 m.) in length. Its volume is 28.3168 litres or about 1/35 of a cubic metre. It is a measure of cargo volume. Gas cargoes are commonly expressed per cubic metres or cubic feet.

- **CU.M. or CBM: Cubic Metre:** *(cargo)* A volume that is made by a cube that is 1 metre on each side. Its symbol is m³. It is equal to 1,000 litres. It is a measure of cargo volume. Gas cargoes are commonly expressed per cubic metres or cubic feet.
- **CVS or C/Vs or Consecs: Consecutive Voyages:** *(charterparty)* It refers to the performance of consecutive voyages from a port A to a port B. The return from B to A is usually made in ballast.
- **CY: Container Yard:** *(charterparty)* Containers' base, located in a "container terminal". It is typically under control and management of a liner operator.
- **D: Dirty or Derrick:** *(cargo, ship)* Depending on the context it may mean "dirty" (e.g. dirty products) or "derrick" (e.g. ship's derricks = lifting gear).
- **DAF: Delivered At Frontier:** *(sale of goods)* Incoterms® 2000 rule eliminated from the version of Incoterms® 2010 rule.
- **DANRVAOCLONL: Discountless And Not Returnable, Vessel And/ Or Cargo Lost Or Not Lost:** *(charterparty, voyage charter)* Charterparty term used in cases of "freight prepaid" or "advance freight". It indicates that the agreed freight prepaid will not be reduced or refunded under any circumstances, even if the ship or cargo is lost. This applies as long as the owner is consistent with its contractual obligations.
- **DAP: Days All Purposes:** *(laytime, voyage charter)* Synonym to "reversible laytime".
- **DAP: Delivered At Place:** *(sale of goods)* Incoterms® 2010 rule which together with "DAT" replaced the Incoterms® 2000 rule "DAF", "DES", "DEQ" and "DDU". It is used in all modes of transport. The seller delivers when the goods are placed at the disposal of the buyer on the arriving means of transport ready for unloading at the named place of destination. The seller bears all risks involved in bringing the goods to the named place.
- **DAT: Delivered At Terminal:** *(sale of goods)* Incoterms® 2010 rule which together with "DAP" replaced the Incoterms® 2000 rule "DAF", "DES", "DEQ" and "DDU". It is used in all modes of transport. The seller delivers when the goods, once unloaded from the arriving means of transport, are placed at the disposal of the buyer at a named terminal at the named port or place of destination. "Terminal" includes a place, whether covered or not, such as a quay, warehouse, container yard or road, rail or air cargo terminal. The seller bears all risks involved in bringing the goods to and unloading them at the terminal at the named port or place of destination.
- **Day:** *(laytime, voyage charter)* See appendix 3, "Laytime Definitions for Charter Parties 2013", term 8.
- **DBEATS: Despatch payable at Both Ends on All Time Saved:** *(laytime, voyage charter)* Synonym to "ATSBENDS".
- **DBELTS: Despatch payable at Both Ends on Laytime Saved:** *(laytime, voyage charter)* Synonym to "AWTSBENDS".

- **DDO: Despatch Discharge Only:** *(laytime, voyage charter)* It is agreed that despatch amount is to be paid only at the discharging port, if indeed unloading is finished earlier than the allowed time (laytime).
- **DDP: Delivered Duty Paid:** *(sale of goods)* Incoterms® 2010 rule used in all modes of transport. Seller is responsible for delivering the goods to the named place in the country of the buyer, and pays all costs in bringing the goods to the destination including import duties and taxes. The seller is not responsible for unloading. This term is often used in place of the non-Incoterms® rule "Free In Store (FIS)". This term places the maximum obligations on the seller and minimum obligations on the buyer. All the risks and responsibilities are not transferred to the buyer upon delivery of the goods at the named place of destination.
- **DDU: Delivered Duty Unpaid:** *(sale of goods)* Incoterms® 2000 rule eliminated from the version of 2010.
- **Deadfreight:** *(charterparty, voyage charter)* The so-called "dead-freight" is payable by the charterers to the shipowners for the part of the cargo which, while it had been agreed in the charterparty to be loaded and transported to the destination, it was not actually loaded on the ship due to a cause attributed to the charterers or shippers. However, the "deadfreight" is not only a compensation paid to the owner if the shipper loads a smaller amount than the agreed in the charterparty, but also in case that the nature of the loaded cargo prevents the use of the full carrying capacity of the vessel. The second case is related to the term "broken stowage".
- **DELY and REDELY: Delivery and Redelivery:** *(charterparty, time charter)* Vessel's delivery and redelivery at a time charter.
- **Demurrage:** *(laytime, voyage charter)* See appendix 3, "Laytime Definitions for Charter Parties 2013", term 30.
- **DEQ: Delivered Ex Quay:** *(sale of goods)* Incoterms® 2000 rule eliminated from the version of 2010.
- **DER: Derricks:** *(cargo, ship)* A cargo ship can have its own handling equipment (gearing). Ship's cranes are called "derricks".
- **DES: Delivered Ex Ship:** *(sale of goods)* Incoterms® 2000 rule eliminated from the version of 2010.
- **Despatch or Dispatch or Despatch Money:** *(laytime, voyage charter)* See appendix 3, "Laytime Definitions for Charter Parties 2013", term 31.
- **Despatch on All Time Saved (ATS):** *(laytime, voyage charter)* See appendix 3, "Laytime Definitions for Charter Parties 2013", term 33.
- **Despatch on All Working Time Saved (WTS) or on All Laytime Saved:** *(laytime, voyage charter)* See appendix 3, "Laytime Definitions for Charter Parties 2013", term 32.
- **DFD: Demurrage/Free Despatch:** *(laytime, voyage charter)* The owner is entitled to "demurrage" (if it arises), but the charterer does not have the right to receive "despatch" (if it arises).

- **DHD: Demurrage/Half Despatch:** *(laytime, voyage charter)* The daily rate of "despatch" will be half of the agreed daily rate of "demurrage".
- **Disbursements:** *(port, ship)* Term describing all payments made in ports by the ship agents on behalf of the shipowners. Such payments usually concern port charges, stevedore expenses, towing costs, custom expenses, supplies and spares, fuel costs, water supplies, etc. The agents charge commission on the "disbursements", which typically is set at 2.5% of total expenses paid by the agent.
- **Disponent Owner:** *(bareboat)* The charterer at a bareboat charter may be called "disponent owner", because on the one hand the ship comes at his disposal and secondly because he acquires operational control and commercial management of the vessel as if he was the shipowner.
- **DISPORT: Discharging Port:** *(port, voyage charter)* The unloading port in a voyage charter
- **Distance Freight:** *(voyage charter)* In a voyage charter, if the cargo needs to be discharged at a port other than the port of destination indicated in the charterparty and the extra distance brings about additional risk or cost, then the owner may require extra freight called "distance freight".
- **Ditto:** *(general)* It is used to indicate that an item is repeated, often expressed with the ditto mark (″) under the word or figure to be repeated.
- **DLO: Despatch Loading Only:** *(laytime, voyage charter)* It is agreed that despatch amount is to be paid only at the loading port, if indeed loading is finished earlier than the allowed time (laytime).
- **DLOSP: Dropping Last Outward Sea Pilot:** *(charterparty, time charter)* Term similar to "DOP". Here it is stressed that the place of redelivery of the ship in a time charter shall be the point of disembarkation of the last pilot.
- **DNV: Det Norske Veritas:** *(general)* Norwegian classification society.
- **DOP: Dropping Outward Pilot:** *(charterparty, time charter)* Time charter term for the redelivery of the ship to the shipowner. It refers to a location, usually outside the port limits, where it is customary to disembark the pilot. At this geographical point of the port and consequently at this point of time the ship is considered as redelivered from the charterer to the owner.
- **DPP: Dirty Petroleum Products:** *(cargo, oil)* Liquid products refined from crude oil, whose colour is greater than 2.5 on the US National Petroleum Association scale. Dirty products usually require heating during a voyage, because their viscosity or waxiness makes discharge difficult at ambient temperatures.
- **Draught or Draft:** *(ship)* The distance from the sea surface to the lowest sunken point of the ship.
- **DRI/DRIP: Direct Reduced Iron Ore/Direct Reduced Iron Ore Pellets:** *(cargo)* Type of iron ore cargo.
- **DTD: Dated:** *(general)* Marked with a date or old (outdated).

- **Dunnage:** *(cargo)* The fixation/stabilisation of general cargo parts (cartons, packages, boxes, etc.) into the holds of the ship, by using wooden sections or other items in order to avoid cargo movement and protect the floor of the ship's hull.
- **DWAT: Dead Weight All Told:** *(ship, cargo)* The total deadweight of the ship. It is the total weight that a ship can carry when sinking up to its loadline (Plimsoll Line). "DWAT" includes cargo, food, fuel, water, supplies, crew, spare parts, luggage, ballast etc. Alternatively, it is defined as the difference between the loaded displacement and the light displacement (LDT) of the ship.
- **DWCC: Dead Weight Cargo Capacity:** *(ship, cargo)* The deadweight of the vessel concerning only the cargo it can carry. The quantities of fuel, water, supplies, etc. are not included. Synonym: "net capacity".
- **DWCT: Dead Weight Cargo Tonnage:** *(ship, cargo)* Synonym to "DWCC".
- **DWT: Dead Weight Tonnes or Tonnage:** *(ship, cargo)* Major measurement of ship's carrying capacity in weight terms.
- **E Af: East Africa:** *(geography)* The eastern region of the African continent, variably defined by geography or geopolitics.
- **East Coast Africa:** *(geography)* It includes the region of the East Coast of Africa from Cape Guardafui in the north to Maputo in the south.
- **East Coast India:** *(geography)* It includes the East Coast of India from Calcutta to Cape Comorin. It excludes Sri Lanka.
- **East Med.: East Mediterranean:** *(geography)* It includes ports located in the East Mediterranean Sea. To the west, the notional line is from Cape Passero in Sicily to Misurata in Libya, while in the east the boundary is the Dardanelles. The Adriatic Sea and the Aegean Sea are thus included.
- **EC: East Coast:** *(geography)* General geographical description.
- **ECCA: East Coast Central America:** *(geography)* It includes ports in the countries Belize, Guatemala, Honduras, Nicaragua, Costa Rica, Panama, which are located at the eastern coast of Central America, bordering the Caribbean Sea. Panama Canal is included.
- **ECCAN: East Coast Canada:** *(geography)* Ports or places in the East Coast of Canada.
- **ECCP: East Coast Coal Port:** *(geography)* Term denoting that the loading of coal will take place in one of the ports of eastern England.
- **ECI: East Coast of Ireland:** *(geography)* Ports or places in this area.
- **ECNA: East Coast North America:** *(geography)* US and Canada land that runs along the Atlantic Ocean.
- **ECSA: East Coast South America:** *(geography)* It includes ports or places at the East Coast of South America, from Georgetown in the north to Punta Dungeness in the south.
- **ECUK: East Coast United Kingdom:** *(geography)* Ports or places of England and Scotland in the eastern coast of UK.

- **ECUS: East Coast United States of America:** *(geography)* It describes ports or places in this area.
- **EIU: Even If Used:** *(laytime, voyage charter)* The time spent on loading and unloading of the ship in excepted periods (e.g. Sundays or public holidays) shall not count as laytime, even if used.
- **E&OE: Errors and Omissions Excepted:** *(general)* Excluding misstatement. Term used in bills and invoices to indicate that the person or company that prepares the account is ready to correct errors and/or omissions that may occur in this.
- **ETA: Expected or Estimated Time of Arrival:** *(ship)* It concerns the time that the ship is estimated to arrive at a port/berth.
- **ETB: Expected or Estimated Time of Berthing:** *(ship)* It concerns the time that the ship is estimated to berth.
- **ETC: Expected or Estimated Time of Commencement/Completion:** *(ship)* It concerns the time that the ship is estimated to commence or complete loading or unloading
- **ETD: Expected or Estimated Time of Departure:** *(ship)* It concerns the time that the ship is estimated to depart from a port/berth.
- **ETS: Expected or Estimated Time of Sailing:** *(ship)* It concerns the time that the ship is estimated to sail from a port.
- **Eur: Europe:** *(geography)* The continent which comprises the westernmost part of Eurasia. It is bordered by the Arctic Ocean to the north, the Atlantic Ocean to the west and the Mediterranean Sea to the south. To the east and southeast, it is separated from Asia by Ural and Caucasus mountains, the Ural river, the Caspian and the Black Sea and the Bosphorus straits.
- **Euromed: Mediterranean Europe:** *(geography)* European countries bordering the Mediterranean Sea.
- **Excepted or Excluded:** *(laytime, voyage charter)* See appendix 3, "Laytime Definitions for Charter Parties 2013", term 19.
- **EXW: Ex Works:** *(sale of goods)* Incoterms® 2010 rule used in all modes of transport. The seller makes the goods available at his premises. This term places the maximum obligation on the buyer and minimum obligations on the seller. It is often used when making an initial quotation for the sale of goods without any costs included. EXW means that a buyer incurs the risks for bringing the goods to their final destination. Either the seller does not load the goods on collecting vehicles and does not clear them for export, or if the seller does load the goods, he does so at buyer's risk and cost.
- **FA or FAS or FAQ: Free Alongside or Free Alongside Ship or Free Alongside Quay:** *(sale of goods)* Incoterms® 2010 rule rule used in sea transport. "Free Alongside Ship" means that the seller delivers when the goods are placed alongside the vessel (e.g. on a quay or a barge) nominated by the buyer at the named port of shipment. The risk of loss of or damage to the goods passes when the goods are alongside the ship, and the buyer bears all costs from that moment onwards.

- **FAC: Fast As Can or As Fast As the Vessel Can Receive/Deliver:** *(laytime, voyage charter, ship, cargo)* Laytime will be calculated in accordance with the maximum loading rate that can be achieved by the ship. In other words, it is the duty of the charterer to load or unload the ship at the maximum speed without undue delays.
- **FC: Fully Containerised:** *(cargo)* It refers to cargo carried only in containers or a trade carried out only by pure (fully cellular) containerships.
- **FCA: Free Carrier:** *(sale of goods)* Incoterms® 2010 rule used in all modes of transport. The seller delivers the goods to the carrier or another person nominated by the buyer at the seller's premises or another named place. The parties are well advised to specify as clearly as possible the point within the named place of delivery, as the risk passes to the buyer at that point.
- **FCC: Fully Cellular Containership:** *(ship)* A ship with cell guides (specific positions) for the placement of containers in the holds. It is a vessel which carries exclusively containers.
- **FCL: Full Container Load:** *(cargo, liner)* This expression describes the cargo shipment by a shipper, which occupies the entire space of a container. It is an opposite term to "LCL" which concerns different cargo shipments from different shippers, which are transported to a common destination within the same "container". The freight for an "FCL" cargo is generally lower than the freight for an "LCL" cargo.
- **FD: Free of Despatch:** *(laytime, voyage charter)* No despatch amount is to be paid even if cargo-handling operations are finished earlier than the allowed time (laytime).
- **FE: Far East:** *(geography)* It includes all the Far East ports which are on the coast, from Burma to southwest to Vostochny in the northeast. Also included are all maritime areas of Singapore, Japan, Philippines, Taiwan, Malaysia, Brunei, Indonesia and Papua New Guinea.
- **FEU: Forty-foot Equivalent Unit:** *(cargo, liner)* The 40-foot container or its equivalent.
- **FFA: Forward Freight Agreement:** *(freight, derivatives)* A forward contract of charter. It is a typical financial product of the shipping derivatives market. It allows shipowners, charterers and speculators to hedge or speculate against the volatility of freight rates. The underlying object may be a freight index or the freight of a single shipping route or the average freight/hire of a basket of routes/charters. FFAs are traded "over the counter" on a principal-to-principal basis and can be cleared through a clearing house.
- **FHEX: Fridays Holidays Excluded:** *(laytime, voyage charter)* Fridays and holidays do not count as laytime.
- **FHINC: Fridays Holidays Included:** Fridays and holidays are included in the laytime.
- **FI: Free In:** *(charterparty, negotiation, voyage charter)* Voyage charter term. All cargo loading expenses are borne by the charterer (or shipper). The owner shall not bear the cost of cargo loading.

- **FILO: Free In Liner Out:** *(charterparty, negotiation, voyage charter)* Voyage charter term. Cargo loading expenses are borne by the charterer (or shipper), whilst the owner shall bear the cost of cargo discharging.
- **FILTD: Free In / Liner Terms Discharge:** *(charterparty, negotiation, voyage charter)* Voyage charter term, synonym to "FILO".
- **FIO: Free In and Out:** *(charterparty, negotiation, voyage charter)* Voyage charter term. All costs of cargo handling (loading and unloading) are carried by the charterer and/or the shipper and/or the recipient respectively. The ship and the owner are not obliged to pay such costs.
- **FIOS: Free In, Out and Stowed:** *(charterparty, negotiation, voyage charter)* Voyage charter term. All costs of cargo loading, unloading and stowage are not carried by the owner. Term used mostly in general cargoes.
- **FIOSPT: Free, In, Out and Spout-Trimmed:** *(charterparty, negotiation, voyage charter)* Voyage charter term. The term is typically used in the transport of dry bulk cargoes (e.g. bulk grain) which are handled through special pumps. It indicates that the costs of cargo handling (loading/unloading) and arrangement of cargo in holds through these pumps will not be charged to the owner.
- **FIOST: Free, In, Out, Stowed and Trimmed:** *(charterparty, negotiation, voyage charter)* Voyage charter term. Some cargoes, usually in dry bulk form, need stowage and arrangement (trimming) through the holds. Under this term it is agreed that the costs of loading, unloading, stowage and trimming of the cargo will not be borne by the shipowner. For certain other goods, different in nature, similar terms can be used, for example in car transport the term may be formulated as *"free in, out, lashed, secured and unlashed"* which refers to the risk and expense of the secure fastening of the cargo on board.
- **FIOT: Free, In, Out and Trimmed:** *(charterparty, negotiation, voyage charter)* Voyage charter term. All costs of cargo loading, unloading and trimming are not carried by the owner. Term used mostly in dry bulk cargoes.
- **Firm for Reply or Firm for Immediate Reply:** *(general)* Terminology used mainly by shipbrokers of the negotiating parties in the beginning of a charter negotiation. It is commonly used to present an offer (for cargo or vessel) and examine the possibility of closing a chartering business.
- **Firm Offer:** *(general)* Commonly used by the owner's shipbroker during a charter negotiation to indicate that the owner is committed to provide his vessel for a future charter business. If the charterer is interested for the vessel, he may make a "counter-offer", thus commencing the charterparty negotiations.
- **Firm Order:** *(general)* Phrase used by charterers to denote the existence of a cargo to be transported and their interest to charter a ship, either for a voyage charter or a time charter.

- **Fixture:** *(general)* The "closing" or "fixing" of a chartering business. It means that the charter negotiations between the involved parties (shipowner – charterer) have been completed and the agreement has come.

- **Flat Rate:** *(freight, tanker)* It is a fixed freight rate agreed to be paid by the charterer or the shipper to the carrier regardless of fluctuations that may occur in the freight market during a charter. It appears mainly in cases where the shipment includes various types of cargo, the nature of which is not known at the closing of the charter or in cases where there are many loading and discharging ports in the charter. Generally, an advantage for the consignee is that the final price of the product can easily be estimated. Also, the term "flat rate" describes the reference freight rates of the "Worldscale", namely the basis for calculating and negotiating spot freight rates in the tanker market.

- **FO: Free Out:** *(charterparty, negotiation, voyage charter)* Voyage charter term. The cargo discharging costs are not included in the freight rate (i.e. not borne by the owner), but are payable separately by the charterer or the shipper or the holder of the bill of lading (receiver or recipient or consignee) depending on the agreement.

- **FOB: Free On Board:** *(sale of goods)* Incoterms® 2010 rule used in sea transport. The seller delivers the goods on board the vessel nominated by the buyer at the named port of shipment or procures the goods already so delivered. The risk of loss of or damage to the goods passes when the goods are on board the vessel, and the buyer bears all costs from that moment onwards.

- **FOLL: Following, Follows:** *(general)* Consequent, next.

- **FONASBA: Federation of National Associations of Shipbrokers and Agents:** *(general)* Organisation founded in 1969 consisting of national associations of shipbrokers and agents. The organisation's work focuses on agency and shipbroking matters.

- **FOQ or FOW: Free On Quay or Free On Wharf:** Similar to "Free Alongside Ship" (FAS).

- **Force Majeure:** *(general)* Unforeseen situations and events beyond the reasonable control of the involved parties in a contract.

- **FOW: First Open Water:** *(port)* If works at a port have stopped due to ice, this term indicates that the earliest possible resumption of the ship's procedures should be achieved, once the port is "reopened" from the ice.

- **FP: Free of Pratique:** *(ship, port)* The ship has been tested successfully by the health authorities of the port and received authorisation to proceed in cargo operations.

- **FPA: Free of Particular Average:** *(general)* The ship is not insured against a partial loss.

- **FPSO: Floating Production Storage Offloading:** *(ship)* Type of an offshore vessel.

- **FPT: Fore Peak Tank:** *(ship)* Fresh water or ballast water tank located in the forward (fore) of the vessel. It is considered important to the stability and seaworthiness of the ship and for arranging the cargo on board.

- **FRT: Freight:** *(freight, voyage charter)* The amount paid by the charterer to the shipowner as compensation for the cargo carriage in a voyage charter. It is typically payable before the cargo is unloaded in the discharging port.

- **FRT P.P.: Freight Prepaid:** *(freight, voyage charter)* The freight is payable in advance, before it is loaded on board.

- **Fumigation:** *(ship, port)* The act of disinfecting the cabins and compartments of a ship. Essential precaution taken by owners to protect their vessels and ensure the health of persons living on board.

- **FWA: Fresh Water Allowance:** *(sea trading, port, ship)* The induced change in the vessel's draught when it is moved from sea water having a higher density (1,025 kg/cbm) to the fresh water which has a lower density (1,000 kg/cbm). In other words, it is the additional draught permitted for the ship under international loading rules, when the ship is loading in fresh water conditions.

- **FWAD: Fresh Water Arrival Draught:** *(sea trading, port, ship)* The maximum draught of a ship on arrival at a port with "fresh water". See also "BWAD" and "SWAD".

- **G/A: General Average:** *(general)* An internationally accepted rule of the sea. When a ship is in danger of total loss, the master has the right to sacrifice property and/or incur reasonable expenditure to prevent the total loss.

- **GD: Good:** *(general)* Of high quality, of high standard, satisfactory, in order etc.

- **GIB: Gibraltar:** *(geography)* A British overseas territory on the southern end of the Iberian peninsula at the entrance of the Mediterranean Sea.

- **GL: Germanischer Lloyd:** *(general)* The German classification society.

- **GL: Great Lakes:** *(geography)* A series of five interconnected freshwater lakes located in northeastern North America, on the Canada – USA border. They are connected to the Atlantic Ocean through the Saint Lawrence River, forming the largest group of freshwater lakes on Earth. Due to their sea-like characteristics (waves, winds, currents, great depths, distant horizons) they are also referred to as "inland seas". The Saint Lawrence Seaway and Great Lakes Waterway make the Great Lakes accessible to ocean-going vessels, but shifts to wider ocean-going containerships have limited container shipping on the lakes. Most Great Lakes trade is of bulk material. Large sections of the Great Lakes freeze over in winter, interrupting most shipping from January to March. The Great Lakes Waterway connects all the lakes; the smaller Saint Lawrence Seaway connects the lakes to the Atlantic Ocean.

- **GLESS: Gearless:** *(ship)* Term referring to a ship which does not have its own cargo-handling equipment. Opposite: geared.
- **GMT: Greenwich Mean Time:** *(general)* The time of the meridian of Greenwich (UK).
- **GR: Grain Capacity or Grain Space Capacity:** *(ship, cargo)* The cargo capacity of the ship's holds, measured in cubic feet or cubic metres. This measurement takes into account the "broken stowage" of the holds, i.e. it includes empty spaces in the holds created from the uneven shape of the cargo or the shape of the holds. Grain capacity is a key factor for the calculation of a bulk cargo which a ship can load, when the stowage factor of this cargo is known.
- **GRD: Geared:** *(ship)* Term referring to a ship which has its own cargo-handling equipment. Opposite: gearless.
- **Gross terms:** *(charterparty, negotiation, voyage charter)* Voyage charter term. In this case the owner is responsible for all costs resulting from the commencement of cargo loading until the end of discharging. Owner must arrange and pay for the execution of cargo loading, unloading, tallying (counting, measuring), stowage, stacking and other voyage costs. Thus, under "gross terms" the freight rate earned by the owner will include all the above. Opposed terms are "fio", "fiot", "fiost" etc. However, either in "gross terms" or in "fio terms", port expenses are always payable by the ship (owner) in a voyage charter.
- **GRT: Gross Registered Tonnage:** *(ship, cargo)* The gross tonnage of the vessel expressed in gross registered tons. GRT equals to 100 cubic feet or 2.831 cubic metres. This capacity includes all enclosed spaces of a ship.
- **G.S.S.L.: Genova, Savone, Spezia, Leghorn:** *(geography)* Italian ports.
- **HA: Hatches:** *(ship)* The lids of the holds of the ship.
- **H.A.D.: Havre/Antwerp/Dunkirk:** *(geography)* Selection of European ports of call. Le Havre or Antwerp or Dunkirk.
- **HA Dims:** *(ship)* Dimensions of hatches.
- **Handymax:** *(ship)* Typically, a bulk carrier of about 35,000–50,000 dwt. The term may be less often used to describe a tanker of about 40,000–60,000 dwt.
- **Handysize:** *(ship)* A bulk carrier of about 20,000–35,000 dwt, or a tanker of about 20,000–40,000 dwt. All tankers ranging between 20,000–60,000 dwt may be called "handy tankers".
- **Haw: Hawaian Islands:** *(geography)* An archipelago of eight major islands, several atolls, numerous smaller islets and undersea seamounts in the North Pacific Ocean, extending some 1,500 miles (2,400 kilometres) from the island of Hawaii.
- **HFO: Heavy Fuel Oil:** *(fuel, ship)* Type of fuel of high density and low processing, used in the main engine of the ship.
- **H/H: Havre to Hamburg:** *(geography)* The area from Havre to Hamburg, including both of them.

GLOSSARY AND ABBREVIATIONS

- **HHDWS: Heavy Handy Deadweight Scrap:** *(cargo)* It is a cargo type concerning "scrap" metals which may be usually exported from the US. The word "handy" indicates that the cargo does not fall to the category of very light cargoes (stowage factor of about 90 cb.ft. per mt), but neither to the category of very heavy cargoes (stowage factor of about 20–40 cb.ft. per mt). The stowage factor of "HHDWS" ranges around 50 cb.ft. per mt.
- **HO: Holds:** *(ship)* Vessel's holds.
- **Holiday:** *(laytime)* See appendix 3, "Laytime Definitions for Charter Parties 2013", term 14.
- **HP: Horse Power:** *(ship, engine)* The horsepower of the ship's main engine.
- **HR: Hampton Roads:** *(geography)* A region that contains a set of ports on the East Coast of the USA. See term "Roads".
- **HSS: Heavy Grains, Soya Beans and Sorghums:** *(cargo, voyage charter)* Term used in grain voyage charters, referring to the transport of heavy grains, such as wheat or soya. Heavy grains have a low stowage factor, as the higher the density and weight of the cargo, the lower the respective stowage factor. For example, wheat has a stowage factor of between 44–49 cb.ft. per mt, while soybeans from 48–52 cb.ft. per mt. On the other hand, barley and oats are considered light grains.
- **IFO: Intermediate Fuel Oil:** *(fuel, ship)* Type of semi-processed fuel with its density ranging between that of the "HFO" and "MDO".
- **IGS: Inert Gas System:** *(tanker)* A technical system of gas neutralisation applying to all tankers to avoid accidents from fire explosions.
- **I.L.O: In Lieu of:** *(general)* Against. Amount paid for/against a work. For example, "ILOHC" means "In Lieu of Hold Cleaning" or an amount to be paid against cleaning the ship's holds.
- **ILO: International Labour Organisation:** *(general)* International organisation which supports and defends human and labour rights.
- **IMO: International Maritime Organisation:** *(general)* It is the largest maritime organisation worldwide, forming a specialised part of United Nations. It mainly deals with the safety of maritime navigation and the prevention from pollution of the marine environment. IMO influence on "chartering" matters is limited to the extent that the terms of a charter-party require ships' compliance with international navigation and anti-pollution rules.
- **In Geographical Rotation:** *(geography, voyage charter)* If on a voyage charter the charterer has the option to direct the vessel at more than one loading or unloading ports, it is important that the charterparty establishes a particular (the most reasonable) geographical order of ship's approach at these ports.
- **INCL: Including:** *(general)* Comprising.
- **INCLOT:** Including Overtime.

- **Ind Sub: Indian Subcontinent:** *(geography)* A southern region of Asia, mostly situated on the Indian Plate and projecting southwards into the Indian Ocean from the Himalayas. Definitions of the extent of the Indian subcontinent differ but it usually includes the core lands of India, Pakistan and Bangladesh; Nepal, Bhutan, Sri Lanka and the Maldives are often included as well. The region is also called by a number of other names including South Asia, a name that is increasingly popular.
- **Indo: Indonesia:** *(geography)* A sovereign island country in Southeast Asia and Oceania. Indonesia is the largest island country in the world by the number of islands, with more than 14,000 islands. The Indonesian archipelago has been an important trade region since at least the seventh century.
- **INL: International Navigating Limits:** *(sea trading)* They are the official geographical restrictions placed on the ships' trading by the British Institute of Marine Underwriters. Until 2003 they were known as "Institute Warranty Limits" (IWL). If the owners or charterers wish to send a ship to the excluded areas, they should pay additional premium to the insurers of the ship.
- **ITF: International Transport (Workers') Federation:** *(seamen)* An international organisation dedicated to the defence of seafarers' interests.
- **KN: Knot:** *(ship)* Unit of measuring vessels' speed. A knot is equal to a mile per hour.
- **LAT: Latitude:** *(geography)* Latitude (φ) is a geographic coordinate that specifies the north–south position of a point on the Earth's surface. Latitude is an angle which ranges from $0°$ at the Equator to $+90°$ at the North Pole and $-90°$ at the South Pole. Lines of constant (same) latitude are the so-called "parallels" which run east–west as circles parallel to the Equator. Latitude is used together with longitude to uniquely define the precise location of features on the surface of the Earth (e.g. ships' geographical position).
- **Laydays:** *(laytime, voyage charter)* The days of "laytime". In other words, the agreed number of days allocated to the charterer for completion of the loading or unloading of the ship.
- **Laytime:** *(laytime, voyage charter)* See appendix 3, "Laytime Definitions for Charter Parties 2013", term 5.
- **LBP: Length Between Perpendiculars:** *(ship)* The length between vessel's perpendiculars.
- **L/C: Lay/Can: Laydays/Cancelling:** *(laytime, voyage charter, time charter)* This term gives the owner an amount of time to present his ship ready for loading in a voyage charter, for example "*Laydays 1st October/Cancelling 15th October*". If the ship reaches the loading port earlier than the first date, it probably should wait. If the ship arrives after the second date, then the charterer is entitled to cancel the charter. The term is also used in time charters to denote the agreed time that is provided to the owner in order to present his ship ready for delivery to the time charterer.

547

- **L/C: Letter of Credit:** *(international trade)* See LOC.
- **LCL: Less (than a) Container Load:** *(cargo, liner)* Term opposed to "FCL". It describes a cargo despatch whose size is not large enough to fill an entire "container". For example, a shipper may need to transport a small amount of packed cargo, able to be carried either as "break bulk cargo" or as "general cargo". This cargo shipment is delivered to the sea carrier directly or indirectly through a freight forwarder. Independent small amounts of "LCL" cargoes coming from different shippers/senders but directed to a common destination, are incorporated in one cargo shipment and transported in the same container under a joint bill of lading. It is a process typically called "groupage". Consolidation of "LCL" cargoes and stuffing of containers take place in special areas of the container terminals (called "container freight stations" / "CFS" or "container yards" / "CY"). Finally, the freight for an "LCL" cargo is generally higher than the freight of a similar cargo as "FCL", as the former takes into account the additional cost of unification (consolidation) of different cargoes and the stuffing of containers.
- **LD: Loading Port:** *(port, voyage charter)* The loading port in a voyage charter.
- **LDT: Light Displacement Tonnage or Light Weight:** *(ship)* The lightship displacement (weight) of a vessel is formed by the weight of the hull, the machinery, the equipment and the spare parts on board. The "light displacement" is usually the parameter by which the scrap value of a ship is calculated at the end of its commercial life. The difference between the loaded displacement (weight) of the ship and the lightship displacement (weight) of the ship is the deadweight of the ship (loaded displacement – light displacement = deadweight tonnage).
- **L.H.A.R.: London, Hull, Antwerp and/or Rotterdam:** *(geography)* Geographical order of European ports, where discharging of grain usually takes place.
- **LIFO: Liner In Free Out:** *(charterparty, negotiation, voyage charter)* Voyage charter term. Cargo loading costs are carried by the owner, whilst the cost of unloading is borne by the charterer or the consignee.
- **Liner terms:** *(charterparty, negotiation, voyage charter)* Synonym to "gross terms". "Liner terms" is a wording mainly used to liner trades, whereas "gross terms" is commonly used in the open market (bulk cargo and tramp trades).
- **LMAA: London Maritime Association of Arbitrators:** *(general)* A maritime arbitration association based in London.
- **LNG: Liquefied Natural Gas:** *(ship, cargo)* Type of gas cargo and type of the respective gas carrier (vessel) which carries such cargo.
- **LOA: Length Overall:** *(ship)* The maximum length of a vessel.
- **Loaded Displacement:** *(ship)* The loaded displacement (weight) of the vessel is the sum of the lightship displacement (light displacement) and the deadweight of the ship (deadweight tonnage).

- **Loading/Discharging Rate:** *(laytime, voyage charter, ship, cargo)* Rate of loading/unloading the ship. It is critical for laytime purposes.
- **LOC: Letter of Credit:** *(international trade)* A legal and financial document issued by a bank at the request of a cargo consignee (buyer of the goods), guaranteeing payment to the shipper (seller of the goods) if certain terms and cargo delivery conditions are fulfilled. In the event that the buyer of the goods is unable to make payment on the purchase, the bank will cover the outstanding amount. Normally, the letter of credit contains a brief description of the goods, documents required, a shipping date and an expiration date after which payment will not longer be made.
- **LOG: Letter of Guarantee:** *(international trade)* A written undertaking issued by a guarantor (a bank) at the request of the "applicant" (one party of a commercial deal, or one part of a contractual or economic relationship) to the "beneficiary" (the other part), guaranteeing the fulfillment of certain economic obligations under the deal or the contract signed between the applicant and the beneficiary. The sum is paid to the "beneficiary" by the bank, if the "applicant" does not fulfil the stipulated obligations under the contract. This can be used for example to essentially insure a buyer or seller of goods from loss or damage due to non-performance by the other party in a sales contract. LOG must clearly specify the amount and the valid period of the guarantee.
- **LOH: Loss of Hire:** *(general)* Insurance against loss of ship's income.
- **LOI: Letter of Indemnity:** *(general)* Letter of compensation. A written undertaking by a third party, on behalf of one of the parties (the first party) to a transaction or contract, to cover the other party (the second party) against specific loss or damage arising out of the action (or a failure to act) of the first party. For example, when a ship has arrived at the delivery port before the original bills of lading reach there, the shipper may instruct the ship's master to deliver the goods to a specific recipient without the appearance of the bill of lading. In such case, the master requests from the shipper to sign a letter of indemnity (compensation), i.e. an attestation that he undertakes himself to indemnify the owner for any damage that may arise if it is proved that this recipient was not entitled to the goods.
- **LO/LO: Lift On/Lift Off:** *(ship, cargo)* System of cargo handling, used mainly for loading and unloading of containers. It comprises technical methods which hoist and draw down the cargo to and from the ship by cranes or other lifting devices (e.g. fork lifts).
- **LONG: Longitude:** *(geography)* Longitude (λ) is a geographic co-ordinate that specifies the east–west position of a point on the Earth's surface. Longitude is defined through "meridians", which are imaginary half-circle lines running from pole to pole. Points with the same longitude lie in the same meridian. Longitude is an angular distance, usually measured in degrees east or west on the earth's surface, expressing the angle contained between the meridian of a particular place and

549

a reference meridian, so-called "the Prime Meridian". By convention, the Prime Meridian passes through the Royal Observatory, Greenwich, England, establishing the position of zero degrees longitude. The longitude of other places is measured as the angle east or west from the Prime Meridian, ranging from 0° at the Prime Meridian to +180° eastward and −180° westward. The +180 and −180 degrees longitude meridians coincide directly opposite the Prime Meridian. Difference in longitude may also be expressed by some corresponding difference in time.

- **LPG: Liquefied Petroleum Gas:** *(ship, cargo)* Type of gas cargo and type of the respective gas carrier (vessel) which carries such cargo.
- **LR: Lloyd's Register of Shipping:** *(general)* The British classification society.
- **LR: Long Range Product Tanker:** *(tanker)* A tanker carrying petroleum products and trading in long sea distances. Generally, tankers of this type may be defined as those having a size between 50/60,000 and 160,000 dwt. There are three sub-categories. Smaller vessels are called LR1 and range between 50/60,000 and 80/90,000 dwt, while larger vessels are called LR2 and range between 80/90,000 and 120,000 dwt, or LR3 reaching up to 160,000 dwt.
- **LT: Long Ton:** *(cargo)* Weight measurement unit used in the Anglo-Saxon system, consisting of 2,240 lbs (pounds) and equivalent to 1,016 kgs (kilograms). One pound equals to 453 gms (grams).
- **LTBENDS: Liner Terms Both Ends:** *(charterparty, negotiation, voyage charter)* Voyage charter term. The costs of cargo loading and unloading are carried by the owner, so they are included in the freight rate.
- **Lumpsum** or **Lump Sum Freight:** *(freight, voyage charter)* Freight agreed to be paid as a fixed amount, instead of being calculated according to the amount of cargo carried (as it is the most common practice).
- **MDO: Marine Diesel Oil:** *(fuel, ship)* Fuel type of relatively low density and high processing, used mainly in the ship's diesel generators.
- **ME: Middle East:** *(geography)* A rather vague term used to describe a trans-continental region centered on Western Asia and Egypt.
- **MED: Mediterranean:** *(geography)* It includes the Mediterranean ports from the Strait of Gibraltar in the west, to the Dardanelles in the northeast. The Adriatic Sea and the Aegean Sea are included, but the Suez Canal is excluded.
- **MEG: Middle East Gulf:** *(geography)* Synonym to "Persian" or "Arabian Gulf".
- **MGO: Marine Gas Oil:** *(fuel, ship)* Fuel type.
- **MIC: Man in Charge:** *(general)* The person responsible for a task.
- **Miss: Mississippi River:** *(geography)* The chief river of the largest drainage system on the North American continent. Being the fourth longest and ninth largest river in the world, it flows entirely in the USA (though its drainage basin reaches into Canada), rising in northern Minnesota and meandering slowly southwards for 2,320 miles

(3,730 km) to the Mississippi River Delta at the Gulf of Mexico. From the perspective of modern commercial navigation, the Mississippi River System, is a mostly riverine network of the US which includes the Mississippi River and inland waterways which are connected by artificial means. The system is maintained by the US Army Corps of Engineers with a project depth of between 9 and 12 feet (2.7–3.7 m.) as per 2015 to accommodate barge transportation and navigation by small commercial vessels, primarily of bulk commodities. It is one of the greatest commercial waterways of the world, facilitating a great percentage of annual US shipments in grain, oil, gas and coal.

- **M/M or Min/Max: Minimun/Maximum:** *(cargo, voyage charter)* It determines a specific minimum and a specific maximum quantity of cargo to be loaded. If however the term reads for example "*10,000 tons min/max*" in essence the agreed quantity of cargo to be loaded is fixed and there is no margin for loading more or less than that.
- **MOL: More Or Less:** *(cargo, voyage charter)* It refers to an option on the determination of the exact amount of cargo to be carried, e.g. "*10.000 tons, 5% more or less*". Typically, the term stipulates which party has this option. For example:
  a) **MOLCO: More or Less Charterer's Option:** Here the charterer decides for the amount of cargo.
  b) **MOLOO: More or Less Owner's Option:** Here the owner decides for the amount of cargo.
- **MPC or MPP: Multi-Purpose Cargoship:** *(ship)* A dry cargo vessel capable of carrying both dry bulk cargoes and general cargo or containers.
- **MR: Medium Range product tanker:** *(tanker)* A tanker carrying petroleum products and trading in medium-haul sea routes. Generally, tankers of this category range from 25,000–50/60,000 dwt.
- **MSG: Message:** *(general)* Exchange of commercial information.
- **MT: Metric Ton or Tonne:** *(cargo)* Weight measurement unit. It consists of 1,000 kilograms (kgs) or 2,204 lb (pounds). Equivalent to 0.9842 "long ton".
- **N Af: North Africa:** *(geography)* It is the northernmost region of Africa. Geopolitically, the United Nations definition includes seven countries or territories; Algeria, Egypt, Libya, Morocco, Sudan, Tunisia, and Western Sahara.
- **N At: North Atlantic islands:** *(geography)* The islands of the North Atlantic Ocean.
- **NAABSA: Not Always Afloat But Safely Aground:** *(charterparty, port)* In some ports, due to a limited depth, it is customary for the ship to deliberately run ashore in the muddy seabed to reach and load/unload. In this case the term "NAABSA" is agreed in the charterparty. Opposite: "AA" or "ASA". Synonym: "sitting aground" or "safely aground".
- **NCSA: North Coast South America:** *(geography)* It includes the ports or places located in the North Coast of South America, from Turbo in the west to Georgetown in the east.

- **NCNA: North Coast North America:** *(geography)* The northern part of North America (Canada and Alaska).
- **NDFCAPMQS: No Dead Freight for Charterers Account Provided Minimum Quantity Supplied:** *(freight, voyage charter)* The charterer is not required to pay "dead freight" to the owner, as long as he provides the minimum quantity of cargo as agreed in the charterparty.
- **n.E.: not East of:** *(geography)* Geographical description.
- **NEOBIG: Not East Of But Including Greece:** *(geography)* Greece is the eastern geographical limit.
- **Net terms:** *(charterparty, negotiation, voyage charter)* Voyage charter term, not common nowadays. In this case the owner receives a net freight rate. All cargo-handling expenses are borne by the charterer or the shipper or the consignee. Opposite to "gross terms".
- **NEWCI: Not East of West Coast Italy:** *(geography)* West coast of Italy is the eastern geographical limit.
- **n.N.: not North of:** *(geography)* Geographical description.
- **N Pac: North Pacific islands:** *(geography)* The islands of the North Pacific Ocean.
- **n.S.: not South of:** *(geography)* Geographical description.
- **n.W.: not West of:** *(geography)* Geographical description.
- **NK: Nippon Kaiji Kyokai:** *(general)* The Japanese classification society.
- **NOR: Notice of Readiness:** *(laytime, voyage charter)* See appendix 3, "Laytime Definitions for Charter Parties 2013", term 25.
- **Northern Range: US ports of Norfolk, Newport News, Philadelphia, Baltimore, New York, Boston, Portland:** *(geography)* It is the region of the East Coast of the USA, which includes these ports.
- **NR: Number:** *(general)* Arithmetic measure.
- **NRT: Net Registered Tonnage:** *(ship, cargo)* The net capacity of the vessel measured in registered tons. It includes all enclosed spaces of the ship that are available for cargo.
- **NWE: Northwest Europe:** *(geography)* Geographically, it usually consists of Ireland, Great Britain, Belgium, the Netherlands, northern Germany, Denmark, Norway, Sweden and Iceland. Luxembourg, northern France, southern Germany and Switzerland are also usually considered part of the grouping.
- **OA: Overaged:** *(general)* Aged, old.
- **OABE: Owners Agents Both Ends:** *(general)* Owners appoint agents in both ports (loading/unloading). Opposite: "CHABE".
- **OBO: Oil/Bulk/Ore:** *(ship)* The so-called "combination carriers" are outdated vessels able to transport either oil or iron ore or other dry bulk cargoes.
- **OCIMF: Oil Companies International Marine Forum:** *(general)* An association of oil companies having an interest in the shipment and terminalling of crude oil and oil products.

- **OECD: Organisation for Economic Co-operation and Development:** *(general)* An international economic organisation of 35 countries, founded in 1961 to stimulate economic progress and world trade.
- **OO: Oil/Ore:** *(ship)* Similar to "OBO", but able to transport either oil or iron ore.
- **OPEC: Organisation of Petroleum Exporting Countries:** *(general)* An international organisation representing the interests of major petroleum exporting countries. It is now headquartered in Austria, but first established in Baghdad, Iraq in 1960. OPEC was formed when the international oil market was largely dominated by a group of multi-national oil companies known as the "Seven Sisters", thus its formation represented a collective act of sovereignty by petroleum-exporting nations, as it ensured that oil companies could not any more determine oil prices. Nowadays, OPEC's mission is to coordinate and unify the petroleum policies of its member countries and ensure the stabilisation of oil markets, in order to secure an efficient, economic and regular supply of petroleum to consumers, a steady income to producers and a fair return on capital for those investing in the petroleum industry. As of May 2017, OPEC had 14 members: Algeria, Angola, Ecuador, Equatorial Guinea, Indonesia, Iran, Iraq, Kuwait, Libya, Nigeria, Qatar, Saudi Arabia (the de facto leader), the United Arab Emirates and Venezuela. As of 2014, approximately 80% of the world's proven oil reserves were located in OPEC member countries and two-thirds of OPEC's reserves were located in the Middle East. According to the US Energy Information Administration (EIA), OPEC crude oil production is an important factor affecting global oil prices.
- **OPT: Option:** *(charterparty)* Selection, decision, alternative.
- **Panamax:** *(ship)* Those ships which have the maximum dimensions allowing passage through the Panama Canal. Currently, the term may refer either to a bulk carrier of about 60,000–100,000 dwt or a tanker of about 60,000–80,000 dwt. However, after the construction of the third, wider lane in the Panama Canal in 2016, the size of vessels able to cross the Panama Canal is expected to adjust.
- **PANDI: Protection and Indemnity Club or Insurance:** *(general)* A P&I Club is a mutual insurance association that provides risk pooling, information and representation for its members. Unlike a marine insurance company, which reports to its shareholders, a P&I Club reports only to its members. Originally, P&I Club members were typically shipowners, ship operators or demise charterers, but more recently freight forwarders and warehouse operators have been able to join. P&I Clubs provide cover against third-party liabilities encountered in the commercial operation of vessels. Examples of main risks covered are liabilities, expenses and costs related to loss of life, injury and illness of crew, passengers and other persons, cargo loss, collision, damage to docks, pollution etc. P&I is to complement a vessel's hull and machinery

insurance and related covers. It is distinguished from ordinary marine insurance in that it is based on the not-for-profit principle of mutuality where members of the P&I Club are both the insurers and the insureds. Whereas in "Hull & Machinery" (H&M) insurance the assured pays a premium to an underwriter for cover which lasts for a particular time (e.g. a year or a voyage), a P&I Club member instead pays a "call". This is a sum of money that is put into the Club's pool. If at the end of the year there are still funds in the pool, each member will pay a reduced call the following year; but if the Club has made a major payout (e.g. after an oil spillage) Club members will immediately have to pay a further call to replenish the pool. Major Clubs are coordinated through the "International Group of P&I Clubs" based in London.

- **PC: Part Cargo:** *(cargo)* Goods which do not cover the entire cargo capacity of a particular ship, but whose quantity is sufficient to be carried on charter terms.
- **PC: Port Charges:** *(port, voyage charter)* Charges levied on the ship by a port authority for the use of the port.
- **PCC or PCTC: Pure Car Carrier or Pure Car/Truck Carrier:** *(ship)* A type of specialised vessel carrying exclusively cars, trucks and vehicles in general.
- **PCT: Per Cent (%):** *(general)* Number or amount expressed per hundred.
- **PD: Per Day:** *(freight)* Daily.
- **PDPR: Per Day Pro Rata:** *(freight)* Daily and in proportion.
- **PDWP: Per Day Weather Permitting:** *(laytime, voyage charter)* See "(working day) weather permitting".
- **Per Hatch Per Day:** *(laytime, voyage charter)* See appendix 3, "Laytime Definitions for Charter Parties 2013", term 6.
- **PG: Persian Gulf or Arabian Gulf:** *(geography)* It includes the ports of the Persian (Arabian or Middle East) Gulf. The one end of the Gulf will be Basrah in the north, while the other end will be given by the notional line joining Bandar Abbas with the Musandam Peninsula in the southeast of the Gulf.
- **PIC: Person in Charge:** *(general)* Synonym to "MIC".
- **PICO: Port In Charterers' Option:** *(port)* Port determination to be made by the charterer.
- **PLT: Per Long Ton:** *(general)* By "long ton", a weight unit used in anglo-saxon systems equals to 1,016 kgs.
- **PMT: Per Metric Tonne (or Metric Ton in the US):** *(general)* By tonne or metric tonne (or metric ton in the US) consisting of 1,000 kgs.
- **POA: Payment on Account:** *(general)* Payment against a work in progress or to be performed. The final amount of total expenses will be cleared in a later stage, on the completion of this work. After the despatch of relevant supporting documents and the monitoring of all accounts (disbursements), final settlement should be made to determine whether an additional payment of money or a return is required.

- **Port:** *(laytime, voyage charter, port)* See appendix 3, "Laytime Definitions for Charter Parties 2013", term 1.
- **PPT: Prompt:** *(cargo, ship)* It indicates that the cargo or the ship will be readily available or in time.
- **PR: Pro Rata:** *(freight, general)* In proportion.
- **Pratique or Free Pratique:** *(ship, port)* Upon arrival at a port of call, the ship is inspected by the health authorities of the port to confirm that it is a "healthy ship", no infectious diseases are carried, living conditions are appropriate and therefore the ship may enter the port and proceed to the cargo-handling operations.
- **PROBO: Products/Bulk/Oil:** *(ship)* A type of a combined carrier which is able to transport either oil products or crude oil or dry bulk cargoes.
- **Prod: Product Carrier:** *(ship)* A tanker able to carry oil products.
- **P/STN: Pilot Station:** *(general)* At seaports, the office or headquarters of marine pilots; the place where the services of a pilot may be obtained; On board, position on the bridge of a ship where the pilot stands to steer or to give directions for steering a ship into and out of a harbour.
- **PT: Per Ton:** *(general)* Term which needs to be interpreted according to the context. It may mean: (a) A unit of internal capacity for ships equal to 100 cubic feet (called also "register ton"). (b) A unit approximately equal to the volume of a long ton weight of seawater used in reckoning the displacement of ships and equal to 35 cubic feet. (c) A unit of volume for cargo freight usually reckoned at 40 cubic feet (called also "measurement ton"). (d) A unit of weight meaning a tonne or a metric tonne (or metric ton in the US) composed of 1,000 kgs (e) A unit of weight meaning either a short ton of 2,000 pounds (about 907 kgs) or a long ton of 2,240 pounds (about 1,016 kgs), with the short ton being more frequently used in the US and Canada and long ton in the UK. Where accuracy is required in terms of weight, the correct term must be used, but for many purposes this is not necessary as the metric and long tons differ by only 1.6%, and the short ton is within 11% of both. From 1965 the UK embarked upon a programme of metrication and gradually introduced metric units, including the tonne (metric ton in the US), defined as 1,000 kgs (2,204.6 lbs). The UK Weights and Measures Act 1985 explicitly excluded from use for trade the ton ("short" or "long") and the term "metric ton", replacing them for "tonne".
- **RE: Regarding – Related to:** *(general)* Typical way of starting a business correspondence message.
- **Reachable on Arrival or Always Accessible:** *(laytime, voyage charter)* See appendix 3, "Laytime Definitions for Charter Parties 2013", term 3.
- **RECAP TLX or MSG: Recapitulation Telex or Message:** *(general)* Telex or message confirming and summarising the main terms of a charter agreement.

- **Reefer: Refrigerated Cargoship:** *(ship)* A type of specialised vessel able to carry frozen or chilled cargo.
- **RESP: Respectively:** *(general)* Accordingly, in the relative order.
- **Reversible laytime:** *(laytime, voyage charter)* See appendix 3, "Laytime Definitions for Charter Parties 2013", term 24.
- **RNR: Rate Not Reported:** *(general)* The amount of the freight rate has not been reported to the market.
- **RO/RO: Roll On/Roll Off:** *(ship, cargo)* System of cargo handling and respective type of vessel. The cargo is transported in wheeled vehicles, loaded and unloaded to and from the ship through ramps. The respective ferries that specialise in this kind of transport are called "Ro-Ro vessels" or "Ro-Pax" if they are able to carry both wheeled cargoes and passengers.
- **Roads: US ports of Hampton Roads – Norfolk, Newport News, Sewells Point:** *(geography)* It is the region of the East Coast of the USA, so-called "Hampton Roads", which includes the above ports.
- **ROB: Remaining On Board:** *(cargo, bunker, ship, charterparty)* Term possibly related to the quantity of cargo, fuel or fresh water remaining on board at a time.
- **ROC or ROM or ROT: Regarding our Cable or Regarding our Message or Regarding our Telex:** *(general)* With reference to our message. . .
- **RPM: Revolutions Per Minute:** *(ship, engine)* Term referring to the operating speed of a ship's engine.
- **RS or R Sea: Red Sea:** *(geography)* It includes ports and places at the Red Sea, from the Suez Canal in the north to the Strait of Bab el Mandeb in the south.
- **RS: Register of Shipping of Russia:** *(general)* The Russian classification society.
- **Running Days (RD) or Consecutive Days (CD):** *(laytime, voyage charter)* See appendix 3, "Laytime Definitions for Charter Parties 2013", term 12.
- **Running Hours or Consecutive Hours:** *(laytime, voyage charter)* See appendix 3, "Laytime Definitions for Charter Parties 2013", term 13.
- **RYC or RYM or RYT: Regarding your Cable or Regarding your Message or Regarding your Telex:** *(general)* With reference to your message. . .
- **S Af: South Africa:** *(geography)* The Republic of South Africa. See also "Southern Africa".
- **S At: South Atlantic islands:** *(geography)* The islands of the South Atlantic Ocean.
- **SA or SB: Safe Anchorage or Safe Berth:** *(laytime, voyage charter)* Anchorage or berth where the ship during the stipulated by the charterparty time it can reach, stay and depart from there safely without, in the absence of some abnormal occurrence, being exposed to danger which

cannot be avoided by good navigation and seamanship. See also "safe port" as long as the "safety" principles apply either in a berth or in a port context.

- **SATPMSHEX: Saturdays Post Meridiem Sundays Holidays Excluded:** *(laytime, voyage charter)* Saturdays after noon, Sundays and holidays are excluded from laytime.
- **SBT: Segregated Ballast Tanks:** *(ship)* Independent tanks of ballast sea water in a tanker. By using separate ballast tanks, mixing of cargo and ballast is avoided and the risk of consequent pollution of the sea is restricted.
- **Scandinavia:** *(geography)* It includes ports located in Norway, Denmark, Sweden and Finland, including the islands of the Baltic Sea.
- **SD or SDS or SDBC: Single Decker or Single Deck Ship or Single Decker Bulk Carrier:** *(ship)* Type of a multi-purpose ship with a single deck. The holds of these ships are not separated horizontally into two or more levels as occurs with "tweendeckers" or "multi-deckers".
- **SD or SLD: Sailed:** *(ship)* The vessel has sailed from the port.
- **SD: Short Delivery:** *(cargo, voyage charter)* Delivery of incomplete cargo. The delivered quantity of cargo to the recipient is less than that agreed and indicated on the relevant bill of lading.
- **SEA: Southeast Asia:** *(geography)* A sub-region of Asia, consisting of the countries that are geographically south of China, east of India, west of New Guinea and north of Australia. Southeast Asia consists of two geographic regions: Maritime Southeast Asia comprising Indonesia, East Malaysia, Singapore, Philippines, East Timor, Brunei and Christmas Island; and Mainland Southeast Asia (also known as "Indochina") comprising Cambodia, Laos, Myanmar (Burma), Thailand, Vietnam and West Malaysia.
- **SF: Stowage Factor:** *(dry cargo, voyage charter)* A coefficient which shows the relation between the volume and the weight of a cargo, expressed in cubic feet per long ton or cubic metres per metric ton (or tonne). The stowage factor is a measure that examines how much space (volume) is occupied in the hold of a ship from a certain amount of weight of a cargo. It is used in conjunction with the "grain capacity" or "bale capacity" of the ship to determine the total amount (weight) of cargo that can be loaded and plays a key role in how each cargo may be stowed. Cargoes with a s.f. less than 50 cubic feet per long ton are considered heavy cargoes, while those with a s.f. greater than 50 cubic feet per long ton are considered light cargoes. The role of stowage factor is crucial in the dry cargo market, but not so important in other chartering business (e.g. tankers, gas carriers, containerships).
- **SHEX: Sundays Holidays Excluded:** *(laytime, voyage charter)* Sundays and holidays are excluded from laytime.
- **SHINC: Sundays Holidays Included:** *(laytime, voyage charter)* Sundays and holidays are included in the laytime.

- **Singapore/Japan:** *(geography)* It includes the Far East ports located in the area which is determined by Singapore in the south to Japan in the north, through the South Sea in China. Singapore, Philippines, Taiwan and Japan are included, but Malaysia, Brunei, Indonesia and Papua New Guinea are excluded.

- **Sitting Aground or Safely Aground:** *(charterparty, port)* The owner agrees to enable the ship to run aground safely to the bottom of the loading or unloading port at low tide period, so as to load or unload. See also "NAABSA". Opposite: "AA" or "ASA".

- **SOF: Statement of Fact:** *(general, laytime, voyage charter)* A statement, prepared by the ship's agents at the loading and discharging ports, which shows the date and times of arrival of the ship and the commencement and completion of loading and discharging. It details the quantity of cargo loaded or discharged each day, the hours worked and the hours stopped with the reasons for the stoppages, such as bad weather, a strike or breakdown of equipment.

- **SOL: Shipowners' Liability:** *(general)* Owners' responsibility.

- **Sous Palan:** *(voyage charter, port, ship, dry cargo)* A voyage charter term. It is a French wording equivalent to the English expression "*under the hook*" or "*under ship's tackle*". It indicates that the shipowner's liability for the cargo begins when the cargo has just been delivered alongside the vessel at the stipulated berth of the loading port, and it ends when the ship unloads and delivers the cargo just alongside at the stipulated berth of the discharging port.

- **Southern Africa:** *(geography)* It includes all the ports on the South Coast of Africa from Maputo in the east to Lüderitz in the west, excluding both.

- **S&P: Sale and Purchase:** *(general)* The market of buying and selling second-hand ships.

- **S Pac: South Pacific islands:** *(geography)* The islands of the South Pacific Ocean.

- **SP: Safe Port:** *(laytime, voyage charter, port)* A port where the ship during the stipulated by the charterparty time it can reach, stay and depart from there safely without, in the absence of some abnormal occurrence, being exposed to danger which cannot be avoided by good navigation and seamanship. Charterers' obligation is to nominate a port (or berth) which, when the order is given, is prospectively safe (i.e. is expected to be safe at the time of vessel's call). Charterers will not be in breach of safe port warranty if the immediate and proximate cause of the loss is the negligence of the master, owners or their servants or agents. Charterers will not be in breach either if loss is caused by some abnormal occurence.

- **SP range or Skaw/Cape Passero:** *(geography)* It covers the entire area of the European continent, outlined from the Skaw, the northernmost point of Denmark, ending at Cape Passero on the eastern side of Sicily.

It includes all the Atlantic Ocean, southern from Cape Skaw and the entire Western Mediterranean, including the Balearic Islands, Sardinia, Corsica and Malta, but excluding North African coast and the Adriatic Sea.

- **SPM: Single Point Mooring:** *(tanker, port)* Floating anchorage installed in deep water off a shallow port in order to facilitate large tankers to load or unload their cargo.
- **Spot:** *(freight, voyage charter, ship, cargo)* It indicates that a ship or a cargo is immediately available. "Spot rate" is also the freight rate paid usually in USD/mt of cargo carried in a voyage charter.
- **SSW: Summer Salt Water:** *(ship)* It refers to the ship's draught when it is loaded up to its summer load line in seawater conditions.
- **STBC/LAKER: Self Trimmer Bulk Carrier/Laker:** *(ship, dry bulk)* A type of bulk carrier in which the shape of the holds allows the direct settlement of dry bulk cargo within them.
- **STEM: Subject to Existence of Merchandise:** *(cargo)* See subject stem.
- **STN: Station:** *(port)* Terminal, depot, pilot's waiting place.
- **Strike:** *(laytime, voyage charter)* A term defined in "Voylayrules '93", but removed from "Laytime Definitions for Charter Parties 2013". According to "Voylayrules '93" it shall mean a concerted industrial action by workmen causing a complete stoppage of their work which directly interferes with the working of the vessel. Refusal to work over-time, go-slow or working to rule and comparable actions not causing a complete stoppage shall not be considered a strike. A strike shall be understood to exclude its consequences when it has ended, such as con-gestion in the port or effects upon the means of transportation bringing or taking the cargo to or from the port.
- **Subject details:** *(charter)* Term denoting that the final conclusion of a charter (fixture) is subject to the agreement of certain details (matters) between the parties. Under US law, a "subject details" agreement is con-sidered sufficient to create (or to have created) the charter contract.
- **Subject Managers' approval or Subject Board's approval:** *(charter)* The charter fixture is subject to approval by the charterers' highest level of management.
- **Subject open or Subject free:** *(charter)* The owner states to the char-terer, during chartering negotiations, that the ship is also in negotiations with other charterers. Therefore, the closing of the charter will depend on whether the ship will still be "open" to get chartered when the char-terer accepts the proposed terms, i.e. no other charter agreement will have arisen between the owner and another charterer in the meanwhile.
- **Subject Owners' approval of Charterers:** *(charter)* The fixture is subject to the approval of charterers' quality from the highest level of shipowners' management. It is a condition favourable to the owner, as opposed to the term "subject Board's approval". It is used when

charterer is somewhat unknown and the owner wishes to collect some more details on his identity and track record.

- **Subject Receivers'/Shippers' approval:** *(voyage charter)* The closure of a voyage charter is subject to the approval and acceptance of the vessel by the recipients/shippers of the cargo.
- **Subject Stem (STEM: Subject To Existence of Merchandise):** *(cargo)* The word "stem" refers to the amount and availability of cargo on the date it is to be loaded on board. The phrase suggests that the charter will be considered as fixed only when charterers confirm that the agreed cargo will be available on the specified dates. Otherwise, if charterers are not in a position to provide the cargo at the stipulated dates, then the charter is frustrated, even if there is full agreement on all the remaining negotiating matters.
- **Subject to contract:** *(charter)* Fixture is considered to have been made only upon the signature of the final charter contract. The existing agreement between the two parties is deemed temporary (provisional agreement) and in any case it is not binding until the charterparty or other contract of carriage is signed.
- **Subject to Government approval:** *(charter)* The fixture is subject to approval and acceptance of the vessel by government echelons in the country of exporters/charterers. The term is mainly used in cases where the charterer is based at a developing country or the charter (voyage or period) concerns the transport of state cargoes.
- **Subject to signing charterparty:** *(charter)* Synonym to "subject to contract".
- **Suezmax:** *(ship)* A tanker vessel typically ranging between 120,000–200,000 dwt.
- **Supramax or Super-handymax or Ultra-handymax:** *(ship)* A bulk carrier of about 50,000–60,000 dwt.
- **SWAD: Salt Water Arrival Draught:** *(sea trading, port, ship)* The maximum draught of a ship on arrival at a port with "salt/sea water". See also "BWAD" and "FWAD".
- **SWL: Safe Working Load:** *(cargo)* The maximum cargo that can be lifted safely by a cargo-handling mechanism, e.g. a crane or a winch. The maximum lifting ability of each machine is specific and should not be violated.
- **Tallying:** *(cargo)* The counting of the quantities of cargo before it is loaded on board or unloaded from it.
- **TBL: To Be Lifted:** *(general)* a. To be removed. In chartering matters "lifting" is mainly related with "subjects", i.e. matters needing resolution before the charter can be agreed. When a fixture is concluded with "subjects", it is up to the brokers to ensure that both principals "lift subjects" as soon as possible. It is important to note that no fixture has been concluded until "all subjects have been lifted", i.e. all laid conditions have been met (satisfied, cured) and "subjects" are removed.

If all subjects are in order ("lifted"), the vessel stands "clean fixed", i.e. the charter contract is enforceable and parties are bound by the terms agreed. Precise and reasonable times should be determined for the lifting of subjects, b. To be carried, transported, elevated. The word "lifting" may also refer to the cargo carriage.

- **TBN: To Be Nominated:** *(general)* To be named, called or determined ... It is commonly used in the chartering negotiations when something has not been revealed yet (e.g. the name of the ship or the charterer).
- **TBR: To Be Renamed:** *(general)* Something is going to be called or named again (e.g. the ship is going to change name).
- **T/C: Time Charter:** *(charter)* The hiring of a ship from a shipowner to a charterer for a period of time. The owner places his ship, with crew and equipment, at the disposal of the charterer, for which the charterer pays hire money. Subject to any restrictions in the contract, the charterer decides the type and quantity of cargo to be carried and the ports of loading and discharging. He is responsible for supplying the ship with bunkers and for the payment of cargo-handling operations, port charges, pilotage, towage and ship's agency. The technical operation and navigation of the ship remain the responsibility of the shipowner. A ship hired in this way is said to be on time charter.
- **TD or TDS or TDBC: Tween Decker or Tween Deck Ship or Tween Decker Bulk Carrier:** *(ship)* Type of a multi-purpose ship with a double deck. The holds of these ships are separated horizontally into two levels.
- **TEU: Twenty-foot Equivalent Unit:** *(cargo, liner)* The 20-foot container or its equivalent. TEU is the common measurement unit of a ship's carrying capacity in containers.
- **THERE4: Therefore:** *(general)* Consequently, thus.
- **Time Lost Waiting for Berth to Count as Loading or Discharging Time or as Laytime:** *(laytime, voyage charter, port)* See appendix 3, "Laytime Definitions for Charter Parties 2013", term 26.
- **TIP: Taking Inward Pilot:** *(charterparty, time charter)* Time charter term for the delivery of the ship to the charterer. The ship is deemed to have been delivered by the owner to the time charterer once it has reached the agreed place of delivery and the pilot has embarked on board. The term "TIP" is advantageous for the charterer, compared with the term "APS", because it implies that the owner bears the risk and the expense of a delayed boarding of the pilot. It is therefore not enough for the owner to deliver the ship at the pilot station, as it is the case under the term "APS". See also "APS".
- **TKS: Thanks:** *(general)* Typical expression of gratitude.
- **TL: Total Loss:** *(ship)* The ship's loss.
- **TLX: Telex:** *(general)* An outdated way of exchanging business information.
- **Touching Soft Ground:** *(charterparty, port)* See "sitting aground".

- **TPC: Tonnes Per Centimetre Immersion:** *(ship, cargo)* It shows the quantity in metric tonnes (e.g. of cargo or fuel) to be loaded on board to immerse the ship one further centimetre. This quantity varies not only ship by ship, but also according to the quantity already on board, the draught and the water density.
- **TPI: Tons Per Inch Immersion:** *(ship, cargo)* Similar to TPC, but it shows the quantity in imperial long tons (e.g. of cargo or fuel) to be loaded on board to immerse the ship one further inch.
- **TS: Time Sheet:** *(laytime, voyage charter)* Statement, drawn up by the ship's agent at the loading and discharging ports, which details the time worked in loading or discharging the cargo, together with the amount of laytime used. This latter figure, when compared with the time allowed in the voyage charterparty, is used by the shipowner and charterer to calculate demurrage or despatch, as the case may be.
- **TSA: Transpacific Stabilisation Agreement:** *(liner)* It is a research and discussion forum of major ocean container shipping lines that serve the transpacific trade in both directions between Asia and the US. TSA member carriers are authorised under the applicable shipping laws of US and Asian governments to exchange market information, represent carrier interests in consultations with government regulatory bodies and with designated shipper organisations, develop voluntary, non-binding guidelines for rates and charges, discuss ways members can manage costs and improve efficiency, establish common terms of service and standards for certain documentation, information systems development and other activities in the public interest, also on a voluntary, non-binding basis.
- **TTL: Total Commission:** *(charterparty, freight, hire)* The total amount paid as commission by the shipowner for the closing of a charter. It usually includes the commission payable to the shipbroker known as "brokerage" and the "address commission" which is due to the charterer by the shipowner as a form of rebate granted by the latter under the charter agreement.
- **TTL/CGO: Total Cargo:** *(cargo)* The total quantity of cargo.
- **UCAE: Unforeseen Circumstances Always Excepted:** *(general)* An agreement will be materialised if it is not frustrated by abnormal events and conditions.
- **UK: United Kingdom:** *(geography)* Ports in England, Wales, Scotland and North Ireland.
- **UKC: United Kingdom and/or Continent:** *(geography)* Ports or places in the United Kingdom and/or Continent.
- **UK/Cont. (B.H.): United Kingdom and/or Continent (Bordeaux – Hamburg range):** *(geography)* Selection of European ports among United Kingdom and *Continent* in Bordeaux – Hamburg range.
- **UK/Cont. (G.H.): United Kingdom and/or Continent (Gibraltar – Hamburg range):** *(geography)* Selection of European ports among United Kingdom and *Continent* in Gibraltar – Hamburg range.

- **UK/Cont. (H.H.): United Kingdom and/or Continent (Havre – Hamburg range):** *(geography)* Selection of European ports among United Kingdom and *Continent* in Havre – Hamburg range.
- **UKHH: United Kingdom or Havre or Hamburg:** *(geography)* Selection of European ports.
- **ULCC: Ultra Large Crude Carrier:** *(ship)* A huge crude oil tanker of over 320,000 dwt.
- **Unless Sooner Commenced:** *(laytime, voyage charter)* See appendix 3, "Laytime Definitions for Charter Parties 2013", term 20.
- **Unless Sooner Commenced, in which case actual time used to count:** *(laytime, voyage charter)* See appendix 3, "Laytime Definitions for Charter Parties 2013", term 21.
- **USAC: United States Atlantic Coast:** *(geography)* Synonym to "USEC".
- **USEC: United States East Coast:** *(geography)* It includes the ports of the East Coast of USA from Miami in the south to Calais in the north, including Chesapeake bay, Delaware bay, Delaware river up to Philadelphia and including Hudson River up to Albany. Synonym: USAC (United States Atlantic Coast).
- **USGC: US Gulf Coast:** *(geography)* It includes the ports of the United States located in the Gulf of Mexico, from Key West in the east to Brownsville in the west. It also includes Mississippi River up to Baton Rouge.
- **USNH: United States North of Cape Hatteras:** *(geography)* It includes the area from Cape Hatteras in the south to Calais in the north. It also includes Chesapeake bay, Delaware bay, Delaware river not north from Philadelphia, as well as Hudson River not north from Albany.
- **USNOPAC: United States North Pacific Coast:** *(geography)* It includes the US ports located in North Pacific Coast, from Seattle in the north to Brookings in the south. It includes rivers Columbia and Willamette, as well as Puget Sound bay.
- **USPAC: United States Pacific Coast:** *(geography)* It includes US ports bordering the Pacific ocean. The region is outlined from Seattle in the north and San Diego in the south. It also includes the bay of San Francisco, the Columbia and Willamette rivers and the Puget Sound bay.
- **USSH: United States South of Cape Hatteras:** *(geography)* It describes the area south from Cape Hatteras.
- **USWC: United States West Coast:** *(geography)* The term "West Coast" or "Pacific Coast" is used for ports or places situated at the westernmost coastal states of the US.
- **UU: Unless Used:** *(laytime, voyage charter)* See appendix 3, "Laytime Definitions for Charter Parties 2013", term 22.
- **UWRS: Underwriters:** *(general)* Insurers.
- **Vessel being in Free Pratique:** *(laytime, voyage charter, ship, port)* See appendix 3, "Laytime Definitions for Charter Parties 2013", term 29.

- **VLCC: Very Large Crude Carrier:** *(ship)* A very big crude oil tanker with a capacity typically ranging between 200,000–320,000 dwt.
- **VLGC: Very Large Gas Carrier:** *(ship)* A very big gas carrier with a cargo capacity of over 70,000 cbm.
- **VLOO: Very Large Ore Oiler:** *(ship)* A combined transport big vessel able to ship either iron ore or oil with a carrying capacity of more than 200,000 dwt.
- **VLPC: Very Large Product Carrier:** *(ship)* A big product tanker with carrying capacity of over 80,000 dwt.
- **VPD: Vessel Pays Dues:** *(charterparty, negotiation, voyage charter)* Charterparty term which specifies that owners will pay for all dues charged for the ship. Opposite term: "C.P.D.".
- **VSL: Vessel:** *(ship)* An abbreviation for the vessel.
- **Waiver:** *(general)* When someone is voluntarily relinquished from his rights and privileges. The waiver of a right may be an "express waiver" or an "implied waiver".
- **W.C.: West Coast:** *(geography)* General geographical description.
- **WCCA: West Coast Central America:** *(geography)* It includes Pacific ports located on the West Coast of Central America and specifically in the countries Guatemala, El Salvador, Honduras, Nicaragua, Costa Rica, Panama. The Panama Canal is also included.
- **WCCON: Whether Customs Cleared Or Not or Vessel Having Been Entered at the Custom House Or Not:** *(laytime, voyage charter, ship, port)* The term means that the ship does not have to wait for completion of the custom formalities to give notice of readiness (NOR). However, any time lost due to a delay in this process will not count as laytime.
- **WCNA: West Coast North America:** *(geography)* It is meant to describe a contiguous region of North America bordering the Pacific Ocean, including the respective US states, parts of Canada, parts of Mexico, parts of the Central American countries of Guatemala, El Salvador, Honduras, Nicaragua, Costa Rica and Panama, as well as the eastern islands of the Pacific Ocean off the west coast.
- **WCSA: West Coast South America:** *(geography)* It includes Pacific ports located on the West Coast of South America, from Turbo in the north to Punta Arenas in the south.
- **WD: Working Day:** *(laytime, voyage charter)* See appendix 3, "Laytime Definitions for Charter Parties 2013", term 11.
- **Wear and Tear:** *(general)* The physical damage of an object or equipment, which inevitably results from the passage of time and/or the use of the article.
- **Weather Permitting:** *(laytime, voyage charter)* See (Working Day) Weather Permitting.
- **Weather Working Day of 24 Hours:** *(laytime, voyage charter)* See appendix 3, "Laytime Definitions for Charter Parties 2013", term 17.

- **Weather Working Day of 24 Consecutive Hours:** *(laytime, voyage charter)* See appendix 3, "Laytime Definitions for Charter Parties 2013", term 16.
- **West Coast Africa:** *(geography)* It includes ports on the West Coast of Africa, from Dakar in the north to Douala in the south.
- **West Coast India:** *(geography)* It includes the ports of the West Coast of India, from Kandla in the north to Cape Comorin in the south.
- **West Indies:** *(geography)* It includes ports located in Cuba, Bahamas and the islands Great Inagua, Turks and Caicos. It is an area in the Caribbean Sea which should not be confused with India.
- **West Med: West Mediterranean:** *(geography)* It includes the Western Mediterranean region, outlined from the Straits of Gibraltar in the west to Cape Passero (Sicily) in the east. The dividing notional line in the west joins Gibraltar to Ceuta, while in the east it joins Cape Passero to Misurata (Libya). Thus, North and Southwest coast of Sicily are included in the Western Mediterranean Sea.
- **WHD: Per Working Hatch Per Day or Per Workable Hatch Per Day:** *(laytime, voyage charter, ship, cargo)* See appendix 3, "Laytime Definitions for Charter Parties 2013", term 7.
- **WIBON: Whether In Berth Or Not or Berth Or No Berth:** *(laytime, voyage charter ship, port)* See appendix 3, "Laytime Definitions for Charter Parties 2013", term 27.
- **WIFPON: Whether In Free Pratique Or Not or Vessel Being In Free Pratique Or Not:** *(laytime, voyage charter, ship, port)* The term means that the ship does not have to wait for the completion of the pratique to give notice of readiness (NOR). However, any time lost due to a delay in this process will not count as laytime.
- **WIPON: Whether In Port Or Not:** *(laytime, voyage charter, ship, port)* See appendix 3, "Laytime Definitions for Charter Parties 2013", term 28.
- **Without Prejudice (wp) to my rights:** *(general)* Reserving all my rights. Term that can be used in negotiations to ensure that an act, a fact or an omission does not affect one's rights. It is a term denoting that someone preserves his rights, not "waiving" them (waiver = one's act of voluntarily withdrawing from his rights).
- **WOG: Without Guarantee:** *(general)* Term denoting that information provided is not absolute and binding, e.g. the vessel's speed when negotiating a time charter.
- **(Working Day) Weather Permitting:** *(laytime, voyage charter)* See appendix 3, "Laytime Definitions for Charter Parties 2013", term 18.
- **WS: Worldscale:** *(tanker, freight, voyage charter)* It is a complicated freight scale typically used as a basis for the expression and negotiation of spot tanker rates. See analytically in section 14.3.
- **WSHTC or WHTC: Worldscale Hours Terms and Conditions:** *(tanker, freight, voyage charter)* The phrase is typically used to provide

that a tanker spot charter should comply with the hours, terms and conditions described in the current version of the "Worldscale".
- **WWD: Weather Working Day:** *(laytime, voyage charter)* See appendix 3, "Laytime Definitions for Charter Parties 2013", term 15.
- **W/WO or W/O: With/Without:** *(general)* Having/Not having.
- **WWReady: When and Where Ready:** *(time charter)* It refers to the determination of the time and place of redelivery of the vessel by the charterer to the shipowner.
- **YAR: York-Antwerp Rules:** *(general)* The international rules which constitute the legal framework for the settlement ("adjustment") of general average ("GA").

APPENDIX 1

Gencon '94*

1. Shipbroker	RECOMMENDED THE BALTIC AND INTERNATIONAL MARITIME COUNCIL UNIFORM GENERAL CHARTER (AS REVISED 1922, 1976 and 1994) (To be used for trades for which no specially approved form is in force) CODE NAME: "GENCON"		
			Part I
	2. Place and date		
3. Owners/Place of business (Cl. 1)	4. Charterers/Place of business (Cl. 1)		
5. Vessel's name (Cl. 1)	6. GT/NT (Cl. 1)		
7. DWT all told on summer load line in metric tons (abt.) (Cl. 1)	8. Present position (Cl. 1)		
9. Expected ready to load (abt.) (Cl. 1)			
10. Loading port or place (Cl. 1)	11. Discharging port or place (Cl. 1)		
12. Cargo (also state quantity and margin in Owners' option, if agreed; if full and complete cargo not agreed state "part cargo") (Cl. 1)			
13. Freight rate (also state whether freight prepaid or payable on delivery) (Cl. 4)	14. Freight payment (state currency and method of payment; also beneficiary and bank account) (Cl. 4)		
15. State if vessel's cargo handling gear shall not be used (Cl. 5)	16. Laytime (if separate laytime for load. and disch. is agreed, fill in a) and b). If total laytime for load. and disch., fill in c) only) (Cl. 6)		
17. Shippers/Place of business (Cl. 6)	a) Laytime for loading		
18. Agents (loading) (Cl. 6)	b) Laytime for discharging		
19. Agents (discharging) (Cl. 6)	c) Total laytime for loading and discharging		
20. Demurrage rate and manner payable (loading and discharging) (Cl. 7)	21. Cancelling date (Cl. 9)		
	22. General Average to be adjusted at (Cl. 12)		
23. Freight Tax (state if for the Owners' account) (Cl. 13 (c))	24. Brokerage commission and to whom payable (Cl. 15)		
25. Law and Arbitration (state 19 (a), 19 (b) or 19 (c) of Cl. 19; if 19 (c) agreed also state Place of Arbitration) (if not filled in 19 (a) shall apply) (Cl. 19)			
(a) State maximum amount for small claims/shortened arbitration (Cl. 19)	26. Additional clauses covering special provisions, if agreed		

It is mutually agreed that this Contract shall be performed subject to the conditions contained in this Charter Party which shall include Part I as well as Part II. In the event of a conflict of conditions, the provisions of Part I shall prevail over those of Part II to the extent of such conflict.

Signature (Owners)	Signature (Charterers)

Printed by The BIMCO Charter Party Editor

---

* Reproduced by kind permission of BIMCO.

1. It is agreed between the party mentioned in Box 3 as the Owners of the Vessel 1
named in Box 5, of the GT/NT indicated in Box 6 and carrying about the number 2
of metric tons of deadweight capacity all told on summer loadline stated in Box 3
7, now in position as stated in Box 8 and expected ready to load under this 4
Charter Party about the date indicated in Box 9, and the party mentioned as the 5
Charterers in Box 4 that: 6
The said Vessel shall, as soon as her prior commitments have been completed, 7
proceed to the loading port(s) or place(s) stated in Box 10 or so near thereto as 8
she may safely get and lie always afloat, and there load a full and complete 9
cargo (if shipment of deck cargo agreed same to be at the Charterers' risk and 10
responsibility) as stated in Box 12, which the Charterers bind themselves to 11
ship, and being so loaded the Vessel shall proceed to the discharging port(s) or 12
place(s) stated in Box 11 as ordered on signing Bills of Lading, or so near 13
thereto as she may safely get and lie always afloat, and there deliver the cargo. 14

2. **Owners' Responsibility Clause** 15
The Owners are to be responsible for loss of or damage to the goods or for 16
delay in delivery of the goods only in case the loss, damage or delay has been 17
caused by personal want of due diligence on the part of the Owners or their 18
Manager to make the Vessel in all respects seaworthy and to secure that she is 19
properly manned, equipped and supplied, or by the personal act or default of 20
the Owners or their Manager. 21
And the Owners are not responsible for loss, damage or delay arising from any 22
other cause whatsoever, even from the neglect or default of the Master or crew 23
or some other person employed by the Owners on board or ashore for whose 24
acts they would, but for this Clause, be responsible, or from unseaworthiness of 25
the Vessel on loading or commencement of the voyage or at any time 26
whatsoever. 27

3. **Deviation Clause** 28
The Vessel has liberty to call at any port or ports in any order, for any purpose, 29
to sail without pilots, to tow and/or assist Vessels in all situations, and also to 30
deviate for the purpose of saving life and/or property. 31

4. **Payment of Freight** 32
(a) The freight at the rate stated in Box 13 shall be paid in cash calculated on the 33
intaken quantity of cargo. 34
(b) *Prepaid.* If according to Box 13 freight is to be paid on shipment, it shall be 35
deemed earned and non-returnable, Vessel and/or cargo lost or not lost. 36
Neither the Owners nor their agents shall be required to sign or endorse bills of 37
lading showing freight prepaid unless the freight due to the Owners has 38
actually been paid. 39
(c) *On delivery.* If according to Box 13 freight, or part thereof, is payable at 40
destination it shall not be deemed earned until the cargo is thus delivered. 41
Notwithstanding the provisions under (a), if freight or part thereof is payable on 42
delivery of the cargo the Charterers shall have the option of paying the freight 43
on delivered weight/quantity provided such option is declared before breaking 44
bulk and the weight/quantity can be ascertained by official weighing machine, 45
joint draft survey or tally. 46
Cash for Vessel's ordinary disbursements at the port of loading to be advanced 47
by the Charterers, if required, at highest current rate of exchange, subject to 48
two (2) per cent to cover insurance and other expenses. 49

5. **Loading/Discharging** 50
(a) *Costs/Risks* 51
The cargo shall be brought into the holds, loaded, stowed and/or trimmed, 52
tallied, lashed and/or secured and taken from the holds and discharged by the 53
Charterers, free of any risk, liability and expense whatsoever to the Owners. 54
The Charterers shall provide and lay all dunnage material as required for the 55
proper stowage and protection of the cargo on board, the Owners allowing the 56
use of all dunnage available on board. The Charterers shall be responsible for 57
and pay the cost of removing their dunnage after discharge of the cargo under 58
this Charter Party and time to count until dunnage has been removed. 59
(b) *Cargo Handling Gear* 60
Unless the Vessel is gearless or unless it has been agreed between the parties 61
that the Vessel's gear shall not be used and stated as such in Box 15, the 62
Owners shall throughout the duration of loading/discharging give free use of 63
the Vessel's cargo handling gear and of sufficient motive power to operate all 64
such cargo handling gear. All such equipment to be in good working order. 65
Unless caused by negligence of the stevedores, time lost by breakdown of the 66
Vessel's cargo handling gear or motive power - pro rata the total number of 67
cranes/winches required at that time for the loading/discharging of cargo 68
under this Charter Party - shall not count as laytime or time on demurrage. 69
On request the Owners shall provide free of charge cranemen/winchmen from 70
the crew to operate the Vessel's cargo handling gear, unless local regulations 71
prohibit this, in which latter event shore labourers shall be for the account of the 72
Charterers. Cranemen/winchmen shall be under the Charterers' risk and 73
responsibility and as stevedores to be deemed as their servants but shall 74

always work under the supervision of the Master. 75
(c) *Stevedore Damage* 76
The Charterers shall be responsible for damage (beyond ordinary wear and 77
tear) to any part of the Vessel caused by Stevedores. Such damage shall be 78
notified as soon as reasonably possible by the Master to the Charterers or their 79
agents and to their Stevedores, failing which the Charterers shall not be held 80
responsible. The Master shall endeavour to obtain the Stevedores' written 81
acknowledgement of liability. 82
The Charterers are obliged to repair any stevedore damage prior to completion 83
of the voyage, but must repair stevedore damage affecting the Vessel's 84
seaworthiness or class before the Vessel sails from the port where such 85
damage was caused or found. All additional expenses incurred shall be for the 86
account of the Charterers and any time lost shall be for the account of and shall 87
be paid to the Owners by the Charterers at the demurrage rate. 88

6. **Laytime** 89
(a) *Separate laytime for loading and discharging* 90
The cargo shall be loaded within the number of running days/hours as 91
indicated in Box 16, weather permitting, Sundays and holidays excepted, 92
unless used, in which event time used shall count. 93
The cargo shall be discharged within the number of running days/hours as 94
indicated in Box 16, weather permitting, Sundays and holidays excepted, 95
unless used, in which event time used shall count. 96
(b) *Total laytime for loading and discharging* 97
The cargo shall be loaded and discharged within the number of total running 98
days/hours as indicated in Box 16, weather permitting, Sundays and holidays 99
excepted, unless used, in which event time used shall count. 100
(c) *Commencement of laytime (loading and discharging)* 101
Laytime for loading and discharging shall commence at 13.00 hours, if notice of 102
readiness is given up to and including 12.00 hours, and at 06.00 hours next 103
working day if notice given during office hours after 12.00 hours. Notice of 104
readiness at loading port to be given to the Shippers named in Box 17 or if not 105
named, to the Charterers or their agents named in Box 18. Notice of readiness 106
at the discharging port to be given to the Receivers or, if not known, to the 107
Charterers or their agents named in Box 19. 108
If the loading/discharging berth is not available on the Vessel's arrival at or off 109
the port of loading/discharging, the Vessel shall be entitled to give notice of 110
readiness within ordinary office hours on arrival there, whether in free pratique 111
or not, whether customs cleared or not. Laytime or time on demurrage shall 112
then count as if she were in berth and in all respects ready for loading/ 113
discharging provided that the Master warrants that she is in fact ready in all 114
respects. Time used in moving from the place of waiting to the loading/ 115
discharging berth shall not count as laytime. 116
If, after inspection, the Vessel is found not to be ready in all respects to load/ 117
discharge time lost after the discovery thereof until the Vessel is again ready to 118
load/discharge shall not count as laytime. 119
Time used before commencement of laytime shall count. 120
* Indicate alternative (a) or (b) as agreed, in Box 16. 121

7. **Demurrage** 122
Demurrage at the loading and discharging port is payable by the Charterers at 123
the rate stated in Box 20 in the manner stated in Box 20 per day or pro rata for 124
any part of a day. Demurrage shall fall due day by day and shall be payable 125
upon receipt of the Owners' invoice. 126
In the event the demurrage is not paid in accordance with the above, the 127
Owners shall give the Charterers 96 running hours written notice to rectify the 128
failure. If the demurrage is not paid at the expiration of this time limit and if the 129
vessel is in or at the loading port, the Owners are entitled at any time to 130
terminate the Charter Party and claim damages for any losses caused thereby. 131

8. **Lien Clause** 132
The Owners shall have a lien on the cargo and on all sub-freights payable in 133
respect of the cargo, for freight, deadfreight, demurrage, claims for damages 134
and for all other amounts due under this Charter Party including costs of 135
recovering same. 136

9. **Cancelling Clause** 137
(a) Should the Vessel not be ready to load (whether in berth or not) on the 138
cancelling date indicated in Box 21, the Charterers shall have the option of 139
cancelling this Charter Party. 140
(b) Should the Owners anticipate that, despite the exercise of due diligence, 141
the Vessel will not be ready to load by the cancelling date, they shall notify the 142
Charterers thereof without delay stating the expected date of the Vessel's 143
readiness to load and asking whether the Charterers will exercise their option 144
of cancelling the Charter Party, or agree to a new cancelling date. 145
Such option must be declared by the Charterers within 48 running hours after 146
the receipt of the Owners' notice. If the Charterers do not exercise their option 147
of cancelling, then this Charter Party shall be deemed to be amended such that 148

the seventh day after the new readiness date stated in the Owners' notification 149
to the Charterers shall be the new cancelling date. 150
The provisions of sub-clause (b) of this Clause shall operate only once, and in 151
case of the Vessel's further delay, the Charterers shall have the option of 152
cancelling the Charter Party as per sub-clause (a) of this Clause. 153

10. Bills of Lading 154
Bills of Lading shall be presented and signed by the Master as per the 155
"Congenbill" Bill of Lading form, Edition 1994, without prejudice to this Charter 156
Party, or by the Owners' agents provided written authority has been given by 157
Owners to the agents, a copy of which is to be furnished to the Charterers. The 158
Charterers shall indemnify the Owners against all consequences or liabilities 159
that may arise from the signing of bills of lading as presented to the extent that 160
the terms or contents of such bills of lading impose or result in the imposition of 161
more onerous liabilities upon the Owners than those assumed by the Owners 162
under this Charter Party. 163

11. Both-to-Blame Collision Clause 164
If the Vessel comes into collision with another vessel as a result of the 165
negligence of the other vessel and any act, neglect or default of the Master, 166
Mariner, Pilot or the servants of the Owners in the navigation or in the 167
management of the Vessel, the owners of the cargo carried hereunder will 168
indemnify the Owners against all loss or liability to the other or non-carrying 169
vessel or her owners in so far as such loss or liability represents loss of, or 170
damage to, or any claim whatsoever of the owners of said cargo, paid or 171
payable by the other or non-carrying vessel or her owners to the owners of said 172
cargo and set-off, recouped or recovered by the other or non-carrying vessel 173
or her owners as part of their claim against the carrying Vessel or the Owners. 174
The foregoing provisions shall also apply where the owners, operators or those 175
in charge of any vessel or vessels or objects other than, or in addition to, the 176
colliding vessels or objects are at fault in respect of a collision or contact. 177

12. General Average and New Jason Clause 178
General Average shall be adjusted in London unless otherwise agreed in Box 179
22 according to York-Antwerp Rules 1994 and any subsequent modification 180
thereof. Proprietors of cargo to pay the cargo's share in the general expenses 181
even if same have been necessitated through neglect or default of the Owners' 182
servants (see Clause 2). 183
If General Average is to be adjusted in accordance with the law and practice of 184
the United States of America, the following Clause shall apply: "In the event of 185
accident, danger, damage or disaster before or after the commencement of the 186
voyage, resulting from any cause whatsoever, whether due to negligence or 187
not, for which, or for the consequence of which, the Owners are not 188
responsible, by statute, contract or otherwise, the cargo, shippers, consignees 189
or the owners of the cargo shall contribute with the Owners in General Average 190
to the payment of any sacrifices, losses or expenses of a General Average 191
nature that may be made or incurred and shall pay salvage and special charges 192
incurred in respect of the cargo. If a salving vessel is owned or operated by the 193
Owners, salvage shall be paid for as fully as if the said salving vessel or vessels 194
belonged to strangers. Such deposit as the Owners, or their agents, may deem 195
sufficient to cover the estimated contribution of the goods and any salvage and 196
special charges thereon shall, if required, be made by the cargo, shippers, 197
consignees or owners of the goods to the Owners before delivery.". 198

13. Taxes and Dues Clause 199
(a) *On Vessel* -The Owners shall pay all dues, charges and taxes customarily 200
levied on the Vessel, howsoever the amount thereof may be assessed. 201
(b) *On cargo* -The Charterers shall pay all dues, charges, duties and taxes 202
customarily levied on the cargo, howsoever the amount thereof may be 203
assessed. 204
(c) *On freight* -Unless otherwise agreed in Box 23, taxes levied on the freight 205
shall be for the Charterers' account. 206

14. Agency 207
In every case the Owners shall appoint their own Agent both at the port of 208
loading and the port of discharge. 209

15. Brokerage 210
A brokerage commission at the rate stated in Box 24 on the freight, dead-freight 211
and demurrage earned is due to the party mentioned in Box 24. 212
In case of non-execution 1/3 of the brokerage on the estimated amount of 213
freight to be paid by the party responsible for such non-execution to the 214
Brokers as indemnity for the latter's expenses and work. In case of more 215
voyages the amount of indemnity to be agreed. 216

16. General Strike Clause 217
(a) If there is a strike or lock-out affecting or preventing the actual loading of the 218
cargo, or any part of it, when the Vessel is ready to proceed from her last port or 219

at any time during the voyage to the port or ports of loading or after her arrival 220
there, the Master or the Owners may ask the Charterers to declare, that they 221
agree to reckon the laydays as if there were no strike or lock-out. Unless the 222
Charterers have given such declaration in writing (by telegram, if necessary) 223
within 24 hours, the Owners shall have the option of cancelling this Charter 224
Party. If part cargo has already been loaded, the Owners must proceed with 225
same, (freight payable on loaded quantity only) having liberty to complete with 226
other cargo on the way for their own account. 227
(b) If there is a strike or lock-out affecting or preventing the actual discharging 228
of the cargo on or after the Vessel's arrival at or off port of discharge and same 229
has not been settled within 48 hours, the Charterers shall have the option of 230
keeping the Vessel waiting until such strike or lock-out is at an end against 231
paying half demurrage after expiration of the time provided for discharging 232
until the strike or lock-out terminates and thereafter full demurrage shall be 233
payable until the completion of discharging, or of ordering the Vessel to a safe 234
port where she can safely discharge without risk of being detained by strike or 235
lock-out. Such orders to be given within 48 hours after the Master or the 236
Owners have given notice to the Charterers of the strike or lock-out affecting 237
the discharge. On delivery of the cargo at such port, all conditions of this 238
Charter Party and of the Bill of Lading shall apply and the Vessel shall receive 239
the same freight as if she had discharged at the original port of destination, 240
except that if the distance to the substituted port exceeds 100 nautical miles, 241
the freight on the cargo delivered at the substituted port to be increased in 242
proportion. 243
(c) Except for the obligations described above, neither the Charterers nor the 244
Owners shall be responsible for the consequences of any strikes or lock-outs 245
preventing or affecting the actual loading or discharging of the cargo. 246

17. War Risks ("Voywar 1993") 247
(1) For the purpose of this Clause, the words: 248
(a) The "Owners" shall include the shipowners, bareboat charterers, 249
disponent owners, managers or other operators who are charged with the 250
management of the Vessel, and the Master; and 251
(b) "War Risks" shall include any war (whether actual or threatened), act of 252
war, civil war, hostilities, revolution, rebellion, civil commotion, warlike 253
operations, the laying of mines (whether actual or reported), acts of piracy, 254
acts of terrorists, acts of hostility or malicious damage, blockades 255
(whether imposed against all Vessels or imposed selectively against 256
Vessels of certain flags or ownership, or against certain cargoes or crews 257
or otherwise howsoever), by any person, body, terrorist or political group, 258
or the Government of any state whatsoever, which, in the reasonable 259
judgement of the Master and/or the Owners, may be dangerous or are 260
likely to be or to become dangerous to the Vessel, her cargo, crew or other 261
persons on board the Vessel. 262
(2) If at any time before the Vessel commences loading, it appears that, in the 263
reasonable judgement of the Master and/or the Owners, performance of 264
the Contract of Carriage, or any part of it, may expose, or is likely to expose, 265
the Vessel, her cargo, crew or other persons on board the Vessel to War 266
Risks, the Owners may give notice to the Charterers cancelling this 267
Contract of Carriage, or may refuse to perform such part of it as may 268
expose, or may be likely to expose, the Vessel, her cargo, crew or other 269
persons on board the Vessel to War Risks; provided always that if this 270
Contract of Carriage provides that loading or discharging is to take place 271
within a range of ports, and at the port or ports nominated by the Charterers 272
the Vessel, her cargo, crew, or other persons onboard the Vessel may be 273
exposed, or may be likely to be exposed, to War Risks, the Owners shall 274
first require the Charterers to nominate any other safe port which lies 275
within the range for loading or discharging, and may only cancel this 276
Contract of Carriage if the Charterers shall not have nominated such safe 277
port or ports within 48 hours of receipt of notice of such requirement. 278
(3) The Owners shall not be required to continue to load cargo for any voyage, 279
or to sign Bills of Lading for any port or place, or to proceed or continue on 280
any voyage, or on any part thereof, or to proceed through any canal or 281
waterway, or to proceed to or remain at any port or place whatsoever, 282
where it appears, either after the loading of the cargo commences, or at 283
any stage of the voyage thereafter before the discharge of the cargo is 284
completed, that, in the reasonable judgement of the Master and/or the 285
Owners, the Vessel, her cargo (or any part thereof), crew or other persons 286
on board the Vessel (or any one or more of them) may be, or are likely to be, 287
exposed to War Risks. If it should so appear, the Owners may by notice 288
request the Charterers to nominate a safe port for the discharge of the 289
cargo or any part thereof, and if within 48 hours of the receipt of such 290
notice, the Charterers shall not have nominated such a port, the Owners 291
may discharge the cargo at any safe port of their choice (including the port 292
of loading) in complete fulfilment of the Contract of Carriage. The Owners 293
shall be entitled to recover from the Charterers the extra expenses of such 294
discharge and, if the discharge takes place at any port other than the 295
loading port, to receive the full freight as though the cargo had been 296

carried to the discharging port and if the extra distance exceeds 100 miles, 297
to additional freight which shall be the same percentage of the freight 298
contracted for as the percentage which the extra distance represents to 299
the distance of the normal and customary route, the Owners having a lien 300
on the cargo for such expenses and freight. 301

(4) If at any stage of the voyage after the loading of the cargo commences, it 302
appears that, in the reasonable judgement of the Master and/or the 303
Owners, the Vessel, her cargo, crew or other persons on board the Vessel 304
may be, or are likely to be, exposed to War Risks on any part of the route 305
(including any canal or waterway) which is normally and customarily used 306
in a voyage of the nature contracted for, and there is another longer route 307
to the discharging port, the Owners shall give notice to the Charterers that 308
this route will be taken. In this event the Owners shall be entitled, if the total 309
extra distance exceeds 100 miles, to additional freight which shall be the 310
same percentage of the freight contracted for as the percentage which the 311
extra distance represents to the distance of the normal and customary 312
route. 313

(5) The Vessel shall have liberty:- 314
(a) to comply with all orders, directions, recommendations or advice as to 315
departure, arrival, routes, sailing in convoy, ports of call, stoppages, 316
destinations, discharge of cargo, delivery or in any way whatsoever which 317
are given by the Government of the Nation under whose flag the Vessel 318
sails, or other Government to whose laws the Owners are subject, or any 319
other Government which so requires, or any body or group acting with the 320
power to compel compliance with their orders or directions; 321
(b) to comply with the orders, directions or recommendations of any war 322
risks underwriters who have the authority to give the same under the terms 323
of the war risks insurance; 324
(c) to comply with the terms of any resolution of the Security Council of the 325
United Nations, any directives of the European Community, the effective 326
orders of any other Supranational body which has the right to issue and 327
give the same, and with national laws aimed at enforcing the same to which 328
the Owners are subject, and to obey the orders and directions of those who 329
are charged with their enforcement; 330
(d) to discharge at any other port any cargo or part thereof which may 331
render the Vessel liable to confiscation as a contraband carrier; 332
(e) to call at any other port to change the crew or any part thereof or other 333
persons on board the Vessel when there is reason to believe that they may 334
be subject to internment, imprisonment or other sanctions; 335
(f) where cargo has not been loaded or has been discharged by the 336
Owners under any provisions of this Clause, to load other cargo for the 337
Owners' own benefit and carry it to any other port or ports whatsoever, 338
whether backwards or forwards or in a contrary direction to the ordinary or 339
customary route. 340

(6) If in compliance with any of the provisions of sub-clauses (2) to (5) of this 341
Clause anything is done or not done, such shall not be deemed to be a 342
deviation, but shall be considered as due fulfilment of the Contract of 343
Carriage. 344

18. General Ice Clause 345
Port of loading 346
(a) In the event of the loading port being inaccessible by reason of ice when the 347
Vessel is ready to proceed from her last port or at any time during the voyage or 348
on the Vessel's arrival or in case frost sets in after the Vessel's arrival, the 349
Master for fear of being frozen in is at liberty to leave without cargo, and this 350
Charter Party shall be null and void. 351
(b) If during loading the Master, for fear of the Vessel being frozen in, deems it 352
advisable to leave, he has liberty to do so with what cargo he has on board and 353
to proceed to any other port or ports with option of completing cargo for the 354
Owners' benefit for any port or ports including port of discharge. Any part 355
cargo thus loaded under this Charter Party to be forwarded to destination at the 356
Vessel's expense but against payment of freight, provided that no extra 357
expenses be thereby caused to the Charterers, freight being paid on quantity 358
delivered (in proportion if lumpsum), all other conditions as per this Charter 359
Party. 360
(c) In case of more than one loading port, and if one or more of the ports are 361
closed by ice, the Master or the Owners to be at liberty either to load the part 362
cargo at the open port and fill up elsewhere for their own account as under 363
section (b) or to declare the Charter Party null and void unless the Charterers 364
agree to load full cargo at the open port. 365

Port of discharge 366
(a) Should ice prevent the Vessel from reaching port of discharge the 367
Charterers shall have the option of keeping the Vessel waiting until the re- 368
opening of navigation and paying demurrage or of ordering the Vessel to a safe 369
and immediately accessible port where she can safely discharge without risk of 370
detention by ice. Such orders to be given within 48 hours after the Master or the 371
Owners have given notice to the Charterers of the impossibility of reaching port 372

of destination. 373
(b) If during discharging the Master for fear of the Vessel being frozen in deems 374
it advisable to leave, he has liberty to do so with what cargo he has on board and 375
to proceed to the nearest accessible port where she can safely discharge. 376
(c) On delivery of the cargo at such port, all conditions of the Bill of Lading shall 377
apply and the Vessel shall receive the same freight as if she had discharged at 378
the original port of destination, except that if the distance of the substituted port 379
exceeds 100 nautical miles, the freight on the cargo delivered at the substituted 380
port to be increased in proportion. 381

19. Law and Arbitration 382
* (a) This Charter Party shall be governed by and construed in accordance with 383
English law and any dispute arising out of this Charter Party shall be referred to 384
arbitration in London in accordance with the Arbitration Acts 1950 and 1979 or 385
any statutory modification or re-enactment thereof for the time being in force. 386
Unless the parties agree upon a sole arbitrator, one arbitrator shall be 387
appointed by each party and the arbitrators so appointed shall appoint a third 388
arbitrator, the decision of the three-man tribunal thus constituted or any two of 389
them, shall be final. On the receipt by one party of the nomination in writing of 390
the other party's arbitrator, that party shall appoint their arbitrator within 391
fourteen days, failing which the decision of the single arbitrator appointed shall 392
be final. 393
For disputes where the total amount claimed by either party does not exceed 394
the amount stated in Box 25** the arbitration shall be conducted in accordance 395
with the Small Claims Procedure of the London Maritime Arbitrators 396
Association. 397
* (b) This Charter Party shall be governed by and construed in accordance with 398
Title 9 of the United States Code and the Maritime Law of the United States and 399
should any dispute arise out of this Charter Party, the matter in dispute shall be 400
referred to three persons at New York, one to be appointed by each of the 401
parties hereto, and the third by the two so chosen; their decision or that of any 402
two of them shall be final, and for purpose of enforcing any award, this 403
agreement may be made a rule of the Court. The proceedings shall be 404
conducted in accordance with the rules of the Society of Maritime Arbitrators, 405
Inc.. 406
For disputes where the total amount claimed by either party does not exceed 407
the amount stated in Box 25** the arbitration shall be conducted in accordance 408
with the Shortened Arbitration Procedure of the Society of Maritime Arbitrators, 409
Inc. 410
* (c) Any dispute arising out of this Charter Party shall be referred to arbitration at 411
the place indicated in Box 25, subject to the procedures applicable there. The 412
laws of the place indicated in Box 25 shall govern this Charter Party. 413
(d) If Box 25 in Part 1 is not filled in, sub-clause (a) of this Clause shall apply. 414
* (a), (b) and (c) are alternatives; indicate alternative agreed in Box 25. 415
** Where no figure is supplied in Box 25 in Part 1, this provision only shall be void but 416
the other provisions of this Clause shall have full force and remain in effect. 417

APPENDIX 2

Shellvoy 6*

Issued March 2005, Version 1.1 Apr06

Code word for this Charter Party
"SHELLVOY 6"

VOYAGE CHARTER PARTY
LONDON,   20

PREAMBLE	1

IT IS THIS DAY AGREED between 2

of .... (hereinafter referred to as "Owners"), being owners /disponent owners of the 3

motor/steam tank vessel called .... with an IMO number of 4

(hereinafter referred to as "the vessel") 5

and .... of 6

(hereinafter referred to as "Charterers"): 7

that the service for which provision is herein made shall be subject to the terms and conditions of this Charter which includes Part I, ... 8
Part II and Part III. In the event of any conflict between the provisions of Part I, Part II and Part III hereof. the provisions of Part I shall prevail. 9

PART I 10

(A) Description of vessel

(I) vessel   Owners warrant that at the date hereof, and from the time when the obligation to proceed to the loadport(s) attaches, the 11 12

(i)   Is classed 13

(ii) (a)   Has a deadweight of .... tonnes (1000 kg) on a salt-water draft on assigned summer freeboard of .... m. and if 14
applicable, ... 15

(b)   Has on board documentation showing the following additional drafts and deadweights 16

(iii)   Has capacity for cargo of .... m³ 17

(iv)   Is fully fitted with heating systems for all cargo tanks capable of maintaining cargo at a temperature of up to 18
degrees Celsius and can accept a cargo temperature on loading of up to a maximum of .... degrees Celcius. 19

(v)   Has tanks coated as follows: 20

(vi)   Is equipped with cranes/derricks capable of lifting to and supporting at the vessel's port and starboard manifolds submarine 21
hoses of up to .... tonnes (1000 kg) in weight. 22

(vii)   Can discharge a full cargo (whether homogenous or multi grade) either within 24 hours, or can maintain a back pressure 23
of 100 PSI at the vessel's manifold and Owners warrant such minimum performance provided receiving facilities permit 24
and subject always to the obligation of utmost despatch set out in <u>Part II, clause 3 (1)</u> 25
The discharge warranty shall only be applicable provided the kinematic viscosity does not exceed 600 centistokes at the 26
discharge temperature required by Charterers. If the kinematic viscosity only exceeds 600 centistokes on part of the cargo 27
or particular grade(s) then the discharge warranty shall continue to apply to all other cargo/grades. 28

(viii)   Has or will have carried, for the named Charterers, the following three cargoes (all grades to be identified) immediately 29
prior to loading under this Charter:- 30
Last Cargo/charterer 31
2nd Last Cargo/charterer 32
3rd Last Cargo/charterer 33

(ix)   Has a crude oil washing system complying with the requirements of the International Convention for the 34
Prevention of Pollution from Ships 1973 as modified by the Protocol of 1978 ("MARPOL 73/78"). 35

(x)   Has an operational inert gas system and is equipped for and able to carry out closed sampling/ullaging/loading and 36
discharging operations in full compliance with the International Safety Guide for Oil Tankers and Terminals ("ISGOTT") 37
guidelines current at the date of this Charter. 38

(xi)   Has on board all papers and certificates required by any applicable law, in force as at the date of this Charter, to enable the 39
vessel to perform the charter service without any delay. 40

* Reproduced by kind permission of Shell International Trading & Shipping Company Limited.

(xii)	Is entered in the	P&I Club, being a member of the International Group of P&I Clubs.	41

(xiii)   Has in full force and effect Hull and Machinery insurance placed through reputable Brokers on Institute Time   42
Clauses-Hull dated   for the value of   43

(xiv)   Complies with the latest edition of the Oil Companies International Marine Forum ("OCIMF") standards for oil tankers'   44
manifolds and associated equipment applicable to its size for cargo manifolds and vapour recovery systems.   45

(xv)   Is equipped to comply with, and is operated in accordance with, and has on board, the latest edition of the International   46
Chamber of Shipping ("ICS") and/or OCIMF guidelines / publications covering: 47
       (a) Ship to Ship Operations   48
       (b) ISGOTT   49
       (c) Clean Seas Guide for Oil Tankers   50
       (d) Bridge Procedure Guide   51

(II)   Throughout the charter service, Owners shall ensure that the vessel shall be maintained, or that they take all steps   52
necessary to promptly restore vessel to be, within the description in Part I clause (A)(I) and any questionnaires requested by   53
Charterers or within information provided by Owners.   54

(III)   Owners warrant that any information provided on any Questionnaire(s) requested by Charterers or any other vessel   55
information/details provided by Owners to Charterers is always complete and correct as at the date hereof, and from the time when   56
the obligation to proceed to the loadport attaches and throughout the charter service. This information is an integral part of this   57
Charter but if there is any conflict between the contents of the Questionnaire(s), or information provided by Owners, and any other   58
provisions of this Charter then such other provisions shall govern.   59

(B) Position/ Readiness   Now   Expected ready to load   60

In addition to the above details on the position of the vessel Owners will advise Charterers of the known programme, including any   61
contractual options available to the Charterers in Part I clause (A)(I) (viii) above between current position up to expected ready to   62
load date at Charterers nominated or indicated first load port/area. Owners will not, unless with Charterers' prior consent, negotiate   63
or enter into any business or give current Charterers any further options that may affect or alter the programme of the vessel as given   64
in this clause.   65

(C) Laydays   Commencing Noon Local Time on   (Commencement Date)   66

Terminating Noon Local Time on   (Termination Date)   67

(D) Loading port(s)/ Range   68

(E) Discharging port(s)/ Range   69

(F) Cargo description   Charterers' option   70

Owners warrant that where different grades of cargo are carried pursuant to this Part I clause (F), they will be kept in complete   71
segregation from each other during loading, transit, and discharge, to include the use of different pumps/lines for each grade. If,   72
however, Charterers so require it, the vessel may be required to: 73

(a) co-mingle different grades of cargo providing such grades fall within the cargo description set out in this Part I clause (F);   74
(b) otherwise breach the vessel's natural segregation;   75
(c) add dye to the cargo after loading, and/or   76
(d) carry out such other cargo operations as Charterers may reasonably require as long as the vessel is capable of such operations   77

provided that the Charterers will indemnify Owners for any loss damage delay or expense caused by following Charterers'   78
instructions, except to the extent that such loss damage delay or expense could have been avoided by the exercise of due diligence   79
by Owners.   80

(G) Freight   At   % of the rate for the voyage as provided for in the New Worldwide Tanker Nominal Freight Scale current at the date of   81

rate	commencement of loading (hereinafter referred to as "Worldscale") per ton (2240 lbs)/tonne (1000 Kg) or, if agreed, the following	82
	lumpsum amount(s)/or freight per tonne for named load and discharge area(s)/port(s) combinations	83
(H) Freight		84
payable to		
(I) Laytime	running hours	85
(J) Demurrage		86
per day (or		
pro rata)		
(K) ETAs	All radio/telex/e-mail messages sent by the master to Charterers shall be addressed to	87
	All telexes must begin with the vessel name at the start of the subject line (no inverted commas, or use of MT / SS preceding the	88
	vessel name)	89
(L) Speed	The vessel shall perform the ballast passage with utmost despatch and the laden passage at knots weather and safe navigation	90
	permitting at a consumption of tonnes of Fueloil (state grade) per day.	91
	Charterers shall have the option to instruct the vessel to increase speed with Charterers reimbursing Owners for the additional	92
	bunkers consumed, at replacement cost.	93
	Charterers shall also have the option to instruct the vessel to reduce speed on laden passage. Additional voyage time caused by such	94
	instructions shall count against laytime or demurrage, if on demurrage, and the value of any bunkers saved shall be deducted from	95
	any demurrage claim Owners may have under this Charter with the value being calculated at original purchase price.	96
	Owners shall provide documentation to fully support the claims and calculations under this clause.	97
(M) Worldscale	Worldscale Terms and Conditions apply / do not apply to this Charter. [delete as applicable]	98
(N) Casualty/	In the event of an accident / marine casualty involving the vessel, Owners' technical managers can be contacted on a 24 hour basis	99
Accident	as follows:	100
contacts	Company Full Name:	101
	Contact Person:	102
	Full Address:	103
	Telephone Number:	104
	Fax Number:	105
	Telex Number:	106
	Email Address:	107
	24 Hour Emergency Telephone number:	108
(O) Special		109
provisions		
Signatures	IN WITNESS WHEREOF, the parties have caused this Charter consisting of the Preamble, Parts I, II and III to be executed as of the	110
	day and year first above written.	111
	By	112
	By	113

PART II

Condition of vessel	1. Owners shall exercise due diligence to ensure that from the time when the obligation to proceed to the	1

Condition of
vessel

1. Owners shall exercise due diligence to ensure that from the time when the obligation to proceed to the   1
loading port(s) attaches and throughout the charter service -   2
    (a)   the vessel and her hull, machinery, boilers, tanks, equipment and facilities are in good order and   3
          condition and in every way equipped and fit for the service required; and   4
    (b)   the vessel has a full and efficient complement of master, officers and crew and the senior officers shall   5
          be fully conversant in spoken and written English language   6
and to ensure that before and at the commencement of any laden voyage the vessel is in all respects fit to carry the   7
cargo specified in Part I clause (F). For the avoidance of doubt, references to equipment in this Charter shall include   8
but not be limited to computers and computer systems, and such equipment shall (inter alia) be required to continue   9
to function, and not suffer a loss of functionality and accuracy (whether logical or mathematical) as a result of the   10
run date or dates being processed.   11

Cleanliness
of tanks

2. Whilst loading, carrying and discharging the cargo the master shall at all times keep the tanks, lines and   12
pumps of the vessel always clean for the cargo. Unless otherwise agreed between Owners and Charterers the vessel   13
shall present for loading with cargo tanks ready and, subject to the following paragraphs, if vessel is fitted with Inert   14
Gas System ("IGS"), fully inerted.   15
      Charterers shall have the right to inspect vessel's tanks prior to loading and the vessel shall abide by   16
Charterers' instructions with regard to tank or tanks which the vessel is required to present ready for entry and   17
inspection. If Charterer's inspector is not satisfied with the cleanliness of the vessel's tanks, Owners shall clean   18
them in their time and at their expense to the satisfaction of Charterers' inspector, provided that nothing herein shall   19
affect the responsibilities and obligations of the master and Owners in respect of the loading, carriage and care of   20
cargo under this Charter nor prejudice the rights of Charterers, should any contamination or damage subsequently be   21
found, to contend that the same was caused by inadequate cleaning and/or some breach of this or any other clause   22
of this Charter.   23
      Notwithstanding that the vessel, if equipped with IGS, shall present for loading with all cargo tanks fully   24
inerted, any time used for de-inerting (provided that such de-inerting takes place after laytime or demurrage time has   25
commenced or would, but for this clause, have commenced) and/or re-inerting those tanks that at Charterers'   26
specific request were gas freed for inspection, shall count as laytime or if on demurrage as demurrage, provided the   27
tank or tanks inspected are found to be suitable. In such case Charterers will reimburse Owners for bunkers   28
consumed for de-inerting/re-inerting, at replacement cost.   29
      If the vessel's tanks are inspected and rejected, time used for de-inerting shall not count towards laytime or   30
demurrage, and laytime or demurrage time shall not commence or recommence, as the case may be, until the tanks   31
have been re-inspected, approved by Charterers' inspector, and re-inerted.   32

Voyage

3. (1) Subject to the provisions of this Charter the vessel shall perform her service with utmost despatch and   33
shall proceed to such berths as Charterers may specify, in any port or ports within Part I clause (D) nominated by   34
Charterers, or so near thereunto as she may safely get and there, always safely afloat, load the cargo specified in   35
Part I clause (F) of this Charter, but not in excess of the maximum quantity consistent with the International Load   36
Line Convention for the time being in force and, being so loaded, proceed as ordered on signing bills of lading to   37
such berths as Charterers may specify, in any port or ports within Part I clause (E) nominated by Charterers, or so   38
near thereunto as she may safely get and there, always safely afloat, discharge the cargo.   39
      Charterers shall nominate loading and discharging ports, and shall specify loading and discharging berths   40
and, where loading or discharging is interrupted, shall provide fresh orders in relation thereto.   41
In addition Charterers shall have the option at any time of ordering the vessel to safe areas at sea for wireless orders.   42
Any delay or deviation arising as a result of the exercise of such option shall be compensated by Charterers in   43
accordance with the terms of Part II clause 26 (1).   44
      (2) Owners shall be responsible for and indemnify Charterers for any time, costs, delays or loss including but   45
not limited to use of laytime, demurrage, deviation expenses, replacement tonnage, lightening costs and associated   46
fees and expenses due to any failure whatsoever to comply fully with Charterers' voyage instructions and clauses in   47
this Charter which specify requirements concerning Voyage Instructions and/ or Owners'/masters' duties including,   48
without limitation to the generality of the foregoing, loading more cargo than permitted under the International Load   49
Line Convention, for the time being in force, or for not leaving sufficient space for expansion of cargo or loading   50
more or less cargo than Charterers specified or for not loading/discharging in accordance with Charterers'   51
instructions regarding the cargo quantity or draft requirements.   52
This clause 3(2) shall have effect notwithstanding the provision of Part II clause 32 (a) of this Charter or Owners'   53
defences under the Hague-Visby Rules.   54
      (3) Owners shall always employ pilots for berthing and unberthing of vessels at all ports and/or berths under   55
this Charter unless prior exemption is given by correct and authorised personnel. Owners to confirm in writing if   56
they have been exempt from using a pilot and provide Charterers with the details, including but not limited to, the   57
authorising organisation with person's name.   58
      (4) Without prejudice to the provisions of sub-clause (2) of this clause, and unless a specific prior agreement   59

	exists, if a conflict arises between terminal orders and Charterers' voyage instructions, the master shall stop cargo	60
	operations, and/or other operations under dispute, and contact Charterers immediately. Terminal orders shall never	61
	supersede Charterers' voyage instructions and any conflict shall be resolved prior to resumption of cargo, or other,	62
	operations in dispute. Where such a conflict arises the vessel shall not sail from the port or resume cargo operations,	63
	and/or other operations under dispute, until Charterers have directed the vessel to do so.	64
	Time spent resolving the vessel/terminal conflict will count as laytime or demurrrage except that failure of	65
	Owners/master to comply with the procedure set forth above shall result in the deduction from laytime or	66
	demurrage time of the time used in resolving the vessel/terminal instruction conflict	67
	(5) In this Charter, "berth" means any berth, wharf, dock, anchorage, submarine line, a position alongside	68
	any vessel or lighter or any other loading or discharging point whatsoever to which Charterers are entitled to order	69
	the vessel hereunder, and "port" means any port or location at sea to which the vessel may proceed in accordance	70
	with the terms of this Charter.	71
Safe berth	4. Charterers shall exercise due diligence to order the vessel only to ports and berths which are safe for	72
	the vessel and to ensure that transhipment operations conform to standards not less than those set out in the latest	73
	edition of ICS/OCIMF Ship-to-Ship Transfer Guide (Petroleum). Notwithstanding anything contained in this	74
	Charter, Charterers do not warrant the safety of any port, berth or transhipment operation and Charterers shall	75
	not be liable for loss or damage arising from any unsafety if they can prove that due diligence was exercised in the	76
	giving of the order or if such loss or damage was caused by an act of war or civil commotion within the trading	77
	areas defined in Part 1 clauses (D/E).	78
Freight	5. (1) Freight shall be earned concurrently with delivery of cargo at the nominated discharging port or ports	79
	and shall be paid by Charterers to Owners without any deductions, except as may be required in the Singapore	80
	Income Tax Act and/or under Part II clause 48 and/or under clause 55 and/or under Part III clause 4(a), in United	81
	States Dollars at the rate(s) specified in Part I clause (G) on the gross bill of lading quantity as furnished by the	82
	shipper (subject to Part II clauses 8 and 40), upon receipt by Charterers of notice of completion of final discharge of	83
	cargo, provided that no freight shall be payable on any quantity in excess of the maximum quantity consistent with	84
	the International Load Line Convention for the time being in force.	85
	If the vessel is ordered to proceed on a voyage for which a fixed differential is provided in Worldscale, such	86
	fixed differential shall be payable without applying the percentage referred to in Part I clause (G).	87
	If cargo is carried between ports and/or by an agreed route for which no freight rate is expressly quoted in	88
	Worldscale, then the parties shall, in the absence of agreement as to the appropriate freight rate, apply to	89
	Worldscale Association (London) Ltd., or Worldscale Association (NYC) Inc., for the determination of an	90
	appropriate Worldscale freight rate. If Owners or master unilaterally elect to proceed by a route that is different to	91
	that specified in Worldscale, or different to a route agreed between Owners and Charterers, freight shall always be	92
	paid in accordance with the Worldscale rate as published or in accordance with any special rate applicable for the	93
	agreed route.	94
	Save in respect of the time when freight is earned, the location of any transhipment at sea pursuant to Part II	95
	clause 26(2) shall not be an additional nominated port, unless otherwise agreed, for the purposes of this Charter	96
	(including this clause 5) and the freight rate for the voyage shall be the same as if such transhipment had not taken	97
	place.	98
	(2) If the freight in Part I clause (G) is a lumpsum amount and such lumpsum freight is connected with a	99
	specific number of load and discharge ports given in Part I clause (L) and Owners agree that Charterers may order	100
	the vessel to additional load and/or discharge ports not covered by the agreed lumpsum freight, the following shall	101
	apply:	102
	(a) the first load port and the final discharge port shall be deemed to be the port(s) that form the voyage and	103
	on which the lumpsum freight included in Part I clause (G) refers to;	104
	(b) freight for such additional ports shall be calculated on basis of deviation. Deviation shall be calculated	105
	on the difference in distance between the specified voyage (for which freight is agreed) and the voyage	106
	actually performed.	107
	BP Shipping Marine Distance Tables (2004), produced by AtoBriac shall be used in both cases.	108
	Deviation time/bunker consumption shall be calculated using the charter speed and bunker consumption as per the	109
	speed and consumptions given in Part I clause(L) of this Charter.	110
	Deviation time and time spent in port shall be charged at the demurrage rate in Part I clause (J) of this Charter	111
	except that time used in port which would otherwise qualify for half rate laytime and/or demurrage under Part II	112
	clause (15) (2) of this Charter will be charged at half rate.	113
	Additional bunkers consumed shall be paid at replacement cost, and actual port costs shall be paid as incurred.	114
	Such deviation costs shall be paid against Owners' fully documented claim.	115
Claims, dues and other	6. (1) Dues and other charges upon the vessel, including those assessed by reference to the quantity of cargo	116
	loaded or discharged, and any taxes on freight whatsoever shall be paid by Owners, and dues and other charges	117

PART II

| charges | upon the cargo shall be paid by Charterers. However, notwithstanding the foregoing, where under a provision of | 118 |

charges — upon the cargo shall be paid by Charterers. However, notwithstanding the foregoing, where under a provision of Worldscale a due or charge is expressly for the account of Owners or Charterers then such due or charge shall be payable in accordance with such provision. 118–120

(2) Any costs including those itemised under applicable "Worldscale" as being for Charterers' account shall, unless otherwise instructed by Charterers, be paid by Owners and reimbursed by Charterers against Owners' fully documented claim. 121–123

(3) Charterers shall be discharged and released from all liability in respect of any charges/claims (other than demurrage and Worldscale charges/dues and indemnity claims) including but not limited to additional bunkers, detention, deviation, shifting, heating, deadfreight, speed up, slow down, drifting, port costs, additional freight, insurance, Owner may send to Charterers under this Charter unless any such charges/claims have been received by Charterer in writing, fully and correctly documented, within ninety (90) days from completion of discharge of the cargo concerned under this Charter. Part II clause 15 (3) of this Charter covers the notification and fully documented claim procedure for demurrage. 124–130

(4) If, after disconnection of hoses, the vessel remains at berth for vessel's purposes, Owners shall be responsible for all direct and indirect costs whether advised to Owners in advance or not, and including charges by Terminal/Suppliers/Receivers. 131–133

Loading and discharging cargo — 7. The cargo shall be loaded into the vessel at the expense of Charterers and, up to the vessel's permanent hose connections, at Charterers' risk. The cargo shall be discharged from the vessel at the expense of Owners and, up to the vessel's permanent hose connections, at Owners' risk. Owners shall, unless otherwise notified by Charterers or their agents, supply at Owners' expense all hands, equipment and facilities required on board for mooring and unmooring and connecting and disconnecting hoses for loading and discharging. 134–138

Deadfreight — 8. Charterers need not supply a full cargo, but if they do not freight shall nevertheless be paid as if the vessel had been loaded with a full cargo. 139–140

The term "full cargo" as used throughout this Charter means a cargo which, together with any collected washings (as defined in Part II clause 40) retained on board pursuant to the requirements of MARPOL 73/78, fills the vessel to either her applicable deadweight or her capacity stated in Part I clause (A) (I) (iii), whichever is less, while leaving sufficient space in the tanks for the expansion of cargo. If under Part I clause (F) vessel is chartered for a minimum quantity and the vessel is unable to load such quantity due to having reached her capacity as stated in Part I clause (A) (I) (iii), always leaving sufficient space for expansion of cargo, then without prejudice to any claims which Charterers may have against Owners, no deadfreight between the quantity loaded and the quantity shown in Part I clause (F) shall be due. 141–148

Shifting — 9. Charterers shall have the right to require the vessel to shift at ports of loading and/or discharging from a loading or discharging berth within port limits and/or to a waiting place inside or outside port limits and back to the same or to another such berth/place once or more often on payment of all additional expenses incurred. For the purposes of freight payment and shifting the places grouped in Port and Terminal Combinations in Worldscale are to be considered as berths within a single port. If at any time before cargo operations are completed it becomes dangerous for the vessel to remain at the specified berth as a result of wind or water conditions, Charterers shall pay all additional expenses of shifting from any such berth and back to that or any other specified berth within port limits (except to the extent that any fault of the vessel contributed to such danger). 149–156

Subject to Part II clause 14(a) and (c) time spent shifting shall count against laytime or if the vessel is on demurrage for demurrage. 157–158

Charterers' failure to give orders — 10. If the vessel is delayed due to Charterers' breach of Part II clause 3 Charterers shall, subject to the terms hereof, compensate Owners in accordance with Part II clause 15(1) and (2) as if such delay were time exceeding the laytime. Such compensation shall be Owners' sole remedy in respect of such delay. 159–161

The period of such delay shall be calculated:
(i) from 6 hours after Owners notify Charterers that the vessel is delayed awaiting nomination of loading or discharging port until such nomination has been received by Owners, or 162–164
(ii) from 6 hours after the vessel gives notice of readiness at the loading or discharging port until commencement of loading or discharging, 165–166

as the case may be, subject always to the same exceptions as those set out in Part II clause 14. Any period of delay in respect of which Charterers pay compensation pursuant to this clause 10 shall be excluded from any calculation of time for laytime or demurrage made under any other clause of this Charter. 167–169

Periods of delay hereunder shall be cumulative for each port, and Owners may demand compensation after the vessel has been delayed for a total of 20 running days, and thereafter after each succeeding 5 running days of delay and at the end of any delay. Each such demand shall show the period in respect of which compensation is claimed and the amount due. Charterers shall pay the full amount due within 14 days after receipt of Owners' demand. Should Charterers fail to make any such payments Owners shall have the right to terminate this Charter 170–174

by giving written notice to Charterers or their agents, without prejudice to any claims which Charterers or   175
Owners may have against each other under this Charter or otherwise.   176

Laydays/
Termination

11.   Should the vessel not be ready to load by noon local time on the termination date set out in Part I clause   177
(C) Charterers shall have the option of terminating this Charter unless the vessel has been delayed due to Charterers'   178
change of orders pursuant to Part II clause 26, in which case the laydays shall be extended by the period of   179
such delay.   180
As soon as Owners become aware that the vessel will not be ready to load by noon on the termination date,   181
Owners will give notice to Charterers declaring a new readiness date and ask Charterers to elect whether or not to   182
terminate this Charter.   183
Within 4 days after such notice, Charterers shall either: 184
     (i)   declare this Charter terminated or   185
     (ii) confirm a revised set of laydays which shall be amended such that the new readiness date stated shall   186
           be the commencement date and the second day thereafter shall be the termination date or,   187
     (iii) agree a new set of laydays or an extension to the laydays mutually acceptable to Owners and Charterers   188
           The provisions of this clause and the exercise or non-exercise by Charterers of their option to terminate   189
shall not prejudice any claims which Charterers or Owners may have against each other.   190

Laytime

12. (1) The laytime for loading, discharging and all other Charterers' purposes whatsoever shall be the   191
number of running hours specified in Part I clause (I). Charterers shall have the right to load and discharge at all   192
times, including night, provided that they shall pay for all extra expenses incurred ashore.   193
        (2) If vessel is able to, and Charterers so instruct, the vessel shall load earlier than the commencement of   194
of laydays and Charterers shall have the benefit of such time saved by way of offset from any demurrage incured.   195
Such benefit shall be the time between commencement of loading until the commencement of the original laydays.   196

Notice of
readiness/
Running
time

13. (1) Subject to the provisions of Part II clauses 13(3) and 14,   197
     (a)   Time at each loading or discharging port shall commence to run 6 hours after the vessel is in   198
           all respects ready to load or discharge and written notice thereof has been tendered by the   199
           master or Owners' agents to Charterers or their agents and the vessel is securely moored at   200
           the specified loading or discharging berth. However, if the vessel does not proceed   201
           immediately to such berth time shall commence to run 6 hours after (i) the vessel is lying in   202
           the area where she was ordered to wait or, in the absence of any such specific order, in a   203
           usual waiting area and (ii) written notice of readiness has been tendered and (iii) the   204
           specified berth is accessible. A loading or discharging berth shall be deemed inaccessible   205
           only for so long as the vessel is or would be prevented from proceeding to it by bad weather,   206
           tidal conditions, ice, awaiting daylight, pilot or tugs, or port traffic control requirements   207
           (except those requirements resulting from the unavailability of such berth or of the cargo).   208
           If Charterers fail to specify a berth at any port, the first berth at which the vessel loads or   209
           discharges the cargo or any part thereof shall be deemed to be the specified berth at such   210
           port for the purposes of this clause.   211
           Notice shall not be tendered before commencement of laydays and notice tendered by radio   212
           shall qualify as written notice provided it is confirmed in writing as soon as reasonably   213
           possible.   214
           Time shall never commence before six hours after commencement of laydays unless loading   215
           commences prior to this time as provided in clause 13 (3).   216
           If Owners fail;   217
          (i)   to obtain Customs clearance; and/or   218
          (ii)   to obtain free pratique unless this is not customary prior to berthing; and/or   219
          (iii) to have on board all papers/certificates required to perform this Charter, either within   220
               the 6 hours after notice of readiness originally tendered or when time would otherwise   221
               normally commence under this Charter, then the original notice of readiness shall not   222
               be valid. A new notice of readiness may only be tendered when Customs clearance and/or   223
               free pratique has been granted and/or all papers/certificates required are in order in accordance   224
               with relevant authorities' requirements. Laytime or demurrage, if on demurrage, would then   225
               commence in accordance with the terms of this Charter. All time, costs and expenses as a   226
               result of delays due to any of the foregoing shall be for Owners' account.   227
     (b)   Time shall: 228
          (i)   continue to run until the cargo hoses have been disconnected.   229
          (ii)   recommence two hours after disconnection of hoses if the vessel is delayed for Charterers'   230
               purposes and shall continue until the termination of such delay provided that if the vessel waits   231
               at any place other than the berth, any time or part of the time on passage to such other place that   232

PART II

occurs after two hours from disconnection of hoses shall not count.	233
(2) If the vessel loads or discharges cargo by transhipment at sea time shall commence in accordance with	234
Part II clause 13 (I) (a), and run until transhipment has been completed and the vessels have separated. always	235
subject to Part II clause 14.	236
(3) Notwithstanding anything else in this clause 13, if Charterers start loading or discharging the	237
vessel before time would otherwise start to run under this Charter, time shall run from commencement of such	238
loading or discharging.	239
(4) For the purposes of this clause 13 and of Part II clause 14 and Part II clause 15 "time" shall mean laytime	240
or time counting for demurrage, as the case may be.	241

Suspension of time

14. Time shall not count when: — 242

    (a)   spent on inward passage from the vessel's waiting area to the loading or discharging berth — 243
         specified by Charterers, even if lightening occurred at such waiting area; or — 244

    (b)   spent in carrying out vessel operations, including but not limited to bunkering, discharging — 245
         slops and tank washings, and handling ballast, except to the extent that cargo operations are — 246
         carried on concurrently and are not delayed thereby; or — 247

    (c)   lost as a result of: — 248
         (i)   breach of this Charter by Owners; or — 249
         (ii) any cause attributable to the vessel, (including but not limited to the warranties in Part I — 250
             (A) of this Charter) including breakdown or inefficiency of the vessel; or — 251
         (iii) strike, lock-out, stoppage or restraint of labour of master, officers or crew of the vessel or — 252
             tug boats or pilot. — 253

Demurrage

15. (1) Charterers shall pay demurrage at the rate specified in Part I clause (J). — 254
If the demurrage rate specified in Part I clause (J) is expressed as a percentage of Worldscale such percentage — 255
shall be applied to the demurrage rate applicable to vessels of a similar size to the vessel as provided in Worldscale — 256
or, for the purpose of clause 10 and/or if this Charter is terminated prior to the commencement of loading, in — 257
Worldscale current at the termination date specified in Part I clause (J). — 258
Demurrage shall be paid per running day or pro rata for part thereof for all time which, under the provisions — 259
of this Charter, counts against laytime or for demurrage and which exceeds the laytime specified in Part I clause (I). — 260
Charterers' liability for exceeding the laytime shall be absolute and shall not in any case be subject to the — 261
provisions of Part II clause 32. — 262

(2) If, however, all or part of such demurrage arises out of or results from fire or explosion or strike or — 263
failure/breakdown of plant and/or machinery at ports of loading and/or discharging in or about the plant of — 264
Charterers, shippers or consignees of the cargo (not being a fire or explosion caused by the negligence or wilful act — 265
or omission of Charterers, shippers or consignees of the cargo or their respective servants or agents), act of God, act — 266
of war, riot, civil commotion, or arrest or restraint of princes, rulers or peoples, the laytime used and/or the rate of — 267
demurrage shall be reduced by half for such laytime used and/or for such demurrage or such parts thereof. — 268

(3) Owners shall notify Charterers within 60 days after completion of discharge if demurrage has — 269
been incurred and any demurrage claim shall be fully and correctly documented, and received by Charterers, within — 270
90 days after completion of discharge . If Owners fail to give notice of or to submit any such claim with — 271
documentation, as required herein, within the limits aforesaid, Charterers' liability for such demurrage shall be — 272
extinguished. — 273

(4) If any part cargo for other charterers, shippers or consignees (as the case may be) is loaded or discharged — 274
at the same berth, then any time used by the vessel waiting at or for such berth and in loading or discharging which — 275
would otherwise count as laytime or if the vessel is on demurrage for demurrage, shall be pro-rated in the proportion — 276
that Charterers' cargo bears to the total cargo to be loaded or discharged at such berth. If however, the running of — 277
laytime or demurrage, if on demurrage, is solely attributable to other parties' cargo operations then such time shall — 278
not count in calculating laytime or demurrage, if on demurrage, against Charterers under this Charter. — 279

Vessel inspection

16. Charterers shall have the right, but no duty, to have a representative attend on board the vessel at any — 280
loading and/or discharging ports and the master and Owners shall co-operate to facilitate his inspection — 281
of the vessel and observation of cargo operations. However, such right, and the exercise or non-exercise — 282
thereof, shall in no way reduce the master's or Owners' authority over, or responsibility to — 283
Charterers and third parties for, the vessel and every aspect of her operation, nor increase Charterers' — 284
responsibilities to Owners or third parties for the same. — 285

Cargo inspection

17. This clause 17 is without prejudice to Part II clause 2 hereof. Charterers shall have the right to require — 286
inspection of the vessel's tanks at loading and/or discharging ports to ascertain the quantity and quality of the cargo, — 287
water and residues on board. Depressurisation of the tanks to permit inspection and/or ullaging shall be carried out — 288
in accordance with the recommendations in the latest edition of the ISGOTT guidelines. Charterers shall also have — 289

PART II

the right to inspect and take samples from the bunker tanks and other non-cargo spaces. Any delay to the vessel 290
caused by such inspection and measurement or associated depressurising/repressurising of tanks shall count against 291
laytime, or if the vessel is on demurrage, for demurrage. 292

Cargo measure-ment
18.   The master shall ascertain the contents of all tanks before and after loading and before and after 293
discharging, and shall prepare tank-by-tank ullage reports of the cargo, water and residues on board which shall 294
be promptly made available to Charterers or their representative if requested. Each such ullage report shall show 295
actual ullage/dips, and densities at observed and standard temperature (15° Celsius). All quantities shall be 296
expressed in cubic metres at both observed and standard temperature. 297

Inert gas
19.   The vessel's inert gas system (if any) shall comply with Regulation 62, Chapter II-2 of the 1974 Safety of 298
Life at Sea Convention as modified by the Protocol of 1978, and any subsequent amendments, and Owners warrant 299
that such system shall be operated (subject to the provisions of Part II clause 2), during loading, throughout the 300
voyage and during discharge, and in accordance with the guidance given in the IMO publication "Inert Gas System 301
(1983)". Should the inert gas system fail, Section 8 (Emergency Procedures) of the said IMO publication shall be 302
strictly adhered to and time lost as a consequence of such failure shall not count against laytime or, if the vessel is 303
on demurrage, for demurrage. 304

Crude oil washing
20.   If the vessel is equipped for crude oil washing Charterers shall have the right to require the vessel to 305
crude oil wash, concurrently with discharge, those tanks in which Charterers' cargo is carried. If crude oil washing 306
is required by Charterers any additional discharge time thereby incurred, always subject to the next succeeding 307
sentences, shall count against laytime or, if the vessel is on demurrage, for demurrage. The number of hours 308
specified in Part I clause (A) (1) (vii) shall be increased by 0.6 hours per cargo tank washed, always subject 309
to a maximum increase of 8 hours. If vessel fails to maintain 100 PSI throughout the discharge then any time over 310
24 hours, plus the additional discharge performance allowance under this clause, shall not count as laytime or 311
demurrage, if on demurrage. This clause 20 does not reduce Owners' liability for the vessel to perform her service 312
with utmost despatch as set out in Part II, clause 3(1). The master shall provide Charterers with a crude oil washing log 313
identifying each tank washed, and stating whether such tank has been washed to the MARPOL minimum standard 314
or has been the subject of additional crude oil washing and whether requested by Charterers or otherwise. 315

Overage insurance
21.   Any additional insurance on the cargo required because of the age of the vessel shall be for Owners' 316
account. 317

Ice
22.   The vessel shall not be required to force ice or to follow icebreakers. If the master finds that a 318
nominated port is inaccessible due to ice, the master shall immediately notify Charterers requesting revised 319
orders and shall remain outside the ice-bound area; and if after arrival at a nominated port there is danger of the 320
vessel being frozen in, the vessel shall proceed to the nearest safe and ice free position and at the same time 321
request Charterers to give revised orders. 322
      In either case if the affected port is: 323
      (i)   the first or only loading port and no cargo has been loaded, Charterers shall either nominate 324
             another port,or give notice cancelling this Charter in which case they shall pay at the demurrage 325
             rate in Part I clause (J) for the time from the master's notification aforesaid or from notice 326
             of readiness on arrival, as the case may be,until the time such cancellation notice is given; 327
      (ii)   a loading port and part of the cargo has been loaded, Charterers shall either nominate another 328
             port, or order the vessel to proceed on the voyage without completing loading in which case 329
             Charterers shall pay for any deadfreight arising therefrom; 330
      (iii) a discharging port, Charterers shall either nominate another port or order the vessel to proceed to or 331
             return to and discharge at the nominated port. If the vessel is ordered to proceed to or return to a 332
             nominated port, Charterers shall bear the risk of the vessel being damaged whilst proceeding to or 333
             returning to or at such port, and the whole period from the time when the master's request for revised 334
             orders is received by Charterers until the vessel can safely depart after completion of discharge shall 335
             count against laytime or, if the vessel is on demurrage, for demurrage. 336
      If, as a consequence of Charterers revising orders pursuant to this clause, the nominated port(s) or the 337
number or rotation of ports is changed, freight shall nevertheless be paid for the voyage which the vessel would 338
otherwise have performed had the orders not been so revised, such freight to be increased or reduced by the 339
amount by which, as a result of such revision of orders, 340
      (a)   the time used including any time awaiting revised orders (which shall be valued at the demurrage rate 341
             in Part I clause (J)), and 342
      (b)   the bunkers consumed, at replacement cost and 343
      (c)   the port charges 344
             for the voyage actually performed are greater or less than those that would have been incurred on the 345

PART II

	voyage which, but for the revised orders under this clause, the vessel would have performed.	346
Quarantine	23. Time lost due to quarantine shall not count against laytime or for demurrage unless such quarantine	347
	was in force at the time when the affected port was nominated by Charterers.	348
Agency	24. The vessel's agents shall be nominated by Charterers at nominated ports of loading and discharging.	349
	Such agents, although nominated by Charterers, shall be employed and paid by Owners.	350

Charterers'
obligation at
shallow draft
port/
Lightening
in port

25.(1) If the vessel, with the quantity of cargo then on board, is unable due to inadequate depth of   351
water in the port safely to reach any specified discharging berth and discharge the cargo there always safely afloat,   352
Charterers shall specify a location within port limits where the vessel can discharge sufficient cargo into vessels or   353
lighters to enable the vessel safely to reach and discharge cargo at such discharging berth, and the vessel shall   354
lighten at such location.   355

(2) If the vessel is lightened pursuant to clause 25(1) then, for the purposes of the calculation   356
of laytime and demurrage, the lightening place shall be treated as the first discharging berth within the port where   357
such lightening occurs.   358

Charterers'
orders/
Change of
orders/ Part
cargo
transhipment

26. (1) If, after loading and/or discharging ports have been nominated, Charterers wish to vary such   359
nominations or their rotation, Charterers may give revised orders subject to <u>Part I clause (D)</u> and/or <u>(E)</u>, as the case   360
may be. Charterers shall reimburse Owners at the demurrage rate provided in <u>Part I clause (J)</u> for any deviation or   361
delay which may result therefrom and shall pay at replacement cost for any extra bunkers consumed.   362
Charterers shall not be liable for any other loss or expense which is caused by such variation.   363

(2) Subject to Part II clause 33(6), Charterers may order the vessel to load and/or discharge any part of the   364
cargo by transhipment at sea in the vicinity of any nominated port or en route between two nominated ports, in   365
which case unless Charterers elect, (which they may do at any time) to treat the place of such transhipment as a load   366
or discharge port (subject to the number of ports and ranges in <u>Part I clauses (D)</u> and <u>(E)</u> of this Charter), Charterers   367
shall reimburse Owners at the demurrage rate specified in <u>Part I clause (J)</u> for any additional steaming time and/or   368
delay which may be incurred as a consequence of proceeding to and from the location at sea of such transhipment   369
and, in addition, Charterers shall pay at replacement cost for any extra bunkers consumed.   370

(3) Owners warrant that the vessel, master, officers and crew are, and shall remain during this Charter,   371
capable of safely carrying out all the procedures in the current edition of the ICS/ OCIMF Ship to Ship Transfer   372
Guide (Petroleum). Owners further warrant that when instructed to perform a ship to ship transfer the master,   373
officers and crew shall, at all times, comply with such procedures. Charterers shall provide, and pay for,   374
the necessary equipment and, if necessary, mooring master, for such ship to ship operation.   375

Heating of
cargo

27. If Charterers require cargo heating the vessel shall, on passage to and whilst at discharging port(s),   376
maintain the cargo at the loaded temperature or at the temperature stated in <u>Part I clause (A) (I) (iv)</u>, whichever is   377
the lower. Charterers may request that the temperature of the cargo be raised above or lowered below that at which   378
it was loaded, in which event Owners shall use their best endeavours to comply with such request and Charterers   379
shall pay at replacement cost for any additional bunkers consumed and any consequential delay to the vessel   380
shall count against laytime or, if the vessel is on demurrage, for demurrage.   381

ETA

28. (1) Owners shall give Charterers a time and date of expected arrival at the first load port or if the loading   382
range is in the Arabian Gulf, the time of her expected arrival off Quoin Island (hereinafter called"load port"   383
in this clause) at the date of this Charter. Owners shall further advise Charterers at any time between the   384
Charter date and arrival at load port of any variation of 6 hours or more in vessel's expected arrival   385
time/date at the load port.   386

(2) Owners undertake that, unless Charterers require otherwise, the master shall: 387

(a)   advise Charterers immediately on leaving the final port of call on the previous voyage   388
of the time and date of the vessel's expected arrival at the first loading port and shall further   389
advise Charterers 72, 48, 36, and 24 hours before the expected arrival time/date.   390

(b)   advise Charterers immediately after departure from the final loading port, of the vessel's   391
expected time of arrival at the first discharging port or the area at sea to which the vessel has been   392
instructed to proceed for wireless orders, and confirm or amend such advice not later than 72, 48,   393
36 and 24 hours before the vessel is due at such port or area;   394

(c)   advise Charterers immediately of any variation of more than six hours from expected times of arrival   395
at loading or discharging ports, Quoin Island or such area at sea to Charterers;   396

(d)   address all messages as specified in <u>Part I clause (K)</u>.   397

Owners shall be responsible for any consequences or additional expenses arising as a result of non-compliance   398
with this clause.   399

(3) If at any time prior to the tender of notice of readiness at the first load port, the vessel ceases to comply   400
with the description set out in <u>Part I clause (A)</u> and in any questionnaire(s), the Owners shall immediately notify   401

PART II

Charterers of the same, providing full particulars, and explaining what steps Owners are taking to ensure that the vessel will so comply. Any silence or failure on the part of Charterers to respond to or any inaction taken in respect of any such notice shall not amount to a waiver of any rights or remedies which Charterers may have in respect of the matters notified by Owners.   402–405

Packed cargo

29. Charterers have the option of shipping products and/or general cargo in available dry cargo space, the quantity being subject to the master's discretion. Freight shall be payable at the bulk rate in accordance with Part II clause 5 and Charterers shall pay in addition all expenses incurred solely as a result of the packed cargo being carried. Delay occasioned to the vessel by the exercise of such option shall count against laytime or, if the vessel is on demurrage, for demurrage.   406–410

Subletting/ Assignment

30. Charterers shall have the option of sub-chartering the vessel and/or of assigning this Charter to any person or persons, but Charterers shall always remain responsible for the due fulfilment of all the terms and conditions of this Charter. Additionally Charterers may novate this charter to any company of the Royal Dutch/ Shell Group of Companies.   411–414

Liberty

31. The vessel shall be at liberty to tow or be towed, to assist vessels in all positions of distress and to deviate for the purpose of saving life or property. On the laden voyage the vessel shall not take on bunkers or deviate or stop, except as allowed in this clause 31, without prior permission of Charterers , Cargo Insurers, and Owners' P&I Club.   415–418

Exceptions

32. (1) The vessel, her master and Owners shall not, unless otherwise in this Charter expressly provided, be liable for any loss or damage or delay or failure arising or resulting from any act, neglect or default of the master, pilots, mariners or other servants of Owners in the navigation or management of the vessel; fire, unless caused by the actual fault or privity of Owners; collision or stranding; dangers and accidents of the sea; explosion, bursting of boilers, breakage of shafts or any latent defect in hull, equipment or machinery; provided, however, that Part I clause (A) and Part II clauses 1 and 2 hereof shall be unaffected by the foregoing. Further, neither the vessel, her master or Owners, nor Charterers shall, unless otherwise in this Charter expressly provided, be liable for any loss or damage or delay or failure in performance hereunder arising or resulting from act of God, act of war, act of public enemies, seizure under legal process, quarantine restrictions, strikes, lock-outs, restraints of labour, riots, civil commotions or arrest or restraint of princes, rulers or people.   419–428

(2) Nothing in this Charter shall be construed as in any way restricting, excluding or waiving the right of Owners or of any other relevant persons to limit their liability under any available legislation or law.   429–430

(3) Clause 32(1) shall not apply to or affect any liability of Owners or the vessel or any other relevant person in respect of   431–432

    (a) loss or damage caused to any berth, jetty, dock, dolphin, buoy, mooring line, pipe or crane or other works or equipment whatsoever at or near any port to which the vessels may proceed under this Charter, whether or not such works or equipment belong to Charterers,   433–435

or   436

    (b) any claim (whether brought by Charterers or any other person) arising out of any loss of or damage to or in connection with the cargo. Any such claim shall be subject to the Hague-Visby Rules or the Hague Rules, or the Hamburg Rules as the case may be, which ought pursuant to Part II clause 37 hereof to have been incorporated in the relevant bill of lading (whether or not such Rules were so incorporated) or, if no such bill of lading is issued, to the Hague-Visby rules unless the Hamburg Rules compulsory apply in which case to the Hamburg Rules.   437–443

Bills of lading

33. (1) Subject to the provisions of this clause Charterers may require the master to sign lawful bills of lading for any cargo in such form as Charterers direct.   444–445

(2) The signing of bills of lading shall be without prejudice to this Charter and Charterers hereby indemnify Owners against all liabilities that may arise from signing bills of lading to the extent that the same impose liabilities upon Owners in excess of or beyond those imposed by this Charter.   446–448

(3) All bills of lading presented to the master for signature, in addition to complying with the requirements of Part II clauses 35, 36 and 37, shall include or effectively incorporate clauses substantially similar to the terms of Part II clauses 22, 33(7) and 34.   449–451

(4) All bills of lading presented for signature hereunder shall show a named port of discharge. If when bills of lading are presented for signature discharging port(s) have been nominated hereunder, the discharging port(s) shown on such bills of lading shall be in conformity with the nominated port(s). If at the time of such presentation no such nomination has been made hereunder, the discharging port(s) shown on such bills of lading must be within Part I clause (E) and shall be deemed to have been nominated hereunder by virtue of such presentation.   452–457

PART II

(5) Article III Rules 3 and 5 of the Hague-Visby Rules shall apply to the particulars included in the   458
bills of lading as if Charterers were the shippers, and the guarantee and indemnity therein contained shall apply to   459
the description of the cargo furnished by or on behalf of Charterers.   460

(6) Notwithstanding any other provisions of this Charter, Owners shall be obliged to comply with   461
any orders from Charterers to discharge all or part of the cargo provided that they have received from Charterers   462
written confirmation of such orders.   463

If Charterers by telex, facsimile or other form of written communication that specifically refers to this clause request   464
Owners to discharge a quantity of cargo either: 465

    (a)   without bills of lading and/or   466
    (b)   at a discharge place other than that named in a bill of lading and/or   467
    (c)   that is different from the bill of lading quantity   468

then Owners shall discharge such cargo in accordance with Charterers' instructions in consideration of receiving the   469
following indemnity which shall be deemed to be given by Charterers on each and every such occasion and which is limited   470
in value to 200 per cent of the C.I.F. value of the cargo on board: 471

    (i)   Charterers shall indemnify Owners, and Owners' servants and agents in respect of any liability loss or damage   472
         of whatsoever nature (including legal costs as between attorney or solicitor and client and associated expenses)   473
         which Owners may sustain by reason of delivering such cargo in accordance with Charterers' request.   474

    (ii)   If any proceeding is commenced against Owners or any of Owners' servants or agents in connection with the   475
         vessel having delivered cargo in accordance with such request, Charterers shall provide Owners or any of   476
         Owners' servants or agents from time to time on demand with sufficient funds to defend the said proceedings.   477

    (iii)   If the vessel or any other vessel or property belonging to Owners should be arrested or detained, or if the arrest   478
         or detention thereof should be threatened, by reason of discharge in accordance with Charterers' instruction as   479
         aforesaid, Charterers shall provide on demand such bail or other security as may be required to prevent such arrest   480
         or detention or to secure the release of such vessel or property and Charterers shall indemnify Owners in respect   481
         of any loss, damage or expenses caused by such arrest or detention whether or not the same may be justified.   482

    (iv)   Charterers shall, if called upon to do so at any time while such cargo is in Charterers' possession, custody or   483
         control, redeliver the same to Owners.   484

    (v)   As soon as all original bills of lading for the above cargo which name as discharge port the place where   485
         delivery actually occurred shall have arrived and/or come into Charterers' possession, Charterers shall   486
         produce and deliver the same to Owners, whereupon Charterers' liability hereunder shall cease.   487

         Provided however, if Charterers have not received all such original bills of lading by 24.00 hours on the day   488
         36 calendar months after the date of discharge, then this indemnity shall terminate at that time unless before   489
         that time Charterers have received from Owners written notice that: 490

        (a)   some person is making a claim in connection with Owners delivering cargo pursuant to Charterers'   491
             request or

        (b)   legal proceedings have been commenced against Owners and/or carriers and/Charterers and/or   492
             any of their respective servants or agents and/or the vessel for the same reason.   493

When Charterers have received such a notice, then this indemnity shall continue in force until such claim or legal   494
proceedings are settled. Termination of this indemnity shall not prejudice any legal rights a party may have   495
outside this indemnity.   496

    (vi)   Owners shall promptly notify Charterers if any person (other than a person to whom Charterers ordered   497
         cargo to be delivered) claims to be entitled to such cargo and/or if the vessel or any other property belonging   498
         to Owners is arrested by reason of any such discharge of cargo.   499

    (vii)   This indemnity shall be governed and construed in accordance with the English law and each and any dispute   500
         arising out of or in connection with this indemnity shall be subject to the jurisdiction of the High Court of   501
         Justice of England.   502

(7) The master shall not be required or bound to sign bills of lading for any blockaded port or for any port which the   503
master or Owners in his or their discretion consider dangerous or impossible to enter or reach.   504

(8) Charterers hereby warrant that on each and every occasion that they issue orders under <u>Part II clauses 22</u>, <u>26</u>, <u>34</u>   505
or <u>38</u> they will have the authority of the holders of the bills of lading to give such orders, and that such bills of lading will not   506
be transferred to any person who does not concur therein.   507

(9) Owners hereby agree that original bill(s) of lading, if available, will be allowed to be placed on board.   508
If original bill(s) of lading are placed on board, Owners agree that vessel will discharge cargo against such bill(s) of lading   509
carried on board, on receipt of receivers' proof of identity.   510

War risks   34.(1) If   511

    (a)   any loading or discharging port to which the vessel may properly be ordered under the provisions of this Charter   512
         or bills of lading issued pursuant to this Charter be blockaded, or   513

    (b)   owing to any war, hostilities, warlike operation, civil commotions, revolutions, or the operation of international   514
         law (i) entry to any such loading or discharging port or the loading or discharging of cargo at any such port be   515
         considered by the master or Owners in his or their discretion dangerous or prohibited or (ii) it be considered   516

PART II

by the master or Owners in his or their discretion dangerous or impossible or prohibited for the vessel to reach 517
any such loading or discharging port, 518
Charterers shall have the right to order the cargo or such part of it as may be affected to be loaded or discharged at any other 519
loading or discharging port within the ranges specified in <u>Part I clause (D)</u> or <u>(E)</u> respectively (provided such other port is not 520
blockaded and that entry thereto or loading or discharging of cargo thereat or reaching the same is not in the master's or Owners' 521
opinion dangerous or impossible or prohibited). 522
(2) If no orders be received from Charterers within 48 hours after they or their agents have received from Owners a 523
request for the nomination of a substitute port, then 524
(a)   if the affected port is the first or only loading port and no cargo has been loaded, this Charter shall terminate 525
forthwith; 526
(b)   if the affected port is a loading port and part of the cargo has already been loaded, the vessel may proceed on 527
passage and Charterers shall pay for any deadfreight so incurred; 528
(c)   if the affected port is a discharging port, Owners shall be at liberty to discharge the cargo at any port which they 529
or the master may in their or his discretion decide on (whether within the range specified in <u>Part I clause (E)</u> 530
or not) and such discharging shall be deemed to be due fulfilment of the contract or contracts of affreightment 531
so far as cargo so discharged is concerned. 532
(3) If in accordance with clause 34(1) or (2) cargo is loaded or discharged at any such other port, freight shall be paid 533
as for the voyage originally nominated, such freight to be increased or reduced by the amount by which, as a result of loading 534
or discharging at such other port, 535
(a)   the time on voyage including any time awaiting revised orders (which shall be valued at the demurrage rate in 536
<u>Part I clause (J)</u>), and 537
(b)   the bunkers consumed, at replacement cost, and 538
(c)   the port charges 539
for the voyage actually performed are greater or less than those which would have been incurred on the voyage originally 540
nominated save as aforesaid, the voyage actually performed shall be treated for the purpose of this Charter as if it were the 541
voyage originally nominated. 542
(4) The vessel shall have liberty to comply with any directions or recommendations as to departure, arrival, routes, ports 543
of call, stoppages, destinations, zones, waters, delivery or in any otherwise whatsoever given by the government of the nation 544
under whose flag the vessel sails or any other government or local authority including any de facto government or local authority 545
or by any person or body acting or purporting to act as or with the authority of any such government or authority or by any 546
committee or person having under the terms of the war risks insurance on the vessel the right to give any such directions 547
or recommendations. If by reason of or in compliance with any such directions or recommendations anything is done or is not 548
done, such shall not be deemed a deviation. 549
If, by reason of or in compliance with any such directions or recommendations as are mentioned in clause 34 (4), the vessel does 550
not proceed to the discharging port or ports originally nominated or to which she may have been properly ordered under the 551
provisions of this Charter or bills of lading issued pursuant to this Charter, the vessel may proceed to any discharging port on 552
which the master or Owners in his or their discretion may decide and there discharge the cargo. Such discharging shall be 553
deemed to be due fulfilment of the contract or contracts of affreightment and Owners shall be entitled to freight as if discharging 554
had been effected at the port or ports originally nominated or to which the vessel may have been properly ordered under the 555
provisions of this Charter or bills of lading issued pursuant to this Charter. All extra expenses involved in reaching and 556
discharging the cargo at any such other discharging port shall be paid by Charterers and Owners shall have a lien on the cargo for 557
all such extra expenses. 558
(5) Owners shall pay for all additional war risk insurance premiums, both for annual periods and also for the specific 559
performance of this Charter, on the Hull and Machinery value, as per <u>Part I clause (A) (I) (xiii)</u> applicable at the date of this 560
Charter,or the date the vessel was fixed "on subjects" (whichever is the earlier), and all reasonable crew war bonus. The period 561
of voyage additional war risks premium shall commence when the vessel enters a war risk zone as designated by the London 562
insurance market and cease when the vessel leaves such zone. If the vessel is already in such a zone the period shall commence 563
on tendering notice of readiness under this Charter. 564
Any increase or decrease in voyage additional war risk premium and any period in excess of the first fourteen days shall be for 565
Charterers' account and payable against proven documentation. Any discount or rebate refunded to Owners for whatever reason 566
shall be passed on to Charterers. Any premiums, and increase thereto, attributable to closure insurance (i.e. blocking and 567
trapping)shall be for Owners' account. 568

Both to blame clause   35. If the liability for any collision in which the vessel is involved while performing this Charter falls to be determined in 569
accordance with the laws of the United States of America, the following clause, which shall be included in all bills of lading 570
issued pursuant to this Charter shall apply: 571
"If the vessel comes into collision with another vessel as a result of the negligence of the other vessel and any act, neglect or 572
default of the master, mariner, pilot or the servants of the Carrier in the navigation or in the management of the vessel, the 573
owners of the cargo carried hereunder will indemnify the Carrier against all loss or liability to the other or non-carrying vessel 574
or her owners in so far as such loss or liability represents loss of, or damage to, or any claim whatsoever of the owners of the said 575

PART II

cargo, paid or payable by the other or non-carrying vessel or her owners to the owners of the said cargo and set off, recouped or 576
recovered by the other or non-carrying vessel or her owners as part of their claim against the carrying vessel or the Carrier. 577
    The foregoing provisions shall also apply where the owners, operators or those in charge of any vessel or vessels or objects 578
other than, or in addition to, the colliding vessels or objects are at fault in respect of a collision or contact." 579

General average/ New Jason clause	36. General average shall be payable according to the York/Antwerp Rules 1994, as amended from time to time, and shall 580 be adjusted in London. All disputes relating to General Average shall be resolved in London in accordance with English Law. 581 Without prejudice to the foregoing, should the adjustment be made in accordance with the Law and practice of the United States 582 of America, the following clause, which shall be included in all bills of lading issued pursuant to this Charter, shall apply: 583

    "In the event of accident, danger, damage or disaster before or after the commencement of the voyage, resulting from any 584
cause whatsoever, whether due to negligence or not, for which, or for the consequence of which, the Carrier is not responsible, 585
by statute, contract or otherwise, the cargo, shippers, consignees or owners of the cargo shall contribute with the Carrier in 586
general average to the payment of any sacrifices, losses or expenses of a general average nature that may be made or incurred and 587
shall pay salvage and special charges incurred in respect of the cargo. 588
    If a salving vessel is owned or operated by the Carrier, salvage shall be paid for as fully as if the said salving vessel or 589
vessels belonged to strangers. Such deposit as the Carrier or its agents may deem sufficient to cover the estimated contribution of 590
the cargo and any salvage and special charges thereon shall, if required, be made by the cargo, shippers, consignees or owners of 591
the cargo to the Carrier before delivery." 592

Clause Paramount	37. The following clause shall be included in all bills of lading issued pursuant to this Charter: 593

    (1) Subject to sub-clauses (2) or (3) hereof, this bill of lading shall be governed by, and have effect subject to the rules 594
contained in the International Convention for the Unification of Certain Rules relating to bills of lading signed at Brussels on 25th 595
August 1924 (hereafter the "Hague Rules") as amended by the Protocol signed at Brussels on 23rd February 1968 (hereafter the 596
"Hague-Visby Rules"). Nothing contained herein shall be deemed to be either a surrender by the carrier of any of his rights or 597
immunities or any increase of any of his responsibilities or liabilities under the Hague-Visby Rules. 598
    (2) If there is governing legislation which applies the Hague Rules compulsorily to this bill of lading, to the exclusion of 599
the Hague-Visby Rules, then this bill of lading shall have effect subject to the Hague Rules. Nothing herein contained shall be 600
deemed to be either a surrender by the carrier of any of his rights or immunities or an increase of any of his responsibilities or 601
liabilities under the Hague Rules. 602
    (3) If there is governing legislation which applies the United Nations Convention on the Carriage of Goods By Sea 1978 603
(hereafter the "Hamburg Rules") compulsorily to this bill of lading to the exclusion of the Hague-Visby Rules, then this bill of 604
lading shall have effect subject to the Hamburg Rules. Nothing herein contained shall be deemed to be either a surrender by the 605
carrier of any of his rights or immunities or an increase of any of his responsibilities or liabilities under the Hamburg Rules. 606
    (4) If any term of this bill of lading is repugnant to the Hague-Visby Rules, or Hague Rules or Hamburg Rules, if 607
applicable,such term shall be void to that extent but no further. 608
    (5) Nothing in this bill of lading shall be construed as in any way restricting, excluding or waiving the right of any 609
relevant party or person to limit his liability under any available legislation and/or law. 610

Back loading	38. Charterers may order the vessel to discharge and/or backload a part or full cargo at any nominated port within the 611 loading / discharging ranges specified within <u>Part I clauses (D/E)</u> and within the rotation of the ports previously nominated, 612 provided that any cargo loaded is of the description specified in <u>Part I clause (F)</u> and that the master in his reasonable discretion 613 determines that the cargo can be loaded, segregated and discharged without risk of contamination by, or of any other cargo. 614

    Charterers shall pay in respect of loading, carrying and discharging such cargo as follows: 615
    (a)   a lumpsum freight calculated at the demurrage rate specified in <u>Part I clause (J)</u> on any additional port time used 616
               by the vessel; and 617
    (b)   any additional expenses, including bunkers consumed (at replacement cost) over above those required to load and 618
               discharge one full cargo and port costs which included additional agency costs: and
    (c)   if the vessel is fixed on a Worldscale rate in <u>Part I clause (G)</u> then freight shall always be paid for the whole 619
               voyage at the rate(s) specified in <u>Part I clause (G)</u> on the largest cargo quantity carried on any ocean leg. 620

Bunkers	39. Owners shall give Charterers or any other company in the Royal Dutch/Shell Group of Companies first option to quote 621 for the supply of bunker requirements for the performance of this Charter. 622

Oil pollution prevention/ Ballast management	40.(1) Owners shall ensure that the master shall: 623

    (a)   comply with MARPOL 73/78 including any amendments thereof; 624
    (b)   collect the drainings and any tank washings into a suitable tank or tanks and, after maximum separation 625
               of free water, discharge the bulk of such water overboard, consistent with the above regulations; and 626
    (c)   thereafter notify Charterers promptly of the amounts of oil and free water so retained on board and details 627
               of any other washings retained on board from earlier voyages (together called the "collected washings"). 628
    (d)   not to load on top of such 'collected washings' without specific instructions from Charterers. 629
    (e)   provide Charterers with a slops certificate to be made up and signed by the master and an independent 630

PART II

surveyor/terminal representative. The certificate shall indicate:	631
Origin and composition of slops, Volume, Free water and API measured in barrels at 60 deg F.	632

(2) On being so notified, Charterers, in accordance with their rights under this clause (which shall include without 633
limitation the right to determine the disposal of the collected washings), shall before the vessel's arrival at the loading berth 634
(or if already arrived as soon as possible thereafter) give instructions as to how the collected washings shall be dealt with. 635
Owners shall ensure that the master on the vessel's arrival at the loading berth (or if already arrived as soon as possible thereafter) 636
shall arrange in conjunction with the cargo suppliers for the measurement of the quantity of the collected washings and shall 637
record the same in the vessel's ullage record. 638

(3) Charterers may require the collected washings to be discharged ashore at the loading port, in which case no freight 639
shall be payable on them. 640

(4) Alternatively Charterers may require either that the cargo be loaded on top of the collected washings and the 641
collected washings be discharged with the cargo, or that they be kept separate from the cargo in which case Charterers shall pay 642
for any deadfreight incurred thereby in accordance with Part II clause 8 and shall, if practicable, accept discharge of the collected 643
washings at the discharging port or ports. 644
In either case, provided that the master has reduced the free water in the collected washings to a minimum consistent with the 645
retention on board of the oil residues in them and consistent with sub-clause (1)(a) above, freight in accordance with Part II 646
clause 5 shall be payable on the quantity of the collected washings as if such quantity were included in a bill of lading and the 647
figure therefore furnished by the shipper provided, however, that 648

    (i)   if there is a provision in this Charter for a lower freight rate to apply to cargo in excess of an agreed quantity, 649
            freight on the collected washings shall be paid at such lower rate (provided such agreed quantity of cargo has been 650
            loaded) and 651
    (ii)   if there is provision in this Charter for a minimum cargo quantity which is less than a full cargo, then whether or 652
            not such minimum cargo quantity is furnished, freight on the collected washings shall be paid as if such minimum 653
            cargo quantity had been furnished, provided that no freight shall be payable in respect of any collected washings 654
            which are kept separate from the cargo and not discharged at the discharge port. 655

(5) Whenever Charterers require the collected washings to be discharged ashore pursuant to this clause, Charterers shall 656
provide and pay for the reception facilities, and the cost of any shifting there for shall be for Charterers' account. Any time lost 657
discharging the collected washings and/or shifting therefore shall count against laytime or, if the vessel is on demurrage, for 658
demurrage. 659

(6) Owners warrant that the vessel will arrive at the load port with segregated/ clean ballast as defined by Annex I of 660
MARPOL 73/78 including any amendments thereof. 661

Oil response pollution and insurance
41. (1) Owners warrant that throughout the duration of this Charter the vessel will be: 662
    (i)   owned or demise chartered by a member of the 'International Tanker Owners Pollution Federation 663
    (ii)   Limited, and entered in the Protection and Indemnity (P&I) Club stated in Part I clause (A) 1 (xii) . 664
(2) It is a condition of this Charter that Owners have in place insurance cover for oil pollution for the maximum on offer 665
through the International Group of P&I Clubs but always a minimum of United States Dollars1,000,000,000 (one thousand million). 666
If requested by Charterers, Owners shall immediately furnish to Charterers full and proper evidence of the coverage. 667
(3) Owners warrant that the vessel carries on board a certificate of insurance as required by the Civil Liability 668
Convention for Oil Pollution damage. Owners further warrant that said certificate will be maintained effective throughout the 669
duration of performance under this Charter. All time, costs and expense as a result of Owners' failure to comply with the 670
foregoing shall be for Owners' account. 671
(4) Owners warrant that where the vessel is a "Relevant Ship", they are a "Participating Owner" as defined, as applicable, 672
in the Small Tanker Oil Pollution Indemnification Agreement ("STOPIA") or in the Tanker Oil Pollution Indemnification 673
Agreement ("TOPIA"), and that the vessel is entered in STOPIA or TOPIA (as applicable) and shall so remain during the currency 674
of this Charter provided always that STOPIA or TOPIA (as applicable) is not terminated in accordance with its provisions.

Lien
42. Owners shall have an absolute lien upon the cargo and all subfreights for all amounts due under this 675
charter and the cost of recovery thereof including any expenses whatsoever arising from the exercise of such lien. 676

Drugs and alcohol
43. Owners are aware of the problem of drug and alcohol abuse and warrant that they have a written policy in force, 677
covering the vessel, which meets or exceeds the standards set out in the "Guidelines for the Control of Drugs and Alcohol on 678
board Ship" as published by OCIMF dated June 1995. 679
Owners further warrant that this policy shall remain in force during the period of this Charter and such policy shall be adhered to 680
throughout this Charter. 681

ITWF
44. Owners warrant that the terms of employment of the vessel's staff and crew will always remain acceptable to the 682
International Transport Workers Federation on a worldwide basis. All time, costs and expenses incurred as a result of Owners' 683
failure to comply with foregoing shall be for Owners' account. 684

Letters of protest/
45. It is a condition of this Charter that from the time the vessel sails to the first load port there will be no Letter(s) of 685
Protest ("LOP"'s) or deficiencies outstanding against the vessel. This refers to LOP's or deficiencies issued by Terminal 686

PART II

Deficiencies	Inspectorate or similar Port or Terminal or Governmental Authorities.	687

Documen-
tation

46. Owners shall ensure that the master and agents produce documentation and provide Charterers with copies of all such 688
documentation relevant to each port and berth call and all transhipments at sea, including but not limited to: 689
Notice of Readiness / Statement of Facts / Shell Form 19x (if Charterers nominate agents under <u>Part II clause 24</u>) / Time sheet(s) 690
/ LOPs/ Hourly pumping logs /crude oil washing performance logs by facsimile (to the number advised in the voyage 691
instructions). These documents to be faxed within 48 hours from sailing from each load or discharge port or transhipment area. If 692
the vessel does not have a facsimile machine on board the master shall advise Charterers, within 48 hours from sailing from each 693
port under this Charter, of the documents he has available and ensure copies of such documents are faxed by agents to Charterers 694
from the relevant port of call or at latest from the next port of call. Complying with this clause does not affect the terms of Part II 695
<u>clause 15(3)</u> with regard to notification and submission of a fully documented claim for demurrage or a claim described in Part II 696
<u>clause 6(3)</u> of this Charter. Any documents to be faxed under this clause may be, alternatively, scanned and e-mailed to 697
Charterers.If any actions or facilities of Suppliers / Receivers / Terminal/ Transhipment vessels or Charterers, as applicable, 698
impinge on the vessel's ability to perform the warranties and / or guarantees of performance under this Charter the master must 699
issue a LOP to such effect. If the master fails to issue such LOP then Owners shall be deemed to have waived any rights to claim. 700
Master and agents shall ensure that all documents concerning port/berth and cargo activities at all ports/berths and transhipment 701
at sea places are signed by both an officer of the vessel and a representative of either Suppliers / Receivers / Terminal / 702
Transhipment vessels or Charterers, as applicable. 703
If such a signature from Suppliers / Receivers / Terminal/ Transhipment vessels or Charterers, as applicable, is not obtainable the 704
master or his agents should issue a LOP to such effect. 705
All LOP's issued by master or his agents or received by master or his agents must be forwarded to Charterers as per the terms of this clause. 706

Administra-
tion

47. The agreed terms and conditions of this Charter shall be recorded and evidenced by the production of a fixture note sent 707
to both Charterers and Owners within 24 hours of the fixture being concluded. This fixture note shall state the name and date of 708
the standard pre-printed Charter Party Form, on which the Charter is based, along with all amendments / additions/ deletions to 709
such charter party form. All further additional clauses agreed shall be reproduced in the fixture note with full wording. This 710
fixture note shall be approved and acknowledged as correct by both Owners and Charterers to either the Ship Broker through 711
whom they negotiated or, if no Ship Broker was involved, to each other within two working days after fixture concluded. 712
No formal written and signed Charter Party will be produced unless specifically requested by Charterers or Owners or is required 713
by additional clauses of this Charter. 714

Cargo
retention

48. If on completion of discharge any liquid cargo of a pumpable nature remains on board (the presence and quantity of 715
such cargo having been established, by application of the wedge formula in respect of any tank the contents of which do not 716
reach the forward bulkhead, by an independent surveyor, appointed by Charterers and paid jointly by Owners and Charterers), 717
Charterers shall have the right to deduct from freight an amount equal to the FOB loading port value of such cargo, cargo 718
insurance plus freight thereon; provided, however, that any action or lack of action hereunder shall be without prejudice to any 719
other rights or obligations of Charterers, under this Charter or otherwise, and provided further that if Owners are liable to any 720
third party in respect of failure to discharge such pumpable cargo, or any part thereof, Charterers shall indemnify Owners against 721
such liability up to the total amount deducted under this clause. 722

Hydrogen
sulphide

49. Owners shall comply with the requirements in ISGOTT (as amended from time to time) concerning Hydrogen Sulphide 723
and shall ensure that prior to arrival at the load port the Hydrogen Sulphide (ppm by volume in vapour) level in all 724
ballast and empty cargo spaces is below the Threshold Limit Value ("TLV") - Time Weighted Average ("TWA"). 725
If on arrival at the loading terminal, the loading authorities, inspectors or other authorised and qualified personnel declare that 726
the Hydrogen Sulphide levels in the vessels' tanks exceed the TLV- TWA and request the vessel to reduce the said level to 727
within the TLV-TWA then the original notice of readiness shall not be valid. A valid notice of readiness can only be tendered 728
and laytime, or demurrage time, if on demurrage, can only start to run in accordance with <u>Part II clause 13</u> when the 729
TLV-TWA is acceptable to the relevant authorities. 730
If the vessel is unable to reduce the levels of Hydrogen Sulphide within a reasonable time Charterers shall have the option of 731
cancelling this Charter without penalty and without prejudice to any claims which Charterers may have against Owners under 732
this Charter. 733

Port
regulations

50. Owners warrant that the vessel will fully comply with all port and terminal regulations at any named port in this Charter, 734
and any ports to which Charterers may order the vessel to under this Charter in accordance with <u>Part I clauses (D/E)</u> provided 735
that Owners have a reasonable opportunity to acquaint themselves with the regulations at such ports. 736

Single Point/
Buoy and
jetty
mooring

51. (1) Owners warrant that: 737
    (a)   the vessel complies with the OCIMF recommendations, current at the date of this Charter, 738
            for equipment employed in the mooring of ships at single point moorings in particular 739
            for tongue type or hinged bar type chain stoppers and that the messenger from the Chain Stopper(s) 740
    .   is secured on a winch drum (not a drum end) and that the operation is totally hands free 741
    (b)   the vessel complies and operates in accordance with the recommendations, current at the date 742

(left margin, rotated) Printed by BIMCO's *idea*

PART II

	of this Charter, contained in the latest edition of OCIMF's "Mooring Equipment Procedures"	743
	(2) If requested by Charterers, or in the event of an emergency situation arising whilst the vessel is at a	744

Single Buoy Mooring ("SBM"), the vessel shall pump sea water, either directly from the sea or from vessel's 745
clean ballast tanks, to flush SBMs floating hoses prior to, during or /after loading and/or discharge of the 746
cargo; this operation to be carried out at Charterers' expense and with time counting against laytime, or 747
demurrage, if on demurrage. Subject to Owners exercising due diligence in carrying out such an operation 748
Charterers hereby indemnify Owners for any cargo loss or contamination directly resulting from this request. 749
If master or Owners are approached by Suppliers/Receivers or Terminal Operators to undertake such an 750
operation Owners shall obtain Charterers' agreement before proceeding. 751

ISPS/MTSA 　52. (1) (a) From the date of coming into force of the International Code for the Security of Ships and of Port 752
Facilities and the relevant amendments to Chapter XI of SOLAS ("ISPS Code") and the US Maritime 753
Transportation Security Act 2002 ("MTSA") in relation to the vessel, and thereafter during the currency of 754
this Charter, Owners shall procure that both the vessel and "the Company" (as defined by the ISPS Code) 755
and the "owner" (as defined by the MTSA) shall comply with the requirements of the ISPS Code relating to 756
the vessel and "the Company" and the requirements of MTSA relating to the vessel and the "owner". 757
Upon request Owners shall provide a copy of the relevant International Ship Security Certificate to 758
Charterers. Owners shall provide documentary evidence of compliance with this clause 52 (1) (a). 759
(b) Except as otherwise provided in this Charter, loss, damage, expense or delay caused by failure on the part 760
of Owners or "the Company"/"owner" to comply with the requirements of the ISPS Code/MTSA or this 761
clause shall be for Owners' account. 762
　(2) (a) Charterers shall provide the Owners with their full style contact details and other relevant information 763
reasonably required by Owners to comply with the requirements of the ISPS Code/MTSA. Additionally, 764
Charterers shall ensure that the contact details of any sub-charterers are likewise provided to Owners. 765
Furthermore, Charterers shall ensure that all sub-charter parties they enter into shall contain the following 766
provision: 767
"The Charterers shall provide the Owners with their full style contact details and, where sub-letting is permitted 768
under the terms of the charter party, shall ensure that contact details of all sub-charterers are likewise provided to the Owners". 769
(b) Except as otherwise provided in this Charter, loss, damage, expense or delay caused by failure on the part 770
of Charterers to comply with this sub clause (2) shall be for Charterers' account. 771
　(3) (a) Without prejudice to the foregoing, Owners right to tender notice of readiness and Charterers' liability 772
for demurrage in respect of any time delays caused by breaches of this clause 52 shall be dealt with in 773
accordance with Part II clauses 13, (Notice of readiness/Running time), 14, (Suspension of Time), and 774
15,(Demurrage), of the charter. 775
(b) Except where the delay is caused by Owners and/or Charterers failure to comply, respectively, with 776
clauses (1) and (2) of this clause 52, then any delay arising or resulting from measures imposed by a port 777
facility or by any relevant authority, under the ISPS Code/MTSA, shall count as half rate laytime, or, if the 778
vessel is on demurrage, half rate demurrage. 779
　(4) Except where the same are imposed as a cause of Owners and/or Charterers failure to comply, respectively, 780
with clauses (1) and (2) of this clause 52 , then any costs or expenses related to security regulations or 781
measures required by the port facility or any relevant authority in accordance with the ISPS Code/MTSA 782
including, but not limited to, security guards, launch services, tug escorts, port security fees or taxes and 783
inspections, shall be shared equally between Owners and Charterers. All measures required by the Owners to 784
comply with the Ship Security Plan shall be for Owners' account. 785
　(5) If either party makes any payment which is for the other party's account according to this clause, the other 786
party shall indemnify the paying party. 787

Business 　53.　Owners will co-operate with Charterers to ensure that the "Business Principles", as amended from time to 788
principles time, of the Royal Dutch/Shell Group of Companies, which are posted on the Shell Worldwide Web 789
(www.Shell.com), are complied with. 790

Law and 　54. (a) This Charter shall be construed and the relations between the parties determined in accordance 791
litigation with the laws of England. 792
Arbitration 　　(b)　All disputes arising out of this Charter shall be referred to Arbitration in London in accordance 793
　　　　with the Arbitration Act 1996 (or any re-enactment or modification thereof for the time being 794
　　　　in force) subject to the following appointment procedure: 795
　　　　(i)　The parties shall jointly appoint a sole arbitrator not later than 28 days after service of a request by 796
　　　　　　in writing by either party to do so. 797
　　　　(ii)　If the parties are unable or unwilling to agree the appointment of a sole arbitrator in accordance with (i) 798
　　　　　　then each party shall appoint one arbitrator, in any event not later than 14 days after receipt of a further 799
　　　　　　request in writing by either party to do so. The two arbitrators so appointed shall appoint a third arbitrator 800

587

PART II

		before any substantive hearing or forthwith if they cannot agree on a matter relating to the arbitration.	801
	(iii)	If a party fails to appoint an arbitrator within the time specified in (ii) (the "Party in Default"), the	802
		party who has duly appointed his arbitrator shall give notice in writing to the Party in Default that he	803
		proposes to appoint his arbitrator to act as sole arbitrator.	804
	(iv)	If the Party in Default does not within 7 days of the notice given pursuant to (iii) make the required	805
		appointment and notify the other party that he has done so the other party may appoint his arbitrator as	806
		sole arbitrator whose award shall be binding on both parties as if he had been so appointed by agreement.	807
	(v)	Any award of the arbitrator(s) shall be final and binding and not subject to appeal.	808
	(vi)	For the purposes of this clause 54 any requests or notices in writing shall be sent by fax, e-mail or	809
		telex and shall be deemed received on the day of transmission.	810
(c)		It shall be a condition precedent to the right of any party to a stay of any legal proceedings in which	811
		maritime property has been, or may be, arrested in connection with a dispute under this Charter, that that party	812
		furnishes to the other party security to which that other party would have been entitled in such legal	813
		proceedings in the absence of a stay.	814

Small claims   (d)   In cases where neither the claim nor any counterclaim exceeds the sum of United States Dollars 50,000 — 815
(or such other sum as Owners/Charterers may agree) the arbitration shall be conducted in accordance with the — 816
London Maritime Arbitrators' Association Small Claims Procedure current at the time when the arbitration — 817
proceedings are commenced. — 818

Address — 819
commission   55. Charterers shall deduct address commission of 1.25% from all payments under this Charter. — 820

Construction   56. The side headings have been included in this Charter for convenience of reference and shall in no — 821
way affect the construction hereof. — 822

Australia	(1) (a)	The vessel shall not transit the Great Barrier Reef Inner Passage, whether in ballast en route to a	1

Australia   (1) (a)   The vessel shall not transit the Great Barrier Reef Inner Passage, whether in ballast en route to a   1
loadport or laden, between the Torres Strait and Cairns, Australia. If the vessel transits the Torres Strait,   2
the vessel shall use the outer reef passage as approved by the Australian Hydrographer. Owners shall   3
always employ a pilot, when transiting the Torres Strait and for entry and departure through the Reef   4
for ports north of Brisbane.   5

(b)   The vessel shall discharge all ballast water on board the vessel and take on fresh ballast water,   6
always in accordance with safe operational procedures, prior to entering Australian waters.   7

(c)   On entering, whilst within and whilst departing from the port of Sydney Owners and master shall   8
ensure that the water line to highest fixed point distance does not exceed 51.8 (fifty one point eight) metres.   9

(d)   If Charterers or Terminal Operators instruct the vessel to slow the cargo operations down or stop   10
entirely the cargo operations in Sydney during the hours of darkness due to excessive noise caused by the   11
vessel then all additional time shall be for Owners' account.   12

Goods Services Tax   (e) (i)   Goods Services Tax ("GST") imposed in Australia has application to any supply made under   13
this Charter, the parties agree that the Charterer shall account for GST in accordance with Division   14
83 of the GST Act even if the Owner becomes registered. The Owner acknowledges that it will not   15
recover from the Charterer an additional amount on account of GST.   16

(ii)   The Owner acknowledges that it is a non-resident and that it does not make supplies through an   17
enterprise carried on in Australia as defined in section 995-1 of the Income Tax Assessment Act 1997.   18

(iii)   The Charterer acknowledges that it is registered. Where appropriate, terms in this clause   19
have the meaning set out in section 195-1 of the GST Act.   20

Brazil   (2) (a)   Owners acknowledge the vessel will have, if Charterers so require, to enter a port or place of   21
clearance within mainland Brazil, to obtain necessary clearance from the Brazilian authorities and/or to   22
pick-up personnel required to be on board during the loading of the cargo at Fluminense FPSO.   23
The vessel then proceeds to the Fluminense FPSO where she can tender her notice of readiness.   24
Time at the port of clearance, taken from arrival at pilot station to dropping outward pilot to be for   25
Charterers' account and payable at the agreed demurrage rate together with freight.   26
However this time not to count as laytime or demurrage if on demurrage.   27

(b)   Freight payment under Part II clause 5 of this Charter shall be made within 5 banking days of   28
receipt by Charterers of notice of completion of final discharge   29

Canada   (3) Owners warrant that the vessel complies with all the Canadian Oil Spill response regulations currently   30
in force and that the Owner is a member of a certified oil spill response organisation and that the   31
Owners/vessel shall continue to be members of such organisation and comply with the regulations and   32
requirements of such organisation throughout the period of this Charter.   33

Egypt   (4) (a)   Any costs incurred by Charterers for vessel garbage or in vessel deballasting at Sidi Kerir shall be   34
for Owners' account and Charterers shall deduct such costs from freight   35

(b)   Charterers shall have the option for the discharge range Euromed and/or United Kingdom/ Continent   36
(Gibraltar Hamburg range) to instruct the vessel to transit via Suez Canal. In the event that Charterers   37
exercise this option the following shall apply: 38
Charterers option to part discharge Ain Sukhna and reload Sidi Kerir.   39
Charterers will pay the following with freight against Owners' fully documented claim: 40

(c)   time incurred at the demurrage rate on the passage from the point at which the vessel deviates from the   41
direct sailing route between last loadport and Port Suez, till the tendering of notice of readiness at Ain   42
Sukhna, less any time lost by reason of delay beyond Charterers' reasonable control;   43

(d)   time incurred at the demurrage rate on the passage from disconnection of hoses at Sidi Kerir to the   44
point at which the vessel rejoins the direct sailing route between Port Said and the first discharge port UK   45
Continent or Mediterranean, less any time lost by reason of delay beyond Charterers' reasonable control;   46

(e)   time incurred at the demurrage rate between tendering of notice of readiness at Ain Sukhna and   47
disconnection of hoses there;   48

(f)   time incurred at the demurrage rate between tendering of notice of readiness at Sidi Kerir and   49
disconnection of hoses there: 50

(g)   all bunkers consumed during the periods (c) to (f) above at replacement cost;   51

(h)   all port charges incurred at Ain Sukhna and Sidi Kerir.   52
Freight rate via Suez shall be based on the Suez/Suez flat rate without the fixed Suez rate differential, other   53
than as described below (the Worldscale rates in Part I clause (G) of this Charter to apply). All canal dues   54
related to Suez laden transit, including Suez Canal port costs, agency fees and expenses, including but not   55
limited to escort tugs and other expenses for canal laden transit, to be for Charterers' account and to be   56
settled directly by them. Charterers' to pay Owners the 'ballast transit only' fixed rate differential as per   57
Worldscale together with freight.   58

India	(5) (a)	In assessing the pumping efficiency under this Charter at ports in India, Owners agree to accept the	59
		record of pressure maintained as stated in receiver's statement of facts signed by the ship's representative.	60
	(b)	Owners shall be aware of and comply with the mooring requirements of Indian ports. All time,	61
		costs and expenses as a result of Owners' failure to comply with the foregoing shall be for Owners'	62
		account.	63
	(c)	Charterers shall not be liable for demurrage unless the following conditions are satisfied:	64
		(i) the requirements of <u>Part II clause 15 (3)</u> are met in full; and	65
		(ii) a copy of this Charter signed by Owners is received by Charterers at least 2 (two) working days	66
		prior to the vessel's arrival in an Indian port.	67

Charterers undertake to pay agreed demurrage liabilities promptly if the above conditions have been   68
satisfied.   69

Japan	(6) (a)	Owners shall supply Charterers with copies of:-	70
		(i) General Arrangement/Capacity plan; and	71
		(ii) Piping/Fire Fighting Diagrams	72
		as soon as possible, but always within 4 working days after subjects lifted on this Charter.	73
	(b)	If requested by Charterers, Owners shall ensure a Superintendent, fully authorised by Owners to	74
		act on Owners' and/or master's behalf, is available at all ports within Japan to attend safety meetings	75
		prior to vessel's arrival at the port(s) and be in attendance throughout the time in each port and during	76
		each cargo operation.	77
	(c)	Vessel to record and print out the position with date/time by Global Positioning System when vessels	78
		enters Japanese Territorial Waters ("JTW") in order to perform vessel's declaration of entering	79
		JTW for crude oil stock piling purpose.	80
	(d)	If under <u>Part I clause (E)</u> of this Charter Japan, or in particular ports or berths in Tokyo Bay and/or	81
		the SBM at UBE Refinery, are discharge options and if the vessel is over 220,000 metric tons	82
		deadweight and has not previously discharged in Tokyo Bay or the SBM at UBE Refinery then:	83
		(i) Owners shall submit an application of Safety Pledge Letter confirming that all safety	84
		measures will be complied with; and	85
		(ii) Present relevant ship data to the Japanese Maritime Safety Agency.	86

Owners shall comply with the above requirements as soon as possible but always within 4 working days   87
after subjects lifted on this Charter.   88

	(e)	If Charterers instruct the vessel to make adjustment to vessel's arrival date/time at discharge port(s)	89
		in Japan, any adjustments shall be compensated in accordance with <u>Part I clause (L)</u> of this Charter.	90
		If vessel is ordered to drift off Japan, at a location in Owners'/master's option, then the following	91
		shall apply:-	92
		(i) Time from vessel's arrival at drifting location to the time vessel departs, on receipt of	93
		Charterers'instructions, from such location shall be for Charterers' account at the	94
		demurrage rate stipulated in <u>Part I clause (J)</u> of this Charter.	95
		(ii) Bunkers consumed whilst drifting as defined in sub clause (e)(i) above shall be for	96
		Charterers'account at replacement cost.	97

Owners shall provide full documentation to support any claim under this clause.   98

New Zealand	(7) (a)	Owners of vessels carrying Persistent Oil - as defined by the International Group of P&I Clubs -	99
		which shall always incorporate Crude and Fuel Oil, Non Persistent Oil as defined by the International	100
		Group of P&I Clubs - which shall always incorporate Petroleum Products; and Chemicals, warrant	101
		that the vessel shall comply at all times with the Maritime Safety Authority of New Zealand's	102
		Voluntary Routeing Code for Shipping whilst transiting the New Zealand coast and / or en route to	103
		or from ports in New Zealand and whether laden or in ballast.	104
	(b)	the following voyage routing will apply:	105
		(i) vessel is to keep a minimum of 5 miles off the New Zealand coast (and outlying islands) until	106
		approaching the port's pilot station, with the following exceptions:	107
		a) to pass a minimum of 4 miles off the coast when transiting Cook Strait;	108
		b) to pass a minimum of 5 miles to the east of Poor Knights Islands and High Peaks Rocks;	109
		c) to pass a minimum of 3 miles from land when transiting the Colville or Jellicoe Channels.	110

If due to safe navigation and or other weather related reasons the vessel proceeds on a different route to   111
those set out above, the Owners and master shall immediately advise Charterers and Owner's agents in   112
New Zealand of the route being followed and the reasons for such deviation from the above warranted route.   113

Thailand	(8)	If <u>Part I clause (E)</u> of this Charter includes option to discharge at a port/berth in Thailand then the	114
		following, which is consistent with industry practice for ships discharging in Thailand, shall apply	115
		over and above any other terms contained within this Charter:-	116
		(a) Laytime shall be 96 running hours	117

590

	(b)	Freight payment under Part II clause 5 of this Charter shall be made within 15 days	118
		of receipt by Charterers of notice of completion of final discharge of cargo.	119
	(c)	Cargo quantity and quality measurements shall be carried out at load and discharge	120
		ports by mutually appointed independent surveyors, with costs to be shared equally between	121
		Owners and Charterers.	

This is additional to any independent surveyors used for the Cargo Retention clause 48 in Part II of this | 122
Charter. | 123

United | (9) (a) | It is a condition of this Charter that Owners ensure that the vessel fully complies with the latest | 124
Kingdom | | Sullom Voe regulations, including but not limited to: | 125
| | (i) | current minimum bulk loading rates; and | 126
| | (ii) | pilot boarding ladder arrangements. | 127

Owners shall also comply with Charterers' instructions regarding the disposal of ballast from the vessel. | 128
Charterers shall accept any deadfreight claim that may arise by complying with such instructions. | 129

| | (b) | It is also a condition of this Charter that Owners ensure that the vessel fully complies with the | 130
| | | latest Tranmere and Shellhaven regulations, including but not limited to: | 131
| | (i) | being able to ballast concurrently with discharge ; or | 132
| | (ii) | maintaining double valve segregation at all times between cargo and ballast if the vessel | 133
| | | has to part discharge, stop to ballast, then resume discharge. | 134
| | (c) | In the event of loading or discharge at Tranmere, Shell U.K. Ltd. shall appoint tugs, pilots and | 135
| | | boatmen on behalf of Owners. The co-ordinator of these services shall be OBC., who will submit | 136
| | | all bills to Owners direct, irrespective of whether OBC are appointed agents or not. Owners warrant | 137
| | | they will put OBC in funds accordingly. | 138

United | (10)(a) | It is a condition of this Charter that in accordance with U.S. Customs Regulations, 19 CFR 4.7a | 139
States of | | and 178.2 as amended, Owners have obtained a Standard Carrier Alpha Code (SCAC) and shall | 140
America | | include same in the Unique Identifier which they shall enter, in the form set out in the above Customs | 141
| | | Regulations,on all the bills of lading, Cargo manifest, Cargo declarations and other cargo documents | 142
| | | issued under this Charter allowing carriage of goods to ports in the U.S. | 143

Owners shall be liable for all time, costs and expenses and shall indemnify Charterers against all | 144
consequences whatsoever arising directly or indirectly from Owners' failure to comply with the above | 145
provisions of this clause. | 146

Owners warrant that they are aware of the requirements of the U.S Bureau of Customs and Border | 147
Protection ruling issued on December 5th 2003 under Federal Register Part II Department of | 148
Homeland Security 19 CFR Parts 4, 103, et al. and will comply fully with these requirements for | 149
entering U.S ports. | 150

Coastguard | (b) | Owners warrant that during the term of this Charter the vessel will comply with all | 151
compliance | | applicable U.S. Coast Guard (USCG) Regulations in effect as of the date the vessel is tendered for | 152
| | | first loading hereunder. If waivers are held to any USCG regulation Owners to advise Charterers of | 153
| | | such waivers, including period of validation and reason(s) for waiver. All time costs and expense as a | 154
| | | result of Owners' failure to comply with the foregoing shall be for Owners' account. | 155

| | (c) | Owners warrant that they will | 156
| | (i) | comply with the U.S. Federal Water Pollution Control Act as amended, and any | 157
| | | amendments or successors to said Act | 158

Laws and | (ii) | comply with all U.S. State Laws and regulations applicable during this Charter, as they apply | 159
regulation | | to the U.S. States that Charterers may order vessel to under Part I clauses (D/E) of this Charter. | 160
| | (iii) | have secured, carry aboard the vessel, and keep current any certificates or other evidence of | 161
| | | financial responsibility required under applicable U.S. Federal or State Laws and regulations | 162
| | | and documentation recording compliance with the requirements of OPA 90, any amendments | 163
| | | or succeeding legislation, and any regulations promulgated thereunder. Owners shall confirm | 164
| | | that these documents will be valid throughout this Charter. | 165

W-8BEN | (d) | If the recipient of the freight due under this Charter does not file taxes within the US, then such | 166
| | | recipient shall complete an IRS Form W-8BEN and forward the original by mail to Charterers, attention | 167
| | | "Freight Payments". Should this not he received in a timely manner, then Charterers shall not be liable | 168
| | | for interest on late payment of freight, or be in default of this Charter for such late payment. | 169

Vapour Recovery | | Owners warrant that the vessel's vapour recovery system complies with the requirements of the United | 170
System | | States Coastguard. | 171

Vietnam | (11) | If required by Charterers, when loading Bach Ho crude oil, Owners will instruct the master to start the | 172
| | | cargo heating system(s) prior to loading commencing. | 173

Laytime Definitions for Charter Parties 2013*

Words, phrases, acronyms and abbreviations ("Words and Phrases") used in a Charter Party shall be defined, for the purposes of Laytime only, in accordance with the corresponding Words and Phrases set out below, when any or all such definitions are expressly incorporated into the Charter Party.

"Charter Party" shall include any form of contract of carriage or affreightment including contracts evidenced by bills of lading.

Singular/Plural

The singular includes the plural and vice versa as the context admits or requires.

List of Definitions

1. PORT shall mean any area where vessels load or discharge cargo and shall include, but not be limited to, berths, wharves, anchorages, buoys and offshore facilities as well as places outside the legal, fiscal or administrative area where vessels are ordered to wait for their turn no matter the distance from that area.
2. BERTH shall mean the specific place where the Vessel is to load or discharge and shall include, but not be limited to, any wharf, anchorage, offshore facility or other location used for that purpose.
3. REACHABLE ON ARRIVAL shall mean that the charterer undertakes that an available loading or discharging Berth be provided to the Vessel on arrival at the Port which the Vessel can reach safely without delay.
4. ALWAYS ACCESSIBLE shall mean that the charterer undertakes that an available loading or discharging Berth be provided to the Vessel on arrival at the Port which the Vessel can reach safely without delay. The charterer additionally undertakes that the Vessel will be able to depart safely from the Berth and without delay at any time before, during or on completion of loading or discharging.
5. LAYTIME shall mean the period of time agreed between the parties during which the owner will make and keep the Vessel available for loading or discharging without payment additional to the freight.

---

* Reproduced by kind permission of BIMCO.

6. PER HATCH PER DAY shall mean that the Laytime is to be calculated by dividing the quantity of cargo by the result of multiplying the agreed daily rate per hatch by the number of the Vessel's hatches. Thus:

$$\text{Laytime} = \frac{\text{Quantity of cargo}}{\text{Daily rate} \times \text{Number of hatches}} = \text{Days}$$

Each pair of parallel twin hatches shall count as one hatch. Nevertheless, a hatch that is capable of being worked by two gangs simultaneously shall be counted as two hatches.

7. PER WORKING HATCH PER DAY or PER WORKABLE HATCH PER DAY shall mean that the Laytime is to be calculated by dividing the quantity of cargo in the hold with the largest quantity by the result of multiplying the agreed daily rate per working or workable hatch by the number of hatches serving that hold. Thus:

$$\text{Laytime} = \frac{\text{Largest quantity in one hold}}{\substack{\text{Daily rate per hatch} \times \\ \text{Number of hatches serving that hold}}} = \text{Days}$$

Each pair of parallel twin hatches shall count as one hatch. Nevertheless, a hatch that is capable of being worked by two gangs simultaneously shall be counted as two hatches.

8. DAY shall mean a period of twenty-four (24) consecutive hours. Any part of a Day shall be counted pro rata.

9. CALENDAR DAY shall mean a period of twenty-four (24) consecutive hours running from 0000 hours to 2400 hours. Any part of a Calendar Day shall be counted pro rata.

10. CONVENTIONAL DAY shall mean a period of twenty-four (24) consecutive hours running from any identified time. Any part of a Conventional Day shall be counted pro rata.

11. WORKING DAY shall mean a Day when by local law or practice work is normally carried out.

12. RUNNING DAYS or CONSECUTIVE DAYS shall mean Days which follow one immediately after the other.

13. RUNNING HOURS or CONSECUTIVE HOURS shall mean hours which follow one immediately after the other.

14. HOLIDAY shall mean a Day other than the normal weekly Day(s) of rest, or part thereof, when by local law or practice work during what would otherwise be ordinary working hours is not normally carried out.

15. WEATHER WORKING DAY shall mean a Working Day or part of a Working Day during which it is or, if the Vessel is still waiting for her turn, it would be possible to load/discharge the cargo without interruption due to the weather. If such interruption occurs (or would have occurred if work had been in progress), there shall be excluded from

the Laytime a period calculated by reference to the ratio which the duration of the interruption bears to the time which would have or could have been worked but for the interruption.

16. WEATHER WORKING DAY OF 24 CONSECUTIVE HOURS shall mean a Working Day or part of a Working Day of 24 consecutive hours during which it is or, if the vessel is still waiting for her turn, it would be possible to load/discharge the cargo without interruption due to the weather. If such interruption occurs (or would have occurred if work had been in progress) there shall be excluded from the Laytime the period during which the weather interrupted or would have interrupted work.

17. WEATHER WORKING DAY OF 24 HOURS shall mean a period of 24 hours made up of one or more Working Days during which it is or, if the Vessel is still waiting for her turn, it would be possible to load/discharge the cargo without interruption due to the weather. If such interruption occurs (or would have occurred if work had been in progress), there shall be excluded from Laytime the actual period of such interruption.

18. (WORKING DAY) WEATHER PERMITTING shall have the same meaning as WEATHER WORKING DAY OF 24 CONSECUTIVE HOURS.

19. EXCEPTED or EXCLUDED shall mean that the Days specified do not count as Laytime even if loading or discharging is carried out on them.

20. UNLESS SOONER COMMENCED shall mean that if turn-time has not expired but loading or discharging is carried out, Laytime shall commence.

21. UNLESS SOONER COMMENCED, IN WHICH CASE ACTUAL TIME USED TO COUNT shall mean that actual time used during turn-time shall count as Laytime.

22. UNLESS USED shall mean that if Laytime has commenced but loading or discharging is carried out during excepted periods, actual time used shall count as Laytime.

23. TO AVERAGE LAYTIME shall mean that separate calculations are to be made for loading and discharging and that any time saved in one operation is to be set off against any excess time used in the other.

24. REVERSIBLE LAYTIME shall mean an option given to the charterer to add together the time allowed for loading and discharging. Where the option is exercised the effect is the same as a total time being specified to cover both operations.

25. NOTICE OF READINESS shall mean the notice to the charterer, shipper, receiver or other person as required by the CharterParty that the Vessel has arrived at the Port or Berth, as the case may be, and is ready to load or discharge.

26. TIME LOST WAITING FOR BERTH TO COUNT AS LOADING OR DISCHARGING TIME or AS LAYTIME shall mean that if no

loading or discharging Berth is available and the Vessel is unable to tender Notice of Readiness at the waiting-place then any time lost to the Vessel is counted as if Laytime were running, or as time on Demurrage if Laytime has expired. Such time ceases to count once the Berth becomes available. When the Vessel reaches a place where she is able to tender Notice of Readiness, Laytime or time on Demurrage resumes after such tender and, in respect of Laytime, on expiry of any notice time provided in the CharterParty.

27. WHETHER IN BERTH OR NOT (WIBON) or BERTH OR NO BERTH shall mean that if the designated loading or discharging Berth is not available on arrival, the Vessel on reaching any usual waiting place at the Port, shall be entitled to tender Notice of Readiness from it and Laytime shall commence in accordance with the Charter Party.

28. WHETHER IN PORT OR NOT (WIPON) shall mean that if the designated loading or discharging Berth and the usual waiting place at the Port are not available on arrival, the Vessel shall be entitled to tender Notice of Readiness from any recognised waiting place off the Port and Laytime shall commence in accordance with the Charter Party.

29. VESSEL BEING IN FREE PRATIQUE shall mean that the Vessel complies with port health requirements.

30. DEMURRAGE shall mean an agreed amount payable to the owner in respect of delay to the Vessel once the Laytime has expired, for which the owner is not responsible. Demurrage shall not be subject to exceptions which apply to Laytime unless specifically stated in the Charter Party.

31. DESPATCH MONEY or DESPATCH shall mean an agreed amount payable by the owner if the Vessel completes loading or discharging before the Laytime has expired.

32. DESPATCH ON ALL WORKING TIME SAVED or ON ALL LAYTIME SAVED shall mean that Despatch Money shall be payable for the time from the completion of loading or discharging until the expiry of the Laytime excluding any periods excepted from the Laytime.

33. DESPATCH ON ALL TIME SAVED shall mean that Despatch Money shall be payable for the time from the completion of loading or discharging to the expiry of the Laytime including periods excepted from the Laytime.

APPENDIX 4

Gentime*

Ship Brokers	THE BALTIC AND INTERNATIONAL MARITIME COUNCIL (BIMCO) GENERAL TIME CHARTER PARTY CODE NAME: "GENTIME"
	PART I
	1. Place and Date of Charter
2. Owners/Disponent Owners/Place of business (State full name, address, telex, and fax. No.)	3. Charterers/Place of business (State full name, address, telex and fax. No.)
4. Vessel's Name	5. Vessel's Description
	Flag:
6. Period of Charter (Cl. 1(a))	Year Built:
6(a). Margin on Final Period (Cl. 1(a))	Class:
	M/tons Deadweight (Summer):
7. Optional Period and Notice (Cl. 1(a))	GT/NT:
8. Delivery Port/Place or Range (Cl. 1(b))	Grain/Bale Capacity:
	Speed capability in knots (about):
9. Earliest Delivery Date/Time (Cl. 1(c)) / 10. Cancellation Date/Time (Cl. 1(c)(d))	Consumption in m/tons at above speed (about):
11. Notices of Delivery (Cl. 1(e)) / 12. Intended First Cargo (Cl. 1(f))	(Speed and Consumption on Summer dwt in good weather, max. windspeed 4Bft)
13. Trading Limits and Excluded Countries (Cl. 2(a))	
14. Excepted Countries (Cl. 2(b))	

(continued overleaf)

Printed by The BIMCO Charter Party Editor

Copyright, published by The Baltic and International Maritime Council (BIMCO), Copenhagen Issued September 1999

* Reproduced by kind permission of BIMCO.

597

15. Excluded Cargoes (Cl. 3(b))		

16. Hazardous Cargo Limit (Cl. 3(c))	17. Redelivery Port/Place or Range (Cl. 4(a))	18. Notices of Redelivery (Cl. 4(c))

19. Fuel Quantity on Delivery (Cl. 6(a))	20. Fuel Quantity on Redelivery (Cl. 6(a))	21. Fuel Price on Delivery (Cl. 6(c))	22. Fuel Price on Redelivery (Cl. 6(c))

23. Fuel Specifications (Cl. 6(d))

24. Hire (Cl. 8(a))	25. Owner's Bank Account (Cl. 8(b))

26. Grace Period (Cl. 8(c))	27. Max. Period for Requisition (Cl. 9(c))	28. General Average Adjustment (Cl. 14(b))

29. Supercargo (Cl. 15(f))	30. Victualling (Cl. 15(g))	31. Representation (Cl. 15(h))	32. Hold Cleaning by Crew (Cl. 15(m))

33. Lumpsum for Hold Cleaning on Redelivery (Cl. 15(m))	34. Vessel's Insured Value (Cl. 20(a))

35. Law and Arbitration (state Cl. 22(a), 22(b) or 22(c) of Cl. 22 as agreed; if 22(c) agreed, place of arbitration must be stated (Cl. 22))	36. Commission and to whom payable (Cl. 23)

37. Additional Clauses

It is agreed that this Contract shall be performed subject to the conditions contained in this Charter Party consisting of PART I including any additional clauses agreed and stated in Box 37 and PART II as well as Appendix A attached thereto. In the event of any conflict of conditions, the provisions of PART I and Appendix A shall prevail over those of PART II to the extent of such conflict but no further.

Signature (Owners)	Signature (Charterers)

Printed by The BIMCO Charter Party Editor

"GENTIME" - General Time Charter Party
Index

599

It is agreed on the date shown in Box 1 between the party named in Box 2 as Owners/ 1
Disponent Owners (hereinafter called "the Owners") of the Vessel named in Box 4, of 2
the description stated in Box 5 and the party named in Box 3 as Charterers as follows: 3

1. Period and Delivery
(a) *Period* - In consideration of the hire stated in Box 24 the Owners let and the 5
Charterers hire the Vessel for the period/trip(s) stated in Box 6. 6
The Charterers shall have the option to extend the Charter Party by the period(s)/ 7
trip(s) stated in Box 7 which option shall be exercised by giving written notice to the 8
Owners on or before the date(s) stated in Box 7. 9
Unless otherwise agreed, the Charterers shall have the option to increase or to 10
reduce the final period of the Charter Party by up to the number of days stated in 11
Box 6(a), which shall be applied only to the period finally declared. 12
(b) *Delivery Place* - The Owners shall deliver the Vessel to the Charterers at the port or 13
place stated in Box 8 or a port or place within the range stated in Box 8. 14
(c) *Delivery Time* - Delivery shall take place no earlier than the date/time stated in Box 15
9 and no later than the date/time stated in Box 10. Delivery shall be effected at any 16
time day or night, Saturdays, Sundays and holidays included. 17
(d) *Cancellation* - Should the Vessel not be delivered by the date/time stated in Box 10 18
the Charterers shall have the option to cancel the Charter Party without prejudice 19
to any claims the Charterers may otherwise have on the Owners under the Charter 20
Party. If the Owners anticipate that, despite their exercise of due diligence, the 21
Vessel will not be ready for delivery by the date/time stated in Box 10, they may 22
notify the Charterers in writing, stating the anticipated new date of readiness for 23
delivery, proposing a new cancelling date/time and requiring the Charterers to 24
declare whether they will cancel or will take delivery of the Vessel. Should the 25
Charterers elect to cancel or should they fail to reply within two (2) working 26
days (as applying at the Charterers' place of business) of receipt of such notification, 27
then unless otherwise agreed, the proposed new cancelling date/time will replace 28
the date/time stated in Box 10. This provision shall operate only once and should 29
the Vessel not be ready for delivery at the new cancelling date/time the Charterers 30
shall have the option of cancelling this Charter Party 31
(e) *Notice(s)* - The Owners shall give the Charterers not less than the number of days 32
notice stated in Box 11 of the date/time on which the Vessel is expected to be 33
delivered and shall keep the Charterers closely advised of possible changes in the 34
Vessel's expected date/time of delivery. The Owners shall give the Charterers and/or 35
their local agents notice of delivery when the Vessel is in a position to come on hire. 36
(f) *Vessel's Condition* - On arrival at the first port or place of loading the Vessel's holds 37
shall be clean and in all respects ready to receive the intended cargo identified in 38
Box 12, failing which the Vessel shall be off-hire from the time of rejection until she 39
is deemed ready. 40
(g) *Charterers' Acceptance* - Acceptance of delivery of the Vessel by the Charterers 41
shall not prejudice their rights against the Owners under this Charter Party. 42

2. Trading Areas
(a) *Trading Limits* - The Vessel shall be employed in lawful trades within Institute Warranty 44
Limits (IWL) and within the trading limits as stated in Box 13 between safe ports or 45
safe places where she can safely enter, lie always afloat, and depart. 46
(b) *Excepted Countries* - The Owners warrant that at the time of delivery the Vessel will 47
not have traded to any of the countries listed in Box 14. 48
(c) *Ice* - The Vessel shall not be required to enter or remain in any icebound port or 49
area, nor any port or area where lights, lightships, markers or buoys have been or 50
are about to be withdrawn by reason of ice, nor where on account of ice there is risk 51
that, in the ordinary course of events, the Vessel will not be able safely to enter and 52
leave the port or area or to depart after completion of loading or discharging. 53
The Vessel shall not be obliged to force ice but, subject to the Owners' prior approval, 54
may follow ice-breakers when reasonably required, with due regard to her size, 55
construction and class. If, on account of ice the Master considers it dangerous to 56
remain at the port or place of loading or discharging for fear of the Vessel being 57
frozen in and/or damaged he shall be at liberty to sail to any convenient place and 58
there await the Charterers' new instructions. 59

3. Cargo - Restrictions and Exclusions
(a) *Lawful Cargoes* - The Vessel shall be employed in carrying lawful cargo. Cargo of 60
a hazardous, injurious, or noxious nature or IMO-classified cargo shall not be carried 61
without the Owners' prior consent in which case it shall be carried only in accordance 62
with the provisions of sub-clause (c) of this Clause. 63
(b) *Excluded Cargoes* - Without prejudice to the generality of the foregoing, the following 64
cargoes shall be excluded: livestock, arms, ammunition, explosives, nuclear and 65
radioactive material other than radio-isotopes as described in sub-clause (d) of this 66
clause and any other cargoes enumerated in Box 15. 67
(c) *Hazardous Cargoes* - If the Owners agree that the Charterers may carry hazardous, 68
injurious, noxious or IMO-classified cargo, the amount of such cargo shall be limited 69
to the quantity indicated in Box 16 and the Charterers shall provide the Master with 70
evidence that the cargo has been packed, labelled and documented and shall be 71
loaded and stowed in accordance with IMO regulations, any mandatory local 72
requirements and regulations and/or recommendations of the competent authorities 73
of the country of the Vessel's registry. Failure to observe the foregoing shall entitle 74
the Master to refuse such cargo or, if already loaded, to discharge it in the Charterers' 75
time and at their risk and expense. 76
(d) *Radio-active Cargoes* - Radio-isotopes, used or intended to be used for industrial, 77
commercial, agricultural, medical or scientific purposes, may be carried subject to 78
prior consent by the Owners and the Master, provided that they are not of such a 79
category as to invalidate the Vessel's P & I cover. 80
(e) *Containers* - If cargo is carried in ISO-containers such containers shall comply with 81
the International Convention for Safe Containers. 82
(f) *Deck Cargo* - Subject to the Master's prior approval, which shall not be unreasonably 83
withheld, cargo may be carried on deck in accordance with the provisions of Clauses 84
17 (c) and 18. 85

4. Redelivery
(a) *Redelivery Place* - The Charterers shall redeliver the Vessel to the Owners at 87
the port or place stated in Box 17 or a port or place within the range stated in Box 17, 88
in the same order and condition as when the Vessel was delivered, fair wear and 89
tear excepted. 90
(b) *Acceptance of Redelivery* - Acceptance of redelivery of the Vessel by the Owners 91
shall not prejudice their rights against the Charterers under this Charter Party. 92
(c) *Notice* - The Charterers shall give the Owners not less than the number of days 93
notice stated in Box 18 indicating the port or place of redelivery and the expected 94
date on which the Vessel is to be ready for redelivery. 95
(d) *Last Voyage* - The Charterers warrant that they will not order the Vessel to commence 96
a voyage (including any preceding ballast voyage) which cannot reasonably be 97
expected to be completed in time to allow redelivery of the Vessel within the period 98
agreed and declared as per Clause 1(a). If, nevertheless, such an order is given, the 99
Owners shall have the option: (i) to refuse the order and require a substitute order 100
allowing timely redelivery; or (ii) to perform the order without prejudice to their rights 101
to claim damages for breach of charter in case of late redelivery. In any event, for 102
the number of days by which the period agreed and declared as per Clause 1(a) is 103
exceeded, the Charterers shall pay the market rate if this is higher than the rate 104
stated in Box 24. 105

5. On/Off-hire Surveys
Joint on-hire and off-hire surveys shall be conducted by mutually acceptable surveyors 107
at ports or places to be agreed. The on-hire survey shall be conducted without loss of 108
time to the Charterers, whereas the off-hire survey shall be conducted in the Charterers' 109
time. Survey fees and expenses shall be shared equally between the Owners and the 110
Charterers. 111
Both surveys shall cover the condition of the Vessel and her equipment as well as 112
quantities of fuels remaining on board. The Owners shall instruct the Master to co- 113
operate with the surveyors in conducting such surveys. 114

6. Bunkers
(a) *Quantity at Delivery/Redelivery* - The Vessel shall be delivered with about the quantity 116
of fuels stated in Box 19 and, unless indicated to the contrary in Box 20, the Vessel 117
shall be redelivered with about the same quantity, provided that the quantity of 118
fuels at redelivery is at least sufficient to allow the Vessel to safely reach the nearest 119
port at which fuels of the required type or better are available. 120
(b) *Bunkering prior to Delivery and Redelivery* - Provided that it can be accomplished 121
at scheduled ports, without hindrance to the operation of the Vessel, and by prior 122
arrangement between the parties, the Owners shall allow the Charterers to bunker 123
for the account of the Charterers prior to delivery and the Charterers shall allow the 124
Owners to bunker for the account of the Owners prior to redelivery. 125
(c) *Purchase Price* - The Charterers shall purchase the fuels on board at delivery at 126
the price stated in Box 21 and the Owners shall purchase the fuels on board at 127
redelivery at the price stated in Box 22. The value of the fuel on delivery shall be 128
paid together with the first instalment of hire. 129
(d) *Bunkering* - The Charterers shall supply fuel of the specifications and grades stated 130
in Box 23. The fuels shall be of a stable and homogeneous nature and unless 131
otherwise agreed in writing, shall comply with ISO standard 8217: 1996 or any 132
subsequent amendments thereof as well as with the relevant provisions of Marpol. 133
The Chief Engineer shall co-operate with the Charterers' bunkering agents and 134
fuel suppliers and comply with their requirements during bunkering, including but 135
not limited to checking, verifying and acknowledging sampling, readings or 136
soundings, meters etc. before, during and/or after delivery of fuels. During delivery 137
four representative samples of all fuels shall be taken at a point as close as possible 138
to the Vessel's bunker manifold. The samples shall be sealed and 139
signed by suppliers, Chief Engineer and the Charterers or their agents. Two samples 140
shall be retained by the suppliers and one each by the Vessel and the Charterers 141
If any claim should arise in respect of the quality or specification or grades of the 142
fuels supplied, the samples of the fuels retained as aforesaid shall be analysed by 143
a qualified and independent laboratory. 144
(e) *Liability* - The Charterers shall be liable for any loss or damage to the Owners 145
caused by the supply of unsuitable fuels or fuels which do not comply with the 146
specifications and grades set out in Box 23 and the Owners shall not be held liable 147
for any reduction in the Vessel's speed performance and/or increased bunker 148
consumption nor for any time lost and any other consequences arising as a result 149
of such supply. 150

7. Vessel's Gear and Equipment
(a) *Regulations* - The Vessel's cargo gear, if any, and any other related equipment 152
shall comply with the law and national regulations of the countries to which the 153
Vessel may be employed and the Owners shall ensure that the Vessel is at all times 154
in possession of valid certificates to establish compliance with such regulations. If 155
stevedores are not permitted to work due to failure of the Master and/or the Owners 156
to comply with the aforementioned regulations or because the Vessel is not in 157
possession of such valid certificates, then the Charterers may suspend hire for the 158
time lost thereby and the Owners shall pay all expenses incurred incidental to and 159
resulting from such failure (see Clause 11(d)). 160
(b) *Breakdown of Vessel's Gear* - All cargo handling gear, including derricks/cranes/ 161
winches if any, shall be kept in good working order and the Owners shall exercise 162
due diligence in maintaining such gear. In the event of loss of time due to a breakdown 163
of derrick(s) crane(s) or winch(es) for any period by reason of disablement or 164
insufficient power, the hire shall be reduced for the actual time lost thereby during 165
loading/discharging unless the lost time is caused by negligence of the Charterers 166
or their servants. If the Charterers continue working by using shore-crane(s) the 167
Owners shall pay the cost of shore craneage, to an amount not exceeding the 168
amount of hire payable to the Owners for such period. 169
(c) *Suez and Panama Canal* - During the currency of this Charter Party the Vessel 170

shall be equipped with all necessary fittings in good working order for Suez and Panama Canal transit . 172

(d) *Lighting* - The Owners shall ensure that the Vessel will supply, free of expense to the Charterers, sufficient lighting on deck and in holds to permit 24 hour working. 173-175

8. Hire 176

(a) *Rate* - The Charterers shall pay hire per day or pro rata for any part of a day from the time the Vessel is delivered until her redelivery to the Owners, in the currency and at the rate stated in Box 24. In the event that additional hire is payable in accordance with Clause 9(d) such hire shall be based on the rate applicable at the time of redelivery. All calculation of hire shall be made by reference to UTC (Universal Time Coordinated). 177-182

(b) *Payment* - Subject to sub-clause (d) payment of hire shall be made in advance in full, without discount every 15 days to the Owners' bank account designated in Box 25 or to such other account as the Owners may from time to time designate in writing, in funds available to the Owners on the due date. 183-186

(c) *Default* - In default of punctual and regular payment of hire the Owners shall have the right to withdraw the Vessel without prejudice to any other claim the Owners may have against the Charterers under this Charter Party. 187-189

Where there is a failure to make punctual and regular payment of hire due to oversight, negligence, errors or omissions on the part of the Charterers or their bankers, the Owners shall give the Charterers written notice of the number of clear banking days stated in Box 26 (as recognized at the agreed place of payment) in which to rectify the failure, and when so rectified within such number of days following the Owners' notice, the payment shall stand as regular and punctual. Failure by the Charterers to pay hire within the number of days stated in Box 26 of their receiving the Owners' notice as provided herein, shall entitle the Owners to withdraw the Vessel without further notice and without prejudice to any other claim they may have against the Charterers. 190-199

Further, at any time after the period stated in Box 26, as long as hire remains unpaid, the Owners shall, without prejudice to their right to withdraw, be entitled to suspend the performance of any and all of their obligations hereunder and shall have no responsibility whatsoever for any consequences thereof in respect of which the Charterers hereby agree to indemnify the Owners. Notwithstanding the provisions of Clause 9(a)(ii), hire shall continue to accrue and any extra expenses resulting from such suspension shall be for the Charterers' account. 200-206

(d) *Deductions* - On production of supporting vouchers the Charterers shall be entitled to deduct from the next hire due any expenditure incurred on behalf of the Owners which is for the Owners' account under this Charter Party. If such expenditure is incurred in a currency other than that in which hire is payable, conversion into such currency for the purpose of deduction shall be effected at the rate of exchange prevailing on the date the expenditure was incurred. 207-212

(e) *Redelivery Adjustment* - Should the Vessel be on her voyage towards the port or place of redelivery at the time payment of hire becomes due, said payment shall be made for the estimated time necessary to complete the voyage, less the estimated value of the fuels remaining on board at redelivery. When the Vessel is redelivered to the Owners any difference shall be refunded to or paid by the Charterers as appropriate but not later than thirty days after redelivery of the Vessel. 213-218

9. Off-hire 219

After delivery in accordance with Clause 1 hereof the Vessel shall remain on hire until redelivered in accordance with Clause 4, except for the following periods: 220-221

(a) *Inability to Perform Services* 222

If the Vessel is unable to comply with the instructions of the Charterers on account of: 223

(i) any damage, defect, breakdown, deficiency of, or accident to the Vessel's hull, machinery, equipment or repairs or maintenance thereto, including drydocking, excepting those occasions when Clauses 7(b) and 16(b) apply; 224-226

(ii) any deficiency of the Master, Officers and/or Crew, including the failure or refusal or inability of the Master, Officers and/or Crew to perform services when required; 227-228

(iii) Arrest of the Vessel at the suit of a claimant except where the arrest is caused by, or arises from, any act or omission of the Charterers, their servants, agents or sub-contractors; 229-231

(iv) the terms of employment of the Master, Officers and/or Crew; 232

then the Vessel shall be off-hire for the time thereby lost. 233

(b) *Deviation* - In the event of the Vessel deviating (which expression includes putting back, or putting into any port or place other than that to which she is bound under the instructions of the Charterers) for reasons other than to save life or property the Vessel shall be off-hire from the commencement of such deviation until the time when the Vessel is again ready to resume her service from a position not less favourable to the Charterers than that at which the deviation commenced, provided always that due allowance shall be given for any distance made good towards the Vessel's destination and any bunkers saved. However, should the Vessel alter course to avoid bad weather or be driven into port or anchorage by stress of weather, the Vessel shall remain on hire and all costs thereby incurred shall be for the Charterers' account. 234-243

(c) *Requisitions* - Should the Vessel be requisitioned by any government or governmental authority during the period of this Charter Party, the Owners shall immediately notify the Charterers. The Vessel shall be off-hire during the period of such requisition and any hire or compensation paid by any government or governmental authority in respect of such requisition shall be paid to the Owners. However, if the period of requisition exceeds the number of days stated in Box 27, either party shall have the option of cancelling the balance period of the Charter Party, by giving 14 days notice of cancellation to the other. 244-251

(d) *Addition to Charter Period* - Any time during which the Vessel is off-hire under this Charter Party may be added, at the option of the Charterers, to the charter period as determined in accordance with Clause 1(a). Such option shall be declared in writing not less than one month before the expected date of redelivery, or latest one week after the event if such event occurs less than one month before the expected date of redelivery. 252-257

10. Loss of Vessel 258

This Charter Party shall terminate and hire shall cease at noon on the day the Vessel is lost or becomes a constructive total loss and if missing, at noon on the date when last heard of. Any hire paid in advance and not earned shall be returned to the Charterers and payment of any hire due shall be deferred until the Vessel is reported safe. 259-262

11. Owners' Obligations 263

Except as provided elsewhere in this Charter Party, the Owners shall deliver the Vessel in the Class indicated in Box 5 and in a thoroughly efficient state of hull and machinery and shall exercise due diligence to maintain the Vessel in such Class and in every way fit for the service throughout the period of the Charter Party. 264-267

Nothing contained in this Charter Party shall be construed as a demise of the Vessel to the Charterers and the Owners remain at all times responsible for her navigation and for the due performance of related services, including but not limited to pilotage and towage even if paid for by the Charterers. 268-271

Unless otherwise agreed, the Owners shall provide and pay for the costs of the following:- 272

(a) *Wages* - Master's, Officers' and Crew's wages. 273

(b) *Stores* - All provisions, deck and engine-room stores, including lubricants. 274

(c) *Insurance of the Vessel* (See Clause 20). 275

(d) *Crew's assistance in*- 276

(i) preparing the Vessel's cranes, derricks, winches and/or cargo handling gear for use, 277-278

(ii) opening and closing any hatches (other than pontoon type hatches), ramps and other means of access to cargo, 279-280

(iii) docking, undocking and shifting operations in port, 281

(iv) bunkering, 282

(v) maintaining power during loading and discharging operations, 283

(vi) instructing crane drivers and winchmen in the use of the Vessel's gear, 284

The above services will be rendered by the crew if required, provided port and local regulations permit; otherwise charges for such services shall be for the Charterers' account. 285-287

(e) *Documentation* - Any documentation relating to the Vessel as required at the commencement of the Charter Party to permit the Vessel to trade within the limits provided in Box 13, including but not limited to international tonnage certificate, Suez and Panama tonnage certificates, certificate of registry, certificates relating to the strength, safety and/or serviceability of the Vessel's gear and certificates of financial responsibility for oil pollution as long as such oil pollution certificates can be obtained by the Owners in the market on ordinary commercial terms. 288-294

Such documentation shall be maintained during the currency of the Charter Party as necessary. 295-296

(f) *Deratisation* - A deratisation certificate at the commencement of the Charter Party and any renewal thereof throughout the Charter Party, except if certification is required as a result of the cargo carried or ports visited under this Charter Party in which case all expenses in connection therewith shall be for the account of the Charterers. 297-300

(g) *Smuggling* - Any fines, taxes or imposts levied in the event of smuggling by the Master, Officers and/or Crew. The Vessel shall be off-hire for any time lost as a result thereof. See also Clause 13(f). 301-303

12. Master 304

The Master shall be conversant with the English language and, although appointed by the Owners, shall at all times during the currency of this Charter Party be under the orders and directions of the Charterers as regards employment, agency or other arrangements. The Master shall prosecute all voyages with due dispatch and supervise loading and discharging operations to ensure that the seaworthiness of the Vessel is not affected. 305-310

The Charterers recognise the principles stated in IMO Resolution A.443 (XI) as regards maritime safety and protection of the marine environment and shall not prevent the Master from taking any decision in this respect which in his professional judgement is necessary. 311-314

13. Charterers' Obligations 315

The Charterers shall keep and care for the cargo at loading and discharging ports, be responsible for the stevedoring operations enumerated under sub-clause 13(d), arrange any transhipment and properly deliver the cargo at destination. 316-318

The Charterers shall furnish the Master with full and timely instructions and unless otherwise agreed, they shall provide and pay for the costs of the following throughout the currency of this Charter Party: 319-321

(a) *Voyage Expenses* - All port charges (including compulsory charges for shore watchmen and garbage removal), light and canal dues, pilotage, towage, consular charges, and all other charges and expenses relating to the cargo and/or to the Vessel as a result of her employment hereunder, other than charges or expenses provided for in Clause 11. 322-326

(b) *Bunker Fuel* (See Clause 6). - All fuels except for quantities consumed while the Vessel is off-hire. 327-328

(c) *Agency Costs* - All agency fees for normal ship's husbandry at all ports or places of call. 329-330

(d) *Stevedoring* - All stevedoring operations during the currency of this Charter Party including receipt, loading, handling, stuffing containers, stowing, lashing, securing, unsecuring, unlashing, discharging, stripping containers, tallying and delivering of all cargo. 331-334

(e) *Advances to Master* - Reasonable funds which, upon request by the Owners, are to be made available by Charterers' local agents to the Master for disbursements. The Charterers may deduct such advance funds from hire payments. 335-337

(f) *Contraband* - Any fines, taxes or imposts levied in the event that contraband and/or unmanifested drugs and/or cargoes are found to have been shipped as part of the cargo and/or in containers on board. The Vessel shall remain on hire during any time lost as a result thereof. However, if it is established that the Master, Officers and/or Crew are involved in smuggling then any security required shall be provided by the Owners. See also Clause 11(g). 338-343

601

14. Owners' Requirements 344

(a) *Maintenance* - Without prejudice to the provisions of Clause 9(a)(i), the Owners 345
shall have the right to take the Vessel out of service at any time for emergency 346
repairs, and by prior arrangement with the Charterers for routine maintenance, 347
including drydocking. 348

(b) *General Average* - General Average shall be adjusted, stated and settled at the 349
place shown in Box 26 according to the York-Antwerp Rules 1994 or any 350
subsequent modification thereto by an adjuster appointed by the Owners. Charter 351
hire shall not contribute to General Average. 352
General Average shall be adjusted in any currency at the sole option of the Owners. 353
Exchange into the currency of adjustment shall be calculated at the rate prevailing 354
on the date of payment for disbursements and on the date of completion of 355
discharge of the Vessel for allowances, contributory values etc. 356
The Charterers agree to co-operate with the Owners and their appointed adjuster 357
by supplying manifest and other information and, where required, to endeavour 358
to secure the assistance of the Charterers' local agents in the collection of security, 359
at the Owners' expense. 360

(c) *Salvage* - All salvage and assistance to other vessels shall be for the Owners' 361
and the Charterers' equal benefit after deducting the Master's and Crew's 362
proportion and all legal and other expenses including hire paid under the Charter 363
Party for time lost in the salvage, damage to the Vessel and fuel consumed. The 364
Charterers shall be bound by all measures taken by the Owners in order to secure 365
payment of salvage and to settle its amount. 366

(d) *Lien* - The Charterers warrant that they will not suffer, nor permit to be continued, 367
any lien or encumbrance incurred by them or their agents, which might have 368
priority over the title and interest of the Owners in the Vessel. In no event shall 369
the Charterers procure, nor permit to be procured, for the Vessel, any supplies, 370
necessaries or services without previously obtaining a statement signed by an 371
authorised representative of the furnisher thereof, acknowledging that such 372
supplies, necessaries or services are being furnished on the credit of the 373
Charterers and not on the credit of the Vessel or of the Owners and that the 374
furnisher claims no maritime lien on the Vessel therefor. 375
The Owners shall have a lien on all shipped cargo before or after discharge and 376
on all sub-freights and/or sub-hire including deadfreight and demurrage, for any 377
amount due under this Charter Party including but not limited to unpaid charter 378
hire, unreimbursed Charterers' expenses initially paid by the Owners, and 379
contributions in general average properly due. 380
The Charterers shall ensure that such lien is incorporated in all documents 381
containing or evidencing Contracts of Carriage issued by them or on their behalf. 382

15. Charterers' Requirements 383

(a) *Plans* - On concluding this Charter Party or as soon as practical thereafter the 384
Owners shall provide the Charterers with copies of any operational plans or 385
documents that the Charterers may reasonably request and which are necessary 386
for the safe and efficient operation of the Vessel. All documents received by the 387
Charterers shall be returned to the Owners on redelivery. 388

(b) *Flag and Funnel* - If they so require, the Charterers shall, during the currency of 389
this Charter Party, be allowed to fly their house flag and/or paint the funnel in the 390
Charterers' colours. All alterations including re-instatement shall be effected in 391
the Charterers' time and at cost. 392

(c) *Communications Facilities* - The Owners shall permit the Charterers' use of the 393
Vessel's communication facilities at cost. 394

(d) *Logs* - The Owners shall maintain full deck and engine room logs during the 395
currency of this Charter Party and the Charterers shall have full access to all the 396
Vessel's logs, rough and official, covering this period. The Owners undertake to 397
produce all such documentation promptly upon written request of the Charterers 398
and to allow them to make copies of relevant entries. 399

(e) *Replacement of Master and Officers* - If the Charterers shall have reason to be 400
dissatisfied with the conduct of the Master or Officers, the Owners shall, on 401
receiving particulars of the complaint in writing, investigate same and, if necessary, 402
replace the offending party or parties at their expense. 403

(f) *Supercargo* - The Owners shall provide and maintain a clean and adequate room 404
for the Charterers' Supercargo if any, furnished to the same standard as officers' 405
accommodation. The Supercargo shall be victualled with the Vessel's officers. 406
The Charterers shall pay at the daily rate shown in Box 29 for his accommodation and 407
victualling. The Supercargo shall be on board at the risk and expense of the 408
Charterers and both Charterers and Supercargo shall sign the customary indemnity 409
forms. 410

(g) *Victualling* - The Owners shall, when requested and authorised in writing by the 411
Charterers or their agents, victual other officials and servants of the Charterers at 412
the rate per person per meal shown in Box 30. 413

(h) *Representation* - Expenses for representation incurred by the Master for the 414
Charterers' account and benefit shall be settled by the Charterers. Payment of the 415
amount stated in Box 31, per month or pro rata. The Charterers shall indemnify the 416
Owners against all consequences and/or liabilities including customs fines which 417
may result from such representation. 418

(i) *Sub-Letting* - The Charterers shall have the right to sub-let all or part of the Vessel 419
whilst remaining responsible to the Owners for the performance of this Charter 420
Party. 421

(j) *Inspections* - The Charterers shall, upon giving reasonable notice, have the right to 422
a superficial inspection of the Vessel in their time and the Master shall within reason 423
co-operate with the Charterers to facilitate their inspection of the Vessel. The 424
Charterers shall pay for any and all expenses associated with such inspection and 425
the Owners shall be entitled to receive a copy of the report. 426

(k) *Weather Routeing* - The Charterers may supply the Master with weather routeing 427
information during the currency of this Charter Party. In this event the Master, though 428
not obliged to follow routeing information, shall comply with the reporting procedure 429
of the Charterers' weather routeing service. 430

(l) *Laying up* - At the written request of the Charterers, the Owners shall at any time 431
provide an estimate of any economies which may be possible in the event of laying- 432
up the Vessel. The Charterers shall then have the right to order the laying-up of the 433
Vessel at any time and for any period of time at a safe berth or safe place in their 434
option, and in the event of such laying-up the Owners shall promptly take reasonable 435
steps to effect all the economies in operating costs. The laying-up port or place and 436
laid-up arrangements shall be subject to approval by the Owners' insurers. Laying- 437
up preparation and reactivation cost, and all expenses incurred shall be for the 438
Charterers' account. The Charterers shall give sufficient notice of their intention in 439
this respect to enable the Owners to make necessary arrangements for 440
decommissioning and recommissioning. The Owners must give prompt credit to 441
the Charterers for all economies achieved. 442

(m) *Cleaning* - The Charterers may request the Owners to direct the crew to sweep 443
and/or wash and/or clean the holds between voyages and/or between cargoes 444
against payment at the rate per hold stated in Box 32, provided the crew is able to 445
undertake such work and is allowed to do so by local regulations. In connection 446
with any such operation the Owners shall not be responsible if the Vessel's holds 447
are not accepted or passed. 448
In lieu of cleaning the Charterers shall have the option to re-deliver the Vessel with 449
unclean/unswept holds against the lump sum payment stated in Box 33 excluding 450
the disposal of dunnage and/or waste, which shall be for Charterers' account. 451

16. Sundry Matters 452

(a) *Stowaways* 453

(i) The Charterers shall exercise due care and diligence in preventing stowaways 454
from gaining access to the Vessel by means of secreting away in cargo or 455
containers shipped by the Charterers. 456

(ii) if, despite the exercise of due care and diligence by the Charterers, stowaways 457
have gained access to the Vessel by means of secreting away in the cargo 458
and/or containers shipped by the Charterers, this shall amount to breach of 459
charter for the consequences of which the Charterers shall be liable and shall 460
hold the Owners harmless and shall keep them indemnified against all claims 461
whatsoever which may arise and be made against them. Furthermore, all time 462
lost and all expenses whatsoever and howsoever incurred, including fines, 463
shall be for the Charterers' account and the Vessel shall remain on hire. 464

(iii) Should the Vessel be arrested as a result of the Charterers' breach of charter 465
according to sub-clause (ii) above, the Charterers shall take all reasonable 466
steps to secure that within a reasonable time, the Vessel is released and at 467
their expense post bail or other security to obtain release of the Vessel. 468

(iv) If, despite the exercise of due care and diligence by the Owners, stowaways 469
have gained access to the Vessel by means other than secreting away in the 470
cargo and/or containers shipped by the Charterers, all time lost and all expenses 471
whatsoever and howsoever incurred, including fines, shall be for the Owners' 472
account. 473

(v) Should the Vessel be arrested as a result of stowaways having gained access 474
to the Vessel by means other than secreting away in the cargo and/or containers 475
shipped by the Charterers, the Owners shall take all reasonable steps to secure 476
that within a reasonable time, the Vessel is released and at their expense post 477
bail or other security to obtain release of the Vessel. 478

(b) *Stevedore Damage* - Notwithstanding anything contained herein to the contrary, 479
the Charterers shall be liable for any and all damage to the Vessel caused by 480
stevedores, provided the Master has notified the Charterers or their agents, in writing, 481
within 24 hours of the occurrence or as soon as possible thereafter but latest when 482
the damage could have been discovered by the exercise of due diligence. 483
The Master shall use his best efforts to obtain written acknowledgment by the party 484
or parties causing damage unless the damage has been made good in the 485
meantime. 486

(i) Stevedore damage affecting the Vessel's seaworthiness and/or the safety of 487
the crew, proper working of the Vessel and/or her equipment, shall be repaired 488
immediately by the Charterers and the Vessel is to remain on hire until such 489
repairs are completed and, if required, passed by the Vessel's classification 490
society. 491

(ii) Stevedore damage not affecting the Vessel's seaworthiness and/or the safety 492
of the crew shall be repaired, at the Charterers' option, before or after redelivery 493
concurrently with Owners' work. In the latter case no hire will be paid to the 494
Owners except in so far as the time required for the repairs for which the Charterers 495
are liable exceeds the time necessary to carry out the Owners' work. 496

(iii) The Owners shall have the option of requiring that stevedore damage affecting 497
the trading capabilities of the Vessel is repaired before redelivery. 498

(c) *Fumigation* - Expenses in connection with fumigations and/or quarantine ordered 499
because of cargo carried or ports visited while the Vessel is employed under this 500
Charter Party shall be for the Charterers' account. Expenses in connection with all 501
other fumigations and/or quarantine shall be for the Owners' account. 502

(d) *Anti-drug Clause* - The Charterers warrant to exercise the highest degree of care 503
and diligence in preventing unmanifested narcotic drugs and/or any other illegal 504
substances being loaded or concealed on board the Vessel. 505
Non-compliance with the provisions of this Clause shall amount to breach of warranty 506
for the consequences of which the Charterers shall be liable and shall hold the 507
Owners, the Master and the crew of the Vessel harmless and shall keep them 508
indemnified against all claims whatsoever which may arise and be made against them 509
individually or jointly. Furthermore, all time lost and all expenses incurred, 510
including fines, as a result of the Charterers' breach of the provisions of this Clause 511
shall be for the Charterers' account and the Vessel shall remain on hire. 512
Should the Vessel be arrested as a result of the Charterers' non-compliance with 513
the provisions of this Clause, the Charterers shall at their expense take all reasonable 514
steps to secure that within a reasonable time the Vessel is released and at their 515
expense post bail to secure release of the Vessel. 516
The Owners shall remain responsible for all time lost and all expenses incurred, 517
including fines, in the event that unmanifested narcotic drugs and other illegal 518

substances are found in the possession or effects of the Vessel's personnel. 519

17. Bills of Lading, Waybills and Other Contracts of Carriage 520

(a) *Signing Contracts of Carriage* 521

    (i) The Master shall sign bills of lading or waybills as presented in conformity with 522
mate's receipts. If requested, the Owners may authorise the Charterers and/or 523
their agents in writing to sign bills of lading, waybills, through bills of lading, or 524
multimodal bills of lading [hereafter collectively referred to as Contracts of 525
Carriage] on the Owners' and/or Master's behalf in conformity with mate's 526
receipts without prejudice to the terms and conditions of the Charter Party. 527

    (ii) In the event the Charterers and/or their agents, pursuant to the provisions of 528
sub-clause 17(a)(i) above, sign Contracts of Carriage which extend the Owners' 529
responsibility beyond the period during which the cargo is on board the Vessel 530
the Charterers shall indemnify the Owners against any claims for loss, damage 531
or expense which may result therefrom. 532

    (iii) Neither the Charterers nor their agents shall permit the issue of any Contract 533
of Carriage (whether or not signed on behalf of the Owners or on behalf of the 534
Charterers or on behalf of any Sub-Charterers) incorporating, where not 535
compulsorily applicable, the Hamburg Rules or any other legislation giving 536
effect to the Hamburg Rules or any other legislation imposing liabilities in excess 537
of Hague or Hague-Visby Rules. 538

(b) *Protective Clauses* - The Charterers warrant that Contracts of Carriage issued in 539
respect of cargo under this Charter Party shall incorporate the clauses set out in 540
Appendix A. 541

(c) *Deck Cargo* - Unless the cargo is stowed in fully closed containers, placed on 542
board the Vessel in areas designed for the carriage of containers with class-approved 543
container fittings, and secured to the Vessel by means of class-approved Vessel's 544
lashing gear or material, Contracts of Carriage covering cargo carried on deck 545
shall be claused: "Agreed to be shipped on deck at Charterers', Shippers' and 546
Receivers' risk, and responsibility for loss, damage or expense howsoever caused". 547

(d) *Defence of Claims* - Should the Charterers issue or cause to be issued a Contract 548
of Carriage in default of the provisions of this Clause 17, they shall be obliged upon 549
written request by the Owners to take over, pay for the defence and pay any 550
liability established in respect of any claim brought against the Vessel and/or the 551
Owners as a result of such default. 552

(e) *Payment and Indemnity* - The Charterers shall pay for, and/or indemnify the Owners 553
against any loss, damage or expense which results from any breach of the provisions 554
of this Clause 17. 555

18. Responsibilities 556

(a) *Cargo Claims* 557

    (i) *Definition* - For the purpose of this Clause 18(a), Cargo Claim means a 558
claim for loss, damage, shortage, (including slackage, ullage or pilferage), 559
overcarriage of or delay to cargo including customs fines or fines in respect 560
of such loss, damage, shortage, overcarriage or delay and includes: 561
(1) any legal costs or interest claimed by the original claimant making such a 562
claim: 563
(2) all legal, Club correspondents' and experts' costs reasonably incurred in 564
the defence of or in the settlement of the claim made by the original claim- 565
ant, but shall not include any costs of whatsoever nature incurred in making 566
a claim or in seeking an indemnity under this Charter Party. 567

    (ii) *Claim Settlement* - It is a condition precedent to the right of recovery by either 568
party under this Clause 18(a) that the party seeking indemnity shall have first 569
properly settled or compromised and paid the claim. 570

    (iii) *Owners' Liability* - The Owners shall be liable for any Cargo Claim arising or 571
resulting from: 572
(1) failure of the Owners or their servants to exercise due diligence before or 573
at the beginning of each voyage to make the Vessel seaworthy; 574
(2) failure of the Owners or their servants properly and carefully to carry, 575
keep and care for the cargo while on board; 576
(3) unreasonable deviation from the voyage described in the Contract of 577
Carriage unless such deviation is ordered or approved by the Charterers; 578
(4) errors in navigation or the management of the Vessel solely where the 579
Contract of Carriage is subject to mandatory application of legislation 580
giving effect to the Hamburg Rules. 581

    (iv) *Charterers' Liability* - The Charterers shall be liable for any Cargo Claim arising 582
or resulting from: 583
(1) the stevedoring operations enumerated under Clause 13(d) unless the 584
Charterers prove that such Cargo Claim was caused by the unseaworthi- 585
ness of the Vessel, in which case the Owners shall be liable; 586
(2) any transhipment in connection with through-transport or multimodal 587
transport save where the Charterers can prove that the circumstances 588
giving rise to the Cargo Claim occurred after commencement of the 589
loading of the cargo onto the Vessel and prior to its discharge; 590
(3) the carriage of cargo on deck unless such cargo is stowed in fully closed 591
containers, placed on board the Vessel in areas designed for the carriage 592
of containers with class-approved container fittings and secured to the 593
Vessel by means of class-approved Vessel's lashing gear or material. 594

    (v) *Shared Liability* - All Cargo Claims arising from other causes than those 595
enumerated under sub-clauses (iii) and (iv), shall be shared equally between 596
the Owners and the Charterers unless there is clear and irrefutable evidence 597
that the claim arose out of pilferage or the act or neglect of one or the other 598
party or their servants or sub-contractors, in which case that party shall bear 599
the full claim. 600

    (vi) *Charterers' Own Cargo* - If the cargo is the property of the Charterers, the 601
Owners shall have the same responsibilities and benefits as they would have 602
had under this Clause had the cargo been the property of a third party and 603
carried under a Bill of Lading incorporating the Hague-Visby Rules. 604

(b) *Fines, etc.* - The Charterers shall also be liable to the Owners for any losses, 605

damages, expenses, fines, penalties, or claims which the Owners may incur or 606
suffer by reason of the cargo or the documentation relating thereto failing to comply 607
with any relevant laws, regulations, directions or notices of port authorities or other 608
authorities, or by reason of any infestation, contamination or condemnation of the 609
cargo or of infestation, damage or contamination of the Vessel by the cargo. 610

(c) *Deck cargo* - The Charterers shall be liable to the Owners for any loss, damage, 611
expense or delay to the Vessel howsoever caused and resulting from the carriage 612
of cargo on deck save where the Charterers can prove that such loss, damage, 613
expense or delay was the result of negligence on the part of the Owners and/or 614
their servants. 615

(d) *Death or Personal injury* - Claims for death or personal injury having a direct 616
connection with the operation of the Vessel shall be borne by the Owners unless 617
such claims are caused by defect of the cargo or by the act, neglect or default of the 618
Charterers, their servants, agents or sub-contractors. 619

(e) *Agency* - The Owners authorise and empower the Charterers to act as the Owners' 620
agents solely to ensure that, as against third parties, the Owners will have the 621
benefit of any immunities, exemptions or liberties regarding the cargo or its carriage. 622
Subject to the provisions of Clause 17 the Charterers shall have no authority to 623
make any contracts imposing any obligations whatsoever upon the Owners in respect 624
of the cargo or its carriage. 625

(f) *Indemnity and Limitation* - The Owners and the Charterers hereby agree to indemnify 626
each other against all loss, damage or expenses arising or resulting from any 627
obligation to pay claims, fines or penalties for which the other party is liable in 628
accordance with this Charter Party. Both the Owners and the Charterers shall retain 629
their right to limit their liability against the other party in respect of any claim brought 630
by way of indemnity, notwithstanding that the other party has been denied the right 631
to limit against any third party or has failed in whatever manner to exercise its rights 632
of limitation. 633

(g) *Time Bar* - In respect of any Cargo Claims as between the Owners and the 634
Charterers, brought under sub-clause 18(a), unless extensions of time have been 635
sought or obtained from one party by the other or notice of arbitration has been 636
given by either party, such claim(s) shall be deemed to be waived and absolutely 637
time barred upon the expiry of two years reckoned from the date when the cargo 638
was or should have been delivered. When the Hamburg Rules apply compulsorily 639
the above time bar shall be extended to three years. 640

19. Exceptions 641

As between the Charterers and the Owners, responsibility for any loss, damage, delay 642
or failure of performance under this Charter Party not dealt with in Clause 18(a), shall 643
be subject to the following mutual exceptions: 644
Act of God, act of war, civil commotions, strikes, lockouts, restraint of princes and rulers, 645
and quarantine restrictions. 646
In addition, any responsibility of the Owners not dealt with in Clause 18(a) shall be 647
subject to the following exceptions: 648
Any act, neglect or default by the Master, pilots or other servants of the Owners in the 649
navigation or management of the Vessel, fire or explosion not due to the personal fault 650
of the Owners or their Manager, collision or stranding, unforeseeable breakdown of or 651
any latent defect in the Vessel's hull, equipment or machinery. 652
The above provisions shall in no way affect the provisions as to off-hire in this Charter 653
Party. 654

20. Insurances 655

(a) *Hull and Machinery* - The Owners warrant that the Vessel is insured for Hull, 656
Machinery and basic War Risks purposes at the value stated in Box 34. 657

(b) *Protection and Indemnity (P & I)* - The Owners warrant that throughout the period 658
of the Charter Party the Vessel will be fully covered for P&I risks, including through 659
transport cover, with underwriters approved by the Charterers which approval shall 660
not be unreasonably withheld. 661
The Charterers warrant that throughout the period of the Charter Party they will be 662
covered for Charterers' liability risk by underwriters approved by the Owners which 663
approval will not be unreasonably withheld. 664

21. War Risks ("Conwartime 1993") 665

(a) For the purpose of this Clause, the words: 666
    (i) "Owners" shall include the shipowners, bareboat charterers, disponent owners, 667
managers or other operators who are charged with the management of the 668
Vessel, and the Master; and 669
    (ii) "War Risks" shall include any war (whether actual or threatened), act of war, 670
civil war, hostilities, revolution, rebellion, civil commotion, warlike operations, 671
the laying of mines (whether actual or reported), acts of piracy, acts of terrorists, 672
acts of hostility or malicious damage, blockades (whether imposed against all 673
vessels or imposed selectively against vessels of certain flags or ownership, or 674
against certain cargoes or crews or otherwise howsoever), by any person, 675
body, terrorist or political group, or the Government of any state whatsoever, 676
which, in the reasonable judgement of the Master and/or the Owners, may be 677
dangerous or are likely to be or to become dangerous to the Vessel, her cargo, 678
crew or other persons on board the Vessel. 679

(b) The Vessel, unless the written consent of the Owners be first obtained, shall not be 680
ordered to or required to continue to or through, any port, place, area or zone 681
(whether of land or sea), or any waterway or canal, where it appears that the Vessel, 682
her cargo, crew or other persons on board the Vessel, in the reasonable judgement 683
of the Master and/or the Owners, may be, or are likely to be, exposed to War Risks. 684
Should the Vessel be within any such place as aforesaid, which only becomes 685
dangerous, or is likely to be or to become dangerous, after her entry into it, she 686
shall be at liberty to leave it. 687

(c) The Vessel shall not be required to load contraband cargo, or to pass through any 688
blockade, whether such blockade be imposed on all vessels, or is imposed selectively 689
in any way whatsoever against vessels of certain flags or ownership, or against 690
certain cargoes or crews or otherwise howsoever, or to proceed to an area where 691

she shall be subject, or is likely to be subject to a belligerent's right of search and/ or confiscation. 692 / 693

(d) (i) The Owners may effect war risks insurance in respect of the Hull and Machinery of the Vessel and their other interests (including, but not limited to, loss of earnings and detention, the crew and their Protection and Indemnity Risks), and the premiums and/or calls therefor shall be for their account. 694 / 695 / 696 / 697

(ii) If the Underwriters of such insurance should require payment of premiums and/or calls because, pursuant to the Charterers' orders, the Vessel is within, or is due to enter and remain within, any area or areas which are specified by such Underwriters as being subject to additional premiums because of War Risks, then such premiums and/or calls shall be reimbursed by the Charterers to the Owners at the same time as the next payment of hire is due. 698 / 699 / 700 / 701 / 702 / 703

(e) If the Owners become liable under the terms of employment to pay to the crew any bonus or additional wages in respect of sailing into an area which is dangerous in the manner defined by the said terms, then such bonus or additional wages shall be reimbursed to the Owners by the Charterers at the same time as the next payment of hire is due. 704 / 705 / 706 / 707 / 708

(f) The Vessel shall have liberty:- 709

(i) to comply with all orders, directions, recommendations or advice as to departure, arrival, routes, sailing in convoy, ports of call, stoppages, destinations, discharge of cargo, delivery, or in any other way whatsoever, which are given by the Government of the Nation under whose flag the Vessel sails, or other Government to whose laws the Owners are subject, or any other Government, or any other body or group whatsoever acting with the power to compel compliance with their orders or directions; 710 / 711 / 712 / 713 / 714 / 715 / 716

(ii) to comply with the order, directions or recommendations of any war risks underwriters who have the authority to give the same under the terms of the war risks insurance; 717 / 718 / 719

(iii) to comply with the terms of any resolution of the Security Council of the United Nations, any directives of the European Community, the effective orders of any other Supranational body which has the right to issue and give the same, and with national laws aimed at enforcing the same to which the Owners are subject, and to obey the orders and directions of those who are charged with their enforcement; 720 / 721 / 722 / 723 / 724 / 725

(iv) to divert and discharge at any other port any cargo or part thereof which may render the Vessel liable to confiscation as a contraband carrier; 726 / 727

(v) to divert and call at any other port to change the crew or any part thereof or other persons on board the Vessel when there is reason to believe that they may be subject to internment, imprisonment or other sanctions. 728 / 729 / 730

(g) If in accordance with their rights under the foregoing provisions of this Clause, the Owners refuse to proceed to the loading or discharging ports, or any one or more of them, they shall immediately inform the Charterers. No cargo shall be discharged at any alternative port without first giving the Charterers notice of the Owners' intention to do so and requesting them to nominate a safe port for such discharge. Failing such nomination by the Charterers within 48 hours of the receipt of such notice and request, the Owners may discharge the cargo at any safe port of their own choice. 731 / 732 / 733 / 734 / 735 / 736 / 737 / 738

(h) If in compliance with any of the provisions of sub-clauses (b) to (g) of this Clause anything is done or not done, such shall not be deemed a deviation, but shall be considered as due fulfilment of this Charter Party. 739 / 740 / 741

22. Law and Arbitration
742

*) (a) This Charter Party shall be governed by and construed in accordance with English law and any dispute arising out of or in connection with this Charter Party shall be referred to arbitration in London in accordance with the Arbitration Act 1996 or any statutory modification or re-enactment thereof save to the extent necessary to give effect to the provisions of this Clause. 743 / 744 / 745 / 746 / 747

The arbitration shall be conducted in accordance with the London Maritime Arbitrators Association (LMAA) Terms current at the time when the arbitration proceedings are commenced. 748 / 749 / 750

The reference shall be to three arbitrators. A party wishing to refer a dispute to arbitration shall appoint its arbitrator and send notice of such appointment in writing to the other party requiring the other party to appoint its own arbitrator within 14 calendar days of that notice and stating that it will appoint its arbitrator as sole arbitrator unless the other party appoints its own arbitrator and gives notice that it has done so within the 14 days specified. If the other party does not appoint its own arbitrator and give notice that it has done so within the 14 days specified, the party referring a dispute to arbitration may, without the requirement of any further prior notice to the other party, appoint its arbitrator as sole arbitrator and shall advise the other party accordingly. The award of a sole arbitrator shall be binding on both parties as if he had been appointed by agreement. 751 / 752 / 753 / 754 / 755 / 756 / 757 / 758 / 759 / 760 / 761 / 762

Nothing herein shall prevent the parties agreeing in writing to vary these provisions to provide for the appointment of a sole arbitrator. 763 / 764

In cases where neither the claim nor any counterclaim exceeds the sum of USD 50,000 (or such other sum as the parties may agree) the arbitration shall be conducted in accordance with the LMAA Small Claims Procedure current at the time when the arbitration proceedings are commenced. 765 / 766 / 767 / 768

*) (b) This Charter Party shall be governed by and construed in accordance with Title 9 of the United States Code and the Maritime Law of the United States and any dispute arising out of or in connection with this Charter Party shall be referred to three persons at New York, one to be appointed by each of the parties hereto, and the third by the two so chosen; their decision or that of any two of them shall be final, and for the purposes of enforcing any award, judgement may be entered on an award by any court of competent jurisdiction. The proceedings shall be conducted in accordance with the rules of the Society of Maritime Arbitrators, Inc. 769 / 770 / 771 / 772 / 773 / 774 / 775 / 776 / 777

In cases where neither the claim nor any counterclaim exceeds the sum of USD 50,000 (or such other sum as the parties may agree) the arbitration shall 778 / 779

be conducted in accordance with the Shortened Arbitration Procedure of the Society of Maritime Arbitrators, Inc. current at the time when the arbitration proceedings are commenced. 780 / 781 / 782

*) (c) This Charter Party shall be governed by and construed in accordance with the laws of the place mutually agreed by the parties and stated in Box 35 and any dispute arising out of or in connection with this Charter Party shall be referred to arbitration at the place stated in Box 35, subject to the procedures applicable there. 783 / 784 / 785 / 786 / 787

(d) If Box 35 in Part I is not appropriately filled in, sub-clause (a) of this Clause shall apply. 788 / 789

*) (a), (b) and (c) are alternatives; indicate alternative agreed in Box 35 790

23. Commission
791

The Owners shall pay a commission at the rate stated in Box 36 to the Broker(s) stated in Box 36 on any hire paid under this Charter Party or any continuation or extension thereof. If the full hire is not paid owing to breach of Charter Party by either of the parties the party liable therefor shall indemnify the Brokers against their loss of commission. 792 / 793 / 794 / 795 / 796

Should the parties agree to cancel this Charter Party, the Owners shall indemnify the Brokers against any loss of commission but in such case the commission shall not exceed the brokerage on one year's hire. 797 / 798 / 799

In signing this Charter Party the Owners acknowledge their agreement with the brokers to pay the commissions described in this Clause. 800 / 801

24. Notices
802

Any notices as between the Owners and the Charterers shall be in writing and sent to the addresses stated in Boxes 2 and 3 as the case may be or to such other addresses as either party may designate to the other in writing. 803 / 804 / 805

"GENTIME" General Time Charter Party
Appendix A - Protective Clauses

A. WAR RISKS ("Voywar 1993")

(1) For the purpose of this Clause, the words:

(a) "Owners" shall include the shipowners, bareboat charterers, disponent owners, managers or other operators who are charged with the management of the Vessel, and the Master; and

(b) "War Risks" shall include any war (whether actual or threatened), act of war, civil war, hostilities, revolution, rebellion, civil commotion, warlike operations, the laying of mines (whether actual or reported), acts of piracy, acts of terrorists, acts of hostility or malicious damage, blockades (whether imposed against all vessels or imposed selectively against vessels of certain flags or ownership, or against certain cargoes or crews or otherwise howsoever), by any person, body, terrorist or political group, or the Government of any state whatsoever, which, in the reasonable judgement of the Master and/or the Owners, may be dangerous or are likely to be or to become dangerous to the Vessel, her cargo, crew or other persons on board the Vessel.

(2) If at any time before the Vessel commences loading, it appears that, in the reasonable judgement of the Master and/or the Owners, performance of the Contract of Carriage, or any part of it, may expose, or is likely to expose, the Vessel, her cargo, crew or other persons on board the Vessel to War Risks, the Owners may give notice to the Charterers cancelling this Contract of Carriage, or may refuse to perform such part of it as may expose, or may be likely to expose, the Vessel, her cargo, crew or other persons on board the Vessel to War Risks; provided always that if this Contract of Carriage provides that loading or discharging is to take place within a range of ports, and at the port or ports nominated by the Charterers the Vessel, her cargo, crew, or other persons on board the Vessel may be exposed, or may be likely to be exposed, to War Risks, the Owners shall first require the Charterers to nominate any other safe port which lies within the range for loading or discharging, and may only cancel this Contract of Carriage if the Charterers shall not have nominated such safe port or ports within 48 hours of receipt of notice of such requirement.

(3) The Owners shall not be required to continue to load cargo for any voyage, or to sign Bills of Lading for any port or place, or to proceed or continue on any voyage, or on any part thereof, or to proceed through any canal or waterway, or to proceed to or remain at any port or place whatsoever, where it appears, either after the loading of the cargo commences, or at any stage of the voyage thereafter before the discharge of the cargo is completed, that, in the reasonable judgement of the Master and/or the Owners, the Vessel, her cargo (or any part thereof), crew or other persons on board the Vessel (or any one or more of them) may be, or are likely to be, exposed to War Risks. If it should so appear, the Owners may by notice request the Charterers to nominate a safe port for the discharge of the cargo or any part thereof, and if within 48 hours of the receipt of such notice, the Charterers shall not have nominated such a port, the Owners may discharge the cargo at any safe port of their choice (including the port of loading) in complete fulfilment of the Contract of Carriage. The Owners shall be entitled to recover from the Charterers the extra expenses of such discharge and, if the discharge takes place at any port other than the loading port, to receive the full freight as though the cargo had been carried to the discharging port and if the extra distance exceeds 100 miles, to additional freight which shall be the same percentage of the freight contracted for as the percentage which the extra distance represents to the distance of the normal and customary route, the Owners having a lien on the cargo for such expenses and freight.

(4) If at any stage of the voyage after the loading of the cargo commences, it appears that, in the reasonable judgement of the Master and/or the Owners, the Vessel, her cargo, crew or other persons on board the Vessel may be, or are likely to be, exposed to War Risks on any part of the route (including any canal or waterway) which is normally and customarily used in a voyage of the nature contracted for, and there is another longer route to the discharging port, the Owners shall give notice to the Charterers that this route will be taken. In this event the Owners shall be entitled, if the total extra distance exceeds 100 miles, to additional freight which shall be the same percentage of the freight contracted for as the percentage which the extra distance represents to the distance of the normal and customary route.

(5) The Vessel shall have liberty:-

(a) to comply with all orders, directions, recommendations or advice as to departure, arrival, routes, sailing in convoy, ports of call, stoppages, destinations, discharge of cargo, delivery or in any way whatsoever which are given by the Government of the Nation under whose flag the Vessel sails, or other Government to whose laws the Owners are subject, or any other Government which so requires, or any body or group acting with the power to compel compliance with their orders or directions;

(b) to comply with the orders, directions or recommendations of any war risks underwriters who have the authority to give the same under the terms of the war risks insurance;

(c) to comply with the terms of any resolution of the Security Council of the United Nations, any directives of the European Community, the effective orders of any other Supranational body which has the right to issue and give the same, and with national laws aimed at enforcing the same to which the Owners are subject, and to obey the orders and directions of those who are charged with their enforcement;

(d) to discharge at any other port any cargo or part thereof which may render the Vessel liable to confiscation as a contraband carrier;

(e) to call at any other port to change the crew or any part thereof or other persons on board the Vessel when there is reason to believe that they may be subject to internment, imprisonment or other sanctions;

(f) where cargo has not been loaded or has been discharged by the Owners under any provisions of this Clause, to load other cargo for the Owners' own benefit and carry it to any other port or ports whatsoever, whether backwards or forwards or in a contrary direction to the ordinary or customary route.

(6) If in compliance with any of the provisions of sub-clauses (2) to (5) of this Clause anything is done or not done, such shall not be deemed to be a deviation, but shall be considered as due fulfilment of the Contract of Carriage.

B. CLAUSE PARAMOUNT

The International Convention for the Unification of Certain Rules of Law relating to Bills of Lading signed at Brussels on 24 August 1924 ("the Hague Rules") as amended by the Protocol signed at Brussels on 23 February 1968 ("the Hague-Visby Rules") and as enacted in the country of shipment shall apply to this Contract. When the Hague-Visby Rules are not enacted in the country of shipment, the corresponding legislation in the country of destination shall apply, irrespective of whether such legislation may only regulate outbound shipments.

When there is no enactment of the Hague-Visby Rules in either the country of shipment or in the country of destination, the Hague-Visby Rules shall apply to this Contract, save where the Hague Rules as enacted in the country of shipment or if no such enactment is in place the Hague Rules as enacted in the country of destination apply compulsorily to this Contract.

The Protocol signed at Brussels on 21 December 1979 ("the SDR Protocol 1979") shall apply where the Hague-Visby Rules apply whether mandatorily or by this Contract.

The Carrier shall in no case be responsible for loss of or damage to cargo arising prior to loading, after discharging, or while the cargo is in the charge of another carrier, or with respect to deck cargo and live animals.

C. GENERAL AVERAGE

General Average shall be adjusted and settled at a port or place in the option of the Carrier according to the York-Antwerp Rules, 1994 or any subsequent amendment thereto.

D. HIMALAYA CLAUSE

It is hereby expressly agreed that no servant or agent of the Carrier (including every independent contractor from time to time employed by the Carrier) shall in any circumstances whatsoever be under any liability whatsoever to the Charterers, Shippers, Consignees, owner of the goods or to any holder of a Bill of Lading issued under this Charter Party, for any loss, damage or delay of whatsoever kind arising or resulting directly or indirectly from any act, neglect or default on his part while acting in the course of or in connection with his employment.

Without prejudice to the generality of the foregoing provisions in this clause, every exemption, limitation, condition and liberty herein contained and every right, exemption from liability, defence and immunity of whatsoever nature applicable to the Carrier or to which the Carrier is entitled hereunder, shall also be available and shall extend to protect every such servant or agent of the Carrier acting as aforesaid.

For the purpose of all the foregoing provisions of this clause the Carrier is or shall be deemed to be acting as agents or trustees on behalf of and for the benefit of all persons who might be his servants or agents from time to time (including independent contractors as aforesaid) and all such persons shall to this extent be or be deemed to be parties to this contract.

E. NEW JASON CLAUSE

In the event of accident, danger, damage or disaster before or after the commencement of the voyage resulting from any cause whatsoever, whether due to negligence or not, for which, or for the consequences of which, the Carrier is not responsible, by statute, contract, or otherwise, the goods, shippers, consignees, or owners of the goods shall contribute with the Carrier in general average to the payment of any sacrifices, losses, or expenses of a general average nature that may be made or incurred, and shall pay salvage and special charges incurred in respect of the goods.

If a salving vessel is owned or operated by the Carrier, salvage shall be paid for as fully as if salving vessel or vessels belonged to strangers. Such deposit as the Carrier, or his agents may deem sufficient to cover the estimated contribution of the goods and any salvage and special charges thereon shall, if required, be made by the goods, shippers, consignees or owners of the goods to the Carrier before delivery.

F.   BOTH-TO-BLAME COLLISION CLAUSE

If the Vessel comes into collision with another vessel as a result of the negligence of the other vessel and any act, neglect or default of the master, mariner, pilot or the servants of the Carrier in the navigation or in the management of the vessel, the owners of the goods carried hereunder will indemnify the Carrier against all loss or liability to the other or non-carrying vessel or her owners insofar as such loss or liability represents loss of, or damage to, or any claim whatsoever of the owners of said goods, paid or payable by the other or non-carrying vessel or her owners to the owners of said goods and set-off, recouped or recovered by the other or non-carrying vessel or her owners as part of their claim against the carrying Vessel or Carrier.

The foregoing provisions shall also apply where the owners, operators or those in charge of any vessels or objects other than, or in addition to, the colliding vessels or objects are at fault in respect to a collision or contact.

APPENDIX 5

Shelltime 4*

Code word for this Charter Party
"SHELLTIME4"

Issued December 1984 amended December 2003

Time Charter Party
LONDON   20

	IT IS THIS DAY AGREED between	1
	of (hereinafter referred to as "Owners"), being owners	2
	of the good motor/steam* vessel called	3
	(hereinafter referred to as "the vessel") described as per <u>Clause 1</u> hereof and	4
	of (hereinafter referred to as "Charterers"):	5
Description	1. At the date of delivery of the vessel under this charter and throughout the charter period:	6
And	(a) she shall be classed by a Classification Society which is a member of the International	7
Condition of	Association of Classification Societies;	8
Vessel	(b) she shall be in every way fit to carry crude petroleum and/or its products;	9
	(c) she shall be tight, staunch, strong, in good order and condition, and in every way fit for the	10
	service, with her machinery, boilers, hull and other equipment (including but not limited to hull	11
	stress calculator, radar, computers and computer systems) in a good and efficient state;	12
	(d) her tanks, valves and pipelines shall be oil-tight;	13
	(e) she shall be in every way fitted for burning, in accordance with the grades specified in <u>Clause</u>	14
	<u>29</u> hereof:	15
	(i) at sea, fuel oil for main propulsion and fuel oil/marine diesel oil* for auxiliaries;	16
	(ii) in port, fuel oil/marine diesel oil* for auxiliaries;	17
	(f) she shall comply with the regulations in force so as to enable her to pass through the Suez and	18
	Panama Canals by day and night without delay;	19
	(g) she shall have on board all certificates, documents and equipment required from time to time by	20
	any applicable law to enable her to perform the charter service without delay;	21
	(h) she shall comply with the description in the OCIMF Harmonised Vessel Particulars Questionnaire appended	22
	hereto as Appendix A, provided however that if there is any conflict between the provisions of	23
	this questionnaire and any other provision, including this <u>Clause 1</u>, of this charter such other	24
	provisions shall govern;	25
	(i) her ownership structure, flag, registry, classification society and management company shall	26
	not be changed;	27
Safety	(j) Owners will operate:	28
Management	(i) a safety management system certified to comply with the International Safety	29
	Management Code (ISM Code) for the Safe Operation of Ships and for	30
	Pollution Prevention;	31
	(ii) a documented safe working procedures system (including procedures for the	32
	identification and mitigation of risks);	33
	(iii) a documented environmental management system;	34
	(iv) documented accident/incident reporting system compliant with flag state	35
	requirements;	36
	(k) Owners shall submit to Charterers a monthly written report detailing all accidents/incidents and	37
	environmental reporting requirements, in accordance with the Shell Safety and Environmental	38
	Monthly Reporting Template appended hereto as Appendix B;	39
	(l) Owners shall maintain Health Safety Environmental (HSE) records sufficient to demonstrate	40
	compliance with the requirements of their HSE system and of this charter. Charterers reserve	41
	the right to confirm compliance with HSE requirements by audit of Owners.	42
	(m) Owners will arrange at their expense for a SIRE inspection to be carried out at intervals of six	43
	months plus or minus thirty days.	44
Shipboard	2. (a) At the date of delivery of the vessel under this charter and throughout the charter period:	45
Personnel	(i) she shall have a full and efficient complement of master, officers and crew for a	46
And their	vessel of her tonnage, who shall in any event be not less than the number required	47
Duties	by the laws of the flag state and who shall be trained to operate the vessel and her	48
	equipment competently and safely;	49
	(ii) all shipboard personnel shall hold valid certificates of competence in accordance	50
	with the requirements of the law of the flag state;	51
	(iii) all shipboard personnel shall be trained in accordance with the relevant	52
	provisions of the International Convention on Standards of Training, Certification	53
	and Watchkeeping for Seafarers, 1995 or any additions, modifications or	54
	subsequent versions thereof;	55

* Delete as appropriate

* Reproduced by kind permission of Shell International Trading & Shipping Company Limited.

Code word for this Charter Party
"SHELLTIME4"

Issued December 1984 amended December 2003

	(iv)	there shall be on board sufficient personnel with a good working knowledge of the English language to enable cargo operations at loading and discharging places to be carried out efficiently and safely and to enable communications between the vessel and those loading the vessel or accepting discharge there from to be carried out quickly and efficiently;
	(v)	the terms of employment of the vessels staff and crew will always remain acceptable to The International Transport Workers Federation and the vessel will at all times carry a Blue Card;
	(vi)	the nationality of the vessels officers given in the OCIMF Vessel Particulars Questionnaire referred to in <u>Clause 1(h)</u> will not change without Charterers prior agreement.

(b) Owners guarantee that throughout the charter service the master shall with the vessel's officers and crew, unless otherwise ordered by Charterers;
  (i)   prosecute all voyages with the utmost despatch;
  (ii) render all customary assistance; and
  (iii) load and discharge cargo as rapidly as possible when required by Charterers or their agents to do so, by night or by day, but always in accordance with the laws of the place of loading or discharging (as the case may be) and in each case in accordance with any applicable laws of the flag state.

Duty to Maintain   3. (a) Throughout the charter service Owners shall, whenever the passage of time, wear and tear or any event (whether or not coming within <u>Clause 27</u> hereof) requires steps to be taken to maintain or restore the conditions stipulated in <u>Clauses 1</u> and <u>2(a)</u>, exercise due diligence so to maintain or restore the vessel.

(b) If at any time whilst the vessel is on hire under this charter the vessel fails to comply with the requirements of <u>Clauses 1</u>, <u>2(a)</u> or <u>10</u> then hire shall be reduced to the extent necessary to indemnify Charterers for such failure. If and to the extent that such failure affects the time taken by the vessel to perform any services under this charter, hire shall be reduced by an amount equal to the value, calculated at the rate of hire, of the time so lost.
Any reduction of hire under this <u>sub-Clause (b)</u> shall be without prejudice to any other remedy available to Charterers, but where such reduction of hire is in respect of time lost, such time shall be excluded from any calculation under <u>Clause 24</u>.

(c) If Owners are in breach of their obligations under <u>Clause 3(a)</u>, Charterers may so notify Owners in writing and if, after the expiry of 30 days following the receipt by Owners of any such notice, Owners have failed to demonstrate to Charterers' reasonable satisfaction the exercise of due diligence as required in <u>Clause 3(a)</u>, the vessel shall be off-hire, and no further hire payments shall be due, until Owners have so demonstrated that they are exercising such due diligence.

(d) Owners shall advise Charterers immediately, in writing, should the vessel fail an inspection by, but not limited to, a governmental and/or port state authority, and/or terminal and/or major charterer of similar tonnage. Owners shall simultaneously advise Charterers of their proposed course of action to remedy the defects which have caused the failure of such inspection.

(e) If, in Charterers reasonably held view:
failure of an inspection, or,
any finding of an inspection,
referred to in <u>Clause 3 (d)</u>, prevents normal commercial operations then Charterers have the option to place the vessel off-hire from the date and time that the vessel fails such inspection, or becomes commercially inoperable, until the date and time that the vessel passes a re-inspection by the same organisation, or becomes commercially operable, which shall be in a position no less favourable to Charterers than at which she went off-hire.

(f) Furthermore, at any time while the vessel is off-hire under this <u>Clause 3</u> (with the exception of <u>lause 3(e)(ii)</u>), Charterers have the option to terminate this charter by giving notice in writing with effect from the date on which such notice of termination is received by Owners or from any later date stated in such notice. This <u>sub-Clause (f)</u> is without prejudice to any rights of Charterers or obligations of Owners under this charter or otherwise (including without limitation Charterers' rights under <u>Clause 21</u> hereof).

Period Trading Limits and Safe Places   4. (a) Owners agree to let and Charterers agree to hire the vessel for a period of
plus or minus   days in Charterers option, commencing from the time and date of delivery of the vessel, for the purpose of carrying all lawful merchandise (subject always to <u>Clause 28</u>) including in particular;
_____

in any part of the world, as Charterers shall direct, subject to the limits of the current British Institute Warranties and any subsequent amendments thereof. Notwithstanding the foregoing, but subject to <u>Clause 35</u>, Charterers may order the vessel to ice-bound waters or to any part of the world outside such limits provided that Owners consent thereto (such consent not to be unreasonably withheld) and that Charterers pay for any insurance premium required by the vessel's underwriters as a consequence of such order.

(b) Any time during which the vessel is off-hire under this charter may be added to the charter

	period in Charterers option up to the total amount of time spent off-hire. In such cases the rate of hire will be that prevailing at the time the vessel would, but for the provisions of this Clause, have been redelivered.	122 123 124
	(c) Charterers shall use due diligence to ensure that the vessel is only employed between and at safe places (which expression when used in this charter shall include ports, berths, wharves, docks, anchorages, submarine lines, alongside vessels or lighters, and other locations including locations at sea) where she can safely lie always afloat. Notwithstanding anything contained in this or any other clause of this charter, Charterers do not warrant the safety of any place to which they order the vessel and shall be under no liability in respect thereof except for loss or damage caused by their failure to exercise due diligence as aforesaid. Subject as above, the vessel shall be loaded and discharged at any places as Charterers may direct, provided that Charterers shall exercise due diligence to ensure that any ship-to-ship transfer operations shall conform to standards not less than those set out in the latest published edition of the ICS/OCIMF Ship-to-Ship Transfer Guide.	125 126 127 128 129 130 131 132 133 134 135
	(d) Unless otherwise agreed, the vessel shall be delivered by Owners dropping outward pilot at a port in	136 137
	_____	138
	at Owners' option and redelivered to Owners dropping outward pilot at a port in	139 140
	_____	
	at Charterers' option.	141
	(e) The vessel will deliver with last cargo(es) of and will redeliver with last cargo(es) of	142
	(f) Owners are required to give Charterers days prior notice of delivery and Charterers are required to give Owners days prior notice of redelivery.	143 144
Laydays/ Cancelling	5. The vessel shall not be delivered to Charterers before and Charterers shall have the option of cancelling this charter if the vessel is not ready and at their disposal on or before	145 146 147
Owners to Provide	6. Owners undertake to provide and to pay for all provisions, wages (including but not limited to all overtime payments), and shipping and discharging fees and all other expenses of the master, officers and crew; also, except as provided in Clauses 4 and 34 hereof, for all insurance on the vessel, for all deck, cabin and engine-room stores, and for water; for all drydocking, overhaul, maintenance and repairs to the vessel; and for all fumigation expenses and de-rat certificates. Owners' obligations under this Clause 6 extend to all liabilities for customs or import duties arising at any time during the performance of this charter in relation to the personal effects of the master, officers and crew, and in relation to the stores, provisions and other matters aforesaid which Owners are to provide and pay for and Owners shall refund to Charterers any sums Charterers or their agents may have paid or been compelled to pay in respect of any such liability. Any amounts allowable in general average for wages and provisions and stores shall be credited to Charterers insofar as such amounts are in respect of a Period when the vessel is on-hire.	148 149 150 151 152 153 154 155 156 157 158 159
Charterers to Provide	7. (a) Charterers shall provide and pay for all fuel (except fuel used for domestic services), towage and pilotage and shall pay agency fees, port charges, commissions, expenses of loading and unloading cargoes, canal dues and all charges other than those payable by Owners in accordance with Clause 6 hereof, provided that all charges for the said items shall be for Owners' account when such items are consumed, employed or incurred for Owners' purposes or while the vessel is off-hire (unless such items reasonably relate to any service given or distance made good and taken into account under Clause 21 or 22); and provided further that any fuel used in connection with a general average sacrifice or expenditure shall be paid for by Owners.	160 161 162 163 164 165 166 167
	(b) In respect of bunkers consumed for Owners purposes these will be charged on each occasion by Charterers on a first-in-first-out basis valued on the prices actually paid by Charterers.	168 169
	(c) If the trading limits of this charter include ports in the United States of America and/or its protectorates then Charterers shall reimburse Owners for port specific charges relating to additional premiums charged by providers of oil pollution cover, when incurred by the vessel calling at ports in the United States of America and/or its protectorates in accordance with Charterers orders.	170 171 172 173 174
Rate of Hire	8. Subject as herein provided, Charterers shall pay for the use and hire of the vessel at the rate of United States Dollars per day, and pro rata for any part of a day, from the time and date of her delivery (local time) to Charterers until the time and date of redelivery (local time) to Owners.	175 176 177 178
Payment of Hire	9. Subject to Clause 3 (c) and 3 (e), payment of hire shall be made in immediately available funds to:	179 180
	_____	181
	Account:	182
	_____	183 184
	in United States Dollars per calendar month in advance, less:	185
	(i) any hire paid which Charterers reasonably estimate to relate to off-hire periods; and;	186

609

	(ii) any amounts disbursed on Owners' behalf, any advances and commission thereon, and charges which are for Owners' account pursuant to any provision hereof, and;	187 188
	(iii) any amounts due or reasonably estimated to become due to Charterers under <u>Clause 3 (c)</u> or <u>24</u> hereof,	189 190

any such adjustments to be made at the due date for the next monthly payment after the facts have been ascertained. Charterers shall not be responsible for any delay or error by Owners' bank in crediting Owners' account provided that Charterers have made proper and timely payment.

In default of such proper and timely payment:

(a) Owners shall notify Charterers of such default and Charterers shall within seven days of receipt of such notice pay to Owners the amount due, including interest, failing which Owners may withdraw the vessel from the service of Charterers without prejudice to any other rights Owners may have under this charter or otherwise; and;

(b) Interest on any amount due but not paid on the due date shall accrue from the day after that date up to and including the day when payment is made, at a rate per annum which shall be 1% above the U.S. Prime Interest Rate as published by the Chase Manhattan Bank in New York at 12.00 New York time on the due date, or, if no such interest rate is published on that day, the interest rate published on the next preceding day on which such a rate was so published, computed on the basis of a 360 day year of twelve 30-day months, compounded semi-annually.

Space Available to Charterers
10. The whole reach, burthen and decks on the vessel and any passenger accommodation (including Owners' suite) shall be at Charterers' disposal, reserving only proper and sufficient space for the vessel's master, officers, crew, tackle, apparel, furniture, provisions and stores, provided that the weight of stores on board shall not, unless specially agreed, exceed   tonnes at any time during the charter period.

Segregated Ballast
11. In connection with the Council of the European Union Regulation on the Implementation of IMO Resolution A747(18) Owners will ensure that the following entry is made on the International Tonnage Certificate (1969) under the section headed "remarks":
"The segregated ballast tanks comply with the Regulation 13 of Annex 1 of the International Convention for the prevention of pollution from ships, 1973, as modified by the Protocol of 1978 relating thereto, and the total tonnage of such tanks exclusively used for the carriage of segregated water ballast is   The reduced gross tonnage which should be used for the calculation of tonnage based fees is   ".

Instructions And Logs
12. Charterers shall from time to time give the master all requisite instructions and sailing directions, and the master shall keep a full and, correct log of the voyage or voyages, which Charterers or their agents may inspect as required. The master shall when required furnish Charterers or their agents with a true copy of such log and with properly completed loading and discharging port sheets and voyage reports for each voyage and other returns as Charterers may require. Charterers shall be entitled to take copies at Owners' expense of any such documents which are not provided by the master.

Bills of Lading
13. (a) The master (although appointed by Owners) shall be under the orders and direction of Charterers as regards employment of the vessel, agency and other arrangements, and shall sign Bills of Lading as Charterers or their agents may direct (subject always to <u>Clauses 35 (a)</u> and <u>40</u>) without prejudice to this charter. Charterers hereby indemnify Owners against all consequences or liabilities that may arise;
(i) from signing Bills of Lading in accordance with the directions of Charterers or their agents, to the extent that the terms of such Bills of Lading fail to conform to the requirements of this charter, or (except as provided in <u>Clause 13 (b)</u> from the master otherwise complying with Charterers' or their agents' orders;
(ii) from any irregularities in papers supplied by Charterers or their agents.
(b) If Charterers by telex, facsimile or other form of written communication that specifically refers To this Clause request Owners to discharge a quantity of cargo either without Bills of Lading and/or at a discharge place other than that named in a Bill of Lading and/or that is different from the Bill of Lading quantity, then Owners shall discharge such cargo in accordance with Charterer's instructions in consideration of receiving the following indemnity which shall be deemed to be given by Charterers on each and every such occasion and which is limited in value to 200% of the CIF value of the cargo carried on board;
"(i) Charterers shall indemnify Owners and Owners' servants and agents in respect of any liability loss or damage of whatsoever nature (including legal costs as between attorney or solicitor and client and associated expenses) which Owners may sustain by reason of delivering such cargo in accordance with Charterers' request.
(ii) If any proceeding is commenced against Owners or any of Owners' servants or agents in connection with the vessel having delivered cargo in accordance with such request, Charterers shall provide Owners or any of Owners' servants or agents from time to time on demand with sufficient funds to defend the said proceedings.
(iii) If the vessel or any other vessel or property belonging to Owners should be arrested or detained, or if the arrest or detention thereof should be threatened, by reason of discharge in accordance with Charterers instruction as aforesaid, Charterers shall provide on demand such

	bail or other security as may be required to prevent such arrest or detention or to secure the	253
	release of such vessel or property and Charterers shall indemnify Owners in respect of any loss,	254
	damage or expenses caused by such arrest or detention whether or not same may be justified.	255
	(iv) Charterers shall, if called upon to do so at any time while such cargo is in Charterers'	256
	possession, custody or control, redeliver the same to Owners.	257
	(v) As soon as all original Bills of Lading for the above cargo which name as discharge port the	258
	place where delivery actually occurred shall have arrived and/or come into Charterers'	259
	possession, Charterers shall produce and deliver the same to Owners whereupon Charterers'	260
	liability hereunder shall cease.	261
	Provided however, if Charterers have not received all such original Bills of Lading by 24.00	262
	hours on the day 36 calendar months after the date of discharge, that this indemnity shall	263
	terminate at that time unless before that time Charterers have received from Owners written	264
	notice that:	265
	aaa) Some person is making a claim in connection with Owners delivering cargo pursuant to	266
	Charterers' request or,	267
	bbb) Legal proceedings have been commenced against Owners and/or carriers and/or	268
	Charterers and/or any of their respective servants or agents and/or the vessel for the same	269
	reason.	270
	When Charterers have received such a notice, then this indemnity shall continue in force until	271
	such claim or legal proceedings are settled. Termination of this indemnity shall not prejudice	272
	any legal rights a party may have outside this indemnity.	273
	(vi) Owners shall promptly notify Charterers if any person (other than a person to whom	274
	Charterers ordered cargo to be delivered) claims to be entitled to such cargo and/or if the vessel	275
	or any other property belonging to Owners is arrested by reason of any such discharge of cargo.	276
	vii) This indemnity shall be governed and construed in accordance with the English law and	277
	each and any dispute arising out of or in connection with this indemnity shall be subject to the	278
	jurisdiction of the High Court of Justice of England.	279
	(c) Owners warrant that the Master will comply with orders to carry and discharge against one or	280
	more Bills of Lading from a set of original negotiable Bills of Lading should Charterers so	281
	require.	282
Conduct Vessel's Personnel	14. If Charterers complain of the conduct of the master or any of the officers or crew, Owners shall	283
	immediately investigate the complaint. If the complaint proves to be well founded, Owners shall,	284
	without delay, make a change in the appointments and Owners shall in any event communicate the	285
	result of their investigations to Charterers as soon as possible.	286
Bunkers at Delivery and Redelivery	15. Charterers shall accept and pay for all bunkers on board at the time of delivery, and Owners shall on	287
	redelivery (whether it occurs at the end of the charter or on the earlier termination of this charter)	288
	accept and pay for all bunkers remaining on board, at the price actually paid, on a first-in-first-out	289
	basis. Such prices are to be supported by paid invoices.	290
	Vessel to be delivered to and redelivered from the charter with, at least, a quantity of bunkers on board	291
	sufficient to reach the nearest main bunkering port.	292
	Notwithstanding anything contained in this charter all bunkers on board the vessel shall, throughout the	293
	duration of this charter, remain the property of Charterers and can only be purchased on the terms	294
	specified in the charter at the end of the charter period or, if earlier, at the termination of the	295
	charter.	296
Stevedores Pilots, Tugs	16. Stevedores, when required, shall be employed and paid by Charterers, but this shall not relieve Owners	297
	from responsibility at all times for proper stowage, which must be controlled by the master who shall	298
	keep a strict account of all cargo loaded and discharged. Owners hereby indemnify Charterers, their	299
	servants and agents against all losses, claims, responsibilities and liabilities arising in any way	300
	whatsoever from the employment of pilots, tugboats or stevedores, who although employed by	301
	Charterers shall be deemed to be the servants of and in the service of Owners and under their	302
	instructions (even if such pilots, tugboat personnel or stevedores are in fact the servants of Charterers	303
	their agents or any affiliated company); provided, however, that;	304
	(a) the foregoing indemnity shall not exceed the amount to which Owners would have been	305
	entitled to limit their liability if they had themselves employed such pilots, tugboats or	306
	stevedores, and;	307
	(b) Charterers shall be liable for any damage to the vessel caused by or arising out of the use of	308
	stevedores, fair wear and tear excepted, to the extent that Owners are unable by the exercise of	309
	due diligence to obtain redress therefor from stevedores.	310
Super-Numeraries	17. Charterers may send representatives in the vessel's available accommodation upon any voyage made	311
	under this charter, Owners finding provisions and all requisites as supplied to officers, except alcohol.	312
	Charterers paying at the rate of United States Dollars 15 (fifteen) per day for each representative while	313
	on board the vessel.	314
Sub-letting/ Assignment/ Novation	18. Charterers may sub-let the vessel, but shall always remain responsible to Owners for due fulfilment of	315
	this charter. Additionally Charterers may assign or novate this charter to any company of the Royal	316
	Dutch/ Shell Group of Companies.	317
Final Voyage	19. If when a payment of hire is due hereunder Charterers reasonably expect to redeliver the vessel before	318
	the next payment of hire would fall due, the hire to be paid shall be assessed on Charterers' reasonable	319

	estimate of the time necessary to complete Charterers' programme up to redelivery, and from which	320
	estimate Charterers may deduct amounts due or reasonably expected to become due for;	321
	(a) disbursements on Owners' behalf or charges for Owners' account pursuant to any provision	322
	hereof, and;	323
	(b) bunkers on board at redelivery pursuant to Clause 15.	324
	Promptly after redelivery any overpayment shall be refunded by Owners or any underpayment made	325
	good by Charterers.	326
	If at the time this charter would otherwise terminate in accordance with Clause 4 the vessel is on a	327
	ballast voyage to a port of redelivery or is upon a laden voyage, Charterers shall continue to have the	328
	use of the vessel at the same rate and conditions as stand herein for as long as necessary to complete	329
	such ballast voyage, or to complete such laden voyage and return to a port of redelivery as provided by	330
	this charter, as the case may be.	331

Loss of
Vessel

20. Should the vessel be lost, this charter shall terminate and hire shall cease at noon on the day of her
loss; should the vessel be a constructive total loss, this charter shall terminate and hire shall cease at
noon on the day on which the vessel's underwriters agree that the vessel is a constructive total loss;
should the vessel be missing, this charter shall terminate and hire shall cease at noon on the day on
which she was last heard of. Any hire paid in advance and not earned shall be returned to Charterers
and Owners shall reimburse Charterers for the value of the estimated quantity of bunkers m on board at
the time of termination, at the price paid by Charterers at the last bunkering port.

Off-hire

21. (a) On each and every occasion that there is loss of time (whether by way of interruption in the
vessel's service or, from reduction in the vessel's performance, or in any other manner);
    (i) due to deficiency of personnel or stores; repairs; gas-freeing for repairs; time in and
waiting to enter dry dock for repairs; breakdown (whether partial or total) of machinery,
boilers or other parts of the vessel or her equipment (including without limitation tank
coatings); overhaul, maintenance or survey; collision, stranding, accident or damage to
the vessel; or any other similar cause preventing the efficient working of the vessel; and
such loss continues for more than three consecutive hours (if resulting from interruption
in the vessel's service) or cumulates to more than three hours (if resulting from partial
loss of service); or;
    (ii) due to industrial action, refusal to sail, breach of orders or neglect of duty on the part of
the master, officers or crew; or;
    (iii) for the purpose of obtaining medical advice or treatment for or landing any sick or
injured person (other than a Charterers' representative carried under Clause 17 hereof) or
for the purpose of landing the body of any person (other than a Charterers'
representative), and such loss continues for more than three consecutive hours; or;
    (iv) due to any delay in quarantine arising from the master, officers or crew having had
communication with the shore at any infected area without the written consent or
instructions of Charterers or their agents, or to any detention by customs or other
authorities caused by smuggling or other infraction of local law on the part of the master,
officers, or crew; or;
    (v) due to detention of the vessel by authorities at home or abroad attributable to legal
action against or breach of regulations by the vessel, the vessel's owners, or Owners
(unless brought about by the act or neglect of Charterers); then;
without prejudice to Charterers' rights under Clause 3 or to any other rights of Charterers
hereunder, or otherwise, the vessel shall be off-hire from the commencement of such loss of
time until she is again ready and in an efficient state to resume her service from a position not
less favourable to Charterers than that at which such loss of time commenced; provided,
however, that any service given or distance made good by the vessel whilst off-hire shall be
taken into account in assessing the amount to be deducted from hire.

    (b) If the vessel fails to proceed at any guaranteed speed pursuant to Clause 24, and such failure
arises wholly or partly from any of the causes set out in Clause 21(a) above, then the period for
which the vessel shall be off-hire under this Clause 21 shall be the difference between;
    (i) the time the vessel would have required to perform the relevant service at such
guaranteed speed, and;
    (ii) the time actually taken to perform such service (including any loss of time arising from
interruption in the performance of such service).
For the avoidance of doubt, all time included under (ii) above shall be excluded from any
computation under Clause 24.

    (c) Further and without prejudice to the foregoing, in the event of the vessel deviating (which
expression includes without limitation putting back, or putting into any port other than that to
which she is bound under the instructions of Charterers) for any cause or purpose mentioned in
Clause 21(a), the vessel shall be off-hire from the commencement of such deviation until the
time when she is again ready and in an efficient state to resume her service from a position not
less favourable to Charterers than that at which the deviation commenced, provided, however,
that any service given or distance made good by the vessel whilst so off-hire shall be taken into
account in assessing the amount to be deducted from hire. If the vessel, for any cause or
purpose mentioned in Clause 21 (a), puts into any port other than the port to which she is

Line numbers: 332–386

	bound on the instructions of Charterers, the port charges, pilotage and other expenses at such port shall be borne by Owners. Should the vessel be driven into any port or anchorage by stress of weather hire shall continue to be due and payable during any time lost thereby.	387 388 389
	(d) If the vessel's flag state becomes engaged in hostilities, and Charterers in consequence of such hostilities find it commercially impracticable to employ the vessel and have given Owners written notice thereof then from the date of receipt by Owners of such notice until the termination of such commercial impracticability the vessel shall be off-hire and Owners shall have the right to employ the vessel on their own account.	390 391 392 393 394
	(e) Time during which the vessel is off-hire under this charter shall count as part of the charter period except where Charterers declare their option to add off-hire periods under Clause 4 (b)).	395 396
	(f) All references to time in this charter party shall be references to local time except where otherwise stated.	397 398

Periodical Drydocking	22. (a)	Owners have the right and obligation to drydock the vessel at regular intervals of On each occasion Owners shall propose to Charterers a date on which they wish to drydock the vessel, not less than before such date, and Charterers shall offer a port for such periodical drydocking and shall take all reasonable steps to make the vessel available as near to such date as practicable.	399 400 401 402 403
		Owners shall put the vessel in drydock at their expense as soon as practicable after Charterers place the vessel at Owners' disposal clear of cargo other than tank washings and residues.	404 405
		Owners shall be responsible for and pay for the disposal into reception facilities of such tank washings and residues and shall have the right to retain any monies received therefor, without prejudice to any claim for loss of cargo under any Bill of Lading or this charter.	406 407 408
	(b)	If a periodical drydocking is carried out in the port offered by Charterers (which must have suitable accommodation for the purpose and reception facilities for tank washings and residues), the vessel shall be off-hire from the time she arrives at such port until drydocking is completed and she is in every way ready to resume Charterers' service and is at the position at which she went off-hire or a position no less favourable to Charterers, whichever she first attains. However;	409 410 411 412 413 414
	(i)	provided that Owners exercise due diligence in gas-freeing, any time lost in gas-freeing to the standard required for entry into drydock for cleaning and painting the hull shall not count as off-hire, whether lost on passage to the drydocking port or after arrival there (notwithstanding Clause 21), and;	415 416 417 418
	(ii)	any additional time lost in further gas-freeing to meet the standard required for hot work or entry to cargo tanks shall count as off-hire, whether lost on passage to the drydocking port or after arrival there.	419 420 421
		Any time which, but for sub-Clause (i) above, would be off-hire, shall not be included in any calculation under Clause 24.	422 423
		The expenses of gas-freeing, including without limitation the cost of bunkers, shall be for Owners account.	424 425
	(c)	If Owners require the vessel, instead of proceeding to the offered port, to carry out periodical drydocking at a special port selected by them, the vessel shall be off-hire from the time when she is released to proceed to the special port until she next presents for loading in accordance with Charterers' instructions, provided, however, that Charterers shall credit Owners with the time which would have been taken on passage at the service speed had the vessel not proceeded to drydock. All fuel consumed shall be paid for by Owners but Charterers shall credit Owners with the value of the fuel which would have been used on such notional passage calculated at the guaranteed daily consumption for the service speed, and shall further credit Owners with any benefit they may gain in purchasing bunkers at the special port.	426 427 428 429 430 431 432 433 434
	(d)	Charterers shall, insofar as cleaning for periodical drydocking may have reduced the amount of tank-cleaning necessary to meet Charterers' requirements, credit Owners with the value of any bunkers which Charterers calculate to have been saved thereby, whether the vessel drydocks at an offered or a special port.	435 436 437 438

Ship Inspection	23.	Charterers shall have the right at any time during the charter period to make such inspection of the vessel as they may consider necessary. This right may be exercised as often and at such intervals as Charterers in their absolute discretion may determine and whether the vessel is in port or on passage.	439 440 441
		Owners affording all necessary co-operation and accommodation on board provided, however:	442
	(a)	that neither the exercise nor the non-exercise, nor anything done or not done in the exercise or non-exercise, by Charterers of such right shall in any way reduce the master's or Owners' authority over, or responsibility to Charterers or third parties for, the vessel and every aspect of her operation, nor increase Charterers' responsibilities to Owners or third parties for the same; and;	443 444 445 446 447
	(b)	that Charterers shall not be liable for any act, neglect or default by themselves, their servants or agents in the exercise or non-exercise of the aforesaid right.	448 449

Detailed Description and	24. (a)	Owners guarantee that the speed and consumption of the vessel shall be as follows:-	450
		Average speed Maximum average bunker consumption per day in knots main propulsion auxiliaries	451 452

Performance		fuel oil/ diesel oil	fuel oil/diesel oil	
	Laden	tonnes	tonnes	453
				454
	_____	_____/_____	_____/_____	455
	_____	_____/_____	_____/_____	456
	_____	_____/_____	_____/_____	457
	Ballast			458
	_____	_____/_____	_____/_____	459
	_____	_____/_____	_____/_____	460
	_____	_____/_____	_____/_____	461

The foregoing bunker consumptions are for all purposes except cargo heating and tank cleaning 462
and shall be pro-rated between the speeds shown. 463

The service speed of the vessel is   knots laden and   knots in ballast and in the absence 464
of Charterers' orders to the contrary the vessel shall proceed at the service speed. However if 465
more than one laden and one ballast speed are shown in the table above Charterers shall have 466
the right to order the vessel to steam at any speed within the range set out in the table (the 467
"ordered speed"). 468

If the vessel is ordered to proceed at any speed other than the highest speed shown in the 469
table, and the average speed actually attained by the vessel during the currency of such order 470
exceeds such ordered speed plus 0.5 knots (the "maximum recognised speed"), then for the 471
purpose of calculating a decrease of hire under this Clause 24 the maximum recognised speed 472
shall be used in place of the average speed actually attained. 473

For the purposes of this charter the "guaranteed speed" at any time shall be the then-current 474
ordered speed or the service speed, as the case may be. 475

The average speeds and bunker consumptions shall for the purposes of this Clause 24 be 476
calculated by reference to the observed distance from pilot station to pilot station on all sea 477
passages during each period stipulated in Clause 24 (c), but excluding any time during which 478
the vessel is (or but for Clause 22 (b) (i) would be) off-hire and also excluding "Adverse 479
Weather Periods", being; 480

(i)   any periods during which reduction of speed is necessary for safety in congested waters 481
       or in poor visibility; 482

(ii)   any days, noon to noon, when winds exceed force 8 on the Beaufort Scale for more than 483
       12 hours. 484

(b) If during any year from the date on which the vessel enters service (anniversary to anniversary) 485
    the vessel falls below or exceeds the performance guaranteed in Clause 24 (a) then if such 486
    shortfall or excess results; 487

    (i)   from a reduction or an increase in the average speed of the vessel, compared to the speed 488
           guaranteed in Clause 24 (a), then an amount equal to the value at the hire rate of the time 489
           so lost or gained, as the case may be, shall be included in the performance calculation; 490

    (ii)   from an increase or a decrease in the total bunkers consumed, compared to the total 491
           bunkers which would have been consumed had the vessel performed as guaranteed in 492
           Clause 24 (a), an amount equivalent to the value of the additional bunkers consumed or 493
           the bunkers saved, as the case may be, based on the average price paid by Charterers for 494
           the vessel's bunkers in such period, shall be included in the performance calculation. 495

    The results of the performance calculation for laden and ballast mileage respectively shall be 496
    adjusted to take into account the mileage steamed in each such condition during Adverse Weather 497
    Periods, by dividing such addition or deduction by the number of miles over which the 498
    performance has been calculated and multiplying by the same number of miles plus the miles 499
    steamed during the Adverse Weather Periods, in order to establish the total performance 500
    calculation for such period. 501

    Reduction of hire under the foregoing sub-Clause (b) shall be without prejudice to any other 502
    remedy available to Charterers. 503

(c) Calculations under this Clause 24 shall be made for the yearly periods terminating on each 504
    successive anniversary of the date on which the vessel enters service, and for the period 505
    between the last such anniversary and the date of termination of this charter if less than a year. 506

    Claims in respect of reduction of hire arising under this Clause during the final year or part 507
    year of the charter period shall in the first instance be settled in accordance with Charterers' 508
    estimate made two months before the end of the charter period. Any necessary adjustment 509
    after this charter terminates shall be made by payment by Owners to Charterers or by 510
    Charterers to Owners as the case may require. 511

(d) Owners and Charterers agree that this Clause 24 is assessed on the basis that Owners are not 512
    entitled to additional hire for performance in excess of the speeds and consumptions given in 513
    this Clause 24. 514

Salvage 25. Subject to the provisions of Clause 21 hereof, all loss of time and all expenses (excluding any 515
    damage to or loss of the vessel or tortious liabilities to third parties) incurred in saving or attempting 516
    to save life or in successful or unsuccessful attempts at salvage shall be borne equally by Owners and 517
    Charterers provided that Charterers shall not be liable to contribute towards any salvage payable by 518

Issued December 1984 amended December 2003

	Owners arising in any way out of services rendered under this <u>Clause 25</u>.	519
	All salvage and all proceeds from derelicts shall be divided equally between Owners and Charterers	520
	after deducting the master's, officers' and crew's share.	521
Lien	26. Owners shall have a lien upon all cargoes and all freights, sub-freights and demurrage for any	522
	amounts due under this charter; and Charterers shall have a lien on the vessel for all monies paid in	523
	advance and not earned, and for all claims for damages arising from any breach by Owners of this	524
	charter.	525
Exceptions	27. (a) The vessel, her master and Owners shall not, unless otherwise in this charter expressly	526
	provided, be liable for any loss or damage or delay or failure arising or resulting from any	527
	act, neglect or default of the master, pilots, mariners or other servants of Owners in the	528
	navigation or management of the vessel; fire, unless caused by the actual fault or privity of	529
	Owners; collision or stranding; dangers and accidents of the sea; explosion, bursting of	530
	boilers, breakage of shafts or any latent defect in hull, equipment or machinery; provided,	531
	however, that <u>Clauses 1, 2, 3</u> and <u>24</u> hereof shall be unaffected by the foregoing. Further,	532
	neither the vessel, her master or Owners, nor Charterers shall, unless otherwise in this charter	533
	expressly provided, be liable for any loss or damage or delay or failure in performance	534
	hereunder arising or resulting from act of God, act of war, seizure under legal process,	535
	quarantine restrictions, strikes, lock-outs, riots, restraints of labour, civil commotions or arrest	536
	or restraint of princes, rulers or people.	537
	(b) The vessel shall have liberty to sail with or without pilots, to tow or go to the assistance of	538
	vessels in distress and to deviate for the purpose of saving life or property.	539
	(c) <u>Clause 27(a)</u> shall not apply to, or affect any liability of Owners or the vessel or any other	540
	relevant person in respect of;	541
	(i) loss or damage caused to any berth, jetty, dock, dolphin, buoy, mooring line, pipe or	542
	crane or other works or equipment whatsoever at or near any place to which the vessel	543
	may proceed under this charter, whether or not such works or equipment belong to	544
	Charterers, or;	545
	(ii) any claim (whether brought by Charterers or any other person) arising out of any loss	546
	of or damage to or in connection with cargo. Any such claim shall be subject to the	547
	Hague-Visby Rules or the Hague Rules or the Hamburg Rules, as the case may be,	548
	which ought pursuant to <u>Clause 38</u> hereof to have been incorporated in the relevant	549
	Bill of Lading (whether or not such Rules were so incorporated) or, if no such Bill of	550
	Lading is issued, to the Hague-Visby Rules unless the Hamburg Rules compulsorily	551
	apply in which case to the Hamburg Rules.	552
	(d) In particular and without limitation, the foregoing <u>subsections (a)</u> and <u>(b)</u> of this Clause	553
	shall not apply to or in any way affect any provision in this charter relating to off-hire or to	554
	reduction of hire.	555
Injurious	28. No acids, explosives or cargoes injurious to the vessel shall be shipped and without prejudice to the	556
Cargoes	foregoing any damage to the vessel caused by the shipment of any such cargo, and the time taken to	557
	repair such damage, shall be for Charterers' account. No voyage shall be undertaken, nor any goods	558
	or cargoes loaded, that would expose the vessel to capture or seizure by rulers or governments.	559
Grade of	29. Charterers shall supply fuel oil with a maximum viscosity of centistokes at 50 degrees	560
Bunkers	centigrade and/or marine diesel oil for main propulsion and fuel oil with a maximum viscosity of	561
	centistokes at 50 degrees centigrade and/or diesel oil for the auxiliaries. If Owners	562
	require the vessel to be supplied with more expensive bunkers they shall be liable for the extra cost	563
	thereof.	564
	Charterers warrant that all bunkers provided by them in accordance herewith shall be of a quality	565
	complying with ISO Standard 8217 for Marine Residual Fuels and Marine Distillate Fuels as	566
	applicable.	567
Disbursements	30. Should the master require advances for ordinary disbursements at any port, Charterers or their agents	568
	shall make such advances to him, in consideration of which Owners shall pay a commission of two and	569
	a half per cent, and all such advances and commission shall be deducted from hire.	570
Laying-up	31. Charterers shall have the option, after consultation with Owners, of requiring Owners to lay up the	571
	vessel at a safe place nominated by Charterers, in which case the hire provided for under this charter	572
	shall be adjusted to reflect any net increases in expenditure reasonably incurred or any net saving	573
	which should reasonably be made by Owners as a result of such lay up. Charterers may exercise the	574
	said option any number of times during the charter period.	575
Requisition	32. Should the vessel be requisitioned by any government, de facto or de jure, during the period of this	576
	charter, the vessel shall be off-hire during the period of such requisition, and any hire paid by such	577
	governments in respect of such requisition period shall be for Owners' account. Any such requisition	578
	period shall count as part of the charter period.	579
Outbreak of	33. If war or hostilities break out between any two or more of the following countries: U.S.A., the	580
War	countries or republics having been part of the former U.S.S.R (except that declaration of war or	581
	hostilities solely between any two or more of the countries or republics having been part of the	582
	former USSR shall be exempted), P.R.C., U.K., Netherlands, then both Owners and Charterers shall	583
	have the right to cancel this charter.	584

Issued December 1984 amended December 2003

Additional War Expenses	34.	If the vessel is ordered to trade in areas where there is war (de facto or de jure) or threat of war, Charterers shall reimburse Owners for any additional insurance premia, crew bonuses and other expenses which are reasonably incurred by Owners as a consequence of such orders, provided that Charterers are given notice of such expenses as soon as practicable and in any event before such expenses are incurred, and provided further that Owners obtain from their insurers a waiver of any subrogated rights against Charterers in respect of any claims by Owners under their war risk insurance arising out of compliance with such orders.

Any payments by Charterers under this clause will only be made against proven documentation. Any discount or rebate refunded to Owners, for whatever reason, in respect of additional war risk premium shall be passed on to Charterers.

War Risks 35. (a) The master shall not be required or bound to sign Bills of Lading for any place which in his or Owners' reasonable opinion is dangerous or impssible for the vessel to enter or reach owing to any blockade, war, hostilities, warlike operations, civil war, civil commotions or revolutions.

(b) If in the reasonable opinion of the master or Owners it becomes, for any of the reasons set out in Clause 35(a) or by the operation of international law, dangerous, impossible or prohibited for the vessel to reach or enter, or to load or discharge cargo at, any place to which the vessel has been ordered pursuant to this charter (a "place of peril"), then Charterers or their agents shall be immediately notified in writing or by radio messages, and Charterers shall thereupon have the right to order the cargo, or such part of it as may be affected, to be loaded or discharged, as the case may be, at any other place within the trading limits of this charter (provided such other place is not itself a place of peril). If any place of discharge is or becomes a place of peril, and no orders have been received from Charterers or their agents within 48 hours after dispatch of such messages, then Owners shall be at liberty to discharge the cargo or such part of it as may be affected at any place which they or the master may in their or his discretion select within the trading limits of this charter and such discharge shall be deemed to be due fulfilment of Owners' obligations under this charter so far as cargo so discharged is concerned.

(c) The vessel shall have liberty to comply with any directions or recommendations as to departure, arrival, routes, ports of call, stoppages, destinations, zones, waters, delivery or in any other wise whatsoever given by the government of the state under whose flag the vessel sails or any other government or local authority or by any person or body acting or purporting to act as or with the authority of any such government or local authority including any de facto government or local authority or by any person or body acting or purporting to act as or with the authority of any such government or local authority or by any committee or person having under the terms of the war risks insurance on the vessel the right to give any such directions or recommendations. If by reason of or in compliance with any such directions or recommendations anything is done or is not done, such shall not be deemed a deviation.

If by reason of or in compliance with any such direction or recommendation the vessel does not proceed to any place of discharge to which she has been ordered pursuant to this charter, the vessel may proceed to any place which the master or Owners in his or their discretion select and there discharge the cargo or such part of it as may be affected. Such discharge shall be deemed to be due fulfilment of Owners' obligations under this charter so far as cargo so discharged is concerned.

Charterers shall procure that all Bills of Lading issued under this charter shall contain the Chamber of Shipping War Risks Clause 1952.

Both to Blame Collision Clause 36. If the liability for any collision in which the vessel is involved while performing this charter falls to be determined in accordance with the laws of the United States of America, the following provision shall apply:

"If the ship comes into collision with another ship as a result of the negligence of the other ship and any act, neglect or default of the master, mariner, pilot or the servants of the carrier in the navigation or in the management of the ship, the owners of the cargo carried hereunder will indemnify the carrier against all loss, or liability to the other or non-carrying ship or her owners in so far as such loss or liability represents loss of, or damage to, or any claim whatsoever of the owners of the said cargo, paid or payable by the other or non-carrying ship or her owners to the owners of the said cargo and set off, recouped or recovered by the other or non-carrying ship or her owners as part of their claim against the carrying ship or carrier."

"The foregoing provisions shall also apply where the owners, operators or those in charge of any ship or ships or objects other than, or in addition to, the colliding ships or objects are at fault in respect of a collision or contact."

Charterers shall procure that all Bills of Lading issued under this charter shall contain a provision in the foregoing terms to be applicable where the liability for any collision in which the vessel is involved falls to be determined in accordance with the laws of the United States of America.

New Jason Clause 37. General average contributions shall be payable according to York/Antwerp Rules, 1994, as amended from time to time, and shall be adjusted in London in accordance with English law and practice but should adjustment be made in accordance with the law and practice of the United States of America, the following position shall apply:

Issued December 1984 amended December 2003

"In the event of accident, danger, damage or disaster before or after the commencement of the 652
voyage, resulting from any cause whatsoever, whether due to negligence or not, for which, or for the 653
consequence of which, the carrier is not responsible by statute, contract or otherwise, the cargo, 654
shippers, consignees or owners of the cargo shall contribute with the carrier in general average to the 655
payment of any sacrifices, losses or expenses of a general average nature that may be made or 656
incurred and shall pay salvage and special charges incurred in respect of the cargo." 657
"If a salving ship is owned or operated by the carrier, salvage shall be paid for as fully as if the said 658
salving ship or ships belonged to strangers. Such deposit as the carrier or his agents may deem 659
sufficient to cover the estimated contribution of the cargo and any salvage and special charges 660
thereon shall, if required, be made by the cargo, shippers, consignees or owners of the cargo to the 661
carrier before delivery." 662
Charterers shall procure that all Bills of Lading issued under this charter shall contain a provision in 663
the foregoing terms, to be applicable where adjustment of general average is made in accordance 664
with the laws and practice of the United States of America. 665

Clause Paramount 38. Charterers shall procure that all Bills of Lading issued pursuant to this charter shall contain the 666
following: 667
"(1)Subject to sub-clause (2) or (3) hereof, this Bill of Lading shall be governed by, and have 668
effect subject to, the rules contained in the International Convention for the Unification of Certain 669
Rules relating to Bills of Lading signed at Brussels on 25th August 1924 (hereafter the "Hague 670
Rules") as amended by the Protocol signed at Brussels on 23rd February 1968 (hereafter the 671
"Hague-Visby Rules"). Nothing contained herein shall be deemed to be either a surrender by the 672
carrier of any of his rights or immunities or any increase of any of his responsibilities or liabilities 673
under the Hague-Visby Rules." 674
"(2)If there is governing legislation which applies the Hague Rules compulsorily to this Bill of 675
Lading, to the exclusion of the Hague-Visby Rules, then this Bill of Lading shall have effect subject 676
to the Hague Rules. Nothing therein contained shall be deemed to be either a surrender by the carrier 677
of any of his rights or immunities or an increase of any of his responsibilities or liabilities under the 678
Hague Rules." 679
(3) If there is governing legislation which applies the United Nations Convention on the Carriage 680
of Goods by Sea 1978 (hereafter the Hamburg Rules) compulsorily to this Bill of Lading, to the 681
exclusion of the Hague-Visby Rules, then this Bill of Lading shall have effect subject to the Hamburg 682
Rules. Nothing therein contained shall be deemed to be either a surrender by the carrier of any of his 683
rights or immunities or an increase of any of his responsibilities or liabilities under the Hamburg 684
Rules." 685
"(4)If any term of this Bill of Lading is repugnant to the Hague-Visby Rules, or Hague Rules, or 686
Hamburg Rules, as applicable, such term shall be void to that extent but no further." 687
"(5)Nothing in this Bill of Lading shall be construed as in any way restricting, excluding or 688
waiving the right of any relevant party or person to limit his liability under any available legislation 689
and/or law." 690

Insurance/ ITOPF 39. Owners warrant that the vessel is now, and will, throughout the duration of the charter: 691
(a) be owned or demise chartered by a member of the International Tanker Owners Pollution 692
Federation Limited; 693
(b) be properly entered in ____ P & I Club, being a member of 694
the International Group of P and I Clubs; 695
(c) have in place insurance cover for oil pollution for the maximum on offer through the 696
International Group of P&I Clubs but always a minimum of United States Dollars 697
1,000,000.000 (one thousand million); 698
(d) have in full force and effect Hull and Machinery insurance placed through reputable brokers 699
on Institute Time Clauses or equivalent for the value of United States Dollars   as from 700
time to time may be amended with Charterers approval, which shall not be unreasonably 701
withheld. 702
Owners will provide, within a reasonable time following a request from Charterers to do so, 703
documented evidence of compliance with the warranties given in this Clause 39. 704

Export Restrictions 40. The master shall not be required or bound to sign Bills of Lading for the carriage of cargo to any 705
place to which export of such cargo is prohibited under the laws, rules or regulations of the country 706
in which the cargo was produced and/or shipped. 707
Charterers shall procure that all Bills of Lading issued under this charter shall contain the following 708
clause: 709
"If any laws rules or regulations applied by the government of the country in which the cargo was 710
produced and/or shipped, or any relevant agency thereof, impose a prohibition on export of the cargo 711
to the place of discharge designated in or ordered under this Bill of Lading, carriers shall be entitled 712
to require cargo owners forthwith to nominate an alternative discharge place for the discharge of the 713
cargo, or such part of it as may be affected, which alternative place shall not be subject to the 714
prohibition, and carriers shall be entitled to accept orders from cargo owners to proceed to and 715
discharge at such alternative place. If cargo owners fail to nominate an alternative place within 72 716
hours after they or their agents have received from carriers notice of such prohibition, carriers shall 717

		be at liberty to discharge the cargo or such part of it as may be affected by the prohibition at any safe	718

be at liberty to discharge the cargo or such part of it as may be affected by the prohibition at any safe place on which they or the master may in their or his absolute discretion decide and which is not subject to the prohibition, and such discharge shall constitute due performance of the contract contained in this Bill of Lading so far as the cargo so discharged is concerned". 718–721

The foregoing provision shall apply mutatis mutandis to this charter, the references to a Bill of Lading being deemed to be references to this charter. 722–723

Business Principles 41. Owners will co-operate with Charterers to ensure that the Business Principles, as amended from time to time, of the Royal Dutch/Shell Group of Companies, which are posted on the Shell Worldwide Web (www.Shell.com), are complied with. 724–726

Drugs and Alcohol 42. (a) Owners warrant that they have in force an active policy covering the vessel which meets or exceeds the standards set out in the "Guidelines for the Control of Drugs and Alcohol On Board Ship" as published by the Oil Companies International Marine Forum (OCIMF) dated January 1990 (or any subsequent modification, version, or variation of these guidelines) and that this policy will remain in force throughout the charter period, and Owners will exercise due diligence to ensure the policy is complied with. 727–732

(b) Owners warrant that the current policy concerning drugs and alcohol on board is acceptable to ExxonMobil and will remain so throughout the charter period. 733–734

Oil Major Acceptability 43. If, at any time during the charter period, the vessel becomes unacceptable to any Oil Major, Charterers shall have the right to terminate the charter. 735–736

Pollution and Emergency Response 44. Owners are to advise Charterers of organisational details and names of Owners personnel together with their relevant telephone/facsimile/e-mail/telex numbers, including the names and contact details of Qualified Individuals for OPA 90 response, who may be contacted on a 24 hour basis in the event of oil spills or emergencies. 737–740

ISPS Code/US MTSA 2002 45. (a) (i) From the date of coming into force of the International Code for the Security of Ships and of Port Facilities and the relevant amendments to Chapter XI of SOLAS (ISPS Code) and the US Maritime Transportation Security Act 2002 (MTSA) in relation to the Vessel and thereafter during the currency of this charter, Owners shall procure that both the Vessel and "the Company" (as defined by the ISPS Code) and the owner(as defined by the MTSA) shall comply with the requirements of the ISPS Code relating to the Vessel and "the Company" and the requirements of MTSA relating to the vessel and the owner. Upon request Owners shall provide documentary evidence of compliance with this Clause 45(a) (i). 741–749

(ii) Except as otherwise provided in this charter, loss, damage, expense or delay, caused by `failure on the part of Owners or "the Company"/owner to comply with the requirements of the ISPS Code/MTSA or this Clause shall be for Owners' account. 750–752

(b) (i) Charterers shall provide Owners/Master with their full style contact details and shall ensure that the contact details of all sub-charterers are likewise provided to Owners/Master. Furthermore, Charterers shall ensure that all sub-charter parties they enter into during the period of this charter contain the following provision: "The Charterers shall provide the Owners with their full style contact details and, where sub-letting is permitted under the terms of the charter party, shall ensure that the contact details of all sub-charterers are likewise provided to the Owners". 753–759

(ii) Except as otherwise provided in this charter, loss, damage, expense or delay, caused by failure on the part of Charterers to comply with this sub-Clause 45(b) shall be for Charterers' account. 760–762

(c) Notwithstanding anything else contained in this charter costs or expenses related to security regulations or measures required by the port facility or any relevant authority in accordance with the ISPS Code/MTSA including, but not limited to, security guards, launch services, tug escorts, port security fees or taxes and inspections, shall be for Charterers' account, unless such costs or expenses result solely from Owners' negligence in which case such costs or expenses shall be for Owners account. All measures required by Owners to comply with the security plan required by the ISPS Code/MTSA shall be for Owners' account. 763–769

(d) Notwithstanding any other provision of this charter, the vessel shall not be off-hire where there is a loss of time caused by Charterers failure to comply with the ISPS Code/MTSA(when in force). 770–772

(e) If either party makes any payment which is for the other party's account according to this Clause, the other party shall indemnify the paying party. 773–774

Law and Litigation 46. (a) This charter shall be construed and the relations between the parties determined in accordance with the laws of England. 775–776

(b) All disputes arising out of this charter shall be referred to Arbitration in London in accordance with the Arbitration Act 1996 (or any re-enactment or modification thereof for the time being in force) subject to the following appointment procedure: 777–779

(i) The parties shall jointly appoint a sole arbitrator not later than 28 days after service of a request in writing by either party to do so. 780–781

(ii) If the parties are unable or unwilling to agree the appointment of a sole arbitrator in accordance with (i) then each party shall appoint one arbitrator, in any event not later than 14 days after receipt of a further request in writing by either party to do so. The 782–784

	two arbitrators so appointed shall appoint a third arbitrator before any substantive hearing or forthwith if they cannot agree on a matter relating to the arbitration.	785 786
	(iii) If a party fails to appoint an arbitrator within the time specified in (ii) (the Party in Default), the party who has duly appointed his arbitrator shall give notice in writing to the Party in Default that he proposes to appoint his arbitrator to act as sole arbitrator.	787 788 789
	(iv) If the Party in Default does not within 7 days of the notice given pursuant to (iii) make The required appointment and notify the other party that he has done so the other party may appoint his arbitrator as sole arbitrator whose award shall be binding on both parties as if he had been so appointed by agreement.	790 791 792 793
	(v) Any Award of the arbitrator(s) shall be final and binding and not subject to appeal.	794
	(vi) For the purposes of this clause 46(b)any requests or notices in writing shall be sent by fax, e-mail or telex and shall be deemed received on the day of transmission.	795 796
	(c) It shall be a condition precedent to the right of any party to a stay of any legal proceedings in which maritime property has been, or may be, arrested in connection with a dispute under this charter, that that party furnishes to the other party security to which that other party would have been entitled in such legal proceedings in the absence of a stay.	797 798 799 800
Confidentiality	47. All terms and conditions of this charter arrangement shall be kept private and confidential	801
Construction	48. The side headings have been included in this charter for convenience of reference and shall in no way affect the construction hereof.	802 803
	Appendix A: OCIMF Vessel Particulars Questionnaire for the vessel, as attached, shall be incorporated herein.	804 805
	Appendix B: Shell Safety and Environmental Monthly Reporting Template, as attached, shall be incorporated herein.	806 807
	Additional Clauses: As attached, shall be incorporated herein.	808
	SIGNED FOR OWNERS SIGNED FOR CHARTERERS	809
	FULL NAME _____ FULL NAME _____	810
	POSITION POSITION	811

SHELLTIME4

Shell Safety and Environmental Monthly Reporting Template	Return to:_____ Charterers marked for the attention of:_____ Fax:_____ Phone:_____ Email:_____

Time Chartered Vessel Name	_____
Management Company	_____
Month	_____

OIL SPILLS INCIDENTS (Any amount entering the water) Approximate volume in barrels and brief details	_____
ANY OTHER INCIDENTS resulting in or having potential for injury, damage or loss	_____

FOR DEFINITIONS OF INCIDENT CLASSIFICATION AND EXPOSURE HOURS PLEASE SEE OIL COMPANIES INTERNATIONAL MARINE FORUM (OCIMF) BOOKLET "Marine Injury Reporting Guidlines" (February 1997) or any subsequent version, amendment, or variation to them

A. No. Of Crew:	_____
B. Days in month / period:	_____
EXPOSURE HOURS (A x B x 24):	_____

LOST TIME INJURIES (LTI'S) including brief details / any treatments

_____

TOTAL RECORDABLE CASE INJURIES (TRC'S) including brief details / any treatments

_____

PLEASE CONFIRM YOUR RETURN CONTACT DETAILS:

Name: _____
Phone: _____
Fax: _____
Email: _____

Return for each calendar month - by 10th of following month.

Shell Safety and Environmental Monthly Reporting Template	Return to: ____ Charterers marked for the attention of: _____ Fax: ____ Phone: _____ Email: _____

Time Chartered Vessel Name	_____
Management Company	_____
Month	_____

Notes: Please enter zero i.e."0" where any amount is nil (rather than entering "Nil" or N/A")
Please do not enter a % sign in the entry boxes for Fuel Sulphur content i.e. if it is 3% then just enter "3".
Cargo loaded for LNG vessels should also be reported as tonnes and not as m3.

Monthly Consumption - Fuel Oil mt	_____
Sulphur content of Fuel Oil (percentage weight)	_____
Monthly Consumption - Diesel and/or Gas Oil mt	_____
Monthly Consumption (LNG ships only) - Fuel Gases mt	_____

Please do not enter a % sign in the entry boxes for Fuel Sulphur content i.e. if it is 3% then just enter 3".
Cargo loaded for LNG vessels should also be reported as tonnes and not as m3.

Monthly Distance Steamed	_____
Monthly Cargo Loaded - mt	_____

Refrigerant Gas Consumption - Type	_____
Refrigerant Gas Consumption - Quantity (litres)	_____

Garbage Disposal m3 - At Sea	_____
Garbage Disposal m3 - Incinerated on Board	_____
Garbage Disposal m3 - Sent Ashore	_____

OIL SPILL INCIDENTS	_____
(Other than those entering the water) Approx. volume & brief details	

Return for each calendar month - by 10th of following month

NYPE 2015 (New York Produce Exchange Form)*

ASBA

BIMCO

Printed by BIMCO's IDEA-2

NYPE 2015
TIME CHARTER
New York Produce Exchange Form®
November 6th, 1913 – Amended October 20th, 1921; August 6th, 1931; October 3rd, 1946;
Revised June 12th 1981; September 14th 1993; June 3rd, 2015.

© 2015, the Association of Ship Brokers and Agents (U.S.A.), Inc. (ASBA).
Jointly authored by ASBA, BIMCO and the SMF

1 **THIS CHARTER PARTY**, made and concluded in Click here to enter text.. this Click here to enter text.. day of Click here to
2 enter text. 20 Click here to enter text.

3 Between **Choose an item.** of Click here to enter text.

4 as *Registered Owners/*Disponent Owners/*Time Chartered Owners (the "Owners") of the Vessel
5 described below

6 *delete as applicable

7 Name: **Choose an item.**

8 IMO Number: Click here to enter text.

9 Flag: Click here to enter text.

10 Built (year): Click here to enter text.

11 Deadweight All Told: Click here to enter text. metric tons

12 (For Vessel's charter party description see Appendix A (Vessel Description)),

13 and **Choose an item.** Charterers of Click here to enter text. (the "Charterers")

14 This Charter Party shall be performed subject to all the terms and conditions herein consisting of this
15 main body including any additional clauses and addenda, if applicable, as well as Appendix A attached
16 hereto. In the event of any conflict of conditions, the provisions of any additional clauses and Appendix A
17 shall prevail over those of the main body to the extent of such conflict, but no further.

1

* Reproduced by kind permission of the Association of Ship Brokers and Agents (U.S.A.) Inc.

1. Duration/Trip Description

(a) The Owners agree to let, and the Charterers agree to hire, the Vessel from the time of delivery, for Click here to enter text.. within below mentioned trading limits.

(b) Trading Limits - The Vessel shall be employed in such lawful trades between safe ports and safe places within the following trading limits Click here to enter text. as the Charterers shall direct.

(c) Berths - The Vessel shall be loaded and discharged in any safe anchorage or at any safe berth or safe place that the Charterers or their agents may direct, provided the Vessel can safely enter, lie and depart always afloat.

(d) The Vessel during loading and/or discharging may lie safely aground at any safe berth or safe place where it is customary for vessels of similar size, construction and type to lie at the following areas/ports Click here to enter text. (*if this space is left blank then this sub-clause 1(d) shall not apply*), if so requested by the Charterers, provided it can do so without suffering damage.

The Charterers shall indemnify the Owners for any loss, damage, costs, expenses or loss of time, including any underwater inspection required by class, caused as a consequence of the Vessel lying aground at the Charterers' request.

(e) Sublet - The Charterers shall have the liberty to sublet the Vessel for all or any part of the time covered by this Charter Party, but the Charterers remain responsible for the fulfillment of this Charter Party.

2. Delivery

(a) The Vessel shall be delivered to the Charterers at Click here to enter text. (state port or place).

(b) The Vessel on delivery shall be seaworthy and in every way fit to be employed for the intended service, having water ballast and with sufficient power to operate all cargo handling gear simultaneously, and, with full complement of Master, officers and ratings who meet the Standards for Training, Certification and Watchkeeping for Seafarers (STCW) requirements for a vessel of her tonnage.

(c) The Vessel's holds shall be clean and in all respects ready to receive the intended cargo, or if no intended cargo, any permissible cargo:

(i) On *delivery; or

(ii) On *arrival at first loading port if different from place of delivery. If the Vessel fails hold inspection then the Vessel shall be off-hire from the time of rejection until the Vessel has passed a subsequent inspection.

*(c)(i) and (c)(ii) are alternatives; delete as appropriate. If no deletion then Sub-clause (c)(i) shall apply.

(d) The Owners shall keep the Charterers informed of the Vessel's itinerary. Prior to the arrival of the Vessel at the delivery port or place, the Owners shall serve the Charterers with Click here to enter text. days' approximate and Click here to enter text. days' definite notices of the Vessel's delivery. Following the tender of any such notice the Owners shall give or allow to be given to the Vessel only such further employment orders, if any, as are reasonably expected when given to allow delivery to occur on or before the date notified. The Owners shall give the Charterers and/or their local agents notice of delivery when the Vessel is in a position to come on hire.

Printed by BIMCO's iDEA·2

© 2015, the Association of Ship Brokers and Agents (U.S.A.), Inc. (ASBA). Jointly authored by ASBA, BIMCO and the SMF

2

59   Vessel itinerary prior to delivery: Click here to enter text..

60 (e)   Acceptance of delivery of the Vessel by the Charterers shall not prejudice their rights against the
61   Owners under this Charter Party.

62 **3.**   **Laydays/Cancelling**

63   If required by the Charterers, time on hire shall not commence before Click here to enter text. (local time)
64   and should the Vessel not have been delivered on or before Click here to enter text. (local time) at the port
65   or place stated in Sub-clause 2(a), the Charterers shall have the option of cancelling this Charter
66   Party at any time but not later than the day of the Vessel's notice of delivery.

67 **4.**   **Redelivery**

68 (a)   The Vessel shall be redelivered to the Owners in like good order and condition, ordinary wear and
69   tear excepted, at Click here to enter text. (*state port or place*)

70 (b)   The Charterers shall keep the Owners informed of the Vessel's itinerary. Prior to the arrival of the
71   Vessel at the redelivery port or place, the Charterers shall serve the Owners with Click here to enter text.
72   days' approximate and Click here to enter text. days' definite notices of the Vessel's redelivery. Following
73   the tender of any such notices the Charterers shall give or allow to be given to the Vessel only such
74   further employment orders, if any, as are reasonably expected when given to allow redelivery to
75   occur on or before the date notified.

76 (c)   Acceptance of redelivery of the Vessel by the Owners shall not prejudice their rights against the
77   Charterers under this Charter Party.

78 **5.**   **On/Off-Hire Survey**

79   Prior to delivery and redelivery the parties shall, unless otherwise agreed, each appoint surveyors,
80   for their respective accounts, who shall not later than at first loading port/last discharging port
81   respectively, conduct joint on-hire/off-hire surveys, for the purpose of ascertaining the quantity of
82   bunkers on board and the condition of the Vessel. A single report shall be prepared on each
83   occasion and signed by each surveyor, without prejudice to his right to file a separate report setting
84   forth items upon which the surveyors cannot agree.

85   If either party fails to have a representative attend the survey and sign the joint survey report, such
86   party shall nevertheless be bound for all purposes by the findings in any report prepared by the
87   other party.

88   Any time lost as a result of the on-hire survey shall be for the Owners' account and any time lost as
89   a result of the off-hire survey shall be for the Charterers' account.

90 **6.**   **Owners to Provide**

91 (a)   The Owners shall provide and pay for the insurances of the Vessel, except as otherwise provided,
92   and for all provisions, cabin, deck, engine-room and other necessary stores, boiler water and
93   lubricating oil; shall pay for wages, consular shipping and discharging fees of the crew and charges
94   for port services pertaining to the crew/crew visas; shall maintain the Vessel's class and keep her in
95   a thoroughly efficient state in hull, machinery and equipment for and during the service, and have a
96   full complement of Master, officers and ratings.

97 (b)   The Owners shall provide any documentation relating to the Vessel as required to permit the
98   Vessel to trade within the agreed limits, including but not limited to International Tonnage

Printed by BIMCO's IDEA-2

© 2015, the Association of Ship Brokers and Agents (U.S.A.), Inc. (ASBA).
Jointly authored by ASBA, BIMCO and the SMF

3

99 Certificate, Suez and Panama tonnage certificates, Certificates of Registry, and certificates relating
100 to the strength, safety and/or serviceability of the Vessel's gear. Such documentation shall be
101 maintained during the currency of the Charter Party as necessary.

102 Owners shall also provide and maintain such Certificates of Financial Responsibility for oil pollution
103 to permit the Vessel to trade within the agreed limits as may be required at the commencement of
104 the Charter Party. However, in the event that, at the time of renewal, a Certificate of Financial
105 Responsibility is unavailable in the market place, or, the premium for same increases significantly
106 over the course of the Charter Party, then Owners and Charterers shall discuss each with the other
107 to find a mutually agreeable solution for same, failing such solution the port(s) that require said
108 Certificate of Financial Responsibility are to be considered as added to the Vessel's trading
109 exclusions. (See also Clause 18 (Pollution)).

110 (c) The Vessel to work night and day if required by the Charterers, with crew opening and closing
111 hatches, when and where required and permitted by shore labor regulations, otherwise shore labor
112 for same shall be for the Charterers' account.

113 **7. Charterers to Provide**

114 (a) The Charterers, while the Vessel is on-hire, shall provide and pay for all the bunkers except as
115 otherwise agreed; shall pay for port charges (including compulsory garbage disposal), compulsory
116 gangway watchmen and cargo watchmen, compulsory and/or customary pilotages, canal dues,
117 towages, agencies, commissions, consular charges (except those pertaining to individual crew
118 members or flag of the Vessel), and all other usual expenses except those stated in Clause 6, but
119 when the Vessel puts into a port for causes for which the Vessel is responsible (other than by
120 stress of weather), then all such charges incurred shall be paid by the Owners.

121 (b) Fumigations ordered because of illness of the crew or for infestations prior to delivery under this
122 Charter Party shall be for the Owners' account. Fumigations ordered because of cargoes carried or
123 ports visited while the Vessel is employed under this Charter Party shall be for the Charterers'
124 account.

125 (c) The Charterers shall provide and pay for necessary dunnage, lashing materials and also any extra
126 fittings requisite for a special trade or unusual cargo, but the Owners shall allow them the use of
127 any dunnage already aboard the Vessel. Prior to redelivery the Charterers shall remove their
128 dunnage, fittings and lashing materials at their cost and in their time.

129 **8. Performance of Voyages**

130 (a) Subject to Clause 38 (Slow Steaming) the Master shall perform the voyages with due despatch and
131 shall render all customary assistance with the Vessel's crew. The Master shall be conversant with
132 the English language and (although appointed by the Owners) shall be under the orders and
133 directions of the Charterers as regards employment and agency; and the Charterers shall perform
134 all cargo handling, including but not limited to loading, stowing, trimming, lashing, securing,
135 dunnaging, unlashing, discharging, and tallying, at their risk and expense, under the supervision of
136 the Master.

137 (b) If the Charterers shall have reasonable cause to be dissatisfied with the conduct of the Master or
138 officers, the Owners shall, on receiving particulars of the complaint, investigate the same, and, if
139 necessary, make a change in appointments.

4

140   **9.   Bunkers**

141   (a)   Bunker quantities and prices

142   *(i) The Charterers on delivery, and the Owners on redelivery or any termination of this Charter
143   Party, shall take over and pay for all bunkers remaining on board the Vessel as hereunder. The
144   Vessel's bunker tank capacities shall be at the Charterers' disposal. Bunker quantities and prices
145   on delivery /redelivery to be Click here to enter text..

146   *(ii) The Owners shall provide sufficient bunkers onboard to perform the entire time charter trip.
147   The Charterers shall not bunker the Vessel, and shall pay with the first hire payment for the
148   mutually agreed estimated bunker consumption for the trip, namely Click here to enter text. metric tons at
149   Click here to enter text. (price). Upon redelivery any difference between estimated and actual
150   consumption shall be paid by the Charterers or refunded by the Owners as the case may be.

151   *(iii) The Charterers shall not take over and pay for bunkers Remaining On Board at delivery but
152   shall redeliver the Vessel with about the same quantities and grades of bunkers as on delivery. Any
153   difference between the delivery quantity and the redelivery quantity shall be paid by the Charterers
154   or the Owners as the case may be. The price of the bunkers shall be the net contract price paid by
155   the receiving party, as evidenced by suppliers' invoice or other supporting documents.

156   *(i), (ii) and (iii) are alternatives; delete as applicable. If neither Sub-clause (i), (ii) nor (iii) is deleted
157   then Sub-clause (i) shall apply.

158   (b)   Bunkering Prior to Delivery/Redelivery

159   Provided that it can be accomplished at ports of call, without hindrance to the working or operation
160   of or delay to the Vessel, and subject to prior consent, which shall not be unreasonably withheld,
161   the Owners shall allow the Charterers to bunker for their account prior to delivery and the
162   Charterers shall allow the Owners to bunker for their account prior to redelivery. If consent is given,
163   the party ordering the bunkering shall indemnify the other party for any delays, losses, costs and
164   expenses arising therefrom.

165   (c)   Bunkering Operations and Sampling

166   (i) The Chief Engineer shall co-operate with the Charterers' bunkering agents and fuel suppliers
167   during bunkering. Such cooperation shall include connecting/disconnecting hoses to the Vessel's
168   bunker manifold, attending sampling, reading gauges or meters or taking soundings, before, during
169   and/or after delivery of fuels.

170   (ii) During bunkering a primary sample of each grade of fuels shall be drawn in accordance with the
171   International Maritime Organization (IMO) Resolution Marine Environment Protection Committee
172   (MEPC) MEPC.182(59) Guidelines for the Sampling of Fuel Oil for Determination of Compliance
173   with the Marine Pollution Convention (MARPOL) 73/78 Annex VI or any subsequent amendments
174   thereof. Each primary sample shall be divided into no fewer than five (5) samples; one sample of
175   each grade of fuel shall be retained on board for MARPOL purposes and the remaining samples of
176   each grade distributed between the Owners, the Charterers and the bunker suppliers.

177   (iii) The Charterers warrant that any bunker suppliers used by them to bunker the Vessel shall
178   comply with the provisions of Sub-clause (c)(ii) above.

179   (iv) Bunkers of different grades, specifications and/or suppliers shall be segregated into separate
180   tanks within the Vessel's natural segregation. The Owners shall not be held liable for any restriction
181   in bunker capacity as a result of segregating bunkers as aforementioned.

5

182 (d) Bunker Quality and Liability

183 (i) The Charterers shall supply bunkers of the agreed specifications and grades: Click here to enter text.
184 The bunkers shall be of a stable and homogeneous nature and suitable for burning in the Vessel's
185 engines and/or auxiliaries and, unless otherwise agreed in writing, shall comply with the
186 International Organization for Standardization (ISO) standard 8217:2012 or any subsequent
187 amendments thereof. If ISO 8217:2012 is not available then the Charterers shall supply bunkers
188 which comply with the latest ISO 8217 standard available at the port or place of bunkering.

189 (ii) The Charterers shall be liable for any loss or damage to the Owners or the Vessel caused by
190 the supply of unsuitable fuels and/or fuels which do not comply with the specifications and/or
191 grades set out in Sub-clause (d)(i) above, including the off-loading of unsuitable fuels and the
192 supply of fresh fuels to the Vessel. The Owners shall not be held liable for any reduction in the
193 Vessel's speed performance and/or increased bunker consumption nor for any time lost and any
194 other consequences arising as a result of such supply.

195 (e) Fuel Testing Program

196 Should the Owners participate in a recognized fuel testing program one of the samples retained by
197 the Owners shall be forwarded for such testing. The cost of same shall be borne by the Owners
198 and if the results of the testing show the fuel not to be in compliance with ISO 8217:2012, or any
199 subsequent amendment thereof, or such other specification as may be agreed, the Owners shall
200 notify the Charterers and provide a copy of the report as soon as reasonably possible.

201 In the event the Charterers call into question the results of the testing, a fuel sample drawn in
202 accordance with IMO Resolution MEPC.96(47) Guidelines for the Sampling of Fuel Oil for
203 Determination of Compliance with Annex VI of MARPOL 73/78 or any subsequent amendments
204 thereof, shall be sent to a mutually agreed, qualified and independent laboratory whose analysis as
205 regards the characteristics of the fuel shall be final and binding on the parties concerning the
206 characteristics tested for. If the fuel sample is found not to be in compliance with the specification
207 as agreed in the paragraph above, the Charterers shall meet the cost of this analysis, otherwise
208 same shall be for the Owners' account.

209 (f) Bunker Fuel Sulphur Content

210 (i) Without prejudice to anything else contained in this Charter Party, the Charterers shall supply
211 fuels of such specifications and grades to permit the Vessel, at all times, to comply with the
212 maximum sulphur content requirements of any emission control area when the Vessel is ordered to
213 trade within that area.

214 The Charterers also warrant that any bunker suppliers, bunker craft operators and bunker
215 surveyors used by the Charterers to supply such bunkers shall comply with Regulations 14 and 18
216 of MARPOL Annex VI, including the Guidelines in respect of sampling and the provision of bunker
217 delivery notes.

218 The Charterers shall indemnify, defend and hold harmless the Owners in respect of any loss,
219 liability, delay, fines, costs or expenses arising or resulting from the Charterers' failure to comply
220 with this Sub-clause (f)(i).

221 (ii) Provided always that the Charterers have fulfilled their obligations in respect of the supply of
222 fuels in accordance with Sub-clause (f)(i), the Owners warrant that:

223 1. the Vessel shall comply with Regulations 14 and 18 of MARPOL Annex VI and with the
224 requirements of any emission control area; and

6

225   2. the Vessel shall be able to consume fuels of the required sulphur content,

226   when ordered by the Charterers to trade within any such area.

227   Subject to having supplied the Vessel with fuels in accordance with Sub-clause (f)(i), the
228   Charterers shall not otherwise bear any loss, liability, delay, fines, costs or expenses arising or
229   resulting from the Vessel's failure to comply with Regulations 14 and 18 of MARPOL Annex VI.

230   (iii) For the purpose of this Clause, "emission control area" shall mean an area as stipulated in
231   MARPOL Annex VI and/or an area regulated by regional and/or national authorities such as, but
232   not limited to, the European Union (EU) and the United States (US) Environmental Protection
233   Agency.

234 (g)   Grades and Quantities of Bunkers on Redelivery

235   Unless agreed otherwise, the Vessel shall be redelivered with the same grades and about the
236   same quantities of bunkers as on delivery; however, the grades and quantities of bunkers on
237   redelivery shall always be appropriate and sufficient to allow the Vessel to reach safely the nearest
238   port at which fuels of the required types are available.

239 **10.**   **Rate of Hire; Hold Cleaning; Communications; Victualing and Expenses**

240 (a)   The Charterers shall pay for the use and hire of the said Vessel at the rate of Click here to enter text. per
241   day or pro rata for any part of a day, commencing on and from the time of her delivery, as
242   aforesaid, including the overtime of crew; hire to continue until the time of her redelivery to the
243   Owners as per Clause 4 (Redelivery) (unless Vessel lost).

244   Unless otherwise mutually agreed, the Charterers shall have the option to redeliver the Vessel with
245   unclean/unswept holds against a lumpsum payment of Click here to enter text. in lieu of hold cleaning, to
246   the Owners (unless Vessel lost).

247   The Owners shall victual pilots and such other persons as authorized by the Charterers or their
248   agents. While on-hire, the Charterers shall pay the Owners along with the hire payments, Click here to
249   enter text. per thirty (30) days or pro rata, to cover all Communications, Victualing and Expenses
250   properly incurred by the Vessel under the Charterers' employment.

251   For the purpose of hire calculations, the times of delivery, redelivery or termination of this Charter
252   Party shall be adjusted to Coordinated Universal Time (UTC).

253 (b)   Hold Cleaning/Residue Disposal

254   (i) The Charterers may request the Owners to direct the crew to sweep and/or wash and/or clean
255   the holds between voyages and/or between cargoes against payment at the rate of Click here to enter
256   text. per hold, provided the crew is able safely to undertake such work and is allowed to do so by
257   local regulations. In connection with any such operation the Owners shall not be responsible if the
258   Vessel's holds are not accepted or passed. Time for cleaning shall be for the Charterers' account.

259   (ii) Unless this Charter Party is concluded for a single laden leg, all cleaning agents and additives
260   (including chemicals and detergents) required for cleaning cargo holds shall be supplied and paid
261   for by the Charterers. The Charterers shall provide the Owners with a dated and signed statement
262   identifying cleaning agents and additives that, in accordance with IMO Resolution 219(63)
263   Guidelines for the Implementation of MARPOL Annex V, are not substances harmful to the marine
264   environment and do not contain any component known to be carcinogenic, mutagenic or
265   reprotoxic.

7

This document is a computer generated NYPE 2015 published by BIMCO and jointly authored by ASBA, BIMCO and the SMF. Any insertion or deletion to the form must be clearly visible. In the event of any modification being made to the pre-printed text of this document which is not clearly visible, the original BIMCO approved document shall apply. BIMCO assumes no responsibility for any loss, damages or expenses as a result of discrepancies between the original BIMCO approved document and this computer generated document.

266 (iii) Throughout the currency of this Charter Party and at redelivery, the Charterers shall remain
267 responsible for all costs and time, including deviation, if any, associated with the removal and
268 disposal of cargo related residues and/or hold washing water and/or cleaning agents and
269 detergents and/or waste. Removal and disposal as aforesaid shall always be in accordance with
270 and as defined by MARPOL Annex V, or other applicable rules.

271 **11. Hire Payment**

272 (a) Payment

273 Payment of Hire shall be made without deductions due to Charterers' bank charges so as to be
274 received by the Owners or their designated payee into the bank account as follows Click here to enter text.
275 in the currency stated in Clause 10 (Rate of Hire; Hold Cleaning; Communications; Victualing and
276 Expenses), in funds available to the Owners on the due date, fifteen (15) days in advance, and for
277 the last fifteen (15) days or part of same the approximate amount of hire, and should the same not
278 cover the actual time, hire shall be paid for the balance day by day as it becomes due, if so
279 required by the Owners. The first payment of hire shall be due on delivery.

280 (b) Grace Period

281 Where there is failure to make punctual payment of hire due, the Charterers shall be given by the
282 Owners three (3) Banking Days (as recognized at the agreed place of payment) written notice to
283 rectify the failure, and when so rectified within those three (3) Banking Days (as recognized at the
284 agreed place of payment and the place of currency of the Charter Party) following the Owners'
285 notice, the payment shall stand as punctual.

286 (c) Withdrawal

287 Failure by the Charterers to pay hire due in full within three (3) Banking Days of their receiving a
288 notice from Owners under Sub-clause 11(b) above shall entitle the Owners, without prejudice to
289 any other rights or claims the Owners may have against the Charterers:

290 (i) to withdraw the Vessel from the service of the Charterers;

291 (ii) to damages, if they withdraw the Vessel, for the loss of the remainder of the Charter Party.

292 (d) Suspension

293 At any time while hire is outstanding, the Owners shall, without prejudice to the liberty to withdraw,
294 be entitled to withhold the performance of any and all obligations hereunder and shall have no
295 responsibility whatsoever for any consequences thereof, and Charterers hereby indemnify the
296 Owners for all legitimate and justifiable actions taken to secure their interests, and hire shall
297 continue to accrue and any extra expenses resulting from such withholding shall be for the
298 Charterers' account.

299 (e) Last Hire Payment

300 Should the Vessel be on her voyage towards port/place of redelivery at the time the last
301 payment(s) of hire is/are due, said payment(s) is/are to be made for such length of time as the
302 estimated time necessary to complete the voyage, including the deduction of estimated
303 disbursements for the Owners' account before redelivery. Should said payments not cover the
304 actual time, hire is to be paid for the balance, day by day, as it becomes due.

305 Unless Sub-clause 9(a)(ii) or (iii) has been agreed, the Charterers shall have the right to deduct the
306 value of bunkers on redelivery from last sufficient hire payment(s).

307 When the Vessel has been redelivered, any difference in hire and bunkers is to be refunded by the
308 Owners or paid by the Charterers within five (5) Banking Days, as the case may be.

309 (f) Cash Advances

310 Cash for the Vessel's ordinary disbursements at any port may be advanced by the Charterers, as
311 required by the Owners, subject to two and a half (2.5) per cent commission and such advances
312 shall be deducted from the hire. The Charterers, however, shall in no way be responsible for the
313 application of such advances.

314 **12. Speed and Consumption**

315 (a) Upon delivery and throughout the duration of this Charter Party the Vessel shall be capable of
316 speed and daily consumption rates as stated in Appendix A in good weather on all sea passages
317 with wind up to and including Force four (4) as per the Beaufort Scale and sea state up to and
318 including Sea State three (3) as per the Douglas Sea Scale (unless otherwise specified in
319 Appendix A). Any period during which the Vessel's speed is deliberately reduced to comply with the
320 Charterers' orders/requirements (unless slow steaming or eco speed warranties have been given in
321 Appendix A) or for reasons of safety or while navigating within narrow or restricted waters or when
322 assisting a vessel in distress or when saving or attempting to save life or property at sea, shall be
323 excluded from performance calculations.

324 (b) The Charterers shall have the option of using their preferred weather routing service. The Master
325 shall comply with the reporting procedure of the Charterers' weather routing service and shall
326 follow routing recommendations from that service provided that the safety of the Vessel and/or
327 cargo is not compromised.

328 (c) The actual route taken by the Vessel shall be used as the basis of any calculation of the Vessel's
329 performance.

330 (d) If the speed of the Vessel is reduced and/or fuel oil consumption increased, the Charterers may
331 submit to the Owners a documented claim limited to the estimated time lost and/or the additional
332 fuel consumed, supported by a performance analysis from the weather routing service established
333 in accordance with this Clause. The cost of any time lost shall be off-set against the cost of any fuel
334 saved and vice versa.

335 (e) In the event that the Owners contest such claim then the Owners shall provide copies of the
336 Vessel's deck logs for the period concerned and the matter shall be referred to an independent
337 expert or alternative weather service selected by mutual agreement, whose report shall take
338 Vessel's log data and the Charterers' weather service data into consideration and whose
339 determination shall be final and binding on the parties. The cost of such expert report shall be
340 shared equally.

341 **13. Spaces Available**

342 (a) The whole reach of the Vessel's holds, decks, and other cargo spaces (not more than she can
343 reasonably and safely stow and carry), also accommodation for supercargo, if carried, shall be at
344 the Charterers' disposal, reserving only proper and sufficient space for the Vessel's Master,
345 officers, ratings, tackle, apparel, furniture, provisions, stores and bunkers.

9

346 (b) In the event of deck cargo being carried, the Owners are to be and are hereby indemnified by the
347 Charterers for any loss and/or damage and/or liability of whatsoever nature howsoever caused to
348 the deck cargo which would not have arisen had the deck cargo not been loaded. Bills of Lading
349 shall be issued as per Clause 31(c).

350 **14. Supercargo**

351 The Charterers are entitled to appoint a supercargo, who shall accompany the Vessel at the
352 Charterers' risk and see that voyages are performed with due despatch. He is to be furnished with
353 free accommodation and meals same as provided for the Master's table. The Charterers and the
354 supercargo are required to sign the standard letter of waiver and indemnity recommended by the
355 Vessel's Protection and Indemnity Association before the supercargo comes on board the Vessel.

356 **15. Sailing Orders and Logs**

357 The Charterers shall furnish the Master from time to time with all requisite instructions and sailing
358 directions, in writing, in the English language, and the Master shall keep full and correct deck and
359 engine logs of the voyage or voyages, which are to be patent to the Charterers or their agents, and
360 shall furnish the Charterers, their agents or supercargo, when required, with a true copy of such
361 deck and engine logs, showing the course of the Vessel, distance run and the consumption of
362 bunkers. Any log extracts required by the Charterers shall be in the English language.

363 **16. Cargo Exclusions**

364 The Vessel shall be employed in carrying lawful merchandise, excluding any goods of a
365 dangerous, injurious, flammable or corrosive nature unless carried in accordance with the
366 requirements or recommendations of the competent authorities of the country of the Vessel's
367 registry, and of ports of loading and discharge, and of any intermediate countries or ports through
368 whose waters the Vessel must pass. Without prejudice to the generality of the foregoing in addition
369 the following are specifically excluded: livestock of any description, arms, ammunition, explosives,
370 nuclear and radioactive material. Click here to enter text..

371 **17. Off-Hire**

372 In the event of loss of time from deficiency and/or default and/or strike of officers or ratings, or
373 deficiency of stores, fire, breakdown of, or damage to hull, machinery or equipment, grounding,
374 detention by the arrest of the Vessel, (unless such arrest is caused by events for which the
375 Charterers, their sub-charterers, servants, agents or sub-contractors are responsible), or detention
376 by Port State control or other competent authority for Vessel deficiencies, or detention by average
377 accidents to the Vessel or cargo, unless resulting from inherent vice, quality or defect of the cargo,
378 drydocking for the purpose of examination, cleaning and/or painting of underwater parts and/or
379 repair, or by any other similar cause preventing the full working of the Vessel, the payment of hire
380 and overtime, if any, shall cease for the time thereby lost. Should the Vessel deviate or put back
381 during a voyage, contrary to the orders or directions of the Charterers, for any reason other than
382 accident to the cargo or where permitted in Clause 22 (Liberties) hereunder, the hire to be
383 suspended from the time of her deviating or putting back until she is again in the same or
384 equidistant position from the destination and the voyage resumed therefrom. All bunkers used by
385 the Vessel while off-hire shall be for the Owners' account. In the event of the Vessel being driven
386 into port or to anchorage through stress of weather, trading to shallow harbors or to rivers or ports
387 with bars, any detention of the Vessel and/or expenses resulting from such detention shall be for
388 the Charterers' account. If upon the voyage the speed be reduced by defect in, or breakdown of,
389 any part of her hull, machinery or equipment, the time so lost, and the cost of any extra bunkers
390 consumed in consequence thereof, and all extra proven expenses may be deducted from the hire.

10

391 Bunkers used by the Vessel while off-hire and the cost of replacing same shall be for the Owners'
392 account and therefore deducted from the hire.

393 **18. Pollution**

394 The Owners shall provide for standard oil pollution coverage equal to the level customarily offered
395 by the International Group of P&I Clubs, together with the appropriate certificates to that effect.
396 (See also Clause 6 (Owners to Provide)).

397 **19. Drydocking**

398 The Vessel was last drydocked Click here to enter text..

399 Except in case of emergency or under Clause 52(b), no drydocking shall take place during the
400 currency of this Charter Party.

401 **20. Total Loss**

402 Should the Vessel be lost, money paid in advance and not earned (reckoning from the date of loss
403 or being last heard of) shall be returned to the Charterers at once.

404 **21. Exceptions**

405 The act of God, enemies, fire, restraint of princes, rulers and people, and all dangers and accidents
406 of the seas, rivers, machinery, boilers and navigation, and errors of navigation throughout this
407 Charter Party, always mutually excepted.

408 **22. Liberties**

409 The Vessel shall have the liberty to sail with or without pilots, to tow and be towed, to assist vessels
410 in distress, and to deviate for the purpose of saving life and property.

411 **23. Liens**

412 The Owners shall have a lien upon all cargoes, sub-hires and sub-freights (including deadfreight
413 and demurrage) belonging or due to the Charterers or any sub-charterers, for any amounts due
414 under this Charter Party, including general average contributions, and the Charterers shall have a
415 lien on the Vessel for all monies paid in advance and not earned, and any overpaid hire or excess
416 deposit to be returned at once.

417 The Charterers will not directly or indirectly suffer, nor permit to be continued, any lien or
418 encumbrance, which might have priority over the title and interest of the Owners in the Vessel. The
419 Charterers undertake that during the period of this Charter Party, they will not procure any supplies
420 or necessaries or services, including any port expenses and bunkers, on the credit of the Owners.

421 **24. Salvage**

422 All derelicts and salvage shall be for the Owners' and the Charterers' equal benefit after deducting
423 the Owners' and the Charterers' expenses and crew's proportion.

424 **25. General Average**

425 General average shall be adjusted according to York-Antwerp Rules 1994 and settled in US dollars
426 in the same place as stipulated in Clause 54 (Law and Arbitration). The Charterers shall procure

11

427 that all bills of lading issued during the currency of this Charter Party will contain a provision to the
428 effect that general average shall be adjusted according to York-Antwerp Rules 1994 and will
429 include the "New Jason Clause" as per Clause 33(c). Time charter hire will not contribute to general
430 average.

431 **26. Navigation**

432 Nothing herein stated is to be construed as a demise of the Vessel to the Charterers. The Owners
433 shall remain responsible for the navigation of the Vessel, acts of pilots and tug boats, insurance,
434 crew, and all other matters, same as when trading for their own account.

435 **27. Cargo Claims**

436 Cargo claims as between the Owners and the Charterers shall be settled in accordance with the
437 Inter-Club NYPE Agreement 1996 (as amended 1 September 2011), or any subsequent
438 modification or replacement thereof.

439 **28. Cargo Handling Gear and Lights**

440 The Owners shall maintain the cargo handling gear of the Vessel providing lifting capacity as
441 described in Appendix A (Vessel Description). The Owners shall also provide on the Vessel for
442 night work lights as on board, but all additional lights over those on board shall be at the
443 Charterers' expense. The Charterers shall have the use of any cargo handling gear on board the
444 Vessel. If required by the Charterers, the Vessel shall work night and day and all cargo handling
445 gear shall be at the Charterers' disposal during loading and discharging. In the event of disabled
446 cargo handling gear, or insufficient power to operate the same, the Vessel is to be considered to be
447 off-hire to the extent that time is actually lost to the Charterers and the Owners to pay stevedore
448 stand-by charges occasioned thereby, unless such disablement or insufficiency of power is caused
449 by the Charterers' stevedores. If required by the Charterers, the Owners shall bear the cost of
450 hiring shore gear in lieu thereof, in which case the Vessel shall remain on-hire, except for actual
451 time lost.

452 **29. Solid Bulk Cargoes/Dangerous Goods**

453 (a) The Charterers shall provide appropriate information on the cargo in advance of loading in
454 accordance with the requirements of the IMO International Maritime Solid Bulk Cargoes (IMSBC)
455 Code to enable the precautions which may be necessary for proper stowage and safe carriage to
456 be put into effect. The information shall be accompanied by a cargo declaration summarising the
457 main details and stating that the cargo is fully and accurately described and that, where applicable,
458 the test results and other specifications can be considered as representative for the cargo to be
459 loaded.

460 (b) If a cargo listed in the IMO International Maritime Dangerous Goods (IMDG) Code (website:
461 www.imo.org) is agreed to be carried, the Charterers shall provide a dangerous goods transport
462 document and, where applicable, a container/vehicle packing certificate in accordance with the
463 IMDG Code requirements. The dangerous goods transport document shall include a certificate or
464 declaration that the goods are fully and accurately described by the Proper Shipping Name, are
465 classified, packaged, marked and labelled/placarded correctly and are in all respects in proper
466 condition for transport according to applicable international and national government regulations.

467 (c) The Master shall be entitled to refuse cargoes or, if already loaded, to unload them at the
468 Charterers' risk and expense if the Charterers fail to fulfil their IMSBC Code or IMDG Code
469 obligations as applicable.

12

30. BIMCO Hull Fouling Clause for Time Charter Parties

(a) If, in accordance with the Charterers' orders, the Vessel remains at or shifts within a place, anchorage and/or berth for an aggregated period exceeding:

(i) a period as the parties may agree in writing in a Tropical Zone or Seasonal Tropical Zone*; or

(ii) a period as the parties may agree in writing outside such Zones*

any warranties concerning speed and consumption shall be suspended pending inspection of the Vessel's underwater parts including, but not limited to, the hull, sea chests, rudder and propeller.

If no such periods are agreed the default periods shall be 15 days.

(b) In accordance with Sub-clause (a), either party may call for inspection which shall be arranged jointly by the Owners and the Charterers and undertaken at the Charterers' risk, cost, expense and time.

(c) If, as a result of the inspection either party calls for cleaning of any of the underwater parts, such cleaning shall be undertaken by the Charterers at their risk, cost, expense and time in consultation with the Owners.

(i) Cleaning shall always be under the supervision of the Master and, in respect of the underwater hull coating, in accordance with the paint manufacturers' recommended guidelines on cleaning, if any. Such cleaning shall be carried out without damage to the Vessel's underwater parts or coating.

(ii) If, at the port or place of inspection, cleaning as required under this Sub-clause (c) is not permitted or possible, or if the Charterers choose to postpone cleaning, speed and consumption warranties shall remain suspended until such cleaning has been completed.

(iii) If, despite the availability of suitable facilities and equipment, the Owners nevertheless refuse to permit cleaning, the speed and consumption warranties shall be reinstated from the time of such refusal.

(d) Cleaning in accordance with this Clause shall always be carried out prior to redelivery. If, nevertheless, the Charterers are prevented from carrying out such cleaning, the parties shall, prior to but latest on redelivery, agree a lump sum payment in full and final settlement of the Owners' costs and expenses arising as a result of or in connection with the need for cleaning pursuant to this Clause.

(e) If the time limits set out in Sub-clause (a) have been exceeded but the Charterers thereafter demonstrate that the Vessel's performance remains within the limits of this Charter Party the Vessel's speed and consumption warranties will be subsequently reinstated and the Charterers' obligations in respect of inspection and/or cleaning shall no longer be applicable.

31. Bills of Lading

(a) The Master shall sign bills of lading or waybills for cargo as presented in conformity with mates' receipts. However, the Charterers or their agents may sign bills of lading or waybills on behalf of the Master, with the Owners'/Master's prior written authority, always in conformity with mates' receipts.

Printed by BIMCO's IDEA•2

© 2015, the Association of Ship Brokers and Agents (U.S.A.), Inc. (ASBA). Jointly authored by ASBA, BIMCO and the SMF

13

508 (b) All bills of lading or waybills shall be without prejudice to this Charter Party and the Charterers shall
509 indemnify the Owners against all consequences or liabilities which may arise from any
510 inconsistency between this Charter Party and any bills of lading or waybills signed by the
511 Charterers or their agents or by the Master at their request.

512 (c) Bills of lading covering deck cargo shall be claused: "Shipped on deck at the Charterers', Shippers'
513 and Receivers' risk, expense and responsibility, without liability on the part of the Vessel or her
514 Owners for any loss, damage, expense or delay howsoever caused."

515 **32. BIMCO Electronic Bills of Lading Clause**

516 (a) At the Charterers' option, bills of lading, waybills and delivery orders referred to in this Charter
517 Party shall be issued, signed and transmitted in electronic form with the same effect as their paper
518 equivalent.

519 (b) For the purpose of Sub-clause (a) the Owners shall subscribe to and use Electronic (Paperless)
520 Trading Systems as directed by the Charterers, provided such systems are approved by the
521 International Group of P&I Clubs. Any fees incurred in subscribing to or for using such systems
522 shall be for the Charterers' account.

523 (c) The Charterers agree to hold the Owners harmless in respect of any additional liability arising from
524 the use of the systems referred to in Sub-clause (b), to the extent that such liability does not arise
525 from Owners' negligence.

526 **33. Protective Clauses**

527 The following protective clauses shall be deemed to form part of this Charter Party and all Bills of
528 Lading or waybills issued under this Charter Party shall contain the following clauses.
529

530 (a) **General Clause Paramount**

531 This bill of lading shall have effect subject to the provisions of the Carriage of Goods by Sea Act of
532 the United States, the Hague Rules, or the Hague Visby Rules, as applicable, or such other similar
533 national legislation as may mandatorily apply by virtue of origin or destination of the bill of lading,
534 (or if no such enactments are mandatorily applicable, the terms of the Hague Rules shall apply)
535 which shall be deemed to be incorporated herein, and nothing herein contained shall be deemed a
536 surrender by the carrier of any of its rights or immunities or an increase of any of its responsibilities
537 or liabilities under said Act. If any term of this bill of lading be repugnant to said Act to any extent,
538 such term shall be void to that extent, but no further.

539 and

540 (b) **Both-to-Blame Collision Clause**

541 "If the ship comes into collision with another ship as a result of the negligence of the other ship and
542 any act, neglect or default of the master, mariner, pilot or the servants of the carrier in the
543 navigation or in the management of the ship, the owners of the goods carried hereunder will
544 indemnify the carrier against all loss or liability to the other or non-carrying ship or her owners
545 insofar as such loss or liability represents loss of, or damage to, or any claim whatsoever of the
546 owners of said goods, paid or payable by the other or non-carrying ship or her owners to the
547 owners of said goods and set-off, recouped or recovered by the other or non-carrying ship or her
548 owners as part of their claim against the carrying ship or carrier.

14

549 The foregoing provisions shall also apply where the owners, operators or those in charge of any
550 ships or objects other than, or in addition to, the colliding ships or objects are at fault in respect to a
551 collision or contact."

552 and

553 (c) **New Jason Clause**

554 "In the event of accident, danger, damage or disaster before or after the commencement of the
555 voyage, resulting from any cause whatsoever, whether due to negligence or not, for which, or for
556 the consequences of which, the carrier is not responsible, by statute, contract, or otherwise, the
557 goods, shippers, consignees, or owners of the goods shall contribute with the carrier in general
558 average to the payment of any sacrifices, losses or expenses of a general average nature that may
559 be made or incurred, and shall pay salvage and special charges incurred in respect of the goods. If
560 a salving ship is owned or operated by the carrier, salvage shall be paid for as fully as if salving
561 ship or ships belonged to strangers. Such deposit as the carrier or his agents may deem sufficient
562 to cover the estimated contribution of the goods and any salvage and special charges thereon
563 shall, if required, be made by the goods, shippers, consignees or owners of the goods to the
564 Carrier before delivery."

565 **34. BIMCO War Risks Clause CONWARTIME 2013**

566 (a) For the purpose of this Clause, the words:

567 (i) "Owners" shall include the shipowners, bareboat charterers, disponent owners, managers or
568 other operators who are charged with the management of the Vessel, and the Master; and

569 (ii) "War Risks" shall include any actual, threatened or reported:

570 war, act of war, civil war or hostilities; revolution; rebellion; civil commotion; warlike operations;
571 laying of mines; acts of piracy and/or violent robbery and/or capture/seizure (hereinafter "Piracy");
572 acts of terrorists; acts of hostility or malicious damage; blockades (whether imposed against all
573 vessels or imposed selectively against vessels of certain flags or ownership, or against certain
574 cargoes or crews or otherwise howsoever), by any person, body, terrorist or political group, or the
575 government of any state or territory whether recognized or not, which, in the reasonable judgement
576 of the Master and/or the Owners, may be dangerous or may become dangerous to the Vessel,
577 cargo, crew or other persons on board the Vessel.

578 (b) The Vessel shall not be obliged to proceed or required to continue to or through, any port, place,
579 area or zone, or any waterway or canal (hereinafter "Area"), where it appears that the Vessel,
580 cargo, crew or other persons on board the Vessel, in the reasonable judgement of the Master
581 and/or the Owners, may be exposed to War Risks whether such risk existed at the time of entering
582 into this Charter Party or occurred thereafter. Should the Vessel be within any such place as
583 aforesaid which only becomes dangerous, or may become dangerous, after entry into it, the
584 Vessel shall be at liberty to leave it.

585 (c) The Vessel shall not be required to load contraband cargo, or to pass through any blockade as set
586 out in Sub-clause (a), or to proceed to an Area where it may be subject to search and/or
587 confiscation by a belligerent.

588 (d) If the Vessel proceeds to or through an Area exposed to War Risks, the Charterers shall reimburse
589 to the Owners any additional premiums required by the Owners' insurers and the costs of any
590 additional insurances that the Owners reasonably require in connection with War Risks.

15

591 (e) All payments arising under Sub-clause (d) shall be settled within fifteen (15) days of receipt of
592   Owners' supported invoices or on redelivery, whichever occurs first.

593 (f) If the Owners become liable under the terms of employment to pay to the crew any bonus or
594   additional wages in respect of sailing into an Area which is dangerous in the manner defined by the
595   said terms, then the actual bonus or additional wages paid shall be reimbursed to the Owners by
596   the Charterers at the same time as the next payment of hire is due, or upon redelivery, whichever
597   occurs first.

598 (g) The Vessel shall have liberty:

599   (i) to comply with all orders, directions, recommendations or advice as to departure, arrival, routes,
600   sailing in convoy, ports of call, stoppages, destinations, discharge of cargo, delivery, or in any other
601   way whatsoever, which are given by the government of the nation under whose flag the Vessel
602   sails, or other government to whose laws the Owners are subject, or any other government of any
603   state or territory whether recognized or not, body or group whatsoever acting with the power to
604   compel compliance with their orders or directions;

605   (ii) to comply with the requirements of the Owners' insurers under the terms of the Vessel's
606   insurance(s);

607   (iii) to comply with the terms of any resolution of the Security Council of the United Nations, the
608   effective orders of any other Supranational body which has the right to issue and give the same,
609   and with national laws aimed at enforcing the same to which the Owners are subject, and to obey
610   the orders and directions of those who are charged with their enforcement;

611   (iv) to discharge at any alternative port any cargo or part thereof which may expose the Vessel to
612   being held liable as a contraband carrier;

613   (v) to call at any alternative port to change the crew or any part thereof or other persons on board
614   the Vessel when there is reason to believe that they may be subject to internment, imprisonment,
615   detention or similar measures.

616 (h) If in accordance with their rights under the foregoing provisions of this Clause, the Owners shall
617   refuse to proceed to the loading or discharging ports, or any one or more of them, they shall
618   immediately inform the Charterers. No cargo shall be discharged at any alternative port without first
619   giving the Charterers notice of the Owners' intention to do so and requesting them to nominate a
620   safe port for such discharge. Failing such nomination by the Charterers within forty-eight (48) hours
621   of the receipt of such notice and request, the Owners may discharge the cargo at any safe port of
622   their own choice. All costs, risk and expenses for the alternative discharge shall be for the
623   Charterers' account.

624 (i) The Charterers shall indemnify the Owners for claims arising out of the Vessel proceeding in
625   accordance with any of the provisions of Sub-clauses (b) to (h) which are made under any bills of
626   lading, waybills or other documents evidencing contracts of carriage.

627 (j) When acting in accordance with any of the provisions of Sub-clauses (b) to (h) of this Clause
628   anything is done or not done, such shall not be deemed a deviation, but shall be considered as due
629   fulfilment of this Charter Party.

630 **35. Ice**

631   The Vessel shall not be obliged to force ice but, subject to the Owners' prior approval having due
632   regard to its size, construction and class, may follow ice-breakers. The Vessel shall not be required

16

This document is a computer generated NYPE 2015 published by BIMCO and jointly authored by ASBA, BIMCO and the SMF. Any insertion or deletion to the form must be clearly visible. In the event of any modification being made to the pre-printed text of this document which is not clearly visible, the original BIMCO approved document shall apply. BIMCO assumes no responsibility for any loss, damages or expenses as a result of discrepancies between the original BIMCO approved document and this computer generated document.

633 to enter or remain in any icebound port or area, nor any port or area where lights or lightships have
634 been or are about to be withdrawn by reason of ice, nor where there is risk that in the ordinary
635 course of things the Vessel will not be able on account of ice to safely enter and remain in the port
636 or area or to get out after having completed loading or discharging.

637 **36. Requisition**

638 Should the Vessel be requisitioned by the government of the Vessel's flag or other government to
639 whose laws the Owners are subject during the period of this Charter Party, the Vessel shall be
640 deemed to be off-hire during the period of such requisition, and any hire paid by the said
641 government in respect of such requisition period shall be retained by Owners. The period during
642 which the Vessel is on requisition to the said government shall count as part of the period provided
643 for in this Charter Party.

644 If the period of requisition exceeds ninety (90) days, either party shall have the option of cancelling
645 this Charter Party and no consequential claim in respect thereof may be made by either party.

646 **37. Stevedore Damage**

647 Notwithstanding anything contained herein to the contrary, the Charterers shall pay for any and all
648 damage to the Vessel caused by stevedores provided the Master has notified the Charterers
649 and/or their agents in writing within twenty-four (24) hours of the occurrence but in case of hidden
650 damage latest when the damage could have been discovered by the exercise of due diligence.
651 Such notice to describe the damage and to invite Charterers to appoint a surveyor to assess the
652 extent of such damage.

653 (a) In case of any and all damage affecting the Vessel's seaworthiness and/or the safety of the crew
654 and/or affecting the trading capabilities of the Vessel, the Charterers shall immediately arrange for
655 repairs of such damage at their expense and the Vessel is to remain on-hire until such repairs are
656 completed and if required passed by the Vessel's classification society.

657 (b) Any and all damage not described under Sub-clause (a) above shall be repaired, at the Charterers'
658 option, before or after redelivery concurrently with the Owners' work. In such case no hire and/or
659 expenses will be paid to the Owners except and insofar as the time and/or expenses required for
660 the repairs for which the Charterers are responsible, exceed the time and/or expenses necessary
661 to carry out the Owners' work.

662 **38. Slow Steaming**

663 (a) The Charterers may at their discretion provide, in writing to the Master, instructions to reduce
664 speed or Revolutions Per Minute (main engine RPM) and/or instructions to adjust the Vessel's
665 speed to meet a specified time of arrival at a particular destination.

666 (i) *Slow Steaming – Where the Charterers give instructions to the Master to adjust the speed or
667 RPM, the Master shall, subject always to the Master's obligations in respect of the safety of the
668 Vessel, crew and cargo and the protection of the marine environment, comply with such written
669 instructions, provided that the engine(s) continue(s) to operate above the cut-out point of the
670 Vessel's engine(s) auxiliary blower(s) and that such instructions will not result in the Vessel's
671 engine(s) and/or equipment operating outside the manufacturers'/designers' recommendations as
672 published from time to time.

673 (ii) *Ultra-Slow Steaming – Where the Charterers give instructions to the Master to adjust the speed
674 or RPM, regardless of whether this results in the engine(s) operating above or below the cut-out
675 point of the Vessel's engine(s) auxiliary blower(s), the Master shall, subject always to the Master's

17

676 obligations in respect of the safety of the Vessel, crew and cargo and the protection of the marine
677 environment, comply with such written instructions, provided that such instructions will not result in
678 the Vessel's engine(s) and/or equipment operating outside the manufacturers'/designers'
679 recommendations as published from time to time. If the manufacturers'/designers'
680 recommendations issued subsequent to the date of this Charter Party require additional physical
681 modifications to the engine or related equipment or require the purchase of additional spares or
682 equipment, the Master shall not be obliged to comply with these instructions.

683 *Sub-clauses (a)(i) and (a)(ii) are alternatives; delete whichever is not applicable. In the absence of
684 deletions, alternative (a)(i) shall apply.

685 (b) At all speeds the Owners shall exercise due diligence to ensure that the Vessel is operated in a
686 manner which minimises fuel consumption, always taking into account and subject to the following:

687 (i) the Owners' warranties under this Charter Party relating to the Vessel's speed and consumption;

688 (ii) the Charterers' instructions as to the Vessel's speed and/or RPM and/or specified time of arrival
689 at a particular destination;

690 (iii) the safety of the Vessel, crew and cargo and the protection of the marine environment; and

691 (iv) the Owners' obligations under any bills of lading, waybills or other documents evidencing
692 contracts of carriage issued by them or on their behalf.

693 (c) For the purposes of Sub-clause (b), the Owners shall exercise due diligence to minimise fuel
694 consumption:

695 (i) when planning voyages, adjusting the Vessel's trim and operating main engine(s) and auxiliary
696 engine(s);

697 (ii) by making optimal use of the Vessel's navigation equipment and any additional aids provided by
698 the Charterers, such as weather routing, voyage optimization and performance monitoring
699 systems; and

700 (iii) by directing the Master to report any data that the Charterers may reasonably request to
701 further improve the energy efficiency of the Vessel.

702 (d) The Owners and the Charterers shall share any findings and best practices that they may have
703 identified on potential improvements to the Vessel's energy efficiency.

704 (e) For the avoidance of doubt, where the Vessel proceeds at a reduced speed or with reduced RPM
705 pursuant to Sub-clause (a), then provided that the Master has exercised due diligence to comply
706 with such instructions, this shall constitute compliance with, and there shall be no breach of, any
707 obligation requiring the Vessel to proceed with utmost and/or due despatch (or any other such
708 similar/equivalent expression).

709 (f) The Charterers shall procure that this Clause be incorporated into all sub-charters and contracts of
710 carriage issued pursuant to this Charter Party. The Charterers shall indemnify the Owners against
711 all consequences and liabilities that may arise from bills of lading, waybills or other documents
712 evidencing contracts of carriage being issued as presented to the extent that the terms of such bills
713 of lading, waybills or other documents evidencing contracts of carriage impose or result in breach
714 of the Owners' obligation to proceed with due despatch or are to be held to be a deviation or the
715 imposition of more onerous liabilities upon the Owners than those assumed by the Owners
716 pursuant to this Clause.

18

Printed by BIMCO's IDEA-2

© 2015, the Association of Ship Brokers and Agents (U.S.A.), Inc. (ASBA). Jointly authored by ASBA, BIMCO and the SMF

39. BIMCO Piracy Clause for Time Charter Parties 2013

(a) The Vessel shall not be obliged to proceed or required to continue to or through, any port, place, area or zone, or any waterway or canal (hereinafter "Area") which, in the reasonable judgement of the Master and/or the Owners, is dangerous to the Vessel, her cargo, crew or other persons on board the Vessel due to any actual, threatened or reported acts of piracy and/or violent robbery and/or capture/seizure (hereinafter "Piracy"), whether such risk existed at the time of entering into this Charter Party or occurred thereafter. Should the Vessel be within any such place as aforesaid which only becomes dangerous, or may become dangerous, after her entry into it, she shall be at liberty to leave it.

(b) If in accordance with Sub-clause (a) the Owners decide that the Vessel shall not proceed or continue to or through the Area they must immediately inform the Charterers. The Charterers shall be obliged to issue alternative voyage orders and shall indemnify the Owners for any claims from holders of the Bills of Lading caused by waiting for such orders and/or the performance of an alternative voyage. Any time lost as a result of complying with such orders shall not be considered off-hire.

(c) If the Owners consent or if the Vessel proceeds to or through an Area exposed to the risk of Piracy the Owners shall have the liberty:

(i) to take reasonable preventative measures to protect the Vessel, crew and cargo including but not limited to re-routeing within the Area, proceeding in convoy, using escorts, avoiding day or night navigation, adjusting speed or course, or engaging security personnel and/or deploying equipment on or about the Vessel (including embarkation/disembarkation);

(ii) to comply with underwriters' requirements under the terms of the Vessel's insurance(s);

(iii) to comply with all orders, directions, recommendations or advice given by the Government of the Nation under whose flag the Vessel sails, or other Government to whose laws the Owners are subject, or any other Government, body or group (including military authorities) whatsoever acting with the power to compel compliance with their orders or directions; and

(iv) to comply with the terms of any resolution of the Security Council of the United Nations, the effective orders of any other Supranational body which has the right to issue and give the same, and with national laws aimed at enforcing the same to which the Owners are subject, and to obey the orders and directions of those who are charged with their enforcement;

and the Charterers shall indemnify the Owners for any claims from holders of Bills of Lading or third parties caused by the Vessel proceeding as aforesaid, save to the extent that such claims are covered by additional insurance as provided in Sub-clause (d)(iii).

(d) Costs

(i) if the Vessel proceeds to or through an Area where due to risk of Piracy additional costs will be incurred including but not limited to additional personnel and preventative measures to avoid Piracy, such reasonable costs shall be for the Charterers' account. Any time lost waiting for convoys, following recommended routeing, timing, or reducing speed or taking measures to minimise risk, shall be for the Charterers' account and the Vessel shall remain on hire;

(ii) if the Owners become liable under the terms of employment to pay to the crew any bonus or additional wages in respect of sailing into an area which is dangerous in the manner defined by the said terms, then the actual bonus or additional wages paid shall be reimbursed to the Owners by the Charterers;

19

This document is a computer generated NYPE 2015 published by BIMCO and jointly authored by ASBA, BIMCO and the SMF. Any insertion or deletion to the form must be clearly visible. In the event of any modification being made to the pre-printed text of this document which is not clearly visible, the original BIMCO approved document shall apply. BIMCO assumes no responsibility for any loss, damages or expenses as a result of discrepancies between the original BIMCO approved document and this computer generated document.

Printed by BIMCO's IDEA·2

760   (iii) if the Vessel proceeds to or through an Area exposed to the risk of Piracy, the Charterers shall
761   reimburse to the Owners any additional premiums required by the Owners' insurers and the costs
762   of any additional insurances that the Owners reasonably require in connection with Piracy risks
763   which may include but not be limited to War Loss of Hire and/or maritime Kidnap and Ransom
764   (K&R); and

765   (iv) all payments arising under Sub-clause (d) shall be settled within fifteen (15) days of receipt of
766   the Owners' supported invoices or on redelivery, whichever occurs first.

767   (e)   If the Vessel is attacked by pirates any time lost shall be for the account of the Charterers and the
768   Vessel shall remain on hire.

769   (f)   If the Vessel is seized by pirates the Owners shall keep the Charterers closely informed of the
770   efforts made to have the Vessel released. The Vessel shall remain on hire throughout the seizure
771   and the Charterers' obligations shall remain unaffected, except that hire payments shall cease as
772   of the ninety-first (91st) day after the seizure until release. The Charterers shall pay hire, or if the
773   Vessel has been redelivered, the equivalent of Charter Party hire, for any time lost in making good
774   any damage and deterioration resulting from the seizure. The Charterers shall not be liable for late
775   redelivery under this Charter Party resulting from the seizure of the Vessel.

776   (g)   If in compliance with this Clause anything is done or not done, such shall not be deemed a
777   deviation, but shall be considered as due fulfilment of this Charter Party. In the event of a conflict
778   between the provisions of this Clause and any implied or express provision of the Charter Party,
779   this Clause shall prevail.

780   **40.**   **Taxes**

781   Charterers are to pay all local, State, National taxes and/or dues assessed on the Vessel or the
782   Owners resulting from the Charterers' orders herein, whether assessed during or after the currency
783   of this Charter Party including any taxes and/or dues on cargo and/or freights and/or sub-freights
784   and/or hire (excluding taxes levied by the country of the flag of the Vessel or the Owners). In the
785   event the Owners/Vessel/her flag state are exempt from any taxes, the Owners shall seek such
786   exemption and filing costs for such exemption, if any, shall be for the Charterers' account and no
787   charge for such taxes shall be assessed to the Charterers.

788   **41.**   **Industrial Action**

789   In the event of the Vessel being delayed or rendered inoperative by strikes, labor stoppages or
790   boycotts or any other difficulties arising from the Vessel's ownership, crew or terms of employment
791   of the crew of the chartered Vessel or any other vessel under the same ownership, operation and
792   control, any time lost is to be considered off-hire. The Owners guarantee that on delivery the
793   minimum terms and conditions of employment of the crew of the Vessel are in accordance with the
794   International Labour Organization Maritime Labour Convention (MLC) 2006, and will remain so
795   throughout the duration of this Charter Party.

796   **42.**   **Stowaways**

797   (a)   If stowaways have gained access to the Vessel by means of secreting away in the goods and/or
798   containers or by any other means related to the cargo operation, this shall amount to breach of this
799   Charter Party. The Charterers shall be liable for the consequences of such breach and hold the
800   Owners harmless and keep them indemnified against all claims; costs (including but not limited to
801   victualing costs for stowaways whilst on board and repatriation); losses; and fines or penalties,
802   which may arise and be made against them. The Charterers shall, if required, place the Owners in

20

803 funds to put up bail or other security. The Vessel shall remain on hire for any time lost as a result of
804 such breach.

805 (b) Save for those stowaways referred to in Sub-clause (a), if stowaways have gained access to the
806 Vessel this shall amount to a breach of this Charter Party. The Owners shall be liable for the
807 consequences of such breach and hold the Charterers harmless and keep them indemnified
808 against all claims; costs; losses; and fines or penalties, which may arise and be made against
809 them. The Vessel shall be off-hire for any time lost as a result of such breach.

810 **43. Smuggling**

811 (a) In the event of smuggling by the Master, other Officers and/or ratings, this shall amount to a breach
812 of this Charter Party. The Owners shall be liable for the consequences of such breach and hold the
813 Charterers harmless and keep them indemnified against all claims, costs, losses, and fines and
814 penalties which may arise and be made against them. The Vessel shall be off-hire for any time lost
815 as a result of such breach.

816 (b) If unmanifested narcotic drugs and/or any other illegal substances are found secreted in the goods
817 and/or containers or by any other means related to the cargo operation, this shall amount to a
818 breach of this Charter Party. The Charterers shall be liable for the consequences of such breach
819 and hold the Owners, Master, officers and ratings of the Vessel harmless and keep them
820 indemnified against all claims, costs, losses, and fines and penalties which may arise and be made
821 against them individually or jointly. The Charterers shall, if required, place the Owners in funds to
822 put up bail or other security. The Vessel shall remain on hire for any time lost as a result of such
823 breach.

824 **44. International Safety Management (ISM)**

825 During the duration of this Charter Party, the Owners shall procure that both the Vessel and "the
826 Company" (as defined by the ISM Code) shall comply with the requirements of the ISM Code.
827 Upon request the Owners shall provide a copy of the relevant Document of Compliance (DOC) and
828 Safety Management Certificate (SMC) to the Charterers. Except as otherwise provided in this
829 Charter Party, loss, damage, expense or delay caused by failure on the part of the Owners or "the
830 Company" to comply with the ISM Code shall be for the Owners' account.

831 **45. International Ship and Port Facility Security Code (ISPS Code)/Maritime Transportation**
832 **Security Act (MTSA)**

833 (a) (i) The Owners shall comply with the requirements of the ISPS and the relevant amendments to
834 Chapter XI of Safety of Life at Sea (SOLAS) (ISPS Code) relating to the Vessel and "the Company"
835 (as defined by the ISPS Code). If trading to or from the US or passing through US waters, the
836 Owners shall also comply with the requirements of the MTSA relating to the Vessel and the
837 "Owner" (as defined by the MTSA).

838 (ii) Upon request the Owners shall provide the Charterers with a copy of the relevant International
839 Ship Security Certificate (ISSC) (or the interim ISSC) and the full style contact details of the
840 Company Security Officer (CSO).

841 (iii) Loss, damages, expense or delay (excluding consequential loss, damages, expense or delay)
842 caused by failure on the part of the Owners or "the Company"/"Owner" to comply with the
843 requirements of the ISPS Code/MTSA or this Clause shall be for the Owners' account, except as
844 otherwise provided in this Charter Party.

Printed by BIMCO's IDEA-2

© 2015, the Association of Ship Brokers and Agents (U.S.A.), Inc. (ASBA).
Jointly authored by ASBA, BIMCO and the SMF

21

845 (b) (i) The Charterers shall provide the Owners and the Master with their full style contact details and,
846 upon request, any other information the Owners require to comply with the ISPS Code/MTSA.
847 Where sub-letting is permitted under the terms of this Charter Party, the Charterers shall ensure
848 that the contact details of all sub-charterers are likewise provided to the Owners and the Master.
849 Furthermore, the Charterers shall ensure that all sub-charter parties they enter into during the
850 period of this Charter Party contain the following provision:

851 *"The Charterers shall provide the Owners with their full style contact details and, where sub-letting*
852 *is permitted under the terms of the charter party, shall ensure that contact details of all sub-*
853 *charterers are likewise provided to the Owners".*

854 (ii) Loss, damages, expense or delay (excluding consequential loss, damages, expense or delay)
855 caused by failure on the part of the Charterers to comply with this Clause shall be for the
856 Charterers' account, except as otherwise provided in this Charter Party.

857 (c) Notwithstanding anything else contained in this Charter Party all delay costs or expenses
858 whatsoever arising out of or related to security regulations or measures required by the port facility
859 or any relevant authority in accordance with the ISPS Code/MTSA including, but not limited to,
860 security guards, launch services, vessel escorts, security fees or taxes and inspections, shall be for
861 the Charterers' account, unless such costs or expenses result solely from the negligence of the
862 Owners, Master or crew or the previous trading of the Vessel, the nationality of the crew, crew
863 visas, the Vessel's flag or the identity of the Owners' managers. All measures required by the
864 Owners to comply with the Ship Security Plan shall be for the Owners' account.

865 (d) If either party makes any payment which is for the other party's account according to this Clause,
866 the other party shall indemnify the paying party.

867 **46. Sanctions**

868 (a) The Owners shall not be obliged to comply with any orders for the employment of the Vessel in any
869 carriage, trade or on a voyage which, in the reasonable judgement of the Owners, will expose the
870 Vessel, Owners, managers, crew, the Vessel's insurers, or their re-insurers, to any sanction or
871 prohibition imposed by any State, Supranational or International Governmental Organization.

872 (b) If the Vessel is already performing an employment to which such sanction or prohibition is
873 subsequently applied, the Owners shall have the right to refuse to proceed with the employment
874 and the Charterers shall be obliged to issue alternative voyage orders within forty-eight (48) hours
875 of receipt of the Owners' notification of their refusal to proceed. If the Charterers do not issue such
876 alternative voyage orders the Owners may discharge any cargo already loaded at any safe port
877 (including the port of loading). The Vessel to remain on hire pending completion of the Charterers'
878 alternative voyage orders or delivery of cargo by the Owners and the Charterers to remain
879 responsible for all additional costs and expenses incurred in connection with such orders/delivery
880 of cargo. If in compliance with this Sub-clause (b) anything is done or not done, such shall not be
881 deemed a deviation.

882 (c) The Charterers shall indemnify the Owners against any and all claims whatsoever brought by the
883 owners of the cargo and/or the holders of Bills of Lading and/or sub-charterers against the Owners
884 by reason of the Owners' compliance with such alternative voyage orders or delivery of the cargo in
885 accordance with Sub-clause (b).

886 (d) The Charterers shall procure that this Clause shall be incorporated into all sub-charters issued
887 pursuant to this Charter Party.

22

888 **47. BIMCO Designated Entities Clause for Charter Parties**

889 (a) The provisions of this clause shall apply in relation to any sanction, prohibition or restriction
890 imposed on any specified persons, entities or bodies including the designation of specified vessels
891 or fleets under United Nations Resolutions or trade or economic sanctions, laws or regulations of
892 the European Union or the United States of America.

893 (b) The Owners and the Charterers respectively warrant for themselves (and in the case of any sublet,
894 the Charterers further warrant in respect of any sub-charterers, shippers, receivers, or cargo
895 interests) that at the date of this fixture and throughout the duration of this Charter Party they are
896 not subject to any of the sanctions, prohibitions, restrictions or designation referred to in Sub-
897 clause (a) which prohibit or render unlawful any performance under this Charter Party or any sublet
898 or any Bills of Lading. The Owners further warrant that the nominated vessel, or any substitute, is
899 not a designated vessel.

900 (c) If at any time during the performance of this Charter Party either party becomes aware that the
901 other party is in breach of warranty as aforesaid, the party not in breach shall comply with the laws
902 and regulations of any Government to which that party or the Vessel is subject, and follow any
903 orders or directions which may be given by any body acting with powers to compel compliance,
904 including where applicable the Owners' flag State. In the absence of any such orders, directions,
905 laws or regulations, the party not in breach may, in its option, terminate the Charter Party forthwith
906 or, if cargo is on board, direct the Vessel to any safe port of that party's choice and there discharge
907 the cargo or part thereof.

908 (d) If, in compliance with the provisions of this Clause, anything is done or is not done, such shall not
909 be deemed a deviation but shall be considered due fulfilment of this Charter Party.

910 (e) Notwithstanding anything in this Clause to the contrary, the Owners or the Charterers shall not be
911 required to do anything which constitutes a violation of the laws and regulations of any State to
912 which either of them is subject.

913 (f) The Owners or the Charterers shall be liable to indemnify the other party against any and all
914 claims, losses, damage, costs and fines whatsoever suffered by the other party resulting from any
915 breach of warranty as aforesaid.

916 (g) The Charterers shall procure that this Clause is incorporated into all sub-charters, contracts of
917 carriage and Bills of Lading issued pursuant to this Charter Party.

918 **48. BIMCO North American Advance Cargo Notification Clause for Time Charter Parties**

919 (a) If the Vessel loads or carries cargo destined for the US or Canada or passing through US or
920 Canadian ports in transit, the Charterers shall comply with the current US Customs regulations (19
921 CFR 47) or the Canada Border Services Agency regulations (Memorandum D3-5-2) or any
922 subsequent amendments thereto and shall undertake the role of carrier for the purposes of such
923 regulations and shall, in their own name, time and expense:

924 (i) have in place a Standard Carrier Alpha Code (SCAC)/Canadian Customs Carrier Code;

925 (ii) for US trade, have in place an International Carrier Bond (ICB);

926 (iii) provide the Owners with a timely confirmation of (i) and (ii) above as appropriate; and

927 (iv) submit a cargo declaration by Automated Manifest System (AMS) to the US Customs or by ACI
928 Automated Commercial Information (ACI) to the Canadian customs, and provide the Owners at the
929 same time with a copy thereof.

930 (b) The Charterers assume liability for and shall indemnify, defend and hold harmless the Owners
931 against any loss and/or damage whatsoever (including consequential loss and/or damage) and/or
932 any expenses, fines, penalties and all other claims of whatsoever nature, including but not limited
933 to legal costs, arising from the Charterers' failure to comply with any of the provisions of Sub-clause
934 (a). Should such failure result in any delay then, notwithstanding any provision in this Charter Party
935 to the contrary, the Vessel shall remain on hire.

936 (c) If the Charterers' ICB is used to meet any penalties, duties, taxes or other charges which are solely
937 the responsibility of the Owners, the Owners shall promptly reimburse the Charterers for those
938 amounts.

939 (d) The assumption of the role of carrier by the Charterers pursuant to this Clause and for the purpose
940 of the US Customs Regulations (19 CFR 4.7) shall be without prejudice to the identity of carrier
941 under any bill of lading, other contract, law or regulation.

942 **49. BIMCO U.S. Census Bureau Mandatory Automated Export System (AES) Clause for Time**
943 **Charter Parties**

944 (a) If the Vessel loads cargo in any US port or place, the Charterers shall comply with the current US
945 Census Bureau Regulations (15 CFR 30) or any subsequent amendments thereto and shall
946 undertake the role of carrier for the purposes of such regulations and shall, in their own name, time
947 and expense:

948 (i) have in place a SCAC (Standard Carrier Alpha Code);

949 (ii) have in place an ICB (International Carrier Bond);

950 (iii) provide the Owners with a timely confirmation of (i) and (ii) above; and

951 (iv) submit an export ocean manifest by Automated Export System (AES) to the US Census Bureau
952 and provide the Owners at the same time with a copy thereof.

953 (b) The Charterers assume liability for and shall indemnify, defend and hold harmless the Owners
954 against any loss and/or damage whatsoever (including consequential loss and/or damage) and/or
955 any expenses, fines, penalties and all other claims of whatsoever nature, including but not limited
956 to legal costs, arising from the Charterers' failure to comply with any of the provisions of Sub-clause
957 (a). Should such failure result in any delay then, notwithstanding any provision in this Charter Party
958 to the contrary, the Vessel shall remain on hire.

959 (c) If the Charterers' ICB is used to meet any penalties, duties, taxes or other charges which are solely
960 the responsibility of the Owners, the Owners shall promptly reimburse the Charterers for those
961 amounts.

962 (d) The assumption of the role of carrier by the Charterers pursuant to this Clause and for the purpose
963 of the US Census Bureau Regulations (15 CFR 30) shall be without prejudice to the identity of
964 carrier under any bill of lading, other contract, law or regulation.

Printed by BIMCO's IDEA•2

24

50. BIMCO EU Advance Cargo Declaration Clause for Time Charter Parties 2012

965

(a) If the Vessel loads cargo in any EU port or place destined for a port or place outside the EU ("Exported") or loads cargo outside the EU destined for an EU port or place or passing through EU ports or places in transit ("Imported"), the Charterers shall, for the purposes of this Clause, comply with the requirements of the EU Advance Cargo Declaration Regulations (the Security Amendment to the Community Customs Code, Regulations 648/2005; 1875/2006; and 312/2009) or any subsequent amendments thereto and shall, in their own name, and in their time and at their expense:

(i) have in place an Economic Operator Registration and Identification (EORI) number;

(ii) provide the Owners with a timely confirmation of (i) above as appropriate; and

(iii) where the cargo is being:

1. Exported: Submit, or arrange for the submission of, a customs declaration for export or, if a customs declaration or a re-export notification is not required, an exit summary declaration; or

2. Imported: Submit, or arrange for the submission of, an entry summary declaration.

Unless otherwise permitted by the relevant customs authorities, such declarations shall be submitted to them electronically.

(b) The Charterers assume liability for and shall indemnify, defend and hold harmless the Owners against any loss and/or damage and/or any expenses, fines, penalties and all other claims of whatsoever nature, including but not limited to legal costs, arising from the Charterers' failure to comply with any of the provisions of Sub-clause (a). Should such failure result in any delay then, notwithstanding any provision in this Charter Party to the contrary, the Vessel shall remain on hire.

51. Ballast Water Exchange Regulations

If ballast water exchanges are required by any coastal state where the vessel is trading, the Owners/Master shall comply with same at the Charterers' time, risk, and expense.

52. Period Applicable Clauses

If the minimum period of this Charter Party exceeds five (5) months, the following Sub-clauses shall apply:

(a) Should the Vessel at the expiry of the described employment period be on a ballast voyage to the place of redelivery or on a laden voyage, reasonably expected to be completed within the employment period when commenced, the Charterers shall have the use of the Vessel on the same conditions and at the same rate or the prevailing market rate, whichever is higher, for any extended time as may be necessary for the completion of the last voyage of the Vessel to the place of redelivery.

(b) Drydocking

The Owners shall have the option to place the Vessel in drydock during the currency of this Charter Party at a convenient time and place, to be mutually agreed upon between the Owners and the Charterers, for bottom cleaning and painting and/or repair as required by class or dictated by circumstances. (see also Clause 19 (Drydocking)).

25

Printed by BIMCO's IDEA-2

© 2015, the Association of Ship Brokers and Agents (U.S.A.), Inc. (ASBA).
Jointly authored by ASBA, BIMCO and the SMF

1003 (c) Off-hire

1004 The Charterers to have the option of adding any time the Vessel is off-hire to the Charter period.
1005 Such option shall be declared in writing not less than one (1) month before the expected date of
1006 redelivery, or latest one (1) week after the event if such event occurs less than one (1) month
1007 before the expected date of redelivery.

1008 (d) Charterers' Colors

1009 The Charterers shall have the privilege of flying their own house flag and painting the Vessel with
1010 their own markings. The Vessel shall be repainted in the Owners' colors before termination of the
1011 Charter Party. Cost and time of painting, maintaining and repainting those changes effected by the
1012 Charterers shall be for the Charterers' account.

1013 **53. Commissions**

1014 A commission of Click here to enter text. per cent is payable by the Vessel and the Owners to Click here to
1015 enter text. on hire earned and paid under this Charter Party, and also upon any continuation or
1016 extension of this Charter Party.

1017 An address commission of Click here to enter text. per cent on the hire earned shall be deducted by the
1018 Charterers on payment of the hire earned under this Charter Party.

1019 **54. Law and Arbitration**

1020 *(a) **New York**. This Charter Party shall be governed by United States maritime law. Any dispute arising
1021 out of or in connection with this Charter Party shall be referred to three persons at New York, one
1022 to be appointed by each of the parties hereto, and the third by the two so chosen. The award of the
1023 arbitrators or any two of them shall be final, and for the purposes of enforcing any award, judgment
1024 may be entered on an award by any court of competent jurisdiction. The proceedings shall be
1025 conducted in accordance with the rules of the Society of Maritime Arbitrators, Inc. (SMA) current at
1026 the time this Charter Party was entered into.

1027 In cases where neither the claim nor any counter claim exceeds the sum of US$ 100,000 (or such
1028 other sum as the parties may agree), the arbitration shall be conducted before a sole arbitrator in
1029 accordance with the Shortened Arbitration Procedure of the SMA current at the time this Charter
1030 Party was entered into. (www.smany.org).

1031 *(b) **London**. This Charter Party shall be governed by and construed in accordance with English law
1032 and any dispute arising out of or in connection with this Charter Party shall be referred to arbitration
1033 in London in accordance with the Arbitration Act 1996 or any statutory modification or re-enactment
1034 thereof save to the extent necessary to give effect to the provisions of this Clause.

1035 The arbitration shall be conducted in accordance with the London Maritime Arbitrators Association
1036 (LMAA) Terms current at the time when the arbitration proceedings are commenced.

1037 The reference shall be to three arbitrators. A party wishing to refer a dispute to arbitration shall
1038 appoint its arbitrator and send notice of such appointment in writing to the other party requiring the
1039 other party to appoint its own arbitrator within fourteen (14) calendar days of that notice and stating
1040 that it will appoint its arbitrator as sole arbitrator unless the other party appoints its own arbitrator
1041 and gives notice that it has done so within the fourteen (14) days specified. If the other party does
1042 not appoint its own arbitrator and give notice that it has done so within the fourteen (14) days
1043 specified, the party referring a dispute to arbitration may, without the requirement of any further
1044 prior notice to the other party, appoint its arbitrator as sole arbitrator and shall advise the other

26

1045 party accordingly. The award of a sole arbitrator shall be binding on both parties as if he had been
1046 appointed by agreement.

1047 Nothing herein shall prevent the parties agreeing in writing to vary these provisions to provide for
1048 the appointment of a sole arbitrator.

1049 In cases where neither the claim nor any counterclaim exceeds the sum of US$ 100,000 (or such
1050 other sum as the parties may agree) the arbitration shall be conducted in accordance with the
1051 LMAA Small Claims Procedure current at the time when the arbitration proceedings are
1052 commenced. (www.lmaa.org.uk)

*(c) **Singapore.** This Charter Party shall be governed by and construed in accordance with
1053
1054 Singapore**/English** law.

1055 Any dispute arising out of or in connection with this Charter Party, including any question regarding
1056 its existence, validity or termination shall be referred to and finally resolved by arbitration in
1057 Singapore in accordance with the Singapore International Arbitration Act (Chapter 143A) and any
1058 statutory modification or re-enactment thereof save to the extent necessary to give effect to the
1059 provisions of this Clause.

1060 The arbitration shall be conducted in accordance with the Arbitration Rules of the Singapore
1061 Chamber of Maritime Arbitration (SCMA) current at the time when the arbitration proceedings are
1062 commenced.

1063 The reference to arbitration of disputes under this clause shall be to three arbitrators. A party
1064 wishing to refer a dispute to arbitration shall appoint its arbitrator and send notice of such
1065 appointment in writing to the other party requiring the other party to appoint its own arbitrator and
1066 give notice that it has done so within fourteen (14) calendar days of that notice and stating that it
1067 will appoint its own arbitrator as sole arbitrator unless the other party appoints its own arbitrator and
1068 gives notice that it has done so within the fourteen (14) days specified. If the other party does not
1069 give notice that it has done so within the fourteen (14) days specified, the party referring a dispute
1070 to arbitration may, without the requirement of any further prior notice to the other party, appoint its
1071 arbitrator as sole arbitrator and shall advise the other party accordingly. The award of a sole
1072 arbitrator shall be binding on both parties as if he had been appointed by agreement.

1073 Nothing herein shall prevent the parties agreeing in writing to vary these provisions to provide for
1074 the appointment of a sole arbitrator.

1075 In cases where neither the claim nor any counterclaim exceeds the sum of US$ 150,000 (or such
1076 other sum as the parties may agree) the arbitration shall be conducted before a single arbitrator in
1077 accordance with the SCMA Small Claims Procedure current at the time when the arbitration
1078 proceedings are commenced. (www.scma.org.sg)

(d) This Charter Party shall be governed by and construed in accordance with the laws of the place
1079
1080 mutually agreed by the parties and any dispute arising out of or in connection with this Charter
1081 Party shall be referred to arbitration at a mutually agreed place, subject to the procedures
1082 applicable there.

1083 *Sub-clauses (a), (b), (c) and (d) are alternatives; indicate alternative agreed. If alternative (d)
1084 agreed also state the place of arbitration. If no alternative agreed and clearly indicated then Sub-
1085 clause (a) shall apply by default.

1086 **Singapore and English law are alternatives; if Sub-clause (c) agreed also indicate choice of
1087 Singapore or English law. If neither or both are indicated, then English law shall apply by default.

27

1088 **55. Notices**

1089 All notices, requests and other communications required or permitted by any clause of this Charter
1090 Party shall be given in writing and shall be sufficiently given or transmitted if delivered by hand,
1091 email, express courier service or registered mail and addressed if to the Owners, to Click here to
1092 enter text. or such other address or email address as the Owners may hereafter designate in
1093 writing, and if to the Charterers to Click here to enter text. or such other address or email address
1094 as the Charterers may hereafter designate in writing. Any such communication shall be deemed to
1095 have been given on the date of actual receipt by the party to which it is addressed.

1096 **56. Headings**

1097 The headings in this Charter Party are for identification only and shall not be deemed to be part
1098 hereof or be taken into consideration in the interpretation or construction of this Charter Party.

1099 **57. Singular/Plural**

1100 The singular includes the plural and vice-versa as the context admits or requires.

1101 Clauses Click here to enter text. to Click here to enter text., both inclusive, as attached hereto are fully incorporated in
1102 this Charter Party.

1103 **OWNERS:**   **CHARTERERS:**

1104 Name: **Choose an item.**   Name: **Choose an item.**
1105 Title: Click here to enter text.   Title: Click here to enter text..

28

NYPE 2015 APPENDIX A (VESSEL DESCRIPTION)

GENERAL INFORMATION

1.1	Vessel's name	Choose an item.
1.2	Type of vessel	Click here to enter text.
1.3	IMO number	Click here to enter text.
1.4	Year of build	Click here to enter text.
1.5	Name of shipyard/where built	Click here to enter text. / Click here to enter text.
1.6	Flag	Click here to enter text.
1.7	Port of Registry	Click here to enter text.
1.8	Classification Society	Click here to enter text.
1.9	Protection & Indemnity Club – full name	Click here to enter text.
1.10	Hull & Machinery insured value	Click here to enter text.
1.11	Date and place of last drydock	Click here to enter text.
1.12	Vessel's Call Sign	Click here to enter text.
1.13	Vessel's INMARSAT number(s)	Click here to enter text.
1.14	Vessel's fax number	Click here to enter text.
1.15	Vessel's email address	Click here to enter text.

LOADLINE INFORMATION

2.1	Loadline	Deadweight	Draft	TPC
	Winter	Click here to enter text.	Click here to enter text.	Click here to enter text.
	Summer	Click here to enter text.	Click here to enter text.	Click here to enter text.
	Tropical	Click here to enter text.	Click here to enter text.	Click here to enter text.
	Fresh Water	Click here to enter text.	Click here to enter text.	Click here to enter text.
	Tropical Fresh Water	Click here to enter text.	Click here to enter text.	Click here to enter text.
2.2	Constant Excluding Fresh Water	Click here to enter text.		
2.3	Freshwater Capacity	Click here to enter text.		

TONNAGES

3.1	Gross Tonnage (GT)	Click here to enter text.	
3.2	Net Tonnage (NT)	Click here to enter text.	
3.3	Panama Canal Net Tonnage (PCNT)	Click here to enter text.	
3.4	Suez Canal Tonnage	Gross (SCGT)	Net (SCNT)
		Click here to enter text.	Click here to enter text.
3.5	Lightweight	Click here to enter text.	

DIMENSIONS

4.1	Number of holds	Click here to enter text.		
4.2	Hold dimensions	1. Click here to enter text.	2. Click here to enter text.	3. Click here to enter text.
		4. Click here to enter text.	5. Click here to enter text.	6. Click here to enter text.
		7. Click here to enter text.	8. Click here to enter text.	9. Click here to enter text.
4.3	Height of holds	Click here to enter text.		
4.4	Number of hatches	Click here to enter text.		
4.5	Manufacturer and type of hatch covers	Click here to enter text.		
4.6	Hatch dimensions	1. Click here to enter text.	2. Click here to enter text.	3. Click here to enter text.
		4. Click here to enter text.	5. Click here to enter text.	6. Click here to enter text.
		7. Click here to enter text.	8. Click here to enter text.	9. Click here to enter text.
4.7	Is vessel strengthened for the carriage of heavy cargoes?	Click here to enter text.		
4.8	If yes, state which holds may be left empty	Click here to enter text.		
4.9	Main deck strength	Click here to enter text.		
4.10	Tanktop strength	Click here to enter text.		
4.11	Strength of hatch covers	Click here to enter text.		
4.12	Cubic grain capacity, by hold	1. Click here to enter text.	2. Click here to enter text.	3. Click here to enter text.
		4. Click here to enter text.	5. Click here to enter text.	6. Click here to enter text.
		7. Click here to enter text.	8. Click here to enter text.	9. Click here to enter text.
4.13	Cubic bale capacity, by hold	1. Click here to enter text.	2. Click here to enter text.	3. Click here to enter text.
		4. Click here to enter text.	5. Click here to enter text.	6. Click here to enter text.
		7. Click here to enter text.	8. Click here to enter text.	9. Click here to enter text.
4.14	Length overall	Click here to enter text.		
4.15	Length between perpendiculars	Click here to enter text.		
4.16	Extreme breadth (beam):	Click here to enter text.		
4.17	Keel to Masthead (KTM):	Click here to enter text.		
4.18	Distance from waterline to top of hatch coamings or hatch covers if side rolling hatches	No. 1 hatch	Midships	Last hatch
		Click here to enter text.	Click here to enter text.	Click here to enter text.
	Ballast condition (ballast holds not flooded, basis 50% bunkers)	Click here to enter text.	Click here to enter text.	Click here to enter text.

30

	Full ballast condition (ballast holds flooded, basis 50% bunkers)	Click here to enter text.	Click here to enter text.	Click here to enter text.
	Light condition (basis 50% bunkers)	Click here to enter text.	Click here to enter text.	Click here to enter text.
	Fully laden condition	Click here to enter text.	Click here to enter text.	Click here to enter text.
4.19	Vessel's temporary ballast hold(s)	Click here to enter text.		
4.20	Vessel's ballasting time/rate of ballasting	Click here to enter text.		
4.21	Vessel's de-ballasting time/rate of de-ballasting	Click here to enter text.		
4.22	If geared state manufacturer and type	Click here to enter text.		
4.23	Number & location of cranes	Click here to enter text.		
4.24	If vessel has power outlets for grabs – state number and power	Click here to enter text.		
4.25	Maximum outreach of cranes beyond ship's rail	Click here to enter text.		
4.26	Are winches electro-hydraulic?	Click here to enter text.		
4.27	If vessel has grabs on board, state:	Click here to enter text.		
	Type	Click here to enter text.		
	Number/Capacity	Click here to enter text.		
4.28	Are holds CO2 fitted?	Click here to enter text.		
4.29	Are holds vessel fitted with Australian type approved hold ladders?	Click here to enter text.		
4.30	Is vessel fitted for carriage of grain in accordance with Chapter VI of SOLAS 1974 and amendments without requiring bagging, trapping and securing when loading a full cargo (deadweight) of heavy grain in bulk (stowage factor 42 cubic feet) with ends untrimmed?	Click here to enter text.		
4.31	Is vessel logs fitted?	Click here to enter text.		
4.32	If yes, state number, type and height of stanchions on board and which stanchions are collapsible. Also state number and type of sockets on board	Click here to enter text.		

BUNKERS, SPEED AND CONSUMPTION

5.1	What type/viscosity of fuel is used for main propulsion?	Click here to enter text.
5.2	Capacity of main engine bunker tanks (excluding unpumpables):	Click here to enter text.
5.3	Number of bunker tanks	Click here to enter text.
5.4	What type/viscosity of fuel is used in the generating plant	Click here to enter text.
	Capacity of auxiliary (aux.)engine(s) bunker tanks (excluding unpumpables)	Click here to enter text.

31

Speed on sea passage	Knots ballast	Knots laden	On tons (main)	On tons (aux.)
	Click here to enter text.	Click here to enter text.	Click here to enter text.	Click here to enter text.
	Click here to enter text.	Click here to enter text.	Click here to enter text.	Click here to enter text.
	Click here to enter text.	Click here to enter text.	Click here to enter text.	Click here to enter text.
Consumption in Port	Tons (main)		Tons (aux.)	
Working	Click here to enter text.		Click here to enter text.	
Idle	Click here to enter text.		Click here to enter text.	

CREW

6.1	Number of Officers	Click here to enter text.
6.2	Number of Ratings	Click here to enter text.
6.3	Name and nationality of Master	Click here to enter text.
6.4	Nationality of Officers	Click here to enter text.
6.5	Nationality of Ratings	Click here to enter text.

CERTIFICATE EXPIRY DATES

7.1	P&I	Click here to enter text.
7.2	H&M	Click here to enter text.
7.3	Class	Click here to enter text.
7.4	Gear	Click here to enter text.
7.5	Document of Compliance (DOC)	Click here to enter text.
7.6	Safety Management Certificate (SMC)	Click here to enter text.
7.7	International Ship Security Certificate	Click here to enter text.

32

FONASBA Time Charter Interpretation Code 2000*

FONASBA

The Federation of National Associations of Ship Brokers and Agents

TIME CHARTER INTERPRETATION CODE 2000

Disclaimer

Where any of this code conflicts with any of the terms of the relevant time charter, those of the latter shall prevail to that extent, but no further:

Introduction:

AIMS AND OBJECTS

In commercial practice many aims and objectives for standardisation are often frustrated by the laws in different jurisdictions and where the legal understanding and interpretation may differ the one from the other.

The main jurisdictions applicable to maritime disputes are:

    a) The Common Law countries – mainly England and the USA.

    b) The Civil Law countries such as France, Germany, Italy, etc.

The endeavour is not going to be the alter-ego of the Laytime Definitions for Voyage Charters; nor is this an attempt to create new charter party clauses, but merely a Code of how to interpret existing charter party clauses as well as to assist disputing parties where charter parties are silent or non-determining.

There is a vast difference between definition and interpretation, but in some ways and sometimes they may compliment one another. For example, nobody in shipping needs a definition of what speed and consumption are or mean, but how should one deal with a speed claim, if any?

The chief objective of the Code is to try to eliminate many often occurring and avoidable maritime charter parties disputes in the field of time charter.

---

* Reproduced by kind permission of the Federation of National Associations of Ship Brokers and Agents (FONASBA).

The following is to apply to any dry cargo time charter not containing a performance clause, and to any combination carrier when engaged in dry cargo trading:

The speed and consumption warrantees of the time charter are to apply for its duration and whether the vessel is fully, partly loaded or in ballast, and shall be computed from pilot station to pilot station on all sea passages while the vessel is on hire, **excluding:**

a)   Any day on which winds of Beaufort Wind Scale 4 or above are encountered for more than six (6) consecutive hours;

b)   Any time during which speed is deliberately reduced for reasons of safety, or on charterers' orders to steam at economical or reduced speed, or when the vessel is navigating within confined waters, or when assisting vessels in distress;

c)   Any complete sea passage of less than 24 hours duration from pilot station to pilot station;

d)   Periods in which time is lost on charterers' instructions or due to causes expressly excepted under terms of the time charter;

e)   Periods when the vessels' speed is reduced by reason of hull fouling caused by charterers' trading orders.

When specific figures have been agreed to for the vessel in ballasted condition these shall be taken into consideration as shall agreed specifics for reduced or economical speed and consumption, when computations are made.

The mileage made good during qualifying periods shall be divided by the warranted speed and compared to the time actually spent. Any excess is to be treated as off-hire. If the word 'about' precedes the speed and consumption, same will be understood to mean ½ knot less in the speed and 5% more in the consumption, not be cumulative.

As to consumption, the recorded qualifying periods, as above shall be multiplied by the warranted consumption on the qualifying days and compared to the actual consumption. In case of any excess, the charterers are be to compensated by the owners for such excess in cost to the charterers calculated at the prices at the last port bunkers were supplied during the time charter, or those at delivery whichever applicable. Such amount may be deducted from hire.

The immediate financial consequences of a speed deficiency shall be set-off with any saving caused by under-consumption.

The computations shall be made sea passage by sea passage. The vessel's speed and consumption shall be reviewed at the end of each twelve months, or other lesser period as appropriate.

If in respect of any such review period it is found that the vessel's speed has fallen below the warranted speed, hire shall be reduced by an amount equivalent to the loss in time involved at the rate of hire. And if in respect of any review period it is found that the vessel's consumption has exceeded the warranted consumption, the additional costs shall be borne by the owners.

The foregoing is without prejudice to any other claim(s) that a party may have on the other.

2. Withdrawal for late/non payment of hire

Except where otherwise specifically permitted in the provisions of the charter party, the charterers shall have no right to make arbitrary deductions from hire which shall remain payable punctually and regularly as stipulated therein. Nothing in the charter party shall, however, prejudice the charterers' right to make any equitable set-off against a hire payment due provided that the calculation is reasonable, made bona fide, and that it is in respect of a claim arising directly out of their deprivation of the use of the vessel in whole or in part.

Except as provided herein, the owners shall have a right of permanent withdrawal of their vessel when payment of hire has not been received by their bankers by the due date by reason of oversight, negligence, errors or omissions of charterers or their bankers. In such cases prior to effecting a withdrawal of the vessel, the owners shall put the charterers on preliminary notice of their failure to pay hire on the due date, following which the charterers shall be given two clear banking days to remedy the default. Where the breach has been cured the payment shall be deemed to have been made punctually.

In respect to a payment of hire made in due time, but insufficient in amount, the owners shall be permitted a reasonable time to verify the correctness of a deduction. If, thereafter, there is found to be disagreement on the amount of the deduction, then the amount in dispute shall be placed in escrow by the charterers and the matter referred to immediate arbitration in accordance with the terms of the charter party's arbitration clause. In that event there shall be no right of withdrawal.

Except as provided heretofore, withdrawal of the vessel may be made by the owners, which shall be without prejudice to any other claim they may otherwise have on the charterers.

3. Off-hire

Any period of time qualifying as off-hire under terms of the charter party shall be allowed to the charterers for any time lost in excess of three consecutive hours for each occurrence.

In addition to matters referred to as off-hire in the charter party, shall be included time lost to the charterers caused by interference by a legal, port of governmental authority, resulting in the charterers being deprived of their unfettered use of the vessel at any given time during the currency of the charter party, or in the vessel being prevented from leaving the jurisdiction contrary to charterers' requirements.

4. Deviation

All periods of off-hire due to deviation shall run from the commencement of the loss of time to charterers, deviation or putting back, and shall continue until the vessel is again in a fully efficient state to resume her service from a position not less favourable to the charterers than that at which the loss of time, deviation or putting back occurred.

5. Legitimacy of the Last Voyage

In the absence of any specific provision in the time charter relating to redelivery and orders for the final voyage, the following shall apply:

Charterers undertake to arrange the vessel's trading so as to permit redelivery within the period and permissible redelivery area as contained in the charter party. As soon as the charterers have arranged the final voyage they shall immediately so inform the owners giving a realistic estimated itinerary up to redelivery time. The owners shall notify the charterers within two working days thereafter as to whether they agree or disagree with charterers' estimate. Should they disagree and consider the vessel will overlap the maximum period, they shall nonetheless allow the voyage to be undertaken at the time charter rate of the charter party without prejudice to their ultimate right to compensation for additional hire at the market rate should an overlap subsequently have proven to have occurred, and should the market rate be higher than the charter party rate of hire.

APPENDIX 8

Barecon 2001*

1. Shipbroker	**BIMCO STANDARD BAREBOAT CHARTER** **CODE NAME: "BARECON 2001"** PART I
	2. Place and date
3. Owners/Place of business (Cl. 1)	4. Bareboat Charterers/Place of business (Cl. 1)
5. Vessel's name, call sign and flag (Cl. 1 and 3)	
6. Type of Vessel	7. GT/NT
8. When/Where built	9. Total DWT (abt.) in metric tons on summer freeboard
10. Classification Society (Cl. 3)	11. Date of last special survey by the Vessel's classification society
12. Further particulars of Vessel (also indicate minimum number of months' validity of class certificates agreed acc. to Cl. 3)	
13. Port or Place of delivery (Cl. 3)	14. Time for delivery (Cl. 4) 15. Cancelling date (Cl. 5)
16. Port or Place of redelivery (Cl. 15)	17. No. of months' validity of trading and class certificates upon redelivery (Cl. 15)
18. Running days' notice if other than stated in Cl. 4	19. Frequency of dry-docking (Cl. 10(g))
20. Trading limits (Cl. 6)	
21. Charter period (Cl. 2)	22. Charter hire (Cl. 11)
23. New class and other safety requirements (state percentage of Vessel's insurance value acc. to Box 29)(Cl. 10(a)(ii))	
24. Rate of interest payable acc. to Cl. 11(f) and, if applicable, acc. to PART IV	25. Currency and method of payment (Cl. 11)

Printed and sold by Fr. G. Knudtzons Bogtrykkeri A/S,
Vallensbaekvej 61, DK-2625 Vallensbaek, Fax: +45 4366 0701

continued

First issued by
The Baltic and International Maritime Council (BIMCO), Copenhagen, in 1974
as "Barecon A" and "Barecon B". Revised and amalgamated 1989. Revised 2001

Copyright, published by
The Baltic and International Maritime Council (BIMCO), Copenhagen, issued November 2001

* Reproduced by kind permission of BIMCO.

26. Place of payment; also state beneficiary and bank account (Cl. 11)	27. Bank guarantee/bond (sum and place)(Cl. 24)(optional)
28. Mortgage(s), if any (state whether 12(a) or (b) applies; if 12(b) applies state date of Financial Instrument and name of Mortgagee(s)/Place of business)(Cl. 12)	29. Insurance (hull and machinery and war risks)(state value acc. to Cl. 13(f) or, if applicable, acc. to Cl. 14(k))(also state if Cl. 14 applies)
30. Additional insurance cover, if any, for Owners' account limited to (Cl. 13(b) or, if applicable, Cl. 14(g))	31. Additional insurance cover, if any, for Charterers' account limited to (Cl. 13(b) or, if applicable, Cl. 14(g))
32. Latent defects (only to be filled in if period other than stated in Cl. 3)	33. Brokerage commission and to whom payable (Cl. 27)
34. Grace period (state number of clear banking days)(Cl. 28)	35. Dispute Resolution (state 30(a), 30(b) or 30(c); if 30(c) agreed Place of Arbitration must be stated (Cl. 30)
36. War cancellation (indicate countries agreed)(Cl. 26(f))	
37. Newbuilding Vessel (indicate with "yes" or "no" whether PART III applies)(optional)	38. Name and place of Builders (only to be filled in if PART III applies)
39. Vessel's Yard Building No. (only to be filled in if PART III applies)	40. Date of Building Contract (only to be filled in if PART III applies)
41. Liquidated damages and costs shall accrue to (state party acc. to Cl. 1) a) b) c)	
42. Hire/Purchase agreement (indicate with "yes" or "no" whether PART IV applies)(optional)	43. Bareboat Charter Registry (indicate "yes" or "no" whether PART V applies)(optional)
44. Flag and Country of the Bareboat Charter Registry (only to be filled in if PART V applies)	45. Country of the Underlying Registry (only to be filled in if PART V applies)
46. Number of additional clauses covering special provisions, if agreed	

PREAMBLE - It is mutually agreed that this Contract shall be performed subject to the conditions contained in this Charter which shall include PART I and PART II. In the event of a conflict of conditions, the provisions of PART I shall prevail over those of PART II to the extent of such conflict but no further. It is further mutually agreed that PART III and/or PART IV and/or PART V shall only apply and only form part of this Charter if expressly agreed and stated in the Boxes 37, 42 and 43. If PART III and/or PART IV and/or PART V apply, it is further agreed that in the event of a conflict of conditions, the provisions of PART I and PART II shall prevail over those of PART III and/or PART IV and/or PART V to the extent of such conflict but no further.

Signature (Owners)	Signature (Charterers)

660

1. Definitions 1

In this Charter, the following terms shall have the 2
meanings hereby assigned to them: 3
'The Owners' shall mean the party identified in Box 3; 4
'The Charterers' shall mean the party identified in Box 4; 5
'The Vessel' shall mean the vessel named in Box 5 and 6
with particulars as stated in Boxes 6 to 12. 7
'Financial Instrument' means the mortgage, deed of 8
covenant or other such financial security instrument as 9
annexed to this Charter and stated in Box 28. 10

2. Charter Period 11

In consideration of the hire detailed in Box 22, the 12
Owners have agreed to let and the Charterers have 13
agreed to hire the Vessel for the period stated in Box 21 14
("The Charter Period"). 15

3. Delivery 16

(not applicable when Part III applies, as indicated in Box 37) 17
(a) The Owners shall before and at the time of delivery 18
exercise due diligence to make the Vessel seaworthy 19
and in every respect ready in hull, machinery and 20
equipment for service under this Charter. 21
The Vessel shall be delivered by the Owners and taken 22
over by the Charterers at the port or place indicated in 23
Box 13 in such ready safe berth as the Charterers may 24
direct. 25
(b) The Vessel shall be properly documented on 26
delivery in accordance with the laws of the flag State 27
indicated in Box 5 and the requirements of the 28
classification society stated in Box 10. The Vessel upon 29
delivery shall have her survey cycles up to date and 30
trading and class certificates valid for at least the number 31
of months agreed in Box 12. 32
(c) The delivery of the Vessel by the Owners and the 33
taking over of the Vessel by the Charterers shall 34
constitute a full performance by the Owners of all the 35
Owners' obligations under this Clause 3, and thereafter 36
the Charterers shall not be entitled to make or assert 37
any claim against the Owners on account of any 38
conditions, representations or warranties expressed or 39
implied with respect to the Vessel but the Owners shall 40
be liable for the cost of but not the time for repairs or 41
renewals occasioned by latent defects in the Vessel, 42
her machinery or appurtenances, existing at the time of 43
delivery under this Charter, provided such defects have 44
manifested themselves within twelve (12) months after 45
delivery unless otherwise provided in Box 32. 46

4. Time for Delivery 47

(not applicable when Part III applies, as indicated in Box 37) 48
The Vessel shall not be delivered before the date 49
indicated in Box 14 without the Charterers' consent and 50
the Owners shall exercise due diligence to deliver the 51
Vessel not later than the date indicated in Box 15. 52
Unless otherwise agreed in Box 18, the Owners shall 53
give the Charterers not less than thirty (30) running days' 54
preliminary and not less than fourteen (14) running days' 55
definite notice of the date on which the Vessel is 56
expected to be ready for delivery. 57
The Owners shall keep the Charterers closely advised 58
of possible changes in the Vessel's position. 59

5. Cancelling 60

(not applicable when Part III applies, as indicated in Box 37) 61
(a) Should the Vessel not be delivered latest by the 62
cancelling date indicated in Box 15, the Charterers shall 63
have the option of cancelling this Charter by giving the 64

Owners notice of cancellation within thirty-six (36) 65
running hours after the cancelling date stated in Box 66
15, failing which this Charter shall remain in full force 67
and effect. 68
(b) If it appears that the Vessel will be delayed beyond 69
the cancelling date, the Owners may, as soon as they 70
are in a position to state with reasonable certainty the 71
day on which the Vessel should be ready, give notice 72
thereof to the Charterers asking whether they will 73
exercise their option of cancelling, and the option must 74
then be declared within one hundred and sixty-eight 75
(168) running hours of the receipt by the Charterers of 76
such notice or within thirty-six (36) running hours after 77
the cancelling date, whichever is the earlier. If the 78
Charterers do not then exercise their option of cancelling, 79
the seventh day after the readiness date stated in the 80
Owners' notice shall be substituted for the cancelling 81
date indicated in Box 15 for the purpose of this Clause 5. 82
(c) Cancellation under this Clause 5 shall be without 83
prejudice to any claim the Charterers may otherwise 84
have on the Owners under this Charter. 85

6. Trading Restrictions 86

The Vessel shall be employed in lawful trades for the 87
carriage of suitable lawful merchandise within the trading 88
limits indicated in Box 20. 89
The Charterers undertake not to employ the Vessel or 90
suffer the Vessel to be employed otherwise than in 91
conformity with the terms of the contracts of insurance 92
(including any warranties expressed or implied therein) 93
without first obtaining the consent of the insurers to such 94
employment and complying with such requirements as 95
to extra premium or otherwise as the insurers may 96
prescribe. 97
The Charterers also undertake not to employ the Vessel 98
or suffer her employment in any trade or business which 99
is forbidden by the law of any country to which the Vessel 100
may sail or is otherwise illicit or in carrying illicit or 101
prohibited goods or in any manner whatsoever which 102
may render her liable to condemnation, destruction, 103
seizure or confiscation. 104
Notwithstanding any other provisions contained in this 105
Charter it is agreed that nuclear fuels or radioactive 106
products or waste are specifically excluded from the 107
cargo permitted to be loaded or carried under this 108
Charter. This exclusion does not apply to radio-isotopes 109
used or intended to be used for any industrial, 110
commercial, agricultural, medical or scientific purposes 111
provided the Owners' prior approval has been obtained 112
to loading thereof. 113

7. Surveys on Delivery and Redelivery 114

(not applicable when Part III applies, as indicated in Box 37) 115
The Owners and Charterers shall each appoint 116
surveyors for the purpose of determining and agreeing 117
in writing the condition of the Vessel at the time of 118
delivery and redelivery hereunder. The Owners shall 119
bear all expenses of the On-hire Survey including loss 120
of time, if any, and the Charterers shall bear all expenses 121
of the Off-hire Survey including loss of time, if any, at 122
the daily equivalent to the rate of hire or pro rata thereof. 123

8. Inspection 124

The Owners shall have the right at any time after giving 125
reasonable notice to the Charterers to inspect or survey 126
the Vessel or instruct a duly authorised surveyor to carry 127
out such survey on their behalf:- 128
(a) to ascertain the condition of the Vessel and satisfy 129

661

themselves that the Vessel is being properly repaired 130
and maintained. The costs and fees for such inspection 131
or survey shall be paid by the Owners unless the Vessel 132
is found to require repairs or maintenance in order to 133
achieve the condition so provided; 134

(b) in dry-dock if the Charterers have not dry-docked 135
her in accordance with Clause 10(g). The costs and fees 136
for such inspection or survey shall be paid by the 137
Charterers; and 138

(c) for any other commercial reason they consider 139
necessary (provided it does not unduly interfere with 140
the commercial operation of the Vessel). The costs and 141
fees for such inspection and survey shall be paid by the 142
Owners. 143

All time used in respect of inspection, survey or repairs 144
shall be for the Charterers' account and form part of the 145
Charter Period. 146

The Charterers shall also permit the Owners to inspect 147
the Vessel's log books whenever requested and shall 148
whenever required by the Owners furnish them with full 149
information regarding any casualties or other accidents 150
or damage to the Vessel. 151

9.   Inventories, Oil and Stores 152
A complete inventory of the Vessel's entire equipment, 153
outfit including spare parts, appliances and of all 154
consumable stores on board the Vessel shall be made 155
by the Charterers in conjunction with the Owners on 156
delivery and again on redelivery of the Vessel. The 157
Charterers and the Owners, respectively, shall at the 158
time of delivery and redelivery take over and pay for all 159
bunkers, lubricating oil, unbroached provisions, paints, 160
ropes and other consumable stores (excluding spare 161
parts) in the said Vessel at the then current market prices 162
at the ports of delivery and redelivery, respectively. The 163
Charterers shall ensure that all spare parts listed in the 164
inventory and used during the Charter Period are 165
replaced at their expense prior to redelivery of the 166
Vessel. 167

10. Maintenance and Operation 168
(a)(i) Maintenance and Repairs - During the Charter 169
Period the Vessel shall be in the full possession 170
and at the absolute disposal for all purposes of the 171
Charterers and under their complete control in 172
every respect. The Charterers shall maintain the 173
Vessel, her machinery, boilers, appurtenances and 174
spare parts in a good state of repair, in efficient 175
operating condition and in accordance with good 176
commercial maintenance practice and, except as 177
provided for in Clause 14(l), if applicable, at their 178
own expense they shall at all times keep the 179
Vessel's Class fully up to date with the Classification 180
Society indicated in Box 10 and maintain all other 181
necessary certificates in force at all times. 182

(ii) New Class and Other Safety Requirements - In the 183
event of any improvement, structural changes or 184
new equipment becoming necessary for the 185
continued operation of the Vessel by reason of new 186
class requirements or by compulsory legislation 187
costing (excluding the Charterers' loss of time) 188
more than the percentage stated in Box 23, or if 189
Box 23 is left blank, 5 per cent. of the Vessel's 190
insurance value as stated in Box 29, then the 191
extent, if any, to which the rate of hire shall be varied 192
and the ratio in which the cost of compliance shall 193
be shared between the parties concerned in order 194
to achieve a reasonable distribution thereof as 195

between the Owners and the Charterers having 196
regard, inter alia, to the length of the period 197
remaining under this Charter shall, in the absence 198
of agreement, be referred to the dispute resolution 199
method agreed in Clause 30. 200

(iii) Financial Security - The Charterers shall maintain 201
financial security or responsibility in respect of third 202
party liabilities as required by any government, 203
including federal, state or municipal or other division 204
or authority thereof, to enable the Vessel, without 205
penalty or charge, lawfully to enter, remain at, or 206
leave any port, place, territorial or contiguous 207
waters of any country, state or municipality in 208
performance of this Charter without any delay. This 209
obligation shall apply whether or not such 210
requirements have been lawfully imposed by such 211
government or division or authority thereof. 212

The Charterers shall make and maintain all arrange- 213
ments by bond or otherwise as may be necessary to 214
satisfy such requirements at the Charterers' sole 215
expense and the Charterers shall indemnify the Owners 216
against all consequences whatsoever (including loss of 217
time) for any failure or inability to do so. 218

(b) Operation of the Vessel - The Charterers shall at 219
their own expense and by their own procurement man, 220
victual, navigate, operate, supply, fuel and, whenever 221
required, repair the Vessel during the Charter Period 222
and they shall pay all charges and expenses of every 223
kind and nature whatsoever incidental to their use and 224
operation of the Vessel under this Charter, including 225
annual flag State fees and any foreign general 226
municipality and/or state taxes. The Master, officers and 227
crew of the Vessel shall be the servants of the Charterers 228
for all purposes whatsoever, even if for any reason 229
appointed by the Owners. 230

Charterers shall comply with the regulations regarding 231
officers and crew in force in the country of the Vessel's 232
flag or any other applicable law. 233

(c) The Charterers shall keep the Owners and the 234
mortgagee(s) advised of the intended employment, 235
planned dry-docking and major repairs of the Vessel, 236
as reasonably required. 237

(d) Flag and Name of Vessel - During the Charter 238
Period, the Charterers shall have the liberty to paint the 239
Vessel in their own colours, install and display their 240
funnel insignia and fly their own house flag. The 241
Charterers shall also have the liberty, with the Owners' 242
consent, which shall not be unreasonably withheld, to 243
change the flag and/or the name of the Vessel during 244
the Charter Period. Painting and re-painting, instalment 245
and re-instalment, registration and re-registration, if 246
required by the Owners, shall be at the Charterers' 247
expense and time. 248

(e) Changes to the Vessel – Subject to Clause 10(a)(ii), 249
the Charterers shall make no structural changes in the 250
Vessel or changes in the machinery, boilers, appurten- 251
ances or spare parts thereof without in each instance 252
first securing the Owners' approval thereof. If the Owners 253
so agree, the Charterers shall, if the Owners so require, 254
restore the Vessel to its former condition before the 255
termination of this Charter. 256

(f) Use of the Vessel's Outfit, Equipment and 257
Appliances - The Charterers shall have the use of all 258
outfit, equipment, and appliances on board the Vessel 259
at the time of delivery, provided the same or their 260
substantial equivalent shall be returned to the Owners 261
on redelivery in the same good order and condition as 262
when received, ordinary wear and tear excepted. The 263

662

Charterers shall from time to time during the Charter 264
Period replace such items of equipment as shall be so 265
damaged or worn as to be unfit for use. The Charterers 266
are to procure that all repairs to or replacement of any 267
damaged, worn or lost parts or equipment are effected 268
in such manner (both as regards workmanship and 269
quality of materials) as not to diminish the value of the 270
Vessel. The Charterers have the right to fit additional 271
equipment at their expense and risk but the Charterers 272
shall remove such equipment at the end of the period if 273
requested by the Owners. Any equipment including radio 274
equipment on hire on the Vessel at time of delivery shall 275
be kept and maintained by the Charterers and the 276
Charterers shall assume the obligations and liabilities 277
of the Owners under any lease contracts in connection 278
therewith and shall reimburse the Owners for all 279
expenses incurred in connection therewith, also for any 280
new equipment required in order to comply with radio 281
regulations. 282

(g) Periodical Dry-Docking - The Charterers shall dry- 283
dock the Vessel and clean and paint her underwater 284
parts whenever the same may be necessary, but not 285
less than once during the period stated in Box 19 or, if 286
Box 19 has been left blank, every sixty (60) calendar 287
months after delivery or such other period as may be 288
required by the Classification Society or flag State. 289

11. Hire 290

(a) The Charterers shall pay hire due to the Owners 291
punctually in accordance with the terms of this Charter 292
in respect of which time shall be of the essence. 293
(b) The Charterers shall pay to the Owners for the hire 294
of the Vessel a lump sum in the amount indicated in 295
Box 22 which shall be payable not later than every thirty 296
(30) running days in advance, the first lump sum being 297
payable on the date and hour of the Vessel's delivery to 298
the Charterers. Hire shall be paid continuously 299
throughout the Charter Period. 300
(c) Payment of hire shall be made in cash without 301
discount in the currency and in the manner indicated in 302
Box 25 and at the place mentioned in Box 26. 303
(d) Final payment of hire, if for a period of less than 304
thirty (30) running days, shall be calculated proportionally 305
according to the number of days and hours remaining 306
before redelivery and advance payment to be effected 307
accordingly. 308
(e) Should the Vessel be lost or missing, hire shall 309
cease from the date and time when she was lost or last 310
heard of. The date upon which the Vessel is to be treated 311
as lost or missing shall be ten (10) days after the Vessel 312
was last reported or when the Vessel is posted as 313
missing by Lloyd's, whichever occurs first. Any hire paid 314
in advance to be adjusted accordingly. 315
(f) Any delay in payment of hire shall entitle the 316
Owners to interest at the rate per annum as agreed in 317
Box 24. If Box 24 has not been filled in, the three months 318
interbank offered rate in London (LIBOR or its successor) 319
for the currency stated in Box 25, as quoted by the British 320
Bankers' Association (BBA) on the date when the hire 321
fell due, increased by 2 per cent., shall apply. 322
(g) Payment of interest due under sub-clause 11(f) 323
shall be made within seven (7) running days of the date 324
of the Owners' invoice specifying the amount payable 325
or, in the absence of an invoice, at the time of the next 326
hire payment date. 327

12. Mortgage 328
(only to apply if Box 28 has been appropriately filled in) 329

*) **(a)** The Owners warrant that they have not effected 330
any mortgage(s) of the Vessel and that they shall not 331
effect any mortgage(s) without the prior consent of the 332
Charterers, which shall not be unreasonably withheld. 333
*) **(b)** The Vessel chartered under this Charter is financed 334
by a mortgage according to the Financial Instrument. 335
The Charterers undertake to comply, and provide such 336
information and documents to enable the Owners to 337
comply, with all such instructions or directions in regard 338
to the employment, insurances, operation, repairs and 339
maintenance of the Vessel as laid down in the Financial 340
Instrument or as may be directed from time to time during 341
the currency of the Charter by the mortgagee(s) in 342
conformity with the Financial Instrument. The Charterers 343
confirm that, for this purpose, they have acquainted 344
themselves with all relevant terms, conditions and 345
provisions of the Financial Instrument and agree to 346
acknowledge this in writing in any form that may be 347
required by the mortgagee(s). The Owners warrant that 348
they have not effected any mortgage(s) other than stated 349
in Box 28 and that they shall not agree to any 350
amendment of the mortgage(s) referred to in Box 28 or 351
effect any other mortgage(s) without the prior consent 352
of the Charterers, which shall not be unreasonably 353
withheld. 354
*) (Optional, Clauses 12(a) and 12(b) are alternatives; 355
indicate alternative agreed in Box 28). 356

13. Insurance and Repairs 357

(a) During the Charter Period the Vessel shall be kept 358
insured by the Charterers at their expense against hull 359
and machinery, war and Protection and Indemnity risks 360
(and any risks against which it is compulsory to insure 361
for the operation of the Vessel, including maintaining 362
financial security in accordance with sub-clause 363
10(a)(iii)) in such form as the Owners shall in writing 364
approve, which approval shall not be un-reasonably 365
withheld. Such insurances shall be arranged by the 366
Charterers to protect the interests of both the Owners 367
and the Charterers and the mortgagee(s) (if any), and 368
the Charterers shall be at liberty to protect under such 369
insurances the interests of any managers they may 370
appoint. Insurance policies shall cover the Owners and 371
the Charterers according to their respective interests. 372
Subject to the provisions of the Financial Instrument, if 373
any, and the approval of the Owners and the insurers, 374
the Charterers shall effect all insured repairs and shall 375
undertake settlement and reimbursement from the 376
insurers of all costs in connection with such repairs as 377
well as insured charges, expenses and liabilities to the 378
extent of coverage under the insurances herein provided 379
for. 380
The Charterers also to remain responsible for and to 381
effect repairs and settlement of costs and expenses 382
incurred thereby in respect of all other repairs not 383
covered by the insurances and/or not exceeding any 384
possible franchise(s) or deductibles provided for in the 385
insurances. 386
All time used for repairs under the provisions of sub- 387
clause 13(a) and for repairs of latent defects according 388
to Clause 3(c) above, including any deviation, shall be 389
for the Charterers' account. 390
(b) If the conditions of the above insurances permit 391
additional insurance to be placed by the parties, such 392
cover shall be limited to the amount for each party set 393
out in Box 30 and Box 31, respectively. The Owners or 394
the Charterers as the case may be shall immediately 395
furnish the other party with particulars of any additional 396

insurance effected, including copies of any cover notes 397
or policies and the written consent of the insurers of 398
any such required insurance in any case where the 399
consent of such insurers is necessary. 400

(c) The Charterers shall upon the request of the 401
Owners, provide information and promptly execute such 402
documents as may be required to enable the Owners to 403
comply with the insurance provisions of the Financial 404
Instrument. 405

(d) Subject to the provisions of the Financial Instru- 406
ment, if any, should the Vessel become an actual, 407
constructive, compromised or agreed total loss under 408
the insurances required under sub-clause 13(a), all 409
insurance payments for such loss shall be paid to the 410
Owners who shall distribute the moneys between the 411
Owners and the Charterers according to their respective 412
interests. The Charterers undertake to notify the Owners 413
and the mortgagee(s), if any, of any occurrences in 414
consequence of which the Vessel is likely to become a 415
total loss as defined in this Clause. 416

(e) The Owners shall upon the request of the 417
Charterers, promptly execute such documents as may 418
be required to enable the Charterers to abandon the 419
Vessel to insurers and claim a constructive total loss. 420

(f) For the purpose of insurance coverage against hull 421
and machinery and war risks under the provisions of 422
sub-clause 13(a), the value of the Vessel is the sum 423
indicated in Box 29. 424

14. Insurance, Repairs and Classification 425
(Optional, only to apply if expressly agreed and stated 426
in Box 29, in which event Clause 13 shall be considered 427
deleted). 428

(a) During the Charter Period the Vessel shall be kept 429
insured by the Owners at their expense against hull and 430
machinery and war risks under the form of policy or 431
policies attached hereto. The Owners and/or insurers 432
shall not have any right of recovery or subrogation 433
against the Charterers on account of loss of or any 434
damage to the Vessel or her machinery or appurt- 435
enances covered by such insurance, or on account of 436
payments made to discharge claims against or liabilities 437
of the Vessel or the Owners covered by such insurance. 438
Insurance policies shall cover the Owners and the 439
Charterers according to their respective interests. 440

(b) During the Charter Period the Vessel shall be kept 441
insured by the Charterers at their expense against 442
Protection and Indemnity risks (and any risks against 443
which it is compulsory to insure for the operation of the 444
Vessel, including maintaining financial security in 445
accordance with sub-clause 10(a)(iii)) in such form as 446
the Owners shall in writing approve which approval shall 447
not be unreasonably withheld. 448

(c) In the event that any act or negligence of the 449
Charterers shall vitiate any of the insurance herein 450
provided, the Charterers shall pay to the Owners all 451
losses and indemnify the Owners against all claims and 452
demands which would otherwise have been covered by 453
such insurance. 454

(d) The Charterers shall, subject to the approval of the 455
Owners or Owners' Underwriters, effect all insured 456
repairs, and the Charterers shall undertake settlement 457
of all miscellaneous expenses in connection with such 458
repairs as well as all insured charges, expenses and 459
liabilities to the extent of coverage under the insurances 460
provided for under the provisions of sub-clause 14(a). 461
The Charterers to be secured reimbursement through 462
the Owners' Underwriters for such expenditures upon 463

presentation of accounts. 464

(e) The Charterers to remain responsible for and to 465
effect repairs and settlement of costs and expenses 466
incurred thereby in respect of all other repairs not 467
covered by the insurances and/or not exceeding any 468
possible franchise(s) or deductibles provided for in the 469
insurances. 470

(f) All time used for repairs under the provisions of 471
sub-clauses 14(d) and 14(e) and for repairs of latent 472
defects according to Clause 3 above, including any 473
deviation, shall be for the Charterers' account and shall 474
form part of the Charter Period. 475

The Owners shall not be responsible for any expenses 476
as are incident to the use and operation of the Vessel 477
for such time as may be required to make such repairs. 478

(g) If the conditions of the above insurances permit 479
additional insurance to be placed by the parties such 480
cover shall be limited to the amount for each party set 481
out in Box 30 and Box 31, respectively. The Owners or 482
the Charterers as the case may be shall immediately 483
furnish the other party with particulars of any additional 484
insurance effected, including copies of any cover notes 485
or policies and the written consent of the insurers of 486
any such required insurance in any case where the 487
consent of such insurers is necessary. 488

(h) Should the Vessel become an actual, constructive, 489
compromised or agreed total loss under the insurances 490
required under sub-clause 14(a), all insurance payments 491
for such loss shall be paid to the Owners, who shall 492
distribute the moneys between themselves and the 493
Charterers according to their respective interests. 494

(i) If the Vessel becomes an actual, constructive, 495
compromised or agreed total loss under the insurances 496
arranged by the Owners in accordance with sub-clause 497
14(a), this Charter shall terminate as of the date of such 498
loss. 499

(j) The Charterers shall upon the request of the 500
Owners, promptly execute such documents as may be 501
required to enable the Owners to abandon the Vessel 502
to the insurers and claim a constructive total loss. 503

(k) For the purpose of insurance coverage against hull 504
and machinery and war risks under the provisions of 505
sub-clause 14(a), the value of the Vessel is the sum 506
indicated in Box 29. 507

(l) Notwithstanding anything contained in sub-clause 508
10(a), it is agreed that under the provisions of Clause 509
14, if applicable, the Owners shall keep the Vessel's 510
Class fully up to date with the Classification Society 511
indicated in Box 10 and maintain all other necessary 512
certificates in force at all times. 513

15. Redelivery 514
At the expiration of the Charter Period the Vessel shall 515
be redelivered by the Charterers to the Owners at a 516
safe and ice-free port or place as indicated in Box 16, in 517
such ready safe berth as the Owners may direct. The 518
Charterers shall give the Owners not less than thirty 519
(30) running days' preliminary notice of expected date, 520
range of ports of redelivery or port or place of redelivery 521
and not less than fourteen (14) running days' definite 522
notice of expected date and port or place of redelivery. 523
Any changes thereafter in the Vessel's position shall be 524
notified immediately to the Owners. 525

The Charterers warrant that they will not permit the 526
Vessel to commence a voyage (including any preceding 527
ballast voyage) which cannot reasonably be expected 528
to be completed in time to allow redelivery of the Vessel 529
within the Charter Period. Notwithstanding the above, 530

should the Charterers fail to redeliver the Vessel within 531
the Charter Period, the Charterers shall pay the daily 532
equivalent to the rate of hire stated in Box 22 plus 10 533
per cent. or to the market rate, whichever is the higher, 534
for the number of days by which the Charter Period is 535
exceeded. All other terms, conditions and provisions of 536
this Charter shall continue to apply. 537
Subject to the provisions of Clause 10, the Vessel shall 538
be redelivered to the Owners in the same or as good 539
structure, state, condition and class as that in which she 540
was delivered, fair wear and tear not affecting class 541
excepted. 542
The Vessel upon redelivery shall have her survey cycles 543
up to date and trading and class certificates valid for at 544
least the number of months agreed in Box 17. 545

16. Non-Lien 546
The Charterers will not suffer, nor permit to be continued, 547
any lien or encumbrance incurred by them or their 548
agents, which might have priority over the title and 549
interest of the Owners in the Vessel. The Charterers 550
further agree to fasten to the Vessel in a conspicuous 551
place and to keep so fastened during the Charter Period 552
a notice reading as follows: 553
"This Vessel is the property of (name of Owners). It is 554
under charter to (name of Charterers) and by the terms 555
of the Charter Party neither the Charterers nor the 556
Master have any right, power or authority to create, incur 557
or permit to be imposed on the Vessel any lien 558
whatsoever." 559

17. Indemnity 560
(a) The Charterers shall indemnify the Owners against 561
any loss, damage or expense incurred by the Owners 562
arising out of or in relation to the operation of the Vessel 563
by the Charterers, and against any lien of whatsoever 564
nature arising out of an event occurring during the 565
Charter Period. If the Vessel be arrested or otherwise 566
detained by reason of claims or liens arising out of her 567
operation hereunder by the Charterers, the Charterers 568
shall at their own expense take all reasonable steps to 569
secure that within a reasonable time the Vessel is 570
released, including the provision of bail. 571
Without prejudice to the generality of the foregoing, the 572
Charterers agree to indemnify the Owners against all 573
consequences or liabilities arising from the Master, 574
officers or agents signing Bills of Lading or other 575
documents. 576
(b) If the Vessel be arrested or otherwise detained by 577
reason of a claim or claims against the Owners, the 578
Owners shall at their own expense take all reasonable 579
steps to secure that within a reasonable time the Vessel 580
is released, including the provision of bail. 581
In such circumstances the Owners shall indemnify the 582
Charterers against any loss, damage or expense 583
incurred by the Charterers (including hire paid under 584
this Charter) as a direct consequence of such arrest or 585
detention. 586

18. Lien 587
The Owners to have a lien upon all cargoes, sub-hires 588
and sub-freights belonging or due to the Charterers or 589
any sub-charterers and any Bill of Lading freight for all 590
claims under this Charter, and the Charterers to have a 591
lien on the Vessel for all moneys paid in advance and 592
not earned. 593

19. Salvage 594
All salvage and towage performed by the Vessel shall 595
be for the Charterers' benefit and the cost of repairing 596
damage occasioned thereby shall be borne by the 597
Charterers. 598

20. Wreck Removal 599
In the event of the Vessel becoming a wreck or 600
obstruction to navigation the Charterers shall indemnify 601
the Owners against any sums whatsoever which the 602
Owners shall become liable to pay and shall pay in 603
consequence of the Vessel becoming a wreck or 604
obstruction to navigation. 605

21. General Average 606
The Owners shall not contribute to General Average. 607

22. Assignment, Sub-Charter and Sale 608
(a) The Charterers shall not assign this Charter nor 609
sub-charter the Vessel on a bareboat basis except with 610
the prior consent in writing of the Owners, which shall 611
not be unreasonably withheld, and subject to such terms 612
and conditions as the Owners shall approve. 613
(b) The Owners shall not sell the Vessel during the 614
currency of this Charter except with the prior written 615
consent of the Charterers, which shall not be unreason- 616
ably withheld, and subject to the buyer accepting an 617
assignment of this Charter. 618

23. Contracts of Carriage 619
*) (a) The Charterers are to procure that all documents 620
issued during the Charter Period evidencing the terms 621
and conditions agreed in respect of carriage of goods 622
shall contain a paramount clause incorporating any 623
legislation relating to carrier's liability for cargo 624
compulsorily applicable in the trade; if no such legislation 625
exists, the documents shall incorporate the Hague-Visby 626
Rules. The documents shall also contain the New Jason 627
Clause and the Both-to-Blame Collision Clause. 628
*) (b) The Charterers are to procure that all passenger 629
tickets issued during the Charter Period for the carriage 630
of passengers and their luggage under this Charter shall 631
contain a paramount clause incorporating any legislation 632
relating to carrier's liability for passengers and their 633
luggage compulsorily applicable in the trade; if no such 634
legislation exists, the passenger tickets shall incorporate 635
the Athens Convention Relating to the Carriage of 636
Passengers and their Luggage by Sea, 1974, and any 637
protocol thereto. 638
*) Delete as applicable. 639

24. Bank Guarantee 640
(Optional, only to apply if Box 27 filled in) 641
The Charterers undertake to furnish, before delivery of 642
the Vessel, a first class bank guarantee or bond in the 643
sum and at the place as indicated in Box 27 as guarantee 644
for full performance of their obligations under this 645
Charter. 646

25. Requisition/Acquisition 647
(a) In the event of the Requisition for Hire of the Vessel 648
by any governmental or other competent authority 649
(hereinafter referred to as "Requisition for Hire") 650
irrespective of the date during the Charter Period when 651
"Requisition for Hire" may occur and irrespective of the 652
length thereof and whether or not it be for an indefinite 653

or a limited period of time, and irrespective of whether it 654
may or will remain in force for the remainder of the 655
Charter Period, this Charter shall not be deemed thereby 656
or thereupon to be frustrated or otherwise terminated 657
and the Charterers shall continue to pay the stipulated 658
hire in the manner provided by this Charter until the time 659
when the Charter would have terminated pursuant to 660
any of the provisions hereof always provided however 661
that in the event of "Requisition for Hire" any Requisition 662
Hire or compensation received or receivable by the 663
Owners shall be payable to the Charterers during the 664
remainder of the Charter Period or the period of the 665
"Requisition for Hire" whichever be the shorter. 666
  (b) In the event of the Owners being deprived of their 667
ownership in the Vessel by any Compulsory Acquisition 668
of the Vessel or requisition for title by any governmental 669
or other competent authority (hereinafter referred to as 670
"Compulsory Acquisition"), then, irrespective of the date 671
during the Charter Period when "Compulsory Acqui- 672
sition" may occur, this Charter shall be deemed 673
terminated as of the date of such "Compulsory 674
Acquisition". In such event Charter Hire to be considered 675
as earned and to be paid up to the date and time of 676
such "Compulsory Acquisition". 677

26. **War** 678
  (a) For the purpose of this Clause, the words "War 679
Risks" shall include any war (whether actual or 680
threatened), act of war, civil war, hostilities, revolution, 681
rebellion, civil commotion, warlike operations, the laying 682
of mines (whether actual or reported), acts of piracy, 683
acts of terrorists, acts of hostility or malicious damage, 684
blockades (whether imposed against all vessels or 685
imposed selectively against vessels of certain flags or 686
ownership, or against certain cargoes or crews or 687
otherwise howsoever), by any person, body, terrorist or 688
political group, or the Government of any state 689
whatsoever, which may be dangerous or are likely to be 690
or to become dangerous to the Vessel, her cargo, crew 691
or other persons on board the Vessel. 692
  (b) The Vessel, unless the written consent of the 693
Owners be first obtained, shall not continue to or go 694
through any port, place, area or zone (whether of land 695
or sea), or any waterway or canal, where it reasonably 696
appears that the Vessel, her cargo, crew or other 697
persons on board the Vessel, in the reasonable 698
judgement of the Owners, may be, or are likely to be, 699
exposed to War Risks. Should the Vessel be within any 700
such place as aforesaid, which only becomes danger- 701
ous, or is likely to be or to become dangerous, after her 702
entry into it, the Owners shall have the right to require 703
the Vessel to leave such area. 704
  (c) The Vessel shall not load contraband cargo, or to 705
pass through any blockade, whether such blockade be 706
imposed on all vessels, or is imposed selectively in any 707
way whatsoever against vessels of certain flags or 708
ownership, or against certain cargoes or crews or 709
otherwise howsoever, or to proceed to an area where 710
she shall be subject, or is likely to be subject to a 711
belligerent's right of search and/or confiscation. 712
  (d) If the insurers of the war risks insurance, when 713
Clause 14 is applicable, should require payment of 714
premiums and/or calls because, pursuant to the 715
Charterers' orders, the Vessel is within, or is due to enter 716
and remain within, any area or areas which are specified 717
by such insurers as being subject to additional premiums 718
because of War Risks, then such premiums and/or calls 719
shall be reimbursed by the Charterers to the Owners at 720

the same time as the next payment of hire is due. 721
  (e) The Charterers shall have the liberty: 722
  (i) to comply with all orders, directions, recommend- 723
      ations or advice as to departure, arrival, routes, 724
      sailing in convoy, ports of call, stoppages, 725
      destinations, discharge of cargo, delivery, or in any 726
      other way whatsoever, which are given by the 727
      Government of the Nation under whose flag the 728
      Vessel sails, or any other Government, body or 729
      group whatsoever acting with the power to compel 730
      compliance with their orders or directions; 731
  (ii) to comply with the orders, directions or recom- 732
      mendations of any war risks underwriters who have 733
      the authority to give the same under the terms of 734
      the war risks insurance; 735
  (iii) to comply with the terms of any resolution of the 736
      Security Council of the United Nations, any 737
      directives of the European Community, the effective 738
      orders of any other Supranational body which has 739
      the right to issue and give the same, and with 740
      national laws aimed at enforcing the same to which 741
      the Owners are subject, and to obey the orders 742
      and directions of those who are charged with their 743
      enforcement. 744
  (f) In the event of outbreak of war (whether there be a 745
declaration of war or not) (i) between any two or more 746
of the following countries: the United States of America; 747
Russia; the United Kingdom; France; and the People's 748
Republic of China, (ii) between any two or more of the 749
countries stated in Box 36, both the Owners and the 750
Charterers shall have the right to cancel this Charter, 751
whereupon the Charterers shall redeliver the Vessel to 752
the Owners in accordance with Clause 15, if the Vessel 753
has cargo on board after discharge thereof at 754
destination, or if debarred under this Clause from 755
reaching or entering it at a near, open and safe port as 756
directed by the Owners, or if the Vessel has no cargo 757
on board, at the port at which the Vessel then is or if at 758
sea at a near, open and safe port as directed by the 759
Owners. In all cases hire shall continue to be paid in 760
accordance with Clause 11 and except as aforesaid all 761
other provisions of this Charter shall apply until 762
redelivery. 763

27. **Commission** 764
The Owners to pay a commission at the rate indicated 765
in Box 33 to the Brokers named in Box 33 on any hire 766
paid under the Charter. If no rate is indicated in Box 33, 767
the commission to be paid by the Owners shall cover 768
the actual expenses of the Brokers and a reasonable 769
fee for their work. 770
If the full hire is not paid owing to breach of the Charter 771
by either of the parties the party liable therefor shall 772
indemnify the Brokers against their loss of commission. 773
Should the parties agree to cancel the Charter, the 774
Owners shall indemnify the Brokers against any loss of 775
commission but in such case the commission shall not 776
exceed the brokerage on one year's hire. 777

28. **Termination** 778
  (a) Charterers' Default 779
The Owners shall be entitled to withdraw the Vessel from 780
the service of the Charterers and terminate the Charter 781
with immediate effect by written notice to the Charterers if: 782
  (i) the Charterers fail to pay hire in accordance with 783
      Clause 11. However, where there is a failure to 784
      make punctual payment of hire due to oversight, 785
      negligence, errors or omissions on the part of the 786

Charterers or their bankers, the Owners shall give 787
the Charterers written notice of the number of clear 788
banking days stated in Box 34 (as recognised at 789
the agreed place of payment) in which to rectify 790
the failure, and when so rectified within such 791
number of days following the Owners' notice, the 792
payment shall stand as regular and punctual. 793
Failure by the Charterers to pay hire within the 794
number of days stated in Box 34 of their receiving 795
the Owners' notice as provided herein, shall entitle 796
the Owners to withdraw the Vessel from the service 797
of the Charterers and terminate the Charter without 798
further notice; 799

(ii) the Charterers fail to comply with the requirements of: 800
    (1) Clause 6 (Trading Restrictions) 801
    (2) Clause 13(a) (Insurance and Repairs) 802
    provided that the Owners shall have the option, by 803
    written notice to the Charterers, to give the 804
    Charterers a specified number of days grace within 805
    which to rectify the failure without prejudice to the 806
    Owners' right to withdraw and terminate under this 807
    Clause if the Charterers fail to comply with such 808
    notice; 809

(iii) the Charterers fail to rectify any failure to comply 810
    with the requirements of sub-clause 10(a)(i) 811
    (Maintenance and Repairs) as soon as practically 812
    possible after the Owners have requested them in 813
    writing so to do and in any event so that the Vessel's 814
    insurance cover is not prejudiced. 815

(b) Owners' Default 816
If the Owners shall by any act or omission be in breach 817
of their obligations under this Charter to the extent that 818
the Charterers are deprived of the use of the Vessel 819
and such breach continues for a period of fourteen (14) 820
running days after written notice thereof has been given 821
by the Charterers to the Owners, the Charterers shall 822
be entitled to terminate this Charter with immediate effect 823
by written notice to the Owners. 824

(c) Loss of Vessel 825
This Charter shall be deemed to be terminated if the 826
Vessel becomes a total loss or is declared as a 827
constructive or compromised or arranged total loss. For 828
the purpose of this sub-clause, the Vessel shall not be 829
deemed to be lost unless she has either become an 830
actual total loss or agreement has been reached with 831
her underwriters in respect of her constructive, 832
compromised or arranged total loss or if such agreement 833
with her underwriters is not reached it is adjudged by a 834
competent tribunal that a constructive loss of the Vessel 835
has occurred. 836
(d) Either party shall be entitled to terminate this 837
Charter with immediate effect by written notice to the 838
other party in the event of an order being made or 839
resolution passed for the winding up, dissolution, 840
liquidation or bankruptcy of the other party (otherwise 841
than for the purpose of reconstruction or amalgamation) 842
or if a receiver is appointed, or if it suspends payment, 843
ceases to carry on business or makes any special 844
arrangement or composition with its creditors. 845
(e) The termination of this Charter shall be without 846
prejudice to all rights accrued due between the parties 847
prior to the date of termination and to any claim that 848
either party might have. 849

29. Repossession 850
In the event of the termination of this Charter in 851
accordance with the applicable provisions of Clause 28, 852
the Owners shall have the right to repossess the Vessel 853
from the Charterers at her current or next port of call, or 854
at a port or place convenient to them without hindrance 855
or interference by the Charterers, courts or local 856
authorities. Pending physical repossession of the Vessel 857
in accordance with this Clause 29, the Charterers shall 858
hold the Vessel as gratuitous bailee only to the Owners. 859
The Owners shall arrange for an authorised represent- 860
ative to board the Vessel as soon as reasonably 861
practicable following the termination of the Charter. The 862
Vessel shall be deemed to be repossessed by the 863
Owners from the Charterers upon the boarding of the 864
Vessel by the Owners' representative. All arrangements 865
and expenses relating to the settling of wages, 866
disembarkation and repatriation of the Charterers' 867
Master, officers and crew shall be the sole responsibility 868
of the Charterers. 869

30. Dispute Resolution 870
*) (a) This Contract shall be governed by and construed 871
in accordance with English law and any dispute arising 872
out of or in connection with this Contract shall be referred 873
to arbitration in London in accordance with the Arbitration 874
Act 1996 or any statutory modification or re-enactment 875
thereof save to the extent necessary to give effect to 876
the provisions of this Clause. 877
The arbitration shall be conducted in accordance with 878
the London Maritime Arbitrators Association (LMAA) 879
Terms current at the time when the arbitration proceed- 880
ings are commenced. 881
The reference shall be to three arbitrators. A party 882
wishing to refer a dispute to arbitration shall appoint its 883
arbitrator and send notice of such appointment in writing 884
to the other party requiring the other party to appoint its 885
own arbitrator within 14 calendar days of that notice and 886
stating that it will appoint its arbitrator as sole arbitrator 887
unless the other party appoints its own arbitrator and 888
gives notice that it has done so within the 14 days 889
specified. If the other party does not appoint its own 890
arbitrator and give notice that it has done so within the 891
14 days specified, the party referring a dispute to 892
arbitration may, without the requirement of any further 893
prior notice to the other party, appoint its arbitrator as 894
sole arbitrator and shall advise the other party 895
accordingly. The award of a sole arbitrator shall be 896
binding on both parties as if he had been appointed by 897
agreement. 898
Nothing herein shall prevent the parties agreeing in 899
writing to vary these provisions to provide for the 900
appointment of a sole arbitrator. 901
In cases where neither the claim nor any counterclaim 902
exceeds the sum of US$50,000 (or such other sum as 903
the parties may agree) the arbitration shall be conducted 904
in accordance with the LMAA Small Claims Procedure 905
current at the time when the arbitration proceedings are 906
commenced. 907
*) (b) This Contract shall be governed by and construed 908
in accordance with Title 9 of the United States Code 909
and the Maritime Law of the United States and any 910
dispute arising out of or in connection with this Contract 911
shall be referred to three persons at New York, one to 912
be appointed by each of the parties hereto, and the third 913
by the two so chosen; their decision or that of any two 914
of them shall be final, and for the purposes of enforcing 915
any award, judgement may be entered on an award by 916
any court of competent jurisdiction. The proceedings 917
shall be conducted in accordance with the rules of the 918
Society of Maritime Arbitrators, Inc. 919
In cases where neither the claim nor any counterclaim 920

exceeds the sum of US$50,000 (or such other sum as 921
the parties may agree) the arbitration shall be conducted 922
in accordance with the Shortened Arbitration Procedure 923
of the Society of Maritime Arbitrators, Inc. current at 924
the time when the arbitration proceedings are commenced. 925
*) **(c)** This Contract shall be governed by and construed 926
in accordance with the laws of the place mutually agreed 927
by the parties and any dispute arising out of or in 928
connection with this Contract shall be referred to 929
arbitration at a mutually agreed place, subject to the 930
procedures applicable there. 931
(d) Notwithstanding (a), (b) or (c) above, the parties 932
may agree at any time to refer to mediation any 933
difference and/or dispute arising out of or in connection 934
with this Contract. 935
In the case of a dispute in respect of which arbitration 936
has been commenced under (a), (b) or (c) above, the 937
following shall apply:- 938
(i) Either party may at any time and from time to time 939
elect to refer the dispute or part of the dispute to 940
mediation by service on the other party of a written 941
notice (the "Mediation Notice") calling on the other 942
party to agree to mediation. 943
(ii) The other party shall thereupon within 14 calendar 944
days of receipt of the Mediation Notice confirm that 945
they agree to mediation, in which case the parties 946
shall thereafter agree a mediator within a further 947
14 calendar days, failing which on the application 948
of either party a mediator will be appointed promptly 949
by the Arbitration Tribunal ("the Tribunal") or such 950
person as the Tribunal may designate for that 951
purpose. The mediation shall be conducted in such 952
place and in accordance with such procedure and 953
on such terms as the parties may agree or, in the 954
event of disagreement, as may be set by the 955
mediator. 956
(iii) If the other party does not agree to mediate, that 957

fact may be brought to the attention of the Tribunal 958
and may be taken into account by the Tribunal when 959
allocating the costs of the arbitration as between 960
the parties. 961
(iv) The mediation shall not affect the right of either 962
party to seek such relief or take such steps as it 963
considers necessary to protect its interest. 964
(v) Either party may advise the Tribunal that they have 965
agreed to mediation. The arbitration procedure shall 966
continue during the conduct of the mediation but 967
the Tribunal may take the mediation timetable into 968
account when setting the timetable for steps in the 969
arbitration. 970
(vi) Unless otherwise agreed or specified in the 971
mediation terms, each party shall bear its own costs 972
incurred in the mediation and the parties shall share 973
equally the mediator's costs and expenses. 974
(vii) The mediation process shall be without prejudice 975
and confidential and no information or documents 976
disclosed during it shall be revealed to the Tribunal 977
except to the extent that they are disclosable under 978
the law and procedure governing the arbitration. 979
(Note: The parties should be aware that the mediation 980
process may not necessarily interrupt time limits.) 981
(e) If Box 35 in Part I is not appropriately filled in, sub-clause 982
30(a) of this Clause shall apply. Sub-clause 30(d) shall 983
apply in all cases. 984
*) *Sub-clauses 30(a), 30(b) and 30(c) are alternatives;* 985
indicate alternative agreed in Box 35. 986

31. Notices 987
(a) Any notice to be given by either party to the other 988
party shall be in writing and may be sent by fax, telex, 989
registered or recorded mail or by personal service. 990
(b) The address of the Parties for service of such 991
communication shall be as stated in Boxes 3 and 4 992
respectively. 993

PART III
PROVISIONS TO APPLY FOR NEWBUILDING VESSELS ONLY
(Optional, only to apply if expressly agreed and stated in Box 37)

1. Specifications and Building Contract

(a) The Vessel shall be constructed in accordance with the Building Contract (hereafter called "the Building Contract") as annexed to this Charter, made between the Builders and the Owners and in accordance with the specifications and plans annexed thereto, such Building Contract, specifications and plans having been counter-signed as approved by the Charterers. 1-8

(b) No change shall be made in the Building Contract or in the specifications or plans of the Vessel as approved by the Charterers as aforesaid, without the Charterers' consent. 9-12

(c) The Charterers shall have the right to send their representative to the Builders' Yard to inspect the Vessel during the course of her construction to satisfy themselves that construction is in accordance with such approved specifications and plans as referred to under sub-clause (a) of this Clause. 13-18

(d) The Vessel shall be built in accordance with the Building Contract and shall be of the description set out therein. Subject to the provisions of sub-clause 2(c)(ii) hereunder, the Charterers shall be bound to accept the Vessel from the Owners, completed and constructed in accordance with the Building Contract, on the date of delivery by the Builders. The Charterers undertake that having accepted the Vessel they will not thereafter raise any claims against the Owners in respect of the Vessel's performance or specification or defects, if any. Nevertheless, in respect of any repairs, replacements or defects which appear within the first 12 months from delivery by the Builders, the Owners shall endeavour to compel the Builders to repair, replace or remedy any defects or to recover from the Builders any expenditure incurred in carrying out such repairs, replacements or remedies. However, the Owners' liability to the Charterers shall be limited to the extent the Owners have a valid claim against the Builders under the guarantee clause of the Building Contract (a copy whereof has been supplied to the Charterers). The Charterers shall be bound to accept such sums as the Owners are reasonably able to recover under this Clause and shall make no further claim on the Owners for the difference between the amount(s) so recovered and the actual expenditure on repairs, replacement or remedying defects or for any loss of time incurred. Any liquidated damages for physical defects or deficiencies shall accrue to the account of the party stated in Box 41(a) or if not filled in shall be shared equally between the parties. The costs of pursuing a claim or claims against the Builders under this Clause (including any liability to the Builders) shall be borne by the party stated in Box 41(b) or if not filled in shall be shared equally between the parties. 19-51

2. Time and Place of Delivery

(a) Subject to the Vessel having completed her acceptance trials including trials of cargo equipment in accordance with the Building Contract and specifications to the satisfaction of the Charterers, the Owners shall give and the Charterers shall take delivery of the Vessel afloat when ready for delivery and properly documented at the Builders' Yard or some other safe and readily accessible dock, wharf or place as may be agreed between the parties hereto and the Builders. Under the Building Contract the Builders have estimated that the Vessel will be ready for delivery to the Owners as therein provided but the delivery date for the purpose of this Charter shall be the date when the Vessel is in fact ready for delivery by the Builders after completion of trials whether that be before or after as indicated in the Building Contract. The Charterers shall not be entitled to refuse acceptance of delivery of the Vessel 52-68

and upon and after such acceptance, subject to Clause 1(d), the Charterers shall not be entitled to make any claim against the Owners in respect of any conditions, representations or warranties, whether express or implied, as to the seaworthiness of the Vessel or in respect of delay in delivery. 69-74

(b) If for any reason other than a default by the Owners under the Building Contract, the Builders become entitled under that Contract not to deliver the Vessel to the Owners, the Owners shall upon giving to the Charterers written notice of Builders becoming so entitled, be excused from giving delivery of the Vessel to the Charterers and upon receipt of such notice by the Charterers this Charter shall cease to have effect. 75-82

(c) If for any reason the Owners become entitled under the Building Contract to reject the Vessel the Owners shall, before exercising such right of rejection, consult the Charterers and thereupon 83-86

(i) if the Charterers do not wish to take delivery of the Vessel they shall inform the Owners within seven (7) running days by notice in writing and upon receipt by the Owners of such notice this Charter shall cease to have effect; or 87-90

(ii) if the Charterers wish to take delivery of the Vessel they may by notice in writing within seven (7) running days require the Owners to negotiate with the Builders as to the terms on which delivery should be taken and/or refrain from exercising their right to rejection and upon receipt of such notice the Owners shall commence such negotiations and/or take delivery of the Vessel from the Builders and deliver her to the Charterers; 91-98

(iii) in no circumstances shall the Charterers be entitled to reject the Vessel unless the Owners are able to reject the Vessel from the Builders; 99-101

(iv) if this Charter terminates under sub-clause (b) or (c) of this Clause, the Owners shall thereafter not be liable to the Charterers for any claim under or arising out of this Charter or its termination. 102-105

(d) Any liquidated damages for delay in delivery under the Building Contract and any costs incurred in pursuing a claim therefor shall accrue to the account of the party stated in Box 41(c) or if not filled in shall be shared equally between the parties. 106-110

3. Guarantee Works 111

If not otherwise agreed, the Owners authorise the Charterers to arrange for the guarantee works to be performed in accordance with the building contract terms, and hire to continue during the period of guarantee works. The Charterers have to advise the Owners about the performance to the extent the Owners may request. 112-117

4. Name of Vessel 118

The name of the Vessel shall be mutually agreed between the Owners and the Charterers and the Vessel shall be painted in the colours, display the funnel insignia and fly the house flag as required by the Charterers. 119-122

5. Survey on Redelivery 123

The Owners and the Charterers shall appoint surveyors for the purpose of determining and agreeing in writing the condition of the Vessel at the time of re-delivery. Without prejudice to Clause 15 (Part II), the Charterers shall bear all survey expenses and all other costs, if any, including the cost of docking and undocking, if required, as well as all repair costs incurred. The Charterers shall also bear all loss of time spent in connection with any docking and undocking as well as repairs, which shall be paid at the rate of hire per day or pro rata. 124-133

669

"BARECON 2001" Standard Bareboat Charter

PART IV
HIRE/PURCHASE AGREEMENT
(Optional, only to apply if expressly agreed and stated in Box 42)

On expiration of this Charter and provided the Charterers have fulfilled their obligations according to Part I and II as well as Part III, if applicable, it is agreed, that on payment of the final payment of hire as per Clause 11 the Charterers have purchased the Vessel with everything belonging to her and the Vessel is fully paid for 1 2 3 4 5 6 7

In the following paragraphs the Owners are referred to as the Sellers and the Charterers as the Buyers. 8 9

The Vessel shall be delivered by the Sellers and taken over by the Buyers on expiration of the Charter. 10 11

The Sellers guarantee that the Vessel, at the time of delivery, is free from all encumbrances and maritime liens or any debts whatsoever other than those arising from anything done or not done by the Buyers or any existing mortgage agreed not to be paid off by the time of delivery. Should any claims, which have been incurred prior to the time of delivery be made against the Vessel, the Sellers hereby undertake to indemnify the Buyers against all consequences of such claims to the extent it can be proved that the Sellers are responsible for such claims. Any taxes, notarial, consular and other charges and expenses connected with the purchase and registration under Buyers' flag, shall be for Buyers' account. Any taxes, consular and other charges and expenses connected with closing of the Sellers' register, shall be for Sellers' account. 12 13 14 15 16 17 18 19 20 21 22 23 24 25 26 27

In exchange for payment of the last month's hire instalment the Sellers shall furnish the Buyers with a Bill of Sale duly attested and legalized, together with a certificate setting out the registered encumbrances, if any. On delivery of the Vessel the Sellers shall provide for deletion of the Vessel from the Ship's Register and deliver a certificate of deletion to the Buyers. 28 29 30 31 32 33 34

The Sellers shall, at the time of delivery, hand to the Buyers all classification certificates (for hull, engines, anchors, chains, etc.), as well as all plans which may be in Sellers' possession. 35 36 37 38

The Wireless Installation and Nautical Instruments, unless on hire, shall be included in the sale without any extra payment. 39 40 41

The Vessel with everything belonging to her shall be at Sellers' risk and expense until she is delivered to the Buyers, subject to the conditions of this Contract and the Vessel with everything belonging to her shall be delivered and taken over as she is at the time of delivery, after which the Sellers shall have no responsibility for possible faults or deficiencies of any description. 42 43 44 45 46 47 48

The Buyers undertake to pay for the repatriation of the Master, officers and other personnel if appointed by the Sellers to the port where the Vessel entered the Bareboat Charter as per Clause 3 (Part II) or to pay the equivalent cost for their journey to any other place. 49 50 51 52 53

670

OPTIONAL PART

PART V
PROVISIONS TO APPLY FOR VESSELS REGISTERED IN A BAREBOAT CHARTER REGISTRY
(Optional, only to apply if expressly agreed and stated in Box 43)

1. Definitions — 1
For the purpose of this PART V, the following terms shall — 2
have the meanings hereby assigned to them: — 3
"The Bareboat Charter Registry" shall mean the registry — 4
of the State whose flag the Vessel will fly and in which — 5
the Charterers are registered as the bareboat charterers — 6
during the period of the Bareboat Charter. — 7
"The Underlying Registry" shall mean the registry of the — 8
State in which the Owners of the Vessel are registered — 9
as Owners and to which jurisdiction and control of the — 10
Vessel will revert upon termination of the Bareboat — 11
Charter Registration. — 12

2. Mortgage — 13
The Vessel chartered under this Charter is financed by — 14
a mortgage and the provisions of Clause 12(b) (Part II) — 15
shall apply. — 16

3. Termination of Charter by Default — 17
If the Vessel chartered under this Charter is registered — 18
in a Bareboat Charter Registry as stated in Box 44, and — 19
if the Owners shall default in the payment of any amounts — 20
due under the mortgage(s) specified in Box 28, the — 21
Charterers shall, if so required by the mortgagee, direct — 22
the Owners to re-register the Vessel in the Underlying — 23
Registry as shown in Box 45. — 24
In the event of the Vessel being deleted from the — 25
Bareboat Charter Registry as stated in Box 44, due to a — 26
default by the Owners in the payment of any amounts — 27
due under the mortgage(s), the Charterers shall have — 28
the right to terminate this Charter forthwith and without — 29
prejudice to any other claim they may have against the — 30
Owners under this Charter. — 31

Gencoa*

<table>
<tr>
<td colspan="2">1. Shipbroker</td>
<td>BIMCO
STANDARD CONTRACT OF AFFREIGHTMENT
FOR DRY BULK CARGOES
CODE NAME: GENCOA</td>
<td>PART I</td>
</tr>
<tr>
<td colspan="2"></td>
<td colspan="2">2. Place and Date of Contract</td>
</tr>
<tr>
<td colspan="2">3. Owners (indicate name, address and telex number)</td>
<td colspan="2">4. Charterers (indicate name, address and telex number)</td>
</tr>
<tr>
<td colspan="4">5. Description of Cargoes (Cl. 1)</td>
</tr>
<tr>
<td colspan="2">6. Loading Port(s) or Range(s) (Cl. 1)</td>
<td colspan="2">7. Discharging Port(s) or Range(s) (Cl. 1)</td>
</tr>
<tr>
<td colspan="2">8. Total Quantity/Number of Shipments (Cl. 2)

If option (a) applies state min./max. quantities and at whose option:

OR

If option (b) applies state number of shipments:</td>
<td colspan="2">9. Period of Contract (state period, first layday for initial vessel and cancelling date for final vessel) (Cl. 3)</td>
</tr>
<tr>
<td colspan="2">10. Quantity per Shipment (state min./max. quantity at Owners' option) (Cl. 4)</td>
<td colspan="2">11. Final Shipment (state min. quantity) (Cl. 5)</td>
</tr>
<tr>
<td colspan="4">12. Shipment Periods/Programme of Shipments/Scheduling/Nomination (Cl. 6 & 7)</td>
</tr>
<tr>
<td colspan="4">13. Performing Vessels/Description (Cl. 10)</td>
</tr>
</table>

continued

Copyright, published by BIMCO
Copenhagen, November 2004

Printed and sold by Fr. G. Knudtzons Bogtrykkeri A/S, Vallensbaekvej 61, DK-2625 Vallensbaek. Fax: +45 4366 0708

* Reproduced by kind permission of BIMCO.

14. Freight Rate (Cl. 12)	15. Freight Payment (currency and when/where payable; also state beneficiary and bank account) (Cl. 12)

16. Demurrage/Despatch Money (state rate(s) or scale) (Cl. 13)	17. Applicable Charter Party (Preamble)

18. Bunker Price Adjustment (Cl. 16)

(a) Bunker price (USD per metric ton) _____

(b) Type and grade of oil (indicate whether gas oil, diesel or fuel oil) _____

(c) Port or place (also supplier or published index) _____

(d) (i) Bunker price higher limit _____

(d) (ii) Bunker price lower limit _____

(e) Bunker consumption _____

19. War Cancellation (indicate other countries, if any, agreed) (Cl. 17)

20. Dispute Resolution (state 18(a), 18(b) or 18(c) of Cl. 18, as agreed; if 18(c) agreed state place of arbitration) (if not filled in 18(a) shall apply) (Cl. 18)	21. Commission and to whom payable (Cl. 19)

22. Names and Addresses for Nominations/Notifications by the Owners	23. Names and Addresses for Nominations/Notifications by the Charterers

24. Additional Clauses

It is mutually agreed between the party mentioned in Box 3 (hereinafter referred to as "the Owners") and the party mentioned in Box 4 (hereinafter referred to as "the Charterers") that this Contract shall be performed in accordance with the conditions contained in PART I including additional clauses, if any agreed and stated in Box 24, and PART II. In the event of a conflict of conditions, the provisions of PART I shall prevail over those of PART II to the extent of such conflict but no further.

Signature (Owners)	Signature (Charterers)

Preamble 1

For the purpose of interpretation: 2

"Form" means PARTS I and II of this GENCOA form. 3

"Contract" means the Form including the attached 4
voyage charter party stated in Box 17. 5

This Form is intended for use with a voyage charter 6
party. Each and every voyage under this Contract shall 7
be governed by the terms and conditions of the attached 8
voyage charter party, as stated in Box 17, which shall 9
be deemed incorporated in this Contract. 10

In the event of any conflict between the terms and 11
conditions of the attached voyage charter party and this 12
Form, the latter shall prevail. 13

1. Subject of Contract 14

The Charterers undertake to provide for shipment and 15
the Owners undertake to carry the cargoes as described 16
in Box 5 from the port(s) or range(s) stated in Box 6 to 17
the port(s) or range(s) stated in Box 7. 18

2. Total Quantity/Number of Shipments 19

*)(a) The total quantity to be shipped shall be within 20
the limits and at the option of the party stated in Box 8. 21
For the purpose of calculating the total quantity shipped 22
under this Contract, the intaken quantity for each 23
shipment shall apply. 24

*)(b) The number of shipments under this Contract shall 25
be as stated in Box 8. 26

*) (a) and (b) are options. Please state applicable option 27
in Box 8. 28

3. Period of Contract 29

This Contract is made for the period stated in Box 9. 30
The first layday for the initial shipment shall not be 31
before the commencement of the period stated in Box 32
9. The cancelling date for the final shipment shall not 33
fall later than the final date of the Contract period stated 34
in Box 9. 35

4. Quantity per Shipment 36

The quantity of each and every shipment shall be at 37
the Owners' option within the limits stated in Box 10. 38

5. Final Shipment 39

The Owners shall not be bound to carry any balance of 40
the total quantity which would be under the minimum 41
quantity stated in Box 11. 42

6. Programme of Shipments 43

(a) Unless otherwise specified in Box 12, the 44
Charterers' programme of shipments shall be fairly 45
evenly spread over the period of the Contract. 46

(b) The Charterers shall advise the Owners of their 47
programme of shipments no later than the number of 48
days stated in Box 12 before the commencement of 49
each period as stated in Box 12 giving their preferred 50
dates for each shipment within the stated period. 51

7. Scheduling/Nomination 52

(a) The Charterers shall give the Owners the following 53
Scheduling notices for each shipment: 54

(i) *Provisional Notice* 55

The Charterers shall give the Owners a provisional 56
notice nominating a spread of laydays of the 57
number of days stated in Box 12, no later than the 58
number of days stated in Box 12 before the 59
opening layday. 60

(ii) *Definite Notice* 61

The Charterers shall give the Owners a definite 62
notice narrowing the laydays to the number of 63
days stated in Box 12, within the original spread 64
of laydays, no later than the number of days stated 65
in Box 12 prior to the opening layday. 66

(b) The Owners shall nominate a vessel or substitute 67
latest within the number of days stated in Box 12 of the 68
Charterers' definite declaration of laydays. 69

(c) The actual performing vessel shall be nominated 70
latest by the number of days stated in Box 12 prior to 71
the opening layday with estimated time of arrival at the 72
load port and the approximate quantity of cargo required. 73

(d) Acceptance of the actual performing vessel shall 74
be given by the Charterers within 24 hours of nomination 75
Sundays and holidays excluded, failing receipt of which 76
the vessel shall be deemed accepted. 77

8. Declaration of Loading Port(s) 78

Where various loading ports or a range or ranges are 79
agreed and stated in Box 6, the Charterers shall declare 80
the definite loading port(s) for each shipment latest on 81
giving the definite notice as stated in Clause 7(a). 82

9. Declaration of Discharging Port(s) 83

The Charterers shall declare the discharging port(s) for 84
each shipment so as not to delay the Vessel and in 85
sufficient time to permit, if necessary, the preparation 86
of the discharging plan and adjustment of the vessel's 87
draft and trim. 88

10. Performing Vessels 89

The Owners shall nominate vessels only of the descrip- 90
tion stated in Box 13 suitable for the intended trade. 91

11. Cancelling of Shipment 92

If a shipment is cancelled by virtue of the appropriate 93
cancelling provisions of the attached charter party, other 94
than by default, the cancellation applies to that shipment 95
only and the corresponding quantity of cargo shall be 96
deducted from the outstanding balance of the total 97
contracted quantity. 98

12. Freight 99

For each and every voyage under this Contract, the 100
freight shall be paid at the applicable rate stated in Box 101
14 to the party and in the manner indicated in Box 15. 102
The Charterers shall not be entitled to make any 103
deductions from the freight unless specifically agreed. 104

13. Demurrage/Despatch Money 105

Demurrage and, if applicable, despatch money shall 106
be computed according to the terms of the attached 107
charter party and settled at the rate(s) stated in Box 16. 108

14. Late Payment of Freight and Demurrage 109

(a) *Interest*: Any freight or part thereof received after 110
the due date shall bear interest at 2 (two) per cent. per 111
month or pro rata for part of a month. 112

Demurrage due or any part thereof received later than 113
15 days after the Charterers' receipt of the Owners' 114
documented invoice shall bear interest at the same rate 115
from the 16th day. 116

(b) *Suspension*: As long as any freight, deadfreight or 117
demurrage due under this Contract is unpaid, the 118
Owners shall not be obliged to: 119

(i) nominate further tonnage hereunder; 120

(ii) send any vessel to the loading port; 121

(iii) commence loading of any vessel. 122

Time lost thereby to any vessel held ready for loading 123
or for nomination shall be paid by the Charterers to 124
the Owners at the applicable demurrage rate. The 125
Owners' right to suspend performance under this 126
Clause shall be without prejudice to any right to cancel 127
the Contract. 128

(c) *Cancelling*: If the Charterers have failed to pay 129
freight, deadfreight or demurrage when such freight, 130
deadfreight or demurrage is due, the Owners may give 131
notice to the Charterers that unless they pay within 120 132
running hours (the "Grace Period") of receipt of the 133
Owners' notice, the Owners shall be entitled to cancel 134
the remaining part of this Contract without prejudice to 135
any other claims the Owners may have against the 136
Charterers. The right to cancel this Contract on the 137
expiry of the Grace Period shall be exercised promptly 138
by written notice from the Owners to the Charterers 139
stating that the Contract is cancelled with immediate 140
effect. The receipt by the Owners of a payment from 141
the Charterers after the Grace Period has expired but 142
prior to the notice of cancellation shall not be deemed a 143
waiver of the Owners' right to cancel the Contract. 144

(d) *Liability*: Whether or not the Owners exercise their 145
rights under sub-clauses 14(b) or 14(c), no claim 146
whatsoever that they may have on the Charterers shall 147
be prejudiced thereby. 148

(e) *Lien*: The Owners shall have a lien on all cargoes 149
carried hereunder for all claims and costs of recovering 150
same. 151

15. Interruption of Performance 152

Neither the Owners nor the Charterers shall, except as 153
otherwise provided in the attached charter party, be 154
responsible for any loss, damage, delay or failure in 155
performance hereunder arising or resulting from act of 156
God, act of war, act of terrorism, seizure under legal 157
process; quarantine restrictions; strikes; boycotts; 158
lockouts; riots, civil commotions and arrest or restraint 159
of princes, rulers or people. Quantities not carried as a 160
result cannot be demanded to be shipped. 161

16. BIMCO Bunker Price Adjustment Clause 162

This Contract is concluded on the basis of the bunker 163
price stated in Box 18(a) for oil of the type and grade 164
stated in Box 18(b). If the bunker price per metric ton at 165
the port or place stated in Box 18(c) on the first day of 166
loading is higher than the figure stated in Box 18(d)(i) or 167
lower than the figure stated in Box 18(d)(ii), any amount 168
in excess of such increase or decrease shall be payable 169
to Owners or Charterers as the case may be. 170
The agreed bunker consumption for each voyage is as 171
stated in Box 18(e). 172

17. BIMCO War Cancellation Clause 2004 173

Either party may cancel this Contract on the outbreak 174
of war (whether there be a declaration of war or not) (i) 175
between any two or more of the following countries: 176
the United States of America; Russia; the United 177
Kingdom; France; and the People's Republic of China, 178
or, (ii) between two or more of the countries stated in 179
Box 19. 180

18. BIMCO Dispute Resolution Clause 181

*)**(a)** This Contract shall be governed by and construed 182
in accordance with English law and any dispute arising 183
out of or in connection with this Contract shall be referred 184
to arbitration in London in accordance with the 185
Arbitration Act 1996 or any statutory modification or re- 186

enactment thereof save to the extent necessary to give 187
effect to the provisions of this Clause. 188
The arbitration shall be conducted in accordance with 189
the London Maritime Arbitrators Association (LMAA) 190
Terms current at the time when the arbitration 191
proceedings are commenced. 192
The reference shall be to three arbitrators. A party wishing 193
to refer a dispute to arbitration shall appoint its arbitrator 194
and send notice of such appointment in writing to the 195
other party requiring the other party to appoint its own 196
arbitrator within 14 calendar days of that notice and stating 197
that it will appoint its arbitrator as sole arbitrator unless 198
the other party appoints its own arbitrator and gives notice 199
that it has done so within the 14 days specified. If the 200
other party does not appoint its own arbitrator and give 201
notice that it has done so within the 14 days specified, 202
the party referring a dispute to arbitration may, without 203
the requirement of any further prior notice to the other 204
party, appoint its arbitrator as sole arbitrator and shall 205
advise the other party accordingly. The award of a sole 206
arbitrator shall be binding on both parties as if he had 207
been appointed by agreement. 208
Nothing herein shall prevent the parties agreeing in 209
writing to vary these provisions to provide for the 210
appointment of a sole arbitrator. 211
In cases where neither the claim nor any counterclaim 212
exceeds the sum of US$50,000 (or such other sum as 213
the parties may agree) the arbitration shall be conducted 214
in accordance with the LMAA Small Claims Procedure 215
current at the time when the arbitration proceedings 216
are commenced. 217

*)**(b)** This Contract shall be governed by and construed 218
in accordance with Title 9 of the United States Code 219
and the Maritime Law of the United States and any 220
dispute arising out of or in connection with this Contract 221
shall be referred to three persons at New York, one to 222
be appointed by each of the parties hereto, and the 223
third by the two so chosen; their decision or that of any 224
two of them shall be final, and for the purposes of 225
enforcing any award, judgement may be entered on an 226
award by any court of competent jurisdiction. The 227
proceedings shall be conducted in accordance with the 228
rules of the Society of Maritime Arbitrators, Inc. 229
In cases where neither the claim nor any counterclaim 230
exceeds the sum of US$50,000 (or such other sum as 231
the parties may agree) the arbitration shall be conducted 232
in accordance with the Shortened Arbitration Procedure 233
of the Society of Maritime Arbitrators, Inc. current at 234
the time when the arbitration proceedings are 235
commenced. 236

*)**(c)** This Contract shall be governed by and construed 237
in accordance with the laws of the place mutually agreed 238
by the parties and any dispute arising out of or in 239
connection with this Contract shall be referred to 240
arbitration at a mutually agreed place, subject to the 241
procedures applicable there. 242

(d) Notwithstanding 18(a), 18(b) or 18(c) above, the 243
parties may agree at any time to refer to mediation any 244
difference and/or dispute arising out of or in connection 245
with this Contract. 246
In the case of a dispute in respect of which arbitration 247
has been commenced under 18(a), 18(b) or 18(c) 248
above, the following shall apply:- 249
(i) Either party may at any time and from time to time 250
elect to refer the dispute or part of the dispute to 251
mediation by service on the other party of a written 252
notice (the "Mediation Notice") calling on the other 253
party to agree to mediation. 254

676

(ii) The other party shall thereupon within 14 calendar days of receipt of the Mediation Notice confirm that they agree to mediation, in which case the parties shall thereafter agree a mediator within a further 14 calendar days, failing which on the application of either party a mediator will be appointed promptly by the Arbitration Tribunal ("the Tribunal") or such person as the Tribunal may designate for that purpose. The mediation shall be conducted in such place and in accordance with such procedure and on such terms as the parties may agree or, in the event of disagreement, as may be set by the mediator.

(iii) If the other party does not agree to mediate, that fact may be brought to the attention of the Tribunal and may be taken into account by the Tribunal when allocating the costs of the arbitration as between the parties.

(iv) The mediation shall not affect the right of either party to seek such relief or take such steps as it considers necessary to protect its interest.

(v) Either party may advise the Tribunal that they have agreed to mediation. The arbitration procedure shall continue during the conduct of the mediation but the Tribunal may take the mediation timetable into account when setting the timetable for steps in the arbitration.

(vi) Unless otherwise agreed or specified in the mediation terms, each party shall bear its own costs incurred in the mediation and the parties shall share equally the mediator's costs and expenses.

(vii) The mediation process shall be without prejudice and confidential and no information or documents disclosed during it shall be revealed to the Tribunal except to the extent that they are disclosable under the law and procedure governing the arbitration.

(Note: The parties should be aware that the mediation process may not necessarily interrupt time limits.)

(e) If Box 20 in PART I is not appropriately filled in, sub-clause 18(a) of this Clause shall apply. Sub-clause 18(d) shall apply in all cases.

*) Sub-clauses 18(a), 18(b) and 18(c) are alternatives; indicate alternative agreed in Box 20.

19. Commission
The Owners shall pay commission on freight, deadfreight and demurrage earned and paid at the rate indicated and to the party mentioned in Box 21.

20. BIMCO Notices Clause
(a) All notices given by either party or their agents to the other party or their agents in accordance with the provisions of this Contract shall be in writing.
(b) For the purposes of this Contract, "in writing" shall mean any method of legible communication. A notice may be given by any effective means including, but not limited to, cable, telex, fax, e-mail, registered or recorded mail, or by personal service.

Standard Charterparties*

1. Voyage Charterparties

   1.1 Animal Oils
       BISCOILVOY '86

   1.2 Cement
       CEMENTVOY 2006

   1.3 Chemicals
       ASBACHEMVOY / BIMCHEMVOY 2008 / CHEMTANKVOY

   1.4 Coal
       AMWELSH '93 / AUSCOAL / BALTCON / COAL-OREVOY /
       GERMANCON-NORTH / NIPPONCOAL / POLCOALVOY /
       RICHARDS BAY / SAFANCHART No. 2 / SOVCOAL 1987

   1.5 Fats
       BISCOILVOY '86

   1.6 Fertilisers
       AFRICANPHOS / FERTICON 2007 / FERTISOV / FERTIVOY
       '88 / QAFCOCHARTER / MUNTAJATCHARTER

   1.7 Gas
       GASVOY 2005 / LNGVOY

   1.8 General
       GENCON '94 / MULTIFORM / NUVOY '84 / SCANCON /
       WORLDFOOD '99

   1.9 Grain
       AUSTWHEAT 1990 / AUSBAR / BFC (BALTIMORE FORM
       "C") / BULKON / CENTROCON / GRAINCON / GRAINVOY /
       NORGRAIN '89 / SYNACOMEX 2000

---

* The list is indicative, not exhaustive. Numbers, where they exist in the name of the document, may indicate either the year of the last revision of the charterparty (e.g. NYPE 2015) or the serial number of last version of the charterparty (e.g. BPVOY 5).

1.10 Heavy & Voluminous Cargoes
HEAVYCON

1.11 Nitrate
HYDROCHARTER / YARACHARTER

1.12 Nuts
ARACON

1.13 Oil
ASBA II / ASBATANKVOY / BPVOY 5 / EXXONMOBILVOY 2012 / EXXONVOY '90 / INTERTANKVOY '76 / MOBILVOY / OMVOY / SHELLVOY 6 / STBVOY / TANKERVOY '87 / TEXACOVOY '94

1.14 Ore
COAL-OREVOY / C (ORE) 7 / MURMAPATIT 1987 / NIPPON-ORE / SOVORECON 1987

1.15 Salt
COASTSALT

1.16 Stone
PANSTONE

1.17 Sugar
AUSTRALIA-JAPAN BULK RAW SUGAR / BULK SUGAR CHARTER PARTY U.S.A. / CUBASUGAR / FIJI SUGAR / MSS FORM / SUGAR CHARTER PARTY

1.18 Vegetable Oil
BISCOILVOY '86

1.19 Wood/Timber
BALDRIA / BLACKSEAWOOD / NANYOZAI 1997 / NUBALT-WOOD / RUSSWOOD / SOVCONROUND

2. Time Charterparties

2.1 Chemicals
BIMCHEMTIME 2005

2.2 Containers & Liner
BOXTIME 2004 / LINERTIME 2015

2.3 Dry Cargo & General
ASBATIME / BALTIME 1939 (revised 2001) / FONASBATIME / GENTIME / NYPE 2015 / SUPPLYTIME / ROPAXTIME

Conlinebooking 2016*

First published 1952, revised 1974, 1976, 1978, 2000, 2016

BIMCO

CONLINEBOOKING 2016
LINER BOOKING NOTE
Page 1

Agents	Place and date
	Vessel
Carrier	Time for shipment (about)
	Port of loading**
Merchant*	Port of discharge
	Merchant's representatives at loading port

Container No./Seal No./Marks and Nos. (if available)	Number and kind of packages, description of cargo	Gross weight, kg (if available)	Measurement, m³ (if available)

Freight details and charges	Special terms, if agreed
Freight (state pre-payable or payable at destination)	

Sample Copy (watermark)

It is hereby agreed that this Contract shall be performed subject to the terms contained on Page 1 and 2 hereof which shall prevail over any previous arrangements and which shall in turn be superseded (except as to deadfreight) by the terms of the Bill of Lading.

Signature (Merchant)	Signature (Carrier)

* As defined hereinafter (Cl. 1)
** (or so near thereunto as the Vessel may safely get and lie always afloat)

* Reproduced by kind permission of BIMCO.

FULL TERMS OF THE CARRIER'S BILL OF LADING FORM*

Page 2

1. Definition.

"Merchant" includes the shipper, the receiver, the consignor, the consignee, the holder of the Bill of Lading, the owner of the cargo and any person entitled to possession of the cargo.

2. Notification.

Any mention in this Bill of Lading of parties to be notified of the arrival of the cargo is solely for the information of the Carrier and failure to give such notification shall not involve the Carrier in any liability nor relieve the Merchant of any obligation hereunder.

3. Liability for Carriage Between Port of Loading and Port of Discharge.

(a) The International Convention for the Unification of Certain Rules of Law relating to Bills of Lading signed at Brussels on 25 August 1924 ("the Hague Rules") as amended by the Protocol signed at Brussels on 23 February 1968 ("the Hague-Visby Rules") and as enacted in the country of shipment shall apply to this Contract. When the Hague-Visby Rules are not enacted in the country of shipment, the corresponding legislation of the country of destination shall apply, irrespective of whether such legislation may only regulate outbound shipments.

When there is no enactment of the Hague-Visby Rules in either the country of shipment or in the country of destination, the Hague-Visby Rules shall apply to this Contract save where the Hague Rules as enacted in the country of shipment or, if no such enactment is in place, the Hague Rules as enacted in the country of destination apply compulsorily to this Contract.

The Protocol signed at Brussels on 21 December 1979 ("the SDR Protocol 1979") shall apply where the Hague-Visby Rules apply, whether mandatorily or by this Contract.

The Carrier shall in no case be responsible for loss of or damage to cargo arising prior to loading, after discharging, or with respect to deck cargo and live animals.

(b) If the Carrier is held liable in respect of delay, consequential loss or damage other than loss of or damage to the cargo, the liability of the Carrier shall be limited to the freight for the carriage covered by this Bill of Lading, or to the limitation amount as determined in sub-clause 3(a), whichever is the lesser.

(c) The aggregate liability of the Carrier and/or any of its servants, agents or independent contractors under this Contract shall, in no circumstances, exceed the limits of liability for the total loss of the cargo under sub-clause 3(a) or, if applicable, the Additional Clause.

4. Law and Jurisdiction.

Disputes arising out of or in connection with this Bill of Lading shall be exclusively determined by the courts and in accordance with the law of the place where the Carrier has its principal place of business, as stated on Page 1, except as provided elsewhere herein.

5. The Scope of Carriage.

The intended carriage shall not be limited to the direct route but shall be deemed to include any proceeding or returning to or stopping or slowing down at or off any ports or places for any reasonable purpose connected with the carriage including bunkering, loading, discharging, or other cargo operations and maintenance of Vessel and crew.

6. Substitution of Vessel.

The Carrier shall be at liberty to carry the cargo or part thereof to the Port of discharge by the said or other vessel or vessels either belonging to the Carrier or others, or by other means of transport, proceeding either directly or indirectly to such port.

7. Transhipment.

The Carrier shall be at liberty to tranship, lighter, land and store the cargo either on shore or afloat and reship and forward the same to the Port of discharge.

8. Liability for Pre- and On-Carriage.

When the Carrier arranges pre-carriage of the cargo from a place other than the Vessel's Port of loading or on-carriage of the cargo to a place other than the Vessel's Port of discharge, the Carrier shall contract as the Merchant's Agent only and the Carrier shall not be liable for any loss or damage arising during any part of the carriage other than between the Port of loading and the Port of discharge even though the freight for the whole carriage has been collected by him.

9. Loading and Discharging.

(a) Loading and discharging of the cargo shall be arranged by the Carrier or its Agent.

(b) The Merchant shall, at its risk and expense, handle and/or store the cargo before loading and after discharging.

(c) Loading and discharging may commence without prior notice.

(d) The Merchant or its Agent shall tender the cargo when the Vessel is ready to load and as fast as the Vessel can receive including, if required by the Carrier, outside ordinary working hours notwithstanding any custom of the port. If the Merchant or its Agent fails to tender the cargo when the Vessel is ready to load or fails to load as fast as the Vessel can receive the cargo, the Carrier shall be relieved of any obligation to load such cargo, the Vessel shall be entitled to leave the port without further notice and the Merchant shall be liable to the Carrier for deadfreight and/or any overtime charges, losses, costs and expenses incurred by the Carrier.

(e) The Merchant or his Agent shall take delivery of the cargo as fast as the Vessel can discharge including, if required by the Carrier, outside ordinary working hours notwithstanding any custom of the port. If the Merchant or its Agent fails to take delivery of the cargo the Carrier's discharging of the cargo shall be deemed fulfilment of the contract of carriage. Should the cargo not be applied for within a reasonable time, the Carrier may sell the same privately or by auction. If the Merchant or its Agent fails to take delivery of the cargo as fast as the Vessel can discharge, the Merchant shall be liable to the Carrier for any overtime charges, losses, costs and expenses incurred by the Carrier.

(f) The Merchant shall accept its reasonable proportion of unidentified loose cargo.

10. Freight, Charges, Costs, Expenses, Duties, Taxes and Fines.

(a) Freight, whether paid or not, shall be considered as fully earned upon loading and non-returnable in any event. Unless otherwise specified, freight and/or charges under this Contract are payable by the Merchant to the Carrier on demand. Interest at Libor (or its successor) plus 2 per cent. shall run from fourteen days after the date when freight and charges are payable.

(b) The Merchant shall be liable for all costs and expenses of fumigation, gathering and sorting loose cargo and weighing onboard, repairing damage to and replacing packing due to excepted causes, and any extra handling of the cargo for any of the aforementioned reasons.

(c) The Merchant shall be liable for any dues, duties, taxes and charges which under any denomination may be levied, *inter alia*, on the basis of freight, weight of cargo or tonnage of the Vessel.

(d) The Merchant shall be liable for all fines, penalties, costs, expenses and losses which the Carrier, Vessel or cargo may incur through non-observance of Customs House and/or import or export regulations.

(e) The Carrier is entitled in case of incorrect declaration of contents, weights, measurements or value of the cargo to claim double the amount of freight which would have been due if such declaration had been correctly given. For the purpose of ascertaining the actual facts, the Carrier shall have the right to obtain from the Merchant the original invoice and to have the cargo inspected and its contents, weight, measurement or value verified.

11. Lien.

The Carrier shall have a lien on all cargo for any amount due under this contract and the costs of recovering the same and shall be entitled to sell the cargo privately or by auction to satisfy any such claims.

12. General Average and Salvage.

General Average shall be adjusted, stated and settled in London according to the York-Antwerp Rules 2016, in respect of all cargo, whether carried on or under deck. In the event of accident, danger, damage or disaster before or after commencement of the voyage resulting from any cause whatsoever, whether due to negligence or not, for which or for the consequence of which the Carrier is not responsible by statute, contract or otherwise, the Merchant shall contribute with the Carrier in General Average to the payment of any sacrifice, losses or expenses of a General Average nature that may be made or incurred, and shall pay salvage and special charges incurred in respect of the cargo. If a salving vessel is owned or operated by the Carrier, salvage shall be paid for as fully as if the salving vessel or vessels belonged to strangers.

13. Both-to-Blame Collision Clause.

If the Vessel comes into collision with another vessel as a result of the negligence of the other vessel and any act, negligence or default of the Master, Mariner, Pilot or the servants of the Carrier in the navigation or in the management of the Vessel, the Merchant will indemnify the Carrier against all loss or liability to the other or non-carrying vessel or her Owner in so far as such loss or liability represents loss of or damage to or any claim whatsoever of the owner of the cargo paid or payable by the other or non-carrying vessel or her Owner to the owner of the cargo and set-off, recouped or recovered by the other or non-carrying vessel or her Owner as part of its claim against the carrying vessel or Carrier. The foregoing provisions shall also apply where the Owner, operator or those in charge of any vessel or vessels or objects other than, or in addition to, the colliding vessels or objects are at fault in respect of a collision or contact.

14. Government directions, War, Epidemics, Ice, Strikes, etc.

(a) The Master and the Carrier shall have liberty to comply with any order or directions or recommendations in connection with the carriage under this contract given by any Government or Authority, or anybody acting or purporting to act on behalf of such Government or Authority, or having under the terms of the insurance on the Vessel the right to give such orders or directions or recommendations.

(b) Should it appear that the performance of the carriage would expose the Vessel or any cargo onboard to risk of seizure, damage or delay, in consequence of war, warlike operations, blockade, riots, civil commotions or piracy, or any person onboard to risk of loss of life or freedom, or that any such risk has increased, the Master may discharge the cargo at the Port of loading or any other safe and convenient port.

(c) Should it appear that epidemics; quarantine; ice; labour troubles, labour obstructions, strikes, lockouts (whether onboard or on shore); difficulties in loading or discharging would prevent the Vessel from leaving the Port of loading or reaching or entering the Port of discharge or there discharging in the usual manner and departing therefrom, all of which safely and without unreasonable delay, the Master may discharge the cargo at the Port of loading or any other safe and convenient port.

(d) The discharge, under the provisions of this Clause, of any cargo shall be deemed due fulfilment of the contract of carriage.

(e) If in connection with the exercise of any liberty under this Clause any extra expenses are incurred they shall be paid by the Merchant in addition to the freight, together with return freight, if any, and a reasonable compensation for any extra services rendered to the cargo.

15. International Group of P&I Clubs/BIMCO Himalaya Clause for bills of lading and other contracts 2014

(a) For the purposes of this contract, the term "Servant" shall include the owners, managers, and operators of vessels (other than the Carrier); underlying carriers; stevedores and terminal operators; and any direct or indirect servant, agent, or subcontractor (including their own subcontractors), or any other party employed by or on behalf of the Carrier, or whose services or equipment have been used to perform this contract whether in direct contractual privity with the Carrier or not.

(b) It is hereby expressly agreed that no Servant shall in any circumstances whatsoever be under any liability whatsoever to the Merchant or other party to this contract (hereinafter termed "Merchant") for any loss, damage or delay of whatsoever kind arising or resulting directly or indirectly from any act, neglect or default on the Servant's part while acting in the course of or in connection with the performance of this contract.

(c) Without prejudice to the generality of the foregoing provisions in this clause, every exemption, limitation, condition and liberty contained herein (other than Art III Rule 8 of the Hague/Hague-Visby Rules if incorporated herein) and every right, exemption from liability, defence and immunity of whatsoever nature applicable to the carrier or to which the carrier is entitled hereunder including the right to enforce any jurisdiction or arbitration provision contained herein shall also be available and shall extend to every such Servant of the carrier, who shall be entitled to enforce the same against the Merchant.

(d) (i) The Merchant undertakes that no claim or allegation whether arising in contract, bailment, tort or otherwise shall be made against any Servant of the carrier which imposes or attempts to impose upon any of them or any vessel owned or chartered by any of them any liability whatsoever in connection with this contract whether or not arising out of negligence on the part of such Servant. The Servant shall also be entitled to enforce the foregoing covenant against the Merchant; and

(ii) The Merchant undertakes that if any such claim or allegation should nevertheless be made, it will indemnify the carrier against all consequences thereof.

(e) For the purpose of sub-paragraphs (a)-(d) of this clause the Carrier is or shall be deemed to be acting as agent or trustee on behalf of and for the benefit of all persons mentioned in sub-clause (a) above who are its Servant and all such persons shall to this extent be or be deemed to be parties to this contract.

16. Stowage.

(a) The Carrier shall have the right to stow cargo by means of containers, trailers, transportable tanks, flats, pallets, or similar articles of transport used to consolidate goods.

(b) The Carrier shall have the right to carry containers, trailers, transportable tanks and covered flats, whether stowed by the Carrier or received by him in a stowed condition from the Merchant, on or under deck without notice to the Merchant.

17. Shipper-Packed Containers, trailers, transportable tanks, flats and pallets.

(a) If a container has not been filled, packed or stowed by the Carrier, the Carrier shall not be liable for any loss of or damage to its contents and the Merchant shall cover any loss or expense incurred by the Carrier, if such loss, damage or expense has been caused by:

(i) negligent filling, packing or stowing of the container;

(ii) the contents being unsuitable for carriage in container; or

(iii) the unsuitability or defective condition of the container unless the container has been supplied by the Carrier and the unsuitability or defective condition would not have been apparent upon reasonable inspection at or prior to the time when the container was filled, packed or stowed.

(b) The provisions of sub-clause (i) of this Clause also apply with respect to trailers, transportable tanks, flats and pallets which have not been filled, packed or stowed by the Carrier.

(c) The Carrier does not accept liability for damage due to the unsuitability or defective condition of reefer equipment or trailers supplied by the Merchant.

18. Return of Containers.

(a) Containers, pallets or similar articles of transport supplied by or on behalf of the Carrier shall be returned to the Carrier in the same order and condition as handed over to the Merchant, normal wear and tear excepted, with interiors clean and within the time prescribed in the Carrier's tariff or elsewhere.

(b) The Merchant shall be liable to the Carrier for any loss, damage to, or delay, including demurrage and detention incurred by or sustained to containers, pallets or similar articles of transport during the period between handing over to the Merchant and return to the Carrier.

ADDITIONAL CLAUSE

U.S. Trade. Period of Responsibility.

(i) In case the Contract evidenced by this Bill of Lading is subject to the Carriage of Goods by Sea Act of the United States of America, 1936 (U.S. COGSA), then the provisions stated in said Act shall govern before loading and after discharge and throughout the entire time the cargo is in the Carrier's custody and in which event freight shall be payable on the cargo coming into the Carrier's custody.

(ii) If the U.S. COGSA applies, and unless the nature and value of the cargo has been declared by the shipper before the cargo has been handed over to the Carrier and inserted in this Bill of Lading, the Carrier shall in no event be or become liable for any loss or damage to the cargo in an amount exceeding USD 500 per package or customary freight unit.

* BIMCO LINER BILL OF LADING
Code name: CONLINEBILL 2016
First published 1949, revised 1950, 1952, 1973, 1974, 1976, 1978, 2000 and 2016.

Letter of Credit – the function of the Bill of Lading

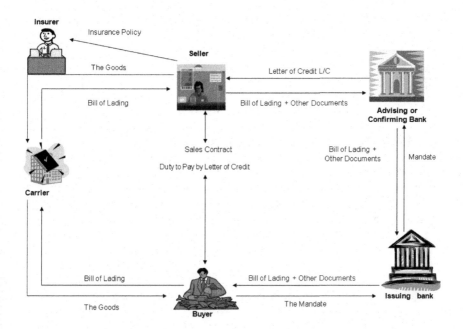

APPENDIX 13

Congenbill 2016*

First published 1946, revised 1964, 1978, 1994, 2007, 2016

BIMCO

CONGENBILL 2016		
	BILL OF LADING	
	To be used with charter parties	
	Page 1	

Shipper	Bill of Lading No.	Reference No.
Consignee	Vessel	
Notify address	Port of loading	
	Port of discharge	
Shipper's description of goods		Gross weight

(of which   on deck at shipper's risk; the Carrier not being responsible for loss or damage howsoever arising)

Freight payable as per CHARTER PARTY dated:	**SHIPPED** at the Port of Loading in apparent good order and condition on the Vessel for carriage to the Port of Discharge or so near thereto as the Vessel may safely get the goods specified above.
	Weight, measure, quality, quantity, condition, contents and value unknown.
FREIGHT ADVANCE Received on account of freight:	IN WITNESS whereof the Master or Owner or Charterer or Agent of the said vessel has signed the number of Bills of Lading indicated below all of this tenor and date, any one of which being accomplished the others shall be void.
	FOR CONDITIONS OF CARRIAGE SEE PAGE 2

Date shipped on board	Place and date of issue	Number of original Bills of Lading

Signature:...(Master*/Agent*/Owner*/Charterer*)

*Delete as appropriate

If signed by an Agent indicate with a tick ☑ whether for and on behalf of:

☐ Master; or

☐ Owner ....(insert name); or

☐ Charterer ....(insert name)

Agent ....(insert name)

* Reproduced by kind permission of BIMCO.

CONGENBILL 2016

BILL OF LADING

To be used with charter parties

Page 2

Conditions of Carriage

(1) All terms and conditions, liberties and exceptions of the Charter Party, dated as overleaf, including the Law and Arbitration Clause/Dispute Resolution Clause, are herewith incorporated.

(2) **General Paramount Clause**

The International Convention for the Unification of Certain Rules of Law relating to Bills of Lading signed at Brussels on 25 August 1924 ("the Hague Rules") as amended by the Protocol signed at Brussels on 23 February 1968 ("the Hague-Visby Rules") and as enacted in the country of shipment shall apply to this Contract. When the Hague-Visby Rules are not enacted in the country of shipment, the corresponding legislation of the country of destination shall apply, irrespective of whether such legislation may only regulate outbound shipments.

When there is no enactment of the Hague-Visby Rules in either the country of shipment or in the country of destination, the Hague-Visby Rules shall apply to this Contract save where the Hague Rules as enacted in the country of shipment or if no such enactment is in place, the Hague Rules as enacted in the country of destination apply compulsorily to this Contract.

The Protocol signed at Brussels on 21 December 1979 ("the SDR Protocol 1979") shall apply where the Hague-Visby Rules apply, whether mandatorily or by this Contract.

The Carrier shall in no case be responsible for loss of or damage to cargo arising prior to loading, after discharging, or while the cargo is in the charge of another carrier, or with respect to deck cargo and live animals.

(3) **General Average**

General Average shall be adjusted, stated and settled according to York-Antwerp Rules 2016 in London unless another place is agreed in the Charter Party.

Cargo's contribution to General Average shall be paid to the Carrier even when such average is the result of a fault, neglect or error of the Master, Pilot or Crew.

(4) **New Jason Clause**

In the event of accident, danger, damage or disaster before or after the commencement of the voyage, resulting from any cause whatsoever, whether due to negligence or not, for which, or for the consequence of which, the Carrier is not responsible, by statute, contract or otherwise, the cargo, shippers, consignees or the owners of the cargo shall contribute with the Carrier in General Average to the payment of any sacrifices, losses or expenses of a General Average nature that may be made or incurred and shall pay salvage and special charges incurred in respect of the cargo. If a salving vessel is owned or operated by the Carrier, salvage shall be paid for as fully as if the said salving vessel or vessels belonged to strangers. Such deposit as the Carrier, or its agents, may deem sufficient to cover the estimated contribution of the goods and any salvage and special charges thereon shall, if required, be made by the cargo, shippers, consignees or owners of the goods to the Carrier before delivery.

(5) **Both-to-Blame Collision Clause**

If the Vessel comes into collision with another vessel as a result of the negligence of the other vessel and any act, neglect or default of the Master, Mariner, Pilot or the servants of the Carrier in the navigation or in the management of the Vessel, the owners of the cargo carried hereunder will indemnify the Carrier against all loss or liability to the other or non-carrying vessel or her owners in so far as such loss or liability represents loss of, or damage to, or any claim whatsoever of the owners of said cargo, paid or payable by the other or non-carrying vessel or her owners to the owners of said cargo and set-off, recouped or recovered by the other or non-carrying vessel or her owners as part of their claim against the carrying Vessel or the Carrier.

The foregoing provisions shall also apply where the owners, operators or those in charge of any vessel or vessels or objects other than, or in addition to, the colliding vessels or objects are at fault in respect of a collision or contact.

(6) **International Group of P&I Clubs/BIMCO Himalaya Clause for bills of lading and other contracts 2014**

(a) For the purposes of this contract, the term "Servant" shall include the owners, managers, and operators of vessels (other than the Carrier); underlying carriers; stevedores and terminal operators; and any direct or indirect servant, agent, or subcontractor (including their own subcontractors), or any other party employed by or on behalf of the Carrier, or whose services or equipment have been used to perform this contract whether in direct contractual privity with the Carrier or not.

(b) It is hereby expressly agreed that no Servant shall in any circumstances whatsoever be under any liability whatsoever to the shipper, consignee, receiver, holder, or other party to this contract (hereinafter termed "Merchant") for any loss, damage or delay of whatsoever kind arising or resulting directly or indirectly from any act, neglect or default on the Servant's part while acting in the course of or in connection with the performance of this contract.

(c) Without prejudice to the generality of the foregoing provisions in this clause, every exemption, limitation, condition and liberty contained herein (other than Art III Rule 8 of the Hague/Hague-Visby Rules if incorporated herein) and every right, exemption from liability, defence and immunity of whatsoever nature applicable to the carrier or to which the carrier is entitled hereunder including the right to enforce any jurisdiction or arbitration provision contained herein shall also be available and shall extend to every such Servant of the carrier, who shall be entitled to enforce the same against the Merchant.

(d)

(i) The Merchant undertakes that no claim or allegation whether arising in contract, bailment, tort or otherwise shall be made against any Servant of the carrier which imposes or attempts to impose upon any of them or any vessel owned or chartered by any of them any liability whatsoever in connection with this contract whether or not arising out of negligence on the part of such Servant. The Servant shall also be entitled to enforce the foregoing covenant against the Merchant; and

(ii) The Merchant undertakes that if any such claim or allegation should nevertheless be made, it will indemnify the carrier against all consequences thereof.

(e) For the purpose of sub-paragraphs (a)-(d) of this clause the Carrier is or shall be deemed to be acting as agent or trustee on behalf of and for the benefit of all persons mentioned in sub-clause (a) above who are its Servant and all such persons shall to this extent be or be deemed to be parties to this contract.

For particulars of cargo, freight, destination, etc., see Page 1

688

APPENDIX 14

Conlinebill 2016*

First published 1949, revised 1950, 1952, 1973, 1974, 1976, 1978, 2000, 2016

BIMCO

CONLINEBILL 2016
LINER BILL OF LADING
Page 1

Shipper	Bill of Lading No.	Reference No.

Consignee or Order	Notify address	Vessel

Pre-carriage by**	Port of loading

Place of receipt by pre-carrier**	Port of discharge

Place of delivery by on-carrier**	

Container No./Seal No./Marks and Nos.	Number and kind of packages, description of cargo	Gross weight, kg	Measurement, m³

PARTICULARS DECLARED BY THE SHIPPER BUT NOT ACKNOWLEDGED BY THE CARRIER

Total number of Containers/Packages or Units received by the Carrier	SHIPPED on board in apparent good order and condition (unless otherwise stated herein) the total number of Containers/Packages or Units indicated in the Box opposite entitled "Total number of Containers/Packages or Units received by the Carrier" and the cargo as specified above, weight, measure, marks, numbers, quality, contents and value unknown, for carriage to the Port of discharge or so near thereto as the vessel may safely get and lie always afloat, to be delivered in the like good order and condition at the Port of discharge unto the lawful holder of the Bill of Lading, on payment of freight as indicated to the left plus other charges incurred in accordance with the provisions contained in this Bill of Lading. In accepting this Bill of Lading the Merchant† expressly accepts and agrees to all its stipulations on both Page 1 and Page 2, whether written, printed, stamped or otherwise incorporated, as fully as if they were all signed by the Merchant.
Shipper's declared value	
Declared value charge	One original Bill of Lading must be surrendered duly endorsed in exchange for the cargo or delivery order, whereupon all other Bills of Lading to be void. IN WITNESS whereof the Carrier, Master or their Agent has signed the number of original Bills of Lading stated below right, all of this tenor and date.

Freight details and charges	Date shipped on board	Place and date of issue	Number of original Bills of Lading

Carrier:...(insert name, principal place of business)

Signature:...(Carrier*/Master*/Agent*)

Delete as appropriate

If signed by an Agent indicate with a tick ☑ whether for and on behalf of:

☐ Master; or

☐ Carrier

Agent...(insert name)

** Applicable only when pre-/on-carriage is arranged in accordance with Clause 8.
† As defined hereinafter (Cl. 1).

* Reproduced by kind permission of BIMCO.

CONLINEBILL 2016
NEGOTIABLE LINER BILL OF LADING

Page 2

1. Definition.
"Merchant" includes the shipper, the receiver, the consignor, the consignee, the holder of the Bill of Lading, the owner of the cargo and any person entitled to possession of the cargo.

2. Notification.
Any mention in this Bill of Lading of parties to be notified of the arrival of the cargo is solely for the information of the Carrier and failure to give such notification shall not involve the Carrier in any liability nor relieve the Merchant of any obligation hereunder.

3. Liability for Carriage Between Port of Loading and Port of Discharge.
(a) The International Convention for the Unification of Certain Rules of Law relating to Bills of Lading signed at Brussels on 25 August 1924 ("the Hague Rules") as amended by the Protocol signed at Brussels on 23 February 1968 ("the Hague-Visby Rules") and as enacted in the country of shipment shall apply to this Contract. When the Hague-Visby Rules are not enacted in the country of shipment, the corresponding legislation of the country of destination shall apply, irrespective of whether such legislation may only regulate outbound shipments.
When there is no enactment of the Hague-Visby Rules in either the country of shipment or in the country of destination, the Hague-Visby Rules shall apply to this Contract save where the Hague Rules as enacted in the country of shipment or, if no such enactment is in place, the Hague Rules as enacted in the country of destination apply compulsorily to this Contract.
The Protocol signed at Brussels on 21 December 1979 ("the SDR Protocol 1979") shall apply where the Hague-Visby Rules apply, whether mandatorily or by this Contract.
The Carrier shall in no case be responsible for loss of or damage to cargo arising prior to loading, after discharging, or with respect to deck cargo and live animals.
(b) If the Carrier is held liable in respect of delay, consequential loss or damage other than loss of or damage to the cargo, the liability of the Carrier shall be limited to the freight for the carriage covered by this Bill of Lading, or to the limitation amount as determined in sub-clause 3(a), whichever is the lesser.
(c) The aggregate liability of the Carrier and/or any of its servants, agents or independent contractors under this Contract shall, in no circumstances, exceed the limits of liability for the total loss of the cargo under sub-clause 3(a) or, if applicable, the Additional Clause.

4. Law and Jurisdiction.
Disputes arising out of or in connection with this Bill of Lading shall be exclusively determined by the courts and in accordance with the law of the place where the Carrier has its principal place of business, as stated on Page 1, except as provided elsewhere herein.

5. The Scope of Carriage.
The intended carriage shall not be limited to the direct route but shall be deemed to include any proceeding or returning to or stopping or slowing down at or off any ports or places for any reasonable purpose connected with the carriage including bunkering, loading, discharging, or other cargo operations and maintenance of Vessel and crew.

6. Substitution of Vessel.
The Carrier shall be at liberty to carry the cargo or part thereof to the Port of discharge by the said or other vessel or vessels either belonging to the Carrier or others, or by other means of transport, proceeding either directly or indirectly to such port.

7. Transhipment.
The Carrier shall be at liberty to tranship, lighter, land and store the cargo either on shore or afloat and reship and forward the same to the Port of discharge.

8. Liability for Pre- and On-Carriage.
When the Carrier arranges pre-carriage of the cargo from a place other than the Vessel's Port of loading or on-carriage of the cargo to a place other than the Vessel's Port of discharge, the Carrier shall contract as the Merchant's Agent only and the Carrier shall not be liable for any loss or damage arising during any part of the carriage other than between the Port of loading and the Port of discharge even though the freight for the whole carriage has been collected by him.

9. Loading and Discharging.
(a) Loading and discharging of the cargo shall be arranged by the Carrier or its Agent.
(b) The Merchant shall, at its risk and expense, handle and/or store the cargo before loading and after discharging.
(c) Loading and discharging may commence without prior notice.
(d) The Merchant or its Agent shall tender the cargo when the Vessel is ready to load and as fast as the Vessel can receive including, if required by the Carrier, outside ordinary working hours notwithstanding any custom of the port. If the Merchant or its Agent fails to tender the cargo when the Vessel is ready to load or fails to load as fast as the Vessel can receive the cargo, the Carrier shall be relieved of any obligation to load such cargo, the Vessel shall be entitled to leave the port without further notice and the Merchant shall be liable to the Carrier for deadfreight and/or any overtime charges, losses, costs and expenses incurred by the Carrier.
(e) The Merchant or his Agent shall take delivery of the cargo as fast as the Vessel can discharge including, if required by the Carrier, outside ordinary working hours notwithstanding any custom of the port. If the Merchant or its Agent fails to take delivery of the cargo the Carrier's discharging of the cargo shall be deemed fulfilment of the contract of carriage. Should the cargo not be applied for within a reasonable time, the Carrier may sell the same privately or by auction. If the Merchant or its Agent fails to take delivery of the cargo as fast as the Vessel can discharge, the Merchant shall be liable to the Carrier for any overtime charges, losses, costs and expenses incurred by the Carrier.

(f) The Merchant shall accept its reasonable proportion of unidentified loose cargo.

10. Freight, Charges, Costs, Expenses, Duties, Taxes and Fines.
(a) Freight, whether paid or not, shall be considered as fully earned upon loading and non-returnable in any event. Unless otherwise specified, freight and/or charges under this Contract are payable by the Merchant to the Carrier on demand. Interest at Libor (or its successor) plus 2 per cent. shall run from fourteen days after the date when freight and charges are payable.
(b) The Merchant shall be liable for all costs and expenses of fumigation, gathering and sorting loose cargo and weighing onboard, repairing damage to and replacing packing due to excepted causes, and any extra handling of the cargo for any of the aforementioned reasons.
(c) The Merchant shall be liable for any dues, duties, taxes and charges which under any denomination may be levied, inter alia, on the basis of freight, weight of cargo or tonnage of the Vessel.
(d) The Merchant shall be liable for all fines, penalties, costs, expenses and losses which the Carrier, Vessel or cargo may incur through non-observance of Customs House and/or import or export regulations.
(e) The Carrier is entitled in case of incorrect declaration of contents, weights, measurements or value of the cargo to claim double the amount of freight which would have been due if such declaration had been correctly given. For the purpose of ascertaining the actual facts, the Carrier shall have the right to obtain from the Merchant the original invoice and to have the cargo inspected and its contents, weight, measurement or value verified.

11. Lien.
The Carrier shall have a lien on all cargo for any amount due under this contract and the costs of recovering the same and shall be entitled to sell the cargo privately or by auction to satisfy any such claims.

12. General Average and Salvage.
General Average shall be adjusted, stated and settled in London according to the York-Antwerp Rules 2016, in respect of all cargo, whether carried on or under deck. In the event of accident, danger, damage or disaster before or after commencement of the voyage resulting from any cause whatsoever, whether due to negligence or not, for which or for the consequence of which the Carrier is not responsible by statute, contract or otherwise, the Merchant shall contribute with the Carrier in General Average to the payment of any sacrifice, losses or expenses of a General Average nature that may be made or incurred, and shall pay salvage and special charges incurred in respect of the cargo. If a salving vessel is owned or operated by the Carrier, salvage shall be paid for as fully as if the salving vessel or vessels belonged to strangers.

13. Both-to-Blame Collision Clause.
If the Vessel comes into collision with another vessel as a result of the negligence of the other vessel and any act, negligence or default of the Master, Mariner, Pilot or the servants of the Carrier in the navigation or in the management of the Vessel, the Merchant will indemnify the Carrier against all loss or liability to the other or non-carrying vessel or her Owner in so far as such loss or liability represents loss of or damage to or any claim whatsoever of the owner of the cargo paid or payable by the other or non-carrying vessel or her Owner to the owner of the cargo and set-off, recouped or recovered by the other or non-carrying vessel or her Owner as part of its claim against the carrying vessel or Carrier. The foregoing provisions shall also apply where the Owner, operator or those in charge of any vessel or vessels or objects other than, or in addition to, the colliding vessels or objects are at fault in respect of a collision or contact.

14. Government directions, War, Epidemics, Ice, Strikes, etc.
(a) The Master and the Carrier shall have liberty to comply with any order or directions or recommendations in connection with the carriage under this contract given by any Government or Authority, or anybody acting or purporting to act on behalf of such Government or Authority, or having under the terms of the insurance on the Vessel the right to give such orders or directions or recommendations.
(b) Should it appear that the performance of the carriage would expose the Vessel or any cargo onboard to risk of seizure, damage or delay, in consequence of war, warlike operations, blockade, riots, civil commotions or piracy, or any person onboard to risk of loss of life or freedom, or that any such risk has increased, the Master may discharge the cargo at the Port of loading or any other safe and convenient port.
(c) Should it appear that epidemics; quarantine; ice; labour troubles, labour obstructions, strikes, lockouts (whether onboard or on shore); difficulties in loading or discharging would prevent the Vessel from leaving the Port of loading or reaching or entering the Port of discharge or there discharging in the usual manner and departing therefrom, all of which safely and without unreasonable delay, the Master may discharge the cargo at the Port of loading or any other safe and convenient port.
(d) The discharge, under the provisions of this Clause, of any cargo shall be deemed due fulfilment of the contract of carriage.
(e) If in connection with the exercise of any liberty under this Clause any extra expenses are incurred they shall be paid by the Merchant in addition to the freight, together with return freight, if any, and a reasonable compensation for any extra services rendered to the cargo.

15. International Group of P&I Clubs/BIMCO Himalaya Clause for bills of lading and other contracts 2014
(a) For the purposes of this contract, the term "Servant" shall include the owners, managers, and operators of vessels (other than the Carrier); underlying carriers; stevedores and terminal operators; and any direct or indirect servant, agent, or subcontractor (including their own subcontractors), or any other party employed by or on behalf of the Carrier, or whose services or equipment have been used to perform this contract whether in direct contractual privity with the Carrier or not.
(b) It is hereby expressly agreed that no Servant shall in any circumstances whatsoever be under any liability whatsoever to the Merchant or other party to this contract (hereinafter termed "Merchant") for any loss, damage or delay of whatsoever kind arising or resulting directly or indirectly from any act, neglect or default on the Servant's part while acting in the course of or in connection with the performance of this contract.
(c) Without prejudice to the generality of the foregoing provisions in this clause, every exemption, limitation, condition and liberty contained herein (other than Art III Rule 8 of the Hague/Hague-Visby Rules if incorporated herein) and every right, exemption from liability, defence and immunity of whatsoever nature applicable to the carrier or to which the carrier is entitled hereunder including the right to enforce any jurisdiction or arbitration provision contained herein shall also be available and shall extend to every such Servant of the carrier, who shall be entitled to enforce the same against the Merchant.
(d) (i) The Merchant undertakes that no claim or allegation whether arising in contract, bailment, tort or otherwise shall be made against any Servant of the carrier which imposes or attempts to impose upon any of them or any vessel owned or chartered by any of them any liability whatsoever in connection with this contract whether or not arising out of negligence on the part of such Servant. The Servant shall also be entitled to enforce the foregoing covenant against the Merchant; and
(ii) The Merchant undertakes that if any such claim or allegation should nevertheless be made, it will indemnify the carrier against all consequences thereof.
(e) For the purpose of sub-paragraphs (a)-(d) of this clause the Carrier is or shall be deemed to be acting as agent or trustee on behalf of and for the benefit of all persons mentioned in sub-clause (a) above who are its Servant and all such persons shall to this extent be or be deemed to be parties to this contract.

16. Stowage.
(a) The Carrier shall have the right to stow cargo by means of containers, trailers, transportable tanks, flats, pallets, or similar articles of transport used to consolidate goods.
(b) The Carrier shall have the right to carry containers, trailers, transportable tanks and covered flats, whether stowed by the Carrier or received by him in a stowed condition from the Merchant, on or under deck without notice to the Merchant.

17. Shipper-Packed Containers, trailers, transportable tanks, flats and pallets.
(a) If a container has not been filled, packed or stowed by the Carrier, the Carrier shall not be liable for any loss of or damage to its contents and the Merchant shall cover any loss or expense incurred by the Carrier, if such loss, damage or expense has been caused by:
(i) negligent filling, packing or stowing of the container;
(ii) the contents being unsuitable for carriage in container; or
(iii) the unsuitability or defective condition of the container unless the container has been supplied by the Carrier and the unsuitability or defective condition would not have been apparent upon reasonable inspection at or prior to the time when the container was filled, packed or stowed.
(b) The provisions of sub-clause (i) of this Clause also apply with respect to trailers, transportable tanks, flats and pallets which have not been filled, packed or stowed by the Carrier.
(c) The Carrier does not accept liability for damage due to the unsuitability or defective condition of reefer equipment or trailers supplied by the Merchant.

18. Return of Containers.
(a) Containers, pallets or similar articles of transport supplied by or on behalf of the Carrier shall be returned to the Carrier in the same order and condition as handed over to the Merchant, normal wear and tear excepted, with interiors clean and within the time prescribed in the Carrier's tariff or elsewhere.
(b) The Merchant shall be liable to the Carrier for any loss, damage to, or delay, including demurrage and detention incurred by or sustained to containers, pallets or similar articles of transport during the period between handing over to the Merchant and return to the Carrier.

ADDITIONAL CLAUSE
U.S. Trade. Period of Responsibility.
(i) In case the Contract evidenced by this Bill of Lading is subject to the Carriage of Goods by Sea Act of the United States of America, 1936 (U.S. COGSA), then the provisions stated in said Act shall govern before loading and after discharge and throughout the entire time the cargo is in the Carrier's custody and in which event freight shall be payable on the cargo coming into the Carrier's custody.
(ii) If the U.S. COGSA applies, and unless the nature and value of the cargo has been declared by the shipper before the cargo has been handed over to the Carrier and inserted in this Bill of Lading, the Carrier shall in no event be or become liable for any loss or damage to the cargo in an amount exceeding USD 500 per package or customary freight unit.

APPENDIX 15

Shipman 2009*

Printed by BIMCO's *idea*

BIMCO

SHIPMAN 2009
STANDARD SHIP MANAGEMENT AGREEMENT

PART I

1. Place and date of Agreement	2. Date of commencement of Agreemen: (Cls. 2, 12, 21 and 25)
3. Owners (name, place of registered office and law of registry) (Cl. 1) (i) Name: (ii) Place of registered office: (iii) Law of registry:	4. Managers (name, place of registered office and law of registry) (Cl. 1) (i) Name: (ii) Place of registered office: (iii) Law of registry:
5. The Company (with reference to the ISM/ISPS Codes) (state name and IMO Unique Company Identification number. If the Company is a third party then also state registered office and principal place of business) (Cls. 1 and 9(c)(i)) (i) Name: (ii) IMO Unique Company Identification number: (iii) Place of registered office: (iv) Principal place of business:	6. Technical Management (state "yes" or "no" as agreed) (Cl. 4)
	7. Crew Management (state "yes" or "no" as agreed) (Cl. 5(a))
	8. Commercial Management (state "yes" or "no" as agreed) (Cl. 6)
9. Chartering Services period (only to be filled in if "yes" stated in Box 8) (Cl 9(a))	10. Crew Insurance arrangements (state "yes" or "no" as agreed) (i) Crew Insurances* (Cl. 5(b)): (ii) Insurance for persons proceeding to sea onboard (Cl. 5(b)(i)): *only to apply if Crew Management (Cl. 5(a)) agreed (see Box 7)
11. Insurance arrangements (state "yes" or "no" as agreed) (Cl. 7)	12. Optional insurances (state optional insurance(s) as agreed, such as piracy, kidnap and ransom, loss of hire and FD & D) (Cl. 10(a)(iv))
13. Interest (state rate of interest to apply after due date to outstanding sums) (Cl. 9(a))	14. Annual management fee (state annual amount) (Cl. 12(a))
15. Manager's nominated account (Cl.12(a))	16. Daily rate (state rate for days in excess of those agreed in budget) (Cl. 12(c))
	17. Lay-up period / number of months (Cl.12(c))
18. Minimum contract period (state number of months) (Cl. 21(a))	19. Management fee on termination (state number of months to apply) (Cl. 22(g))
20. Severance Costs (state maximum amount) (Cl. 22(h)(ii))	21. Dispute Resolution (state alternative Cl. 23(a), 23(b) or 23(c); if Cl. 23(c) place of arbitration must be stated) (Cl. 23)
22. Notices (state full style contact details for serving notice and communication to the Owners) (Cl. 24)	23. Notices (state full style contact details for serving notice and communication to the Managers) (Cl. 24)

Continued

* Reproduced by kind permission of BIMCO

(Continued)

It is mutually agreed between the party stated in <u>Box 3</u> and the party stated in <u>Box 4</u> that this Agreement consisting of PART I and PART II as well as Annexes "A" (Details of Vessel or Vessels), "B" (Details of Crew), "C" (Budget), "D" (Associated Vessels) and "E" (Fee Schedule) attached hereto, shall be performed subject to the conditions contained herein. In the event of a conflict of conditions, the provisions of PART I and Annexes "A", "B", "C", "D" and "E" shall prevail over those of PART II to the extent of such conflict but no further.

Signature(s) (Owners)	Signature(s) (Managers)

InterManager

Approved by the International Ship Managers' Association

First published 1988. Revised 1998 and 2009

Explanatory Notes for SHIPMAN 2009 are available from BIMCO at www.bimco.org

Copyright, published by BIMCO

1. Definitions
In this Agreement save where the context otherwise requires, the following words and expressions shall have the meanings hereby assigned to them:

"Company" (with reference to the ISM Code and the ISPS Code) means the organization identified in Box 5 or any replacement organization appointed by the Owners from time to time (see Sub-clauses 9(b)(i) or 9(c) (ii), whichever is applicable).

"Crew" means the personnel of the numbers, rank and nationality specified in Annex "B" hereto.

"Crew Insurances" means insurance of liabilities in respect of crew risks which shall include but not be limited to death, permanent disability, sickness, injury, repatriation, shipwreck unemployment indemnity and loss of personal effects (see Sub-clause 5(b) (Crew Insurances) and Clause 7 (Insurance Arrangements) and Clause 10 (Insurance Policies) and Boxes 10 and 11).

"Crew Support Costs" means all expenses of a general nature which are not particularly referable to any individual vessel for the time being managed by the Managers and which are incurred by the Managers for the purpose of providing an efficient and economic management service and, without prejudice to the generality of the foregoing, shall include the cost of crew standby pay, training schemes for officers and ratings, cadet training schemes, sick pay, study pay, recruitment and interviews.

"Flag State" means the State whose flag the Vessel is flying.

"ISM Code" means the International Management Code for the Safe Operation of Ships and for Pollution Prevention and any amendment thereto or substitution therefor.

"ISPS Code" means the International Code for the Security of Ships and Port Facilities and the relevant amendments to Chapter XI of SOLAS and any amendment thereto or substitution therefor.

"Managers" means the party identified in Box 4.

"Management Services" means the services specified in SECTION 2 - Services (Clauses 4 through 7) as indicated affirmatively in Boxes 6 through 8, 10 and 11, and all other functions performed by the Managers under the terms of this Agreement.

"Owners" means the party identified in Box 3.

"Severance Costs" means the costs which are legally required to be paid to the Crew as a result of the early termination of any contracts for service on the Vessel.

"SMS" means the Safety Management System (as defined by the ISM Code).

"STCW 95" means the International Convention on Standards of Training, Certification and Watchkeeping for Seafarers, 1978, as amended in 1995 and any amendment thereto or substitution therefor.

"Vessel" means the vessel or vessels details of which are set out in Annex "A" attached hereto.

2. Commencement and Appointment
With effect from the date stated in Box 2 for the commencement of the Management Services and continuing unless and until terminated as provided herein, the Owners hereby appoint the Managers and the Managers hereby agree to act as the Managers of the Vessel in respect of the Management Services.

3. Authority of the Managers
Subject to the terms and conditions herein provided, during the period of this Agreement the Managers shall carry out the Management Services in respect of the Vessel as agents for and on behalf of the Owners. The Managers shall have authority to take such actions as they may from time to time in their absolute discretion consider to be necessary to enable them to perform the Management Services in accordance with sound ship management practice, including but not limited to compliance with all relevant rules and regulations.

1

4. Technical Management 43

(*only applicable if agreed according to* Box 6). 44

The Managers shall provide technical management which includes, but is not limited to, the following 45
services: 46

(a) ensuring that the Vessel complies with the requirements of the law of the Flag State; 47

(b) ensuring compliance with the ISM Code; 48

(c) ensuring compliance with the ISPS Code; 49

(d) providing competent personnel to supervise the maintenance and general efficiency of the Vessel; 50

(e) arranging and supervising dry dockings, repairs, alterations and the maintenance of the Vessel to the 51
standards agreed with the Owners provided that the Managers shall be entitled to incur the necessary 52
expenditure to ensure that the Vessel will comply with all requirements and recommendations of the 53
classification society, and with the law of the Flag State and of the places where the Vessel is required to 54
trade; 55

(f) arranging the supply of necessary stores, spares and lubricating oil; 56

(g) appointing surveyors and technical consultants as the Managers may consider from time to time to be 57
necessary; 58

(h) in accordance with the Owners' instructions, supervising the sale and physical delivery of the Vessel 59
under the sale agreement. However services under this Sub-clause 4(h) shall not include negotiation of the 60
sale agreement or transfer of ownership of the Vessel; 61

(i) arranging for the supply of provisions unless provided by the Owners; and 62

(j) arranging for the sampling and testing of bunkers; 63

5. Crew Management and Crew Insurances 64

(a) *Crew Management* 65

(*only applicable if agreed according to* Box 7) 66

The Managers shall provide suitably qualified Crew who shall comply with the requirements of STCW 95. 67
The provision of such crew management services includes, but is not limited to, the following services: 68

(i) selecting, engaging and providing for the administration of the Crew, including, as applicable, payroll 69
arrangements, pension arrangements, tax, social security contributions and other mandatory dues related 70
to their employment payable in each Crew member's country of domicile; 71

(ii) ensuring that the applicable requirements of the law of the Flag State in respect of rank, qualification 72
and certification of the Crew and employment regulations, such as Crew's tax and social insurance, are 73
satisfied; 74

(iii) ensuring that all Crew have passed a medical examination with a qualified doctor certifying that they are 75
fit for the duties for which they are engaged and are in possession of valid medical certificates issued in 76
accordance with appropriate Flag State requirements or such higher standard of medical examination 77
as may be agreed with the Owners. In the absence of applicable Flag State requirements the medical 78
certificate shall be valid at the time when the respective Crew member arrives on board the Vessel and 79
shall be maintained for the duration of the service on board the Vessel; 80

(iv) ensuring that the Crew shall have a common working language and a command of the English language 81
of a sufficient standard to enable them to perform their duties safely; 82

(v) arranging transportation of the Crew, including repatriation; 83

(vi) training of the Crew; 84

2

694

(vii) conducting union negotiations; and 85

(viii) if the Managers are the Company, ensuring that the Crew, on joining the Vessel, are given proper 86
familiarisation with their duties in relation to the Vessel's SMS and that instructions which are essential 87
to the SMS are identified, documented and given to the Crew prior to sailing. 88

(ix) if the Managers are **not** the Company; 89

    (1) ensuring that the Crew, before joining the Vessel, are given proper familiarisation with their duties 90
in relation to the ISM Code; and 91

    (2) instructing the Crew to obey all reasonable orders of the Company in connection with the operation 92
of the SMS. 93

(x) Where Managers are **not** providing technical management services in accordance with Clause 4 94
(Technical Management): 95

    (1) ensuring that no person connected to the provision and the performance of the crew management 96
services shall proceed to sea on board the Vessel without the prior consent of the Owners (such consent 97
not to be unreasonably withheld); and 98

    (2) ensuring that in the event that the Owners' drug and alcohol policy requires measures to be taken 99
prior to the Crew joining the Vessel, implementing such measures; 100

(b) Crew Insurances 101
(only applicable if Sub-clause 5(a) applies **and** if agreed according to Box 10) 102
The Managers shall throughout the period of this Agreement provide the following services: 103

(i) arranging Crew Insurances in accordance with the best practice of prudent managers of vessels of a 104
similar type to the Vessel, with sound and reputable insurance companies, underwriters or associations. 105
Insurances for any other persons proceeding to sea onboard the Vessel may be separately agreed by 106
the Owners and the Managers (see Box 10); 107

(ii) ensuring that the Owners are aware of the terms, conditions, exceptions and limits of liability of the 108
insurances in Sub-clause 5(b)(i); 109

(iii) ensuring that all premiums or calls in respect of the insurances in Sub-clause 5(b)(i) are paid by their 110
due date; 111

(iv) if obtainable at no additional cost, ensuring that insurances in Sub-clause 5(b)(i) name the Owners as 112
a joint assured with full cover and, unless otherwise agreed, on terms such that Owners shall be under 113
no liability in respect of premiums or calls arising in connection with such insurances. 114

(v) providing written evidence, to the reasonable satisfaction of the Owners, of the Managers' compliance with 115
their obligations under Sub-clauses 5(b)(ii), and 5(b)(iii) within a reasonable time of the commencement 116
of this Agreement, and of each renewal date and, if specifically requested, of each payment date of the 117
insurances in Sub-clause 5(b)(i). 118

6. Commercial Management 119
(only applicable if agreed according to Box 8). 120
The Managers shall provide the following services for the Vessel in accordance with the Owners' instructions, ... 121
which shall include but not be limited to: 122

(a) seeking and negotiating employment for the Vessel and the conclusion (including the execution thereof) 123
of charter parties or other contracts relating to the employment of the Vessel. If such a contract exceeds the 124
period stated in Box 9, consent thereto in writing shall first be obtained from the Owners; 125

(b) arranging for the provision of bunker fuels of the quality specified by the Owners as required for the 126
Vessel's trade; 127

(c) voyage estimating and accounting and calculation of hire, freights, demurrage and/or despatch monies 128
due from or due to the charterers of the Vessel; assisting in the collection of any sums due to the Owners 129

3

related to the commercial operation of the Vessel in accordance with <u>Clause 11</u> (Income Collected and   130
Expenses Paid on Behalf of Owners);   131

If any of the services under Sub-<u>clauses 6(a)</u>, <u>6(b)</u> and <u>6(c)</u> are to be excluded from the Management Fee, remuneration   132
for these services must be stated in Annex E (Fee Schedule). See Sub-<u>clause 12(e)</u>.   133

   (d)   issuing voyage instructions;   134

   (e)   appointing agents;   135

   (f)   appointing stevedores; and   136

   (g)   arranging surveys associated with the commercial operation of the Vessel.   137

7. Insurance Arrangements   138
(only applicable if agreed according to <u>Box 11</u>).   139
The Managers shall arrange insurances in accordance with <u>Clause 10</u> (Insurance Policies), on such terms as   140
the Owners shall have instructed or agreed, in particular regarding conditions, insured values, deductibles,   141
franchises and limits of liability.   142

4

8. Managers' Obligations   143
   (a) The Managers undertake to use their best endeavours to provide the Management Services as agents   144
for and on behalf of the Owners in accordance with sound ship management practice and to protect and   145
promote the interests of the Owners in all matters relating to the provision of services hereunder.   146

   Provided however, that in the performance of their management responsibilities under this Agreement, the   147
Managers shall be entitled to have regard to their overall responsibility in relation to all vessels as may from 148
time to time be entrusted to their management and in particular, but without prejudice to the generality of   149
the foregoing, the Managers shall be entitled to allocate available supplies, manpower and services in such   150
manner as in the prevailing circumstances the Managers in their absolute discretion consider to be fair and   151
reasonable.   152

   (b) Where the Managers are providing technical management services in accordance with Clause 4 (Technical   153
Management), they shall procure that the requirements of the Flag State are satisfied and they shall agree   154
to be appointed as the Company, assuming the responsibility for the operation of the Vessel and taking over   155
the duties and responsibilities imposed by the ISM Code and the ISPS Code, if applicable.   156

9. Owners' Obligations   157
   (a) The Owners shall pay all sums due to the Managers punctually in accordance with the terms of this   158
Agreement. In the event of payment after the due date of any outstanding sums the Manager shall be entitled   159
to charge interest at the rate stated in Box 13.   160

   (b) Where the Managers are providing technical management services in accordance with Clause 4 (Technical   161
Management), the Owners shall: 162

   (i) report (or where the Owners are not the registered owners of the Vessel procure that the registered   163
owners report) to the Flag State administration the details of the Managers as the Company as required   164
to comply with the ISM and ISPS Codes;   165

   (ii) procure that any officers and ratings supplied by them or on their behalf comply with the requirements   166
of STCW 95; and   167

   (iii) instruct such officers and ratings to obey all reasonable orders of the Managers (in their capacity as the   168
Company) in connection with the operation of the Managers' safety management system.   169

   (c) Where the Managers are **not** providing technical management services in accordance with Clause 4   170
(Technical Management), the Owners shall: 171

   (i) procure that the requirements of the Flag State are satisfied and notify the Managers upon execution of   172
this Agreement of the name and contact details of the organization that will be the Company by completing   173
Box 5;   174

   (ii) if the Company changes at any time during this Agreement, notify the Managers in a timely manner of   175
the name and contact details of the new organization;   176

   (iii) procure that the details of the Company, including any change thereof, are reported to the Flag State   177
administration as required to comply with the ISM and ISPS Codes. The Owners shall advise the Managers   178
in a timely manner when the Flag State administration has approved the Company; and   179

   (iv) unless otherwise agreed, arrange for the supply of provisions at their own expense.   180

   (d) Where the Managers are providing crew management services in accordance with Sub-clause 5(a) the   181
Owners shall: 182

   (i) inform the Managers prior to ordering the Vessel to any excluded or additional premium area under   183
any of the Owners' Insurances by reason of war risks and/or piracy or like perils and pay whatever   184
additional costs may properly be incurred by the Managers as a consequence of such orders including,   185
if necessary, the costs of replacing any member of the Crew. Any delays resulting from negotiation   186

5

	with or replacement of any member of the Crew as a result of the Vessel being ordered to such an area	187
	shall be for the Owners' account. Should the Vessel be within an area which becomes an excluded or	188
	additional premium area the above provisions relating to cost and delay shall apply;	189

(ii) agree with the Managers prior to any change of flag of the Vessel and pay whatever additional costs   190
may properly be incurred by the Managers as a consequence of such change. If agreement cannot be   191
reached then either party may terminate this Agreement in accordance with Sub-clause 22(e); and   192

(iii) provide, at no cost to the Managers, in accordance with the requirements of the law of the Flag State,   193
or higher standard, as mutually agreed, adequate Crew accommodation and living standards.   194

(e) Where the Managers are **not** the Company, the Owners shall ensure that Crew are properly familiarised   195
with their duties in accordance with the Vessel's SMS and that instructions which are essential to the SMS   196
are identified, documented and given to the Crew prior to sailing.   197

6

SECTION 4 – Insurance, Budgets, Income, Expenses and Fees

10. Insurance Policies

The Owners shall procure, whether by instructing the Managers under Clause 7 (Insurance Arrangements) or otherwise, that throughout the period of this Agreement: | 198 199 200

(a) at the Owners' expense, the Vessel is insured for not less than its sound market value or entered for its full gross tonnage, as the case may be for: | 201 202

(i) hull and machinery marine risks (including but not limited to crew negligence) and excess liabilities; | 203

(ii) protection and indemnity risks (including but not limited to pollution risks, diversion expenses and, except to the extent insured separately by the Managers in accordance with Sub-clause 5(b)(i), Crew Insurances; | 204 205 206

NOTE: *If the Managers are not providing crew management services under Sub-clause 5(a) (Crew Management) or have agreed not to provide Crew Insurances separately in accordance with Sub-clause 5(b)(i), then such insurances must be included in the protection and indemnity risks cover for the Vessel (see Sub-clause 10(a)(ii) above).* | 207 208 209 210

(iii) war risks (including but not limited to blocking and trapping, protection and indemnity, terrorism and crew risks); and | 211 212

(iv) such optional insurances as may be agreed (such as piracy, kidnap and ransom, loss of hire and FD & D) (see Box 12) | 213 214

Sub-clauses 10(a)(i) through 10(a)(iv) all in accordance with the best practice of prudent owners of vessels of a similar type to the Vessel, with sound and reputable insurance companies, underwriters or associations ("the Owners' Insurances"); | 215 216 217

(b) all premiums and calls on the Owners' Insurances are paid by their due date; | 218

(c) the Owners' Insurances name the Managers and, subject to underwriters' agreement, any third party designated by the Managers as a joint assured, with full cover. It is understood that in some cases, such as protection and indemnity, the normal terms for such cover may impose on the Managers and any such third party a liability in respect of premiums or calls arising in connection with the Owners' Insurances. | 219 220 221 222

If obtainable at no additional cost, however, the Owners shall procure such insurances on terms such that neither the Managers nor any such third party shall be under any liability in respect of premiums or calls arising in connection with the Owners' Insurances. In any event, on termination of this Agreement in accordance with Clause 21 (Duration of the Agreement) and Clause 22 (Termination), the Owners shall procure that the Managers and any third party designated by the Managers as joint assured shall cease to be joint assured and, if reasonably achievable, that they shall be released from any and all liability for premiums and calls that may arise in relation to the period of this Agreement; and | 223 224 225 226 227 228 229

(d) written evidence is provided, to the reasonable satisfaction of the Managers, of the Owners' compliance with their obligations under this Clause 10 within a reasonable time of the commencement of the Agreement, and of each renewal date and, if specifically requested, of each payment date of the Owners' Insurances. | 230 231 232

11. Income Collected and Expenses Paid on Behalf of Owners

(a) Except as provided in Sub-clause 11(c) all monies collected by the Managers under the terms of this Agreement (other than monies payable by the Owners to the Managers) and any interest thereon shall be held to the credit of the Owners in a separate bank account. | 233 234 235 236

(b) All expenses incurred by the Managers under the terms of this Agreement on behalf of the Owners (including expenses as provided in Clause 12(c)) may be debited against the Owners in the account referred to under Sub-clause 11(a) but shall in any event remain payable by the Owners to the Managers on demand. | 237 238 239

(c) All monies collected by the Managers under Clause 6 (Commercial Management) shall be paid into a | 240

7

bank account in the name of the Owners or as may be otherwise advised by the Owners in writing.   241

12. Management Fee and Expenses   242

(a)   The Owners shall pay to the Managers an annual management fee as stated in <u>Box 14</u> for their services   243
as Managers under this Agreement, which shall be payable in equal monthly instalments in advance, the first   244
instalment (pro rata if appropriate) being payable on the commencement of this Agreement (see <u>Clause 2</u>   245
(Commencement and Appointment) and <u>Box 2</u>) and subsequent instalments being payable at the beginning   246
of every calendar month. The management fee shall be payable to the Managers' nominated account stated   247
in <u>Box 15</u>.   248

(b)   The management fee shall be subject to an annual review and the proposed fee shall be presented in   249
the annual budget in accordance with Sub-<u>clause 13</u>(a).   250

(c)   The Managers shall, at no extra cost to the Owners, provide their own office accommodation, office staff,   251
facilities and stationery. Without limiting the generality of this <u>Clause 12</u> (Management Fee and Expenses) the   252
Owners shall reimburse the Managers for postage and communication expenses, travelling expenses, and   253
other out of pocket expenses properly incurred by the Managers in pursuance of the Management Services.   254
Any days used by the Managers' personnel travelling to or from or attending on the Vessel or otherwise used   255
in connection with the Management Services in excess of those agreed in the budget shall be charged at   256
the daily rate stated in <u>Box 16</u>.   257

(d)   If the Owners decide to layup the Vessel and such layup lasts for more than the number of months   258
stated in <u>Box 17</u>, an appropriate reduction of the Management Fee for the period exceeding such period   259
until one month before the Vessel is again put into service shall be mutually agreed between the parties. If   260
the Managers are providing crew management services in accordance with Sub-<u>clause 5(a)</u>, consequential   261
costs of reduction and reinstatement of the Crew shall be for the Owners' account. If agreement cannot be   262
reached then either party may terminate this Agreement in accordance with Sub-<u>clause 22(e)</u>.   263

(e)   Save as otherwise provided in this Agreement, all discounts and commissions obtained by the Managers   264
in the course of the performance of the Management Services shall be credited to the Owners.   265

13. Budgets and Management of Funds   266

(a)   The Managers' initial budget is set out in Annex 'C' hereto. Subsequent budgets shall be for twelve   267
month periods and shall be prepared by the Managers and presented to the Owners not less than three   268
months before the end of the budget year.   269

(b)   The Owners shall state to the Managers in a timely manner, but in any event within one month of   270
presentation, whether or not they agree to each proposed annual budget. The parties shall negotiate in good   271
faith and if they fail to agree on the annual budget, including the management fee, either party may terminate   272
this Agreement in accordance with Sub-<u>clause 22(e)</u>.   273

(c)   Following the agreement of the budget, the Managers shall prepare and present to the Owners their   274
estimate of the working capital requirement for the Vessel and shall each month request the Owners in writing   275
to pay the funds required to run the Vessel for the ensuing month, including the payment of any occasional or   276
extraordinary item of expenditure, such as emergency repair costs, additional insurance premiums, bunkers   277
or provisions. Such funds shall be received by the Managers within ten running days after the receipt by the   278
Owners of the Managers' written request and shall be held to the credit of the Owners in a separate bank   279
account.   280

(d)   The Managers shall at all times maintain and keep true and correct accounts in respect of the Management   281
Services in accordance with the relevant International Financial Reporting Standards or such other standard   282
as the parties may agree, including records of all costs and expenditure incurred, and produce a comparison   283
between budgeted and actual income and expenditure of the Vessel in such form and at such intervals as   284
shall be mutually agreed.   285

The Managers shall make such accounts available for inspection and auditing by the Owners and/or their   286
representatives in the Managers' offices or by electronic means, provided reasonable notice is given by the   287
Owners.   288

(e)   Notwithstanding anything contained herein, the Managers shall in no circumstances be required to use   289

8

or commit their own funds to finance the provision of the Management Services.   290

9

14. Trading Restrictions
If the Managers are providing crew management services in accordance with Sub-clause 5(a) (Crew
Management), the Owners and the Managers will, prior to the commencement of this Agreement, agree on any
trading restrictions to the Vessel that may result from the terms and conditions of the Crew's employment.

291
292
293
294

15. Replacement
If the Managers are providing crew management services in accordance with Sub-clause 5(a) (Crew
Management), the Owners may require the replacement, at their own expense, at the next reasonable
opportunity, of any member of the Crew found on reasonable grounds to be unsuitable for service. If the
Managers have failed to fulfil their obligations in providing suitable qualified Crew within the meaning of Sub-
clause 5(a) (Crew Management), then such replacement shall be at the Managers' expense.

295
296
297
298
299
300

16. Managers' Right to Sub-Contract
The Managers shall not subcontract any of their obligations hereunder without the prior written consent of
the Owners which shall not be unreasonably withheld. In the event of such a sub-contract the Managers
shall remain fully liable for the due performance of their obligations under this Agreement.

301
302
303
304

17. Responsibilities

(a) *Force Majeure*
Neither party shall be liable for any loss, damage or delay due to any of the following force majeure events
and/or conditions to the extent that the party invoking force majeure is prevented or hindered from
performing any or all of their obligations under this Agreement, provided they have made all
reasonable efforts to avoid, minimize or prevent the effect of such events and/or conditions:

305
306
307
308
309
310

(i)　acts of God;

311

(ii)　any Government requisition, control, intervention, requirement or interference;

312

(iii)　any circumstances arising out of war, threatened act of war or warlike operations, acts of terrorism,
sabotage or piracy, or the consequences thereof;

313
314

(iv)　riots, civil commotion, blockades or embargoes;

315

(v)　epidemics;

316

(vi)　earthquakes, landslides, floods or other extraordinary weather conditions;

317

(vii)　strikes, lockouts or other industrial action, unless limited to the employees (which shall not include the
Crew) of the party seeking to invoke force majeure;

318
319

(viii)　fire, accident, explosion except where caused by negligence of the party seeking to invoke force majeure;
and

320
321

(ix)　any other similar cause beyond the reasonable control of either party.

322

(b)　*Liability to Owners*
(i)　Without prejudice to Sub-clause 17(a), the Managers shall be under no liability whatsoever to the Owners
for any loss, damage, delay or expense of whatsoever nature, whether direct or indirect, (including but
not limited to loss of profit arising out of or in connection with detention of or delay to the Vessel) and
howsoever arising in the course of performance of the Management Services UNLESS same is proved
to have resulted solely from the negligence, gross negligence or wilful default of the Managers or their
employees or agents, or sub-contractors employed by them in connection with the Vessel, in which case
(save where loss, damage, delay or expense has resulted from the Managers' personal act or omission
committed with the intent to cause same or recklessly and with knowledge that such loss, damage,
delay or expense would probably result) the Managers' liability for each incident or series of incidents
giving rise to a claim or claims shall never exceed a total of ten (10) times the annual management fee
payable hereunder.

323
324
325
326
327
328
329
330
331
332
333
334

10

(ii)   *Acts or omissions of the Crew* - Notwithstanding anything that may appear to the contrary in this   335
Agreement, the Managers shall not be liable for any acts or omissions of the Crew, even if such acts   336
or omissions are negligent, grossly negligent or wilful, except only to the extent that they are shown to   337
have resulted from a failure by the Managers to discharge their obligations under Clause 5(a) (Crew   338
Management), in which case their liability shall be limited in accordance with the terms of this Clause   339
17 (Responsibilities).   340

(c)   *Indemnity*   341
Except to the extent and solely for the amount therein set out that the Managers would be liable under   342
Sub-clause 17(b), the Owners hereby undertake to keep the Managers and their employees,   343
agents and sub-contractors indemnified and to hold them harmless against all actions, proceedings, claims,   344
demands or liabilities whatsoever or howsoever arising which may be brought against them or incurred or   345
suffered by them arising out of or in connection with the performance of this Agreement, and against and in   346
respect of all costs, loss, damages and expenses (including legal costs and expenses on a full indemnity   347
basis) which the Managers may suffer or incur (either directly or indirectly) in the course of the performance   348
of this Agreement.   349

(d)   *"Himalaya"*   350
It is hereby expressly agreed that no employee or agent of the Managers (including every   351
sub-contractor from time to time employed by the Managers) shall in any circumstances whatsoever be   352
under any liability whatsoever to the Owners for any loss, damage or delay of whatsoever kind arising or   353
resulting directly or indirectly from any act, neglect or default on his part while acting in the course of or in   354
connection with his employment and, without prejudice to the generality of the foregoing provisions in this   355
Clause 17 (Responsibilities), every exemption, limitation, condition and liberty herein contained and every   356
right, exemption from liability, defence and immunity of whatsoever nature applicable to the Managers or to   357
which the Managers are entitled hereunder shall also be available and shall extend to protect every such   358
employee or agent of the Managers acting as aforesaid and for the purpose of all the foregoing provisions   359
of this Clause 17 (Responsibilities) the Managers are or shall be deemed to be acting as agent or trustee   360
on behalf of and for the benefit of all persons who are or might be their servants or agents from time to time   361
(including sub-contractors as aforesaid) and all such persons shall to this extent be or be deemed to be   362
parties to this Agreement.   363

18. General Administration   364
(a)   The Managers shall keep the Owners and, if appropriate, the Company informed in a timely manner of   365
any incident of which the Managers become aware which gives or may give rise to delay to the Vessel or   366
claims or disputes involving third parties.   367

(b)   The Managers shall handle and settle all claims and disputes arising out of the Management Services   368
hereunder, unless the Owners instruct the Managers otherwise. The Managers shall keep the Owners   369
appropriately informed in a timely manner throughout the handling of such claims and disputes.   370

(c)   The Owners may request the Managers to bring or defend other actions, suits or proceedings related   371
to the Management Services, on terms to be agreed.   372

(d)   The Managers shall have power to obtain appropriate legal or technical or other outside expert advice in   373
relation to the handling and settlement of claims in relation to Sub-clauses 18(a) and 18(b) and disputes and   374
any other matters affecting the interests of the Owners in respect of the Vessel, unless the Owners instruct   375
the Managers otherwise.   376

(e)   On giving reasonable notice, the Owners may request, and the Managers shall in a timely manner make   377
available, all documentation, information and records in respect of the matters covered by this Agreement   378
either related to mandatory rules or regulations or other obligations applying to the Owners in respect of   379
the Vessel (including but not limited to STCW 95, the ISM Code and ISPS Code) to the extent permitted by   380
relevant legislation.   381

On giving reasonable notice, the Managers may request, and the Owners shall in a timely manner make   382
available, all documentation, information and records reasonably required by the Managers to enable them   383
to perform the Management Services.   384

11

(f) The Owners shall arrange for the provision of any necessary guarantee bond or other security. 385

(g) Any costs incurred by the Managers in carrying out their obligations according to this Clause 18 (General 386
Administration) shall be reimbursed by the Owners. 387

19. Inspection of Vessel 388
The Owners may at any time after giving reasonable notice to the Managers inspect the Vessel for any reason 389
they consider necessary. 390

20. Compliance with Laws and Regulations 391
The parties will not do or permit to be done anything which might cause any breach or infringement of the 392
laws and regulations of the Flag State, or of the places where the Vessel trades. 393

21. Duration of the Agreement 394
(a) This Agreement shall come into effect at the date stated in Box 2 and shall continue until terminated by 395
either party by giving notice to the other; in which event this Agreement shall terminate upon the expiration 396
of the later of the number of months stated in Box 18 or a period of two (2) months from the date on which 397
such notice is received, unless terminated earlier in accordance with Clause 22 (Termination). 398

(b) Where the Vessel is not at a mutually convenient port or place on the expiry of such period, this Agreement 399
shall terminate on the subsequent arrival of the Vessel at the next mutually convenient port or place. 400

22. Termination 401
(a) *Owners' or Managers' default* 402
If either party fails to meet their obligations under this Agreement, the other party may give notice to the 403
party in default requiring them to remedy it. In the event that the party in default fails to remedy it within a 404
reasonable time to the reasonable satisfaction of the other party, that party shall be entitled to terminate this 405
Agreement with immediate effect by giving notice to the party in default. 406

(b) *Notwithstanding Sub-clause 22(a):* 407

(i) The Managers shall be entitled to terminate the Agreement with immediate effect by giving notice to the 408
Owners if any monies payable by the Owners and/or the owners of any associated vessel, details of 409
which are listed in Annex "D", shall not have been received in the Managers' nominated account within 410
ten (10) days of receipt by the Owners of the Managers' written request, or if the Vessel is repossessed by 411
the Mortgagee(s). 412

(ii) If the Owners proceed with the employment of or continue to employ the Vessel in the carriage of 413
contraband, blockade running, or in an unlawful trade, or on a voyage which in the reasonable opinion 414
of the Managers is unduly hazardous or improper, the Managers may give notice of the default to the 415
Owners, requiring them to remedy it as soon as practically possible. In the event that the Owners fail to 416
remedy it within a reasonable time to the satisfaction of the Managers, the Managers shall be entitled 417
to terminate the Agreement with immediate effect by notice. 418

(iii) If either party fails to meet their respective obligations under Sub-clause 5(b) (Crew Insurances) and 419
Clause 10 (Insurance Policies), the other party may give notice to the party in default requiring them to 420
remedy it within ten (10) days, failing which the other party may terminate this Agreement with immediate 421
effect by giving notice to the party in default. 422

(c) *Extraordinary Termination* 423
This Agreement shall be deemed to be terminated in the case of the sale of the Vessel or, if the Vessel 424
becomes a total loss or is declared as a constructive or compromised or arranged total loss or is requisitioned 425
or has been declared missing or, if bareboat chartered, unless otherwise agreed, when the bareboat charter 426
comes to an end. 427

(d) *For the purpose of Sub-clause 22(c) hereof:* 428

(i) the date upon which the Vessel is to be treated as having been sold or otherwise disposed of shall be 429
the date on which the Vessel's owners cease to be the registered owners of the Vessel; 430

(ii) the Vessel shall be deemed to be lost either when it has become an actual total loss or agreement has 431
been reached with the Vessel's underwriters in respect of its constructive total loss or if such agreement 432

12

with the Vessel's underwriters is not reached it is adjudged by a competent tribunal that a constructive | 433
loss of the Vessel has occurred; and | 434

(iii) the date upon which the Vessel is to be treated as declared missing shall be ten (10) days after the Vessel | 435
was last reported or when the Vessel is recorded as missing by the Vessel's underwriters, whichever | 436
occurs first. A missing vessel shall be deemed lost in accordance with the provisions of Sub-clause 22(d) | 437
(ii). | 438

(e) In the event the parties fail to agree the annual budget in accordance with Sub-clause 13(b), or to agree | 439
a change of flag in accordance with Sub-clause 9(d)(ii), or to agree to a reduction in the Mangement Fee in | 440
accordance with Sub-clause 12(d), either party may terminate this Agreement by giving the other party not | 441
less than one month's notice, the result of which will be the expiry of the Agreement at the end of the current | 442
budget period or on expiry of the notice period, whichever is the later. | 443

(f) This Agreement shall terminate forthwith in the event of an order being made or resolution passed | 444
for the winding up, dissolution, liquidation or bankruptcy of either party (otherwise than for the purpose of | 445
reconstruction or amalgamation) or if a receiver or administrator is appointed, or if it suspends payment, | 446
ceases to carry on business or makes any special arrangement or composition with its creditors. | 447

(g) In the event of the termination of this Agreement for any reason other than default by the Managers the | 448
management fee payable to the Managers according to the provisions of Clause 12 (Management Fee and | 449
Expenses), shall continue to be payable for a further period of the number of months stated in Box 19 as | 450
from the effective date of termination. If Box 19 is left blank then ninety (90) days shall apply. | 451

(h) In addition, where the Managers provide Crew for the Vessel in accordance with Clause 5(a) (Crew | 452
Management): | 453

(i) the Owners shall continue to pay Crew Support Costs during the said further period of the number of | 454
months stated in Box 19; and | 455

(ii) the Owners shall pay an equitable proportion of any Severance Costs which may be incurred, not | 456
exceeding the amount stated in Box 20. The Managers shall use their reasonable endeavours to minimise | 457
such Severance Costs. | 458

(i) On the termination, for whatever reason, of this Agreement, the Managers shall release to the Owners, | 459
if so requested, the originals where possible, or otherwise certified copies, of all accounts and all documents | 460
specifically relating to the Vessel and its operation. | 461

(j) The termination of this Agreement shall be without prejudice to all rights accrued due between the parties | 462
prior to the date of termination. | 463

23. BIMCO Dispute Resolution Clause | 464
(a) This Agreement shall be governed by and construed in accordance with English law and any dispute | 465
arising out of or in connection with this Agreement shall be referred to arbitration in London in accordance with | 466
the Arbitration Act 1996 or any statutory modification or re-enactment thereof save to the extent necessary | 467
to give effect to the provisions of this Clause. | 468

The arbitration shall be conducted in accordance with the London Maritime Arbitrators Association (LMAA) | 469
Terms current at the time when the arbitration proceedings are commenced. | 470

The reference shall be to three arbitrators. A party wishing to refer a dispute to arbitration shall appoint its | 471
arbitrator and send notice of such appointment in writing to the other party requiring the other party to appoint | 472
its own arbitrator within 14 calendar days of that notice and stating that it will appoint its arbitrator as sole | 473
arbitrator unless the other party appoints its own arbitrator and gives notice that it has done so within the | 474
14 days specified. If the other party does not appoint its own arbitrator and give notice that it has done so | 475
within the 14 days specified, the party referring a dispute to arbitration may, without the requirement of any | 476
further prior notice to the other party, appoint its arbitrator as sole arbitrator and shall advise the other party | 477
accordingly. The award of a sole arbitrator shall be binding on both parties as if he had been appointed by | 478
agreement. | 479

Nothing herein shall prevent the parties agreeing in writing to vary these provisions to provide for the | 480

13

appointment of a sole arbitrator. 481

In cases where neither the claim nor any counterclaim exceeds the sum of USD50,000 (or such other sum 482
as the parties may agree) the arbitration shall be conducted in accordance with the LMAA Small Claims 483
Procedure current at the time when the arbitration proceedings are commenced. 484

(b) This Agreement shall be governed by and construed in accordance with Title 9 of the United States Code 485
and the Maritime Law of the United States and any dispute arising out of or in connection with this Agreement 486
shall be referred to three persons at New York, one to be appointed by each of the parties hereto, and the 487
third by the two so chosen; their decision or that of any two of them shall be final, and for the purposes of 488
enforcing any award, judgment may be entered on an award by any court of competent jurisdiction. The 489
proceedings shall be conducted in accordance with the rules of the Society of Maritime Arbitrators, Inc. 490

In cases where neither the claim nor any counterclaim exceeds the sum of USD50,000 (or such other sum 491
as the parties may agree) the arbitration shall be conducted in accordance with the Shortened Arbitration 492
Procedure of the Society of Maritime Arbitrators, Inc. current at the time when the arbitration proceedings 493
are commenced. 494

(c) This Agreement shall be governed by and construed in accordance with the laws of the place mutually 495
agreed by the parties and any dispute arising out of or in connection with this Agreement shall be referred 496
to arbitration at a mutually agreed place, subject to the procedures applicable there. 497

(d) Notwithstanding Sub-clauses 23(a), 23(b) or 23(c) above, the parties may agree at any time to refer to 498
mediation any difference and/or dispute arising out of or in connection with this Agreement. 499

(i) In the case of a dispute in respect of which arbitration has been commenced under Sub-clauses 23(a), 500
23(b) or 23(c) above, the following shall apply: 501

(ii) Either party may at any time and from time to time elect to refer the dispute or part of the dispute to 502
mediation by service on the other party of a written notice (the "Mediation Notice") calling on the other 503
party to agree to mediation. 504

(iii) The other party shall thereupon within 14 calendar days of receipt of the Mediation Notice confirm that 505
they agree to mediation, in which case the parties shall thereafter agree a mediator within a further 14 506
calendar days, failing which on the application of either party a mediator will be appointed promptly by 507
the Arbitration Tribunal ("the Tribunal") or such person as the Tribunal may designate for that purpose. 508
The mediation shall be conducted in such place and in accordance with such procedure and on such 509
terms as the parties may agree or, in the event of disagreement, as may be set by the mediator. 510

(iv) If the other party does not agree to mediate, that fact may be brought to the attention of the Tribunal 511
and may be taken into account by the Tribunal when allocating the costs of the arbitration as between 512
the parties. 513

(v) The mediation shall not affect the right of either party to seek such relief or take such steps as it considers 514
necessary to protect its interest. 515

(vi) Either party may advise the Tribunal that they have agreed to mediation. The arbitration procedure shall 516
continue during the conduct of the mediation but the Tribunal may take the mediation timetable into 517
account when setting the timetable for steps in the arbitration. 518

(vii) Unless otherwise agreed or specified in the mediation terms, each party shall bear its own costs incurred 519
in the mediation and the parties shall share equally the mediator's costs and expenses. 520

(viii) The mediation process shall be without prejudice and confidential and no information or documents 521
disclosed during it shall be revealed to the Tribunal except to the extent that they are disclosable under 522
the law and procedure governing the arbitration. 523

(Note: The parties should be aware that the mediation process may not necessarily interrupt time limits.) 524

(e) If Box 21 in Part I is not appropriately filled in, Sub-clause 23(a) of this Clause shall apply. 525

Note: Sub-clauses 23(a), 23(b) and 23(c) are alternatives; indicate alternative agreed in Box 21. Sub-clause 526

14

23(d) shall apply in all cases.   527

24. Notices   528

(a) All notices given by either party or their agents to the other party or their agents in accordance with the   529
provisions of this Agreement shall be in writing and shall, unless specifically provided in this Agreement to   530
the contrary, be sent to the address for that other party as set out in Boxes 22 and 23 or as appropriate or   531
to such other address as the other party may designate in writing.   532

A notice may be sent by registered or recorded mail, facsimile, electronically or delivered by hand in accordance   533
with this Sub-clause 24(a).   534

(b) Any notice given under this Agreement shall take effect on receipt by the other party and shall be deemed   535
to have been received: 536

(i) if posted, on the seventh (7th) day after posting;   537

(ii) if sent by facsimile or electronically, on the day of transmission; and   538

(iii) if delivered by hand, on the day of delivery.   539

And in each case proof of posting, handing in or transmission shall be proof that notice has been given,   540
unless proven to the contrary.   541

25. Entire Agreement   542

This Agreement constitutes the entire agreement between the parties and no promise, undertaking,   543
representation, warranty or statement by either party prior to the date stated in Box 2 shall affect this   544
Agreement. Any modification of this Agreement shall not be of any effect unless in writing signed by or on   545
behalf of the parties.   546

26. Third Party Rights   547

Except to the extent provided in Sub-clauses 17(c) (Indemnity) and 17(d) (Himalaya), no third parties may   548
enforce any term of this Agreement.   549

27. Partial Validity   550

If any provision of this Agreement is or becomes or is held by any arbitrator or other competent body to be   551
illegal, invalid or unenforceable in any respect under any law or jurisdiction, the provision shall be deemed   552
to be amended to the extent necessary to avoid such illegality, invalidity or unenforceability, or, if such   553
amendment is not possible, the provision shall be deemed to be deleted from this Agreement to the extent   554
of such illegality, invalidity or unenforceability, and the remaining provisions shall continue in full force and   555
effect and shall not in any way be affected or impaired thereby.   556

28. Interpretation   557

In this Agreement: 558

(a) *Singular/Plural*   559
The singular includes the plural and vice versa as the context admits or requires.   560

(b) *Headings*   561
The index and headings to the clauses and appendices to this Agreement are for convenience only and shall not affect   562
its construction or interpretation.   563

(c) *Day*   564
"Day" means a calendar day unless expressly stated to the contrary.   565

15

InterManager

Approved by the International Ship Managers' Association

First published 1988. Revised 1998 and 2009

Explanatory Notes for SHIPMAN 2009 are available from BIMCO at www.bimco.org

Copyright, published by BIMCO

ANNEX "A" (DETAILS OF VESSEL OR VESSELS)
TO THE BIMCO STANDARD SHIP MANAGEMENT AGREEMENT
CODE NAME: SHIPMAN 2009

Date of Agreement:

Name of Vessel(s):

Particulars of Vessel(s):

Continued

ANNEX "B" (DETAILS OF CREW)
TO THE BIMCO STANDARD SHIP MANAGEMENT AGREEMENT
CODE NAME: SHIPMAN 2009

Date of Agreement:

Details of Crew:

Numbers   Rank   Nationality

Continued

ANNEX "C" (BUDGET)
TO THE BIMCO STANDARD SHIP MANAGEMENT AGREEMENT
CODE NAME: SHIPMAN 2009

Date of Agreement:

Managers' Initial budget with effect from the commencement date of this Agreement (see **Box 2**):

Continued

InterManager

Approved by the International Ship Managers' Association

First published 1988. Revised 1998 and 2009

Explanatory Notes for SHIPMAN 2009 are available from BIMCO at www.bimco.org

Copyright, published by BIMCO

ANNEX "D" (ASSOCIATED VESSELS)
TO THE BIMCO STANDARD SHIP MANAGEMENT AGREEMENT
CODE NAME: SHIPMAN 2009

NOTE: PARTIES SHOULD BE AWARE THAT BY COMPLETING THIS ANNEX "D" THEY WILL BE SUBJECT TO THE PROVISIONS OF SUB-CLAUSE 22(b)(i) OF THIS AGREEMENT.

Date of Agreement:

Details of Associated Vessels:

Continued

ANNEX "E" (FEE SCHEDULE)
TO THE BIMCO STANDARD SHIP MANAGEMENT AGREEMENT
CODE NAME: SHIPMAN 2009

Continued

Measurements

Conversion Factors*

Weight (GB & US)

1 English or long ton = 2,240 pounds (lb) = 1.12 American or short tons = 1.01605 tonnes or metric tonnes (or metric tons in the USA) = 1016.05 kilograms (kg)

1 American or short ton = 2000 pounds (lb) = 0.892857 English or long tons = 0.90718 tonnes or metric tonnes (or metric tons in the USA)

1 tonne or metric tonne (or metric ton in the USA) = 1000 kilograms = 2204.621 pounds (lb) = 0.98421 English or long ton = 1.10231 American or short tons

1 stone = 14 pounds (lb) = 6.356 kilograms

1 pounds (lb) = 16 ounces = 0.454 kilogram

1 ounce = 28.35 grams

1 gram = 0.035 ounce

1 kilogram = 1000 grams = 2.205 pounds (lb)

Length (GB & US)

1 league = 3 miles = 4.828 kilometres

1 mile = 8 furlongs = 1,760 yards = 1.609 kilometres

1 furlong = 220 yards = 201.17 metres

1 yard = 3 feet = 0.914 metre

1 foot = 12 inches = 30.48 centimetres

1 inch = 2.54 centimetres

1 kilometre = 0.621 mile

1 metre = 1.094 yards = 3.281 feet

1 centimetre = 0.394 inch = 0.033 foot

---

* Source: Rankin, K. (1995) *Thomas' Stowage: The Properties and Stowage of Cargoes* (p. 363); Hornby, A.S. (1989) *Oxford Advanced Learner's Dictionary* (pp. 1529–1530); Packard, W. (1985) *Sea – Trading: Cargoes* (pp. 142–143) (www.clarksons.net); Giziakis K., Papadopoulos A. and Plomaritou E. (2010) *Chartering* (3rd edition, pp. 1257–1258).

1   millimetre = 0.0394 inch
1   nautical mile = 1.852 kilometres

Volume (GB & US)

1   cubic foot = 1,728 cubic inches = 0.028 cubic metre
1   cubic metre = 35.315 cubic feet
1   cubic inch = 16.387 cubic centimetres
1   cubic centimetre = 0.061 cubic inch

Liquid Volume (GB & US)

1   imperial gallon (GB) = 8 imperial pints = 4.546 litres
1   US gallon = 8 US pints = 3.785 litres
1   litre = 0.220 imperial gallons = 0.264 US gallons
1   oil barrel (bbl) = 42 US gallons = 159 litres = 35 imperial gallons
1   tonne = between 6 and 8 barrels (bbl) depending on density of the petro-
    leum variety

Stowage Factors*

The stowage factor of any commodity is the figure which expresses the number
of cubic metres per tonne (metric) or cubic feet per ton of 2,240 lb, which will
occupy in stowage and should include a proper allowance for broken stowage
and dunnage. On the other hand, liquids fill the tank into which they are put.
For this reason the number of tonnes (metric) per cubic metre (specific gravity)
for the temperatures of the liquid is considered in preference to the stowage
factor.

Commodity	cub. ft/long ton	cub. mt/metric tonne
Asphalt (bulk)	33–36	0.94–0.98
Bauxite (bulk)	25–31	0.70–0.85
Cement (bulk)	20–36	0.60–1.00
Coal (bulk)	38–50	1.08–1.39
Coke (bulk)	45–65	1.25–1.80
Cork (pressed bales)	200	5.57
Fertilizers (bags)	50–60	1.39–1.67
Grain – Barley (bulk)	48–54	1.34–1.50
Grain – Barley (bags)	52–60	1.45–1.67

* Source: Rankin, K. (1995) *Thomas' Stowage: The Properties and Stowage of Cargoes* (pp. 125–
350); Alderton, P. (1984) *Sea Transport: Operations and Economics* (p. 238); Baroutakis, M. (1991)
Shipping Guide and Manual (pp. 164–180); Giziakis, K., Papadopoulos, A. and Plomaritou, E.
(2010) *Chartering* (3rd edition, p. 1259).

Commodity	cub. ft/long ton	cub. mt/metric tonne
Grain – Wheat (bulk)	45–50	1.25–1.39
Grain – Wheat (bags)	48–53	1.34–1.48
Grain (heavy)	45	1.30
Iron Ore (bulk)	14	0.40
Iron, Pig (bulk)	10–12	0.28–0.33
Pulpwood (average)	120–150	3.34–4.18
Salt	29–40	0.81–1.12
Wood Chips	110–160	3.07–4.46
Containers (TEU)	56–105	1.6–3.0
Cars	150	4.2
Light Crude Oil	37.6	1.07
Heavy Crude Oil	33.7	0.95
Water	35.3	1

1 cubic foot per ton = 0.02788 cubic metres per tonne
1 cubic metre per tonne = 35.88 cubic feet per ton

Distance Table*

Route		Distance (miles)	
Gibraltar to	Piraeus	1481	miles
	Port Said	1313	"
	Panama	4340	"
	New York	3145	"
	Cape Town	5190	"
Suez to	Kuwait	3199	miles
	Calcutta	4604	"
	Sydney	8233	"
	Tokyo	7853	"
Panama to	San Francisco	3245	miles
	Yokohama	7680	"
	Hong Kong	9194	"
	Sydney	7680	"
	Vancouver	4022	"
London to	Panama	4720	miles
	New York	3200	"
	Gibraltar	1301	"
	Buenos Aires	6330	"
	Cape Horn	7510	"
New York to	Panama	1972	miles
	New Orleans	1707	"
	Hong Kong	11230	"
	Montevideo	5750	"

* Source: Alderton, P. (1984) *Sea Transport: Operations and Economics* (p. 257); Giziakis, K., Papadopoulos, A. and Plomaritou E. (2010) *Chartering* (3rd edition, p. 1260).

Decimal Parts of a Day

Hours		Minutes							
1	.041666	1	.000694	25	.017361	49	.034027
2	.083333	2	.001388	26	.018055	50	.034722
3	.125	3	.002083	27	.018749	51	.035416
4	.166666	4	.002777	28	.019444	52	.036111
5	.208333	5	.003472	29	.020138	53	.036805
6	.25	6	.004166	30	.020833	54	.037499
7	.291666	7	.004861	31	.021527	55	.038194
8	.333333	8	.005555	32	.022222	56	.038888
9	.375	9	.006249	33	.022916	57	.039583
10	.416666	10	.006944	34	.023611	58	.040277
11	.458333	11	.007638	35	.024305	59	.040972
12	.5	12	.008333	36	.024999	60	.041666
13	.541666	13	.009027	37	.025694		
14	.583333	14	.009722	38	.026388		
15	.625	15	.010416	39	.027083		
16	.666666	16	.011111	40	.027777		
17	.708333	17	.011805	41	.028472		
18	.75	18	.012499	42	.029166		
19	.791666	19	.013194	43	.029861		
20	.833333	20	.013888	44	.030555		
21	.875	21	.014583	45	.031249		
22	.916666	22	.015277	46	.031944		
23	.958333	23	.015972	47	.032638		
24	1.0	24	.016666	48	.033333		

BIBLIOGRAPHY

- ABB (2014) *Shaft Generator Drive for Marine: Decreasing Emissions, Improving Safety* (www.abb.com/marine)
- Alderton, P. (2011) *Sea Transport: Operations and Economics* (Thomas Reed Publications)
- Baughen, S. (2015) *Shipping Law* (Routledge-Cavendish, 6th edition)
- Baltic Exchange (2014) *The Baltic Code 2014* (www.balticexchange.com)
- Baltic Exchange (2015) *Manual for Panellists: A Guide to Freight Reporting and Index Production* (www.balticexchange.com, January 2015)
- BBC Chartering (2015) *Chartering Terms* (www.bbc-chartering.com)
- BIMCO (1993) *BIMCO Bulletin* (vol. 2/93)
- BIMCO (1995) *BIMCO Bulletin* (vol. 90, No. 3/95)
- BIMCO (2005) *BIMCO Ice Clauses* (BIMCO Special Circular No. 1, 24 February 2005)
- BIMCO (1998) *BIMCO Standard ISM Clause for Voyage and Time Charterparties* (BIMCO Special Circular No. 1, 4 February 1998)
- BIMCO (1992) *Check Before Fixing* (Denmark, BIMCO Informatique A/S)
- BIMCO (2017) *Check Before Fixing* (Denmark, BIMCO Informatique A/S)
- BIMCO (2013) *Laytime Definitions for Charter Parties 2013* (Special Circular No. 8, 10 September 2013)
- BIMCO (2013) *Revised Piracy Clauses* (BIMCO Special Circular No. 7, 19 July 2013)
- BIMCO, CMI, FONASBA, INTERCARGO (1993) *Voylarules '93* (Voyage Charter Party Laytime Interpretation Rules 1993)
- Bishop, B. (2004) "Key Operational Issues Facing the Tanker Industry Today" *Intertanko Seminar: The Tanker World Today*
- Black, J., Hashimzade, N., Myles, G. (2009) *Contango. A Dictionary of Economics* (Oxford University Press, 3rd edition)
- Bolero International (2016) *Electronic Bills of Lading are Part of the Quiet Revolution in World Trade* (www.bolero.net, accessed 21 November 2016)

- Bonnick, S. (1988) *Gram on Chartering Documents* (London, Lloyd's of London Press Ltd., 2nd edition)
- Branch, A. and Robarts, M. (2014) *Branch's Elements of Shipping* (London, Routledge, 9th edition)
- Branch, A. (1988) *Economics of Shipping Practice & Management* (Chapman and Hall, 2nd edition)
- Branch, A. (1995) *Dictionary of Shipping, International Business, Trade Terms and Abbreviations* (London, Witherby, 4th edition)
- Branch, A. (1998) *Maritime Economics* (Cheltenham, Stanley Thornes Ltd., 3rd edition)
- Brodie, P. (2013) *Commercial Shipping Handbook* (London, Routledge, 2nd edition)
- Cambridge Academy of Transport (2000) *Anatomy of Shipping* (seminar proceedings, 10–22 September 2000)
- Cariou, P. and Wolff F-C. (2011) "Ship-owners' Decision to Outsource Vessel Management" *Transport Reviews* (31[6], 709–724)
- Carpenter, W. (2015) *The World's Biggest State Owned Oil Companies* (www.investopedia.com)
- Carr, I. and Stone, P. (2014) *International Trade Law* (England, Routledge, 5th edition)
- Chitty, J.W. (2008) Bareboat Charters: Can a Shipowner Limit Liability to Third Parties? *Georgia State University Law Review* (Vol. 25, Issue 2, Article 2)
- Clarksons Research Services *Container Intelligence Monthly* (https://sin.clarksons.net)
- Clarksons Research Services *Dry Bulk Trade Outlook* (https://sin.clarksons.net)
- Clarksons Research Services *Oil and Tanker Trades Outlook* (https://sin.clarksons.net)
- Clarkson Research Services *Shipping Intelligence Weekly* (https://sin.clarksons.net)
- Clarksons Research Services *Shipping Review and Outlook* (https://sin.clarksons.net)
- Collins, N. (2000) *The Essential Guide to Chartering and the Dry Freight Market* (London, Clarkson Research Studies)
- Cooke, J., Young, T., Ashcroft, M., Taylor, A., Kimball, J., Martowski, D., Lambert, L.R. and Sturley M. (2014) *Voyage Charters* (England, Informa Law from Routledge, 4th edition)
- Cooke, J., Young, T., Taylor, A., Kimball, J., Martowski, D. Lambert, L.R. and Sturley M. (1993) *Voyage Charters* (London, Lloyd's of London Press)
- Coulson, E.C. (1995) *A Guide for Tanker Brokers* (London, Clarkson Research Studies)
- Coulter, D., Coulter, B., Darden, W. and Brown, G. (1989) "Freight Transportation Carrier Selection Criteria: Identification of Service

Dimensions for Competitive Positioning" *Journal of Business Research* (Vol. 19)

- De Zwarte, E. (2007) *There is so Much More in Laytime* (Ireland, Arklow Co. Wicklow)
- Dickie, J.W. (2014) *21st Century Ship Management* (London, Bloomsbury Publishing)
- Drewry Maritime Research (2015) *Ship Operating Costs 2015–2016. Annual Review & Forecast.* (www.drewry.co.uk)
- Drewry Shipping Consultants *Shipping Market Reports* (www.drewry.co.uk)
- Drewry Shipping Consultants *Shipping Insight* (www.drewry.co.uk)
- Eder, B., Bennett, H., Berry, S., Foxton, D. and Smith, C. (2011) *Scrutton on Charterparties and Bills of Lading* (London, Sweet & Maxwell, 22nd edition)
- Evans, J.J. and Marlow, P.B. (1990) *Quantitative Methods in Maritime Economics* (London, Fairplay Publications, 2nd edition)
- Eversheds Sutherland (2016) *Shipping: BPVOY5 to Take Effect on 21 March 2016* (United Kingdom, www.eversheds-sutherland.com)
- FONASBA (2012) *The Role, Responsibilities and Obligations of the Ship Agent in the International Transport Chain* (www.fonasba.com/wp-content/uploads/2012/10/Role-of-Agent-Final1.pdf)
- Furmston, O. and Hosking, B. (2015) *Speed and Performance Claims* (The Standard Club, March 2015, www.standard-club.com)
- Gaskell, N.J.J., Debatista, C. and Swatton, R.J. (1992) *Chorley and Giles' Shipping Law* (London, Pitman Publishing, 8th edition)
- Giziakis, K., Papadopoulos, A. and Plomaritou, E. (2010) *Chartering* (Athens, Stamoulis Publications, 3rd edition, in Greek)
- Gorton, L. and Ihre, R. (1990) *A Practical Guide to Contracts of Affreightment and Hybrid Contracts* (Lloyd's of London Press Limited)
- Haugen Consulting (2017) *What is Demurrage?* (15 June 2017, www.haugenconsulting.com)
- Heaver, T. (2002) "Supply Chain and Logistics Management: Implications for Liner Shipping" in Grammenos, C.T. *The Handbook of Maritime Economics and Business* (London, Lloyd's of London Press Ltd., 1st edition)
- Hess, J. (2004) "Tanker Management and Self Assessment: ISM is not Enough" *Safety Management Systems*, (LLC, 12 October 2004)
- Hill Dickinson (2009) *Cargo Conventions: Comparing Hague, Hague-Visby, Hamburg and Rotterdam Rules* (Hill Dickinson LLP, www.lmalloyds.com and www.hilldickinson.com)
- Hill, C. (1998) *Maritime Law* (London, Lloyd's of London Press Ltd., 5th edition)
- Hosking, B. and Furmston, O. (2016) *The Inter-Club Agreement* (The Standard Club Ltd, www.standard-club.com)

- Hudson, N.G. and Harvey, M.D. (2010) *The York-Antwerp Rules: The Principles and Practice of General Average Adjustment* (England, Informa Law from Routledge, 3rd edition)
- IMO (2016) *Carriage of Chemicals by Ship and IBC Code* (www.imo. org, 12 November 2016)
- International Chamber of Commerce (2006) *ICC's New Rules on Documentary Credits Now Available* (www.iccwbo.org, Paris, 4 December 2006)
- International Chamber of Commerce (2017) *The Incoterms® Rules* (www.iccwbo.org, 1 January 2017)
- Intertanko (2011) *Shifting off a Berth due to Weather/Sea Conditions – Charterparty Provisions Compared* (www.intertanko.com, 3 October 2011)
- Ivamy, H. (1989) *Payne and Ivamy's Carriage of Goods by Sea* (London, Butterworths, 13th edition)
- Kapoor, P. (1993) *The Fairplay Book of Shipping Abbreviations* (Fairplay Publications Ltd)
- Kemp, J.F., Barrass, C.B. and Young, P. (2001) *Ship Stability. Notes & Examples* (Oxford, Butterworth-Heinmann, 3rd edition)
- Lopez, J.N. (1992) *Bes' Chartering and Shipping Terms* (London, Barker & Howard Ltd, 11th edition)
- Marsoft *Container Market Report* (www.marsoft.com)
- Marsoft *Dry Bulk Market Report* (www.marsoft.com)
- Marsoft *Tanker Market Report* (www.marsoft.com)
- Mayer, R.A. (2013) *International Business Law: Text, Cases and Readings* (England, Harlow Pearson, 6th edition)
- McConville, J. (1999) *Economics of Maritime Transport – Theory and Practice* (London, Witherby and Co. Ltd, 1st edition)
- Mocatta, A., Mustill, M. and Boyd, S. (1984) *Scrutton on Charterparties and Bills of Lading* (London, Sweet & Maxwell, 9th edition)
- Norwegian Hull Club (2016) *York Antwerp Rules 2016 Finally Approved* (www.norclub.no, 12 May 2016)
- Packard, W. (1986) *Sea Trading: Trading* (Surrey, Fairplay Publications)
- Packard, W. (1993) *Laytime Calculating* (Surrey, Fairplay Publications)
- Packard, W. (1996) *Voyage Estimating* (Surrey, Fairplay Publications)
- Plomaritou, E. (2004) "Marketing of Shipping Companies: A Necessity in Modern Shipping Business" *Economic Outlook* (December 2004, Issue 4696, No. 87, p. 14)
- Plomaritou, E. (2005) *Marketing of Shipping Companies as a Tool for Improvement of Chartering Policy. A Comparative Analysis of Marketing Implementation in Bulk and Liner Shipping Companies Worldwide and in Greece: A Case Study in Containership Market and Tanker Market* (PhD Thesis, University of Piraeus)
- Plomaritou, E. (2005) "Marketing: The Greek Way" *Shipping Network* (London, Institute of Chartered Shipbrokers, No 1, Issue 6)

- Plomaritou, E. (2006) "An Empirical Research of Marketing Strategies of the Leading Shipping Companies in the World" *International Shipping Conference: Shipping in the Era of Social Responsibility* (University of Piraeus, Ionian University, University of the Aegean, Cephalonia, 14–16 November 2006)
- Plomaritou, E. (2006) *Marketing of Shipping Companies* (Athens, Stamoulis Publications, in Greek)
- Plomaritou, E. (2006) "The Application of Marketing Philosophies and Policies to Shipping Companies" *Cyprus Journal of Science and Technology* (Vol. 5, No. 4)
- Plomaritou, E. (2006) "The Differentiation Strategies of the Leading Shipping Companies in the World" *Economic Outlook* (April 2006, No. 102)
- Plomaritou, E. (2007) "A Quantitative Research of Marketing Implementation in the Greek Shipping Company" *Cyprus Journal of Science and Technology* (Vol. 5, No. 4)
- Plomaritou, E. (2008) "A Proposed Application of the Marketing Mix Concept to Tramp and Liner Shipping Companies" *Management – Journal of Contemporary Management Issues* (Vol. 13, No. 1)
- Plomaritou, E. (2008) *Marketing of Shipping Companies: A Tool for Improvement of Chartering Policy* (Recommended by the Institute of Chartered Shipbrokers, Athens, Stamoulis Publications)
- Plomaritou, E. (2014) "A Review of Shipowner's & Charterer's Obligations in Various Types of Charter" *Journal of Shipping & Ocean Engineering* (Vol. 4, Issue 11–12)
- Plomaritou, E. (2015) *Charterparty Contract* (London, Lloyd's Maritime Academy, Module 4 of Distance Learning Course "Postgraduate Diploma in Maritime Law")
- Plomaritou, E. (2015) *Calculating Laytime* (London, Lloyd's Maritime Academy, Module 3 of Distance Learning Course "Certificate in Laytime and Demurrage")
- Plomaritou, E. (2015) *Demurrage, Damages for Detention, Despatch* (London, Lloyd's Maritime Academy, Module 4 of Distance Learning Course "Certificate in Laytime and Demurrage")
- Plomaritou, E. (2015) *Earning Revenue from Ships* (London, Lloyd's Maritime Academy, Module 5 of Distance Learning Course "Diploma in Shipping Commercial Management")
- Plomaritou, E. (2015) *Vessels and Voyage Operations* (London, Lloyd's Maritime Academy, Module 2 of Distance Learning Course "Certificate in Ship Operations")
- Plomaritou, E. (2015) *What Agents Need to Know about Chartering* (London, Lloyd's Maritime Academy, Module 6 of Distance Learning Course "Diploma for Ship and Port Agents")
- Plomaritou, E. (2017) *Commercial Risks Arising from Charterparties, Operations and Claim Issues* (London, Lloyd's Maritime Academy,

Module 2 of Distance Learning Course "Certificate in Commercial Risks in Shipping")

- Plomaritou, E. (2017) *Chartering Policy of Shipping Companies* (London, Lloyd's Maritime Academy, Module 7 of Distance Learning Course "Diploma in Maritime Business Management")
- Plomaritou, E. (2017) *Marketing Strategy of Shipping Companies* (London, Lloyd's Maritime Academy, Module 7 of Distance Learning Course "Diploma in Maritime Business Management")
- Plomaritou, E. and Goulielmos, A. (2009) "A Review of Marketing in Tramp Shipping" *International Journal of Shipping and Transport Logistics* (Vol. 1, No. 2)
- Plomaritou, E. and Goulielmos, A. (2014) "The Shipping Marketing Strategies within the Framework of Complexity Theory" *British Journal of Economics, Management & Trade* (Vol. 4, Issue 7)
- Plomaritou, E. and Nikolaides, M. (2016) "Commercial Risks Arising from Chartering" Vessels *Journal of Shipping & Ocean Engineering* (Vol. 6, Issue 4)
- Plomaritou, E., Plomaritou, V. and Giziakis, K. (2011) "Shipping Marketing and Customer Orientation: The Psychology and Buying Behaviour of Charterer and Shipper" in Tramp and Liner Market *Management – Journal of Contemporary Management Issues* (Vol. 16, No. 1)
- Rankin, K. (2002) *Thomas' Stowage: The Properties and Stowage of Cargoes* (Glasgow, Brown, Son & Ferguson Ltd, 3rd edition)
- Raoust, J.B. (2003) "Broking Better Times. Learning to Cope With Change" *Fairplay International Shipping Weekly* (July 2003)
- Reay, J., Rees, C. (2016) *International Navigating Limits* (The Standard Club Ltd, www.standard-club.com)
- Sarll, R. and Kemp, A. (2016) *York-Antwerp Rules 2016: A Summary* (Shipping & Trade Law, England, Informa plc., 15 July 2016)
- Schofield, J. (2016) *Laytime and Demurrage* (Informa Law from Routledge, 7th edition)
- Scrutton, T.E., Boyd, S.C., Burrows, A.S. and Foxton, D. (1996) *Scrutton on Charterparties and Bills of Lading* (London, Sweet & Maxwell, 20th edition)
- Sjostrom, W. (2002) "Liner Shipping: Modelling Competition and Collusion" in Grammenos C.T. *The Handbook of Maritime Economics and Business* (London, Lloyd's of London Press Ltd, 1st edition)
- Spruyt J. (1994) *Ship Management* (London, Lloyd's of London Press Ltd)
- The Standard Club *Cargo Conventions* (www.standard-club.com, London, accessed 6 January 2017)
- Steamship Mutual (2014) *The Carriage of Goods by Sea Conventions* (www.steamshipmutual.com)

- Stephens, K. (2014) *Glossary: Chartering & Shipping Terms* (www. rickmers-linie.com)
- Stopford, M. (2009) *Maritime Economics* (London, Routledge Publications, 3rd edition)
- Sullivan, E. (1988) *The Marine Encyclopaedic Dictionary* (London, Lloyd's of London Press Ltd, 2nd edition)
- The Swedish Club *Deviation Insurance* (www.swedishclub.com)
- Swift, P. (2005) "TMSA Well Received With a Few Reservations" *Tanker Operator Journal* (September 2005)
- Tallack, L.R. (1996) *Commercial Management for Ship Masters* (London, Nautical Institute)
- Tiberg, H. (2013) *Law of Demurrage* (London, Sweet & Maxwell, 5th edition)
- Todd, P. (2015) *Principles of the Carriage of Goods by Sea* (NY, Routledge)
- Todd, P., Gaskell, N., Clarke, M., Glass, D. and Hughes, A. (1993) *Contracts for the Carriage of Goods* (London, Lloyd's of London Press)
- Todd, P., Glass, D., Yates, D., Hughes, N., Clarke, M. and Gaskell, N. (1995) *Contracts for the Carriage of Goods by Land, Sea and Air* (London, Lloyd's of London Press Ltd)
- UK P&I Club (2011) *Inter-Club Agreement as Amended 1 September 2011* (www.ukpandi.com, 25 August 2011)
- UNCTAD (1988) *UNCTAD Minimum Standards for Shipping Agents* (Distr. GENERAL UNCTAD/ST/SHIP / 13)
- United Nations (1994) *United Nations Convention on the Carriage of Goods by Sea, 1978 (Hamburg Rules)*
- United Nations (2008) *United Nations Convention on Contracts for the International Carriage of Goods Wholly or Partly by Sea (Rotterdam Rules)*
- US Department of Transportation, Maritime Administration (2013) *Panama Canal Expansion Study* (November 2013)
- Uttmark, G. (2016) *Worldscale and the Zen of Tanker Forecasting* (www.marinemoneyoffshore.com/node/6032)
- Willingale, M. (1998) *Ship Management* (London, Lloyd's of London Press Ltd, 3rd edition)
- Wilson, J. (2010) *Carriage of Goods by Sea* (England, Pearson Education Ltd, 7th edition)
- Wood, P. (2000) *Tanker Chartering* (London, Witherby & Co Ltd)
- Zarate, J.A.F. (2009) "Risk of Delay in Charterparties: Like a Ping-Pong Game?" *Revista E-Mercatoria* (Vol. 8, No. 1, 2009)

INTERNET SOURCES / FURTHER RESEARCH

- http://law.justia.com/cases/federal/appellate-courts
- http://ports.com/sea-route
- http://www.ics-shipping.org/shipping-facts/shipping-facts
- www.abb.com/marine
- www.abcmaritime.ch
- www.acf.gr
- www.asba.org
- www.atobviaconline.com
- www.axs-alphaliner.com/top100/index.php
- www.balticexchange.com
- www.bancosta.com
- www.bbc-chartering.com/fileadmin/user_upload/Downloads/BBC_Chartering_Terms.pdf
- www.bimco.org
- www.bloomberg.com
- www.bluewater-offshore.com
- www.bp.com/en/global/corporate/about-bp/energy-economics/statistical-review-of-world-energy.html
- www.braemaracm.com
- www.brsbrokers.com
- www.businessdictionary.com
- www.butterworth.com
- www.calculator.org
- www.carrierschartering.com
- www.ci-online.co.uk
- www.clarksons.net
- www.cnbc.com/2015/01/13/oil-traders-to-store-millions-of-barrels-at-sea-as-prices-slump.html#
- www.comitemaritime.org
- www.crweber.com
- www.dietze-assoc.com
- www.doric.gr
- www.drewry.co.uk
- www.eia.gov

- www.energy.ca.gov
- www.energydigital.com
- www.eversheds-sutherland.com
- www.fearnleys.com
- www.fleetship.com
- www.fonasba.com
- www.fta.co.uk
- www.fta.co.uk/policy_and_compliance/sea/long_guide/demise_identity. html
- www.galbraiths.co.uk
- www.gard.no
- www.gibsons.co.uk
- www.greatlakes-seaway.com
- www.hamburg-shipbrokers.de
- www.haugenconsulting.com
- www.ibc-academy.com
- www.iccwbo.org
- www.iccwbo.org/incoterms
- www.iea.org
- www.ifchor.com
- www.igc.int
- www.igpandi.org
- www.ihrdc.com
- www.exchange.imarex.com
- www.imf.org
- www.imo.org
- www.inderscience.com/info/inarticle.php?artid=24492
- www.indexmundi.com/commodities
- www.intercargo.org
- www.intertanko.com
- www.investopedia.com
- www.iopcfunds.org
- www.jus.uio.no/lm/sea.carriage.hague.visby.rules.1968
- www.law.berkeley.edu/library/robbins/CommonLawCivilLawTraditions. html
- www.lawandsea.net/supplements/TheHarterAct_1893.html
- www.lchclearnet.com
- www.legislation.gov.uk/ukpga/1996/23/contents
- www.liffe.com
- www.liquefiedgascarrier.com
- www.lloydslist.com
- www.lloydslistintelligence.com
- www.lloydsmaritimeacademy.com
- www.lorstem.com
- www.maerskbroker.com

- www.marinemoneyoffshore.com
- www.marineterms.com
- www.marsoft.com
- www.mcquilling.com
- www.naturalgas.org
- www.newyorkconvention.org
- www.norclub.no
- www.nordisk.no
- www.nos.no
- www.nymex.com
- www.oceanweather.com
- www.ocimf.org
- www.odingroup.com
- www.oecd.org
- www.opec.org
- www.optimashipbrokers.com
- www.pareto.no/p.-f.-bassoe
- www.platou.com
- www.platts.com
- www.portinfo.co.uk
- www.poten.com
- www.providenceship.com/images/publications/Shipping-Terms.pdf
- www.rickmers-linie.com
- www.rimship.no/abb/abbreviation.html
- www.schultegroup.com
- www.scorpiotankers.com/glossary
- www.scribd.com/doc/58589958/Mv-Vale-Brasil-Ship-s-Particulars
- www.sea-distances.org
- www.sgx.com
- www.shi.samsung.co.kr/eng
- www.ship.gr/shipbroker/cargoope.htm
- www.shipbroking.com
- www.shipinspection.eu
- www.ship-management.net
- www.shipping-markets.com
- www.shippingonline.cn/chartering/index.asp
- www.shippingtimes.co.uk
- www.ship-technology.com
- www.skuld.com
- www.skuld.com/topics/legal/clauses/clause-library1/both-to-blame-collision-clause
- www.ssyonline.com
- www.standard-club.com
- www.statista.com

- www.steamshipmutual.com/publications/Articles/Articles/Safe_Port.asp
- www.suezcanal.gov.eg
- www.swedishclub.com
- www.tc.gc.ca/eng/marinesafety/tp-tp14609-3-stability-180.htm
- www.theguardian.com
- www.theshippinglawblog.com
- www.tradewinds.no
- www.ukpandi.com
- www.uncitral.org/uncitral/en/uncitral_texts/sale_goods/1980CISG.html
- www.uncitral.org/uncitral/en/uncitral_texts/transport_goods/Hamburg_rules.html
- www.unctad.org/en/Pages/Publications.aspx
- www.wci-coal.com
- www.westpandi.com/publications
- www.wilhelmsen.com
- www.worldcoal.org
- www.worldscale.co.uk
- www.worldshipping.org

INDEX

Printed in the United States
by Baker & Taylor Publisher Services